Students:
Looking to improve your grades?

ACCESS FREE STUDY TOOLS AT edge.sagepub.com/barbour9e

- Study your way with mobile-friendly **FLASHCARDS** and **QUIZZES** for anywhere, anytime studying.

- Watch **VIDEOS** that illustrate key chapter concepts in action.

- Listen to engaging podcasts and **AUDIO** resources.

- Access influential **RESEARCH IN YOUR FIELD** via selected SAGE journal articles.

$SAGE edge™
for CQ Press

SAGE
Premium
Video

BOOST COMPREHENSION. BOLSTER ANALYSIS.

- SAGE Premium Video **EXCLUSIVELY CURATED FOR THIS TEXT**
- **BRIDGES BOOK CONTENT** with application and critical thinking
- Includes short, auto-graded quizzes that **DIRECTLY FEED TO YOUR LMS GRADEBOOK**
- Premium content is **ADA COMPLIANT WITH TRANSCRIPTS**
- Comprehensive media guide to help you **QUICKLY SELECT MEANINGFUL VIDEO** tied to your course objectives

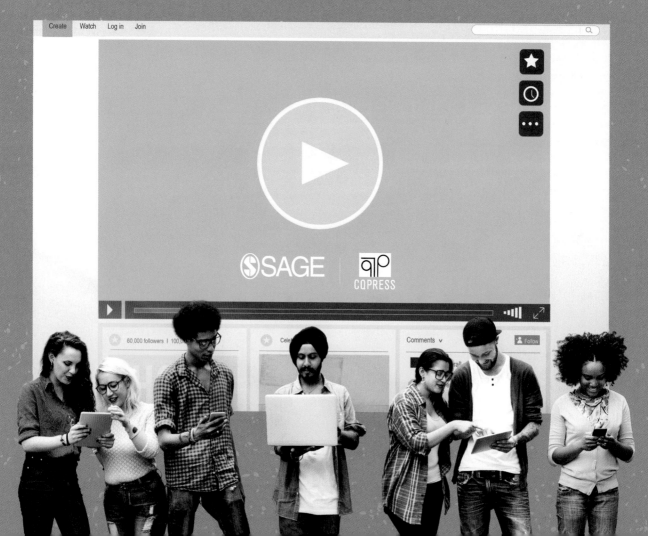

The
Hallmark
Features

A COMPLETE LEARNING PACKAGE

The dynamic features in **Keeping the Republic** show students how to think critically about "who gets what and how" in American politics. These features improve students' critical thinking skills through application and encourages them to be savvy consumers of political information.

- **THE *POWER & CITIZENSHIP* THEMES** emphasize politics as a struggle not just over who gets power and resources in society but also how the narrative that defines that struggle is controlled.

- **WHAT'S AT STAKE FEATURES** push students to consider people's struggle with our system of government, what the people in our society need, and how the rules affect the outcome of that struggle.

- **SNAPSHOT OF AMERICA GRAPHICS** focus on demographics and invite students to explore the connections between data and politics.

- **THE BIG PICTURE GRAPHICS** present rich, poster-worthy infographic displays that broaden students' understanding of big processes, big concepts, and big data.

SAGE Outcomes:
MEASURE RESULTS, TRACK SUCCESS

FOR STUDENTS, understanding the objectives for each chapter and the goals for the course is essential for getting the grade you deserve!

FOR INSTRUCTORS, being able to track your students' progress allows you to more easily pinpoint areas of improvement and report on success.

This title was crafted around specific chapter objectives and course outcomes, vetted by experts, and adapted from renowned syllabi. Tracking student progress can be challenging. Promoting and achieving success should never be. We are here for you.

COURSE **OUTCOMES** FOR AMERICAN GOVERNMENT:

ARTICULATE the foundations of American government, including its history, critical concepts, and important documents and achievements.

EXAMINE the main institutions of American government, including their roles and interrelationships.

DESCRIBE the roles and relative importance of major entities and influences in American political life.

ANALYZE the development and impact of important governmental policies.

Want to see how these outcomes tie in with this book's chapter-level objectives?
Visit us at edge.sagepub.com/barbour9e for complete outcome-to-objective mapping.

Keeping the
REPUBLIC

the essentials

9th Edition

Keeping the
REPUBLIC

Power and Citizenship in
AMERICAN POLITICS

the essentials

CHRISTINE BARBOUR & GERALD C. WRIGHT

Indiana University

FOR INFORMATION:

CQ Press
SAGE Publications, Inc.
2455 Teller Road
Thousand Oaks, California 91320
E-mail: order@sagepub.com

SAGE Publications Ltd.
1 Oliver's Yard
55 City Road
London EC1Y 1SP
United Kingdom

SAGE Publications India Pvt. Ltd.
B 1/I 1 Mohan Cooperative Industrial Area
Mathura Road, New Delhi 110 044
India

SAGE Publications Asia-Pacific Pte Ltd
18 Cross Street #10-10/11/12
China Square Central
Singapore 048423

Printed in Canada

ISBN 978-1-5443-2606-1

Executive Publisher: Monica Eckman
Development Editors: Sarah Calabi,
                       Anna Villarruel
Editorial Assistant: Sam Rosenberg
Production Editors: Kelly DeRosa,
                      Tori Mirsadjadi
Copy Editor: Amy Marks
Typesetter: C&M Digitals (P) Ltd.
Proofreader: Theresa Kay
Indexer: Judy Hunt
Cover Designer: Gail Buschman
Marketing Manager: Erica DeLuca

This book is printed on acid-free paper.

19 20 21 22 23 10 9 8 7 6 5 4 3 2 1

We dedicate this book with love to our parents,
Patti Barbour and John Barbour and
Doris and Gerry Wright,
To our kids, Andrea and Monica,
To our grandkids, Liam, Elena, Paloma, and Asher,
And to each other.

ABOUT THE AUTHORS

CHRISTINE BARBOUR

Christine Barbour teaches in the Political Science Department and the Hutton Honors College at Indiana University, where she has become increasingly interested in how teachers of large classes can maximize what their students learn. She is working with online course designers to create an online version of her Intro to American Politics class. At Indiana, Professor Barbour has been a Lilly Fellow, working on a project to increase student retention in large introductory courses, and a member of the Freshman Learning Project, a university-wide effort to improve the first-year undergraduate experience. She has served on the *New York Times* College Advisory Board, working with other educators to develop ways to integrate newspaper reading into the undergraduate curriculum. She has won several teaching honors, but the two awarded by her students mean the most to her: the Indiana University Student Alumni Association Award for Outstanding Faculty and the Indiana University Chapter of the Society of Professional Journalists Brown Derby Award. When not teaching or writing textbooks, Professor Barbour enjoys playing with her dogs, traveling with her coauthor, and writing about food. She is the food editor for *Bloom Magazine* of Bloomington and is a coauthor of *Indiana Cooks!* (2005) and *Home Grown Indiana* (2008). She also makes jewelry from precious metals and rough gemstones. If she ever retires, she will open a jewelry shop in a renovated Airstream on the beach in Apalachicola, Florida, where she plans to write another cookbook and a book about the local politics, development, and fishing industry.

GERALD C. WRIGHT

Gerald C. Wright has taught political science at Indiana University since 1981, and he is currently the chair of the Political Science Department. An accomplished scholar of American politics, and the 2010 winner of the State Politics and Policy Association's Career Achievement Award, his books include *Statehouse Democracy: Public Opinion and Policy in the American States* (1993), coauthored with Robert S. Erikson and John P. McIver. He has published more than fifty articles on elections, public opinion, and state politics. Professor Wright has long studied the relationship among citizens, their preferences, and public policy.

He is currently conducting research funded by grants from the National Science Foundation and the Russell Sage Foundation on the factors that influence the equality of policy representation in the states and in Congress. He is also writing a book about representation in U.S. legislatures. He has been a consultant for Project Vote Smart in the past several elections. Professor Wright is a member of Indiana University's Freshman Learning Project, a university-wide effort to improve the first-year undergraduate experience by focusing on how today's college students learn and how teachers can adapt their pedagogical methods to best teach them. In his nonworking hours, Professor Wright also likes to spend time with his dogs, travel, eat good food, fish, and play golf.

BRIEF CONTENTS

CONTENTS

PREFACE

WHEN one of us was a freshman journalism major in college, more years ago now than she cares to remember, she took an introduction to American politics course—mostly because the other courses she wanted were already full. But the class was a revelation. The teacher was terrific, the textbook provocative, and the final paper assignment an eye opener. "As Benjamin Franklin was leaving Independence Hall," the assignment read, "he was stopped by a woman who asked, 'What have you created?' Franklin replied, 'A Republic, Madam, if you can keep it'." Have we succeeded in keeping our republic? Had we been given a democracy in the first place? These questions sparked the imagination, the writing of an impassioned freshman essay about the limits and possibilities of American democracy, and a lifetime love affair with politics. If we have one goal in writing this textbook, it is to share the excitement of discovering humankind's capacity to find innovative solutions to those problems that arise from our efforts to live together on a planet too small, with resources too scarce, and with saintliness in too short a supply. In this book we honor the human capacity to manage our collective lives with peace and even, at times, dignity. And, in particular, we celebrate the American political system and the founders' extraordinary contribution to the possibilities of human governance.

WHERE WE ARE GOING

Between the two of us, we have been teaching American politics for way more than half a century. We have used a lot of textbooks in that time. Some of them have been too difficult for introductory students (although we have enjoyed them as political scientists!), and others have tried excessively to accommodate the beginning student and have ended up being too light in their coverage of basic information. We wanted our students to have the best and most complete treatment of the American political system we could find, presented in a way that would catch their imagination, be easy to understand, and engage them in the system about which they were learning.

This book is the result of that desire. It covers essential topics with clear explanations, but it is also a thematic book, intended to guide students through a wealth of material and to help them make sense of the content both academically and personally. To that end we develop two themes that run throughout every chapter: an analytic theme to assist students in organizing the details and connecting them to the larger ideas and concepts of American politics and an evaluative theme to help them find personal meaning in the American political system and develop standards for making judgments about how well the system works. Taken together, these themes provide students a framework on which to hang the myriad complexities of American politics.

The analytic theme we chose is a classic in political science: politics is a struggle over limited power and resources, as gripping as a sporting event in its final minutes, but much more vital. The rules guiding that struggle influence who will win and who will lose, so that often the struggles with the most at stake are over the rule making itself. In short, and in the words of a famous political scientist, *politics is about who gets what, and how they get it.* To illustrate this theme, we begin and end every chapter with a feature called **What's at Stake . . . ?** that poses a question about what people want from politics—what they are struggling to get and how the rules affect who gets it. At the end of every major chapter section, we **Pause and Review** to revisit Harold Laswell's definition in context and ask **Who, What, How**. This periodic analytic summary helps solidify the conceptual work of the book and gives students a sturdy framework within which to organize the facts and other empirical information we want them to learn. For the evaluative theme, we focus on the "who" in the formulation of "who gets what, and how." Who are the country's citizens? What are the ways they engage in political life? To "keep" a republic, citizens must shoulder responsibilities as well as exercise their rights. We challenge students to view democratic participation among the diverse population as the price of maintaining liberty.

Working in concert with the Who, What, How summary are the **In Your Own Words** goals that provide each chapter's major points up front to help students organize the material they read. Who, What, How summaries provide the opportunity for students to pause and review these goals and gauge how well they're understanding and retaining the information.

Our citizenship theme has three dimensions. First, in our **Profiles in Citizenship** feature, present in every chapter, we introduce students to important figures in American politics and ask the subjects why they are involved in public service or some aspect of political life. Based on personal interviews with these people, the profiles model republic-keeping behavior for students, helping them to see what is expected of them as members of a democratic polity. We feel unabashedly that a primary goal of teaching introductory politics is not only to create good scholars but also to create good citizens. Second, at the end of nearly every chapter, the feature *The Citizens and . . .* provides a critical view of what citizens can or cannot do in American politics, evaluating how democratic various aspects of the American system actually are and what possibilities exist for change. Third, we premise this book on the belief that the skills that make good students and good academics are the same skills that make good citizens: the ability to think critically about and process new information and the ability to be actively engaged in one's subject. Accordingly, in our **CLUES to Critical Thinking** feature, we help students understand what critical thinking looks like by modeling it for them, and guiding them through the necessary steps as they examine current and classic readings about American politics. Similarly, the **Don't Be Fooled by . . .** feature assists students to critically examine the various kinds of political information they are bombarded with—from information in textbooks like this one, to information from social networks, to information from their congressional representative or political party. **Thinking Outside the Box** questions prompt students to take a step back and engage in some big-picture thinking about what they are learning.

The book's themes are further illustrated through two unique features that will enhance students' visual literacy and critical thinking skills. Each chapter includes a rich, poster-worthy display called **The Big Picture** that focuses on a key element in the book, complementing the text with a rich visual that grabs students' attention and engages them in understanding *big processes* like how cases get to the Supreme Court, *big concepts* such as when the law can treat people differently, and *big data*, including who has immigrated to the United States and how they have assimilated. In addition, an innovative feature called **Snapshot of America**, reimagined from the Who Are We feature of past editions, describes through graphs, charts, and maps just who we Americans are and where we come from, what we believe, how educated we are, and how much money we make. This recurring feature aims at exploding stereotypes, and **Behind the Numbers** questions lead students to think critically about the political consequences of America's demographic profile. These visual features are the result of a partnership with award-winning designer, educator, and artist Mike Wirth, who has lent his expert hand in information design and data visualization to craft these unique, informative, and memorable graphics.

Marginal definitions of the key terms as they occur and chapter summary material—vocabulary and summaries—help to support the book's major themes and to reinforce the major concepts and details of American politics.

HOW WE GET THERE

In many ways this book follows the path of most American politics texts: there are chapters on all the subjects that instructors scramble to cover in a short amount of time. But in keeping with our goal of making the enormous amount of material here more accessible to our students, we have made some changes to the typical format. After our introductory chapter, we have included a chapter not found in every book: "American Citizens and Political Culture." Given our emphasis on citizens, this chapter is key. It covers the history and legal status of citizens and immigrants in America and the ideas and beliefs that unite us as Americans as well as the ideas that divide us politically.

Another chapter that breaks with tradition is Chapter 4, "Federalism and the U.S. Constitution," which provides an analytic and comparative study of the basic rules governing this country—highlighted up front because of our emphasis on the *how* of American politics. This chapter covers the essential elements of the Constitution: federalism, the three branches, separation of powers and checks and balances, and amendability. In each case we examine the rules the founders provided, look at the alternatives they might have chosen, and ask what difference the rules make to who wins and who loses in America. This chapter is explicitly comparative. For each rule change considered, we look at a country that does things differently. We drive home early the idea that understanding the rules is crucial to understanding how and to whose advantage the system works. Throughout the text we look carefully at alternatives to our system of government as manifested in other countries—and among the fifty states.

Because of the prominence we give to rules—and to institutions—this book covers Congress, the presidency, the bureaucracy, and the courts before looking at public opinion, parties, interest groups, voting, and the media—the inputs or processes of politics that are shaped by those rules. While this approach may seem counterintuitive to instructors who have logged many miles teaching it the other way around, we have found that it is not counterintuitive to students, who have an easier time grasping the notion that the rules make a difference when they are presented with those rules in the first half of the course. We have, however, taken care to write the chapters so that they will fit into any organizational framework.

We have long believed that teaching is a two-way street, and we welcome comments, criticisms, or just a pleasant chat about politics or pedagogy. You can email us directly at barbour@indiana.edu and wright1@indiana.edu.

WHAT'S NEW IN THE NINTH EDITION

These are strange days in American politics. We have tried to deal with that strangeness bluntly, objectively, and clearly. We are in a "moment." Whether that moment becomes the "new normal" or remains a historical blip, we have no way of knowing. Writing about it in real time, we take it as it comes. We are political scientists, not magicians, and thus have a hard bias toward the scientific, the empirical, the observable. Distinguishing between truth and falsity is central to what we do. We can make projections and predictions but our crystal ball has been particularly hazy lately, and we make no pretense of knowing the future.

The 2016 election only exacerbated divisions that have been building for decades, the product of economic displacement, demographic change and a widening gap between those with college educations and those without. Somedays it really does feel like there are two Americas, and the challenge of writing a textbook for both of them has been heavy at times. We have worked hard to explain the nature of our ideological divisions as objectively as possible, and I suspect we have ruffled a few feathers, including our own. That's as it should be. No one likes to be described as a statistic or a faceless member of a demographic group or have opinions ascribed to them that they may not even knowingly hold, or may actively reject. It's a good thing if this book inspires debate, disagreement, and discovery.

Ideological polarization is not the only characteristic of American politics that has been a challenge to deal with in this edition. We have a president who likes the limelight and, love him or hate him (it's hard to be indifferent), he delights in shattering the norms that underlie the rules of American politics. Indeed, that is his appeal to many Americans who would like to see the system turned upside down. That means we have had to be more careful about focusing on those norms and explaining the roles they play in supporting the Constitution, so that we can fully understand the consequences as we decide whether they matter.

Finally, as we say later in this book, if we have a bias, it is unquestionably toward diversity, toward the whole crazy salad of Americans. We can't write effectively for our students unless they can see themselves mirrored in the pages. This book has to belong to them, and so we have deplored the movement to return to an America where women, people of color, immigrants, members of the LGBTQ community, and other minority groups are marginalized. In the last two years, some Americans have felt more free to voice disparaging or degrading remarks about members of all those groups. We reject that view.

Writing the ninth edition also gave us an opportunity to revitalize the book's theme to reflect the influences of modern technology on power and citizenship, in particular the ways that citizenship is mediated by third parties. To do that, we looked at the ways that controlling the political narrative has translated into political power and how that power has shifted with the advent of new and social media. This coverage is integrated throughout each chapter and is especially notable in **The Citizens and . . .** sections and the **Don't Be Fooled By . . .** boxes' focus on digital media.

Reviews for this edition helped guide some key changes that we hope will make the text even more useful to you and your students. We have sought to streamline both the main narrative and its features to provide a more focused reading experience. Three new **CLUES to Critical Thinking** boxes teach students to think carefully about the news of the day, including the late John McCain's speech on the attempted repeal of Obamacare and articles on Donald Trump's relationship with corporate America and the rise of tribalism in America politics. One new **Profiles in Citizenship** interview appears in this edition—we had the opportunity to interview Senator Tammy Duckworth before the 2018 midterms.

New **What's at Stake . . . ?** vignettes examine such topics as the activism of the students of Marjorie Stoneman Douglas High School, the rise of the alt right and the Make America Great Again movement, what happens when outsiders challenge party establishment, the consequences of overturning executive action on climate change, and the unusual presidency of Donald Trump.

DIGITAL RESOURCES

We know how important good resources can be in the teaching of American government. Our goal has been to create resources that not only support but also enhance the text's themes and features. **SAGE edge** offers a robust online environment featuring an impressive array of tools and resources for review, study, and further exploration, keeping both instructors and students on the cutting edge of teaching and learning. SAGE edge content is open access and available on demand. Learning and teaching has never been easier! We gratefully acknowledge Graphic World and Alicia Fisher of California State University, Fullerton for developing the digital resources on this site.

SAGE COURSE OUTCOMES: MEASURE RESULTS, TRACK SUCCESS

The journey to retaining and applying course content differs for every student. To successfully navigate this journey, course goals should remain clear, consistent, and constructive. For instructors, the ability to track and measure individual progress is vital to ensuring student success.

SAGE/CQ Press is invested in mapping measurable course outcomes to chapter-level learning objectives for all introductory textbook offerings through **SAGE course outcomes**. Each title is crafted with specific course outcomes in mind, vetted by leading advisors in the field, and adapted from renowned syllabi from across the country.

Students Benefit

- **A clear path for learners:** Understanding the objectives for each chapter and how those objectives are tied to the goals of the course is essential for getting the grade students want.
- **Meaningful context for skills**: course outcomes emphasize the skills learned in the course and highlight how they can be applied in the real world after graduation.
- **More targeted instruction:** Students receive better, more targeted feedback when instructors can track and measure individual progress based on course-specific expectations.

Instructors Benefit

- **Effective measuring mechanism:** Being able to track student progress allows you to more easily pinpoint specific areas of improvement, increases course efficacy, allows you to report out on success, and aligns student learning with course and institutional goals.
- **Personalized instruction and feedback:** Promoting student success through targeted and individualized instruction improves retention and increases the likelihood of achieving course mastery.
- **Standardized benchmarking:** Formative and summative assessment is more effective and actionable when assessing student progress against standard course outcome benchmarks.

Course Outcomes for American Government:

- ✓ ARTICULATE the foundations of American government, including its history, critical concepts, and important documents and achievements.
- ✓ EXPLAIN the main institutions of American government, including their roles and interrelationships.
- ✓ DESCRIBE the roles and relative importance of major entities and influences in American political life.
- ✓ ANALYZE the development and impact of important governmental policies.

INSTRUCTOR RESOURCES

SAGE Coursepacks and SAGE edge online resources are included FREE with this text. For a brief demo, contact your sales representative today.

SAGE COURSEPACKS FOR INSTRUCTORS makes it easy to import our quality content into your school's learning management system (LMS). Intuitive and simple to use, it allows you to

Say NO to . . .

- required access codes
- learning a new system

Say YES to . . .

- using only the content you want and need
- high-quality assessment and multimedia exercises

For use in: Blackboard, Canvas, Brightspace by Desire2Learn (D2L), and Moodle

Don't use an LMS platform? No problem, you can still access many of the online resources for your text via SAGE edge.

With SAGE coursepacks, you get:

- Quality textbook content delivered **directly into your LMS**;
- An **intuitive, simple format** that makes it easy to integrate the material into your course with minimal effort;
- **Assessment tools** that foster review, practice, and critical thinking, including:
  - Diagnostic chapter **pre tests and post tests** that identify opportunities for improvement, track student progress, and ensure mastery of key learning objectives
  - **Test banks** built on Bloom's Taxonomy and SAGE Course Outcomes that provide a diverse range of test items with ExamView test generation
  - **Activity and quiz options** that allow you to choose only the assignments and tests you want
  - **Instructions** on how to use and integrate the comprehensive assessments and resources provided

- **Assignable SAGE Premium video** (available via the interactive eBook version, linked through SAGE Coursepacks) that is tied to learning objectives, created and curated exclusively for this text, featuring:
  - **Corresponding multimedia assessment options** that automatically feed to your gradebook
  - SAGE original *Topics in American Government* recap the fundamentals of American politics
  - *American Government News Clips* bring current events into the book, connecting brief, 2- to 4-minute news clips with core chapter content
  - Comprehensive, downloadable, easy-to-use *Media Guide in the Coursepack* for every video resource, listing the chapter to which the video content is tied, matching learning objective(s), a helpful description of the video content, and assessment questions.
- **Assignable data exercises** build students' data literacy skills with interactive data visualization tools from **SAGE Stats** and **U.S. Political Stats**, offering a dynamic way to analyze real-world data and think critically of the narrative behind the numbers;
- **Chapter-specific discussion questions** help launch engaging classroom interaction while reinforcing important content;
- Exclusive, influential **SAGE journal and reference content**, built into course materials and assessment tools, that ties influential research and scholarship to chapter concepts;
- Editable, chapter-specific **PowerPoint® slides** offer flexibility when creating multimedia lectures so you don't have to start from scratch;
- **Integrated links to the interactive eBook** make it easy for your students to maximize their study time with this "anywhere, anytime" mobile-friendly version of the text. It also offers access to more digital tools and resources, including SAGE Premium Video;
- **All tables and figures** from the textbook.

SAGE EDGE FOR STUDENTS

http://edge.sagepub.com/barbour9e

SAGE edge for students enhances learning, it's easy for students to use, and offers:

- An open-access site that makes it easy for students to maximize their study time, any-time, anywhere;

- **eFlashcards** that strengthen understanding of key terms and concepts;
- **Practice quizzes** that allow students to practice and assess how much they've learned and where they need to focus their attention;
- **Video resources** that bring concepts to life, are tied to learning objectives, and curated exclusively for this text;
- **Exclusive access to influential SAGE journal and reference content**, that ties important research and scholarship to chapter concepts to strengthen learning.

ACKNOWLEDGMENTS

Africans say that it takes a village to raise a child—it is certainly true that it takes one to write a textbook! We could not have done it without a community of family, friends, colleagues, students, reviewers, and editors who supported us, nagged us, maddened us, and kept us on our toes. Not only is this a better book because of their help and support, but it would not have been a book at all without them.

On the home front, we thank our families and our friends. We are forever grateful for the unconditional love and support, not to mention occasional intellectual revelation (Hobbes was wrong: it is not a dog-eat-dog world after all!), offered up gladly by Ollie, Gracie, Giuseppe, Bay Cat and Mags. (Though we lost Max, Clio, Daphne, Gina, Zoë, Ginger, Bandon, Maggie, and Spook along the way, they were among our earliest and strongest supporters and we miss them still.)

Colleagues now or once in the Political Science Department at Indiana University have given us invaluable help on details beyond our ken: Yvette Alex Assensoh, Bill Bianco, Jack Bielasiak, Doris Burton, Ted Carmines, Dana Chabot, Mike Ensley, Chuck Epp, Judy Failer, Russ Hanson, Margie Hershey, Bobbi Herzberg, Virginia Hettinger, Fenton Martin, Burt Monroe, Rich Pacelle, Karen Rasler, Leroy Rieselbach, Jean Robinson, Steve Sanders, Pat Sellers, and the late Lin Ostrom and John Williams. IU colleagues from other schools and departments have been terrific: Trevor Brown, Dave Weaver, and Cleve Wilhoit from the Journalism School; Bill McGregor and Roger Parks from the School of Public and Environmental Affairs; John Patrick from the School of Education; and Julia Lamber and Pat Baude from the Law School have all helped out on substantive matters. Many IU folks have made an immeasurable contribution by raising to new levels our consciousness about teaching: Joan Middendorf and David Pace, as well as all the Freshman Learning Project people. James Russell and Bob Goelhert, and all the librarians in the Government Publications section of our library have done yeoman service for us. We are also grateful to colleagues from other institutions: Joe Aistrup, Shaun Bowler, Bob Brown, Tom Carsey, Kisuk Cho, E. J. Dionne, Todd Donovan, Diana Dwyre, Bob Erikson, David Hobbs, Kathleen Knight, David Lee, David McCuan, John McIver, Dick Merriman, Glenn Parker, Denise Scheberle, John Sislin, Dorald Stoltz, and Linda Streb. Rich Pacelle and Robert Sahr were particularly helpful.

Special thanks to all our students—undergraduate and graduate, past and present—who inspired us to write this book in the first place. Many students helped us in more concrete ways, working tirelessly as research assistants. On previous editions these former students, now colleagues at other universities, helped enormously: Nate Birkhead, Tom Carsey, Jessica Gerrity, Dave Holian, Tracy Osborn, Brian Schaffner, and Mike Wagner. Jon Winburn, Laura Bucci, Trish Gibson, Katelyn Stauffer, and Ben Toll have been super helpful in the creation of the electronic version of the book. We are also grateful to Hugh Aprile, Liz Bevers, Christopher McCollough, Rachel Shelton, Jim Trilling, and Kevin Willhite for their help with the earliest editions of the book.

Thanks also to Mike Stull, for taking us seriously in the first place; and to Jean Woy, for the vision that helped shape the book. Ann West in particular was a friend, a support, and a fabulous editor. We will love her forever. Ann Kirby-Payne is another development editor who loved the book as her own and made it better over the course of multiple editions. We miss our Anns.

We have also benefited tremendously from the help of the folks at Project Vote Smart and the many outstanding political scientists across the country who have provided critical reviews of the manuscript at every step of the way. We'd like to thank the following people who took time away from their own work to critique and make suggestions for the improvement of ours. They include all the reviewers—Sheldon Appleton, Paul Babbitt, Harry Bralley, Scott Brown, Peter Carlson, David Holian, Carol Humphrey, Glen Hunt, Marilyn Mote-Yale, and Craig Ortsey—and also:

Yishaiya Abosch, California State University, Fresno
Amy Acord, Wharton County Junior College
Danny M. Adkison, Oklahoma State University
Ellen Andersen, University of Vermont
Alicia Andreatta, Cisco College
Don Arnold, Laney College
Kevin Bailey, former member, Texas House of Representatives, District 140
Bethany Blackstone, University of North Texas

James Borders, United States Air Force Academy
Jeffrey A. Bosworth, Mansfield University
Ralph Edward Bradford, University of Central Florida
James Bromeland, Winona State University
Jenny Bryson Clark, South Texas College
Scott E. Buchanan, The Citadel, the Military College of South Carolina
John F. Burke, Trinity University
Charity Butcher, Kennesaw State University
Anne Marie Cammisa, Georgetown University
David Campbell, University of Notre Dame
Francis Carleton, University of Nevada, Las Vegas
Michael Ceriello, Clark College
Betty Chan, Sierra College
Jennifer B. Clark, South Texas Community College
Diana Cohen, Central Connecticut State University
Kimberly H. Conger, Iowa State University
Albert Craig, Augusta State University
Renee Cramer, Drake University
Paul Davis, Truckee Meadows Community College
Christine L. Day, University of New Orleans
Mary C. Deason, University of Mississippi
William Delehanty, Missouri Southern State University
Lisa DeLorenzo, St. Louis Community College–Wildwood
Robert E. DiClerico, West Virginia University
Robert Dillard, Texas A&M University–Corpus Christi
Robert L. Dion, University of Evansville
Price Dooley, University of Illinois Springfield
Lois Duke-Whitaker, Georgia Southern University
Johanna Dunaway, Texas A&M University
Richard Ellis, Willamette University
C. Lawrence Evans, William and Mary College
Heather K. Evans, Sam Houston State University
Victoria Farrar-Myers, Southern Methodist University
Femi Ferreira, Hutchinson Community College
Richard Flanagan, College of State Island
Daniel Franklin, Georgia State University
Savanna Garrity, Madisonville Community College
Heidi Getchell-Bastien, Northern Essex Community College
Patrick Gilbert, Lone Star College–Tomball
Dana K. Glencross, Oklahoma City Community College
Abe Goldberg, University of South Carolina Upstate
Larry Gonzalez, Houston Community College-Southwest
Eugene Goss, Long Beach City College
Heidi Jo Green, Lone Star College–Cyfair
Richard Haesly, California State University, Long Beach
Bill Haltom, University of Puget Sound
Victoria Hammond, Austin Community College–Northridge

Patrick J. Haney, Miami University

Sally Hansen, Daytona State College

Charles A. Hantz, Danville Area Community College

Virginia Haysley, Lone Star College–Tomball

David M. Head, John Tyler Community College

Paul Herrnson, University of Connecticut

Erik Herzik, University of Nevada–Reno

Ronald J. Hrebenar, University of Utah

Tseggai Isaac, Missouri University of Science and
Technology

William G. Jacoby, Michigan State University

W. Lee Johnston, University of North Carolina
Wilmington

Philip Edward Jones, University of Delaware

Kalu N. Kalu, Auburn University Montgomery

Kelechi A. Kalu, Ohio State University

Joshua Kaplan, University of Notre Dame

John D. Kay, Santa Barbara City College

Ellen Key, Appalachian State University

Richard J. Kiefer, Waubonsee College

Kendra A. King Momon, Oglethorpe University

Tyson King-Meadows, University of Maryland–
Baltimore County

Elizabeth Klages, Augsburg College

Bernard D. Kolasa, University of Nebraska at Omaha

John F. Kozlowicz, University of Wisconsin–
Whitewater

Geoffrey Kurtz, Borough of Manhattan Community
College–CUNY

Lisa Langenbach, Middle Tennessee State University

Jeff Lee, Blinn College–Bryan

Angela K. Lewis, University of Alabama at Birmingham

Ted Lewis, Naval Postgraduate School

Kara Lindaman, Winona State University

Brad Lockerbie, East Carolina University

Paul M. Lucko, Murray State University

Jack Adam MacLennan, Park University

Vincent N. Mancini, Delaware County Community
College

Jonathan Martin, Texas Tech University

Tom McInnis, University of Central Arkansas

Amy McKay, Georgia State University

Tim McKeown, University of North Carolina at
Chapel Hill

Sam Wescoat McKinstry, East Tennessee State
University

Utz Lars McKnight, University of Alabama

David McCuan, Sonoma State University

Lauri McNown, University of Colorado at Boulder

Bryan McQuide, Grand View University

Eric Miller, Blinn College–Bryan Campus

Lawrence Miller, Collin County Community College–
Spring Creek

Maureen F. Moakley, University of Rhode Island

Sara Moats, Florida International University

Theodore R. Mosch, University of Tennessee at Martin

T. Sophia Mrouri, Lone Star College, CyFair

Melinda A. Mueller, Eastern Illinois University

Steven Neiheisel, University of Dayton

Adam Newmark, Appalachian State University

David Nice, Washington State University

Zane R. Nobbs, Delta College

James A. Norris, Texas A&M International University

Susan Orr, College at Brockport, SUNY

Tracy Osborn, University of Iowa

William Parent, San Jacinto College

Gerhard Peters, Citrus College

Mike Pickering, University of New Orleans

Paul Thomas Rabchenuk, Salem State University

Darrial Reynolds, South Texas College

David Robinson, University of Houston–Downtown

Jason Robles, Colorado State University

Dario Albert Rozas, Milwaukee Area Technical College

Trevor Rubenzer, University of South Carolina, Upstate

Raymond Sandoval, Richland College

Thomas A. Schmeling, Rhode Island College

Paul Scracic, Youngstown State University

Todd Shaw, University of South Carolina

Daniel M. Shea, Allegheny College

Neil Snortland, University of Arkansas at Little Rock

Michael W. Sonnleitner, Portland Community College–
Sylvania

Robert E. Sterken Jr., University of Texas at Tyler

Atiya Kai Stokes-Brown, Bucknell University

James W. Stoutenborough, Idaho State University

Ruth Ann Strickland, Appalachian State University

Tom Sweeney, North Central College

Bill Turini, Reedley College

Richard S. Unruh, Fresno Pacific University

Anip Uppal, Alpena Community College

Lynn Vacca, Lambuth University

Jan P. Vermeer, Nebraska Wesleyan University

Elizabeth A. Wabindato, Northern Arizona University

Julian Westerhout, Illinois State University

Matt Wetstein, San Joaquin Delta College

Cheryl Wilf, Kutztown University

Shawn Williams, Campbellsville University

David C. Wilson, University of Delaware

David E. Woodard, Concordia University–St. Paul

Shoua Yang, St. Cloud State University

Kimberly Zagorski, University of Wisconsin–Stout

David J. Zimny, Los Medanos College

We are also incredibly indebted to the busy public servants who made the *Profiles in Citizenship* possible. We are gratified and humbled that they believed in the project enough to give us their valuable time.

Finally, it is our great privilege to acknowledge and thank all the people at CQ Press who believed in this book and made this edition possible. In this day and age of huge publishing conglomerates, it has been such a pleasure to work with a small, committed team dedicated to top-quality work. Brenda Carter, now at the American Psychological Association, more than anyone, saw the potential of this book and made it what it is today. Michele Sordi has been a great source of advice, inspiration, and good food. Charisse Kiino earned our instant gratitude for so thoroughly and immediately "getting" what this book is about. She has worked tirelessly with us and we have relied heavily on her good sense, her wisdom, her patience, and her friendship. We can't do without her. Thanks to Linda Trygar and her team of field reps across the country who sometimes seem to know the book better than we do ourselves. We appreciate their enthusiasm and commitment. For putting this beautiful book together and drawing your attention to it, we thank the folks on the design, editorial, marketing, and production teams: Gail Buschman, Anna Villarruel, Sam Rosenberg, Sarah Christensen, Lauren Younker, Joseph McManus, Dom Shank, Erica DeLuca, Eric Garner, and especially Kelly DeRosa and Tori Mirsadjadi for their good production management, and to Amy Marks, for her always gentle and miraculous copyediting.

Very special mention goes to two people on this edition. Monica Eckman walked into this project cold as a new editor, and we are still trying to figure out what hit us. She is a dynamo—smart as a whip and astute about publishing but constantly full of encouragement, chortling amusement, CAPITAL LETTERS, and good spirits. We loved her instantly and hope for a long and laugher-filled friendship.

Lastly, Sarah Calabi. How she put up with us, twice now, I don't know. She is everything we are not—focused, organized, and full of good Maine sense. She managed to help us juggle and finish two projects in the timespan available for just one and did all of this with the demands of two small daughters. Her dry humor and wickedly acerbic view of the world made working with her fun, even when it was tough. This book is way better than it should be, and that's on her.

Christine Barbour
Gerald C. Wright

TO THE STUDENT

SUGGESTIONS ON HOW TO READ THIS TEXTBOOK

1. As they say in Chicago about voting, do it **early and often**. If you open the book for the first time the night before the exam, you will not learn much from it and it won't help your grade. Start reading the chapters in conjunction with the lectures, and you'll get so much more out of class.

2. Pay attention to the **chapter headings** and **In Your Own Words** goals. They tell you what we think is important, what our basic argument is, and how all the material fits together. Often, chapter subheadings list elements of an argument that may show up on a quiz. Be alert to these clues.

3. **Read actively.** Constantly ask yourself: Why is this important? How do these different facts fit together? What are the broad arguments here? How does this material relate to class lectures? How does it relate to the broad themes of the class? When you stop asking these questions, you are merely moving your eyes over the page, and that is a waste of time.

4. **Highlight or take notes.** Some people prefer highlighting because it's quicker than taking notes, but others think that writing down the most important points helps in recalling them later. Whichever method you choose (and you can do both), be sure you're doing it properly.

   - **Highlighting.** An entirely highlighted page will not give you any clues about what is important. Read each paragraph and ask yourself: What is the basic idea of this paragraph? Highlight that. Avoid highlighting all the examples and illustrations. You should be able to recall them on your own when you see the main idea. Beware of highlighting too little. If whole pages go by with no marking, you are probably not highlighting enough.

   - **Outlining.** Again, the key is to write down enough, but not too much. Go for key ideas, terms, and arguments.

5. **Note all key terms**, and be sure you understand the definition and significance.

6. Do not skip **tables and figures**. These things are there for a purpose, because they convey crucial information or illustrate a point in the text. After you read a chart or graph or *Big Picture* infographic, make a note in the margin about what it means.

7. **Do not skip the boxes.** They are not filler! The *Don't Be Fooled by . . .* boxes provide advice on becoming a critical consumer of the many varieties of political information that come your way. Each *Profile in Citizenship* box highlights the achievements of a political actor pertinent to that chapter's focus. They model citizen participation and can serve as a beacon for your own political power long after you've completed your American government course. And the *Snapshot of America* boxes help you understand who Americans are and how they line up on all sorts of dimensions.

8. Make use of the book's web site at **http://edge.sage pub.com/barbour9e**. There you will find chapter summaries, flashcards, and practice quizzes that will help you prepare for exams.

9th
Edition

Keeping the
REPUBLIC

the essentials

Spencer Platt/Getty Images

In Your Own Words

After you've read this chapter, you will be able to

1.1 Describe the role that politics plays in determining how power and resources, including control of information, are distributed in a society.

1.2 Compare how power is distributed between citizens and government in different economic and political systems.

1.3 Explain the historical origins of American democracy and the ways that the available media controlled the political narrative.

1.4 Describe the enduring tension in the United States between self-interested human nature and public-spirited government and the way that has been shaped in a mediated world.

1.5 Apply the five steps of critical thinking to this book's themes of power and citizenship in American politics.

1
POLITICS: WHO GETS WHAT, AND HOW?

What's at Stake . . . in "Hashtag Activism"?

THE LAST THING THEY WANTED to do was become famous. Not this way, not now. But when seventeen of their classmates and teachers were murdered on February 14, 2018, by a disturbed former student, the students of Marjory Stoneman Douglas High School in Parkland, Florida, decided to make some noise.

They had seen this movie before. There had been mass shootings. Ever since they were little they had practiced what to do if someone showed up with a gun in their classrooms. There was even an armed guard on their campus. And still, it happened again. So they knew the ritual that would follow.

Every time this nation experiences a mass shooting, a grimly familiar routine follows. First there is unrelenting press coverage—of the dead, of the bereaved, of the shooter. Then those who lost loved ones make impassioned calls for more gun control and those who oppose gun control make equally

1

impassioned declarations that we should not politicize tragedy, that it is too soon to talk about it. There are funerals. The president (usually) makes a speech. Then the press moves on to the next big news and only the grieving are left to testify before Congress, create foundations in the names of their loved ones, and implore people not to forget. Lather, rinse, repeat.

But the MSD students knew the drill and were media savvy enough to figure out how to hack it. They were ready. Some, in the drama club, comfortable on stage; some, school journalists, eloquent and at ease with words; others, bright, articulate, privileged to attend a school with an embarrassment of extracurricular activities that had prepared them for their futures. Smart enough to know that their moment in the spotlight would be brief, they were determined to make it count.

The shooting was on a Wednesday. Cameron Kasky was so angry he took to Facebook, first to announce that he and his brother were safe and then to vent. "I just want people to understand what happened and understand that doing nothing will lead to nothing. Why is that so hard to grasp?" His social media posts caught the eye of CNN, which asked him to write an op-ed piece on Thursday, which led to television appearances. It became apparent to Kasky that his words were helping to shape the story of what had happened and what it meant. "People are listening and people care," Kasky wrote. "They're reporting the right things."[1]

To capitalize on that fickle national attention before it turned away, Kasky and several of his friends met that night to plan a social media campaign. By midnight they had a hashtag, #NeverAgain, social media accounts, and a message for politicians: legislate better background checks on gun buyers, or we will vote you out.

Meanwhile, MSD student Jaclyn Corin took to her own social media accounts to express her grief and anger at the loss of her friends. She, a girl who had never been political, also began to strategize. With the help of Florida Democratic congresswoman Debbie Wasserman Schultz, she planned a bus trip for one hundred students to Tallahassee to lobby state lawmakers.

By Friday, Corin and Kasky had joined forces, and on Saturday they added David Hogg, a student journalist who had conducted interviews while they were under fire, Sarah Chadwick, already famous for her angry, grief-filled tweets, and Emma González, whose speech at a local rally went viral. On Sunday they hit the morning talk shows to proclaim that the Never Again movement was planning the first March for Our Lives in Washington, D.C., on March 24.

Two weeks later (forever in the typical media cycle), the kids were still making news. Boycotts were organized to put pressure on companies doing business with the National Rifle Association (NRA), which blocked background checks.

A National School Walkout was planned for the one-month anniversary of the shooting. Thousands of students across the nation participated. Famous people donated large sums to help fund the March 24 March for Our Lives. As Dahlia Lithwick wrote in *Slate*, "These teens have—by most objective measures—used social media to change the conversation around guns and gun control in America."[2]

The March for Our Lives, when it happened, defied expectations. Huge crowds assembled not just in Washington but in eight hundred places around the world. The only adults who appeared on the D.C. stage were entertainers. The Parkland kids, knowing they had created a unique platform, had invited other kids whose lives had been touched by gun violence. Yolanda King, the nine-year-old granddaughter of Martin Luther King, confidently stood before tens of thousands to lead the crowd in a call and response:

> Spread the word.
> Have you heard?
> All across the nation.
> We
> Are going to be
> A great generation.

The event highlight was not words, eloquent as many of them were, but silence—four minutes and twenty-six seconds of uneasy, suspenseful silence as Emma González stood like a sculpture, tears tracking down her face, so that the crowd would experience the duration of the shooting that ended seventeen of her friends' and teachers' lives.

Just like the 2017 and 2018 Women's Marches, which brought out millions of pink-hatted women marching for human rights around the world; like Black Lives Matter, founded in 2013 to protest the unwarranted deaths of black men at the hands of police; like Occupy Wall Street, a 2011 movement to protest the unequal distribution of wealth in the United States; and like the It Gets Better Project, which works to convince LGBTQ youths that life does get better after the high school years, #NeverAgain was fueled and spread by social media.

Of course some older people know their way around the Internet, but #NeverAgain was the first mass movement planned and executed by digital natives, people who have never *not* known the world of digital media, for whom navigating digital terrain is second nature. It's not clear what the generation—what Yolanda King called "a great generation"—will be called by history. Gen Z, maybe? iGen? Generational divides are blurry, and few social scientists agree where the dividing lines fall. But the post-millennial generation—those born since the mid-1990s or thereabouts—has an amazing political skill set to use if, like the Parkland students, they choose to do so. They have the ability, as Lithwick said, to "change the conversation," or create a powerful political narrative that they can disseminate and that helps level the playing field with powerful opponents like the NRA.

Marching for Their Lives

At the March for Our Lives in Washington, D.C., student Emma González riveted the nation with her powerful speech. After her two-minute-long introductory remarks, she stood silent, with tears rolling down her face, for four and a half minutes, to mark the roughly six minutes and twenty seconds it took for the gunman to do so much damage. Despite the churn of the news cycle, she and her classmates held the nation's attention for weeks, working to change the narrative on gun control.

No movement can create change or defeat an opponent if it is only hashtag activism. Eventually, you have to put your vote where your # is. What is especially remarkable about the Never Again movement is that it emphasizes not just marching but voting. March for Our Life rallies throughout the summer gave them the chance to hone the narrative, register people to vote, and activate other students. Youth participation in the 2018 midterms soared.[3] Some writers are calling for the vote to be extended to those who are sixteen years old. Political scientist Jonathan Bernstein says that is a good idea because voting is "the training wheels of political participation."[4] By the time they are eighteen, kids are distracted by the drama of their lives and they tend not to want to be bothered.

In fact, since the military draft ended in 1973, young people have been notoriously uninvolved in politics, often seeing it as irrelevant to their lives and the things they really care about. Knowing that they pay little attention and tend not to vote in large numbers, politicians feel free to ignore their concerns, reinforcing their cynicism and apathy. Young people have turned out in larger numbers since the 2008 election of Barack Obama, however, and the Never Again movement promises to energize even more.

The American founders weren't crazy about the idea of mass movements, political demonstrations, or even political parties, but they did value political engagement and they knew that democracies needed care and attention in order to survive. In 1787, when Benjamin Franklin was asked by a woman what he and other founders of the Constitution had created, he replied, "A republic, madam, if you can keep it." Today, many commentators worry that we are not "keeping the republic" and that, as new generations who find politics a turn-off become disaffected adults, the system will start to unravel. As one writer says, "a nation that hates politics will not long thrive as a democracy."[5]

Yet protesters like Cameron Kasky, Emma González, David Hogg, and Yolanda King sound as committed to democracy as Benjamin Franklin could have wished, even though their efforts are not focused solely on voting or traditional methods of political engagement. Is a nation of these young activists a nation in trouble, or can movements begun via technology Franklin could not have imagined help to keep the republic? What, exactly, is at stake in *hashtag activism*—what one writer called a "netroots outcry" to follow an online call to political action? We return to this question after we learn more about the meaning of politics and the difference it makes in our lives. **≪**

HAVE you got grand ambitions for your life?

Do you want to found an Internet start-up and sell it for millions, be the investment banker that funds the project, achieve a powerful position in business, gain influence in high places, and spend money to make things happen? Perhaps you would like to make a difference in the world, heal the sick, fight for peace, feed the poor. Maybe you want to travel the world, learning languages and immersing yourself in new cultures and working abroad. Or maybe what you want from life is a good education; a well-paying job; a healthy family; a comfortable home; and a safe, prosperous, contented existence. Think politics has nothing to do with any of those things? Think again.

All the things that make those goals attainable—a strong national defense, good relations with other countries, student loans, economic prosperity, favorable mortgage rates, secure streets and neighborhoods, cheap and efficient public transportation, affordable health care and family leave protections—are influenced by or are the products of politics.

Yet, if you pay attention to the news, politics may seem like one long and crazy reality show: eternal bickering and finger-pointing by public servants who seem more interested in gaining power over their ideological opponents than actually solving our collective problems. Increasingly, it appears that political actors with the big bucks have more influence over the process than those of us with normal bank accounts. Public service, which we would like to think of as a noble activity, can take on all the worst characteristics of the business world, where we expect people to be greedy and self-interested. Can this America really be the heritage of Thomas Jefferson and Abraham Lincoln? Can this be the "world's greatest democracy" at work?

In this chapter, we get to the heart of what politics is, how it relates to other concepts such as power, government, rules, norms, economics, and citizenship, and how all of these things are mediated by the ever-present channels of information that define the way we live in the digital age. We propose that politics can best be understood as the struggle over who gets power and resources in society, and that a major resource is control of the narrative, or story, that defines each contestant. There is not enough of all that power and influence to go around, so inevitably politics produces winners and losers. Much of the reason it can look so ugly is that people fight desperately to be the former and to create and perpetuate narratives that celebrate their wins and put the best face possible on their losses. It can get pretty confusing for the average observer.

As we will see, it is the beauty of a democracy that *all* the people, including everyday people like us, get to fight for what they want. Not everyone can win, of course, and many never come close. There is no denying that some people bring resources to the process that give them an edge, and that the rules give advantages to some groups of people over others. But as the *What's at Stake . . . ?* shows, what makes living today so different from previous eras is that we all have some access to the multiple channels of information through which battles over political narratives take place. The people who pay attention, who learn the rules and how to use those communication channels effectively, can increase their chances of getting what they want, whether it is restrictions on ownership of assault weapons, a lower personal tax bill, greater pollution controls, a more aggressive foreign policy, safer streets, a better-educated population, or more public parks. If they become very skilled citizens, they can even begin to change the rules so that people like them have more control of the rules and narratives and a greater chance to end up winners in the high-stakes game we call politics.

The government our founders created for us gives us a remarkable playing field on which to engage in that game. Like any other politicians, the designers of the American system were caught up in the struggle to create a narrative that justified their claim to power and resources, and in the desire to write laws that would maximize the chances that they, and people like them, would be winners in the new system. Nonetheless, they crafted a government impressive for its ability to generate compromise and stability, and also for its potential to realize freedom and prosperity for its citizens.

balancing act btwn order + freedom

WHAT IS POLITICS?

A peaceful means of determining who gets power and influence in society

Over two thousand years ago, the Greek philosopher Aristotle said that we are political animals, and political animals we seem destined to remain. The truth is that politics is a fundamental and complex human activity. In some ways it is our capacity to be political—to cooperate, bargain, and compromise—that helps distinguish us from all the other animals out there. Politics may have its baser moments, but it also allows us to reach more exalted heights than we could ever achieve alone, from dedicating a new public library or building a national highway system, to curing deadly diseases or exploring the stars.

Since this book is about politics, in all its glory as well as its disgrace, we need to begin with a clear understanding of the word. One of the most famous definitions, put forth by the well-known late political scientist Harold Lasswell, is still one of the best, and we use it to frame our discussion throughout this book. Lasswell defined **politics** as "who gets what when and how."[6] Politics is a way of determining, without recourse to violence, who gets power and resources in society, and how they get them. **Power** is the ability to get other people to do what you want them to do. The resources in question here might be government jobs, tax revenues, laws that help you get your way, or public policies that work to your advantage. A major political resource that helps people to gain and maintain power is the ability to control the **media**, not just the press and television but also the multiple channels created by companies like Google, Facebook, and Apple through which people get information about politics and that may actually affect the information we get. These days we live in a world of so many complex information networks that sorting out and keeping track of what is happening around us is a task in itself. Anyone who can influence the stories that are told has a big advantage.

Politics provides a process through which we can try to arrange our collective lives in some kind of **social order** so that we can live without crashing into each other at every turn, and to provide ourselves with goods and services we could not obtain alone. But politics is also about getting our own way. The way we choose may be a noble goal for society or pure self-interest, but the struggle we engage in is a political struggle. Because politics is about power and other scarce resources, there will always be winners and losers in

politics who gets what, when, and how; a process of determining how power and resources are distributed in a society without recourse to violence

power the ability to get other people to do what you want

media the channels—including television, radio, newspapers, and the Internet—through which information is sent and received

social order the way we organize and live our collective lives

politics. If we could always get our own way, politics would disappear. It is because we cannot always get what we want that politics exists.

Our capacity to be political gives us tools with which to settle disputes about the social order and to allocate scarce resources. The tools of politics are compromise and cooperation; discussion and debate; deal making, bargaining, storytelling; even, sometimes, bribery and deceit. We use those tools to agree on the principles that should guide our handling of power and other scarce resources and to live our collective lives according to those principles. Because there are many competing narratives about how to manage power—who should have it, how it should be used, how it should be transferred—agreement on those principles can break down.

The tools of politics do not include violence. When people drop bombs, blow themselves up, or fly airplanes into buildings, they have tried to impose their ideas about the social order through nonpolitical means. That may be because the channels of politics have failed, because they cannot agree on basic principles, because they don't share a common understanding of what counts as negotiation and so cannot craft compromises, because they are unwilling to compromise, or because they don't really care about deal making at all—they just want to impose their will or make a point. The threat of violence may be a political tool used as leverage to get a deal, but when violence is employed, politics has broken down. Indeed, the human history of warfare attests to the fragility of political life.

It is easy to imagine what a world without politics would be like. There would be no resolution or compromise between conflicting interests, because those are political activities. There would be no agreements struck, bargains made, or alliances formed. Unless there were enough of every valued resource to go around, or unless the world were big enough that we could live our lives without coming into contact with other human beings, life would be constant conflict—what the philosopher Thomas Hobbes called in the seventeenth century a "war of all against all." Individuals, unable to cooperate with one another (because cooperation is essentially political), would have no option but to resort to brute force to settle disputes and allocate resources. Politics is essential to our living a civilized life.

> **government** a system or organization for exercising authority over a body of people
>
> **authority** power that is recognized as legitimate, or right
>
> **legitimate** accepted as "right" or proper

Water Under the Bridge
Political parties and their leaders frequently clash on issues and ideology—but when politics is out of the picture, the nature of the game can change. President Barack Obama and House Speaker John Boehner lampooned their retirement from public life in a viral video for the White House Correspondents' Dinner in 2016.

POLITICS AND GOVERNMENT

Although the words *politics* and *government* are sometimes used interchangeably, they refer to different things. Politics, we know, is a process or an activity through which power and resources are gained and lost. **Government**, by contrast, is a system or organization for exercising authority over a body of people.

American politics is what happens in the halls of Congress, on the campaign trail, at Washington cocktail parties, and in neighborhood association meetings. It is the making of promises, deals, and laws. American government is the Constitution and the institutions set up by the Constitution for the exercise of authority by the American people, over the American people.

Authority is power that citizens view as **legitimate**, or "right"—power to which we have given our implicit consent. Think of it this way: as children, we probably did as our parents told us, or submitted to their punishment if we didn't, because we recognized their authority over us. As we became adults, we started to claim that our parents had less authority over us, that we could do what we wanted. We no longer saw their power as wholly legitimate or appropriate. Governments exercise authority because people recognize them as legitimate even if they often do not like doing what they are told (paying taxes, for instance). When governments cease to be regarded as legitimate, the result may be revolution or civil war, unless the state is powerful enough to suppress all opposition.

RULES AND INSTITUTIONS

Government is shaped by the process of politics, but it in turn provides the rules and institutions that shape the way politics continues to operate. The rules and institutions of government have a profound effect on how power is distributed and who wins and who loses in the political arena. Life is different for people in other countries not only because they speak different languages and eat different foods but also because their governments establish rules that cause life to be lived in different ways.

Rules can be thought of as the *how* in the definition "who gets what . . . and how." They are directives that determine how resources are allocated and how collective action takes place—that is, they determine how we try to get the things we want. The point of the rules is to provide some framework for us to solve without violence the problems that our collective lives generate.

Because the rules we choose can influence which people will get what they want most often, understanding the rules is crucial to understanding politics. Consider for a moment the impact a change of rules would have on the outcome of the sport of basketball, for instance. What if the average height of the players could be no more than 5'10"? What if the baskets were lowered? What if foul shots counted for two points rather than one? Basketball would be a very different game, and the teams recruited would look quite unlike the teams for which we now cheer. So it is with governments and politics: change the people who are allowed to vote or the length of time a person can serve in office, and the political process and the potential winners and losers change drastically.

Rules can be official—laws that are passed, signed, and entered into the books; amendments that are ratified; decisions made by bureaucrats; or judgments handed down by the courts. Less visible but no less important are **norms**, the tacitly understood rules about acceptable political behavior, ways of doing things, boundaries between the branches, and traditional practices that grease the wheels of politics and keep them running smoothly. Because norms are understood but not explicitly written down, we often don't even recognize them until they are broken.

Let's take an example close to home. Say it's Thanksgiving dinner time and your brother decides he wants the mashed potatoes on the other side of the table. Instead of asking to have them passed, imagine that he climbs up on the table and walks across the top of it with his big, dirty feet, retrieves the potatoes, clomps back across the table, jumps down, takes his seat, and serves himself some potatoes. Everyone is aghast, right? What he has just done just isn't done. But when you challenge him, he says, "What, there's a rule against doing that? I got what I wanted, didn't I?" and you have to admit there isn't and he did. But the reason there is no broken rule is because nobody ever thought one would be necessary. You never imagined that someone would walk across the table because everyone knows there is a norm against doing that, and until your brother broke that norm, no one ever bothered to articulate it. And getting what you want is not generally an acceptable justification for bad behavior.

Just because norms are not written down doesn't mean they are not essential for the survival of a government or the process of politics. In some cases they are far more essential than written laws. A family of people who routinely stomp across the table to get the food they want would not long want to share meals; eating alone would be far more comfortable.

We can think of **institutions** as the *where* of the political struggle, though Lasswell didn't include a "where" in his definition. They are the organizations where government power is exercised. In the United States, our rules provide for the institutions of a representative democracy—that is, rule by the elected representatives of the people, and for a federal political system. Our Constitution lays the foundation for the institutions of Congress, the presidency, the courts, and the bureaucracy as a stage on which the drama of politics plays itself out. Other systems might call for different institutions— perhaps an all-powerful parliament, or a monarch, or even a committee of rulers.

These complicated systems of rules and institutions do not appear out of thin air. They are carefully designed by the founders of different systems to create the kinds of society they think will be stable and prosperous, but also where people like themselves are likely to be winners. Remember that not only the rules but also the institutions we choose influence who most easily and most often get their own way.

POWER, NARRATIVES, AND MEDIA

From the start of human existence, an essential function of communication has been recording events, giving meaning to them and creating a story, or narrative, about how they fit into the past and stretch into the future. It is human nature to tell stories, to capture our experiential knowledge and

---

rules directives that specify how resources will be distributed or what procedures govern collective activity

norms informal, unwritten expectations that guide behavior and support formal rule systems; often most noticeable when broken

institutions organizations in which government power is exercised

beliefs and weave them together in ways that give larger meaning to our lives. Native peoples of many lands do it with their legends; the Greeks and Romans did it with their myths; the Jews, Christians, Muslims, and other major religious groups do it with their holy texts; and the Grimms did it with their fairy tales. Human beings tell stories. It's what we do, and it gives us our history and a way of passing that history down to new generations.

A major part of politics is about competing to have your narrative accepted as the authoritative account. Control of political information has always been a crucial resource when it comes to making and upholding a claim that one should be able to tell other people how to live their lives, but it used to be a power reserved for a few. Creation and dissemination of **political narratives**—the stories that people believe about who has power, who wants power, who deserves power, and what someone has done to get and maintain power—were the prerogative of authoritative sources like priests, kings, and their agents.

Through much of our common history, the storytellers of those narratives were given special status. They were wise men or women, shamans, prophets, oracles, priests, and rabbis. And they were frequently in the service of chiefs, kings, emperors, and other people of enormous power. It's no accident that the storytellers frequently told narratives that bolstered the status quo and kept the power structure in place. The storytellers and the power holders had a monopoly on control for so much of human history because books were in scarce supply and few people could read in any case or had the leisure to amass facts to challenge the prevailing narratives. The **gatekeepers** of information—those who determined what news got reported and how—were very few.

Before the seventeenth-century era known as the Enlightenment, there may have been competing narratives about who had claims to power, but they were not that hard to figure out. People's allegiance to power was based on tribal loyalties, religious faith, or conquest. Governments were legitimate through the authority of God or the sword, and that was that. Because most people then were illiterate, that narrative was *mediated*, that is, passed to people through channels that could shape and influence it. Information flowed mostly through medieval clergy and monarchs, *the very people who had a vested interest in getting people to believe it.*

Even when those theories of legitimacy changed, information was still easily controlled because literacy rates were low and horses and wind determined the speed of communication until the advent of steam engines and radios. Early newspapers were read aloud, shared, and reshared, and a good deal of the news of the day was delivered from the pulpit. As we will see when we discuss the American founding, there were lively debates about whether independence was a good idea and what kind of political system should replace the colonial power structure, but by the time information reached citizens, it had been largely processed and filtered by those higher up the power ladder. Even the American rebels were elite and powerful men who could control their own narratives. Remember the importance of this when we read the story behind the Declaration of Independence in Chapter 3.

These days, we take for granted the ease with which we can communicate ideas to others all over the globe. Just a hundred years ago, radio was state of the art and television had yet to be invented. Today many of us carry access to a world of information and instant communication in our pockets.

When we talk about the channels through which information flows, and the ways that the channel itself might alter or control the narrative, we are referring to media. Just like a medium is a person through whom some people try to communicate with those who have died, media (the plural of medium) are channels of communication, as mentioned earlier. The integrity of the medium is critical. A scam artist

> **political narrative** a persuasive story about the nature of power, who should have it, and how it should be used
>
> **gatekeepers** journalists and the media elite who determine which news stories are covered and which are not

FIGURE 1.1
A Comparison of Economic Systems

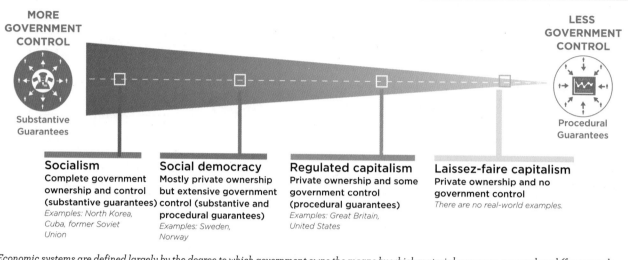

MORE GOVERNMENT CONTROL

Substantive Guarantees

LESS GOVERNMENT CONTROL

Procedural Guarantees

Socialism
Complete government ownership and control (substantive guarantees)
Examples: North Korea, Cuba, former Soviet Union

Social democracy
Mostly private ownership but extensive government control (substantive and procedural guarantees)
Examples: Sweden, Norway

Regulated capitalism
Private ownership and some government control (procedural guarantees)
Examples: Great Britain, United States

Laissez-faire capitalism
Private ownership and no government control
There are no real-world examples.

Economic systems are defined largely by the degree to which government owns the means by which material resources are produced (for example, factories and industry) and controls economic decision making. On a scale ranging from socialism—complete government ownership and control of the economy (on the left)—to laissez-faire capitalism—complete individual ownership and control of the economy (on the right)—social democracies would be located in the center. These hybrid systems are characterized by mostly private ownership of the means of production but considerable government control over economic decisions.

might make money off the desire of grieving people to contact a lost loved one by making up the information she passes on. The monarch and clergy who channeled the narrative of the Holy Roman Empire were motivated by their wish to hold on to power. Think about water running through a pipe. Maybe the pipe is made of lead, or is rusty, or has leaks. Depending on the integrity of the pipe, the water we get will be toxic or colored or limited. *In the same way, the narratives and information we get can be altered by the way they are mediated, by the channels, or the media, through which we receive them.*

As we will see, in today's digital world, there are so many channels of information that it is all the more important that people check the integrity of the media they use in order to understand the narratives those media may be pushing.

POLITICS AND ECONOMICS

Whereas politics is concerned with the distribution of power and resources and the control of information in society, **economics** is concerned specifically with the production and distribution of society's wealth—material goods such as bread, toothpaste, and housing, and services such as medical care, education, and entertainment. Because both politics and economics focus on the distribution of society's resources, political and economic questions often get confused in contemporary life. Questions about how to pay for government, about government's role in the economy, and about whether

government or the private sector should provide certain services have political and economic dimensions. Because there are no clear-cut distinctions here, it can be difficult to keep these terms straight. The various forms of possible economic systems are shown in Figure 1.1.

The processes of politics and economics can be engaged in procedurally or substantively. In procedural political and economic systems, the legitimacy of the outcome is based on the legitimacy of the process that produced it. In substantive political and economic systems, the legitimacy of the outcome depends on how widely accepted is the narrative the government tells about who should have what. The outcome is based on the decision of a powerful person or people, not a process people believe is impartial. In procedural systems, the means (process) justifies the ends; in substantive systems, the ends justify the means.

CAPITALISM Capitalism is a procedural economic system based on the working of the *market*—the process of supply and demand. In a pure **capitalist economy**, all the means

> **economics** production and distribution of a society's material resources and services
>
> **capitalist economy** an economic system in which the market determines production, distribution, and price decisions, and property is privately owned

used to produce material resources (industry, business, and land, for instance) are owned privately, and decisions about production and distribution are left to individuals operating through the free-market process. Capitalist economies rely on the market to decide how much of a given item to produce or how much to charge for it. In capitalist countries, people do not believe that the government is capable of making such judgments (like how much toothpaste to produce), so they want to keep such decisions out of the hands of government and in the hands of individuals who they believe know best what they want. The most extreme philosophy that corresponds with this belief is called **laissez-faire capitalism**, from a French term that, loosely translated, means "let people do as they wish." The government has no economic role at all in such a system.

Building a Better Rocket?

SpaceX, headed by Tesla Motors CEO Elon Musk, is a private company that hopes in the near future to send manned missions to Mars. As part of a test of its new rocket technology, SpaceX launched this Tesla (with a dummy in the driver's seat) into orbit around the sun in 2018. Capitalism enables ambitious entrepreneurs like Musk, but technological advances like space travel would not be possible (or profitable) without the years—and billions of dollars—of previous government investment in space technology.

SpaceX via Getty Images

Like most other countries today, the United States has a system of **regulated capitalism**. It maintains a capitalist economy and individual freedom from government interference remains the norm, but it allows government to step in and regulate the economy to guarantee individual rights and to provide **procedural guarantees** that the rules will work smoothly and fairly. Although in theory the market ought to provide everything that people need and want, and should regulate itself as well, sometimes it fails. The notion that the market, an impartial process, has "failed" is a somewhat substantive one—it is the decision of a government that the outcome is not acceptable and should be replaced or altered to fit a substantive vision of what the outcome should be. When markets have ups and downs—periods of growth followed by periods of slowdown or recession—individuals and businesses look to government for economic security. If the market fails to produce some goods and services, like schools or highways, individuals expect the government to step in to produce them (using taxpayer funds). It is not very substantive—the market process still largely makes all the distributional decisions—but it is not laissez faire capitalism, either.

SOCIALISM In a **socialist economy** like that of the former Soviet Union, economic decisions are made not by individuals through the market but rather by politicians, based on their judgment of what society needs. In these systems the state often owns the factories, land, and other resources necessary to produce wealth. Rather than trusting the market process to determine the proper distribution of material resources among individuals, politicians decide what the distribution ought to be—according to some principle like equality, need, or political reward—and then create economic policy to bring about that outcome. In other words, they emphasize not procedural guarantees of fair rules and process, but rather **substantive guarantees** of what they believe to be fair outcomes.

The societies that have tried to put these theories into practice have ended up with very repressive political systems, even though Karl Marx, the most famous of the theorists associated with socialism, hoped that eventually humankind

---

laissez-faire capitalism an economic system in which the market makes all decisions and the government plays no role

regulated capitalism a market system in which the government intervenes to protect rights and make procedural guarantees

procedural guarantees government assurance that the rules will work smoothly and treat everyone fairly, with no promise of particular outcomes

socialist economy an economic system in which the state determines production, distribution, and price decisions, and property is government owned

substantive guarantees government assurance of particular outcomes or results

AP Photo/Mark Schiefelbein

President for Life

In March 2018, China's legislature, the National People's Congress, voted to change the country's constitution to eliminate the existing ten-year presidential term limit. This step reaffirmed the authoritarianism in China's political culture and set up President Xi Jinping as a president for life.

would evolve to a point where each individual had control over his or her own life—a radical form of democracy. Since the socialist economies of the former Soviet Union and Eastern Europe have fallen apart, socialism has been left with few supporters, although some nations, such as China, North Korea, and Cuba, still claim allegiance to it. Even China, however, introduced market-based reforms in the 1970s and in 2015 ranked as the world's second largest economy, after the United States.

SOCIAL DEMOCRACY Some countries in Western Europe, especially the Scandinavian nations of Norway, Denmark, and Sweden, have developed hybrid economic systems. As noted in Figure 1.1, these systems represent something of a middle ground between socialist and capitalist systems. Primarily capitalist, in that they trust the market process and they believe most property can be held privately, proponents of **social democracy** argue nonetheless that the equitable outcomes often promoted by socialism are attractive and can be brought about by democratic reform. Believing that the economy does not have to be owned by the state for its effects to be controlled by the state, social democratic countries attempt to strike a difficult balance between providing substantive guarantees of fair outcomes and procedural guarantees of fair rules.

Since World War II, the citizens of many Western European nations have elected social democrats to office, where they have enacted policies to bring about more equality—for instance, the elimination of poverty and unemployment, better housing, and adequate health care for all. Even where social democratic governments are voted

out of office, such programs have proved so popular that it is often difficult for new leaders to alter them. Few people in the United States would identify themselves with social democracy, as presidential candidate Bernie Sanders found out in 2016, although his campaign did help people understand that some versions of socialism did not require a wholesale elimination of capitalism and some of his proposals found their way into the Democratic Party platform.

In Your Own Words Describe the role that politics plays in determining how power and resources, including control of information, are distributed in a society.

POLITICAL SYSTEMS AND THE CONCEPT OF CITIZENSHIP

Competing ideas about power and the social order, different models of governing

Just as there are different kinds of economic systems on the substantive to procedural scale, there are many sorts of political systems, based on competing ideas about who should have power and what the social order should be—that is, how much substantive regulation there should be over individual decision-making. For our purposes, we can divide political systems into two types: those in which the government has the substantive power to impose a particular social order, deciding how individuals ought to behave, and those procedural systems in which individuals exercise personal power over most of their own behavior and ultimately over government as well. These two types of systems are different not just in a theoretical sense. The differences have very real implications for the people who live in them; the notion of citizenship (or the lack of it) is tied closely to the kind of political system a nation has.

Figure 1.2 compares these systems, ranging from the more substantive authoritarian governments that potentially have total power over their subjects to more procedural nonauthoritarian governments that permit citizens to limit the state's power by claiming rights that the government must protect. Figure 1.3 shows what happens when we overlie our economic and political figures, giving us a model of most of the world's political/economic systems. Note that when we say *model*, we are talking about abstractions from reality used as a tool to help us understand. We

> **social democracy** a hybrid system combining a capitalist economy and a government that supports equality

FIGURE 1.2
A Comparison of Political Systems

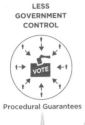

LESS GOVERNMENT CONTROL

Procedural Guarantees

Anarchy
No government or manmade laws; individuals do as they please.
There are no real-world examples.

Nonauthoritarian system
(such as democracy)
Individuals (citizens) decide how to live their lives. Government role is limited to procedural guarantees of individual rights.
Examples: United States, Sweden, Japan, South Korea, India

Authoritarian system
Government decides how individuals (subjects) should live their lives and imposes a substantive vision.
Examples: China, North Korea, Cuba, Saudi Arabia

MORE GOVERNMENT CONTROL
Substantive Guarantees

Political systems are defined by the extent to which individual citizens or governments decide what the social order should look like—that is, how people should live their collective, noneconomic lives. Except for anarchies, every system allots a role to government to regulate individual behavior—for example, to prohibit murder, rape, and theft. But beyond such basic regulation, they differ radically on who gets to determine how individuals live their lives, and whether government's role is simply to provide procedural guarantees that protect individuals' rights to make their own decisions or to provide a much more substantive view of how individuals should behave.

---

authoritarian governments systems in which the state holds all power over the social order

totalitarian a system in which absolute power is exercised over every aspect of life

authoritarian capitalism a system in which the state allows people economic freedom but maintains stringent social regulations to limit noneconomic behavior

---

don't pretend that all the details of the world are captured in a single two-dimensional figure, but we can get a better idea of the similarities and differences by looking at them this way.

AUTHORITARIAN SYSTEMS

Authoritarian governments give ultimate power to the state rather than to the people to decide how they ought to live their lives. By "authoritarian governments," we usually mean those in which the people cannot effectively claim rights against the state; where the state chooses to exercise its power, the people have no choice but to submit to its will.

Authoritarian governments can take various forms: sovereignty can be vested in an individual (dictatorship or monarchy), in God (theocracy), in the state itself (fascism), or in a ruling class (oligarchy). When a system combines an authoritarian government with a socialist economy, we say that the system is **totalitarian** (in the lower-left quadrant of Figure 1.3). As in the earlier example of the former Soviet Union, a totalitarian system exercises its power over every part of society—economic, social, political, and moral—leaving little or no private realm for individuals.

But an authoritarian state may also limit its own power. In such cases, it may deny individuals rights in those spheres where it chooses to act, but it may leave large areas of society, such as a capitalist economy, free from government interference. China and Singapore are examples of this type of **authoritarian capitalism**, in the lower-right quadrant of Figure 1.3. In these systems, people have considerable economic freedom but stringent social regulations limit their noneconomic behavior.

Authoritarian governments often pay lip service to the people, but when push comes to shove, as it usually does in such states, the people have no effective power against the government. Again, to use the terminology we introduced earlier, government does not provide guarantees of fair processes for individuals; it guarantees a substantive vision of what life will be like—what individuals will believe, how they will act, what they will choose. Consequently, in authoritarian governments, the narrative is not up for debate. The rulers set the narrative and control the flow of information so that it supports their version of why they should have power. Subjects of these governments accept the narrative for a variety of reasons: there is no free media, communication with the outside world is limited, or they may be afraid to do otherwise. Authoritarian rulers often use punishment to coerce uncooperative subjects into obedience.

FIGURE 1.3

Political and Economic Systems

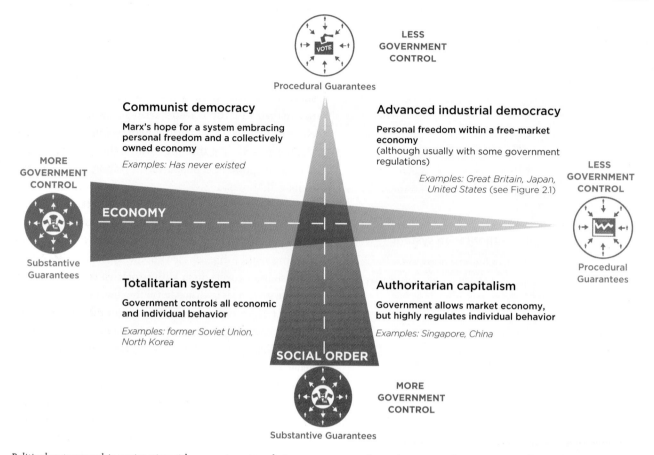

Procedural Guarantees

LESS GOVERNMENT CONTROL

MORE GOVERNMENT CONTROL

LESS GOVERNMENT CONTROL

MORE GOVERNMENT CONTROL

Substantive Guarantees

Procedural Guarantees

Substantive Guarantees

Communist democracy

Marx's hope for a system embracing personal freedom and a collectively owned economy

Examples: Has never existed

Advanced industrial democracy

Personal freedom within a free-market economy
(although usually with some government regulations)

Examples: Great Britain, Japan, United States (see Figure 2.1)

ECONOMY

Totalitarian system

Government controls all economic and individual behavior

Examples: former Soviet Union, North Korea

Authoritarian capitalism

Government allows market economy, but highly regulates individual behavior

Examples: Singapore, China

SOCIAL ORDER

Political systems work in conjunction with economic systems, but government control over the economy does not necessarily translate into tight control over the social order. We have identified four possible combinations of these systems, signified by the labeled points in each quadrant. These points are approximate, however, and some nations cannot be classified so easily. Sweden is an advanced industrial democracy by most measures, for instance, but because of its commitment to substantive economic values, it would be located much closer to the vertical axis.

NONAUTHORITARIAN SYSTEMS

In nonauthoritarian systems, ultimate power rests with individuals to make decisions concerning their lives. The most extreme form of nonauthoritarianism is called **anarchy**. Anarchists would do away with government and laws altogether. People advocate anarchy because they value the freedom to do whatever they want more than they value the order and security that governments provide by forbidding or regulating certain kinds of behavior. Few people are true anarchists, however. Anarchy may sound attractive in theory, but the inherent difficulties of the position make it hard to practice. For instance, how could you even organize a revolution to get rid of government without some rules about who is to do what and how decisions are to be made?

DEMOCRACY A less extreme form of nonauthoritarian government, and one much more familiar to us, is **democracy** (from the Greek *demos*, meaning "people"). In democracies, government is not external to the people, as it is in authoritarian systems; in a fundamental sense, government *is* the people. Democracies are based on the principle of **popular sovereignty**; that is, there is no power higher than the people and, in the United States, the document

> **anarchy** the absence of government and law
>
> **democracy** government that vests power in the people
>
> **popular sovereignty** the concept that the citizens are the ultimate source of political power

establishing their authority, the Constitution. The central idea here is that no government is considered legitimate unless the governed consent to it, and people are not truly free unless they live under a law of their own making.

Recognizing that collective life usually calls for some restrictions on what individuals may do (laws forbidding murder or theft, for instance), democracies nevertheless try to maximize freedom for the individuals who live under them. Although they generally make decisions through some sort of majority rule, democracies still provide procedural guarantees to preserve individual rights—usually protections of due process and minority rights. This means that if individuals living in a democracy feel their rights have been violated, they have the right to ask government to remedy the situation.

There are many institutional variations on democracy. Some democracies make the legislature (the representatives of the people) the most important authority; some retain a monarch with limited powers; and some hold referenda at the national level to get direct feedback on how the people want the government to act on specific issues.

Most democratic forms of government, because of their commitment to procedural values, practice a capitalist form of economics. Fledgling democracies may rely on a high degree of government economic regulation, but **advanced industrial democracies** (in the upper-right quadrant of Figure 1.3) combine a considerable amount of personal freedom with a free-market (though still usually regulated) economy.

The people of many Western countries have found the idea of democracy persuasive enough to found their governments on it. Especially since the mid-1980s, democracy has been spreading rapidly through the rest of the world as the preferred form of government. No longer the primary province of industrialized Western nations, attempts at democratic governance now extend into Asia, Latin America, Africa, Eastern Europe, and the republics of the former Soviet Union.

It is rare to find a country that is truly committed to democratic freedom that also tries to regulate the economy

> **advanced industrial democracy** a system in which a democratic government allows citizens a considerable amount of personal freedom and maintains a free-market (though still usually regulated) economy
>
> **communist democracy** a utopian system in which property is communally owned and all decisions are made democratically
>
> **populism** social movements based on the idea that power has been concentrated illegitimately among elites at the people's expense

heavily. The philosopher Karl Marx believed that radical democracy would coexist with communally owned property, in a form of **communist democracy** (in the upper-left quadrant of Figure 1.3), but such a system has never existed, and most real-world systems fall elsewhere in Figure 1.3.

DEMOCRATIC NARRATIVES Generally, the narrative of democracy is based on the idea that power comes from the people. This is misleadingly simple, however. Some democratic narratives hold that all the people should agree on political decisions. This rule of unanimity makes decision making very slow, and sometimes impossible, since everyone has to be persuaded to agree. Even when majority rule is the norm, there are many ways of calculating the majority. Is it 50 percent plus one? Two-thirds? Three-fourths? Decision making becomes increasingly difficult as the number of people who are required to agree grows. And, of course, majority rule brings with it the problem of minority rights. If the majority gets its way, what happens to the rights of those who disagree?

Not surprisingly, there are multiple narratives about how much and in what ways popular power should be exercised in a democracy. They argue for power at the top, in groups, and for individuals. For instance, *elite democracy* is a narrative that sees democracy merely as a process of choosing among competing leaders; for the average citizen, input ends after the leader is chosen.[7]Advocates of the narrative of *pluralist democracy* argue that what is important is not so much individual participation but rather membership in groups that participate in government decision making on their members' behalf.[8] Supporters of the narrative of *participatory democracy* claim that individuals have the right to control *all* the circumstances of their lives, and direct democratic participation should take place not only in government but in industry, education, and community affairs as well.[9] For advocates of this view, democracy is more than a way to make decisions: it is a way of life, an end in itself. In practice, those who argue for democratic government probably include elements of more than one of these democratic narratives; they are not mutually exclusive.

Ironically, some present-day democracies are now experiencing backlashes of **populism**—social movements that promote the narrative that democracy has concentrated power at an elite level and neglected the concerns of ordinary people. Because populism is a narrative based on the grievances of people who believe they are getting less than they deserve, it is relatively easy for an authoritarian figure to exploit. Often these movements backfire on the people who support them and result in the seizing of authoritarian power by an individual or group who claims to wield it in the name of the people but does not. Turkey and Venezuela are extreme examples of this, but there are serious populist movements in many democratic countries today, including the United States.

THE ROLE OF THE PEOPLE

What is important about the political and economic systems we have been sorting out here is that they have a direct impact on the lives of the people who live in them. So far we have given a good deal of attention to the latter parts of Lasswell's definition of politics. But easily as important as the *what* and the *how* in Lasswell's formulation is the *who*. Underlying the different political theories we have looked at are fundamental differences in the powers and opportunities possessed by everyday people.

THE PEOPLE AS SUBJECTS In authoritarian systems, the people are **subjects** of their government. They possess no rights that protect them from that government; they must do whatever the government says or face the consequences, without any other recourse. They have obligations to the state but no rights or privileges to offset those obligations. They may be winners or losers in government decisions, but they have very little control over which it may be.

THE PEOPLE AS CITIZENS Everyday people in democratic systems have a potentially powerful role to play. They are more than mere subjects; they are **citizens**, or members of a political community with rights as well as obligations. Democratic theory says that power is drawn from the people, that the people are sovereign, that they must consent to be governed, and that their government must respond to their will. In practical terms, this may not seem to mean much, since not consenting doesn't necessarily give us the right to disobey government. It does give us the option of leaving, however, and seeking a more congenial set of rules elsewhere.

Theoretically, democracies are ruled by "the people," but different democracies have at times been very selective about whom they count as citizens. Just because a system is called a democracy is no guarantee that all or even most of its residents possess the status of citizen.

In democratic systems, the rules of government can provide for all sorts of different roles for those they designate as citizens. At a minimum, citizens possess certain rights, or powers to act, that government cannot limit, although these rights vary in different democracies. Citizens of democracies also possess obligations or responsibilities to the public realm. They have the obligation to obey the law, for instance, once they have consented to the government (even if that consent amounts only to not leaving); they may also have the obligation to pay taxes, serve in the military, or sit on juries. Some theorists argue that truly virtuous citizens should put community interests ahead of personal interests.

In Your Own Words Compare how power is distributed between citizens and government in different economic and political systems.

ORIGINS OF DEMOCRACY IN AMERICA

From divine right to social contract

Government in the United States is the product of particular decisions the founders made about the who, what, and how of American politics. There was nothing inevitable about those decisions and, had the founders decided otherwise, our system would look very different indeed.

Given the world in which the founders lived, democracy was not an obvious choice for them, and many scholars argue that in some respects the system they created is not very democratic. We can see this more clearly if we understand the intellectual heritage of the early Americans, their historical experience, and the theories about government that informed them.

EUROPEAN SOURCES OF DEMOCRATIC THOUGHT AND PRACTICE

The heyday of democracy, of course, was ancient Athens, from about 500 to 300 BCE. Even Athenian democracy was a pretty selective business. To be sure, it was rule by "the people," but "the people" was defined narrowly to exclude women, slaves, youth, and resident aliens. Athenian democracy was not built on values of equality, even of opportunity, except for the 10 percent of the population defined as citizens.

subjects individuals who are obliged to submit to a government authority against which they have no rights

citizens members of a political community with both rights and responsibilities

We can see parallels here to early colonial American democracy, which restricted participation in political affairs to a relatively small number of white men with wealth and particular religious beliefs.

Limited as Athenian democracy was, it was positively wide open compared to most forms of government that existed during the Middle Ages, from roughly AD 600 to 1500. During this period, monarchs gradually consolidated their power over their subjects, and some even challenged the greatest political power of the time, the Catholic Church. Authoritarianism was a lot easier to pull off when few people could read; maintaining a single narrative about power that enforced authoritarian rule was relatively simple. For instance, as we see in Chapter 3, the narrative of

ANIS MILI/AFP/Getty Images

Democracy Is Messy

The "Arab Spring" uprisings that spread across the Middle East in 2011 fueled hopes that democracy would take root in Middle Eastern countries, but they also illustrate just how difficult it can be to establish and maintain democracy. In 2018, demonstrators in Tunis, Tunisia, mark the seventh anniversary of the Tunisian Revolution. The years following the revolution were marked by terrorist attacks and declared states of emergency, before the country achieved successful elections in 2014.

the **divine right of kings** kept monarchs in Europe on their thrones by insisting that those rulers were God's representatives on earth and that to say otherwise was not just a crime but a sin.

Following the development of the printing press in 1439, more people gained literacy. Information could be mediated independently of those in power, and competing narratives could grab a foothold. Martin Luther promoted the narrative behind the Protestant Reformation (1517–1648) to weaken the power of the Catholic Church. Luther's ideas spread and were embraced by a number of European monarchs, leading to a split between Catholic and Protestant countries. Where the Catholic Church was seen as unnecessary, it lost political as well as religious clout, and its decline paved the way for new ideas about the

world. Those new ideas came with the Enlightenment period of the late 1600s and 1700s, when ideas about science and the possibilities of knowledge began to blow away the shadows and cobwebs of medieval superstition. Enlightenment philosophy said that human beings were not at the mercy of a world they could not understand, but rather, as rational human beings, they could learn the secrets of nature and harness the world to do their bidding. The political narratives of **classical liberalism** that emerged from the Enlightenment emphasized individual rights, and nonauthoritarianism.

> ### Do subjects enjoy any advantages that citizens don't have?

THE SOCIAL CONTRACT

One of the key classical liberal narratives was the **social contract**, a story that said power is derived not from God but from the consent of the governed. Philosopher John Locke argued that before government comes into being, people have natural rights. They give up some of those rights in order to have the convenience of government but retain enough of them to rebel against that government if it fails to protect their rights. For it to work, the social

divine right of kings the principle that earthly rulers receive their authority from God

classical liberalism a political ideology dating from the seventeenth century emphasizing individual rights over the power of the state

social contract the notion that society is based on an agreement between government and the governed in which people agree to give up some rights in exchange for the protection of others

Dan Savage

Dan Savage could not tell us about the start of his It *Gets Better Project* without choking up, and we could not hear about it without tears of our own. It started with the desperation of a young man named Steven Lucas, who had been bullied because kids said he was gay, and his ultimate suicide, which filled Savage with rage that day in New York in 2010. It grieved Savage that Lucas did not have someone to reassure him and tell him in concrete ways how to survive the crappy, terrorized years so that he could have caught a glimpse of the full life that would have one day been his.

Savage, a journalist and the author of the advice column and podcast *Savage Love* at the Seattle indie paper *The Stranger*, survived the tough, bullying years of high school because, "I never regarded my homosexuality as something damaged, or wrong, or sinful about myself. I regarded the homophobia, and the hatred, and the discrimination, and the violence as the problem."

That confidence in who he is and his Catholic upbringing and education also fueled a fiery sense of social justice and a steely patience that made Savage realize change happened slowly, one doable action at a time. He had come of age as an activist in Act Up, which, he says, ". . . . It was really hyper-organized and included this structure where people could show up and participate and then melt back into the crowd and go home . . . I've always felt that one of the jobs from people like me, who still considers himself an activist, is not to guilt, and not to harangue, and not to 'where were you' when you weren't at the meeting; it's to identify the doable thing that people who can't be active 24/7 can do, and say, 'Here's this doable thing. Do it.'"

The "one doable thing" philosophy informed Savage's work in Seattle, where he acquired an army of devoted *Savage Love* followers by basically entertaining them most of the time and urging them to action a tiny bit of the time.

So sitting on that train in 2010, fuming with anger at the kids who had tormented Billy Lucas and then taken to his Facebook page to continue the bullying after his death, there *was* that one, doable thing. He and his husband, Terry Miller, sat in front of their computer and recorded a simple message to those kids:

"It Gets Better." It told of the misery of the bullying they faced as kids and the joyful family and love-filled moments of the lives they live today, the promise that the intolerance of others would one day fade in importance, if they could just endure and look forward. He and Terry posted their video on YouTube and it went viral —"Here's a doable thing. You can sit in front of your computer for ten minutes and you can talk." In time all kinds of people added their own stories until today there are more than fifty thousand videos on the itgetsbetter.org website.

Billy Lucas had become a catalyst for the saving of so many others. And in the process, it accelerated the normalization of being LGBT as a simple part of being human. The nature of single doable acts is that they don't work alone. They build and they gather speed and they don't require the organization of armies, just the willingness of one person to carry the sword. It is Savage's genius to take advantage of that and to use social media to avoid the pitfalls and infighting and burnout that political organization in pursuit of social change so often falls victim to.

On patriotism

"We're an idea, and we're a document, and we're a promise . . . I do believe that the United States is the last best hope on Earth, as Lincoln said . . . because the United States, in its founding documents, in its founding idea, was an idea about creating a more perfect union . . . That's what fills me with kind of patriotic fervor. It's the political process and the idea that America is an unfinished thing that is imperfect and will never be perfect, but that we can keep working on making more perfect.".

On keeping the republic

"You're either going to be the person who can identify the doable thing, which I think is the most effective kind of activism, or be a person who is willing to jump in when asked to do the doable thing. Those are your options. Pick one or pick the other. Don't be that person who does nothing: doesn't pitch in, doesn't help, can't be bothered to do the doable thing, and then sit there and complain about the state of the world . . . "

Source: Dan Savage spoke with Christine Barbour and Gerald C. Wright on September 9, 2016.

contract requires that people have freedom to criticize the government (that is, to create counternarratives) and that information and narratives flow through channels that are protected from the influence of those in power.

As we will see in Chapter 3, Thomas Jefferson was clearly influenced by Locke's work. The Declaration of Independence is itself a founding narrative of the rights of Americans: it tells a story about how the British violated those rights and was designed to combat the British narrative that America should remain part of its colonial empire.

AS THE FOUNDERS SAW IT

While philosophers in Europe were beginning to explore the idea of individual rights and democratic governance, there had long been democratic stirrings on the founders' home continent. The Iroquois Confederacy was an alliance of five (and eventually six) East Coast Native American nations whose constitution, the "Great Law of Peace," impressed American leaders such as Benjamin Franklin with its suggestions of federalism, separation of powers, checks and balances, and consensus building. Although historians are not sure that these ideas had any direct influence on the founders' thinking about American governance, they were clearly part of the stew of ideas that the founders could dip into, and some scholars make the case that their influence was significant.[10]

Meanwhile, literacy among average citizens remained limited. Political elites still played a major role in mediating information, but new channels also started to play a part—newspapers, pastors, and publicans all began to shape narratives. For our purposes, the most important thing about these ideas about politics is that they were prevalent at the same time the American founders were thinking about how to build a new government. Locke particularly influenced the writings of James Madison, a major author of our Constitution. Like Locke, Madison thought government had a duty to protect property. At first he was hopeful that, with a fresh start in a new country, citizens would be driven by innate notions of *republican virtue* to put the interests of the public over their own self-interests.

Public behavior after the Revolution disillusioned him, however, and Madison ended up rejecting notions of "pure democracy," in which all citizens would have direct power to control government, opting instead for what he called a "republic." A **republic**, according to Madison, would differ from a democracy by relying on representation and would be more appropriate in a large polity where there would be a lot of citizens to be heard. It also limited the involvement of those citizens to choosing their representatives, not doing any actual governing.

In Your Own Words Explain the historical origins of American democracy and the ways that the available media controlled the political narrative.

THE EVOLUTION OF AMERICAN CITIZENSHIP

Redefining American citizenship from the founding era to the digital age

Unlike the founders, certainly, but even unlike most of the people currently running this country (who are, let's face it, kind of old), people born in this century are almost all **digital natives**. They have been born in an era in which not only are most people hooked up to electronic media, but they also live their lives partly in cyberspace as well as in "real space." For many of us, the lives we live are almost entirely mediated—that is, most of our relationships, our education, our news, our travel, our sustenance, our purchases, our daily activities, our job seeking, and our very sense of ourselves are influenced by, experienced through, or shared via electronic media.

Essentially we are conducting our lives through channels that, like that water pipe we talked about earlier, may be made of lead, may be rusty, or may be full of holes. When we search online, certain links are offered first according to the calculations made by the search engine we use. When we shop online, we are urged to buy certain products that an algorithm thinks we will like or that people like us have purchased. When we travel, certain flights and hotels are flagged, and when we use social media, certain posts appear while others don't. Most of us don't check very hard to ensure that the information on which we base our choices isn't emerging from the cyberequivalent of lead pipes.

A mediated world has all kinds of implications for everyday living and loving and working. The implications we care about here are the political implications for our roles as

> **republic** a government in which decisions are made through representatives of the people
>
> **digital native** an individual born after the advent of digital technology who is proficient in and dependent on its use

Citizens Stepping Up

Americans may be individualists, but that doesn't mean they don't pitch in to help others in need—at least some of the time. When Hurricane Maria struck Puerto Rico in 2017, Washington, D.C.-based chef José Andrés jumped into action via his organization World Central Kitchen to provide meals to people across the islands who had lost power, or even their homes.

citizens—the ones to do with how we exercise and are impacted by power. We will be turning to these implications again and again throughout this book.

Even though Americans today still largely adhere to the basic governing narrative the founders promoted, the country is now light years removed from the founding era, when communication was limited by illiteracy and the scarcity of channels through which it could pass. Consider the timeline in Figure 1.4. It follows the development of the media through which we get information, receive narratives, and send out our own information (see also *Snapshot of America: How Do We Engage Politically Online?*). Being a citizen in a mediated world is just flat out different from being one in the world in which James Madison wrote the Constitution. It's the genius of the Constitution that it has been able to navigate the transition successfully, so far. The mediated world we live in gives us myriad new ways to keep the republic and some pretty high-tech ways to lose it. That puts a huge burden on us as **mediated citizens**, and also opens up a world of opportunity.

Among the things we disagree on in this country is what it means to be a citizen. James Madison obviously had ideas about this. As mentioned earlier, he hoped people would be so filled with what he called republican virtue that they would readily sacrifice their self-interest to advance the public interest. As we will see in Chapter 3,

this **public-interested citizenship** proved not to be the rule, much to Madison's disappointment. Instead, early Americans demonstrated **self-interested citizenship**, trying to use the system to get the most they could for themselves. This was a dilemma for Madison because he was designing a constitution that depended on the nature of the people being governed. He believed he had solved that dilemma by creating a political system that would check our self-interested nature and produce laws that would support the public interest.

Still, the Constitution has not put that conflict to rest. Today there are plenty of people who put country first—who enlist in the armed services, sometimes giving their lives for their nation, or who go into law enforcement or teaching or other lower paying careers because they want to serve. There are people who cheerfully pay their taxes because it's a privilege to live in a free democracy where you can climb the ladder of opportunity. Especially in moments of national trouble—after the terrorist attacks on the World Trade Center and the Pentagon in September 2001, for instance—Americans willingly help their fellow citizens.

At the same time, the day-to-day business of life turns most people inward. Many people care about self and family and friends, but most don't have the energy or inclination to get beyond that. John Kennedy challenged his "fellow Americans" in 1961 to "ask not what your country can do for you—ask what you can do for your country," but only a rare few have the time or motivation to take up that challenge.

Unlike the citizens Madison and his colleagues designed a constitution for, mediated citizens experience the world through multiple channels of information and interaction. That doesn't change whether citizens are self-interested or public-interested, but it does give them more opportunities and raise more potential hazards for being both.

mediated citizens those for whom most personal and commercial relationships; access to information about the world and recreational or professional activities; and communication with others passes through third-party channels, which may or may not modify or censor that information

public-interested citizenship a view of citizenship focused on action to realize the common good

self-interested citizenship a view of citizenship focused on action to realize an individual citizen's interests

Snapshot of America: *How Do We Engage Politically Online?*

 "Like" or promote material related to politics or social issues that others have posted — **38%**   45%

 Use a social networking site to encourage people to vote — **35%**

 Post one's own comments on political/social issues — **34%**

 Repost content related to political/social issues that was originally posted by someone else — **33%**

 Encourage other people to take action on a political/social issue — **31%**

Post links to political stories or articles for others to read — **28%**

Follow elected officials and candidates for office — **20%**

Impacts of Online Political Engagement

25%   **16%**   **0.09%**

 Became more active in a political issue after discussing/reading about it online

 Changed views about a political issue after discussing/reading about it online

Became less involved in a political issue after encountering it online

Behind the Numbers

Social media enable citizens to engage with their government, the news media, and each other much more efficiently than in previous decades. But widespread and easy access to political information comes to us with few quality checks. Did you engage politically during the 2016 presidential election in any of the ways listed above? In what ways might social media affect political outcomes?

Source: Pew Research Center: Internet, Science & Tech, "Politics Fact Sheet," www.pewinternet.org/fact-sheets/politics-fact-sheet/ (accessed March 15, 2016).

FIGURE 1.4
Media Timeline

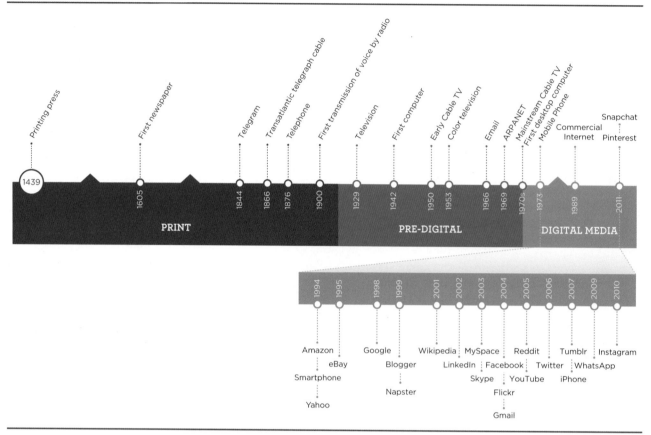

Many older Americans who are not digital natives nonetheless experience political life through television or through web surfing and commenting, usually anonymously and often rudely. This is not always a positive addition to our civil discourse, but they are trying to adapt. You may have grandparents who fit this description. They probably want to know why you are not on Facebook.

But younger, more media-savvy digital natives—the Marjory Stoneman Douglas students we discussed in *What's at Stake . . . ?*, millennials, Gen Xers, even some tech-savvy Baby Boomers—not only have access to traditional media if they choose but also are accustomed to interacting, conducting friendships and family relationships, and generally attending to the details of their lives through electronic channels. Their digital selves exist in networks of friends and acquaintances who take for granted that they can communicate in seconds. They certainly get their news digitally

and increasingly organize, register to vote, enlist in campaigns, and call each other to action that way.

> **When, if ever, should individuals be asked to sacrifice their own good for that of their country?**

In fact, as we saw earlier, **hashtag activism**, the forming of social movements through viral calls to act politically—whether to march, to boycott, to contact politicians, or to vote—has become common enough that organizers warn that action has to go beyond cyberspace to reach the real world or

hashtag activism a form of political engagement that occurs by organizing individuals online around a particular issue

it will have limited impact. #BlackLivesMatter, #ItGetsBetter, and #NeverAgain are just three very different, very viral, very successful ways of using all the channels available to us to call attention to a problem and propose solutions.

Although living an intensely mediated life has the potential to broaden our horizons and expose us to multiple views and cultures, it does not automatically produce public-interested citizens. People can easily remain self-interested in this digital world. We can customize our social media to give us only news and information that confirms what we already think. We can live in an **information bubble** where everything we see and hear reinforces our narratives. That makes us more or less sitting ducks for whatever media narrative is directed our way, whether from inside an online media source or from a foreign power that weaponizes social media to influence an election, as the Russians did in 2016. Without opening ourselves up to multiple information and action channels, we can live an unexamined mediated life.

But mediated citizenship also creates enormous opportunities that the founders never dreamed of. Truth to tell, Madison wouldn't have been all that thrilled about the multiple ways to be political that the mediated citizen possesses. He thought citizens should be seen on election day, but not heard most of the time, precisely because he thought we would push our own interests and destabilize the system. He was reassured by the fact that it would take days for an express letter trying to create a dissenting political organization to reach Georgia from Maine. Our mediated world has blown that reassuring prospect to smithereens.

Mediated citizens are not only the receivers and distributors of narratives from powerful people, like the TV-watching couch potato or headphone-wearing student with her eyes fixed on Insta. We can be the creators and disseminators of our own narratives, something that would have terrified the old monarchs comfortably ensconced in their divine right narrative. Even the founders would have been extremely nervous about what the masses might get up to.

As mediated citizens, we have unprecedented access to power, but we are also targets of the use of unprecedented power—attempts to shape our views and control our experi-

> **information bubble** a closed cycle, sometimes self-created, in which all the information we get reinforces the information we already have, solidifying our beliefs without reference to outside reality checks

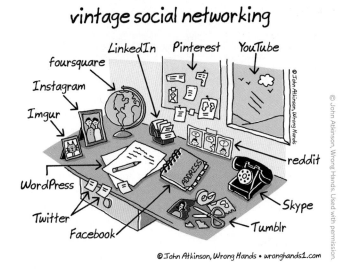

vintage social networking

foursquare · LinkedIn · Pinterest · YouTube · Instagram · Imgur · reddit · WordPress · Skype · Twitter · Tumblr · Facebook

©John Atkinson, Wrong Hands • wronghands1.com

ences. That means it is up to us to pay critical attention to what is happening in the world around us.

In Your Own Words Describe the enduring tension in the United States between self-interested human nature and public-spirited government and the way that has been shaped in a mediated world.

THINKING CRITICALLY ABOUT AMERICAN POLITICS

How to use the themes and features in this book

Our primary goal in this book is to get you thinking critically about American politics, especially about the political narratives that you encounter every day. Critical thinking is the analysis and evaluation of ideas and arguments based on reason and evidence—it means digging deep into what you read and what you hear and asking tough questions. Critical thinking is what all good scholars do, and it is also what savvy citizens do.

Our analytic and evaluative tasks in this book focus on the twin themes of power and citizenship. We have adopted the classic definition of politics proposed by the late political scientist Harold Lasswell that politics is "who gets what when and how." We simplify his understanding by dropping the "when" and focusing on politics as the struggle by citizens

Your Own Information Bubble

Technologies that enable citizens to connect with one another, to engage in lively debate, and to organize for common purposes hold great promise for democracy. The power to communicate on a massive scale was once held only by governments and those with access to print or broadcast media outlets, but today it is in the hands of anyone with a cell phone. As every superhero learns, with great power comes great responsibility. There is no guarantee that what you learn through social media is true, and if you are sharing information that isn't reality based, you are helping to perpetuate a false narrative.

In addition, your social media feeds and even your browser are working against you, ensuring that the news that comes your way is tailored to your interests and preconceptions, creating what one observer calls a filter bubble.[11] Whether your news feed is custom made or crowd sourced, always look before you "like" since social media algorithms can channel information to you that reinforces the narrative you get about "who gets what and how" in today's political world.

What to Watch Out For

- **Don't create your own echo chamber.** Social networking sites and other tools make it easy to create your own custom news channel, ensuring that you see stories from sources you like, about subjects that interest you. Important stories can easily slip past you, and your understanding of political matters will suffer. But if you follow only the political sources you like, that will get you in trouble, too. So open yourself up to alternative sources of news and opinions that you might find offensive or wrong. If what's showing up in your news feed does not challenge your ideas and beliefs from time to time, consider whether you've been censoring news that you don't like. Make sure you're getting all sides of the story, not just the one that you want to hear.[12]

- **Don't trust your browser.** It's not just your self-selected social media feeds that are shaping your information diet: every link you click and word you search is fed into complex algorithms that tailor your results into a custom feed of "things you might like." Just as Amazon knows what items to suggest based on your browsing and purchase history, your Google results are similarly parsed and packaged for your viewing pleasure. Two people searching on a particular topic will get very different results.[13] Search around—don't just click on the first links offered to you.

- **Separate truth from truthiness.** Some of the most compelling (and viral) political material on the Internet comes from people who are intent on selling you on their narrative. Their arguments may be valid, and their evidence may be strong—but bear in mind that an opinion piece is different from a statement of fact. Take care to seek out news sources that strive for objectivity and don't have an ax to grind (such as the Associated Press or the *news* pages of the *New York Times*, the *Wall Street Journal,* or Politico) alongside those that offer analysis and argument.

- **Don't be complacent about conventional news sources.** While you are watching your social networks and second-guessing Google algorithms, don't neglect old-fashioned news sources. If you watch television news, make a point of changing the channel often, especially if one of the stations has an ideological agenda like Fox or MSNBC. Ditto on the radio shows and late-night comedy. In fact, try to have political discussions with different groups of people, too. The more sources you use to gather information, the harder it will be for you to lose touch with political reality.

over who gets power and resources in society and how they get them, but we also consider how the struggle for power and resources can change dramatically over time.

ANALYSIS

Lasswell's definition of politics gives us a framework of analysis for this book; that is, it outlines how we break down politics into its component parts in order to understand it. Analysis helps us understand how something works, much like taking apart a car and putting it back together again helps us understand how it runs. Lasswell's definition provides a strong analytic framework because it focuses our attention on questions we can ask to figure out what is going on in politics.

The Critical Importance of Critical Thinking

This book is an introduction to American politics, and in a way it is also an introduction to political science. Political science is not exactly the same kind of science as biology or geology. Not only is it difficult to put our subjects (people and political systems) under a microscope to observe their behavior, but we are also somewhat limited in our ability to test our theories. We cannot replay World War II to test our ideas about what caused it, for example. A further problem is our subjectivity; we are the phenomena under investigation, and so we may have stronger feelings about our research and our findings than we would about, say, cells and rocks.

These difficulties do not make a science of politics impossible, but they do mean we must proceed with caution. Even among political scientists, disagreement exists about whether a rigorous science of the political world is a reasonable goal. We can agree, however, that it is possible to advance our understanding of politics beyond mere guessing or debates about political preferences. Although we use many methods in our work (statistical analysis, mathematical modeling, case studies, and philosophical reasoning, to name only a few), what political scientists have in common is an emphasis on critical thinking about politics.

Critical thinking means challenging the conclusions of others, asking why or why not, and exploring alternative interpretations. It means considering the sources of information—not accepting an explanation just because someone in authority offers it, or because you have always been told that it is the true explanation, but because you have discovered independently that there are good reasons for accepting it. You may emerge from reading this textbook with the same ideas about politics that you have always had; it is not our goal to change your mind. But as a critical thinker, you will be able to back up your old ideas with new and persuasive arguments of your own, or to move beyond your current ideas to see politics in a new light.

Becoming adept at critical thinking has a number of benefits:

- **We learn to be good democratic citizens.** Critical thinking helps us sort through the barrage of information that regularly assails us, and it teaches us to process this information thoughtfully. Critical awareness of what our leaders are doing and the ability to understand and evaluate what they tell us is the lifeblood of democratic government.
- **We are better able to hold our own in political (or other) arguments.** We think more logically and clearly, we are more persuasive, and we impress people with our grasp of reason and fact. There is not a career in the world that is not enhanced by critical thinking skills.
- **We become much better students.** The skills of the critical thinker are the skills of the scholar. When we

read critically, we figure out what is important quickly and easily, we know what questions to ask to tease out more meaning, we can decide whether what we are reading is worth our time, and we know what to take with us and what to discard.

It may sound a little dull and dusty, but critical thinking can be a vital and enjoyable activity. When we are good at it, it empowers and liberates us. We are not at the mercy of others' conclusions and decisions. We can evaluate facts and arguments for ourselves, turning conventional wisdom upside down and exploring the world of ideas with confidence.

How does one learn to think critically?

The trick to learning how to think critically is to do it. It helps to have a model to follow, however, and we provide one in *The Big Picture*, which traces this process. The focus of critical thinking here is on understanding political argument. Argument in this case refers not to a confrontation or a fight, but rather to a contention, based on a set of assumptions, supported by evidence, and leading to a clear, well-developed conclusion with consequences for how we understand the world.

Critical thinking involves constantly asking questions about the arguments we read: Who has created it, what is the basic case and what values underlie it, what evidence is used to back it up, what conclusions are drawn, and what difference does the whole thing make? To help you remember the questions to ask, we have used a mnemonic device that creates an acronym from the five major steps of critical thinking. Until asking these questions becomes second nature, thinking of them as CLUES to critical thinking about American politics will help you keep them in mind. To help you develop the critical thinking habit, readings featured in each chapter of this book will provide a CLUES model for you to follow.

This is what CLUES stands for:

- Consider the source and the audience
- Lay out the argument and the underlying values and assumptions
- Uncover the evidence
- Evaluate the conclusion
- Sort out the political implications

When you read each of the *CLUES to Critical Thinking* features in the book, keep in mind *The Big Picture*.

Source: Adapted from the authors' "Preface to the Student," in Christine Barbour and Matthew J. Streb, eds., *Clued in to Politics: A Critical Thinking Reader in American Government*, 3rd ed. (Washington, DC: CQ Press, 2010).

Follow the CLUES
to Critical Thinking

START
Your Comfort Zone

CONSIDER THE SOURCE

ASK YOURSELF

- *Where does this information come from?*
- *Who is the author?*
- *Who is he or she talking to?*
- *How do the source and the audience shape the author's perspective?*

LAY OUT THE ARGUMENT

ASK YOURSELF

- *What argument is the author asking you to accept?*
- *If you accept the argument, what values are you also buying?*
- *Does the argument hold together logically?*

UNCOVER THE EVIDENCE

ASK YOURSELF

- *Did the author do research to back up the conclusions?*
- *Is there any evidence or data that is not provided that should be there?*
- *If there is no evidence provided, does there need to be?*

I read it on the Internet. It must be true.

My parents always watch this TV station. Of course it's reliable.

OCEAN OF EXCUSES

Arguments sound like conflict. I hate conflict.

Values are private. It's rude to pry.

Logic gives me hives!

Data means numbers. Numbers freak me out.

BRIDGE to ENLIGHTENMENT

What, do I look like some kind of detective?

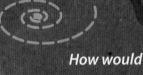

Who cares? What do I need to know for the test?

SEA OF CONFUSION

There is no way to know what conclusions are right.

Ouch! Thinking is hard work. Wake me up when it's over.

How would I know?

These ideas make me really uncomfortable. They don't click with anything I think I know. Time for a beer!

I don't like this person's values. Why should I care about his or her conclusions?

WISDOM HAPPINESS

GOAL

SUCCESS BIG BUCKS

ASK YOURSELF

- *What difference does this argument make to your understanding of the political world?*
- *How does it affect who gets what and how they get it?*
- *Was getting this information valuable to you or did it waste your time?*

SORT OUT THE POLITICAL SIGNIFICANCE

ASK YOURSELF

- *What's the punch line here?*
- *Did the author convince you that he or she is correct?*
- *Does accepting the conclusion to this argument require you to change any of your ideas about the world?*

EVALUATE THE CONCLUSIONS

Accordingly, in this book, we analyze American politics in terms of three sets of questions:

- Who are the parties involved? What resources, powers, and rights do they bring to the struggle?
- What do they have at stake? What do they stand to win or lose? Is it power, influence, position, policy, or values?
- How do the rules shape the outcome? Where do the rules come from? What strategies or tactics do the political actors employ to use the rules to get what they want?

If you know who is involved in a political situation, what is at stake, and how (under what rules) the conflict over resources will eventually be resolved, you will have a pretty good grasp of what is going on, and you will probably be able to figure out new situations, even when your days of taking a course in American government are far behind you. To get you in the habit of asking those questions, we have designed several features in this text explicitly to reinforce them.

As you found at the start of your reading, each chapter opens with key tasks that we expect you to be able to perform, *In Your Own Words*, which will help you to set goals for your reading and evaluate whether or not you've accomplished them. Each chapter begins with a *What's at Stake . . . ?* feature that analyzes a political situation in terms of what various groups of citizens stand to win or lose, and ends with *Let's Revisit . . .* , in which we reconsider those issues once you have the substantive material of the chapter under your belt. We also focus our analysis along the way by closing each major chapter section, beginning in Chapter 2, with a *Pause and Review* feature that explicitly addresses the questions of who gets what, and how they get it; concisely summarizes what you have learned; and asks you to put your understanding in your own words.

We reinforce the task of analysis with a *Don't Be Fooled by . . .* feature that discusses ways you can improve your critical thinking skills by analyzing (that is, taking apart) different kinds of sources of information about politics. Similarly, *CLUES to Critical Thinking* readings in each chapter provide a text that is central to the material you are learning to give you some practice in using the critical thinking model we described in *The Big Picture*.

In addition to focusing on analysis of what you read, we offer graphics that will help you visualize processes and data that affect and are affected by politics. *The Big Picture* infographics relate the book's themes to the big concepts, big processes, and big data that will help you make sense of American politics. *Snapshots of America* provide you with a lot more data to help you understand who the American people are and to help you dig into the question of what challenges our diversity poses for the task of governance. Finally, we highlighted key questions throughout each chapter, challenging you to take the analysis one step further: What if the rules or the actors or the stakes were different? What would be the impact on American politics? How would it work differently?

EVALUATION

As political scientists, however, we want not only to understand how the system works but also to assess how well it works. A second task of critical thinking is evaluation, or seeing how well something measures up according to a standard or principle. We could choose any number of standards by which to evaluate American politics, but the most relevant, for most of us, is the principle of democracy and the role of citizens.

We can draw on the traditions of self-interested and public-interested citizenship and the opportunities offered by digital citizenship to evaluate the powers, opportunities, and challenges presented to American citizens by the system of government under which they live. In addition to the two competing threads of citizenship in America, we can also look at the kinds of action that citizens engage in and whether they take advantage of the options available to them. For instance, citizen action might be restricted by the rules, or by popular interest, to merely choosing between competing candidates for office, as in the model of elite democracy described earlier. Alternatively, the rules of the system might encourage citizens to band together in groups to get what they want, as they do in pluralist democracy. Or the system might be open and offer highly motivated citizens a variety of opportunities to get involved, as they do in participatory democracy. American democracy has elements of all three of these models, and one way to evaluate citizenship in America is to look at what opportunities for each type of participation exist and whether citizens take advantage of them.

> **Why does critical thinking feel like so much more work than "regular thinking"?**

To evaluate how democratic the United States is, we include in most chapters a section called *The Citizens and . . .* , which looks at the changing concept and practice of citizenship in this country with respect to the chapter's subject matter. That feature looks at citizenship from many angles, considering the following types of questions: What role do "the people" have in American politics? How has that role expanded or diminished over time? What kinds of political participation do the rules of American politics (formal and informal) allow, encourage, or require citizens to take? What kinds of political participation are discouraged, limited, or forbidden? Do citizens take advantage of the opportunities for political action that the rules provide them? How do they react to the rules that limit their participation? How have citizens in different times exercised their rights and responsibilities? What do citizens need to do to keep the republic? How democratic is the United States?

To put all this in perspective, the book uses two features to give you a more concrete idea of what citizen participation might mean on a personal level. *Profiles in Citizenship* introduce you to individuals who have committed a good part of their lives to public service and focus on what citizenship means to those people and what inspired them to take on a public role. The *Snapshots of America*, described earlier, provide demographic data to bring the diversity of the American citizenry front and center and to highlight the difficulties inherent in uniting into a single nation individuals and groups with such different and often conflicting interests.

We have outlined several features that recur throughout this book. Remember that each is designed to help you to think critically about American politics, either by analyzing power in terms of who gets what, and how, or by evaluating citizenship to determine how well we are following Benjamin Franklin's mandate to keep the republic. And remember that further exploration of the book's themes is always available on the companion web site at **edge.sagepub .com/barbour9e.**

In Your Own Words Apply the five steps of critical thinking to this book's themes of power and citizenship in American politics.

LET'S REVISIT: *What's at Stake . . . ?*

We began this chapter by looking at the power of hashtag activism in response to the phenomenal seffort of the Parkland students to change the prevailing narrative about guns, increase the involvement of young people in politics, and bring about political change. We asked whether Benjamin Franklin would consider such movements as fulfilling his admonishment to keep the republic. Since then, we have covered a lot of ground, arguing that politics is fundamental to human life and, in fact, makes life easier for us by giving us a nonviolent way to resolve disputes. We pointed out that politics is a method by which power and resources get distributed in society: politics is who gets what and how they get it. Citizens who are aware and involved stand a much better chance of getting what they want from the system than do those who check out or turn away. One clear consequence when young people disregard politics, then, is that they are far less likely to get what they want from the political system. This is exactly what happens.

But the hashtag activists we met in this chapter have been instrumental in changing the narrative of contemporary American politics. As Occupy protester Matt Brandi says:

The objective of Occupy was to change the direction of the national dialogue and debate. . . . By appearing in strong numbers and generating media interest (both new/social and commercial/mass), Occupy was able to influence the national dialogue. We protested about inequality and exploitation, the corruption of our government by wealth and influence; and while we did not make "demands," people began to talk about inequality, exploitation, and the corruption of democracy. The very way people talked and thought about these issues changed.

What Matt is suggesting was at stake for the Occupy protesters was, in the language of political scientists, agenda setting. A problem not defined as a problem, or not on the national agenda, cannot be solved by public action. It worked for the Occupy protestors who saw income inequality become a major issue between President Obama and his 2012 Republican challenger, Mitt Romney

It was that effort to change the narrative, and to put real political effort behind it, that encouraged the kids in the March for Our Lives project to spend the summer registering young people and getting them fired up to vote for changes in the gun laws. Although the gun laws remain stubbornly the same, the narrative has begun to change. Young people voted in huge numbers for a midterm election and the policy change is likely to follow the change in narrative.

FIGURE 1.5
Politics and Young Americans

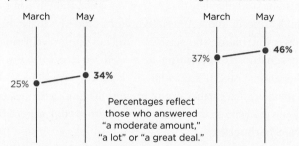

Percentage saying elected public officials care what people like them think:

March   May

25% ●——————● **34%**

Percentage saying people like them can affect what the government does:

March   May

37% ●——————● **46%**

Percentages reflect those who answered "a moderate amount," "a lot" or "a great deal."

Results based on interviews with 939 U.S. residents ages 15–34. Margin of error is ±4.3 percentage points for the full sample, higher for subgroups.

Younger Americans, typically the least likely to vote, are increasingly feeling empowered to influence politics, according to an AP-NORC Center/MTV poll.

Source: From "MTV/AP-NORC: Comparing the Political Views of Young People and Their Parents' Generation," The Associated Press-NORC Center for Public Affairs Research, June, 2018.

In the same way, the It Gets Better Project helped change the narrative on both bullying and gay rights. In the years since the movement began in 2011, as more and more "mainstream" people have posted videos promising LGBT youth that it does indeed get better, the world in fact *has* gotten better. Certainly, the It Gets Better Project was not solely responsible for these changes, but in significant ways it helped change the narrative that made the changes possible.

And the debates over systemic racism and intersectionality in the 2016 election, at least on the Democratic side, make clear that Black Lives Matter had changed the narrative on race, too. President Obama had been cautious about making race a centerpiece of his administration, but his presidency and the BLM movement freed Hillary Clinton, as candidate, to address it in a more comprehensive way.

These movements highlight the value of grassroots action, and the power of stepping outside the system to put pressure on the status quo to respond to unmet and even previously unvoiced needs. It might not have been what Benjamin Franklin had in mind, but occupying the republic may very well be another means of keeping it.

CLUES to Critical Thinking

Excerpts from President Barack Obama's Howard University commencement address, May 7, 2016

President Obama gave a moving address at Howard University his final spring in office, calling for the class of 2016 to be aware of how much the world had changed, how "If you had to choose one moment in history *in which you could be born, and you didn't know ahead of time who you were going to be—what nationality, what gender, what race, whether you'd be rich or poor, gay or straight, what faith you'd be born into—you wouldn't choose 100 years ago. You wouldn't choose the fifties, or the sixties, or the seventies. You'd choose right now. If you had to choose a time to be, in the words of Lorraine Hansberry, 'young, gifted,*

and black' in America, you would choose right now."
He offered graduates three pieces of advice: to be
confident in the many ways there were to be black
today, to be aware of the struggle that came before
them and the structural racism that still pervades the
system, and finally, this call for action.

You have to go through life with more than just passion for change; you need a strategy. I'll repeat that. I want you to have passion, but you have to have a strategy. Not just awareness, but action. Not just hashtags, but votes.

You see, change requires more than righteous anger.... And I'm so proud of the new guard of black civil rights leaders who understand this. It's thanks in large part to the activism of young people like many of you, from Black Twitter to Black Lives Matter, that America's eyes have been opened—white, black, Democrat, Republican—to the real problems, for example, in our criminal justice system.

But to bring about structural change, lasting change, awareness is not enough. It requires changes in law, changes in custom. If you care about mass incarceration, let me ask you: How are you pressuring members of Congress to pass the criminal justice reform bill now pending before them? If you care about better policing, do you know who your district attorney is? Do you know who your state's attorney general is? Do you know the difference? Do you know who appoints the police chief and who writes the police training manual? Find out who they are, what their responsibilities are. Mobilize the community, present them with a plan, work with them to bring about change, hold them accountable if they do not deliver. Passion is vital, but you've got to have a strategy.

And your plan better include voting—not just some of the time, but all the time. It is absolutely true that 50 years after the Voting Rights Act, there are still too many barriers in this country to vote. There are too many people trying to erect new barriers to voting. This is the only advanced democracy on Earth that goes out of its way to make it difficult for people to vote. And there's a reason for that. There's a legacy to that.

But let me say this: Even if we dismantled every barrier to voting, that alone would not change the fact that America has some of the lowest voting rates in the free world. In 2014, only 36 percent of Americans turned out to vote in the midterms—the second lowest participation rate on record. Youth turnout—that would be you—was less than 20 percent. Less than 20 percent. Four out of five did not vote. In 2012, nearly two in three African Americans turned out. And then, in 2014, only two in five turned out. You don't

think that made a difference in terms of the Congress I've got to deal with? And then people are wondering, well, how come Obama hasn't gotten this done? How come he didn't get that done? You don't think that made a difference? What would have happened if you had turned out at 50, 60, 70 percent, all across this country? People try to make this political thing really complicated. Like, what kind of reforms do we need? And how do we need to do that? You know what, just vote. It's math. If you have more votes than the other guy, you get to do what you want. It's not that complicated.

And you don't have excuses. You don't have to guess the number of jellybeans in a jar or bubbles on a bar of soap to register to vote. You don't have to risk your life to cast a ballot. Other people already did that for you. Your grandparents, your great grandparents might be here today if they were working on it. What's your excuse? When we don't vote, we give away our power, disenfranchise ourselves—right when we need to use the power that we have; right when we need your power to stop others from taking away the vote and rights of those more vulnerable than you are—the elderly and the poor, the formerly incarcerated trying to earn their second chance.

So you've got to vote all the time, not just when it's cool, not just when it's time to elect a President, not just when you're inspired. It's your duty. When it's time to elect a member of Congress or a city councilman, or a school board member, or a sheriff. That's how we change our politics—by electing people at every level who are representative of and accountable to us. It is not that complicated. Don't make it complicated.

And, finally, change requires more than just speaking out—it requires listening, as well. In particular, it requires listening to those with whom you disagree, and being prepared to compromise. When I was a state senator, I helped pass Illinois's first racial profiling law, and one of the first laws in the nation requiring the videotaping of confessions in capital cases. And we were successful because, early on, I engaged law enforcement. I didn't say to them, oh, you guys are so racist, you need to do something. I understood, as many of you do, that the overwhelming majority of police officers are good, and honest, and courageous, and fair, and love the communities they serve....

And I can say this unequivocally: Without at least the acceptance of the police organizations in Illinois, I could never have gotten those bills passed. Very simple. They would have blocked them.

——

The point is, you need allies in a democracy...—democracy requires compromise, even when you are 100 percent right. This is hard to explain sometimes. You can be completely right, and you still are going to have to engage folks who disagree with you. If you think that the only way forward is to be as uncompromising as possible, you will feel good about yourself, you will enjoy a certain moral purity, but you're not going to get what you want. And if you don't get what you want long enough, you will eventually think the whole system is rigged. And that will lead to more cynicism, and less participation, and a downward spiral of more injustice and more anger and more despair. And that's never been the source of our progress. That's how we cheat ourselves of progress....

So don't try to shut folks out, don't try to shut them down, no matter how much you might disagree with them. There's been a trend around the country of trying to get colleges to disinvite speakers with a different point of view, or disrupt a politician's rally. Don't do that—no matter how ridiculous or offensive you might find the things that come out of their mouths. Because as my grandmother used to tell me, every time a fool speaks, they are just advertising their own ignorance. Let them talk. Let them talk. If you don't, you just make them a victim, and then they can avoid accountability.

That doesn't mean you shouldn't challenge them. Have the confidence to challenge them, the confidence in the rightness of your position. There will be times when you shouldn't compromise your core values, your integrity, and you will have the responsibility to speak up in the face of injustice. But listen. Engage. If the other side has a point, learn from them. If they're wrong, rebut them. Teach them. Beat them on the battlefield of ideas. And you might as well start practicing now, because one thing I can guarantee you—you will have to deal with ignorance, hatred, racism, foolishness, trifling folks. I promise you, you will have to deal with all that at every stage of your life. That may not seem fair, but life has never been completely fair. Nobody promised you a crystal stair. And if you want to make life fair, then you've got to start with the world as it is.

So that's my advice. That's how you change things. Change isn't something that happens every four years or eight years; change is not placing your faith in any particular politician and then just putting your feet up and saying, okay, go. Change is the effort of committed citizens who hitch their wagons to something bigger than themselves and fight for it every single day.

Consider the source and the audience: In the last year of his presidency, Obama is speaking to an audience at a black university that has graduated some notable political figures. He is tailoring his remarks to an African American audience. Is that the only audience he is speaking to? Who else might he expect to be listening?

Lay out the argument and the underlying values and assumptions: The part of the speech we focus on here is about the importance of taking action, going beyond the kind of hashtag activism we talked about early in this chapter. "Not just hashtags, but votes," says Obama. What kind of democracy is he advocating here? What are the values that support democracy?

Uncover the evidence: In parts of the speech we had to cut for length, Obama gives many examples of people, primarily Howard grads, who were able to change the world they lived in by practicing the principles he calls for. Would that kind of anecdotal evidence be sufficient to persuade you that he is right? He also draws on his own personal experience. Is that persuasive?

Evaluate the conclusion: Obama wants the class of 2016 to understand that they won't get the change they seek in the world without taking action, especially voting and working with others. Are you persuaded? What alternatives might there be to effecting political change?

Sort out the political significance: What is the historical context in which Obama is writing? Have the Republicans he has had to deal with in Congress practiced democracy as he defines it? What would have been the political results if they had? What fate does he worry will befall movements like Black Lives Matter if they are not backed by action, hard work, and votes?

Review

What Is Politics?

Politics may appear to be a grubby, greedy pursuit, filled with scandal and backroom dealing. In fact, despite its shortcomings and sometimes shabby reputation, politics is an essential means for resolving differences and determining how power and resources, including control of information through the creation of political narratives, are distributed in society. Politics is about who gets power and resources in society—and how they get them. Increasingly we get them through channels that are mediated, or controlled, by forces external to us.

Government, by contrast, is the system established for exercising authority over a group of people. In the United States, the government is embodied in the Constitution and the institutions set up by the Constitution. Government is shaped not only by politics but also by economics, which is concerned specifically with the distribution of wealth and society's resources.

politics (p. 4)
power (p. 4)
media (p. 4)
social order (p. 4)
government (p. 5)
authority (p. 5)
legitimate (p. 5)

rules (p. 6)
norms (p. 6)
institutions (p. 6)
political narrative (p. 7)
gatekeepers (p. 7)
economics (p. 8)
capitalist economy (p. 8)

laissez-faire capitalism (p. 9)
regulated capitalism (p. 9)
procedural guarantees (p. 9)
socialist economy (p. 9)
substantive guarantees (p. 9)
social democracy (p. 10)

Political Systems and the Concept of Citizenship

Political systems dictate how power is distributed among leaders and citizens, and these systems take many forms. Authoritarian governments give ultimate power to the state. Nonauthoritarian systems, like democracy, place power largely in the hands of the people. Democracy is based on the principle of popular sovereignty, giving the people the ultimate power to govern. The meaning of citizenship is key to the definition of democracy. Citizens are believed to have rights protecting them from government as well as responsibilities to the public realm.

authoritarian governments (p. 11)
totalitarian (p. 11)
authoritarian capitalism (p. 11)
anarchy (p. 12)

democracy (p. 12)
popular sovereignty (p. 12)
advanced industrial democracy (p. 13)
communist democracy (p. 13)

populism (p. 13)
subjects (p. 14)
citizens (p. 14)

Origins of Democracy in America

Democracy was not an obvious choice for the founders—their decisions were based on their own intellectual heritage, their historical experience, and the theories about government that informed them.

divine right of kings (p. 15)
classical liberalism (p. 15)

social contract (p. 15)
republic (p. 17)

The Evolution of American Citizenship

At the time of our nation's founding, two competing views of citizenship emerged. The first view, articulated by James Madison, sees the citizen as fundamentally self-interested; this view led the founders to fear too much citizen participation in government. The second view puts faith in citizens' ability to act for the common good, to put their obligation to the public ahead of their own self-interest. Both views are still alive and well today, and we can see evidence of both sentiments at work in the mediated era, where citizenship is not experienced so much directly as through channels controlled by others. Ironically, this both limits our freedom and enhances our opportunities to take control.

digital native (p. 17)
mediated citizens (p. 18)

public-interested citizenship (p. 18)
self-interested citizenship (p. 18)

hashtag activism (p. 20)
information bubble (p. 21)

Thinking Critically About American Politics

In this textbook, we rely on two underlying themes to analyze how our American political system works, and to evaluate how well it works. The first theme is power, and how it functions in our system: we look at political events in terms of who the actors are, what they have to win or lose, and how the rules shape the way these actors engage in their struggle. The second theme is citizenship, specifically, how diverse citizens participate in political life to improve their own individual situations and to promote the interests of the community at large. Throughout this book, we will evaluate citizenship carefully as a means to determine how well the American system is working.

Sam Hodgson/Bloomberg via Getty Images

In Your Own Words

After you've read this chapter, you will be able to

2.1 Analyze the role of immigration and citizenship in U.S. politics.

2.2 Explain how shared core values define the United States as a country and a culture.

2.3 Describe the competing narratives that drive partisan divisions in American politics.

2.4 Describe the gap between the ideal American democratic narrative and its practice.

2

AMERICAN CITIZENS AND POLITICAL CULTURE

What's at Stake . . . in Our Immigration Policy?

DONALD TRUMP opened his campaign for the presidency in 2015 with a dramatic descent down an escalator in Trump Tower, followed by a speech best remembered for the words denouncing immigration: "When Mexico sends its people, they're not sending their best . . . . They're sending people that have lots of problems, and they're bringing those problems with us. They're bringing drugs. They're bringing crime. They're rapists. And some, I assume, are good people." He followed that up by vowing to build a "huge, beautiful wall" between here and Mexico, and forcing Mexico to pay for it. By the midterm elections he was warning of foreign caravans filled with terrrorists and murderers were coming north to "invade our borders."

It's hard to imagine that only six short years ago, immigration reform looked like the biggest no-brainer on earth. The Republicans had lost the 2012 presidential election by almost five million votes and the powers that be in the party concluded that immigration reform was central to a future presidential win for the party.

John Moore/Getty Images

On the Edge of the American Dream

Reforms that would provide undocumented immigrants with a path to citizenship have stalled repeatedly in Congress and provide one of the biggest sources of conflict in American politics today. Here, a deported Mexican immigrant walks along the U.S.-Mexico border in Nogales, Mexico.

After all, Mitt Romney had won the votes of only 27 percent of Latinos—a group that was 10 percent of the electorate in 2012 and sure to get bigger. Immigration reform is an important issue to the Latino community, but, unfortunately for the Republican Party, its base rejects any solution other than returning the estimated eleven million undocumented immigrants in the United States to their homes. To get the presidential nomination, Romney had run so far to the right, talking about something he called "self deportation," that he was never able to find his way back to the middle. The party leadership, meeting after the election to assess the damage, determined that that had to change.[1]

Other Republicans, especially business leaders, echoed that message and Democrats were on board too. In June 2013, the Senate, with a bipartisan majority scarcely heard of in these polarized times, passed an extensive immigration reform bill with a vote of 68–32.[2] The bill provided for tougher border security measures but also for a thirteen-year path to citizenship for those in this country without proper documentation. The ball was in then–Speaker of the House John Boehner's court.

And there it sat. Any path to citizenship for those who had initially broken the law by their arrival in this country was too much for conservative Republicans who had scuttled Boehner's legislative plans many times before. When limited immigration reform finally came, it was done by President Barack Obama, who took executive action without Congress to single-handedly defer the deportation of young undocumented immigrants who had been brought to this country as small children, and to similarly spare the parents of citizens or legal residents from being deported and to allow them to apply for work permits. In September, 2017, the Trump administration canceled the Obama DACA policy, leaving thousands of young people in legal limbo. A year later, in November 2018, the 9th Circuit Court of Appeals upheld a previous ruling that blocked Trump's action, making it likely that the issue will end up in the Supreme Court.[3]

In fact, it was as if the Republican angst over the issue had never been. In 2016 and the midterms two years later, the Republican candidates were once again running to the right, vying to outdo each other in their promises to voters that they would remove every undocumented immigrant from the country. Donald Trump affirmed his intention to secure the nation's borders, with a "beautiful wall" and was furious with Congress for not including its full cost in their budget. Under his administration, the U.S. Department of Homeland Security Immigration and Customs Enforcement (ICE) has had a tighter rule on deportations, deporting many long-time residents who did not have documentation.[4]

On the other side, Democrats were again promising reform with a path to citizenship. When the vote totals were counted in November 2016 and 2018, the Latino vote was again lopsided, helping to solidify the partisan division between the more diverse Democratic Party and the whiter, older Republicans.

How had immigration come to be such a toxic issue for Republicans and such a difficult challenge for the country as a whole? How had immigration reform gone from a win-win sure thing to a no-win risk? Had the Republicans changed their minds about the importance of immigration reform, or did they know (or care) that they were committing electoral suicide? Why was there no risk for the Democrats in promising a path to citizenship for undocumented workers? What was at stake for all these actors in passing—or not passing—immigration reform? **«**

OVER the years, American schoolchildren have grown up hearing two conflicting narratives about who we are as a nation. Neither disputes that we are nation of immigrants, but they tell very different stories about the consequences of immigration. The first, that we are a melting pot, implies that the United States is a vast cauldron into which go many cultures and ethnicities, all of which are boiled down into some sort of homogenized American stew.

The other origin story, so to speak, is that we are a multicultural nation in which each individual ethnic and religious identity should be preserved and honored, lest its distinctive nature be lost. The first vision sees the effect of immigration as something that should disappear, leaving only generic "Americans"; the other sees it as worthy of recognition and celebration. We learned in Chapter 1 that being able to get one's preferred narrative accepted is a form of political power, and that is certainly the case with those who are promoting these competing narratives about American diversity. Not surprisingly, reality, as typically happens, falls somewhere between the two extremes.

The rich diversity of the American people is one of the United States' greatest strengths, combining talents, tradition, culture, and custom from every corner of the world. Just to take one example, half of the current *Fortune* 500 (*Fortune* magazine's list of the nation's richest companies) were founded by immigrants or their kids. But our diversity has also contributed to some of the nation's deepest conflicts. We cannot possibly understand the drama that is American politics without an in-depth look at *who* the actors are that in many ways shape the *what* and *how* of politics.

Politics—what we want from government and how we try to get it—stems from who we are. Understanding where American citizens have come from and what they have brought with them, what their lives look like and how they spend their time and money, and what they believe and how they act on those beliefs is critically important to understanding what they choose to fight for politically and how they elect to carry out the fight. As a nation, we have a choice to include those groups with their own stories as valued parts of the national narrative, or to face the tumult of **identity politics**—political conflicts based on the claims of groups who feel their interests are being ignored or undervalued because of who they are. Identity politics includes not just new immigrant groups but also white Americans whose families have long been here and who see the waves of new immigrants, especially immigrants of color, as threats to their status. In a mediated world, every one of those groups has a chance to speak out and try to create a compelling narrative.

Since we cannot, of course, meet all the Americans out there, we settle for the next best thing: statistics, which provide us with relevant details about a large and complex population. Throughout this book we use statistics, in the form of charts and graphs, to examine the demographic trends that shape our national culture—political and otherwise. We'll use this information not only to understand better who we are but also to consider how the characteristics, habits, and lives of real people relate to the political issues that shape our society. (Be sure to read *Don't Be Fooled by . . . Big Data* for a discussion of the uses and limits of statistics in politics. It will serve you well as you read this book.)

In this chapter's *Snapshots of America*, you will see that our population is changing. Older people, whose pensions and nursing home care must be funded, compete for scarce resources with younger families, who want better schools and health care for children, and with college students, who want cheaper educations and better terms for their loans and who have a longer term investment in how we care for the environment. The white population in the United States will soon be outnumbered by ethnic and racial minority populations that traditionally support affirmative action, changes in law enforcement, immigration reform, and other social policies (less popular with whites) designed to protect them and raise them up from the lower end of the socioeconomic scale. As a result of these demographic changes, the prospect of becoming a minority population has some whites feeling threatened and fearful about the future of the country, sometimes feeling like strangers in their own towns.[5] Our population is in constant flux, and every change in the makeup of the people brings a change in what we try to get from government and how we try to get it.

As you look at these depictions of the American people and American life, try to imagine the political complexities that arise from such incredible diversity. How can a single government represent the interests of people with such varied backgrounds, needs, and preferences? How does who we are affect what we want and how we go about getting it?

WHO IS AN AMERICAN?

Native-born and naturalized citizens

In Chapter 1 we said that citizenship exacts obligations from individuals and also confers rights on them. We saw that the American concept of citizenship contains both self-interested and public-spirited elements, and is challenged in new ways by the mediated lives we live. But citizenship is not only a prescription for how governments ought to treat residents and how those residents ought to act; it is also a very precise legal status. A fundamental element of democracy is not just the careful specification of the rights and obligations of citizenship but also an equally careful legal description of just who is a citizen and how that status can be acquired by immigrants who choose to switch their allegiance to a new country. In this section we look at the legal definition of American citizenship and at the long history of immigration that has shaped our body politic.

---

identity politics the assertion of power, or discrimination, *by* a group—or an appeal for support *to* a group—based on their common perception of who they are

---

Should it be possible to lose one's citizenship under any circumstances?

Snapshot of America: *Who Are We and Who Will We Be by 2050?*

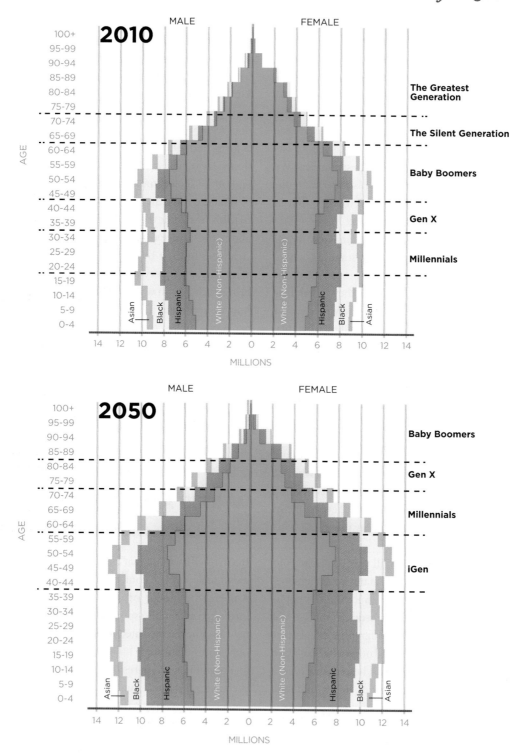

2010

MALE | FEMALE

The Greatest Generation

The Silent Generation

Baby Boomers

Gen X

Millennials

AGE

Asian | Black | Hispanic | White (Non-Hispanic) | White (Non-Hispanic) | Hispanic | Black | Asian

14 12 10 8 6 4 2 0 2 4 6 8 10 12 14

MILLIONS

2050

MALE | FEMALE

Baby Boomers

Gen X

Millennials

iGen

AGE

Asian | Black | Hispanic | White (Non-Hispanic) | White (Non-Hispanic) | Hispanic | Black | Asian

14 12 10 8 6 4 2 0 2 4 6 8 10 12 14

MILLIONS

Behind the Numbers

By 2050 most of the Baby Boomers will have died, and today's younger generations will be collecting Social Security; the working population will be predominately non-white. What will this increasing racial and ethnic diversity mean for American politics? What do you think the two political parties will look like in 2050?

Source: Pew Research Center Social & Demographic Trends, U.S. Population Projections: 2005–2050.

Big Data

The United States is a big country, so when we talk about American politics, we are usually talking about huge numbers: of people, of votes, of incomes, of ages, of policy preferences or opinions. Statistics are bandied about every day in the media. Depending on the source, they can be used as evidence to support arguments about everything from baseball to gun control. As critical consumers of American politics, it's crucial that we be able to sort through the barrage of numbers thrown at us daily through multiple media channels—to interpret their meaning, judge their veracity, and make sense of the ways in which they are displayed.

What to Watch Out For

- **Pay attention to the baseline.** When looking at a line graph or bar chart, take time to scrutinize the way numbers are plotted on the axes. Typically the numbers that go up the vertical axis begin at zero and move up at regular intervals. The real relationship between the numbers on each axis can be disguised, however, if the baseline is not zero—especially if it is below zero. Do not take for granted that you know what the baseline is. Check the scale or timeframe plotted on the axes, too. A set of numbers (for example, the Dow Jones Industrial Average) can look erratic over a series of hours, days, or even weeks, but when the data are plotted over years, patterns seem more predictable and far less volatile.

- **Remember the difference between the median and the mean.** Back in middle school, you learned that the *mean* is the average—calculated by adding up a series of values and dividing by the number of values. The mean is often used to provide a midrange estimate, but it can be skewed dramatically by *outlying values*, the ones far off at the top or bottom. For example, a small influx of multimillionaires moving into an impoverished neighborhood can raise the mean income into the middle-class range—even though many residents are struggling. For this reason, political scientists usually prefer to use the *median*, calculated by sorting all the values numerically and then finding the one in the physical middle. In our hypothetical neighborhood study, the median income would show that most residents are near the poverty line, even though a few residents live far, far above it.

- **Notice how the data are broken down.** Statisticians typically break down data into chunks for comparison. For example, you might divide a population into five or seven or ten segments, to see how they differ in terms of earnings, grades, and so on. But the way those data are chunked can skew a graph one way or another. For example, if you wanted to assess income inequality by comparing the incomes of the rich and the poor, you might compare the top 10 percent with the bottom 10 percent and you would find the top group earns about nine times as much as the low-income group. That is a lot, but what if you compare the top 0.1 percent with the same bottom 10 percent group? In this case, the top group makes 184 times as much per household as the bottom group, yielding a much more severe assessment of income inequality.[1]

- **Ask yourself what a graph is *not* showing you.** Graphs and visual displays can show you only a small part of the picture. Because they are usually limited to just a few variables, there is always more context to consider when you look at them. For example, population charts will often show growth in the numbers of a group without relating the group to the population as a whole. In such cases, a large influx of immigrants or refugees can look dramatic, but if the entire population is growing as well, the percentage of foreign-born people may remain the same.

- **Make sure that graphs focused on prices or money are using constant dollars.** A graph comparing the minimum wage over the past fifty years is useless if it is based on *nominal dollars*—because a dollar in 2017 buys a lot less than it did in 1965. Whenever a graph deals with prices or money, make sure that values are in *constant dollars*, which are adjusted for inflation, so that each dollar has a consistent value for all years (some graphs might note the value by a specific year, for example, "in 2016 dollars").

- **Beware of cause-and-effect claims.** The fact that two variables shift at the same time does not mean that one has caused the other. Causality is difficult to prove, and generally the best you can hope to do is to see if there might be a relationship between two variables.

- **Don't let the design fool you.** Numbers may have concrete meaning, but design choices like color, icons, and even typeface can imply meaning beyond what the numbers actually say. In accounting, for example, the color red denotes debt, whereas the color black denotes a favorable balance; in political science, the color red typically refers to the Republican Party, whereas blue refers to the Democratic Party. Any one or a combination of these design elements can intentionally or unintentionally influence the perception of the data when they are visualized.

---

1. Institute for Policy Studies, "Income Inequality," inequality .org/income-inequality/.

How Immigration Has Changed the Face of America

Immigration to the United States reflects both historical events outside our borders and policy decisions made within them. Each wave of arrivals triggered public anxiety about changing demographics, prompting policies that limited the number of incoming immigrants and often targeted specific ethnic or racial groups. We may be a nation of immigrants, but immigrants quickly assimilate, often closing the door behind them.

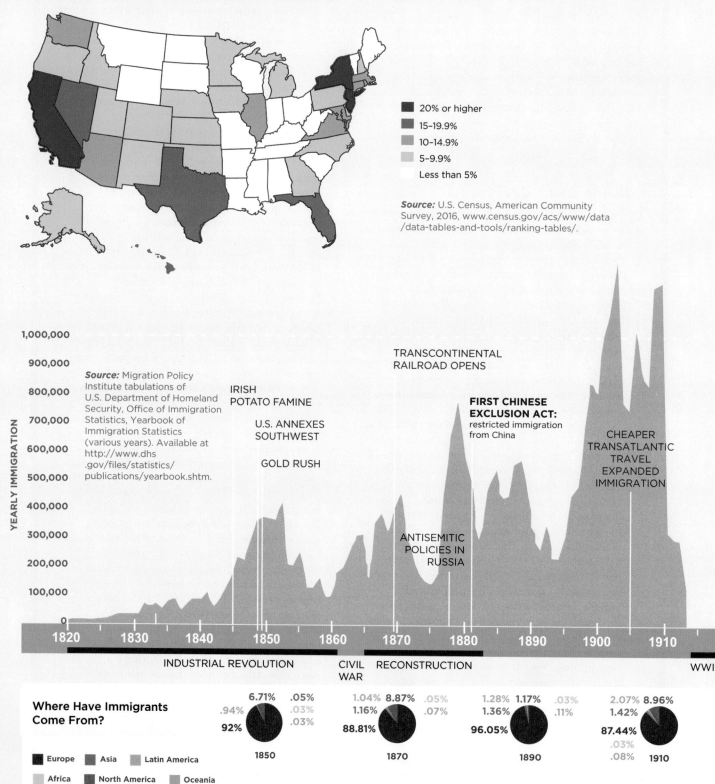

Foreign-Born Population as a Percentage of State Population: 2016

- ■ 20% or higher
- ■ 15–19.9%
- ■ 10–14.9%
- ■ 5–9.9%
- □ Less than 5%

Source: U.S. Census, American Community Survey, 2016, www.census.gov/acs/www/data/data-tables-and-tools/ranking-tables/.

Source: Migration Policy Institute tabulations of U.S. Department of Homeland Security, Office of Immigration Statistics, Yearbook of Immigration Statistics (various years). Available at http://www.dhs.gov/files/statistics/publications/yearbook.shtm.

TRANSCONTINENTAL RAILROAD OPENS

IRISH POTATO FAMINE

U.S. ANNEXES SOUTHWEST

GOLD RUSH

FIRST CHINESE EXCLUSION ACT: restricted immigration from China

ANTISEMITIC POLICIES IN RUSSIA

CHEAPER TRANSATLANTIC TRAVEL EXPANDED IMMIGRATION

YEARLY IMMIGRATION: 1,000,000 / 900,000 / 800,000 / 700,000 / 600,000 / 500,000 / 400,000 / 300,000 / 200,000 / 100,000 / 0

1820 1830 1840 1850 1860 1870 1880 1890 1900 1910

INDUSTRIAL REVOLUTION CIVIL WAR RECONSTRUCTION WWI

Where Have Immigrants Come From?

- ■ Europe
- ■ Asia
- ■ Latin America
- ■ Africa
- ■ North America
- ■ Oceania

1850: 6.71% / .05% / .94% / .03% / .03% / 92%

1870: 1.04% / 8.87% / .05% / 1.16% / .07% / 88.81%

1890: 1.28% / 1.17% / .03% / 1.36% / .11% / 96.05%

1910: 2.07% / 8.96% / 1.42% / .03% / .08% / 87.44%

How Immigrants Fare in Successive Generations

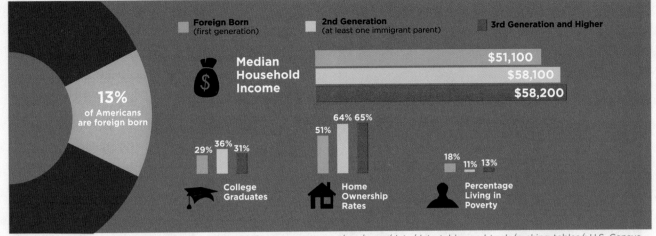

Foreign Born (first generation) | 2nd Generation (at least one immigrant parent) | 3rd Generation and Higher

13% of Americans are foreign born

Median Household Income
- $51,100
- $58,100
- $58,200

College Graduates: 29% 36% 31%

Home Ownership Rates: 51% 64% 65%

Percentage Living in Poverty: 18% 11% 13%

Source: U.S. Census, American Community Survey, 2016, www.census.gov/acs/www/data/data-tables-and-tools/ranking-tables/; U.S. Census Bureau, 2017 National Population Projections, www.census.gov/content/dam/Census/library/publications/2018/demo/P25_1144.pdf.

Nineteen out of twenty Hispanic children in the United States under the age of 18 were born in the United States and are citizens.

40% FORTUNE 500

About 40% of Fortune 500 firms were founded by immigrants or their children.

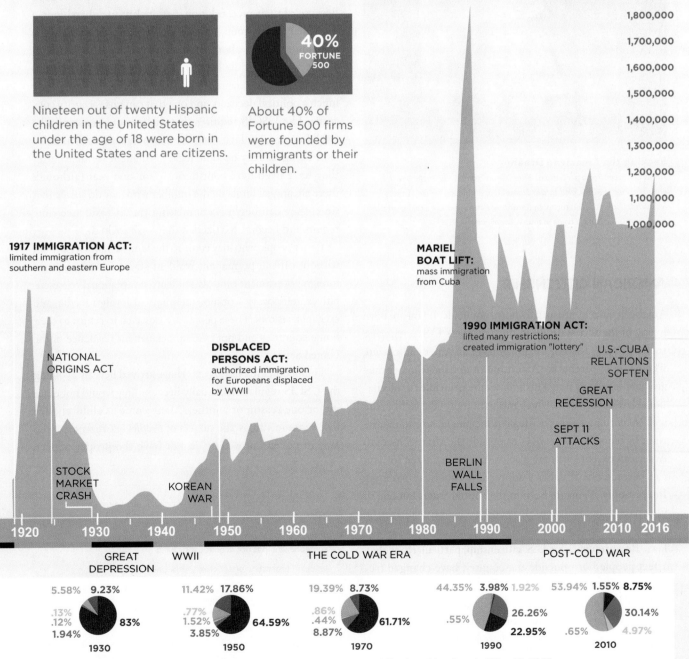

1917 IMMIGRATION ACT: limited immigration from southern and eastern Europe

NATIONAL ORIGINS ACT

STOCK MARKET CRASH

DISPLACED PERSONS ACT: authorized immigration for Europeans displaced by WWII

KOREAN WAR

MARIEL BOAT LIFT: mass immigration from Cuba

1990 IMMIGRATION ACT: lifted many restrictions; created immigration "lottery"

U.S.-CUBA RELATIONS SOFTEN

GREAT RECESSION

SEPT 11 ATTACKS

BERLIN WALL FALLS

1,800,000
1,700,000
1,600,000
1,500,000
1,400,000
1,300,000
1,200,000
1,100,000
1,000,000

1920 1930 1940 1950 1960 1970 1980 1990 2000 2010 2016

GREAT DEPRESSION | WWII | THE COLD WAR ERA | POST-COLD WAR

1930: 5.58% | 9.23% | .13% | .12% | 1.94% | 83%

1950: 11.42% | 17.86% | .77% | 1.52% | 3.85% | 64.59%

1970: 19.39% | 8.73% | .86% | .44% | 8.87% | 61.71%

1990: 44.35% | 3.98% | 1.92% | .55% | 26.26% | 22.95%

2010: 53.94% | 1.55% | 8.75% | .65% | 4.97% | 30.14%

Source: Pew Research Center, "Latino Children: A Majority Are U.S. Born Offspring of Immigrants," May 28, 2009, www.pewhispanic.org/2009/05/28/ii-the-legal-and-generational-status-of-hispanic-children/.

Universal History Archive/UIG via Getty Images

Seeking the American Dream
Anna Schiacchitano arriving at Ellis Island from Sicily in 1908 with her children Paolo, Mary, and infant Domenico, intending to join Anna's husband, Giovanni Gustozzo, in Scranton, Pennsylvania. Stories similar to theirs fill the family trees of many Americans.

AMERICAN CITIZENSHIP

American citizens are usually born, not made. If you are born in any of the fifty states or in most overseas U.S. territories, such as Puerto Rico or Guam, you are an American citizen, whether your parents are Americans or not and whether they are here legally or not. This follows the principle of international law called *jus soli*, which means literally "the right of the soil." According to another legal principle, *jus sanguinis* ("the right by blood"), if you are born outside the United States to American parents, you are also an American citizen (or you can become one if you are adopted by American parents). Interestingly, if you are born in the United States but one of your parents holds citizenship in another country, you may be able to hold dual citizenship, depending on that country's laws. Requirements for U.S. citizenship, particularly as they affect people born outside the country, have changed frequently over time.

Since before its birth America has been attractive to **immigrants**, who are citizens or subjects of another country who come here to live and work. If these immigrants come here legally on permanent resident visas—that is, if they follow the rules and regulations of the U.S. Citizenship and Immigration Services (USCIS)—they may be eligible to apply for citizenship through a process called **naturalization**. Although almost all American citizens are themselves immigrants or have descended from immigrants, they have, ironically, clamored for strict limits on who else can come in behind them.

NONIMMIGRANTS

Many people who come to the United States do not come as legal permanent residents. The USCIS refers to these people as nonimmigrants. Some arrive seeking **asylum**, or protection. These are political **refugees**, who are allowed into the United States if they face or are threatened with persecution because of their race, religion, nationality, membership in a particular social group, or political opinions. As we see in the continuing debate about whether Syrian and other Muslim refugees from Middle Eastern strife should be allowed into the United States, who can be considered a refugee is very much a political decision, and one that can raise security concerns. The USCIS requires that the fear of persecution be "well founded," and it is itself the final judge of a well-founded fear. Refugees may become legal permanent residents after they have lived here continuously for one year (although there are annual limits on the number who may do so). At that time, they can begin accumulating the in-residence time required to become a citizen, if they wish to do so.

Other people who may come to the United States legally but without official permanent resident status include visitors, foreign government officials, students, international representatives, temporary workers, members of foreign media, and exchange visitors. These people are expected to return to their home countries and not take up permanent residence in the United States.

Undocumented immigrants have arrived here by avoiding the USCIS regulations, usually because they would not qualify for one reason or another. Many come as children, like Jose Antonio Vargas, the subject of *Profiles in Citizenship*, who may not even know they do not have the proper papers.

immigrants citizens or subjects of one country who move to another country to live or work

naturalization the legal process of acquiring citizenship for someone who has not acquired it by birth

asylum protection or sanctuary, especially from political persecution

refugees individuals who flee an area or a country because of persecution on the basis of race, nationality, religion, group membership, or political opinion

American laws have become increasingly harsh with respect to undocumented immigrants, but for years that did not stop them from coming in search of a better life. Even before the 2016 election of President Trump, with his harsh anti-immigrant rhetoric, levels of undocumented immigration had actually fallen off, although this does not fit well with many of the prevailing narratives about the issue.[6] In particular, more Mexicans have been leaving the United States, generally to reunite with their families, than have been seeking to enter it.[7]

Even people who are not legal permanent residents of the United States have rights and responsibilities here, just as we do when we travel in other countries. The rights that immigrants enjoy are primarily legal protections; they are entitled to due process in the courts (guarantee of a fair trial, right to a lawyer, and so on), and the U.S. Supreme Court has ruled that it is illegal to discriminate against immigrants in the United States.[8] Nevertheless, their rights are limited. They cannot, for instance, vote in our national elections (although some communities allow them to vote in local elections[9]) or decide to live here permanently without permission. In addition, immigrants, even legal ones, are subject to the decisions of the USCIS, which is empowered by Congress to exercise authority in immigration matters.

U.S. IMMIGRATION POLICY

Immigration law is generally made by Congress with the approval of the president. In the wake of September 11, 2001, security issues came to play a central role in deciding who may enter the country, and new legislation took the federal agency tasked with implementing immigration law out of the Department of Justice, where it was formerly located. The new agency, named the U.S. Citizenship and Immigration Services, was placed under the jurisdiction of the newly formed Department of Homeland Security.

WHOM TO ADMIT No country, not even the huge United States, can manage to absorb every impoverished or threatened

> **nativism** the belief that the needs of citizens ought to be met before those of immigrants

HISTORY MARCHES ON; NATIVISM MARCHES IN PLACE

global resident who wants a better or safer life. Deciding whom to admit is a political decision—like all political decisions, it results in winners and losers. Especially when times are tough, **nativism**, or the belief that the needs of citizens ought to be met before those of immigrants, can take on political force, as it did in Donald Trump's campaign in 2016. For instance, jobs are just the sort of scarce resource over which political battles are fought. If times are good and unemployment is low, newcomers, who are often willing to do jobs Americans reject in prosperous times, may be welcomed with open arms. When the economy hits hard times, immigration can become a bitter issue among jobless Americans. It's also the case that immigrants, especially the very young and the very old, are large consumers of social services and community resources. Immigrants do contribute to the economy through their labor and their taxes, but because they are distributed disproportionately throughout the population, some areas find their social service systems more burdened than others, and immigration can be a much more controversial issue in places where immigrants settle. In addition, large numbers of immigrants can change the demographic balance, as we have already seen by the fact that whites will be a minority group in this country by 2050. For some people, being a part of the majority is a status and a source of political power worth fighting for.

Nations typically want to admit immigrants who can do things the country's citizens are unable or unwilling to do. During and after World War II, when the United States wanted to develop a rocket program, German scientists with the necessary expertise were desirable immigrants. At times in our history when our labor force was insufficient for the demands of industrialization and railroad building and when western states wanted larger populations, immigrants were welcomed. Today, immigration law allows for temporary workers to come to work in agriculture when our own labor force falls short or is unwilling to work for low wages. As a rule, however, our official immigration policy expects immigrants to be skilled and financially stable so that they do not become a burden on the American social services system. Remember that politics is about how power and resources are distributed in society; who gets to consume government services is a hotly contested issue.

REGULATING THE BORDER Some areas of the country, particularly those near the Mexican-American border, like Texas and California, have often had serious problems brought on by unregulated immigration. This is one reason undocumented immigration is a hot-button issue. Communities can find themselves swamped with new residents, often poor and unskilled. Because their children must be educated and they themselves may be entitled to receive social services, they can pose a significant financial burden on those communities. Some undocumented immigrants work off the books, meaning they do not contribute to the tax base. Furthermore, most income taxes are federal, and federal money is distributed back to states and localities to fund social services based on the population count in the census. Since undocumented immigrants are understandably reluctant to come forward to be counted, their communities are typically underfunded in that respect as well.

At the same time, many undocumented immigrants act just like citizens, obeying laws, paying taxes, and sending their children to school. Some have lived here for decades, perhaps since they were children themselves, and their own children and grandchildren may be citizens. They are well integrated into their communities, which makes the prospect and challenge of finding and repatriating them a formidable one for those who believe that is the best political solution. It is also why many others think providing some sort of amnesty or path to citizenship is more practical.

Whether motivated by cultural stereotypes, global events, or domestic economic circumstances, Americans have decided at times that we have allowed "enough" immigrants to settle here, or that we are admitting too many of the "wrong" kind of immigrants, and we have encouraged politicians to enact restrictions. When this happens, narratives emerge in which immigrants are scapegoated for the nation's problems and demonized as a threat to American culture. This occurred from 1882 to 1943 with Chinese immigrants and in the late 1800s and early 1900s with southern and eastern Europeans. Legislation in the 1920s limited immigration by creating a quota system that favored the northern and

western nationalities, seen as more desirable immigrants.[10] Today's debate over undocumented immigration taps into some of the same emotions and passions as earlier efforts to limit legal immigration.

Congress abolished the existing immigration quota system in 1965 with the Immigration and Nationality Act. This act doubled the number of people allowed to enter the country, set limits on immigration from the Western Hemisphere, and made it easier for families to join members who had already immigrated. More open borders meant immigration was increasingly hard to control. Reacting to the waves of undocumented immigrants who entered the country in the 1970s and 1980s, Congress passed the Immigration Reform and Control Act in 1986, granting amnesty to undocumented immigrants who had entered before 1982 and attempting to tighten controls on those who came after. Although this law included sanctions for those who hired undocumented immigrants, people continued to cross the border illegally from Mexico looking for work. The 1965 act was reformed with the Immigration Act of 1990, which, among other things, admitted even more immigrants. In the 1990s, legislation under President Bill Clinton strengthened the power of the Immigration and Naturalization Service (the precursor to the USCIS).

IMMIGRATION LAW TODAY As we saw in *What's at Stake . . . ?*, in recent years the immigration debate has come to be defined by the tension between two opposing political camps. On the one hand are those who seek to grapple with the issue of the estimated eleven million undocumented immigrants already in this country and the demands of American business for the cheap labor that immigrants provide; on the other hand are those who prioritize the rule of law and believe undocumented immigrants should be sent home and the borders tightened against the arrival of any more. Although under Barack Obama's administration, deportations of undocumented workers, especially those with criminal backgrounds, rose sharply, Obama tried hard to get Congress to pass immigration reform, especially the Development, Relief and Education for Alien Minors (DREAM) Act. This policy would have granted relief to young adults who were brought here without documentation as children. Unwilling to leave the job unfinished, Obama decided to take executive action. In 2012, he announced the Deferred Action for Childhood Arrivals (DACA) policy that allowed children brought in without documentation to apply for a two-year, renewable exemption from deportation during which time they would be eligible for work permits.

As we saw in *What's at Stake . . . ?*, opposition to undocumented immigration has been a cornerstone of Donald Trump's campaign and presidential rhetoric. For many of

Snapshot of America: *What Do Our Two Largest Immigrant Groups Look Like?*

Latino Immigrants

32% of Latino immigrants are foreign born. **The majority (65.6%) are born in the United States.**

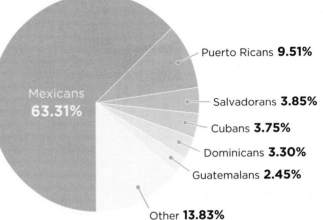

Mexicans **63.31%**
Puerto Ricans **9.51%**
Salvadorans **3.85%**
Cubans **3.75%**
Dominicans **3.30%**
Guatemalans **2.45%**
Other **13.83%**

Asian Immigrants

41% of Asian immigrants are born in the United States. **The majority (59%) are foreign born.**

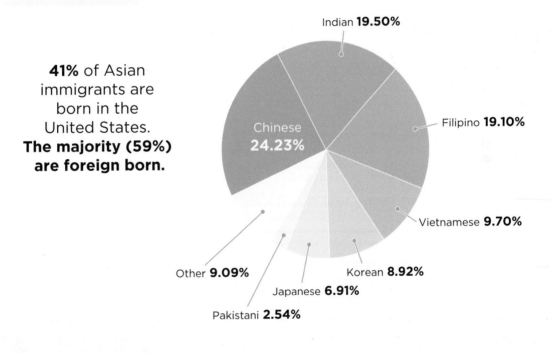

Indian **19.50%**
Filipino **19.10%**
Chinese **24.23%**
Vietnamese **9.70%**
Korean **8.92%**
Japanese **6.91%**
Pakistani **2.54%**
Other **9.09%**

Behind the Numbers

America is changing. Looking toward the future, we will see growth in the numbers of Asians and Latinos. Will diversity within these groups affect their political cohesion? How will whites, the traditional majority, adapt to their coming minority status?

Source: Mark Hugo Lopez, Ana Gonzalez-Barrera, and Danielle Cuddington, "Diverse Origins: The Nation's 14 Largest Hispanic-Origin Groups," Pew Research Hispanic Trends Project, http://www.pewhispanic.org/2013/06/19/diverse-origins-the-nations-14-largest-hispanic-origin-groups/; Pew Research Center Social & Demographic Trends, U.S. Population Projections: 2005–2050.

FIGURE 2.1

Sanctuary Cities

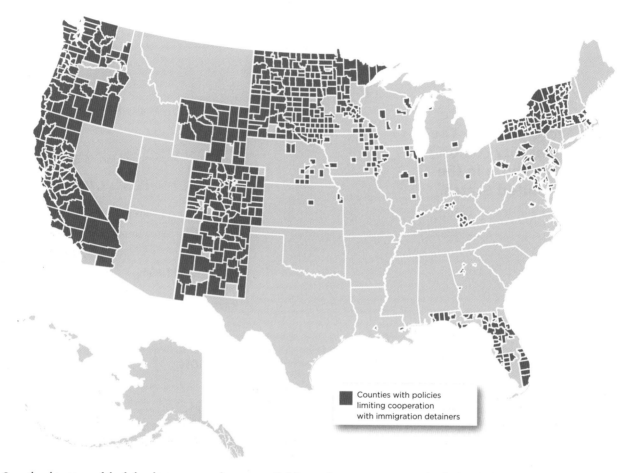

Counties with policies limiting cooperation with immigration detainers

Over the objections of the federal government, five states—California, Connecticut, New York, Rhode Island, and Vermont—as well as many other counties and cities nationwide, have passed laws limiting local authorities' obligation to cooperate with immigration officials. Whether this constitutes an illegal infringement on the federal government's ability to set immigration policy is likely to be decided by the courts.

Source: "What Are Sanctuary Cities?" *New York Times,* February 6, 2017, https://www.nytimes.com/interactive/2016/09/02/us/sanctuary-cities.html.

his supporters, the building of a wall along the southern border would be a visual sign that the United States intends to crack down on undocumented entrants, but it is not clear that a wall has more than symbolic value. Still, Trump has made funding the wall and stricter laws on *legal* as well as illegal immigration the price of his support for immigration reform. He has said he wants to limit the family members legal immigrants can bring in with them (so-called chain migration) and limit the number of immigrants from what he called "shithole" countries, referring to Haiti and the nations of Africa. Although he initially said he would support the DREAM Act, as we noted in *What's at Stake* he tried to end DACA in 2017; in 2018 the District Court in

Washington, D.C., said that the program had to resume taking applications and that ruling was upheld in November. As of this writing, DACA stays in place, but the Justice Department has asked the Supreme Court to hear the issue quickly. There is unquestionably a conservative majority on the Court but whether that will translate into the ruling Trump wants is not yet clear (although it may be by the time you read this). In the meantime, raids by Immigration and Customs Enforcement (ICE) agents under Trump have risen so much so that even Trump supporters are having second thoughts.[11]

At the state and local levels, some places are resisting the Trump administration's efforts by creating sanctuary

Jose Antonio Vargas

Gerry Salva-Cruz

Born in the Philippines, Jose Antonio Vargas was sent by his mother to the United States at age twelve to live with his grandparents, both naturalized U.S. citizens. Until he went to get his driver's license, Vargas had no idea that the papers that had gotten him into the country were fake, paid for by his family in the hopes of giving him a better life.

And his life was great, except for the weight of the secret he carried, forcing him into a virtual closet, afraid to let anyone, except for a few trusted confidants, close enough to know him. Even when he became a successful journalist and part of a Pulitzer Prize–winning team at the *Washington Post*, his anxiety about having his secret revealed was so debilitating that in 2011 he decided to come out of the shadows in a long and moving essay in the *New York Times Sunday Magazine*. (The *Post* was afraid to publish the essay because of possible legal repercussions for having hired him.)

So far, Vargas is still here, for the most part left to himself by immigration authorities, and he has made himself a voice for the voice-less, founding the nonprofit Define American and working as an immigration-rights activist and a filmmaker. He has become an entrepreneur because, as an undocumented worker, he can employ others but cannot be hired himself.

On living in the shadows

I was risking my sanity, I think. And I think I was risking my sense of self. It was almost as if I had to create a different person that had to lie to all of my friends. You know I was the kind of person who, if you had known me six years ago, I just never talked about my family, there were no photos of them anywhere in my house. I never talked about where I was from because, if you talk about where you're from, then it's gonna come up. Well, how'd you get here?

On the meaning of citizenship

I just hope that young people in this country do not take their citizenship for granted. And I hope that they realize what was paid for it—literally and figuratively, what paved the way for them to be free. And that freedom isn't comfortable . . . . [T]here's this quote from Toni Morrison and I didn't realize she got it from [James] Baldwin. The quote was, "Your crown has been bought and paid for. Your ancestors already gave it up for you. It's already done. Now you can love yourself. It's possible."

On keeping the republic

To me, this country has always been an experiment. It was and it is still an experiment. So these questions of how we define what an American is, I think, especially in this age of globalization, during the migrant crisis that is enveloping all of Europe. I think this question of how we define "American" is at the very core of this republic and how we keep it. Is it laws? Is it papers? One last thing. So I was in North Carolina a few months ago and I showed my film [*White People*]. It was a pretty sizeable black crowd that went to the screening and this black woman—I guess she saw me on television—so she came. She was elderly. She said, "Ah, Mr. Vargas. I was fascinated hearing you say in an interview that your life is subjected to pieces of papers that you don't have. And I thought about my great, great, great, great grandmother who landed in South Carolina, was given a piece of paper—a bill of sale saying she's a slave. So can you connect the piece of paper that my great, great, great, great grandmother got to the pieces of paper that you and millions of people like you can't seem to get." I didn't know what to tell her. That's America to me.

Source: Jose Antonio Vargas spoke with Christine Barbour and Gerald C. Wright on May 13, 2016.

Support and Defend

An immigrant from Haiti, Alix Schoelcher Idrache earned his citizenship while serving in the Maryland National Guard before being accepted into the nation's most prestigious military school. This photo, capturing his intense emotion during commencement at West Point in 2016, quickly went viral.

cities where local officials do not comply with the federal effort to deport undocumented workers. Approximately three hundred states, cities, and local governments have declared themselves to be sanctuaries (see Figure 2.1). The Supreme Court made clear in a 2012 Arizona case that although a state was within its rights to require police officers to verify the status of people they had reason to believe were here illegally, it could not infringe on the federal right to set immigration policy.[12] When Trump tried to defund sanctuary cities by executive order, however, several federal judges said such action was unconstitutional. These issues have yet to be untangled by the courts. As we will see in Chapter 4, federalism issues can be very complicated.

Although the reasons for declaring a locality to be a sanctuary city are generally humanitarian, there can be an awareness of economic consequences as well. One Alabama study, for instance, found that in the wake of the passage of a strict immigration bill, 40,000 to 80,000 workers had left the state, reducing demand for goods and services and costing the state between 70,000 and 140,000 jobs.[13]

PAUSE AND REVIEW Who, What, How

There are competing narratives about how immigrants are assimilated into American society—one sees them blending into a melting pot, the other sees a crazy salad of diversity, and the view you accept has real implications for your stance on immigration issues, issues in which the political and humanitarian stakes are very high.

For non-Americans who are threatened or impoverished in their native countries, the stakes are sanctuary, prosperity, and an

improved quality of life, which they seek to gain through acquiring asylum or by becoming legal or undocumented immigrants. People who are already American citizens have a stake here as well. At issue is the desire to be sensitive to humanitarian concerns, as well as to fill gaps in the nation's pool of workers and skills, and to meet the needs of current citizens. These often-conflicting goals are turned into law by policymakers in Congress and the White House, and their solutions are implemented by the bureaucracy of the USCIS.

In Your Own Words Analyze the role of immigration and the meaning of citizenship in U.S. politics.

THE IDEAS THAT UNITE US

A common culture based on shared values

Making a single nation out of such a diverse people is no easy feat. It is possible only because, despite all our differences, most Americans share some fundamental attitudes and beliefs about how the world works and how it should work. These ideas, our political culture, pull us together and, indeed, provide a framework in which we can also disagree politically without resorting to violence and civil war.

Political culture refers to the general political orientation or disposition of a nation—the shared values and beliefs about the nature of the political world that give us a common language with which to discuss and debate political ideas. **Values** are ideals or principles that most people agree are important, even if they disagree on exactly how the value—such as "equality" or "freedom"—ought to be defined.

Statements about values and beliefs are not descriptive of how the world actually is, but rather are prescriptive, or **normative**, statements about how the value-holders believe the world ought to be. Our culture consists of deep-seated, collectively held ideas, handed down through the generations—through the process of *political socialization*, which we will read about in Chapter 11—about how life *should* be lived. Normative statements aren't true or false but depend for their worth on the arguments that are made to back them up.

Often we take our own culture (that is, our common beliefs about how the world should work) so much for granted that we aren't even aware of it; we just think we have the correct outlook and those who live elsewhere are simply mistaken about

> **political culture** the broad pattern of ideas, beliefs, and values that a population holds about its citizens and government
>
> **values** the central ideas, principles, or standards that most people agree are important
>
> **normative** a term used to describe beliefs or values about how things should be or what people ought to do rather than what actually is

how things should be done. For that reason, it is often easier to see our own political culture by contrasting it to another's.

Political culture is shared, although certainly some individuals find themselves at odds with it. When we say, "Americans think . . . ," we mean that most Americans hold those views, not that there is unanimous agreement on them. To the extent that we get more polarized—that is, to the extent that our political differences get farther apart and the channels through which we get information become more easily manipulated—the political culture itself may begin to break down and we may lose the common language that enables us to settle those differences through conventional political means. The 2016 election campaign showed us just how fragile the cultural ties that bind us can be when our differences are stoked and the legitimacy of our system is challenged.

FAITH IN RULES AND INDIVIDUALS

In American political culture, our expectations of government have traditionally focused on rules and processes rather than on results, what we called in Chapter 1 an insistence on **procedural guarantees**. For example, we think government should guarantee a fair playing field but not guarantee equal outcomes for all the players. We also tend to believe that individuals are responsible for their own welfare and that what is good for them is good for society as a whole, a perspective called **individualism**. American culture is not wholly procedural and individualistic—indeed, differences on these matters constitute some of the major partisan divisions in American politics—but these characteristics are more prominent in the United States than they are in most other nations.

To illustrate this point, we can compare American culture to the more social democratic cultures of Scandinavia, such as Sweden, Denmark, and Norway. In many ways, the United States and the countries in Scandinavia are more similar than they are different: they are all capitalist democracies, and they essentially agree that individuals ought to make most of the decisions about their own lives. Recall our comparison of political and economic systems from Chapter 1. The United States and Scandinavia, which reject substantial government control of both the social order and the economy, would all fit into the upper-right quadrant of Figure 1.3, along with other advanced industrial democracies such as Japan and Great Britain.

> **procedural guarantees** government assurance that the rules will work smoothly and treat everyone fairly, with no promise of particular outcomes
>
> **individualism** the belief that what is good for society is based on what is good for individuals

Free Speech, Even When It's Ugly
Americans don't agree on much, but they do cherish their right to disagree. Most citizens have little tolerance for censorship and expect the government to protect even the most offensive speech. Here, a police officer flanks a marcher at a Ku Klux Klan rally in South Carolina in 2015.

These countries do differ in some important ways, however. All advanced industrial democracies repudiate the wholehearted substantive guarantees of communism, but the Scandinavian countries have a greater tolerance for substantive economic policy than does the more procedural United States. We explore these differences here in more detail so that we can better understand what American culture supports and what it does not.

PROCEDURAL GUARANTEES As we have noted, when we say that American political culture is procedural, we mean that Americans generally think government should guarantee fair processes—such as a free market to distribute goods, majority rule to make decisions, due process to determine guilt and innocence—rather than specific outcomes. The social democratic countries of Sweden, Denmark, and Norway, however, as we saw in Chapter 1, believe that government should actively seek to realize the values of equality—perhaps to guarantee a certain quality of life (shelter, jobs, and health) to all citizens or to increase equality of income. Government can then be evaluated by how well it produces those substantive outcomes, not just by how well it guarantees fair processes.

American politics does set some substantive goals for public policy, but Americans are generally more comfortable ensuring that things are done in a fair and proper way, and trusting that the outcomes will be good ones because the rules are fair. Although the American government is involved in social programs and welfare, and took a big step in a substantive direction with passage of the Patient Protection and Affordable Care Act, it aims more at helping individuals get on their feet so that they can participate in the market (fair procedures) than at cleaning up slums or eliminating poverty (substantive goals).

INDIVIDUALISM The individualistic nature of American political culture means that individuals are seen as responsible for their own well-being. This contrasts with a collectivist point of view, which gives government or society some responsibility for individual welfare, and holds that what is good for society may not be the same as what is in the interest of individuals. When Americans are asked by the government to make economic sacrifices, like paying taxes, such requests tend to be unpopular and more modest than in most other countries (even though Americans often give privately, generously, and voluntarily to causes in which they believe). A collective interest that supersedes individual interests is generally invoked in the United States only in times of war or national crisis. This echoes the two American notions of self-interested and public-interested citizenship we discussed in Chapter 1.

For contrast, let's look again at the Scandinavian countries, which tend to have more collectivist political cultures. In fact, one reason Scandinavians have more substantive social policies than are found in the United States is because they have a sense of themselves as a collective whole: to help one is to help all. They value *solidarity*, a sense of group identification and unity that allows them to entertain policies we would not consider. For example, at one time, Sweden used pension funds to help equalize the wages of workers so that more profitable and less profitable industries would be more equal, and society, according to the Swedish view, would be better off. Americans would reject this policy as violating their belief in individualism (and proceduralism, as well).

CORE AMERICAN VALUES: DEMOCRACY, FREEDOM, AND EQUALITY

We can see our American procedural and individualistic perspective when we examine the different meanings of three core American values: democracy, freedom, and equality.

DEMOCRACY Democracy in America, as we have seen, means representative democracy, based on consent and majority rule. Basically, Americans believe democracy should be a procedure to make political decisions, to choose political leaders, and to select policies for the nation. It is seen as a fundamentally just or fair way of making decisions because every individual who cares to participate is heard in the process, and all interests are considered. We don't reject a democratically made decision because it is not fair; it is fair precisely because it is democratically made.

FREEDOM Americans also put a very high premium on the value of freedom, defined as freedom for the individual from restraint by the state. This view of freedom is procedural in the sense that it provides that no unfair restrictions should be put in the way of your pursuit of what you want, but it does not guarantee you any help in achieving those things. For instance, when Americans say, "We are all free

to get a job," we mean that no discriminatory laws or other legal barriers are stopping us from applying for any particular position. A substantive view of freedom would ensure us the training to get a job so that our freedom meant a positive opportunity, not just the absence of restraint.

Americans' commitment to procedural freedom can be seen nowhere so clearly as in the Bill of Rights, the first ten amendments to the U.S. Constitution, which guarantees our basic civil liberties, the areas where government cannot interfere with individual action. Those civil liberties include freedom of speech and expression, freedom of belief, freedom of the press, and the right to assemble, just to name a few. (See Chapter 5, "Fundamental American Liberties," for a complete discussion of these rights.)

But Americans also believe in economic freedom, the freedom to participate in the marketplace, to acquire money and property, and to do with those resources pretty much as we please. Americans believe that government should protect our property, not take it away or regulate our use of it too heavily. Our commitment to individualism is apparent here, too. Even if society as a whole would benefit if we paid off the federal debt (the amount our government owes from spending more than it brings in), our individualistic view of economic freedom means that Americans have one of the lowest tax rates in the industrialized world (for a comparison, see *Snapshot of America: How Much Do We Pay in Taxes?*).

EQUALITY Another central value in American political culture is equality. Of all the values we hold dear, equality is probably the one we cast most clearly in procedural versus substantive terms. Equality in America means government should guarantee equality of treatment, of access, of opportunity, but not equality of result. People should have equal access to run the race, but we don't expect everyone to finish in the same place or indeed to start from the same place. Thus we believe in political equality (one person, one vote) and equality before the law—that the law shouldn't make unreasonable distinctions among people the basis for treating them differently, and that all people should have equal access to the legal system.

One problem the courts have faced is deciding what counts as a reasonable distinction. Can the law justifiably discriminate between—that is, treat differently—men and women, minorities and white Protestants, rich and poor, young and old? When the rules treat people differently, even if the goal is to make them more equal in the long run, many Americans get very upset. Witness the controversy surrounding affirmative action policies in this country. The point of such policies is to allow special opportunities to members of groups that have been discriminated against in the past, to remedy the long-term effects of that discrimination. For many Americans, such policies violate our commitment to procedural solutions. They wonder how treating people unequally can be fair.

Snapshot of America: *How Much Do We Pay in Taxes?**

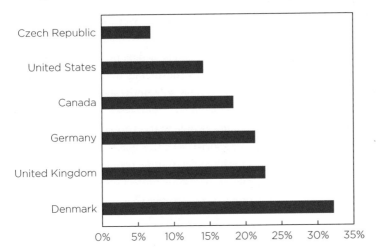

Behind the Numbers

No one, anywhere, likes taxes, and most Americans feel their taxes are too high. But notice that our average tax rate is lower than that in most other industrialized countries. What are the tradeoffs in people keeping more of their income versus government having funds to deal with national problems?

Source: Organization for Economic Cooperation and Development, *Revenue Statistics 2015*, Table 1.7, stats.oecd.org/index.aspx?DataSet Code=TABLE_I1.

Tax rate for family with average national wage. (Married couple with two children and one wage earner.)

PAUSE AND REVIEW Who, What, How

To live as a nation, citizens need to share a view of who they are, how they should live, and what their world should be like. If they have no common culture, they fragment and break apart, like the divided peoples of Ireland and the former Yugoslavia. Political cultures provide coherence and national unity to citizens who may be very different in other ways. Americans achieve national unity through a political culture based on procedural and individualistic visions of democracy, freedom, and equality.

In Your Own Words Explain how shared core values define the United States as a country and a culture.

THE IDEAS THAT DIVIDE US

Differences over how much government control there should be in our lives

Most Americans are united in their commitment at some level to a political culture based on proceduralism and individualism and to the key values of democracy, freedom, and equality. This shared political culture gives us a common political language, a way to talk about politics that keeps us united even though we may use that common language to tell different narratives about who we are, what's important to us, and what direction we feel the country should move in. That is not surprising.

> **ideologies** sets of beliefs about politics and society that help people make sense of their world

Although Americans have much in common, there are more than 300 million of us, and the *Snapshots of America* throughout the book demonstrate graphically how dramatically different we are in terms of our religious, educational, geographic, and professional backgrounds. We have different interests, different beliefs, different prejudices, and different hopes and dreams.

With all that diversity, we are bound to have a variety of beliefs and opinions about politics, the economy, and society that help us make sense of our world but that can divide us into opposing camps. These camps, or different belief systems, are called **ideologies**. Again, like the values and beliefs that underlie our culture, our ideologies are based on normative prescriptions—they depend for their force on the arguments we make to defend them. We cannot even pretend to live in a Norman Rockwell world where we learn our values face to face at our parents' dinner table. In a mediated age there are more and more arguments from more and more channels that are harder and harder to sort out. It might seem clear as a bell to us that our values are right and true, but to a person who disagrees with our prescriptions, we are as wrong as they think we are. So we debate and argue. In fact, anyone who pays attention to American politics knows that we disagree about many specific political ideas and issues, and that our differences have gotten more passionate and polarized (that is, further apart) in recent years.

But because we still share a political culture, our range of debate in the United States is relatively narrow, compared with the ideological spectrum of many countries. We have no successful communist or socialist parties here, for instance, because the ideologies on which those parties are founded seem to most Americans to push the limits of procedural and individualistic culture too far, especially in the economic realm. The two main ideological camps in the United States are the liberals (associated, since the 1930s, with the Democratic Party) and the conservatives (associated with the Republicans), with many Americans falling somewhere in between. Even though Sen. Bernie Sanders, a self-identified democratic socialist, ran for president in 2016, he did it as a Democrat (a party he had joined only briefly, to run), and he lost the nomination to Hillary Clinton.

There are lots of different ways to characterize American ideologies. It is conventional to say that conservatives tend to promote a political narrative based on traditional social values, distrust of government action except in matters of national security, resistance to change, and the maintenance of a prescribed social order. Liberals, in contrast, are understood to tell a narrative based on the potential for progress and change, trust in government, innovations as answers to social problems, and the expansion of individual rights and expression. For a more nuanced understanding of ideology in America, however, we focus on the two main ideological dimensions of economics and social order issues.

THE ECONOMIC DIMENSION

Since the Great Depression in the 1930s and Franklin D. Roosevelt's New Deal (a set of government policies designed to get the economy moving and to protect citizens from the worst effects of the Depression), American conservatives and liberals have diverged on how much they trust government to regulate a market that had demonstrated a marked inability to regulate itself. Conservatives believe that government is not to be trusted with too much power and is not a competent economic actor. Liberals, in contrast, have been willing to trust government more to regulate the economy, arguing that some of the effects of an unregulated market (poverty, hunger, etc.) are substantively unacceptable in a rich, advanced industrial nation. American economic ideological differences are much like those located on our economic continuum in Chapter 1 (see Figure 1.1), although none get anywhere as substantive as those do. Consequently, we say that liberals who advocate a larger role for government in regulating the economy are on the left, and conservatives who think government control should be minimal are on the right.

THE SOCIAL ORDER DIMENSION

In the 1980s and 1990s another ideological dimension became prominent in the United States. Perhaps because, as some researchers have argued, most people are able to meet their basic economic needs and more people than ever before are identifying themselves as middle class, many Americans began to focus less on economic questions and more on issues of morality and quality of life. The new ideological dimension,

which is analogous to the social order dimension we discussed in Chapter 1, divides people on the question of how much government control there should be over the moral and social order—whether government's role should be limited to protecting individual rights and providing procedural guarantees of equality and due process, or whether the government should be involved in making more substantive judgments about how people should live their lives.

Even though few people in the United States want to go so far as to create a social order that makes all moral and political decisions for its subjects, some people hold that it is the government's job to create and protect some version of a preferred social order. A conservative view of the preferred social order usually includes the following:

- An emphasis on religion in public life (prayer in school, public posting of religious documents like the Ten Commandments)
- A rejection of abortion and physician-assisted suicide
- Promotion of traditional family values (including a rejection of gay marriage and other gay rights)
- Emphasis on the "American Way" (favoring the melting pot narrative we mentioned earlier, rejecting the value of diversity for conformity and restricting immigration)
- A hierarchical sense that people should know their place in society
- Censorship of materials that promote alternative visions of the social order

Conservatives are not the only ones who seek to tell individuals how to live their lives. A newer, more liberal vision of the social order prescribes an expanded government role in regulating individual lives, though to achieve different substantive ends, including the following:

- The preservation of the environment (laws that require individuals to recycle or that tax gasoline to encourage conservation)
- The creation of a sense of community based on equality and protection of minorities (rules that urge political correctness and censorship of pornography)
- The promotion of individual safety (laws promoting gun control, seat belts, and motorcycle helmets)

conservatives people who generally favor limited government and are cautious about change

liberals people who generally favor government action and view change as progress

FIGURE 2.2

Paper!

Ideological Beliefs in the United States

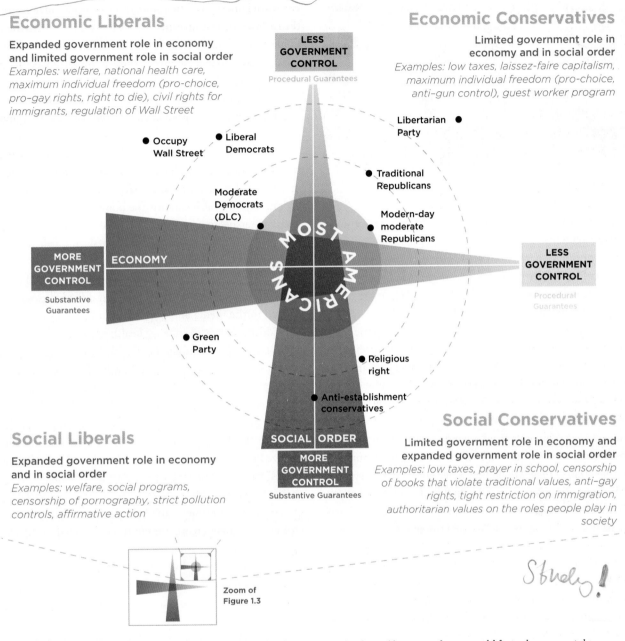

Economic Liberals

Expanded government role in economy and limited government role in social order
Examples: welfare, national health care, maximum individual freedom (pro-choice, pro-gay rights, right to die), civil rights for immigrants, regulation of Wall Street

Economic Conservatives

Limited government role in economy and in social order
Examples: low taxes, laissez-faire capitalism, maximum individual freedom (pro-choice, anti-gun control), guest worker program

LESS GOVERNMENT CONTROL
Procedural Guarantees

● Occupy Wall Street
● Liberal Democrats
Libertarian Party ●
● Traditional Republicans

Moderate Democrats (DLC)
● Modern-day moderate Republicans

MOST AMERICANS

MORE GOVERNMENT CONTROL — ECONOMY
Substantive Guarantees

LESS GOVERNMENT CONTROL
Procedural Guarantees

● Green Party

● Religious right

● Anti-establishment conservatives

SOCIAL ORDER
MORE GOVERNMENT CONTROL
Substantive Guarantees

Social Liberals

Expanded government role in economy and in social order
Examples: welfare, social programs, censorship of pornography, strict pollution controls, affirmative action

Social Conservatives

Limited government role in economy and expanded government role in social order
Examples: low taxes, prayer in school, censorship of books that violate traditional values, anti-gay rights, tight restriction on immigration, authoritarian values on the roles people play in society

Zoom of Figure 1.3

Slowly!

Although committed generally to a procedural and individualistic political culture (this entire figure would fit in the upper-right quadrant of Figure 1.3), Americans still find plenty of room for political disagreement. This figure outlines the two main dimensions of that conflict: beliefs about government's role in the economy and beliefs about government's role in establishing a preferred social order. Those ideological beliefs on the right side of the figure are conservative beliefs, and those on the left side are more liberal. The axes in these figures are continuums and do not represent all-or-nothing positions; most Americans fall somewhere in between.

THE RELATIONSHIP BETWEEN THE TWO IDEOLOGICAL DIMENSIONS

Clearly this social order ideological dimension does not dovetail neatly with the more traditional liberal and conservative orientations toward government action. Figure 2.2 shows some of the ideological positions yielded by these two dimensions. What this figure shows is a detail of the broader political spectrum we saw in Figure 1.3, focused on a small part of the upper-right quadrant we called *advanced industrial democracy*. When you look at the quadrants produced by examining those same dimensions within the United States' procedural and individualistic political culture, you get four distinct American ideological positions that are more explanatory than

By permission of Gary Varvel and Creators Syndicate.

simply saying "left" and "right." Figure 2.2 lays out these positions graphically.

Economic liberals hold views that fall into the upper-left quadrant of the figure because they are willing to allow government to make substantive decisions about the economy, and tend to embrace procedural individualistic positions on the social order dimension. Some economic policies they favor are job training and housing subsidies for the poor, taxation to support social programs, and affirmative action to ensure that *opportunities* for economic success (but not necessarily outcomes) are truly equal. As far as government regulation of individuals' private lives goes, however, these liberals favor a hands-off stance, preferring individuals to have maximum freedom over their noneconomic affairs. They are willing to let government regulate such behaviors as murder, rape, and theft, but they believe that social order issues such as reproductive choices, marijuana usage, gay rights, and assisted suicide are not matters for government regulation. They value diversity, expanding rights for people who have historically been left out of the power structure in the American social order—women, minorities, gays, and immigrants. Their love for their country is tempered by the view that the government should be held to the same strict procedural standard to which individuals are held—laws must be followed, checks and balances adhered to in order to limit government power, and individual rights protected, even when the individuals are citizens of another country.

Economic conservatives, in the upper-right quadrant of the figure, share their liberal counterparts' reluctance to allow government interference in people's private lives, but they combine this with a conviction that government should limit involvement in the economy as well. These economic conservatives prefer government to limit its role in economic decision making to regulation of the market (like changing interest rates and cutting taxes to end recessions), elimination of "unfair" trade practices (like monopolies), and provision of some public goods (like highways and national defense). When it comes to immigration, they favor more open policies since immigrants often work more cheaply and help keep the labor market competitive for business. The most extreme holders of economic conservative views are called **libertarians**, people who believe that only minimal government action in any sphere is acceptable. Consequently, economic conservatives also hold the government accountable for sticking to the constitutional checks and balances that limit its own power.

Social liberals, in the lower-left quadrant of the figure, tend to favor a substantive government role in achieving a more equal distribution of material resources (such as welfare programs and health care for the poor) but carry that substantive perspective into the social order as well. Although they continue to want the freedom to make individual moral choices that economic liberals want, they are happy to see some government action to create a more diverse and more equal power structure (including the way different groups are treated in the media and popular culture) and to regulate individual behavior to enhance health and safety (promoting environmental protections, motorcycle helmets, gun control, food labeling and restrictions on how food is produced, etc.). They endorse social norms to use **political correctness** as a way to name and shame those who do not share their substantive view of a community of disadvantaged groups that struggle against an oppressive power structure, and they believe higher education, in particular, should provide "safe spaces" where hurtful language and offensive popular culture should be banned. The most extreme adherents of social liberalism are sometimes called **communitarians** for their strong commitment to a community based on radical equality of all people. Because American political culture is procedural both economically and socially, not a lot of Americans are strong adherents of an ideology that calls for a substantive

economic liberals those who favor an expanded government role in the economy but a limited role in the social order

economic conservatives those who favor a strictly procedural government role in the economy and the social order

libertarians those who favor a minimal government role in any sphere

social liberals those who favor greater control of the economy and the social order to bring about greater equality and to regulate the effects of progress

political correctness the idea that language shapes behavior and therefore should be regulated to control its social effects

communitarians those who favor a strong, substantive government role in the economy and the social order so that their vision of a community of equals may be realized

government role in both dimensions. Many economic liberals, however, pick up some of the policy prescriptions of social liberals, such as environmentalism, gun control, and political correctness, but do not embrace more extreme forms of communitarianism.

Social conservatives occupy the lower-right quadrant in our ideological scheme. These people share economic conservatives' views on limited government involvement in the economy, but with less force and commitment and perhaps for different reasons (in fact, following the Great Depression, social conservatives, many of whom were members of the working class, were likely to be New Deal liberals). They may very well support government social programs like Social Security or Medicaid for those they consider deserving. Their primary concern is with their vision of the moral tone of life, including an emphasis on fundamentalist religious values, demonstrated, for instance, by government control of reproductive choices, opposition to gay rights, promotion of public prayer, and public display of religious icons. They endorse traditional family roles, and reject change or diversity that they see as destructive to the preferred social order. Immigration is threatening because it brings into the system people who are different and threatens to dilute the majority that keeps the social order in place. Many resent what they view as condemnation by liberal elites of the way they talk about race, gender, ethnicity, and sexual orientation and believe that they are labeled racist, sexist, or politically incorrect by overly sensitive liberal "snowflakes." In a world in which groups make claims of discrimination for historical or social reasons, they believe that they themselves are discriminated against for refusing to be politically correct and in some cases for being white and Christian. Social conservatives seek to protect people's moral character, and they embrace an authoritarian notion of community that emphasizes a hierarchical order (everyone in his or her proper place) rather than equality for all. Since limited government is not valued here, a large and powerful state is appreciated as being a sign of strength on the international stage. Patriotism for social conservatives is not a matter of holding the government to the highest procedural standards, as it is for those in the top half of Figure 2.2. Less worried about limiting government power over individual lives, they adopt more of a "my country right or wrong," "America First" view that sees criticism of the United States as unpatriotic.

> **social conservatives** those who endorse limited government control of the economy but considerable government intervention to realize a traditional social order; based on religious values and hierarchy rather than equality

POLITICAL SCIENCE

"And then there is the 'authoritarian' form of governing, which we'll be using in this class."

WHO FITS WHERE?

Many people, indeed most of us, might find it difficult to identify ourselves as simply "liberal" or "conservative," because we consider ourselves liberal on some issues, conservative on others. In fact, most Americans fall somewhere in the circle in the middle of Figure 2.2—leaning in one direction or another but not too extreme in any of our beliefs.

Others of us have more pronounced views, and the framework in Figure 2.2 allows us to see how major groups in society might line up if we distinguish between economic and social-moral values. We can see, for instance, the real spatial distances that lie among (1) the religious right, who are very conservative on political and moral issues but who were once part of the coalition of southern blue-collar workers who supported Roosevelt on the New Deal; (2) traditional Republicans, who are very conservative on economic issues but often more libertarian on political and moral issues, wanting government to guarantee procedural fairness and keep the peace, but otherwise to leave them alone; and (3) moderate Republicans, who are far less conservative economically and morally. As recent politics has shown, it can be difficult or impossible for a Republican candidate on the national stage to hold together such an unwieldy coalition.

RISE OF THE TEA PARTY/FREEDOM CAUCUS ON THE RIGHT In the summer of 2009, with the nation in economic crisis and the new African American president struggling to pass his signature health care reform in Washington, a wave of populist anger swept the nation. The so-called Tea Party movement (named after the Boston Tea Party rebellion against taxation in 1773) crafted a narrative that was pro-American, anti-corporation, and anti-government (except for programs like Social Security and Medicare, which benefit the Tea Partiers, who tended to be older Americans). Mostly it was angry, fed by emotional appeals of conservative talk show hosts and others, whose narratives took political debate out of the range of logic and analysis and into the world of emotional drama and angry invective. A *New York Times* poll found that Americans who identified as Tea Party supporters were more likely to be Republican, white, married, male, and over forty-five, and to hold views that were more conservative than Republicans generally.[14] In fact, they succeeded in shaking up the Republican Party from 2010 onward, as they supported primary challenges to office-holders who did not share their anti-government ideology. Once in Congress, the new members eventually formed the Freedom Caucus, which is sympathetic to many of the Tea Party values.

As we will see, this shakeup culminated in a rejection of the party establishment in 2016. The election that year signaled a moment of reckoning for a party that had been teetering on the edge of crisis for more than a decade. As establishment candidates fell in the primaries, so too did Tea Party favorites. The split in the party left an opening for the very unconventional candidacy of Donald Trump. Much to the dismay of party leaders like Speaker of the House Paul Ryan and Senate Majority Leader Mitch McConnell, Trump's candidacy proved to be more about his personality and the anger of his followers than it did about the Republican Party, although in the end most party members fell in line to vote for him.

Even before the rise of the Tea Party, Republican leaders had determined that they would not cede any political victories to President Obama. In an effort that goes beyond ideology and approaches tribalism—or the pure desire to see one's own team win at the expense of the other (see *CLUES to Critical Thinking* in Chapter 11)—Republicans simply blocked everything Obama tried to do. In 2010, then–Senate minority leader Mitch McConnell said that the highest priority the party had was to make Obama a one-term president.[15] The members of Congress elected by the Tea Party wave in 2010 enthusiastically committed to this no-compromise stance toward policymaking, demanding the fulfillment of their wish list and refusing to negotiate with the Democrats or President Obama to get things done. That is, rather than participate in the give-and-take, compromise-oriented procedural narrative of American politics, they held out for substantive policy ends. The Freedom Caucus presented then–Speaker of the House John Boehner with serious challenges to his leadership, bringing the country to the brink of economic disaster over their refusal to raise the debt ceiling so that the United States could pay its bills in the summer of 2011. In October 2013, they even shut down the federal government for more than two weeks. Eventually their threats to unseat Boehner succeeded. In 2015, with visible relief, he turned over the Speaker's gavel to a reluctant Representative Paul Ryan and resigned from Congress. Weary from the same battle, Ryan decided to resign the office in 2018.

What has become clear is that many social conservatives are outside the circle that defines mainstream American beliefs, posing a challenge to Republicans who run statewide or nationally because they need to satisfy two divergent constituencies. The late Sen. John McCain discovered this in 2008 when he found himself upstaged by his charismatic vice presidential running mate, Sarah Palin, and her strong social conservative ideas. Mitt Romney rediscovered it during the Republican primary season in 2012, when Tea Party members supported first Rick Perry, then Newt Gingrich, and then Rick Santorum in their effort to pick anybody but (the too moderate) Romney.

TRUMP'S APPEAL TO ANTI-ESTABLISHMENT CONSERVATIVES The escalating anger of social conservatives who felt inadequately represented by the Republican Party's mainstream came to a peak in the anti-establishment fury displayed in 2016. During that primary season, both Donald Trump and Sen. Ted Cruz competed to address the anger that drove that group. They felt used and betrayed, especially by a party that had promised and failed to defeat Barack Obama, a president they viewed, partly because of Trump's challenge to the president's birth certificate, as illegitimate. A mix of populist anger against the economic elite who profited at their expense, nativist anger at the perception that whites seemed to be falling behind while government was reaching out to help people of color, and partisan anger that economic conservative Republicans had been promising them socially conservative accomplishments since the days of Richard Nixon without delivering, the rage of social conservatives seemed to be one of **authoritarian populism**.

Indeed, social scientists trying to understand the surprising phenomenon of the Trump vote found that one particular characteristic predicted it: a commitment to "authoritarian values."[16] These social scientists have found that some social conservatives, when they feel that proper order and power hierarchy is threatened, either physically or existentially, are attracted to authoritarian narratives that seek to secure the old order by excluding the perceived danger. In

authoritarian populism a radical right-wing movement that appeals to popular discontent but whose underlying values are not democratic

the words of one scholar who studies this, the response is, "In case of moral threat, lock down the borders, kick out those who are different, and punish those who are morally deviant."[17] Those who score higher on the authoritarianism scale hold the kind of ideas one would expect from social conservatives seeking to keep faith with a familiar and traditional order—anti-gay sentiment, anti-immigration views, even white supremacy and overt racism. Interestingly, most recently it has also corresponded to narratives that reject the idea of political correctness itself, a reaction to the sense that the expression of their fear and anger is not socially acceptable.[18]

THE DEMOCRATS Although there have been major splits in the Democratic coalition in the past, their current divisions are minor, even after a presidential election season when a self-avowed democratic socialist challenged a more moderate liberal. The Democrats have to satisfy the party's economic liberals, who are very procedural on most political and moral issues (barring affirmative action) but relatively substantive on economic concerns; the social liberals, substantive on both economic and social issues; and the more middle-of-the-road Democratic groups that are fairly procedural on political and moral issues but not very substantive on economic matters at all. In the late 1960s, the party almost shattered under the weight of anti–Vietnam War sentiment, and in 1972, it moved sharply left, putting it out of the American mainstream. It was President Bill Clinton, as a founder of the now-defunct Democratic Leadership Council (DLC), who in the 1990s helped move his party closer to the mainstream from a position that, as we can see in Figure 2.2, is clearly out of alignment with the position taken by most Americans. Compared to those earlier divisions, its current intraparty disputes are relatively minor, although they may deepen in the 2020 race for the Democratic presidential nomination.

Ironically, in the 2000 election, Al Gore's commitment to the DLC position left him vulnerable to attack from Ralph Nader, who, as a representative of the Green Party, came from the lower-left quadrant. This position does not draw huge numbers of supporters, but in an election as close as the one in 2000, it probably drew sufficient support from Gore to cost him the election. In 2004, Democratic candidate John Kerry did not have to worry as much about appealing to voters in that lower-left quadrant since many of them disliked George W. Bush so much that they were willing to vote for a candidate with whom they did not completely agree in order to try to oust Bush from office. Democrat Barack Obama had the same advantage in 2008, drawing support from across his party's ideological spectrum in large part because of Bush's deep unpopularity. When the Occupy movement rose on the president's left flank in 2011, Obama was quick to adopt some of the movement's anti–Wall Street, anti-inequality rhetoric and made it a central part of his campaign, helping to ensure that we would not face an interparty challenge from the left. Similarly, in response to the primary challenge from democratic socialist Bernie Sanders, Hillary Clinton moved to adopt some of his more substantive economic positions. The Democrats have been able to manage the ideological dissension in their ranks more easily than have Republicans, for

FIGURE 2.3
Political Ideology, by Generation

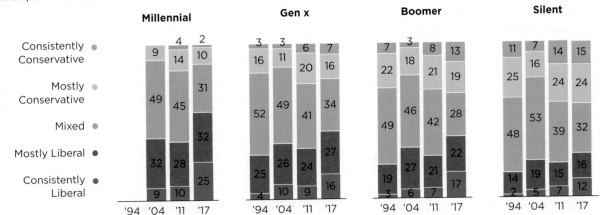

% with political values that are . . .

Source: Pew Research Center, "The Generation Gap in American Politics," March 1, 2018, http://www.people-press.org/2018/03/01/the-generation-gap-in-american-politics/.

whom the challenge is more fundamental, although Clinton's loss of the presidency has caused the party to do some soul-searching about where it goes post-Obama.

WHERE DO YOU FIT? One of the notable aspects of American ideology is that it often shows generational effects. Although we have to be careful when we say that a given generation begins definitively in a certain year (there is much overlap and evolution between generations), it can be helpful to look for patterns in where people stand in order to understand political trends. We know, for instance, that older white Americans tend to be more ideologically conservative, and because they are reliable voters, they get a lot of media attention. But with researchers gathering public opinion data on younger voters, and with those voters promising to turn out on issues they care about, it's a good idea to look at where millennials and post-millennials fall in Figure 2.2.

Keep in mind that all we can do is talk about generalities here—obviously there will be many, many exceptions to the rule, and you may very well be one of them. But as a group, younger voters, especially the *youngest* voters, tend to be economically and socially liberal—that is, they fall in the left-hand side of Figure 2.2.

PAUSE AND REVIEW Who, What, How

Although most Americans share a political culture, deep political differences, underscored and reinforced by the media, can remain about whose view of government should prevail and who should benefit from its actions. These differences have traditionally centered on government's economic role but increasingly also involve views on establishing a preferred social order, and on what the preferred social order should be. In the United States, ideologies generally go by the umbrella labels *liberalism* and *conservatism*, although many differences exist even within these broad perspectives. Ideological conflict can be contentious since what is at stake are fundamental views of what the political world ought to look like and control of the channels that publicize those views. It can be difficult for all the ideological conflict to be contained in a two-party system like ours.

In Your Own Words Describe the competing narratives that drive partisan divisions in American politics.

THE CITIZENS AND AMERICAN POLITICAL BELIEFS

The gap between the democratic narrative and the practice of American politics

One of the core values of American political culture is democracy, an ideal that unites citizens—both those who are born here as well as more newly minted naturalized citizens—in the activity of self-governance. In terms of the right to vote, we have grown more democratic in the past two hundred years. Many more people can participate now—women, African Americans, and eighteen-year-olds. Although it has been subject to some authoritarian battering lately, as have other democracies around the world, our national narrative, one shared by most Americans no matter what our ideological positions, is that we are a strong and active democracy, if not the premier democracy in the world.

The prevailing narrative is that the American notion of democracy doesn't ask much of us except that we pay attention to the news of the day and come together periodically and vote to elect our public officials. But most of us don't even do that. The news we get, as we have seen, is highly mediated by people who are trying to influence our views. American turnout rates (the percentages of people who go to the polls and vote on election days) are abysmally low compared to those of other Western industrialized democracies, and surveys show that many Americans are apathetic toward politics. Even in 2008, a year of unusually high turnout, only about 60 percent of eligible voters cast a vote although, remarkably, that number was almost duplicated in the midterms of 2018.

How does American democracy work with such low rates of participation or interest on the part of the citizenry? One theory, based on the elite notion of democracy described in Chapter 1, claims that it doesn't really matter whether people participate in politics because all important decisions are made by elites—leaders in business, politics, education, the military, and the media. Drawing on the pluralist theory of democracy, another explanation claims that Americans don't need to participate individually because their views are represented in government sufficiently through their membership in various groups. For instance, a citizen may make her views heard through membership in an environmental group, a professional association or labor union, a parent-teacher organization, a veterans' group, a church, or a political party.

By contrast, some educators and social scientists argue that falling levels of involvement, interest, and trust in politics signal a true civic crisis in American politics. They see a swing from the collectivist citizens of republican virtue to the self-interested individualistic citizens of Madisonian theory so severe that the fabric of American political life is threatened. For instance, Benjamin Barber, discussing the tendency of Americans to take their freedoms for granted and to assume that since they were born free they will naturally remain free, says that citizenship is the "price of liberty."[19] For all the importance of presidents and senators and justices in the American political system, it is the people, the citizens, who are entrusted with "keeping the republic."

The question of how democratic the United States is may seem to be largely an academic one—that is, one that has little or no relevance to your personal life—but it is really a question of who has the power, who is likely to be a winner in the political process. Looked at this way, the question has quite a lot to do with your life, especially as government starts to make more demands on you, and you on it. Are you likely to be a winner or a loser? Are you going to get what you want from the political system? How much power do people like you have to get their way in government?

Does it matter to the success of a democracy if relatively few people take an active political role (by paying attention, voting, exchanging political views, and the like)?

In Your Own Words Describe the gap between the ideal American democratic narrative and its practice.

LET'S REVISIT: *What's at Stake . . . ?*

We began this chapter with a look at the political circus surrounding the issue of American immigration reform. After the 2012 election, the Republican leadership determined that they had to pass immigration reform in order to improve their chances with Latino voters. But what had seemed like a slam dunk for everyone had become too toxic to touch by the 2016 Republican primaries and even more so by the 2018 midterm elections. What was really at stake in American immigration policy?

Part of the problem is that, for the Republican Party, the stakes were mixed. For business leaders, a guest worker program meant affordable labor for jobs Americans were not always willing to do. They argued that undocumented workers came here because there were jobs for them and that policies that punished employers for hiring them benefited no one and damaged the economy.

For Republican Party leaders, passing reform meant getting a difficult issue off the agenda, one that portrayed the party in a divisive, unflattering light and sent a negative message to an important and growing voting bloc. They knew that Latinos were key to carrying the vote in battleground states like Colorado, Nevada, and Florida. Furthermore, they believed that the policies of economic individualism and social conservatism they advocated should be attractive to Latino voters but that, until immigration was off the table, they would not get a hearing.

But many conservatives in the party, particularly the supporters of Donald Trump, think reform means giving a pass to law-breakers who would be rewarded for coming here illegally. If you think back to the ideological authoritarianism we discussed earlier, tough economic times and a dwindling white majority are exactly the kinds of threats to the social order that would trigger the slamming of the immigration door and the rejection of outsiders. At its worst, the rhetoric on this side of the argument, with its references to an "illegal invasion," "third world diseases," and "access to terrorists," begins to sound like xenophobia and even racism,[20] part of the reason why the party leadership want to get it behind them. But increasingly, the Republican agenda is becoming Trump's agenda and it is not clear that is going to happen.

For the Democrats, passing immigration reform meant being responsive to one of their core constituencies. For President Obama, in particular, the failure to act meant leaving undone one of his central campaign promises, the major reason he finally used executive action to address the issue. When the Democrats took back control of the House in 2018, immigration reform was on the top of their list, although without the Senate or Trump's support, it is not likely to be successful.

Shortly after the 2012 election, Eliseo Medina, the secretary-treasurer of the Service Employees International Union and a leader of efforts to mobilize Latino voters, said, "The Latino giant is wide awake, cranky and taking names."[21] After 2018, there will be plenty on the list.

CLUES to Critical Thinking

"The New Colossus"

By Emma Lazarus, 1883

Anyone who has ever taken a literature course knows it is just as important to think critically about elegant prose and poetry as the stories in the daily news. At least a part of this poem is familiar to most Americans—it appears on a plaque on the Statue of Liberty, one of the first glimpses of America for millions of immigrants to the United States arriving at Ellis Island. A gift from France celebrating American freedom (the statue holds a torch and a tablet inscribed "July 4, 1776"), the Statue of Liberty itself was not intended to be a symbol of immigration. Yet it has become so, especially because of the words put in her mouth by this poem. Given the decision to associate this poem with a national monument, we should think about it not only as a work of art but also as a political statement.

Not like the brazen giant of Greek fame,
With conquering limbs astride from land to land;
Here at our sea-washed, sunset gates shall stand
A mighty woman with a torch, whose flame
Is the imprisoned lightning, and her name
Mother of Exiles. From her beacon-hand
Glows world-wide welcome; her mild eyes command
The air-bridged harbor that twin cities frame.
"Keep, ancient lands, your storied pomp!" cries she
With silent lips. "Give me your tired, your poor,
Your huddled masses yearning to breathe free,
The wretched refuse of your teeming shore.
Send these, the homeless, tempest-tost to me,
I lift my lamp beside the golden door!"

Consider the source and the audience: The poem was written by Emma Lazarus (1849–1887), a Jewish American poet who became particularly interested in immigration after Russian anti-Semitism drove thousands of refugees to America in the late 1880s. She submitted the poem to an auction to fund the building of a pedestal for the Statue of Liberty, a gift from France to the United States, and it was later placed on a plaque inside the pedestal. How might Lazarus's own feelings have shaped her message? Why would future immigrants seize on those words as a symbol of hope?

Lay out the argument and the underlying values and assumptions: What is Lazarus's vision of Lady Liberty—does she see her as a symbol of national freedom from oppressive governance by England (signified by the date on the statue's tablet) or as a symbol of freedom for individuals from repression by other countries? What does she mean by naming the statue "Mother of Exiles"? What "ancient lands" is the statue talking to when she says, "Give me your tired, your poor"? What role of the United States to those displaced from their homelands is suggested by the poem's words?

Uncover the evidence: Lazarus does not create a political argument here but uses literary techniques to imply that the State of Liberty is a symbol of individual as well as national freedom. By calling her "Mother of Exiles" and having her utter comforting words of compassion and succor, she implies not only that the purpose of the statue is to welcome immigrants but also that such welcome is the policy of the United States. Does she offer anything other than literary skill to back up the claim that this is what the statue symbolizes?

Evaluate the conclusion: Lazarus is clearly offering a glowing "world-wide welcome" to victimized or suffering refugees to come to "the golden door" of America. From what you know about U.S. immigration history, is that an accurate representation of American immigration policy?

Sort out the political significance: Regardless of the political purpose of the French in giving the Statue of Liberty to the United States, or the intention of the American government in accepting it, it has become a near-universal symbol of an open-door immigration policy whereby the United States stands to welcome those immigrants fleeing inhospitable shores. That is due in large part to Lazarus's words. How has this generous and humane poem created a narrative about how the United States receives immigrants, and how has that narrative shaped expectations and public policy? How does it compare to the reality of Americans' sentiments about immigration over time?

Review

Who Is an American?

Citizenship in the United States is both a concept promising certain rights and responsibilities, and a precise legal status. U.S. immigrants are citizens or subjects of another country who come here to live and work. To become full citizens, they must undergo naturalization by fulfilling requirements designated by the U.S. Citizenship and Immigration Services.

Some people come to the United States for other reasons and do not seek permanent residency. In recent years the influx of undocumented immigrants, particularly in the southwestern states, has occupied national debate. Advocates of strict immigration policy complain that undocumented immigrants consume government services without paying taxes. Opponents of these policies support the provision of basic services for people who, like our ancestors, are escaping hardship and hoping for a better future. Congress, with the president's approval, makes immigration law, but these rules change frequently.

identity politics (p. 35) naturalization (p. 40) refugees (p. 40)
immigrants (p. 40) asylum (p. 40) nativism (p. 41)

The Ideas That Unite Us

Americans share common values and beliefs about how the world should work that allow us to be a nation despite our diversity. The American political culture is described as both procedural and individualistic. Because we focus more on fair rules than on the outcomes of those rules, our culture has a procedural nature. In addition, our individualistic nature means that we assume that individuals know what is best for them and that individuals, not government or society, are responsible for their own well-being.

Democracy, freedom, and equality are three central American values. Generally, Americans acknowledge democracy as the most appropriate way to make public decisions. We value freedom for the individual from government restraint, and we value equality of opportunity rather than equality of result.

political culture (p. 46) normative (p. 46) individualism (p. 47)
values (p. 46) procedural guarantees (p. 47)

The Ideas That Divide Us

Although the range of ideological debate is fairly narrow in America when compared to other countries, there exists an ideological division among economic liberals, social liberals, economic conservatives, and social conservatives based largely on attitudes toward government control of the economy and of the social order.

ideologies (p. 49) economic conservatives (p. 52) communitarians (p. 52)
conservatives (p. 50) libertarians (p. 52) social conservatives (p. 53)
liberals (p. 50) social liberals (p. 52) authoritarian populism (p. 54)
economic liberals (p. 52) political correctness (p. 52)

The Citizens and American Political Beliefs

America's growing political apathy is well documented. Yet despite abysmal voting rates, the country continues to function, a fact that may be explained by several theories. However, many people claim that such apathy may indeed signal a crisis of democracy.

3
POLITICS OF THE AMERICAN FOUNDING

What's at Stake . . . in Challenging the Legitimacy of the U.S. Government?

DECLARING WAR ON THE U.S. GOVERNMENT is a risky business. Governments depend for their authority on people believing their power is legitimate—when that legitimacy is challenged, so is their authority. Still, the United States is a democracy that guarantees free speech and the right to assemble peacefully, so handling rebellion can be tricky.

That was why the federal government reacted cautiously when Ammon Bundy, leader of a militia group called Citizens for Constitutional Freedom and the son of anti-government activist Cliven Bundy, responded to what he said was a divine instruction to take over the Malheur National Wildlife Refuge in eastern Oregon on January 2, 2016. Bundy said he was acting to support two ranchers who had been arrested for arson on federal land, though the ranchers disavowed the group. Specifically, Bundy demanded that the wildlife refuge land be given back to the state.

The federal government, which owned the land but was wary of causing a bloody showdown, waited. As various militias came to join the effort, police were able to apprehend Bundy and several of the other leaders traveling in a convoy. Although one person was shot and killed, most surrendered and the siege ended on February 28.[1]

The Malheur National Wildlife Refuge occupation reflected a movement that has gained traction in recent years: declaring that the federal government is abusing the power of the Constitution, and that that power must be returned to the people via the action of private citizens. Timothy McVeigh's 1995 attack on the federal building in Oklahoma City, which killed 168 people, including 19 children, was the bloodiest incident in the anti-government movement, but the broadest and strongest expression is the Tea Party movement, some of whose members have become part of the federal government themselves.

The birth of the Tea Party in 2010 might have been 1773 all over again. Anti-tax and anti-government, the protesters were angry, and if they didn't go as far as to empty shiploads of tea into Boston Harbor, they made their displeasure known in other ways. Though their ire was directed at government in general, the Tea Party had specific targets. In particular, they opposed the George W. Bush administration's bailouts of big financial institutions through the Troubled Asset Relief Program (TARP) in 2008 and other measures taken in response to the economic crisis that began that year, including mortgage assistance for people facing foreclosure, the stimulus bill, and the health reform act, all passed by Congress in 2009 and 2010 with the strong backing of President Barack Obama.

The Tea Party movement was a decentralized mix of many groups—mostly simply frustrated Republicans (the major party that most Tea Partiers identify with or lean toward). Ted Cruz from Texas and Marco Rubio from Florida won seats in the U.S. Senate with Tea Party support and went on to run for the presidency in 2016. Tea Party members elected to Congress caused many headaches for Speaker of the House John Boehner, leading to his resignation in 2015.

But other members of the rebellious faction chose less establishment paths. David Barstow of the *New York Times* wrote in early 2010 that a "significant undercurrent within the Tea Party movement" was less like a part of the Republican Party than it was like "the Patriot movement, a brand of politics historically associated with libertarians, militia groups, anti-immigration advocates and those who argue for the abolition of the Federal Reserve." He quoted a Tea Party leader so worried about the impending tyranny threatening her country that she could imagine being called to violence in its defense: "I don't see us being the ones to start it, but I would give up my life for my country.... Peaceful means are the best way of going about it. But sometimes you are not given a choice."[2]

AP Photo/Joel Page, File

Is That a Gun in Your Pocket?

Outside a 2009 Obama town hall meeting in New Hampshire, an armed demonstrator's sign refers to the Thomas Jefferson quote, "The tree of liberty must be refreshed from time to time with the blood of patriots and tyrants."

Like the extreme Tea Partier quoted above, McVeigh and his associates, the Bundys, and other militia-group members are everyday men and women who say they are the ideological heirs of the American Revolution. They liken themselves to the colonial Sons of Liberty, who rejected the authority of the British government and took it upon themselves to enforce the laws they thought were just. The Sons of Liberty instigated the Boston Massacre and the Boston Tea Party, historical events that we celebrate as patriotic but that would be considered treason or terrorism if they took place today—and were considered as such by the British back when they occurred.

Today's so-called Patriot groups claim that the federal government has become as tyrannical as the British government ever was, that it deprives citizens of their liberty and over-regulates their everyday lives. They reject federal laws that do everything from limiting the weapons that individual citizens can own, to imposing taxes on income, to requiring the registration of motor vehicles, to creating the Federal Reserve Bank, to reforming the health care system. The groups base their claim to legitimate existence on the Constitution's Second Amendment, which reads, "A well regulated Militia, being necessary to the security of a free State, the right of the people to keep and bear Arms, shall not be infringed." Members of state militias, and other groups like them, take this amendment literally and absolutely. The website teaparty.org, though not representative of all Tea Party groups, says "gun ownership is sacred."[3]

Some militias go even further. They may blend their quests for individual liberty with white supremacy or anti-Semitism and see conspiracies aimed at reducing the power of white citizens in the government's actions. In August 2012, with the November election in the offing, a Texas judge, Tom Head, actually called for a tax increase so that police could be prepared for what he anticipated would happen if President Obama were reelected. He said, "He's going to try to hand over the sovereignty of the United States to the UN, and what is going to happen when that happens? . . . I'm thinking the worst. Civil unrest, civil disobedience, civil war maybe."[4]

Although there are some indications that militia membership had declined after the Oklahoma City bombing, it surged after Obama's first election, as did arguments that the federal government (or at least the president) was not legitimate.[5] Donald Trump's loud support for the birther movement, which argued that Obama was not qualified by birth for the presidency, presaged Trump's presidential campaign, which seemed to capitalize on the same anger the Tea Party had

thrived on. A number of writers have argued that some of this increased anger is a panicky reaction of a shrinking white majority to demographic change and the presence of a black man in the White House.[6] In any case, it helped propel Donald Trump there in 2016.

The federal government has reacted strongly to limit the threat presented by state militias and others who believe that its authority is not legitimate. Congress passed an anti-terrorism bill signed by President Bill Clinton in 1996 that would make it easier for federal agencies to monitor the activities of such groups, and these powers were broadened after September 11, 2001. In June 2014, in reaction to the surging numbers of radicalized people within the country, then–attorney general Eric Holder announced that he would revive the domestic terrorism task force that had been formed after the Oklahoma City bombings but had not met since 9/11 turned the nation's attention to terrorism overseas.

How should the federal government respond to these challenges to its legitimacy? Are these groups, as they claim, the embodiment of revolutionary patriotism? Do they support the Constitution, or sabotage it? And where do we draw the line between a Tea Party member who wants to sound off against elected officials and policies she doesn't like, and one who advocates resorting to violence to protect her particular reading of the Constitution? Think about these questions as you read this chapter on the founding of the United States. At the end of this chapter, we revisit the question of what's at stake for American politics in a revolutionary challenge to government authority. ≪

FROM the moment students start coloring in pictures of grateful Pilgrims and cutting out construction paper turkeys in grade school, the founding of the United States is a recurring focus of American education, and with good reason. Democratic societies, as we saw in Chapter 1, rely on the consent of their citizens to maintain lawful behavior and public order. To be committed to the rules and the goals of the American system requires that we feel good about that system. What better way to stir up good feelings and patriotism than by recounting thrilling stories of bravery and derring-do on the part of selfless heroes dedicated to the cause of American liberty? We celebrate the Fourth of July with fireworks and parades, displaying publicly our commitment to American values and our belief that our country is special, in the same way that other nations celebrate their origins all over the world. Bastille Day (July 14) in France, May 17 in Norway, October 1 in China, July 6 in Malawi, Africa—all are days on which people rally together to celebrate their common past and their hopes for the future.

People feel real pride in their countries, and many nations, not only our own, have amazing stories to tell about their

earliest days. But as political scientists, we must separate myth from reality. For us, the founding of the United States is central not because it inspires warm feelings of patriotism but because it can teach us about American politics, the struggles for power that forged the political system that continues to shape our collective struggles today.

The history of the American founding has been told from many points of view. You are probably most familiar with this account: The early colonists escaped from Europe to avoid religious persecution. Having arrived on the shores of the New World, they built communities that allowed them to practice their religions in peace and to govern themselves as free people. When the tyrannical British king made unreasonable demands on the colonists, they had no choice but to protect their liberty by going to war and establishing a new government of their own.

Sound historical evidence suggests that the story is more complicated, and more interesting, than that. A closer look shows that the early Americans were complex beings with economic and political agendas as well as religious and philosophical motives. After much struggle among themselves, the majority of Americans decided that those agendas could be carried out better and more profitably if they broke their ties with England.[7]

Just because a controversial event like the founding is recounted by historians or political scientists one or two hundred years after it happens does not guarantee that there is common agreement on what took place. People write history not from a position of absolute truth but from particular points of view. When we read a historical narrative, as critical thinkers we need to ask the same probing questions we ask about contemporary political narratives: Who is telling the story? What point of view is being represented? What values and priorities lie behind it? If I accept this interpretation, what else will I have to accept?

In this chapter, we talk a lot about history—the history of the American founding and the creation of the Constitution. As we point out in *Don't Be Fooled by . . . Your Textbook*, we, like all other authors, have a particular point of view that affects how we tell the story. True to the first basic theme of this book, we are interested in power and politics. We want to understand American government in terms of who the winners and losers are likely to be. It makes sense for us to begin by looking at the founding to see who the winners and losers were then. We are also interested in how rules and institutions make it more likely that some people will win and others lose. Certainly an examination of the early debates about rules and institutions will help us understand that. Finally, because we are interested in winners and losers, we are interested in understanding how people come to be defined as players in the system in the first place, the focus of the second theme of this book—citizenship. It was during the founding that many of the initial decisions were made about who "We the People" would actually be.

POLITICS IN THE ENGLISH COLONIES

Power struggles in the new world

America was a battlefield—both political and military—long before the war for independence from Britain was fought. Not only did the English settlers have to struggle with brutal winters, harsh droughts, disease, and other unanticipated natural disasters, but they quickly came into conflict with the people who already inhabited the New World when they arrived—Native Americans and Spanish and French colonists.

Declaring that they had a legitimate right to colonize unoccupied territory, the British set about populating the eastern coast of America. Many Native Americans initially helped the British overcome the rigors of life in the New World. But cultural differences between the Indians and the British—and the latter's conviction that their beliefs and practices were superior to Indian ways—made the relationship between the two unpredictable. Some Indians engaged in political dealings with the Europeans, forming military partnerships, trade alliances, and other arrangements. Others were more hostile, particularly in the face of the European assumption that the New World was theirs to subdue and exploit.

The Spanish, too, were an obstacle to English domination. Spain in the sixteenth century seemed to be well on its way to owning the New World. Spanish explorers had laid claim to both eastern and western North America as well as key parts of Central and South America. The ancestors of many of the 41 million Spanish-speaking people in America today were living in what is now New Mexico, California, Colorado, and Texas, for instance, before many people were speaking English in America at all. But the monarchs of England wanted a piece of the treasure that was being exported regularly from the Americas. Spain and England were already in conflict in Europe, and Spain was vulnerable. Despite treaties, Spanish spies, intrigue with Native Americans, and occasional military action, Britain edged Spain out of the colonial picture in eastern America.

REASONS FOR LEAVING ENGLAND

Many British subjects were eager and willing to try their luck across the Atlantic. They came to America to make their fortunes, to practice their religions without interference, to become landowners—to take advantage of a host of opportunities that England, still struggling to throw off the straightjacket of the middle ages, could not offer.

Although the colonists did not know it, England in the 1600s was on the brink of major change. Within the century, political thinkers would begin to reject the idea that monarchs ruled through divine right, would favor increasing the power of Parliament at the expense of the king, and would promote the idea that individuals were not merely subjects but citizens, with rights that government could not violate.

But in the early 1600s, settlers came to America in part because England seemed resistant to change. England also had a national interest in sending colonists to America. They were engaged with other European nations in a competition for the world's resources through trade, and colonies were a primary source of raw materials for manufacturing. Entrepreneurs often supported colonization as an investment, and the government issued charters to companies, giving them the right to settle land as English colonies.

Your Textbook

Consider these two narratives describing the same familiar event: Christopher Columbus's arrival in the Americas.[1]

From a 1947 textbook

At last the rulers of Spain gave Columbus three small ships, and he sailed away to the west across the Atlantic Ocean. His sailors became frightened. They were sure the ships would come to the edge of the world and just fall off into space. The sailors were ready to throw their captain into the ocean and turn around and go back. Then, at last they all saw the land ahead. They saw low green shores with tall palm trees swaying in the wind. Columbus had found the New World. This happened on October 12, 1492. It was a great day for Christopher Columbus—and for the whole world as well.

And from a 1991 text

When Columbus stepped ashore on Guanahani Island in October 1492, he planted the Spanish flag in the sand and claimed the land as a possession of Ferdinand and Isabella. He did so despite the obvious fact that the island already belonged to someone else—the "Indians" who gathered on the beach to gaze with wonder at the strangers who had suddenly arrived in three great, white-winged canoes. He gave no thought to the rights of the local inhabitants. Nearly every later explorer—French, English, Dutch and all the others as well as the Spanish— thoughtlessly dismissed the people they encountered. What we like to think of as the discovery of America was actually the invasion and conquest of America.

Which one of these passages is "true"? The first was the conventional textbook wisdom through the 1960s in America. The latter reflects a growing criticism that traditional American history has been told from the perspective of history's "winners," largely white males of European background. Together they show that history varies depending on who is doing the telling, when, and to whom. What this means to you is that the critical vigilance we urge you to apply to all information should be applied to your textbooks as well. And, yes, that means this textbook, too. In an age of mediated citizenship, you really have your work cut out for you.

There is some truth to the idea that history is written by the winners, but it is also true that the winners change over time. If history was once securely in the hands of white European males, it is now the battleground of a cultural war between those who believe the old way of telling history was accurate, and those who believe it left out the considerable achievements of women and minorities and masked some of the less admirable episodes of our past.[2]

Bias is not reserved for history books; this textbook itself has a point of view. In these pages we have an interest in highlighting power and citizenship, in focusing on the impact of the rules in American politics, and in multiculturalism. We do not think that the outstanding political accomplishments of the traditional heroes of American history warrant ignoring the contributions of people who have not historically been powerful.

The fact that all textbooks have some sort of bias means you must be as careful in what you accept from textbook authors as you are in what you accept from any other source.

What to Watch Out For

Here are some things you should think about when you are reading any textbook:

- **Who selected the book?** Textbooks are chosen by instructors, not the end users. Publishers have tailored the content to appeal to those making the selection. How does the politics of those individuals affect what you have been given to read?
- **What is the book's audience?** If it is a big, colorful book, it is probably aimed at a wide market. If so, what might that say about its content? If it is a smaller book with a narrower focus, who is it trying to appeal to?
- **What is the author's point of view?** Does he or she promote particular values or ideas? Are any points of view left out? Do the authors make an effort to cover both sides of an issue or a controversy? If something troubles you, locate the primary source the authors refer to in the footnotes and read it yourself.
- **What were your own reactions?** Did the book cause you to look at a subject in a new way? What is the source of your reaction? Is it intellectual, or emotional?

1. These two passages accompanied Sam Dillon, "Schools Growing Harsher in Scrutiny of Columbus," *New York Times*, October 12, 1992, www.nytimes.com/1992/10/12/us/schools-growing-harsher-in-scrutiny-of-columbus.html. The first paragraph is from Merlin M. Ames, *My Country* (Sacramento: California State Department of Education, 1947); the second is from John A. Garraty, *The Story of America* (New York: Holt Rinehart Winston, Harcourt Brace Jovanovich, 1991).

2. Frances Fitzgerald, *America Revised* (New York: Vintage Books, 1979); James McKinley Jr., "Texas Conservatives Win Curriculum Change," *New York Times*, March 12, 2010, www.nytimes.com/2010/03/13/education/13texas.html; Laura Moser, "Texas Is Debuting Textbooks That Downplay Jim Crow and Frame Slavery as a Side Issue in the Civil War," *Slate*, July 7, 2015, www.slate.com/blogs/schooled/2015/07/07/texas_textbook_revisionism_new_textbooks_in_the_lone_star_state_downplay.html.

POLITICAL PARTICIPATION IN THE COLONIES

It shouldn't surprise us, therefore, to find that the settlers often created communities that were in some ways as restrictive and repressive as the ones they had left behind in England. The difference, of course, was that they were now the ones doing the repressing rather than the ones being repressed. In other ways, life in America was more open than life in Britain. Land was widely available. Although much of it was inhabited by Native Americans, many of them believed in communal or shared use of property. The Europeans arrived with notions of private property and the sophisticated weaponry to defend the land they took from the Indians. Some colonies set up systems of self-rule, with representative assemblies. Though they had governors, often appointed by the king, the colonies were left largely, though not exclusively, to their own devices at least until the late 1600s.

A useful way to understand who had power in the colonies is to look at the rules regulating political participation—that is, who was allowed to vote in colonial lawmaking bodies, who wasn't, and why. Each colony set its own voting rules, based on such factors as religion, property, gender, and race:

- **Religion.** At least in the earliest days of colonial government, the tightest requirements for voting were moral or religious qualifications. The northern colonies, especially, were concerned about keeping the ungodly out of government. By 1640, for instance, religious tests for voting prevented three-fourths of the Massachusetts population from having any political power. By 1691, however, Massachusetts had moved into line with Virginia and the other colonies that based an individual's political rights on his wealth rather than his character.

- **Property.** Conventional British wisdom held that if you didn't own property, you were unlikely to take a serious interest in government. Gradually the colonies adopted that view and began to require of voters some degree of property ownership or, later, tax-paying status.

- **Gender.** Women weren't officially excluded from political participation in America until the Revolution. Until then, as in England, they occasionally could exercise the vote when they satisfied the property requirement and when there were no voting males in their households. In some localities, widows, in particular, or daughters who had inherited a parent's property could vote or participate in church meetings (which sometimes amounted to the same thing).[8]

- **Race.** Initially, Africans in America were subject to the same laws and codes of behavior as Europeans there.[9] However, the colonies required tremendous amounts of cheap labor to produce the raw materials and goods needed for trade with England, and when English people from the Caribbean island of Barbados settled in South Carolina in 1670, they brought with them the institution of **slavery**. Slavery proved economically profitable even in the more commercial areas of New England, but it utterly transformed the tobacco plantations of Maryland and Virginia.[10]

> **slavery** the ownership, for forced labor, of one people by another

A Political Divide

Under English rule, some women in the American colonies were able to participate in politics. Once the United States was formed, however, the states crafted a firm political divide that restricted voting primarily to wealthy, landowning men.

Not surprisingly, as slavery became accepted in the colonies, the rights of blacks were gradually stripped away. In the 1640s, Maryland denied blacks the right to bear arms. A 1669 Virginia law declared that if a slave "should chance to die" when resisting his or her master or the master's agent, it would not be a felony—a crime that legally required malice—because no one would destroy his own property with malice. Most politically damaging, by the 1680s, free blacks were forbidden to own property, the only access to political power that colonial society recognized.[11]

Reasons for these legal changes are not hard to find. Slavery can work only if slaves are dependent, defenseless, and afraid to escape. Also, an institution as dehumanizing as slavery requires some justification that enables slaveholders to live with themselves, especially in the Enlightenment era, when words like *natural rights* and *liberty* were on everyone's tongue. It was said that the Africans were childlike, lazy, and undisciplined, and that they needed the supervision of slave owners. The worse slaves were treated, the more their humanity was denied. **Racism**, the belief that one race is superior to another, undoubtedly existed before slavery was well established in America, but the institution of slavery made it a part of American political culture. We discuss the issue of race in American politics in more detail in Chapter 6.

PAUSE AND REVIEW   Who, What, How

The English colonists wanted, first and foremost, to find new opportunities in America. But those opportunities were not available to all. Religious and property qualifications for the vote, and the exclusion of women and blacks from political life, meant that the colonial leaders did not feel that simply living in a place or obeying the laws or even paying taxes carried with it the right to

participate in government. Following the rigid British social hierarchy, they wanted rules to ensure that the "right kind" of people could participate, people who could be depended on to make the kind of rules that would ensure their status and maintain the established order. The danger of expanding the vote, of course, is that the new majority might want something very different from what the old majority wanted.

In Your Own Words   Describe the power relationships among different groups in colonial America.

THE SPLIT FROM ENGLAND

Making the transition from British subjects to American citizens

Both England and America accepted as perfectly normal the relationships of colonial power that initially bound them together. Americans, as colonists, were obliged to make England their primary trading partner, and all goods they traded to other countries had to pass through Britain, where a tax was collected on them. The benefits of being a colony, however, including financial support by British corporations, military defense by the British army and navy, and a secure market for their agricultural products, usually outweighed any burdens of colonial obligation. Eventually the relationship started to sour as the colonists developed an identity as Americans rather than as transplanted English people, and as the British became a more intrusive political presence. Even then, they searched painstakingly for a way to fix the relationship before they decided to eliminate it altogether. Revolution was not welcomed on either side.

BRITISH ATTEMPTS TO GAIN CONTROL OF THE COLONIES

Whether the British government had actually become oppressive in the years before 1776 is open to interpretation. Certainly the colonists thought so. Britain was deeply in debt, having won the **French and Indian War**, which effectively forced the French to leave North America and the Spanish to

racism the belief that one race is superior to another

French and Indian War a war fought between France and England, and allied Indians, from 1754 to 1763; resulted in France's expulsion from the New World

vacate Florida and retreat west of the Mississippi. Britain, having done its protective duty as a colonial power and having taxed British citizens heavily to finance the war, turned to its colonies to help pay for their defense. It chose to do that by levying taxes on the colonies and by attempting to enforce more strictly the trade laws that would increase British profits from American resources.

The irony is that, with the British victory in the war, the colonies were largely free of Spanish, French, and Indian threat. No longer in need of British protection, they could afford to resist British efforts to make them help pay for it.[12] The series of acts the British passed to gain revenue infuriated the colonists, who saw them as intolerable violations of their rights, even though the British were being taxed at home too. To show their displeasure with the Tea Act of 1773, they hurled 342 chests of tea into Boston Harbor in the infamous Boston Tea Party. Britain responded by passing the Coercive Acts of 1774, designed to punish the citizens of Massachusetts. In the process, Parliament sowed the seeds that would blossom into revolution in just a few years.

CHANGING IDEAS ABOUT POLITICS

The American reluctance to cooperate with Britain was reinforced by the colonists' changing political culture and the narrative that supported it. Philosophical ideas that were fermenting in England and the European Enlightenment as a whole, especially those of John Locke, were flourishing in America. For the British, the sovereign authority was Parliament, which established the rule of law and constitutional principles. But the colonists rejected that in favor of the principle of **popular sovereignty**; that is, the ultimate authority, the power to govern, belonged in the hands of the people.[13]

These philosophical changes meant that any British colonial authority had begun to seem illegitimate to the colonial elite, and that lack of legitimacy began to figure heavily in the narratives they told about political power. Much has been made in American schoolbooks about the colonists' defiant rejection of British taxation without representation. The British had offered Americans representation in Parliament, however, and they had rejected it in the assemblies of South Carolina and Virginia.[14] It wasn't just taxation the colonists objected to; it was the sovereignty of the British parliament itself. Some loyalists to the Crown continued to support British authority, but for the rest of the colonists, it became

> **popular sovereignty** the concept that the citizens are the ultimate source of political power

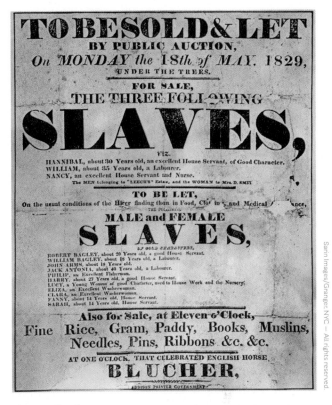

Human Trade

Slaves were used to meet the needs of the South's burgeoning economy in tobacco and cotton, which required plentiful, cheap labor. They were shipped from Africa and sold to farmers alongside rice, books, and other goods. In the eighteenth century, approximately 275,000 slaves were shipped to the American colonies. Many did not survive the harsh conditions of the passage.

harder and harder to recognize British power over them as legitimate authority.

REVOLUTION

From the moment that the unpopularly taxed tea plunged into Boston Harbor in December 1773, it became apparent that the Americans were not going to settle down and behave like proper and orthodox colonists. Even before the Tea Party, mobs in many towns were demonstrating and rioting against British control. Calling themselves the Sons of Liberty, and under the guidance of the eccentric Samuel Adams (cousin to the future president John Adams), rebellious colonists routinely caused extensive damage and, in early 1770, provoked the so-called Boston Massacre, an attack by British soldiers that left six civilians dead and further inflamed popular sentiments.

By the time of the Boston Tea Party, also incited by the Sons of Liberty, passions were at a fever pitch. The American patriots called a meeting in Philadelphia in September 1774.

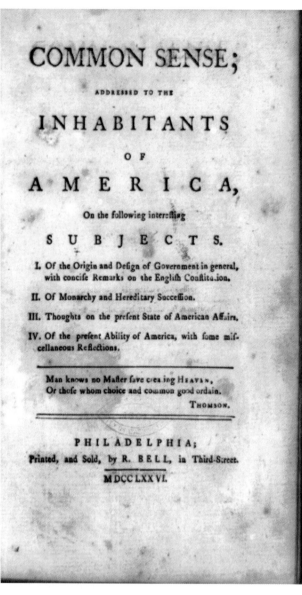

Courtesy of Library of Congress, Prints and Photographs Division

America's First Viral Message

More than 150,000 copies of Thomas Paine's influential essay Common Sense *were sold in 1776 alone, and those were circulated and read aloud in taverns and meeting places throughout the colonies. Eventually more than a half-million copies made their way across the colonies and Europe.*

Known as the First Continental Congress, the meeting declared the Coercive Acts void, announced a plan to stop trade with England, and called for a second meeting in May 1775. Before they could meet again, in the early spring of 1775, the king's army went marching to arrest Samuel Adams and another patriot, John Hancock, and to discover the hiding place of the colonists' weapons. Roused by the silversmith Paul Revere, Americans in Lexington and Concord fired the first shots of rebellion at the British, and revolution was truly under way.

The narrative about where the locus of power should be spread quickly, even given the limited communication channels

of the day. The mobs were not fed by social media or connected electronically—the story was passed by word of mouth and, therefore, could be controlled relatively easily because each person could not disseminate ideas widely. The people who stood to gain the most financially from independence—the propertied and economic elite, the attendees at the Continental Congress—were translating a philosophical explanation for the masses to act on. Because many colonists could not read, they got their news at the tavern or at the Sunday pulpit where it was colored by the interests of the teller, and then passed it on. The vast majority of citizens were passive recipients of the narrative.

THE DECLARATION OF INDEPENDENCE

Even in the midst of war, the colonists did not at first clearly articulate a desire for independence from England. But publication of the pamphlet *Common Sense*, written by the English-born Thomas Paine, turned their old ideas upside-down. In this immensely popular pamphlet, which sold more than 150,000 copies in just a few weeks (the colonial equivalent of "going viral"),[15] Paine called for the rejection of the king, for independence, and for republican government, and his passionate writing crystallized the thinking of the colonial leaders.[16]

In 1776, at the direction of a committee of the Continental Congress, thirty-four-year-old Thomas Jefferson sat down to write a declaration of independence from England. His training as a lawyer at the College of William and Mary, and his service as a representative in the Virginia House of Burgesses, helped prepare him for his task, but he had an impressive intellect in any case. President John F. Kennedy once announced to a group of Nobel Prize winners he was entertaining that they were "the most extraordinary collection of talents that has ever gathered at the White House, with the possible exception of when Thomas Jefferson dined alone."[17] A testimony to Jefferson's capabilities is the strategically brilliant document that he produced.

The **Declaration of Independence** is first and foremost a political document. Having decided to make the break from England, the American founders had to create a narrative that convinced themselves, their fellow colonists, and the rest of the world that they were doing the right thing. Jefferson did not have to hunt further than the writing of John Locke for a good reason for his revolution.

Common Sense the pamphlet written by Thomas Paine in 1776 that persuaded many Americans to support the revolutionary cause

Declaration of Independence the political document that dissolved the colonial ties between the United States and Britain

Recall from Chapter 1 that Locke said that government is based on a contract between the rulers and the ruled. The ruled agree to obey the laws as long as the rulers protect their basic rights to life, liberty, and property. If the rulers fail to do that, they break the contract and the ruled are free to set up another government. This is exactly what the second paragraph of the Declaration of Independence says, except that Jefferson changed "property" to "the pursuit of happiness," perhaps to garner the support of those Americans who didn't own enough property to worry about. Having established that the breaking of the social contract was a good reason for revolution, Jefferson could justify the American Revolution if he could show that Britain had broken such a contract by violating the colonists' rights.

Consequently, he spelled out all the things that King George III had allegedly done to breach the social contract. Take a look at the Declaration in the *CLUES to Critical Thinking* feature at the end of this chapter and notice the extensive list of grievances against the king. For twenty-seven paragraphs, Jefferson documented just how badly the monarch had treated the colonists. Note, however, that many of the things the colonists complained of were the normal acts of a colonial power. No one had told the king that he was a party to a Lockean contract, so it isn't surprising that he violated it at every turn. Furthermore, some of the things he was blamed for were the acts of Parliament, not of the king at all. Perhaps because the colonists intended to have some sort of parliament of their own, or perhaps, as some scholars have argued, because they simply did not recognize Parliament's authority over them, George III was the sole focus of their wrath and resentment. But the clear goal of the document was to discredit George III so thoroughly that this revolution became inevitable in the eyes of every American, and the world.

> **Are there any circumstances in which it would be justifiable for groups in the United States to rebel against the federal government today?**

"... THAT ALL MEN ARE CREATED EQUAL"

The Declaration of Independence begins with a statement of the equality of all men. Since so much of this document relies heavily on Locke, and since clearly the colonists did not mean that all men are created equal, it is worth turning to Locke for some help in seeing exactly what they did mean. In his most famous work, *A Second Treatise on Government*, Locke wrote,

Though I have said above that all men are by nature equal, I cannot be supposed to understand all sorts of equality. Age or virtue may give men a just precedency. Excellency of parts and merit may place others above the common level. Birth may subject some, and alliance or benefits others, to pay an observance to those whom nature, gratitude, or other respects may have made it due.[18]

Men are equal in a natural sense, said Locke, but society quickly establishes many dimensions on which they may be unequal. A particularly sticky point for Locke's ideas on equality is his treatment of slavery, which he did not endorse but ultimately failed to condemn. Here, too, our founders would have been in agreement with him.

The founders' ambivalence about slavery and equality can be seen in a passage that Jefferson included in the original draft of the Declaration, as part of the political indictment of George III. He wrote:

He [George III] has waged cruel war against human nature itself, violating its most sacred rights of life and liberty in the persons of a distant people who never offended him, captivating and carrying them into slavery in another hemisphere or to incur miserable death in their transportation thither.[19]

Blaming King George for the institution of slavery, and including it on a list of behaviors so horrible that they justify revolution, was an amazing act on the part of a man who not only owned slaves himself but also was writing on behalf of many other slave owners. His action shows just how politically confusing and morally ambiguous the issue was at that time. Reflecting the political realities of the time, the passage was eventually deleted.

AFRICAN AMERICANS AND THE REVOLUTION

The Revolution was a mixed blessing for American slaves. On the one hand, many slaves won their freedom as a result of the war; slavery was outlawed north of Maryland, and many slaves in the Upper South also were freed. The British offered freedom in exchange for service in the British army, although the conditions they provided were not always a great improvement over enslavement. The abolitionist, or antislavery, movement gathered steam in some northern cities, expressing moral and constitutional objections to the institution of slavery. Whereas before the Revolution only about 5 percent of American blacks were free, the number grew tremendously with the coming of war.[20]

Many African Americans served in the war. There were probably about twelve blacks in the first battle at Lexington and Concord, in Massachusetts, for example. The South

Women at War

Deborah Sampson and a few other women disguised themselves as males and served in the colonial army. Sampson served under George Washington's command but was dishonorably discharged after the war when it became known she was a woman. Ten years later, after Washington's intervention, she became the first woman in the U.S. Army to receive a soldier's pension.

feared the idea of arming slaves, for obvious reasons, but by the time Congress began to fix troop quotas for each state, southerners were drafting slaves to serve in their masters' places.

In the aftermath of war, however, African Americans did not find their lot greatly improved, despite the ringing rhetoric of equality that fed the Revolution. The economic profitability of slave labor still existed in the South, and slaves continued to be imported from Africa in large numbers. The explanatory narrative—that all men were created equal but that blacks weren't quite men and thus could be treated unequally—spread throughout the new country, including the North, making even free blacks unwelcome in many communities. By 1786 New Jersey prohibited free blacks from entering the state, and within twenty years northern states had started passing laws specifically denying free blacks the right to vote.[21] No wonder the well-known black abolitionist Frederick Douglass said, in 1852: "This Fourth of July is yours, not mine. You may rejoice, I must mourn."

NATIVE AMERICANS AND THE REVOLUTION Native Americans were another group the founders did not consider to be prospective citizens. Not only were they already considered members of their own sovereign nations, but their communal property holding, their non-monarchical political systems, and their divisions of labor between women working in the fields and men hunting for game were not compatible with European political notions. Pushed farther and farther west by land-hungry colonists, the Indians were actively hostile to the American cause in the Revolution. Knowing this, the British hoped to gain their allegiance in the war. But the colonists, having asked in vain for the Indians to stay out of what they called a "family quarrel," were able to suppress early on the Indians' attempts to get revenge for their treatment at the hands of the settlers.[22] There was certainly no suggestion that the claim of equality at the beginning of the Declaration of Independence might include the peoples who had lived on the continent for centuries before the white man arrived.

WOMEN AND THE REVOLUTION Neither was there any question that "all men" might somehow be a generic term for human beings that would include women. The Revolution proved to be a step backward for women politically. It was after the war that states began specifically to prohibit women, even those with property, from voting.[23] That doesn't mean, however, that women did not get involved in the war effort. Within the constraints of society, they contributed what they could to the American cause. They boycotted tea and other British imports, sewed flags, made bandages and clothing, nursed and housed soldiers, and collected money to support the Continental Army. Under the name Daughters of Liberty, women in many towns met publicly to discuss the events of the day, spinning and weaving to make the colonies less dependent on imported cotton and woolens from England, and drinking herbal tea instead of tea that was taxed by the British. Some women moved beyond such mild patriotic activities to outright political behavior, writing pamphlets urging independence, spying on enemy troops, carrying messages, and even, in isolated instances, fighting on the battlefields.[24]

Men's understanding of women's place in early American politics was nicely put by Thomas Jefferson, writing from Europe to a woman in America in 1788:

> But our good ladies, I trust, have been too wise to wrinkle their foreheads with politics. They are contented to soothe & calm the minds of their husbands returning ruffled from political debate. They have the good sense to value domestic happiness above all others. There is no part of the earth where so much of this is enjoyed as in America.[25]

Women's role with respect to politics at the time was plain: they may be wise and prudent, but their proper sphere was the domestic, not the political, world. They were seen as almost "too good" for politics, representing peace and serenity, moral happiness rather than political dissension, the values of the home over the values of the state. This narrative provided a flattering reason for keeping women in "their place," while allowing men to reign in the world of politics.

PAUSE AND REVIEW Who, What, How

By the mid-1700s the interests of the British and the colonists were clearly beginning to separate. If the colonists had played by the rules of imperial politics, England would have been content. It would have taxed the colonies to pay its war debts, but it also would have continued to protect them and rule benignly from across the sea.

The colonial leaders, however, changed the rules. Rejecting British authority, they established new rules based on Enlightenment thought. Then they used impassioned rhetoric and inspiring theory to engage the rest of the colonists in their rebellion, and to create the narrative that fueled American independence. Finally, they used revolution to sever their ties with England.

The Revolution dramatically changed American fortunes, but not everyone's life was altered for the good by political independence. Many of those who were not enfranchised before the war—slaves and free blacks, American Indians, and women—remained powerless afterward, and in some cases voting rules became even more restrictive.

In Your Own Words Outline the events and political motivations that led to the colonies' split from England.

THE ARTICLES OF CONFEDERATION

Political and economic instability under the nation's first constitution

In 1777 the Continental Congress met to try to come up with a framework or constitution for the new government. We use the word *constitution* in the United States almost as if it could refer only to one specific document. In truth, a **constitution** is any establishment of rules that "constitutes"—that is, makes up—a government. It may be written, as in our case, or unwritten, as in Great Britain's. One constitution can endure for over two hundred years, as ours has, or it can change quite frequently, as the French constitution has. What's important about a constitution is that it defines a political body, the rules and institutions for running a government. As we have said

before, those rules have direct consequences for how politics works in a given country, who the winners are and who the losers will be.

The **Articles of Confederation**, our first constitution, created the kind of government the founders, fresh from their colonial experience, preferred. The rules set up by the Articles of Confederation show that the states jealously guarded their own power. Having just won their independence from one large national power, the last thing they wanted to do was create another. They were also extremely wary of one another, and much of the debate over the Articles of Confederation reflected wide concern that the rules not give any states preferential treatment. (See the Appendix for the text of the Articles of Confederation.)

The Articles established a "firm league of friendship" among the thirteen American states, but they did not empower a central government to act effectively on behalf of those states. The Articles were ultimately replaced because, without a strong central government, they were unable to provide the economic and political stability that the founders wanted. Even so, under this set of rules, some people were better off, and some problems, namely the resolution of boundary disputes and the political organization of new territories, were handled extremely well.

THE PROVISIONS OF THE ARTICLES

The government set up by the Articles was called a **confederation** because it established a system in which each state retained almost all the power to do what it wanted. In other words, in a confederation, each state is sovereign, and the central government has only the job of running the collective business of the states. It has no independent source of power and resources for its operations. Another characteristic of a confederation is that, because it is founded on state sovereignty (authority), it says nothing about individuals. It creates neither rights nor obligations for individual citizens, leaving such matters to be handled by state constitutions.

Under the Articles of Confederation, Congress had many formal powers, including the power to establish and direct the armed forces, to decide matters of war and peace, to coin

constitution the rules that establish a government

Articles of Confederation the first constitution of the United States (1777) creating an association of states with weak central government

confederation a government in which independent states unite for common purpose but retain their own sovereignty

money, and to enter into treaties. Its powers, however, were quite limited. For example, although Congress controlled the armed forces, it had no power to draft soldiers or to tax citizens to pay for its military needs. Its inability to tax put Congress—and the central government as a whole—at the mercy of the states. The government could ask, but it was up to the states to contribute or not as they chose. Furthermore, Congress lacked the ability to regulate commerce between states, and between states and foreign powers. It could not establish a common and stable monetary system. In essence, the Articles allowed the states to be thirteen independent units, printing their own currencies, setting their own tariffs, and establishing their own laws with regard to financial and political matters. In every critical case—national security, national economic prosperity, and the general welfare—the U.S. government had to rely on the voluntary goodwill and cooperation of the state governments. That meant that the success of the new nation depended on what went on in state legislatures around the country.

SOME WINNERS, SOME LOSERS

The era of American history following the Revolution was dubbed "this critical period" by John Quincy Adams, nephew of patriot Samuel Adams, son of John Adams, and himself a future president of the country. During this time, while the states were under the weak union of the Articles, the future of the United States was very much up in the air. The lack of an effective central government meant that the country had difficulty conducting business with other countries and enforcing harmonious trade relations and treaties. Domestic politics was equally difficult. Economic conditions following the war were poor. Many people had debts they could not pay. State taxes were high and the economy was depressed, offering farmers few opportunities to sell their produce, for example, and hindering those with commercial interests from conducting business as they had before the war.

The radical poverty of some Americans seemed particularly unjust to those hardest hit, especially in light of the rhetoric of the Revolution about equality for all. This is a difficulty of having a narrative controlled from on high—if it doesn't match up with the reality on the ground, new narratives can develop. Having used "equality" as a rallying cry during the war, the founders were afterward faced with a population that wanted to take equality seriously and eliminate the differences that existed between men.[26]

One of the ways this passion for equality manifested itself was in some of the state legislatures, where laws were passed to ease the burden of debtors and farmers. Often the focus of

the laws was property, but rather than preserving property, as per the Lockean narrative, these laws frequently were designed to confiscate or redistribute property instead. The have-nots in society, and the people acting on their behalf, were using the law to redress what they saw as injustices in early American life. To relieve postwar suffering, they printed paper money, seized property, and suspended "the ordinary means for the recovery of debts."[27] In other words, in those states, people with debts and mortgages could legally escape or postpone paying the money they owed. With so much economic insecurity, naturally those who owned property would not continue to invest and lend money. The Articles of Confederation, in their effort to preserve power for the states, had provided for no checks or limitations on state legislatures. In fact, such action would have been seen under the Articles as infringing on the sovereignty of the states. What you had was a clash between two visions of what America was to be about.

> **How would American politics be different today if we had retained the Articles of Confederation instead of adopting the Constitution?**

The political elite in the new country started to grumble about **popular tyranny**. In a monarchy, one feared the unrestrained power of the king, but perhaps in a republican government one had to fear the unrestrained power of the people. The final straw was **Shays's Rebellion**. Massachusetts was a state whose legislature, dominated by wealthy and secure citizens, had not taken measures to aid the debt-ridden population. In an effort to keep their land from foreclosure (seizure by those to whom they owed money), a mob of angry musket-wielding farmers from western Massachusetts, led by a former officer of the Continental Army, Daniel Shays, stormed a federal armory in Springfield that housed 450 tons of military supplies in January 1787. The mob was turned back after a violent clash with state militia, but the attack frightened and embarrassed the leaders of the United States, who feared that the rebellion foreshadowed the failure of their grand experiment in self-governance, and certainly challenged their story of what it was about. In their minds, it

popular tyranny the unrestrained power of the people

Shays's Rebellion a grassroots uprising (1787) by armed Massachusetts farmers protesting foreclosures

underscored the importance of discovering what James Madison would call "a republican remedy for those diseases most incident to republican government."[28] The leaders had to find a way to contain and limit the will of the people in a government that was to be based on the will of the people. If the rules of government were not producing the "right" winners and losers, then the rules would have to be changed before the elite lost control of their narrative and the power to change the rules.

PAUSE AND REVIEW Who, What, How

The fledgling states had an enormous amount at stake as they forged their new government after the Revolution. Perceiving that alarming abuses of power by the British king had come from a strong national government, they were determined to limit the central power of the new nation. The solution was to form a "firm league of friendship" among the several states but to keep the power of any central institutions as weak as possible.

With widespread land ownership possible and with the need for popular support, most farmers and artisans enjoyed the status of citizenship. Given easy access to the state legislatures under the Articles of Confederation, they were able to use the rules of the new political system to take the edge off the economic hardships they were facing, and to build a power base and create their own narrative about the purpose of government.

But the same rules that made it so easy for the new citizens to influence their state governments made it more difficult for the political and economic leaders of the former colonies to protect their own economic security. In their eyes, new rules were needed that would remove government from the rough-and-ready hands of the farmers and protect it from what they saw as unreasonable demands.

In Your Own Words Explain who won and who lost under the Articles of Confederation.

THE CONSTITUTIONAL CONVENTION

Division and compromise over state power and representation

Even before Shays and his men attacked the Springfield armory, delegates from key states had met in Annapolis, Maryland, to discuss the nation's commercial weaknesses. There they adopted a proposal to have each state send delegates to a national convention to be held in Philadelphia in May 1787. The purpose of the meeting would be to make the national government strong enough to handle the demands of united action.

The Philadelphia Convention was authorized to try to fix the Articles of Confederation, but it was clear that many of the fifty-five state delegates who gathered in May were not interested in saving the existing framework at all. Many of the delegates represented the elite of American society, and thus they were among those most injured under the terms of the Articles. When it became apparent that the **Constitutional Convention** was replacing, not revising, the Articles, some delegates refused to attend, declaring that such a convention was outside the Articles of Confederation and therefore illegal—in fact, it was treason. The convention was in essence overthrowing the government.

"AN ASSEMBLY OF DEMIGODS"

When Thomas Jefferson, unable to attend the convention because he was on a diplomatic mission to Europe, heard about the Philadelphia meeting, he called it "an assembly of demigods."[29] As you'll see from *Snapshot of America: Who Were the Founders?*, the delegates were among the most educated, powerful, and wealthy citizens of the new country. Some leading figures were absent. Not only was Jefferson in Paris, but John Adams was also in Europe. Samuel Adams had not been elected but had declared his general disapproval of the "unconstitutional" undertaking, as had Patrick Henry, another hotheaded revolutionary patriot and advocate of states' rights. But there was George Washington, from Virginia, the general who had led American troops to victory in the Revolution. Also from Virginia were George Mason, Edmund Randolph, and James Madison, the sickly and diminutive but brilliant politician who would make a greater imprint on the final Constitution than all the other delegates combined. Other delegates were also impressive, including eighty-one-year-old Benjamin Franklin, as mentally astute as ever, if increasingly feeble in body; Gouverneur Morris from Pennsylvania; and Alexander Hamilton among the New Yorkers.

These delegates represented the very cream of American society. As the *Snapshot of America* shows, they were well educated in an age when most of the population was not. They were also wealthy, and even though they were, on the whole, a young group, they were politically experienced. Many had been active in revolutionary politics, and they were well read in the political theories of the day.

Members of the delegations met through a sweltering Philadelphia summer to reconstruct the foundations of

Constitutional Convention the assembly of fifty-five delegates in the summer of 1787 to recast the Articles of Confederation; the result was the U.S. Constitution

Snapshot of America: *Who Were the Founders?*

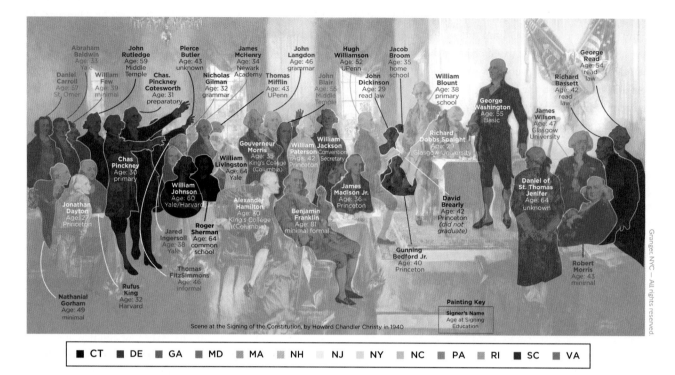

Scene at the Signing of the Constitution, by Howard Chandler Christy in 1940

Painting Key
Signer's Name
Age at Signing
Education

■ CT　■ DE　▨ GA　■ MD　▨ MA　▨ NH　▢ NJ　▢ NY　▨ NC　■ PA　▨ RI　■ SC　▨ VA

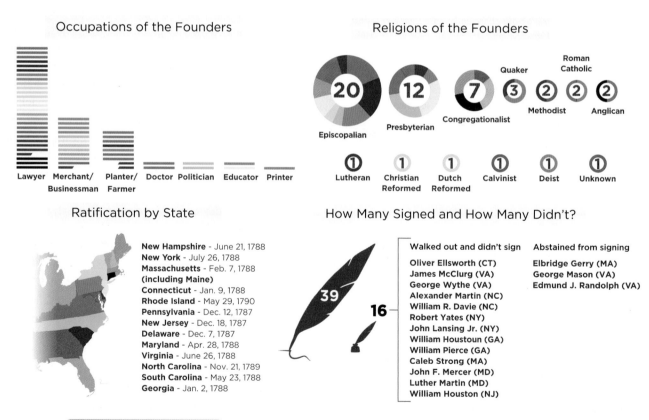

Occupations of the Founders

Lawyer | Merchant/Businessman | Planter/Farmer | Doctor | Politician | Educator | Printer

Religions of the Founders

20 Episcopalian
12 Presbyterian
7 Congregationalist
3 Quaker
2 Roman Catholic
2 Methodist
2 Anglican

1 Lutheran
1 Christian Reformed
1 Dutch Reformed
1 Calvinist
1 Deist
1 Unknown

Ratification by State

New Hampshire - June 21, 1788
New York - July 26, 1788
Massachusetts - Feb. 7, 1788 (including Maine)
Connecticut - Jan. 9, 1788
Rhode Island - May 29, 1790
Pennsylvania - Dec. 12, 1787
New Jersey - Dec. 18, 1787
Delaware - Dec. 7, 1787
Maryland - Apr. 28, 1788
Virginia - June 26, 1788
North Carolina - Nov. 21, 1789
South Carolina - May 23, 1788
Georgia - Jan. 2, 1788

How Many Signed and How Many Didn't?

39

16

Walked out and didn't sign

Oliver Ellsworth (CT)
James McClurg (VA)
George Wythe (VA)
Alexander Martin (NC)
William R. Davie (NC)
Robert Yates (NY)
John Lansing Jr. (NY)
William Houstoun (GA)
William Pierce (GA)
Caleb Strong (MA)
John F. Mercer (MD)
Luther Martin (MD)
William Houston (NJ)

Abstained from signing

Elbridge Gerry (MA)
George Mason (VA)
Edmund J. Randolph (VA)

Behind the Numbers

The founders were clearly an elite group of men. They attended the top schools and most were successful and wealthy. In general, how does one's economic and social status affect one's political views? Are your views shaped by your own circumstances? Can a government created by "an assembly of demigods" work for the rest of us mortals?

American government. The heat and humidity were heightened because the windows of Convention Hall were kept closed against listening ears and, consequently, the possibility of a cooling breeze.[30] We owe most of what we know about the convention today to the notes of James Madison, which he insisted not be published until after the deaths of all the convention delegates.[31]

As the delegates had hoped, the debates at the Constitutional Convention produced a very different narrative about power and a different system of rules than that established by the Articles of Confederation. Many of these rules were compromises to resolve the conflicting interests brought by delegates to the convention. In fact, the importance of political compromise became one of the prevailing narratives that emerged from the convention and that still carries considerable weight today.

Imagine that you face the delegates' challenge—to construct a new government from scratch. You can create all the rules, arrange all the institutions, just to your liking. The only hitch is that you have other delegates to work with. Delegate A, for instance, is a merchant with a lot of property; he has big plans for a strong government that can ensure secure conditions for conducting business and can adequately protect property. Delegate B is a planter. In Delegate B's experience, big governments are dangerous. Big governments are removed from the people, and it is easy for corruption to take root when people can't keep a close eye on what their officials are doing. People like Delegate B think that they do better when power is broken up and localized and there is no strong central government. In fact, Delegate B would prefer a government like that provided by the Articles of Confederation. How do you reconcile these two very different agendas?

The solution adopted under the Articles of Confederation had basically favored Delegate B's position. The new Constitution, given the profiles of the delegates in attendance, was moving strongly in favor of Delegate A's position. Naturally the agreement of all those who followed Delegate B would be important in ratifying, or getting approval for, the final Constitution, so their concerns could not be ignored. The compromise chosen by the founders at the Constitutional

Convention was called **federalism**. Unlike a confederation, in which the states retain the ultimate power over the whole, federalism gives the central government its own source of power, in this case the Constitution of the people of the United States. But unlike a unitary system, which we discuss in Chapter 4, federalism also gives independent power to the states.

Compared to how they fared under the Articles of Confederation, the advocates of states' rights were losers under the new Constitution, but they were better off than they might have been. The states could have had all their power stripped away. The economic elite, people like Delegate A, were clear winners under the new rules. This proved to be one of the central issues during the ratification debates. Those who sided with the federalism alternative, who mostly resembled Delegate A, came to be known as **Federalists**. The people like Delegate B, who continued to hold onto the strong state–weak central government option, were called **Anti-Federalists**. We will return to them shortly.

LARGE STATES, SMALL STATES

Once the convention delegates agreed that federalism would provide the framework of the new government, they had to decide how to allot power among the states. Should all states count the same in decision making, or should the larger states have more power than the smaller ones? The rules chosen here could have a crucial impact on the politics of the country. If small states and large states had equal amounts of power in national government, residents of large states such as Virginia, Massachusetts, and New York would effectively have less voice in the government than would residents of small states, like New Jersey and Rhode Island, since they would have proportionately less influence on how their power was wielded. If power were allocated on the basis of size, however, the importance of the small states would be reduced.

Two plans were offered by convention delegates to resolve this issue. The first, the **Virginia Plan**, was created by James Madison and presented at the convention by Edmund Randolph. The Virginia Plan represented the preference of the large, more populous states. This plan proposed that the country would have a strong national government, run by a bicameral (two-house) legislature. One house would be elected directly by the people, one indirectly by a combination of the state legislatures and the popularly elected national house. But the numbers of representatives would be determined by the taxes paid by the residents of the state, which would reflect the free population in the state. In other words, large states would have more representatives in both houses of the legislature, and national law and policy would be weighted heavily in their favor. Just three large states, Virginia, Massachusetts, and Pennsylvania, would be able to form a

> **federalism** a political system in which power is divided between the central and regional units
>
> **Federalists** supporters of the Constitution who favored a strong central government
>
> **Anti-Federalists** advocates of states' rights who opposed the Constitution
>
> **Virginia Plan** a proposal at the Constitutional Convention that congressional representation be based on population, thus favoring the large states

majority and carry national legislation their way. The Virginia Plan also called for a single executive, to see that the laws were carried out, and a national judiciary, both appointed by the legislature, and it gave the national government power to override state laws.

A different plan, presented by William Paterson of New Jersey, was designed by the smaller states to better protect their interests. The **New Jersey Plan** amounted to a reinforcement, not a replacement, of the Articles of Confederation. It provided for a multiperson executive, so that no one person could possess too much power, and for congressional acts to be the "supreme law of the land." Most significantly, however, the Congress was much like the one that had existed under the Articles. In a unicameral (one-house) legislature, each state got only one vote. The delegates would be chosen by state legislatures. The powers of Congress were stronger than under the Articles, but the national government was still dependent on the states for some of its funding. The large states disliked this plan because small states together could block what the larger states wanted, even though the larger states had more people and contributed more revenue.

The prospects for a new government could have foundered on this issue. The stuffy heat of the closed Convention Hall shortened the tempers of the weary delegates, and frustration made compromise difficult. Each side had too much to lose by yielding to the other's plan. The solution finally arrived at was politics at its best and shows the triumph of the compromise narrative. The **Great Compromise** kept much of the framework of the Virginia Plan. It was a strong federal structure headed by a central government with sufficient power to tax its citizens, regulate commerce, conduct foreign affairs, organize the military, and exercise other central powers. It called for a single executive and a national judicial system. The compromise that allowed the smaller states to live with it involved the composition of the legislature. Like the Virginia Plan, it provided for two houses. The House of Representatives would be based on state population, giving the large states the extra clout they felt they deserved, but in the Senate each state had two votes. This gave the smaller states relatively much more power in the Senate than in the House of Representatives. Members of the House of Representatives would be elected directly by the people, members of the Senate by the state legislatures. Thus the government would be directly binding on the people as well as on the states. A key to the compromise was that most legislation would need the approval of both houses, so that neither large states nor small states could hold the entire government hostage to their wishes. The smaller states were sufficiently happy with this plan that most of them voted to approve, or ratify, the Constitution quickly and easily. *The*

Big Picture compares the Constitution with the Articles of Confederation, and shows how we got there via a number of compromises.

NORTH AND SOUTH

The compromise reconciling the large and small states was not the only one crafted by the delegates. The northern and the southern states, which is to say the non-slave-owning and the slave-owning states, were at odds over how population was to be determined for purposes of representation in the House of Representatives. The southern states wanted to count slaves as part of their populations when determining how many representatives they got, even though they had no intention of letting the slaves vote. Including slaves would give them more representatives and, thus, more power in the House. For exactly that reason, the northern states said that if slaves could not vote, they should not be counted. The compromise, also a triumph of politics if not humanity, is known as the **Three-fifths Compromise**. It was based on a formula developed by the Confederation Congress in 1763 to allocate tax assessments among the states. According to this compromise, for representation purposes, each slave would count as three-fifths of a person, every five slaves counting as three people. Interestingly, the actual language in the Constitution is a good deal cagier than this. It says that representatives and taxes shall be determined according to population, figured "by adding to the whole Number of free Persons, including those bound to Service for a Term of Years, and excluding Indians not taxed, three fifths of all other Persons."

The issue of slavery was divisive enough for the early Americans that the most politically safe approach was not to mention it explicitly at all and thus to avoid having to endorse or condemn it. Implicitly, of course, the silence had the effect of letting slavery continue. Article I, Section 9, of the Constitution, in similarly vague language, allows that "The Migration or Importation of such Persons as any of the States now existing shall think proper to admit, shall not be prohibited by Congress prior to the Year one thousand eight hundred and eight, but a

---

New Jersey Plan a proposal at the Constitutional Convention that congressional representation be equal, thus favoring the small states

Great Compromise the constitutional solution to congressional representation: equal votes in the Senate, votes by population in the House

Three-fifths Compromise the formula for counting five slaves as three people for purposes of representation, which reconciled northern and southern factions at the Constitutional Convention

Tax or duty may be imposed on such Importation, not exceeding ten dollars for each Person." Even more damning, Article IV, Section 2, obliquely provides for the return of runaway slaves: "No Person held to Service or Labour in one State under the Laws thereof, escaping into another, shall, in Consequence of any Law or Regulation therein, be discharged from such Service or Labour, but shall be delivered up on Claim of the Party to whom such Service or Labour may be due." The word *slavery* did not appear in the Constitution until it was expressly outlawed in the Thirteenth Amendment, passed in December 1865, nearly eighty years after the writing of the Constitution.

PAUSE AND REVIEW Who, What, How

Not only the political and economic elite but also the everyday citizens who did not attend the Constitutional Convention stood to gain or lose dramatically from the proceedings. At stake that summer were the very rules that would provide the framework for so many political battles in the future and the stories that justified them.

Differences clearly existed among the founding elites. Those representing large states, of course, wanted rules that would give their states more power, based on their larger population, tax base, and size. Representatives of small states, by contrast, wanted rules that would give the states equal power, so that they would not be squashed by the large states. North and South also differed on the rules. The North wanted representation to be based on the population of free citizens, while the South wanted to include slaves in the population count. The Great Compromise and the Three-fifths Compromise solved both disagreements.

The people at the convention were divided along another dimension as well. The Federalists sought to create a strong central government more resistant to the whims of popular opinion. Opposing them, the Anti-Federalists wanted a decentralized government, closer to the control of the people. It was the Federalists who controlled the agenda at the convention and who ultimately determined the structure of the new government.

In Your Own Words Identify the competing narratives, goals, and compromises that shaped the Constitution.

RATIFICATION

Selling the Constitution to Americans

For the Constitution to become the law of the land, it had to go through the process of **ratification**—being voted on and approved by state conventions in at least nine of the states. As it happens, the Constitution was eventually ratified by all thirteen states, but not until some major political battles had been fought.

FEDERALISTS VERSUS ANTI-FEDERALISTS

So strongly partisan were the supporters and opponents of the Constitution that, if the battle were taking place today, Twitter feeds would be on fire and we would probably find the two sides sniping at each other on cable shows like *The Sean Hannity Show* and *Hardball With Chris Matthews*, and Samantha Bee would be busy mocking both groups. It was a fierce, lively battle to control the narrative of what the new republic would be like, but instead of producing viral videos with the lifespan of a fruit fly, it yielded some of the finest writings for and against the American system.

Those in favor of ratification called themselves the Federalists. The Federalists, like Delegate A in our hypothetical constitution-building scenario, were mostly men with a considerable economic stake in the new nation. Having fared poorly under the Articles, they were certain that if America were to grow as an economic and world power, it needed to be the kind of country in which people with property would want to invest. Security and order were key values, as was popular control. The Federalists thought people like themselves should be in charge of the government, although some of them did not object to an expanded suffrage if government had enough built-in protections. Mostly, these students of the Enlightenment were convinced that a good government could be designed if the underlying principles of human behavior were known. If people were ambitious and tended toward corruption, then government should make use of those characteristics to produce good outcomes.

The Anti-Federalists told a different story. They rejected the notion that ambition and corruption were inevitable parts of human nature. If government could be kept small and local, and popular scrutiny truly vigilant, then Americans could live happy and contented lives without getting involved in the seamier side of politics. If America did not stray from its rural roots and values, it could permanently avoid the creeping corruption that they believed threatened it. The Articles of Confederation were more attractive to the Anti-Federalists than was the Constitution because they did not call for a strong central government that, tucked away from the voters' eyes, could become a hotbed of political intrigue. Instead, the Articles vested power in the state governments, which could be more easily watched and controlled.

---

ratification the process through which a proposal is formally approved and adopted by vote

---

THE BIG PICTURE:
How We Got to the Constitution From the Articles of Confederation

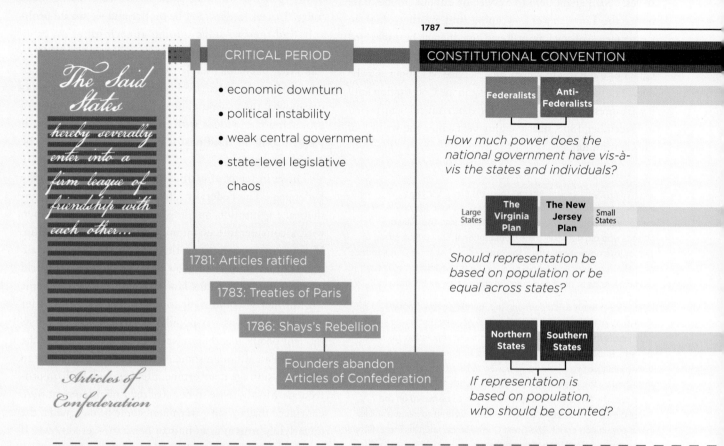

CRITICAL PERIOD

- economic downturn
- political instability
- weak central government
- state-level legislative chaos

The Said States hereby severally enter into a firm league of friendship with each other...

Articles of Confederation

1781: Articles ratified

1783: Treaties of Paris

1786: Shays's Rebellion

Founders abandon Articles of Confederation

1787

CONSTITUTIONAL CONVENTION

| Federalists | Anti-Federalists |

How much power does the national government have vis-à-vis the states and individuals?

| Large States | The Virginia Plan | The New Jersey Plan | Small States |

Should representation be based on population or be equal across states?

| Northern States | Southern States |

If representation is based on population, who should be counted?

Articles of Confederation

State sovereignty

State law is supreme

Unicameral legislature; equal votes for all states

Two-thirds vote to pass important laws

No congressional power to levy taxes, regulate commerce

No executive branch; laws executed by congressional committee

No national judiciary

All states required to pass amendments

The Virginia Plan

Popular sovereignty

National law is supreme

Bicameral legislature; representation in both houses based on population

Majority vote to pass laws

Congressional power to regulate commerce and tax

No restriction on strong single executive

National judiciary

Popular ratification of amendments

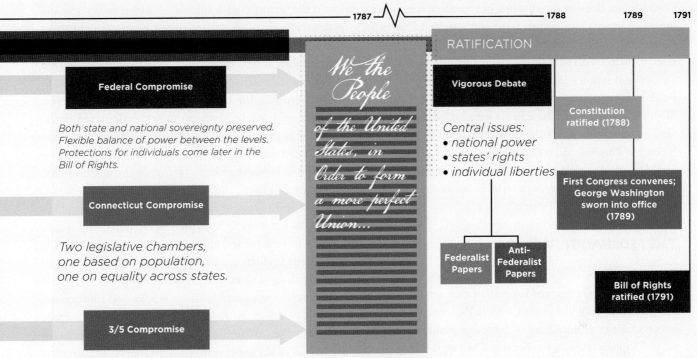

1787   **1788**   **1789**   **1791**

RATIFICATION

Federal Compromise

Both state and national sovereignty preserved. Flexible balance of power between the levels. Protections for individuals come later in the Bill of Rights.

Vigorous Debate

Central issues:
- *national power*
- *states' rights*
- *individual liberties*

Constitution ratified (1788)

Connecticut Compromise

Two legislative chambers, one based on population, one on equality across states.

First Congress convenes; George Washington sworn into office (1789)

Federalist Papers   **Anti-Federalist Papers**

3/5 Compromise

Representation in the House to be based on population, counting all "free Persons" and "three fifths of all other Persons."

Bill of Rights ratified (1791)

We the People of the United States, in Order to form a more perfect Union...

The Constitution

The New Jersey Plan	The Constitution
State sovereignty	**People are sovereign**
State law is supreme	**National law is supreme**
Unicameral legislature; one vote per state	**Bicameral legislature; equal votes in Senate; representation by population in House**
Extraordinary majority to pass laws	**Simple majority to pass laws in Congress; presidential veto**
Congressional power to regulate commerce and tax	**Congressional power to regulate commerce and tax**
Multiple executive	**Strong executive**
No national judiciary	**Federal court system**
All states required to pass amendments	**Amendment process is complex**

Writing under various aliases as well as their own names, the Federalists and Anti-Federalists fired arguments back and forth in pamphlets and newspaper editorials, aimed at persuading undecided Americans to come out for or against the Constitution. Because the channels of communication were limited, the competing ideas were concentrated into two streams. The Federalists were far more aggressive and organized in their "media blitz," hitting New York newspapers with a series of eloquent editorials published under the pen name Publius, but really written by Alexander Hamilton, James Madison, and John Jay. These essays were bound and distributed in other states where the ratification struggle was close. Known as *The Federalist Papers*, they are one of the main texts on early American politics today. In response, the Anti-Federalists published essays written under such names as Cato, Brutus, and The Federal Farmer.[32]

THE FEDERALIST PAPERS

Eighty-five essays were written by Publius. These essays are clever, well thought out, and logical, but they are also tricky and persuasive examples of the hard sell. We take a close look at two of the most important of the essays, numbers 10 and 51, in Chapters 13 and 4, respectively. Their archaic language makes *The Federalist Papers* generally difficult reading for contemporary students. However, the arguments in support of the Constitution are laid out so beautifully that taking the trouble to read them is worthwhile. It would be a good idea to turn to them and read them carefully now.

In *Federalist* No. 10, Madison tried to convince Americans that a large country was no more likely to succumb to the effects of special interests than a small one (preferred by the Anti-Federalists). He explained that the greatest danger to a republic came from **factions**—what we might call interest groups. Factions are groups of people motivated by a common interest, but one different from the interest of the country as a whole. Farmers, for instance, have an interest in keeping food prices high, even though that would make most Americans worse off. Businesspeople prefer high import duties on foreign goods, even though they make both foreign and domestic goods more expensive for the rest of us. Factions are not a particular problem when they constitute a minority of the population because they are offset by majority rule. They become problematic, however, when they are a majority. Factions usually have economic roots, the most basic being between the haves and have-nots in society. One of the majority factions that worried Madison was the mass of propertyless people whose behavior was so threatening to property holders under the Articles of Confederation.

To control the causes of factions would be to infringe on individual liberty. But Madison believed that the effects of factions were easily managed in a large republic. First of all, representation would dilute the effects of factions, and it was in this essay that Madison made his famous distinction between "pure democracy" and a "republic." In addition, if the territory were sufficiently large, factions would be neutralized because there would be so many of them that no one would be likely to become a majority. Furthermore, it would be difficult for people who shared common interests to find one another if some lived in South Carolina, for instance, and others lived in New Hampshire. Clearly Madison never anticipated social media, or even the telegraph. We discuss Madison's argument about factions again in Chapter 13, when we take up the topic of interest groups. In the meantime, however, notice how Madison relied on mechanical elements of politics (size and representation) to remedy a flaw in human nature (the tendency to form divisive factions). This is typical of the Federalists' approach to government, and it reflects the importance of institutions as well as rules in bringing about desired outcomes in politics.

We see the same emphasis on mechanical solutions to political problems in *Federalist* No. 51. Madison argued there that the institutions proposed in the Constitution would lead to neither corruption nor tyranny. The solution was the principles of checks and balances and separation of powers. We discuss these at length in Chapter 4, but it is worth looking at Madison's interesting explanation of why such checks work. Again building his case on a potential defect of human character, he said, "Ambition must be made to counteract ambition."[33] If men tend to be ambitious, give two ambitious men the job of watching over each other, and neither will let the other have an advantage.

Federalist No. 84 was written by Hamilton. It doesn't reflect great principles, but it is interesting politically because the Constitution was ratified in spite of it, not because of it. In this essay, Hamilton argued that a **Bill of Rights**—a listing of the protections against government infringement of individual rights guaranteed to citizens by government itself—was not necessary in a constitution (see the *CLUES to Critical Thinking* in Chapter 5).

The Federalist Papers a series of essays written to build support for ratification of the Constitution

factions groups of citizens united by some common passion or interest and opposed to the rights of other citizens or to the interests of the whole community

Bill of Rights a summary of citizen rights guaranteed and protected by a government; added to the Constitution as its first ten amendments in order to achieve ratification

The original draft of the Constitution contained no Bill of Rights. Some state constitutions had them, and so the Federalists argued that a federal Bill of Rights would be redundant. Moreover, the limited government set up by the federal Constitution didn't have the power to infringe on individual rights anyway, and many of the rights that would be included in a Bill of Rights were already in the body of the text. To the Anti-Federalists, already afraid of the invasive power of the national government, this omission was more appalling than any other aspect of the Constitution.

Hamilton argued that a Bill of Rights was unnecessary, even dangerous. As it stood, Hamilton said, the limited national government didn't have the power to interfere with citizens' lives in many ways, and any interference at all would be suspect. But if the Constitution were prefaced with a list of things government could not do to individuals, then government would assume it had the power to do anything that wasn't expressly forbidden. Therefore, government, instead of being unlikely to trespass on its citizens' rights, would be more likely to do so with a Bill of Rights than without. This argument was so unpersuasive to Americans at that time that the Federalists were forced to give in to Anti-Federalist pressure during the ratification process. The price of ratification exacted by several states was the Bill of Rights, really a Bill of "Limits" on the federal government, added to the Constitution as the first ten amendments. We look at those limits in detail in Chapter 5, on fundamental American liberties.

> **Would we have more freedoms today, or fewer, without the Bill of Rights?**

THE FINAL VOTE

The smaller states, gratified by the compromise that gave them equal representation in the Senate, and believing they would be better off as part of a strong nation, ratified the Constitution quickly. The vote was unanimous in Delaware, New Jersey, and Georgia. In Connecticut (128–40) and Pennsylvania (46–23), the convention votes, though not unanimous, were strongly in favor of the Constitution. This may have helped to tip the balance for Massachusetts, voting much more closely to ratify (187–168). Maryland (63–11) and South Carolina (149–73) voted in favor of ratification in the spring of 1788, leaving only one more state to supply the requisite nine to make the Constitution law.

The battles in the remaining states were much tighter. When the Virginia convention met in June 1788, the Federalists felt that it could provide the decisive vote and threw much of their effort into securing passage. Madison

and his Federalist colleagues debated with such Anti-Federalist advocates as George Mason and Patrick Henry, promising as they had in Massachusetts to support a Bill of Rights. Virginia ratified the Constitution by the narrow margin of 89 to 79, preceded by a few days by New Hampshire, voting 57 to 47. Establishment of the Constitution as the law of the land was ensured with approval of ten states. New York also narrowly passed the Constitution, 30 to 27, but North Carolina defeated it (193–75). Rhode Island, which had not sent delegates to the Constitutional Convention, refused to call a state convention to put it to the vote. Later both North Carolina and Rhode Island voted to ratify and join the union, in November 1789 and May 1790, respectively.[34] The *Snapshot of America* on page 74 summarizes the voting on the Constitution.

Again we can see how important rules are in determining outcomes. The Articles of Confederation had required the approval of all the states. Had the Constitutional Convention chosen a similar rule of unanimity, the Constitution may very well have been defeated. Recognizing that unanimous approval was not probable, however, the Federalists decided to require ratification by only nine of the thirteen, making adoption of the Constitution far more likely.

> **PAUSE AND REVIEW** Who, What, How
>
> The fight over ratification of the Constitution not only had the actual form of government at stake but also represented a conflict between narratives about the nature of human beings and the possibilities of republican government. The Federalists favored the new Constitution. For the Anti-Federalists, the Constitution seemed to present

PROFILES IN CITIZENSHIP
Newt Gingrich

Chip Somodevilla/Getty Images

History is anything but dull when it comes from the mouth of the man who has made so much of it. Newt Gingrich is the architect of the "Contract With America," a document that helped propel the Republicans into the majority in Congress in 1994 for the first time in forty years, and made him Speaker of the U.S. House of Representatives from 1995 to 1998.

But sitting at his desk at the American Enterprise Institute, it is hard to forget that long before he revolutionized American politics in the 1990s, Newt Gingrich was a history professor at Western Georgia College. For the last few years he has resumed the work of a scholar in the American Enterprise Institute, a conservative Washington think tank where, in addition to being a media commentator and adviser to his party, he can play with ideas and talk to other smart people to his heart's content.

Does it mean Gingrich has given up politics for good? Clearly not. It seems to be part of who he is. When he was as young as ten years old, he was flexing his civic muscles by petitioning the Harrisburg (Pennsylvania) City Council to build a zoo. They didn't, but only, he claims with a smile, because his military family moved away before he could persuade them.

Throughout his junior-high years the Gingriches lived in a number of post–World War II European cities. There was no pretending that the atrocities of war "couldn't happen there"; they had happened, and it was apparent to Gingrich that they could happen at home, too. He says, "Out of all that experience I concluded that citizenship was central to our freedom and our safety, and that having civilian leaders who thought about it every day was central to our survival."

What he does—the short answer—is to study history and glean from it insights about human motivation and behavior, and then use those historical insights to make things happen today. He is committed to crafting new ideas out of old lessons, leading his fellow citizens on a mission he believes will restore the country to its fundamental principles.

Ask him to explain just why it's important to study history and he pauses so long you wonder if he's forgotten the question or perhaps thinks it's so obvious that he won't deign to give it an answer. But no, he's just assembling his thoughts; you can almost hear the clicks and whirls of the processors. He opens his mouth and gracefully constructed sentences tumble out, fully formed. No umms, no stumbles; just perfect, elegant prose. Here's what he says:

On why students should study history

"If you've never run out of gas, you may not understand why filling your gas tank matters. And if you've never had your brakes fail, you may not care about having your brakes checked. And if you've never slid on an icy road, you may not understand why learning to drive on ice really matters. For citizens, if you haven't lived in a bombed-out city like Beirut or Baghdad, if you haven't seen a genocidal massacre like Rwanda, if you haven't been in a situation where people were starving to death, like Calcutta, you may not understand why you ought to study history. Because your life is good and it's easy and it's soft.

But for most of the history of the human race, most people, most of the time, have lived as slaves or as subjects to other people. And they lived lives that were short and desperate and where they had very little hope. And the primary breakthroughs have all been historic. It was the Greeks discovering the concept of self-governance, it was the Romans creating the objective sense of law, it was the Jewish tradition of being endowed by God—those came together and fused in Britain with the Magna Carta, and created a sense of rights that we take for granted every day. Because we have several hundred years of history protecting us. And the morning that history disappears, there's no reason to believe we'll be any better than Beirut or Baghdad."

On keeping the republic

"Be responsible, live out your responsibilities as a citizen, dedicate some amount of your time every day or every week to knowing what is going on in the world, be active in campaigns, and if nobody is worthy of your support, run yourself. . . . The whole notion of civil society [is] doing something as a volunteer, doing something, helping your fellow American, being involved with human beings. America only works as an organic society. . . . We're the most stunningly voluntaristic society in the world. And so if voluntarism dries up, in some ways America dries up."

Source: Newt Gingrich spoke with Christine Barbour on March 21, 2005.

innumerable opportunities for corruption to fester. Knowing they had lost the battle for public opinion and for votes, they made the attachment of a Bill of Rights a condition of their acquiescence.

In Your Own Words Summarize the debate over ratification of the Constitution.

THE CITIZENS AND THE FOUNDING

New rights bring obligations

As we said at the beginning of this chapter, there are different narratives to be told about the American founding. We did not want to fall into the oversimplification trap, portraying the founding as a headlong rush to liberty on the part of an oppressed people. Politics is always a good deal more complicated than that, and this is a book about politics. We also wanted to avoid telling a story that errs on the other end of one-sidedness, depicting the American founding as an elite-driven period of history, in which the political, economic, and religious leaders decided they were better off without English rule; inspired the masses to revolt; and then created a Constitution that established rules that benefited people like themselves. Neither of these stories is entirely untrue, but they obscure two very important points.

COMPETING ELITES

The first point is that there was not just one "elite" group at work during the founding period. Although political and economic leaders might have acted together over the matter of the break from England (even then, important elites remained loyal to Britain), once the business of independence was settled, it was clear that competing elite groups existed. These groups included leaders of big states and leaders of small states, leaders of northern states and leaders of southern states, merchant elites and agricultural elites, and elites who found their security in a strong national government and those who found it in decentralized power. The power struggle between all those adversaries resulted in the compromises that form the framework of our government today.

THE RISE OF THE "ORDINARY" CITIZEN

The second point is that not all the actors during the founding period were among the top tier of political, economic, and religious leadership. Just because the Revolution and the government-building that followed it were not the product of ordinary citizens zealous for liberty does not mean that ordinary citizens had nothing to do with it.

Citizenship as we know it today was a fledgling creation at the time of the founding. The British had not been citizens of the English government but subjects of the English Crown. There is a world of difference between a subject and a citizen, as we pointed out in Chapter 1. The subject has a personal tie to the monarch; the citizen has a legal tie to a national territory. The subject has obligations; the citizen has both obligations and rights. The source for these new ideas about citizenship was Enlightenment thinking. We have seen in the ideas of John Locke the concept of the social contract—that citizenship is the product of a contractual agreement between rulers and ruled that makes obeying the law contingent on having one's rights protected by the state.

But having transitioned from subjecthood to citizenship is not to say that citizenship conferred equal rights. Here principle clashed with profound prejudice. We saw throughout this chapter that the rights of citizenship were systematically denied to Native Americans, to African Americans, and to women. The ideals of citizenship that were born during the founding are truly innovative and inspiring, but they were unavailable in practice to a major portion of the population for well over a hundred years. It is conventional today to be appalled at the failure of the founders to practice the principles of equality they preached, and certainly that failure is appalling in light of today's values, but we should remember that the whole project of citizenship was new to the founders and that in many ways they were far more democratic than any who had come before them. One of our tasks in this book will be to trace the evolving narratives and practice of American citizenship, as the conferral of equal rights so majestically proclaimed in the Declaration slowly becomes reality for all Americans. Another related task will be to see the empowerment of individual citizens as their ability to create and share their own narratives is enhanced by technology. The more mediated their world becomes, the harder it will be to shake off dominant narratives but the more possibilities there will be for them to create their own.

In Your Own Words Explain the role of everyday citizens in the founding of the United States.

LET'S REVISIT: *What's at Stake . . . ?*

Having read the history of revolutionary America, what would you say is at stake in the modern militia movement? The existence of state militias and similar groups poses a troubling dilemma for the federal government; and groups whose members are mostly benign, like the Tea Partiers, are even trickier for the government to deal with. Bill Clinton, who was president when Timothy McVeigh bombed the federal building in Oklahoma City, warned at the time of the fifteenth anniversary of those attacks that "there can be real consequences when what you say animates people who do things you would never do." Angry rhetoric and narratives that justify that anger can result in violence that those who goad the anger might not necessarily endorse. The violence at Trump rallies in 2016 was a case in point, and there are those out there, like McVeigh and the Bundys, who "were profoundly alienated, disconnected people who bought into this militant anti-government line."[35]

The dilemma is that, on the one hand, the purpose of government is to protect our rights, and the Constitution surely guarantees Americans freedom of speech and assembly. On the other hand, government must hold the monopoly on the legitimate use of force in society or it will fall, just as the British government fell to the American colonies. If groups are allowed to amass weapons and forcibly resist or even attack U.S. law enforcers, then they constitute "mini-governments," or competing centers of authority, and life for citizens becomes chaotic and dangerous.

The American system was designed to be relatively responsive to the wishes of the American public. Citizens can get involved; they can vote, run for office, change the laws, and amend the Constitution. By permitting these legitimate ways of affecting American politics, the founders hoped to prevent the rise of groups, like the Bundys, that would promote and act toward violence. The founders intended to create a society characterized by political stability, not by revolution, which is why Jefferson's Declaration of Independence is so careful to point out that revolutions should occur only when there is no alternative course of action.

Some militia members reject the idea of working through the system; they say, as did McVeigh, that they consider themselves at war with the federal government. We call disregard for the law at the individual level "crime," at the group level "terrorism" or "insurrection," and at the majority level "revolution." It is the job of any government worth its salt to prevent all three kinds of activities. Thus it is not the existence or the beliefs of the militia groups that government seeks to control but rather their activities.

What's at stake in challenges to the legitimacy of government are the very issues of government authority and the rights of individual citizens. It is difficult to draw the line between the protection of individual rights and the exercise of government authority. In a democracy, we want to respect the rights of all citizens, but this respect can be thwarted when a small number of individuals reject the rules of the game agreed on by the vast majority.

CLUES to Critical Thinking

The Declaration of Independence

By Thomas Jefferson, July 4, 1776

We discuss the Declaration of Independence at length in this chapter, but it is often a good idea to read for yourself the primary sources by which our history has been shaped.

IN CONGRESS, JULY 4, 1776

The unanimous Declaration of the thirteen United States of America

When in the Course of human events it becomes necessary for one people to dissolve the political bands which have connected them with another and to assume among the powers of the earth, the separate and equal station to which the Laws of Nature and of Nature's God entitle them, a decent respect to the opinions of mankind requires that they should declare the causes which impel them to the separation.

We hold these truths to be self-evident, that all men are created equal, that they are endowed by their Creator with certain unalienable Rights, that among these are Life, Liberty and the pursuit of Happiness. — That to secure these rights, Governments are instituted among Men, deriving their just powers from the consent of the governed, — That whenever any Form of Government becomes destructive of these ends, it is the Right of the People to alter or to abolish it, and to institute new Government, laying its foundation on such principles and organizing its powers in such form, as to them shall seem most likely to effect their Safety and Happiness. Prudence, indeed, will dictate that Governments long established should not be changed for light and transient causes; and accordingly all experience hath shewn that mankind are more disposed to suffer, while evils are sufferable than to right themselves by abolishing the forms to which they are accustomed. But when a long train of abuses and usurpations, pursuing invariably the same Object evinces a design to reduce them under absolute Despotism, it is their right, it is their duty, to throw off such Government, and to provide new Guards for their future security. — Such has been the patient sufferance of these Colonies; and such is now the necessity which constrains them to alter their former Systems of Government. The history of the present King of Great Britain is a history of repeated injuries and usurpations, all having in direct object the establishment of an absolute Tyranny over these States. To prove this, let Facts be submitted to a candid world.

He has refused his Assent to Laws, the most wholesome and necessary for the public good.

He has forbidden his Governors to pass Laws of immediate and pressing importance, unless suspended in their operation till his Assent should be obtained; and when so suspended, he has utterly neglected to attend to them.

He has refused to pass other Laws for the accommodation of large districts of people, unless those people would relinquish the right of Representation in the Legislature, a right inestimable to them and formidable to tyrants only.

He has called together legislative bodies at places unusual, uncomfortable, and distant from the depository of their Public Records, for the sole purpose of fatiguing them into compliance with his measures.

He has dissolved Representative Houses repeatedly, for opposing with manly firmness his invasions on the rights of the people.

He has refused for a long time, after such dissolutions, to cause others to be elected, whereby the Legislative Powers, incapable of Annihilation, have returned to the People at large for their exercise; the State remaining in the mean time exposed to all the dangers of invasion from without, and convulsions within.

He has endeavoured to prevent the population of these States; for that purpose obstructing the Laws for Naturalization of Foreigners; refusing to pass others to encourage their migrations hither, and raising the conditions of new Appropriations of Lands.

He has obstructed the Administration of Justice by refusing his Assent to Laws for establishing Judiciary Powers.

He has made Judges dependent on his Will alone for the tenure of their offices, and the amount and payment of their salaries.

He has erected a multitude of New Offices, and sent hither swarms of Officers to harass our people and eat out their substance.

He has kept among us, in times of peace, Standing Armies without the Consent of our legislatures.

He has affected to render the Military independent of and superior to the Civil Power.

He has combined with others to subject us to a jurisdiction foreign to our constitution, and unacknowledged by our laws; giving his Assent to their Acts of pretended Legislation:

For quartering large bodies of armed troops among us:

For protecting them, by a mock Trial from punishment for any Murders which they should commit on the Inhabitants of these States:

For cutting off our Trade with all parts of the world:

For imposing Taxes on us without our Consent:

For depriving us in many cases, of the benefit of Trial by Jury:

For transporting us beyond Seas to be tried for pretended offences:

For abolishing the free System of English Laws in a neighbouring Province, establishing therein an Arbitrary government, and enlarging its Boundaries so as to render it at once an example and fit instrument for introducing the same absolute rule into these Colonies:

For taking away our Charters, abolishing our most valuable Laws and altering fundamentally the Forms of our Governments:

For suspending our own Legislatures, and declaring themselves invested with power to legislate for us in all cases whatsoever.

He has abdicated Government here, by declaring us out of his Protection and waging War against us.

He has plundered our seas, ravaged our coasts, burnt our towns, and destroyed the lives of our people.

He is at this time transporting large Armies of foreign Mercenaries to compleat the works of death, desolation, and tyranny, already begun with circumstances of Cruelty & Perfidy scarcely paralleled in the most barbarous ages, and totally unworthy the Head of a civilized nation.

He has constrained our fellow Citizens taken Captive on the high Seas to bear Arms against their Country, to become the executioners of their friends and Brethren, or to fall themselves by their Hands.

He has excited domestic insurrections amongst us, and has endeavoured to bring on the inhabitants of our frontiers, the merciless Indian Savages whose known rule of warfare, is an undistinguished destruction of all ages, sexes and conditions.

In every stage of these Oppressions We have Petitioned for Redress in the most humble terms: Our repeated Petitions have been answered only by repeated injury. A Prince, whose character is thus marked by every act which may define a Tyrant, is unfit to be the ruler of a free people.

Nor have We been wanting in attentions to our British brethren. We have warned them from time to time of attempts by their legislature to extend an unwarrantable jurisdiction over us. We have reminded them of the circumstances of our emigration and settlement here. We have appealed to their native justice and magnanimity, and we have conjured them by the ties of our common kindred to disavow these usurpations, which would inevitably interrupt our connections and correspondence. They too have been deaf to the voice of justice and of consanguinity. We must, therefore, acquiesce in the necessity, which denounces our Separation, and hold them, as we hold the rest of mankind, Enemies in War, in Peace Friends.

We, therefore, the Representatives of the united States of America, in General Congress, Assembled, appealing to the Supreme Judge of the world for the rectitude of our intentions, do, in the Name, and by Authority of the good People of these Colonies, solemnly publish and declare, That these united Colonies are, and of Right ought to be Free and Independent States, that they are Absolved from all Allegiance to the British Crown, and that all political connection between them and the State of Great Britain, is and ought to be totally dissolved; and that as Free and Independent States, they have full Power to levy War, conclude Peace, contract Alliances, establish Commerce, and to do all other Acts and Things which Independent States may of right do. — And for the support of this Declaration, with a firm reliance on the protection of Divine Providence, we mutually pledge to each other our Lives, our Fortunes, and our sacred Honor.

Source: National Archives, http://www.archives.gov/exhibits/charters/declaration_transcript.html.

Consider the source and the audience: Thomas Jefferson is writing here to rally American colonists as well as to justify the American Revolution to the world. How do those twin goals affect his writing?

Lay out the argument and the underlying values and assumptions: Jefferson painstakingly lays out an argument here that, if the logic holds, leads inescapably to the conclusion that Americans must declare independence. What is that argument? What values about equality, rights, and political legitimacy underlie his argument about the social contract?

Uncover the evidence: What evidence does Jefferson offer for the premise of his argument, that all men are created equal and possess certain rights? To show that George III has broken the social contract, he offers certain "facts" to a "candid world." What are those facts? Are they all evidence of George III's misdeeds?

E_valuate the conclusion:_ Jefferson concludes that the argument he has made and the facts he has presented mean that the colonies are "absolved from allegiance to the British crown." Assuming the facts he presents are true, was it possible to come to any other conclusion?

S_ort out the political implications:_ The political implications of Jefferson's work were obvious and immediate: the colonies launched a war of independence that created the United States. How did this declaration smooth the way for that to happen? What if Jefferson had failed in his task—where would we be today?

Review

Politics in the English Colonies

The politics of the American founding shaped the political compromises embodied in the Constitution. This in turn defined the institutions and many of the rules that do much to determine the winners and losers in political struggles today.

The battle for America involved a number of different groups, including American Indians, the Spanish, the French, and the British colonists. The English settlers came for many reasons, including religious and economic, but then duplicated many of the politically restrictive practices in the colonies that they had sought to escape in England. These included restrictions on political participation and a narrow definition of citizenship.

slavery (p. 65)   racism (p. 66)

The Split From England

The Revolution was caused by many factors, including British attempts to get the colonies to pay for the costs of the wars fought to protect them. The pressures from the Crown for additional taxes coincided with new ideas about the proper role of government among colonial elites. These ideas are embodied in Jefferson's politically masterful writing of the Declaration of Independence.

French and Indian War (p. 66)   _Common Sense_ (p. 68)
popular sovereignty (p. 67)   Declaration of Independence (p. 68)

The Articles of Confederation

The government under the Articles of Confederation granted too much power to the states, which in a number of cases came to serve the interests of farmers and debtors. The Constitutional Convention was called to design a government with stronger centralized powers that would overcome the weaknesses elites perceived in the Articles.

constitution (p. 71)   confederation (p. 71)   Shays's rebellion (p. 72)
Articles of Confederation (p. 71)   popular tyranny (p. 72)

The Constitutional Convention

The new Constitution was derived from a number of key compromises: federalism was set as a principle to allocate power to both the central government and the states; the Great Compromise allocated power in the new national legislature; and the Three-fifths Compromise provided a political solution to the problem of counting slaves in the southern states for purposes of representation in the House of Representatives.

Constitutional Convention (p. 73)   Anti-Federalists (p. 75)   Great Compromise (p. 76)
federalism (p. 75)   Virginia Plan (p. 75)   Three-fifths Compromise (p. 76)
Federalists (p. 75)   New Jersey Plan (p. 76)

Ratification

The politics of ratification of the Constitution provides a lesson in the marriage between practical politics and political principle. *The Federalist Papers* served as political propaganda to convince citizens to favor ratification, and they serve today as a record of the reasoning behind many of the elements of our Constitution.

ratification (p. 77)   factions (p. 80)
The Federalist Papers (p. 80)   Bill of Rights (p. 80)

The Citizens and the Founding

The American founding reflects competition among elites as well as the establishment of a new form of citizenship.

In Your Own Words

After you've read this chapter, you will be able to

4.1 Describe the role of each branch of government.

4.2 Explain why the founders chose to structure each of the three branches of government as they did.

4.3 Identify the rules and interests that keep relations tense between state and national governments.

4.4 Demonstrate how the flexibility built into the Constitution has allowed it to change with the times.

4.5 Discuss whether the Constitution fosters or limits citizen participation in government.

4
FEDERALISM AND THE U.S. CONSTITUTION

What's at Stake . . . When a State Takes Marijuana Laws Into Its Own Hands?

IF YOU ARE READING THIS in Alaska, California, Colorado, Maine, Massachusetts, Michigan, Nevada, Oregon, Vermont, Washington, or the District of Columbia, or in one of the thirty plus states that has legalized some form of marijuana for medical use, be careful—very careful—how you exercise your rights. Due to the crazy patchwork nature of America's marijuana laws, what is legal in your home state might get you jail or prison time and a hefty fine if you take it on the road. You can thank the founding fathers' invention of federalism for this, although it's doubtful this is what they had in mind when they designed it.

Of course, everyone knows that smoking marijuana is against the law in the United States. Among other things, the U.S. Federal Controlled Substances

Weedy Territory

Laws regarding marijuana have changed in several states (including Colorado, where this image was taken), but cannabis consumption remains illegal in many other states, and marijuana use is still a federal offense. The resulting patchwork of state laws and changing federal enforcement from one administration to the next make for a confusing pot market.

Act says so. Under that law, passed in 1970, marijuana is a "schedule I drug," equivalent, in legal terms, to heroin and LSD. But most people also know that, although the U.S. government considers marijuana a drug for which there is "no currently accepted medical use," most of the states beg to differ, and nine say, "Who cares? It's just plain fun" (although Vermont and D.C. won't let you buy it).

So if you live in a state with legal medical marijuana and you have a prescription, or if you stop in at the local pot shop in one of the seven that allow commercial sales, you are good, right?

Well, sort of. Maybe. It depends.

Consider the case of B. J. Patel, a thirty-one-year-old man from Arizona who was traveling through Idaho and was stopped for failing to signal by a police officer using license plate recognition software to target out-of-state drivers. The officer saw the medical marijuana card in his wallet, asked where the pot was, and, when shown by Patel, promptly arrested him. No matter how law-abiding Patel had been when he bought the pot, he was breaking the law in Idaho.

Idaho law provides for imprisonment and a $1,000 fine for under three ounces of pot and up to five years in prison and a $10,000 fine for more than three ounces. "Come on vacation, leave on probation," says a Coeur d'Alene, Idaho lawyer.[1]

Or consider the case of the five brothers in Colorado who sold an oil made from a strain of marijuana that doesn't even get you high. The plant is rich in a substance, CBD, that is used to treat seizures. It's legal in Colorado, of course, but there is a global demand for the oil, and

the brothers want to expand to meet that demand.[2] The fly in their ointment is that, even though the oil is not an intoxicant, it is made from marijuana and marijuana is illegal under federal law. So the brothers got their product classified as "industrial hemp," which is okay by Colorado, but not necessarily by the United States, although it will be if Senate majority leader Mitch McConnell manages to get the Hemp Farming Act of 2018 passed.[3]

Generally, federal law trumps state law when there is a conflict. The Obama administration, however, followed a policy under which the federal government wouldn't prosecute for marijuana use in the states where it was legal, as long as the sale of marijuana was regulated.[4] Try to sell that marijuana, however, or any product made from it, across state lines and the feds would seize it and possibly put the seller in jail. That policy stayed in place until January 2018, when the Trump administration's attorney general, Jeff Sessions, rescinded it. Colorado senator Cory Gardner took the issue straight to Trump, who assured him Colorado's pot smokers were safe from federal action. Trump has stood by that position, although his Department of Justice, led by Sessions, has not. Now that he has fired Sessions that may change, although Sessions had White House allies determined to enforce the federal law.[5]

Finally, consider the case of a Minnesota mom who was arrested in 2014 for giving her fifteen-year-old son marijuana oil on a doctor's advice to relieve chronic pain and muscle spasms from a brain injury. The pot was purchased legally in Colorado but administered in Minnesota, which had passed a law allowing medical marijuana. The catch? It didn't come into effect until July 2015. Said Bob Capecchi, who works for the Marijuana Policy Project in Washington, D.C., "Stunned was my initial reaction. I can't think of an instance where an individual has been brought up on charges like this simply because the effective date hasn't come around yet for the law that has already been passed. Let's not forget, there is a medical marijuana law that has been endorsed by the legislature and by the Governor."[6]

Why is there so much legal turmoil surrounding the use of marijuana, something that a majority of Americans now think should be legal?[7] Why can an activity that is legal in one state get you fined and thrown in jail in another? Why can the federal government forbid an activity but turn a blind eye to it unless you carry it across state lines? How do the laws get so complicated and tangled that you can get yourself arrested in one state for an activity that is legal in the state where you engaged in it, even if it is soon to be legal in the place where you are arrested? What is at stake when states decide to pass their own laws legalizing marijuana? We will return to this question at the end of the chapter, when we have a better grasp of the complex relationships generated by American federalism. **«**

IMAGINE

IMAGINE that you are playing Monopoly, but you've lost the rule book. You and your friends decide to play anyway and make up the rules as you go along. Even though the game still looks like Monopoly, and you're using the Monopoly board, and the money, and the game pieces, and the little houses and hotels, if you aren't following the official Monopoly rules, you aren't really playing Monopoly.

In the same way, imagine that the United States becomes afflicted with a sort of collective amnesia so that all the provisions of the Constitution are forgotten. Or perhaps the whole country gets fed up with politics as usual in America and votes to replace our Constitution with, say, the French Constitution. Even if we kept all our old politicians, and the White House and the Capitol, and the streets of Washington, what went on there would no longer be recognizable as American politics. What is distinctive about any political system is not just the people or the buildings, but also the rules, the ideas, and the narratives that lie behind them and give them life and meaning.

Now imagine that you found the rulebook! Yay. You are playing by the rules of Monopoly, but one of the players continually cheats. You know he is cheating, he's not even hiding it. But all of the rest of you keep on playing by the rules. Maybe one of you sees what he is getting away with and starts to cheat also. Those of you who value the game are frustrated and angry. The cheater wins, as you might expect, and the rest of you lose. What just happened?

It happened because, although you found the rule book, not all of you committed to following the rules, or to banishing a player who refused. It happened because, although the official rules are important, so is the commitment to play by them. In Chapter 1 we discussed the power of norms—the unspoken understandings about how to behave that underlie the rule of law. One hugely important norm, the one that makes the rules meaningful, is the commitment not to cheat by breaking, bending, or skirting the rules, and the obligation to report anyone who does break them. Another important norm is to accept the results of the rules, even if it means you lose. If we tolerate the breaking of norms, then the bad behavior becomes "normal" and the rules become meaningless. What makes rules work is the norm that most of us agree to follow them and penalize anyone who doesn't.

In politics, as in games, rules are crucial. The rules set up the institutions and the procedures that are the heart of the political system, and these institutions and procedures help determine who will be the winners and the losers in politics, what outcomes will result, and how resources will be distributed. Political rules are themselves the product of a political process, as we saw in Chapter 3. Rules do not

drop from the sky, all written and ready to be implemented. Instead they are created by human beings, determined to establish procedures that will help them, and people like them, get what they want from the system. If you change the rules, you change the people who will be advantaged and disadvantaged by those rules.

The founders were not in agreement about the sorts of rules that should be the basis of American government. Instead they were feeling their way, balancing historical experience against contemporary reality. They had to craft new rules to achieve their goal of a government whose authority came from the people but whose power was limited so as to preserve the liberty of those people. Rules that failed to meet that test would be inconsistent with the narrative of liberty and self-rule that they were promoting. Even rules that did limit self-rule had to be couched in terms that made them seem to be strengthening freedom.

The questions that consumed the founders may surprise us. We know about the debate over how much power should belong to the national government and how much to the states. But discussions ranged far beyond issues of federalism versus states' rights. How should laws be made, and by whom? Should the British parliament be a model for the new legislature, with the "lords" represented in one house and the "common people" in the other? Or should there even be two houses at all? What about the executive? Should it be a king, as in England? Should it be just one person, or should several people serve as executive at the same time? How much power should the executive have, and how should he or they be chosen? And what role would the courts play? How could all these institutions be designed so that no one could become powerful enough to destroy the others? How could the system change with the times and yet still provide for stable governance?

The founders' answers to those questions are contained in the official rule book for who gets what and how in America, which is, of course, the Constitution. In Chapter 3 we talked about the political forces that produced the Constitution, the preferences of various groups for certain rules, the compromises these groups evolved to arrive at a final document, and the narratives they created to get the document ratified. In this chapter, we look at the Constitution from the inside. Since rules are so important for producing certain kinds of outcomes in the political system, it is essential that we understand not only what the rules provide for but also what the choice of those rules means, what other kinds of rules exist that the founders did not choose, and what outcomes the founders rejected by not choosing those alternative rules. We also need to understand the norms that underlie the rules they created. Remember that norms are unspoken and unwritten, so we can only infer from the rules the founders

chose, and the rules they did not, what kinds of behavior it would take to support them. In this chapter, we focus on the founders' concerns, the constitutional provisions they established, the alternatives they might have chosen, the norms we can infer, and how their choices affect who gets what, and how, in American politics.

THE THREE BRANCHES OF GOVERNMENT

Making, executing, and interpreting the laws

All governments must have the power to do three things: (1) legislate, or make the laws; (2) administer, or execute the laws; and (3) adjudicate, or interpret the laws. The kinds of institutions they create to manage those powers vary widely. Because of our system of separation of powers, which we discuss later in this chapter, separate branches of government handle the legislative, executive, and judicial powers. Article I of the Constitution sets up Congress, our legislature; Article II establishes the presidency, our executive; and Article III outlines the federal court system, our judiciary.

THE LEGISLATIVE BRANCH

Legislative power is lawmaking power. Laws can be created by a single ruler or by a political party, they can be divined from natural or religious principles, or they can be made by the citizens who will have to obey the laws or by representatives working on their behalf. Most countries that claim to be democratic choose the last method of lawmaking. The body of government that makes laws is called the **legislature**.

Legislatures themselves can be set up in different ways: they can have one or two chambers, or houses; members can be elected, appointed, or hereditary; and if elected, they can be chosen by the people directly or by some other body. A variety of electoral rules can apply. The U.S. Congress is a **bicameral legislature**, meaning there are two chambers, and the legislators are elected directly by the people for terms of two or six years, depending on the house.

> **legislature** the body of government that makes laws
>
> **bicameral legislature** a legislature with two chambers

THE CASE FOR REPRESENTATION In *Federalist* No. 10, James Madison argued that American laws should be made by representatives of the people rather than by the people themselves. He rejected what he called "pure democracies," small political systems in which the citizens make and administer their own laws. Instead Madison recommended a **republic**, a system in which a larger number of citizens delegate, or assign, the tasks of governing to a smaller body. A republic claims two advantages: the dangers of factions are reduced, and the people running the government are presumably the best equipped to do so. Representation, said Madison, helps to "refine and enlarge the public views by passing them through the medium of a chosen body of citizens," distinguished by their wisdom, patriotism, and love of justice.[8] Notice that, motivated by his disillusionment with the Articles of Confederation, Madison basically set up a system in which the few have more power than the many, and he justified that system with a narrative that claimed a goal of enhancing freedom for all.

Of course, Americans were already long accustomed to the idea of representation. All the states had legislatures. The Articles of Confederation had provided for representation as well, and even Britain had representation of a sort in Parliament.

WHAT DOES THE CONSTITUTION SAY? Article I sets out the framework of the legislative branch of government. Since the founders expected the legislature to be the most important part of the new government, they spent the most time specifying its composition, the qualifications for membership, its powers, and its limitations.

The best known part of Article I is the famous Section 8, which spells out the specific powers of Congress. This list is followed by the provision that Congress can do anything "necessary and proper" to carry out its duties. The Supreme Court has interpreted this clause so broadly that there are few effective restrictions on what Congress can do.

The House of Representatives, where representation is based on population, was intended to be truly the representative of all the people, the "voice of the common man," as it were. To be elected to the House, a candidate need be only twenty-five years old and a citizen for seven years. Since House terms last two years, members run for reelection often and can be ousted fairly easily, according to public whim. The founders intended this office to be accessible to and easily influenced by citizens and to reflect frequent changes in public opinion.

> republic a government in which decisions are made through representatives of the people
>
> unicameral legislature a legislature with one chamber

> *Are there any advantages to making up the rules as you go along instead of sticking to a rule book?*

The Senate is another matter. Candidates have to be at least thirty years old and citizens for nine years—older, wiser, and, the founders hoped, more stable than the representatives in the House. Because senatorial terms last for six years, senators are not so easily swayed by changes in public sentiment. In addition, senators were originally elected not directly by the people, but by members of their state legislatures. Election by state legislators, themselves already a "refinement" of the general public, would ensure that senators were a higher caliber of citizen: more in tune with "the commercial and monied interest," as Massachusetts delegate Elbridge Gerry put it at the Constitutional Convention.[9] The Senate would thus be a more aristocratic body; that is, it would look more like the British House of Lords, where members are admitted on the basis of their birth or achievement, not by election.

POSSIBLE ALTERNATIVES: A UNICAMERAL LEGISLATURE? The Congress we have is not the only Congress the founders could have given us. Instead of establishing the House of Representatives and the Senate, for instance, they could have established one legislative chamber only, what we call a unicameral legislature. Many countries today have **unicameral legislatures** and although forty-nine of the fifty United States have followed the national example with bicameral state legislatures, Nebraska has chosen a unicameral, nonpartisan legislature.

Proponents of unicameral systems claim that lawmaking is faster and more efficient when laws are debated and voted on in only one chamber. They say such laws are also more responsive to changes in public opinion, which at least theoretically is a good thing in a democracy. On the national level, a unicameral system can help encourage citizens to feel a sense of identity with their government, since it implies that the whole country shares the same fundamental interests and can thus be represented by a single body.

In Europe, governments originally had different legislative chambers to represent different social classes or estates in society. We can see the remnants of this system in the British parliament, whose upper chamber is called the House of Lords, and lower, the House of Commons, or the common people. The French once had five houses in their legislature, and the Swedish four. As countries become more democratic—that is, as their governments become more representative of the people as a whole and not of social classes—the legislatures become more streamlined. Sweden eventually

Unicameral or Bicameral?

Although the founders were convinced a bicameral system was the way to go, Nebraska, alone of all the states, chose to adopt a one-house system in the 1930s. Advocates argued that one house offered more transparency, simplicity, and economy. The legislative body meets in this room in the Nebraska State Capitol.

George Washington explained that, just as one would pour one's coffee into the saucer to cool it off (a common practice of the day), "we pour legislation into the senatorial saucer to cool it." In reality, each chamber has served to cool the passions of the other; this requirement that laws be passed twice has helped keep the American legislature in check.[11]

WHAT THE CONSTITUTION DOESN'T SAY: NORMS THAT SUPPORT THE LEGISLATURE

The Constitution created two bodies that have to agree on a law in the exact same form for it to pass. That condition is likely to demand that opposing sides compromise at times. If the founders hadn't wanted to force compromise, a unicameral legislature would have been an easier way to go. They rejected that.

Given that the authors of the Constitution themselves had to compromise with those who preferred the Articles of Confederation, we can infer that *compromise* is an important democratic norm. The founders also set up the Senate to be the older and more stable chamber. As Washington implied, the founders expected more from senators, that they behave with more *dignity* than the more unruly House. That expectation is apparent in the extra responsibilities the Senate is given, such as the approval of members of the president's cabinet. Senators are expected to act like the adults in the room. Finally, the members of Congress were to be elected, so they intended that the results of fair elections would be recognized by all parties. It implies the norm of *good sportsmanship*, another way of saying that one occasionally has to be a good loser. When one side loses, it doesn't take its marbles and go home. It doesn't call the other side a cheater or say the win is illegitimate (unless it is). Instead, it accepts the loss knowing it will have another chance, another day.

moved to two legislative houses, and in 1971 it adopted a unicameral legislature. France now has two. Britain still has the Lords and the Commons, but increasing democratization has meant less legislative power for the House of Lords, which now can only delay, not block, laws made by the House of Commons.[10] In that sense, the fewer chambers a legislature has, the more representative it is of the people as a whole.

The founders rejected unicameralism for several reasons, however. Such a system makes it difficult for the legislature to represent more than one set of interests, and the framers preferred bicameralism in part because the two houses could represent different interests in society—the people's interests in the House and the more elite interests in the Senate. Bicameral legislatures could also represent the different levels of the federal government in the legislative process. Federal governments that preserve a bicameral structure typically do so with the intention of having the "people" represented in one house and the individual regions—in our case, the states—in another.

Finally, the founders were convinced that bicameralism was better than unicameralism for the young republic because it fit their narrative that the smaller the units of government power, the safer the government would be from those who would abuse its power. The quick legislative responsiveness of a unicameral legislature can have some drawbacks. Changes in public opinion are often only temporary, and perhaps a society in a calmer moment would not want the laws to be changed so hastily. When asked by Thomas Jefferson, who had been in France during the Constitutional Convention, why the delegates had adopted a bicameral legislature,

THE EXECUTIVE BRANCH

The **executive** is the part of government that "executes" the laws, or sees they are carried out. Although technically executives serve in an administrative role, many end up with some decision-making or legislative power as well. National executives are the leaders of their countries, and they participate, with varying amounts of power, in making laws and policies. That

> **executive** the branch of government responsible for putting laws into effect

role can range from the U.S. president, who, while not a part of the legislature itself, can propose, encourage, and veto legislation, to European prime ministers, who are part of the legislature and may have, as in the British case, the decisive power to dissolve the entire legislature and call a new election.

FEARS OF THE FOUNDERS That the Articles of Confederation provided for no executive power at all was a testimony to the founders' conviction that such a power threatened their liberty. The chaos that resulted under the Articles, however, made it clear that a stronger government was called for—not only a stronger legislature, but a stronger executive as well. The constitutional debates reveal that many of the founders were haunted by the idea that they might inadvertently reestablish the same tyrannical power over themselves that they had escaped only recently with the Revolution. The central controversies focused on whether the executive should be more than one person, whether he should be able to seek reelection as many times as he wanted, and whether he should be elected directly by the people or indirectly by the legislature.

The founders were divided.[12] Some, fearing a strong executive, believed its power could be limited by dividing it among several officeholders, but they eventually lost to those who believed there should be a single president.

The issue of whether the executive should be allowed to run for reelection for an unlimited number of terms was more complicated because it got tangled up with the question of just how the president was to be elected. If, as some founders argued, he were chosen by Congress rather than by the people, then he should be limited to one term. Since he would be dependent on Congress for his power, he might fail to provide an adequate check on that body, perhaps currying favor with Congress in order to be chosen for additional terms. At the same time, the founders had no great trust in "the people," as we have seen, so popular election of the president was considered highly suspect, even though it would free the executive from dependence on Congress and allow him to be elected for multiple terms. Alexander Hamilton wanted to go so far as to have the president serve for life, thereby eliminating the problem of being dependent on Congress or on the popular will.

That these diverse ideas were resolved and consensus was achieved is one of the marvels of the American founding. The final provision of presidential authority was neither as powerful as Hamilton's kinglike lifetime executive nor as constrained as Randolph's multiple executive. Still, it was a much stronger office than many of the founders, particularly the Anti-Federalists, wanted.

Electoral College an intermediary body that elects the president

WHAT DOES THE CONSTITUTION SAY? The solution chosen by the founders was a complex one, but it satisfied all the concerns raised at the convention. The president, a single executive, would serve an unlimited number of four-year terms. (A constitutional amendment in 1951 limited the president to two elected terms.) In addition, the president would be chosen neither by Congress nor directly by the people. Instead the Constitution provides for his selection by an intermediary body called the **Electoral College**. Citizens vote not for the presidential candidates, but for a slate of electors who cast their votes for the candidates about six weeks after the general election. The founders believed that this procedure would ensure a president elected by well-informed delegates who, having no other lawmaking power, could not be bribed or otherwise influenced by candidates. We will say more about how this process works in Chapter 14, on elections.

Article II of the Constitution establishes the executive. The four sections of that article make the following provisions:

- Section 1 sets out the four-year term and the manner of election (that is, the details of the Electoral College). It also provides for the qualifications for office: that the president must be a natural-born citizen of the United States, at least thirty-five years old, and a resident of the United States for at least fourteen years. The vice president serves if the president cannot, and Congress can make laws about the succession if the vice president is incapacitated.

- Section 2 establishes the powers of the chief executive. He is commander-in-chief of the armed forces and of the state militias when they are serving the nation, and he has the power to grant pardons for offenses against the United States. With the advice and consent of two-thirds of the Senate, the president can make treaties, and with a simple majority vote of the Senate the president can appoint ambassadors, ministers, consuls, Supreme Court justices, and other U.S. officials whose appointments are not otherwise provided for.

- Section 3 says that the president will periodically tell Congress how the country is doing (the State of the Union address given every January) and will propose to the members those measures he thinks appropriate and necessary. Under extraordinary circumstances, the president calls Congress into session or, if the two houses of Congress cannot agree on when to end their sessions, may adjourn them. The president also receives ambassadors and public officials, executes the laws, and commissions all officers of the United States.

- Section 4 specifies that the president, vice president, and other civil officers of the United States (such as Supreme Court justices) can be impeached, tried, and convicted for "Treason, Bribery, or other High Crimes and Misdemeanors."

POSSIBLE ALTERNATIVES: A PARLIAMENTARY SYSTEM?

As the debates over the American executive clearly show, many options were open to the founders as they designed the office. They chose what is referred to today as a **presidential system**, in which a leader is chosen independently of the legislature to serve a fixed term that is unaffected by the success or failure of the legislature. The principal alternative to a presidential system among contemporary democracies is called a **parliamentary system**, in which the executive is a member of the legislature, chosen by the legislators themselves, *not* by a national electorate. When the founders briefly considered the consequences of having a president chosen by Congress, they were discussing something like a parliamentary system. The fundamental difference between a parliamentary system and a presidential system is that in the former the legislature and the executive are merged, but in the latter they are separate. In parliamentary systems the executive is accountable to the legislature, but in a presidential system he or she is independent.

Generally speaking, the executive or prime minister in a parliamentary system is the chosen leader of the majority party in the legislature. This would be roughly equivalent to allowing the majority party in the House of Representatives to install its leader, the Speaker of the House, as the national executive. If the parliament does not think the prime minister is doing a good job, it can replace him or her without consulting the country's voters.

This process is very different from the American provision for impeachment of the president for criminal activity. Parliaments can remove executives for reasons of political or ideological disagreement. Although there may be political disagreement over the grounds for impeachment in the American case, as there was in the impeachment of President Bill Clinton, there must be at least an allegation of criminal activity, which need not exist for removal in a parliamentary system. (If the United States had a parliamentary system, then a legislative vote of "no confidence" could have ousted Clinton at the beginning of the process.) Consequently the executive in a parliamentary system is dependent on the legislature and cannot provide any effective check if the legislature abuses its power. In Germany the parliamentary government is constrained by an independent court, but the British system has no check on parliament at all. The French split the executive functions between a prime minister and a president so that there is an executive check on the legislature, even though it is a parliamentary system.

Politics is very different in a parliamentary system than it is in a presidential system. Leadership is clearly more concentrated in the former case. Because the prime minister usually chooses his or her cabinet from the legislature, the executive and legislative branches truly overlap. It is much easier for a prime minister to get his or her programs and laws passed by the legislature because, under normal circumstances, he or she already has the party votes to pass them. If the party has a serious loss of faith or "confidence" in the prime minister, it can force the prime minister out of office. Thus the prime minister has a strong incentive to cooperate with the legislature. In some cases, like the British, the prime minister has some countervailing clout of his or her own. The British prime minister has the power to call parliamentary elections at will within a five-year period and consequently can threaten the jobs of uncooperative members of parliament or, conversely, can time the elections to take place when the party's fortunes are high. One result of this close relationship between executive and legislative is that the ties of political party membership are strong in a parliamentary system.

No "Hail to the Chief" Here

When the president of the United States appears before Congress, it is usually a formal affair. But in the United Kingdom the prime minister is afforded no such luxury. Here, British prime minister Theresa May and supporters laugh over pointed comments she made to an opposition leader during a typical parliamentary session. Prime ministers regularly subject themselves to being peppered by queries from the opposition in a British tradition known as "Question Time."

presidential system government in which the executive is chosen independently of the legislature and the two branches are separate

parliamentary system government in which the executive is chosen by the legislature from among its members and the two branches are merged

WHAT THE CONSTITUTION DOESN'T SAY: NORMS THAT SUPPORT THE EXECUTIVE The founders knew what kind of man they wanted to hold the presidency; George Washington was right in front of them, a model executive. But they left that description unspoken. Implied by the rules are the norm of *independence*—a separate executive and legislature make it difficult to ram through legislation, and the Constitution guards against any allegiance to another country (hence the requirement of natural-born citizenship and the complicated emoluments clause, which forbids the president from taking expensive gifts from another country). They also wanted the president to demonstrate *dignity*. The office combines the jobs of the head of government (the political role) and the head of state (the symbolic role). Truth to tell, they never imagined a government as large and complex as ours is today, so the head-of-government role didn't loom as large. But the head-of-state role, representing the country as a whole, was key. So the founders implied the norm of *unity*, of representing the entire country. Only Lincoln has had to oversee an actual split of the country, and holding the country together was his chief goal in the Civil War. Finally, it is clear from the impeachment powers of Congress and from limits such as the emoluments clause that the founders had created a limited executive who could be removed from office by Congress for "Treason, Bribery, or other high Crimes and Misdemeanors." So another executive norm is that the president is bound by *the rule of law*.

THE JUDICIAL BRANCH

Judicial power is the power to interpret the laws and to judge whether the laws have been broken. Naturally, by establishing how a given law is to be understood, the courts (the agents of judicial power) end up making law as well. Our constitutional provisions for the establishment of the judiciary are brief and vague; much of the American federal judiciary under the Supreme Court is left to Congress to arrange. But the founders left plenty of clues as to how they felt about judicial power in their debates and their writings, particularly in *The Federalist Papers*.

THE "LEAST DANGEROUS" BRANCH In *Federalist* No. 78, Hamilton made clear his view that the judiciary was the least threatening branch of power. The executive and the legislature might endanger liberty, but not so the judiciary.

Hamilton created a reassuring narrative that, as long as government functions are separate from one another (that is, as long as the judiciary is not part of the executive or the legislature), then the judiciary "will always be the least dangerous to the political rights of the Constitution; because it has the least capacity to annoy or injure them." The executive "holds the sword," and the legislature "commands the purse." The judiciary, controlling neither sword nor purse, neither "strength nor wealth of the society," has neither "FORCE nor WILL but merely judgment."[13]

Although the founders were not particularly worried, then, that the judiciary would be too *powerful*, they did want to be sure it would not be too *political*—that is, caught up in the fray of competing interests and influence. The only federal court they discussed in much detail was the Supreme Court, but the justices of that Court were to be appointed for life, provided they maintain "good behavior," in part to preserve them from politics. Instead of trying to do what is popular, they could concentrate on doing what is just, or constitutional.

Even though the founders wanted to keep the Court out of politics, they did make it possible for the justices to get involved when they considered it necessary. The most powerful tool of the Court is not even mentioned in the Constitution. Judicial review allows the Supreme Court to rule that an act of Congress or the executive branch (or of a state or local government) is unconstitutional, that it runs afoul of constitutional principles. This practice is introduced through the back door, first by Hamilton in *Federalist* No. 78 and then institutionalized by the Supreme Court itself, with Chief Justice John Marshall's 1803 ruling in *Marbury v. Madison*. In that case, Marshall ruled that the Supreme Court is the ultimate interpreter of when laws are unconstitutional. It is fascinating that this gigantic grant of power to the Court was made by the Court itself and remains unchallenged by the other branches. The irony is that the sort of empire-building the founders hoped to avoid appears in the branch they took the least care to safeguard. We return to *Marbury v. Madison* and judicial review in Chapter 10, on the court system. Note, however, that this review process is not an automatic part of lawmaking; the Court does not examine every law that Congress passes or every executive order to be sure that it does not violate the Constitution. Rather, if a law is challenged as unconstitutional by an individual or a group, and if it is appealed all the way to the Supreme Court, then the justices may decide to rule on it.

---

judicial power the power to interpret laws and judge whether a law has been broken

judicial review the power of the Supreme Court to rule on the constitutionality of laws

---

Which really is the least dangerous branch of the federal government?

WHAT DOES THE CONSTITUTION SAY? Article III of the Constitution is very short. It says that the judicial power of the United States is to be "vested in one Supreme Court, and in such inferior courts as the Congress may from time to time ordain and establish," and that judges serve as long as they demonstrate "good behavior." It also explains that the Supreme Court has original jurisdiction in some types of cases and appellate jurisdiction in others. That is, in some cases the Supreme Court is the only court that can rule; much more often, inferior courts try cases, but their rulings can be appealed to the Supreme Court. Article III provides for jury trials in all criminal cases except impeachment, and it defines the practice of and punishment for acts of treason. Because the Constitution is so silent on the role of the courts in America, that role has been left to be defined by Congress and, in some cases, by the courts themselves.

POSSIBLE ALTERNATIVES: LEGISLATIVE SUPREMACY? Clearly one alternative to judicial review is to allow the legislature's laws to stand unchallenged. This system of **legislative supremacy** underlies British politics. The British have no written constitution. Acts of Parliament are the final law of the land and cannot be reviewed or struck down by the courts. They become part of the general collection of acts, laws, traditions, and court cases that make up the British "unwritten constitution." Our Court is thus more powerful, and our legislature correspondingly less powerful, than the same institutions in the British system. We are accustomed to believing that judicial review is an important limitation on Congress and a protection of individual liberty. Britain is not remarkably behind the United States, however, in terms of either legislative tyranny or human rights. Think about how much difference judicial review really makes, especially if you consider the experience of a country like Japan, where judicial review usually results in upholding government behavior over individual rights and liberties.[14]

Yet another alternative to our system would be to give judicial review more teeth. The German Constitutional Court also reviews legislation to determine if it fits with the German Basic Law, but it does not need to wait for cases to come to it on appeal. National and state executives, the lower house of the legislature (the Bundestag), or even citizens can ask the German high court to determine whether a law is constitutional.

WHAT THE CONSTITUTION DOESN'T SAY: NORMS THAT SUPPORT THE JUDICIARY It's a little more difficult to make inferences about the judiciary because the founders didn't spell out the details in the Constitution. They wanted a judiciary to have *independence* from political and public influence, hence the grant of lifetime tenure. And it's pretty clear that the Federalists, at least, wanted it to be *powerful.*

Hamilton's argument in *Federalist* No. 78 laid the groundwork for John Marshall's decision in *Marbury v. Madison* granting the Court the power of judicial review. They also wanted the federal judiciary to be supreme, something they spelled out gently because it was still a sore spot with Anti-Federalists, but that was reinforced with subsequent rulings. But they also wanted the Court to be perceived as above politics, and one way to achieve that illusion was for the court to remain *nonpartisan* in its rulings. Rulings would undoubtedly have political impact but not show blatant support for the agenda of one party over another. As we will see in Chapter 10, popular rejection of Franklin Roosevelt's court-packing scheme showed that the public has internalized this norm, even when they favor the cause the Court would be championing.

> ### PAUSE AND REVIEW   Who, What, How
>
> The founders' goal was to devise a legislature, an executive, and a judiciary that would correct the flaws of the Articles of Confederation while balancing the rights and powers of citizens against the need for the government to be secure from abuse and corruption. The means they employed were unusual—they had the unique opportunity to write the rule book, the Constitution, from scratch, constrained only by the necessity of gaining the approval of sufficient states to allow the Constitution to be ratified and thus seen as legitimate.

In Your Own Words   Describe the role of each branch of government.

SEPARATION OF POWERS AND CHECKS AND BALANCES

Mechanical arrangements to limit abuses of power

Separation of powers means that the legislature, the executive, and the judicial powers are not exercised by the same person or group of people, lest they abuse the considerable amount of power they hold. We are indebted to the French Enlightenment philosopher the Baron de Montesquieu for explaining this notion.[15] Essentially, he argued, putting all political power into one set of hands is like putting all our eggs in one basket. If the person or body of people entrusted with all the power becomes corrupt or dictatorial, the whole

---

legislative supremacy an alternative to judicial review; the acceptance of legislative acts as the final law of the land

separation of powers the institutional arrangement that assigns legislative, executive, and judicial powers to different persons or groups, thereby limiting the powers of each

FIGURE 4.1
Separation of Powers and Checks and Balances

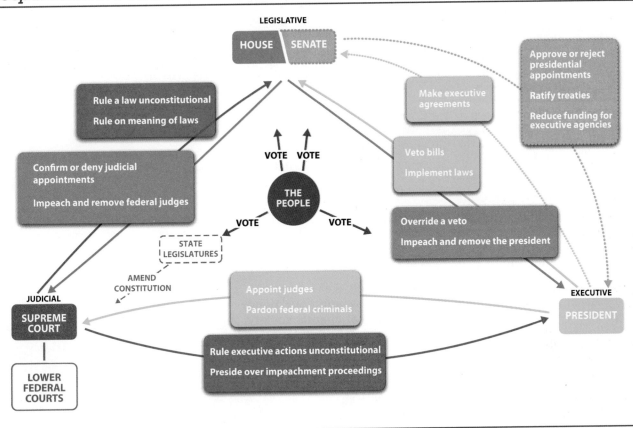

system will go bad. If, however, power is divided so that each branch is in separate hands, one may go bad while leaving the other two intact. The principle of separation of powers gives each of the branches authority over its own domain.

A complementary principle, **checks and balances**, allows each of the branches to police the others, checking any abuses and balancing the powers of government. The purpose of this additional authority is to ensure that no branch can exercise power tyrannically. In our case, the president can veto an act of Congress, Congress can override a veto, the Supreme Court can declare a law of Congress unconstitutional, Congress can—with the help of the states—amend the Constitution itself, and so on. Figure 4.1 illustrates these relationships.

REPUBLICAN REMEDIES

As we see in the first *The Big Picture* in this chapter and in the *CLUES to Critical Thinking* feature at the end of the chapter, James Madison wrote in *Federalist* No. 51 that "If men were

> **checks and balances** the principle that allows each branch of government to exercise some form of control over the others

angels, no government would be necessary. If angels were to govern men, neither external nor internal controls on government would be necessary."[16] Alas, we are not angels, nor are we governed by angels. Since human nature is flawed and humans are sometimes ambitious, greedy, and corruptible, precautions must be taken to create a government that will make use of human nature, not be destroyed by it. Continuing with the narrative he crafted so successfully in *Federalist* No. 10, Madison argued that a republic, which offers so many people the opportunity to take advantage of political power, requires special controls. The job, according to Madison, was to find a "republican remedy for those diseases most incident to republican government."[17] He said, "In framing a government which is to be administered by men over men, the great difficulty is this: you must first enable the government to control the governed; and in the next place oblige it to control itself."[18] The founders used separation of powers and checks and balances to oblige government to control itself, to impose internal limitations on government power in order to safeguard the liberty of the people.

The founders were generally supportive of separation of powers, some form of which appeared in all the state governments. The notion of checks and balances—that once

power was separated, it should be shared somehow—was not accepted so readily. Having carefully kept the executive from taking on a legislative role, the founders were reluctant to return any of it to him, although they eventually agreed. As Madison put it in *Federalist* No. 51: "Ambition must be made to counteract ambition."[19] Thus there was no danger in sharing some control over the branches because jealous humans would always be looking over their shoulders for potential abuses. Madison's elegant argument is still the basis of the narrative we use to justify checks and balances today.

WHAT DOES THE CONSTITUTION SAY?

The Constitution establishes separation of powers with articles setting up a different institution for each branch of government. We have already examined Article I, establishing Congress as the legislature; Article II, establishing the president as the executive; and Article III, outlining the court system. Checks and balances are provided by clauses within each of those articles:

- Article I sets up a bicameral legislature. Because both houses must agree on all legislation, each can check the other. Article I also describes the presidential veto, with which the president can check Congress, and the override provision, by which two-thirds of Congress can check the president. Congress can also use impeachment to check abuses of the executive or judicial branch.
- Article II empowers the president to execute the laws and to share some legislative function by "recommending laws." He has some checks on the judiciary through his power to appoint judges, but his appointment power is checked by the requirement that a majority of the Senate must confirm his choices. The president can also check the judiciary by granting pardons. The president is commander-in-chief of the armed forces, but his ability to exercise his authority is checked by the Article I provision that only Congress can declare war.
- Article III creates the Supreme Court. The Court's ruling in the case of *Marbury v. Madison* fills in some of the gaps in this vague article by establishing judicial review, a true check on the legislative and executive branches. Congress can countercheck judicial review by amending the Constitution (with the help of the states).

The Constitution wisely ensures that no branch of the government can act independently of the others, yet none is wholly dependent on the others, either. This approach results in a structure of separation of powers and checks and balances that is distinctly American.

POSSIBLE ALTERNATIVES: FUSION OF POWERS?

An alternative way to deal with the different branches of government is to fuse rather than separate them. We have already discussed what this might look like when we compared a parliamentary system with a presidential system. A parliamentary system involves a clear **fusion of powers**. Because the components of government are not separate, no formal internal checks can curb the use of power. That is not to say that the flaws in human nature might not still encourage members of the government to keep a jealous eye on one another, but no deliberate mechanism exists to bring these checks into being. In a democracy, external checks may still be provided by the people, through either the ballot box or public opinion polls. Where the government is not freely and popularly elected, or, more rarely these days, when all the components are fused into a single monarch, even the checks of popular control are missing.

WHAT THE CONSTITUTION DOESN'T SAY: NORMS THAT SUPPORT CHECKS AND BALANCES

What the Constitution doesn't say about checks and balances is that the branches have to make it work for it to work. The two houses of Congress have to *compromise* and to hold the president to account through *oversight* and by withholding consent to unqualified appointments. The president has to veto bills he disagrees with on policy grounds or that the country cannot afford in some way. The Courts have to truly be *independent*—not loyal to the person who appointed them but loyal to the country and the Constitution. The founders expected checks and balances to hold even if a single party held Congress and the White House; they would have chosen a parliamentary system if they wanted the Congress to rubberstamp executive action or the Courts to take partisan sides.

| PAUSE AND REVIEW | Who, What, How |

The founders wanted, for themselves and the public, a government that would not succumb to the worst of human nature. The viability and stability of the American system would be jeopardized if they could not find a way to tame the jealousy, greed, and ambition that

---

fusion of powers an alternative to separation of powers, combining or blending branches of government

might threaten the new republic. The remedy they chose to save the American Constitution from its own leaders and citizens is the set of rules called separation of powers and checks and balances. Whether the founders were right or wrong about human nature, the principles of government they established have been remarkably effective at guaranteeing the long-term survival of the American system.

In Your Own Words Explain why the founders chose to structure each of the three branches of government as they did.

FEDERALISM

Balancing power between national and state governments

Federalism, as we said in Chapter 3, is a political system in which authority is divided between different levels of government. In the United States, federalism refers to the relationship between the national government (also frequently, but confusingly, called the federal government) and the states. Each level has some power independent of the other levels so that no level is entirely dependent on another for its existence. For the founders, federalism was a significant compromise in the bitter dispute between those who wanted stronger state governments and those who preferred a stronger national government. Both sides knew that the rules dividing power between the states and the federal government were crucial to determining who would be the winners and the losers in the new country. Even though, ultimately, the Constitution makes clear that the national government trumps the states, the narrative of shared power allowed both sides to come together around this novel concept.

Today the effects of federalism are all around us. We pay income taxes to the national government, which parcels out the money to the states, under certain conditions, to be spent on programs such as welfare, health care, highways, and education. In most states, local schools are funded by local property taxes and run by local school boards (local governments are created under the authority of the state), and state universities are supported by state taxes and influenced by the state legislatures. Even so, both state and local governments are subject to national legislation, such as the requirement that schools be open to students of all races, and both can be affected by national decisions about funding various programs. Sometimes the lines of responsibility can be extremely unclear. Witness the simultaneous presence, in many areas, of city police, county police, state police, and, at the national level, the Federal Bureau of Investigation (FBI), all coordinated, for some purposes, by the national Department of Homeland Security.

Even when a given responsibility lies at the state level, the national government frequently finds a way to enforce its will. For instance, it is up to the states to decide on the minimum drinking age for their citizens. In the 1970s, many states required people to be only eighteen or nineteen before they could legally buy alcohol; today all the states have a uniform drinking age of twenty-one. The change came about because interest groups persuaded officials in the federal (that is, national) government that the higher age would lead to fewer alcohol-related highway accidents and greater public safety. The federal government couldn't pass a law setting a nationwide drinking age of twenty-one, but it could control the flow of highway money to the states. By withholding 5 percent of federal highway funds, which every state wants and needs, until a state raised the drinking age to twenty-one, Congress prevailed.

WHAT DOES THE CONSTITUTION SAY?

No single section of the Constitution deals with federalism. Instead the provisions dividing up power between the states and the national government appear throughout the Constitution. Local government is not mentioned in the Constitution at all, because it is completely under the jurisdiction of the states. Most of the Constitution is concerned with establishing the powers of the national government. Since Congress is the main lawmaking arm of the national government, many of the powers of the national government are the powers of Congress. The strongest statement of national power is a list of the **enumerated powers of Congress** (Article I, Section 8). This list is followed by a clause that gives Congress the power to make all laws that are "necessary and proper" to carry out its powers. The **necessary and proper clause** (also called the "elastic clause" because the Supreme Court has interpreted it broadly) has been used to justify giving Congress many powers never mentioned in the Constitution. National power is also based on the **supremacy clause** of Article VI, which says that the Constitution and laws made in accordance with it are "the supreme law of the land." This means that when national and state laws conflict, the national laws will be followed. The Constitution also sets some limitations on the national government. Article I, Section 9, lists specific powers not granted to Congress, and the Bill of Rights (the first ten amendments to the Constitution) limits the power of the national government over individuals.

enumerated powers of Congress congressional powers specifically named in the Constitution (Article I, Section 8)

necessary and proper clause constitutional authorization for Congress to make any law required to carry out its powers

supremacy clause constitutional declaration (Article VI) that the Constitution and laws made under its provisions are the supreme law of the land

The Constitution says considerably less about the powers granted to the states. The Tenth Amendment says that all powers not given to the national government are reserved for the states, although, as we will soon see, the Court's interpretation of the necessary and proper clause as elastic makes it difficult to see which powers are withheld from the national government. The states are given the power to approve the Constitution itself and any amendments to it. The Constitution also limits state powers. Article I, Section 10, denies the states certain powers, mostly the kinds they possessed under the Articles of Confederation. The Fourteenth Amendment limits the power of the states over individual liberties, essentially a Bill of Rights that protects individuals from state action, since the first ten amendments apply only to the national government.

What these constitutional provisions mean is that the line between the national government and the state governments is not clearly drawn. We can see from Figure 4.2 that the Constitution designates specific powers as national, state, or concurrent. **Concurrent powers** are those that both levels of government may exercise. But the federal relationship is a good deal more complex than this figure would lead us to believe. The Supreme Court has become crucial to establishing the exact limits of such provisions as the necessary and proper clause, the supremacy clause, the Tenth Amendment, and the Fourteenth Amendment. The Court's interpretation has changed over time, especially as historical demands have forced it to think about federalism in new ways.

TWO VIEWS OF FEDERALISM

Political scientists have also changed the way they think about federalism. For many years the prevailing academic narrative, known as **dual federalism**, basically argued that the relationship between the two levels of government was like a layer cake. That is, the national and state governments were to be understood as two self-contained layers, each essentially separate from the other and carrying out its functions independently. In its own area of power, each level was supreme. Dual federalism reflects the formal distribution of powers in the Constitution, and perhaps it was an accurate portrayal of the judicial interpretation of the federal system for our first hundred years or so.

But the theory of dual federalism was criticized for not describing realistically the way the federal relationship was evolving in the twentieth century. It certainly did not take into account the changes brought about by the New Deal. The layer cake image was replaced by a new bakery metaphor. According to the new narrative of **cooperative federalism**, rather than being two distinct layers, the national and state levels were swirled together like the chocolate and vanilla batter in a marble cake.[20] National and state powers were interdependent, and each level required the cooperation of the other to get things done. In fact, federalism came to be seen by political scientists as a partnership in which the dominant partner was, more often than not, the national government.

POSSIBLE ALTERNATIVES TO FEDERALISM

The federal system was not the only alternative available to our founders for organizing the relationship between the central government and the states. In fact, as we know, it wasn't even their first choice as a framework for government. The Articles of Confederation, which preceded the Constitution, handled the relationship quite differently. We can look at federalism as a compromise system that borrows some attributes from a unitary system and some from a confederal system, as shown in Figure 4.3. Had the founders chosen either of these alternatives, American government would look very different today.

UNITARY SYSTEMS In a **unitary system** the central government ultimately has all the power. Local units (states or counties) may have some power at some times, but basically they are dependent on the central unit, which can alter or even abolish them. Many contemporary countries, like Great Britain, have unitary systems, which means that national and local politics in Britain unfold very differently from federal politics in the United States. Most important decisions are made in London, from foreign policy to housing policy—even the details of what ought to be included in the school curriculum. Even local taxes are determined centrally. In 1972, when the legislature in Northern Ireland (a part of Great Britain) could not resolve its religious conflicts, the central government suspended the local lawmaking body and ruled Northern Ireland from London. These actions are tantamount to a Republican president's dissolving a Democratic state that disagreed with his policies, or the national government's deciding during the days of segregation to suspend the state legislature in Alabama and run the state from Washington. Such an arrangement has been impossible in the United States except during the chaotic state of emergency following the Civil War. What is commonplace under a unitary system is unimaginable under our federal rules.

concurrent powers powers that are shared by the federal and state governments

dual federalism the federal system under which the national and state governments are responsible for separate policy areas

cooperative federalism the federal system under which the national and state governments share responsibilities for most domestic policy areas

unitary system government in which all power is centralized

FIGURE 4.2

The Constitutional Division of Powers Between the National Government and the States

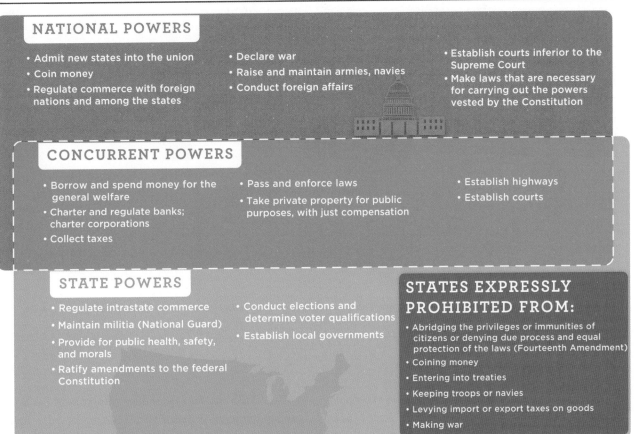

NATIONAL POWERS

- Admit new states into the union
- Coin money
- Regulate commerce with foreign nations and among the states
- Declare war
- Raise and maintain armies, navies
- Conduct foreign affairs
- Establish courts inferior to the Supreme Court
- Make laws that are necessary for carrying out the powers vested by the Constitution

CONCURRENT POWERS

- Borrow and spend money for the general welfare
- Charter and regulate banks; charter corporations
- Collect taxes
- Pass and enforce laws
- Take private property for public purposes, with just compensation
- Establish highways
- Establish courts

STATE POWERS

- Regulate intrastate commerce
- Maintain militia (National Guard)
- Provide for public health, safety, and morals
- Ratify amendments to the federal Constitution
- Conduct elections and determine voter qualifications
- Establish local governments

STATES EXPRESSLY PROHIBITED FROM:

- Abridging the privileges or immunities of citizens or denying due process and equal protection of the laws (Fourteenth Amendment)
- Coining money
- Entering into treaties
- Keeping troops or navies
- Levying import or export taxes on goods
- Making war

CONFEDERAL SYSTEMS Confederal systems provide an equally sharp contrast to federal systems, even though the names sound quite similar. In a **confederal system** the local units hold all the power, and the central government is dependent on them for its existence. The local units remain sovereign, and the central government has only as much power as those units allow it to have. Examples of confederal systems include America under the Articles of Confederation and associations such as the United Nations and the European Union, twenty-eight European nations that have joined economic and political forces. The European Union has been experiencing problems much like ours after the Revolutionary War, debating whether it ought to move in a federal direction. Some of the nations involved, jealous of their sovereignty, have been reluctant, and in 2016, amid immigration worries,

British voters chose to leave the union in a referendum referred to by the press as "Brexit."

WHAT DIFFERENCE DOES FEDERALISM MAKE?

That our founders settled on federalism, rather than a unitary or a confederal system, makes a great deal of difference to American politics. Federalism gave the founders a government that could take effective action, restore economic stability, and regulate disputes among the states, while still allowing the states considerable autonomy and possession of a narrative that they have, in many cases, more power than they actually do. Several specific consequences of that autonomy, both good and bad, deserve discussion.

ALLOWING FLEXIBILITY AT THE LOCAL LEVEL

Federalism gives government considerable flexibility to preserve local standards and to respond to local needs—that is, to solve problems at the levels at which they occur. Examples include local traffic laws, community school policies, and city

> **confederal system** government in which local units hold all the power

FIGURE 4.3

The Division and Flow of Power in Three Systems of Government

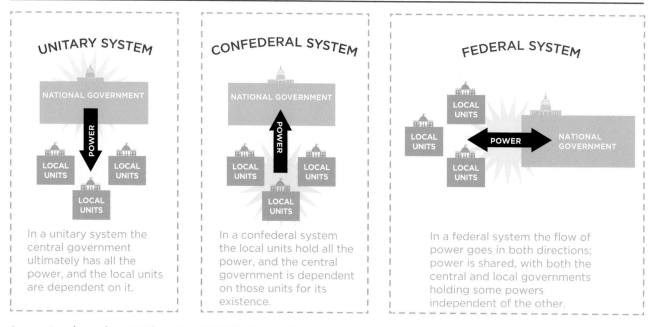

UNITARY SYSTEM

In a unitary system the central government ultimately has all the power, and the local units are dependent on it.

CONFEDERAL SYSTEM

In a confederal system the local units hold all the power, and the central government is dependent on those units for its existence.

FEDERAL SYSTEM

In a federal system the flow of power goes in both directions; power is shared, with both the central and local governments holding some powers independent of the other.

Source: Based on Robert S. Erikson, Gerald C. Wright, and John McIver, *Statehouse Democracy* (New York: Cambridge University Press, 1993).

and county housing codes. Federalism also allows experimentation with public policy. If all laws and policies need not be uniform across the country, then different states may try different solutions to common problems and share the results of their experiments, making states "laboratories of democracy," in the words of one Supreme Court Justice.[21] For instance, the popularity and success of the health care policy passed in Massachusetts under Governor Mitt Romney in 2006 became the model for President Obama's Affordable Care Act four years later.

The flexibility that federalism provides can also be helpful when Congress cannot or will not act. As recent polarization in the nation's capital has essentially paralyzed legislative action for most purposes, enterprising states can take advantage of the resulting power vacuum. For example, in the face of congressional gridlock over the development of fossil fuel resources, the states have leapt into the breach with their own energy policies, many times reflecting the political proclivities of the dominant party in the states. Republican-controlled Pennsylvania has encouraged fracking (the process of pumping water and chemicals into subterranean rock formations to free bound-up natural gas and oil), whereas neighboring New York and, to a lesser extent, Ohio—which share the giant Marcellus Shale deposit—have taken a much more environmentally cautious approach to the development of shale deposits.[22]

The flexibility that federalism offers states has disadvantages as well. Where policies are made and enforced locally, all economies of scale are lost. Many functions are repeated across the country as states locally administer national programs. Making and enforcing laws can be troublesome as well under federalism. Different penalties for the same crime can make it difficult to gauge the consequences of one's behavior across states, as we saw in the *What's at Stake . . . ?* in this chapter. Most problematic is the fact that federalism permits, even encourages, local prejudices to find their way into law. LGBTQ Americans, for example, do not have the same rights in all localities of the United States today.

PROVIDING INCREASED ACCESS TO GOVERNMENT
Federalism also makes a difference in the lives of citizens. It provides real power at levels of government that are close to the citizens. Citizens can thus have access to officials and processes of government that they could not have if there were just one distant, national unit. Federalism also enhances the power of interest groups in that it provides a variety of government levels at which different groups can try to gain political advantage. Often a group that is not successful at one level can try again at another and "shop" for institutions or agencies that are more receptive to its requests. The states vary considerably in their political

Snapshot of America: *How Do We Differ From State to State?*

Ideologies in the States

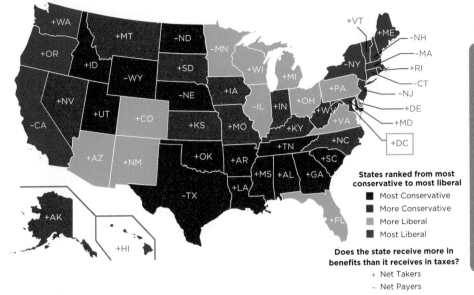

Behind the Numbers

This map shows how states vary in political ideology. Notice how states that are most conservative typically receive the most benefits. Is the ideological classification for your state consistent with your experience? What kinds of federal expenditures might account for whether a state is a net winner or a net loser?

States ranked from most conservative to most liberal

- ■ Most Conservative
- ■ More Conservative
- ■ More Liberal
- ■ Most Liberal

Does the state receive more in benefits than it receives in taxes?

- \+ Net Takers
- – Net Payers

Source: Based on Robert S. Erikson, Gerald C. Wright, and John McIver, *Statehouse Democracy* (New York: Cambridge University Press, 1993), and updated through 2016 by authors; "States' Federal Spending and Taxes," *Huffington Post*, December 11, 2017, www .huffingtonpost.com/entry/states-federal-spending-and-taxes_us_5a2e78d3e4b04e0bc8f3b699.

---

ideologies and thus in the policies they are likely to adopt (see *Snapshot of America: How Do We Differ From State to State?*). For example, African Americans were unable to achieve significant political influence in the South as long as the southern states, with their segregationist traditions, were allowed to control access to the voting booths. When the national government stepped in to stop segregation with the Civil Rights Act of 1964, the balance of power began to become less lopsided. Conversely, when women were unable to get the vote at the national level, they turned their attention to the states and won their suffrage there first. More recently, in the face of laxer federal rules on auto emissions, California has adopted tougher standards and, in the wake of the 2018 midterm election results, looks to be followed soon by Illinois and New Mexico.[23]

CREATING COMPETITION AMONG THE STATES

The federal relationship also has an impact on state politics by placing the states in competition with one another for scarce resources. "Smokestack chasing" happens as states bid against one another to get both domestic and foreign industries to locate within their borders by providing them with tax breaks, loan financing, and educational training for workers, and by assuming the costs of roads, sewers, and other infrastructure that new industries would otherwise

have to pay for themselves. Even though much modern industry is no longer manufacturing and thus has no actual smokestacks, we can see this phenomenon as cities raced in 2017 and 2018 to outdo each other in bidding to house Amazon's second headquarters.[24] The consequence is that states, in a race to lure businesses, may give away more than they will eventually gain.

Federalism is not a perfect system, but overall it has proved to be a flexible and effective compromise for American government. The United States is not the only federal nation, although other countries may distribute power among their various units differently than we do. Germany, Canada, Mexico, Australia, and Switzerland are all examples of federal systems.

THE CHANGING BALANCE: AMERICAN FEDERALISM OVER TIME

Although the Constitution provides for both national and state powers (as well as some shared powers), the balance between the two and the narratives that justify it have changed considerably since it was written. Because of the founders' disagreement over how power should be distributed in the new country, the final wording about national and state powers was kept vague intentionally, which probably helped the Constitution get ratified.

Because it wasn't clear how much power the different levels held, it has been possible ever since for both ardent Federalists and states' rights advocates to find support for their positions in the document. That very vagueness has opened the door for the Supreme Court to decide to interpret the Constitution's meaning. Those interpretations have varied along with the people sitting on the Court and with historical circumstances. Consequently, the norms underlying federalism provide less of a fixed standard against which we can measure actual behavior; the norm is that while the federal government is supreme, the relationship is characterized by *flexibility*.

The circumstances themselves have helped to alter the balance of state and national powers over time. The context of American life has been transformed periodically through major events such as the end of slavery and the Civil War, the process of industrialization and the growth of big business, the economic collapse of the Great Depression in the 1930s, world wars (both hot and cold) followed by the fall of communism in the 1980s, the devastating terrorist attacks of September 11, 2001, and the huge economic recession that began in 2008 with the mortgage crisis and that resulted in a massive federal government economic stimulus program to stem the economy's downward spiral. With these events come shifts in the demands made on the different levels of government. When we talk about federalism in the United States, we are talking about specific constitutional rules and provisions, but we are also talking about a continuously changing context in which those rules are understood.

Two trends are apparent when we examine American federalism throughout our history. One is that American government in general is growing in size, at both the state and national levels. We make many more demands than did, say, the citizens of George Washington's time, or Abraham Lincoln's, and the apparatus to satisfy those demands has grown accordingly. But within that overall growth, a second trend has been the gradual, but uneven, strengthening of the national government at the expense of the states.

The increase in the size of government shouldn't surprise us. One indisputable truth about the United States is that, over the years, it has gotten bigger, more industrialized, more urban, and more technical. As the country has grown, so have our expectations of what the government will do for us. We want to be protected from the fluctuations of the market, from natural disasters, from terrorists, from unfair business practices, and from unsafe foods and drugs. We want government to protect our "rights," but our concept of those rights has expanded beyond the first ten amendments to the Constitution to include things like economic security in old age, a minimum standard of living for all citizens, a safe interstate highway system, and crime-free neighborhoods. These new demands and expectations create larger government at all levels but particularly at the national level, where the resources and will to accomplish such broad policy goals are more likely to exist.

Traditionally, liberals have preferred to rely on a strong central government to solve many social problems that the states have not solved, such as discrimination and poverty. Conservatives have tended to believe that "big government" causes more problems than it solves. Like the Anti-Federalists at the founding, they have preferred to see power and government services located at the state or local level, closer to the people being governed. From 2000 to 2006, and again after 2016, however, with Republicans holding the reins of power in both the legislative and executive branches, the conservative distaste for big government waned somewhat as they were the ones dictating the actions of that government. President Bush's No Child Left Behind Act, for instance, took away many of the prerogatives of local school districts to decide whether to engage in regular testing of students, and yet it enjoyed the support of many conservatives. Some Republicans themselves noted that, once they come to Washington, conservatives can be "as bad as liberals" about enforcing the national will on states.[25] Once President Barack Obama was elected and the Democrats passed the economic stimulus bill and health care reform, however, Republicans quickly returned to their traditional views and decried the return of "big government." Both Democrats and Republicans are more willing to entertain the possibility of national government action when they are the ones controlling the national government.

The growth of the national government's power over the states can be traced by looking at four moments in our national history: the early judicial decisions of Chief Justice John Marshall (1801–1835), the Civil War, the New Deal, and the civil rights movement and the expanded use of the Fourteenth Amendment from the 1950s through the 1970s. Since the late 1970s we have seen increasing opposition to the growth of what is called "big government" on the part of citizens and officials alike, but most of the efforts to cut it back in size and to restore power to the states have been mixed.

JOHN MARSHALL: STRENGTHENING THE CONSTITUTIONAL POWERS OF THE NATIONAL GOVERNMENT

John Marshall, the third chief justice of the United States, was a man committed to the Federalist narrative about strong national power. His rulings did much to strengthen the power of the national government both during his lifetime and after. The 1819 case of *McCulloch v. Maryland* set the tone. In resolving this dispute about whether Congress had the power to charter a bank and whether the

McCulloch v. Maryland Supreme Court ruling (1819) confirming the supremacy of national over state government

state of Maryland had the power to tax that bank, Marshall had plenty of scope for exercising his preference for a strong national government. Congress did have the power, he ruled, even though the Constitution didn't spell it out, because Congress was empowered to do whatever was necessary and proper to fulfill its constitutional obligations.

Marshall did not interpret the word *necessary* to mean "absolutely essential," but rather he took a looser view, holding that Congress could do whatever was "appropriate" to execute its powers. If that meant chartering a bank, then the necessary and proper clause could be stretched to include chartering a bank. Furthermore, Maryland could not tax the federal bank because "the power to tax involves the power to destroy."[26] If Maryland could tax the federal bank, that would imply the state had the power to destroy the bank, making Maryland supreme over the national government and violating the Constitution's supremacy clause, which makes the national government supreme.

Marshall continued this theme in *Gibbons v. Ogden* in 1824.[27] In deciding that New York did not have the right to create a steamboat monopoly on the Hudson River, Marshall focused on the part of Article I, Section 8, that allows Congress to regulate commerce "among the several states." He interpreted commerce very broadly to include almost any kind of business, creating a justification for a national government that could freely regulate business and that was dominant over the states.

Gibbons v. Ogden did not immediately establish national authority over business. Business interests were far too strong to meekly accept government authority, and subsequent Court decisions recognized that strength and a prevailing public philosophy of laissez-faire. The national government's power in general was limited by cases such as *Cooley v. Board of Wardens of Port of Philadelphia* (1851),[28] which gave the states greater power to regulate commerce if local interests outweigh national interests, and *Dred Scott v. Sanford* (1857),[29] which held that Congress did not have the power to outlaw slavery in the territories.

THE CIVIL WAR: NATIONAL DOMINATION OF THE STATES

The Civil War represented a giant step in the direction of a stronger national government. The war itself was fought for a variety of reasons. Besides the issue of slavery and the conflicting economic and cultural interests of the North and the South, the war was fought to resolve the question of national versus state supremacy. When the national government, dominated by the northern states, passed legislation that would have furthered northern interests, the southern states tried to maintain their own preferred narrative of states' rights by invoking the doctrine of nullification. **Nullification** was the idea that states could render national laws null if they disagreed with them, but the national government never recognized this doctrine. The southern states also seceded, or withdrew from the United States, as a way of rejecting national authority, but the Union's victory in the ensuing war showed decisively that states did not retain their sovereignty under the Constitution.

THE NEW DEAL: NATIONAL POWER OVER BUSINESS

The Civil War did not settle the question of the proper balance of power between national government and business interests. In the years following the war, the courts struck down both state and national laws regulating business. For example, *Pollock v. Farmer's Loan and Trust Company* (1895) held that the federal income tax was unconstitutional[30] (until it was legalized by the Sixteenth Amendment in 1913). *Lochner v. New York* (1905) said that states could not regulate working hours for bakers.[31] This ruling was used as the basis for rejecting state and national regulation of business until the middle of the New Deal in the 1930s. *Hammer v. Dagenhart* (1918) said that national laws prohibiting child labor were outside Congress' power to regulate commerce and therefore were unconstitutional.[32]

Throughout the early years of Franklin Roosevelt's New Deal, designed amid the devastation of the Great Depression of the 1930s to recapture economic stability through economic regulations, the Supreme Court maintained its anti-regulation stance. But the president berated the Court for striking down his programs, and public opinion backed the New Deal and Roosevelt himself against the interests of big business. Eventually the Court had a change of heart. Once established as constitutional, New Deal policies redefined the purpose of American government and thus the scope of national and state powers. The relationship between the nation and the states became more cooperative as the government became employer, provider, and insurer of millions of Americans in times of hardship. Our Social Security system was born during the New Deal, as were many other national programs designed to get America back to work and back on its feet. A sharper contrast to the laissez-faire policies of the turn of the century can hardly be imagined.

Gibbons v. Ogden Supreme Court ruling (1824) establishing national authority over interstate business

nullification declaration by a state that a federal law is void within its borders

> **What would the U.S. government be like today if states had the power of nullification?**

Federalism **109**

Redefining American Government

This highly partisan contemporary cartoon shows President Franklin Roosevelt cheerfully steering the American ship of state toward economic recovery, despite detractors in big business. New Deal policies redefined the scope of both national and state powers.

FEDERALISM TODAY

Clearly federalism is a continually renegotiated compromise between advocates of strong national government on the one hand and advocates of state power on the other. Making the job of compromise more complex, however, is that, as we have suggested, federalism is not a purely ideological issue but also reflects pragmatic politics. If a party dominates the federal government for a long time, its members become accustomed to looking to that government to accomplish their aims. Those whose party persists in the minority on the federal level tend to look to the states.[33] In short, most of the time people will fight to have decisions made in the arena (national or state) where they are most likely to prevail, or where the opposition will have the greatest difficulty achieving their policy goals.

Although the Supreme Court, since the days of *Marbury v. Madison*, had endorsed an extension of the range of the national government, the conservative Supreme Court under Chief Justice William Rehnquist passed down a set of decisions beginning in 1991 that signaled a rejection of congressional encroachment on the prerogatives of the states—a power shift that was dubbed **devolution**. However, that movement came to an abrupt stop in 2002 following the terrorist attacks of September 11, 2001. The Court continued to have a conservative majority under Chief Justice John Roberts, and that is unlikely to change as long as Donald Trump is president.[34]

Whether or not the Supreme Court's decisions give the federal government greater latitude in exercising its powers, the states are still responsible for the policies that most affect our lives. For instance, the states retain primary responsibility for everything from education to regulation of funeral parlors, from licensing physicians to building roads and telling us how fast we can drive on them. Most questions of contemporary federalism involve the national government trying to influence how the states and localities go about providing the goods and services and regulating the behaviors that have traditionally been within their jurisdictions.

Why should the national government care so much about what the states do? There are several reasons. First, from a Congress member's perspective, it is easier to solve many social and economic problems at the national level, especially

CIVIL RIGHTS: NATIONAL PROTECTION AGAINST STATE ABUSE The national government picked up a host of new roles as American society became more complex, including that of guarantor of individual rights against state abuse. The Fourteenth Amendment to the Constitution was passed after the Civil War to make sure southern states extended all the protections of the Constitution to the newly freed slaves. In the 1950s and 1960s the Supreme Court used the amendment to strike down a variety of state laws that maintained segregated, or separate, facilities for whites and African Americans, from railway cars to classrooms. By the 1970s the Court's interpretation of the Fourteenth Amendment had expanded, allowing it to declare unconstitutional many state laws that it said deprived state citizens of their rights as U.S. citizens. For instance, the Court ruled that states had to guarantee those accused of state crimes the same protections that the Bill of Rights guaranteed those accused of federal crimes. As we will see in more detail in Chapter 5, the Fourteenth Amendment has come to be a means for severely limiting the states' powers over their own citizens.

The trend toward increased national power has not killed the narrative that states should have more power. In the 1970s and 1980s, Presidents Richard Nixon and Ronald Reagan tried hard to return some responsibilities to the states, mainly by giving them more control over how they spend federal money. In the next section, we look at recent efforts to alter the balance of federal power in favor of the states.

devolution the transfer of powers and responsibilities from the federal government to the states

when those problems, like race discrimination or air pollution, affect the populations of multiple states. In some instances, national problem solving involves redistributing resources from one state or region to another, which individual states, on their own, would be unwilling or unable to do. Second, members of Congress profit electorally by passing laws and regulations that bring to their states resources, such as highway funds; welfare benefits; urban renewal money; and assistance to farmers, ranchers, miners, and educators. Doing well by constituents gets incumbents reelected.[35] Third, sometimes members of Congress prefer to adopt national legislation to preempt what states may be doing or planning to do. In some cases they might object to state laws, as Congress did when it passed civil rights legislation against the strong preferences of the southern states. In other cases they might enact legislation to prevent states from making fifty different regulatory laws for the same product. If Congress makes a set of nationally binding regulations, businesses or corporations—generally large contributors to politicians—do not have to incur the expense of altering their products or services to meet different state standards.

To deliver on their promises, national politicians must have the cooperation of the states. Although some policies, such as Social Security, can be administered easily at the national level, others, such as changing educational policy or altering the drinking age, remain under state authority and cannot be legislated in Washington. This creates one of federal policymakers' biggest challenges: how to get the states to do what federal officials have decided they should do.

HOW THE NATIONAL GOVERNMENT TRIES TO INFLUENCE THE STATES Congress makes two key decisions when it attempts to influence what the states are doing. The first concerns the character of the rules and regulations that are issued: Will they be broad enough to allow the states flexibility, or narrow and specific to guarantee that policy is executed as Washington wishes? The other is about whether the cost of the new programs will be paid for by the national government and, if so, how much of the cost the government will cover. The combination of these two decisions yields the four general congressional strategies for influencing the states that we see in second *The Big Picture* in this chapter.

---

categorical grant federal funds provided for a specific purpose and restricted by detailed instructions, regulations, and compliance standards

block grant federal funds provided for a broad purpose and unrestricted by detailed requirements and regulations

---

- **Option One (No National Government Influence).** When the national government chooses to leave a state's authority unchallenged, it provides no instructions (either broad or specific) and no funding (second column, second row in *The Big Picture*). When there is no national government influence, states can act as they wish in the given policy area.

- **Option Two (Categorical Grants).** Sometimes Congress decides that the nation's interests depend on all the states taking actions to solve some particular problem—perhaps the provision of early childhood education, food security for the disadvantaged, or health care for low-income individuals. The most popular tool Congress has devised for this purpose is the categorical grant (first column, first row in *The Big Picture*), which provides detailed instructions, regulations, and compliance requirements for the states (and sometimes for local governments, as well) in specific policy areas. If a state complies with the requirements, federal money is released for those specified purposes. If a state doesn't comply with the detailed provisions of the categorical grant, it doesn't get the money. In many cases the states also have to provide some funding themselves.

  The states, like most governments, never have enough money to meet all their citizens' demands, so categorical grants can look very attractive, at least on the surface. The grants can be refused, but that rarely happens. In fact, state and local governments have become so dependent on federal grants that these subsidies now make up more than a quarter of all state and local spending.[36] State politicians, however, chafe under the requirements and all the paperwork that the federal government imposes with categorical grants. States and localities also frequently argue that federal regulations prevent them from doing a good job. They want the money, but they also want more flexibility. Most members of Congress, by contrast, like to use categorical grants—they receive credit for sponsoring specific grant programs, which in turn helps establish them as national policy leaders, building their reputations with their constituents for bringing "home" federal money.

- **Option Three (Block Grants).** State politicians understandably want the maximum amount of freedom possible. They want to control their own destinies, not just carry out political deals made in Washington, and they want to please the coalitions of interests and voters that put them in power in the states. Their preferred policy tool, the block grant (first column, second row in *The Big Picture*), combines broad (rather than detailed) program requirements and regulations with

THE BIG PICTURE:
How the National Government Influences the States

Public demands, policy complexities, and electoral politics all put pressures on the national government to expand its powers beyond those enumerated in the Constitution. To get the states to do its will, Congress has to decide if it is willing to pay for what it wants and how much it trusts the states to comply voluntarily.

FEDERAL GRANTS

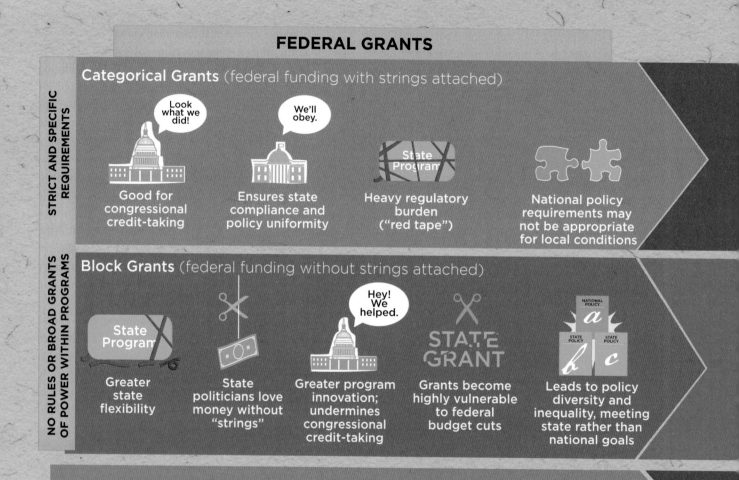

STRICT AND SPECIFIC REQUIREMENTS

Categorical Grants (federal funding with strings attached)

Look what we did!

Good for congressional credit-taking

We'll obey.

Ensures state compliance and policy uniformity

State Program

Heavy regulatory burden ("red tape")

National policy requirements may not be appropriate for local conditions

NO RULES OR BROAD GRANTS OF POWER WITHIN PROGRAMS

Block Grants (federal funding without strings attached)

State Program

Greater state flexibility

State politicians love money without "strings"

Hey! We helped.

Greater program innovation; undermines congressional credit-taking

STATE GRANT

Grants become highly vulnerable to federal budget cuts

NATIONAL POLICY *a* — STATE POLICY *b* — STATE POLICY *c*

Leads to policy diversity and inequality, meeting state rather than national goals

Categorical Grants *in real life*:
The Environmental Protection Agency makes categorical grants to states specifically to fund state partnerships in enforcing the Clean Water Act, the Clean Air Act, and the Safe Drinking Water Act. States have no flexibility in how to spend the funds they receive from EPA.

Block Grants *in real life*:
Since 1974, Housing and Urban Development has offered Community Development Block Grants to local government units of the states to provide affordable housing, to deliver services to the disadvantaged, and to draw businesses and jobs to poorer urban areas. Communities have a great deal of flexibility in how they use the funds to meet these needs.

NO FEDERAL GRANTS

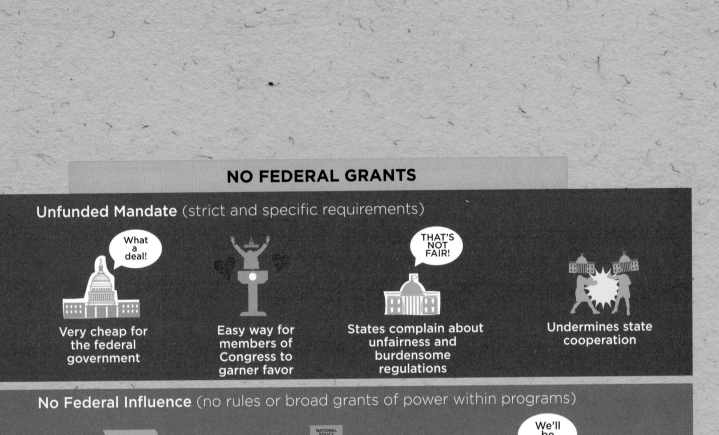

Unfunded Mandate (strict and specific requirements)

What a deal!

Very cheap for the federal government

Easy way for members of Congress to garner favor

THAT'S NOT FAIR!

States complain about unfairness and burdensome regulations

Undermines state cooperation

No Federal Influence (no rules or broad grants of power within programs)

States have autonomy and pay for their own programs

Results in high diversity of policies, including inequality; promotes state competition and its outcomes

We'll be good.

Calls for congressional and presidential restraint in exercising their powers

Unfunded Mandates *in real life*:
The No Child Left Behind Act of 2001 required that public schools administer state-wide standardized tests to students. If schools did not show yearly improvement on the tests, they had to take steps at their own expense to raise the quality of the education they provided.

No Federal Influence *in real life*:
Martin Luther King Jr. Day was established as a federal holiday (most federal employees get a paid day off) in 1968. But that was not binding on the states and a number resisted. It took until 2000 for all the states to recognize it, and some states used other names for a time, like Civil Rights Day (New Hampshire) or Lee-Jackson-King Day (Virginia).

funding from the federal treasury. Block grants give the states considerable freedom in using the funds in broad policy areas. State officials find support here from conservative politicians at the national level who, despite the electoral advantages to be gained from them, have long balked at the detailed, Washington-centered nature of categorical grants.

Congress has generally resisted the block grant approach for both policy and political reasons. In policy terms, many members of Congress fear that the states will pursue their own agendas instead of what Congress intends. One member characterized the idea of putting federal money into block grants as "pouring money down a rat hole,"[37] because it is impossible to control how the states deal with particular problems under block grants. Congress also has political objections to block grants. When federal funds are not attached to specific programs, members of Congress can no longer take credit for the programs. From their standpoint, it does not make political sense to take the heat for taxing people's income, only to return those funds to the states as block grants, leaving governors and mayors to get the credit for how the money is spent. In addition, interest groups contribute millions of dollars to congressional campaigns when members of Congress have control over program specifics. If Congress allows the states to assume that control, interest groups have less incentive to make congressional campaign contributions. As a result, the tendency in Congress has been to place more conditions on block grants with each annual appropriation,[38] and categorical grants remain the predominant form of federal aid, amounting to about 80 percent of all aid to state and local governments.

- **Option Four (Unfunded Mandates).** The politics of federalism yields one more strategy, shown in the second column, first row of *The Big Picture*. When the federal government issues an unfunded mandate, it imposes specific policy requirements on the states but does not provide funds to pay for those activities. Rather, Congress forces states to comply either by threatening criminal or civil penalties or by promising to cut off other, often unrelated, federal funds if the states do not follow its directions. Unfunded mandates are more attractive to members of Congress in periods of ballooning national deficits, when the national government has no money to spend.[39] In large part due to complaints from the states, Congress passed the Unfunded Mandate Act of 1995, which promised to reimburse the states for expensive unfunded mandates or to pass a separate law acknowledging the cost of an unfunded mandate. This act has limited congressional efforts to pass "good laws" that cost the U.S. Treasury nothing. However, because Congress can define what the states see as an unfunded mandate in several different ways—classifying a directive as a simple "clarification of legislative intent," for example—Congress has continued to push some policy costs on to the states.[40]

Fears of large unfunded mandates played a role in the debates leading up to health care reform in 2008. A version of the reform that expanded Medicaid for low-income people prompted instant criticism from governors because significant portions of Medicaid (varying from about 25 to 50 percent) are paid for from the state treasuries.[41] Congress later backed down and provided assistance to the states to fund the new policy, but that did not stop the states from challenging the act in court, which resulted in the Supreme Court's ruling that states could not be forced to expand coverage under the Medicaid program.

THE CONTINUING TENSION BETWEEN NATIONAL AND STATE GOVERNMENT The current status of federalism is a contradictory mix of narratives about returning power to the states and new national initiatives (and program requirements) in the areas of health, education, and the environment (see *Don't Be Fooled by . . . Political Rhetoric*). Although many actors in the states and even the national government say they want the states to have more power, or simply that they want all levels of government to do less, the imperatives of effective policy solutions and congressional and presidential electoral calculations combine to create strong pressures for national solutions to our complex problems.

Advocates for the national government and supporters of the states are engaged in a constant struggle for power, as they have been since the days of the Articles of Confederation. The power of the federal government is enhanced through the mechanisms of cooperative federalism, which gives the federal government an increasing role in domestic policy. As the federal government has used the restrictive rules of categorical grants and the economic threats that provide the muscle of unfunded mandates, critics have claimed that cooperative federalism has been transformed into "coercive federalism," in which the states are pressured to adopt national solutions to their local problems with minimal state input.

Remember, however, that members of Congress who pass the laws are elected in the states and have their primary loyalties to their local constituencies, not to any national audience. Their states have traditionally been only too happy to

---

unfunded mandate a federal order mandating that states operate and pay for a program created at the national level

Political Rhetoric

You are a hot commodity. Every day, politicians, pundits, advertisers, bloggers, and politically minded folks in your social networks are vying for your attention, your support, your votes, and possibly your dollars, and they employ an entire arsenal of weapons—eloquent words, seductive arguments, tempting promises—designed to get you to buy their political narrative.

As a critical consumer of information, it's important that you understand what you're up against. Learning to identify logical fallacies (forms of faulty reasoning) and to understand different types of persuasive appeals not only can make you a better consumer of political information but also can help you to articulate your own arguments in a way that is both persuasive and ethical.

What to Watch Out For

- **The post-hoc fallacy.** From the Latin *post hoc ergo propter hoc* (meaning "after this, therefore because of this"), the post hoc fallacy occurs when one draws a cause-and-effect relationship between two events simply because one follows the other. You might observe, for example, that students who take notes on laptops do well on exams. But if you assert that the digital note-taking causes better grades, then you're falling victim to the post hoc fallacy.

- **Appeals to tradition.** Historical evidence is important, but using tradition as a litmus test for what is right or wrong is not always sound. When a pundit points to the way things have always been, it's your job to carefully evaluate whether or not the way things have always been is the way things ought to be. Such appeals are particularly effective in persuading people who are nervous about change, which is one reason they come up so frequently in political narratives relating to things like marriage and family.

- **Emotional appeals.** One surefire way to get lots of attention fast is to go for the heart: stirring up anger, fear, disgust, or empathy gets a quick reaction. It's impossible to ignore your emotions when something is upsetting, but it pays to take a moment to evaluate whether you are being persuaded by evidence, or just by your own emotions.

- **The "straw man" fallacy.** One way to make an argument appear stronger is to show that competing ideas are weaker. That can be fine when evaluating the strengths and weaknesses of two viable options. However, it's not uncommon for pundits to pit their argument not against actual alternatives, but rather against a simplified, weaker counterargument (or "straw man") that can easily be knocked down. When someone presents a weak or even ludicrous counterargument, check to see whether the counterargument is even real. Unfortunately, when a straw man argument is also an emotional appeal, it can take on a narrative life of its own. Consider, for example, the hysteria over government "death panels" during the fight over the Patient Protection and Affordable Care Act.

- **The slippery slope.** You've heard this one a million times, on both sides of such contentious issues as gun control and freedom of speech: If you limit or allow one thing, that will eventually lead us down a "slippery slope" to anarchy, tyranny, or some other unthinkable outcome. It's often possible that one will lead to another, but when someone presents such connections as inevitable, without any proof, you should take their arguments with the proverbial grain of salt.

- **The false dilemma.** Beware any argument that implies that limited options are available, especially when it comes to policy. Just because the narrative implies there are no compromises or alternatives doesn't mean that's true.

- **Bandwagoning.** The United States may be a democracy governed by, for, and of the people—but facts remain facts whether they are widely held or not. If a writer or commentator is using the popularity of a statement as proof of its validity, you should immediately take a second look. Opinions and beliefs are not credible evidence, even if they are widely agreed upon.

- **Anecdotal evidence and hasty generalizations.** Anecdotes liven up speeches and can lend support to arguments—but they're of limited use when making a point and should never be used as evidence of a trend. One story does not carry as much weight as real statistics that come from systematic research.

- **Red herrings.** Take care to sort out and ignore irrelevant or unrelated information, which can be insinuated into arguments purely for the sake of distracting you from the matter at hand.

- **Cherry picking evidence.** Deciding what evidence to use—and what to leave out—is a crucial step in developing any argument. In the process, it may be tempting to select only the evidence that supports one's own opinion and to ignore evidence that contradicts it. This tendency, which social scientists call confirmation bias, often occurs unconsciously, so it is especially important to be vigilant in weeding it out of any arguments you encounter—including your own.

"In Two Words, Yes And No"

FEDERAL BENEFITS

FEDERAL AUTHORITY

"STATES RIGHTS"

HERBLOCK
©1949 THE WASHINGTON POST Co

accept federal funds to meet the needs of their residents (and voters) for everything from education to highways to welfare and health care for the poor. However, they also chafe under the rules and regulations that typically come with federal dollars, and especially since 2009, the powerful anti-government rhetoric emerging from the Republican Party and its Tea Party wing strongly opposes the growth of the federal government. All of this opposition can override even the electoral incentives that members of Congress have for supporting policies that bring federal money to their states, as evidenced by the roughly one-third of the states that have still not accepted federal funds to expand Medicaid under the Affordable Care Act.

This tension is currently playing out in the aftermath of the slower growth that followed the country's longest and worst economic recession since the Great Depression. The states were particularly hard hit as revenues from sales, income, and property taxes dropped dramatically. Federal stimulus funds helped the states deal with about 40 percent of their budget shortfalls, but many conservative governors and legislatures rejected the funds, seeing them as encroachments by a power-hungry federal government rather than as necessary short-term help in hard times.[42] In any case, those funds began drying up in 2010, leaving the states with continuing insufficient funds and forcing them to lay off workers to make up the difference.[43] The recovery of the states continued to lag behind that of the general economy, with the result that

many citizens still faced decreased services from the states in the areas of education, health, and public security.[44]

As we suggested earlier, as the national policymaking machinery can grind to a halt under divided government, an opportunity has opened up for states to take more action on their own. For several years, a conservative Republican-controlled Congress resisted virtually every initiative put forth by the Obama administration, and similarly, President Obama was not shy about using the veto when Congress sent him bills that did not fit with his agenda. National inaction has left a policy vacuum being filled with state policy initiatives. Even though President Trump does not face divided government, the Republican caucus itself is split, causing inactivity at the national level that can be countered at the state level.

Three-fifths of the states are under unified control—both houses of the state legislature are controlled by the same party as the governor. This has given them the ability to move where gridlocked Washington cannot; and unlike Washington action that moves policy in the same direction nationwide, the states go their own, separate ways. Take immigration policy, for example. Some Republican-led states, such as Alabama and Arizona, have passed restrictive immigration legislation. Others states, where the Democrats are in control, have passed legislation to make life easier for undocumented workers and their families.

Gridlock between the president and Congress has also elevated the role of interexecutive negotiations in making changes in the major areas of education and health care. Republican governors have negotiated "waivers" with the federal bureaucracy (individualized changes in specific laws) to achieve politically workable solutions to problems in Medicaid and other federally mandated programs. The trend of hyperpartisanship and polarization that has led to gridlock at the national level has taken Congress out of the game as a significant actor in many policy areas, while executives (state and federal) make deals, and the states take the initiative to implement policy that fits with their voters' (very different) preferences.[45]

PAUSE AND REVIEW   Who, What, How

Where decisions are made—in Washington, D.C., or in the state capitals—makes a big difference in who gets what, and how they get it. The compromise of federalism as it appears in the Constitution, and as it has been interpreted by the Supreme Court, allows the nation, the states, and the citizens to get political benefits that would not be possible under either a unitary or a confederal system, but the balance of power has swung back and forth over the years. Much of the current battle is fought in the halls of Congress, where states pull for more autonomy in the form of block grants and devolution, and the national government holds out for categorical grants and unfunded mandates. Underlying the ideological battle is the political truth that the contestants generally favor the level of government most likely to give them what they want. Ironically, as Congress has found itself politically unable to act because of gridlock, it has created more space for states to take action on their own.

In Your Own Words Identify the rules and interests that keep relations tense between state and national governments.

AMENDING THE CONSTITUTION

Making it difficult but not impossible

If a constitution is a rule book, then its capacity to be changed over time is critical to its remaining a viable political document. A rigid constitution runs the risk of ceasing to seem legitimate to citizens who have no prospect of changing the rules according to shifting political realities and visions of the public good. A constitution that is revised too easily, however, can be seen as no more than a political tool in the hands of the strongest interests in society. A final feature of the U.S. Constitution that deserves mention here is its **amendability**—that is, the founders' provision for a method of amendment, or change, that allows the Constitution to grow and adapt to new circumstances. In fact, the founders provided for two methods: the formal amendment process outlined in the Constitution, and an informal process that results from the vagueness of the document and the evolution of the role of the courts.

In the more than two hundred years since the U.S. Constitution was written, over 10,000 amendments have been introduced, but it has been formally amended only twenty-seven times. We have passed amendments to expand the protections of civil liberties and rights—to protect freedom of speech and religion; to provide guarantees against abuses of the criminal justice system; to guarantee citizenship rights to African Americans; and to extend the right to vote to blacks, women, and eighteen-year-olds.

We have also passed amendments on more mechanical matters—to tinker with the rules of the political institutions the Constitution sets up in order to better control the outcomes. To that end, we have made senatorial elections direct, we have limited presidents to two terms in office, and we have provided for a succession order for presidents unable to serve out their terms.

On at least one occasion we have also used the Constitution to make a policy that could more easily have been made

> **amendability** the provision for the Constitution to be changed, so as to adapt to new circumstances

Not So Happy Hours

Amending the U.S. Constitution is no easy task, but Americans' love-hate relationship with alcohol was intense enough to do it twice in a mere fourteen years. Temperance advocates succeeded in banning the sale of "intoxicating liquors" with the Eighteenth Amendment in 1919; prohibition opponents, many of whom voiced their opinions during protests like this one, managed to have it repealed in 1933.

through normal legislative channels. With the ratification of the Eighteenth Amendment in 1919, we instituted Prohibition, making the production and sale of alcohol illegal. When our national views on temperance changed, we repealed the amendment in 1933, having to pass a new amendment to do so.

But the Constitution can be changed in more subtle ways by the Supreme Court without an amendment's ever being passed. As we will see in the next chapter, in the name of interpreting the Constitution the Supreme Court has extended many Bill of Rights protections to state citizens via the Fourteenth Amendment, permitted the national government to regulate business, prohibited child labor, and extended equal protection of the laws to women. In some cases, amendments had earlier been introduced to accomplish these goals but failed to be ratified (like the child labor amendment and the Equal Rights Amendment), and sometimes the Court has simply decided to interpret the Constitution in a new way. Judicial interpretation is at times quite controversial.

But these views about whether the Constitution should be changed by amendment or by interpretation are not just matters for academics to solve—they also have political implications and tend to break down along partisan lines. For instance, many recent calls to amend the Constitution have focused on banning abortion, banning gay marriage, banning flag burning, or permitting prayer in school. For the most part, people split into partisan camps in their support of or opposition to those amendments. Democrats tend to oppose such amendments, believing they curtail fundamental individual rights, and Republicans tend to support them, claiming they promote important traditional values.

But one can go even further in drawing partisan lines around this issue. Democrats, in general, as liberals who believe that change is inevitable and probably a good thing, are more willing to see the Constitution as a flexible, living document that can be altered continually in small, nonpermanent ways by judicial interpretation. By contrast, Republicans share for the most part the conservative suspicion of change and a belief that the words of the founders ought not to be tampered with by unelected judges. They are willing to change the Constitution, and even to change it in deep and fundamental ways, but they prefer to do it by amendment. We return to this controversy when we look more closely at the courts in Chapter 10.

WHAT DOES THE CONSTITUTION SAY?

The Constitution is silent on the subject of judicial interpretation, but the courts have been able to evolve their own role in part because of this silence. At the same time, however, Article V spells out in detail the rather confusing procedures for officially amending the Constitution. These procedures are federal; that is, they require the involvement and approval of the states as well as the national government. The procedures boil down to this: amendments may be proposed either by a two-thirds vote of the House and the Senate or, when two-thirds of the states request it, by a constitutional convention. Amendments must be approved either by the legislatures of three-fourths of the states or by conventions of three-fourths of the states (see Figure 4.4). Two interesting qualifications are contained in Article V. No amendment affecting slavery could be made before 1808, and no amendment can deprive a state of its equal vote in the Senate without that state's consent. We can easily imagine the North-South and large state–small state conflicts that produced those compromises.

The constitutional convention method of amendment, where change is initiated by the states, has never been used, although states have frequently tried to initiate a such a movement. In fact, an effort to create a balanced budget amendment in this way is currently in the works. Twenty-seven of the necessary thirty-four states (all Republican-led) have passed resolutions calling on Congress to hold a constitutional convention to pass a balanced budget amendment. Several other efforts are right behind it that would try to put in extra protections for religious freedom (and perhaps defining citizenship as beginning at conception) or limitations on government action. Opponents argue that once a convention is convened, it might be hard to contain the urge to make multiple changes to the Constitution, although three-quarter of the states would still need to approve the resulting amendments.[46]

POSSIBLE ALTERNATIVES: MAKING THE CONSTITUTION EASIER OR HARDER TO AMEND

The fifty states provide some interesting examples of alternative rules for amending constitutions. Compared to the national government, some states make it harder to amend their own constitutions. For instance, twelve states require amendments to pass in more than one session of the legislature—that is, in successive years.

Rules can also make it much easier to amend constitutions. Some states require only simple legislative majorities (50 percent plus one) to propose amendments, and unlike the national Constitution, some states give their citizens a substantial role in the process through mechanisms called referenda and initiatives, which we discuss in the next section. The method by which an amendment is proposed can affect the success of the amendment itself. For instance, amendments limiting the number of terms legislators can serve have been passed in several states with the citizen-controlled initiative, but they have not fared well in states that depend on state legislatures to propose amendments. With opinion polls showing large public majorities favoring term limits, we can safely assume that term limits for Congress would pass much faster if the U.S. Constitution had a provision for a national constitutional initiative. Congress has proven, not surprisingly, reluctant to put restrictions on congressional careers.

One problem with making it too easy to amend a constitution is that public opinion can be fickle, and we might not always want the constitution to respond too hastily to changes in public whim. A second problem is that where amendments can be made easily, special interests push for amendments that give them tax breaks or other protections and can often manipulate the debate by creating narratives based on misleading logic or language that is intentionally difficult to comprehend. Constitutional status of their special treatment protects those interests from having to periodically justify that treatment to the public and the legislature.

Finally, where constitutions can be amended more easily, they are amended more frequently. The initiative process in California permits relatively easy translation of citizen concerns into constitutional issues. Compared to just twenty-seven amendments to our national Constitution, California's constitution has been amended more than five hundred times with everything from putting a cap on taxes, to limiting legislative terms, to withholding public services from undocumented immigrants. Such matters would be the subject of ordinary legislation in states where amending is more difficult and thus would not have "higher law" status. Some critics feel that the fundamental importance of a constitution is trivialized by cluttering it with many additions that could be dealt with in other ways.

The U.S. Constitution has weathered the passing of time so well for two good reasons, then. First, it is not too detailed and

FIGURE 4.4
Amending the Constitution

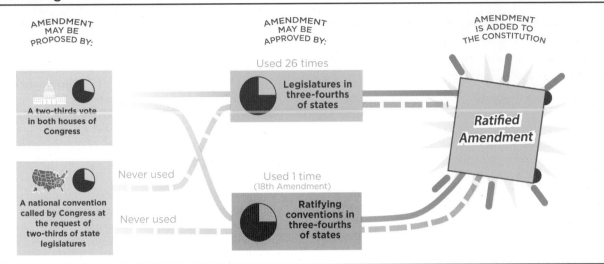

AMENDMENT MAY BE PROPOSED BY:

A two-thirds vote in both houses of Congress

A national convention called by Congress at the request of two-thirds of state legislatures

Never used

Never used

AMENDMENT MAY BE APPROVED BY:

Used 26 times

Legislatures in three-fourths of states

Used 1 time
(18th Amendment)

Ratifying conventions in three-fourths of states

AMENDMENT IS ADDED TO THE CONSTITUTION

Ratified Amendment

---

explicit, and second, its amendment procedure, in Madison's words, "guards equally against that extreme facility, which would render the Constitution too mutable; and the extreme difficulty, which might perpetuate its discovered faults."[47]

PAUSE AND REVIEW Who, What, How

The founders and the American public had an enormous stake in a Constitution that would survive. The founders had their own reputations as nation-builders at stake, but they and the public also badly wanted their new experiment in self-governance to prove successful, to validate the Enlightenment view of the world. For the Constitution to survive, it had to be able to change, but to change judiciously. The amendment process provided in the Constitution allows for just such change. But occasionally this process is too slow for what the courts consider justice, and they use their broad powers to interpret the existing words of the Constitution in light of the changed circumstances of the modern day. That is, they focus not so much on what the founders meant at the time, but on what they would intend if they were alive today. The founders would have been as mixed in support of this practice as are contemporary scholars. Perhaps the focus of so many critical eyes on the Court has served as an informal check on this power.

In Your Own Words Demonstrate how the flexibility built into the Constitution has allowed it to change with the times.

THE CITIZENS AND THE CONSTITUTION

Limited participation at the national level, enhanced opportunities beyond

Remember Benjamin Franklin's reply to the woman who asked him what he and his colleagues had created? "A Republic, Madam, if you can keep it." In fact, however, the Constitution assigns citizens only the slimmest of roles in keeping the republic. The founders wrote a constitution that in many respects profoundly limits citizen participation.

The political role available to "the people" moved from "subject" to "citizen" with the writing of the Constitution, and especially with the addition of the Bill of Rights, but the citizens' political options were narrow. It is true that they could vote if they met the tight restrictions that the states might require. Their constitutional roles as voters, however, were—and are still—confined to choosing among competing political elites. The founders did not trust human beings, either to know their own best interests or to handle power without being corrupted. They wanted popular power to serve as a potential check on the elected leaders, but they wanted to impose strict checks on popular power as well, to prevent disturbances like Shays's Rebellion from threatening the system. The Constitution was the republic's insurance policy against chaos and instability.

But the Constitution enhances opportunities for participation by leaving considerable power at the state and local levels, where citizens participate in local government, on school boards and in parent-teacher organizations, in charitable groups, and in service organizations. Our mediated culture offers multiple opportunities to get involved in congressional and presidential election campaigns (volunteers can make phone calls for candidates over the Internet and help get out the vote without leaving their own homes). Citizens run for office, serve as magistrates, circulate petitions, take part in fundraising drives, and participate in neighborhood associations. They file lawsuits, they belong to interest groups, and they march in parades and demonstrations. They read papers and watch the news, they call in to radio talk shows, and they write letters to the editor. They blog, they

Susana Martinez

Courtesy of the office of Governor Susana Martinez

It has always been important to Susana Martinez that everyone play by the same rules. As a child, when she and her family played a game, she assembled all the cousins and said, "We're going to play this game and these are the rules. This is how you play and you're not allowed to cheat and if you cheat you're not going to play." Her grandmother called her *abogadita*— a "little lawyer." That is pretty much what you need to know about how Governor Martinez ran the state of New Mexico from 2011 to 2018.

From the time that the teachers at school had the students do an exercise where they imagined where they would be in five years, in ten, and in fifteen, she has had an eye on the bigger picture, and it involved public service. "I enjoyed watching the news where we would watch senators and congressmen debate each other and argue their points. That I really enjoyed; who would make the better point, and why." But being a senator didn't appeal. She says, "I thought the best place to cause the greatest change was being a governor, so that became my goal."

Raised in a conservative Catholic family in Texas, she kept her focus on those goals. From college at University of Texas at El Paso she headed to law school in Oklahoma and into the courtroom, working for the district attorney. "I was a talker, so I knew I wanted to be in the courtroom. . . . I went to court every day for twenty-five years because that's where the action is. . . . I loved it. I loved the ability to debate and argue my position." She carved out a niche for herself as a tough prosecutor, specializing in cases of child murder and abuse.

She began to think of running for the office of district attorney herself. Although she had been raised as a Democrat she realized after a lunch with local Republicans that her values aligned more closely with theirs. She got into the car with her husband after the lunch and said, "I'll be damned, we're Republicans!" For a woman with political ambitions in New Mexico, a blue state, this was not necessarily a good thing. But she ran for D.A., against her old boss, and won the way she had done most things in her life—by doing her homework, being prepared, and having a clear vision of where she wanted to go.

When the opportunity came around to run for governor in 2010, she took the same approach. Martinez worked hard, ran hard, and won, determined to clean up a state government that she felt had gotten sloppy. When you talk to her about it, it is clear she is enjoying every minute.

On patriotism

"I would define patriotism as love of one's country and being loyal to it. I also believe it is important to acknowledge our history and God's providence. I think believing in something and having faith is very important. When I was a prosecutor, I remember before I went into the courtroom and after studying all the information—I believed in the case I was prosecuting and in the facts I had collected, and in the end, everything just gelled. Sure there were moments when things weren't always perfect, maybe a piece of information just didn't fit as neatly as we would like or something was said by someone that changed things slightly, but I would assemble all the available information and evidence, and have confidence in what we were pursuing."

On keeping the republic

"I think to keep the republic, people must stay informed, particularly youth. With the world of technology, it can play both ways as there is an abundance of information, but also a dearth of attention. On my iPhone and iPad, I can access every piece of news I could ever want. From what's happening in the Middle East in *The New York Times* to developments in Congress in *The Washington Post* to our local newspapers, it's all at my fingertips. But at the same time, all that access to information, including movies and other things can take away from—for instance—watching the six o'clock news, which is very important to stay informed. Consuming information is not enough, in that discussion is required, whether you agree with someone's viewpoint or not. A cup of coffee at Starbucks, where the kids hang out, can go a long way to receiving a diversity of opinion. In the end, if we are discussing important issues, we can have more control over determining our own future and crafting our destinies as individuals, as a community and as a nation."

Source: Susana Martinez spoke with Christine Barbour and Gerald C. Wright on September 23, 2014.

engage in political debate on the Internet, and they use their social networks as a means of grassroots organization to rally others behind causes in which they believe.

There are also three formal mechanisms of direct democracy at the state level that are enhanced by the possibilities of mediated citizenship: the initiative, the referendum, and the recall.

With the **initiative**, citizens can force a constitutional amendment or state law to be placed on the ballot. This is accomplished by getting a sufficient number of signatures on petitions, typically between 3 and 15 percent of those voting in the last election for governor. A ballot initiative that receives a majority vote is adopted and becomes law, completely bypassing the state legislature. About half of the states have provisions for the initiative, and in California it has become the principal way to make significant changes to state law. Initiatives offer a way for citizens to change state marijuana laws, expand state Medicaid coverage through the Affordable Care Act, or enact local state pollution controls.

The **referendum** is an election in which bills passed by the state legislatures or localities are submitted to the voters for their approval. In most states, constitutional amendments have to be submitted for a referendum vote, and in some states questions of taxation do also. A number of states allow citizens to call for a referendum (by petition) on controversial laws passed by the state legislature, and in many cases the state legislatures themselves can ask for a referendum on matters they believe the voters should decide directly. Laws on marijuana, school board funding, and term limits are all issues that voters have weighed in on.

Recall elections are a way for citizens to remove elected officials from office before their terms are up. These, too, require petitions, usually with more signatures than are needed for an initiative (frequently 25 percent of the electorate). Statewide recalls are infrequent, but some are quite notable, like the one that removed Gray Davis as governor of California in 2003, clearing the way for Arnold Schwarzenegger's election, and the 2012 effort to recall Wisconsin governor Scott Walker and Republican members of the state legislature. Although enough of the recalls were successful to switch control of the Wisconsin Senate to the Democrats, Walker held on to his office. Officials may be subject to recall elections for ethical violations, or for other issues on which voters feel the official has broken faith with them. For instance, when a concerted social media campaign to expose what was happening to the

AP Photo/John Minchillo

Taking It Into Their Own Hands

Concerned that the state legislature was drawing overly partisan congressional districts, Ohio voters decided in May 2018, by an overwhelming 75–25 percent bipartisan majority, to make the district drawing a more neutral process. Sometimes measures of direct democracy are necessary to make decisions that run counter to the interests of those entrenched in power.

Flint, Michigan, water supply came to the attention of MSNBC's Rachel Maddow, she made it a national issue. The mayor of Flint subsequently avoided recall in a field of seventeen other candidates seeking to unseat her.

The record of these three measures of direct democracy is mixed, but the point is that they do enhance opportunities for individuals to participate, and they give citizens more control over what their government does. However, many citizens do not take advantage of these opportunities, leaving greater power concentrated in the hands of the intense minority who do. Furthermore, many of the details of lawmaking can be complicated and hard to understand without careful study—something most citizens don't have time to give them. As a result, the people who do vote can be misled or manipulated by complex or obscure wording, and it is hard for them to know exactly what they are voting on. Finally, direct democracy, by eliminating the checks the founders thought important, makes government more responsive to short-term fluctuations in public opinion, sometimes denying politicians the time needed to take a long-term approach to problem solving and policymaking.

In twenty-first-century mediated America, many of those limitations can be avoided with the help of various forms of electronic media in unraveling complicated issues and organizing people who normally would not be reached by political messages. What mediated citizenship does not do is eliminate the possibility that people can be manipulated—in fact, it multiplies the opportunities for that to happen, making critical thinking and fact checking all the more important.

> **initiative** citizen petitions to place a proposal or constitutional amendment on the ballot, to be adopted or rejected by majority vote, bypassing the legislature
>
> **referendum** an election in which a bill passed by the state legislature is submitted to voters for approval
>
> **recall elections** votes to remove elected officials from office

In Your Own Words Discuss whether the Constitution fosters or limits citizen participation in government.

LET'S REVISIT: *What's at Stake . . . ?*

As we have seen in this chapter, the issue of what powers go to the federal government and what powers are reserved to the states has been a hotly contested one since the founding, and one that has no clean, crisp, right answer. As the country and the composition of the Supreme Court have changed, so too have interpretations of states' rights and federal power. All of that means the issue of medical marijuana use, which currently is legal in more than half the country, and recreational marijuana, which is legal in nine states plus the District of Columbia, is an excellent example of the messiness that can characterize federal issues in the United States, where national law dictates that any kind of marijuana is illegal.

The states and the national government both have a stake in protecting their turf against the other when it comes to marijuana laws. One of the chief virtues of federalism is that it gives the states the flexibility to experiment and to respond to their citizens' demands for policy change. Policies are frequently incubated in the states before they are ready for launching on the national stage, or before the national stage is ready to receive them. The trouble when it comes to legalizing marijuana—medical or recreational—is that there is already a binding federal policy in place. The federal government under the George W. Bush administration claimed that its law trumped state laws because of the commerce clause, the part of Article I, Section 8, of the Constitution that gives Congress the power to regulate commerce among the states. The Supreme Court backed that view in 2005, voting six to three in *Gonzales v. Raich*, a case concerning a California medical marijuana law.[48] Defenders of the laws responded that growing, selling, or smoking marijuana for personal medical use within a single state has nothing to do with interstate commerce. Fourteen states passed laws decriminalizing the use of marijuana for medical purposes by prescription, and slowly, federal law swung in their direction. In May 2009 the Supreme Court refused to hear a case challenging the California law, essentially handing a victory to medical marijuana proponents, and that October, the Justice Department, then under the Barack Obama administration, signaled that, as long as use was consistent with state laws, marijuana use by those holding a prescription for it would not be prosecuted.[49] Reading these cues, more states followed suit, only to see the Trump administration rescind the Obama policy, although the policy's current status remains unclear.

State law can conflict, of course, not just with national law but with the laws of other states, and here it is the states that have a stake in enforcing their own marijuana laws—either because their citizens deeply disagree with the laws of other states or because there is profit to be had in prosecuting people from other states who violate the law. As the Idaho example in *What's at Stake . . . ?* suggested, states with different laws and policies can provide treacherous terrain for their citizens and nice cash cows for the states collecting fines for violations of their laws. The flip side of federalism's ability to permit experimentation and innovation is that on some issues you can end up with fifty different policies regulating the same behavior. As the Idaho example indicates, citizens from one state can be caught flat-footed when visiting another if they don't take care to learn the laws of their destination.

It is not just states that have a stake in setting their own laws on things like marijuana policy; businesses also have a stake in what states do and in resolving the legal confusion that can result from federalism. As is evident in the experience of the brothers who grow nonintoxicating marijuana for medical purposes, but who faced barriers to transporting the medicinal oil across state lines, businesses can face expensive and exasperating delays and roadblocks when they have to accommodate fifty separate state laws. Throw the federal law into the mix as well, and federalism can be an entrepreneur's nightmare.

Finally, citizens have a stake in how the states manage their policies on marijuana. For some supporters of the medical marijuana laws, what is at stake is the ability of ill patients to receive the most effective treatment possible. But they are allied with those who want to put limits on national power, some of whom might not approve of medical marijuana on its own merits. In his dissent in *Gonzales v. Raich*, Justice Clarence Thomas said, "No evidence from the founding suggests that 'commerce' included the mere possession of a good or some purely personal activity that did not involve trade or exchange for value. In the early days of the Republic, it would have been unthinkable that Congress could prohibit the local cultivation, possession, and consumption of marijuana." If the national government can regulate this, it can regulate anything.[50]

Opponents of the medical marijuana laws say that as long as the Court has ruled that the state laws violate the commerce clause, the national law should be enforced. Further, some argue that it does touch the issue of interstate commerce because the provision and purchase of medical marijuana "affects the marijuana market generally," and they worry that if the federal government cannot regulate this, then perhaps the government will be hampered in other areas, like child pornography.[51]

That there is no clear constitutional resolution of such issues, that it is possible for the Court to produce conflicting rulings on this policy, and that the Bush, Obama, and Trump administrations would take such variable stances on it explains both how our federal system has found the flexibility to survive so long and so well, and why the debates over where power resides can be so bitterly fought.

CLUES to Critical Thinking

Federalist *No. 51*

By James Madison, *The Federalist Papers*

Federalist No. 51 is James Madison's famous justification of the principles of federalism, separation of powers, and checks and balances. It is based on his notion that if people are too ambitious and self-interested to produce good government, then government will have to be adapted to the realities of human nature. A mechanism must be created by which the product of government will be good, even if the nature of the human beings participating in it cannot be counted on to be so. The solution, according to Madison, is to create a government that prevents one person or one group from obtaining too much power. How does he make human nature, warts and all, work for the public interest in the Constitution? We present Madison's Federalist No. 51, slightly abridged, in order to throw into sharper relief his argument about the constitutional protections of liberty.

In order to lay a due foundation for that separate and distinct exercise of the different powers of government, which to a certain extent is admitted on all hands to be essential to the preservation of liberty, it is evident that each department should have a will of its own; and consequently should be so constituted, that the members of each should have as little agency as possible in the appointment of the members of the others. Were this principle rigorously adhered to, it would require that all the appointments for the supreme executive, legislative, and judiciary magistracies should be drawn from the same fountain of authority, the people, through channels having no communication whatever with one another. Perhaps such a plan of constructing the several departments would be less difficult in practice than it may in contemplation appear. Some difficulties, however, and some additional expense would attend the execution of it. Some deviations, therefore, from the principle must be admitted. In the constitution of the judiciary department in particular, it might be inexpedient to insist rigorously on the principle; first, because peculiar qualifications being essential in the members, the primary consideration ought to be to select that mode of choice which best secures these qualifications; secondly, because the permanent tenure by which the appointments are held in that department, must soon destroy all sense of dependence on the authority conferring them.

It is equally evident that the members of each department should be as little dependent as possible on those of the others, for the emoluments annexed to their offices. Were the executive magistrate, or the judges, not independent of the legislature in this particular, their independence in every other would be merely nominal.

But the great security against a gradual concentration of the several powers in the same department, consists in giving to those who administer each department the necessary constitutional means and personal motives to resist encroachments of the others. The provision for defense must in this, as in all other cases, be made commensurate to the danger of attack. Ambition must be made to counteract ambition. The interest of the man must be connected with the constitutional right of the place. It may be a reflection on human nature, that such devices should be necessary to control the abuses of government. But what is government itself, but the greatest of all reflections on human nature? If men were angels, no government would be necessary. If angels were to govern men, neither external nor internal controls on government would be necessary. In framing a government which is to be administered by men over men, the great difficulty lies in this: You must first enable the government to control the governed; and in the next place, oblige it to control itself. A dependence on the people is, no doubt, the primary control on the government; but experience has taught mankind the necessity of auxiliary precautions.

This policy of supplying, by opposite and rival interests, the defect of better motives, might be traced through the whole system of human affairs, private as well as public. We see it particularly displayed in all the subordinate distributions of power, where the constant aim is to divide and arrange the several offices in such a manner as that each may be a check on the other that the private interest of every individual, may be a sentinel over the public rights. These inventions of prudence cannot be less requisite in the distribution of the supreme powers of the state.

But it is not possible to give each department an equal power of self defense. In republican government, the legislative authority necessarily predominates. The remedy for this inconvenience is to divide the legislative into different branches; and to render them, by different modes of election and different principles of action, as little connected with each other as the nature of their common functions and their common dependence on the society will admit. It may even be necessary to guard against dangerous encroachments by still further precautions. As the weight of the legislative authority requires that it should be thus divided, the weakness of the executive may require, on the other hand, that it should be fortified. An absolute negative on the legislature appears, at first view, to be the natural defense with which the executive magistrate should be armed. But perhaps it would be neither altogether safe nor alone sufficient. On ordinary occasions it might not be exerted with the requisite firmness, and on extraordinary occasions it might be perfidiously abused. May not this defect of an absolute negative be supplied by some qualified connection between this weaker department and the weaker branch of the stronger department, by which the latter may be led to support the constitutional rights of the former, without being too much detached from the rights of its own department?

If the principles on which these observations are founded be just, as I persuade myself they are, and they be applied as a criterion to the several State constitutions, and to the federal Constitution, it will be found that if the latter does not perfectly correspond with them, the former are infinitely less able to bear such a test.

There are, moreover, two considerations particularly applicable to the federal system of America, which place the system in a very interesting point of view.

First. In a single republic, all the power surrendered by the people is submitted to the administration of a single government; and usurpations are guarded against by a division of the government into distinct and separate departments. In the compound republic of America, the power surrendered by the people is first divided between distinct governments, and then the portion allotted to each subdivided among distinct and separate departments. Hence a double security arises to the rights of the people. The different governments will control each other; at the same time that each will be controlled by itself.

Second. It is of great importance in a republic not only to guard the society against the oppression of its rulers, but to guard one part of the society against the injustice of the other part. Different interests necessarily exist in different classes of citizens. If a majority be united by a common interest, the rights of the minority will be insecure. There are but two methods of providing against this evil: The one by creating a will in the community independent of the majority that is, of the society itself; the other, by comprehending in the society so many separate descriptions of citizens as will render an unjust combination of a majority of the whole very improbable, if not impracticable. The first method prevails in all governments possessing an hereditary or self-appointed authority. This, at best, is but a precarious security; because a power independent of the society may as well espouse the unjust views of the major, as the rightful interests of the minor party, and may possibly be turned against both parties. The second method will be exemplified in the federal republic of the United States. While all authority in it will be derived from and dependent on the society, the society itself will be broken into so many parts, interests, and classes of citizens, that the rights of individuals, or of the minority, will be in little danger from interested combinations of the majority.... In the extended republic of the United States, and among the great variety of interests, parties, and sects which it embraces, a coalition of a majority of the whole society could seldom take place on any other principles than those of justice and the general good; whilst there being thus less danger to a minor from the will of the major party, there must be less pretext, also, to provide for the security of the former, by introducing into the government a will not dependent on the latter, or, in other words, a will independent of the society itself. It is no less certain than it is important, notwithstanding the contrary opinions which have been entertained, that the larger the society, provided it lie within a practicable sphere, the more duly capable it will be of self-government. And happily for the *republican cause*, the practicable sphere may be carried to a very great extent, by a judicious modification and mixture of the *federal principle.*

Consider the source and the audience: This piece was originally published in a New York newspaper in 1788, at a time when New Yorkers were debating whether to ratify the new Constitution. What was its political purpose? Who was Madison arguing against?

Lay out the argument and the underlying values and assumptions: What two ways did Madison think the Constitution would undertake to preserve liberty? What assumptions did he make about the purpose of government?

Uncover the evidence: What sort of evidence did Madison rely on to make his case? Was any other evidence available to him at that time?

Evaluate the conclusion: Was Madison right about the best way to preserve liberty in a republic? How would the other authors we've read in this chapter answer this question?

Sort out the political implications: What will the political process be like in a political system that is divided between national and state levels, and at each level among executive, legislative, and judicial branches? Will policymaking be quick and efficient, gradual and judicious, or slow and sluggish? Why? How much power do everyday citizens end up having in such a system? Why didn't Madison give us more power?

Review

The Three Branches of Government

The Constitution is the rule book of American politics. The great decisions and compromises of the founding were really about the allocation of power among the branches of the government, between the national and state governments, and between government and citizens.

Congress is given broad lawmaking responsibilities in the Constitution. It is composed of two houses, the House of Representatives and the Senate, each with different qualifications, terms of office, and constituencies. Having two houses of the legislature that are constitutionally separated from the president means that more interests are involved in policymaking and that it takes longer to get things done in the United States than under a parliamentary system.

The president is elected indirectly by the Electoral College. Compared to the chief executive of parliamentary systems, the U.S. president has less power.

The Supreme Court today has much greater powers than those named in the Constitution. This expansion derives from the adoption of the principle of judicial review, which gives the Court much more power than its counterparts in most other democracies and also acts as a check on the powers of the president, Congress, and the states.

legislature (p. 92)	executive (p. 94)	judicial power (p. 97)
bicameral legislature (p. 92)	Electoral College (p. 95)	judicial review (p. 97)
republic (p. 93)	presidential system (p. 96)	legislative supremacy (p. 98)
unicameral legislature (p. 93)	parliamentary system (p. 96)	

Separation of Powers and Checks and Balances

The scheme of checks and balances prevents any branch from overextending its own power. It grew out of the founders' fears of placing too much trust in any single source. The system provides a great deal of protection from abuses of power, but it also makes it difficult to get things done.

separation of powers (p. 98)	checks and balances (p. 99)	fusion of powers (p. 102)

Federalism

The Constitution is ambiguous in defining federalism, giving "reserved powers" to the states but providing a "necessary and proper clause" that has allowed tremendous growth of national powers. Our understanding of federalism in the United States has evolved from a belief in dual federalism, with distinct policy responsibilities for the national and state governments, to the more realistic cooperative federalism, in which the different levels share responsibility in most domestic policy areas.

Alternatives to our federal arrangement are unitary systems, which give all effective power to the central government, and confederal systems, in which the individual states (or other subunits) have primary power. The balance of power adopted between central and subnational governments directly affects the national government's ability to act on large policy problems and the subnational units' flexibility in responding to local preferences.

Federalism creates competition among the states, connects citizens with government, and offers flexibility in governing at the local level. The growth of national power can be traced to the early decisions of Chief Justice John Marshall, the constitutional consequences of the Civil War, the establishment of national supremacy in economics with the New Deal, and new national responsibilities in protecting citizens' rights that are associated with the civil rights movement.

Devolution has required new, and sometimes difficult, agreements between state governments and their citizens. For the most part, state institutions (legislature, courts, governor) have become stronger and more efficient in the process.

enumerated powers of Congress (p. 103)	cooperative federalism (p. 104)	nullification (p. 109)
necessary and proper clause (p. 103)	unitary system (p. 104)	devolution (p. 110)
supremacy clause (p. 103)	confederal system (p. 105)	categorical grant (p. 111)
concurrent powers (p. 104)	*McCulloch v. Maryland* (p. 108)	block grant (p. 111)
dual federalism (p. 104)	*Gibbons v. Ogden* (p. 109)	unfunded mandate (p. 114)

Amending the Constitution

The founders sought to ensure the long-term stability of their new nation, and so they created a Constitution that could be adapted over time to meet new needs and new realities but that could not change too quickly or erratically. Two basic avenues exist for changing the Constitution. The first is the amendment process, which is the formal and intentionally difficult process for changing the rules as outlined in the Constitution itself. The second is a less formal process of judicial interpretation, which arises from the vague language of the Constitution and the evolving role of the courts.

amendability (p. 117)

The Citizens and the Constitution

The Constitution does not create a democratic society in which the people make laws directly. In a republic, the role of national lawmaking is left to representatives elected by the people to act on their behalf. However, citizens do have many opportunities to shape laws in substantial ways at the state and local levels.

initiative (p. 121)   referendum (p. 121)   recall elections (p. 121)

In Your Own Words

After you've read this chapter, you will be able to

5.1 Define rights and liberties and their role in a democratic society.

5.2 Explain how the Bill of Rights relates to the federal government and to the states.

5.3 Describe how the First Amendment protects both church and state, as well as individuals' religious freedom.

5.4 Explain the value of freedom of expression and how its protections have been tested.

5.5 Give examples of different interpretations of the Second Amendment's meaning.

5.6 Describe the protections afforded criminal defendants under the Constitution.

5.7 Discuss the extent of an individual's right to privacy.

5.8 Compare the idea of civil rights with that of civil obligations.

5
FUNDAMENTAL AMERICAN LIBERTIES

What's at Stake . . . in Regulating the Internet?

NET NEUTRALITY. It's the kind of free expression issue the founders never dreamed of.

Even the founders of the Internet had no idea what they were starting. The early days of the Internet were the wild, wild West—the frontier of information technology. People communicated freely, individuals wrote their own rules, and freewheeling entrepreneurs could take off on exciting adventures, make their fortunes, and create empires. (Hello, Jeff Bezos and Mark Zuckerberg, we are looking at you!) There was no lawman in town, mostly because there were no laws.

In those formative years of anything-goes-online life, it was hard to imagine that one day we would be asked to pay for access to news sites, have to pay sales tax on purchases made online, or be limited by profit-minded Internet providers in where we could go and how fast we could get there. The world was our electronic oyster.

That was then.

Today the Internet isn't just a quirky place where academics or gamers or other nerdy types hang out. It is a virtual public square that an increasing number of us visit daily, hourly, or constantly, a line of communication on which most of us depend to mediate our social ties, our business lives, our creative work, our faith, and our entertainment. Of course we expect to pay for an Internet provider, but having our online access limited beyond that—to pay different amounts to access sites depending on whether the sites have economic or political clout—seems at once outrageous and fundamentally unfair, as if we were being asked to pay for access to the air we breathe or the ground we walk on.

And that is the issue at the heart of **net neutrality**: the idea that Internet providers should provide the same access to all sites, regardless of content or source. Providers should not favor or promote some sites over others, or offer them at a premium speed, and no sites should be discriminated against by a provider's tax or penalty. In other words, the government should regulate Internet providers so that they provide users equal access to all sites.

Many groups, from the libertarian right to the progressive left, have been in favor of net neutrality. Then-candidate Barack Obama endorsed the idea in 2007, and under his administration the Federal Communications Commission (FCC) adopted a net neutrality policy in 2010.

Obama claimed that net neutrality was necessary for "lowering the cost of a new idea, igniting new political movements, and bringing communities closer together."[1] Other supporters said it was about freedom of expression (one Democratic commissioner said that the rule was "no more a plan to regulate the Internet 'than the First Amendment is a plan to regulate free speech'").[2]

The FCC ruling was challenged by Verizon Communications in court, where the FCC order was overturned in 2014. In response to a citizens' petition on the White House's "We the People" site, signed by 105,572 people, the FCC classified Internet providers as "common carriers," which allowed them to be regulated as public utilities under the 1934 Communications Law designed to deal with the new media of radio and television. During a required public comment period, almost four million Americans chimed in on the subject, an FCC record. On February 26, 2015, the FCC voted in favor of the principle that all Internet traffic should be treated the same.[3]

Not surprisingly, the vote was immediately controversial. In April 2016, the House of Representatives passed a bill along party lines that banned the FCC from reviewing the rates that Internet service providers charge, an effort to blunt the effect of the FCC rule change. Although it had no chance of becoming law (even if it got through the Senate, the president would have vetoed it), it was seen as a victory by Republicans who had been trying to strike down net neutrality.[4] A Republican commissioner on the FCC who voted against the new rule said that it would lead to a "monumental shift" toward "government control of the Internet." He argued that rates would go up, service would slow as more users accessed the system for free, and it would open the doors to "billions of dollars in new taxes."[5] A Republican House member who voted for the congressional legislation said, "The last thing we want to throw on there is the cold water of Washington bureaucracy, after the fact regulation, that will stifle competition and innovation."[6]

And then, when Donald Trump became president in 2017, he appointed Republicans to the FCC who overturned the Obama-era policy, allowing Internet service providers to charge what they wanted. Within months, Democratic-backed legislation to overturn the FCC regulations had passed in the Senate with some Republican support. It had no hope of passing in the House, however, and President Trump would have almost certainly vetoed it anyway. Democrats hoped to leverage their position, popular with the public, into electoral advantage in November 2018.[7]

Polls showed that 83 percent of the public favored the Obama-era net neutrality, including a large majority of Republicans.[8] Given our constitutional guarantees of free speech and free press in this country, not to mention the right of the people to assemble, which is the kind of engagement that could easily be promoted, or stifled, on the Internet, it's hard to see where the force of the objections come from. Why the controversy about a principle that on its face just makes the Internet a more fair and open channel of communication? We'll take a closer look at this issue after we explore the political battles Americans have fought to secure all of their freedoms. «

> **net neutrality** the idea that Internet providers should provide access to all websites without preference or prejudice

"GIVE me liberty," declared patriot Patrick Henry at the start of the Revolutionary War, "or give me death." "Live Free or Die," proudly proclaims the message on the New Hampshire license plate. Americans have always put a lot of stock in their freedom. Certain that they live in the least restrictive country in the world, Americans celebrate their freedoms and are proud of the Constitution, the laws, and the traditions that preserve them.

And yet, living collectively under a government means that we aren't free to do whatever we want. Limits on our freedoms allow us to live peacefully with others, minimizing the conflict that would result if we all did exactly what we pleased. John Locke said that liberty does not equal license; that is, the freedom to do some things doesn't mean the freedom to do everything. Deciding what rights we give up to join civilized society, and what rights we retain, is one of the great challenges of democratic government.

What are these things called "rights" or "liberties," so precious that some Americans are willing to lay down their lives to preserve them? On the one hand, the answer is very simple. Rights and liberties are synonyms; they mean freedoms or privileges to which one has a claim. In that respect, we use the words more or less interchangeably. But when prefaced by the word *civil*, both *rights* and *liberties* take on more specific meanings and no longer mean quite the same thing.

Our civil liberties are individual freedoms that place limitations on the power of government. In general, civil liberties protect our right to think and act without government interference. Some of these rights are spelled out in the Constitution, particularly in the Bill of Rights. These include the rights to express ourselves and to choose our own religious beliefs. Others, like the right to privacy, rest on the shakier ground of judicial decision making. Although government is prevented from limiting these freedoms per se, they are often limited anyway, even if only by another citizen's rights.

Whereas civil liberties refer to restrictions on government action, civil rights refer to the extension of government action to secure citizenship rights to all members of society. When we speak of civil rights, we most often mean that the government must treat all citizens equally, apply laws fairly, and not discriminate unjustly against certain groups of people. Most of the rights we consider civil rights are guaranteed by the Thirteenth, Fourteenth, Fifteenth, Nineteenth, and Twenty-sixth Amendments. These amendments lay out fundamental rights of citizenship, most notably the right to vote.

> **civil liberties** individual freedoms guaranteed to the people primarily by the Bill of Rights
>
> **civil rights** citizenship rights guaranteed to the people (primarily in the Thirteenth, Fourteenth, Fifteenth, Nineteenth, and Twenty-sixth Amendments) and protected by the government

but also the right to equal treatment before the law and the right to due process of law. They forbid government from making laws that treat people differently on the basis of race, and they ensure that the right to vote cannot be denied on the basis of race or gender.

Not all people live under governments whose rules guarantee them fundamental liberties. We argued in Chapter 1 that one way of distinguishing between authoritarian and nonauthoritarian governments is that nonauthoritarian governments, including democracies, give citizens the power to challenge government if they believe it has denied them their basic rights. In fact, democracies depend on the existence of rights in at least two ways. First, civil liberties provide rules that keep government limited, so that it cannot become too powerful. Second, civil rights help define who "we, the people" are in a democracy, and they give those people the power necessary to put some controls on their governments.

We take two chapters to explore the issues of civil liberties and civil rights in depth. In this chapter we begin with a general discussion of the meaning of rights or liberties in a democracy, and then focus on the traditional civil liberties that provide a check on the power of government. In Chapter 6 we focus on civil rights and the continuing struggle of some groups of Americans—like women, African Americans, and other minorities—to be fully counted and empowered in American politics.

RIGHTS IN A DEMOCRACY

Limiting government to empower people

The freedoms we consider indispensable to the working of a democracy are part of the everyday language of politics in America. We take many of them for granted: we speak confidently of our freedoms of speech, of the press, of religion, and of our rights to bear arms, to a fair trial, and to privacy. There is nothing inevitable about these freedoms, however.

In fact there is nothing inevitable about the idea of rights at all. Until the writing of Enlightenment figures such as John Locke, it was rare for individuals to talk about claiming rights against government. The prevailing narrative was that governments had all the power, giving their subjects only such privileges as they were willing to bestow. Locke argued that the rights to life, liberty, and the pursuit of property were conferred on individuals by nature, and that one of the primary purposes of government was to preserve the natural rights of its citizens. This notion of natural rights and limited government was central to the founders of the American system.

Practically speaking, of course, any government can make its citizens do anything it wishes, regardless of their rights, as long as it is in charge of the military and the police. But in nonauthoritarian governments like the United States, public opinion is usually outraged at the invasion of individual rights. Unless the government is willing to dispense with its reputation as a democracy, it must respond in some way to pacify public opinion. Public opinion and the narrative of natural rights can be a powerful guardian of citizens' liberties in a democracy.

RIGHTS AND THE POWER OF THE PEOPLE

Just as rights limit government, they also empower its citizens. To claim a right is to embrace a powerful narrative—power over a government that wants to collect data on its citizens for security purposes; power over a school board that wants children to say a Christian prayer in school, regardless of their religious affiliation; power over a state legal system that wants to charge suspects with a crime without guaranteeing that a lawyer can be present; power over a state legislature that says residents can't vote because of the color of their skin or because they were born female.

A person who can successfully claim that he or she has rights that must be respected by government is a citizen of that government; a person who is under the authority of a government but cannot claim rights is merely a subject, bound by the laws but without any power to challenge or change them. This does not mean, as we will see, that a citizen can always have things his or her own way. Nor does it mean that noncitizens have no rights in a democracy. It does mean, however, that citizens have special protections and powers that allow them to stand up to government and plead their cases when they believe an injustice is being done.

WHEN RIGHTS CONFLICT

Because rights represent power, they are, like all other forms of power, subject to conflict and controversy. Often for one person to get his or her own way, someone else must lose out.

There are two major rights conflicts that concern citizens in a democracy. Because power to claim a right is one of the scarce resources people wrestle to win in politics, there will be winners and losers in those conflicts. The first type of rights conflict occurs between individuals. One person's right to share a prayer with classmates at the start of the school day conflicts with another student's right not to be subjected to a religious practice against his or her will. Our right as citizens to know about the individuals we elect to office might conflict with a given candidate's right to privacy. The second way rights conflict is when the rights of individuals are pitted against the needs of society and the demands of collective living. The decision to wear a motorcycle helmet or a seat belt, for instance, might seem like one that should be left up to

individuals. But society also has an interest in regulating these behaviors because jeopardizing one's safety is costly to society in terms of the loss of talent or social contributions the individual might have made, the wasted public investment in education and training, and the cost of medical care.

One of the most important aspects of claiming and defending a right against the claims of others is building and perpetuating a narrative that the right you claim exists and that you deserve to have it. Many disputed rights claims are really battles between competing narratives: gun ownership is a sacred right protected by the Constitution versus gun ownership is a conditional privilege that the Constitution allows to be regulated; a woman has a right to make her personal health decisions without government interference versus the government must protect the lives of unborn (or even unconceived) children; religious freedom means we can do whatever our deeply held beliefs dictate versus others have rights that our public behavior has to respect regardless of our beliefs. Telling a compelling story and using all the available media to reinforce it is central to winning disputes over rights.

WHEN RIGHTS CONFLICT—
THE CASE OF NATIONAL SECURITY

One clear example of how individual rights can conflict with the needs of society is the case of national security. After the terrorist attacks of September 11, 2001, Americans were deeply afraid. Determined to prevent a repeat of the horrific attacks, the government federalized airport security and began screening passengers, searching luggage, and allowing armed agents on airplanes. Officials scrutinized the backgrounds of tourists and students from the Middle East and kept a close eye on Arab Americans they suspected of having ties to terrorist organizations.

In October 2001, Congress passed and President George W. Bush signed the USA Patriot Act, which, among other things, made it easier for law enforcement to intercept email and conduct roving wiretaps, gave it access to library records and bookstore purchases, and allowed immigrants suspected of terrorist activity to be held for up to seven days (and sometimes indefinitely) without being charged. The Bush administration, fearful that the evidence required in a U.S. court of law might not be forthcoming to convict a suspected terrorist, issued an executive order that non-U.S. citizens arrested on grounds of terrorism could be subject to trial in a military tribunal, where usual rules of due process need not apply. The National Security Agency (NSA) began to collect enormous amounts of data from the phone and electronic communications of both foreign and domestic individuals.

All these measures may have increased the security of U.S. citizens, but they also reduced their civil liberties. In times of perceived threat, such a trade-off strikes most Americans as worthwhile; we are susceptible to calls for locking down our liberties if we believe that doing so can help lock out threats. Somehow a reduction in freedom does not seem like an unreasonable price to pay for a reduction in fear.

But not all Americans endorse the sacrifice of their rights in favor of a potentially safer society. Immediately after the Patriot Act was passed, organizations such as the American Civil Liberties Union (ACLU) criticized the legislation for infringing on Americans' privacy, violating due process, and being discriminatory. Although their efforts failed, some members of Congress tried to repeal sections of the act. Even support among the public began to wane as the events of September 11 became more distant. Nonetheless, Congress voted to reauthorize the 2001 Patriot Act under Presidents Bush and Obama, although the NSA's ability to collect phone data has been limited following the whistleblower revelations of Edward Snowden, who revealed the scope of the practice in 2013.

> **In the delicate balance between security and freedom, on which side should we err?**

Americans are more willing to tolerate the reduction in liberties when they come at the expense of non-U.S. citizens. After 9/11, those accused of terrorism or of being enemy combatants were tortured by the U.S. government, imprisoned in ways that violate the Geneva Conventions on the treatment of prisoners of war, and denied the rights of due process that Americans accused of crimes are guaranteed. Although the Obama administration stopped the practice of waterboarding and large numbers of Americans object to torture, support for providing terrorists with trials in civilian courts is far less widespread. It is notable that, when terror events take place overseas, significant portions of the public want to put limits on the ability of Muslims to enter the country, something that several candidates running for the Republican presidential nomination in 2016 supported, including the one who eventually won the presidency.

The balancing of public safety with individuals' rights is complex. We could ensure our safety from most threats, perhaps, if we were willing to give up all our freedom. With complete control over our movements, with the ability to monitor all our communications, and with information on all our spending decisions, government could keep itself informed

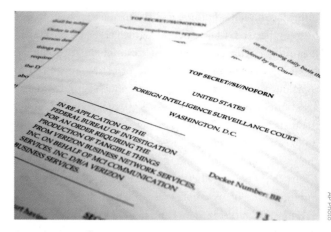

Security or Liberty?

The United States Foreign Intelligence Surveillance Court was created in the 1970s to authorize warrants from agencies like the FBI or the National Security Agency to investigate suspected foreign spies inside the United States. In 2013 it was revealed that the court had authorized the collection of metadata on millions of Americans' phone records, raising a question of what, exactly, is protected by the Fourth Amendment's prohibition of unreasonable searches and seizures.

about which of us was likely to endanger others. The ultimate problem, of course, is that without our civil liberties, we have no protection from government itself.

HOW DO WE RESOLVE CONFLICTS ABOUT RIGHTS?

Much of the conflict over rights in this country is between competing visions of what is fair. Because so much is at stake, the resulting battles are often politics at its messiest. Adding to the general political untidiness is the fact that so many actors get involved in the process: the courts, Congress, the president, and the people themselves. Although we focus on these actors in depth later in this book, we now look briefly at the role each one plays in resolving conflicts over rights.

THE COURTS One of the jobs of the judiciary system is to arbitrate disputes among individuals about such things as rights. Even though we typically think of the Supreme Court as the ultimate judge of what is fair in the United States, the truth is that its rulings have varied as the membership of the Court has changed. There is no guarantee that the Court will reach some unarguably "correct" answer to a legal dilemma; as we will see in Chapter 10, the justices are human beings influenced by their own values, ideals, and biases in interpreting and applying the laws. In addition, although the founders had hoped that the Supreme Court justices would be above the political fray, they are in fact subject to all sorts of political pressures, from the ideology of the presidents who appoint them to the steady influence of public opinion and the media. At times in our history the Court has championed what seem like underdog interests that fight the mainstream of American public opinion—for example, ruling in favor of those who refuse to salute the American flag on religious grounds.[9] It has also tempered some of the post-9/11 legislation by ruling, for instance, that U.S. citizens held as enemy combatants do have some due process rights.[10] The Court also rejected the Bush administration's argument that the Supreme Court had no jurisdiction over military tribunals for foreign-born enemy combatants, holding that such tribunals must be authorized by Congress, not executive order.[11] At other times the Supreme Court has been less expansionary in its interpretation of civil liberties, and its rulings have favored the interests of big business over the rights of ordinary Americans, blocked the rights of racial minorities, and even put the stamp of constitutional approval on the World War II incarceration of Japanese Americans in internment camps,[12] an action for which we, as a nation, have since apologized.

CONGRESS Another actor involved in the resolution of conflicts over rights in this country is Congress. Sometimes Congress has chosen to stay out of disputes about rights. At other times it has taken decisive action either to limit or to expand the rights of many Americans. For example, the Smith Act, passed by Congress in 1940, made it illegal to advocate the overthrow of the U.S. government by force or to join any organization that advocated government subversion. A decade later, in the name of national security, the House Un-American Activities Committee investigated and ruined the reputations of many Americans suspected of having sympathy for the Communist Party, sometimes on the flimsiest of evidence.[13] But Congress has also acted on the side of protecting rights. When the courts became more conservative in the 1980s and 1990s, with appointments made by Republican presidents Ronald Reagan and George H. W. Bush, for example, the judiciary narrowed its protections of civil rights issues. The Democratic-led Congress of the time countered with the Civil Rights Act of 1991, which broadened civil rights protection in the workplace. Similarly, Congress held hearings in 2010 on "don't ask, don't tell," a policy that prevented gay men and lesbians from serving openly in the military, and the policy was repealed in December of that year.

THE PRESIDENT Presidents as well can be involved in resolving disputes over rights. They can get involved by having administration officials lobby the Supreme Court to encourage outcomes they favor. Popular presidents can also try to persuade Congress to go along with their policy initiatives by bringing public pressure to bear. Their influence can be used to expand or contract the protection of individual rights. In the 1950s, President Dwight Eisenhower was reluctant to enforce desegregation in the South, believing that it was the job of the states, not the federal government.[14] President John F. Kennedy chose more active involvement when he sent Congress a civil rights bill in 1963 (it was signed by Lyndon Johnson in 1964). More recently, President Obama moved to close the detention center at Guantánamo Bay that had been at the heart of so much controversy, but Congress blocked the funds for the transfer of detainees to mainland prisons, leaving the center open, and Obama turned his attention to making some improvements in the prisoners' lives, including the banning of brutal interrogations.

THE PEOPLE Finally, the American people themselves are actors in the struggle over rights. Individual Americans may use the courts to sue for what they perceive as their rights, but more often individuals act in groups. One of the best known of these groups is the ACLU. The ACLU's goal is to defend the liberties of Americans, whatever their ideological position. Thus the ACLU would be just as likely to fight for the right of the American Nazi Party to stage a march as it would be to support a group of parents and students challenging the removal of books with gay themes from a high school library, and in fact it has been critical of both the Bush and Obama administrations for their support of wiretapping and surveillance of individuals.[15] Other interest groups that get involved in the effort to resolve rights conflicts include the National Association for the Advancement of Colored People (NAACP), the National Organization for Women (NOW), the Christian Coalition, Common Cause, environmental groups like the Sierra Club, AARP (formerly the American Association of Retired Persons), and the National Rifle Association (NRA). These groups and many others like them engage in fundraising and public relations activities to publicize their views and work to influence government directly, by meeting with lawmakers and testifying at congressional hearings. Even though individuals may not feel very effective in trying to change what government does, their efforts are magnified in groups, and the effects can be considerable.

PAUSE AND REVIEW Who, What, How

Citizens of democracies have a vital stake in the issue of fundamental rights. What they stand to gain is more power for themselves and less for government. But citizens also have at stake the resolution of the very real conflicts that arise as all citizens try to exercise their rights simultaneously. And as citizens try to maximize their personal freedoms, they are likely to clash with government rules that suppress some individual freedom in exchange for public order.

The means for resolving these conflicts are to be found in the Constitution, in the exercise of judicial review by the Supreme Court, in congressional legislation and presidential persuasion, and in the actions of citizens themselves, engaging in interest group activities and litigation.

In Your Own Words Define rights and liberties and their role in a democratic society.

THE BILL OF RIGHTS AND INCORPORATION

Keeping Congress and the state governments in check

The Bill of Rights looms large in any discussion of American civil liberties, but the document that today seems so inseparable from American citizenship had a stormy birth. Controversy raged over whether a bill of rights was necessary in the first place, deepening the split between Federalists and Anti-Federalists during the founding. And the controversy did not end once it was firmly established as the first ten amendments to the Constitution. Over a century passed before the Supreme Court agreed that at least some of the restrictions imposed on the national government by the Bill of Rights should be applied to the states as well.

WHY IS A BILL OF RIGHTS VALUABLE?

Recall from Chapter 3 that we came very close to not having any Bill of Rights in the Constitution at all. The Federalists had argued that the Constitution itself was a bill of rights, that individual rights were already protected by many of the state constitutions, and that to list the powers that the national government did not have was dangerous, because doing so implied that the government had every other power. Alexander Hamilton had spelled out this argument in *Federalist* No. 84 (see the *CLUES to Critical Thinking* feature at the end of this chapter), and James Madison agreed, at least initially, calling the effort to pass such "parchment barriers," as he called the first ten amendments, a "nauseous project."[16]

But Madison, in company with some of the other Federalists, came to agree with such Anti-Federalists as Thomas Jefferson, who wrote, "A bill of rights is what the people are entitled to against every government on earth."[17] Even though, as the Federalists argued, the national government was limited in principle by popular sovereignty (the concept that ultimate authority rests with the people), it could not hurt to limit it in practice as well. A specific list of the rights held by the people would give the judiciary a more effective check on the other branches.

To some extent, Hamilton was correct in calling the Constitution a bill of rights in itself. Protection of some very specific rights is contained in the text of the document. The national government may not suspend writs of **habeas corpus**, which means that it cannot fail to bring prisoners, at their request, before a judge and inform them why they are being held and what evidence exists against them. This provision protects people from being imprisoned solely for political reasons. Both the national and state governments are forbidden to pass **bills of attainder**, which are laws that single out a person or group as guilty and impose punishment without trial. Neither can they pass **ex post facto laws**, which are laws that make an action a crime after the fact, even though it was legal when carried out. States may not impair or negate the obligation of contracts; here the founders obviously had in mind the failings of the Articles of Confederation. And the citizens of each state are entitled to "the privileges and immunities of the several states," which prevents any state from discriminating against citizens of other states. This provision protects a nonresident's right to travel freely, conduct business, and have access to state courts while visiting another state.[18] Of course, nonresidents are discriminated against when they have to pay a higher nonresident tuition to attend a state college or university, but the Supreme Court has ruled that this type of "discrimination" is not a violation of the privileges and immunities clause.

For the Anti-Federalists, these rights, almost all of them restrictions on the national and state governments with respect to criminal laws, did not provide enough security against potential abuse of government power. The first ten amendments add several more categories of restrictions on government. Although twelve amendments had been proposed, two were not ratified: one concerned the apportionment of members of Congress, and the other barred midterm pay raises for them. (The congressional pay raise

habeas corpus the right of an accused person to be brought before a judge and informed of the charges and evidence against him or her

bills of attainder laws under which specific persons or groups are detained and sentenced without trial

ex post facto laws laws that criminalize an action after it occurs

Americans like to think that the founders were so concerned with our personal freedoms that they created a bedrock of liberty for us to stand on. But, of course, the Bill of Rights is a political document, and the founders weren't motivated so much by concern for us as by fear of a powerful national government that might use the coercive power of the state for its own ends. Notice that not one of our liberties—even the right to life—is absolute.

1ST FREEDOMS OF PRESS, RELIGION, ASSEMBLY & PETITION

YOU CAN go to a church of your own choosing, observe your religious traditions, express your opinions, publish them as you wish, get together with like-minded people, and convey your collective sentiment to the government.

BUT YOU CAN'T...

practice religion in conflict with the law or in the public sphere with public support, taunt people to pick fights with them, threaten national security, or maliciously ruin a reputation.

2ND RIGHT TO BEAR ARMS

YOU CAN own a gun, just in case the government should find itself in the need of a well-trained militia.

BUT YOU CAN'T...

own a gun without background checks or registration (in some places). Can't just shoot at random, either. Murder and mayhem are still against the law.

3RD QUARTERING OF SOLDIERS

YOU CAN be free from the government forcing you to let soldiers stay in your house without permission.

BUT YOU CAN'T...

get off so easily if your relatives overstay their welcome. ☺

4TH ARRESTS AND SEARCHES

YOU CAN be protected from unreasonable searches and seizures by the police.

BUT YOU CAN'T...

be protected from all searches. Generally, police need a warrant to search your stuff, including using your cell phone to track your movements. But be 'darned careful what you carry in your car or say on or text from your phone.

5TH RIGHTS OF PERSONS ACCUSED OF CRIMES

YOU CAN be safe from arrest, imprisonment, self-incrimination, having your stuff confiscated, and being put to death without due process of law.

BUT YOU CAN'T...

take back a confession given before you were read your Miranda rights. The cat's out of the bag and the confession usually counts.

Turn to the appendix, p. A-14, for the full text of the Constitution's first ten amendments.

GOVERNMENT
WITNESSES
IMPARTIAL PROCESS
SPEEDY CRIMINAL
LAW
ACCUSATION
CONFRONTED DEFENSE

6TH RIGHTS OF PERSONS ON TRIAL FOR CRIMES

YOU CAN expect a speedy trial, to be told what you are accused of, and to have a lawyer to help you sort it all out.

BUT YOU CAN'T...

assume a "speedy trial" won't take years, or that your overworked public defense lawyer won't be something less than crackerjack.

RE-EXAMINED
COMMON
SUITS COURT
LAW TRIAL
ASSEMBLE
STATES JURY

7TH JURY TRIALS IN CIVIL CASES

YOU CAN have a trial by jury.

BUT YOU CAN'T...

avoid jury duty forever. It's an obligation implied by the right to a jury trial.

PUNISHMENT
EXCESSIVE
UNUSUAL FINES
CRUEL INFRINGED
INFLICTED
SECURITY BAIL

8TH AVOID CRUEL AND UNUSUAL PUNISHMENT

YOU CAN hope you never have to ponder what "cruel" and "unusual" mean. Even SCOTUS isn't entirely sure.

BUT YOU CAN'T...

avoid punishments if you've earned them. So don't push your luck.

ENUMERATION
RIGHTS
OTHERS RETAINED
DENY CERTAIN
DISPARAGE
CONSTITUTION
PEOPLE

9TH RIGHTS KEPT BY THE PEOPLE

YOU CAN have more rights than just the ones listed here (this is what Hamilton was talking about in *Federalist* 78).

BUT YOU CAN'T...

rely on that completely. Some Supreme Court justices think you have only the rights listed here and no more.

STATES
CONSTITUTION
PEOPLE PROHIBITED
UNITED
RESERVED
SECURITY POWERS

10TH POWERS KEPT BY THE STATES OR THE PEOPLE

YOU CAN, if you're a state, get all powers not needed by Congress to carry out its duties (see Article 1, Section 8).

BUT YOU CAN'T...

avoid being subject to 50 sets of state laws, which means that joint you packed in Colorado could get you arrested when you're back in Indiana.

amendment, which prevents members of Congress from voting themselves a salary increase effective during that term of office, was passed as the Twenty-seventh Amendment in 1992.) Amendments One through Ten were ratified on December 15, 1791. See *The Big Picture* for details on the provisions of the Bill of Rights.

APPLYING THE BILL OF RIGHTS TO THE STATES

Most of the limitations on government action are directed toward Congress. Nothing in the text of the first ten amendments would prevent the legislatures of Oregon or Georgia or Texas, for instance, from passing a law restricting the freedoms of local newspaper editors to criticize the government. Until about the turn of the twentieth century, the Supreme Court clearly stipulated that the Bill of Rights applied only to the national government and not to the states.[19]

Not until the passage of the Fourteenth Amendment in 1868 did the Supreme Court have a tool that made it possible for the Court to require that states protect their citizens' basic liberties. That post–Civil War amendment was designed specifically to force southern states to extend the rights of citizenship to African Americans, but its wording left it open to other interpretations. The amendment says, in part,

No state shall make or enforce any law which shall abridge the privileges and immunities of citizens of the United States; nor shall any state deprive any person of life, liberty, or property, without due process of law; nor deny to any person within its jurisdiction the equal protection of the laws.

TABLE 5.1

Applying the Bill of Rights to the States

AMENDMENT	ADDRESSES	CASE	YEAR
Fifth	Just compensation	*Chicago, Burlington & Quincy v. Chicago*	1897
First	Freedom of speech	*Gilbert v. Minnesota*	1920
	Freedom of the press	*Gitlow v. New York*	1925
		Fiske v. Kansas	1927
		Near v. Minnesota	1931
Sixth	Counsel in capital cases	*Powell v. Alabama*	1932
First	Religious freedom (generally)	*Hamilton v. Regents of California*	1934
	Freedom of assembly	*DeJonge v. Oregon*	1937
	Free exercise	*Cantwell v. Connecticut*	1940
	Religious establishment	*Everson v. Board of Education*	1947
Sixth	Public trial	*In re Oliver*	1948
Fourth	Unreasonable search and seizure	*Wolf v. Colorado*	1949
	Exclusionary rule	*Mapp v. Ohio*	1961
Eighth	Cruel and unusual punishment	*Robinson v. California*	1962
Sixth	Counsel in felony cases	*Gideon v. Wainwright*	1963
Fifth	Self-incrimination	*Malloy v. Hogan*	1964
Sixth	Impartial jury	*Parker v. Gladden*	1966
	Speedy trial	*Klopfer v. North Carolina*	1967
	Jury trial in serious crimes	*Duncan v. Louisiana*	1968
Fifth	Double jeopardy	*Benton v. Maryland*	1969
Second	Right to bear arms	*McDonald v. Chicago*	2010

In 1897 the Supreme Court tentatively began the process of selective nationalization, or **incorporation**, of most (but not all) of the protections of the Bill of Rights into the states' Fourteenth Amendment obligations to guarantee their citizens due process of law. But it was not until the case of *Gitlow v. New York* (1925) that the Court reversed almost a century of ruling by assuming that some rights are so fundamental that they deserve protection by the states as well as the federal government.[20] This was a clear shift of power from the states to the national government to determine what rights states had to protect, a shift that came as it so often does at the hands of the Supreme Court. But it did not at first mean that all rights necessarily qualified for incorporation. The Court had to consider each right on a case-by-case basis to see how fundamental it was. Over the years, almost all the rights in the first ten amendments have been incorporated (see Table 5.1).

Keep in mind that since incorporation is a matter of interpretation rather than an absolute constitutional principle, it is a judicial creation. Like all other judicial creations, the process of incorporation is subject to reversal if the justices change their minds or if the Court's composition changes, and it is possible that such a reversal may currently be under way as today's more conservative Court narrows its understanding of the rights that states must protect.

PAUSE AND REVIEW Who, What, How

Because rights are so central to a democracy, citizens clearly have a stake in seeing that they are guaranteed these rights at every level of government. The Bill of Rights guarantees them at the federal level, but it is through the process of incorporation into the Fourteenth Amendment that they are guaranteed at the state level unless the state constitution also provides guarantees. Incorporation, as a judicial creation, is not on as firm ground as the Bill of Rights because it can be reversed if the Supreme Court changes its mind.

The Supreme Court also has a stake here. It has considerably expanded its power over the states and within the federal government by virtue of its interpretation of the Fourteenth Amendment and its creation of the process of incorporation.

In Your Own Words Explain how the Bill of Rights relates to the federal government and to the states.

---

incorporation Supreme Court action making the protections of the Bill of Rights applicable to the states

FREEDOM OF RELIGION

Limiting Congress to protect both church and state, as well as the individual's right to believe

The First Amendment reads, "Congress shall make no law respecting an establishment of religion, or prohibiting the free exercise thereof; or abridging the freedom of speech, or of the press; or the right of the people peaceably to assemble, and to petition the government for a redress of grievances." These are the "democratic freedoms," the liberties that the founders believed to be so necessary to ensuring the free and unfettered people required by a representative democracy that they crammed them all into the very first of the amendments. For all that, none of these liberties has escaped controversy, and none has been interpreted by the Supreme Court to be absolute or unlimited. Beginning with freedom of religion, we will look at each clause of the First Amendment, the controversy and power struggles surrounding it, and the way the courts have interpreted and applied it.

WHY IS RELIGIOUS FREEDOM VALUABLE?

The briefest look around the world tells us what happens when politics and religion are allowed to mix. When it comes to conflicts over religion, over our fundamental beliefs about the world and the way life should be lived, the stakes are enormous. Passions run deep, and compromise is difficult.

So far the United States has been spared the sort of violent conflict that arises when one group declares its religion to be the one true faith for the whole polity. One reason for this is that Americans are largely Christian, although they belong to many different sects (see *Snapshot of America: What Do We Believe?*), so there hasn't been too much disagreement over basic beliefs. But another reason is the First Amendment, whose first line guarantees that "Congress shall make no law respecting an establishment of religion or prohibiting the free exercise thereof." Although this amendment has generated a tremendous amount of controversy, it has at the same time established general guidelines with which most people can agree and a venue (the courts) where conflicts can be aired and addressed.

Not all the founders endorsed religious freedom for everyone, but some of them, notably Jefferson and Madison, cherished the notion of a universal freedom of conscience, the right of all individuals to believe as they pleased. Jefferson wrote that the First Amendment built "a wall of separation between church and state."[21] They based their view of religious freedom on two main arguments. First, history has shown, from the Holy Roman Empire to the Church of England, that linking church and state can have a negative impact on secular life. It generally puts all individual

Snapshot of America: *What Do We Believe?*

Our Religious Identities

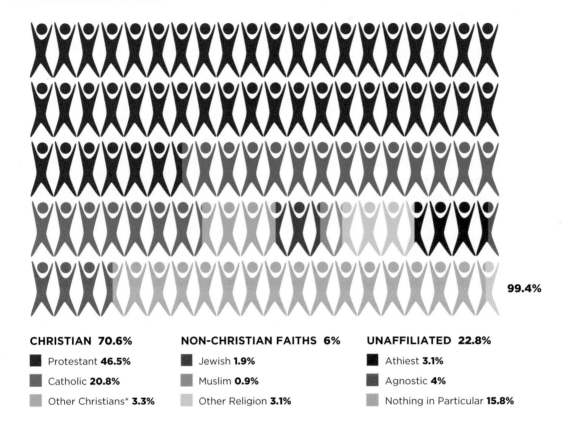

99.4%

CHRISTIAN 70.6%
- ■ Protestant **46.5%**
- ■ Catholic **20.8%**
- ■ Other Christians* **3.3%**

NON-CHRISTIAN FAITHS 6%
- ■ Jewish **1.9%**
- ■ Muslim **0.9%**
- ■ Other Religion **3.1%**

UNAFFILIATED 22.8%
- ■ Athiest **3.1%**
- ■ Agnostic **4%**
- ■ Nothing in Particular **15.8%**

Other Christians includes Mormons, Jehovah's Witnesses, Orthodox Christians, and other Christian religions

How Religious Are We?

26% SOMEWHAT IMPORTANT **53%** VERY IMPORTANT

79% of Americans say that religion is important in their lives.

65% of Americans of all faiths feel that many religions can lead to eternal life.

88% of unaffiliated Americans indicated that they were not looking for a faith that would be right for them.

Behind the Numbers

America has always been a religious nation, and as this infographic shows, it is also an overwhelmingly Christian nation. Americans of Jewish, Muslim, Hindu, and Buddhist faiths, in total, make up less than 10 percent of the population even in diverse cities like New York. Meanwhile, the number of non-religious Americans—those who are not affiliated with any religion—is growing, especially among the youngest Americans. Does the First Amendment provide adequate protection for people of faith? How does it affect those who do not adhere to a specific faith?

Source: Pew Research Center, "America's Changing Religious Landscape," May 12, 2015, www.pewforum.org/2015/05/12/americas-changing-religious-landscape/.

freedoms in jeopardy and reduces the population to subjecthood. After all, if government is merely the arm of God, what power of government cannot be justified? Furthermore, religion divides society into the factions that Madison saw as the primary threat to republican government.

A second argument for religious freedom is based on the effect that politics can have on religious concerns. Early champions of a separation between politics and religion worried that the spiritual purity and sanctity of religion would be ruined if it mixed with the worldly realm of politics, with its emphasis on power and influence.[22] History has given us more than one example of religious organizations becoming corrupt when they have become entwined with secular power. If religion became dependent on government, in Madison's words, it would result in "pride and indolence in the clergy; ignorance and servility in the laity; in both, superstition, bigotry and persecution."[23]

THE ESTABLISHMENT CLAUSE: SEPARATIONISTS VERSUS ACCOMMODATIONISTS

The beginning of the First Amendment, forbidding Congress to make laws that would establish an official religion, is known as the establishment clause. Americans have fought over the meaning of the establishment clause almost since its inception. Although founders like Jefferson and Madison were clear on their position that church and state should be separate realms, other early Americans were not. After independence, for instance, all but two of the former colonies had declared themselves to be "Christian states."[24] Non-Christian minorities were rarely tolerated or allowed to participate in politics. Jews could not hold office in Massachusetts until 1848.[25] It may be that the founders were sometimes less concerned with preserving the religious freedom of others than with guaranteeing their own.

A similar division continues today between the separationists, who believe that a "wall" should exist between church and state, and the nonpreferentialists, or accommodationists, who contend that the state should not be separate from religion but rather should accommodate it, without showing a preference for one religion over another. These accommodationists argue that the First Amendment should not prevent government aid to religious groups, prayer in school or in public ceremonies, public aid to parochial schools, the posting of religious documents such as the Ten Commandments in public places, or the teaching of the Bible's story of creation along with evolution in public schools. Adherents of this position claim that a rigid interpretation of separation of church and state amounts to intolerance of their religious rights or, in the words of Supreme Court Justice Anthony Kennedy, to "unjustified hostility to religion."[26] President Reagan, both Presidents Bush, and many Republicans have shared this view, as have many powerful interest groups.

A lot is clearly at stake in the battle between the separationists and the accommodationists. On one side of the dispute is the separationists' image of a society in which the rights of all citizens, including minorities, receive equal protection by the law. In this society, private religions abound, but they remain private, not matters for public action or support. Very different is the view of the accommodationists, which emphasizes the sharing of community values, determined by the majority and built into the fabric of society and political life.

JUDICIAL RULINGS ON THE ESTABLISHMENT CLAUSE Today U.S. practice stands somewhere between these two views. Sessions of Congress open with prayers, for instance, but a schoolchild's day does not. Although religion is not kept completely out of our public lives, the Court has generally leaned toward a separationist stance.[27] The Court in the 1960s, under the leadership of Chief Justice Earl Warren, was known for its liberal views, even though Warren, himself a Republican, had been appointed to the Court by President Eisenhower. As the more conservative appointments of Republican presidents Richard Nixon and Reagan began to shape the Court, the Court's rulings moved in a more accommodationist direction. In *Lemon v. Kurtzman* (1971), the Court required that a law not foster "an excessive government entanglement with religion."[28] Under the new *Lemon* **test** the justices had to decide how much entanglement there was between politics and religion, leaving much to their own discretion.

As the current rule in deciding establishment cases, the *Lemon* test is not used consistently, primarily because the justices have not settled among themselves the underlying issue of whether religion and politics should be separate, or whether state support of religion is permissible.[29] The justices still lean in a separationist direction, but their rulings occasionally nod at accommodationism.[30]

THE GAP BETWEEN CONSTITUTIONAL LAW AND STATE PRACTICE Clearly, religion is a subject about which people feel strongly; however, and despite the separationist tilt of the Court's rulings, many Americans have found a way to bring their religions into their public lives, even

establishment clause the First Amendment guarantee that the government will not create and support an official state church

separationists supporters of a "wall of separation" between church and state

accommodationists supporters of government nonpreferential accommodation of religion

Lemon test the three-pronged rule used by the courts to determine whether the establishment clause is violated

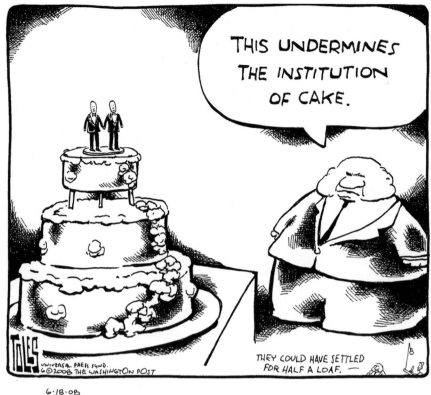

THIS UNDERMINES THE INSTITUTION OF CAKE.

THEY COULD HAVE SETTLED FOR HALF A LOAF. —

UNIVERSAL PRESS SYND. ©2008 THE WASHINGTON POST

6·18·08

into the schoolroom. Some communities simply ignore the law, allowing children to begin the school day with prayer or to gather in religious clubs and associations at school. In addition, many state legislatures are testing the limits by passing laws that blur the lines between secular and nonsecular activities at school. A Florida law, signed in 2012, allows school boards to encourage students to give "inspirational messages" at school events; other states are considering similar bills. Georgia, Texas, Tennessee, and South Carolina passed bills allowing schools to offer Bible classes, but setting no parameters to ensure that the teachers of such courses are qualified or that the courses offered are academic rather than religious in nature. And some states, like Louisiana and Tennessee, have passed legislation that requires teachers to clarify the "strengths and weaknesses" of evolution and other subjects held to be controversial by some members of the religious community.[31] These practices and laws are the new battlefield over religious establishment, and the Court will no doubt be called on to weigh in before long.

THE FREE EXERCISE CLAUSE: WHEN CAN STATES REGULATE RELIGIOUS BEHAVIOR?

Religious freedom is controversial in the United States not just because of the debate between the separationists and the accommodationists. Another question that divides the public and justices alike is what to do when religious beliefs and practices conflict with state goals. The second part of the First

Amendment grant of religious freedom guarantees that Congress shall make no law prohibiting the free exercise of religion. Seemingly straightforward, the **free exercise clause**, as it is called, has generated as much controversy as the establishment clause. For example, what is the solution when a religious belief against killing clashes with compulsory military service during a war, or when religious holy days are ignored by state legislation about the days on which individuals should be expected to work? When is the state justified in regulating religions? The Court decided in 1940 that there is a difference between the freedom to believe and the freedom to act on those beliefs.[32] Americans have an absolute right to believe whatever they want, but their freedom to act is subject to government regulation. The state's **police power** allows it to protect its citizens, providing social order and security. If it needs to regulate behavior, it may. These two valued goods of religious freedom and social order are bound to conflict, and the Court has had an uneasy time trying to draw the line between them. Although it waffled a bit before doing so, the Court has said that schoolchildren cannot be required to salute the American flag if it violates their religious principles to do so (as it does for Jehovah's Witnesses).[33]

The Court has gone back and forth on other religious freedom issues, as well, as it has struggled to define what actions the state might legitimately seek to regulate. For a while the Court held that any incidental burden placed on religious freedom must be justified by a **compelling state interest**; that is, the state must show that it is absolutely necessary for some fundamental state purpose that the religious freedom be limited.[34] How the Court determines what is and what is not a compelling state interest is examined in Chapter 6. The Court rejected this compelling state interest test, however, in *Employment Division, Department of Human Resources v. Smith*

> **free exercise clause** the First Amendment guarantee that citizens may freely engage in the religious activities of their choice
>
> **police power** the ability of the government to protect its citizens and maintain social order
>
> **compelling state interest** a fundamental state purpose, which must be shown before the law can limit some freedoms or treat some groups of people differently

(1990).[35] Under the *Smith* ruling, a number of religious practices have been declared illegal by state laws on the grounds that the laws do not unfairly burden any particular religion.

Religious groups consider the *Smith* ruling a major blow to religious freedom because it places the burden of proof on the individual or church to show that its religious practices should not be punished, rather than on the state to show that the interference with religious practice is absolutely necessary. In response to the *Smith* decision, Congress in 1993 passed the Religious Freedom Restoration Act (RFRA). This act, supported by a coalition of ninety religious groups, restored the compelling state interest test for state action limiting religious practice and required that when the state did restrict religious practice, it be carried out in the least burdensome way. However, in the 1997 case of *City of Boerne v. Flores*, the Court held that the RFRA was an unconstitutional exercise of congressional power.[36] Congress amended the act in 2003 to apply only to the federal government, and the Supreme Court in 2006 affirmed the amended federal RFRA when it ruled that the act protected a New Mexico church's use of tea containing an illegal substance for sacramental purposes, reinstating the compelling state interest test.[37]

Supporters of greater freedom for religious institutions were further heartened in 2012, when the Supreme Court issued a unanimous ruling in *Hosanna-Tabor Evangelical Lutheran Church and School v. Equal Employment Opportunity Commission*, which the *New York Times* called perhaps "its most significant religious liberty decision in two decades."[38] In *Hosanna-Tabor*, the Court held that the hiring practices of religious groups could not be regulated by federal employment law (in this case, law that prohibited discrimination against an employee with a disability), because that would essentially give government the right to tell such groups whom they could hire. Chief Justice John Roberts wrote the unanimous opinion, saying, "The Establishment Clause prevents the government from appointing ministers and the Free Exercise Clause prevents it from interfering with the freedom of religious groups to select their own." Still, the sweeping decision has not stopped critics of the Court's earlier *Boerne* ruling from arguing that to really protect religious freedom, the Constitution should be amended to make RFRA the law of the land.[39]

Concern over religious freedom among church members was renewed after the full implementation of the Patient Protection and Affordable Care Act (ACA) in 2014. The Obama administration interpreted the ACA requirements as meaning that employer-based health insurance should provide birth control coverage, but in 2012 the Supreme Court ruled, in *Burwell v. Hobby Lobby*, that corporations that are not publicly traded (so-called closely held corporations) did not have to provide such coverage if it violated the owners' religious beliefs. This case not only upheld the right of employers not to provide contraception coverage if it conflicted with the employer's religious beliefs, but it also affirmed that right for some kinds of corporations as well as for individuals.

Meanwhile, when the federal law appeared to be in jeopardy, many states passed their own RFRAs to protect religious practices at the state level, and they have been used to protect a variety of controversial practices on religious grounds, including the denial of services and rights to those in the LGBTQ community. Such laws proliferated again in 2015 and 2016 in the wake of the Supreme Court's ruling that constitutionalized marriage equality. States such as Indiana, Mississippi, and North Carolina suffered serious blowback from companies that considered the intent of such laws to be discriminatory and chose to take their business elsewhere. (This topic is covered in more depth in Chapter 6.)

PAUSE AND REVIEW Who, What, How

All citizens have a stake in a society where they are not coerced to practice a religion in which they do not believe, and where they cannot be prevented from practicing the religion in which they do believe. The rules that help them get what they want here are the establishment clause and the free exercise clause of the First Amendment. There is, however, an inherent conflict between those two clauses. If there truly is a wall of separation between church and state, as the separationists want, then restrictions on religious practice are permissible, which is the opposite of what the accommodationists seek. The only solution is to find a level of separation that the separationists can tolerate that is compatible with a level of protection to which accommodationists can agree.

In Your Own Words Describe how the First Amendment protects both church and state, as well as individuals' religious freedom.

FREEDOM OF EXPRESSION

Checking government by protecting speech and the press

Among the most cherished of American values is the right to free speech. The First Amendment reads that "Congress shall make no law . . . abridging the freedoms of speech, or of the press" and, at least theoretically, most Americans agree.[40] When it comes to actually practicing free speech, however, our national record is less impressive. In fact, time and again, Congress has made laws abridging freedom of expression, often with the enthusiastic support of much of the American public. As a nation we have never had a great deal of difficulty restricting speech we don't like, admire, or respect. The challenge of the First Amendment is to protect the speech we despise.

The ongoing controversy surrounding free speech has kept the Supreme Court busy. Against claims that the right to speak freely should be absolute are demands that speech should be limited—perhaps because it threatens national security or unity or certain economic interests; because it is offensive, immoral, or hurtful; because it hinders the judicial process; or because it injures reputations. The Supreme Court has had to navigate a maze of conflicting arguments as it has assessed the constitutionality of a variety of congressional and state laws that do, indeed, abridge the freedom of speech and of the press.

WHY IS FREEDOM OF EXPRESSION VALUABLE?

It is easier to appreciate what is at stake in the battles over when and what kind of speech should be protected if we think about just why we value free speech so much in the first place. Freedom of speech can help to empower citizens and limit government in four ways:

- In a democracy, citizens are responsible for participating in their government's decisions. Democratic theory holds that, to participate wisely, citizens must be informed about what their government is doing. This requires, at the least, a **free press**, able to report fully on government's activities. Otherwise, citizens are easily manipulated by those people in government who control the flow of information. Mediated citizenship gives us many more channels through which to access information, but that also means many more channels to monitor for truth and reliability. The imperative to maintain a free press is more critical than ever in an age in which the president of the United States feels free to label unflattering or critical news coverage "fake news."

- By being free to voice criticism of government, to investigate its actions, and to debate its decisions, both citizens and journalists are able to exercise an additional check on government that supplements our valued principle of checks and balances. This watchdog function of freedom of expression, again, potentially raised to new levels in a hypermediated age, helps keep government accountable and less likely to step on our other rights.

- Allowing free speech in society—even (or especially) speech of which we do not approve—avoids setting a dangerous precedent of censorship. Censorship occurs when a powerful entity—whether a dictator or a group—decides what information can pass through the channels or even what channels are allowed. Censorship in a democracy usually allows the voice of the majority to prevail, although we also see examples of elite minorities developing monopolies on information. One of the reasons to support minority rights as well as majority rule, however, is that we never know when we may fall into the minority on an issue. If we make censorship a legitimate activity of government, we too will be potentially vulnerable to it.

- Political theorist John Stuart Mill argued that the free traffic of all ideas, those known to be true as well as those suspected to be false, is essential in a society that values truth. By allowing the expression of all ideas, we discover truths that we had previously believed to be false, and we develop strong defenses against known falsehoods like racist and sexist ideas. Imagining John Stuart Mill grappling with the possibilities of the wild west of the Internet is a priceless vision.

If free speech is so valuable, why is it so controversial? Like freedom of religion, free speech requires tolerance of ideas and beliefs other than our own, even ideas and beliefs that we find personally repugnant. Those who are convinced that their ideas are absolutely and eternally true see no real reason to practice tolerance, especially if they are in the majority. It is clear to them that language they view as false or objectionable should be silenced to create the sort of society they believe should exist. For them, there is really only one ultimate channel of information that counts. In addition, conflicting ideas about what constitutes the public interest—well-meaning or engineered by a third party—can sometimes lead reasonable people to disagree about whether speech ought to be protected or restricted.[41]

It is the Supreme Court that generally has to balance the claims of those who defend the rights of all speakers and those who think they should be limited. The Court has had to make difficult decisions about how to apply the First Amendment to speech that criticizes government, symbolic speech, obscenity, and other offensive speech, as well as about freedom of the press and censorship on the Internet. How the Court arrived at the very complex and rich interpretation that it generally uses today is a political tale.

> **free press** a press that is able to report fully on government's activities

SPEECH THAT CRITICIZES THE GOVERNMENT

Speech that criticizes the government to promote rebellion, called sedition, has long been a target of restrictive legislation, and most of the founders were quite content that it should be so. Of course, all the founders had engaged daily in the practice of criticizing their government when they were inciting their countrymen to revolution against England, so they were well aware of the potential consequences of seditious activity. Now that the shoe was on the other foot, and they *were* the government, many were far less willing to encourage dissent. It was felt that criticism of government undermined authority and destroyed patriotism, especially during wartime.

EARLY RESTRICTIONS ON SPEECH

Early in our history it was easy enough for those in government to control the information that they felt threatened their power. It didn't take long for American "revolutionaries" to pass the Alien and Sedition Act of 1798, which outlawed "any false, scandalous writing against the government of the United States." In the early 1800s, state governments in the South punished speech advocating the end of slavery and even censored the mail to prevent the distribution of abolitionist literature. Throughout that century and into the next, all levels of government, with the support and encouragement of public opinion, squashed the views of radical political groups, labor activists, religious sects, and other minorities.[42]

By World War I, freedom of speech and of the press were a sham for many Americans, particularly those holding unorthodox views or views that challenged the status quo. War in Europe was seen as partly due to the influence of evil ideas, and leaders in America were determined to keep those ideas out of the United States. Government clamped down hard on people promoting socialism, anarchism, revolution, and even labor unions. In 1917 the U.S. Congress had passed the Espionage Act, which made it a crime to engage in "any disloyal . . . scurrilous, or abusive language about the form of government of the United States, . . . or any language intended to bring the form of government of the United States . . . into contempt, scorn, contumely, or disrepute."[43] Such sweeping prohibitions made it possible to arrest people on the flimsiest of pretexts.

sedition speech that criticizes the government to promote rebellion

bad tendency test the rule used by the courts that allows speech to be punished if it leads to punishable actions

clear and present danger test the rule used by the courts that allows language to be regulated only if it presents an immediate and urgent danger

THE ROLE OF THE SUPREME COURT

Those arrested and imprisoned under the new sedition laws looked to the Supreme Court to protect their freedom to criticize their government, but the Court did not dispute the idea that speech criticizing the government could be punished. The question it dealt with was just how bad the speech had to be before it could be prohibited. In four cases upholding the Espionage Act, the Court used a measure it called the bad tendency test, which simply required that, for the language to be regulated, it must have "a natural tendency to produce the forbidden consequences." This test is pretty easy for prosecutors to meet, so most convictions under the act were upheld.[44]

But in two of those cases, *Schenck v. United States* (1919) and *Abrams v. United States* (1919), Justice Oliver Wendell Holmes began to articulate a new test, which he called the clear and present danger test. This test, as Holmes conceived it, focused on the circumstances in which language was used.[45] If no immediately threatening circumstances existed, then the language in question would be protected and Congress could not regulate it. But Holmes's views did not represent the majority opinion of the Court, and the clear and present danger test was slow to catch on.

With the tensions that led to World War II, Congress again began to fear the power of foreign ideas, especially communism, which was seen as a threat to the American way of life. The Smith Act of 1940 made it illegal to advocate for the violent overthrow of the government or to belong to an organization that did so. Similarly, as the communist scare picked up speed after the war, the McCarran Act of 1950 required members of the Communist Party to register with the U.S. attorney general. At the same time, Sen. Joseph McCarthy was conducting investigations of American citizens to search out communists, and the House Un-American Activities Committee was doing the same thing. The suspicion or accusation of being involved in communism was enough to stain a person's reputation irreparably, even if there were no evidence to back up the claim. Many careers and lives were ruined in the process.

The clear and present danger test did not protect them. The Supreme Court upheld convictions under both the Smith and McCarran Acts even though by Holmes's formulation there was no danger of imminent harm. The clear and present danger test had come to be seen as a kind of balancing test in which society's interests in prohibiting the speech were weighed against the value of free speech; the emphasis on an obvious and immediate danger was lost.

The Court's record as a supporter of sedition laws finally ended with the personnel changes that brought Earl Warren to the position of chief justice. In 1969 the Court overturned the conviction of Charles Brandenburg, a Ku Klux Klan

one disputes that government has the right to regulate actions and behavior if it believes it has sufficient cause, but what happens when that behavior is also expression? When is an action a form of expression? Is burning a draft card, or wearing an armband to protest a war, or torching the American flag an action or an expression? All these questions, and more, have come before the Court, which generally has been more willing to allow regulation of symbolic speech than of speech alone, especially if the regulation is not a direct attempt to curtail the speech.[47]

One of the most divisive issues of symbolic speech that has confronted the Supreme Court, and indeed the American public, concerns that ultimate symbol of our country, the American flag. There is probably no more effective way of showing one's dissatisfaction with the United States or its policies than by burning the Stars and Stripes. In 1969 the Court split five to four when it overturned the conviction of a person who had broken a New York law making it illegal to deface or show disrespect for the flag (he had burned it).[48] Twenty years later, with a more conservative Court in place, the issue was raised again by a similar Texas law. Again the Court divided five to four, voting to protect the burning of the flag as symbolic expression.[49] Because the patriotic feelings of so many Americans were fired up by this ruling, Congress passed the federal Flag Protection Act in 1989, making it a crime to desecrate the flag. In *United States v. Eichman*, the Court declared the federal law unconstitutional for the same reasons it had overturned the New York and Texas laws: all were aimed specifically at "suppressing expression."[50] The only way to get around a Supreme Court ruling of unconstitutionality is to amend the Constitution. Efforts to pass an amendment failed by a fairly small margin in the House and the Senate, meaning that despite the strong feeling of many, flag burning is still considered protected speech in the United States.

The Court has proved willing to restrict symbolic speech, however, if it finds that the speech goes beyond expression of a view. In a 2003 ruling, the Court held that cross burning, a favored practice of the Ku Klux Klan and other segregationists that it had previously held to be protected speech, was not protected under the First Amendment if it was intended as a threat of violence. "When a cross burning is used to intimidate, few if any messages are more powerful," wrote Justice Sandra Day O'Connor, speaking

Un-American Activity

Preying on American anxieties about communism, Sen. Joseph McCarthy led an aggressive investigation of suspected communists in the government during the 1950s. Though his investigations, with their sensational and clever tactics, ruined many careers, McCarthy failed to find evidence of even one "card-carrying communist" in the government. He was censured by the Senate in 1954 and died in disgrace in 1957.

leader who had been arrested under Ohio's criminal syndicalism law. In this case the Court ruled that abstract teaching of violence is not the same as incitement to violence. In other words, political speech could be restricted only if it was aimed at producing or was likely to produce "imminent lawless action." Mere advocacy of specific illegal acts was protected unless it led to immediate illegal activity. In a concurring opinion, Justice William O. Douglas pointed out that it was time to get rid of the clear and present danger test because it was so subject to misuse and manipulation. Speech, except when linked with action, he said, should be immune from prosecution.[46] The **imminent lawless action test** continues to be the standard for regulating political speech today.

SYMBOLIC SPEECH

The question of what to do when speech is linked to action, of course, remained. Many forms of expression go beyond mere speech or writing. Should they also be protected? No

imminent lawless action test the rule used by the courts that restricts speech only if it is aimed at producing or is likely to produce imminent lawless action

for a six-to-three majority. "A state may choose to prohibit only those forms of intimidation that are most likely to inspire fear of bodily harm," if the intent to stir up such fear is clear.[51] The Court noted that cross burning would still be protected as symbolic speech in certain cases, such as at a political rally.

Closely related to symbolic speech is an additional First Amendment guarantee, **freedom of assembly**, or "the right of the people peaceably to assemble, and to petition the government for a redress of grievances." The courts have interpreted this provision to mean not only that people can meet and express their views collectively, but also that their very association is protected as a form of political expression. So, for instance, they have ruled that associations like the NAACP cannot be required to make their membership lists public[52] (although groups deemed to have unlawful purposes do not have such protection) and that teachers do not have to reveal the associations to which they belong.[53] In addition, the Court has basically upheld people's rights to associate with whom they please, although it held that public[54] and, in some circumstances, private groups cannot discriminate on the basis of race or sex.[55]

OBSCENITY AND PORNOGRAPHY

Of all the forms of expression, obscenity has probably presented the Court with its biggest headaches. In attempting to define it in 1964, Justice Potter Stewart could only conclude, "I know it when I see it."[56] The Court has used a variety of tests for determining whether material is obscene, but until the early 1970s, only the most hard-core pornography was regulated.

Coming into office in 1969, however, President Nixon made it one of his administration's goals to control pornography in America. Once the Court began to reflect the ideological change that came with Nixon's appointees, rulings became more restrictive. In 1973 the Court developed the *Miller* test, which returned more control over the definition of obscenity to state legislatures and local standards. Under the *Miller* test, the Court asks "whether the work depicts or describes, in a patently offensive way, sexual conduct specifically defined by state law" and "whether the

work, taken as a whole, lacks serious literary, artistic, political or scientific value" (called the SLAPS test).[57] These provisions have also been open to interpretation, and the Court has tried to refine them over time. The emphasis on local standards has meant that pornographers can look for those places with the most lenient definitions of obscenity in which to produce and market their work, and the Court has let this practice go on.

Still, the question of whether obscenity should be protected speech raises some fundamental issues, chief among them defining what is obscene. Justice John Marshall Harlan was quite right when he wrote that "one man's vulgarity is another man's lyric,"[58] raising the inescapable possibility of majorities enforcing decisions on minorities. People offended by what they consider to be obscenity might advocate banning adult bookstores, nude dancing at bars, and naked women on magazine covers at the supermarket. Many feminists argue that pornography represents aggression toward women and should be banned primarily because it perpetuates stereotypes and breeds violence. And some people carry the notion of obscenity further, arguing that selling violent video games to minors is obscene. (The Court has ruled it is not.[59])

FIGHTING WORDS AND OFFENSIVE SPEECH

Among the categories of speech that the Court has ruled may be regulated is one called **fighting words**, words whose express purpose is to create a disturbance and incite violence in the person who hears the speech.[60] However, the Court rarely upholds legislation designed to limit fighting words unless the law is written very carefully. Consequently it has held that threatening and provocative language is protected unless it is likely to "produce a clear and present danger of serious substantive evil that rises far above public inconvenience, annoyance, or unrest."[61]

The Court has also ruled that offensive language, while not protected by the First Amendment, may occasionally contain a political message, in which case constitutional protection applies. For instance, the Court overturned the conviction of a young California man named Paul Cohen who was arrested for violating California's law against "maliciously and willfully disturb[ing] the peace or quiet of any neighborhood or person . . . by . . . offensive conduct." Cohen had worn a jacket in a Los Angeles courthouse that had "Fuck the Draft" written across the back, in protest of the Vietnam War. The Court held that this message was not directed to any specific person who was likely to see the jacket and, further, there was no evidence that Cohen was in

---

freedom of assembly the right of the people to gather peacefully and to petition government

Miller test the rule used by the courts in which the definition of obscenity must be based on local standards

fighting words speech intended to incite violence

Bill Maher

Jeff Kravitz/FilmMagic, Inc/Getty Images

Bill Maher is a big fan of the First Amendment. That's because he says what few of us dare to say, what most of us dare not even think. The gasp of laughter that follows the comedian's one-liners is not just shocked amusement; it's shocked recognition that, uncomfortable, unflattering, and unpalatable as his observations are, they're often right on target. Maher has made a career out of mocking the emperor's anatomy, while most of us are still oohing and aahing over the splendor of his new clothes. Usually the First Amendment saves his bacon.

And sometimes it doesn't. On September 17, 2001, he went on his ABC comedy show, *Politically Incorrect,* and said, about the suicide bombing of the World Trade Center: "We have been the cowards, lobbing cruise missiles from miles away. That's cowardly. Staying in the airplane when it hits the building—say what you want about it, it's not cowardly."

Predictably, in those shaky days of national trouble, all hell broke loose. Asked about Maher's comment at a White House press briefing, then–press secretary Ari Fleischer replied: "All Americans . . . need to watch what they say, watch what they do." Advertisers balked, and Maher's show was canceled.

He's back now, with a cable show called *Real Time With Bill Maher,* where he continues to speak his mind. Still, there are limits. He says: "I can't get up there every week and just rail about the environment and global warming and whatever is going on that I think is most important. But I push it as far as I can. You've got to try to find entertaining ways to get the message through. I always say, in America if you want to teach somebody something, it's got to be like a pill in the dog's food. You've got to wrap it in the bologna . . . stick it right at the back of his throat so he doesn't even know it's there."

The trouble, as he sees it, is that Americans want to fit their beliefs into tidy categories of "liberal" and "conservative" as if that sums up the whole debate. Maher wants us to dig our way out of our comfortable platitudes to reach new truths, even if they're unpopular. He recalls getting booed once on the *Tonight Show* after he berated an animal trainer who had appeared with his tiger.

"They're like, please, Mr. Comedown. We just enjoyed a delightful animal show, and I pointed out that animals really don't want to be in show business." New rule, as Maher would say today.

Maher is a libertarian, but, true to his own creed, he is also a bit of everything else, believing fiercely in causes like animal rights, the environment, personal responsibility, and civic education. Today, he says, we've lost the thread to the things that matter. Raised by parents who served in World War II, Maher grew up thinking that there was a common good worth sacrificing for, "that the world had been to the brink and good citizenship was responsible for saving it. And we have nothing like that today. Nothing." Here's more Maher:

On patriotism

"Well, it means being loyal to your country above other countries. And I am . . . . [But] it has to be put in context and also it has to be put side by side with a greater humanity . . . . Americans who say, 'This is the greatest country in the world,' without having any clue what goes on in any other countries, are just pulling it out of nowhere. There are many things that I'm proud of in this country. I'm proud of how my parents and other people stopped fascism and communism. I'm certainly proud of what we started in 1776. It was a new dawn of freedom and liberty in the world. But I'm not proud of slavery. I'm not proud of the genocide of the Indians. I'm not proud of much of what goes on today. So I still believe in the promise of America, but most of America looks at itself through rose-colored glasses. And that's not healthy."

On keeping the republic

"Take it upon [yourself] to learn the basics . . . . [K]ids need . . . to learn history. Because kids say to me all the time when I say something from history: 'How should I know about that? I wasn't born.' Oh, really? So nothing happened before you were born? . . . Kids need to learn history so they can put themselves in the proper place, which is of great insignificance . . . . The problem with kids today is not too little self-esteem, it's too much. And history, I think, learning a big picture, is very important in that."

Source: Bill Maher spoke with Christine Barbour and Gerald C. Wright on May 9, 2005.

fact inciting anyone to a disturbance. Those who were offended by the message on Cohen's jacket did not have to look at it.[62]

These cases have taken on modern-day significance in the wake of the **political correctness** movement that swept the country in the late 1980s and 1990s, especially on college campuses. As mentioned in Chapter 2, political correctness refers to an ideology, held primarily by some liberals, including some civil rights activists and feminists, that language shapes society in critical ways, and therefore racist, sexist, homophobic, or any other language that demeans any group of individuals should be silenced to minimize its social effects. An outgrowth of the political correctness movement is the adoption of speech codes on college campuses, banning speech that might be offensive to women and ethnic and other minorities. Critics of speech codes, and of political correctness in general, argue that such practices unfairly repress free speech, which should flourish, of all places, on college campuses. In 1989 and 1991, federal district court judges agreed, finding speech codes on two campuses, the University of Michigan and the University of Wisconsin, in violation of students' First Amendment rights.[63] Neither school appealed. The Supreme Court spoke on a related issue in 1992 when it struck down a Minnesota "hate crime law" that prohibited activities that "arouse anger, alarm or resentment in others on the basis of race, color, creed, religion or gender." The Court held that it is unconstitutional to outlaw such broad categories of speech based on its content.[64]

Political correctness has had its impact outside of campus politics as well. Immediately after September 11, some conservatives treated any criticism of the United States as something close to treason, and commentators who disagreed with U.S. foreign policy had to be particularly careful lest they find themselves on the wrong end of a boycott. Liberal comedian Bill Maher (see *Profiles in Citizenship*) had a television show on ABC called *Politically Incorrect*, where very few topics escaped his scathing tongue. When he suggested that it took courage

Freedom of the Press in Action

The reporting of journalists Bob Woodward (center) and Carl Bernstein (second from left) drives home the importance of a free press. The pair's investigation into the Watergate break-in and cover-up resulted in congressional inquiries and, ultimately, President Richard Nixon's 1974 resignation on the brink of his impeachment. Here, they discuss story developments with publisher Katherine Graham, managing editor Howard Simons, and executive editor Benjamin Bradlee.

to fly a plane into a building, the outcry was so loud that he soon found himself without a job on network television.

More recently, political correctness was the target of several Republican candidates for the presidency in 2016, including the eventual Republican nominee. Their argument is that overly sensitive liberals have stifled people's ability to express themselves. Although there are many good reasons to deplore the effects of political correctness (particularly that it prevents people from developing the skills of defending themselves and their beliefs), the 2016 campaign unfortunately resulted in an upsurge of nativist and racist language, as supporters followed the Republican candidate's exuberance in smashing through what they saw as the cultural insult of political correctness.

FREEDOM OF THE PRESS

The First Amendment covers not only freedom of speech but also freedom of the press. Many of the controversial issues we have already covered apply to both of these areas, but some problems are confronted exclusively, or primarily, by the press: the issue of prior restraint, libel restrictions, and the conflict between a free press and a fair trial.

PRIOR RESTRAINT The founders modeled their ideas about freedom of expression on British common law, which held that it is acceptable to censor writing and

political correctness the idea that language shapes behavior and therefore should be regulated to control its social effects

speech about the government as long as the censorship occurs after publication. **Prior restraint**, a restriction on the press before its message is actually published, was seen as a more dangerous form of censorship since the repressed ideas never entered the public domain and their worth could not be debated. The Supreme Court has shared the founders' concern that prior restraint is a particularly dangerous form of censorship and almost never permits it. Two classic judgments illustrate their view. In *Near v. Minnesota* (1931), the Court held that a Minnesota law infringed on a newspaper publisher's freedom of the press. While an extreme emergency, such as war, might justify previous restraint on the press, wrote Justice Charles Evans Hughes, the purpose of the First Amendment was to limit it to those rare circumstances.[65] Similarly, and more recently, in *New York Times Company v. United States*, the Court prevented the Nixon administration from stopping the publication by the *New York Times* and the *Washington Post* of the *Pentagon Papers*, a "top secret" document about U.S. involvement in Vietnam. The Court held that "security" is too vague to be allowed to excuse the violation of the First Amendment; to grant such power to the president, it ruled, would be to run the risk of destroying the liberty that the government is trying to secure.[66]

LIBEL Freedom of the press also collides with the issue of libel, the written defamation of character (verbal defamation is called *slander*). Obviously it is crucial to the watchdog and information-providing roles of the press that journalists be able to speak freely about the character and actions of those in public service. At the same time, because careers and reputations are easily ruined by rumors and innuendo, journalists ought to be required to "speak" responsibly. The Supreme Court addressed this issue in *New York Times v. Sullivan*, which revolutionized libel law in the United States.[67] No longer simply a state matter, libel became a constitutional issue under the First Amendment. The Court held that public officials, as opposed to private individuals, when suing for libel, must show that a publication acted with "actual malice," which means not that the paper had an evil intent but only that it acted with "knowledge that [what it printed] was false or with reckless disregard for whether it was false or not."[68] Shortly afterward, the Court extended the ruling to include public figures such as celebrities and political candidates—anyone whose actions put them in a public position.

Of course, suing for libel has to have real news as its target. Especially in an age in which "fake news" is a regular rallying cry, finding out if news is legit is particularly important if you intend to sue. Libel laws don't apply when the whole point of the publication is to make things up (see *Don't Be Fooled by . . . Parody News Sites*). In 2013, Donald Trump's personal lawyer threatened the satirical site *The Onion* with legal action for writing a parody article in Trump's voice. Five years later, *The Onion* released the email as part of another satirical piece but confirmed for *Newsweek* that the email itself was "the real deal."[69]

The Court's rulings attempt to give the press some leeway in its actions. Without *Sullivan*, investigative journalism would never have been able to uncover the U.S. role in Vietnam, for instance, or the Watergate cover-up. Freedom of the press, and thus the public's interest in keeping a critical eye on government, is clearly the winner here. The Court's view is that when individuals put themselves into the public domain, the public's interest in the truth outweighs the protection of those individuals' privacy.

THE RIGHT TO A FAIR TRIAL Freedom of the press also confronts head-on another Bill of Rights guarantee, the right to a fair trial. Media coverage of a crime can make it very difficult to find an "impartial jury," as required by the Sixth Amendment. On the other side of this conflict, however, is the "public's right to know." The Sixth Amendment promises a "speedy and public trial," and many journalists interpret this provision to mean that the proceedings ought to be open. On the whole the Court has ruled in favor of media access to most stages of legal proceedings, and courts have been extremely reluctant to uphold gag orders, which would impose prior restraint on the press during those proceedings.[70]

CENSORSHIP ON THE INTERNET

We opened this chapter with a discussion of net neutrality—the effort to keep the channels of the Internet open without allowing providers to favor or discriminate against sites or sources of information. One of the central arguments in favor of net neutrality is that without it providers can effectively control our access to certain sites, if not censoring them, then making it difficult to connect. Such arguments are premised on the idea that the Internet is a public

---

prior restraint censorship of or punishment for the expression of ideas before the ideas are printed or spoken

libel written defamation of character

Parody News Sites

The First Amendment is an essential tool for keeping the republic. Americans who wish to speak truth to power are protected—whether they do it in a pamphlet, online, in a song, or on a stage. But what happens when they employ made-up facts or exaggerations as a vehicle to speak truth to power? That is: when a story is fabricated around what seems like a grain of truth, stretched to its absurd limits to make a political point? That's the nature of satire, a form of writing, art, or drama that uses irony, exaggeration, and humor to shed light on specific—and often political—issues.

It can be tricky telling stories that seem like they *could be* true, because it can be remarkably easy to fool people into thinking *they are* true. Consider the web site *Daily Currant*, which during the Obama administration posted fake news stories with no punchlines or discernible humor to be found. It presented completely false headlines (for example, "Obama Nominates Abortion Doctor to Replace Scalia on the Supreme Court" or "Donald Trump: 'I Have the Greatest Toenails in the History of Mankind'") that at some level seem reasonable to at least some readers. Although most folks get the joke, at least a few will invariably click, like, or share, believing the story to be true.[71]

If you've been fooled by a *Daily Currant* piece, don't feel bad: It's also happened to reporters at the *New York Times* and the *Washington Post*.[72] In a warning to his own staff, one editor described the *Currant*'s stories as "semi-believable political wish-fulfillment articles distinguished by a commitment to a complete absence of what most people would recognize as 'jokes.'"[73]

What to Watch Out For

It's not always easy to tell the difference between real news and fake news, but there are a few steps you can take to critically assess whether something is real or satire. Whether or not you actually find it funny is wholly up to you.

- **Notice the presentation.** Fake new sites take great pains to look and sound like authentic journalism while "reporting" stories that are completely untrue.

Site names like *Daily Currant*, *National Report*, *Empire News*, and *World News Daily Report* sound like legitimate news sources, and their format and style mimic hard news. Even the well-known satire site *The Onion*, despite its silly name and often hilarious headlines, still gets mistaken for real news often enough that, by 2015, Facebook was considering adding a "satire" tag to *Onion* stories shared on the site.[74] Remember that if something looks like news and sounds like news . . . it still might not be news. Googling the site's name will usually tell you if it's true.

- **Know your satire sources.** Most people know satire when they see it, and stories from traditional comedy sites (like *Saturday Night Live*'s "Weekend Update" or *The Daily Show*) are hard to mistake as real news. But as a consumer of news from Internet sources, it's up to you to know which "news" sites are real and which are satire. Further muddying the waters are blogs connected to more traditional news publications, such as *The New Yorker*'s "Borowitz Report," which, other than the inclusion of the word "humor" in the site's URL, is not always recognizable as satire.

- **Follow the links.** Is what you are reading original reporting, or is it a story about a story from another web site or news source? If the source of a story is a link to another story, check the original source.

- **Don't make laughter your guide.** Remember that satire doesn't have to be funny to be fake: some news satire sites are, for the most part, completely devoid of anything you might call a "joke," depending on shock value or sheer unlikeliness for their appeal.

- **Beware news reports that seem to skewer someone you already don't like.** When individuals come across something that seems to support their preferred narrative, they tend to want to believe it. In 2013, for example, a *Daily Currant* report that liberal economist Paul Krugman had filed for bankruptcy was quickly picked up by conservative blogs, and another *Daily Currant* story that Sarah Palin had joined *Al Jazeera* was reposted to liberal ones.[75] If something you read seems to "prove" you were right all along about celebrity X or politician Y, consider whether you are perhaps too eager to believe.

space and that people should be able to interact on it freely. Of course, private utilities limiting access is not exactly government censorship, but if the space itself is a public one, then private actors should not deny us access any more than they should stop us from attending a protest or rally or prevent us from going into the voting booth.

The truth is that lawmakers do not always know how to deal with new outlets for expression as they become available. Modern technology has presented the judiciary with a host of free speech issues the founders never anticipated. Sometimes, just as there are books and magazines whose explicit content is not protected free speech, some web sites contain explicit sexual material, obscene language, and other content that many people find objectionable. Since children often find their way onto the Internet on their own, parents and groups of other concerned citizens have clamored for regulation of this medium. Congress obliged in 1996 with the Communications Decency Act (CDA), which made it illegal to knowingly send or display indecent material over the Internet. In 1997 the Supreme Court ruled that such provisions constituted a violation of free speech, and that communication over the Internet, which it called a modern "town crier," is subject to the same protections as nonelectronic expression.[76] When Congress tried again with a more narrowly tailored bill, the Child Online Protection Act, the Court struck it down, too.[77]

The Court has not always ruled on the side of a completely unregulated Internet. While not restricting the creation of content, the Supreme Court in 2003 upheld the Children's Internet Protection Act, which required public libraries that received federal funds to use filtering software to block material deemed harmful to minors, such as pornography.[78] However, these filters can create some problems. Many companies and institutions use them to screen offensive incoming email, but such filters often have unwanted consequences. Since the filters cannot evaluate the material passing through, they can end up blocking even legitimate messages and publications. One editor of a newsletter on technology has resorted to intentionally misspelling words (for example, writing "sez" instead of "sex") to avoid the automatic sensors that screen many of his readers' messages.[79]

The Internet can also have the effect of freeing people from censorship, however. As many people who have worked on their high school newspapers know, the Court has ruled that student publications are subject to censorship by school officials if the restrictions serve an educational purpose. The Internet, however, offers students an alternative medium of publication that the courts say is not subject to censorship. As a result, students have been able to publish stories on investigations into school elections and campus violence, among other topics that have been excluded from the hard-copy newspaper.[80]

We can probably expect some flux in the laws on Internet censorship as the courts become more familiar with the medium itself and the issues surrounding it, including not only open access to information but also protection of the intellectual property rights of those who create the content that people seek to share on the Internet. In fact, the increasing use of the Internet not just as a source of information but also as a mechanism for people to download books, music, movies, and other forms of entertainment has set up another clash of rights. This conflict is between authors and creators—even the manufacturers of medication—who claim a copyright to their works, and the public, who wants to access those works, frequently without paying full fare for their use. Two bills, one in the House (the Stop Online Piracy Act, or SOPA) and one in the Senate (the Protect IP Act, or PIPA), attempted to address this issue in 2012 by requiring Internet providers to monitor their users and block access to international sites that share files. Companies like Google, Yahoo, Bing, Facebook, Twitter, and Tumblr, which depend on open Internet access, opposed the legislation, claiming it would require them to censor their users' practices and stifle free speech and innovation. Many of them went dark or threatened to do so in protest of the bills, and leaders in both houses postponed votes, effectively killing the proposed legislation in its current form.[81] The issue of the protection of intellectual property rights on the Internet remains unresolved.

The question of whether the Internet needs to be regulated to ensure protection of people's personal data privacy has become an important one in Congress, especially since we have learned that users of some sites, such as Facebook, have been manipulated into giving up their own data as well as information about everyone in their address books to firms like the now-defunct Cambridge Analytica. Unfortunately, congressional hearings revealed that members of Congress know next to nothing about how social media works, making it likely that we will leave the wolves in charge of the digital henhouse.

How much free speech do we need on our college campuses?

No less than the success of free democratic government is at stake in the issue of freedom of expression. This First Amendment liberty, we have argued, produces information about government, limits corruption, protects minorities, and helps maintain a vigorous defense of the truth. But something else is at stake as well—preservation of social order; stable government; and protection of civility, decency, and reputation.

It has been left to the courts, using the Constitution, to balance these two desired goods: freedom of expression on the one hand, and social and moral order on the other. The courts have devised several rules, or tests, to try to reconcile the competing claims. Thus we have had the bad tendency test, the clear and present danger test, the *Miller* test, and revised libel laws. The tension between freedom and order lends itself not to a permanent solution, since the circumstances of American life are constantly in flux, but rather to a series of uneasy truces and revised tests.

In Your Own Words   Explain the value of freedom of expression and how its protections have been tested.

THE RIGHT TO BEAR ARMS

Providing for militias to secure the state or securing an individual right?

The Second Amendment to the Constitution reads, "A well-regulated militia, being necessary to the security of a free state, the right of the people to keep and bear arms, shall not be infringed." This amendment has been the subject of some of the fiercest debates in American politics. Originally it was a seemingly straightforward effort by opponents of the Constitution to keep the federal government in check by limiting the power of standing, or permanent, armies. Over time it has become a rallying point for those who want to engage in sporting activities involving guns, those who believe that firearms are necessary for self-defense, those who believe an armed citizenry is necessary to check government that might become tyrannical, and those who simply don't believe that it is government's business to make decisions about who can own guns (see *Snapshot of America: Who Owns the Guns?*).

Although various kinds of gun control legislation have been passed at the state and local levels, powerful interest groups like the National Rifle Association (NRA) have kept it to a minimum at the federal level. The 1990s, however, saw the passage of three federal bills that affect the right to bear arms: the 1993 Brady Bill, requiring background checks on potential handgun purchasers; the 1994 Crime Bill, barring semiautomatic assault weapons; and a 1995

bill making it illegal to carry a gun near a school. The 1995 law and the interim provisions of the Brady Bill, which imposed a five-day waiting period for all gun sales, with local background checks until a national background check system could be established, were struck down by the Supreme Court on the grounds that they were unconstitutional infringements of the national government into the realm of state power.[82] In September 2004, Congress let the ban on semiautomatic weapons expire. While some Democrats in Congress promised to reintroduce the ban, action proved impossible because the powerful NRA has framed the conversation around guns in terms of rights. The narrative they have persuaded some Americans to believe is that the Second Amendment unequivocally guarantees all Americans the right to own guns (when even a cursory reading disputes that) and that any limitation on that right is an assault on the Constitution and the beginning of the slippery slope to the end of American liberty. *Business Insider* says the NRA is "a juggernaut of influence in Washington" because it is simultaneously "a lobbying firm, a campaign operation, a popular social club, a generous benefactor and an industry group."[83] By *industry group*, the author means that the NRA not only represents gun owners but that much of its financial and political clout comes from gun manufacturers who stand to make considerable money when people feel their guns or lives are threatened. In part, its strength also comes from its members, not because they are a majority of Americans, but because they are an intense minority, passionately unwilling to tolerate any compromise in the protection of what they believe is an essential right.

The NRA's narrative has proved powerful. In the wake of the shootings of twenty children and six adults at Sandy Hook Elementary School in December 2012, President Barack Obama promised to do everything he could to prevent another school shooting. By early January, he had formed a task force on gun violence, with Vice President Joe Biden at the helm, and he had proposed that Congress pass legislation banning assault weapons, requiring universal background checks on gun purchases, and limiting magazine capacity to ten cartridges. Interest groups rallied to pressure members of Congress to move forward. Congresswoman Gabrielle Giffords, herself shot in the head in a mass shooting in Tucson, Arizona, announced the formation of Americans for Responsible Solutions, which raised $6 million in its first year. The newly formed Moms Demand Action for Gun Sense organized chapters across the country. Former New York City mayor Michael Bloomberg founded Everytown for Gun Safety, an umbrella group that quickly

Snapshot of America: *Who Owns the Guns?*

Why Do Americans Say They Own Guns?

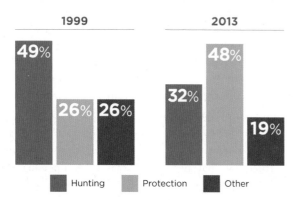

1999

49% 26% 26%

2013

32% 48% 19%

■ Hunting ■ Protection ■ Other

Source: Hannah Fingerhut, "Five Facts About Guns in the United States," Pew Research Center, January 5, 2016, http://www.pewresearch.org/fact-tank/2016/01/05/5-facts-about-guns-in-the-united-states/.

Americans Are Sharply Divided by Gun Debate

Percent saying it is more important to:

Protect Gun Rights   Control Gun Ownership

2000

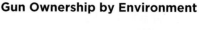

29%   66%

Protect Gun Rights   Control Gun Ownership

2017

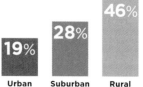

47%   51%

Source: Pew Research Center, America's Complex Relationship With Guns, June 22, 2017 http://www.pewsocialtrends.org/2017/06/22/americas-complex-relationship-with-guns/

Gun Deaths in America

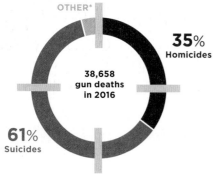

4% OTHER*

35% Homicides

38,658 gun deaths in 2016

61% Suicides

The **U.S. population** owns **1/3** of the guns on the planet.

Americans are **20 times more likely** to be **killed by a gun** than is someone from a developing country.

*includes accidental discharges, police shootings, and undetermined causes.

Source: Drew Desilver, "Suicides Account for Most Gun Deaths," Pew Research Center, May 24, 2013, http://www.pewresearch.org/fact-tank/2013/05/24/suicides-account-for-most-gun-deaths/.

Gun Ownership by Party

41% Republican
16% Democrat
36% Independent

Gun Ownership by Region

32% Midwest
36% South
16% Northeast
31% West

Gun Ownership by Environment

19% Urban
28% Suburban
46% Rural

Source: Pew Research Center, America's Complex Relationship With Guns, June 22, 2017 http://www.pewsocialtrends.org/2017/06/22/americas-complex-relationship-with-guns/.

Behind the Numbers

The Second Amendment protects citizens' right to bear arms, and guns are a way of life for many Americans. But this freedom comes at a high cost. Strict regulations on gun sales exist in only a few states, contributing to a large black market for guns across the country, and a high instance of gun-related homicides and suicides. How does the tension between the civil liberties and public safety play out in the political narrative surrounding the right to bear arms?

claimed more than two million members. The Brady Campaign to Prevent Gun Violence and the Law Center to Prevent Gun Violence also kicked into high gear, reporting record donations. Altogether, gun control groups said they spent five times as much in federal lobbying in 2013 as they had the year before.[84]

And still, nothing happened. The NRA and its spokespeople argued that the issue was mental health, not guns, and that more guns, not fewer, were necessary to stop gun violence in schools. Frustrated with his inability to make good on his promises after the school shootings at Sandy Hook and angry with Congress for not acting, President Obama promoted a counternarrative in the final year of his presidency. He took executive action to close the loopholes that allowed guns to be purchased at gun shows without a background check and that allowed purchasers to skirt restrictions on the acquisition of some especially dangerous weapons.[85]

Between the Sandy Hook shootings in 2012 and the Marjory Stoneman Douglas shootings in 2018, more than four hundred additional people were killed in more than two hundred school shootings.[86] The Parkland deaths added seventeen to that total. As we saw in *What's at Stake . . . ?* in Chapter 1, the students from Parkland, Florida, created a much more effective counternarrative in response to the NRA: "Why is your right to a gun more important than my right to life?" By the numbers of voluntary surrenders of AR-15s following the shootings at MSD, it was clear that this was a narrative that resonated even among some assault weapon enthusiasts. Unfortunately, it did not resonate quickly enough to save lives. Narratives take time to change and the NRA has lots of money and power behind it. In 2018, many Democratic members were elected to Congress who do not owe the NRA but they cannot pass legislation by themselves. Mass shootings (defined as four or more deaths, not counting the shooter's) have been occurring almost weekly since Parkland. In fact, the 2018 midterm election on Nov. 6 was bookended by a massacre killing eleven people at worship in a Pittsburgh synagogue on October 27 and a shooting at a bar in Thousand Oaks, California, that killed twelve on November 7.

WHY IS THE RIGHT
TO BEAR ARMS VALUABLE?

During the earliest days of American independence, the chief source of national stability was the state militia system—armies of able-bodied men who could be counted on to assemble, with their own guns, to defend their country from external and internal threats, whether from the British, the Native Americans, or local insurrection. Local militias were seen as far less dangerous to the fledgling republic than a standing army under national leadership. Such an army could seize control and create a military dictatorship, depriving citizens of their hard-won rights. Madison, Hamilton, and Jay devoted five *Federalist Papers* to the defense of standing armies and the unreliability of the militia, but they did not persuade the fearful Anti-Federalists. The Second Amendment was designed to guard against just that tyranny of the federal government.

ARGUMENTS IN DEFENSE OF THE SECOND AMENDMENT TODAY The restructuring of the U.S. military, and the growing evidence that under civilian control it did not pose a threat to the liberties of American citizens, caused many people to view the Second Amendment as obsolete. Gun advocates' narrative that the right to bear arms should be unregulated has at least four components: First, they argue that hunting and other leisure activities involving guns are an important part of American culture. Second, they claim that possession of guns is necessary for self-defense. They believe that gun control means that only criminals, who get their guns on the black market, will be armed, making life even more dangerous. Their third argument is that citizens should have the right to arm themselves to protect their families and property from a potentially tyrannical government, just as the American revolutionaries did. Finally, advocates of unregulated gun ownership say that the government's effort to regulate guns constitutes illegitimate use of federal power.

ARGUMENTS AGAINST THE RIGHT TO BEAR ARMS Opponents of these views—such as the groups that emerged after Sandy Hook as well as #NeverAgain, Handgun Control, Inc., and the Coalition to Stop Gun Violence—argue that gun owners want to make this an issue about rights because that gives their claims a higher status in American discourse, when in fact the issue is merely about their wants and preferences. Americans have long held that wants and preferences can be limited and regulated if they have harmful effects on society. If we are arguing within the narrative of "rights" rather than discussing policy solutions to gun violence, it decreases the chance for resolution.[87] Opponents also assemble facts and comparative data to support their claims that countries with stricter gun control laws have less violence and fewer gun deaths. They remind us that none of the rights of Americans, even such fundamental ones as freedoms of speech and of the press, is absolute, so why should the right to bear arms not also carry limitations and exceptions? Finally, they point out the irony of claiming the protection of the Constitution to own weapons that could be used to overthrow the government that the

Constitution supports.[88] As we said earlier, young people who feel threatened at school are beginning to create a strong counternarrative of their own.

JUDICIAL DECISIONS

Until 2008 the Supreme Court had ruled on only a handful of cases that had an impact on gun rights and the Second Amendment, mostly interpreting the Second Amendment as intending to arm state militias, and letting state gun-related legislation stand.[89] In 2008, however, the Supreme Court heard arguments for the first time since 1939 on whether the Constitution guarantees an individual the right to bear arms. In a five-to-four decision, the Court held that it did, striking down a Washington, D.C., law that banned handgun possession in the home. Although the Court held that the D.C. law violated an individual's right to own a gun for self-protection, the majority was careful to say that the right to own guns is not unlimited. For instance, it does not encompass military-grade weapons, and it does not extend to felons and the mentally ill.[90] In 2010 the Court took the ruling a step further, incorporating the Second Amendment by holding not only that the federal government could not violate an individual's right to bear arms, as it had in the D.C. case, but that neither could a state government.[91]

> **PAUSE AND REVIEW** | Who, What, How
>
> Some citizens want a protected right to own whatever guns they choose, and others want some regulation on what guns can be owned by private citizens. The rule that should determine who wins and who loses here is the Second Amendment, but though the Supreme Court has been fairly clear that the amendment does not confer on Americans an unqualified right to gun ownership, it also has been reluctant to allow the federal government to impose its will on the states. Consequently, the battle is played out in state legislatures, in Congress, and, most recently, in the White House.

In Your Own Words Give examples of different interpretations of the Second Amendment's meaning.

THE RIGHTS OF CRIMINAL DEFENDANTS

Protecting the accused from an arbitrary government

A full half of the amendments in the Bill of Rights, and several clauses in the Constitution itself, are devoted to protecting the rights of people who are suspected or accused of committing a crime. These precautions were a particular concern for the founders, who feared an arbitrary government that could accuse and imprison people without evidence or just cause. Governments tend to do such things to shore up their power and to silence their critics. The authors of these amendments believed that, to limit government power, people needed to retain rights against government throughout the process of being accused, tried, and punished for criminal activities. Amendments Four through Eight protect people against unreasonable searches and seizures, self-incrimination, and cruel and unusual punishment, and guarantee them a right to legal advice, a speedy and public trial, and various other procedural protections.

WHY ARE THE RIGHTS OF CRIMINAL DEFENDANTS VALUABLE?

As we indicated earlier, a primary reason for protecting the rights of the accused is to limit government power. One way governments can stop criticism of their actions is by eliminating the opposition, imprisoning them or worse. The guarantees in the Bill of Rights provide checks on government's ability to prosecute its enemies.

Another reason for guaranteeing rights to those accused of crimes is the strong tradition in American culture, coming from our English roots, that a person is innocent until proven guilty. An innocent person, naturally, still has the full protection of the Constitution, and even a guilty person is protected to some degree, for instance, against cruel and unusual punishment. All Americans are entitled to what the Fifth and Fourteenth Amendments call due process of law. **Due process of law** means that laws must be reasonable and fair, and that those accused of breaking the law, and who stand to lose life, liberty, or property as a consequence, have the right to appear before their judges to hear the charges and evidence against them, to have legal counsel, and to present any contradictory evidence in their defense. Due process means essentially that those accused of a crime have a right to a fair trial.

During the 1960s and 1970s, the Supreme Court expanded the protection of the rights of the accused and incorporated them so that the states had to protect them as well. And yet the more conservative 1980s and 1990s witnessed a considerable backlash against a legal system perceived as having gone soft on crime—overly concerned with the rights of criminals at the expense of safe streets, neighborhoods, and cities, and deaf to the claims of victims of violent crimes. We want to protect the innocent, but when the seemingly guilty go free because of a "technicality," the public is often incensed. The Supreme Court has had the heavy responsibility of drawing

> **due process of law** the guarantee that laws will be fair and reasonable and that citizens suspected of breaking the law will be treated fairly

the line between the rights of defendants and the rights of society. We can look at the Court's deliberations on these matters in four main areas: the protection against unreasonable searches and seizures, the protection against self-incrimination, the right to counsel, and the protection against cruel and unusual punishment.

PROTECTION AGAINST UNREASONABLE SEARCHES AND SEIZURES

The Fourth Amendment says,

> The right of the people to be secure in their persons, houses, papers, and effects, against unreasonable searches and seizures, shall not be violated, and no warrants shall issue but upon probable cause, supported by oath or affirmation, and particularly describing the place to be searched, and the persons or things to be seized.

The founders were particularly sensitive on this question because the king of England had had the right to order the homes of his subjects searched without cause, looking for any evidence of criminal activity. For the most part this amendment has been interpreted by the Court to mean that a person's home is private and cannot be invaded by police without a warrant, obtainable only if they have very good reason to think that criminal evidence lies within.

WHAT'S REASONABLE? Under the Fourth Amendment, there are a few exceptions to the rule that searches require warrants. Automobiles present a special case, for example, since by their nature they are likely to be gone by the time an officer appears with a warrant. Cars can be searched without warrants if the officer has probable cause to think a law has been broken, and the Court has gradually widened the scope of the search so that it can include luggage or closed containers in the car.

Modern innovations like wiretapping and electronic surveillance presented more difficult problems for the Court because, of course, they are not mentioned in the Constitution. A "search" was understood legally to require some physical trespass, and a "seizure" involved taking some tangible object. Not until the case of *Katz v. United States* (1967) did the Court require that a warrant be obtained before phones could

Analog Searches Only

Although police can examine personal items in certain circumstances, the Supreme Court in 2014 ruled that the digital information stored on one's cell phone is protected by the Fourth Amendment. If the police want to look at your data, they must get a search warrant first.

be tapped,[92] although, as we noted earlier, the 2001 Patriot Act makes it a good deal easier to get a warrant. In 2012 the Court ruled that a search warrant was needed in order to put a GPS tracking device on a suspect's car.[93]

Physical searches of cell phones have also presented a modern conundrum for the courts, as cell phones have been considered to be part of the contents of one's pockets, which the Supreme Court had determined could be legally searched. But in 2014, writing for a unanimous Court, Chief Justice John Roberts acknowledged that "[t]he average smartphone user has installed 33 apps which together can form a revealing montage of the user's life." Thus, our phones are "mini-computers" that contain the same kind of information about us that our houses have traditionally contained, and just as our houses cannot be searched without a warrant, now neither can our cell phones (at least most of the time). It bears repeating, however, that warrants are not that hard to come by, so people who store information they prefer to keep private on their cell phones or computers should in general be cautious.[94]

Yet another modern area in which the Court has had to determine the legality of searches is mandatory random testing for drug or alcohol use, usually by urine or blood tests. These are arguably a very unreasonable kind of search, but the Court has tended to allow them where the violation of privacy is outweighed by a good purpose, for instance, discovering the cause of a train accident,[95] preventing drug use in schools,[96] or preserving the public safety by requiring drug tests of train conductors and airline pilots.

A Prisoner's Appeal

Clarence Earl Gideon spent much of his time in prison studying the law. His handwritten appeal to the Supreme Court resulted in the landmark decision Gideon v. Wainwright, *which granted those accused of state crimes the right to counsel.*

Finally, in 2012 the Court held, five to four, that the Fourth Amendment is not violated by the requirement that someone arrested for a minor infraction and not suspected of concealing a weapon or drugs could nonetheless be subjected to an invasive strip search. In *Florence v. Board of Chosen Freeholders of County of Burlington,* the majority ruled that the plaintiff could be subjected to a strip search even though he had been arrested for something that he had not in fact done and that would not have been a crime in any case. The key issue was that the plaintiff was going to be held in the general jail population, and correctional officers are rightly concerned with jail security, which outweighs an individual's privacy rights.[97]

THE EXCLUSIONARY RULE By far the most controversial part of the Fourth Amendment rulings has been the exclusionary rule. In a 1914 case, *Weeks v. United States,* the Court confronted the question of what to do with evidence that had been obtained illegally. It decided that such evidence should be excluded from use in the defendant's trial.[98] This **exclusionary rule**, as it came to be known, meant that even though the police might have concrete evidence of criminal activity, if obtained unlawfully, it could not be used to gain a conviction of the culprit.

The exclusionary rule has been controversial from the start. In some countries, including England, illegally obtained evidence can be used at trial, but the defendant is allowed to sue the police in a civil suit or to bring criminal charges against them. The object is clearly to deter misbehavior on the part of the police, while not allowing guilty people to go free. But the American exclusionary rule, while it does serve as a deterrent to police, can help criminals avoid punishment. The Court itself has occasionally seemed uneasy about the rule.[99] Not until the 1961 case of *Mapp v. Ohio* was the exclusionary rule finally incorporated into state as well as federal practice.[100]

But extending the reach of the exclusionary rule did not end the controversy. Although the Warren Court continued to uphold it, the Burger and Rehnquist Courts cut back on the protections it offers. In 1974 they ruled that the exclusionary rule was to be a deterrent to abuse by the police, not a constitutional right of the accused.[101] The Court subsequently ruled that illegally seized evidence could be used in civil trials[102] and came to carve out what it called a good faith exception, whereby evidence is admitted to a criminal trial, even if obtained illegally, if the police are relying on a warrant that appears to be valid at the time or on a law that appears to be constitutional (though either may turn out to be defective),[103] or on a warrant that is obtained in error. In 2009 the Roberts Court ruled that to trigger the exclusionary rule, the police conduct must be deliberate.[104] The Court's more conservative turn on this issue has not silenced the debate, however. Some observers are appalled at the reduction in the protection of individual rights, whereas others do not believe that the Court has gone far enough in protecting society against criminals.

PROTECTION AGAINST SELF-INCRIMINATION

No less controversial than the rulings on illegally seized evidence are the Court's decisions on unconstitutionally obtained confessions. The Fifth Amendment provides for a number of protections for individuals, among them that no

---

exclusionary rule the rule created by the Supreme Court that evidence seized illegally may not be used to obtain a conviction

person "shall be compelled in any criminal case to be a witness against himself." The Supreme Court has expanded the scope of the protection against self-incrimination from criminal trials, as the amendment dictates, to grand jury proceedings, legislative investigations, and even police interrogations. It is this last extension that has proved most controversial.

Court rulings in the early 1900s ordered that police could not coerce confessions, but they did not provide any clear rule for police about what confessions would be admissible. Instead the Court used a case-by-case scrutiny that depended on "the totality of the circumstances" to determine whether confessions had been made voluntarily. This approach was not very helpful to police in the streets trying to make arrests and conduct investigations that would later hold up in court. In 1966 the Warren Court ruled, in *Miranda v. Arizona*, that police had to inform suspects of their rights to remain silent and to have a lawyer present during questioning to prevent them from incriminating themselves. The *Miranda* rights are familiar to viewers of police dramas: "You have the right to remain silent. Anything you say can and will be used against you . . . ." If a lawyer could show that a defendant had not been "read" his or her rights, information gained in the police interrogation would not be admissible in court. Like the exclusionary rule, the *Miranda* ruling could and did result in criminals going free even though the evidence existed to convict them.

Reacting to public and political accusations that the Warren Court was soft on crime, Congress passed the Crime Control and Safe Streets Act of 1968, which allowed confessions to be used in federal courts not according to the *Miranda* ruling but according to the old "totality of the circumstances" rule. *Miranda* was still effective in the states, however. Vowing to change the liberal tenor of the Warren Court, 1968 presidential candidate Richard Nixon pledged to appoint more conservative justices. True to his campaign promise, once elected he appointed Warren Burger as chief justice. Under the Burger Court, and later the Rehnquist Court, the justices have backed off the *Miranda* decision to some degree. In 2000, despite the fact that some justices had been highly critical of the *Miranda* ruling over the years, the Court upheld the 1966 decision, stating that it had become an established part of the culture, and held the 1968 Crime Control Act to be unconstitutional.[105]

RIGHT TO COUNSEL

Closely related to the *Miranda* decision, which upholds the right to have a lawyer present during police questioning, is the Sixth Amendment declaration that the accused shall "have the assistance of counsel for his defense." The founders' intentions on this amendment are fairly clear from the Crimes

Act of 1790, which required courts to provide counsel for poor defendants only in capital cases—that is, in those punishable by death. Defendants in other trials had a right to counsel, but the government had no obligation to provide it. The Court's decisions were in line with that act until 1938, when in *Johnson v. Zerbst* it extended the government's obligation to provide counsel to impoverished defendants in all criminal proceedings in federal courts.[106] Only federal crimes, however, carried that obligation, until 1963. In one of the most dramatic tales of courtroom appeals, a poor man named Clarence Earl Gideon was convicted of breaking and entering a pool hall and stealing money from the vending machine. Gideon asked the judge for a lawyer, but the judge told him that the state of Florida was not obligated to give him one. He tried to defend the case himself but lost to the far more skilled and knowledgeable prosecutor. Serving five years in prison for a crime he swore he did not commit, he filed a handwritten appeal with the Supreme Court. In a landmark decision, *Gideon v. Wainwright*, the Court incorporated the Sixth Amendment right to counsel.[107]

Not just in Florida, but all over the country, poor people in prison who had not had legal counsel had to be tried again or released. Gideon himself was tried again with a court-appointed lawyer, who proved to the jury not only that Gideon was innocent but that the crime had been committed by the chief witness against him. Conservatives believed that *Gideon* went far beyond the founders' intentions. Again, both the Burger and Rehnquist Courts succeeded in rolling back some of the protections won by *Gideon*, ruling, for instance, that the right to a court-appointed attorney does not extend beyond the filing of one round of appeals, even if the convicted indigent person is on death row.[108]

Though the right to counsel is now seen by most people as an essential right, many observers argue that this right is in reality often violated because of overworked public defenders or state laws that limit who can receive court-appointed counsel. According to a study by the National Association of Criminal Defense Lawyers, the Bucks County, Pennsylvania, public defender's office handled 4,173 cases in 1980. "Twenty years later, with the same number of attorneys, the office handled an estimated 8,000 cases." In Wisconsin, "more than 11,000 people go unrepresented annually because anyone with an annual income of more than $3,000 is deemed able to pay a lawyer."[109]

PROTECTION AGAINST CRUEL AND UNUSUAL PUNISHMENT

The final guarantee we look at in this section has also generated some major political controversies. The Eighth Amendment says, in part, that "cruel and unusual punishments"

Snapshot of America: *Where Do We Stand on Capital Punishment?*

U.S. Execution Totals

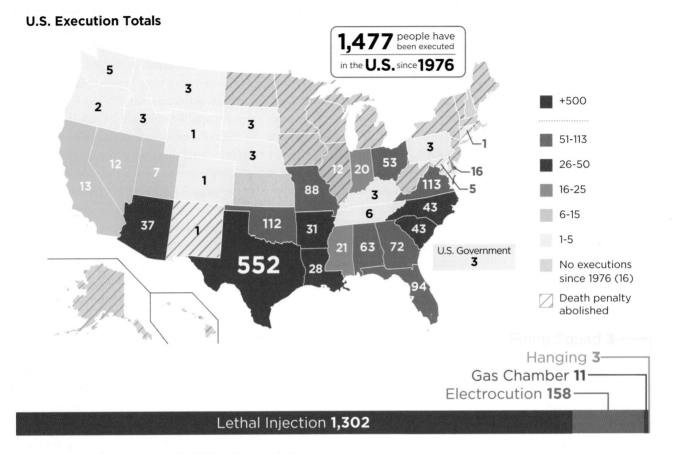

1,477 people have been executed in the **U.S.** since **1976**

Map values:
5, 3, 2, 3, 1, 3, 3, 3, 12, 7, 1, 1, 13, 37, 1, 112, 88, 31, 12, 20, 53, 3, 3, 113, 16, 5, 6, 43, 21, 63, 72, 43, 552, 28, 94

U.S. Government **3**

Legend:
- +500
- 51-113
- 26-50
- 16-25
- 6-15
- 1-5
- No executions since 1976 (16)
- Death penalty abolished

Firing Squad **3**
Hanging **3**
Gas Chamber **11**
Electrocution **158**
Lethal Injection **1,302**

How Americans View the Death Penalty Today

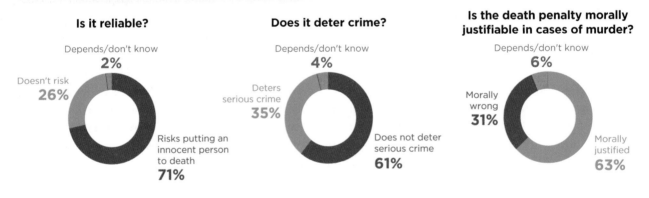

Is it reliable?
- Depends/don't know **2%**
- Doesn't risk **26%**
- Risks putting an innocent person to death **71%**

Does it deter crime?
- Depends/don't know **4%**
- Deters serious crime **35%**
- Does not deter serious crime **61%**

Is the death penalty morally justifiable in cases of murder?
- Depends/don't know **6%**
- Morally wrong **31%**
- Morally justified **63%**

Behind the Numbers

American support for capital punishment declined since a high around 1990, but we can see from the map that its use varies across the states, with Texas standing out from all the rest. Is it somehow "cruel and unusual" that the ultimate punishment applies for certain crimes in some states but not others? What circumstances would make the death penalty "cruel and unusual"?

Sources: Death Penalty Information Center, "Facts about the Death Penalty," updated March 16, 2018. www.deathpenaltyinfo.org/documents/FactSheet.pdf; David Masci, "5 Facts About the Death Penalty," Pew Research Center, May 28, 2015. www.pewresearch.org/fact-tank/2015/05/28/5-facts-about-the-death-penalty/.

shall not be inflicted. Like some of the earlier amendments, this one reflects a concern of English law, which sought to protect British subjects from torture and inhumane treatment by the king. The Americans inherited the concern and wrote it into their Constitution. It is easy to see why it would be controversial, however. What is "cruel"? And what is "unusual"? Can we protect American citizens from cruel and unusual punishment delivered in other countries?

The Court has ruled that not all unusual punishments are unconstitutional, because all new punishments—electrocution or lethal injection, for instance—are unusual when they first appear, but they may be more humane than old punishments like hanging or shooting.[110] Despite intense lobbying on the part of impassioned interest groups, however, the Court has not ruled that the death penalty itself is cruel or unusual (except in the case of mentally retarded individuals,[111] juveniles,[112] and crimes against an individual that do not result in the death of the victim[113]), and the majority of states have death penalty laws (see *Snapshot of America: Where Do We Stand on Capital Punishment?*).

The strongest attack on the death penalty began in the 1970s, when the NAACP Legal Defense Fund joined with the ACLU and the American Bar Association to argue that the death penalty was disproportionately given to African Americans, especially those convicted of rape. They argued that this was a violation of the Eighth Amendment, and also the Fourteenth Amendment guarantee of equal protection of the laws. Part of the problem was that state laws differed about what constituted grounds for imposing the death penalty, and juries had no uniform standards on which to rely. Consequently, unequal patterns of application of the penalty developed.

In *Furman v. Georgia* (1972) and two related cases, the Court ruled that Georgia's and Texas's capital punishment laws were unconstitutional, but the justices were so far from agreement that they all filed separate opinions, totaling 231 pages.[114] Thirty-five states passed new laws trying to meet the Court's objections and to clarify the standards for capital punishment. By 1976 six hundred inmates waited on death row for the Court to approve the new laws. That year the Court ruled in several cases that the death penalty was not unconstitutional, although it struck down laws requiring the death penalty for certain crimes.[115] The Court remained divided over the issue. In 1977 Gary Gilmore became the first person executed after a ten-year break. Executions by state since 1976 are detailed in *Snapshot of America: Where Do We Stand on Capital Punishment?*

In 1987 *McCleskey v. Kemp* raised the race issue again, but by then the Court was growing more conservative.[116] It held, five to four, that statistics showing that blacks who murder whites received the death penalty more frequently than whites who murder blacks did not prove a racial bias in the law or in how it was being applied.[117] The Rehnquist Court continued to knock down procedural barriers to imposing the death penalty. In 2006 the Roberts Court held that death row inmates could challenge state lethal injection procedures in lower courts on cruel and unusual punishment grounds. Several of those courts came to different conclusions. In 2008, in *Baze v. Rees*,[118] the Supreme Court upheld Kentucky's lethal injection practice, and other states, waiting for a sign from the Court, went ahead with their own practices.

In recent years, public support for capital punishment appears to be softening, not because of opposition in principle but because of fears that the system might be putting innocent people on death row. This feeling grew as DNA testing cleared some death row residents, and careful investigation showed that others, too, were innocent. After thirteen death row convicts in his state were exonerated between 1977 and 2000, Illinois governor George Ryan, a moderate Republican who supported the death penalty in principle, called for a statewide halt to executions. "I cannot support a system, which, in its administration, has proven so fraught with error," Ryan explained, "and has come so close to the ultimate nightmare, the state's taking of an innocent life."[119] Following his lead, then–Maryland governor Parris Glendening issued a moratorium in 2002, but that action was quickly reversed by the new governor, Robert Ehrlich, in January 2003. In 2007 the New Jersey legislature banned the death penalty in the state—the first state to do so since the Supreme Court declared capital punishment constitutional in 1976.[120]

Despite misgivings, the American public continues to favor capital punishment. In 2016 a Pew poll found 49 percent of the public supporting the death penalty, with 42 percent opposed, even though majorities of both supporters and opponents thought it meant that sometimes an innocent person would be put to death.[121]

PAUSE AND REVIEW Who, What, How

Every citizen has a huge stake in the protection of the rights of criminal defendants. If the government were allowed to arrest, imprison, and punish citizens at will, without legal protections, in secrecy, and without record, then all of us, criminal or not, would be vulnerable to persecution, perhaps for who we are, how we vote, what we say, or what we believe. It is the rules of due process that protect us from an unpredictable and unaccountable legal system.

In Your Own Words Describe the protections afforded criminal defendants under the Constitution.

THE RIGHT TO PRIVACY

The personal meets the political

One of the most controversial rights in America is not even mentioned in the Constitution or the Bill of Rights: the right to privacy. This right is at the heart of one of the deepest divisions in American politics, the split over abortion rights, and is fundamental to two other controversial areas of civil liberties: gay rights and the right to die.

WHY IS THE RIGHT TO PRIVACY VALUABLE?

Although the right to privacy is not spelled out in the Bill of Rights, it goes hand in hand with the founders' insistence on limited government. Their goal was to keep government from getting too powerful and interfering with the lives and affairs of individual citizens. They certainly implied a right to privacy, and perhaps even assumed such a right, but they did not make it explicit.

The right to privacy, to be left alone to do what we want, is so obviously desirable that it scarcely needs a defense. The problem, of course, is that a right to privacy without any limits is anarchy, the absence of government altogether. Clearly governments have an interest in preventing some kinds of individual behavior—murder, theft, and rape, for example. But what about more subtle behaviors that do not directly affect the public safety but arguably have serious consequences for the public good, like prostitution, drug use, gambling, and even, to take the example we used earlier in this chapter, riding a motorcycle without a helmet? Should these behaviors fall under a right to privacy, or should the state be able to regulate them? The specific issues the Court has dealt with related to this topic are contraception use and abortion, laws restricting the behavior of homosexuals, and laws preventing terminally ill patients from ending their lives.

A right to privacy per se did not enter the American legal system until 1890, when an article titled "The Right to Privacy" appeared in the *Harvard Law Review*.[122] In the years after the article appeared, states began to add a privacy right to their own bodies of statutory or constitutional law. The Supreme Court had dealt with privacy in some respects when it ruled on cases under the Fourth and Fifth Amendments, but it did not "discover" a right to privacy until 1965, and whether such a right exists remains controversial. None of the rights guaranteed by the first ten amendments to the Constitution is absolute. All, as we have seen, include limitations and contradictions. The right to privacy, without firm constitutional authority, is the least certain of all.

As modern technology has exploded the boundaries between the public and the private, the courts have had to grapple with where these boundaries should be. In a 2018 opinion that protected the data in a personal cell phone from searches without a warrant, Chief Justice John Robert pointed out that a GPS-equipped cell phone was a "near perfect" tool for government surveillance, not unlike an electronic monitoring ankle bracelet.[123]

REPRODUCTIVE RIGHTS

Throughout the 1940s, people had tried to challenge state laws that made it a crime to use birth control, or even to give out information about how to prevent pregnancies. The Supreme Court routinely refused to hear these challenges until the 1965 case of *Griswold v. Connecticut*. Connecticut had a law on its books making it illegal to use contraceptive devices or to distribute information about them. Under that law, Estelle Griswold, the Connecticut director of Planned Parenthood, was convicted and fined $100 for counseling married couples about birth control.

The Court held that, while the right to privacy is not explicit in the Constitution, a number of other rights, notably those in Amendments One, Three, Four, Five, and Nine, create a "zone of privacy" in which lie marriage and the decision to use contraception. It said that the specific guarantees in the Bill of Rights have "penumbras," or outlying shadowy areas, in which can be found a right to privacy. The Fourteenth Amendment applies that right to the states, and so Connecticut's law was unconstitutional.[124] In 1972 the Court extended the ruling to cover the rights of unmarried people to use contraception as well.[125]

Because of the Court's insistence that reproductive matters are not the concern of the government, abortion rights advocates saw an opportunity to use the *Griswold* ruling to strike down state laws prohibiting or limiting abortion. Until the Civil War, such laws were uncommon; most states allowed abortions in the early stages of pregnancy. After the war, however, opinion turned, and by 1910 every state except Kentucky had made abortions illegal. In the 1960s, legislation was again becoming more liberal, but abortions were still unobtainable in many places.

The Court had tried to avoid ruling on the abortion issue, but by 1973 it had become hard to escape. In *Roe v. Wade*, the justices held that the right to privacy did indeed encompass the right to abortion. It tried to balance a woman's right to privacy in reproductive matters with the state's interest in protecting human life, however, by treating the three trimesters of pregnancy differently. In the first three months of pregnancy, it held, there can be no compelling state interest that offsets a woman's privacy rights. In the second three months, the state can regulate access to abortions if it does so reasonably. In the last trimester, the state's interest becomes far more compelling, and a state can limit or even prohibit abortions as long as the mother's life is not in danger.[126]

The *Roe* decision launched the United States into an intense and divisive battle over abortion. States continued to try to limit abortions by requiring the consent of husbands or parents, by outlawing clinic advertising, by imposing waiting periods, and by erecting other roadblocks. The Court struck down most of these efforts, at least until 1977, when it allowed some state limitations. But the battle was not confined to statehouses. Congress, having failed to pass a constitutional amendment banning abortions, passed over thirty laws restricting access to abortions in various ways. For instance, it limited federal funding for abortions through Medicaid, a move the Supreme Court upheld in 1980.[127] Presidents got into the fray as well. President Reagan and the first President Bush were staunch opponents of *Roe* and worked hard to get it overturned. Reagan appointed only antiabortion judges to federal courts, and his administration was active in pushing litigation that would challenge *Roe*.

The balance on the Supreme Court was crucial. *Roe* had been decided by a seven-to-two vote, but many in the majority were facing retirement. When Warren Burger retired, Reagan elevated William Rehnquist, one of the two dissenters, to chief justice, and appointed conservative Antonin Scalia in his place. Reagan's appointees did finally move the Court in a more conservative direction, but even they did not overturn *Roe*. The 1973 ruling has been limited in some ways, but Rehnquist did not succeed in gathering a majority to strike it down.[128] In 2007 the Roberts Court upheld a ban on partial-birth abortion, but it has not signaled that it would overturn *Roe*.[129]

The debate over reproductive rights in this country is certainly not over. Indeed, all the vitriolic debate that surrounded the 2014 *Hobby Lobby* case shows that even the idea that contraception use is entirely a matter of private conscience is not wholly settled. Rejection of the notion that there is a constitutional right to privacy has long been a rallying point for the Christian Right, which has become a powerful part of the Republican Party. And although some Democrats also oppose abortion rights, abortion has become largely a partisan issue. Since 1980 the Republicans have included a commitment to a constitutional amendment banning abortion in their presidential party platform. Unable to effect change at a national level, many have directed their efforts to the states. One strategy, pursued by right-to-life groups in Colorado, Mississippi, Oklahoma, and others, is the attempt to pass personhood amendments that would define life as beginning from the moment of conception, making a fetus a legal person possessing citizenship rights. Such amendments would have the effect of making abortion illegal, but also, opponents fear, some forms of birth control and the disposal of fertilized eggs after in vitro fertilization processes.[130] Although no such amendment has yet

"If I wanted the government in my body, I would have asked it out on a date."

passed, and the Oklahoma Supreme Court declared the proposed amendment in that state to be unconstitutional, the strategy continues to have enthusiastic supporters.

A number of state legislatures have focused on making abortions harder to obtain, or more emotionally difficult for women (for instance, by requiring them to view an ultrasound of the fetus).[131] As governor of Indiana, 2016 Republican vice presidential candidate Mike Pence signed a bill making it illegal for women to request abortions for reasons including the fact that a baby would be born with a severe disability and penalizing doctors who performed them. For many poor women without the option to travel to another state, obtaining an abortion had become practically impossible, but in June 2016, in a major victory for supporters of reproductive rights, the Supreme Court struck down a restrictive abortion law in Texas, saying the state could not place an undue burden on women seeking an abortion.[132]

GAY RIGHTS

The *Griswold* and *Roe* rulings have opened up a variety of difficult issues for the Supreme Court. If there is a right to privacy, what might be included under it? On the whole, the Court has been very restrictive in expanding it beyond the reproductive rights of the original cases. Most controversial was its ruling in *Bowers v. Hardwick* (1986).[133]

Michael Hardwick was arrested under a Georgia law outlawing heterosexual and homosexual sodomy. A police officer, seeking to arrest him for failing to show up in court on a minor matter, was let into Hardwick's house by a friend and directed to his room. When the officer entered, he found Hardwick in bed with another man, and arrested him.

Hardwick challenged the law (although he wasn't prosecuted under it), claiming that it violated his right to privacy. The Court disagreed. Looking at the case from the perspective of whether there was a constitutional right to engage in sodomy, rather than from the dissenting view that what took place between consenting adults was a private matter, the Court held five to four that the state of Georgia had a legitimate interest in regulating such behavior.

Justice Lewis Powell, who provided the fifth vote for the majority, said after his retirement that he regretted his vote in the *Bowers* decision, but by then, of course, it was too late. Several states were critical of the Court's ruling. Kentucky's Supreme Court went so far in 1992 as to strike down the state's sodomy law as unconstitutional on the grounds the U.S. Supreme Court refused to use.[134] The Georgia Supreme Court itself struck down Georgia's sodomy law in 1998 on privacy grounds, but in a case involving heterosexual rather than homosexual activity. Not until 2003, in *Lawrence v. Texas*, did the Court, in a six-to-three decision, finally overturn *Bowers* on privacy grounds.[135] Interestingly, despite its longtime reluctance to overturn *Bowers*, the Court in 1996 used the equal protection clause of the Fourteenth Amendment to strike down a Colorado law that would have made it difficult for gays to use the Colorado courts to fight discrimination, and it has used that logic in subsequent cases, as we will see in Chapter 6.[136] Thus the Court can pursue several constitutional avenues to expand the rights of gay Americans, should it want to do so.

THE RIGHT TO DIE

A final right-to-privacy issue that has stirred up controversy for the Court is the so-called right to die. In 1990 the Court ruled on the case of Nancy Cruzan, a woman who had been in a vegetative state and on life-support systems since she was in a car accident in 1983. Her parents asked the doctors to withdraw the life support and allow her to die, but the state of Missouri, claiming an interest in protecting the "sanctity of human life," blocked their request. The Cruzans argued that the right to privacy included the right to die without state interference, but the Court upheld Missouri's position, saying it was unclear that Nancy's wishes in the matter could be known for sure but that when such wishes were made clear, either in person or via a living will, a person's right to terminate medical treatment was protected under the Fourteenth Amendment's due process clause.[137]

The right-to-die issue appeared back on the national agenda in 2005 through a case involving Terri Schiavo, a young woman who had been in a persistent vegetative state for more than fifteen years. Claiming that Schiavo had not wished to be kept alive by artificial measures, her husband asked a state court to have her feeding tube removed. Her parents challenged the decision, but after numerous appeals the court ordered the tube removed in accordance with the precedent set in the Cruzan case. Social conservatives in Congress tried to block the action, but all federal courts, including the Supreme Court, refused to intervene and Schiavo died soon after. Angered by their inability to overturn the state court ruling, conservative groups vowed to fight for federal judicial appointees who would be more likely to intervene in such cases.

The Schiavo case did not change the prevailing legal principles—that this is a matter for individuals to decide and that when their wishes are known they should be respected by the doctors and the courts. In this matter, at least, public opinion seems to be consistent with the law. Polls showed the public strongly opposed to Congress' intervention to prevent Schiavo's death, and large majorities supported the removal of her feeding tube. In the wake of the case, 70 percent of Americans said they were thinking about getting their own living wills.[138]

The question of a person's right to suspend treatment is different from another legal issue—whether individuals

On Her Own Terms
Twenty-nine-year-old Brittany Maynard shocked the country when she publicly announced her decision to end her life. "I do not want to die," she later wrote. "But I am dying. And I want to die on my own terms." Maynard, stricken with terminal brain cancer, moved from California to Oregon to take advantage of that state's right-to-die laws. After she died in 2014, her mother, seen here, and other family members successfully campaigned for a right-to-die law in California.

have the right to have assistance ending their lives when they are terminally ill and in severe pain. Proponents of this right argue that patients should be able to decide whether to continue living with their conditions, and since such patients are frequently incapacitated or lack the means to end their lives painlessly, they are entitled to help if they want to die. Opponents, by contrast, say that a patient's right to die may require doctors to violate their Hippocratic Oath, and that it is open to abuse. Patients, especially those whose illnesses are chronic and costly, might feel obligated to end their lives out of concern for family or financial matters. In 1997 the Supreme Court ruled that the issue be left to the states and kept open the possibility that dying patients might be able to make a claim to a constitutional right to die in the future.[139]

Oregon provided the first test of this policy. In 1997 it passed a referendum allowing doctors under certain circumstances to provide lethal doses of medication to enable terminally ill patients to end their lives. In late 2001, then–U.S. attorney general John Ashcroft effectively blocked the law by announcing that doctors who participated in assisted suicides would lose their licenses to prescribe federally regulated medications, an essential part of medical practice. In 2004 a federal appellate court ruled that Ashcroft overstepped his authority under federal law, and in early 2006 the Supreme Court upheld the Oregon law. In 2015 California passed a law making it the fifth state, after Oregon, Washington, Vermont, and Montana, to allow physician assisted suicide in the United States, although it has faced some legal turmoil.[140]

PAUSE AND REVIEW Who, What, How

What's at stake in the right to privacy seems amazingly simple, given the intensity of the debate about it. In short, the issue is whether citizens have the right to control their own bodies in fundamentally intimate matters like birth, sex, and death. The controversy arises when opponents argue that citizens do not have that right, but rather should be subject to religious rules, natural laws, or moral beliefs that dictate certain behaviors with respect to these matters. They promote legislation and constitutional amendments that seek to bring behavior into conformity with their beliefs. The founders did not act to protect this right, possibly because they did not anticipate that they had created a government strong enough to tell people what to do in such personal matters, or possibly because technology has put choices on the table today that did not exist more than two hundred years ago. In the absence of constitutional protection or prohibition of the right to privacy, the rule that provides for it today derives from a series of Court cases that could just as easily be overturned should the Court change its mind.

In Your Own Words Discuss the extent of an individual's right to privacy.

THE CITIZENS AND CIVIL LIBERTIES

Rights come with obligations

The final section of a chapter on civil liberties is an interesting place to speculate about the duties attached to American citizenship. We have explored the Bill of Rights. What might a Bill of Obligations look like? The Constitution itself suggests the basics. Obligations are very much the flip side of rights; for every right guaranteed, there is a corresponding duty to use it, sometimes in an explicit law and often in an unwritten norm. For instance, the provisions for elected office and the right to vote imply a duty to vote. It's not a law but a norm that democracies depend on for survival. Congress is authorized to collect taxes, duties, and excises, including an income tax; citizens are obligated to pay those taxes. That, of course, is a law. Congress can raise and support armies, provide and maintain a navy, provide for and govern militias; correspondingly, Americans have a duty to serve in the military. That is merely a norm in peacetime, and one that carries more force in wartime, although not enough to have kept us from having a military draft in five military conflicts. The Constitution defines treason as waging war against the states or aiding or abetting their enemies; citizens have an obligation not to betray their country or state. Again, it's a norm and depending on how egregious the treason, a law as well. Amendments Five and Six guarantee grand juries and jury trials to those accused of crimes; it is citizens who must serve on those juries. Though people successfully evade it, there is a heavy presumption that they will serve.

Should the founders have provided a Bill of Obligations as well as a Bill of Rights?

As citizenship obligations around the world go, these are not terribly onerous. In Europe such obligations are explicitly extended to include providing for the welfare of those who cannot take care of themselves, for instance. Tax burdens are much higher in most other industrialized nations than they are in the United States. In some countries the obligation to vote is enforced legally, and others have mandatory military service for all citizens, or at least all male citizens.

Still, many people find the obligations associated with American citizenship to be too harsh. For instance, two *Wall Street Journal* reporters once wrote, "We [Americans] are a nation of law breakers. We exaggerate tax-deductible expenses, lie to customs officials, bet on card games and sports events, disregard jury notices, drive while intoxicated . . . and hire illegal child care workers . . . . Nearly all people violate some laws, and many run afoul of dozens without ever being considered or considering themselves criminals."[141] How much fulfillment of political obligation is enough? Most Americans clearly obey most of the laws, most of the time. When there is a war and a military draft, most draft-aged males have agreed to serve. If we do not pay all the taxes we owe, we pay much of them. If we do not vote, we get involved in our communities in countless other ways. As a nation, we are certainly getting by, at least for now. But perhaps we should consider the long-term political consequences to a democratic republic if the emphasis on preserving civil liberties is not balanced by a corresponding commitment to fulfilling political obligations.

Something else to consider: If citizenship is now more expansive in a mediated age that opens up opportunities for participation, engagement, and action that once did not exist, are the obligations that go with it also different? We have already discussed how the multitude of channels through which we can obtain information obligates us to ensure the information is factual and that we don't get caught in an information bubble of our own or someone else's making. Judging by the comments sections on social media, we could also say that an obligation to civil discourse would enhance our public lives. These are norms only, but following them would vastly improve our collective and individual experiences of mediated citizenship.

In Your Own Words Compare the idea of civil rights with that of civil obligations.

LET'S REVISIT: *What's at Stake . . . ?*

We opened this chapter with a look at the political controversy surrounding the Trump administration's reversal of the FCC's decision to enforce net neutrality—the idea that no Internet provider could provide "fast-lane" service or special access to advertisers or privileged businesses or charge more for access to others. That this was a political hot potato was clear from the fact, first, that there was never sufficient support in Congress to get it passed and, second, that it had to be done by administrative fiat at the urging of a public petition and President Obama, who had campaigned on it. The flood of public comments following the FCC rule change, Trump's flip on it, and the congressional disarray only makes it more apparent that this was a high-stakes issue.

But why? What is at stake in net neutrality? For one thing, as we can guess after reading this chapter, regulation itself, no matter what the subject, is controversial in American politics. Democrats tend to see the government as a benign creature tasked to look out for the welfare of its citizens and increase their freedoms, and Republicans think it is an incompetent monster whose job it is to limit civil liberties, burden business, and slow down the economy. That alone is enough to explain why net neutrality gets people's political juices going.

There is also the fact, however, that lots of money is to be made on the Internet—and while access is free and open, one of the main channels of revenue is closed off to Internet providers. Those providers—Comcast, Viacom, AT&T, and other mega-corporations (as we will see in Chapter 15)—own much of the media in this country and media owners have traditionally acted as gatekeepers, deciding what counts as news, what information about the world we should get. Give them the power to charge companies or otherwise exact costs for faster access, and they'd be foolish not to take the maximum advantage of it. For example, with multiple companies vying to be the top distributor of on-demand movies, the ones that can guarantee faster download times would command a premium. Whether it enhances innovation as its supporters claim, a net neutrality–free world certainly enhances the profitability of Internet providers, powerful actors in the lobbying universe with considerable sway over legislators.

Against the Internet providers' financial stake is the less tangible but equally valuable stake consumers of the Internet have to a right to the free flow of information—a key goal of the founders in creating the Bill of Rights. One of the repeated themes of this book is that access to information and the ability to control or contribute to the narrative about who has and should have power is power itself. The free and open Internet has been a potent force, for good and for bad, in opening up the possibility of narrative control to all of us. Net neutrality preserves that and its loss endangers the democratization of power over the political narrative.

CLUES to Critical Thinking

Federalist *No. 84*

By Alexander Hamilton, *The Federalist Papers*

The original text of the Constitution contained no Bill of Rights, and that would almost be its undoing. Fearful of a strong central government, the Anti-Federalists insisted that they would not vote to ratify the Constitution unless it contained some built-in limitations to its own power. In Federalist No. 84, the second-to-last of The Federalist Papers, Alexander Hamilton was busy tying up loose ends that had not been dealt with in previous essays. It was here that he chose to rebut the Anti-Federalist claim that a Bill of Rights was needed. It was not necessary, he argued, because many of the state constitutions admired by the Anti-Federalists did not have bills of rights, and in any case the text of the Constitution had many rights built in, among them the protection against the suspension of habeas corpus, the prohibition against bills of attainder and ex post facto laws, and the entitlement to trial by jury.

Hamilton went further than arguing that a Bill of Rights was unnecessary, however. In the excerpt reprinted here, he claimed that it was actually dangerous to liberty. Are we freer or less free than we were at the time of the founding?

It has been several times truly remarked that bills of rights are, in their origin, stipulations between kings and their subjects, abridgements of prerogative in favor of privilege, reservations of rights not surrendered to the prince. Such was MAGNA CHARTA, obtained by the barons, sword in hand, from King John. Such were the subsequent confirmations of that charter by succeeding princes. Such was the PETITION OF RIGHT assented to by Charles I, in the beginning of his reign. Such, also, was the Declaration of Right presented by the Lords and Commons to the Prince of Orange in 1688, and afterwards thrown into the form of an act of parliament called the Bill of Rights. It is evident, therefore, that, according to their primitive signification, they have no application to constitutions professedly founded upon the power of the people, and executed by their immediate representatives and servants. Here, in strictness, the people surrender nothing; and as they retain every thing they have no need of particular reservations. "WE, THE PEOPLE of the United States, to secure the blessings of liberty to ourselves and our posterity, do ORDAIN and ESTABLISH this Constitution for the United States of America." Here is a better recognition of popular rights, than volumes of those aphorisms which make the principal figure in several of our State bills of rights, and which would sound much better in a treatise of ethics than in a constitution of government.

But a minute detail of particular rights is certainly far less applicable to a Constitution like that under consideration, which is merely intended to regulate the general political interests of the nation, than to a constitution which has the regulation of every species of personal and private concerns. If, therefore, the loud clamors against the plan of the convention, on this score, are well founded, no epithets of reprobation will be too strong for the constitution of this State. But the truth is, that both of them contain all which, in relation to their objects, is reasonably to be desired.

I go further, and affirm that bills of rights, in the sense and to the extent in which they are contended for, are not only unnecessary in the proposed Constitution, but would even be dangerous. They would contain various exceptions to powers not granted; and, on this very account, would afford a colorable pretext to claim more than were granted. For why declare that things shall not be done which there is no power to do? Why, for instance, should it be said that the liberty of the press shall not be restrained, when no power is given by which restrictions may be imposed? I will not contend that such a provision would confer a regulating power; but it is evident that it would furnish, to men disposed to usurp, a plausible pretense for claiming that power. They might urge with a semblance of reason, that the Constitution ought not to be charged with the absurdity of providing against the abuse of an authority which was not given, and that the provision against restraining the liberty of the press afforded a clear implication, that a power to prescribe proper regulations concerning it was intended to be vested in the national government. This may serve as a specimen of the numerous handles which would be given to the doctrine of constructive powers, by the indulgence of an injudicious zeal for bills of rights.

On the subject of the liberty of the press, as much as has been said, I cannot forbear adding a remark or two: in the first place, I observe, that there is not a syllable concerning it in the constitution of this State; in the next, I contend, that whatever has been said about it in that of any other State, amounts to nothing. What signifies a declaration, that "the liberty of the press shall be inviolably preserved?" What is the liberty of the press? Who can give it any definition which would not leave the utmost latitude for evasion? I hold it to be impracticable; and from this I infer, that its security, whatever fine declarations may be inserted in any constitution respecting it, must altogether depend on public opinion, and on the general spirit of the people and of the government. And here, after all, as is intimated upon another occasion, must we seek for the only solid basis of all our rights.

There remains but one other view of this matter to conclude the point. The truth is, after all the declamations we have heard, that the Constitution is itself, in every rational sense, and to every useful purpose, A BILL OF RIGHTS. The several bills of rights in Great Britain form its Constitution, and conversely the constitution of each State is its bill of rights. And the proposed Constitution, if adopted, will be the bill of rights of the Union. Is it one object of a bill of rights to declare and specify the political privileges of the citizens in the structure and administration of the government? This is done in the most ample and precise manner in the plan of the convention; comprehending various precautions for the public security, which are not to be found in any of the State constitutions. Is another object of a bill of rights to define certain immunities and modes of proceeding, which are relative to personal and private concerns? This we have seen has also been attended to, in a variety of cases, in the same plan. Adverting therefore to the substantial meaning of a bill of rights, it is absurd to allege that it is not to be found in the work of the convention. It may be said that it does not go far enough, though it will not be easy to make this appear; but it can with no propriety be contended that there is no such thing. It certainly must be immaterial what mode is observed as to the order of declaring the rights of the citizens, if they are to be found in any part of the instrument which establishes the government. And hence it must be apparent, that much of what has been said on this subject rests merely on verbal and nominal distinctions, entirely foreign from the substance of the thing.

Consider the source and the audience: Hamilton was directing this essay to staunch opponents of the Constitution, and on this point, at least, they were winning. He was also speaking to citizens of New York who admired their own state constitution. How did these considerations shape the way he framed his argument?

Lay out the argument and the underlying values and assumptions: How powerful a government did Hamilton believe was established by the Constitution? Why did he think a Bill of Rights would be unnecessary? Why did he think it would be dangerous? What mischief would be done if the government were told it was not allowed to do things it didn't have the power to do anyway?

Uncover the evidence: Hamilton used historical evidence to discuss why bills of rights had existed in the past. Did that evidence have anything to do with the case he was discussing? How did he use logic to make the case that a Bill of Rights was dangerous?

Evaluate the conclusion: Did Hamilton persuade you that a Bill of Rights would empower government officials to argue that government had all the powers not specifically listed in a written Bill of Rights? Would the burden be on us to prove that we had any rights other than those listed?

Sort out the political implications: Today many Americans argue that we have a right to privacy. People who interpret the Constitution strictly, as do many conservatives, believe that we have only the rights that are written down in the Constitution. How does this debate relate to Hamilton's argument here?

Review

Rights in a Democracy

Our civil liberties are individual freedoms that place limitations on the power of government. Most of these rights are spelled out in the text of the Constitution or in its first ten amendments, the Bill of Rights, but some have developed over the years through judicial decision making.

Sometimes rights conflict, and when they do, government, guided by the Constitution and through the institutions of Congress, the executive, and the actions of citizens themselves, is called upon to resolve these conflicts.

net neutrality (p. 128)   **civil liberties (p. 129)**   **civil rights (p. 129)**

The Bill of Rights and Incorporation

For much our history the limitations on government outlined in the Bill of Rights applied only to Congress, meaning that although the federal government could not infringe on civil rights, state and local governments could. The passage of the Fourteenth Amendment began the process of nationalizing, or incorporating, the protections of the Bill of Rights at the state level, although not all of the amendments have been incorporated yet.

habeas corpus (p. 133)   **ex post facto laws (p. 133)**
bills of attainder (p. 133)   **incorporation (p. 137)**

Freedom of Religion

According to the establishment and free exercise clauses of the First Amendment, citizens of the United States have the right not to be coerced to practice a religion in which they do not believe, as well as the right not to be prevented from practicing the religion they espouse. Because these rights can conflict, religious freedom has been a battleground ever since the founding of the country. The courts have played a significant role in navigating the stormy waters of religious expression since that time.

establishment clause (p. 139)   ***Lemon* test (p. 139)**   **compelling state interest (p. 140)**
separationists (p. 139)   **free exercise clause (p. 140)**
accommodationists (p. 139)   **police power (p. 140)**

Freedom of Expression

Freedom of expression, also provided for in the First Amendment, is often considered the hallmark of our democratic government. Freedom of expression produces information about government, limits corruption, protects minorities, and helps maintain a vigorous defense of the truth. But this right may at times conflict with the preservation of social order and the protection of civility, decency, and reputation. Again, it has been left to the courts to balance freedom of expression with social and moral order.

free press (p. 142)   **imminent lawless action test (p. 144)**   **political correctness (p. 147)**
sedition (p. 143)   **freedom of assembly (p. 145)**   **prior restraint (p. 148)**
bad tendency test (p. 143)   ***Miller* test (p. 145)**   **libel (p. 148)**
clear and present danger test (p. 143)   **fighting words (p. 145)**

The Right to Bear Arms

The right to bear arms, supported by the Second Amendment, has also been hotly debated—more so in recent years than in the past, as federal gun control legislation has been enacted only recently. Most often the debate over gun laws is carried out in state legislatures.

The Rights of Criminal Defendants

The founders believed that, to limit government power, people needed to retain rights against government throughout the process of being accused, tried, and punished for criminal activities. Thus they devoted some of the text of the

Constitution as well as the Bill of Rights to a variety of procedural protections, including the right to a speedy and public trial, protection from unreasonable search and seizure, and the right to legal advice.

due process of law (p. 154) **exclusionary rule (p. 156)**

The Right to Privacy

Though the right to privacy is not mentioned in either the Constitution or the Bill of Rights—and did not even enter the American legal system until the late 1800s—it has become a fiercely debated right on a number of different levels, including reproductive rights, gay rights, and the right to die. In the absence of constitutional protection, the series of court cases on these matters determines how they are to be resolved. Many of these issues are still on shaky ground, as the states create their own legislation and the courts hand down new rulings.

The Citizens and Civil Liberties

Our political system is concerned with protecting individual rights, which grant freedoms and allow us to make claims on our government. But citizens are also expected to act within certain restrictions—laws and limits designed to protect the collective good. The balance between the freedom to do as we wish and the obligations to do as we should is a continuing challenge, especially in an era of mediated citizenship.

In Your Own Words

After you've read this chapter, you will be able to

6.1 Outline the criteria used by the courts to determine if and when the law can treat people differently.

6.2 Summarize key events and outcomes in the struggle for equality of African Americans.

6.3 Explain the different paths to equality taken by other racial and ethnic groups.

6.4 Describe how women have fought for equality and the changing role of women in American politics.

6.5 Recognize examples of other groups that face discrimination.

6.6 Identify tools used by citizens to expand the promise of civil rights.

6
THE STRUGGLE FOR EQUAL RIGHTS

What's at Stake . . . When a Racial Majority Becomes a Minority?

EVEN BEFORE DONALD TRUMP'S unexpected win in the presidential election, it was apparent that 2016 was a time for coming out of the shadows. At an American Renaissance conference in Tennessee that year, the excitement was palpable. "We're on the winning side for the first time in my experience," said Richard Spencer, the chair of the National Policy Institute, a white nationalist organization. "Even if Trump loses, he's already shown that immigration and economic nationalism and the whole concept of 'America first' works electorally," said Peter Brimelow, the founder of an anti-immigration and white nationalist web site.[1]

More overtly racist espousers of the same views claim a so-called alt-right ideology, an alternative, extremist version of the far right that opposes immigration, multiculturalism, and the classical democratic values that undergird the American political system. Journalist Rosie Gray calls it "white supremacy perfectly tailored for our times: 4chan-esque racist

Joshua Lott/Bloomberg via Getty Images

Great Again for Whom?

More equality means that white Americans face more competition and lose some of the unspoken advantages that come with discrimination against other groups. Donald Trump's "Make America Great Again" appealed primarily to older, less educated, and less wealthy white Republican voters, whose status is threatened by shifting economic and demographic trends.

obscurity of their own, secretive information channels like Breitbart News (whose publisher, Steve Bannon, signed on as Trump campaign CEO and later served in the White House), or in other social media where it often made its presence virulently felt in the comments sections. They gathered physically in out-of-the-way places precisely because they knew their ideas were out of line with mainstream America. One of the things that enraged them was that the expression of their views of misogyny, white supremacy, or anti-Semitism was considered politically incorrect and they felt that mainstream society was censoring their views.

But Trump's popularity changed things. "The success of the Trump campaign just proves that our views resonate with millions," Rachel Pendergraft, organizer of a white supremacist group, told reporters for the progressive journal *Mother Jones*. "They may not be ready for the Ku Klux Klan yet, but as anti-white hatred escalates, they will."[6] The Klan was among the white supremacists marching in an August 2017 Unite the Right rally in Charlottesville, Virginia, where clashes with counterprotesters left thirty people injured and a man affiliated with the white supremacists drove his car into a crowd, killing a woman. Trump refused to condemn the white supremacists, saying there was bigotry on both sides and, later, that there were "very fine people on both sides."[7]

The anger that Trump tapped into is due at least in part to rapid changes across America. The country is becoming ever more diverse, and the groups the white nationalists disdain are slowly becoming the majority, even as they themselves become a smaller and smaller percentage of the American population. Perhaps therein lies the rub. Although the avowed white nationalists were fired up at the prospect of a Trump presidency, they were only a small minority of Trump's supporters.

The majority of his most committed base is the much larger group of white Americans, largely rural males without college educations, who would never think of themselves as racists, who recognize the white privilege they have been born with only in its absence as they compete for a dwindling share of an American Dream they were told was their birthright, and who in fact believe they themselves are the target of racist behavior. Even before he became the widely accepted candidate of a Republican Party that didn't quite know what to do with him, Trump was speaking to the concerns of a gradually shrinking white population who felt that their jobs were being given to immigrants who worked too cheaply; who felt that "Black Lives

rhetoric combined with a tinge of Silicon Valley–flavored philosophizing, all riding on the coattails of the Trump boom."[2]

The Trump boom. Even though the Donald Trump campaign refused to comment for the above-cited articles on the white supremacist movement, members of that movement were convinced he was their guy. After President Barack Obama was elected, Trump was the most prominent member of the birther movement, claiming that Obama's presidency was illegitimate if he wouldn't produce his birth certificate. His remarks on immigrants being rapists, on Jews being focused on making money, on Muslims being dangerous, on various women being fat pigs, or dogs, or disgusting animals (or, if he likes them, "hot") have encouraged their bigotry. His slowness to reject an endorsement from noted Ku Klux Klan member David Duke (who later tweeted on Trump's victory: "GOD BLESS DONALD TRUMP! It's time to do the right thing, it's time to TAKE AMERICA BACK!!!#MAGA #AmericaFirst #LockHerUp #GodBlessAmerica")[3]; his referring to U.S. senator Elizabeth Warren, who claims Native American ancestry, as "Pocahontas"; his dispute with a Gold Star family about their Muslim son's sacrifice; his conviction that "the big problem this country has is being politically correct"[4]; and his claim that his fame makes sexual assault welcome by women, has, intentionally or not, ignited and given hope to a dark side of American politics. If this sounds harsh, political scientists have found that the Trump campaign made deliberate appeals to voters' sense of racial and gender grievance.[5]

Many of the people to whom Trump appealed felt liberated by his campaign. Before 2016, the white supremacist movement had existed largely out of sight of most people, lurking in the

Matter" meant their lives didn't; who believed that a Christian black president in the White House was a Muslim Kenyan, unqualified by birth for the office; who saw policies like the despised "Obamacare" as just another handout of "free stuff" to African Americans at their expense; and who felt that they were struggling to survive in a system that was rigged by the establishment against them and yet offered them no help.

As one observer noted, Trump's very language was keyed to evoke a nostalgia for an America long gone—his frequent use of the words *again* ("Make America Great Again") and *back* (bringing back jobs, law and order, and American power) were speaking to people for whom America is no longer as great as it was. These words appeared on hats, on T-shirts, and as the basis of chants at rallies where they were filmed and shown incessantly on cable TV. Democratic pollster Cornell Belcher says, "It's almost a cultural nostalgia, for when white male culture [was] most dominant.... When women, African American and Hispanic voters hear that ... they get the joke that going back to the past [would be] great for some but at the expense of others."[8]

The frustration and despair of the white, blue-collar, working class is not an imaginary malady, or mere sour grapes that they are no longer on top. Writes one researcher, "The highest costs of being poor in the U.S. are ... in the form of unhappiness, stress, and lack of hope." And it is lower-class, rural whites who feel the relative deprivation the most as the rich get impossibly richer, blacks and Hispanics improve their economic position, and they seem to be stuck or falling even if their incomes are actually above the average.[9] A 2015 study showed that mortality rates for *almost* all groups in the United States were dropping; the exception was for non-college-educated middle-aged whites. They were less healthy and dying younger, and of causes such as suicide, drug overdose, and alcoholism.[10]

Studies by political scientists disagreed on whether you could predict these early Trump supporters by their attitudes toward authoritarianism (an ideology based on the belief that there is a proper hierarchical order in society that a strong leader should enforce)[11] or populism (distrust of elites and experts and advocacy of strong nationalist values).[12] Either way, it boiled down to the idea that some American people were more authentically American and therefore more privileged than others; that is, it boiled down to race. Wrote one political scientist, Trump's core of support in the primaries was among "Republicans who held unfavorable views of African Americans, Muslims, immigrants, and minority groups in general. Perceptions that whites are treated unfairly in the United States and that the country's growing diversity is a bad thing were also significantly associated with Trump in the primaries."[13]

Race has been a permanent thread in the fabric of American politics and perhaps it always will be. But today it confronts some undeniable facts. The fact is that the racial landscape is changing in irreversible ways. The fact is that whites are a diminishing racial group in the United States, as people of color are growing in numbers. The fact is that nearly eleven million undocumented immigrants live and work in the United States, with no easy or affordable way to repatriate them. The fact is that Muslim Americans are deeply integrated into communities throughout the country. The fact is that a black man was elected to and served two terms in the White House and left with a significant majority approving of the job he had done, although the elected Republican government promptly began to dismantle his legacy.

The American landscape is changing in some nonracial ways as well that are relevant to the grievances to which Trump's candidacy spoke. Although the United States did not elect its first woman president in 2016, Hillary Clinton got more popular votes than did Donald Trump. Young people seem to have more open minds not just about race but also about social issues like marriage equality, transgender rights, and legalization of pot. The economy has changed in permanent ways that mean some traditional working-class jobs are gone forever and the government has failed to provide funding and training for alternative sources of employment. We live in a world where global terror threats can be monitored but probably never eliminated. And we live in a mediated world where third parties have powerful motivations to drive their own narratives and more ways than ever to circulate them.

Authoritarianism, populism, and racism are often reactions to perceived threats to a group's security, well-being, and prosperity. Are these facts of modern life—all indicators that the way we live is shifting in significant ways—sufficient threats to bring out the racial animus that seemed to buoy Trump and elate white nationalists? What exactly is at stake when a demographic group that is accustomed to being automatically in power starts to lose its majority status? We take a close look at race, ethnicity, and gender equality in this chapter, and return to this important question after examining what is at stake in civil rights politics in general. **«**

WHEN you consider where we started, the progress toward equality in the United States can look pretty impressive. Nowhere is the change more vivid than in the case of racial equality. In the early 1950s it was still illegal for most blacks and whites to attend the same schools in the American South or to use the same public facilities like swimming pools and drinking fountains. Today, for most of us, the segregated South is a distant memory. On August 28, 2008, forty-five years from the day that civil rights leader Martin Luther King Jr. declared that he had a dream that one day a child would be judged on the content of his character rather than the color of his skin, the nation watched as Barack Hussein Obama, born of a white mother from Kansas and a black father from Kenya, accepted the Democratic Party's nomination to the presidency, an office he would go on to win twice. Such moments, caught in the media spotlight, illuminate a stark contrast between now and then.

But in some ways, the changes highlighted at such moments are only superficial. Though black cabinet members are not uncommon—George W. Bush had two African American secretaries of state, Obama appointed the first two black attorneys general, and Trump has an African American secretary of housing and urban development—there have been remarkably few blacks in national elected office. *USA Today* pointed out in 2002 that "if the U.S. Senate and the National Governors Association were private clubs, their membership rosters would be a scandal. They're virtually lily white,"[14] and not much has changed since then. Out of a total of 1,974 U.S. senators since the founding,[15] only ten have been African Americans. Ironically, Obama's election to the presidency in 2008 removed the only black senator serving at the time. For the first time in our history, there are three African American senators serving simultaneously, Cory Booker, D-N.J., and Tim Scott, R-S.C., both elected in 2014; and Kamala Harris, D-Calif., elected in 2016.

Even though legal discrimination ended more than half a century ago and there are positive signs of improvement in the lives of African Americans, including a newfound optimism about the future,[16] inequality still pervades the American system and continues to be reflected in economic and social statistics. On average, blacks are less educated and much poorer than whites, they experience higher crime rates, they are more likely to be incarcerated and killed in altercations with the police, they live disproportionately in poverty-stricken areas, they score lower on standardized tests, and they rank at the bottom of most social measurements. Life expectancy is lower for African American men and women than for their white counterparts (although recent studies have shown the gap closing), and a greater percentage of African American children live in single-parent homes than do white or Hispanic children. The statistics illustrate what we suggested in Chapter 5—that rights equal power, and long-term deprivation of rights results in powerlessness. Unfortunately, the granting of formal **civil rights**, which we defined in Chapter 5 as the citizenship rights guaranteed by the Thirteenth, Fourteenth, Fifteenth, Nineteenth, and Twenty-sixth Amendments, may not bring about speedy changes in social and economic status.

African Americans are not the only group that shows the effects of having been deprived of its civil rights. Native Americans, Hispanics, and Asian Americans all face or have faced unequal treatment in the legal system, the job market, and the schools. Women, making up over half the population of the United States, have long struggled to gain economic parity with men. People in America are also denied rights, and thus power, on the basis of their sexual orientation, their age, their physical abilities, and their citizenship status. People who belong to multiple groups face the complex issues of intersectionality—the overlapping discrimination and oppression that results when you are black, female, and poor, for instance. (See *CLUES to Critical Thinking* at the end of this chapter for a first-person examination of the intersection of gender and race.) A country once praised by French observer Alexis de Tocqueville as a place of extraordinary equality, the United States today is haunted by traditions of unequal treatment and intolerance that it cannot entirely shake. And, as we noted in *What's at Stake . . . ?*, the growing attention to the various groups that have been denied rights is seen by some white people as diminishing their own rights.

In this chapter we look at the struggles of these groups to gain equal rights and the power to enforce those rights. The struggles are different because the groups themselves, and the political avenues open to them, vary in important ways. But, as we'll examine in this chapter, groups can use different political strategies to change the rules and win power.

THE MEANING OF POLITICAL INEQUALITY

When is different treatment okay?

Despite the deeply held American expectation that the law should treat all people equally, laws by nature must treat some people differently from others. Not only are laws designed in the first place to discriminate between those who abide by society's rules and those who don't,[17] but the laws can also legally treat criminals differently once they are convicted. For instance, in all but two states, Maine and Vermont, felons are denied the right to vote for some length of time, and in some cases, felons forfeit voting rights permanently.[18] But when particular groups are treated differently because of some characteristic like race, religion, gender, sexual orientation, age, or wealth, we say that the law discriminates against them, that they are denied equal protection of the laws. Throughout our history, legislatures, both state and national, have passed laws treating groups differently based on characteristics such as these. Sometimes those laws have seemed just and reasonable, but often they have not. Deciding which characteristics may fairly be the basis for unequal treatment is the job of all three branches of our government, but especially of our court system.

civil rights citizenship rights guaranteed to the people (primarily in the Thirteenth, Fourteenth, Fifteenth, Nineteenth, and Twenty-sixth Amendments) and protected by the government

intersectionality the interdependent discrimination and oppression that results when an individual is a member of more than one oppressed or minority group

WHEN CAN THE LAW TREAT PEOPLE DIFFERENTLY?

The Supreme Court has expended considerable energy and ink on this problem, and its answers have changed over time as various groups have waged the battle for equal rights against a backdrop of ever-changing American values, public opinion, and politics. Before we look at the struggles those groups have endured in their pursuit of equal treatment by the law, we should understand the Court's current formula for determining what sorts of discrimination need what sorts of legal remedy.

LEGAL CLASSIFICATIONS The Court has divided the laws that treat people differently into three tiers (see *The Big Picture*):

- The top tier refers to classifications of people that are so rarely constitutional that they are immediately "suspect." Suspect classifications require the government to have a compelling state interest for treating people differently. Race is a **suspect classification.** To determine whether a law making a suspect classification is constitutional, the Court subjects it to a heightened standard of review called **strict scrutiny.** Strict scrutiny means that the Court looks very carefully at the law and the government interest involved. (The catch, as we will see, is that while laws that discriminate *against* a suspect class are examined carefully, so are laws that discriminate in their favor.) As we saw in Chapter 5, laws that deprived people of some fundamental religious rights were once required to pass the compelling state interest test; at that time, religion was viewed by the Court as a suspect category.
- Classifications that the Court views as less potentially dangerous to fundamental rights fall into the middle tier. These "quasi-suspect" classifications may or may not be legitimate grounds for treating people differently. Such classifications are subject not to strict scrutiny

but to an **intermediate standard of review.** That is, the Court looks to see if the law requiring different treatment of people bears a substantial relationship to an important state interest. An "important interest test" is not as hard to meet as a "compelling interest test." Laws that treat women differently than men fall into this category.

- Finally, the least-scrutinized tier of classifications is that of "nonsuspect" classifications; these are subject to the **minimum rationality test.** The Court asks whether the government had a rational basis for making a law that treats a given class of people differently. Laws that discriminate on the basis of age, such as a curfew for young people, or on the basis of economic level, such as a higher tax rate for those in a certain income bracket, need not stem from compelling or important government interests. The government must merely have had a rational basis for making the law, which is fairly easy for a legislature to show.

THE FIGHT FOR SUSPECT STATUS The significance of the three tiers of classifications and the three review standards is that all groups that feel discriminated against want the Court to view them as a suspect class so that they will be treated as a protected group. Civil rights laws might cover them anyway, and the Fourteenth Amendment, which guarantees equal protection of the laws, may also formally protect them. However, once a group is designated as a suspect class, the Supreme Court is unlikely to permit any laws to treat them differently. Thus gaining suspect status is crucial in the struggle for equal rights.

After over one hundred years of decisions that effectively allowed people to be treated differently because of their race, the Court finally agreed in the 1950s that race is a suspect class. Women's groups, however, have failed to convince the Court, or to amend the Constitution, to make gender a suspect classification. The intermediate standard of review was devised by the Court to express its view that it is a little more dangerous to classify people by gender than by age or wealth, but not as dangerous as classifying them by race or religion. Other groups in America—those in the LGBTQ community, for instance—have struggled to get the Court to consider them in the quasi-suspect category. Although the lower courts have flirted with changing nonsuspect classification status, the Supreme Court didn't specify a standard of review when it struck down the Defense of Marriage Act in 2013. Some states and localities have passed legislation to prevent discrimination on the basis of sexual orientation, but gays can still be treated differently by law as long as the state can demonstrate a rational basis for the law.

suspect classification a classification, such as race, for which any discriminatory law must be justified by a compelling state interest

strict scrutiny a heightened standard of review used by the Supreme Court to assess the constitutionality of laws that limit some freedoms or that make a suspect classification

intermediate standard of review a standard of review used by the Court to evaluate laws that make a quasi-suspect classification

minimum rationality test a standard of review used by the Court to evaluate laws that make a nonsuspect classification

These standards of review make a real difference in American politics—they are part of the rules of politics that determine society's winners and losers. Americans who are treated unequally by the law consequently have less power to use the democratic system to get what they need and want (like legislation to protect and further their interests), to secure the resources available through the system (like education and other government benefits), and to gain new resources (like jobs and material goods). People who cannot claim their political rights have little if any standing in a democratic society.

WHY DO WE DENY RIGHTS?

People deny rights to others for many reasons, although they are not always candid or even self-aware about what those reasons are. People usually explain their denial of others' rights by creating a narrative focused on some group characteristic. They may say that the other group is not "civilized" or does not recognize the "true God," or that its members are in some other way unworthy or incapable of exercising their rights. People feel compelled to justify poor treatment by blaming the group they are treating poorly.

But usually there is something other than simple fault-finding behind the denial of rights. People deny the rights of others because rights are power. To deny people rights is to have power over them and over how they live their lives—to force them to conform to our will. Thus, at various times in our history, people with power in the United States have compelled slaves to work for their profit, they have denied wives the right to divorce their husbands, and they have forcibly removed Native Americans from their ancestral lands so that those lands could be developed. Denying people their rights is an attempt to keep them dependent and submissive. When they find their voice to create a counternarrative and can effectively demand their rights, the laws change and they soon leave their subservience behind.

People also deny rights to others for another reason. Isolating categories of people—be they recent immigrants who speak English poorly, homosexuals whose lifestyle seems threatening, or people whose religious beliefs are unfamiliar—helps groups to build a narrative that defines who they are, who their relevant community is, and who they are not. Such narratives help communities, and those who want to stir them up for political reasons, believe that they—with their culture, values, and beliefs—are superior to people who are different. This belief promotes cohesion and builds loyalty to "people who are like us"; it also intensifies dislike of and hostility to those who are "not our kind." It is only a small step from there to believing that people outside the community do not really deserve the same rights as those "superior" people within.

Strict Scrutiny, Loose Evidence

Executive Order 9066 forced more than 100,000 men, women, and children, most of them American citizens, into internment camps during World War II. When the order was challenged two years later in Korematsu v. United States (1944), the Supreme Court, applying the strict scrutiny standard for the first time, held that the government's need to protect the nation against espionage outweighed the individual rights of Japanese Americans. Four decades later, Fred Korematsu, who had fled the order and was later arrested, was able to clear his name on grounds that the government had knowingly suppressed evidence, but the precedent set in his case remains. He was awarded the Presidential Medal of Freedom in honor of his decades-long fight in 1998.

As *What's at Stake . . . ?* and *Let's Revisit: What's at Stake . . . ?* suggest, all of these elements go into the reaction of less educated white, heterosexual males who feel that demographic trends are against them, that the power and privilege that used to come along with being a member of the majority is gradually slipping away, and that anything they try to say about it is criticized as being politically incorrect.

DIFFERENT KINDS OF EQUALITY

The notion of equality is controversial in the United States. Disputes arise in part because we often think that "equal" must mean "identical" or "the same." Thus equality can seem threatening to the American value system, which prizes people's freedom to be different, to be unique individuals. We can better understand the controversies over the attempts to create political equality in this country if we return briefly to a distinction we made in Chapter 2, between substantive and procedural equality.

In American political culture, we prefer to rely on government to guarantee fair treatment and equal opportunity (a procedural view), rather than to manipulate fair and equal outcomes (a substantive view). We want government to treat everyone the same, and we want people to be free to be different, but we do not want government to treat people differently in order to make them equal at the end. This distinction poses a problem for the civil rights movement in America, the effort to achieve equal treatment by the laws for all Americans. When the laws are changed, which is a procedural solution, substantive action may still be necessary to ensure equal treatment in the future.

> **PAUSE AND REVIEW** Who, What, How

In the struggle for political equality, the people with the most at stake are members of groups that, because of some characteristic beyond their control, have been denied their civil rights. What they seek is equal treatment by the laws. The rules the Supreme Court uses to determine if they should have equal treatment are the three standards of strict scrutiny, the intermediate standard of review, and the minimum rationality test.

But minority groups are not the only ones with a stake in the battle for equal rights. Those who support discrimination want to maintain the status quo, which bolsters their own power and the power of those like them. The means open to them are maintaining discriminatory laws and intimidating those they discriminate against.

In Your Own Words Outline the criteria used by the courts to determine if and when the law can treat people differently.

RIGHTS DENIED ON THE BASIS OF RACE: AFRICAN AMERICANS

The battle to end the legacy of slavery and racism, fought mainly in the courts

We cannot separate the history of our race relations from the history of the United States. Americans have struggled for centuries to come to terms with the fact that citizens of African nations were kidnapped, packed into sailing vessels, exported to America, and sold, often at great profit, into a life that destroyed their families, their spirit, and their human dignity. The narratives of white supremacy and black inferiority, told to numb the sensibilities of European Americans to the horror of their own behavior, have been almost as damaging as slavery itself and have lived on in the American psyche—and in political institutions—much longer than the practice they justified. As we saw in *What's at Stake . . . ?*, these narratives are very much alive today. **Racism**, institutionalized power inequalities in society based on the perception of racial differences, is not a "southern problem" or a "black problem"; it is an American problem, and one that we have not yet managed to eradicate from national culture.

Not only has racism had a decisive influence on American culture, but it also has been central to American politics. From the start, those with power in America have been torn by the issue of race. The framers of the Constitution were so ambivalent that they would not use the word *slavery*, even while that document legalized its existence. Although some early politicians were morally opposed to the institution of slavery, they were, in the end, more reluctant to offend their southern colleagues by taking an antislavery stand. Even the Northwest Ordinance of 1787, which prohibited slavery in the northwestern territories, contained the concession to the South that fugitive slaves could legally be seized and returned to their owners. Sometimes in politics the need to compromise and bargain can cause people to excuse the inexcusable for political gain or expediency.

> *What would a legal system that treated all people exactly the same look like?*

racism institutionalized power inequalities in society based on the perception of racial differences

The Supreme Court has expended considerable energy and ink on this problem, and its answers have changed over time as various groups have waged the battle for equal rights against a backdrop of ever-changing American values, public opinion, and politics. Before we look at the struggles those groups have endured in their pursuit of equal treatment by the law, we should understand the Court's current formula for determining what sorts of discrimination need what sorts of legal remedy.

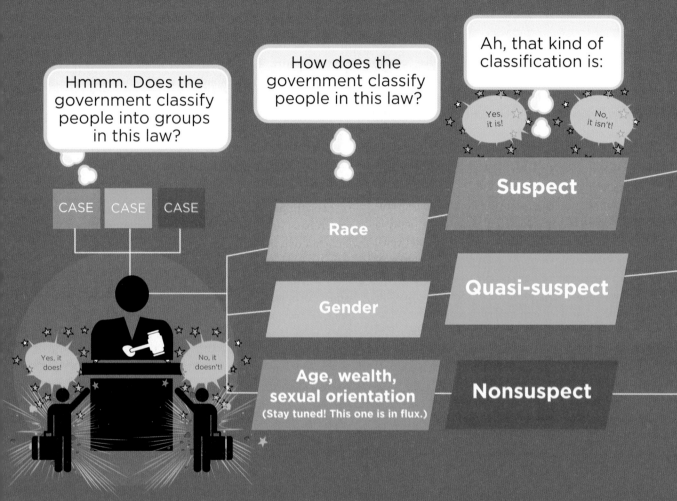

	SUSPECT
EXAMPLE OF CLASSIFICATION UPHELD	Government had a compelling state interest (national security) in relocating Japanese Americans from the West Coast during World War II. *Korematsu v. United States* (1944)
CLASSIFICATION STRUCK DOWN	State government had no compelling reason to segregate schools to achieve state purpose of educating children. *Brown v. Board of Education* (1954)

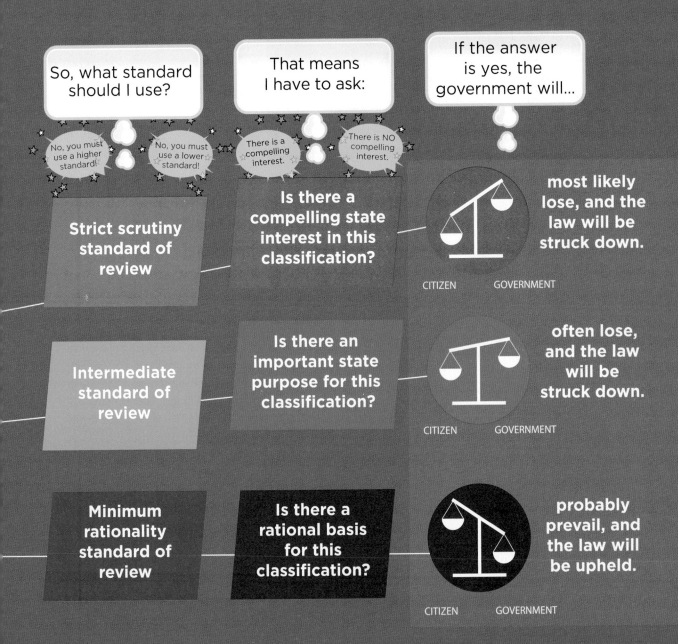

QUASI-SUSPECT
Court upheld federal law requiring males but not females to register for military service (the draft). *Rostker v. Goldberg* (1981)

Court struck down an Alabama law requiring husbands but not wives to pay alimony after divorce. *Orr v. Orr* (1979)

NONSUSPECT
Court found a Missouri law requiring public officials to retire at age seventy to have a rational basis. *Gregory v. Ashcroft* (1991)

Court struck down an amendment to the Colorado constitution that banned legislation to protect people's rights on the basis of their sexual orientation because it had no rational relation to a legitimate state goal. *Romer v. Evans* (1996)

THE CIVIL WAR AND ITS AFTERMATH: WINNERS AND LOSERS

We can't begin to cover here all the causes of the Civil War, which tore the country apart from April 1861 to May 1865. Suffice it to say that the war was not fought simply over the moral evil of slavery. Slavery was an economic and political issue as well as an ethical one. The southern economy depended on slavery, and when, in an effort to hold the Union together in 1863, President Abraham Lincoln issued the Emancipation Proclamation, he was not simply taking a moral stand. He was trying to use economic pressure to keep the country intact. The proclamation, in fact, did not free all slaves, only those in states rebelling against the Union.[20]

It is hard to find any real "winners" in the American Civil War. Indeed the war took such a toll on North and South that neither world war in the twentieth century would claim as many American casualties. The North "won" the war, in that the Union was restored, but the costs would continue to be paid for decades afterward. Politically, the northern Republicans, the party of Lincoln, were in the ascendance, controlling both the House and the Senate, but after Lincoln was assassinated in April 1865, their will was often thwarted by President Andrew Johnson, a Democrat from Tennessee who was sympathetic toward the South.

The Thirteenth Amendment, banning slavery, was passed by Congress in January 1865, under Lincoln, and ratified in December. This was a huge blow to southern white power. In retaliation, and to ensure that their political and social dominance of southern society would continue, the southern white state governments legislated **black codes**. Black codes were laws that sought to keep blacks in a subservient economic and political position by legally restricting most of the freedoms

Murderous Mob

After Reconstruction, the fervor to reestablish and maintain white supremacy in southern and border states led to acts of terror. Between 1882 and 1951, 3,437 African Americans were lynched by mobs. Local authorities usually claimed the killers could not be identified, although the mobs often posed for photographs like this one that were then turned into postcards and saved as macabre souvenirs.

BLACKS IN AMERICA BEFORE THE CIVIL WAR

At the time of the Civil War there were almost four million slaves in the American South and nearly half a million free blacks living in the rest of the country. Even where slavery was illegal, blacks as a rule did not enjoy full rights of citizenship. In fact, in *Dred Scott v. Sanford* (1857), the Supreme Court had ruled that blacks could not be citizens because the founders had not considered them citizens when the Constitution was written.[19]

Congress was no more protective of blacks than the Court was. Laws such as the Fugitive Slave Act of 1850 made life precarious even for free northern blacks. When national institutions seemed impervious to their demands for black rights, the **abolitionists**, a coalition of free blacks and northern whites working to end slavery altogether, tried other strategies. The movement put pressure on the Republican Party to take a stand on political equality and persuaded three state legislatures (Iowa, Wisconsin, and New York) to hold referenda (statewide votes) on black suffrage between 1857 and 1860. The abolitionists lost all three votes by large margins. Even in the North, on the eve of the Civil War, public opinion did not favor rights for blacks.

> **abolitionists** a coalition of free blacks and northern whites working to end slavery prior to the Civil War
>
> **black codes** a series of laws in the post–Civil War South designed to restrict the rights of former slaves before the passage of the Fourteenth and Fifteenth Amendments

(voting, property owning, education) they had gained by becoming citizens.[21]

RECONSTRUCTION AND ITS REVERSAL Congress, led by northern Republicans, tried to check southern obstruction in 1865 by instituting a period of federal control of southern politics called **Reconstruction**. In an attempt to make the black codes unconstitutional, they passed the Fourteenth Amendment, guaranteeing all people born or naturalized in the United States the rights of citizenship, and ensuring that no state could take away those rights. As we saw in Chapter 5, the Supreme Court has made varied use of this amendment, but its original intent was to bring some semblance of civil rights to southern blacks. The Fifteenth Amendment followed in 1870, effectively extending the right to vote to all adult males.

At first Reconstruction worked as the North had hoped. Under northern supervision, southern life began to change. Blacks voted, were elected to some local posts, and cemented Republican dominance with their support. But southern whites responded with violence. Groups like the Ku Klux Klan terrorized blacks in the South. Lynchings, arson, assaults, and beatings made claiming one's rights or associating with Republicans a risky business. Congress fought back vigorously and suppressed the reign of terror for a while, but by 1876, political problems in the North and resurgent white power in the South effectively brought Reconstruction to an end. Shortly after that, southern whites set about the business of stripping blacks of their newfound political power.

SEGREGATION AND THE ERA OF JIM CROW Without the intervention of the northern Republicans, disenfranchising blacks turned out to be easy to accomplish. Under the Fifteenth Amendment the vote could not be denied on the basis of race, color, or previous condition of servitude, so the Democrats, who now controlled the southern state governments, set out to deny it on other, legal, bases. **Poll taxes**, which required the payment of a small tax before voters could cast their votes, effectively took the right to vote away from the many blacks who were too poor to pay, and **literacy tests**, which required potential voters to demonstrate some reading skills, excluded most blacks who, denied an education, could not read. Even African Americans who were literate were often kept from voting because a white registrar administered the test unfairly. To permit illiterate whites to vote, literacy tests were combined with **grandfather clauses**, which required passage of such tests only by those prospective voters whose grandfathers had not been allowed to vote before 1867. Thus, unlike the black codes, these new laws, called **Jim Crow laws**, obeyed the letter of the Fifteenth Amendment, never explicitly saying that they were denying blacks the right to vote because of their race, color, or previous condition of servitude. This strategy proved devastatingly effective, and by 1910, registration of black voters had dropped dramatically, and registration of poor, illiterate whites had fallen as well.[22] Southern Democrats were back in power and had eliminated the possibility of competition.

Jim Crow laws were not just about voting but also concerned many other dimensions of southern life. The 1900s launched a half-century of **segregation** in the South—that is, of separate facilities for blacks and whites for leisure, business, travel, education, and other activities. The Civil Rights Act of 1875 had guaranteed that all people, regardless of race, color, or previous condition of servitude, were to have full and equal accommodation in "inns, public conveyances on land or water, theaters, and other places of public amusement," but the Supreme Court struck down the law, arguing that the Fourteenth Amendment only restricted the behavior of states, not of private individuals.[23] Having survived the legal test of the Constitution, Jim Crow laws continued to divide the southern world in two unequal halves. The whites-only facilities were invariably superior to those intended for blacks; they were newer, cleaner, more comfortable. Before long, the laws were challenged by blacks who asked why equal protection of the law shouldn't translate into some real equality in their lives.

In *Plessy v. Ferguson*, in which a Louisiana statute requiring blacks and whites to travel in separate railway cars was challenged, the Court held that enforced separation of the races did not mean that one race was inferior to the other. As long as the facilities provided were equal, states were within their rights to require them to be separate. Rejecting the majority view, Justice John Marshall Harlan wrote in a famous dissent, "Our Constitution is color-blind, and neither knows nor tolerates classes among citizens."[24] It would be over fifty years before a majority on the Court shared his view. In the meantime, everyone immediately embraced the "separate," and forgot the "equal," part of the ruling. Segregated facilities for whites and blacks had received the Supreme Court's seal of approval.

> **Reconstruction** the period following the Civil War during which the federal government took action to rebuild the South
>
> **poll taxes** taxes levied as a qualification for voting
>
> **literacy tests** tests requiring reading or comprehension skills as a qualification for voting
>
> **grandfather clauses** provisions exempting from voting restrictions the descendants of those able to vote in 1867
>
> **Jim Crow laws** southern laws designed to circumvent the Thirteenth, Fourteenth, and Fifteenth Amendments and to deny blacks rights on bases other than race
>
> **segregation** the practice and policy of separating races
>
> *Plessy v. Ferguson* the Supreme Court case that established the constitutionality of the principle "separate but equal"

THE LONG BATTLE TO OVERTURN *PLESSY*: THE NAACP AND ITS LEGAL STRATEGY

The years following the *Plessy* decision were bleak ones for African American civil rights. The formal rules of politics giving blacks their rights had been enacted at the national level, but no branch of government at any level was willing to enforce them. The Supreme Court had firmly rejected attempts to give the Fourteenth Amendment more teeth. Congress was not inclined to help once the Republican fervor for reform had worn off. Nor were the southern state governments likely to support black rights.

In the early days of the twentieth century, African Americans themselves did not agree on the best political strategy to follow. They were divided between taking an accommodationist approach that gave up demands for political and social equality, in exchange for economic opportunity on the one hand, and a far more assertive approach that demanded rights and refused to settle for second-class treatment on the other.[25]

Advocates of the latter position started the **National Association for the Advancement of Colored People (NAACP)** in 1910 to help individual blacks but also to raise white society's awareness of the atrocities of contemporary race relations and, most important, to change laws and court rulings that kept blacks from true equality. The NAACP, over time, was able to develop a legal strategy that was ultimately the undoing of Jim Crow and the segregated South.

By the 1930s, blacks had made some major political advances in the North, not so much by convincing Republicans to support them again, but by joining the coalition that supported Democratic president Franklin Roosevelt's New Deal. Wanting to woo black voters from the Republican Party, the Democrats gave as much influence to blacks as they dared without alienating powerful southern Democratic congressmen. The Supreme Court had even taken some tentative steps in the direction of civil rights, such as striking down grandfather clauses in 1915.[26] But after four decades, the *Plessy* judgment was still intact.

LAYING THE FOUNDATION FOR SCHOOL DESEGREGATION The NAACP, with the able assistance of a young lawyer named Thurgood Marshall, decided to launch its attack in the key area of education. Segregation in education was particularly disastrous for blacks because the poor quality of their educations in turn reinforced southern beliefs about their inferiority. Knowing that a loss reinforcing *Plessy* would be a major setback, the lawyers at the NAACP chose their cases carefully. Rather than trying to force the immediate integration of elementary schools, a goal that would have terrified and enraged whites, they began with law schools. Not only would this approach fly under most people's radar, but law schools were clearly discriminatory (most states didn't even have black law schools) and were an educational institution the justices on the Court knew well. The NAACP decision to lead with law school cases proved a masterful legal strategy.

Because the justices shared the experience of attending law school, it proved impossible for them to refute the NAACP lawyers' arguments that separate legal education was unequal. In *Missouri ex rel Gaines*[27] and *Sweatt vs. Painter*,[28] their rulings knocked a hole in the *Plessy* conviction that separate facilities would be equal. The ruling striking down "separate but equal" laws was aided by an unrelated case that, ironically, had the effect of depriving Japanese American citizens of many of their civil rights during World War II. In *Korematsu v. United States* (1944), Justice Hugo Black articulated the strict scrutiny test described earlier in this chapter: "All legal restrictions which curtail the civil rights of a single racial group are immediately suspect. That is not to say that all such restrictions are unconstitutional. It is to say that courts must subject them to the most rigid scrutiny."[29] After applying strict scrutiny, the Court allowed the laws that limited the civil rights of Japanese Americans to stand because it felt that the racial classification was justified by considerations of national security. The ruling was disastrous for Japanese Americans, but it would give blacks more ammunition in their fight for equal rights. From that point on, a law that treated people differently on the basis of race had to be based on a compelling government interest, or it could not stand.

BROWN V. BOARD OF EDUCATION By the early 1950s the stage was set for tackling the issue of education more broadly. The Court heard four pending cases under the case name *Brown v. Board of Education of Topeka* (1954). The NAACP used the arguments it had developed in the law school cases to emphasize the intangible aspects of education, including how black students felt when made to go to a separate school. They cited sociological evidence of the low self-esteem of black schoolchildren and argued that it resulted from a system that made black children feel inferior by treating them differently.

Under the new leadership of Chief Justice Earl Warren, the Court ruled unanimously in favor of Linda Brown and the other black students. Without explicitly denouncing segregation or overturning *Plessy*, hoping to keep the South from erupting in violent outrage again, the Warren Court held that separate schools, by their very definition, could never be equal

National Association for the Advancement of Colored People (NAACP) an interest group founded in 1910 to promote civil rights for African Americans

Brown v. Board of Education of Topeka the Supreme Court case that rejected the idea that separate could be equal in education

Apologies: Better Late Than Never

The scene was chaotic and ugly in 1957 when Elizabeth Eckford and eight other black students integrated Central High School in Little Rock, Arkansas. Forty years later, Eckford and a member of the mob that had taunted her, Hazel Bryan Massery, met again in front of the school, this time on friendly terms (Massery had telephoned Eckford in 1962 to apologize for her part in the disturbance).

because it was the fact of separation itself that made black children feel unequal. Segregation in education was inherently unconstitutional.[30]

The *Brown* decision did not bring instant relief to the southern school system.[31] The most public and blatant attempt to avoid compliance took place in Little Rock, Arkansas, in September 1957, when Governor Orval Faubus posted the National Guard at the local high school to prevent the attendance of nine African American children. Rioting white parents showed the faces of southern bigotry on the nightly news. It took one thousand federal troops sent by President Dwight Eisenhower to guarantee the safe passage of the nine black children through the angry mob of white parents who threatened to lynch them rather than let them enter the school. The *Brown* case, and the attempts to enforce it, proved to be a catalyst for a civil rights movement that would change the whole country.

THE CIVIL RIGHTS MOVEMENT

In 1955, the same year that the Court ordered school desegregation to proceed "with all deliberate speed," a woman

---

boycott the refusal to buy certain goods or services as a way to protest policy or force political reform

---

named Rosa Parks sat down on a bus in Montgomery, Alabama, and started a chain of events that would end with a Court order to stop segregation in all aspects of southern life. When Parks refused to yield her seat to a white passenger, as the law required, she was arrested and sent to jail.

Overnight, local groups in the black community organized a **boycott** of the Montgomery bus system. A boycott seeks to put economic pressure on a business to do something by encouraging people to stop purchasing its goods or services. Montgomery blacks, who formed the base of the bus company's clientele, wanted the bus company to lose so much money that it would force the local government to change the bus laws. Against all expectations, the bus boycott continued for over a year. In the meantime, the case wound its way through the legal system, and a little over a year after the boycott began, the Supreme Court affirmed a lower court's judgment that Montgomery's law was unconstitutional.[32] Separate bus accommodations were not equal. (The Montgomery bus boycott was portrayed in the movie *The Long Walk Home*. Watching a historical film—especially one based on a real person or an event—requires critical thinking skills similar to those needed to read a newspaper or surf the web. See *Don't Be Fooled by . . . the Movies* for some suggestions on how to get the most out of the political movies you view.)

The Movies

Throughout this book, we've suggested films that offer some insights into the events that have shaped our history and politics. Movies and other popular culture artifacts both reflect and affect the times in which they were made, offering a glimpse into the prevailing political narrative—and occasionally changing the narrative along the way. This relationship between art and politics is especially evident when you look at films depicting the African American experience. Compare, for example, the romantic depiction of slavery in *Gone With the Wind* (1939) with the harsh realities shown in *Twelve Years a Slave* (2013). Both films were critical and box office successes, turning the narratives they tell into the prevailing narratives for different generations.

As a critical consumer, it's your duty to pair your enjoyment of movies with some consideration of what is being left out of the story—and what might be misrepresented in it—and of what impact the story will have on the prevailing political narrative.

What to Watch Out For

Here are a few questions to ask yourself the next time you watch a movie about historical events:

- **Who is the intended audience?** Big Hollywood releases are meant to draw in huge crowds and make lots of money. That business model has historically meant that even movies about the African American experience were made by white filmmakers, in hopes of attracting large—and largely white—audiences. Thus popular films (such as 1988's *Mississippi Burning* or 2011's *The Help*) approached the civil rights movement from the perspective of white protagonists.

- **Who is telling the story?** Consider whether the filmmakers have a stake in a particular interpretation of events. How might a film like *Twelve Years a Slave* (2013) have been different had it been made by a white director rather than by Steve McQueen, an African American man? Would the story told by Gus Van Sant, a gay man, in the 2008 biopic *Milk* have been told differently by a straight director? You should also bear in mind the filmmakers' reputation: directors like Michael Moore, Oliver Stone, and Tyler Perry are known for promoting their own political or cultural agendas in their films.

- **Where and when was it made?** Films are informed by the times in which they were produced and must be viewed with that in mind. Movies that were considered progressive at the time they were released—such as *Woman of the Year* (1942) or *Guess Who's Coming to Dinner* (1967)—would likely seem sexist or racist to modern audiences. Consider the way the prevailing narratives of the 2010s play into the films coming out of Hollywood today, and what might change the way they are viewed in the future. For example, how do you think a film like Spike Lee's anti-gun-violence film *Chi-Raq* (2015) might be viewed in twenty years? Would this movie have been made twenty years ago?

- **What is the scope of the story?** When putting together a biopic or trying to tell a very long historical story, the nature of film means that many details will be changed, characters will be eliminated, and events will be changed in order to ramp up the drama. In recent years, many filmmakers seeking to tell "true stories" have jettisoned the "whole story" in order to tell one part of the story more accurately: Ava DuVernay's *Selma* focuses not on Martin Luther King Jr.'s entire life, but on the historic voting rights marches that King led in 1965; likewise, Brian Helgeland chose to focus his film *42* (2013) on Jackie Robinson's groundbreaking first season with the Brooklyn Dodgers. As a viewer, it's important for you to be aware of the parts of the story that are being left out—and perhaps do a little research to get some context after you leave the theater.

- **What is the source for historical material?** Even films with no commercial ambitions whatsoever—independent documentaries, for example—are shot and edited by filmmakers who inevitably have their own agendas, and who are limited by time, budget, and available evidence. Ken Burns's *Civil War* (1990), for example, is a critically acclaimed, thorough, and fact-based documentation of the war between the states. It is, however, colored not only by Burns's own feelings about the war and by the culture in which it was produced but also to some degree by the limitations of the historical record. Letters from soldiers on the battlefront, for example, were typically treasured and preserved, and so Burns had access to many first-person accounts from white soldiers. But first-person narratives from black Americans at that time are relative rare, as most slaves were kept intentionally illiterate—meaning that the *whole* truth of the era remains elusive.

TWO KINDS OF DISCRIMINATION The civil rights movement launched by the Montgomery bus boycott confronted two different types of discrimination. **De jure discrimination** (discrimination by law) is created by laws that treat people differently based on some characteristic like race. This is the sort of discrimination most blacks in the South faced. Especially in rural areas, blacks and whites lived and worked side by side, but by law they used separate facilities. Although the process of changing the laws was excruciatingly painful, once the laws were changed and the new laws were enforced, the result was integration.

The second sort of discrimination, called **de facto discrimination** (discrimination in fact), however, produces a kind of segregation that is much more difficult to eliminate. Segregation in the North was of this type because blacks and whites did not live and work in the same places to begin with. It was not laws that kept them apart, but past discrimination, tradition, custom, economic status, and residential patterns. This kind of segregation is hard to remedy because there are no laws to change; the segregation is woven more complexly into the fabric of society.

We can look at the civil rights movement in America as having two stages. The initial stage involved the battle to change the laws so that blacks and whites would be equally protected by the laws, as the Fourteenth Amendment guarantees. The second stage, and one that is ongoing today, is the fight against the aftereffects of those laws, and of centuries of discrimination, that leave many blacks and whites still living in communities that are worlds apart.

CHANGING THE RULES: FIGHTING DE JURE DISCRIMINATION Rosa Parks and the Montgomery bus boycott launched a new strategy in blacks' fight for equal rights. Although it took the power of a court judgment to move the city officials, blacks themselves had exercised considerable power through peaceful protest and massive resistance to the will of whites. One of the leaders of the boycott, a young Baptist minister named Martin Luther King Jr., became known for his nonviolent approach to political protest. This philosophy of peacefully resisting enforcement of laws perceived to be unjust, and marching or "sitting in" to express political views, captured the imagination of supporters of black civil rights in both the South and the North. Black college students, occasionally joined by whites, staged peaceful demonstrations, called sit-ins, to desegregate lunch counters in southern department stores and other facilities.

de jure discrimination discrimination that arises from or is supported by the law

de facto discrimination discrimination that is the result not of law but rather of tradition and habit

The protest movement was important not just for the practices it challenged directly—such as segregation in motels and restaurants, on beaches, and in other recreational facilities—but also for the pressure it brought to bear on elected officials and the effect it had on public opinion, particularly in the North, which had been largely unaware of southern problems.

The nonviolent resistance movement, in conjunction with the growing political power of northern blacks, brought about remarkable social and political change in the 1960s. The administration of Democratic president John F. Kennedy, not wanting to alienate the support of southern Democrats, tried at first to limit its active involvement in civil rights work. But the political pressure of black interest groups forced Kennedy to take a more visible stand. The Reverend King was using his tactics of nonviolent protest to great advantage in the spring of 1963. Kennedy responded to the political pressure so deftly orchestrated by King by sending to Birmingham federal mediators to negotiate an end to segregation, and then by sending to Congress a massive package of civil rights legislation.

Kennedy did not live to see his proposals become law, but they became the top priority of his successor, Lyndon Johnson. During the Johnson years, the president, bipartisan majorities in Congress (southern Democrats split off to vote against their president and started a slow process of leaving the party altogether), and the Supreme Court were in agreement on civil rights issues, and their joint legacy is impressive. The Kennedy-initiated Civil Rights Act of 1964 reinforced the voting laws, allowed the attorney general to file school desegregation lawsuits, permitted the president to deny federal money to state and local programs that practiced discrimination, prohibited discrimination in public accommodations and in employment, and set up the Equal Employment Opportunity Commission (EEOC) to investigate complaints about job discrimination. Johnson also sent to Congress the Voting Rights Act of 1965, which, when passed, disallowed discriminatory tests like literacy tests and provided for federal examiners to register voters throughout much of the South. The Supreme Court, still the liberal Warren Court that had ruled in *Brown*, backed up this new legislation.[33] In addition, the Twenty-fourth Amendment, outlawing poll taxes in federal elections, was ratified in 1964.

Because of the unusual cooperation among the three branches of government, by the end of the 1960s, life in the South, though far from perfect, was radically different for blacks. In 1968, 18 percent of southern black students went to schools with a majority of white students; in 1970 the percentage rose to 39, and in 1972 to 46. The comparable figure for black students in the North was only 28 percent in 1972.[34] Voter registration had also improved dramatically: from 1964 to 1969, black voter registration in the South nearly doubled, from 36 to 65 percent of adult blacks.[35]

AP Photo/Bill Hudson, File

Nonviolence as a Strategy for Change

In Birmingham, Alabama, a seventeen-year-old demonstrator is attacked by a police dog after defying a city antiparade ordinance on May 3, 1963. This photograph, running on the front page of the New York Times *the next day, would draw the attention of President John F. Kennedy. As stories and images of such events spread across the country, more and more people demanded that the violence end and blacks be given equal rights and opportunities.*

CHANGING THE OUTCOMES: FIGHTING DE FACTO DISCRIMINATION Political and educational advances did not translate into substantial economic gains for blacks. As a group, they remained at the very bottom of the economic hierarchy, and ironically, the problem was most severe not in the rural South but in the industrialized North. Many southern blacks who had migrated to the North in search of jobs and a better quality of life found conditions not much different from those they had left behind. Abject poverty, discrimination in employment, and segregated schools and housing led to frustration and inflamed tempers. In the summers of 1966 and 1967, race riots flashed across the northern urban landscape. Impatient with the passive resistance of the nonviolent protest movement in the South, the Black Muslims, led by Malcolm X until his assassination in 1965; the Black Panthers; and the Student Nonviolent Coordinating Committee all demanded "black power" and radical change. These activists rejected the King philosophy of working peacefully through existing political institutions to bring about gradual change.

Northern whites who had applauded the desegregation of the South grew increasingly nervous as angry African Americans began to target segregation in the North. Although the de facto segregation in the North was not the product of laws that treated blacks and whites differently, black inner-city schools and white suburban schools were often as segregated as if the hand of Jim Crow had been at work. But the different residential patterns, socioeconomic trends, and years of traditions and customs that subtly discriminated against blacks and caused these patterns were in some ways harder to change than actual laws in the South had been.

In the 1970s the courts and some politicians, believing that they had a duty not only to end segregation laws in education but also to integrate all the nation's schools, instituted a policy of **busing** in some northern cities. Students from majority-white schools would be bused to mostly black schools, and vice versa. The policy was immediately controversial; riots in South Boston in 1974 resembled those in Little Rock seventeen years earlier.

Not all opponents of busing were reacting from racist motives. Busing students from their homes to a distant school strikes many Americans as fundamentally unjust. Parents who move to better neighborhoods so that they can send their children to better schools do not want to see those children bused back to their old schools. Parents want their children to be part of a local community and its activities, which is hard when the children must leave the community for the better part of each day. Even many African American families were opposed to busing because of fears for their children's safety and because of the often long bus rides into predominantly white neighborhoods.

The Supreme Court has shared America's ambivalence about busing. Although it endorsed busing as a remedy for segregated schools in 1971,[36] three years later it ruled that busing plans could not merge inner-city and suburban districts unless officials could prove that the district lines had been drawn in a racially discriminatory manner.[37] Since many whites were moving out of the cities, there were fewer white students to bus, and busing did not really succeed in integrating schools in many urban areas. More than sixty years after the *Brown* decision, many schools, especially those in urban areas, remain largely segregated.[38]

> **busing** achieving racial balance by transporting students to schools across neighborhood boundaries

EARLY EFFORTS AT AFFIRMATIVE ACTION Civil rights activists and policymakers have faced the difficult problem of deciding whether the Fourteenth Amendment guarantee of equal protection simply requires that the states not sanction discrimination or whether it imposes an active obligation on them to integrate blacks and whites. As the northern experience shows, the absence of legal discrimination does not mean equality. In 1965 President Johnson issued an executive order that prohibited discrimination in firms doing business with the government and ordered them to take **affirmative action** to compensate for past discrimination. In other words, if a firm had no black employees, it wasn't enough not to have a policy against hiring them; the firm now had to actively recruit and hire blacks. The test would not be the law or the hiring procedure, but the actual outcome of that procedure—the racial mix of employees.

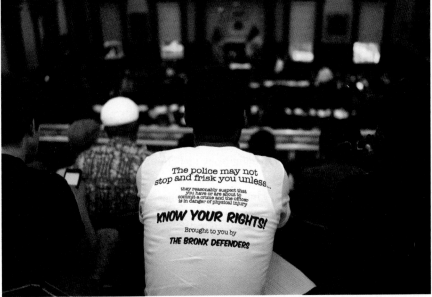

Random, but Not Equal

Police departments claim that because they stop individuals at random, stop-and-frisk checks are not discriminatory in nature. But African Americans are stopped at much higher rates than are other Americans—leading to concerns that the practice is discriminatory. The subject has been a matter of much debate, including during this New York City Council hearing and the 2016 presidential campaign, when Donald Trump came out in support of the policy, recommending that it be used in Chicago.

Johnson's call for affirmative action was taken seriously not only in employment situations but also in university decisions. Patterns of discrimination in employment and higher education showed the results of decades of decisions by white males to hire or admit other white males. Blacks, as well as other minorities and women, were relegated to low-paying, low-status jobs. After Johnson's executive order, the EEOC decided that the percentage of blacks working in firms should reflect the percentage of blacks in the labor force. Many colleges and universities reserved space on their admissions lists for minorities, sometimes accepting minority applicants with grades and test scores lower than those of whites.

Like busing, affirmative action has proved controversial among the American public. We have talked about the tension in American politics between procedural and substantive equality, between equality of treatment and equality of results. That is precisely the tension that arises when Americans are faced with policies of busing and affirmative action, both of which are instances of American policy attempting to bring about substantive equality. The end results seem attractive, but the means to get there—treating people differently—seem inherently unfair in the American value system.

The Court reflected the public's unease with these affirmative action policies when it ruled in *Regents of the University of California v. Bakke* in 1978 that it was a violation of the equal protection clause for the medical school at the University of California, Davis, to have a quota system that held sixteen of one hundred spots for minorities. But it did not reject the idea of affirmative action, holding that schools can have a legitimate interest in having a diversified student body, and that they can take race into account in admissions decisions, just as they can take into account geographic location, athletic ability, or alumni parents, for instance.[39] In this and several later cases, the Court signaled its approval of the intent of affirmative action, even though it occasionally took issue with specific implementations.[40]

Such judicial tolerance for affirmative action was the standard until the Reagan years. That administration lobbied the Court strenuously to change its rulings on the constitutionality of affirmative action and the message fell on fertile ground. In 1989 the Court fulfilled civil rights advocates' most pessimistic expectations, striking down a variety of civil rights laws.[41] The Democratic-led Congress sought to undo some of the Court's late-1980s rulings by passing the Civil Rights Act of 1991, which made it easier for workers to seek redress against employers who discriminate, but the country had turned rightward and the civil rights era was over.

> **affirmative action** a policy of creating opportunities for members of certain groups as a substantive remedy for past discrimination

BLACKS IN CONTEMPORARY AMERICAN POLITICS

The Supreme Court's use of strict scrutiny on laws that discriminate on the basis of race has put an end to most de jure discrimination. However, de facto discrimination remains, with all the consequences that stem from the fact that tradition and practice in the United States endorse a fundamental inequality of power. Although groups like Black Lives Matter have called public attention to the fact that young black men are often racially profiled, killed by police without justification, and incarcerated at higher rates than whites, there are other, more subtle ways that we fall short of true racial equality.

THE ECONOMIC OUTLOOK FOR BLACKS Although there is a large and growing black middle class in many parts of the country, blacks lag behind whites on most socioeconomic indicators. The median household income for African Americans in 2014 was $35,398; for whites, it was $60,256. Blacks trail whites in businesses owned, small business loans received, homeownership, and other indicators of achieving the promises of the American Dream.[42] (See *Snapshot of America: Poverty, Prosperity, and Education, by Race and Ethnicity* for more comparisons.)

One study by two sociologists uncovered the dispiriting fact that, all other things being equal, African American doctors, lawyers, and real estate managers make less than their white counterparts. Those in securities and financial services fields make seventy-two cents for every dollar earned by a white man in the same job. They speculate that perhaps the gap is due to blacks tending to be assigned by employers to black clients, who are often less financially well off than whites.[43] Such studies show how subtle and yet how pervasive economic inequities can be.[44] *Snapshot of America: Poverty, Prosperity, and Education, by Race and Ethnicity* also provides data on educational disparities that still exist.

POLITICAL GAINS AND LOSSES In 2008 the nation elected its first African American president. Barack Obama served two terms and left office a popular president. It's tempting to think that that signals the end of racial discrimination in politics, and it is true that when Obama was on the ballot, African American voter turnout was way up. Due in large part to President Obama's effective voter mobilization effort, African American turnout in 2012 was a robust 13 percent of the electorate, but it was only 12 percent of a smaller electorate in 2016. Obama's administration promised to usher in a much more relaxed attitude toward race, but he faced unprecedented obstruction from Congress and a significant percentage of Americans who believed he was not born in the United States and thus was never qualified to be president. As we saw in *What's at Stake . . . ?*, his election may have served to ratchet up the anxiety of whites who felt their status was threatened, making them ripe targets for the high-strung, racially tinged rhetoric of right-wing entertainer-commentators and ultimately resulting in the election of Donald Trump.

It's an open question whether Obama's presidency will have an overall effect on the numbers of African Americans in U.S. politics, especially if black turnout in elections remains below the levels in 2008 and 2012. In the wake of Obama's election, African Americans appeared to be more optimistic about black progress. A majority (53 percent) said life will be better for blacks in the future (compared to 44 percent who said so in 2007), and 54 percent of blacks said Obama's election had improved race relations, but by 2013, only 32 percent said that a lot of progress had been made toward Martin Luther King's dream of racial equality.[45] By 2015 the Black Lives Matter movement had formed to protest the killings of young black men by police officers in the wake of teenage Trayvon Martin's murder in Florida and the killing of Michael Brown in Ferguson, Missouri. Even Obama had begun to speak out more on race. Racial tensions were further inflamed in the wake of Trump's election, causing one commentator to call it a "whitelash" to Obama's presidency.[46]

Because people of lower income and education levels are less likely to vote, African Americans' economic disadvantage had, until 2008, translated into a political limitation as well, especially in a country with a history of suppressing the black vote. The Voting Rights Act of 1965 put protections in place, but in 2013, in a five-to-four decision, the Supreme Court threw out a part of the law that it claims requires updating: the clause that requires nine southern states to "pre-clear" with the Department of Justice any changes they make to their voting laws to be sure they are race neutral. The ruling left the door open for new congressional legislation to qualify states for pre-clearance, but so far, although Democrats have pushed for such legislation, Republican stalling tactics have held it off.[47] It remains to be seen how Democrats will fare in future years in the face of more restrictive voting rules. In the meantime, the courts have continued to push back at what they see as more egregious attempts to limit voting rights. In 2017, for instance, the Supreme Court let stand a 2016 federal appeals court decision that struck down a North Carolina voter ID law that was unconstitutional because it targeted African American voters with almost "surgical precision."[48] In 2018 the Supreme Court refrained from taking a clear stand against gerrymandering.

African Americans have had difficulty overcoming barriers not just on the voting side of the democratic equation. In terms of elected officials, progress has been mixed. By 2001 there were slightly more than nine thousand black elected

Snapshot of America: *Poverty, Prosperity, and Education, by Race and Ethnicity*

Population and Poverty

HISPANIC **ASIAN**

AFRICAN AMERICANS **WHITE**

12.7%

% of U.S. Population in Poverty

19% 10% 22% 8.8%

% of each group in poverty

Source: U.S. Census Bureau, *Current Population Reports: Income and Poverty in the United States: 2016,* Table 3, www.census.gov/content/dam/Census/library/publications/2017/demo/P60-259.pdf.

Education and Median Income

Didn't Graduate[1]		High School[2]	Associate's[3]	Bachelor's	Advanced
33%		42%	8%	12%	5%
$29,000		$35,000	$39,000	$53,000	$80,000

Didn't Graduate	High School	Associate's	Bachelor's	Advanced
10%	29%	6%	31%	24%
$29,000	$32,000	$42,000	$67,000	**$105,000**

Didn't Graduate	High School	Associate's	Bachelor's	Advanced
16%	50%	10%	15%	9%
$22,000	$30,000	$39,000	$58,000	$80,000

Didn't Graduate	High School	Associate's	Bachelor's	Advanced
14%	42%	11%	22%	13%
$26,000	$39,000	$46,000	$70,000	$97,000

Sources: U.S. Census Bureau, "Educational Attainment in the United States: 2017," www.census.gov/data/tables/2017/demo/education-attainment/cps-detailed-tables.html, table 3; Current Population Survey Tables for Personal Income. PINC-04. Educational Attainment--People 18 Years Old and Over, by Total Money Earnings, Work Experience, Age, Race, Hispanic Origin, and Sex, www.census.gov/data/tables/time-series/demo/income-poverty/cps-pinc/pinc-04.html.

Notes: 1. Includes GED. 2. Includes those with high school diploma, as well as those with some college but no degree. 3 Includes both vocational and academic associate's degrees.

Behind the Numbers

There are sizable racial and ethnic group differences in income and those living in poverty. Twice as many African Americans, Hispanics, and Native Americans live in poverty as whites and Asians. What explanations might account for these differences? Should government play a role in bringing about more equality?

officials in the United States, in posts ranging from local education and law enforcement jobs to the U.S. Congress. But the number of African Americans is much higher at local levels of government, where the constituents who elect them are more likely to be African American themselves. As the constituencies grow larger and more diverse, the task of black candidates gets tougher. In 2016 there were well over 500 black mayors[49] but no African American governors. This seems likely to continue in 2018, with two African American gubernatorial candidates facing razor thin deficits in their races as of this writing. In the 116th Congress, elected in 2018, more than 50 of 435 members of the House of Representatives were black, and there were three black senators.

AFFIRMATIVE ACTION TODAY Affirmative action continues to be a controversial policy in America. The American public remains divided: opinion polls show support for the ideals behind affirmative action, but not if it is perceived to be giving minorities preferential treatment.[50] Some states have taken matters into their own hands. In 1996, voters in California declared affirmative action illegal in their state, and voters in Washington did the same in 1998. Michigan voted to ban affirmative action in the state's public colleges and government contracting in 2006, and affirmative action was on the ballot in Colorado and Nebraska in 2008. Although the ban passed in Nebraska with 58 percent of the vote, it was defeated narrowly in Colorado. Arizona passed a constitutional ban on government-sponsored affirmative action programs in 2010.

A number of cases have come before the federal courts and, in general, while respecting that universities seek diverse student bodies, the courts have taken the notion that race is a suspect classification to mean that any laws treating people differently according to race must be given strict scrutiny. Even though strict scrutiny has traditionally been used to support the rights of racial minorities, when applied consistently across the board, it can also preclude laws that give them special treatment or preferences, even if those preferences are meant to create more equality. That doesn't necessarily mean that the courts throw out the laws, but they do hold them to a higher standard. In a 2001 case rejecting a University of Michigan Law School affirmative action policy, a federal district court judge stated the principle bluntly: "All racial distinctions are inherently suspect and presumptively invalid. . . . Whatever solution the law school elects to pursue, it must be race-neutral."[51] A few months later, a federal appeals court held that the University of Georgia's affirmative action policy was unconstitutional. It said that although a university can strive to achieve a diverse student body, race could not be the only factor used to define diversity.[52]

The University of Michigan Law School case eventually found its way to the Supreme Court, along with another that dealt with Michigan's undergraduate admissions policy. The Court threw out the university's undergraduate admissions policy because it was tantamount to racial quotas.[53] In a five-to-four decision, however, the Court held that the law school's holistic approach of taking into account the race of the applicant was constitutional because of the importance of creating a diverse student body.[54] Just ten years later, however, in 2013, a considerably more conservative Court than the one in 2003 held that race-based admissions standards had to be given strict scrutiny and, in a separate ruling, upheld a Michigan ban on using race in admissions decisions.[55] Supporters of affirmative action were surprised and pleased when the Court reaffirmed in June 2016 that race can be considered in college admissions decisions.[56]

The issues raised by the affirmative action debate in the United States deserve to be taken seriously by students of American politics. Unlike many earlier debates in American civil rights politics, this one cannot be reduced to questions of racism and bigotry. What is at stake are two competing images of what America ought to be about. On one side is a vision of an America whose discriminatory past is past and whose job today is to treat all citizens the same. This view, shared by many minorities as well as many white Americans, argues that providing a set of lower standards for some groups is not fair to anybody. Ward Connerly, an African American businessman and a former member of the University of California Board of Regents, whose American Civil Rights Institute is a strong opponent of affirmative action, says that "people tend to perform at the level of competition. When the bar is raised, we rise to the occasion. That is exactly what black students will do in a society that has equal standards for all."[57]

On the other side of the debate are those who argue that affirmative action programs have made a real difference in equalizing chances in society, and although they are meant to be temporary, their work is not yet done. These advocates claim that the old patterns of behavior are so ingrained that they can be changed only by conscious effort. *New York Times* writer David Shipler says, "White males have long benefited from unstated preferences as fraternity brothers, golfing buddies, children of alumni and the like—unconscious biases that go largely unrecognized until affirmative action forces recruiters to think about how they gravitate toward people like themselves."[58]

PAUSE AND REVIEW Who, What, How

All Americans have had a great deal at stake in the civil rights movement. Blacks have struggled, first, to be recognized as American citizens and, then, to exercise the rights that go along with citizenship. Lacking fundamental rights, they also lacked economic and social power. Those who fought to withhold their rights knew

Tammy Duckworth

U.S. Senate Photographic Studio: Renee Bouchard

For Senator Tammy Duckworth, her steel and titanium legs are a sign of strength, her wheel chair is a badge of honor. This woman, who followed her father and a long line of relatives into the military was willing to give her life for her country, but she doesn't look at November 12 (the day the helicopter she was piloting in Iraq was attacked) as a day of self-pity. On that day in 2018, coincidently when Veteran's Day was observed, she tweeted:

"Today is my Alive Day, the anniversary of the day I almost died but didn't. On this day 14 years ago, an RPG tore through the cockpit of the helicopter I was flying over Iraq, taking my legs and partial use of my right arm with it.

I was quite literally in pieces, but my buddies risked their lives and refused to leave me behind. Every day I think about what they did for me and what I can do to repay them. Making sure I don't let them down is what drives me to do everything I can for our Veterans and troops."

That is what a commitment to service looks like. Duckworth, the daughter of an American soldier and an Asian mom, grew up all over Southeast Asia. Her father worked first in the Marines, then for the UN. She was struck by the fact that, even though we had just lost a war there, Americans were revered—primarily because of our involvement in President John F. Kennedy's Peace Corps program. Pictures of Kennedy adorned the walls of homes—the country saw the U.S. as a partner who could be trusted for equal treatment and fairness. Duckworth wanted to represent that spirit and those values.

She attended George Washington University in Washington, D.C., intending to head for the Foreign Service, but she hung out with a military crowd and they convinced her to take a ROTC class or two, where she studied with members of the Reserve Officer Training Corps. She "fell in love with the Army." She was always part-time, working toward a Ph.D. in political science (a degree she completed several years ago while serving as a Member of Congress). In the middle of writing her dissertation she was deployed to Iraq. When she came home, it was to Walter Reed hospital.

Life takes odd turns. As the highest ranking amputee at Walter Reed, Duckworth was already taking a leadership position among her fellow wounded

warriors. Senator Dick Durbin from Illinois came to visit and was impressed. He invited her to one of President George W. Bush's State of the Union addresses as his guest and he realized she was tougher than he thought when he found out she had an IV tucked under her sleeve.

He talked her into running for Congress and, although she lost her first congressional campaign, she got to know Durbin and a young senator from Illinois, Barack Obama. After running the Illinois Department of Veterans Affairs, she went to work for then-President Obama in the U.S. Department of Veterans Affairs. She ran for Congress again a few years later, won, and ended up in the Senate where she makes a significant impact as a strong advocate for her fellow veterans.

One of the main issues she is focused on and one that comes straight from her life experience, is the creation of a national community service program that she hopes will get to the floor for a vote soon. Her bill is an invitation for Americans of all backgrounds to serve in a variety of non-mandatory capacities. Every person would get a letter in the mail detailing the opportunities available to them when they turn 18. Under current law, serving in the Armed Forces gets you four years of college, but Duckworth is keen to show young people that there are multiple ways to show ones commitment to the country, from Teach for America to AmeriCorps, to opportunities not yet invented—from the national to the local level. Unless you opt out, a letter would continue to arrive every two years until you are thirty, to see if your life has changed in a way that makes service feasible and attractive.

On the importance of service

"I don't know that young people know that they can serve. I feel like there is a disconnect between military families who know about serving and they serve and the same ones serve over and over again, and poor families know about service often times because it's the only way out."

On keeping the republic

"Vote. Really. Vote. Because not voting is just ceding your voice to someone who may not truly represent you."

Source: Tammy Duckworth spoke with Christine Barbour and Gerald C. Wright on September 27, 2018.

that recognizing them would inevitably upset the traditional power structure in both the South and the North.

The formal citizenship rights granted African Americans by way of the Thirteenth, Fourteenth, and Fifteenth Amendments should have changed the rules of American politics sufficiently to allow blacks to enter the political world on an equal footing with whites. Yet when Congress and the courts failed to enforce the Reconstruction amendments, southern blacks were at the mercy of discriminatory state and local laws for nearly a century. Those laws were finally changed by a combination of tactics that succeeded in eliminating much of the de jure discrimination that had followed the Civil War. However, they were not very effective in remedying the de facto discrimination that persisted, particularly in the North. Efforts to get rid of de facto discrimination generally involve substantive remedies like affirmative action, which remain controversial with procedure-loving Americans. The remnants of past discrimination, in the form of greater poverty and lower education levels for blacks, mean that increased political rights are not easily translated into equal economic and social power.

In Your Own Words Summarize key events and outcomes in the struggle for equality of African Americans.

RIGHTS DENIED ON THE BASIS OF OTHER RACIAL AND ETHNIC IDENTITIES

Different paths to equality for Native Americans, Hispanics, and Asian Americans

African Americans are by no means the only Americans whose civil rights have been denied on racial or ethnic grounds. Native Americans, Hispanics, and Asian Americans have all faced their own particular kind of discrimination. For historical and cultural reasons, these groups have had different political resources available to them, and thus their struggles have taken shape in different ways.

NATIVE AMERICANS

Native Americans of various tribes shared the so-called New World for centuries before it was "discovered" by Europeans. The relationship between the original inhabitants of this continent and the European colonists and their governments has been difficult, marked by the new arrivals' clear intent to settle and develop the Native Americans' ancestral lands, and complicated by the Europeans' failure to understand the Indians' cultural, spiritual, and political heritage. The lingering effects of these centuries-old conflicts continue to color the political, social, and economic experience of Native Americans today.

NATIVE AMERICANS AND THE U.S. GOVERNMENT

The precise status of Native American tribes in American politics and in constitutional law is complicated. The Indians always saw themselves as sovereign independent nations, making treaties, waging war, and otherwise dealing with the early Americans from a position of strength and equality. But that sovereignty has not been recognized consistently by the United States. The commerce clause of the Constitution (Article I, Section 8) gives Congress the power to regulate trade "with foreign nations, among the several states, and with the Indian tribes." The U.S. perception of Indian tribes as neither foreign countries nor states was underscored by Chief Justice John Marshall in 1831. Denying the Cherokees the right to challenge a Georgia law in the Supreme Court, as a foreign nation would be able to do, Marshall declared that the Indian tribes were "domestic dependent nations."[59]

Until 1871, however, Congress continued to treat the tribes outwardly as if they were sovereign nations, making treaties with them to buy their land and relocate them. The truth is that regardless of the treaties, the commerce clause was interpreted as giving Congress guardianship over Indian affairs. The tribes were often forcibly moved from their traditional lands; by the mid-1800s, most were living in western territories on land that had no spiritual meaning for them, where their hunting and farming traditions were ineffective, leaving them dependent on federal aid. The creation of the Bureau of Indian Affairs in 1824 as part of the Department of War (moved, in 1849, to the Department of the Interior) institutionalized that guardian role, and the central issues became what the role of the federal government would be and how much self-government the Indians should have.[60]

Modern congressional policy toward the Native Americans has varied from trying to assimilate them into the broader, European-based culture to encouraging them to develop economic independence and self-government. The combination of these two strategies—stripping them of their native lands and cultural identity, and reducing their federal funding to encourage more independence—has resulted in tremendous social and economic dislocation in the Indian communities. Poverty, joblessness, and alcoholism have built communities of despair and frustration for many Native Americans. Their situation has been aggravated as Congress has denied them many of the rights promised in their treaties in order to exploit the natural resources so abundant in the western lands they have been forced onto, or as they have been forced to sell rights to those resources in order to survive.

POLITICAL STRATEGIES The political environment in which Native Americans found themselves in the mid-twentieth century was very different from the one faced by African Americans. What was at stake were Indians' civil rights and their enforcement, and the fulfillment of old promises and the preservation of a culture that did not easily coexist with modern American economic and political beliefs and practice. For cultures that emphasized the spirituality of living in harmony with lands that cannot really "belong" to anyone, haggling over mining and fishing rights seems the ultimate desecration. But the government they rejected in their quest for self-determination and tribal traditions was the same government they depended on to keep poverty at bay.

Essentially, Native American tribes find themselves in a relationship with the national government that mimics elements of federalism, what some scholars have called "fry-bread federalism."[61] Although that relationship has evolved over time, the gist of it is that American Indians are citizens of tribes as well as citizens of the United States, with rights coming from each. It was not clear what strategy the Native Americans should follow in trying to get their U.S. rights recognized. State politics did not provide any remedies, not merely because of local prejudice but also because the Indian reservations were separate legal entities under the federal government. Because Congress itself has been largely responsible for denying the rights of Native Americans, it was not a likely source of support for their expansion. Too many important economic interests with influence in Congress have had a lot at stake in getting their hands on Indian-held resources. In 1977 a federal review commission found the Bureau of Indian Affairs guilty of failing to safeguard Indian legal, financial, and safety interests. Nor were the courts anxious to extend rights to Native Americans. Most noticeably in cases concerning religious freedom, the Supreme Court has found compelling state interests to outweigh most Indian claims to religious freedom. In 1988, for instance, the Court ruled that the Forest Service could allow roads and timber cutting in national forests that had been used by Indian tribes for religious purposes.[62] And in 1990 the Court held that two Native American drug counselors who had been dismissed for using peyote, a hallucinogenic drug traditionally used in Native American religious ceremonies, were not entitled to unemployment benefits from the state of Oregon.[63]

Like many other groups shut out from access to political institutions, Native Americans took their political fate into their own hands. Focusing on working outside the system to change public opinion and to persuade Congress to alter public policy, the Indians formed interest groups like the National Congress of American Indians (NCAI), founded in 1944, and the American Indian Movement (AIM), founded in 1968, to

Economics Over Indian Rights?
Native Americans march on Washington, D.C., in 2017 to protest the construction of the Dakota Access Pipeline (DAPL) near the Standing Rock Sioux reservation in North Dakota. The protestors say the construction is a threat to their sacred grounds and water.

Justin Sullivan/Getty Images

fight for their cause. AIM, for example, staged dramatic demonstrations, such as the 1969 takeover of Alcatraz Island in San Francisco Bay and the 1973 occupation of a reservation at Wounded Knee (the location of an 1890 massacre of Sioux Indians). AIM drew public attention to the plight of many Native Americans and, at the same time, to the divisions within the Indian community on such central issues as self-rule, treaty enforcement, and the role of the federal government.

CONTEMPORARY CHALLENGES For all the militant activism of the 1960s and 1970s, Native Americans have made no giant strides in redressing the centuries of dominance by white people. They remain at the bottom of the income scale in America, earning less than African Americans on average, and their living conditions are often poor. In 2016, 26.2 percent of American Indians lived in poverty, compared to only 14.0 percent of the total U.S. population.[64] And in 2016 only 79.9 percent of adult Native Americans (aged twenty-five years or older) held a high school diploma, compared to 87.5 percent of the overall adult population.[65] Consider, for example, the individuals on the Pine Ridge Indian Reservation in Pine Ridge, South Dakota. Some 70 percent are unemployed, fewer than 10 percent have graduated from high school, and life expectancy is somewhere in the high forties, much lower than the national average, which approaches eighty years.[66]

Since the 1980s, however, an ironic twist of legal interpretation has enabled some Native Americans to parlay their status as semisovereign nations into a foundation for economic

A Rising Tide

Turnout among Hispanic Americans has been historically low, but as a group Hispanics carry considerable—and growing—political clout. Large and highly organized groups like Voto Latino have focused on getting eligible Hispanic voters registered and mobilized to vote, and they can have a strong impact on elections in key regions of the country.

prosperity. As a result of two court cases,[67] and Congress' 1988 Indian Gaming Regulatory Act, if a state allows any form of legalized gambling at all, even a state lottery, then Indian reservations in that state may allow all sorts of gambling, subject only to the regulation of the Bureau of Indian Affairs. Many reservations now have casinos that rival Las Vegas in gaudy splendor, and the money is pouring into their coffers. Close to thirty states now allow Indian gambling casinos, which in 2016 brought in more than $31 billion, more than Native Americans received in federal aid.[68] In 2016, Native American gaming revenue represented 44.5 percent of all casino gambling revenue nationwide,[69] although many tribes and individuals have no share in it.

Casino gambling is controversial on several counts. Native Americans themselves are of two minds about it—some see gambling as their economic salvation and others as spiritually ruinous. The revenue created by the casinos has allowed Indian tribes to become major donors to political campaigns in states such as California, which has increased their political clout though leaving them open to criticism for making big money donations while many reservations remain poverty stricken. Many other Americans object for economic reasons. Opponents like President Donald Trump, a casino owner, claim that Congress is giving special privileges to Native Americans that may threaten their own business interests. Regardless of the moral and economic questions unleashed by the casino boom, for many Native Americans it is a way to recoup at least some of the resources that were lost in the past.

Politically, there is the potential for improvement as well. Although recent Supreme Court cases failed to support religious freedom for Native Americans, some lower court orders have supported their rights. In 1996 President Bill Clinton issued an executive order that requires federal agencies to protect and provide access to sacred religious sites of American Indians, which has been a major point of contention in Indian-federal relations. Until the Supreme Court ruled in 1996 that electoral districts could not be drawn to enhance the power of particular racial groups, Native Americans had been gaining strength at the polls, to better defend their local interests. Still, the number of American Indian state representatives has increased slightly in the past few years[70]; two American Indians, Tom Cole and Markwayne Mullin, both Republicans from Oklahoma, are currently serving in the House of Representatives and Sharice Davids, a Democrat from Kansas, became the first American Indian woman elected to the House in 2018. Democratic senator Elizabeth Warren of Massachusetts also claims American Indian ancestry.

HISPANIC AMERICANS

Hispanic Americans, often also called Latinos, are a diverse group with yet another history of discrimination in the United States. They did not have to contend with the tradition of slavery that burdened blacks, and they don't have the unique legal problems of Native Americans, but they face peculiar challenges of their own in trying to fight discrimination and raise their standing in American society. Among the reasons that the Hispanic experience is different are the diversity within the Hispanic population; the language barrier that many face; and the political reaction to immigration, particularly undocumented immigration, from Mexico into the United States that often spills over to legal immigrants or citizens of Hispanic ancestry who have lived in the United States for generations. The contentious nature of the immigration debate means the narratives driving the debate are mediating people's opinions about the people involved.

Hispanics are the largest minority group in the United States today, making up over 16 percent of the population. Their numbers have more than tripled in recent years, from 14.6 million in 1980 to 57.5 million in 2016.[71] Between the 2000 and 2010 censuses, the Hispanic population grew at a rate that is four times the U.S. average.[72] Clearly, issues concerning Hispanics will become much more central to the country as a whole as the twenty-first century continues to unfold.

DIVERSITY As we said, a striking feature of the Hispanic population is its diversity. Hispanics have in common their Spanish heritage, but they have arrived in the United States traveling different routes, at different times. The vast majority of the current Hispanic population is Mexican. Americans with Mexican backgrounds, called Chicanos or Chicanas, do not necessarily share the concerns and issues of more recent Mexican-born immigrants, so there is diversity even within this group. Immigrants from U.S. territories like Puerto Rico or from different countries—Costa Rica, Colombia, Argentina, and any number of other Latin American nations—have settled across the United States. Mexican Americans are concentrated largely in California, Texas, Arizona, and New Mexico; Puerto Ricans tend to settle in New York, New Jersey, and other northern states; and Cubans are clustered in South Florida.

These groups differ in more than place of origin and settlement. Cubans are much more likely to have been political refugees, escaping the communist government of Fidel Castro, whereas those from other countries tend to be economic refugees looking for a better life. Because educated, professional Cubans are the ones who fled, they have largely regained their higher socioeconomic status in this country. For instance, almost 24 percent of Cuban Americans are college educated, a percentage comparable to that found in the U.S. population as a whole, but only 9 percent of Mexican Americans and 16 percent of Puerto Ricans are college graduates.[73] Consequently, Cuban Americans also hold more professional and managerial jobs, and their standard of living, on average, is much higher. What this diversity means is that there is little reason for Hispanics to view themselves as a single ethnic group with common interests and thus to act in political concert. Their numbers suggest that if they acted together they would wield considerable clout. However, college attendance among Hispanics has increased sharply in recent years, so some of those differences may even out in time.[74]

THE ENGLISH-ONLY MOVEMENT Language has also presented a special challenge to Hispanics. The United States today ranks sixth in the world in the number of people who consider Spanish a first language, with an active and important Spanish-language media of radio, television, and press. This preponderance of Spanish speakers is probably due less to a refusal on the part of Hispanics to learn English than to the arrival of new immigrants.[75] Nonetheless, especially in areas with large Hispanic populations, white Anglos feel threatened by what they see as the encroachment of Spanish. Many communities have launched **English-only movements** to make English the official language, precluding foreign languages from appearing on ballots and official documents. The English-only controversy is clearly about more than language—it is about national and cultural identity, a struggle to lay claim to the voice of America.

THE CONTROVERSY OVER IMMIGRATION A final concern that makes the Hispanic struggle for civil rights unique in America is the reaction against immigration, particularly undocumented immigration from Mexico. As we saw in Chapter 2, undocumented immigration is a critical problem in some areas of the country. A backlash against undocumented or even legal immigration has serious consequences for Hispanic American citizens, who may be indistinguishable in appearance, name, and language from recent immigrants. They have found themselves suspected, followed, and challenged by the police; forced to show proof of legal residence on demand; and subjected to unpleasant reactions from non-Hispanic citizens who blame an entire ethnic group for the perceived behavior of a few of its members. All this makes acceptance into American society more difficult for Hispanics; encourages segregation; and makes the subtle denial of equal rights in employment, housing, and education, for instance, easier to carry out.

POLITICAL STRATEGIES Though Hispanics have faced formidable barriers to assimilation, their political position is improving. Like African Americans, they have had some success in organizing and calling public attention to their circumstances. Cesar Chavez, as leader of the United Farm Workers in the 1960s, drew national attention to the conditions under which farm workers labored. Following the principles of the civil rights movement, he highlighted concerns of social justice in his call for a nationwide boycott of grapes and lettuce picked by nonunion labor, and in the process he became a symbol of the Hispanic struggle for equal rights. More recently groups like the National Council of La Raza, the Mexican American Legal Defense and Education Fund (MALDEF), and the League of United Latin American Citizens (LULAC) continue to lobby for immigration reform, for Latino civil engagement, and for the end of discrimination against Hispanic Americans.

For much of our history, the voter turnout rate for Hispanics has been low because they are disproportionately poor and poor people are less likely to vote, but this situation is changing. Where the socioeconomic status of Hispanics is

> **English-only movements** efforts to make English the official language of the United States

high and where their numbers are concentrated, as in South Florida, their political clout is considerable. Presidential candidates, mindful of Florida's twenty-nine electoral votes, regularly make pilgrimages to South Florida to denounce Cuba's communist policies, a position popular among the Cuban American voters there. Although President Obama resumed relations with Cuba assuming that a policy of disengagement and sanctions had not worked, the politics of that may be changing. Grassroots political organization has also paid off for Hispanic communities, especially registration drives in states like California, Texas, and New Mexico. Such movements have increased registration of Hispanic voters. Turnout has been creeping up in general elections, and was up in 2018 as well, with Latino voters comprising and estimated 11 percent of the electorate, up from 9 percent in 2008. Issues like immigration have helped to politicize Hispanic Americans and, as the Republican base has become solidly against immigration reform, Hispanics have increasingly voted Democratic.

Because of the increase in the number of potential Hispanic voters, and because of the prominence of the Hispanic population in battleground states such as Florida, New Mexico, Colorado, Nevada, and even in places such as Iowa, where one might not expect a significant Hispanic population, candidates generally court Hispanic voters, as Barack Obama and Mitt Romney did in 2012. Although at one time there was bipartisan consensus on immigration reform, in recent years it has become a partisan issue, with Democrats proposing more generous immigration policies, and Republicans seeking to tighten them. Republicans made it a point to defeat the DREAM (Development, Relief, and Education for Alien Minors) Act, different versions of which would have provided a path to permanent residency and even citizenship for the children of undocumented immigrants who came to this country as minors, but who have completed high school here and maintained a good moral character. In 2012 President Obama took matters into his own hands, announcing that his administration would grant a special immigration status to young people who fit the DREAM profile, deferring any deportation action against them for two years. Ultimately, the 2012 Latino vote broke for Obama, 71 to 27 percent. In the immediate aftermath of the election, Republicans held a "post-mortem" to see where their voter outreach efforts needed to be beefed up. The initial consensus was that they needed to join Democrats behind immigration reform or they would lose the Latino vote for a generation or more. Such a plan proved too much for the Tea Party faction of the party, however, and the efforts of more moderate party members came to nothing. Donald Trump made opposition to immigration the original plank of his campaign, and Hillary Clinton won the Latino vote handily. Despite the presence of an immigration opponent on the ballot, however, Hispanic turnout wasn't up enough to cost Trump the election.

There were roughly forty Hispanic representatives in the 116th Congress and four Hispanic senators. There are three Hispanic governors (Brian Sandoval of Nevada, Susana Martinez of New Mexico and Chris Sununu of New Hampshire). In 2004 President Bush appointed Alberto Gonzales to be the first Hispanic attorney general, and in 2009 President Obama appointed Sonia Sotomayor to be the first Hispanic justice on the U.S. Supreme Court.

ASIAN AMERICANS

Asian Americans share some of the experiences of Hispanics, facing cultural prejudice as well as racism and absorbing some of the public backlash against immigration. Yet the history of Asian American immigration, the explosive events of World War II, and the impressive educational and economic success of many Asian Americans mean that the Asian experience is also in many ways unique.

DIVERSITY Like Hispanics, the Asian American population is diverse. There are Americans with roots in China, Japan, Korea, the Philippines, India, Vietnam, Laos, and Cambodia, to name just a few. Asian Americans vary not only by their country of origin but also by the time of their arrival in the United States. There are Chinese and Japanese Americans whose families have lived here for nearly two centuries, arriving in the early 1800s with the waves of immigrants who came to work in the frontier West. In part because of the resentment of white workers, whose wages were being squeezed by the low pay the immigrants would accept, Congress passed the Chinese Exclusion Act in 1882, halting immigration from China, and the National Origin Act of 1925, barring the entry of the Japanese. It was 1943 before Congress repealed the Chinese Exclusion Act, and 1965 before Asian immigrants were treated the same as those of other nationalities. Asians and Pacific Islanders are currently the fastest-growing immigrant group in America, arriving from all over Asia but in particular from Vietnam, Laos, and Cambodia.

Today Asian Americans live in every region of the United States. In 2015, Asians comprised 56 percent of the population in Hawaii, and six million were living in California.[76] As of 2015, Asians were the fastest growing racial or ethnic group in the country, with 60 percent of their growth coming from international migration.[77] Los Angeles had the largest Asian population of any U.S. county. The more recent immigrants are spread unevenly throughout the country, with increasing numbers in the south.

DISCRIMINATION Asians have faced discrimination in the United States since their arrival. The fact that they are identifiable by their appearance has made assimilation into the larger European American population difficult. While most immigrants dream of becoming citizens in their new country, and eventually gaining political influence through the right to vote, that option was at first not open to Asians. The Naturalization Act of 1790 provided only for white immigrants to become naturalized citizens, and with few exceptions—for Filipino soldiers in the U.S. Army during World War II, for example—the act was in force until 1952. Branded "aliens ineligible for citizenship," not only were Asians permanently disenfranchised, but in many states they could not even own or rent property. Female citizens wishing to marry Asian "aliens" lost their own citizenship. The exclusionary immigration laws of 1882 and 1925 reflect this country's hostility to Asians, but at no other time was anti-Asian sentiment so painfully evident than in the white American reaction to Japanese Americans during World War II.

As we saw earlier in this chapter, in our discussion of *Korematsu v. United States*, when the United States found itself at war with Japan, there was a strong backlash against Asian Americans.[78] In 1942 the U.S. government began to round up Japanese Americans, forcing them to abandon or sell their property, and putting them in detention camps for purposes of "national security." While the government was worried about security threats posed by those with Japanese sympathies, two-thirds of the 120,000 incarcerated were American citizens. Neither German Americans nor Italian Americans, both of whose homelands were also at war with the United States, were stripped of their rights. Remarkably, after they were incarcerated, young Japanese men were asked to sign oaths of loyalty to the American government so that they could be drafted into military service. Those who refused in outrage over their treatment were imprisoned. The crowning insult was the *Korematsu* case, when the Supreme Court approved of curfews and detention camps for Japanese Americans.[79] Though the government later backed down and, in fact, in 1988 paid $1.25 billion as reparation to survivors of the ordeal, the Japanese internment camps remain a major scar on America's civil rights record.

THE PRICE OF PROSPERITY One unusual feature of the Asian American experience is their overall academic success and corresponding economic prosperity. Although all Asian groups have not been equally successful (groups that have immigrated primarily as refugees—like the Vietnamese—have higher rates of poverty than do others), median household income in 2014 was $74,297 for Asian and Pacific Islanders, compared with $60,256 for whites, $42,491 for Hispanics, and $35,398 for blacks.[80] A number of factors probably account for this success. Forced out of wage labor in the West in the 1880s by resentful white workers, Asian immigrants developed entrepreneurial skills and many came to own their own businesses and restaurants. A cultural emphasis on hard work and high achievement lent itself particularly well to success in the American education system and culture of equality of opportunity. Furthermore, many Asian immigrants were highly skilled and professional workers in their own countries and passed on the values of their achievements to their children.

High school and college graduation rates are higher among Asian Americans than among other ethnic groups, and are at least as high as, and in some places higher than, those of whites. In 2018, 22.9 percent of incoming freshmen at Harvard were Asian, as were 23 percent at Stanford, 37 percent at MIT, and 33 percent at the University of California, Berkeley.[81] What their high levels of academic success sometimes mean for Asian Americans is that they become the targets of racist attacks by resentful whites.[82] Asian Americans have accused schools like Stanford, Brown, Harvard, and Berkeley of "capping" the number of Asians they admit, and white alumni who feel that slots at these elite schools should be reserved for their children have complained about the numbers of Asians in attendance. Their success also means that Asian Americans stand in an odd relationship to affirmative action, a set of policies that usually helps minorities blocked from traditional paths to economic prosperity. While affirmative action policies might benefit them in hiring situations, they actually harm Asian Americans seeking to go to universities or professional schools. Because these students are generally so well qualified, more of them would be admitted if race were not taken into account to permit the admission of Hispanic and African American students. A case against Harvard is currently pending on these grounds.[83] Policies that pit minority groups against each other in this way do not promote solidarity and community among them and make racist attitudes even harder to overcome.

POLITICAL STRATEGIES According to our conventional understanding of what makes people vote in the United States, participation among Asian Americans ought to be quite high. Voter turnout usually rises along with education and income levels, yet Asian American voter registration and turnout rates have been among the lowest in the nation. Particularly in states with a sizable number of Asian Americans such as California, where they constitute 16 percent of the population, their political representation and influence do not reflect their numbers.[84] Although in recent years they are more likely to vote Democratic than Republican, they tend to register as independents.

Political observers account for this lack of participation in several ways. Until after World War II, as we saw, immigration laws restricted the citizenship rights of Asian Americans. In addition, the political systems that many Asian immigrants left behind did not have traditions of democratic political participation. Also, many Asian Americans came to the United States for economic reasons and have focused their attentions on building economic security rather than on learning to navigate an unfamiliar political system.[85] Finally, some observers argue that the parties don't compete for the Asian American vote the way they do for the Hispanic vote—in other words, they may not vote simply because no one asks them to.[86]

Some evidence indicates, however, that this trend of nonparticipation is changing. Researchers have found that where Asian Americans do register, they tend to vote at rates higher than those of other groups.[87] In 2018 there was only one Asian American governor (David Ige of Hawaii). The 116th Congress saw eleven Asian Pacific American members of the House of Representatives, and two Asian Pacific American senators (Mazie Hirono of Hawaii and Tammy Duckworth of Illinois). Asian American turnout has generally lagged behind its numbers in the population, but early turnout was up in 2016 and the vote went overwhelmingly to Hillary Clinton.

PAUSE AND REVIEW Who, What, How

Native Americans' rights have been denied through the Supreme Court's interpretation of the commerce clause, giving Congress power over them and their lands. Because neither Congress nor the courts have been receptive to the claims of Native Americans, they have sought to force the American government to fulfill its promises to them and to gain political rights and economic well-being by working outside the system and using the resources generated from running casinos.

Hispanics too have been denied their rights, partly through general discrimination but partly through organized movements such as the English-only movement and anti-immigration efforts. Because of their diversity and low levels of socioeconomic achievement, Hispanics have not been very successful in organizing to fight for their rights politically. Tactics that Hispanic leaders use include boycotts and voter education and registration drives.

Finally, Asian Americans—long prevented by law from becoming citizens and under suspicion during World War II—have also had to bear the collective brunt of Americans' discriminatory actions. As diverse as Hispanics, Asian Americans have also failed to organize politically. Their socioeconomic fate, however, has been different from that of many Hispanic groups, and as a group, Asian Americans have managed to thrive economically in their own communities despite political discrimination.

In Your Own Words Explain the different paths to equality taken by other racial and ethnic groups.

RIGHTS DENIED ON THE BASIS OF GENDER

Fighting the early battles for equality at the state level

Of all the battles fought for equal rights in the American political system, the women's struggle has been perhaps the most peculiar, because women, while certainly denied most imaginable civil and economic rights, were not outside the system in the same way that racial and ethnic groups have been. Most women lived with their husbands or fathers, and many shared their view that men, not women, should have power in the political world. Women's realm, after all, was the home, and the prevailing narrative was that white women anyway were too good, too pure, too chaste, to deal with the sordid world outside.[88] Today there are still some women as well as men who agree with the gist of this sentiment. That means that the struggle for women's rights not only has failed to win the support of all women but also has been actively opposed by some, as well as by many men whose power, standing, and worldview it has threatened.

WOMEN'S PLACE IN THE EARLY NINETEENTH CENTURY

The legal and economic position of women in the early nineteenth century, though not exactly "slavery," in some ways was not much different. According to English common law, on which our legal system was based, when a woman married, she merged her legal identity with her husband's, which is to say in practical terms she no longer had one. Once married, she could not be a party to a contract, bring a lawsuit, own or inherit property, earn wages for any service, gain custody of her children in case of divorce, or initiate divorce from an abusive husband. If her husband were not a U.S. citizen, she lost her own citizenship. Neither married nor unmarried women could vote. In exchange for the legal identity his wife gave up, a husband was expected to provide security for her, and if he died without a will, she was entitled to one-third of his estate. If he made a will and left her out of it, however, she had no legal recourse to protect herself and her children.[89]

Opportunities were not plentiful for women who preferred to remain unmarried. Poor women worked in domestic service and, later, in the textile industry. But most married women did not work outside the home. For unmarried women with some education, the professions available were those that fit their supposed womanly nature and that paid too little to be attractive to men, primarily nursing and teaching. Women who tried to break the occupational barriers were usually rebuffed, and for those who prevailed, success was often a mixed blessing as successful professional women were not readily accepted in society.[90]

THE BIRTH OF THE WOMEN'S RIGHTS MOVEMENT

The women's movement is commonly dated from an 1848 convention on women's rights held in Seneca Falls, New York. There, men and women who supported the extension of rights to women issued a Declaration of Principles that deliberately sought to evoke the sentiments of those calling for freedom from political oppression. Echoing the Declaration of Independence, it stated:

> We hold these truths to be self-evident: that all men and women are created equal; that they are endowed by their Creator with certain inalienable rights; that among these are life, liberty and the pursuit of happiness.

Against the advice of many of those present, a resolution was proposed to demand the vote for women. It was the only resolution not to receive the convention's unanimous support—even among supporters of women's rights, the right to vote was controversial. Other propositions were enthusiastically and unanimously approved, among them calls for the right to own property, to have access to higher education, and to receive custody of children after divorce. Some of these demands were realized in New York, but they were not extended to all American women, and progress was slow.

The women's movement picked up steam after Seneca Falls and the victories in New York, but it had yet to settle on a political strategy. The courts were closed to women, of course, much as they had been for Dred Scott; women simply weren't allowed access to the legal arena. For a long time, women's rights advocates worked closely with the antislavery movement, assuming that when blacks received their rights, as they did with the passage of the Fourteenth Amendment, they and the Republican Party would rally to the women's cause. Not only did that fail to happen, but the passage of the Fourteenth Amendment marked the first time the word *male* appeared in the Constitution. There was a bitter split between the two movements, and afterward it was not unheard of, especially in the South, for women's rights advocates to promote their cause with racist appeals, arguing that giving women the right to vote would dilute the impact of black voters. In 1869 the women's movement itself split into two groups, divided by philosophy and strategy, with some determined to focus on change at the federal level and others focused on state-level reform.

THE STRUGGLE IN THE STATES

The state strategy was a smart one for women. Different states have different cultures and traditions, and the Constitution allows them to decide who may legally vote. Women were able to target states that were sympathetic to them and gradually gain enough political clout that their demands were listened to on the national level.

In frontier country, it wasn't possible for women to be as protected as they might be back East, and when they proved capable of taking on a variety of other roles, it was hard to justify a narrative that denied them the same rights as men. Women had been able to vote since 1869 in the Territory of Wyoming. When Wyoming applied for statehood in 1889, Congress tried to impose the disenfranchisement of women as the price of admission to the Union. The Wyoming legislature responded, "We will remain out of the Union a hundred years rather than come in without the women."[91] When Wyoming was finally admitted to the United States, it was the first state to allow women to vote.

That success was not to prove contagious, however. From 1870 to 1910, women waged 480 campaigns in thirty-three states, caused seventeen referenda to be held in eleven states, and won in only two of them: Colorado (1893) and Idaho (1896). The two factions of the women's movement merged, becoming the National American Woman Suffrage Association (NAWSA), and began to refine their state-level strategy. By 1912, women could vote in states, primarily in the West, that controlled 74 of the total 483 Electoral College votes that decided the presidency, but the movement was facing strong external opposition and was being torn apart internally by political differences.

In 1914 an impatient, militant offshoot of NAWSA began to work at the national level again, picketing the White House and targeting the president's party, contributing to the defeat of twenty-three of forty-three Democratic candidates in the western states where women could vote. The appearance of political power gave momentum to the state-level efforts. In 1917 North Dakota gave women presidential suffrage; then Ohio, Indiana, Rhode Island, Nebraska, and Michigan followed suit. Arkansas and New York joined the list later that year. NAWSA issued a statement to members of Congress that if they would not pass the Susan B.

MAP 6.1

Women's Right to Vote Before the Nineteenth Amendment (1920)

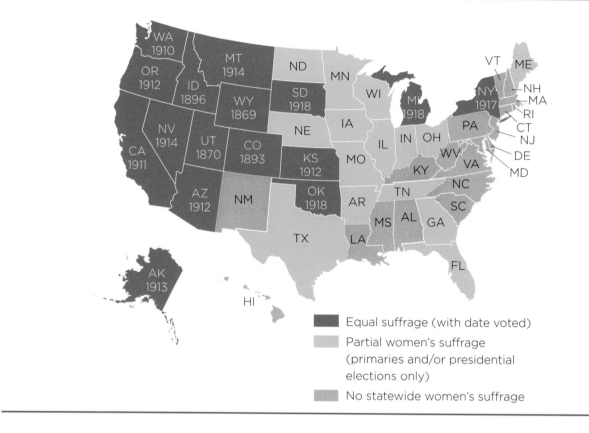

■ Equal suffrage (with date voted)

▢ Partial women's suffrage (primaries and/or presidential elections only)

▢ No statewide women's suffrage

Anthony Amendment granting women the right to vote, it would work to defeat every legislator who opposed it. The amendment passed in the House, but not the Senate, and NAWSA targeted four senators. Two were defeated, and two held on to their seats by only narrow margins. Nine more states gave women the right to vote in presidential elections (see Map 6.1).

In 1919 the Susan B. Anthony Amendment, regularly defeated from 1878 to 1896, was reintroduced into Congress with the support of President Woodrow Wilson and passed by the necessary two-thirds majority in both houses. When, in August 1920, Tennessee became the thirty-sixth state to ratify the Nineteenth Amendment, for the required total of three-fourths of the state legislatures, women finally had the vote nationwide. Unlike the situation faced by African Americans, the legal victory ended the battle. Enforcement was not as difficult as enforcement of the Fifteenth Amendment, although many women were not inclined to use their newly won right. But until the end, the opposition had been petty and virulent, and the victory was only narrowly won.

WINNERS AND LOSERS IN THE SUFFRAGE MOVEMENT

The debate over women's suffrage, like the fight over black civil rights, hit bitter depths because so much was at stake. If women were to acquire political rights, opponents feared, an entire way of life would be over. And, of course, in many ways they were right.

The opposition to women's suffrage came from a number of different directions. In the South, white men rejected women's suffrage for fear that women would encourage enforcement of the Civil War amendments, giving political power to blacks. And if women could vote, then of course black women could vote, further weakening the white male position. Believing that women would force temperance on the nation, brewing and liquor interests fought the women's campaign vigorously. In the East, industrial and business interests opposed suffrage because they were concerned that voting women would pass enlightened labor legislation. For some well-to-do women, the status quo was comfortable, and changing expectations about women's roles could only threaten that security.[92]

Everything these opponents feared came to pass eventually, although not necessarily as the result of women voting. In fact, in the immediate aftermath of the Nineteenth Amendment, the results of women's suffrage were disappointing to supporters. Blacks and immigrants were still being discriminated against in many parts of the country, effectively preventing both men and women from voting. Political parties excluded women, and most women lacked the money, political contacts, and experience to get involved in politics. Perhaps most important, general cultural attitudes worked against women's political participation. Politically active women were ostracized and accused of being unfeminine, making political involvement costly to many women.[93] While the women's rights advocates were clear winners in the suffrage fight, it took a long time for all the benefits of victory to materialize. As the battle over the Equal Rights Amendment (ERA) was to show, attitudes toward women were changing at a glacial pace.

THE EQUAL RIGHTS AMENDMENT

The Nineteenth Amendment gave women the right to vote, but it did not ensure the constitutional protection against discrimination. Even though the Fourteenth Amendment technically applied to women as well as men, the courts did not interpret it that way. It was not unconstitutional to treat people differently on account of gender. Since the ratification of the Nineteenth Amendment in 1920, some women's groups had been working for the passage of an additional **Equal Rights Amendment** that would ban discrimination on the basis of sex and guarantee women equal protection of the laws.

Objections to the proposed amendment again came from many different directions. Traditionalists, both men and women, opposed changing the status quo and giving more power to the federal government. But there were also women, and supporters of women's rights, who feared that requiring laws to treat men and women the same would actually make women worse off by nullifying legislation that sought to protect women. Many social reformers, for instance, had worked for laws that would limit working hours or establish minimum wages for women, which now would be in jeopardy. Opponents also feared that an ERA would strike down laws preventing women from being drafted and sent into combat. Many laws in American society treat men and women differently, and few, if any, would survive under such an amendment

Going to the Dance
In 1919, with the Nineteenth Amendment headed toward final ratification, women began to sense the first signs of real political power.

(the double-edged sword of strict scrutiny that we mentioned earlier in this chapter). Nonetheless, an ERA was proposed in Congress on a fairly regular basis.

In the 1960s the political omens started to look more hopeful for expanding women's rights. Support for women's rights more generally came from an unlikely quarter, however. Title VII of the Civil Rights Act of 1964, intended to prohibit job discrimination on the basis of race, was amended to include discrimination on the basis of gender, as well, in the hopes that the addition would doom the bill's passage. Unexpectedly, the amended bill passed.

In 1967 the National Organization for Women (NOW) was organized to promote women's rights and lent its support to the ERA. Several pieces of legislation that passed in the early seventies signaled that public opinion was favorable to the idea of expanding women's rights. Title IX of the Education Amendments of 1972 banned sex discrimination in schools receiving federal funds, which meant, among other things, that schools had to provide girls with the equal opportunity and support to play sports in school. The Revenue Act of 1972 provided for tax credits for child care.

> **Equal Rights Amendment** a constitutional amendment passed by Congress but never ratified that would have banned discrimination on the basis of gender

Title IX Evens the Score

Title IX of the Higher Education Act, passed in 1972, sought to end discrimination in athletic programs at institutions receiving federal funding. It has resulted in more sports programs and scholarships for young women and a stronger field of female athletes. Here, the University of Connecticut's women's team plays against the men's team. Since 1999, UConn's women Huskies have won the NCAA championship ten times; the men, four.

In 1970 the ERA was again introduced in the House, and this time it passed. But the Senate spent the next two years debating provisions that would have kept women from being drafted. Arguing that such changes would not amount to true equality, advocates of equal rights for women managed to defeat them. Finally, on March 22, 1972, the ERA passed in the Senate. The exact language of the proposed amendment read:

1. Equality of rights under the law shall not be denied or abridged by the United States or by any State on account of sex.

2. The Congress shall have the power to enforce, by appropriate legislation, the provisions of this article.

3. This amendment shall take effect two years after the date of ratification.

When both houses of Congress passed the final version of the amendment, the process of getting approval of three-quarters of the state legislatures began. Thirty states had ratified the amendment by early 1973. But while public opinion polls showed support for the idea of giving constitutional protection to women's rights, the votes at the state level began to go the other way. By 1977 only thirty-five states had voted to ratify, three short of the necessary thirty-eight. Despite the extension of the ratification deadline from 1979 to 1982, the amendment died unratified (although Illinois recently ratified the amendment in a largely symbolic gesture).

Why did a ratification process that started out with such promise fizzle so abruptly? First, although most people supported the idea of women's rights in the abstract, they weren't sure what the consequences of such an amendment would be, and people feared the possibility of radical social change. Second, the ERA came to be identified in the public's mind with the 1973 Supreme Court ruling in *Roe v. Wade* that women have abortion rights in the first trimester of their pregnancies. One scholar has argued that conservative opponents of the ERA managed to link the two issues, claiming that the ERA was a rejection of motherhood and traditional values, and turning ERA votes into referenda on abortion.[94]

> ## Is it possible to have too much equality?

Finally, the Supreme Court had been striking down some (though not all) laws that treated women differently from men using the equal protection clause of the Fourteenth Amendment, something it had previously declined to do.[95] Some people took this as a sign that the ERA was unnecessary, which probably reassured those who approved of the principle of equality but had no desire to turn society upside-down.

GENDER DISCRIMINATION TODAY

Despite the failure of the ERA, today most of the legal barriers to women's equality in this country have been eliminated. But because the ERA did not pass, and there is no constitutional amendment specifically guaranteeing equal protection of the laws regardless of gender, the Supreme Court has not been willing to treat gender as a suspect classification, although it has come close at times. Laws that treat men and women differently are subject only to the intermediate standard of review, not the strict scrutiny test. Examples of laws that have failed that test, and thus have been struck down by the Court, include portions of the Social Security Act that give benefits to widows but not to widowers, and laws that require husbands but not wives to be liable for alimony payments.[96] Some laws that do treat men and women differently—for instance, statutory rape laws and laws requiring that only males be drafted—have been upheld by the Court.

Having achieved formal equality, women still face some striking discrimination in the workplace (see *Snapshot of America: How Equal Are We, by Gender?*). Women today earn seventy-seven cents for every dollar earned by men, and the National Committee on Pay Equity, a nonprofit

Snapshot of America: *How Equal Are We, by Gender?*

Gender Wage Gap for Different Professions: Annual Earnings

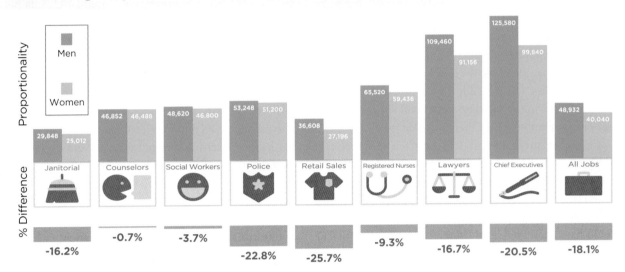

Proportionality

	Men	Women

Profession	Men	Women
Janitorial	29,848	25,012
Counselors	46,852	46,488
Social Workers	48,620	46,800
Police	53,248	51,200
Retail Sales	36,608	27,196
Registered Nurses	65,520	59,436
Lawyers	109,460	91,156
Chief Executives	125,580	99,840
All Jobs	48,932	40,040

% Difference

-16.2% -0.7% -3.7% -22.8% -25.7% -9.3% -16.7% -20.5% -18.1%

Average Women's Salary as a Percentage of Men's, 1979–2016

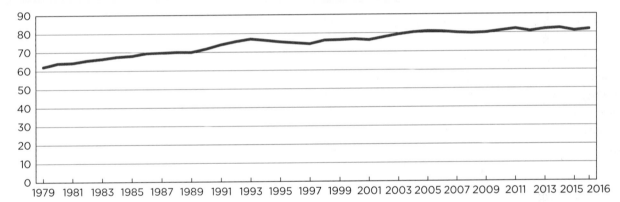

Closing the Gap?

Rising number of stay-at-home dads

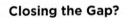

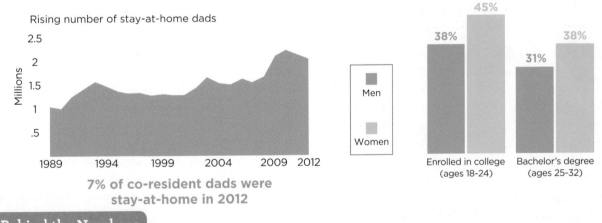

7% of co-resident dads were stay-at-home in 2012

	Men	Women

Millennial women outpace men in educational attainment

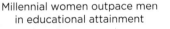

	Men	Women
Enrolled in college (ages 18-24)	38%	45%
Bachelor's degree (ages 25-32)	31%	38%

Behind the Numbers

Men make more than women overall, but the size of the pay gap varies by profession and by racial and ethnic group. What factors might account for these differences in the pay gap? With more stay-at-home dads, and more women attending and finishing college, will this pay inequality be a concern for the millennial generation?

Sources: U.S. Bureau of Labor Statistics, "Highlights of Women's Earnings," August 2017, www.bls.gov/opub/reports/womensearnings/2016/home.htm; U.S. Census Bureau Historical Family Tables, www.census.gov/data/tables/time-series/demo/families/families.html.

group in Washington, calculates that the pay gap may cost women almost a half-million dollars over the course of their work lives.[97] Women's ability to seek remedies for this discrimination has been limited by law. In 2007 the U.S. Supreme Court ruled in a five-to-four decision that a female worker's right to sue for discrimination was constrained by the statutes of limitations in existing civil rights law.[98] On January 29, 2009, the first bill signed into law by President Obama was the Lilly Ledbetter Act, extending the time frame so that workers could still sue even if the wage discrimination against them revealed itself over time. A companion piece to this legislation, the Paycheck Fairness Act, would prohibit discrimination and retaliation against workers who bring discrimination claims. It passed in the House in 2009 but stalled in the Senate. It remains a controversial proposal, with Democrats claiming women should have increased legal protection in the workplace, and Republicans arguing that women make less money

than men for reasons other than discrimination (like the decision to leave the labor market to have children), and that market forces ought to prevail without regulation. In 2017 the Trump administration halted an Obama policy that would have required companies with more than one hundred employees to disclose salaries by gender and race so that people would know whether they were making less than their colleagues.[99] In the meantime, some states, such as New Jersey, have passed strong equal pay acts of their own, and in 2018 the U.S. Court of Appeals for the Ninth Circuit held that employers could not ask about a woman's pay history in setting current salary, preventing a history of unequal pay from being perpetuated.[100]

In addition to falling behind on the pay scale, women are tremendously underrepresented on the power scale as well, having a harder time getting hired at the upper levels of corporate management, academic administration, and other top echelons of authority. Some people argue that women fail to achieve levels of power and salary on a par with men because many women may leave and enter the job market several times or put their careers on hold to have children. The so-called Mommy track has been blamed for much of the disparity between men's and women's positions in the world. Others argue, however, that there is an enduring difference in the hiring and salary patterns of women that has nothing to do with childbearing, or else reflects male inflexibility when it comes to incorporating motherhood and corporate responsibility. These critics claim that there is a "glass ceiling" in the corporate world, invisible to the eye but impenetrable, that prevents women from rising to their full potential. The Civil Rights Act of 1991 created the Glass Ceiling Commission to study this phenomenon, and among the commission's conclusions was the observation that business is depriving itself of a large pool of talent by denying leadership positions to women.

Ever since President Johnson's executive order of 1965 on affirmative action was amended in 1968 to include gender, the federal government has had not only to stop discriminating against women in its hiring practices but also to take positive steps to make sure that women are hired. Many other levels of government take gender into consideration when they hire, and the Supreme Court has upheld the practice.[101] But it is hard to mandate change in leadership positions when the number of jobs is few to begin with and the patterns of discrimination appear across corporations, universities, and foundations.

Some analysts have argued that the glass ceiling is a phenomenon that affects relatively few women, and that most women today are less preoccupied with moving up the corporate ladder than with making a decent living, or getting off what one observer has called the "sticky floor" of low-paying

Courtesy of Sally Bonn

A Gesture of Gratitude

The passage of the Nineteenth Amendment in 1920 gave women the right to vote, but it would take nearly a century for them to be able to cast a vote for a member of their own gender in a presidential race. After casting ballots for Hillary Clinton in the 2016 presidential primary, female voters paid their respects to Susan B. Anthony, peppering the trailblazing suffragist's gravestone in Rochester, New York, with "I Voted" stickers.

jobs.[102] While the wage gap between men and women with advanced education is narrowing, women still tend to be excluded from the more lucrative blue-collar positions in manufacturing, construction, communication, and transportation.[103]

Getting hired, maintaining equal pay, and earning promotions are not the only challenges women face on the job. They are often subject to unwelcome sexual advances, comments, or jokes that make their jobs unpleasant, offensive, and unusually stressful. Now technically illegal, **sexual harassment** is often difficult to define and document, and women have traditionally faced retribution from employers and fellow workers for calling attention to such practices. The much-publicized cases of sexual harassment in the military show that progress toward gender equality in the armed forces still has a long way to go.

Sexual harassment in the civilian world came to the national stage with an explosion during the 2016 campaign, where in one surreal moment candidate Donald Trump—accused of sexual assault by several women and on the basis of his own tape-recorded words—invited to the presidential debate women who had accused President Bill Clinton of sexual assault in an effort to intimidate Hillary Clinton, the first serious woman candidate for president. Women's reaction to Trump's election resulted in the Women's Marches held across the country the day after his inauguration—numbers of marchers in Washington alone far exceeded the number who had attended the ceremonies the day before. The March was reprised in 2018, and the gathering anger of women at what they saw as a disrespectful culture designed to peel away their rights resulted in record numbers of women on the ballots (and winning) at all levels in 2018.

The #MeToo movement in 2017–2018 showed that the problem is pervasive not just in politics but in the entertainment, news, culinary, and many other fields. The male power advantage persists, however. In 2018, Dr. Christine Blasey Ford, a California psychologist, testified during the confirmation hearings on Judge Brett Kavanaugh for the Supreme Court that he had attempted to rape her in high school. Her story was persuasive enough to call for a serious investigation, but received only a cursory one (neither she nor Kavanaugh were even questioned). Kavanaugh called her a liar and the Republicans closed ranks to ensure his confirmation along near party lines.

Another form of employment discrimination is highlighted in the recent dramatic rise in the number of cases of discrimination reported by pregnant women. In one

---

Alyssa Milano ✓
@Alyssa_Milano

Follow ∨

If you've been sexually harassed or assaulted write 'me too' as a reply to this tweet.

Me too.

Suggested by a friend: "If all the women who have been sexually harassed or assaulted wrote 'Me too.' as a status, we might give people a sense of the magnitude of the problem."

1:21 PM - 15 Oct 2017

24,063 Retweets   52,452 Likes

◯ 66K   ⇄ 24K   ♡ 52K

A Movement Begins
In October 2017, prompted by the wave of accusations against movie producer Harvey Weinstein, actress Alyssa Milano suggested people tweet the words "me too" to emphasize the scale of the problem of sexual harassment and assault. Within the first seven hours, she had more than 30,000 responses to her tweet. The hashtag #MeToo became a shorthand for the movement, which emboldened a number of survivors of sexual abuse to come out of the shadows.

study, roughly half of the sample of pregnant women stated that their bosses had had negative reactions to the pregnancies. The Supreme Court weighed in on the issue in 2015, ruling that even if a business was not intentionally discriminating against a pregnant woman, it could not impose significant burdens on her in violation of the Pregnancy Discrimination Act without a sufficient justification. The EEOC has issued guidelines on when and how women can file complaints if they are the object of such discrimination.[104]

WOMEN IN CONTEMPORARY POLITICS

Women still face discrimination not only in the boardroom but in politics as well. Although 2016 nearly saw the election of the first woman president, it was a campaign fraught with sexism. In part as a reaction to Clinton's treatment and to the #MeToo Movement, women won seats to Congress and state legislatures in record numbers in 2018.

Women have traditionally been underrepresented in government for many reasons. Some observers argue that women may be less likely to have access to the large amounts of money needed to run a successful campaign. A study of U.S. House candidates from the 1970s to the 1990s shows that women candidates raised and spent about three-fourths of what male candidates did between 1974 and 1980. However, by 1990, women candidates for the House raised and spent

---

sexual harassment unwelcome sexual speech or behavior that creates a hostile work environment

more money than did male candidates; women candidates raised 111 percent of what male candidates did for the 1992 race.[105] Others argue that women are not as likely as men to want to go in to politics. For instance, more women candidates for state legislative office reported waiting to wage a campaign until after they were asked to run by a party or legislative official.[106]

However, the representation of women in government is clearly better than it was. In 1971, women comprised only 2 percent of Congress members and less than 5 percent of state legislators. By 2014, 18.5 percent of Congress members and 24.2 percent of state legislators were female, both all-time highs. In 2014, women held 22.6 percent of all statewide executive offices, including five governorships and eleven lieutenant governorships.[107] In addition, 249, or 18.4 percent, of the cities with populations of more than 30,000 had female mayors.[108] In 2014 the state of New Hampshire had elected an all-female congressional delegation (two members of the House and two senators) as well as a female governor. After unprecedented electoral gains by women following the confirmation hearings of Clarence Thomas under the cloud of credible claims of sexual harassment, 1992 had been known as "The Year of the Woman." The 2018 midterms outdid it, putting over 100 women in the House (the previous high had been 84) and at least 23 in the Senate (the count is still going on at the time of writing). Many of them were first time candidates. They and their supporters were moved to action not only by a Supreme Court confirmation hearing that failed to give credence to a woman's credible testimony, but the entire #MeToo Movement and the sexist behavior of President Trump. But they did not portray themselves as a feminist movement; time and again, women said they were persuaded to run on local issues—health care, clean water, safe highways.

Michigan chose a female governor, US senator, attorney general, and secretary of state. More than 12 states added women to their delegations, although that number was limited structurally by the existing gerrymandering so that their numbers were not reflected in seats won. The gendered nature of American politics is changing, albeit slowly. In 2018, Tammy Duckworth, D-Ill., became the first U.S. senator to become pregnant while in office, forcing the once all-male Senate to deal with the issue of accommodating a nursing mother. (See *Profile in Citizenship* in this chapter.)

Americans, of course, have still failed to elect a female president, despite Hillary Clinton's winning of the popular vote in 2016. It was her concession speech in 2008, when she lost the primary to Barack Obama, that most clearly put her candidacies into context:

Now, on a personal note—when I was asked what it means to be a woman running for president, I always gave the same answer: that I was proud to be running as a woman but I was running because I thought I'd be the best president. But I am a woman, and like millions of women, I know there are still barriers and biases out there, often unconscious.

I want to build an America that respects and embraces the potential of every last one of us.

I ran as a daughter who benefited from opportunities my mother never dreamed of. I ran as a mother who worries about my daughter's future and a mother who wants to lead all children to brighter tomorrows. To build that future I see, we must make sure that women and men alike understand the struggles of their grandmothers and mothers, and that women enjoy equal opportunities, equal pay, and equal respect. Let us resolve and work toward achieving some very simple propositions: There are no acceptable limits and there are no acceptable prejudices in the twenty-first century.

You can be so proud that, from now on, it will be unremarkable for a woman to win primary state victories, unremarkable to have a woman in a close race to be our nominee, unremarkable to think that a woman can be the president of the United States. And that is truly remarkable.[109]

Although no woman has yet attained the presidency, in 2007 (and again in 2019) Nancy Pelosi became the first female Speaker of the House, and three of the last four secretaries of state have been women. In fact, in 2010 the second and fourth officials in the line of succession to the president of the United States were women (the Speaker of the House follows the vice president, and the secretary of state comes after the president pro tempore of the Senate).

It is difficult to know if the underrepresentation of women throughout government has real policy consequences, but a variety of decisions affecting women—ranging from issues concerning women in the marketplace to women's health—are often made without a significant female voice contributing to the discussion. In the past few years alone, we have seen political battles over whether all women should be provided with services that help protect them against domestic violence, whether they should be able to sue easily for discrimination in the workplace, whether they should be guaranteed equal pay for equal work, whether they should have access to all forms of birth control, whether they are entitled to have that birth control covered by their health insurance policies, whether they should have to undergo an invasive form of ultrasound in order to have a legal abortion, and other similar issues. The Democrats' victory in the House in 2018, however, may keep these issues of the table. Some research suggests that states that have a stronger female presence in the government may enact more "women-friendly" policies, although other political factors matter as well.[110]

| PAUSE AND REVIEW | Who, What, How |

Supporters and opponents of the women's movement struggled mightily over the extension of rights to women. As in the battles we discussed earlier, at stake were not just civil rights but social and economic power as well.

Because the courts and Congress were at first off-limits to the women's movement, women took their fight to the states, with their more accepting cultures and less restrictive rules. Having finally gained the vote in enough states to put electoral pressure on national officials, women got the national vote in 1920. The Nineteenth Amendment, however, did not give them the same equal protection of the laws that the Fourteenth Amendment had given blacks. Today the courts give women greater protection of the law, but the failure of the ERA to be ratified means that laws that discriminate against them are still subject to only an intermediate standard of review.

In Your Own Words   Describe how women have fought for equality and the changing role of women in American politics.

RIGHTS DENIED ON OTHER BASES

Challenging other classifications in the courts

Race, ethnicity, and gender, of course, are not the only grounds on which the laws treat people differently in the United States. Four other classifications that provide interesting insights into the politics of rights in America are sexual orientation, age, disability, and lack of citizenship.

SEXUAL ORIENTATION

Gays and lesbians have faced two kinds of legal discrimination in this country. On the one hand, overt discrimination simply prohibits some behaviors: until 2011, gays could not serve openly in the military, for instance, and in some states they cannot adopt children or teach in public schools. But a more subtle kind of discrimination doesn't forbid their actions or behavior; it simply fails to recognize them legally. Thus until 2015, when the Supreme Court ruled that marriage equality is

the law of the land in *Obergefell v. Hodges*, many states made it impossible for gays to marry or claim the rights that married people share, such as collecting their partner's Social Security, being covered by a partner's insurance plan, being each other's next of kin, or having a family. Being gay, unlike being black or female or Asian, is something that can be hidden from public view, and until the 1970s many gays escaped overt discrimination by denying or concealing who they were, but that too is a serious deprivation of civil rights.[111]

POLITICAL STRATEGIES: THE COURTS As we discussed in Chapter 5, the case of *Bowers v. Hardwick* (1986) failed to advance the rights of gays and lesbians. The Court ruled that a Georgia statute against sodomy was a legitimate exercise of the state's power and that it met the minimum rationality test described earlier in this chapter.[112] The Court required that a law that treated people differently on the basis of sexual orientation merely had to be a reasonable use of state power. The four justices who dissented from that opinion did not want to tackle the issue of whether homosexuality was right or wrong. Rather they claimed that, as a privacy issue, what consenting adults do is none of the government's business.

A number of cases followed *Bowers*, most of them reinforcing the message that sexual orientation was provided no protections by the law. By 2003, however, public opinion on gay rights, as well as the Court's opinion on the subject, were changing. First, in *Lawrence v. Texas*, the Supreme Court overturned the *Bowers* decision, ruling that state sodomy laws were a violation of the right to privacy.[113] Even though many states had already repealed their sodomy laws, or failed to enforce them, the *Lawrence* decision was substantively and symbolically a break with previous judicial opinion that allowed the states to regulate the sexual behavior of gays and lesbians. Also in 2003, the Massachusetts Supreme Judicial Court ruled, in an extremely controversial four-to-three decision, that marriage was a civil right and that the state's law banning homosexual marriage violated the equal protection and due process clauses in the Massachusetts constitution.[114] The Massachusetts court ruling sent shockwaves throughout the country as the nation's first legal gay marriages were performed in Massachusetts.

Almost immediately after the ruling, President George W. Bush announced his support for an amendment to the Constitution defining marriage as a union between a man and a woman. However, because Congress had already passed a Defense of Marriage Act (DOMA) in 1996 asserting that states need not recognize gay marriages performed in other states, the amendment failed to garner much immediate congressional support.

In 2013 the Supreme Court struck down DOMA as well, followed by *Obergefell* two years later to the day. Conservatives

Equal Access to the Wedding Aisle
When Representative Barney Frank wed his longtime partner James Brady in the summer of 2012, their marriage was not recognized in many states. The Supreme Court struck down the Defense of Marriage Act the following year, ensuring marriage equality for all Americans.

were furious with what they saw as an activist Court, but marriage equality was legal across all the states. Although the Court did not clearly say that sexual orientation was a suspect class, some members hinted that their thinking might be going in that direction.

Opponents of gay rights did find solace in the *Masterpiece Cakeshop* decision that backed a baker who refused to bake a wedding cake for a gay couple for religious reasons, but the seven-to-two opinion was based on narrow grounds, which means it was decided on a technical issue that does not necessary apply to other similar cases.[115]

POLITICAL STRATEGIES: ELECTIONS The courts were not the only political avenue open to gays in their struggle for equal rights. Gays have also been effective in parlaying their relatively small numbers into a force to be reckoned with electorally. It is difficult to gain an accurate idea of the size of the gay population in the United States,[116] although some estimates say between 4 and 5 percent of the electorate self-identifies as gay, lesbian, or bisexual. Gays wield political power not just as individuals, however. They began to organize politically in 1969, after riots following police harassment at a gay bar in New York City, the Stonewall Inn. Today many interest groups are organized around issues of concern to the gay community. Although in the past gays have primarily supported the Democratic Party, a growing number identify themselves as independent, and a group of conservative gays calling themselves the Log Cabin Republicans have become active on the political right. Openly gay members of Congress have been elected from both sides of the partisan divide, and in 2016 the Senate confirmed Eric Fanning as the first openly gay Secretary of the Army.

In 1992, acting on a campaign promise made to gays, President Clinton decided to end the ban on gays in the military with an executive order, much as President Truman had ordered the racial integration of the armed forces in 1948. Clinton, however, badly miscalculated the public reaction to his move. In the ensuing storm, Clinton settled instead for a "don't ask, don't tell" (DADT) policy: members of the armed forces did not need to disclose their sexual orientation, but if they revealed it, or the military otherwise found out, they could still be disciplined or discharged. In 2008 Barack Obama campaigned on the repeal of DADT, and in 2010 Congress voted to repeal the policy in a lame-duck session before Democrats handed control of the House over to the Republicans.

Gays have also tried to use their political power to fend off the earlier-mentioned legislation banning gay marriage, but in 1996 Congress, fearing gay victories in the states, passed DOMA to prevent federal recognition of gay marriage and to allow states to pass laws denying its legality. President Clinton, who opposed the idea of gay marriage, signed the bill under protest, claiming the bill was politically motivated and mean-spirited. Although the Obama administration continued to enforce the law, it stopped defending it in federal courts, arguing that it did not think part of the law was constitutional. Speaking for the Republican majority in the House, John Boehner said that they would hire the necessary staff to defend the law in court itself. The Supreme Court's decision in 2013, essentially agreeing with the Obama administration, made the issue moot, and the 2015 decision settled it.

Another issue of active concern to gays is workplace discrimination. The Employment Non-Discrimination Act (ENDA) would make it illegal to discriminate on the basis of sexual orientation in hiring, firing, pay, and promotion decisions. Despite repeated efforts to pass the bill (since 1994 it has been introduced in every Congress except one), it has so far failed to get through both houses. As it became clear that the 113th Congress would once again refuse to act, President Obama signed an executive order in 2014 that would make it illegal for federal contractors and subcontractors to discriminate against LGBTQ employees.[117]

The issue of gay rights has come to the forefront of the American political agenda not only because of gays' increasing political power but also because of the fierce opposition of the Christian Right. Their determination to banish what they see as an unnatural and sinful lifestyle—and their conviction that protection of the basic rights of homosexuals means that they will be given "special privileges"—has focused tremendous public attention on issues that most of the public would rather remained private. The spread of AIDS and the political efforts of gay groups to fight for increased resources to battle the disease have also heightened public awareness of gay issues.

Public opinion has remained mixed on the subject for some time, but, driven by more accepting values among young people, it has changed more rapidly on the issue of the acceptance of gay rights than on practically any issue. For instance, in 2001, 57 percent of Americans opposed gay marriage; but in 2017, 62 percent approved of it.[118]

AGE

In 1976 the Supreme Court ruled that age is not a suspect classification.[119] That means that if governments have rational reasons for doing so, they may pass laws that treat younger or older people differently from the rest of the population, and courts do not have to use strict scrutiny when reviewing those laws. Young people are often not granted the full array of rights of adult citizens, being subject to curfews or locker searches at school; nor are they subject to the laws of adult justice if they commit a crime. Some observers have argued that children should have expanded rights to protect them in dealings with their parents.

Older people face discrimination most often in the area of employment. Compulsory retirement at a certain age, regardless of an individual's capabilities or health, may be said to violate basic civil rights. The Court has generally upheld mandatory retirement requirements.[120]

Congress, however, has sought to prevent age discrimination with the Age Discrimination in Employment Act of 1967, outlawing discrimination against people up to seventy years of age in employment or in the provision of benefits, unless age can be shown to be relevant to the job in question. In 1978 the act was amended to prohibit mandatory retirement before seventy, and in 1986 all mandatory retirement policies were banned except in special occupations.

Unlike younger people, who can't vote until they are eighteen and don't vote in great numbers after that, older people defend their interests very effectively. Voter participation rates rise with age, and older Americans are also extremely well organized politically. AARP (formerly the American Association of Retired Persons), a powerful interest group with nearly 38 million members, has been active in pressuring the government to preserve policies that benefit older people. In the debates in the mid-1990s about cutting government services, AARP was very much present, and in the face of the organization's advice and voting power, programs like Social Security and Medicare (providing health care for older Americans) remained virtually untouched.

DISABILITY

People with physical and mental disabilities have also organized politically to fight for their civil rights. Advocates for the disabled include people with disabilities themselves, people

A Minor Thing
School lockers can be searched without a warrant because discrimination on the basis of age is not considered a violation of civil rights. Because age is a nonsuspect classification, it is not unconstitutional to treat Americans under the age of eighteen differently from others.

who work in the social services catering to the disabled, and veterans' groups. Even though laws do not prevent disabled people from voting, staying in hotels, or using public phones, circumstances often do. Inaccessible buildings, public transportation, and other facilities can pose barriers as insurmountable as the law, as can public attitudes toward and discomfort around disabled people.

The 1990 Americans with Disabilities Act (ADA), modeled on the civil rights legislation that empowers racial and gender groups, protects the rights of the more than 44 million mentally and physically disabled people in this country. Disabilities covered under the act need not be as dramatic or obvious as confinement to a wheelchair or blindness. People with AIDS, those recovering from drug or alcohol addiction, and patients with heart disease or diabetes are among those covered. The act provides detailed guidelines for access to buildings, mass transit, public facilities, and communication systems. It also guarantees protection from bias in employment; the EEOC is authorized to handle cases of job discrimination because of disabilities, as well as race and gender. The act was controversial because many of the required changes in physical accommodations, such as ramps and elevators, are extremely expensive to install. Advocates for the disabled respond that these expenses will be offset by increased business from disabled people and by the added productivity and skills that the disabled bring to the workplace. The reach of the act was limited in 2001, when the Supreme Court ruled that state employees could not sue their states for damages under the ADA because of the seldom discussed, but extremely important, Eleventh Amendment, which limits lawsuits that can be filed against the states.[121] The Court's five-to-four decision was criticized by disability rights advocates as severely limiting the ADA.

CITIZENSHIP

The final category of discrimination we discuss is discrimination against people who are not citizens. Should noncitizens have the same rights as U.S. citizens? Should all noncitizens have those rights? Illegal visitors as well as legal? Constitutional law has been fairly clear on these questions, granting both citizens and noncitizens most of the same constitutional rights, except the right to vote. (Even documented aliens who serve in the military are unable to vote.) Politics and the Constitution have not always been in sync on these points, however. Oddly for a nation of immigrants, the United States has periodically witnessed backlashes against the flow of people arriving from other countries, often, as we noted in *What's at Stake . . . ?*, triggered by fear that the newcomers' needs will mean fewer resources, jobs, and benefits for those who arrived earlier. During these backlashes, politicians have vied for public favor by cutting back on immigrants' rights. The Supreme Court responded in 1971 by declaring that alienage, like race and religion, is a suspect classification, and that laws that discriminate against aliens must be backed by a compelling government purpose.[122] To be sure, the Court has upheld some laws restricting the rights of immigrants, but it has done so only after a strict scrutiny of the facts. In light of the ruling, it has even supported the rights of undocumented immigrants to a public education.[123]

Among the groups that fight for the rights of immigrants are the Coalition for Humane Immigrant Rights and many politically active Hispanic groups. The people they represent, however, are often among the poorest, and the most politically silent, in society. Undocumented immigrants, especially, do not have much money or power, and they are thus an easy target for disgruntled citizens and hard-pressed politicians. However, considerable evidence suggests that although immigrants, particularly the larger groups like Mexicans, tend to be poor, they do become assimilated into American society. The average wages of second- and third-generation Mexican Americans, for instance, rise to about 80 percent of the wages of whites.[124] And their wage levels do not necessarily depress the overall wage levels. In the 1980s, wages rose faster in parts of the country with higher immigrant populations.[125] Although many immigrant groups are certainly poor, and a gap remains between their average standards of living and those of longer-term residents, the reaction against immigration in this country may be out of proportion to the problem.

Even groups that already enjoy basic civil rights can face considerable discrimination. Opposition to the extension of more comprehensive rights to these groups comes from a variety of directions.

In the case of gays and lesbians, opponents claim that providing a heightened standard of review for laws that discriminate on the basis of sexual orientation would be giving special rights to gays. Gays and lesbians are politically sophisticated and powerful, however, and the techniques they use are often strategies that had originally been closed off to minorities and women. Both they and their opponents use the courts, form interest groups, lobby Congress, and support presidential candidates to further their agendas.

In terms of age discrimination, opponents are motivated not by moral concerns but by issues of social order and cost-efficiency. Older people are able to protect their rights more effectively than younger people because of their higher voter turnout.

People resist giving rights to the disabled generally out of concern for the expense of making buildings accessible and the cost-efficiency of hiring disabled workers. Organization into interest groups and effective lobbying of Congress have resulted in considerable protection of the rights of the disabled.

Finally, noncitizens seeking rights face opposition from a variety of sources. Although immigrants themselves are not usually well organized, the biggest protection of their rights comes from the Supreme Court, which has ruled that alienage is a suspect classification and, therefore, laws that discriminate on the basis of citizenship are subject to strict scrutiny.

In Your Own Words Recognize examples of other groups that face discrimination.

THE CITIZENS AND CIVIL RIGHTS

The power of group action

The stories of America's civil rights struggles are the stories of citizen action. But clearly, citizens acting individually have not been able to bring about all the changes that civil rights groups have achieved. Although great leaders and effective organizers have played an important role in the battles for rights, the battles themselves have been part of a group movement.

> *Can we end de facto discrimination without imposing substantive solutions?*

In Chapter 1 we discussed three models of democracy that define options for citizen participation: elite, pluralist, and participatory. Of the three, the pluralist model best describes the actions that citizens have taken to gain the government's protection of their civil rights. Pluralism emphasizes the ways that citizens can increase their individual power by organizing into groups. The civil rights movements in the United States have been group movements, and to the extent that groups have been unable to organize effectively to advance their interests, their civil rights progress has been correspondingly slowed.

As we will see in Chapter 13, what have come to be known as interest groups play an increasingly important role in American politics. In fact, from the 1960s through the end of the twentieth century, the number of national associations in the United States grew by over 250 percent, to about 23,000, and the number of groups organized specifically to advocate for the rights of African Americans, Hispanics, Asian Americans, and women multiplied by six times during that period.[126] Scholars do not agree on whether this proliferation of groups increases the quality of democracy or skews its results. Groups that are well organized, well financed, and well informed and that have particularly passionate members (who put their votes where their hearts are) are likely to carry greater weight with lawmakers than are groups that are less focused and less well to do. They are also more likely to control the channels of information in which narratives are built and disseminated. On the one hand, money, information, and intensity of opinion can make interest groups more powerful than their numbers would indicate, a fact that seems at odds with notions of political equality and democracy. On the other hand, as we have seen, individuals can accomplish things together in groups that they can only dream of doing alone. In the case of the civil rights movement, democracy would have clearly been impoverished without the power of groups to work on distributing citizenship rights more broadly. We return to the question of how democratic a pluralist society can be in Chapter 13, when we investigate in more depth the role of interest groups in American politics.

In Your Own Words Identify tools used by citizens to expand the promise of civil rights.

LET'S REVISIT: *What's at Stake . . . ?*

We began this chapter with a look at the white supremacy and xenophobia (fear of strangers) that were given new life by Donald Trump's candidacy for the presidency. We saw that he generated huge enthusiasm among avowed white supremacist groups but also possessed a strong appeal for much larger groups of everyday white voters who felt that they were losing some vague but real racial privilege and economic status. We asked what was at stake when a majority group in society faces minority status.

As we now know, rights are power, and racism and sexism have never been too far below the surface of American politics. The difference is that today, with sites like Breitbart or other alt-right media channels, it is easier to find people who agree with you and to build a collective sense of grievance. When you have an economic system based on slavery or when you deny half the population any legal rights, you have to develop a moral narrative that allows you to live with what you are doing and still believe that you are a good person. The idea that Africans are uncivilized savages, or lazy and stupid, that immigrants are rapists or criminals or imbeciles for not speaking English, that women are delicate and incapable and need the sheltering protection of men, or that gays and lesbians live godless lives are all narratives that have been told and retold in the tapestry of American history. These narratives allow the people perpetuating them to maintain a narrative about themselves—that they are deserving, and superior, and righteous in keeping the other groups in their place. That is power.

But as we have seen, the facts and the narratives of American power have changed and continue to change dramatically. Where once even such civil rights giants as Abraham Lincoln and Lyndon Johnson held views at odds with racial equality, even as they recognized racial injustice, it is now viewed as racially insensitive at best—or racist at worst—to express the views that regularly came out of these men's mouths. For some white people, particularly white men, privilege was once seen as so natural that they didn't even know it was privilege. It can then be deeply unnerving and confusing for them to hear other people weave narratives in which not only are they no longer the heroes, but all too frequently they are the villains, especially when they can't tell what it is they are supposed to have done wrong.

It is easy to laugh at a figure like the buffoonish, blue-collar worker Archie Bunker, the anti-hero of the groundbreaking 1970s sitcom *All in the Family,* who railed at a world in which diverse groups were claiming rights, each of which meant that he lost a little bit of power that he considered his. But it must be jarring to actually *be* Archie Bunker, almost fifty years later, confronting not just the claims for equal treatment that drove him crazy but also the loss of the majority status that made his own claims to power legitimate in his eyes in the first place.

For people like Archie Bunker, race is for other groups; the majority group doesn't have to think of itself as a race because it is the dominant group. If whites are just one group among many, then they begin to experience race in a way they have not had to do before. They might indeed wonder why people are talking about reparations for past discrimination against other groups when it feels to them like they are being discriminated against today. And it might be hard to understand why people are getting excited about the election of presidents who don't look like them, precisely *because* they don't look like them. And it might indeed be infuriating to find that they have no language with which to talk about what is happening to them because, when they complain about what they perceive as their unjust treatment, they are told they are "politically incorrect," insensitive, and racist. Right-wing radio host Rush Limbaugh has made a career of stirring up just such resentment, and it is now a potent political force.

Many European countries have thriving right-wing political parties that base their appeal on nationalism and on keeping the "other" out. We have had such movements in our past, and we have one now, culminating in Donald Trump's election to the presidency in 2016, tellingly won by the Electoral College even as he was outnumbered in the popular vote. The demographic trends that are reconstituting the American population and reducing whites to minority status can only be anxiety-producing for them, especially when they feel economically marginalized and threatened by external events. The rhetoric of a candidate like Donald Trump, inflaming but also validating the unease and concern they have already experienced, must have been a breath of fresh air to the people feeling downtrodden. To white supremacists, it was as if the power they seek was finally in sight. To Trump supporters who were not white supremacists, but who were nonetheless a beleaguered and bewildered group hemorrhaging numbers and power, it must have felt as if someone, finally, was listening.

As difficult and even unjust as it might seem, given the racial atrocities of our American history, acknowledging that feeling of white disorientation and grievance might be necessary for us to fully understand the stakes in civil rights politics today and the challenges it will have to meet in the future. Nativist movements in other countries have successfully played off such emotions where the culture has not found a way to respond.

CLUES to Critical Thinking

"Ain't I a Woman?"

By Sojourner Truth, speaking at the Women's Rights Convention in Akron, Ohio, 1851

There were both women and men at the Women's Rights Convention in Akron in 1851, but the convention was dominated by impassioned arguments from men who believed that women were not capable of doing the things men did and were not made equal by God. Sojourner Truth was an emancipated slave from New York with a commanding presence and a spellbinding speaking voice. When she rose to speak, her listeners found themselves torn between cheers and tears. Though Truth herself has become the stuff of legend, her speech remains today a brief but powerful comment on gender roles.

Well, children, where there is so much racket there must be something out of kilter. I think that 'twixt the negroes of the South and the women at the North, all talking about rights, the white men will be in a fix pretty soon. But what's all this here talking about?

That man over there says that women need to be helped into carriages, and lifted over ditches, and to have the best place everywhere. Nobody ever helps me into carriages, or over mud-puddles, or gives me any best place! And ain't I a woman? Look at me! Look at my arm! I have ploughed and planted, and gathered into barns, and no man could head me! And ain't I a woman? I could work as much and eat as much as a man—when I could get it—and bear the lash as well! And ain't I a woman? I have borne thirteen children, and seen most all sold off to slavery, and when I cried out with my mother's grief, none but Jesus heard me! And ain't I a woman?

Then they talk about this thing in the head; what's this they call it? [member of audience whispers, "intellect"] That's it, honey. What's that got to do with women's rights or negroes' rights? If my cup won't hold but a pint, and yours holds a quart, wouldn't you be mean not to let me have my little half measure full?

Then that little man in black there, he says women can't have as much rights as men, 'cause Christ wasn't a woman! Where did your Christ come from? Where did your Christ come from? From God and a woman! Man had nothing to do with Him.

If the first woman God ever made was strong enough to turn the world upside down all alone, these women together ought to be able to turn it back, and get it right side up again! And now they is asking to do it, the men better let them.

Obliged to you for hearing me, and now old Sojourner ain't got nothing more to say.

Source: Sojourner Truth Institute, http://www .sojournertruth.org/Library/Speeches/AintI AWoman.htm.

Consider the source and the audience: How might Sojourner Truth's audience have affected how she presented her message? Most contemporary accounts of her speech come to us from her supporters. How might this fact shape the context in which we read her words today?

Lay out the argument and the underlying values and assumptions: Truth was a slave until New York freed all its slaves in 1828, when she was approximately thirty years old. To what extent did her personal experience fit with the notions that women were too weak and needed too much pampering to be equal to men? What idea of equality does she seem to be working with? Does she think equal means identical? What is her image of God? Does God have a gender?

Uncover the evidence: What is Truth's evidence that women can be as strong and tough as men? Is it compelling? Can she prove God's will? Can her opponents? Can anyone win that part of the argument? If so, how?

Evaluate the conclusion: Is Truth's claim that all people should be allowed to develop to their capacity convincing today? Why would anyone ever have opposed it?

Sort out the political significance: Truth's contention that the mystique of feminine weakness and delicacy didn't apply to slave women and thus probably didn't apply to white women must have been shocking at the time. Do we still have different expectations of people according to gender and race?

Review

The Meaning of Political Equality

Throughout U.S. history, various groups, because of some characteristic beyond their control, have been denied their civil rights and have fought for equal treatment under the law. All three branches of the government have played an important role in providing remedies for the denial of equal rights.

Groups that are discriminated against may seek procedural remedies, such as changing the law to guarantee equality of opportunity, or substantive remedies, such as the institution of affirmative action programs, to guarantee equality of outcome.

civil rights (p. 172)

intersectionality (p. 172)

suspect classification (p. 173)

strict scrutiny (p. 173)

intermediate standard of review (p. 173)

minimum rationality test (p. 173)

Rights Denied on the Basis of Race: African Americans

African Americans have experienced both de jure discrimination, created by laws that treat people differently, and de facto discrimination, which occurs when societal tradition and habit lead to social segregation.

African Americans led the first civil rights movement in the United States. By forming interest groups such as the NAACP and developing strategies such as nonviolent resistance, African Americans eventually defeated de jure discrimination.

De facto discrimination persists in America, signified by the education and wage gap between African Americans and whites. Programs like affirmative action, which could remedy such discrimination, remain controversial. Although African Americans have made great strides in the past several decades, much inequality remains.

racism (p. 175)
abolitionists (p. 178)
black codes (p. 178)
Reconstruction (p. 179)
poll taxes (p. 179)
literacy tests (p. 179)
grandfather clauses (p. 179)

Jim Crow laws (p. 179)
segregation (p. 179)
Plessy v. Ferguson (p. 179)
National Association for the Advancement of Colored People (NAACP) (p. 180)
Brown v. Board of Education of Topeka (p. 180)

boycott (p. 181)
de jure discrimination (p. 183)
de facto discrimination (p. 183)
busing (p. 184)
affirmative action (p. 185)

Rights Denied on the Basis of Other Racial and Ethnic Identities

Native Americans, Hispanics, and Asian Americans have also fought to gain economic and social equality. Congressional control over their lands has led Native Americans to assert economic power through the development of casinos. Using boycotts and voter education drives, Hispanics have worked to stem the success of English-only movements and anti-immigration efforts. Despite their smaller numbers, Asian Americans also aim for equal political clout, but it is through a cultural emphasis on scholarly achievement that they have gained considerable economic power.

English-only movements (p. 193)

Rights Denied on the Basis of Gender

Women's rights movements represented challenges to power, to a traditional way of life, and to economic profit. Early activists found success through state politics because they were restricted from using the courts and Congress; efforts now focus on the courts to give women greater protection of the law.

Equal Rights Amendment (p. 199)   sexual harassment (p. 203)

Rights Denied on Other Bases

Gays, youth, the elderly, and the disabled enjoy the most fundamental civil rights, but they still face de jure and de facto discrimination. While laws concerning gays, lesbians, and transgender individuals are usually motivated by moral beliefs, social order and cost-efficiency concerns mark the restrictions against youth, the elderly, and disabled Americans. The rights of noncitizens, especially undocumented Americans, remain somewhat unclear, and discrimination on the basis of citizenship status continues to be an issue in the United States.

The Citizens and Civil Rights

The progression of civil rights in the United States has been propelled largely by group action, an example of the pluralist model of democracy. Through collective action, those seeking change and equality are able to put pressure on lawmakers and on the courts to remedy unequal treatment.

In Your Own Words

After you've read this chapter, you will be able to

7.1 Describe the tensions between local representation and national lawmaking.

7.2 Explain how checks and balances work between Congress and the executive and judicial branches.

7.3 Identify the ways that politics influences how congressional districts are defined and who runs for Congress.

7.4 Summarize the central role that the parties play in Congress.

7.5 Describe the process of congressional policymaking.

7.6 Discuss the relationship between the people and Congress.

7
CONGRESS

What's at Stake . . . in the Senate's Obligation to Give Advice and Consent to the President?

WITHIN HOURS OF THE FEBRUARY 13, 2016, announcement that Supreme Court justice Antonin Scalia had died unexpectedly, even before the proper condolences to the family had been voiced, politics set in.

Of course, politics always surrounds the appointment of a new Supreme Court justice, as the Brett Kavanaugh hearings demonstrated so dramatically in 2018. The Constitution sets it up that way, giving the president the power to nominate a new justice "with the Advice and Consent of the Senate." "Advice and Consent" is purposely vague—it's intended to put a legislative check on presidents while keeping primary control in their hands.

This new Supreme Court vacancy was more political than many. Scalia, after all, had been the larger than life, gregarious and outspoken justice who defined the conservative end of the Court, which often broke five-to-four on significant cultural and political issues. If President Barack Obama replaced him with someone closer

DUTY CALLS

to the president's own more progressive values, as he could be expected to do (see Chapter 10), then the balance of the Court would swing the other way. And besides, Republicans had been making it a point of pride to thwart Obama wherever they could. Blocking his opportunity to leave a lasting legacy on the Court was an opportunity too good to be missed.

And it wasn't. With the stakes so high, the gloves came off quickly and completely. Senate majority leader Mitch McConnell, in his first public announcement in the hour after the announcement of Scalia's death, concluded his expression of sorrow to the Scalia family with this opening gambit: "The American people should have a voice in the selection of their next Supreme Court Justice. Therefore, this vacancy should not be filled until we have a new president."[1] What he meant, he later explained, is not that the Senate would refuse to confirm the president's as-yet-unnamed nominee, but that they would not even hold hearings or a vote on his candidate for the Court.

Of course, 2016 was an election year, which brings out crazy politics in the best of times and, arguably, nothing about 2016 was the best. But Supreme Court justices have been nominated and even confirmed in election years many times before. The Constitution does not give the president the power to make nominations to the Court only through the first three years of a term but through all four. And so in time, President Obama gave his own speech, in which he implicitly responded to McConnell:

> I plan to fulfill my constitutional responsibilities to nomi-
> nate a successor in due time. There will be plenty of time
> for me to do so, and for the Senate to fulfill its responsibility
> to give that person a fair hearing and a timely vote. These
> are responsibilities that I take seriously, as should everyone.
> They're bigger than any one party.

They are about our democracy. They're about the institution to which Justice Scalia dedicated his professional life, and making sure it continues to function as the beacon of justice that our Founders envisioned.

Thus began a battle of narratives over how to understand the meaning of "advice and consent": a proxy for what was clearly a power struggle to decide the future of the Court. After considering various candidates, conducting interviews, and talking to advisors in the White House, Obama nominated Merrick Garland, a well-liked and respected judge on the D.C. Circuit Court whose rulings tended to be somewhat left of center but hardly the liberal counterpart of Scalia. The nomination angered progressives who wanted to see Obama nominate a liberal firebrand, but it was meant to appease conservatives, many of whom had spoken favorably of Garland, and convince them to give the nominee a hearing.[2]

The strategy didn't work. Two warring narratives took over the communication networks—according to the Republican narrative, presidents in their last year in office should not impose their choices on the people about to vote for their replacement, which meant the job of advising and giving consent meant ignoring the nomination entirely. Although some senators agreed to chat with Judge Garland, only two thought he should be given the usual hearings. The Democratic narrative said that presidents were elected for four-year, not three-year terms, and that the Senate was within its rights to deny Garland confirmation, but that "advice and consent" meant they had to give him a hearing.

By early summer, polls showed that most of the American people were buying the Democratic version of the story, though that did not move McConnell, who risked infuriating the Republican base if he went back on his decision. But Republicans in close races for the Senate began to see their polls tighten, putting pressure on McConnell, who wanted to keep the Senate majority in his party's hands. By June, the nomination was in a standoff that lasted through the fall.

Why was what is usually a routine, if consequential, part of Senate business so fraught with drama in 2016? Why did the Republicans go to such lengths to construct and stick to a narrative that most people did not buy? What exactly is at stake in the constitutional obligation of Congress to give advice and consent to the president? We will be better able to answer these questions after examining the precarious relationship between Congress and the White House and this chapter's *CLUES to Critical Thinking.* ◀◀

THE U.S. Congress is the world's longest-running and most powerful democratic legislature. If politics is all about who gets what, and how, then Congress is arguably also the center of American national politics. Not only does it often decide exactly who gets what, but Congress also has the power to alter many of the rules that determine who wins and who loses in American political life and the narratives that define the conflicts. Social media have enhanced dramatically the way representatives can reach out to constituents—to convey messages, exchange opinions, inform them of actions taken in Congress, and solicit funds. In a mediated political world, the power of the representative's narrative is strengthened but so is the power of the constituent to break out of that narrative and represent his or her own views.

The Capitol building in Washington, D.C., home to both the House of Representatives and the Senate, has become as much a symbol of America's democracy as are the Stars and Stripes or the White House. We might expect Americans to express considerable pride in their national legislature, with its long tradition of serving democratic government. But if we did, we would be wrong.

Congress is generally distrusted, seen by the American public as incompetent, corrupt, torn by partisanship, and at the beck and call of special interests.[3] Yet despite their contempt for the institution of Congress as a whole, Americans typically like their representatives and senators and generally reelect them often enough that critics have long been calling for term limits to get new people into office (see *Snapshot of America: How Do We Hate Congress?*). How can we understand this bizarre paradox?[4]

There are two main reasons for America's love-hate relationship with Congress. The first is that the behaviors that help a member of Congress keep his or her job—creating satisfied constituents and supporting partisan positions—don't always make the institution more popular. On the one hand, voters want their representatives in Washington to take care of their local or state interests and to ensure that their home districts get a fair share of national resources. Parties want their members to be loyal to the party itself and not to "go rogue"—voting with the other party, for instance, or being seen as independent. On the other hand, citizens also want Congress to take care of the nation's business, and to look like a mature, deliberative, and collegial body, a goal not necessarily furthered by individual legislators' efforts to keep their jobs.

The second reason for citizens' love-hate relationship with Congress is that the rules that determine how Congress works were designed by the founders to produce slow, careful lawmaking based on compromise that can often seem motionless to an impatient public. When citizens are looking to Congress to produce policies that they favor or to distribute national resources, the built-in slowness can look like intentional foot-dragging and partisan bickering, especially when those behaviors are also taking place. That it is instead part of the constitutional safeguard of checks and balances is a civics lesson most Americans have long forgotten.

Keeping in mind these two dynamics—our legislators' struggle to keep their jobs while meeting national expectations and our own frustration with Congress' institutionalized slowness—will take us a long way toward understanding our mixed feelings about our national legislature. In this chapter we explore those dynamics as we look at who—including citizens, other politicians, and members of Congress themselves—gets the results they want from Congress, and how the rules of legislative politics help or hinder them.

UNDERSTANDING CONGRESS

The essential tensions among representation, lawmaking, and partisanship

We have traditionally counted on our elected representatives in both the House and the Senate to perform two major roles: representation and lawmaking. By **representation**, we mean that those we elect should represent, or look out for, our local interests and carry out our will. Representatives know far more about what we want in a mediated age, and they might have to respond to constituents who are informed and passionate. At the same time, we expect our legislators to address the country's social and economic problems by **national lawmaking**—passing laws that serve the interest of the entire nation.

Because the roles of representation and lawmaking often conflict (what is good for us and our local community may not serve the national good), scholars have long noted that members of Congress would usually favor their roles as representatives since the way they get reelected is by pleasing voters in their districts. Thus national problems go unaddressed while local problems get attention, resources, and solutions.

The tension between representation and lawmaking, however, is complicated further by the fact that members of Congress have to be responsive not only to their constituents and the nation, but also to their parties. Since the early days of the republic, **partisanship**—the loyalty to a party that helps shape how members see the world, how they define problems, and how they determine appropriate solutions—has been an important part of how members of Congress identify and organize themselves. They have juggled a commitment to the party with the simultaneous need to represent voters and to solve national problems, usually creating some kind of balance among the three. As we will see in Chapter 12, party identification can be a useful guide for voters as well as politicians.

> **representation** the efforts of elected officials to look out for the interests of those who elect them
>
> **national lawmaking** the creation of policy to address the problems and needs of the entire nation
>
> **partisanship** loyalty to a party that helps shape how members see the world, define problems, and identify appropriate solutions

Snapshot of America: *How Do We Hate Congress? (Let Us Count the Ways.)*

Putting the Unpopularity of Congress Into Perspective

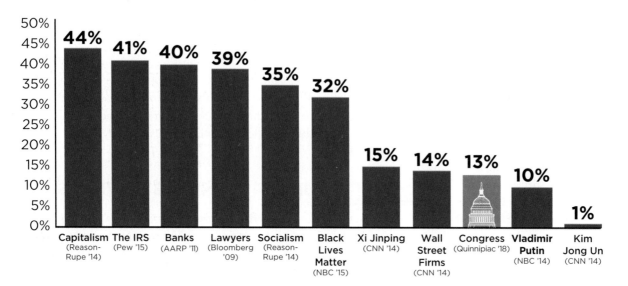

Approval Ratings of How Congress Is Handling Its Job

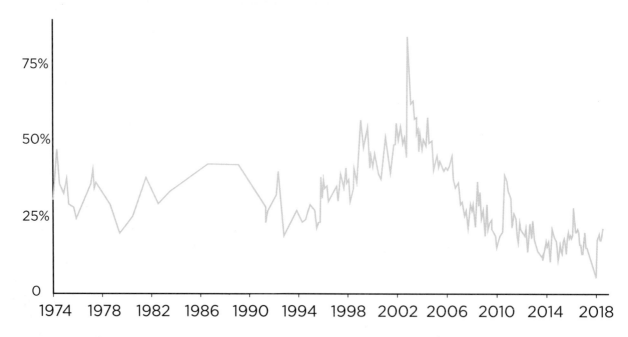

Behind the Numbers

Americans are proud of our form of government, but the data show that we do not approve of how Congress does its job. Moreover, this approval is at an all-time low. Why do you think we are so disappointed? What can Congress do to change the public's attitude?

Source: Congress and the Public, Gallup, www.gallup.com/poll/1600/congress-public.aspx.

REPRESENTATION

Representation means working on behalf of one's **constituency**, the folks back home in the district who voted for the member as well as those who did not. To help us understand this complex job, political scientists often speak about four types of representation.[5] Most members of Congress try to excel at all four functions so that constituents will rate them highly and reelect them.

Policy representation refers to congressional work for laws that advance the economic and social interests of the constituency. For example, House members and senators from petroleum-producing states can be safely predicted to vote in ways favorable to the profitability of the oil companies, members from the Plains states try to protect subsidies for wheat farmers, and so on. It is rarer for a member to champion a national interest, since it is in the local constituency that he or she will face reelection, but some members do focus on such issues as foreign policy, campaign finance reform, or the environment.

Voters have also come to expect a certain amount of **allocative representation**, in which the congressperson gets projects and grants for the district. Such perks traditionally were called "**pork barrel projects**" (or "bringing home the bacon") but now are referred to as **earmarks**. These are provisions in various appropriations documents or the budget that direct funding for quite specific purposes (for example, highway construction or the establishment of a research institution). They are electorally popular because they appear free to the district while the costs are spread to all taxpayers.

Senators and representatives also represent their states or districts by taking care of the individual problems of constituents, especially problems that involve the federal

Meanwhile, Back in the District . . .

Rep. Chellie Pingree, D-Maine, brings pizza to a food tent for striking workers outside Fairpoint Communications in Portland. Members of Congress split their time between Washington, D.C., and their home districts, just as they must divide their attention between national and local needs.

bureaucracy. This kind of representation is called **casework**, or constituency service, and it covers things such as finding out why a constituent's Social Security check has not shown up, sending a flag that has flown over the U.S. Capitol to a high school in the district, or helping with immigration and naturalization problems. To promote their work for constituents, members maintain web pages and send information to the homes of voters through more traditional channels. The congressional privilege of **franking** allows members to use the U.S. mail at no charge, although this perk is less valuable as members take greater advantage of social media to present themselves to their constituents. (See *Don't Be Fooled by . . . Your Elected Officials* for some tips on how to be a savvy consumer of congressional information.)

Another kind of representation is called **symbolic representation**. In this elusive but important function, the member of Congress tries to represent many of the positive values Americans associate with public life and government without seeming too political. Thus members are glad to serve as commencement speakers at high school graduations or to attend town meetings to explain what is happening in Washington. Equally important are the ways members present themselves to their districts—for example, using colloquialisms such as "y'all" even if they are not from the South, or wearing a denim work shirt to the county fair. These appearances are part of a member's "home style" and help to symbolize the message "I am one of you" and "I am a person you can trust; I share your values and interests."[6] Symbolic representation can be in person or virtual—communication around patriotic and regional messages is easy and inexpensive online.

---

constituency the voters in a state or district

policy representation congressional work to advance the issues and ideological preferences of constituents

allocative representation congressional work to secure projects, services, and funds for the represented district

pork barrel projects public works projects and grants for specific districts paid for by general revenues

earmarks legislative provisions to allocate spending to a specific purpose or project

casework legislative work on behalf of individual constituents to solve their problems with government agencies and programs

franking the privilege of free mail service provided to members of Congress

symbolic representation efforts of members of Congress to stand for American ideals or to identify with common constituency values

Your Elected Officials

Being a critical constituent means more than sitting around the dinner table griping about Congress. It means knowing what your representatives are doing so that you can evaluate how well they are representing your interests. You have at your disposal unprecedented access to your representatives in Congress, and to information about just what they are up to. You also have a number of effective ways of helping your representatives get to know you in return.

Elizabeth Warren/Twitter

What to Watch Out For

- **Who is your representative, really?** Every member of Congress has some presence on social media. Their official web sites are great starting points if you want to know what your representatives are doing, how they voted on specific bills, or what your congressional district looks like. Most have Facebook pages as well as Instagram and Twitter feeds. The coverage on these sites, understandably, is glowing—most social media feeds are essentially public relations pages managed by staffers—so you do need to take them with a healthy grain of salt. Do some independent investigation— your friend Google can help you dig deeper to find out what kind of record they have.

- **Can you get some face time?** Members regularly come home for long weekends in part to maintain contact with constituents. Staff will be happy to reply to your phone call or email to tell you of upcoming town meetings or visits to district offices to meet with constituents. This is harder to arrange for a U.S. senator from a large state, but most citizens can meet with their U.S. representative with just a bit of effort.

- **Can you interact with them online?** As we said, most congressional social network feeds are carefully managed, but that doesn't mean you can't use them to your advantage. A well-timed, well-worded tweet or post tagged to your senator or representative, especially on a public forum, can get their attention for an issue or cause that's important to you. An email should at least get you a form letter response.

- **How do his or her facts stack up?** A number of well-run web sites run fact-checks to see if our representatives are stretching, bending, or outright breaking with the truth. Notable here is politifact .com, run by the esteemed *Tampa Bay Times*, which rates politicians' claims on their "Truth-O-Meter," from "True" to "Half True" to "Pants on Fire." Other solid resources are factcheck.org, operated by the University of Pennsylvania's Annenberg Public Policy Center, and the *Washington Post* Fact Checker at www.washingtonpost.com/news/fact-checker/.

- **What do locals think?** Although big, sweeping legislation is national news, bills that could affect you and your neighbors or classmates are often ignored by large news organizations. Your local newspaper or news site will pay close attention to the activities of your congressional representatives, and may offer editorials that can help you decide how well they are serving your community. It's also a great idea to follow your state and local representatives on social media, to keep abreast of what's happening at city hall and in your state capitol—and to get alerts for matters of local interest hitting the floor of Congress.

- **Follow the money.** If you want a good clue about what your congressperson is up to, it will help to see who has been donating to his or her campaigns. Check out www.opensecrets.org, the web site for the Center for Responsive Politics, a nonprofit that tracks campaign contributions to all political candidates. With just a few clicks, you can see how much money a senator or member of the House has raised, and who made the contributions, right down to the last dollar. You can see what industries, groups, or companies have made the largest contributions—the site can even tell you who in your ZIP code area has given how much money to which political causes or candidates.

NATIONAL LAWMAKING

As we explained earlier, representation is not the only business of our senators and representatives. A considerable part of their jobs involves working with one another in Washington to define and solve the nation's problems. We expect Congress to create laws that serve the common good. One scholar calls this view of effective lawmaking "collective responsibility."[7] By this he means that Congress should be responsible for the effectiveness of its laws in solving national problems. A variety of factors are involved in a representative's calculation of how to vote on matters of national interest. He or she might be guided by conscience or ideology, by the demands of constituents, by interest groups, or by party position. These considerations may very well be at odds with the four kinds of representation just described, which frequently makes it difficult, if not impossible, for members to fulfill their collective responsibility.

Imagine, for instance, the dilemma of a Democratic congresswoman representing an oil-producing district in Texas who has to vote yes or no on government support for the development of non-fossil-fuel technologies. What is good for the nation—to decrease our dependence on fossil fuels so that we are less reliant on foreign sources of oil and to reduce global warming—is not necessarily what is good for the economic interests of her district. The bill would mean higher taxes for her constituents to support a technology that makes their main industry less profitable. In deciding how to vote, our congresswoman would have to consider tough questions that affect the public good, her policy goals, and her reelection.

In this case, what's best for the local district clearly clashes with the national interest. And the scenario holds true again and again for every representative and senator. The potential for conflict is great when one works for one's constituents as well as for the entire nation. We all want a Congress that focuses on the nation's problems, but as voters we tend to reward members for putting constituency concerns first.

PARTISANSHIP

As we noted earlier in the chapter, complicating the already difficult balance between representation and lawmaking is

hyperpartisanship a commitment to party so strong that it can transcend other commitments

party polarization greater ideological (liberal versus conservative) differences between the parties and increased ideological consensus within the parties

a commitment to party that we call partisanship. Party affiliations have always been an important part of the identities of members of Congress, but in recent years they have come to trump other considerations in what political scientists refer to as **hyperpartisanship**, or the raising of party above all other commitments. This hyperpartisanship is made worse by increased **party polarization**, which means that the issue positions and ideological stances of Democrats and Republicans have been growing apart and each party has become more internally homogeneous. As a result, bipartisanship (working with members of the opposite party) is increasingly rare, especially when the very act of cooperating with the other side can be seen as a betrayal of one's own. The information bubbles we live in and through which we get our news can exacerbate this by demonizing our opponents without providing any other perspectives.

Hyperpartisanship was last at play to this extent in the early 1900s (we discuss partisan eras in more detail in Chapter 12), but since the mid-1990s partisanship has again become a fierce divider of the American public. In fact, a recent study found that the American public is more divided by party than by race, class, gender, or age,[8] and members of Congress have not been so polarized by party since the Civil War.[9] In practical terms this polarization has real implications for how laws get made in Congress. Voters sort themselves into parties with greater internal ideological purity (that is, dissent is frowned on), and tend to live nearer to those with whom they share values. Add to that the fact that the districts from which members are elected are increasingly drawn by state legislatures (also in the grips of hyperpartisanship) so that they are safe for Democrats or safe for Republicans, with fewer members of the other party. The people running for Congress have little incentive to appeal to more moderate voters, as they used to do. If the hyperpartisan representative wants to keep his or her job and not face a primary election challenge from a candidate viewed by the party as more ideologically pure, he or she has to pick party over what's best for the district or the nation.[10] The results can slow government to a crawl or even bring it to the brink of disaster.

Two influential political scientists, one at the Brookings Institution (a liberal think tank) and one at the American Enterprise Institute (a conservative think tank) but both with solid reputations as impartial scholars, wrote a book in 2012 in which they argued that the problem of hyperpartisanship in the first part of this century has not affected both parties equally. They point out that the Republicans, at least so far, are more prone to internal purity tests and using obstruction to get their way. Their argument is not that there is anything wrong with the substance of what Republicans want or with their policies or with conservative ideology. Rather, the problem is that the recent Republican strategy of putting party first, not tolerating internal dissent, and refusing to compromise has ground American government to a halt.[11] They say, "We have been studying Washington politics and Congress for more than 40 years, and never have we seen them this dysfunctional. In our past writings, we have criticized both parties when we believed it was warranted. Today, however, we have no choice but to acknowledge that the core of the problem lies with the Republican Party."[12]

The consequence, they say, is that American government is in trouble: "Today, thanks to the GOP, compromise has gone out the window in Washington."[13] In fact, instead of following the legislative norm dictated by the procedural orientation that we discussed in Chapter 1 as a part of American political culture—that the process of a free election legitimates the results—the GOP took a more substantive stance—that if the procedures of the government didn't endorse their plan, they would simply block them and hope that the failure of the system would frustrate the public sufficiently that people would vote Republicans into power.

In 2012, voters finally delivered a rebuke to the Republican effort to stalemate government—reelecting President Obama, increasing the Democratic majority in the Senate, and even adding Democrats to the House. Obama believed that his reelection would cool the fervor of Republican opposition efforts, but instead, Tea Party Republicans in Congress, calling themselves the Freedom Caucus, only stiffened their resolve to block the president.[14] Their efforts culminated in a government shutdown in October 2013, another norm broken, when House Republicans refused to pass a continuing budget resolution (which would allow the government to continue operating) unless it defunded the Patient Protection and Affordable Care Act, also known as "Obamacare." The Senate Democrats would not agree to this killing of the administration's signature legislation. After sixteen days and an estimated $10 billion lost to the U.S. economy, the House Republicans agreed to a Senate bill, gaining only a token concession of trivial legislative importance.[15] That defeat didn't cool the fever either, and in September 2015, tired of trying to keep his unruly members on the same page, Speaker of the House John Boehner resigned the speakership and left Congress entirely. After his party scrambled to find someone to take on the job, former vice-presidential candidate Paul Ryan reluctantly took the office, but he did not have much better luck marshalling his troops.

As we saw in *What's at Stake . . . ?*, in February 2016, Senate majority leader Mitch McConnell showed the same hyperpartisanship at work in the Senate, an institution that used to consider itself collegial and bipartisan, when he refused to hold hearings on Merrick Garland, President Obama's nominee to replace Antonin Scalia on the Supreme Court. Denying a president

hearings on his choice to fill a Supreme Court seat in the hopes that a future election would bring a Republican president who would nominate someone more pleasing to Republicans was another stunning breakage of a legislative norm. As we will see in Chapter 12 (and as we mentioned in Chapter 2), a power struggle within the Republican Party has reduced its ability to compromise with Democrats and to get anything done that doesn't have majority Republican support. When the president is the same party as a majority of Congress, that party can and should be able to ease the passage of the president's agenda; but conflict in the party resulted more often in bringing politics to a grinding halt. The same forces frustrated voters to such an extent that they eliminated the Republican majority in the House in the 2018 midterms.

For very committed, very conservative Republicans who fundamentally disagree with liberal goals and policies, it may seem like a perfectly reasonable strategy to refuse to compromise with Democrats in an effort to hold out for what they want. In fact, there is an influential movement by some conservative organizations, including, for example, the Tea Party, the Club for Growth, and Americans for Tax Reform, and individuals like Sheldon Adelson (who pitched in $30 million to help the Republican Party hold the House in 2018), the Koch brothers, or the Mercer family, to punish and replace Republican members who vote the "wrong way" on issues they care about or do not heed the party line.[16] Since they truly believe that what they want for the nation is in its best interest, that is the narrative that they tell: that the nation faces a crisis that can be fixed only by not going further into debt or by repealing Obamacare, which requires closing the government in order to pressure the president to give in; that raising the debt ceiling amounts to giving the president a blank check (it does not); that failing to give the president's nominee to the Supreme Court a hearing is "letting the people's voice be heard"; that supporting the current leadership in Israel is our chief foreign policy obligation; and that repealing environmental protections is removing burdens that hamper economic growth. In each case the Democrats have a competing narrative about what is happening, but for the most part the contention just confuses voters, causing them to blame all establishment politicians for not getting anything done. Sometimes deliberately confusing voters with conflicting media reports can be an effective strategy for getting them to just tune out.

As a consequence, representatives and senators, especially Republicans, have been focused more on representing their party—and especially the most ideologically extreme members of their party—than they are on the compromise and bipartisan activity that enables Congress to make laws that respond to policy needs at the local and particularly the national levels. Sometimes this causes more moderate Republicans to try to satisfy their Tea Party critics, but it leads others to leave public service altogether. Republican senator Olympia Snowe of Maine retired in 2012, decrying the end of bipartisanship in the institution she had served since 1995. Later that same year, Ohio Republican representative Steve LaTourette, who had already won his primary and was almost certainly going to be reelected, decided to leave the House, saying, "I have reached the conclusion that the atmosphere today, and the reality that exists in the House of Representatives, no longer encourages the finding of common ground."[17] In 2018, multiple Republicans decided not to run for reelection. One of the first to make the decision, probably because he had decided he would face a primary from the right and have trouble hanging on to his job, Sen. Jeff Flake of Arizona announced his retirement with an eloquent condemnation of the breaking of essential political norms:

> In this century, a new phrase has entered the language to describe the accommodation of a new and undesirable order, that phrase being the new normal. That we must never adjust to the present coarseness of our national dialogue with the tone set at the top. We must never regard as normal the regular and casual undermining of our democratic norms and ideals. We must never meekly accept the daily sundering of our country. The personal attacks, the threats against principles, freedoms, and institutions, and the flagrant disregard for truth and decency, the reckless provocations, most often for the pettiest and most personal reasons, reasons having nothing whatsoever to do with the fortunes of the people that we have been elected to serve.[18]

Both citizens and their representatives have something serious at stake in the tensions among representation, lawmaking, and hyperpartisanship. Citizens want their local interests protected, and many partisan activists who have contributed time and money have strong policy preferences. But citizens also want sound national policy, and here they are often disappointed. The need to secure reelection by catering to local—and increasingly partisan—interests often means that their representatives have fewer incentives to concentrate on national lawmaking.

In fact, members of the House and the Senate face a true dilemma. On the one hand, they want to serve their constituents' local interests and needs, and they want to be reelected to office by those constituents. But they also must face personal, party, and special interest demands to take stands that might not suit the voters back home. As a result, part of their job ends up being the creation

> **bicameral legislature** a legislature with two chambers

and dissemination of a narrative that satisfies these competing constituencies, with the result that voters often lose faith in their representative institutions.

In Your Own Words Describe the tensions between local representation and national lawmaking.

CONGRESSIONAL POWERS AND RESPONSIBILITIES

Expansive powers held in check by the Constitution

The Constitution gives the U.S. Congress enormous powers, although it is safe to say that the founders could not have imagined the scope of contemporary congressional power since they never anticipated the growth of the federal government to today's size. As we will see, they were less concerned with the conflict between local and national interests we have been discussing than they were with the representation of short-term popular opinion versus long-term national interests. The basic powers of Congress are laid out in Article I, Section 8, of the Constitution (see Chapter 4). They include the powers to tax, to pay debts, to regulate interstate commerce, and to provide for the common defense and welfare of the United States, among many other things.

DIFFERENCES BETWEEN THE HOUSE AND THE SENATE

The term *Congress* refers to the institution that is formally made up of the U.S. House of Representatives and the U.S. Senate. Congresses are numbered so that we can talk about them over time in a coherent way. Each congress covers a two-year election cycle. The 116th Congress was elected in November 2018, and its term runs from January 2019 through the end of 2020. The **bicameral** (two-house) **legislature** is laid out in the Constitution. As we discussed in earlier chapters, the founders wanted two chambers so that they could serve as a restraint on each other, strengthening the principle of checks and balances. The framers' hope was that the smaller, more elite Senate would "cool the passions" of the people represented in the House. Accordingly, although the two houses are equal in their overall power—both can initiate legislation (although tax bills must originate in the House) and both must pass every bill in identical form before it can be signed by the president to become law—there are also some key differences, particularly in the extra responsibilities assigned to the Senate. In addition, the two chambers operate differently, and they have distinct histories and norms.[19] Some of the major differences are outlined in Table 7.1.

The single biggest factor determining the differences between the House and the Senate is size. With 100 members, the Senate is less formal; the 435-person House needs more rules and hierarchy in order to function efficiently. The Constitution also provides for differences in terms: two years for the House, six for the Senate (on a staggered basis—all senators do not come up for reelection at the same time). In the modern context, this means that House members (also referred to as congresspersons or members of Congress, a term that sometimes applies to senators as well) never stop campaigning. Senators, in contrast, can suspend their preoccupation with the next campaign for the first four or five years of their terms and thus, at least in theory, have more time to spend on the affairs of the nation. The minimum age of the candidates is different as well: members of the House must be at least twenty-five years old, senators thirty. This again reflects the founders' expectation that the Senate would be older, wiser, and better able to deal with national lawmaking. This distinction was reinforced in the constitutional provision that senators be elected not directly by the people, as were members of the House, but by state legislatures. Although this provision was changed by constitutional amendment in 1913, its presence in the original Constitution reflects the convictions of its authors that the Senate was a special chamber, one step removed from the people.

Budget bills are initiated in the House of Representatives. In practice this is not particularly significant since the Senate has to pass budget bills as well, and most of the time differences are negotiated between the two houses. The budget process has gotten quite complicated, as demonstrated by congressional struggles to deal with the deficit, which called for reductions in spending at the same time that constituencies and interest groups were pleading for expensive new programs. The budget process illustrates once again the constant tension for members of Congress between being responsive to local or particular interests, supporting the party leadership, and at the same time trying to make laws in the interest of the nation as a whole.

Other differences between the House and the Senate include the division of power on impeachment of public figures such as presidents and Supreme Court justices. The House impeaches, or charges the official with "Treason, Bribery, or other high Crimes and Misdemeanors," and the Senate tries the official. Both Andrew Johnson and Bill Clinton were impeached by the House, but in both cases the Senate failed to find the president guilty of the charges brought by the House.

TABLE 7.1
Differences Between the House and the Senate

DIFFERENCES	HOUSE	SENATE
Constitutional		
Term length	2 years	6 years
Minimum age	25	30
Citizenship required	7 years	9 years
Residency	In state	In state
Apportionment	Changes with population	Fixed; entire state
Impeachment	Impeaches official	Tries the impeached official
Treaty-making power	No authority	2/3 approval
Presidential appointments	No authority	Majority approval
Organizational		
Size	435 members	100 members
Number of standing committees	20	16
Total committee assignments per member	Approx. 6	Approx. 11
Rules Committee	Yes	No
Limits on floor debate	Yes	No (filibuster possible)
Electoral, 2018		
Average incumbent raised	$1,814,000	$15,357,000
Average challenger raised	$904,000	$4,963,000
Most expensive campaign (candidate expenditures)	$20,629,000	$93,853,000
Incumbency advantage	93% (93.1% is 56-year average)	86% (81.4% is 56-year average)

Sources: Roger H. Davidson, Walter J. Oleszek, and Frances E. Lee, *Congress and Its Members*, 13th ed. (Washington, D.C.: CQ Press, 2008), 44, 187; Federal Election Commission data compiled by the Center for Responsive Politics, 2018, https://www.opensecrets.org/overview/index.php.

In addition, only the Senate is given the responsibility of confirming appointments to the executive and judicial branches, and of sharing the treaty-making power with the president, responsibilities we explore in more detail later in the chapter.

CONGRESSIONAL CHECKS AND BALANCES

The founders were concerned about the abuse of power by all branches, but they were most anxious to avoid executive tyranny and so they granted Congress the bulk of the lawmaking power. The Constitution gives Congress the power to regulate commerce; the exclusive power to raise and to spend money for the national government; the power to provide for economic infrastructure (roads, postal service, money, patents); and significant powers in foreign policy, including the powers to declare war, to ratify treaties, and to raise and support the armed forces.

As we discussed in Chapter 4, the Supreme Court has often extended legislative power through a broad interpretation of the necessary and proper clause of Article I, Section 8, of the Constitution. But the Constitution also limits congressional powers through the protection of individual rights and by the watchful eyes of the other two branches of government, with which Congress shares power.

CONGRESS AND THE EXECUTIVE BRANCH Our system of checks and balances means that, to exercise its powers, each branch has to have the cooperation of the others. Thus Congress has the responsibility for passing bills, but the bills do not become law unless (1) the president signs them or, more passively, refrains from vetoing them, or (2) both houses of Congress are able to muster a full two-thirds majority to override a presidential veto. The president cannot vote on legislation or even introduce bills, but the Constitution gives the chief executive a powerful policy formulation role in calling for the president's annual State of the Union address and in inviting the president to recommend to Congress "such measures as he shall judge necessary and expedient."

One of the most important checks on the executive that the Constitution gives to Congress is **congressional oversight** of the executive to ensure that the president and bureaucracy are carrying out the laws as Congress intended. This is usually done through hearings and selective investigations of executive actions and is essential for Congress to be certain its will is being carried out. When Congress and the White House are controlled by opposite parties, however, oversight can become a political weapon in the hands of Congress, with Congress

> **congressional oversight** a committee's investigation of the executive and of government agencies to ensure they are acting as Congress intends

keeping the executive continually on the defensive by requiring it to defend itself against accusations that are frequently made to hamstring that branch. Consequently, the number of congressional investigations of executive behavior increases sharply when the president faces a House of Representatives controlled by the opposition party.[20]

Unlike most of its predecessors, the Obama administration proved to be remarkably scandal-free but that didn't stop the GOP from trying to find a way to tarnish the administration.[21] The United States House Select Committee on Events Surrounding the 2012 Terrorist Attack in Benghazi was convened by Speaker John Boehner in May 2014 to investigate the deaths of four Americans in Benghazi, Libya, with the goal, in the words of then-Speaker John Boehner, of "getting to the truth" about whether the Obama administration misled the public about the deadly attack in Libya. Two years and $7 million later the committee found no wrong-doing on Secretary of State Hillary Clinton's part.[22] The *New York Times*, generally no friend of Clinton's, called it "one of the longest, costliest and most bitterly partisan congressional investigations in history . . . ."[23]

Just as a Congress can be hard on an administration of the opposite party, it can go easy on its own. The Republican House oversight of Russian intervention into the 2016 election was unable to get to the bottom of what the Russian role was because President Trump viewed their charge as implying that his election was illegitimate. Once the Democrats took back control of the House in 2018 they promised to look carefully at the Russian involvement in the 2016 election, Trump's financial relationship with Russia, and his efforts to hamper the free press by targeting the business interests of the owner of the *Washington Post*, Jeff Bezos, and CNN's effort to merge with Time Warner. The Democrats have been careful not to mention impeachment, however, (though Trump has repeatedly warned of it) so that they are not seen as over-reaching.

Oversight also comes into play when Congress delegates authority to regulatory agencies in the executive branch. Often the agencies do what they are supposed to do, which can make the job of keeping an eye on them boring and unrewarding. If Congress does not keep watch, however, the agencies can develop unhealthy relationships with those they are supposed to be regulating. This was the case with the Securities and Exchange Commission, which failed to protect us from the risky investment practices that resulted in the economic meltdown in late 2008, as well as with the Minerals Management Service, whose failure to adequately police offshore drilling procedures contributed to the ecological disaster in the Gulf of Mexico following the 2010 explosion of BP's Deepwater Horizon drilling platform. The Marine Mammal Protection Act and the National

Environmental Policy Act were routinely violated by regulators seeking bonuses for encouraging offshore oil drilling.[24] Since these relationships develop far from public scrutiny, we rely on Congress to ensure, through oversight, that agencies do the job they were set up to do, though there is a strong temptation for members to slight congressional responsibility here in favor of splashier and more electorally rewarding activities.

Another congressional check on the executive is the constitutional requirement that major presidential appointments—for instance, to cabinet posts, ambassadorships, and the federal courts—must be made with the **advice and consent** of the Senate. Beyond a norm, this is an actual constitutional duty. Historically, most presidential appointments have proceeded without incident, but in recent administrations, appointments have become increasingly political. Senators sometimes use their confirmation powers to do more than advise on and consent to the appointment at hand. They frequently tie up appointments, either because they oppose the nominee on account of his or her ideology or because they wish to extract promises and commitments from the president. In today's highly polarized Congress, senators of the opposing party are quick to object to many of a president's appointees. The result is that many appointments languish and high offices in the federal government go unfilled for months or even years.[25] The power to approve appointments can also be used as leverage for individual senators to pressure the administration, as when, for instance, freshman senator Rand Paul, R-Ky., put a hold on a highly qualified Obama court nominee in 2012 to force the president's hand on an unrelated proposal to cut off aid to Egypt.[26]

As *What's at Stake . . . ?* and the events following Justice Anthony Kennedy's retirement in 2018 have made painfully clear, the constitutional duty to provide advice and consent can become political theater with serious consequences. The Senate loses the important norm of cooperation with the president on judicial appointments, setting a dangerous precedent for future appointments under divided government.

And clearly, presidents can find the Senate's ability to block their appointments incredibly frustrating, as it gums up the works of the executive and judicial branches, preventing agencies and courts from taking care of their business. Stymied presidents have sometimes taken advantage of a constitutional provision that allows them to make temporary appointments without Senate approval if a vacancy occurs when the Senate is not in session. These so-called recess appointments were designed to let presidents fill vacancies in an era when it might take the Senate long

weeks to convene, but modern-day presidents sometimes use them to get around Senate opposition. Senators determined to deny a president the opportunity to make a recess appointment have taken to keeping the Senate in session on a technicality, even when they are not in Washington. President Obama, facing such obstruction, argued that Congress was really in recess when its members were not present and made several appointments, some of which were challenged in court. In 2014 the Supreme Court voided recess appointments that Obama had made while the Senate was technically in session although not in Washington, calling it an overreach of his authority because it is up to Congress to decide when it is or is not in session.[27]

A final built-in source of institutional conflict between Congress and the president is the difference in constituencies. Presidents look at each policy in terms of a national constituency and their own policy program, whereas members of Congress necessarily take a narrower view. For example, the president may decide that clean air should be a national priority. For some members of Congress, however, a clean air bill might mean closing factories in their districts because it would not be profitable to bring them up to emissions standards, or shutting down soft coal mines because the bill would kill the market for high-sulfur coal. Increasingly, within an era of hyperpartisanship, opposition members can get their bases excited just by opposing the president's agenda, whatever it may be. Often, public policy looks very different from the perspective of congressional offices than it does from the presidential Oval Office at the other end of Pennsylvania Avenue.

CONGRESS AND THE JUDICIAL BRANCH The constitutional relationship between the federal courts and Congress is simple in principle: Congress makes the laws, and the courts interpret them. The Supreme Court also has the lofty job of deciding whether laws and procedures are consistent with the Constitution, although this power of judicial review is not mentioned in the Constitution.

We think of the judiciary as independent of the other branches, but this self-sufficiency is only a matter of degree. Congress, for example, is charged with setting up the lower federal courts and determining the salaries for judges, with the interesting constitutional provision that a judge's salary

---

advice and consent the constitutional obligation that the Senate approve certain executive appointments

cannot be cut. Congress also has considerable powers in establishing some issues of jurisdiction—that is, deciding which courts hear which cases (Article III, Section 2). And, as we just indicated, in accepting and rejecting presidential Supreme Court and federal court nominees, the Senate influences the long-term operation of the courts.[28]

Congress also exerts power over the courts by passing laws that limit the courts' discretion to rule or impose sentences as judges think best. For example, in the 1980s, Congress passed strict drug laws that required mandatory sentences for offenders; judges could not sentence someone for less than the minimum time that Congress defined in legislation. And finally, though it is hard to do, Congress can remove the ability of federal courts and the Supreme Court to interpret constitutional issues by trying to amend the Constitution itself.

PAUSE AND REVIEW Who, What, How

The Constitution gives great power to both the House and the Senate, but it does so in the curiously backhanded way known as checks and balances. The House and the Senate share most lawmaking functions, but the fact that both must approve legislation gives them a check over each other. They in turn are checked by the power of the president and the courts. The legislature is unable to operate without the cooperation of the other two branches unless it can demonstrate unusual internal strength and consensus, allowing it to override presidential vetoes and, in more extreme circumstances, amend the Constitution and impeach presidents.

In Your Own Words Explain how checks and balances work between Congress and the executive and judicial branches.

CONGRESSIONAL ELECTIONS

Political calculations to define districts and determine who will run

If we want to understand how Congress works, the place to begin is with the election of its members. With House terms of two years and Senate terms of six years, getting elected occupies a great deal of a representative's time. In fact, one

---

reapportionment a reallocation of congressional seats among the states every ten years, following the census

redistricting the process of dividing states into legislative districts

gerrymandering redistricting to benefit a particular group

---

professor argues that most aspects of Congress are designed to aid the reelection goals of its members.[29] Furthermore, the way in which the districts they run in are drawn goes a long way to determining how successful they will be.

THE POLITICS OF DEFINING CONGRESSIONAL DISTRICTS

The Constitution provides that each state will have two senators, which is easy to determine, and that seats in the House of Representatives will be allocated on the basis of population, which is less so because state populations fluctuate over time. **Reapportionment** is the process in which the 435 House seats are reallocated among the states after each ten-year census yields a new population count. States whose populations grow gain seats, which are taken from those whose populations decline or remain steady. Figure 7.1 shows the current apportionment for each state through 2020. The winners are mostly in the rapidly growing Sun Belt states of the South and Southwest; the losers are largely in the Northeast and Midwest.

Since areas that lose population will also lose representatives, just how you count the population becomes critical since many people will not fill out the household questionnaires the Census Bureau sends out. Democrats in 2000 proposed using what they claimed was a more precise statistical sampling technique that would allow census workers to get a better estimate of hard-to-count portions of the population such as poor people and immigrants. Republicans balked, fearing that this would add to the population of Democratic districts and thus increase Democratic representation. The Supreme Court sided with the Republicans, ruling that the Constitution and the legislation on the books required that, for purposes of reapportionment, the census had to reflect an actual count of the population.

Not only must the 435 delegates be apportioned among the fifty states, but, in a process called **redistricting**, districts within the states have to be redrawn to keep them relatively equal in population. In 1964 the Supreme Court decided that, for the U.S. House of Representatives as well as for state legislatures, Americans should be represented under the principle of "one person, one vote" and that the districts therefore must have equal populations.[30] The average size of a house district in the year 2010 was 710,767.[31] Redistricting, which is carried out by the state legislators (or by commissions they empower), can turn into a bitter political battle because how the district lines are drawn will have a lot to do with who gets elected.

Gerrymandering is the process of drawing district lines to benefit one group or another, and it can result in some

FIGURE 7.1

House Apportionment for Elections in 2012–2020

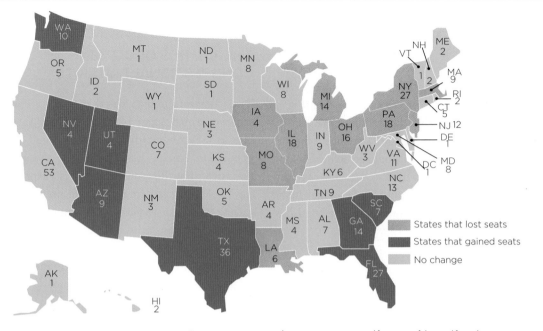

Source: U.S. Census Bureau, "Apportionment Data," www2.census.gov/programs-surveys/decennial/2010/data/apportionment/ ApportionmentPopulation2010.pdf.

extremely strange shapes by the time the state politicians are through. Gerrymandering usually is one of three kinds. **Partisan gerrymandering** is the process in a particular state legislature whereby the majority party draws districts to maximize the number of House seats their party can win. Consequently, Democrats might draw districts that would split a historically Republican district and force an incumbent Republican to run in a new, more liberal district—a tactic called "cracking"—or even draw districts to concentrate as many opposition-party voters as possible—called "packing"—so that the party drawing the districts can more easily win in surrounding districts. As a result of partisan gerrymandering, it is easily possible for a party to win a substantial majority of seats in the legislature while losing the statewide popular vote.

The Republican success in the 2010 elections gave the party control of the redistricting process in a majority of states.[32] In 2012, House Democrats won 1.7 million more votes than House Republicans did but won only 201 seats to the Republicans' 234. While Democrats tried to use their greater vote total as an indication that they truly possessed a popular mandate, that narrative was no substitute for actually controlling the House. Because of the way the districts had been drawn at the congressional level, Democrats probably needed a five percentage point win just to take the House back. Voting is still going on as we write but it looks like their margin of victory may be

closer to 7 or 8 points which could support a majority of 35–40.

Crucially for the Democrats, they gained more control at the state legislative level (also difficult because of gerrymandering), which will give them a say in how the districts are drawn after the 2020 census. In all, Democrats took seven governorships, flipped six legislative chambers (where gerrymandering is done) and added about 300 state-level House and Senate seats.

Meanwhile, the effects of extreme gerrymandering were too much for the judicial system. In Pennsylvania, the state Supreme Court redrew the map to equalize the seats between the party somewhat, since the previous, Republican map had made it possible for the Democrats to carry about half of the statewide vote but win only five of Pennsylvania's 18 seats.[33] In 2018 the districts split with the vote, nine and nine.

A second kind of gerrymandering is pro-incumbent gerrymandering. This happens when legislators agree to create districts to enhance the electoral security of the current members of both parties.[34] Such political outcomes tend to

---

partisan gerrymandering redistricting controlled by the majority party in a state's legislature, to increase the number of districts that party can expect to carry

FIGURE 7.2
Gerrymanders and Earmuffs

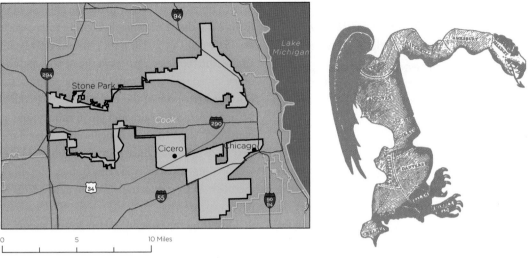

Illinois Fourth Congressional District

Back in 1812, district lines in the state of Massachusetts were drawn to concentrate Federalist support in a few key districts. A contemporary cartoon likened one particularly convoluted district to a long-necked monster, nicknamed the "Gerry-mander" after Massachusetts governor Elbridge Gerry. Redistricting after the 2010 Census proved that the gerrymander is alive and well, as evidenced by the new map of the Illinois Fourth Congressional District, nicknamed the "earmuffs" district, which joins two predominantly Latino areas in Chicago.

Source: *"Congressional District 4," NationalAtlas.gov; Library of Congress.*

occur when a state legislature is divided so closely that neither party can dictate the redistricting process.

Finally, **racial gerrymandering** occurs when district lines are drawn to favor or disadvantage an ethnic or racial group. For many years, states in the Deep South drew district lines to ensure that black voters would not constitute a majority that could elect an African American to Congress. The 1965 Voting Rights Act, as we have seen, was intended to ease the way for African Americans to exercise their voting rights. For a time, states with discriminatory backgrounds were subject to federal supervision to ensure they did not intend their voting laws to discriminate. Since the 1982 Voting Rights Act, the drawing of district lines has been used to maximize the likelihood that African Americans will be elected to Congress. Both Republicans and minority (African American and Latino) political activists have backed the formation of majority-minority districts, in which African Americans or Hispanics constitute majorities. This has the effect of concentrating enough minority citizens to elect one of their own, and at the same time, it takes these (usually Democratic) voters out of the pool of voters in other districts—a process aptly termed "bleaching"—thus making it

> **racial gerrymandering** redistricting to enhance or reduce the chances that a racial or ethnic group will elect members to the legislature

easier for nonminority districts to be won by Republicans.[35] When sufficient numbers of minority voters are not concentrated in a geographic area, majority-minority districts take bizarre shapes. One of many examples is the Fourth Congressional District in Illinois, which joined two Hispanic communities (see Figure 7.2). The district has been named "earmuffs."[36]

Racial gerrymandering, however, remains highly controversial. While politicians and racial and ethnic group leaders continue to jockey for the best district boundaries for their own interests, the courts struggle to find a "fair" set of rules for drawing district lines. In 2013 the Court struck down part of the 1965 Voting Rights Act and directed Congress to update it, which never happened. In 2018 the Court looked at a Texas map that a lower court had found to be intentionally discriminatory. In a five-to-four decision the Court ruled that Texas Republicans had not intentionally drawn their districts to disadvantage minorities and they let most of the map stand. The upshot is that the remaining protections make it very difficult to prove such intentionality in the future, essentially gutting parts of the 1965 Voting Rights Act.[37] Making laws that deal explicitly with race is tricky in any case. Since, as we discussed in Chapter 6, race is a suspect classification, a law that uses race to treat citizens differently is subject to strict scrutiny, and the law must fulfill a compelling state purpose, whether it penalizes them or benefits them.[38] In recent cases the Supreme Court declared that race cannot be the predominant factor in drawing congressional districts. It can be taken into account, but so must other factors, such as neighborhood and community preservation.[39]

> **Why is geography a better basis for congressional representation than, say, race, religion, gender, occupation, or socioeconomic group?**

DECIDING TO RUN

The formal qualifications for Congress are not difficult to meet. In addition to the age and citizenship requirements listed in Table 7.1, the Constitution requires that a member live in the state he or she wants to represent, although state laws vary on how long or when. Custom dictates that if you are running for the House, you live in the actual district. There are no educational requirements for Congress—you don't even need to have graduated from high school. In many ways, the qualifications for Congress are lighter than for most jobs you might apply for when you graduate, but you do have to be prepared to expose yourself to the critical scrutiny of your prospective constituents—not a pleasant prospect if you value your privacy!

WHY WOULD ANYONE WANT THIS JOB? Given the low esteem in which Congress is held by most Americans, it's hard to imagine why anyone would want to be a part of that institution, let alone spend the money, resources, and public effort necessary to win. Some members of Congress, of course, are probably motivated by a desire to serve the public. These days they are also increasingly likely to be motivated by ideology—running for office from a sense of personal conviction and commitment to enact policy that represents strongly held values.

But being a member of Congress is a very attractive job in its own right. First, there is all the fun of being in Washington, living a life that is undeniably exciting and powerful. The salary, $174,000 in 2018, puts representatives and senators among the top wage earners in the nation, and the "perks" of office include generous travel allowances, ample staff, franking privileges (free use of the U.S. mail), free parking at Reagan National Airport, health and life insurance, and a substantial pension.[40] Many of those benefits are designed to help members keep their jobs once they get them; franking privileges, videotaping services, and trips home were all designed by members of Congress to help them get reelected—all at taxpayer expense.

Offsetting the benefits, salary, power, and prestigious title ("The Honorable So-and-So") is the fact that the job security is nonexistent. No matter how hard they work, members of Congress are sure to face an opponent in the next election who claims they did not do enough and declares that it's "time for a change." So they have to work all the harder, raise more money, and be even more popular than they were to begin with, just to keep their job. Also, despite the seemingly high salary, being a member of Congress is expensive. Most members have to maintain two households, one in Washington and one at home, and many find it hard to manage on their congressional salaries.[41] It is also hard on families, who must either divide their time between two homes or live without one parent for part of the year. Finally, like Sen. Olympia Snowe, more and more members are becoming disenchanted with the job. The level of conflict in Congress is so high—especially the bitter partisan infighting—and the interest group pressure and fundraising needs so intense, that for some "the job just isn't any fun anymore."[42]

No Joke

Minnesota senator Al Franken majored in political science at Harvard, but he made his name as a comic writer and occasional performer on Saturday Night Live *before graduating to a career as a political commentator and author. In his second term, accusations of sexual misconduct from earlier in his career arose and, facing pressure from his party, Franken resigned from the Senate.*

WHAT IT TAKES TO WIN To have an outside chance of winning, nonincumbent candidates for Congress need political and financial assets. The key political asset for a potential candidate is experience, such as working for other candidates, serving as a precinct chair, or holding an office in the local party organization. Even more helpful is experience in elective office. Political amateurs without such experience are considered "low-quality" candidates for Congress because, except under unusual circumstances, they almost never win—unless they happen to be famous sports stars, television personalities, or wealthy businesspeople who have personal resources that can help them beat the odds.[43]

"High-quality" candidates with the requisite political assets need to be careful not to squander them. They do not want to use up favors and political credibility in a losing effort, especially if they have to give up something valuable, like money or an office they currently hold, in order to run. **Strategic politicians** act rationally and carefully in deciding whether a race is worth running by asking four key questions:

1. **Is this a district or state I can win?** Liberals do not do well in conservative parts of the South, African Americans have great difficulty getting elected in predominantly white districts, Republicans have a hard time in areas that are mostly Democratic, and so forth.

2. **Who is my opponent likely to be?** Whether an opponent is vulnerable is governed largely by the **incumbency advantage**, which refers to the edge in visibility, experience, organization, and fundraising ability possessed by the people who already hold the job. It can make them hard to defeat (see the box "The 116th Congress"). The best bet from a challenger's perspective is an open seat, but these are likely to draw more than one high-quality candidate.

3. **Can I get the funds necessary to run a winning campaign?** Modern political campaigns are expensive. Winning nonincumbents over the past decade have spent on average over four times as much as nonincumbents who did not win, and even then the winning nonincumbents could not keep up with the spending of incumbents.[44] Incumbents have access to a lot more funds than do nonincumbents.

4. **What kind of year is this?** Some years are good for Democrats, some for Republicans. These tides are a result of such things as presidential popularity, the state of the economy, and military engagements abroad. If it is a presidential election year, enthusiasm for a popular presidential candidate might sweep fellow party members to victory in what is known as the **coattail effect**, but this has been less significant in recent elections.

The strength of coattails might be declining, but there is no arguing with the phenomenon of the **midterm loss**. This is the striking regularity with which the presidential party loses seats in Congress in the midterm elections, also called

> **strategic politicians** office-seekers who base the decision to run on a rational calculation that they will be successful
>
> **incumbency advantage** the electoral edge afforded to those already in office
>
> **coattail effect** the added votes received by congressional candidates of a winning presidential party
>
> **midterm loss** the tendency for the presidential party to lose congressional seats in off-year elections

FIGURE 7.3

Party Control in the House of Representatives, 1925–2018

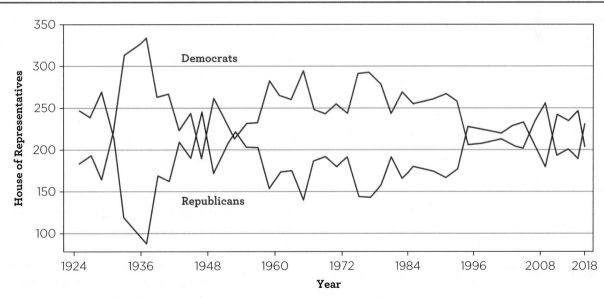

After a long period of uninterrupted dominance by the Democratic Party, Republicans controlled the House of Representatives for twelve years following the "Republican Revolution" of 1994. The Democrats won back control of both houses of Congress in 2006 and extended their control in 2008, but lost control of the House in the 2010 midterm elections and of the Senate in 2014. They regained the House, however, in the 2018 midterms.

Source: U.S. House of Representatives, "Party Divisions of the House of Representatives," history.house.gov/Institution/Party-Divisions/Party-Divisions.

"off-year" elections—those congressional elections that fall between presidential election years. Before 1998 the presidential party lost seats in the House of Representatives in every midterm election of the twentieth century except in 1934. The 1994 election that brought Republicans to power in Congress for the first time in forty years (see Figure 7.3) was a striking example of the midterm loss.[45] In general, the presidential party losses depend on the president's standing with the public and the state of the economy; an unpopular president and a sour economy make the loss worse, but it generally happens regardless. In recent years, only 1998 and 2002 broke the midterm loss pattern, and both of those were unusual circumstances.

In 2010 a sputtering economic recovery, high unemployment, and President Obama's correspondingly low approval ratings cost the Democrats the majority in the House. The GOP gain of sixty-three House seats was the largest for that party in six decades, eclipsing the historic 1994 victory and easily wiping out the Democrats' gains in the previous two election cycles. The Democrats were especially vulnerable because they had won in a large number of Republican districts in 2006 and again in 2008. With fewer seats at stake in the Senate, the Democrats lost only six seats, keeping majority control in that chamber, but not by much. In 2014 the Democrats again lost seats in the House but this time lost control of the Senate as well, giving the coveted leadership spot to Sen. Mitch McConnell from Kentucky. In 2018 the tables were turned. The economy was roaring, but the president remained extremely unpopular. While the Republicans didn't have a lot of exposure in the Senate, they were highly exposed at the House level, making them vulnerable to Democratic takeovers. While Trump did his best to rally his supporters—effectively putting himself on the ballot by saying Democrats would impeach him—Democrats were enthused and motivated. People of color and young people, not always reliable midterm voters, turned out, and an enormous gender gap sent women suburban voters to the Democratic side while men tended to vote Republican. In the end, the Republicans held the Senate and may have picked up a few seats pending the results of recounts, but the Democrats took almost 40 House seats, their biggest gain since Watergate.

BEING A REPRESENTATIVE

The founders intended that the House of Representatives, which was elected directly by the people, would be the "people's house," reflecting the opinions and interests of the mass of American citizenry. The Senate was to be a more elite institution, composed of older men of virtue, education, and property like the founders themselves, whom they believed would have the wisdom to balance the impulses of the popularly elected House. It went without saying that both houses would be filled with white, male, and probably Christian representatives.

Today we assume that representation requires that Congress to some degree reflects the demographics of the American people, that is, that it achieves what we call **descriptive representation**. Founder and president John Adams said a representative assembly "should be in miniature an exact portrait of the people at large. It should think, feel, reason, and act like them."[46] By most measures, Congress fails at this quite miserably. Still, almost as much as in the days following the 1787 Constitutional Convention in Philadelphia, the modern Congress is dominated by relatively well-educated, well-to-do white males. The poor, the less educated, women, and minorities are not represented proportionately to their numbers in the population, although there are several trends in the direction of a more demographically representative Congress. (See *Snapshot of America: Who Represents Us in Congress?*)

OCCUPATIONS Americans work in many kinds of jobs, most as skilled and semiskilled workers, service economy workers, sales representatives, managers, and clerical workers. Congress, however, is dominated by lawyers and businesspeople and, not surprisingly, politicians. Although the occupations tend to split more or less evenly between the parties, the Republicans draw much more heavily from business and banking, and the Democrats are more likely to have come from public service careers.

EDUCATION AND INCOME In the adult population at large, 39.4 percent have a 2- or 4-year college degree and only 12.9 percent have advanced degrees. In contrast, of Congress' 535 members, more than three-quarters have advanced degrees.[47] Their income is well above the average American's income as well. Many House members—and an even greater percentage of senators—are millionaires.[48] By these standards, Congress is an educational, occupational, and income elite. Those lower in the socioeconomic ranks do not have people like themselves in Washington working for them.

RACE AND GENDER Over the long haul, women and minorities have not been well represented in Congress (as indicated in *Snapshot of America: Who Represents Us in Congress?*). Congress, however, is more representative today than it has been through most of our history. Until the civil rights movement in the 1960s, there were hardly any blacks or Hispanics in the House. Women seemed to have

---

descriptive representation the idea that an elected body should mirror demographically the population it represents

fared somewhat better, partly because of the once-common practice of appointing (and sometimes electing) a congressman's widow to office when the member died. This tactic was thought to minimize intraparty battles for the appointment. Not until the 1970s did female candidates begin to be elected and reelected on their own in significant numbers.

In the 1990s, representation of all three groups, especially blacks and women, began to improve. The reasons for the improvements, however, are quite different for each group.

Women have been coming into their own as candidates, as a natural extension of their progress in education and the workplace. Women's political status has also been reinforced by the growing salience of issues that are of particular concern to them, from abortion to family leave policy to sexual harassment. Despite dramatic changes in women's representation since the 1970s, the number of women in office has still not reached the levels that exist in many other countries. These differences exist in part because election rules in some countries, such as Sweden, require parties to run a certain number of women candidates. But new research also highlights the role that the potential pool of women candidates plays. In the United States, women tend to be less likely than men to be "self-starters" in running for office; that is, rather than just deciding to run for office and jumping into the campaign, women are more likely to wait to be asked by a party leader or the community. This difference exists even among a pool of potential women officeholders—like attorneys and local officeholders—that is similar to potential male candidates in all other characteristics. Because this is the case at the local and state legislative levels, these lower levels of government produce fewer women to run for office at higher levels like the U.S. Congress or the presidency.[49] This pattern may have changed in 2018, however, when, following the Women's March after Donald Trump's inauguration and the #MeToo movement, women filed to run for office in unprecedented numbers, and won. More than a hundred women headed to the House in 2019, and at least 23 to the Senate. Winning a quarter of each chamber might not seem like much for a majority of the population, but given where they started and the obstacles they have had to overcome to get elected, it is an accomplishment. At least four more Democratic governors and one Republican won in 2019—an important benchmark since it is often from the gubernatorial ranks that presidential candidates are drawn. The female candidates were notable for breaking other demographic lines as well—the youngest member ever elected to the House (Alexandria Ocasio-Cortez, 29), the first two Muslim women members of the House, and the first two Native American members. One of those Native Americans is a member of the LGBTQ community, as is the new governor of Colorado, the first openly gay U.S. governor.

The pattern of black representation showed steady increases during the 1970s and 1980s, followed by a comparatively large jump in the 1990s with the advent of racial gerrymandering. As we noted, the Supreme Court has refused to approve racially based districting, making the future of this pattern hard to predict.[50] Still, blacks have been far more successful at winning seats in the House than they have at winning statewide elections to the Senate, currently holding 52 seats in the House and 3 in the Senate.

The Underrepresented Majority

More than half of all Americans are female, but women have been historically underrepresented in Congress. Between the two chambers, however, there are at least enough women to field an all-female softball team. Here, the Congressional Women's Softball Team celebrates after a 10–5 victory over female journalists in a charity event to help young women with breast cancer.

Hispanics have been even more underrepresented in Congress than have blacks. Hispanic populations do not tend to be as solidly concentrated geographically as African Americans, they do not vote as consistently for a single party, and many do not vote at all. Underrepresentation of this group may be poised to change, however. Because both the Hispanic and Asian populations are growing so rapidly in America, both parties have pushed for minorities to run for office and have also worked hard to mobilize them to vote. The Democrats have been more successful recently, however, with the Obama campaign winning the Hispanic and Asian American vote in the 2008 and 2012 elections by large margins, especially among the young. What might be temporary Democratic support could be sealed as one-party loyalty, depending on how the issue of immigration plays out. The Republicans' continued support for tough, punitive immigration regulations, as evidenced by the anti-immigration rhetoric of Donald Trump both during his campaign in 2016 and as president, continues to push Hispanics toward the Democratic Party.[51]

DOES IT MATTER? Does it matter if Congress looks like the people it represents? For the poor, the answer is not hard to find. There is little or no descriptive representation for the poor, and this does appear to have a substantive effect on how well their interests are represented. Research suggests that the concerns of the poor do not have equal weight with those of the better off. Constituents with higher income and better education have the resources and skills to communicate their policy preferences to their representatives, and they are more likely to vote and to participate in and contribute to campaigns. The result is that elected officials in general pay less attention to the concerns of the poor in their legislative work. In short, economic inequality carries over to the policymaking process of who gets what.[52]

What limited evidence we have suggests, similarly, that the lack of working people in Congress probably leads to some of their concerns being left off the congressional agenda. Although 50 to 60 percent of the population can be considered "working class" based on occupational status, only 2 percent of those elected to Congress fit this definition. The underrepresentation of working-class interests is reflected in how members vote on economic policies. On economic matters, working-class members are substantially more liberal than Congress as a whole, and if workers were represented proportionately in Congress, it is likely that each Congress would pass at least some significant additional legislation that favors their economic interests.[53]

For race and gender, the answer is that descriptive representation matters, at least at a symbolic level if not in substantive terms. Having "one of our own" as an active participant

Snapshot of America: *Who Represents Us in Congress?*

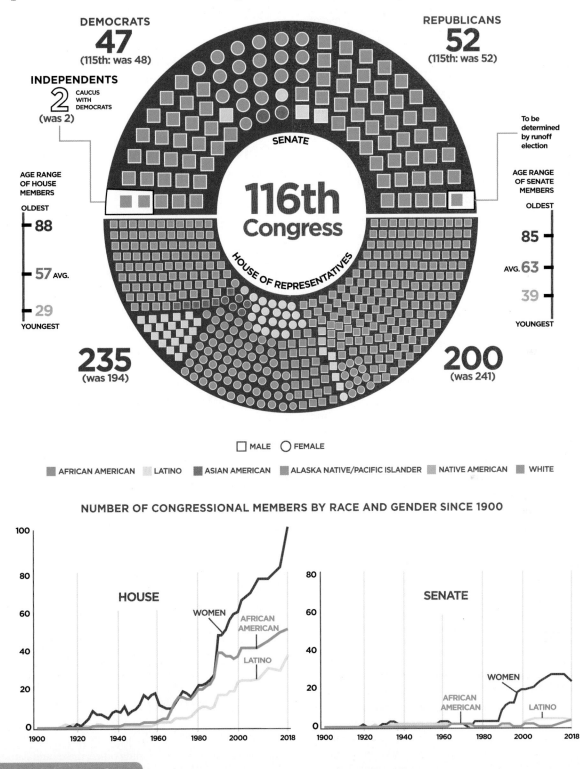

DEMOCRATS
47
(115th: was 48)

INDEPENDENTS
2 CAUCUS WITH DEMOCRATS
(was 2)

REPUBLICANS
52
(115th: was 52)

To be determined by runoff election

SENATE

116th Congress

HOUSE OF REPRESENTATIVES

AGE RANGE OF HOUSE MEMBERS
OLDEST
88
57 AVG.
29
YOUNGEST

AGE RANGE OF SENATE MEMBERS
OLDEST
85
AVG. **63**
39
YOUNGEST

235
(was 194)

200
(was 241)

☐ MALE   ◯ FEMALE

■ AFRICAN AMERICAN   ■ LATINO   ■ ASIAN AMERICAN   ■ ALASKA NATIVE/PACIFIC ISLANDER   ■ NATIVE AMERICAN   ■ WHITE

NUMBER OF CONGRESSIONAL MEMBERS BY RACE AND GENDER SINCE 1900

HOUSE

WOMEN
AFRICAN AMERICAN
LATINO

(x-axis: 1900, 1920, 1940, 1960, 1980, 2000, 2018; y-axis: 0, 20, 40, 60, 80, 100)

SENATE

WOMEN
AFRICAN AMERICAN
LATINO

(x-axis: 1900, 1920, 1940, 1960, 1980, 2000, 2018; y-axis: 0, 20, 40, 60, 80)

Behind the Numbers

Congress has been dominated by white males—and it still is, but less so than in the past (bottom line charts). What difference does it make if more minorities and women are elected to Congress? Does it matter which party they serve?

Source: CQ Weekly Guide to the New Congress, November 12, 2018.

Note: Includes likely winners of races not settled at press time.

in the policy process has positive symbolic meaning for women, Hispanics, and African Americans.[54] This often takes the form of being more informed, having a higher sense of efficacy, and sometimes having higher turnout. Results are mixed, however, as to whether the presence of these groups in the legislative process produces better policies for them. Members of these demographic groups do tend to put issues of concern to the groups on the political agenda, but in terms of how they actually vote, the effect is muted. Women legislators do tend to vote for "women's issues," but they are also Democrats and Republicans, and partisan interest can override gender commitment.[55] The effect of descriptive representation is similarly mixed for minorities. As mentioned earlier, creating majority-minority districts through racial gerrymandering (typically at least 65 percent African American and Hispanic) has the effect of "bleaching" adjacent districts, particularly in the southern states. The result is whiter, more conservative districts that elect more Republicans and make it harder to pass legislation that is friendly to minority interests.[56] And, as is true for women, African American and Hispanic legislators add to the agenda new bills regarding their demographic groups and speak about their issues in floor debate. However, once one takes into account the character of districts, there is little difference in voting on bills between those legislators and their non-Hispanic, white counterparts. The increase in minority legislators elected to Congress has increased the number of bills concerning race, but passage of these bills is contingent on which party is in charge of the legislative process rather than simply the number of minority legislators.[57]

The primary policy effect of descriptive representation seems to be that it brings what might be otherwise neglected perspectives to the legislatures, raising minority-interest issues and anticipating the needs and concerns of fellow minorities when new issues arise.[58] For groups like the poor, who are not represented descriptively, even these limited benefits do not exist.

PAUSE AND REVIEW Who, What, How

Congressional elections are the meeting ground for citizens and their representatives, where each brings his or her own goals and stakes in the process. Citizens want a congressperson who will take care of local affairs, mind the nation's business, and represent them generally on political and social issues. The rules of local representation and electoral politics, however, mean that citizens are more likely to get someone who takes care of local interests and affairs, and who sticks to a partisan line, at the expense of national interests and general representation.

Members of Congress want to be elected and reelected. Because they make many of the rules that control electoral politics, the rules often favor those already in office. Many members may wish to turn

to national affairs, to do what is best for the nation regardless of their local district or state, but they have to return continually to the local concerns and electoral supporters that are crucial to their reelection.

In Your Own Words Identify the ways that politics influences how congressional districts are defined and who runs for Congress.

CONGRESSIONAL ORGANIZATION

The key role of political parties and congressional committees

Despite the imperatives of reelection and the demands of constituency service, the official business of Congress is making laws. Lawmaking is influenced a great deal by the organization of Congress—that is, the rules of the institution that determine where the power is and who can exercise it. In this section we describe how Congress organizes itself and how this structure is influenced by members' goals.

THE CENTRAL ROLE OF PARTY

Political parties are central to how Congress functions for several reasons. First, Congress is organized along party lines. In each chamber, the party with the most members—the **majority party**—decides the rules for the chamber and gets to fill the top leadership posts, such as the Speaker of the House, the majority leader in the Senate, and the chairs of all the committees and subcommittees.

Party is also important in Congress because it is the mechanism for members' advancement. Because all positions are determined by the parties, members have to advance within their party to achieve positions of power in the House or the Senate, whether as a committee chair or in the party leadership.

Finally, party control of Congress matters because the parties stand for very different things. Across a wide range of issues, Democrats embrace more liberal policies, whereas Republicans advocate more conservative ones. Figure 7.4 shows that on issues from abortion to oil exploration, Democratic House candidates are more liberal and Republican House candidates are much more conservative. Upon winning office, these candidates vote very differently from one another. As Figure 7.5 illustrates, Democratic members of the House are increasingly likely to vote with the majority of their party and are opposed by Republican

> **majority party** the party with the most seats in a house of Congress

Jon Tester

Tom Williams/Roll Call/Getty Images

U.S. senator John Tester, D-Mont, is a farmer and former music teacher who served on various local board and committees before moving on to national politics. "I think it keeps you real," he says about his determination to fly home to Montana and get his hands dirty on the farm his family has worked for a century. "... [It] keeps you grounded with what's going on economically in the country. If the farm quits working, I know that right away; if the market disappears, I know it; fuel prices go up, I know it; cost of equipment goes up or down, I know it."

Tester got caught up in public service early. During a high school trip to the state capital, his imagination had been fired by the state Senate—the grandeur of the building, the enthusiasm of the representatives, and a job that looked "very challenging but very fun."

But in a rural community, he says, there is an expectation that citizens will serve on boards and committees. So Tester first did a stint on the school board and his local Soil Conservation Service Committee before following that high school ambition and running for, and winning, a seat in the Montana Senate. "I like public service," says Tester. "There is a lot of negative, sure there is, but there is a feeling of accomplishment different than working in a field, harvesting a field, picking hay bales or rocks or whatever you are doing on the farm."

In 2006, after eight years in the state Senate, he decided to make the leap to national politics. He was a long-shot candidate for the U.S. Senate, and the race was squeaky close—but Tester was philosophical about it, figuring he had done his best and it was in the voters' hands. When the dust settled, he was the new senator from Montana. He narrowly won reelection in 2012 and won another close election in 2018, despite efforts to unseat him. He finds the job good, but challenging.

Down sides? There are those, too, though "there isn't any job out there that doesn't have its ups and downs," he says. The most frustrating part, for him, is the excessive partisanship that the Senate is prone to these days, "I can tell you that there is no doubt in my mind that folks vote in some cases 'yes' or 'no' just to be partisan. That's not what's always best for the country. That's not always best for your constituents, not always what's best for your state." Watching a Senate vote take place along party lines in his office, he points at the screen. "There is only one hope for what we see on that tube right there, and that's the next generation. They're the ones that can fix this, and if they are willing to allow this to happen, it will never get fixed. It just won't. They can fix it."

On running for the Senate

"[When I was running for the Senate] I was running in the primary against a guy who had already won statewide who was a millionaire—I'm not. I just thought, if we work hard, like the way I was brought up—if you work hard, and stick to it, to do what you want to do, the good Lord will open the door or he won't. And if you never try it, trust me—there were many times I wanted to get out of the race, many times. But if you never try it, you never know."

On keeping the republic

"[Benjamin] Franklin is right. This place won't work if everybody sits on their hands. And I think it's critically important and I think it's very rewarding for people to get involved. And there is all too many times that I hear people ... say, 'Oh, I can't make a difference.' You know, 'I can't do this or I can't do that'—well, 'can't' shouldn't be a word in somebody's lexicon. The truth is that you can make a difference and it might not take near as much work as you think it's going to take. And second of all, if you get involved, you'll make your community, your county, your state, your country a better place...It takes some work, but it's very rewarding, and the time I'm talking about is that you don't have to do it eight hours a day. You can do it one evening a month in some cases. And it is very, very important. It's very important to the health of the country, it's very important for you to know what's going on in your community, and it makes life a whole helluva lot more fun."

Source: Senator Jon Tester spoke with Christine Barbour and Gerald Wright on July 27, 2010.

FIGURE 7.4
Party Differences Among House Candidates on Policy Stances, 2016

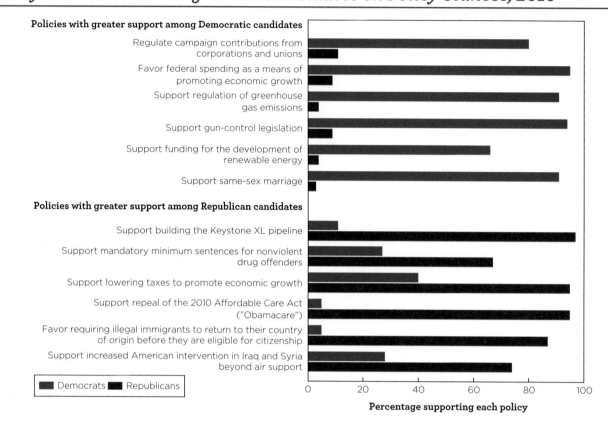

Policies with greater support among Democratic candidates

- Regulate campaign contributions from corporations and unions
- Favor federal spending as a means of promoting economic growth
- Support regulation of greenhouse gas emissions
- Support gun-control legislation
- Support funding for the development of renewable energy
- Support same-sex marriage

Policies with greater support among Republican candidates

- Support building the Keystone XL pipeline
- Support mandatory minimum sentences for nonviolent drug offenders
- Support lowering taxes to promote economic growth
- Support repeal of the 2010 Affordable Care Act ("Obamacare")
- Favor requiring illegal immigrants to return to their country of origin before they are eligible for citizenship
- Support increased American intervention in Iraq and Syria beyond air support

■ Democrats ■ Republicans

Percentage supporting each policy

Source: Responses are from the Project Vote Smart 2016 Political Courage Test and from positions gleaned by Project Vote Smart staff from candidates' public positions. Includes all two-party candidates in the general election. "Unknown" positions are excluded. Calculated by the authors.

representatives similarly voting as a bloc. Thus, although Americans like to downplay the importance of parties in their own lives, political parties are fundamental to the operation of Congress and, hence, to what the national government does.

Parties have become much more significant in Congress in recent years due to the process of party polarization, described earlier in the chapter. Recall that this refers to the growing ideological differences between the two parties, the greater ideological agreement within the parties, and the lack of members falling in between. In today's era of hyperpartisanship, almost all the Democrats in Congress are pretty liberal, and to an even greater extent the vast majority of congressional Republicans are very conservative. The patterns of party-ideological voting are shown in Figure 7.6. The higher the line, the more conservative the party is in its voting. Notice that the parties in both the Senate and the House of Representatives are farther apart ideologically than they have been for over a hundred years. It is also worth noting that the biggest changes have occurred within the Republican Party, which is now more conservative than at any time in its history.[59] This makes it harder for the parties to work together because the two parties' members are committed to such

divergent positions across the whole range of issues with which Congress must deal.

We also noted that hyperpartisanship has become such a force in congressional voting that members will often vote against their own ideological preferences just to vote against the other side. While the Democrats held a majority (before the 2010 election), President Obama was successful in getting his priorities enacted by the House of Representatives, but solid Republican opposition to anything he favored was enough to block his policy initiatives after the midterm. It was also nearly impossible for him to get his policies passed in the Senate, even when the Democrats held a majority, because the Republicans used the filibuster to block him when they could.

THE LEADERSHIP

The majority and minority parties in each house elect their own leaders, who are, in turn, the leaders of Congress. Strong, centralized leadership allows Congress to be more efficient in enacting party or presidential programs, but it gives less independence to members to take care of their own constituencies or to pursue their own policy preferences.[60] Although the nature

FIGURE 7.5

Party Voting in Congress, 1970–2018

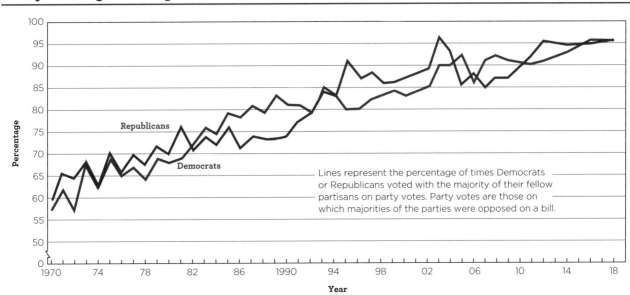

Lines represent the percentage of times Democrats or Republicans voted with the majority of their fellow partisans on party votes. Party votes are those on which majorities of the parties were opposed on a bill.

Sources: Roger H. Davidson, Walter J. Oleszek, and Frances E. Lee, *Congress and Its Members*, 12th ed. (Washington, D.C.: CQ Press, 2010), Figure 9-1; "The U.S. Congress Votes Data Base," *Washington Post*, projects.washingtonpost.com/congress/112/house/party-voters/, updated by author with data from projects.washingtonpost.com/congress/113/house/members/; Keith Poole, "Party Unity Scores for Democrat and Republican Members of Congresses 35–113 (1857–2014)," May 31, 2015, www.voteview.com/party_unity.html.

of leadership in the House of Representatives has varied over time, the current era had been one of considerable centralization of power until recently, when Republican factions began to challenge the leadership. Because the Senate is a smaller chamber and thus easier to manage, its power is more decentralized.

LEADERSHIP STRUCTURE The Constitution provides for the election of some specific congressional officers, but Congress itself determines how much power the leaders of each chamber will have. The main leadership offices in the House of Representatives are the Speaker of the House, the majority leader, the minority leader, and the whips (see Figure 7.7). The real political choice about who the party leader should be occurs within the party groupings in each chamber. The **Speaker of the House** is elected by the majority party and, as the person who presides over floor deliberations, is the most powerful House member. The House majority leader, second in command, is given wide-ranging responsibilities to assist the Speaker.

The leadership organization in the Senate is similar but not as elaborate. The presiding officer of the Senate is the vice president of the United States, who can cast a tie-breaking vote when necessary but otherwise does not vote. When the vice

president is not present, which is almost always the case, the presiding officer is the president pro tempore (an honorific given to the longest-serving senator of the majority party). In practice, however, the role is typically performed by a junior member. Because of the Senate's much freer rules for deliberation on the floor, the presiding officer has less power than in the House, where debate is generally tightly controlled. The locus of real leadership in the Senate is the majority leader and the minority leader. Each is advised by party committees on both policy and personnel matters, such as committee appointments.

In both chambers, Democratic and Republican leaders are assisted by party whips. (The term *whip* comes from an old English hunting expression; the "whipper in" was charged with keeping the dogs together in pursuit of the fox.) Elected by party members, whips find out how people intend to vote so that, on important party bills, the leaders can adjust the legislation, negotiate acceptable amendments, or employ favors (or, occasionally, threats) to line up support. Whips work to persuade party members to support the party on key bills, and they are active in making sure favorable members are available to vote when needed.

LEADERSHIP POWERS Leaders can exercise only the powers that their party members give them. From the members' standpoint, the advantage of a strong leader is that he or she can move legislation along, get the party program passed, do favors for members, and improve the party's standing. The disadvantage is that a strong party

> **Speaker of the House** the leader of the majority party who serves as the presiding officer of the House of Representatives

FIGURE 7.6

Ideological Polarization of the Parties in Congress, 1879–2017

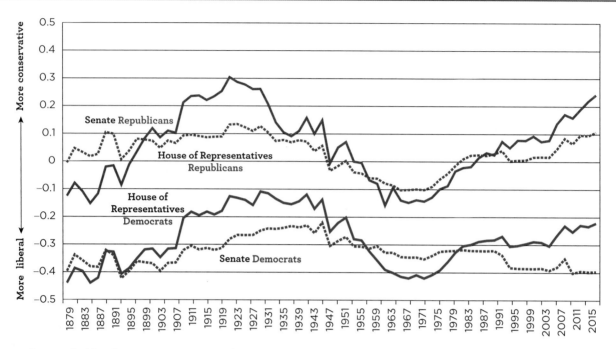

Source: Data on the liberal-conservative measures (DW-NOMINATE scores) developed by Keith Poole and Howard Rosenthal, "The Polarization of the Political Parties," May 18, 2016, voteview.com/political_polarization.asp.

Credit: Jeffrey B. Lewis et al. (2017). Voteview: Congressional Roll-Call Votes Database, https://voteview.com/.

leader can pursue national party (or presidential) goals at the expense of members' pet projects and constituency interests, and he or she can withhold favors.

The power of the Speaker of the House has changed dramatically over time. At the beginning of the twentieth century, the strong "boss rule" of Speaker Joe Cannon greatly centralized power in the House. Members rebelled at this in 1910 and moved to the **seniority system,** which vested great power in committee chairs instead of the Speaker. Power followed seniority, or length of service on a committee, so that once a person assumed the chair of a committee, business was run very much at his or her pleasure.[61] The seniority system itself was reformed in the 1970s by a movement that weakened the grip of chairs and gave some power back to the committees and subcommittees, but especially to the Speaker and the party caucuses.[62]

Speakers' powers were enhanced further with the Republican congressional victories in the 1994 election, when Rep. Newt Gingrich, R-Ga., became Speaker. Gingrich quickly became the most powerful Speaker in the modern era. His House Republican colleagues were willing to give him new powers because his leadership enabled them to take control of the House and to enact the well-publicized conservative agenda that they called the "Contract With America."[63] Gingrich continued as the powerful Republican congressional spokesperson and leader until he resigned in

the wake of the almost unprecedented reversal of the 1998 midterm loss, to be replaced by Dennis Hastert, a Republican from Illinois.

When the Democrats won control of the House in 2006, Nancy Pelosi was elected Speaker, the first woman to hold that position. In response to those who wondered if Pelosi could wield power as effectively as her male counterparts, Pelosi herself stated, "Anybody who's ever dealt with me knows not to mess with me."[64] Pelosi's role in passing Obama's health care reform bill was crucial, and she was effective at maintaining the support and discipline of her Democratic majority in the House, holding on to her leadership position in the party even after the Republicans regained the majority in 2010.[65] One early assessment by a longtime congressional watcher is that she is "entitled to be regarded among the best speakers."[66] Although Republicans tried to make her an issue in the 2018 election, few of the red-state Democrats who repudiated her won. Although she has acknowledged the need for younger leadership, and has called herself a "transitional Speaker," there is little doubt she will lead the Democrats for another term in office starting in 2019.

> **seniority system** the accumulation of power and authority in conjunction with the length of time spent in office

FIGURE 7.7

Structure of the House and Senate Leadership in the 116th Congress

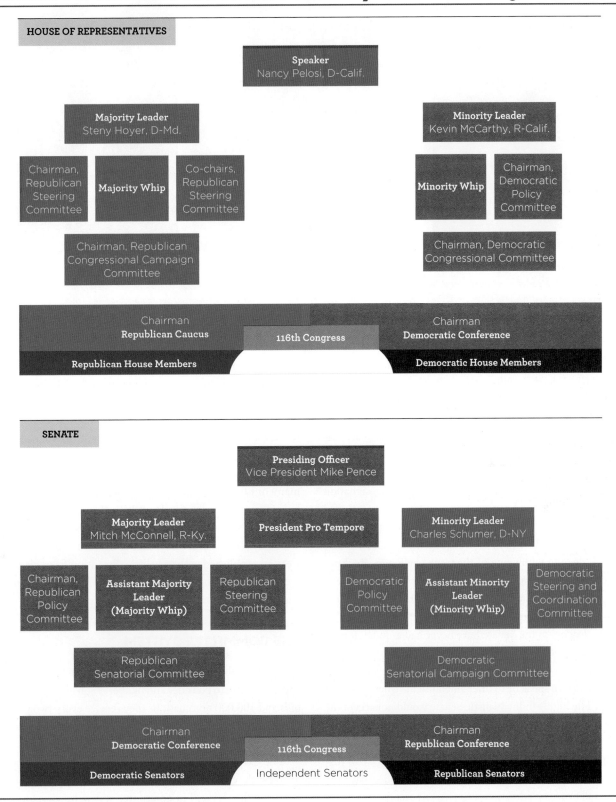

HOUSE OF REPRESENTATIVES

Speaker
Nancy Pelosi, D-Calif.

Majority Leader
Steny Hoyer, D-Md.

Minority Leader
Kevin McCarthy, R-Calif.

Chairman, Republican Steering Committee

Majority Whip

Co-chairs, Republican Steering Committee

Minority Whip

Chairman, Democratic Policy Committee

Chairman, Republican Congressional Campaign Committee

Chairman, Democratic Congressional Committee

Chairman **Republican Caucus**

116th Congress

Chairman **Democratic Conference**

Republican House Members

Democratic House Members

SENATE

Presiding Officer
Vice President Mike Pence

Majority Leader
Mitch McConnell, R-Ky.

President Pro Tempore

Minority Leader
Charles Schumer, D-NY

Chairman, Republican Policy Committee

Assistant Majority Leader (Majority Whip)

Republican Steering Committee

Democratic Policy Committee

Assistant Minority Leader (Minority Whip)

Democratic Steering and Coordination Committee

Republican Senatorial Committee

Democratic Senatorial Campaign Committee

Chairman **Democratic Conference**

116th Congress

Chairman **Republican Conference**

Democratic Senators

Independent Senators

Republican Senators

The Johnson Treatment

As Senate majority leader, and later as president, Lyndon Johnson was legendary for his ability to cajole, charm, bully, and—by any means necessary—persuade others to see things his way. Here, the six foot, four inch tall Johnson makes a point or two, towering over colleagues while invading their personal space.

John Boehner's lot as Speaker was more difficult in many ways. His leadership skills were challenged by the effort of holding together a diverse caucus, divided between traditional Republicans and the newly elected Tea Partiers who came to Congress determined not to compromise in accomplishing their ambitious agenda. Indeed, Speaker Boehner was so battered during the fractious 113th and 114th Congresses that there were continued calls for his resignation from both liberals and conservatives, and he finally resigned in 2015.[67] Paul Ryan replaced him reluctantly, knowing that the caucus would be hard to lead, and immediately found himself dealing with some of the same challenges Boehner faced, even though his own conservative credentials had been impeccable. Ryan had planned to retire at the end of 2018 even if the Democrats had not won the majority.

The leaders of the Senate have never had as much formal authority as those in the House, and that remains true today. The traditions of the Senate, with its much smaller size, allow each senator to speak or to offer amendments when he or she wants. The highly individualistic Senate would not accept the kind of control that some Speakers wield in the House. But though the Senate majority leader cannot control senators, he or she can influence the scheduling of legislation, a factor that can be crucial to a bill's success. The majority leader may even pull a bill from consideration, a convenient exercise of authority when defeat would embarrass the leadership.

The current majority leader, Mitch McConnell of Kentucky, replaced Democrat Harry Reid, a highly effective manager in the biggest legislative victories of Obama's first years as president, shepherding the health care bill through the Senate and also helping to get major legislation passed in the lame-duck session after the 2010 election.[68] McConnell, who had hoped to win the majority leader's seat for several elections in a row, only to see his chances slip away, has used his time in office to push through as much as his party's agenda as he can. His determination to block as many of Obama's policies as possible, his prevention of the hearings on Merrick Garland, his refusal to get behind a bipartisan warning that our electoral system was under attack by Russia, and his breaking of norms on procedure were accomplished with very little dissention from his party. Despite the ideological unruliness of the party, McConnell has kept his eye on the prize of holding power.

THE COMMITTEE SYSTEM

Meeting as full bodies, it would be impossible for the House and the Senate to consider and deliberate on all of the 10,000 bills and 100,000 nominations they receive every two years.[69] Hence, the work is broken up and handled by smaller groups called committees.

The Constitution says nothing about congressional committees; they are completely creatures of the chambers of Congress they serve. The committee system has developed to meet the needs of a growing nation as well as the evolving goals of members of Congress. Initially, congressional committees formed to consider specific issues and pieces of legislation; after they made their recommendations to the full body, they dispersed. As the nation grew, and with it the number of bills to be considered, this ad hoc system became unwieldy and Congress formed a system of more permanent committees. Longer service on a committee permitted members to develop expertise and specialization in a particular policy area, and thus bills could be considered more efficiently. Committees also provide members with a principal source of institutional power and the primary position from which they can influence national policy.

WHAT COMMITTEES DO It is at the committee and, even more, the subcommittee stages that the nitty-gritty details of legislation are worked out. Committees and subcommittees do the hard work of considering alternatives and drafting legislation. Committees are the primary information gatherers for Congress. Through hearings, staff reports, and investigations, members gather information on policy alternatives and discover who will support different policy options. Thus committees act as the eyes, ears, and workhorses of Congress in considering, drafting, and redrafting proposed legislation.

Committees do more, however, than write laws. Committees also undertake the congressional oversight discussed earlier in the chapter. That is, they check to see that the executive and its agencies are carrying out the laws as Congress intended them to. Committee members gather information about agencies from the media, constituents, interest groups, staff, and special investigations (see the discussion of the Government Accountability Office, later in this chapter). A lot of what is learned in oversight is reflected in changes to the laws that give agencies their power and operating funds.

Members and the general public all strongly agree on the importance of congressional oversight; it is part of the "continuous watchfulness" that Congress mandated for itself in the Legislative Reorganization Act of 1946 and reiterated in its Legislative Reorganization Act of 1970. Nevertheless, oversight tends to be slighted in the congressional process. The reasons are not hard to find. Oversight takes a lot of time, and the rewards to individual members are less certain than from other activities like fundraising or grabbing a headline in the district with a new pork project. Consequently, oversight most often takes the form of "fire-alarm" oversight, in which some scandal or upsurge in public interest directs congressional attention to a problem in the bureaucracy, rather than careful and systematic reviews of agencies' implementation of congressional policies.[70] Like so much of our lives in a mediated world, congressional attention is

standing committees permanent committees responsible for legislation in particular policy areas

TABLE 7.2
Standing Committees of the 115th Congress

HOUSE	SENATE
Agriculture (46 members)	Agriculture, Nutrition, and Forestry (21 members)
Appropriations (52 members)	
Armed Services (62 members)	Appropriations (31 members)
Budget (36 members)	Armed Services (27 members)
Education and the Workforce (40 members)	Banking, Housing, and Urban Affairs (25 members)
Energy and Commerce (55 members)	Budget (23 members)
Ethics (10 members)	Commerce, Science, and Transportation (27 members)
Financial Services (60 members)	Energy and Natural Resources (23 members)
Foreign Affairs (47 members)	Environment and Public Works (21 members)
Homeland Security (40 members)	Finance (27 members)
House Administration (9 members)	Foreign Relations (21 members)
Judiciary (41 members)	Health, Education, Labor, and Pensions (23 members)
Natural Resources (43 members)	Homeland Security and Governmental Affairs (15 members)
Oversight and Government Reform (42 members)	Judiciary (21 members)
Rules (13 members)	Rules and Administration (19 members)
Science, Space, and Technology (39 members)	Small Business and Entrepreneurship (19 members)
Small Business (24 members)	
Transportation and Infrastructure (61 members)	Veterans' Affairs (15 members)
Veterans' Affairs (24 members)	Senate Special or Select Committees
Ways and Means (40 members)	Aging
House Select Committee Intelligence (21 members)	Ethics
	Intelligence

herd-like—following the loudest noises and the narratives that catch the eye of their constituents.

TYPES OF COMMITTEES Congress has four types of committees: standing, select, joint, and conference. The vast majority of work is done by the **standing committees**. These are permanent committees, created by statute, that carry over from one session of Congress to the next. They review most

Lordy, I Hope There Are Tapes

Committee hearings often happen far from the public eye but are occasionally major news. In 2017 former FBI director James Comey testified before the Senate Intelligence Committee hearing on Russian interference in the 2016 presidential election.

debated, how long debate can last, how it can be amended, and so on. Because the House is so large, debate would quickly become chaotic without the organization and structure provided by the Rules Committee. Such structure is not neutral in its effects on legislation, however. Since the committees are controlled by the majority party in the House, and especially by the Speaker, the rule that structures a given debate will reflect the priorities of the majority party.

When a problem before Congress does not fall under the jurisdiction of a standing committee, a select committee may be appointed. These committees are usually temporary and do not recommend legislation per se. They are used to gather information on specific issues, like the **Select Committee** on Homeland Security did after the September 11 terror attacks, or to conduct an investigation, as did the Select Bipartisan Committee to Investigate the Preparation for and Response to Hurricane Katrina. As mentioned earlier, the House of Representatives voted in May 2014 to establish a select committee to investigate what happened in the attack on the diplomatic mission in Benghazi, Libya.

Joint committees are made up of members of both houses of Congress. Although each house generally considers bills independently (making for a lot of duplication of effort and staff), in some areas they have coordinated activities to expedite consideration of legislation. The joint committees in the 115th Congress were on printing, economics, taxation, and the library and will probably be similar in the 116th.

Before a bill can become law, it must be passed by both houses of Congress in exactly the same form. But because the legislative process in each house often subjects bills to different pressures, they may be very different by the time they are debated and passed. **Conference committees** are temporary

pieces of legislation that are introduced to Congress. So powerful are the standing committees that they scrutinize, hold hearings on, amend, and, frequently, kill legislation before the full Congress ever gets the chance to discuss it.

The standing committees of the 115th Congress are listed in Table 7.2; most deal with issues in specific policy areas, such as agriculture, foreign relations, or justice, and they vary dramatically in size. Each committee is typically divided into several subcommittees that focus on detailed areas of policy. There are twenty standing committees and 104 subcommittees in the House. The Senate has sixteen committees and seventy-two subcommittees. Not surprisingly, committees are larger in the House, with membership of more than sixty on some committees, compared to thirty or fewer on the Senate committees. The size of the committees and the ratio of majority- to minority-party members on each are determined at the start of each Congress by the majority leadership in the House and by negotiations between the majority and minority leaders in the Senate. Standing committee membership is relatively stable as seniority on the committee is a major factor in gaining subcommittee or committee chairs; the chairs wield considerable power and are coveted positions.

The policy areas represented by the standing committees of the two houses roughly parallel each other, but the **House Rules Committee** exists only in the House of Representatives. (There is a Senate Rules and Administration Committee, but it does not have equivalent powers.) The House Rules Committee provides a "rule" for each bill that specifies when it will be

---

House Rules Committee the committee that determines how and when debate on a bill will take place

select committee a committee appointed to deal with an issue or a problem not suited to a standing committee

joint committees combined House-Senate committees formed to coordinate activities and expedite legislation in a certain area

conference committees temporary committees formed to reconcile differences in House and Senate versions of a bill

committees made up of members of both houses of Congress commissioned to resolve these differences, after which the bills go back to each house for a final vote. Members of the conference committees are appointed by the presiding officer of each chamber, who usually taps the senior members, especially the chair, of the committees that considered the bill. Most often the conferees are members of those committees.

In the past, conference committees have tended to be small (five to ten members). In recent years, however, as Congress has tried to work within severe budget restrictions and across the divide of increased party polarization, it has taken to passing huge "megabills" that collect many proposals into one. Conference committees have expanded in turn, sometimes ballooning into gigantic affairs with many "subconferences."[71] This has given rise to a relatively new process of "omnibus" legislation in which the committees play a less central role and congressional leadership is much more involved, even at early stages. We discuss these changes later in this chapter when we talk about policymaking.

GETTING ON THE RIGHT COMMITTEES Getting on the right standing committee is vital for all members of Congress because so much of what members want to accomplish is realized through their work on these committees. Reelection is paramount for members, and getting on a committee where they can serve their constituents' interests is central.[72] Examples of good matches include the Agriculture Committee for farm states' legislators and the Defense Committee for members with military bases or contractors in their districts.

Some members also like to accumulate influence within their chamber. The House Rules Committee, for instance, is extremely powerful. Because it plays the central "traffic cop" role we discussed earlier, its members are in a position to do a lot of favors for members whose bills have to go through the committee. Almost all senators have the opportunity to sit on one of the four most powerful Senate committees: Appropriations, Armed Services, Finance, and Foreign Relations.[73]

Decisions on who gets on what committee vary by party and chamber. Occasionally the awarding of committee assignments has been used by the parties to reward those who support party positions, but in general both the Democrats and the Republicans accommodate their members when they can, since the goal of both parties is to support their ranks and help them be successful.

COMMITTEE CHAIRS For much of the twentieth century, congressional power rested with the committee chairs of Congress; their power was unquestioned under the seniority system. Seniority remains important today, but

chairs serve at the pleasure of their party caucuses and the party leadership. The committees, under this system, are expected to reflect more faithfully the preferences of the average party member rather than just those of the committee chair or current members.[74]

CONGRESSIONAL RESOURCES

For Congress to guide government lawmaking knowledgeably, it needs expertise and information. Members find, however, that alone they are no match for the enormous amount of information generated by the executive branch, on the one hand, or the sheer informational demands of the policy process—economic, social, military, and foreign affairs—on the other. The need for independent, expert information, along with the ever-present reelection imperative, has led to a big growth in what we call the congressional bureaucracy.

CONGRESSIONAL STAFF The vast majority of congressional staff—secretaries, computer personnel, clericals, and professionals—work for individual members or committees. Representatives average about seventeen staff members; senators' staffs average around forty, but the numbers vary largely with the population of each senator's state. Staff members can be assigned to either legislative work or constituency service, at the member's discretion. Those doing primarily constituency work are usually located in the district or state, close to constituents, rather than in Washington. Most offices also employ interns, frequently college students, whose efforts supplement the full-time staff.

The committees' staffs do much of the committee work, from honing ideas, suggesting policy options to members, scheduling hearings, and recruiting witnesses, to actually drafting legislation.[75] In most committees, each party also has its own staff. Because of the huge workloads, members rely on staff a great deal, which can give them a significant amount of influence.

CONGRESSIONAL BUREAUCRACY Since Vietnam and Watergate, Congress has been reluctant to be dependent on the executive branch for information and has built its own research organizations and agencies to facilitate its work. Unlike personal or committee staffs, these are strictly nonpartisan, providing expert advice and technical assistance. The Congressional Research Service (CRS), a unit of the Library of Congress, does research for members of Congress. For example, if Congress is considering a bill to relax air quality standards in factories, it can have the CRS determine what is known about the effects of air quality on worker health.

The Government Accountability Office (formerly the General Accounting Office but still known as the GAO) audits the books of executive departments and conducts policy evaluation and analysis.[76] These studies are meant to help Congress determine the nature of policy problems, possible solutions, and what government agencies are doing to solve the problems. The GAO studies supplement the already substantial committee staffs working on legislation and oversight.

A third important congressional agency is the Congressional Budget Office (CBO). The CBO is Congress' economic adviser, providing members with economic estimates about the budget, the deficit or surplus, and the national debt, as well as forecasts of how they will be influenced by different tax and spending policies. The CBO's regularly updated estimates on the costs of various versions of the Affordable Care Act were a central element in congressional considerations of the bill. Congress has a stronger and more independent role in the policy process when it is not completely dependent on the executive branch for information and expertise.

HOW CONGRESS WORKS

An already complex process, complicated further by external and internal forces

The policies passed by Congress are a result of both external and internal forces. The external environment includes the problems that are important to citizens at any given time— sometimes the economy, sometimes foreign affairs, at other times national security or the federal deficit or the plight of the homeless, and so forth. The policy preferences of the president loom large in this external environment as well. It is often said, with some exaggeration but a bit of truth, that "the president proposes, the Congress disposes" of important legislation. The role of parties, always important, has increased dramatically in an age of hyperpartisanship, often overriding other pressing concerns.

THE CONTEXT OF CONGRESSIONAL POLICYMAKING

Congress also has a distinct internal institutional environment that shapes the way it carries out its business. Three characteristics of this environment are especially important: the requirement that bills must be passed in identical form in both houses, the fragmentation inherent in policymaking, and the norms of conduct in each house.

SEPARATE HOUSES, IDENTICAL BILLS The Constitution requires that almost all congressional policy has to be passed in identical form by both houses. This requirement, laid out by the founders in the Constitution, makes the policy process difficult because the two houses serve different constituencies and operate under different decision-making procedures. Interests that oppose a bill and lose in one chamber can often be successful at defeating a bill in the other chamber. The opposition has to stop a bill in only one place to win, but the proponents have to win in both. In Congress, it is much easier to play defense than offense.

FRAGMENTATION As you read the next section, on how a bill becomes a law, notice how legislation is broken into bits, each considered individually in committees. This fragmentation makes it difficult to coordinate what one bill does with those laws that are already on the books or with what another committee might be doing in a closely related area. Thus we do such seemingly nonsensical things as simultaneously subsidizing tobacco growers and antismoking campaigns.[77] This fragmentation increases opportunities for constituencies, individual members, well-organized groups, and media pushing particular narratives to influence policy in the niches about which they really care. The process also makes it very hard for national policymakers—the president or the congressional leaders—to take a large-scale, coordinated approach to our major policy problems.

NORMS OF CONDUCT We have discussed repeatedly in this book the importance of norms, or informal rules that establish accepted ways of doing things. As much as anywhere in our government, they are a critical feature of the institutional environment of Congress. These are sometimes called "folkways" and are usually learned quickly by newcomers when they enter Congress. Norms include the idea that members should work hard, develop a specialization, treat other members with the utmost courtesy, reciprocate favors generally, and take pride in their chambers and in Congress. The purpose of congressional norms is to constrain conflict and personal animosity in an arena where disagreements are inevitable, but they also aid in getting business done (see *CLUES to Critical Thinking* at the end of this chapter). Although congressional norms continue to be important, they are less constraining on members today than they were in the 1950s and 1960s.[78] The extent to which the norms of respect and decorum have been stretched in a hyperpartisan Congress was illustrated when Rep. Joe Wilson, R-S.C., yelled out "You lie!" during President Obama's nationally televised health care address before a joint session of Congress in 2009, and we have mentioned other examples in this chapter. Ironically, the norms of collegial deference are even more important in the current era of intense partisan conflict where they struggle to survive. Without those norms, what is frequently tense partisan rhetoric would undoubtedly devolve quickly into some version of the rude and unpleasant vitriol common in the political blogosphere.[79] For instance, Sen. Ted Cruz, R-Texas, broke informal norms when he incited House members to rebel against their leadership on the issue of the government shutdown, earning him the enmity of so many colleagues that he became one of the most disliked men in Washington, a fact that was painfully on display when he ran for the Republican nomination for president in 2016. Former Speaker of the House John Boehner called him "Lucifer in the flesh," saying, "I get along with almost everyone, but I have never worked with a more miserable son of a bitch in my life."[80]

HOW A BILL BECOMES A LAW—SOME OF THE TIME

When we see something personally that seems unfair in business or in the workplace, when we hear through social media or groups that we follow that government is doing something we don't like, when disaster strikes and causes much suffering, or when workers go on strike and disrupt our lives—whenever a crisis occurs, we demand that government do something to solve the problem that we cannot solve on our own. This means government must have a policy, a set of laws, to

---

legislative agenda the slate of proposals and issues that representatives think it worthwhile to consider and act on

---

AP Photo/J. Scott Applewhite

Shutting It Down

Sen. Ted Cruz, center, speaks at a news conference with conservative congressional Republicans who demanded the defunding of the Affordable Care Act in order to prevent a government shutdown in 2013. Cruz's interference in House politics challenged the boundaries of congressional norms and earned him the enmity of many in his party, making his run for the presidency far more challenging.

deal with the problem. Because so many problems seem beyond the ability of individual citizens to solve, there is an almost infinite demand for new laws and policies, often with different groups demanding quite contradictory responses from the government.

This section considers briefly how demands for solutions become laws. We consider two aspects of congressional policy here: (1) the agenda, or the source of ideas for new policies; and (2) the legislative process, or the steps a bill goes through to become law. Very few proposed policies, as it turns out, actually make it into law, and those that do have a difficult path to follow.

SETTING THE AGENDA Before a law can be passed, it must be among the things that Congress thinks it ought to do. There is no official list of actions that Congress needs to take, but when a bill is proposed that would result in a significant change in policy, it must seem like a reasonable thing for members to turn their attention to—a problem that is possible, appropriate, and timely for them to try to solve with a new policy. That is, it must be on the **legislative agenda**. Potential new laws can get on Congress' agenda in several ways. First, because public attention is focused so intently on presidential elections and campaigns, new presidents are especially effective at setting the congressional agenda. Later in their terms, presidents also use their yearly State of the Union addresses to outline the legislative agenda they would like Congress to pursue. Because the media and the public pay attention to the president, Congress does, too. This does not guarantee presidential success, but it means presidents can usually get Congress to give serious attention to their major policy proposals. The proposals may be efforts to fulfill campaign promises, to pay political debts, to realize ideological commitments, or to deal with a crisis.

A second way an issue gets on the legislative agenda is when it is triggered by a well-publicized event—especially one that monopolizes cable news or our social media feeds—even if the problem it highlights is not a new one at all. For example, the 2010 explosion of BP's oil drilling platform Deepwater Horizon and the subsequent release of millions of barrels of crude oil into the Gulf of Mexico drew the nation's attention to energy policy, the adequacy of regulatory procedures, and the need to protect the environment. What leaders in Washington will actually do in response to such an event is hard to predict, especially in circumstances in which they are unable to do much of anything (the federal government had neither the technical know-how nor the equipment to plug the oil well, for instance). Nonetheless, such events create a public demand that the government "do something!"

A third way an idea gets on the agenda is for some member or members to find it in their own interests, either politically or ideologically, to invest time and political resources in pushing the policy. Many members of Congress want to prove their legislative skills to their constituents, key supporters, the media, and fellow lawmakers. The search for the right issue to push at the right time is called **policy entrepreneurship**. Most members of Congress to greater or lesser degrees are policy entrepreneurs. Those with ambition, vision, and luck choose the issues that matter in our lives and that can bring them significant policy influence and recognition, but most successful policy entrepreneurs are not widely recognized outside of the policy communities in which they operate.[81] Policy entrepreneurship by members is important in setting the congressional policy agenda, and it can reap considerable political benefits for those associated with important initiatives.

LEGISLATIVE PROCESS: BEGINNING THE LONG JOURNEY Bills, even those widely recognized as representing the president's legislative program, must be introduced by members of Congress. The formal introduction is done by putting a bill in the "hopper" (a wooden box) in the House, where it goes to the clerk of the House, or by giving it to the presiding officer in the Senate. The bill is then given a number (for example, HR932 in the House or S953 in the Senate) and begins the long journey that might result in its becoming law. Figure 7.8 shows the general route for a bill once it is introduced in either the House or the Senate, but the details can get messy, and there are exceptions (as this chapter's *The Big Picture* shows). A bill introduced in the House goes first through the House and then on to the Senate, and vice versa. However, bills may be considered simultaneously in both houses.

LEGISLATIVE PROCESS: MOVING THROUGH COMMITTEE The initial stages of committee consideration are similar for the House and the Senate. The bill first has to be referred to committee. This is largely automatic for most bills; they go to the standing committee with jurisdiction over the content of the bill. A bill to change the way agricultural subsidies on cotton are considered would start, for example, with the House Committee on Agriculture. In some cases, a bill might logically fall under more than one committee's jurisdiction, and here the Speaker exercises a good deal of power. He or she can choose the committee that will consider the bill or even refer the same bill to more than one committee. This gives the Speaker important leverage in the House because he or she often knows which committees are likely to be more or less favorable to different bills. Senators do not worry

policy entrepreneurship the practice of legislators becoming experts and taking leadership roles in specific policy areas

FIGURE 7.8
How a Bill Becomes a Law: Neat and Tidy Version

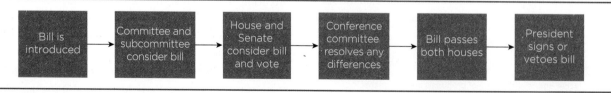

quite as much about where bills are referred because they have much greater opportunity to make changes later in the process than representatives do. We'll see why when we discuss floor consideration.

Bills then move on to subcommittees, where they may, or may not, get serious consideration. Most bills die in committee because the committee members don't care about the issue (it isn't on their agenda) or they actively want to block it. Even if the bill's life is brief, the member who introduced it can still campaign as its champion. In fact, a motivation for the introduction of many bills is not that the member seriously believes the bill has a chance of passing but that the member wants to be seen back home as taking some action on the issue.

Bills that subcommittees decide to consider will have hearings—testimony from experts, interest groups, executive department secretaries and undersecretaries, and even other members of Congress. The subcommittee deliberates and votes the bill back to the full committee. There the committee further considers the bill and makes changes and revisions in a process called markup. If the committee votes in favor of the final version of the bill, it goes forward to the floor. Here, however, a crucial difference exists between the House and the Senate.

GETTING TO THE FLOOR: HOUSE RULES In the House, bills go from the standing committee to the Rules Committee. This committee, highly responsive to the Speaker of the House, gives each bill a "rule," which includes when and how the bill will be considered. Some bills go out under an "open rule," which means that any amendments can be proposed and added as long as they are germane, or relevant, to the legislation under consideration. More typically, especially for important bills, the House leadership gains more control by imposing rules that limit the time for debate and restrict the amendments that can be offered. For example, if the leadership knows that there is a lot of sentiment in favor of action on a tax cut, it can control the form of the tax cut by having a restrictive rule that prohibits any amendments to the committee's bill. In this way, even members who would like to vote for a different kind of tax cut face pressure to go along with the bill because they can't amend it; it is either this tax cut or none at all, and they don't want to vote against a tax cut. Thus,

Talking a Bill to Death
In the classic 1939 film Mr. Smith Goes to Washington, *a naïve man appointed to fill a vacant Senate seat takes to the Senate floor in a long, exhausting filibuster to defend himself against false charges and stop a bill's passage. Mr. Smith's use of the filibuster is a far cry from today's reality, where the mere threat of a filibuster has become a blunt partisan weapon.*

for some bills, not only can the House Rules Committee make or break the bill, but it can also influence the bill's final content.

GETTING TO THE FLOOR: SENATE RULES The Senate generally guarantees all bills an "open rule" by default; thus senators have access to the floor for whatever they want in a way that is denied to representatives. Furthermore, whereas in the House the rule for each bill stipulates how long a member can debate, the Senate's tradition of "unlimited debate" means that a member can talk indefinitely. Senators opposed to a bill can **filibuster** in an effort to tie up the floor of the Senate in nonstop debate to prevent the Senate from voting on the bill or, in the case of the fifteen-hour filibuster by Sen. Chris Murphy, D-Conn., in June 2016, to force a vote. Though Murphy achieved the vote—on gun control—the measures failed to get majority support.[82]

A filibuster can usually be stopped only by **cloture**. Cloture, a vote to cut off debate and end a filibuster, requires an extraordinary three-fifths majority, or sixty votes. A dramatic example of a filibuster occurred when southern senators attempted to derail Minnesota senator Hubert Humphrey's efforts to pass the Civil Rights Act of 1964. First, they filibustered Humphrey's attempt to bypass the Judiciary Committee, whose chair, a southern Democrat, opposed the bill. This was known as the "minibuster," and it

---

filibuster a practice of unlimited debate in the Senate in order to prevent or delay a vote on a bill

cloture a vote to end a Senate filibuster; requires a three-fifths majority, or sixty votes

How does a bill become a law? Sometimes it seems like our lawmakers are playing some goofy game to which no one really understands the rules. In fact, it is not quite that bad, but the process is far more complicated than the *Schoolhouse Rock* cartoon version of poor, dejected Bill, sitting on Capitol Hill, would have you believe. Take a close look at this version of the lawmaking process, and you will not be surprised that so many bills fail to make it to the president's desk. The founders wanted a slow, incremental lawmaking process in which the brakes could be applied at multiple points, and that is exactly what they got.

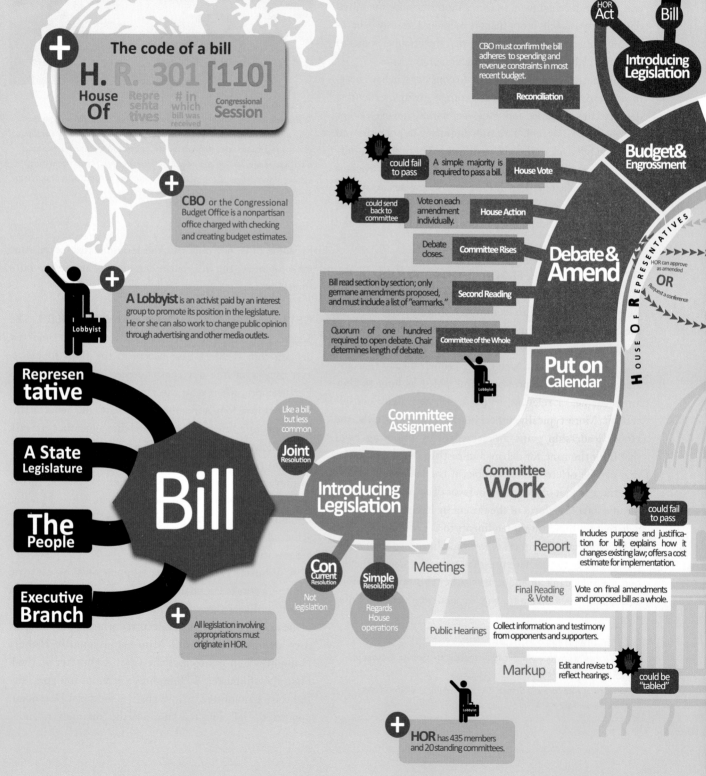

The code of a bill

H. R. 301 [110]

House Of | Representatives | # in which bill was received | Congressional Session

CBO or the Congressional Budget Office is a nonpartisan office charged with checking and creating budget estimates.

A Lobbyist is an activist paid by an interest group to promote its position in the legislature. He or she can also work to change public opinion through advertising and other media outlets.

Lobbyist

Representative

A State Legislature

The People

Executive Branch

All legislation involving appropriations must originate in HOR.

Bill

Like a bill, but less common

Joint Resolution

Con Current Resolution

Not legislation

Simple Resolution

Regards House operations

Introducing Legislation

Committee Assignment

Meetings

Committee Work

HOR has 435 members and 20 standing committees.

Senator

HOR Act

Bill

Introducing Legislation

CBO must confirm the bill adheres to spending and revenue constraints in most recent budget.

Reconciliation

Budget & Engrossment

could fail to pass

A simple majority is required to pass a bill.

House Vote

could send back to committee

Vote on each amendment individually.

House Action

Debate closes.

Committee Rises

Bill read section by section; only germane amendments proposed, and must include a list of "earmarks."

Second Reading

Quorum of one hundred required to open debate. Chair determines length of debate.

Committee of the Whole

Debate & Amend

Put on Calendar

HOUSE OF REPRESENTATIVES

HOR can approve as amended

OR

Request a conference

Lobbyist

could fail to pass

Report

Includes purpose and justification for bill; explains how it changes existing law; offers a cost estimate for implementation.

Final Reading & Vote

Vote on final amendments and proposed bill as a whole.

Public Hearings

Collect information and testimony from opponents and supporters.

Markup

Edit and revise to reflect hearings.

could be "tabled"

Lobbyist

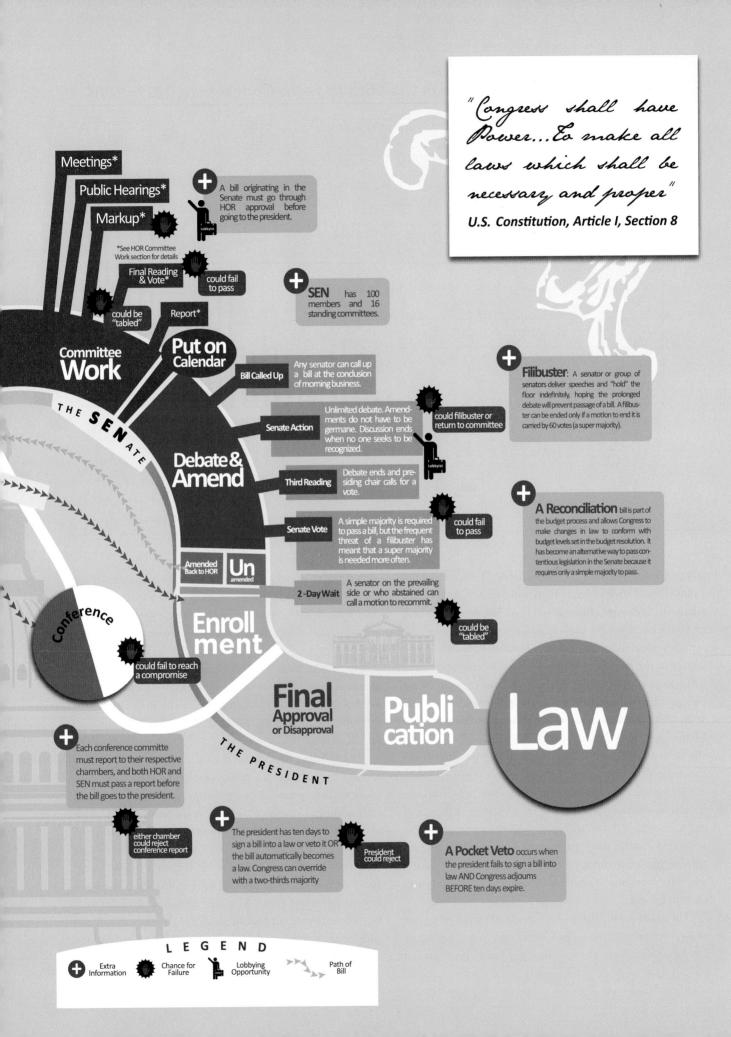

"Congress shall have Power...To make all laws which shall be necessary and proper"

U.S. Constitution, Article I, Section 8

Meetings*

Public Hearings*

Markup*

*See HOR Committee Work section for details

Final Reading & Vote*

➕ A bill originating in the Senate must go through HOR approval before going to the president.

✋ Lobbyist

✋ could fail to pass

✋ could be "tabled"

Report*

Committee **Work**

Put on Calendar

➕ **SEN** has 100 members and 16 standing committees.

Bill Called Up — Any senator can call up a bill at the conclusion of morning business.

THE SENATE

➕ **Filibuster:** A senator or group of senators deliver speeches and "hold" the floor indefinitely, hoping the prolonged debate will prevent passage of a bill. A filibuster can be ended only if a motion to end it is carried by 60 votes (a super majority).

Senate Action — Unlimited debate. Amendments do not have to be germane. Discussion ends when no one seeks to be recognized.

✋ could filibuster or return to committee

✋ Lobbyist

Debate & Amend

Third Reading — Debate ends and presiding chair calls for a vote.

➕ **A Reconciliation** bill is part of the budget process and allows Congress to make changes in law to conform with budget levels set in the budget resolution. It has become an alternative way to pass contentious legislation in the Senate because it requires only a simple majority to pass.

Senate Vote — A simple majority is required to pass a bill, but the frequent threat of a filibuster has meant that a super majority is needed more often.

✋ could fail to pass

Amended Back to HOR | **Un** amended

2-Day Wait — A senator on the prevailing side or who abstained can call a motion to recommit.

✋ could be "tabled"

Conference

✋ could fail to reach a compromise

Enroll ment

Final Approval or Disapproval

Publi cation

Law

THE PRESIDENT

➕ Each conference committee must report to their respective chambers, and both HOR and SEN must pass a report before the bill goes to the president.

✋ either chamber could reject conference report

➕ The president has ten days to sign a bill into a law or veto it OR the bill automatically becomes a law. Congress can override with a two-thirds majority

✋ President could reject

➕ **A Pocket Veto** occurs when the president fails to sign a bill into law AND Congress adjourns BEFORE ten days expire.

LEGEND

➕ Extra Information

✋ Chance for Failure

🧑‍💼 Lobbying Opportunity

»»» Path of Bill

FIGURE 7.9

Cloture Votes to End Filibusters in the 66th to 114th Congresses, 1917–2018

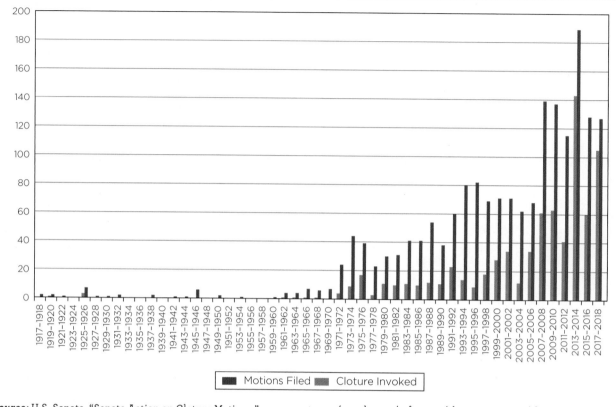

Motions Filed   Cloture Invoked

Source: U.S. Senate, "Senate Action on Cloture Motions," www.senate.gov/pagelayout/reference/cloture_motions/clotureCounts.htm.

stopped Senate business for sixteen days.[83] It was considered "mini" because from March 30 to June 30, 1964, these same southern Democrats filibustered the Civil Rights Act and created a twenty-week backlog of legislation.[84] Often these senators resorted to reading the telephone book in order to adhere to the rules of constant debate. The consequence of a filibuster, as this example suggests, is that a minority in the Senate is able to thwart the will of the majority. Even a single senator can halt action on a bill by placing a hold on the legislation, notifying the majority party's leadership that he or she plans to filibuster a bill. That threat alone often keeps the leadership from going forward with the legislation.[85] With increased polarization and partisanship, recent congressional sessions have seen a striking increase in the use of the filibuster, as shown in Figure 7.9, with congresses now averaging around forty attempts at cloture. Only about a third of these have been successful in mustering the necessary sixty votes, so a minority has prevailed over the majority most of the time.

The use of the filibuster—once reserved for the rarest and most controversial votes—had become so commonplace by 2013 that almost any vote reaching the Senate floor needed sixty votes to pass. In fact, shortly after the Republicans lost their majority in the Senate in 2008, then–Senate minority leader Mitch McConnell spelled it out when he said, "I think we can stipulate once again for the umpteenth time that matters that have any level of controversy about it in the Senate will require 60 votes."[86] The filibuster had become so routine that the minority leader simply informed the majority leader of the intention to filibuster and, if the majority leader couldn't summon sixty votes, the bill or the nomination would be dead.

Republicans proceeded to foil as much of President Obama's agenda as they could, employing the filibuster to block votes on presidential appointments to the bureaucracy, on his judicial nominees, as well as on policies such as an extension of unemployment benefits, immigration, and gun regulation. On November 21, 2013, a year after the president had scored a decisive win over his Republican opponent, many of his judicial appointees were still stuck in the pipeline, unable to get a vote. The heads of federal agencies were left unconfirmed, in part because the Republicans disapproved of their missions, and Democratic frustration hit a high pitch.

The filibuster is not in the Constitution and can be gotten around by legislative maneuvering. After months of being lobbied by members of his party, then–Senate majority leader Harry Reid was ready to pull the trigger on the so-called **nuclear option** to bypass the filibuster.[87] The nuclear option Reid crafted was not designed to do away with the filibuster entirely—he didn't have enough Democratic votes for that. The minority would still retain a veto over legislation and Supreme Court nominees. But for appointments to head up the federal bureaucracy or to fill the vacancies on the lower courts that were resulting in judicial bottlenecks, a simple majority would suffice.

Republicans were furious, calling Reid's move a "power grab" and warning Democrats that when they retook the Senate they would do away with the filibuster for everything, legislation and Supreme Court nominees as well, making the Democrats sorry they had ever thought to change the rules. Said Mitch McConnell, soon to be the majority leader again himself, "I say to my friends on the other side of the aisle: you'll regret this. And you may regret it a lot sooner than you think."[88] After McConnell refused to hold hearings for President Obama's Supreme Court nominee, Merrick Garland, he didn't have a filibuster-proof majority to get Donald Trump's nominee, Neil Gorsuch, approved, so he extended the nuclear option to Supreme Court nominees as well.

In the highly charged partisan atmosphere of the U.S. Senate today, use of the filibuster and the consequent cloture motions has become business as usual with little prospect for change.[89] Now that the nuclear option has been used, we can probably expect to see an increase in its use, especially for votes the majority party considers crucial to the running of the government.

UNORTHODOX LAWMAKING Because the legislative process allows so many interests to weigh in, the bills that emerge frequently can't get majority support because everyone can find some part to object to, because members anticipate a presidential veto, or because of partisan differences. Since the 1980s, congressional leaders have dealt with the logjam of bills by packaging them together in what is usually called **omnibus legislation**, a large bill that contains so many important elements, including the money necessary to fund the government, that members can't afford to defeat it and the president can't afford to veto it, even if the bill contains elements they dislike. This "unorthodox lawmaking"[90] has become the norm for most of the budget and many other difficult-to-pass bills. As a result (1) more power has been concentrated in the party leadership, (2) the White House is more involved than was traditionally the case, and (3) the traditional power of standing committees has waned as they are more frequently bypassed or overridden as the leadership moves legislation along. The overly large bills that sometimes result go unread by some members and are criticized by outsiders as an abuse of the legislative process. And the public, as we have seen, finds the entire process a turn-off (see *Snapshot of America: How Do We Hate Congress?*). It is, nevertheless, an important mechanism that Congress has developed to pass needed legislation and to keep the government running.

FINAL CHALLENGES: A BILL BECOMES A LAW A bill must survive a number of challenges to get out of Congress alive. A bill can be killed, or just left to die, in a subcommittee, the full committee, the House Rules Committee, or any of the corresponding committees in the Senate; and, of course, it has to pass votes on the floors of both houses.

There are multiple ways for the House of Representatives to vote, including a simple voice vote ("all in favor say 'aye'"), but most important legislation requires each member to explicitly vote "yea" or "nay" in what are called **roll call votes**. These are a matter of public record and are monitored by the media, interest groups, and sometimes even constituents. A variety of influences come to bear on the senator or member of Congress as he or she decides how to vote. Studies have long shown that party affiliation is the most important factor in determining roll call voting, but constituency also plays a role, as does presidential politics. Busy representatives often take cues from other members whom they respect and generally agree with.[91] They also consult with their staff, some of whom may be very knowledgeable about certain legislation. Finally, interest groups have an effect on how a member of Congress votes, but studies suggest that their impact is much less than we usually imagine. Lobbying and campaign contributions buy access to members so that the lobbyists can try to make their case, but they do not actually buy votes.[92]

The congressperson or senator who is committed to passing or defeating a particular bill cannot do so alone, however,

> **nuclear option** a controversial Senate maneuver by which a simple majority could decide to allow a majority to bypass the filibuster for certain kinds of votes
>
> **omnibus legislation** a large bill that contains so many important elements that members can't afford to defeat it and the president can't afford to veto it, even if the bill contains elements they dislike
>
> **roll call votes** publicly recorded votes on bills and amendments on the floor of the House or the Senate

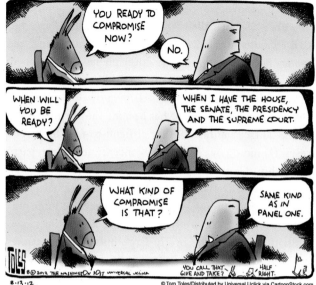

and he or she looks to find like-minded members for political support. Once a representative or senator knows where he or she stands on a bill, there are a variety of methods for influencing the fate of that bill, many of them effective long before the floor vote takes place. Congressional politics— using the rules to get what one wants—can entail many complex strategies, including controlling the agenda (whether a bill ever reaches the floor), proposing amendments to a bill, influencing its timing, and forming coalitions with other members to pass or block a bill. Knowing how to use the rules makes a huge difference in congressional politics.

If a bill emerges from the roll call process in both houses relatively intact, it goes to the president, unless the chambers passed different versions. If the bills differ, then the two versions go to a conference committee made up of members of both houses, usually the senior members of the standing committees that reported the bills. If the conferees can reach an agreement on a revision, then the revised bill goes back to each house to be voted up or down; no amendments are permitted at this point. If the bill is rejected, that chamber sends it back to the conference committee for a second try.

Finally, any bill still alive at this point moves to the president's desk. The president has several choices of action. The simplest choice is to sign the bill, in which case it becomes law. If the president doesn't like it, however, he or she can veto it. In that case, the president sends it back to the originating house of Congress with a short explanation of what he or she does not like about the bill. Congress can then attempt a **veto override**, which requires a two-thirds vote of both houses. Because the president can usually count on the support of at least one-third of one of the houses, the veto is a powerful negative tool; it is hard for Congress to accomplish

legislative goals that the president opposes. They can, however, bundle policies together, so that the bill that arrives on the president's desk contains elements that he or she would typically want to veto, along with legislation that is very hard to turn down. To get around this practice, Congress introduced and passed in 1996 a controversial line-item veto bill, which would have allowed presidents to strike out spending provisions they didn't like, but the Supreme Court ruled in June 1998 that the line-item veto was unconstitutional.[93]

The president can also kill a bill with the **pocket veto**, which occurs when Congress sends a bill to the president within ten days of the end of a session and the president does not sign it. The bill fails simply because Congress is not in session to consider a veto override. The president might choose this option when he or she wants to veto a bill without drawing much public attention to it. Similarly, the president can do nothing, and if Congress remains in session, a bill will automatically become law in ten days, excluding Sundays. This seldom-used option signals presidential dislike for a bill but not enough dislike for the president to use the veto power.

The striking aspect of our legislative process is how many factors have to fall into place for a bill to become law. At every step there are ways to kill bills, and a well-organized group of members in the relatively decentralized Congress has a good chance, in most cases, of blocking a bill to which these members strongly object. In terms of procedures, Congress is better set up to ensure that bills do not impinge on organized interests than it is to facilitate coherent, well-coordinated solutions to the nation's problems. Once again, we see a balance between representation, lawmaking, and partisanship, with the procedures of passage tilted against effective lawmaking.

PAUSE AND REVIEW   Who, What, How

All American political actors, those in Washington and those outside, have something important at stake in the legislative process. Presidents have a huge stake in what Congress does, in terms of fulfilling their own campaign promises, supporting their party's policy goals, and building a political legacy. Presidents can influence the legislative agenda; try to persuade their fellow party members in Congress to support their policies; take their case to the people; or, once the process is under way, threaten to veto or, in fact, use several different veto techniques.

veto override reversal of a presidential veto by a two-thirds vote in both houses of Congress

pocket veto presidential authority to kill a bill submitted within ten days of the end of a legislative session by not signing it

But it is Congress that has the most range and flexibility when it comes to passing or stopping legislation. Members want to satisfy constituents, build national reputations or platforms on which to run for future office, and accomplish ideological and partisan goals. They have a wealth of legislative tools and strategies at their disposal. But success is not just a matter of knowing the rules. It involves personality, luck, timing, and context, as well as political skill in using the rules that make a successful legislator. Repeated filibusters may accomplish a political goal, but if they earn a party a reputation as excessively partisan and obstructionist, they could also cause voter backlash. Legislative politics is a complex balance of rules and processes that favors the skilled politician.

In Your Own Words Describe the process of congressional policymaking.

THE CITIZENS AND CONGRESS

Public frustration with a slow-moving institution

In the tumultuous election season of 2016, it was apparent that a large number of Americans were angry at their government, and for many of them, the target of their anger was Congress. Academics and journalists spend a great deal of time speculating about what the decline in public support for our political institutions means for American democracy.[94] In this final section we look at the implications for citizens of their increasingly negative views of the U.S. Congress. Although public approval of Congress spiked in the wake of September 11, Gallup polls during most of the period since 1974 showed that less than a third of the public "approves of the way Congress is handling its job." In 2014 this proportion dipped below 10 percent, although it recovered slightly afterward. Part of the blame may be attributed to a general decline in respect for societal institutions ranging from government to organized religion to the media.[95] However, the intense partisanship of the contemporary Congress and its repeated legislative crises as the parties are unable to compromise is no doubt a major contributor to our generally low regard for the institution.

At least four factors help to explain why citizens are not always very happy with Congress. First, some candidates encourage a negative image of the institution they want to join—running for Congress by running against it, and declaring their intention to fight against special interests, bureaucrats, and the general incompetence of Washington.[96] We saw this in 2016, evidenced by the fact that Donald Trump, a man with no Washington or government experience at all, captured the Republican nomination and the

presidency. Second, in the post-Watergate wave of investigative reporting, media coverage of Congress has become more negative, more continuous, and harder to avoid. Third, since the 1970s the law requires that information about how much campaigns cost and who contributes to them must be made public, casting a shadow of suspicion on the entire process and raising the concern that congressional influence can be bought. Finally, citizens are turned off by what they see as incessant bickering and partisanship in Congress.

Does it make a difference that Americans dislike Congress so much?

Given the reasons why many Americans are unhappy with Congress, most of the reforms currently on the agenda are not likely to change their minds. One of the most popular reforms being advocated is term limits. The specific proposals vary, but the intent is to limit the number of terms a member of Congress can serve, usually to somewhere between eight and twelve years. Term limits might work if there was evidence that serving in Congress corrupts good people, but there is no such evidence, which makes the reform unlikely to bring about a "cleaner" institution. Other reforms, however, might make a difference in public support for Congress. Campaign finance reform, for instance, could have a significant impact. Institutional reforms might be able to speed up congressional lawmaking and reduce the need to compromise on details.

Such reforms, however, will probably not fundamentally change how the public feels about Congress. Congress does have the power to act, and when it is unified and sufficiently motivated, it usually does. When Congress reflects a sharply divided society, however, it has a harder time getting things done. It is unable to act because it is a representative institution, not because members are inattentive to their districts or in the grip of special interests. Furthermore, Congress has more incentives on a daily basis to be a representative institution than a national lawmaking body. It is important to remember, too, that this slow process is not entirely an accident. It was the founders' intention to create a legislature that would not move hastily or without deliberation. The irony is that the founders' mixed bag of incentives works so well that Congress today often does not move very much at all.

The truth is that democracy is messy. Bickering arises in Congress because members represent many different Americans with varied interests and goals. It has always been this way, and probably always will be. However, it seems

worse today because the parties have come to represent warring ideological armies. The rhetoric is coarse, and bipartisan cooperation is increasingly viewed as a weakness by party activists and outside groups.

It is precisely our bickering, our inefficiency, and the need to compromise—even when that is hard to do—that preserve the freedoms Americans hold dear. It is the nature of our representative government. We conclude where we began. Congress has the conflicting goals of representing constituents, working together to solve national problems, and operating as members of opposing partisan teams. These goals often and necessarily conflict. The practice of congressional politics is fascinating to many close-up observers but looks rather ugly as we average citizens understand it, based on the nightly headlines and our social media feeds. It is important to understand, however, that this view of Congress stems as much from the difficulties inherent in the conflicting incentives of the job as from the failings of the people we send to Washington.

In Your Own Words Discuss the relationship between the people and Congress.

LET'S REVISIT: *What's at Stake . . .?*

We opened this chapter by asking why the constitutional requirement that the Senate provide the president with advice and consent to major appointments had become almost akin to a hostage situation by the middle of 2016. No action was taken on Merrick Garland's nomination, despite the fact that President Obama continued to campaign for him and Democratic nominee Hillary Clinton called on the Senate to take action.

But McConnell dug in, playing out a scenario in which the stakes were high in a politically sophisticated game of risk.

For the Republicans, if Justice Scalia's replacement were to be nominated by a Democrat—either President Obama or a future President Clinton—they stood to lose the majority that they had held in the Court. For the party base, few things were more important than a justice who could be counted on to vote against reproductive rights and for gun rights and religious freedom. That base put enormous pressure on Senate majority leader Mitch McConnell not to hold hearings, and he could not afford to give in, especially before the election.

In an effort to galvanize that base to hold his own seat and campaign for fellow Republicans up for reelection to the Senate, the late Republican senator John McCain pledged that if voters would just choose Republican candidates, they would block all Supreme Court nominations if Hillary Clinton should win the presidency.[97]

The risk McConnell had to juggle, of course, was that the Republicans would lose their thin Senate majority and that a new senate majority leader, Democrat Chuck Schumer, would hold hearings on anyone President Hillary Clinton nominated. If the Democrats voted to dispense with the filibuster for

Supreme Court nominations, a so-called "nuclear option" they had already employed for other nominations in the past, a far more liberal justice than Merrick Garland might join the Court.

Without knowing the election outcome, Democrats, and particularly President Obama, wanted Garland's nomination confirmed because it would help ensure the continuity of the legacy the president had built. But Democrats were torn. Progressives thought that they might get a far more liberal justice if Hillary Clinton became president, and as it looked more and more likely that she would, waiting seemed a reasonable bet.

But the likelihood of a Clinton victory and the possibility of a Senate loss had Republicans scrambling to minimize the damage. Republican Jeff Flake of Arizona, who had staunchly opposed Donald Trump's nomination as president, said he was encouraging his Senate colleagues to go ahead and confirm Merrick Garland in the lame-duck session (the remainder of the term before January 2017, when the new Congress—and president—were to be sworn in), on the assumption that Garland would be far more acceptable to Republicans that anyone Clinton might nominate. His colleague Senate judiciary chair Chuck Grassley said there would be no lame-duck vote but granted that the Senate would at least have to act on a Clinton nominee. "If that new president happens to be Hillary, we can't just simply stonewall," he said before the election.[98]

In the end, McConnell's risky gambit paid off in a nail-biter of an election outcome. Although Hillary Clinton did indeed win the popular vote, she lost the prize and the Democrats lost the ability to appoint Scalia's replacement. The Senate also lost an important norm of cooperation with the executive branch, making the stakes of future appointments under divided government very high indeed.

The absence of norms of bipartisanship and cooperation that John McCain values so highly in the following CLUES to Critical Thinking were again apparent when Justice Anthony Kennedy announced his retirement in 2018 (after a good deal of prompting and deal making with the Trump administration about who his replacement would be). Trump nominated Judge Brett Kavanaugh whose hearings seemed to be going well until Dr. Christine Blasey Ford, a Stanford psychologist, came forth with accusations that she had been attacked by Kavanaugh in high school. She believed he had intended to rape her but was too drunk to prevent her escape. Her testimony before Congress was moving and credible—even President Trump said he found it so—but a well-coached Kavanaugh came out swinging, defending his name and essentially calling Blasey Ford a liar. There was no pretense that this was a nonpartisan hearing. A crucial Kavanaugh vote, Republican Senator Jeff Flake, on the brink of retirement, said he would not vote for confirmation until an investigation had been completed. The White House-controlled investigation proved to be a farce (neither Blasey Ford nor Kavanaugh was interviewed) but the Republicans declared themselves satisfied and confirmed Kavanaugh on a near party-line vote.

The Kavanaugh hearings were reminiscent of the 1991 Clarence Thomas hearings in which law professor Anita Hill accused Thomas of sexual harassment when she had worked for him. Again, the accusations were credible enough to be investigated but were not and Thomas was confirmed after what he called a "high tech lynching." In both cases the men portrayed themselves as the victims and the Senate bought their stories and confirmed them. In both cases, like the case of Merrick Garland, partisan politics defined the stakes for advice and consent.

CLUES to Critical Thinking

John McCain's Speech to the Senate on Regular Order, July 25, 2017

On July 25, 2018, knowing it was likely the last speech he would give in the Senate he had served for more than 30 years, John McCain made an impassioned plea for a return to what he called "regular order." He had just cast a tie-breaking vote that allowed debate to proceed on the issue of repealing Obamacare, only to cast the deciding vote rejecting the repeal hours after the speech. What was the point he wanted to make that was important enough to leave his cancer treatment and travel to D.C.?

Mr. President:

I've stood in this place many times and addressed as president many presiding officers. I have been so addressed when I have sat in that chair, as close as I will ever be to a presidency.

It is an honorific we're almost indifferent to, isn't it. In truth, presiding over the Senate can be a nuisance, a bit of a ceremonial bore, and it is usually relegated to the more junior members of the majority.

But as I stand here today—looking a little worse for wear I'm sure—I have a refreshed appreciation for the protocols and customs of this body, and for the other ninety-nine privileged souls who have been elected to this Senate.

I have been a member of the United States Senate for thirty years. I had another long, if not as long, career before I arrived here, another profession that was profoundly rewarding, and in which I had experiences and friendships that I revere. But make no mistake, my service here is the most important job I have had in my life. And I am so grateful to the people of Arizona for the privilege—for the honor—of serving here and the opportunities it gives me to play a small role in the history of the country I love.

I've known and admired men and women in the Senate who played much more than a small role in our history, true statesmen, giants of American politics. They came from both parties, and from various backgrounds. Their ambitions were frequently in conflict. They held different views on the issues of the day. And they often had very serious disagreements about how best to serve the national interest.

But they knew that however sharp and heartfelt their disputes, however keen their ambitions, they had an obligation to work collaboratively to ensure the Senate discharged its constitutional responsibilities effectively. Our responsibilities are important, vitally important, to the continued success of our Republic. And our arcane rules and customs are deliberately intended to require broad cooperation to function well at all. The most revered members of this institution accepted the necessity of compromise in order to make incremental progress on solving America's problems and to defend her from her adversaries.

That principled mindset, and the service of our predecessors who possessed it, come to mind when I hear the Senate referred to as the world's greatest deliberative body. I'm not sure we can claim that distinction with a straight face today.

I'm sure it wasn't always deserved in previous eras either. But I'm sure there have been times when it was, and I was privileged to witness some of those occasions.

Our deliberations today—not just our debates, but the exercise of all our responsibilities—authorizing government policies, appropriating the funds to implement them, exercising our advice and consent role—are often lively and interesting. They can be sincere and principled. But they are more partisan, more tribal more of the time than any other time I remember. Our deliberations can still be important and useful, but I think we'd all agree they haven't been overburdened by greatness lately. And right now they aren't producing much for the American people.

Both sides have let this happen. Let's leave the history of who shot first to the historians. I suspect they'll find we all conspired in our decline—either by deliberate actions or neglect. We've all played some role in it. Certainly I have. Sometimes, I've let my passion rule my reason. Sometimes, I made it harder to find common ground because of something harsh I said to a colleague. Sometimes, I wanted to win more for the sake of winning than to achieve a contested policy.

Incremental progress, compromises that each side criticize but also accept, just plain muddling through to chip away at problems and keep our enemies from doing their worst isn't glamorous or exciting. It doesn't feel like a political triumph. But it's usually the most we can expect from our system of government, operating in a country as diverse and quarrelsome and free as ours.

Considering the injustice and cruelties inflicted by autocratic governments, and how corruptible human nature can be, the problem solving our system does make possible, the fitful progress it produces, and the liberty and justice it preserves, is a magnificent achievement.

Our system doesn't depend on our nobility. It accounts for our imperfections, and gives an order to our individual strivings that has helped make ours the most powerful and prosperous society on earth. It is our responsibility to preserve that, even when it requires us to do something less satisfying than "winning." Even when we must give a little to get a little. Even when our efforts manage just three yards and a cloud of dust, while critics on both sides denounce us for timidity, for our failure to "triumph."

I hope we can again rely on humility, on our need to cooperate, on our dependence on each other to learn how to trust each other again and by so doing better serve the people who elected us. Stop listening to the bombastic loudmouths on the radio and television and the Internet. To hell with them. They don't want anything done for the public good. Our incapacity is their livelihood.

Let's trust each other. Let's return to regular order. We've been spinning our wheels on too many important issues because we keep trying to find a way to win without help from across the aisle. That's an approach that's been employed by both sides, mandating legislation from the top down, without any support from the other side, with all the parliamentary maneuvers that requires.

We're getting nothing done. All we've really done this year is confirm Neil Gorsuch to the Supreme Court. Our healthcare insurance system is a mess. We all know it, those who support Obamacare and those who oppose it. Something has to be done. We Republicans have looked for a way to end it and replace it with something else without paying a terrible political price. We haven't found it yet, and I'm not sure we will. All we've managed to do is make more popular a policy that wasn't very popular when we started trying to get rid of it.

I voted for the motion to proceed to allow debate to continue and amendments to be offered. I will not vote for the bill as it is today. It's a shell of a bill right now. We all know that. I have changes urged by my state's governor that will have to be included to earn my

support for final passage of any bill. I know many of you will have to see the bill changed substantially for you to support it.

We've tried to do this by coming up with a proposal behind closed doors in consultation with the administration, then springing it on skeptical members, trying to convince them it's better than nothing, asking us to swallow our doubts and force it past a unified opposition. I don't think that is going to work in the end. And it probably shouldn't.

The Obama administration and congressional Democrats shouldn't have forced through Congress without any opposition support a social and economic change as massive as Obamacare. And we shouldn't do the same with ours.

Why don't we try the old way of legislating in the Senate, the way our rules and customs encourage us to act. If this process ends in failure, which seem likely, then let's return to regular order.

Let the Health, Education, Labor, and Pensions Committee under Chairman Alexander and Ranking Member Murray hold hearings, try to report a bill out of committee with contributions from both sides. Then bring it to the floor for amendment and debate, and see if we can pass something that will be imperfect, full of compromises, and not very pleasing to implacable partisans on either side, but that might provide workable solutions to problems Americans are struggling with today.

What have we to lose by trying to work together to find those solutions? We're not getting much done apart. I don't think any of us feels very proud of our incapacity. Merely preventing your political opponents from doing what they want isn't the most inspiring work. There's greater satisfaction in respecting our differences, but not letting them prevent agreements that don't require abandonment of core principles, agreements made in good faith that help improve lives and protect the American people.

The Senate is capable of that. We know that. We've seen it before. I've seen it happen many times. And the times when I was involved even in a modest way with working out a bipartisan response to a national problem or threat are the proudest moments of my career, and by far the most satisfying.

This place is important. The work we do is important. Our strange rules and seemingly eccentric practices that slow our proceedings and insist on our cooperation are important. Our founders envisioned the Senate as the more deliberative, careful body that operates at a greater distance than the other body from the public passions of the hour.

We are an important check on the powers of the Executive. Our consent is necessary for the President to appoint jurists and powerful government officials and in many respects to conduct foreign policy. Whether or not we are of the same party, we are not the President's subordinates. We are his equal!

As his responsibilities are onerous, many and powerful, so are ours. And we play a vital role in shaping and directing the judiciary, the military, and the cabinet, in planning and supporting foreign and domestic policies. Our success in meeting all these awesome constitutional obligations depends on cooperation among ourselves.

The success of the Senate is important to the continued success of America. This country—this big, boisterous, brawling, intemperate, restless, striving, daring, beautiful, bountiful, brave, good and magnificent country—needs us to help it thrive. That responsibility is more important than any of our personal interests or political affiliations.

We are the servants of a great nation, "a nation conceived in liberty and dedicated to the proposition that all men are created equal." More people have lived free and prosperous lives here than in any other nation. We have acquired unprecedented wealth and power because of our governing principles, and because our government defended those principles.

America has made a greater contribution than any other nation to an international order that has liberated more people from tyranny and poverty than ever before in history. We have been the greatest example, the greatest supporter and the greatest defender of that

order. We aren't afraid. We don't covet other people's land and wealth. We don't hide behind walls. We breach them. We are a blessing to humanity.

What greater cause could we hope to serve than helping keep America the strong, aspiring, inspirational beacon of liberty and defender of the dignity of all human beings and their right to freedom and equal justice? That is the cause that binds us and is so much more powerful and worthy than the small differences that divide us.

What a great honor and extraordinary opportunity it is to serve in this body.

It's a privilege to serve with all of you. I mean it. Many of you have reached out in the last few days with your concern and your prayers, and it means a lot to me. It really does. I've had so many people say such nice things about me recently that I think some of you must have me confused with someone else. I appreciate it though, every word, even if much of it isn't deserved.

I'll be here for a few days, I hope managing the floor debate on the defense authorization bill, which, I'm proud to say is again a product of bipartisan cooperation and trust among the members of the Senate Armed Services Committee.

After that, I'm going home for a while to treat my illness. I have every intention of returning here and giving many of you cause to regret all the nice things you said about me. And, I hope, to impress on you again that it is an honor to serve the American people in your company.

Thank you, fellow senators.

Mr. President, I yield the floor.

Source: John McCain, https://www.mccain.senate.gov/public/index .cfm/2017/7/mccain-on-senate-floor-today.

Consider the source and the audience: Senator McCain prided himself on being a maverick, willing to buck his party line to maintain his principles, but he was also an institutionalist. He valued the Senate and the values and norms that had traditionally supported it. What is the significance of his choosing this moment and this vote to make his point that the Senate is dangerously close to being broken?

Lay out the argument and the underlying values and assumptions: McCain is motivated by what he sees as overly partisan behavior to call for a return to compromise, "compromises that each side criticize but also accept," and regular order. Why is compromise valuable to him? Why does he criticize himself just for trying to score points for the purpose of winning? What does regular order mean to him and how does he outline it here?

Uncover the evidence: McCain is not making an empirical argument here, he is criticizing the way senators do business today and saying that they *should* return to the norms that the founders intended for imperfect human beings and that have worked in the past. He uses the debacle of the Obamacare debate to show what happens when those norms are broken. Is that persuasive?

Evaluate the conclusion: Do you agree with McCain that the Senate is broken and should return to its older commitment of bipartisan cooperation, compromise, and regular order? How would the process look different if that were to happen? Would it be better or worse? What yardstick are you using to decide?

Sort out the political implications: If McCain had his way, politicians would put their principles above winning, would give up on hyperpartisanship and would value the reputation of the Senate over their own egos. Why is it hard to imagine that happening? How does the Senate McCain reveres compare to the one that approved Trump's Supreme Court nominees?

Review

Understanding Congress

Members of Congress are responsible for both representation and lawmaking. These two duties are often at odds because what is good for a local district may not be beneficial for the country as a whole. Representation style takes four different forms—policy, allocative, casework, and symbolic—and congresspersons attempt to excel at all four. However, since the legislative process designed by the founders is meant to be very slow, representatives have fewer incentives to concentrate on national lawmaking when reelection interests, and therefore local interests, are more pressing.

representation (p. 215)
national lawmaking (p. 215)
partisanship (p. 215)
constituency (p. 217)
policy representation (p. 217)

allocative representation (p. 217)
pork barrel projects (p. 217)
earmarks (p. 217)
casework (p. 217)
franking (p. 217)

symbolic representation (p. 217)
hyperpartisanship (p. 219)
party polarization (p. 219)

Congressional Power and Responsibilities

The founders created our government with a structure of checks and balances. In addition to checking each other, the House and the Senate may be checked by either the president or the courts. Congress is very powerful but must demonstrate unusual strength and consensus to override presidential vetoes and to amend the Constitution.

bicameral legislature (p. 221)

congressional oversight (p. 223)

advice and consent (p. 224)

Congressional Elections

Citizens and representatives interact in congressional elections, which in turn are profoundly affected by the way in which state legislatures define congressional districts. The incumbency effect is powerful in American politics because those in office often create legislation that makes it difficult for challengers to succeed.

reapportionment (p. 225)
redistricting (p. 225)
gerrymandering (p. 225)
partisan gerrymandering (p. 226)

racial gerrymandering (p. 227)
strategic politicians (p. 229)
incumbency advantage (p. 229)
coattail effect (p. 229)

midterm loss (p. 229)
descriptive representation (p. 230)

Congressional Organization

Representatives want autonomy and choice committee assignments to satisfy constituent concerns. They achieve these goals by joining together into political parties and obeying their leadership and party rules. House and Senate members make their own organizational rules, which means the dominant party in each house has great power over the internal rules of Congress and what laws are made.

majority party (p. 234)

Speaker of the House (p. 237)

seniority system (p. 238)

standing committees (p. 241)

House Rules Committee (p. 242)

select committee (p. 242)

joint committees (p. 242)

conference committees (p. 242)

How Congress Works

The structure of our bicameral legislature and organization of each house can slow the legislative process, yet despite these obstructions, Congress has a wealth of tools and strategies for creating policy. Legislative politics is a complex balance of rules and processes that favors the skilled politician.

legislative agenda (p. 245)

policy entrepreneurship (p. 246)

filibuster (p. 247)

cloture (p. 247)

nuclear option (p. 251)

omnibus legislation (p. 251)

roll call votes (p. 251)

veto override (p. 252)

pocket veto (p. 252)

The Citizens and Congress

Citizens, interest groups, the president, and members of Congress all have a stake in the legislative process. Voters organized into interest groups may have a greater impact on legislative outcomes than may the individual. Yet Congress, with various legislative tools and strategies, holds the most sway over the fate of legislation.

8

THE PRESIDENCY

In Your Own Words

After you've read this chapter, you will be able to

8.1 Describe the tension between the president's role as chief executive and the constitutional checks on presidential power.

8.2 Compare the modern presidency with the founders' expectations for a limited executive.

8.3 Identify strategies and tools presidents employ to overcome the constitutional limitations of the office.

8.4 Describe the organization and functions of the executive office.

8.5 Evaluate the importance of leadership style and image as they relate to presidential power.

8.6 Give examples of ways in which public opinion affects the relationship between citizens and the president.

What's at Stake . . . in Donald Trump's Presidency?

PRESIDENT DONALD J. TRUMP. You may love him. You may hate him. But you can't ignore him.

A polarizing political figure who has taken Washington by storm, he is the elephant in the country's classrooms (and textbooks). With students split between supporters and detractors, every discussion is a potential minefield. It would be easy to talk about nothing but Trump. Imagine your political science instructors turned into cable news hosts. It would be hair-on-fire education in an era of hair-on-fire politics; every tweet a crisis that consumes a class. Exciting for you, maybe, but it would leave very little time for more conventional details like how a bill becomes a law. Yet the alternative—dodging the tweets, the scandals, the media distractions, the next big news, and generally ignoring the elephant—would be to risk normalizing a moment in American politics that is, frankly, not normal at all.

So let us take another route, douse our hair with a fire hose and take a giant step back from the adrenaline-fueled politics to look closely at the political, media, and

261

Going Public by Tweet

President Trump has largely circumvented the traditional media and used Twitter to speak to his supporters, make announcements, respond to news stories, and fight his political opponents. Occasional efforts by staff to limit the practice have been largely abandoned.

entertainment phenomenon that is Donald Trump. The fact that he is such a huge and divisive figure in American politics today suggests that he has tapped into the American psyche in ways that say a lot about who we are and where we might be going as a country. We would be smart to unpack this presidency and figure out what its stakes are for us going forward.

Consider: With no background in politics, Donald Trump cleared a field of more than a dozen establishment Republican candidates to get the nomination. The consummate entertainer, he left no air for the other candidates, who struggled to get out from under whatever childish but searingly effective nickname he had saddled them with. After a scorched earth campaign against Democrat Hillary Clinton, he won the Electoral College vote but failed to gain a majority of the popular vote by three million. Still, 30 percent of Americans stand by him no matter what. As he once said, he could "stand in the middle of Fifth Avenue and shoot somebody" without losing support. That may be one of the few things he hasn't actually tried.

He came into office not only a reality TV host but a businessman, who learned his craft in the anything-goes world of New York real estate. He takes deals where he finds them and has carefully shielded his financial dealings from public scrutiny. He blows through long-established norms—not revealing his tax returns, hiring his own children, and profiting off government use of his many properties, for instance. His administration has not vetted his appointments carefully and has left many positions unfilled.

The turnover in the White House is unprecedented. His preferred management style is chaotic; he likes to pit employees against each other and revels in the competition for his approval. When he upsets a political apple cart, by pulling out of a treaty, pardoning a renegade sheriff, threatening to veto a bill his party passed, making a comment that is ambiguous enough that many Americans are certain it is sexist or racist, or just tweeting something unexpected that throws his staff off their stride, he is happy. People say he can be charming in person and that he just really, really wants to be liked. When people don't like him, he becomes angry and is quick to "fight back" or to call bad news "fake."

To supporters, he is a breath of fresh air, a much needed kick in the pants to elites whose power is entrenched and whose interests seem miles away from theirs. They applaud what they hear as an authentic voice willing to bust through the constraints of political correctness, and for whom no sentiment is too outrageous to say out loud. When he claims victimhood, it echoes the victimhood they feel too, from the elites that look down on them, the government that ignores them, and a future that doesn't seem to have a place for them. When Trump rocks the boat and the elite (but especially the liberal elite) start talking about the threat to democracy, they cheer him on. They wanted change, and, boy, is he ever change!

To his detractors, he is a narcissistic attention-hungry scam artist who got lucky in a presidential election he never seriously thought he would win. Without any background in politics or commitment to democratic values, he endangers the system he finds himself leading by breaking rules that are needed for the long-term health of democracy. His detractors may be Democrats or Republicans—what they have in common is a devotion to constitutional norms that many suspect he does not care much about. Whether they like the status quo or not, they want to see it changed by democratic means, not by blowing it up.

It is probably not possible to say definitively which of these groups is right or wrong—they live in different media worlds, make decisions based on different perceptions of reality, and for the most part think the other is crazy. Americans have not seen a leader like President Trump before. Just what is at stake in such an unusual presidency?[1] ◀◀

AS the American narrative has it, and indeed as much of the world would agree, the most powerful person on the planet is the president of the United States. He or she is the elected leader of the nation that has one of the most powerful economies, one of the greatest military forces, and the longest-running representative government the world has ever seen. Media coverage enforces this narrative; the networks and news services all have full-time reporters assigned to the White House. The 24-hour news cycle keeps us posted on what presidents do every day, even if they only went to church or played a round of golf, and the White House helps feed and control the narrative with a web site, Facebook page, Twitter account, and other social media connections. Today, with the president's own direct media presence and all the public reaction to it, the centrality of the presidency to the nation's political narrative is what one scholar calls the presidency's "monopolization of the public space."[2] In a perfect storm of telegenic personality and social media potential, that has never been more true than it has in the Trump years.

Typically, when anything of significance happens, whether it is a school shooting, a foreign terrorist attack, a natural disaster, or a big drop in the stock market, we, and the media, look to the president to solve our problems and to represent the nation in our times of struggle, tragedy, and triumph. The irony is that the U.S. Constitution provides for a relatively weak chief executive, and one whose job encompasses two roles—head of government and head of state—so often at loggerheads that most countries separate them into two distinct jobs handled by different people. The American public's, and indeed the world's, high expectations of the office constitute a major challenge for modern presidents. That, along with the need to get along with the other two branches with whom they share power and the extensive executive branch they oversee, make the job of being president a prestigious one but one difficult to do well.

> **Should presidents represent the interests of the people who voted for them, or of all Americans?**

THE PRESIDENTIAL JOB DESCRIPTION

The founders' notion of a limited executive

Since the legislature was presumed by all to be the real engine of the national political system, the presidency was not a preoccupation of the framers when they met in Philadelphia in 1787. The breakdown of the national government under the Articles of Confederation, however, demonstrated the need

> **head of state** the apolitical, unifying role of the president as symbolic representative of the whole country
>
> **head of government** the political role of the president as leader of a political party and chief arbiter of who gets what resources

for some form of a central executive. Nervous about trusting the general public to choose the executive, the founders provided for an Electoral College, a group of people who would be chosen by the states for the sole purpose of electing the president. The assumption was that this body would be made up of leading citizens who would exercise care and good judgment in casting their ballots and who would not make postelection claims on him. Because of their experience with King George III, the founders also wished to avoid the concentration of power that could be abused by a strong executive.

Although the majority's concept of a limited executive is enshrined in the Constitution, many of the arguments we hear today for a stronger executive were foreshadowed by the case that Alexander Hamilton made in *Federalist* No. 70 for a more "energetic" president. We can see much of this tension play out in the fact that the job of the presidency combines two very different roles: the more symbolic head of state and the more energetic head of government.

HEAD OF STATE VERSUS HEAD OF GOVERNMENT

Those of the founders who pictured a more limited executive probably had in mind something of a figurehead, someone who would sit at the top of the then very small executive branch, command the armed forces, and represent the nation. This role is known as the **head of state**—the symbol of the hopes and dreams of a people, responsible for enhancing national unity by representing that which is common and good in the nation. In many countries this is an apolitical role, so the head of state is not seen as a divisive figure—in Great Britain it is the queen. That the founders wanted the presidency to carry the dignity, if not the power, of a monarch is evident in George Washington's wish that the president might bear the title "His High Mightiness, the President of the United States and the Protector of Their Liberties."[3]

Americans were not ready for such a pompous title, but we nevertheless do put presidents, as the embodiment of the nation, on a higher plane than other politicians. Consequently the American president's job includes a ceremonial role for activities like greeting other heads of state, attending state funerals, tossing out the first baseball of the season, hosting the annual Easter egg hunt on the White House lawn, and consoling survivors of national tragedies. The vice president can relieve the president of some of these responsibilities, but there are times when only the president's presence will do.

Our system of checks and balances, however, gives the president real political powers, which are intended to help keep the other branches in check. So presidents also serve as the **head of government**, in which capacity they are supposed to run the government, make law, and function as the head of a political

Head of Government, Head of State

The presidency is one office, but the president plays two roles. When President Obama signed his signature health care reform bill, he was leading on a potentially controversial government policy complete with arm twisting and ample use of the bully pulpit—the quintessential head of government. When President Bush visited Ground Zero after September 11, spoke to first responders via bullhorn, and reached out to console them individually, his goal was to unify us and speak for the nation as head of state.

party. These functions will result in some citizens winning more than others, some losing, and some becoming angry—all of which works against the unifying image of the head of state. In Great Britain, as in many other countries, the head of government role is given to the prime minister, who not only can be political but, as the official head of a party in charge, is expected to be. In fact, the prime minister is a much more powerful executive position than the president of the United States, even though the president's political roles have expanded far beyond the founders' intentions since Franklin Roosevelt's New Deal.

Being head of government involves a variety of political activities. Because of the constant attention presidents command, they are uniquely situated to define the nation's policy agenda—that is, to get issues on the unofficial list of business that Congress and the public think should be taken care of. An effective head of government must also broker the deals, line up the votes, and work to pass legislation. This may seem peculiar since Congress makes the laws, but presidents are often critical players in developing political support from the public and Congress to get these laws passed. And of course, presidents are expected to execute the laws, to make government work. When things go well, no one thinks much about it. But when things go wrong, presidents are held accountable even for things outside their control. Reflecting this idea, President Harry Truman kept a sign on his desk that read "The Buck Stops Here."

Like prime ministers, U.S. presidents lead their political party as well. We explore the rest of the president's powers in greater detail later in this chapter. What is important for our

purposes here is that all these roles place presidents in an inherently and unavoidably contradictory position. On the one hand, they are the symbol of the nation, representing all the people (head of state); on the other hand, they have to take the lead in politics that are inherently divisive (head of government). Thus the political requirements of presidents' role as head of government necessarily undermine their unifying role as head of state.

The hyperpartisanship that has infected the U.S. Congress in recent years makes it even more difficult for the president to bridge these conflicting roles. The distinction depends on our ability as a nation to insist on respect for the office even when we disagree with the specific views or actions of the person holding it. When politics leads us to move from criticizing the policies of the president to insulting the office, it is more difficult for the president to act as a unifying figure when the need arises.

QUALIFICATIONS AND CONDITIONS OF OFFICE

The framers' conception of a limited presidency can be seen in the brief attention the office receives in the Constitution. Article II is short and not very precise. It provides some basic details on the office of the presidency:

- The president is chosen by the Electoral College to serve four-year terms. The number of terms was unlimited until 1951 when, in reaction to Franklin Roosevelt's unprecedented four terms in office, the

Constitution was amended to limit the president to two terms.

- The president must be a natural-born citizen of the United States, at least thirty-five years old, and a resident for at least fourteen years.
- The president is succeeded by the vice president if he or she dies or is removed from office.
- The Constitution does not specify who becomes president in the event that the vice president, too, is unable to serve, but in 1947 Congress passed the Presidential Succession Act, which establishes the order of succession after the vice president (see Table 8.1).
- Although the rules for succession following vacancies are clear, the rules for replacing a president because of disability are not. The Twenty-fifth Amendment states that a vice president can take over when either the president or the vice president and a majority of the cabinet report to Congress that the president is unable to serve. If reports are contradictory, two-thirds of Congress must agree that the president is incapacitated.[4]
- The president can be removed from office for reasons of "Treason, Bribery, or other High Crimes and Misdemeanors." The process of removal involves two steps: First, after an in-depth investigation, the House votes to impeach by a simple majority vote, which charges the president with a crime. Second, the Senate tries the president on the articles of **impeachment** and can convict by a two-thirds majority vote.

Only two American presidents, Andrew Johnson and Bill Clinton, have been impeached (in 1868 and 1998, respectively), but neither was convicted. The Senate failed, by one vote, to convict Johnson and could not assemble a majority against Clinton. The power of impeachment is meant to be a check on the president, but it is most often threatened for partisan purposes. Impeachment resolutions were filed against Ronald Reagan (over the invasion of Grenada and the Iran-contra affair), George H. W. Bush (over Iran-contra), and George W. Bush (for a host of offenses ranging from falsifying evidence justifying the war in Iraq to failing to respond adequately to Hurricane Katrina). Republicans called for President Obama's impeachment for causes ranging from supposedly lacking a birth certificate; to covering

up what the administration knew about the terrorist attack on the U.S. diplomatic compound in Benghazi, Libya; to taking executive actions regarding, among other things, immigration and EPA regulations on power plants.[5] Although some Democrats have called for Trump's impeachment, it is not a popular stance in the party, which would rather let Robert Mueller do his job and, now that they are in the House majority, conduct their own oversight of Trump's actions. There are more ways to provide checks and balances than impeachment, and as the Clinton years taught us, impeachments can be expensive, time-consuming, and punishing for the party that conducts them. Few of the impeachment resolutions over the years have made it to the floor for a vote in the House, in part because such actions bring governing virtually to a halt and are not popular with the public.[6]

> ***What political impact might have resulted if, following George Washington's wishes, the president were known as "His High Mightiness"?***

Impeachment has come to be wielded as a weapon in partisan political battles, but the president does sometimes commit actions worthy of impeachment. Richard Nixon would have been impeached had he not resigned in 1974 (the House Judiciary Committee had passed the resolution and there were enough votes to pass the measure on the House floor and to gain conviction in the Senate). In that case there was clear evidence, in the form of conversations taped by the president himself, that Nixon had been involved directly in the cover-up of a burglary at Democratic National Committee headquarters in the Watergate Complex. During the Reagan administration, a seven-year investigation by an independent counsel revealed that many members of Reagan's national security staff directed or knew about a plan to sell arms to Iran in exchange for American hostages, and to use the proceeds from the sale to assist "contra rebels" fighting against the Marxist Sandinista government in Nicaragua, in direct contradiction to Congress' wishes. Although the so-called Iran-contra scandal damaged Reagan's legacy, Reagan himself claimed he knew nothing about it, and no solid evidence surfaced that he did. President George H. W. Bush, calling the investigation a partisan witch-hunt, pardoned six of the fourteen people indicted in the incident. And although the indictments of Trump's associates suggest that Mueller is

> **impeachment** a formal charge by the House that the president (or another member of the executive branch) has committed acts of "Treason, Bribery, or other high Crimes and Misdemeanors," which may or may not result in removal from office

TABLE 8.1

Who Does the President's Job When the President Cannot?

PRESIDENTIAL ORDER OF SUCCESSION
1. Vice President
2. Speaker of the House
3. President Pro Tempore of the Senate
4. Secretary of State
5. Secretary of the Treasury
6. Secretary of Defense
7. Attorney General
8. Secretary of the Interior
9. Secretary of Agriculture
10. Secretary of Commerce
11. Secretary of Labor
12. Secretary of Health and Human Services
13. Secretary of Housing and Urban Development
14. Secretary of Transportation
15. Secretary of Energy
16. Secretary of Education
17. Secretary of Veterans Affairs
18. Secretary of Homeland Security

Note: It seems impossible that all in the line of succession could die simultaneously. Nevertheless, during the State of the Union address, when Congress and the cabinet are present with the president and vice president, one cabinet member does not attend in order to ensure that a catastrophe could not render our government leaderless. Some members of Congress have pushed legislation that would leapfrog the secretary of homeland security to eighth in line (one behind the attorney general), arguing that because of that secretary's particular familiarity with crises, he or she would be best able to lead the country.

getting closer to Trump, we won't know until his report is released if any behavior deserving of impeachment might even have occurred. It is also possible that Trump is such an unusual president that his supporters will never turn on him, no matter what Mueller finds, which would make it politically precarious for Republicans to support an impeachment.

Impeachment is more of a political than a legal process. The definition of an impeachable offense, as laid out in the Constitution, is so vague that it can mean anything a majority of the House of Representatives and two-thirds of the Senate are willing to vote on.

THE CONSTITUTIONAL POWER OF THE PRESIDENT

The Constitution uses vague language to discuss some presidential powers and is silent on the range and limits of others. It is precisely this ambiguity that allowed the Constitution to be ratified by both those who wanted a strong executive power and those who did not. In addition, this vagueness has allowed the powers of the president to expand over time without constitutional amendment. We can think of the president's constitutional powers as falling into three areas: executive authority to administer government, and legislative and judicial powers to check the other two branches.

EXECUTIVE POWERS Article II, Section 1, of the Constitution begins, "The executive power shall be vested in a president of the United States of America." However, the document does not explain exactly what "executive power" entails, and scholars and presidents through much of our history have debated the extent of these powers.[7] Section 3 states the president "shall take care that the laws be faithfully executed." Herein lies much of the executive authority; the president is the **chief administrator** of the nation's laws. This means that the president is the chief executive officer of the country, the person who, more than anyone else, is held responsible for agencies of the national government and the implementation of national policy.

The Constitution also specifies that the president, with the approval of the majority of the Senate, will appoint the heads of departments, who will oversee the work of implementation. These heads, who have come to be known collectively as the **cabinet**, report to the president. Today the president is responsible for the appointments of more than 3,500 federal employees: cabinet and lower administrative officers, federal judges, military officers, and members of the diplomatic corps. These responsibilities place the president at the top of a vast federal bureaucracy. But the president's control of the federal bureaucracy is limited, as we will see in Chapter 9, because although presidents can make a large number of appointments, they are not able to fire many of the people they hire.

chief administrator the president's executive role as the head of federal agencies and the person responsible for the implementation of national policy

cabinet a presidential advisory group selected by the president, made up of the vice president, the heads of the federal executive departments, and other high officials to whom the president elects to give cabinet status

Other constitutional powers place the president, as **commander-in-chief**, at the head of the command structure for the entire military establishment. The Constitution gives Congress the power to declare war, but as the commander-in-chief, the president has the practical ability to wage war. These two powers, meant to check each other, instead provide for a battleground on which Congress and the president struggle for the power to control military operations. Congress passed the War Powers Act of 1973 after the controversial Vietnam War, which was waged by Presidents Lyndon Johnson and Richard Nixon but never officially declared by Congress. The act was intended to limit the president's power to send troops abroad without congressional approval. Most presidents have ignored it, however, when they wished to engage in military action abroad, and since public opinion tends to rally around the president at such times, Congress has declined to challenge popular presidential actions. The War Powers Act remains more powerful on paper than in reality.

Finally, the president's executive powers include the role of **chief foreign policy maker**. This role is not spelled out in the Constitution, but the foundation for it is laid in the provision that the president negotiates **treaties**—formal international agreements with other nations—with the approval of two-thirds of the Senate. The president also appoints ambassadors and receives ambassadors of other nations, a power that essentially amounts to determining what nations the United States will recognize.

Although the requirement of Senate approval for treaties is meant to check the president's foreign policy power, much of U.S. foreign policy is made by the president through **executive agreements** with other heads of state, which avoids the slower and more cumbersome route of treaty making.[8] Executive agreements are used much more frequently than treaties; over 10,000 have been executed since 1970, compared to fewer than 1,000 treaties.[9] This heavy reliance on executive agreements gives the president considerable power and flexibility in foreign policy. Executive agreements are not only used to get around the need for Senate approval. Often they concern routine matters and are issued for the sake of efficiency. If the Senate had to approve each agreement, it would have to act at the rate of one per day, tying up its schedule and keeping the chamber from many more important issues.[10] However, even though the executive agreement is a useful and much-used tool, Congress may still thwart the president's intentions by refusing to approve the funds needed to put an agreement into action.

The framers clearly intended that the Senate would be the principal voice and decision maker in foreign policy, but that objective was not realized even in George Washington's presidency. At subsequent points in our history, Congress has exerted more authority in foreign policy, but for the most part, particularly in the twentieth century, presidents have taken a strong leadership role in dealing with other nations. Part of the reason for this is that Congress has guarded its prerogatives in domestic policy because those are so much more crucial in its members' reelection efforts. This has changed somewhat in recent years as the worldwide economy has greatly blurred the line between domestic and foreign affairs, and in instances where domestic constituencies have a strong interest overseas, as in the Israeli-Palestinian conflict in the Middle East or terrorist ideologies that threaten our shores.

LEGISLATIVE POWERS Even though the president is the head of the executive branch of government, the Constitution also gives the president some legislative power to check Congress, directing that the holder of the office "shall from time to time give to the Congress information of the state of the union, and recommend to their consideration such measures as he shall judge necessary and expedient." Although the framers' vision of this activity was quite limited, today the president's **State of the Union address**, delivered before the full Congress every January, is a major statement of the president's policy agenda. In this chapter's *The Big Picture*, you can see "wordle" images for key State of the Union addresses from different presidents. Notice how this form of rendering the speech allows you to compare the issues that were important to each administration.

The Constitution gives the president the nominal power to convene Congress and, when there is a dispute about when to disband, to adjourn it as well. Before Congress met regularly, this power, though limited, actually meant something. Today we rarely see it invoked. Some executives, such as the British prime minister, who can dissolve Parliament and call new elections, have a much more formidable convening power than that available to the U.S. president.

---

commander-in-chief the president's role as the top officer of the country's military establishment

chief foreign policy maker the president's executive role as the primary shaper of relations with other nations

treaties formal agreements with other countries; negotiated by the president and requiring approval by two-thirds of the Senate

executive agreements presidential arrangements with other countries that create foreign policy without the need for Senate approval

State of the Union address a speech given annually by the president to a joint session of Congress and to the nation announcing the president's agenda

The principal legislative power given the president by the Constitution is the **presidential veto**. A president who objects to a bill passed by the House and the Senate can veto it, sending it back to Congress with a message indicating the reasons. Congress can override a veto with a two-thirds vote in each house, but because mustering the two-thirds support is quite difficult, the presidential veto is a substantial power. Even the threat of a presidential veto can have a major impact in getting congressional legislation to fall in line with the administration's preferences.[11] Table 8.2 shows the number of bills vetoed since 1933 and the number of successful veto overrides by Congress.

As can be seen in the first column of figures in Table 8.2, the number of vetoes has varied a great deal from one president to the next. Most of the time, presidents are successful in having the vetoes sustained. The least successful was President George W. Bush. Although he joined John Quincy Adams and Thomas Jefferson as the only presidents who did not veto a bill during their first terms,[12] following the 2006 midterm elections, Bush vetoed dozens of the new Democratic majority's bills. These were overridden at a record rate that can partially be explained by Bush's falling popularity and by public disenchantment with the war in Iraq. The Democrats in Congress had little concern about their challenging an unpopular president.

Congress has regularly sought to get around the obstacle of presidential vetoes by packaging a number of items together in a bill (the *omnibus legislation* we described in Chapter 7). Traditionally, presidents have had to sign a complete bill or reject the whole thing. Thus, for example, Congress regularly adds such things as a building project or a tax break for a state industry onto, say, a military appropriations bill that the president wants. Often presidents calculate that it is best to accept such add-ons, even if they think them unjustified or wasteful, in order to get passed what they judge to be important legislation.

Before it was ruled unconstitutional by the Supreme Court in 1998, the short-lived line-item veto promised to provide an important new tool for presidents. Favored by conservatives and by President Clinton, the 1996 line-item veto was supposed to save money by allowing presidents to cut some items, like pork barrel projects, from spending bills without vetoing the entire package. The Supreme Court declared the law unconstitutional because the Constitution says that all legislation is to be passed by both houses and then presented as a whole to the president for approval.

Another of the president's key legislative powers comes from the vice president's role as presiding officer of the Senate. Vice presidents rarely preside over the Senate, but according to Article I, Section 3, they may cast a tie-breaking vote when the hundred-member Senate is evenly divided. Some recent examples illustrate just how important this has been to presidential prerogatives. In 1993 Vice President Al Gore voted to break a tie that enabled President Clinton's first budget to pass. The bill included controversial tax increases and spending cuts but ultimately helped create a budget surplus. Eight years later, Vice President Dick Cheney broke a tie vote on Bush's first budget, which ironically undid some of the Clinton tax increases but also included numerous other tax reductions. Both of these pieces of legislation were hallmarks of their respective presidents' agendas. Vice President Mike Pence broke six ties his first year in office—more than any previous vice president in a single year—and continued at a good clip his second year. The fact that the president can count on the vice president to break a tie when the Senate is split over controversial legislation is an often underappreciated legislative power.

Although the Constitution does not grant the president the power to make law, the power to do so has grown over time and now is generally accepted. For instance, presidents can issue **executive orders** (not to be confused with the executive agreements they can make with other nations), which are supposed to clarify how laws passed by Congress are to be implemented by specific agencies. Some of the most significant presidential actions have come from executive orders, including President Franklin Roosevelt's order to hold Japanese Americans in internment camps in World War II, President Truman's order that black and white military troops be integrated, President John F. Kennedy's and President Lyndon Johnson's affirmative action programs, and many of the post–September 11 security measures. Similarly, the use of **signing statements** is a quasi-legislative power that can significantly increase the president's role as a policymaker, independent of Congress. Issued on the signing of a bill, these statements are intended to "clarify" the president's understanding of what the bill means and how it ought to be enforced.[13]

With some exceptions (notably President Obama), executive orders tend to be released at a higher rate at the beginning of a president's term as the president immediately implements key policies and at the end of the term as the

---

presidential veto a president's authority to reject a bill passed by Congress; may be overridden only by a two-thirds majority in each house

executive orders clarifications of congressional policy issued by the president and having the full force of law

signing statements statements recorded along with signed legislation clarifying the president's understanding of the constitutionality of the bill

TABLE 8.2
Presidential Vetoes, Roosevelt to Trump

YEARS	PRESIDENT	TOTAL VETOES	REGULAR VETOES	POCKET VETOES	VETOES OVERRIDDEN	VETO SUCCESS RATE
1933–1945	Franklin Roosevelt	635	372	263	9	97.6%
1945–1953	Harry Truman	250	180	70	12	93.3
1953–1961	Dwight Eisenhower	181	73	108	2	97.3
1961–1963	John F. Kennedy	21	12	9	0	100.0
1963–1969	Lyndon Johnson	30	16	14	0	100.0
1969–1974	Richard Nixon	43	26	17	7	73.1
1974–1977	Gerald Ford	66	48	18	12	75.0
1977–1981	Jimmy Carter	31	13	18	2	84.6
1981–1989	Ronald Reagan	78	39	39	9	76.9
1989–1993	George H. W. Bush	46	29	17*	1	96.6
1993–2001	Bill Clinton	37	36	1	2	96.4
2001–2009	George W. Bush	12	11	1	4	66.7
2009–2017	Barack Obama	12	12	0	1	91.7
2017–2018	Donald Trump	0	0	0	0	

Source: "Summary of Bills Vetoed: 1789–Present," www.senate.gov/reference/Legislation/Vetoes/Vetocounts.htm.

*Although they are counted here, Congress did not recognize two of Bush's pocket vetoes and considered the legislation enacted.

president tries to leave a legacy.[14] Indeed, presidents often release particularly symbolic executive orders on their first days in office. Since executive orders are not Congress-made laws, new presidents can reverse any of their predecessors' orders.[15] Donald Trump has been especially zealous in undoing as many of his predecessor's executive actions as possible.

JUDICIAL POWERS Presidents can have tremendous long-term impact on the judiciary, but in the short run their powers over the courts are meager. Their continuing impact comes from nominating judges to the federal courts, including the Supreme Court. The political philosophies of individual judges influence significantly how they interpret the law, and this is especially important for Supreme Court justices, who are the final arbiters of constitutional meaning. Since judges serve for life, presidential appointments have a long-lasting effect. For instance, today's Supreme Court is distinctly more conservative than its immediate predecessors due to the appointments made by Presidents Reagan and Bush in the 1980s

and early 1990s. Moreover, President Reagan is credited by many observers with having ushered in a "judicial revolution." He, together with his successor, George H. W. Bush, appointed 550 of the 837 federal judges, most of them conservatives. Clinton appointed moderates to the courts, angering many Democrats, who felt that his appointees should have been more liberal. President George W. Bush revived the conservative trend that was halted under Clinton.[16] Although President Obama's pick of Sonia Sotomayor for the Supreme Court pleased liberals, his nomination of Elena Kagan caused some to worry that his selections would follow Clinton's more moderate record.[17] His final nomination, Judge Merrick Garland, also was a more moderate choice, but this was partly in the hopes of encouraging the Republican-led Senate to give him a hearing, which never happened. In general, Obama's choices for the judiciary were fairly liberal. Many of the appointments he made were blocked by Republicans in the Senate, however, and their refusal to recognize his final Supreme Court nominee with hearings was an unprecedented denial of power to shape the Court.[18] Obama's

Visualizing the State of the Union

GEORGE WASHINGTON (1790)

Just after his inauguration, the first American president carefully shepherds the new nation over rocky terrain.

ABRAHAM LINCOLN (1862)

In the second year of the Civil War, the president who hadn't been able to save the Union tries to hold the remnants of his country together.

FRANKLIN D. ROOSEVELT (1944)

The year before he died, the president who saw the country through the Great Depression and into World War II reassures and encourages Americans to hold the course.

JOHN F. KENNEDY (1962)

In the middle of his short time in office, the first president born in the twentieth century faces new challenges.

New Technology and New Ways to Talk to the Nation

First presidential public address (1789)

First presidential press conference (1913)

First presidential radio address (1923)

Fireside Chats (1933–44)

First televised presidential speech (1947)

First presidential whistlestop tour (1948)

LYNDON B. JOHNSON (1965)

In the first year of his own term, the president who came to office because of the murder of another seeks to raise the spirits of a nation and secure his legacy.

RONALD REAGAN (1985)

After a landslide reelection, the president who became a conservative icon lays out his agenda for his second term.

GEORGE W. BUSH (2002)

The year after 9/11, the president who had come to office objecting to nation building rallies the country for war.

DONALD TRUMP (2018)

The president's speech was a nod to a possible "new America moment" and focused on jobs, the economy, infrastructure, immigration, trade, and national security.

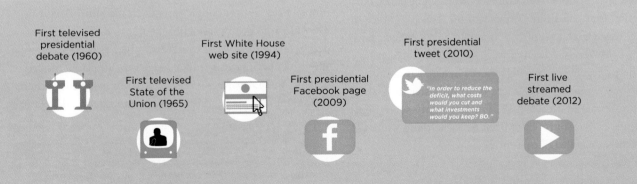

First televised presidential debate (1960)

First televised State of the Union (1965)

First White House web site (1994)

First presidential Facebook page (2009)

First presidential tweet (2010)

"In order to reduce the deficit, what costs would you cut and what investments would you keep? BO."

First live streamed debate (2012)

Bettmann/Getty Images

Speaking From the Bully Pulpit

President Theodore Roosevelt—who famously used the term "Bully!" the way we might use "excellent" or "awesome" today—coined the phrase "bully pulpit" to describe the office of the president. Roosevelt was one of the first to exploit the presidency as a platform from which to leverage both public and legislative support for his policy agenda. He used it to push for Progressive movement reforms and earned his reputation as the "trust buster" for his fight to ensure the rights of the common working man by pushing back against large corporate monopolies.

nominations, however, did produce a more diverse federal judiciary. As we will see in Chapter 10, he nominated more women, Asians, and Hispanics than any previous president as well as twelve openly gay federal judges and the first-ever Native American female judge in the country's history.[19] President Trump's picks for the courts, beginning with his selection of Neil Gorsuch for the Supreme Court position that had been Obama's to fill, and his choice of Brett Kavanaugh to replace retiring Justice Kennedy, have been consistently conservative. He has appointed people to the federal bench quickly and the Senate has as quickly approved them now that there is no filibuster to hold up such votes. As of March 2018, Trump's eighty-seven nominations to the courts have been overwhelming white (92 percent) and male (77 percent).[20]

Presidents cannot always gauge the judicial philosophy of their appointees, however, and they can be sadly disappointed in their choices. Republican president Dwight Eisenhower

appointed Chief Justice Earl Warren and Justice William Brennan, both of whom turned out to be more liberal than the president had anticipated. When asked if he had any regrets as president, Eisenhower answered, "Yes, two, and they are both sitting on the Supreme Court."[21]

The presidential power to appoint is limited to an extent by the constitutional requirement for Senate approval of federal judges. Traditionally, most nominees have been approved, with occasional exceptions. Sometimes rejection stems from questions about the candidate's competence, but in other instances rejection is based more on style and judicial philosophy. The Democratic-led Senate's rejection of President Reagan's very conservative Supreme Court nominee Robert Bork in 1987 is one of the more controversial cases.[22] Some observers believe that the battle over the Bork nomination signaled the end of deference to presidents and opened up the approval process to endless challenges and partisan bickering.[23] Some of the harshest battles between the president and Congress in recent years came from partisan Senate challenges to judicial nominations. The political polarization we discussed in Chapter 7 has infected the nomination process. The frequent threat of the filibuster and the use of anonymous holds in the Senate allowed the party opposing the president to hold up nominations so that many federal judgeships remained open, causing a backlog of cases. With both of those tools now gone, it is much easier for a bare majority to have its way in shaping the courts in a partisan image.

A president's choice of judges for the federal district courts can also be limited by the tradition of **senatorial courtesy**, whereby a senior senator of the president's party or both senators of either party from the state in which the appointees reside have what amounts to a veto power over the president's choice. If presidents should ignore the custom of senatorial courtesy and push a nomination unpopular with one of the home state senators, fellow senators used to refuse to confirm the appointee.[24] In today's era of broken norms, even senatorial courtesy is not a given.

Although presidents can leave a lasting imprint on the judiciary, in the short run they do little to affect court decisions. They do not contact judges to plead for decisions; they do not offer them inducements as they might a fence-sitting member of Congress. When, as happens rarely, a president criticizes a federal judge for a decision, the criticism is usually poorly received. For example, when President Obama used his State of the Union address in

senatorial courtesy the tradition of granting senior senators of the president's party considerable power over federal judicial appointments in their home states

2010 to criticize the Supreme Court majority for its land-mark campaign finance decision (*Citizens United v. Federal Election Commission*), a flood of blogs and editorials suggested that the president had been unduly disrespectful, and one justice, Samuel Alito, sat shaking his head and mouthing the words "not true" as the president spoke.[25] Trump has been much more frequently free-spoken in his criticism of judgments that have gone against him, but although social media reacts, most people seem to have become used to Trump's norm-breaking behavior.

The least controversial way a president can try to influence a court decision is to have the Justice Department invest resources in arguing a case. The third-ranking member of the Justice Department, the **solicitor general**, is a presidential appointee whose job it is to argue cases for the government before the Supreme Court. The solicitor general is thus a bridge between the executive and the judiciary, not only deciding which cases the government will appeal to the Court but also filing petitions stating the government's (usually the president's) position on cases to which the government is not even a party. These petitions, called amicus curiae ("friend of the court") briefs, are taken very seriously by the Court. The government is successful in its litigation more often than any other litigant, winning over two-thirds of its cases in the past half-century, and often having its arguments cited by the justices themselves in their opinions.[26] Elena Kagan, President Obama's second appointment to the Supreme Court, served as his solicitor general before her nomination.

One additional judicial power granted to the president by the Constitution is the **pardoning power**, which allows a president to exempt a person, convicted or not, from punishment for a crime. This power descends from a traditional power of kings as the court of last resort and thus is a check on the courts. Pardons can backfire in dramatic ways. After President Gerald Ford pardoned Richard Nixon, in the hopes that the nation would heal from its Watergate wounds more quickly if it didn't have to endure the spectacle of its former president on trial, Ford experienced a tremendous backlash that may have contributed to his 1976 loss to Jimmy Carter. Subsequent presidents have each run into problems with unpopular pardons. Bill Clinton, in his last day in office, issued an unusually large number of pardons. Some were widely unpopular—like that for fugitive Marc Rich, who was residing in Switzerland, owed millions in

taxes, and was charged with multiple counts of tax fraud—but nevertheless were entirely legal. When pardons like this are motivated by personal, political, or partisan considerations, rather than as a check on the power of the courts, they tend to be seen by the public and the media as presidential abuses of the public trust.[27] This is true of President Trump's pardons of controversial Arizona sheriff Joe Arpaio, long a Trump supporter and fellow opponent of immigration, who had been convicted for refusing to stop profiling Latinos, and of Scooter Libby, former chief of staff to Vice President Dick Cheney, who had been convicted of leaking the identity of CIA agent Valerie Plame for political reasons. Bush had commuted Libby's sentence but refused to pardon him. Unusual for presidents, who have tended to wait until later in their term, Trump issued eleven pardons or commutations in his first two years of office. These actions didn't seem to have an impact on his already low approval ratings, although some critics have suggested that he is hinting to those under investigation by Robert Mueller that he will be ready to pardon them, too.[28]

PAUSE AND REVIEW Who, What, How

The politicians who initially had something important at stake in the rules governing the executive were the founders themselves. Arranged by those, like Alexander Hamilton, who wanted a strong leader and by others who preferred a multiple executive to ensure checks on the power of the office, the constitutional compromise provides for a stronger position than many wanted, but one still limited in significant ways from becoming overly powerful and independent.

Presidents have a tremendous stake in leaving a legacy of which they can be proud, but the Constitution puts an obstacle course in the way of achieving that goal. Navigating around the conflicting roles of the president's job description and the institutions of the bureaucracy, the Congress, and the Court, all of which have their own stakes, is difficult. But that is exactly what the framers had in mind when they set up our system of checks and balances.

In Your Own Words Describe the tension between the president's role as chief executive and the constitutional checks on presidential power.

THE EVOLUTION OF THE AMERICAN PRESIDENCY

From restrained administrator to energetic problem-solver

As we saw, the framers designed a much more limited presidency than the one we have today. The constitutional provisions give most of the policymaking powers to Congress, or

---

solicitor general the Justice Department officer who argues the government's cases before the Supreme Court

pardoning power a president's authority to release or excuse a person from the legal penalties of a crime

at least require power sharing and cooperation. For most of our history, this arrangement was not a problem. As leaders of a rural nation with a relatively restrained government apparatus, presidents through the nineteenth century were largely content with a limited authority that rested on the grants of powers provided in the Constitution. But the presidency of Franklin Roosevelt, beginning in 1932, ushered in a new era in presidential politics.

THE TRADITIONAL PRESIDENCY

The presidency that the founders created and outlined in the Constitution is not the presidency of today. In fact, so clearly have the effective rules governing the presidency changed that scholars speak of two different presidential eras—that before the 1930s and that after. Although the constitutional powers of the president have been identical in both eras, the interpretation of how far the president can go beyond those constitutional powers has changed dramatically.

The **traditional presidency**—the founders' limited vision of the office—survived more or less intact for a little over one hundred years. There were exceptions, however, to their expectations that echoed Hamilton's call for a stronger executive. Several early presidents exceeded the powers granted in the Constitution. Washington expanded the president's foreign policy powers, Jefferson entered into the Louisiana Purchase, and Andrew Jackson developed the role of president as popular leader. In one of the most dramatic examples, Abraham Lincoln, during the emergency conditions of the Civil War, stepped outside his constitutional role to call up state militias, to enlarge the army and use tax money to pay for it, to blockade the southern ports, and to suspend the writ of habeas corpus (see the *CLUES to Critical Thinking* feature at the end of the chapter). Lincoln claimed that his actions, though counter to the Constitution, were necessary to save the nation.[29]

These presidents believed that they had what modern scholars call **inherent powers** to fulfill their constitutional duty to "take care that the laws be faithfully executed." Some presidents, like Lincoln, claimed that national security required a broader presidential role. Others held that the president, as our sole representative in foreign affairs, needed a stronger hand abroad than at home. Inherent powers are not listed explicitly in the Constitution but are implied by the powers that are granted, and they have been supported, to some extent, by the Supreme Court.[30] But most nineteenth- and early-twentieth-century presidents, conforming to the founders' expectations, took a more retiring role, causing one observer to claim that "twenty of the twenty-five presidents of the nineteenth century were lords of passivity."[31] The job of the presidency was seen as a primarily administrative office, in which presidential will was clearly subordinate to the will of Congress.

THE MODERN PRESIDENCY

The **modern presidency**, a time of evolving executive power since the 1930s, is still a work in progress. The simple rural nature of life in the United States changed rapidly in the century and a half after the founding. The country grew westward, and the nation became more industrialized. More people worked in factories, fewer on the land. The postal system expanded greatly, and the federal government became involved in American Indian affairs, developed national parks, and enacted policies dealing with transportation, especially the railroads. Government in the nineteenth century sought bit by bit to respond to the new challenges of its changing people and economy, and as it responded, it grew beyond the bounds of the rudimentary administrative structure supervised by George Washington. With the crisis of the Great Depression and Franklin Roosevelt's New Deal solution, the size of government exploded and popular ideas about government changed radically. From being an exception, as it was in our early history, the use of strong presidential power became an expectation of the modern president.

THE GREAT DEPRESSION Nothing in their prior experience had prepared Americans for the calamity of the Great Depression. Following the stock market crash of October 1929, the economy went into a tailspin. Unemployment soared to 25 percent while the gross national product plunged from around $100 billion in 1928 to under $60 billion in 1932.[32] President Herbert Hoover held that government had only limited powers and responsibility to deal with what was, he believed, a private economic crisis. There was no widespread presumption, as there is today, that government was responsible for the state of the economy or for alleviating the economic suffering of its citizens.

Roosevelt's election in 1932, and his three reelections, initiated an entirely new level of governmental activism. For the first time, the national government assumed responsibility for the economic well-being of its citizens on a substantial scale. Relying on the theory mentioned earlier, that foreign affairs are thought to justify greater presidential power than do domestic affairs, Roosevelt portrayed himself as waging a war against the Depression and sought from Congress the powers "that would be given to me if we were in fact invaded by

traditional presidency the founders' vision of limited executive power

inherent powers presidential powers implied but not stated explicitly in the Constitution

modern presidency the trend toward a higher degree of executive power since the 1930s

a foreign foe."[33] The New Deal programs he put in place tremendously increased the size of the federal establishment and its budget. The number of civilians (nonmilitary personnel) working for the federal government increased by over 50 percent during Roosevelt's first two terms (1933–1941). The crisis of the Great Depression created the conditions for extraordinary action, and Roosevelt's leadership created new responsibilities and opportunities for the federal government. Congress delegated a vast amount of discretionary power to Roosevelt so that he could implement his New Deal programs.

> **How might presidential behavior change if we once again allowed presidents to serve more than two terms?**

PRESIDENTIAL PROMISES, POPULAR EXPECTATIONS

The legacy of the New Deal is that Americans now look to their president and their government to regulate their economy, solve their social problems, and provide political inspiration. No president has had such a profound impact on how Americans live their lives today.[34] Roosevelt's New Deal was followed by Truman's Fair Deal. Eisenhower's presidency was less activist, but it was followed by Kennedy's New Frontier and Johnson's Great Society. All of these comprehensive policy programs did less than they promised, but they reinforced Americans' belief that it is government's and, in particular, the president's job to make ambitious promises. While presidents from Carter to Reagan to Clinton enthusiastically promoted plans for cutting back the size of government, few efforts were successful. Not even President Reagan, more conservative and therefore more hostile to "big government," was able to significantly reduce government size and popular expectations of government action.

"THE IMPERIAL PRESIDENCY" The growth of domestic government is not the only source of the increased power of the modern president, however. As early as 1936, the Supreme Court confirmed in *United States v. Curtiss-Wright Corporation* the idea that the president has more inherent power in the realm of foreign affairs than in domestic politics.[35]

These decisions became more significant as the U.S. role in world politics expanded greatly in the post–World War II years. The ascendance of the United States as a world power, its engagement in the Cold War, and its participation in undeclared wars such as Korea and Vietnam made the office very powerful indeed—what historian Arthur Schlesinger called, in a 1973 book, "the imperial presidency."[36] The philosophy

Underwood Archives/Getty Images

The Policies and Persona of the Modern Presidency
The challenges of the Great Depression and World War II were met with a greatly increased role of the national government in American lives, the economy, and the world. Franklin Roosevelt's New Deal policies, and his central leadership role in the war effort, combined with his use of radio to speak directly to the public, transformed the nature of the office. The president became the central figure in American politics, and politics became more central to the lives of Americans.

behind the imperial presidency was summed up neatly by Richard Nixon, ironically several years after he was forced to resign, when he declared, "When the president does it, that means it's not illegal."[37]

THE BATTLE OVER EXECUTIVE AUTHORITY TODAY

Whether or not the power of the modern presidency ever approached "imperial" status at one time, there is no doubt that the political reaction to the Vietnam War and the Watergate scandal in the 1970s made it harder for the modern president to act. Congress, the media, and the courts check the president in ways they had not done earlier in the era of the modern presidency. Many in Congress felt that neither the Johnson nor the Nixon administrations had been sufficiently forthcoming over the Vietnam War. Frustration with that, as well as with Nixon's abuse of his powers during Watergate and his unwillingness to spend budgeted money as Congress had appropriated it, led Congress to develop its own mechanisms for getting information about public policy to use as a check on presidential power.[38] Congress also weakened the office of the presidency with the passage of the War

Powers Act (1973), which we discussed earlier; the Foreign Intelligence and Surveillance Act (1978), designed to put a check on the government's ability to spy on people within the United States; and the Independent Counsel Act (1978), which was intended to provide an impartial check on a president's activities but was ultimately left open to abuse.

At the same time, fresh from the heady success of the *Washington Post*'s discovery of the Watergate scandal, the Washington press corps abandoned the discretion that had kept them from reporting Franklin Roosevelt's inability to walk or John F. Kennedy's extramarital affairs, and began to subject the president to closer scrutiny. Reporters, eager to make their names as investigative journalists, became far more aggressive in their coverage of the White House.

Even the Supreme Court served to limit the power and stature of the presidency, as when it ruled unanimously in 1997 that a sitting president does not have immunity from civil lawsuits while in office, adding that the process of such a case was unlikely to prove a disruption of the president's duties.[39] Paula Jones's lawsuit against Bill Clinton, of course, proved to be disruptive of his presidency in the extreme, and ended up leading to his impeachment, although on grounds that had nothing to do with the case. Had the Court not made that decision, Clinton's affair with Monica Lewinsky would not have come to light, and he would most likely not have been impeached.

THE BUSH-CHENEY RESTORATION OF THE IMPERIAL PRESIDENCY The modern presidency had been weakened by post-Watergate developments and the Clinton impeachment. When the George W. Bush administration came to power, Bush and his vice president, Dick Cheney, were determined to restore the luster and power of the office. Cheney had been a young staffer in the Nixon White House and chief of staff to Gerald Ford before embarking on a career in Congress. He had seen firsthand the changes in the executive and felt they had gone too far. Thus, many of Bush's early executive orders were designed to bolster presidential powers, as were claims of executive privilege made by his administration.

In addition, Bush expanded the practice of using signing statements. Typically, presidents used the presidential veto to block legislation they didn't like, whereupon Congress could override the veto if the bill had sufficient support. But unlike his predecessors, Bush had not vetoed a single bill by the time he had been in office for five years. Instead he had issued a huge number of signing statements, over 750, compared to 232 by his father in his four years in the White House, and only 140 issued by Bill Clinton in his eight years.

Many of Bush's signing statements reflected a strong commitment to the theory of the unitary executive, a controversial legal view held by members of the Bush administration that the Constitution requires that all executive power be held only by the president and, therefore, that it cannot be delegated to or wielded by any other branch. Consequently, Bush's signing statements reserved the right to ignore, among other things, an antitorture law, a law forbidding him to order troops into combat in Colombia, a law requiring him to inform Congress if he wanted to divert funds from congressionally authorized programs to start up secret operations, a law preventing the military from using intelligence about Americans that was gathered unconstitutionally, a law that required the Justice Department to inform Congress about how the FBI was using domestic wiretapping, laws that created whistleblower protection for federal employees, and laws that required the federal government to follow affirmative action principles.[40]

Critics of the Bush administration howled when they realized what was going on, accusing Bush of doing an end-run around Congress and claiming that he was setting up himself, and thus the executive branch, as the ultimate decider of what is constitutional, a function generally thought to belong to the Supreme Court. "There is no question that this administration has been involved in a very carefully thought-out, systematic process of expanding presidential power at the expense of the other branches of government," said one scholar.[41]

The terror attacks of September 11, 2001, provided Bush and Cheney with a strong and persuasive rationale for their desire to create a more muscular presidency. Bush's extraordinarily high approval ratings in the days following September 11 made Congress unwilling to take him on. The Republicans in Congress were supportive of the administration's efforts, and the Democrats feared being seen as soft on terrorism and so went along with Bush's plans. He was able to initiate the wars in Afghanistan and Iraq, and the Patriot Act passed handily in 2001, and only the Supreme Court, in the 2004 case *Hamdi v. Rumsfeld* and the 2006 case *Hamdan v. Rumsfeld*, attempted to put on the brakes. As we argue in this chapter, high approval ratings can give a president power beyond that granted by the Constitution.

Only after Bush's reelection in 2004, with waning approval ratings, was he seen as vulnerable enough for Congress to criticize him seriously. By 2006 his approval was so low that Democrats easily won back control of both the House and the Senate and began to undertake the job of congressional oversight that had been largely lacking for the previous six years.

The fate of the Bush administration reflects the basic lessons of this chapter. The Constitution does not give

The Post-9/11 Presidency

As the public united behind the president in the aftermath of the terror attacks of 2001, the Bush-Cheney administration was able to take on a more active role in governing and increased the power of the office through the use of presidential signing statements, executive orders, and claims of executive privilege.

presidents sufficient power to meet their promises and to match expectations of domestic and world leadership, so presidents curry public support to engender a more compliant Congress. Bush chose to stick with his ideological agenda and his slim but cooperative majorities in Congress, and to use the levers available to act unilaterally: signing statements, executive orders, claims of executive privilege, and politicizing of the bureaucracy to achieve policy compliance, especially in regard to the Department of Justice. With the decline in his popularity and his party's losses in Congress, his powers waned and he was a reclusive lame duck during the final months of his presidency.

THE OBAMA PRESIDENCY Overall, it is not clear whether the Bush-Cheney efforts to bulk up the executive will have lasting effect. Obama wrestled with the same challenges of office as have all presidents in the modern age. A former constitutional law professor, he seemed to be

aware of the necessity of maintaining checks and balances, and he showed no signs of embracing the Bush philosophy of the unitary executive. Trump, by contrast, with the opportunity to appoint more judges and justices than most presidents, clearly believes in a strong presidency and will probably appoint judges to back up that power.

Still, as relations between the Obama White House and Congress became impossibly strained, with Congress' determination to pass no element of his agenda, the president turned more and more to executive action to get his agenda accomplished.

Although the magazine *Politico* found that most of Obama's actions would take some time to make their impact felt, they included a higher minimum wage for federal workers and antidiscrimination measures in the federal workplace for gays, a new retirement savings plan, new workplace reforms, efforts to halt climate change by boosting fuel efficiency standards and reducing emissions, the creation of a marine sanctuary, assistance repaying student loans, regulation of for-profit colleges, small business assistance, a change in the loophole that allowed those purchasing guns at gun shows to avoid background checks, changes in immigration policy, the institution of net neutrality, and other similar programs that could be accomplished with the executive pen or by encouraging executive agencies to act in a particular way.[42]

As executive actions, few, if any, of these decisions will survive Obama's presidency. Although Obama's political legacy has been significant and his approval ratings as he ended his term were in the mid-50s, Trump's victory has allowed the Republicans to reverse much of Obama's work, including, in all likelihood, his signature health care plan. All presidents and congresses have at least occasionally adversarial relationships, but Obama may be one of the few presidents whose conflict with Congress survives his administration. Donald Trump, in fact, promised to undo as much of Obama's legacy as he could, as quickly as he could, and Congress has helped out where it could.

THE TRUMP PRESIDENCY As we noted in *What's at Stake . . . ?*, there are no models for the Trump presidency. He has pleased his fans and inflamed his critics. Running the executive branch as he ran his business, Donald Trump has chafed at the limits of checks and balances since taking office, pushing against the notion that the president is bound by the rule of law. He views people in the bureaucracy as being there to serve him rather than to serve the Constitution, and he has shown evidence of wanting to use the power of the federal government to punish those he views as his enemies. For instance, he lobbied the U.S. Postal Service to double the rates that would affect clients like Amazon, whose founder, Jeff Bezos, Trump blames for his negative coverage in the *Washington Post*, which Bezos also owns.

TABLE 8.3

Presidents by the Numbers: The First Year of Their First Terms

	DONALD TRUMP	BARACK OBAMA	GEORGE W. BUSH	BILL CLINTON	GEORGE H. W. BUSH	RONALD REAGAN
Cabinet-level departures	3	0	0	0	0	0
Turnover in key staff	34%	9%	6%	11%	7%	17%
Independent counsel investigations	1	0	0	0	0	1
Independent counsel indictments	3	0	0	0	0	0
Bills signed	117	161	134	209	242	157
Executive orders signed	58	41	56	59	33	53
Vacation days (does not include Camp David)	107	26	69	21	40	45
Visits to troops abroad	0	3	1	0	0	0
State dinners	1	1	1	1	7	9
Foreign countries visited	14	21	11	9	16	2
Federal judges appointed	23	13	28	28	15	41
Tweets sent	2,568	0	0	0	0	0
Average approval rating	38%	57%	68%	49%	66%	57%
Solo press conferences	1	11	5	12	28	6

Source: National Archives; congress.gov; D'Angelo Gore, "President Obama's Vacation Days," https://www.factcheck.org/2010/01/president-obamas-vacation-days/; Kyle Kim, "Trump Appointing Judges at Rapid Pace," Los Angeles Times, January 19, 2018, http://www.latimes.com/projects/la-na-pol-trump-federal-judiciary/; "Trump's First-Year Job Approval Worst by 10 Points," Gallup, http://news.gallup.com/poll/226154/trump-first-year-job-approval-worst-points.aspx; American Presidency Project, http://www.presidency.ucsb.edu/data/newsconferences.php.

Trump has differed from other presidents from the beginning by deciding not to forgive those who didn't vote for him. Most presidents reach out to the other side and, especially when dealing with issues of national concern, speak not as a partisan politician but as a nonpolitical head of state. Trump has largely bypassed that role. When the Trumps held their first state dinner, no Democrats (or journalists) were invited. When tragedies like school shootings have occurred, many families of victims say he has not contacted them. When he does speak out, it is often via tweet, which lacks the gravitas of a traditional presidential statement. But if Trump has ignored the head-of-state role, he hasn't spent a lot of time on the head-of-government role, either. He has blown up deals with Congress rather than trying to broker agreements and bring people on board his side. He has shown little interest in the health of the Republican Party he leads, and when that vacuum has been filled by his vice president, his staff has reacted with suspicion about Pence's motives.[43] Table 8.3 compares the first year of the past six presidents' first terms.

Trump's novel approach to governance is based partly on his personality, partly on his reliance on what has worked for him in business, and partly on his refusal to learn the gritty details of how government works. Because of his lack of political background, he entered office with less idea of how to work with the other branches or, indeed, with the rest of the executive branch than have other new presidents. Political scientists have coined the term **weak presidency** to refer to presidents who do not excel at managing their executive offices. The early indications are that Trump joins former president Jimmy Carter in this camp. That term should not be confused with the notion that Trump is necessarily a weak man—he can be very influential with those who seek his favor—but it does mean he isn't a very good manager of the people around him.

> **weak presidency** a term that refers to presidents who do not excel at managing their executive offices

Until the 1930s, presidents were mostly content to live within the confines of their constitutional restrictions, with only occasional excursions into the realm of inherent powers. But since the 1930s, presidents and citizens have entered into a complex relationship, with presidential power fluctuating with the nation's needs and the president's ambition. When the powers of the presidency have seemed to have gotten out of hand, however, Congress, the courts, and the media have been quick to limit it, showing how well the founders' system of checks and balances functions.

In Your Own Words Compare the modern presidency with the founders' expectations for a limited executive.

PRESIDENTIAL POLITICS

The struggle for power in a constitutionally limited office

Presidential responsibilities and the public's expectations of what the president can accomplish have increased greatly since the start of the twentieth century. But, as we have discussed, the Constitution has not been altered to give the president more power, resulting in an **expectations gap** that makes the job inherently challenging. To avoid failure, presidents have to seek power beyond that which is explicitly granted by the Constitution, and even beyond what they can claim as part of their inherent powers. They do that with varying degrees of success.

THE EXPECTATIONS GAP AND THE NEED FOR PERSUASIVE POWER

Even presidents who have drawn enthusiastically on their inherent powers to protect national security or conduct foreign policy or who support the theory of the unitary executive still cannot summon the official clout needed to ensure that their legislation gets through Congress, that the Senate approves their appointments, and that other aspects of their campaign promises are fulfilled. New presidents quickly face

> **expectations gap** the gap between popular expectations of what modern presidents can and should do, and their constitutional powers to get things done
>
> **power to persuade** a president's ability to convince Congress, other political actors, and the public to cooperate with the administration's agenda
>
> **going public** a president's strategy of appealing to the public on an issue, expecting that public pressure will be brought to bear on other political actors

the dilemma of having high visibility and status but limited constitutional authority. Presidential frustration with the limits of the office is captured nicely by President Truman's remarks about his successor, President Eisenhower, a former general. "He'll sit here," Truman would remark (tapping his desk for emphasis), "and he'll say, 'Do this! Do that!' And nothing will happen. Poor Ike—it won't be a bit like the Army. He'll find it very frustrating."[44]

Yet people continue to run for and serve as president, and as we have seen, they deal with the expectations gap by attempting to augment their power with executive orders, executive agreements, claims of executive privilege, signing statements, and the like. All of these give the president some ability to act unilaterally. However, to be successful with larger policy initiatives, presidents seek to develop their primary extraconstitutional power, which is, in one scholar's phrase, the **power to persuade**.[45] To achieve what is expected of them, the argument goes, presidents must persuade others to cooperate with their agendas—most often members of Congress, but also the courts, the media, state and local officials, bureaucrats, foreign leaders, and especially the American public.

Other scholars, however, doubt that it is really persuasion alone that allows a president to get things done. They argue that little evidence indicates that presidents are able to influence important actors, or even the public, to change their policy priorities or preferences, and that presidents' substantial policy successes are due primarily to their ability to see and exploit existing opportunities. These may be political ambitions of members of Congress; latent concerns or yearnings in the public; or changes in public mood or media attention about unexpected events, such as the economic collapse of the 2008 Great Recession or the terrorist attacks of September 11, 2001. Presidents vary in their ability to capitalize on the political context they face as much as on their ability to single-handedly change minds, either in Washington or in the country at large.[46] Whether the power to persuade really works for presidents or not, sometimes it is all they have in their political tool box to get lawmakers to go along with their agendas.

GOING PUBLIC

A central strategy that presidents follow in their efforts to influence people "inside the Beltway" (that is, the Washington insiders) to go along with their agenda is to reach out and appeal to the public directly for support. This strategy of **going public** is based on the expectation that public support will put pressure on other politicians to give presidents what they want.[47] Presidents use their powers as both head of government and head of state to appeal to the public by creating

NICHOLAS KAMM/AFP/Getty Images

Awkward Bedfellows?

President-elect Donald Trump met with House Speaker Paul Ryan, R-Wisc., on November 10, 2016, on his first trip to the U.S. Capitol after the election. Ryan had stopped campaigning for Trump before the election but generally backed him up once he was president.

a narrative that will make what they want seem reasonable and necessary.[48] A president's effort to go public can include a trip to an international summit, a town meeting–style debate on a controversial issue, the president's annual State of the Union address or other nationally televised speeches, or White House conferences drawing experts and leaders together to promote presidential initiatives. The intention is to garner support among specific and strategically situated leaders who have the capacity to move on problems even in the face of continued congressional gridlock.[49]

THE PRESIDENCY AND THE MEDIA At the simplest level of the strategy of going public, presidents just take their case to the people. Consequently, presidential public appearances have increased greatly in the era of the modern presidency. Recent presidents have had some sort of public appearance almost every day of the week, year round. Knowing that the White House press corps will almost always get some airtime on network news, presidents want that coverage to be favorable. Shaping news coverage so that it supports the presidential narrative and generates favorable public opinion for the president is now standard operating procedure.[50] President Trump has largely taken his communications strategy into his own hands and runs it via Twitter and well-placed leaks to members of the media. Although this ensures that the media spotlight is always on him, he does not control the actual message as well as he could. The mainstream media are talking about Trump constantly, to be sure, but they are not always saying what he wants them to say.

THE RATINGS GAME Naturally, only a popular president can use the strategy of going public effectively, so popularity ratings become crucial to how successful a president can be. Since the 1930s the Gallup Organization has been asking people, "Do you approve or disapprove of the way [name of the current president] is handling his job as president?" The public's ratings of the president—that is, the percentage saying they approve of how the president is handling the job—varies from one president to the next and also typically rises and falls within any single presidential term. The president's ratings are a kind of political barometer: the higher they are, the more effective the president is with other political and economic actors; the lower they are, the harder the president finds it to get people to go along. For the modern presidency, the all-important power to persuade is intimately tied to presidential popularity. This is perhaps one of the greatest weaknesses Trump faces. By never reaching out beyond his base, his approval ratings have been remarkably steady but low. His base is with him, but few other Americans support him, which helped account for the blue wave of the 2018 midterm election.

Three factors in particular can affect a president's popularity: a cycle effect, the economy, and unifying or divisive current events:[51]

- The **cycle effect** refers to the tendency for most presidents to begin their terms of office with relatively high popularity ratings, which decline as they move through their four-year terms (see Figure 8.1). During the very early months of this cycle, often called the **honeymoon period**, presidents are frequently most effective with Congress. Often, but not always, presidential ratings rise going into reelection, but this seldom approaches the popularity the president had immediately after being elected the first time.

  The post-honeymoon drop in approval demonstrated in Figure 8.1 may occur because, by then, presidents have begun to try to fulfill the handsome promises on which they campaigned. Fulfilling promises requires political action, and as presidents exercise their head-of-government responsibilities, they lose the head-of-state glow they bring with them from the election. Political change seldom favors everyone equally, and when someone wins, someone else usually loses. Some citizens become disillusioned as the president makes divisive choices, acts as a partisan, or is attacked

---

cycle effect the predictable rise and fall of a president's popularity at different stages of a term in office

honeymoon period the time following an election when a president's popularity is high and congressional relations are likely to be productive

280   Chapter 8: The Presidency

by Congress and interests that do not favor the president's policies. The cycle effect means that presidents need to present their programs early, while they enjoy popular support. Unfortunately, much opportunity available during the honeymoon period can be squandered because of inexperience, as it was at the start of the Clinton administration. In contrast, President Obama chose as his first chief of staff Rahm Emanuel, a veteran Clinton White House staffer then serving in Congress. Emanuel was able to help Obama accomplish an unusually ambitious legislative agenda in the early years of his presidency. Obama continued to be effective with Congress long after his approval ratings left the honeymoon stage, passing in his first two years a major economic stimulus plan, health care reform, and a financial reform bill, along with many less comprehensive pieces of legislation. In fact, his achievements, coming in the context of a highly polarized political environment, probably helped to drive down his approval ratings.

- Another important factor that consistently influences presidential approval is the state of the economy. Since the administration of Franklin Roosevelt, the government has taken an active role in regulating the national economy, and every president promises economic prosperity. In practice, however, presidential power over the economy is quite limited, though we nevertheless hold our presidents accountable for economic performance. George H. W. Bush lost the presidency in large measure because of the prolonged recession in the latter part of his administration. Bill Clinton won it with a campaign focused on his plan for economic recovery. Obama came into office during the worst economic recession to hit the nation since the Great Depression of the 1930s. His ratings reflected a traditional honeymoon effect, but they dropped as unemployment rose and continued to decline as the economic recovery was slower than the public hoped. They rose right before his reelection in 2014 and again as the economy began to pick up real steam in 2016 as his term came to an end. President Trump's approval ratings show one of the anomalies of his presidency. With a thriving economy inherited from Obama, his ratings should be strong. It is because he is seen as such a divisive personality and because Americans are increasingly tribal in their politics that people can approve of the economy and still not give him credit.

- Newsworthy current events can also influence presidential approval. Presidents are judged by their response to events, even those beyond their control. For example, the public and the media looked to President Obama for a response to the BP oil disaster in 2010. Although the government could do little about the spill because it was dependent on BP for equipment and technological know-how to find a solution, Obama's ratings still took a hit as the oil continued to spill into the Gulf. Events like these are opportunities for establishing presidential leadership, and how presidents perform under such unexpected pressures influences their standing with the public and their long-term effectiveness. The disaster that followed Hurricane Maria in Puerto Rico was seen as the federal government's fault, but Trump's approval ratings did not take a hit—possibly because those who were going to disapprove of his handling of the storm's aftermath already disapproved of his job performance. His handling of the separation of refugee families at border controls may have had a greater impact on his ratings. He got a minor bump from the Kavanaugh confirmation, but it was short lived.

Besides being tests of a president's leadership, newsworthy events can be both divisive and unifying. Political controversy, almost by definition, is divisive and generally hurts presidential ratings. Of course, controversy in politics is unavoidable, even though the public at large is reluctant to accept this fact of democratic governance.[52]

On the flip side, unifying events can help presidential ratings. Television footage of the president signing agreements with other heads of state looks "presidential." Similarly, when a president leads the nation in conflict with other countries, the public rallies and the president's approval ratings improve, at least initially. President George H. W. Bush's rating soared during the 1990–1991 Gulf War, but those were topped by his son's ratings following the terrorist attacks of 2001 (see Figure 8.1). George W. Bush's administration framed subsequent legislation in terms of the war on terror, including tax cuts, energy policy, and military spending, all of which were on his agenda before September 11, and his high approval ratings helped him garner support for his agenda even from congressional Democrats. President Obama experienced a small bump in his approval ratings in spring 2011 after he announced the killing of Osama bin Laden, but it did not translate into leverage with the Republican Congress, which soon helped to send Obama's numbers south again in the wake of the debt ceiling crisis later that summer and continued legislative inaction.

Thus modern presidents necessarily play the ratings game.[53] Those who choose not to play suffer the consequences: Truman, Johnson, and Ford tended not to heed

FIGURE 8.1

Average Quarterly Presidential Approval Ratings, Eisenhower to Trump

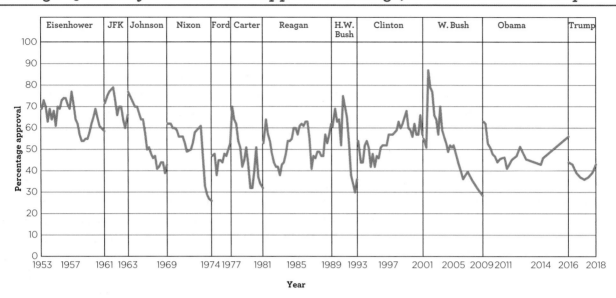

Source: Quarterly data for 1953–2000 provided by Robert S. Erikson; developed for Robert S. Erikson, James A. Stimson, and Michael B. MacKuen, The Macro Polity (Cambridge, U.K.: Cambridge University Press, 2002); data for 2001–2018 calculated by authors from the Gallup Organization.

Note: Respondents were asked, "Do you approve or disapprove of the way [name of the current president] is handling his job as president?"

the polls so closely, and they either had a hard time in office or were not reelected.[54] Trump pays incredibly close attention to the polls, but he is not willing to do the outreach that could raise his standing. Unless he experiences some huge foreign policy success, it is hard to think of what might cause a change in his remarkably steady ratings.

WORKING WITH CONGRESS

Presidents do not always try to influence Congress by going public. They must often deal directly with Congress itself, and sometimes they combine strategies and deal with the public and Congress at the same time. The Constitution gives the primary lawmaking powers to Congress. Thus, to be successful with their policy agendas, presidents need congressional cooperation. This depends in part on the president's reputation with members of that institution and other Washington elites for being an effective leader.[55] Such success varies with several factors, including the compatibility of the president's and Congress' goals and the party composition of Congress.

SHARED POWERS AND CONFLICTING POLICY GOALS Presidents and members of Congress usually

define the nation's problems and possible solutions in different ways. In addition to the philosophical and partisan differences that may exist between the president and members of Congress, each has different constituencies to please. The president, as the one leader elected by the whole nation, needs to take a wider, more encompassing view of the national interest. Members of Congress have relatively narrow constituencies and tend to represent their particular interests. Thus, in many cases, members of Congress do not want the same things the president does.

What can presidents do to get their legislation through a Congress made up of members whose primary concern is with their individual constituencies? For one thing, presidents have a staff of assistants to work with Congress. The **legislative liaison** office specializes in determining what members of Congress are most concerned about, what they need, and how legislation can be tailored to get their support. In some cases, members just want their views to be heard; they do not want to be taken for granted. In other

> **legislative liaison** executive personnel who work with members of Congress to secure their support in getting a president's legislation passed

cases, the details of the president's program have to be explained adequately. It is electorally useful for members to have this done in person, by the president, complete with photo opportunities for release to the papers back home.

Presidential candidates often claim to be running for office as "outsiders," politicians removed from the politics-as-usual world of Washington and therefore untainted by its self-interest and strife. This can just be a campaign ploy, but when presidents such as Jimmy Carter and Bill Clinton were elected who truly did lack experience in Washington politics, they failed to understand the sensitivities of members of Congress and the dynamics of sharing powers. President Carter, even though he had a healthy Democratic majority, had a very difficult time with Congress because he did not realize that, from the perspective of Capitol Hill, what Jimmy Carter believed was good for the nation might not be considered best for each member.[56] Subsequent presidents seem to have learned from Carter's experience. Donald Trump, with less government experience than any previous president and fewer political contacts to rely on, has had special challenges in this respect. He succeeded in getting a tax cut passed and justices confirmed to the Court only because those were also the goals of Republicans in Congress. Other priorities like his border wall have not fared as well.

PARTISANSHIP AND DIVIDED GOVERNMENT

When the president and the majority of Congress are of the same party, the president is more successful at getting programs passed. When presidents face **divided government**—that is, when the president is of a different party than the majority in one or both houses—they do not do as well.[57] Part of the problem is that, in our highly polarized politics today, passage of a bill supported by the president is evaluated not only in terms of policy impact but also as giving a victory to the president, which is something the opposition is loath to do.

An equally important part of the problem of divided government is that members of different parties stand for different approaches and solutions to the nation's problems. Democratic presidents and members of Congress tend to be more liberal than the average citizen, and Republican presidents and members of Congress tend to be more conservative.

Figure 8.2 shows a hypothetical example of the position that a Democratic president would take in dealing with a Democratic-led Congress. When the same party controls Congress and the presidency, the two institutions can cooperate

> **divided government** the situation that exists when political rule is split between two parties, in which one controls the White House and the other controls one or both houses of Congress

relatively easily on ideological issues because the majority party wants to go in the same direction as the president. The president offers his or her own position but is happy to cooperate with the Democratic majority on proposal A because this is much closer to what he or she wants than is the status quo or the opposition party's proposal. This reflects the situation for two years after the 2008 election, when the Democrats had won the presidency along with continuing control of both houses of Congress. With substantial and sympathetic Democratic majorities in Congress, President Obama set a record for getting his bills through Congress (see Figure 8.3).

Consider how drastically the situation changes under divided government. If the hypothetical Republican Congress sent a bill like proposal B to the Democratic president, he or she would veto it, preferring the alternative of no bill, the status quo, to what Congress passed. Under divided government, Congress tends to ignore what the president wants, and the president tends to veto what the opposition majority party in Congress offers. In fact, after the 2014 midterms, both the House and the Senate were in Republican hands and with Obama in the White House, that's exactly how the scenario played out.

Under divided government, presidents are not likely to succeed at getting their agendas met. Figure 8.3 shows the percentage of bills passed that were supported by each president from Eisenhower to Obama. Notice that the success rate is consistently higher under unified government (orange bars). Dramatic examples of the impact of divided government can be seen in Bill Clinton's, George W. Bush's, and Barack Obama's administrations. For his first two years in office, Clinton worked with a Democratic majority in both houses, and Congress passed 86 percent of the bills he supported. The next two years the Republicans had a majority in both houses, and Clinton's success rate dropped to 46 percent.[58] Bush enjoyed impressive success, with an average of more than three-quarters of his favored bills enacted into law when he had Republican majorities in Congress. But when Bush had to deal with a Democratic Congress after the 2006 midterm election, his success rate dropped dramatically. With 96.7 percent of his preferred bills making it into law, Obama in 2009 had the most successful year of any president in the fifty-six years that *Congressional Quarterly* has been keeping track. These results are attributable to the large Democratic majorities in the House and the Senate, coupled with the president's ambitious agenda and a tanking economy that required action.[59] The 2010 midterm elections, which replaced the Democratic majority in the House of Representatives with a conservative Republican majority, spelled an end to Obama's high rate of success, dropping from an average of 91 percent under the Democratic majority to just over 55 percent in his years facing a Republican

FIGURE 8.2

Hypothetical Policy Alternatives Under Unified and Divided Government

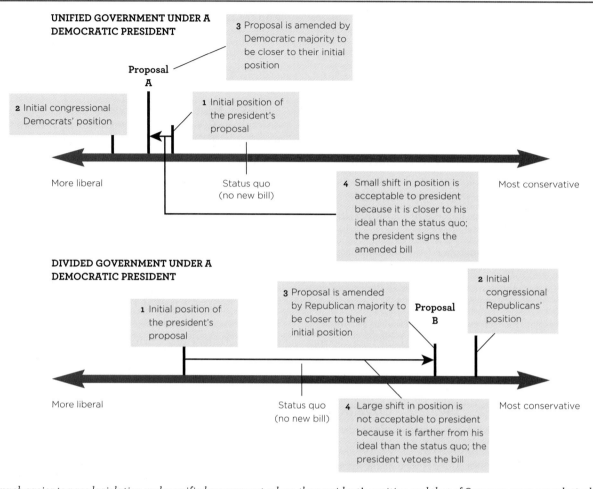

It is much easier to pass legislation under unified government, where the president's position and that of Congress start out relatively close together, than under divided government, where a large gap exists between the initial positions of the president and Congress. Presidential success in getting bills passed is much higher under unified government than it is when the opposition party has a majority in Congress.

House. Although Trump did not face a divided government in his first two years, his party's own divided priorities and the lack of congruence between his agenda and theirs led to a mostly stalemated legislative record. They passed a tax cut and approved a steady stream of federal judges, but most of Congress does not want to build a wall on the border or pass draconian immigration legislation.

Now that Trump does face divided government, he has a choice—either to keep playing to his base or to do what Bill Clinton did and work with the other party to make deals where they could find common ground. It requires a fair amount of consistency and compromise to do that, however, and a willingness to take on one's own base, and Trump has not shown any desire to do that.

Divided government, however, does not doom Washington to inaction. When national needs are pressing or the public mood seems to demand action, the president and opposition majorities have managed to pass important legislation.[60] For example, the government was divided with a Democrat in the White House and Republicans in control of both houses of Congress when major welfare reform was passed with the Personal Responsibility and Work Opportunity Act of 1996. But national needs do not always cause Congress to step up. In 2011 and 2012, Congress was unable to agree on policies to deal with revenue shortfalls and the budget, or even the previously routine extension of the national debt limit to enable it to pay its bills. This brinksmanship has played out repeatedly in an era of polarized politics with one party at odds within itself.

FIGURE 8.3

Presidential Success Under Unified and Divided Government, Eisenhower to Trump

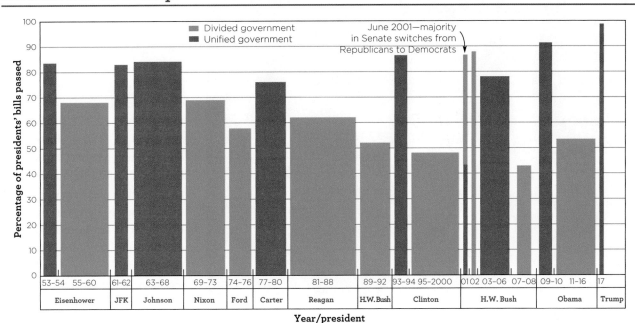

When presidents face divided government—that is, when the opposing party controls one or both houses of Congress—they usually find it harder to get their bills passed.

Source: Data from "Presidential Support Background," *CQ Weekly*, January 11, 2010, 117; "Table 6-7: Presidential Victories on Votes in Congress, 1953–2010," in Harold W. Stanley and Richard G. Niemi, eds., *Vital Statistics on American Politics 2011-2012* (Washington, D.C.: CQ Press, 2011), 246–248; Sam Goldfarb, "2011 Vote Studies: Presidential Support," *CQ Weekly*, January 16, 2012, 98–104; Shawn Zeller, "2012 Vote Studies: Presidential Support," *CQ Weekly*, January 21, 2013; Emily Ethridge, "2013 Vote Studies: Presidential Support," *CQ Weekly*, February 3, 2014; Shawn Zeller, CQ Staff, "2014 Vote Studies: Running on Empty," *CQ Weekly*, March 16, 2015, 26; CQ Staff, "2015 Vote Studies: Presidential Support Hits Low for Obama," *CQ Weekly*, February 8, 2016; CQ Staff, "CQ Vote Studies: Next Hit: Presidential Support— Trump Divided, Conquered," *CQ Weekly*, February 12, 2018.

PAUSE AND REVIEW Who, What, How

Presidents want to get their policy agendas enacted with congressional cooperation and to get and maintain the public approval necessary to keep the expanded powers they need to do their job. They try to accomplish these goals with their constitutional powers, by maintaining their reputation among Washington elites as an effective leader, by building coalitions among members of Congress, by going public, by skillfully using the media, and by trying to keep the economy healthy.

Citizens have an enormous amount of power in this regard because, distant though Washington may seem to most citizens, presidents are driven by the need for public approval to get most of the things they want. Congress too has goals: members want to get policy passed so that they may go home to the voters and claim to have supported their interests and to have brought home the bacon. Legislators need to meet the expectations of a different constituency than does the president, but few members of Congress want to be seen by the voters as an obstacle to a popular president. Presidents who have a strong reputation inside Washington and who have broad popularity outside come to Congress with a distinct advantage, and members of Congress will go out of their way to cooperate and compromise with them.

In Your Own Words Identify strategies and tools presidents employ to overcome the constitutional limitations of the office.

MANAGING THE PRESIDENTIAL ESTABLISHMENT

The challenges of supervising an unwieldy bureaucracy

We tend to think of the president as one person—what one presidential scholar calls the "single executive image."[61] However, despite all the formal and informal powers of the presidency, presidents are limited in what they can accomplish on their own. In fact, the modern president is one individual at the top of a large and complex organization called the presidency, which itself heads the even larger executive branch of government. George Washington got by with no

THE CABINET

Each department in the executive branch is headed by a presidential appointee; collectively these appointees form the president's cabinet. Today the cabinet comprises fifteen posts heading up fifteen departments. The newest cabinet-level department is the Department of Homeland Security, created in 2003. The cabinet is not explicitly set up in the Constitution, though the founders were well aware that the president would need specialty advisers in certain areas. President Washington's cabinet included just secretaries of state, treasury, and war (now called the secretary of defense). The original idea was for the cabinet members to be the president's men overseeing areas for which the president was responsible but that he was unable to supervise personally.

All of that has changed. Today presidents consider the demands of organized interests and the political groups and the stature of their administration in putting together the cabinet. The number of departments has grown as various interests (for example, farmers, veterans, workers) have pressed for cabinet-level representation. Appointments to the cabinet in part serve presidential political goals. Thus the cabinet secretaries typically are chosen with an eye to the constituencies most affected by the departments, and Democrats and Republicans will not always choose the same sort of person to fill a cabinet post. For example, a Democratic president would be likely to choose a labor leader for secretary of labor, whereas a Republican president would be more likely to fill the post with a representative of the business community.

Presidents may also seek ethnic and gender balance in their cabinet choices. Bill Clinton followed through on his promise to appoint a cabinet of exceptional diversity, and George W. Bush's first- and second-term cabinets followed suit. Bush had two Hispanics, two African Americans, and two Asian Americans serving in his second-term cabinet; four cabinet members were women. In addition, the president tends to choose cabinet members who have independent stature and reputation before their appointments. President Obama borrowed from Abraham Lincoln's notion of building a "team of rivals" when he appointed Hillary Clinton (whom he defeated for the 2008 Democratic Party nomination) to be

Cabinet Battle

Presidents choose their cabinet members, but that doesn't mean they all get along. Disagreements between Secretary of State Thomas Jefferson and Secretary of the Treasury Alexander Hamilton were famously fierce during George Washington's administration, as the two locked horns over such issues as national debt and relations with France. Their arguments are presented as rap battles in the hit Broadway musical Hamilton, *shown here.*

staff to speak of and consulted with his small cabinet of just three department heads, but citizens' expectations of government, and consequently the sheer size of the government, have grown considerably since then, and so has the machinery designed to manage that government. We mentioned earlier that a president without the skills to successfully manage this machinery can be seen as weak because running the executive branch is his charge.

Today the executive branch is composed of the cabinet with its fifteen departments, the Executive Office of the President, and the White House staff, amounting altogether to hundreds of agencies and two million civilian employees and almost a million and a half active-duty military employees. Modern presidents require a vast bureaucracy to help them make the complex decisions they face daily, but at the same time the bureaucracy itself presents a major management challenge. The reality of the modern presidency is that presidents are limited in their ability to accomplish what they want by the necessity of dealing with this complex bureaucracy. The executive bureaucracy becomes part of the "how" through which presidents try to get what they want—for the country, their party, or themselves as politicians. But at the same time, the executive branch becomes another "who," a player in government that goes after its own goals and whose goals can conflict with those of the president.

his first secretary of state and when he retained Bush's secretary of defense, Robert Gates. Trump's norm-busting behavior might be most on show in his cabinet choices. Late in making many of his decisions, picking people with no experience, leaving many candidate unvetted, removing people from office after a short time, choosing people best known for working in the industries they would be in charge of regulating, and requiring that cabinet secretaries publicly praise him in meetings, Trump has treated the Cabinet as a less august and more personal board of directors than other presidents. The president's sense of legitimacy is typically underscored by having top-quality people working in the administration, but Trump has seemed unconcerned with this. Generally presidents want people who are ideologically similar to them in the policy areas they will be handling.[62] This is not easily achieved (and may not be possible) given the other considerations presidents must weigh, but Trump has been less shy about putting personal loyalty and getting his own way over other considerations.

The combination of these factors in making cabinet choices—political payoffs to organized interests, and the legitimacy provided by top people in the area—often results in a "team" that may not necessarily be focused on carrying out the president's agenda. There are exceptions to the typically guarded relationship between cabinet members and the president, but they prove the rule. President Kennedy appointed his brother Robert as attorney general. George H. W. Bush appointed his very close friend and personal adviser James Baker as Treasury secretary. In these cases, however, the close relationship with the president preceded appointment to the cabinet. In general, the political considerations of their appointment, coupled with their independent outlook, mean that cabinet members will provide the president with a variety of views and perspectives. They do not usually, as a group, place loyalty to the president's agenda above other considerations in their advice to the president. Consequently, presidents tend to centralize their decision making by

relying more on their advisers in the Executive Office of the President for advice they can trust.[63]

EXECUTIVE OFFICE OF THE PRESIDENT

The **Executive Office of the President** (EOP) is a collection of organizations that form the president's own bureaucracy. Instituted by Franklin Roosevelt in 1939, the EOP was designed specifically to serve the president's interests, supply information, and provide expert advice.[64] Among the organizations established in the EOP is the **Office of Management and Budget** (OMB), which helps presidents to exert control over the departments and agencies of the federal bureaucracy by overseeing all their budgets. The director of OMB works to ensure that the budget reflects the president's own policy agenda. Potential regulations created by the agencies of the national government must be approved by OMB before going into effect. This gives the president an additional measure of control over what the bureaucracy does.

Because modern presidents are held responsible for the performance of the economy, all presidents attempt to bring about healthy economic conditions. The job of the **Council of Economic Advisers** is to predict for presidents where the economy is going and to suggest ways to achieve economic growth without much inflation.

The **National Security Council** (NSC) gives the president daily updates about events around the world. The NSC's job is to provide the president with information and advice about foreign affairs; however, the council's role has expanded at times into actually carrying out policy—sometimes illegally, as in the Iran-contra affair.[65] When the existing federal bureaucracy is less than fully cooperative with the president's wishes, some presidents have simply bypassed the agencies by running policy from the White House. One strategy that presidents since Nixon have followed is to appoint so-called policy czars who have responsibility for supervising policy across agencies. Obama used this strategy extensively to coordinate policy in such areas as health care, energy, and the economy. He made over forty of these appointments in his first term, to establish firm White House control over the bureaucracy.[66]

WHITE HOUSE STAFF

Closest to the president, both personally and politically, are the members of the **White House Office**, which is included as a separate unit of the EOP. White House staffers have offices in the White House, and their appointments do not have to be confirmed by the Senate. Just as the public focus on the presidency has grown, so has the size of the president's staff. The White House staff, around 60 members under Roosevelt, grew to the 300–400 range under Eisenhower and in 2013 rested at about 460.[67] Presidential scholar James P.

Executive Office of the President the collection of organizations that help the president with policy and political objectives

Office of Management and Budget the organization within the Executive Office of the President that oversees the budgets of departments and agencies

Council of Economic Advisers the organization within the Executive Office of the President that advises the president on economic matters

National Security Council the organization within the Executive Office of the President that provides foreign policy advice to the president

White House Office the more than four hundred employees within the EOP who work most closely and directly with the president

FIGURE 8.4

Organization of the White House Office

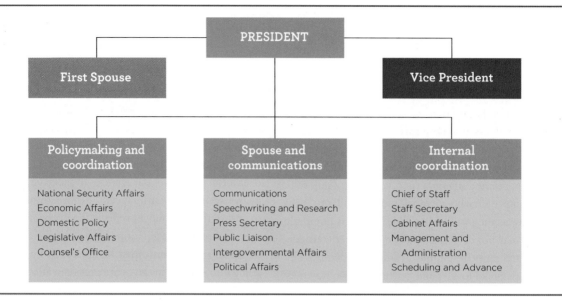

Pfiffner has described this organization generally in terms of the following three functional categories: policymaking and coordination, outreach and communications, and internal coordination (see Figure 8.4).

Central to the White House Office is the president's **chief of staff**, who is responsible for the operation of all White House personnel. Depending on how much power the president delegates, the chief of staff may decide who gets appointments with the president and whose memoranda the president reads. The chief of staff also has a big hand in hiring and firing decisions at the White House. Critics claim that chiefs of staff isolate the presidents they serve by removing them from the day-to-day control of their administrations, but demands on presidents have grown to the point that a chief of staff is now considered a necessity. Presidents Carter and Ford tried to get by without a chief of staff, but each gave up and appointed one in the middle of his term to make his political life more manageable.[68]

The chief of staff and the other top assistants to presidents have to be their eyes and ears, and they act on the president's behalf every day. The criteria for a good staffer are very different from those for a cabinet selection. First and foremost, the president demands loyalty. That is why presidents typically bring along old friends and close campaign staff as personal assistants. Although Donald Trump asked Republican National Committee chair Reince Priebus to be his chief of staff after the 2016 election, Priebus did not last long in a dysfunctional West Wing. He was soon replaced with John Kelly, Trump's Secretary of

Homeland Security. Kelly, with a military background, did a better job of focusing the president's attention and managing HIS schedule, but Trump is a person who notoriously does not like to be managed and it is possible that Kelly's days too will turn out to be numbered. If he had his way, Trump would probably prefer not to have any chief of staff at all.

A general principle that presidents employ is that their staffs exist only to serve them. When things go well, the president gets the credit; when they do not, the staff take the blame, sometimes even being fired or asked to resign. Such replacements are not unusual at all as presidents change personnel and management strategies to maximize their policy effectiveness and political survival.

The different backgrounds, objectives, and constituencies of the White House staff and the cabinet mean that the two groups are often at odds. The cabinet secretaries, dedicated to large departmental missions, want presidential attention for those efforts; the staff want the departments to put the president's immediate political goals ahead of their departmental interests. As a result, the past several decades have seen more centralization of important policymaking in the White House, and more decisions being taken away from the traditional turf of the departments.[69]

> **chief of staff** the person who oversees the operations of all White House staff and is traditionally expected to control access to the president

Right-Hand Man

Vice presidents have only as much power and influence as the president allows, and vice presidents traditionally were relegated to ceremonial duties. But that trend has changed significantly in recent administrations. John F. Kennedy chose former rival Lyndon Johnson as his running mate for political reasons and he never became a trusted advisor. Barack Obama and his vice president, Joe Biden, however, grew to have a close relationship, both personally and professionally.

THE VICE PRESIDENT

For most of our history, vice presidents have not been important actors in presidential administrations. Because the original Constitution awarded the vice presidency to the second-place presidential candidate, these officials were seen as potential rivals to the president and were excluded from most decisions and any meaningful policy responsibility. That was corrected with the Twelfth Amendment (1804), which provided for electors to select both the president and the vice president. However, custom for most of the period since then has put a premium on balancing the ticket in terms of regional, ideological, or political interests, which has meant that the person in the second spot is typically not close to the president. In fact, the vice president has sometimes been a rival even in modern times, as when John F. Kennedy appointed Lyndon Johnson, the Senate majority leader from Texas, as his vice president in 1960 in an effort to gain support from the southern states.

Since the Constitution provides only that the vice president acts as president of the Senate, which carries no power unless there is a tie vote, most vice presidents have tried to make small, generally insignificant jobs seem important, often admitting that theirs was not an enviable post. Thomas Marshall, Woodrow Wilson's vice president, observed in his inaugural address that "I believe I'm entitled to make a few remarks because I'm about to enter a four-year period of silence."[70] Roosevelt's first vice president, John Nance Garner, expressed his disdain for the office

even more forcefully, saying that the job "is not worth a pitcher of warm piss."[71]

Ultimately, however, the job of vice president is what the president wants it to be. President Reagan largely ignored George H. W. Bush, for instance, whereas Al Gore, serving under President Bill Clinton, had a central advisory role.[72] Dick Cheney brought a good deal of Washington experience upon which President George W. Bush relied heavily, so much so that many observers have portrayed Cheney as the real power behind the throne.[73]

President Obama's vice president, Joe Biden, brought the heft of a lengthy résumé from six terms in the U.S. Senate and his longtime service on the Senate Foreign Relations Committee. Obama did not relinquish as much authority to his vice president as Bush did, but Biden proved to be an effective, independent, and valued policy adviser to the president. He was an administration spokesperson on a wide range of issues, including his specialty area of foreign relations.[74] (See *Profiles in Citizenship*.) Donald Trump picked Indiana governor Mike Pence, ostensibly as a gesture to reassure traditional social conservatives. Pence's role as legislator and governor was also a good counterpoint to Trump's lack of governing experience.

Thus, even though the office of the vice presidency is not a powerful one, vice presidents who establish a relationship of trust with the president can have a significant impact on public policy. The office is important as well, of course, because it is the vice president who assumes the presidency if the president dies, is incapacitated, resigns, or is impeached. Many vice presidents also find the office a

PROFILES IN CITIZENSHIP
Joe Biden

Scott Kowalchyk/CBS via Getty Images

Our interview with Vice President Joe Biden took place in the thick of the administration's negotiations with congressional Republicans over extending the tax cuts, and Biden was the negotiator-in-chief. We were slotted in for an appointment in his White House office between cabinet members who wanted to discuss the implications of agreeing to extend the Bush tax cuts for the country's wealthiest citizens, and Nancy Pelosi and Harry Reid, who were adamantly opposed to extending the tax cuts for the wealthy. By late afternoon it would be announced that, due in large part to Biden's bargaining, the White House had gotten much of what it wanted in the tax cut deal.

That day in early December, the vice president clearly relished his role in brokering the deal and he was eloquent and hopeful about the possibilities of using power to good purpose. It's a great time to be in service, he says, what he calls "the single greatest opportunity" in his forty years of public life. "We are in one of those inflection points in history," he says, "I don't think it's occurred in American history but three times, where . . . if we do nothing, the momentum is going to drag us in the direction that makes it increasingly more difficult to correct the course."

Being a key actor in a transformational moment is a pretty heady place to be for someone who started life as a working-class kid from Scranton, Pennsylvania. How he got from there to here is an unlikely story but in some ways a quintessentially American one. Biden was born to a large Irish-Catholic family that moved, in time, to Delaware, but it was in his "Grandpop" Finnegan's kitchen in Scranton that he learned the first principles of politics: that no one and no group is above any other and that politics was a matter of personal honor.[1] Those themes have guided Biden's career, through his college years, law school, a stint on the New Castle County Council, and a long-shot candidacy for the U.S. Senate when he was only twenty-nine years old that launched the thirty-six years he spent in that institution before he joined the Obama ticket and ascended to the vice presidency.

You can tell by his face, as he talks about his career, that it has been fun. He says, "My dad used to have an expression, he'd say it's a lucky person that gets up in the morning, puts both feet on the floor, knows what they are about to do, and thinks it still matters."

He has more power than the traditional vice president, serving as an essential liaison with Congress for the Obama administration (witness his work with McConnell on the tax cut extension) and as a key adviser to the president on foreign policy and issues facing the middle class. Asked whether he can stay optimistic in the face of partisan battles at home and dire challenges abroad, he lights up. "Absolutely, I am absolutely optimistic," he says. "I've been here for eight presidents, and I'm an optimist because I know the history of the story of American progress. I mean the American people have never ever, never shied away when you've given them a vision, a challenge, and you know where you want to take it. They've never let the country down, never. That's not American exceptionalism. I would argue, as a student of history, that that's literally true, literally true; we rise to the occasion."

And the boy from Scranton is right in the middle of it. Here are some other words of advice from the vice president:

On the importance of confidence

"The great advantage I had is that I don't ever remember a time my parents not drilling into me—'You're a man of your word, without your word you're not a man. Joey, nobody is better than you in the whole world, you're no better but nobody is better than you.' My mother gave me absolute confidence. It was a gigantic, gigantic asset."

On keeping the republic

"I'd tell [students] to be engaged. . . . [Y]ou know that old quote from Plato, the penalty good men pay for not being engaged in politics is being governed by men worse than themselves. [Students] have nobody to blame but themselves, zero. My dad used to say never complain and never explain, and . . . that's exactly what I'd tell them . . . stop whining, get engaged. Number two, the political system is so wide open you can drive a Mack truck through it, so the idea that 'Oh, God, I have to come from influence and money to have an impact?' Simply not true."

Source: Joe Biden talked with Christine Barbour, Gerald Wright, and Patrick Haney on December 6, 2010.

---

1. Joe Biden, *Promises to Keep.* (New York: Random House, 2007), xv.

good launching pad for a presidential bid. Four of the last ten vice presidents—Lyndon Johnson, Richard Nixon, Gerald Ford, and George H. W. Bush—ended up in the Oval Office, although Al Gore did not enjoy similar success in 2000.

THE FIRST SPOUSE

The office of the "first lady" is undergoing immense changes that reflect the tremendous flux in Americans' perceptions of the appropriate roles for men and women. Even the term "first lady" seems strangely antiquated in an age when a woman came within a whisper of winning the presidency. The office of first lady contains controversial elements, partly because of conflicts over the role of women in politics, but also because the intimate relationship between husband and wife gives the presidential spouse, an unelected position, unique insight into and access to the president's mind and decision-making processes. For all the checks and balances in the American system, there is no way to check the influence of the first spouse.

Our first ladies' attempts to play a political role are almost as old as the Republic. In fact, as her husband, John, was preparing to help with the writing of the Constitution, future first lady Abigail Adams admonished him to "remember the ladies," although there is no evidence that he actually did. Much later, in 1919, first lady Edith Bolling Galt Wilson virtually took over the White House following the illness of her husband, Woodrow, controlling who had access to him and perhaps even issuing presidential decisions in his name. And Eleanor Roosevelt, like her husband, Franklin, took vigorously to political life and kept up an active public role even after his death.

Since the 1960s and the advent of the women's movement, the role of the first lady is seen by the public as less an issue of individual personality and quirks, and more a national commentary on how women in general should behave. As a surrogate for our cultural confusion on what role women should play, the office of the first lady came under uncommon scrutiny, especially when she took on a more overtly political role, as did Rosalynn Carter, who even attended cabinet meetings at her husband's request. Hillary Rodham Clinton shook up public expectations of the first lady's role even more. A successful lawyer who essentially earned the family income while her husband, Bill, served four low-paid terms as governor of Arkansas, Clinton was the target of both public acclaim and public hatred. Her nontraditional tenure as first lady was capped in 2000 by her election as the junior senator from New York. Eight years later she made her own nearly successful run for the Democratic nomination for president, became Obama's

Writing Their Own Job Description
First Lady Michelle Obama shares a giggle with Secretary of State Hillary Rodham Clinton at an event in 2010. Clinton redefined the role of first lady and served in a number of political capacities before becoming the first female major-party presidential candidate in 2016. Michelle Obama for the most part chose a more traditional path, raising public awareness about health and nutrition and reaching out to military families. She has said she has no political aspirations of her own.

secretary of state, earned the Democratic presidential nomination in 2016, and capped an astonishing career by becoming the first female major-party candidate for the office and winning the popular vote.

Most first spouses have not taken on as overtly a political role as Hillary Clinton. The politically safest strategy for a first spouse appears to be to stick with a noncontroversial moral issue. Lady Bird Johnson beseeched us to support highway beautification; Nancy Reagan suggested, less successfully, that we "just say no" to drugs; and Laura Bush focused on the issues of education, youth, and literacy.

First lady Michelle Obama said flatly that she did not intend to take on an active policymaking role. "I can't do everything," she explained. A committed and active mother to two children still at home, she wanted to keep their lives as normal as possible while living in the White House. Insofar as she took on a public role, it was in the noncontroversial styles of Reagan and Bush, as an advocate for working parents, particularly those in the military, who juggle career loads with the demands of raising families, and as a strong supporter of a healthy diet as an antidote to rising childhood obesity rates.[75] Avoiding policy and partisan conflict, Michelle Obama has had popularity ratings much higher than the president's.[76] Ironically, she was able to parlay that popularity into becoming one of Hillary Clinton's most powerful and eloquent surrogates on the campaign trail.

Melania Trump has been more mysterious than most first ladies. Trump's third wife, she did not move into the White

House right away because she did not want to take their young son Barron out of school in New York. After moving to Washington, she stayed mostly out of the public spotlight, especially during some embarrassing scandals concerning Donald Trump's extramarital behavior. In spring 2018 she launched an initiative called "Be Best" focused on children and aimed specifically at well-being, positive social media use, and the effects of opioid abuse.

PAUSE AND REVIEW Who, What, How

The purpose of the executive bureaucracy is to help presidents to do their job by providing information, expertise, and advice. Although presidents' closest advisers are usually focused on the president's interests, various cabinet officers, staff members, and agency heads may develop agendas of their own that may be at odds with those of the president. The president has an easier time controlling members of the Executive Office of the President, whose job is more clearly to serve the president. The vice president and first spouse are also more likely to find an agenda that is consistent with the president's.

In Your Own Words Describe the organization and functions of the executive office.

THE PRESIDENTIAL PERSONALITY

Translating leadership style and image into presidential power

Effective management of the executive branch is one feature of a successful presidency, but there are many others. Historians and presidential observers regularly distinguish presidential success and failure, even to the extent of actually rating presidential greatness.[77] Political scientists also assess presidential success, usually in terms of how frequently presidents can get their legislative programs passed by Congress.[78] We have already discussed the powers of the president, the challenges to success provided by the need for popularity, the difficulties of dealing with Congress, and the enormous management tasks faced by the president. In this section we look at the personal resources of a president that lead to success or contribute to failure. We begin by exploring what kinds of people are driven to become president in the first place.

CLASSIFYING PRESIDENTIAL CHARACTER

Most presidents share some personality characteristics—giant ambition and large egos, for instance—but this does not mean that they are carbon copies of one another. They clearly differ in fundamental ways. A number of scholars have developed classification schemes of presidential personalities. Each of these schemes is based on the expectation that knowing key dimensions of individual presidential personalities will help explain, or even predict, how presidents will behave in certain circumstances. The most famous of these schemes was developed by James David Barber, who classified presidents on two dimensions: their energy level (passive or active) and their orientation toward life (positive or negative).[79]

Some of our best and most popular presidents have been active-positives. They have had great energy and a very positive orientation toward the job of being president. Franklin Roosevelt, John F. Kennedy, Bill Clinton, and Barack Obama represent this type. Others have had less energy (passives) or have been burdened by the job of being president (negatives). They have acted out their roles, according to Barber, as they thought they should, out of duty or obligation. Ronald Reagan and George W. Bush fit the model of the passive-positive president. They liked being leaders but believed that the job was one of delegating and setting the tone rather than of taking an active policymaking role. Richard Nixon is usually offered as one of the clearest examples of an active-negative president; he had lots of energy but could not enjoy the job of being president. Even after two years it is difficult to classify Donald Trump—he probably falls more toward a passive-negative. He rarely looks as though he is enjoying being president, his tweets reveal a lot of personal disgruntlement, and his frequent weekends playing golf make it clear that he misses his old life very much. Stymied in getting some of his signature domestic programs through Congress, he took on a more active foreign policy stance.

Assessing individual personalities is a fascinating enterprise, but it is fraught with danger. Few politicians fit neatly into Barber's boxes (or the categories of other personality theorists) in an unambiguous way. Although some scholars find that personality analysis adds greatly to their understanding of the differences among presidencies, others discount it altogether, claiming that it leads one to overlook the ways in which rules and external forces have shaped the modern presidency.[80]

PRESIDENTIAL STYLE

In addition to their personality differences, presidents strive to create their own **presidential style**, an image that captures symbolically who the president is for the American people and for leaders of other nations. These personal differences in how presidents present themselves are real, but they are also carefully cultivated. Presidents also strive to distinguish themselves from their predecessors, to set themselves apart, and to give hope for new, and presumably better, presidential leadership.[81]

For example, Harry Truman was known for his straight, sometimes profane, talk and no-nonsense decision making. In contrast, Dwight Eisenhower developed his "Victorious General" image as a statesman above the fray of petty day-to-day politics. John F. Kennedy, whose term followed Eisenhower's, evoked a theme of "getting the country moving again" and embodied this with a personal image of youth and energy.

In the wake of Watergate and Richard Nixon's disgrace, Jimmy Carter hit a winning note with a somewhat austere style promising honesty and competent government. In contrast, an eager public soaked up Ronald Reagan's "it's-morning-in-America" optimism and his calming, grandfatherly presence.

Bill Clinton's style combined the image of the highly intellectual Rhodes scholar with that of a compassionate leader, famous for "feeling America's pain." That carefully managed image could not disguise the fact that Clinton was also a man of large appetites, however, from his jogging breaks to eat at McDonald's to his extramarital affairs. While people approved of Clinton's leadership through the end of his presidency, a majority of citizens noted concerns about his honesty and moral character.

George W. Bush came into office with an opposite set of characteristics. Widely perceived as a nonintellectual who joked that C students could grow up to be president, he cultivated the image of the chief executive officer he was: a president primarily interested in results, not academic debates, who was willing to set a course and leave others to get the job done. Despite a reputation for high living in his youth, Bush's pledge of abstinence, traditional marriage, and frequent references to Jesus Christ helped to put a moral tone on his presidency that Clinton's had lacked.

Barack Obama brought an even-keeled, introvert's disposition to the White House. His calm demeanor (symbolized by the unofficial slogan of his first campaign—"No Drama Obama") remained consistent through the economic and environmental crises of the first term of his presidency. As he said of himself, "I don't get too high when things are going

The Great Communicator

This was the label many people applied to President Ronald Reagan because of his ability to connect with the American public. His effectiveness as a communicator had little to do with explaining complex policy decisions. Rather, he conveyed a sense of confidence, trustworthiness, and warmth. He made people feel good.

well, and I don't get too low when things are going tough."[82] Obama's image incorporated elements of the styles of several of his predecessors, combining Ronald Reagan's optimism, Bill Clinton's braininess, and George W. Bush's faith and commitment to family.

At least one part of his presidential style seemed to be uniquely Obama's own. In his first term, he brought to office a deep commitment to bipartisanship that had given way, by the end of his second term, to a more confrontational posture with respect to congressional Republicans as he fought to solidify his legacy.

As we have seen repeatedly, Donald Trump's presidential style is his own. We have already seen his brash and flamboyant television personality, and his willingness to say whatever comes into his mind, regardless of who might be offended by it. Although his supporters liked what they called his lack of political correctness, commentators kept waiting for Trump to pivot to a more presidential style through his first two

presidential style the image that presidents project that represents how they would like to be perceived at home and abroad

Courtesy of Ronald Reagan Library

Political Comedy

Since America's infancy, mockery has been a weapon of choice for those seeking to speak truth to power. A hundred years later, cartoonist Thomas Nast's ruthless takedowns of New York politician Boss Tweed were so effective that Tweed reportedly offered cartoonist Nast $100,000 to stop drawing cartoons about him (such as the one on page 421 in Chapter 12),[1] complaining, "My constituents can't read. . . . But, damn it, they can see pictures."[2]

By the 1970s, *Saturday Night Live* was broadcasting live caricatures of American presidents into the nation's living rooms, creating enduring narratives about the men in the White House. For many Americans, real presidential personalities were eclipsed by the comic interpretations offered by Chevy Chase (Gerald Ford), Darrell Hammond (Bill Clinton), and Will Ferrell (George W. Bush). By 2008, Amy Poehler and Tina Fey were taking candidates Hillary Clinton and Sarah Palin to task. And the 2016 presidential primary season practically gift wrapped skit-ready personalities (in the form of Larry David's Bernie Sanders and Alec Baldwin's Donald Trump) for comedy writers and performers to have their way with.

It's all in good fun, but such comedy can play an important role in defining the way Americans see their candidates and leaders. As a critical consumer of information, it is your job to consider how the narrative presented via comedy sources like *Saturday Night Live, Full Frontal With Samantha Bee, Funny or Die, The Onion,* and countless viral videos influence perceptions about the personalities at the top of our political food chain.

What to Watch Out For

Here are a few things to consider whenever you find yourself laughing at the folks in power:

- **What's the goal of this piece of comedy?** Some comic skits and cartoons are simply created to poke fun. Dana Carvey created a caricature of George H. W. Bush that was far more fun to watch than the real president, mocking the kind of verbal idiosyncrasies that Will Ferrell would later exploit when mocking Bush's son. In both cases, the goal was pure entertainment. But other comic takes are far more pointed. When *Key & Peele* introduced Barack

Obama's "anger translator" in 2012, they were not merely poking fun at the president's famously cool, calm demeanor—they were also making a statement about the way race influenced perceptions of Obama's behavior.

- **Who is the audience?** *Saturday Night Live* may have begun as edgy, "not ready for primetime" comedy, but after forty-odd seasons, the program is pretty much the definition of mainstream. Basic cable shows might appeal to slightly more niche audiences, and the Internet presents a free-for-all for comics at every level.

- **Where is the truth, and what is the exaggeration?** Like satire, caricature is only effective if it's built around a grain of truth. It's your job to distinguish between that truth and the bluster of humor that is built around it. For example, just two days after Sarah Palin pointed to the fact that "you can actually see Russia from land here in Alaska" as evidence of her foreign policy credentials, Tina Fey's version of Palin exclaimed, "I can see Russia from my house!" Fey took much of her dialogue directly from transcripts of Palin's own words, a practice Alec Baldwin replicated in his devastating impersonations of Donald Trump in 2016.

- **How does this affect the narrative?** It's easy to dismiss comedy as all in good fun, but even the most benign humor can make a lasting impression. In fact, *SNL* in particular—watched by millions of Americans each week, with countless more watching skits that go viral—has proven to have real agenda-setting power.[3] Because many (if not most) of those watching may not be all that interested in politics, the show serves, to some degree, as the primary source of political information for a great many viewers. For those viewers, *SNL* portrayals of Donald Trump's temper tantrums and policy frustrations might make a more lasting impression than any of Trump's real accomplishments or policy proposals.[4]

1. Richard E. Marschall, "The Century in Political Cartoons," *Columbia Journalism Review*, May–June 1999, 54.
2. Ira F. Grant, "Cartoonists Put the Salt in the Stew," *Southland (New Zealand) Times*, February 20, 1999, 7.
3. Jessica Leano, "The Agenda-Setting Power of *Saturday Night Live*," *The Elon Journal of Undergraduate Research in Communications* 5 (2014), www.elon.edu/docs/e-web/academics/communications/research/vol5no1/09leanoejspring14.pdf.
4. Angela D. Abel and Michael Barthel, "Appropriation of Mainstream News: How *Saturday Night Live* Changed the Political Discussion," *Critical Studies in Media Communication* 30 (2013): 1–16.

years in office. Trump himself said that even his family wanted him to be more toned down but that although he could easily be presidential, he didn't want to because "it would be boring as hell."[83] Time will tell how Trump resolves that issue and whether he listens to his own voice or that of his advisors.

Presidential style is an important but subtle means by which presidents communicate. It can be an opportunity for enhancing public support and thereby the president's ability to deal effectively with Congress and the media. But any style has its limitations, and the same behavioral and attitudinal characteristics of a style that help a president at one juncture can prove a liability later. Furthermore, the president does not always have total control over the image the public sees. Political enemies and an investigative press can combine to counter the image the president wants to project. Because public perception is tied so closely to leadership ability, a significant portion of the president's staffers end up concerning themselves with "image management," as we will see in Chapter 15.

AP Photo/LM Otero

A Very Exclusive Club

One of the great innovations of modern democracy is the peaceful transfer of power. In 2017, all five of the living past presidents participated in a benefit in College Station, Texas, to raise money for relief efforts from Hurricanes Harvey, Irma, and Maria, which devastated Texas, Florida, Puerto Rico, and the U.S. Virgin Islands. From left to right are Jimmy Carter, George H. W. Bush, George W. Bush, Bill Clinton, and Barack Obama.

PAUSE AND REVIEW Who, What, How

In the matter of presidential style and personality, the person with the most at stake is undoubtedly the president. Presidents' goals are popularity, legislative success, support for their party, and a favorable judgment in the history books. Presidents function in a number of policy roles as head of government, but they also serve as head of state, a role that is merely symbolic at times but that can be of tremendous importance for presidential power in times of national crisis or in conflicts with other nations. Because presidents' formal powers to fulfill these functions are limited, and their informal powers depend on their popularity with citizens and with the Washington elite, the personality and style that allow them to win popularity are crucial.

In Your Own Words Evaluate the importance of leadership style and image as they relate to presidential power.

THE CITIZENS AND THE PRESIDENCY

The critical role of public opinion

There are more than 300 million American citizens and only one president. Although we all have a reasonable chance of meeting our members of Congress, only the luckiest few will actually shake hands with the president of the United States. With connections this remote, how can we talk about the relationship between the citizens and the president?

Perhaps in the days before technology made mass communication so easy and routine, we could not. But today, although we may never dance at an inaugural ball or even wave at the president from afar, we can know our presidents intimately (and often far more intimately than we want to!). Through the medium of television, we can watch them board airplanes, speak to foreign leaders, swing golf clubs or play basketball, dance with their spouses, and speak directly to us. Skilled communicators, especially like Ronald Reagan and Barack Obama, can touch us personally—inspiring us and infuriating us as if we were family or friends.

Understanding presidential approval ratings is difficult because it is never clear which of the president's roles the public is being asked to evaluate. Americans may have disapproved of President Bill Clinton as head of state, but they

Sexism, the Glass Ceiling, and the 2016 Election

Fighting for Equal Footing

Hillary Clinton, the 2016 Democratic presidential nominee, concedes the election on November 9, 2016.

The United States, unlike most Western democracies and even many developing nations, has yet to put a female chief executive into office. Clinton came as close as anyone has, and if not for the Electoral College she would have pulled it off. Her achievement is singular and historic.

Her loss can still teach us some valuable lessons about how women and leadership are perceived in American culture. Our very notions of leadership are gendered.[1] Think about the words we use to describe a leader—*strong, authoritative, active, decisive, ambitious*—and then think about how our cultural narratives apply those words to men and women.

Strong. Just because it's not politically correct any longer to say that women are the "weaker sex," don't imagine that it's not ingrained into the narrative.

Authoritative. When men wield power, we see them as exercising authority. When women do so, the narrative is that they are "bossy." In a culture in which bosses have traditionally been men, it is curious that the word *bossy* is saved for women who step into a role seen as belonging to men.

Active. Our leadership narratives put a premium on taking action. Trump's slogan "Make America Great Again" was an action statement. Clinton, by contrast, was frequently accused of not having a message. Her slogan, "Stronger Together," presented a cooperative, collaborative vision that focused more on a way of being than on acting. Our notions of leadership are so gendered that unless the message is full of tough action verbs, many of us miss it altogether.

Decisive. There are different ways of making decisions. George W. Bush frequently said, "I am the decider." Trump's convention speech featured the words, "I alone can fix it." Hillary Clinton has said that it took years for her to be able to use the word *I* rather than *we* in a political context, and she is famous for writing a book about raising children called *It Takes a Village*.[2] Researchers have noted that women often use a more collaborative and consultative decision-making style.

Ambitious. The cultural narrative says men are supposed to be ambitious but finds something dubious about women who seek higher goals. Research shows that to be successful, ambitious women have to demonstrate that they can be as assertive and powerful as men, but when they do they are seen as unfeminine and unlikeable.[3]

Consider that a campaign is really a job interview. Clinton clearly won the three presidential debates in 2016. She received 92 percent of newspaper endorsements. Her campaign was well organized, her policy positions clearly articulated. In a way, the story is that of every woman who worked her way to the top through sheer grit, only to lose the plum job to a less qualified man.

Was sexism the only reason? Almost certainly not. But we can't discount it either. Although Hillary Clinton won the popular vote by three million, a poll still shows today that almost two-thirds of Republicans don't want to see a woman president in their lifetime.[4] As the old cigarette commercial had it, women have come a long way, baby, but apparently not long enough.

1. Anne M. Koenig et al., "Are Leader Stereotypes Masculine? A Meta-analysis of Three Research Paradigms," *Psychological Bulletin*, 137 (2011): 616–642, www.uni-klu.ac.at/gender/downloads/FP_Koenig_Eagly_2011.pdf.
2. Emily Crockett, "Why the Word 'I' Causes Hillary Clinton So Much Trouble," *Vox*, April 6, 2016, www.vox.com/2016/4/6/11377220/hillary-clinton-i-pronouns-sexism-trouble.
3. Laurie Rudman et al., "Status Incongruity and Backlash Effects: Defending the Gender Hierarchy Motivates Prejudice Against Female Leaders," *Journal of Experimental Social Psychology*, 48 (2012): 165–179, http://rutgerssocialcognitionlab.weebly.com/uploads/1/3/9/7/13979590/rudman_moss-racusin_phelan__nauts_2012.pdf.
4. Tim Marcin, "Nearly 60 Percent of Republicans Don't Want a Woman President in Their Lifetime, Poll Finds," *Newsweek*, April 26, 2018, www.newsweek.com/nearly-60-percent-republicans-dont-want-woman-president-lifetime-poll-902254.

Justin Sullivan/Getty Images

certainly supported him as head of government. The opposite might be more the case for President George W. Bush. Under everyday circumstances, questions concerning presidential job and personal approval seem straightforward, but the strength of the economy, current political conflicts, external events, and the personal foibles of the president can alter the public's assessment in complex ways that either enhance or limit the president's power. Finally, the institution of the American presidency, like most of the rest of the government designed by the framers, was meant to be insulated from the whims of the public. It is an irony that in contemporary politics presidents are often more indebted to the citizens for their power than they are to the Electoral College, Congress, the courts, or any of the political elites the founders trusted to stabilize American government.

In Your Own Words Give examples of ways in which public opinion affects the relationship between citizens and the president.

LET'S REVISIT: *What's at Stake . . . ?*

We began this chapter with a question that might have seemed a little odd – What is at stake in the unusual presidency of Donald Trump?

Now that we know about the conventional role and powers of the American president, it is probably easier to see why we asked that question. President Trump rejects, in almost every way he can, the established role of the presidency. Presidents have varied at how effective they are at the job, but rarely have they acted without regard for precedent, ignoring the typical expectations the country and the world have for an American president.

To many Americans who feel that the system is rigged or unfair or inaccessible, that is exactly his appeal. An article by a journalist who spent time attending his rallies begins an article this way:

> The instant you attend your first Trump rally you are confronted by an uncomfortable truth: to figure out what's happening you have to acknowledge the love. It may not be pure and selfless. It may be narcissistic and at times even threatening. But love is very much in the air.[84]

People speak of getting positive energy from him, of feeling peaceful among like-minded people who are willing to say what they think without regard for political correctness. They certainly line up to get into these rallies, and it is at these rallies that Trump seems to find his joy. He smiles widely, he embraces the crowd with his arms. He loves rallies, he loves his supporters, and he loves being loved.

This is very reminiscent of the *tribalism* that Laila Lalami describes in the *CLUES to Critical Thinking* article in Chapter 11. To give you a taste of her argument, she says

> The impulse to belong to a clan is deeply human, however, and new tribes continue to form, organized not around ancestry but along fuzzier lines of ideology or demography. . . . They rule over separate territories, listen to different oracles, uphold distinct values and dismiss contradictory information as unreliable propaganda or "fake news." . . . Above all, tribe members protect one another from perceived attacks by outsiders.[85]

By that definition, President Trump sounds less like a textbook American president and more like a tribal leader, which may be why *these* textbook writers, at least, have such difficulty writing about him. There is plenty to say about Trump—he's a fascinating character—but it's a challenge to talk about Trump "the president" when he declines to perform the role in the way we are accustomed to, from highly popular Republican presidents, such as Ronald Reagan, to, more recently, Barack Obama.

One of the main stakes we have discussed throughout this book is the principle that political norms should be respected and observed. Trump isn't concerned with political norms, doesn't always know when he is stepping on them, and often enjoys it when he finds out he is. What do his deviations from these norms mean for the next person to hold this office? Is Trump heralding a new normal or will American democracy return to its less colorful but more stable roots?

Another stake is free speech. Trump's criticism of the mainstream press, including CNN and the *New York Times*, and support for conservative outlets like Fox News indicate that news that flatters Trump is good, news that doesn't is fake. Other presidents might have wanted to give in to this tidy dichotomy—plenty have bent the truth, and some have outright lied—but none has so consistently refused to admit the truth of information that conflicts with his worldview.

The founders put free speech and press in the First Amendment for a reason: being freely able to criticize and debate the actions of politicians is one of the main supports of democratic culture. Trump undermines that right by insulting journalists, barring them from his press room, and sowing doubt about the truth. He isn't bothered or embarrassed by his lies and many of his supporters aren't either. In the article about his rallies we cited earlier, they either believed him or chalked it up to "just joking."

But then, there is the love. The feeling people have of being heard, of belonging. That is something most of us crave and is no less an important stake in politics. Without it, citizens are alienated and angry, and alienated and angry citizens aren't good for democracy either.

The disconcerting part of all of this is that Trump hasn't reached out to include all of us in the love. He has defied the traditional unifying role of head of state. You have to love him first; he won't woo you like most politicians and if you don't love him from the start, he doesn't seem to consider you part of his tribe. If you don't fit his image of an American,

he comes to the same conclusion. Almost all of us have lived through presidencies we didn't choose, under heads of government and state we didn't vote for. And yet, it is rare, if not politically suicidal, for those presidents to so openly disregard those from the other tribe. The job of president has historically included rising above the tribal divisions and having a thick enough skin that being hated is just all in a day's work.

That is not Trump's style. You are in the tribe, or you are not. And what is at stake may be American democracy as we have known it.

CLUES to Critical Thinking

Excerpt From Abraham Lincoln's Speech to Congress, September 15, 1863

In a list of restrictions on the powers of Congress, the U.S. Constitution says in Article I, Section 9, "The Privilege of the Writ of Habeas Corpus shall not be suspended, unless when in Cases of Rebellion or Invasion the public Safety may require it." Habeas corpus, meaning literally "to have the body," is a way of protecting someone from being arrested and held for political reasons. A judge can issue a writ of habeas corpus and have the prisoner delivered before him, to inquire into the legality of the charge. For some people, this writ is so essential to our notion of due process of law that they call it the "writ of liberty."

As the Civil War began, President Abraham Lincoln struggled to suppress the rebellion in the southern states and the activities of its northern sympathizers in the Democratic Party. In April 1861 he was fearful that the state of Maryland, leaning toward secession, would act to prevent the federal army from passing through the state.

To control what he believed to be the subversive speech and actions of Maryland politicians, he suspended the writ of habeas corpus.

John Merryman was arrested in May of the same year. U.S. Supreme Court justice Roger B. Taney issued a writ of habeas corpus to the military to show cause for Merryman's arrest. Under Lincoln's orders, the military refused. Taney issued a judgment saying that under the Constitution only Congress had the power to suspend the writ, and that by taking that power on himself, Lincoln was taking not only the legislative power, but also the judicial power, to arrest and imprison without due process of law. Taney granted that he could not enforce his judgment against the power of the military but said that if the military were allowed to take judicial power in that way, then the people of the United States had ceased to live under the rule of law.

On July 4, Lincoln appeared before Congress and, among other things, attempted to defend his assumption of the power to suspend habeas corpus and his defiance of the Supreme

Court's ordering him to stop. The following is an excerpt from his speech.

Obviously we have survived what Taney saw as an overzealous power grab. Although Lincoln expanded the suspension of habeas corpus in 1862, Congress finally acted to approve it in 1863, and it remained suspended until a Supreme Court ruling in 1866 (Ex Parte Milligan) officially restored it. What did Lincoln risk in defying the Supreme Court? Was it worth it?

Soon after the first call for militia it was considered a duty to authorize the commanding general in proper cases according to his discretion, to suspend the privilege of the writ of habeas corpus, or in other words to arrest and detain, without resort to the ordinary processes and forms of law, such individuals as he might deem dangerous to the public safety. This authority has purposely been exercised but very sparingly. Nevertheless the legality and propriety of what has been done under it are questioned and the attention of the country has been called to the proposition that one who is sworn to "take care that the laws be faithfully executed" should not himself violate them. Of course some consideration was given to the questions of power and propriety before this matter was acted upon. The whole of the laws which were required to be faithfully executed were being resisted and failing of execution in nearly one-third of the States. Must they be allowed to finally fail of execution, even had it been perfectly clear that by the use of the means necessary to their execution some single law, made in such extreme tenderness of the citizen's liberty that practically it relieves more of the guilty than of the innocent, should to a very limited extent be violated? To state the question more directly, are all the laws but one to go unexecuted and the Government itself go to pieces lest that one be violated? Even in such a case would not the official oath be broken if the Government should be overthrown, when it was believed that disregarding the single law would tend to preserve it? But it was not believed that this question was presented. It was not believed that any law was violated. The provision of the Constitution that "the privilege of the writ of habeas corpus shall not be suspended unless when in cases of rebellion or invasion the public safety may require it," is equivalent to a provision—is a provision—that such privilege may be suspended when in cases of rebellion or invasion the public safety does require it. It was decided that we have a case of rebellion, and that the public safety does require the qualified suspension of the privilege of the writ which was authorized to be made. Now, it is insisted that Congress and not the Executive is vested with this power. But the Constitution itself is silent as to which, or who, is to exercise the power; and as the provision was plainly made for a dangerous emergency, it cannot be believed the framers of the instrument intended that in every case the danger should run its course until Congress could be called together, the very assembling of which might be prevented, as was intended in this case, by the rebellion.

Source: Federal Judicial Center, www.fjc.gov/history/home.nsf/page/tu_merryman_doc_5.html.

Consider the source and the audience: Lincoln is speaking to Congress under a state of emergency. How does that fact affect the terms in which he casts his argument? When does urgency become panic? How far should it be resisted?

Lay out the argument and the underlying values and assumptions: What is Lincoln's essential purpose here, which he believes justifies some reduction in due process? What does he see as the trade-off facing him as executor of the laws? Why doesn't he mention the name of the person who has challenged his actions? How does he reason that the founders must not have intended members of Congress to be the ones to decide whether habeas corpus should be suspended?

Uncover the evidence: What does a reading of the Constitution tell us about this matter? Is the Constitution indeed silent?

Evaluate the conclusion: How persuasive is the "ends justify the means" argument in this context? What are its limits? What means might not be justified by a worthy end?

Sort out the political implications: Is Lincoln's argument relevant to the beefing up of executive power after 9/11? What are the similarities between the two situations? What are the differences?

Review

The Presidential Job Description

An American president must function as both a political head of government and an apolitical head of state. Often these two roles conflict.

When it came to defining the functions and powers of the president, the founders devised rules that both empowered and limited the president. Some of the founders argued for a strong leader with far-reaching powers, but others argued for several executives who would check each other's power. The constitutional compromise gives us an executive that has certain powers and independence, yet is checked by congressional and judicial power.

head of state (p. 263)   head of government (p. 263)

The Evolution of the American Presidency

We have seen two periods of presidential leadership so far. The first period, called the traditional presidency, which lasted until the 1930s, describes chief executives who mainly lived within the limits of their constitutional powers. Since then, in the modern presidency, a more complex relationship has existed between the president and the American citizens, in which presidents branch out to use more informal powers yet remain indebted to public approval for this expansion.

impeachment (p. 265)	executive agreements (p. 267)	solicitor general (p. 273)
chief administrator (p. 266)	State of the Union address (p. 267)	pardoning power (p. 273)
cabinet (p. 266)	presidential veto (p. 268)	traditional presidency (p. 274)
commander-in-chief (p. 267)	executive orders (p. 268)	inherent powers (p. 274)
chief foreign policy maker (p. 267)	signing statements (p. 268)	modern presidency (p. 274)
treaties (p. 267)	senatorial courtesy (p. 272)	weak presidency (p. 278)

Presidential Politics

Presidents face an expectations gap when it comes to their relationship with the American public. The gap results because what the president must promise in order to gain office does not align well with the powers granted by the Constitution.

Presidents are in a constant struggle with Congress and the public for the furthering of their legislative agenda. Presidents needs both congressional cooperation and public approval in order to fulfill campaign promises. The chief executive uses several strategies to achieve these goals, including going public and building coalitions in Congress.

expectations gap (p. 279)	cycle effect (p. 280)	divided government (p. 283)
power to persuade (p. 279)	honeymoon period (p. 280)	
going public (p. 279)	legislative liaison (p. 282)	

Managing the Presidential Establishment

The presidential establishment includes the cabinet, the Executive Office of the President, and the White House Office—a huge bureaucracy that has grown considerably since the days of George Washington's presidency. Although the resources are vast, managing such a large and complex organization presents its own problems for the president. The president's closest advisers are generally focused on the chief executive's interests, but the variety of other staff and agency heads—often with their own agendas and often difficult to control—can make life difficult for the president.

Executive Office of the President (p. 287)	Council of Economic Advisers (p. 287)	White House Office (p. 287)
Office of Management and Budget (p. 287)	National Security Council (p. 287)	chief of staff (p. 288)

The Presidential Personality

Personality differences play a role in a president's success or failure. Barber's typology offers one way to characterize these differences, classifying presidents in terms of their energy level and their orientation toward life. Presidents also create their own presidential styles, which distinguish them from their predecessors and influence their ability to communicate with the public, Congress, and the media.

presidential style (p. 293)

The Citizens and the Presidency

Americans get to know the president via the media as much as through any policy the president makes. Public opinion polling connects the president to citizens on an ongoing basis.

Drew Angerer/Getty Images

In Your Own Words

After you've read this chapter, you will be able to

9.1 Explain how the characteristics and features of bureaucracy influence decision making.

9.2 Outline the organization and roles of the federal bureaucracy.

9.3 Describe power struggles between political appointees and professional bureaucrats.

9.4 Outline the relationship between the federal agencies and the three branches of the federal government.

9.5 Analyze the tension between transparency and efficiency in the federal bureaucracy.

9
THE BUREAUCRACY

What's at Stake . . . in Rolling Back Regulations?

IT WAS A REPUBLICAN'S DREAM. Not since Reagan had a president come into office and unraveled the regulatory fabric of the U.S. government with such gusto. Although Donald Trump's campaign rhetoric had been populist and anti-establishment, in one way he was following as traditional a playbook as Republicans have—shrinking the bureaucracy and getting rid of regulations, the rules that limit individual or corporate behavior, generally to protect the public good.[1]

Democrats and Republicans had different views of regulation. The narrative repeated in the media read by Democrats emphasizes the public health benefits of required health insurance, the environmental stakes of emissions controls, the financial stability that resulted from the Consumer Financial Protection Bureau, and the open communication of an unrestricted Internet. That narrative—enforced over and over through progressive blogs, liberal commentators, and thousands of tweets—is that government is benign, not always as efficient as it could be, but a force for the improvement of its citizens' lives.

For Republicans, government is not the "good guy." Prone to inefficiencies and unintended consequences, they think it generally favors the collective good over the individual good. Remember, too, that there is a strong strain in American political culture that puts individual profit over public welfare. In conservative eyes, universal health mandates are restrictions on the freedom *not* to be insured, environmental regulation is costly and an administrative burden for businesses, consumer protection just means limitations on banks and lending, and the Internet is a private utility that can be manipulated like any other commodity. The antiregulation narrative was amplified through conservative media channels until the very science in which the regulations were based came to be seen as false propaganda. Against the best science of the day, Republicans have even claimed there is no human-made climate change needing to be addressed.

The Obama administration, eight years of health care reform, stimulating up an ailing economy, establishing environmental protections, and the like infuriated conservatives and provided a strong motive for Republican voters who were not attracted by Trump's ideology of grievance to vote for him anyway.

They were rewarded. After just nine months with Trump in office, one journalist was already writing about what he called the "Trump Effect"—the use of administrative directives to the bureaucracy to rewrite the rules according to which Americans live their lives.[2]

Fourteen times Trump used the Congressional Review Act, a legislative instrument that had been used only once 16 years

before, to fast track the reversal of regulations Obama had passed in his last months. And just as Obama had turned to executive action in the face of a recalcitrant Congress, Trump used executive directives to undo what Obama had done. One way or another, Trump undid more than 800 Obama regulations in his first six months. In just his first year in office he had issued 47 executive orders to get rid of other regulations.

Among the regulations the Trump administration rolled back and the new guidelines he provided were some that face legal challenges—his Muslim travel ban, his reversal of the DACA, his ban on transgendered members of the military—but others have already begun to shape American life. Here are just a dozen:

- Opened up the Dakota Access oil pipeline

- Stepped up enforcement of deportations on undocumented immigrants

- Withdrew from the Paris Climate Agreement

- Rolled back protections for retirement savings

- Allowed companies that violate labor laws to win federal contracts

- Made it easier to fire federal employees

- Cancelled restrictions on internet providers using private data

- Revised standards for health insurance, allowing lower quality plans back on the market

- Revoked forgiveness programs for student loans taken for fraudulent university programs

- Unveiled plans to roll back anti-pollution and fuel efficiency requirements for automobiles

- Permitted states to re-establish drugs tests for unemployment benefits

- Eased restrictions on for-profit colleges[3]

As you can see, in ways big and small, regulations influence the lives we live—for the better or the worse, depending on your perspective. After we discuss the bureaucracy—the giant regulation-making machine in government, we will return to the question of what is at stake in rolling them back. **«**

KIDS have dramatic aspirations for their futures: they want to be adventurers or sports stars, doctors or lawyers, even president of the United States. Almost no one aspires to be what so many of us become: bureaucrats. But bureaucrats are the people who make national, state, and local government work for us. They are the people who give us our driving tests and renew our licenses, who deliver our mail, who maintain our parks, who order books for our libraries. Bureaucrats send us our Social Security checks, find us jobs through the unemployment office, process our student loans, and ensure that we get our military benefits. In fact, bureaucrats defend our country from foreign enemies, chase our crooks at home, and get us aid in times of natural disasters. We know them as individuals. We greet them, make small talk, laugh with them. They may be our neighbors or friends. But as a profession, the civil service is seldom much admired or esteemed in this country. Indeed, it is often the target of scorn or jokes, and civil servants, the people who work in the organizations we call bureaucracies, are derided as lazy, incompetent, power hungry, and uncaring.

Such a jaded view, like most other negative stereotypes, is based on a few well-publicized bureaucratic snafus and the frustrating experiences we all have at times with the bureaucracy. Filling out financial aid forms, going through customs at the airport, signing up for a new health care policy, or waiting for a package being delivered via the U.S. Postal Service (better known as "snail mail"), all these things can drive us crazy. In addition, the bureaucracy is the source of many of the rules that can help us get what we want from government but that often irritate us with their seeming arbitrariness and rigidity. Though they aren't elected, bureaucrats can have a great deal of power over our lives.

Bureaucracies are essential to running a government. Bureaucracy, in fact, is often the only ground on which citizens and politics meet, the only contact many Americans have with government except for their periodic trips to the voting booth. Bureaucrats are often called "civil servants" because, ultimately, their job is to serve the civil society in which we all live.

WHAT IS BUREAUCRACY?

*A top-down organizational system
aiming for competence and fairness*

In simplest terms, a **bureaucracy** is any organization that is structured hierarchically: those at the top—with responsibility

---

> **bureaucracy** an organization characterized by hierarchical structure, worker specialization, explicit rules, and advancement by merit
>
> **neutral competence** the principle that bureaucracy should be depoliticized by making it more professional

---

for the organization's success—give the orders, and those on the bottom follow them. The classic definition comes to us from German sociologist Max Weber. Weber's model of bureaucracy features the following four characteristics:[4]

- **Hierarchy.** A clear chain of command exists in which all employees know who their bosses or supervisors are, as well as whom they in turn are responsible for.
- **Specialization.** The effectiveness of the bureaucracy is accomplished by having tasks divided and handled by expert and experienced full-time professional staffs.
- **Explicit rules.** Bureaucratic jobs are governed by rules rather than by bureaucrats' own feelings or judgments about how the job should be done. Thus bureaucrats are limited in the discretion they have, and one person in a given job is expected to make pretty much the same decisions as another. This leads to standardization and predictability.
- **Merit.** Hiring and promotions are often based on examinations but also on experience or other objective criteria. Politics, in the form of political loyalty, party affiliation, or dating the boss's son or daughter, is not supposed to play a part.

Political scientist Herbert Kaufman says that the closer governments come to making their bureaucracies look more like Weber's model, the closer they are to achieving "neutral competence."[5] **Neutral competence** represents the effort to depoliticize the bureaucracy, or to take politics out of administration, by having the work of government done expertly, according to explicit standards rather than personal preferences or party loyalties. The bureaucracy in this view should not be a political arm of the president or of Congress, but rather it should be neutral, administering the laws of the land in a fair, evenhanded, efficient, and professional way.

WHY IS BUREAUCRACY NECESSARY?

Much of the world is organized bureaucratically. Large tasks require organization and specialization. The Wright brothers may have been able to construct a rudimentary airplane, but no two people or even small group could put together a Boeing 787 Dreamliner. Similarly, though we idolize individual American heroes, we know that efforts like the D-Day invasion of Europe, putting a man on the moon, or the war on terrorism take enormous coordination and planning. Smaller in scale, but still necessary, are routine tasks like issuing driver's licenses, doing security pre-checks to make air travel easier, stamping a passport, ensuring that

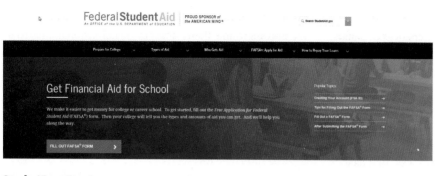

Study Now, Pay Later

Applying for a student loan is never fun. But imagine what the experience would be like if student loan awards were made democratically, rather than through the neutral and impartial bureaucracy that is tasked with the job.

Social Security recipients get their checks, and processing student loans.

Obviously many bureaucracies are public, like those that form part of our government. But the private sector has the same demand for efficient expertise to manage large organizations. Corporations and businesses are bureaucracies, as are universities and hospitals. It is not being public or private that distinguishes a bureaucracy; rather, it is the need for a structure of hierarchical, expert decision making. In this chapter we focus on public bureaucracies, in particular, the federal bureaucracy.

BUREAUCRACY AND DEMOCRACY

Decision making by experts may seem odd to Americans, who cherish the *idea* of democracy, if not always its practice, and it may be why so many Americans dislike so much of our public bureaucracy. If we value democracy and the corresponding idea that public officials should be accountable, or responsible, to the people, how can we also value bureaucracy, in which decisions are often made behind closed doors by unelected "experts" who, because of civil service protections, are difficult to hold accountable?

Bureaucratic decision making in a democratic government presents a real puzzle unless we consider that democracy may not be the best way to make every kind of decision. If we want to ensure that many voices are heard from, then democracy is an appropriate way to make decisions. But those decisions will be made slowly (it takes a long time to poll many people on what they want to do), and though the decisions are likely to be popular, they are not necessarily made by people who know what they are doing. When you're deciding whether to have open heart surgery, you don't want to poll the American people, or even the hospital employees. Instead you want an expert, a heart surgeon, who can make the "right" decision, not the popular decision, and make it quickly.

Democracy could not have designed the rocket ships that formed the basis of America's space program, or decided the level of toxic emissions allowable from a factory smokestack, or determined the temperature at which beef must be cooked in restaurants to prevent food poisoning. Bureaucratic decision making, by which decisions are made at upper levels of an organization and carried out at lower levels, is essential when we require expertise and dispatch.

ACCOUNTABILITY AND RULES

Bureaucratic decision making does leave open the problem of **accountability**: Who is responsible for seeing that things get done, and to whom does that person answer? Where does the buck stop? Unlike private bureaucracies, where the need to turn a profit usually keeps bureaucrats relatively accountable, the lines of accountability are less clear in public bureaucracies. Because the Constitution does not provide specific rules for the operation of the bureaucracy, Congress has filled in a piecemeal framework for it that, generally speaking, ends up promoting the goals of members of Congress and the interests they represent.[6] The president of the United States, nominally the head of the executive branch of government, also has goals and objectives he or she would like the bureaucracy to serve. Thus at the very highest level, the public bureaucracy must answer to several bosses who often have conflicting goals.

> **When does bureaucratic decision making become a threat to democracy?**

The problem of accountability exists at a lower level as well. Even if the lines of authority from the bureaucracy to the executive and legislative branches were crystal clear, no president or congressional committee would be interested in supervising the day-to-day details of bureaucratic

> **accountability** the principle that bureaucratic employees should be answerable for their performance to supervisors, all the way up the chain of command

operations or would have the time to do so. To solve the problem of accountability within the bureaucracy and to prevent the abuse of public power at all levels, we again resort to rules. If the rules of bureaucratic policy are clearly defined and well publicized, it is easier to tell if a given bureaucrat is doing his or her job, and doing it fairly.

What does fairness mean in the context of a bureaucracy? It means, certainly, that the bureaucrat should not play favorites. The personnel officer for a city is not supposed to give special consideration to her neighbors or to her boyfriend's brother. We do not want employees to give preferential treatment to people like themselves, whether that likeness is based on race, ethnicity, religion, partisanship, or sexual orientation, or to discriminate against people who are different from them. And we do not want people to run their organizations at the expense of the public good. In these and many additional ways, we do not want the people carrying out jobs in any bureaucracy to take advantage of the power they have.

CONSEQUENCES OF A RULE-BASED SYSTEM

The centrality of rules in bureaucracies has important trade-offs. According to the goals of neutral competence, we try to achieve fairness and predictability by insisting that the bureaucrats do their work according to certain rules. If everyone follows his or her job description, the supervisor, boss, or policymaker can know what, within some limits, is likely to happen. Similarly, if an important task is left undone, it should be possible to determine who did not do his or her job.

On the negative side, bureaucrats' jobs can quickly become rule-bound; that is, deviations from the rules become unacceptable, and individuality and creativity are stifled. Sometimes the rules that bind bureaucrats do not seem relevant to the immediate task at hand, and the workers are rewarded for following the rules, not for fulfilling the organization's goals. Rigid adherence to rules designed to protect the bureaucracy often results in outcomes that have the opposite effect. Furthermore, compliance with rules has to be monitored, and the best way we have developed to guarantee compliance is to generate a paper or, these days, an electronic record of what has been done. To be sure that all the necessary information will be available if needed, it

has to be standardized—hence the endless forms for which the bureaucracy is so famous.

For the individual citizen applying for a driver's license, a student loan, or food stamps, the process can become a morass of seemingly unnecessary rules, regulations, constraints, forms, and hearings. We call these bureaucratic hurdles **red tape**, after the red tape that seventeenth-century English officials used to bind legal documents.

Rules thus generate one of the great trade-offs of bureaucratic life. If we want strict fairness and accountability, we must tie the bureaucrat to a tight set of rules. If we allow the bureaucrat discretion to try to reach goals with a looser set of rules, or to waive a rule when it seems appropriate, we may gain some efficiency, but we lose accountability. Given the vast number of people who work for the federal government, we have opted for the accountability, even while we howl with frustration at the inconvenience of the rules.[7]

PAUSE AND REVIEW Who, What, How

The American public is strongly committed to democratic governance, but sometimes decisions need to be made that do not lend themselves to democracy. When complex, technical decision making is needed, some form of specialization and expertise is required. Because we also want accountability and fairness among our decision makers, we want them to stick to a prescribed set of rules. Bureaucratic decision making and administration offer possibilities in governance that democracy cannot, but they also bring their own difficulties and challenges.

In Your Own Words Explain how the characteristics and features of bureaucracy influence decision making.

THE AMERICAN FEDERAL BUREAUCRACY

A patchwork of agencies and commissions to meet growing public demands

In 2018 nearly three million civilians worked for the federal government, including about half a million U.S. Postal Service employees and almost a million in the military. Only a relative handful, approximately 63,000 employees, work in the legislative branch or the judiciary. The remaining more than two and a half million are in the executive branch, home of the federal bureaucracy. Another five million or so contract and grant workers make the federal workforce larger than its official numbers would indicate.[8] In this section we look at the evolution of the federal bureaucracy, its present-day organization, and its basic functions.

> **red tape** the complex procedures and regulations surrounding bureaucratic activity

THE SPOILS SYSTEM

Americans have not always been so concerned with the norm of neutral competence in the bureaucracy. Under a form of bureaucratic organization called the spoils system, practiced through most of the nineteenth century in the United States, elected executives—the president, governors, and mayors—were given wide latitude to hire their own friends, family, and political supporters to work in their administrations. They may not have had social media, but the interconnected personal relationships created a similar tightly knit web. The spoils system is often said to have begun with the administration of President Andrew Jackson and gets its name from the adage "To the victor belong the spoils of the enemy," but Jackson was neither the first nor the last politician to see the acquisition of public office as a means of feathering his cronies' nests. Such activity, referred to as patronage, allowed the elected executive to use jobs to pay off political debts as well as to gain cooperation from the officials who were hired this way, thereby strengthening his base of power.

Filling the bureaucracy with political appointees almost guarantees incompetence because those who get jobs for political reasons are more likely to be politically motivated than genuinely skilled in a specific area. Experts who are devoted to the task of the agency soon become discouraged because advancement is based on political favoritism rather than on how well the job is done. America's disgust with the corruption and inefficiency of the spoils system, as well as our collective distrust of placing too much power in the hands of any one person, led Congress to institute various reforms of the American civil service, as it is sometimes called, aimed at achieving a very different sort of organization.

One of the first reforms, and certainly one of the most significant, was the Civil Service Reform Act of 1883. This act, usually referred to as the Pendleton Act, created the initial Civil Service Commission, under which federal employees would be hired and promoted on the basis of merit rather than patronage. It prohibited firing employees for failure to contribute to political parties or candidates.

Protection of the civil service from partisan politicians got another boost in 1939 with the passage of the Hatch Act. This act was designed to take the pressure off civil servants to work for the election of parties and candidates. It forbids pressuring federal employees for contributions to political campaigns, and it prohibits civil servants from taking leadership roles in campaigns. They cannot run for federal political office, head up an election campaign, or make public speeches on behalf of candidates. However, they are permitted to make contributions, to attend rallies, and to work on registration or get-out-the-vote drives that do not focus on just one candidate or party. The Hatch Act seeks to neutralize the political effects of the bureaucracy but, in doing so, it denies federal employees a number of activities that are open to other citizens.

EVOLUTION OF THE FEDERAL BUREAUCRACY

The central characteristic of the federal bureaucracy is that most of its parts developed independently of the others in a piecemeal and political fashion, rather than emerging from a coherent plan. Some government activities are fundamental; from the earliest days of the republic, the government had departments to handle foreign relations, money, and defense. But other government tasks have developed over time as the result of historical forces, as solutions to particular problems, or as a response to different groups that want government to do something for them. Thus the nature and duties of the agencies reflect the politics of their creation and the subsequent politics of their survival and growth.[9] Federal agencies fall into three categories: those designed to serve essential government functions, those crafted to meet the changing needs and problems of the country, and those intended to serve particular clientele groups.[10]

SERVING ESSENTIAL GOVERNMENT FUNCTIONS

Some departments are created to serve essential government functions, the core operations that any viable government performs. For example, the Departments of State, War, and the Treasury were the first cabinet offices because the activities they handle are fundamental to the smooth functioning of government. The Department of State exists to handle diplomatic relations with other nations.

> **spoils system** the nineteenth-century practice of firing government workers of a defeated party and replacing them with loyalists of the victorious party
>
> **patronage** a system in which a successful candidate rewards friends, contributors, and party loyalists for their support with jobs, contracts, and favors
>
> **civil service** nonmilitary employees of the government who are appointed through the merit system
>
> **Pendleton Act** the 1883 civil service reform that required the hiring and promoting of civil servants to be based on merit, not patronage
>
> **Hatch Act** the 1939 law that limited the political involvement of civil servants to protect them from political pressure and keep politics out of the bureaucracy

When diplomacy fails, national interests must be protected by force; the Department of Defense (formerly War) supervises the air force, army, navy, marines, and, in time of war, the coast guard. All nations have expenses and must extract resources in the form of taxes from their citizens to pay for them. The Department of the Treasury, which oversees the Internal Revenue Service (IRS), performs this key tax collection function. Treasury also prints the money we use and oversees the horrendous job of managing the national debt. Imagine the effort to manage a debt that increases $2.4 billion a day![11]

RESPONDING TO CHANGING NATIONAL NEEDS

Other departments and agencies were created to meet the changing needs of the country as we industrialized and evolved into a highly urbanized society. For example, with westward expansion, the growth of manufacturing, and increased commerce came demands for new roles for government. The Department of the Interior was created in 1848 to deal with some of the unforeseen effects of the move westward, including the displacement of Native Americans and the management of western public lands and resources.

Similarly, a number of the negative aspects of industrialization, including child labor abuses, filthy and dangerous working conditions, unsanitary food production, and price gouging by the railroads, led to calls for government intervention to manage the burgeoning marketplace of an industrialized society. Thus began the development of the independent regulatory commissions starting in the late nineteenth century with the Interstate Commerce Commission and continuing into the twentieth century with the Federal Trade Commission, the Federal Reserve System, and others.

Under the New Deal, several new agencies were created and new programs put into place. The federal government's largest single program today, Social Security, was organized under the Social Security Administration as a supplement for inadequate and failed old-age pensions. For the first time, the national government became directly involved in the economic well-being of individual citizens. Americans came to expect that government would play a large role in managing the economy and in ensuring that people could work, eat, and live in decent housing. President Lyndon Johnson's War on Poverty resulted in the creation of the Office of Economic Opportunity in 1964 and the Department of Housing and Urban Development (HUD) in 1965.

A changing international environment also created needs that required government to grow. The Cold War between

Uncle Sam Lends a Hand (and a Brush)

The federal government's response to the Great Depression was Roosevelt's New Deal, which provided assistance to anxious Americans of all professions in need of stable work. The Federal Art Project provided support to struggling artists between 1935 and 1943, creating more than 200,000 works of art for public buildings. This poster is both a product of and publicity for the project.

the United States and the Soviet Union launched a multi-pronged policy effort that included investment in military research (Defense Advanced Research Projects Agency), science (the National Science Foundation), education (the National Defense Education Act), and space exploration (the National Aeronautics and Space Administration). The September 11, 2001, terror attacks on the United States led to the establishment of a new cabinet-level Department of Homeland Security to coordinate efforts to protect the country. The new department created a new bureaucratic structure but also organized under its authority some preexisting agencies and bureaus, including those controlling the

U.S. Secret Service, immigration, and emergency management.

More recently, the Great Recession of 2008 prompted the creation of the Consumer Financial Protection Bureau as part of the 2010 reform legislation known as Dodd–Frank. In the past, it was up to consumers to evaluate investments and if they were taken advantage of, that was tough luck. But as financial products have become more complex, it is increasingly difficult for individual consumers to be sure they aren't being defrauded. After seeing the damage done by shady financial products during the crisis, Congress decided a new regulatory agency was necessary to prevent a repeat. You can imagine new national needs—especially the looming challenges of automation and artificial intelligence in the workplace, for instance—driving new growth of the federal bureaucratic landscape. It is precisely our inability to foresee the consequences of global, economic, and technological changes that lead us to demand that government protect us from them.

RESPONDING TO THE DEMANDS OF CLIENTELE GROUPS

A number of departments and agencies either were created or have evolved to serve distinct clientele groups. These may include interest groups—groups of citizens, businesses, or industry members who are affected by government regulatory actions and who organize to try to influence policy. Or they may include unorganized groups, such as poor people, to which the government has decided to respond. Such departments are sensitive to the concerns of those specific groups rather than focusing on what is good for the nation as a whole. The U.S. Department of Agriculture (USDA), among the first of these, was set up in 1862 to assist U.S. agricultural interests. It began by providing research information to farmers and later arranged subsidies and developed markets for agricultural products. Politicians in today's budget-cutting climate talk about cutting back on agricultural subsidies, but no one expects the USDA to change its focus of looking out, first and foremost, for the farmer. Similar stories can be told of the Departments of Labor, Commerce, Education, and Veterans Affairs.

ORGANIZATION OF THE FEDERAL BUREAUCRACY

The federal bureaucracy consists of four types of organizations: (1) cabinet-level departments, (2) independent agencies, (3) regulatory boards and commissions, and (4) government corporations. Making the job of understanding the bureaucracy more complicated, some agencies can fit into more than one of those classifications. The difficulty in classifying

an agency as one type or another stems partly from Congress' habit of creating hybrids: agencies that act like government corporations, for instance, or cabinet-level departments that regulate. The overall organizational chart of the U.S. government makes this complex bureaucracy look reasonably orderly, but to a large extent the impression of order is an illusion.

DEPARTMENTS The federal government currently has fifteen departments. This chapter's *The Big Picture* shows how and when these departments were created. The heads of departments are known as secretaries—for example, the secretary of state or the secretary of defense—except for the head of the Department of Justice, who is called the attorney general. These department heads collectively make up the president's cabinet, appointed by the president, with the consent of the Senate, to provide advice on critical areas of government affairs such as foreign relations, agriculture, education, and so on. These areas are not fixed, and presidents may propose different cabinet offices. Although the secretaries are political appointees who usually change when the administration changes (or even more frequently), they sit at the heads of the large, more or less permanent, bureaucracies we call departments. Cabinet heads may not have any more actual power than other agency leaders, but their posts do carry more status and prestige.

When a cabinet department is established, it is a sign that the government recognizes its policy area as a legitimate and important political responsibility. Therefore, groups fight hard to get their causes represented at the cabinet level. During Bill Clinton's administration, environmental groups tried to get the Environmental Protection Agency (EPA) raised to the cabinet level. The fact that it was not elevated, despite Clinton's campaign promises on the matter, was a sign that the business and development interests that opposed environmental regulation were stronger politically. Even though the EPA is not a cabinet-level agency, its director has been asked by some presidents to meet with the cabinet, giving him or her cabinet rank and thus more status, even if the agency is not so elevated. In the Obama administration, the EPA director had cabinet-level rank, as did the White House chief of staff, the director of the Office of Management and Budget, the U.S. trade representative, the

---

clientele groups groups of citizens whose interests are affected by an agency or a department and who work to influence its policies

departments one of the major subdivisions of the federal government, represented in the president's cabinet

ambassador to the United Nations, and the chair of the Council of Economic Advisers.[12] Donald Trump's cabinet includes the same officials, but the mission of some, for example, the head of the EPA, has changed dramatically.

INDEPENDENT AGENCIES Congress has established a host of agencies outside the cabinet departments. The independent agencies are structured like the cabinet departments, with a single head appointed by the president. Their areas of jurisdiction, however, tend to be narrower than those of the cabinet departments. Congress does not follow a blueprint for how to make an independent agency or a department. Instead, it expands the bureaucracy to fit the case at hand, given the mix of political forces of the moment—that is, given what groups are demanding what action, and with what resources. As a result, the independent agencies vary tremendously in size, ranging from fewer than 320 employees in the Federal Election Commission (FEC) to over 62,000 in the Social Security Administration.[13]

These agencies are called independent because of their independence from cabinet departments, but they vary in their independence from the president. This is not accidental, but political. When Congress is not in agreement with the current president, it tends to insulate new agencies from presidential control by making the appointments for fixed terms that do not overlap with the president's, or they remove budgetary oversight from the Office of Management and Budget.[14] Thus some agency heads serve at the president's discretion and can be fired at any time; others serve fixed terms, and the president can appoint a new head or commissioner only when a vacancy occurs. Independent agencies also vary in their freedom from judicial review. Congress has established that some agencies' rulings cannot be challenged in the courts, whereas others' can be.[15]

INDEPENDENT REGULATORY BOARDS AND COMMISSIONS Independent regulatory boards and commissions make regulations for various industries, businesses, and sectors of the economy. Regulations are simply limitations or restrictions on the behavior of an individual or a business; they are bureaucratically

A Rough Road to Success
The initial roll-out of HealthCare.gov was hampered by technological glitches, but once the bugs were worked out, the system took off. By the end of 2016, an estimated 20 million Americans were newly insured—among them many young people who were able to remain on their parents' plans.

determined prescriptions for how business is to take place. This chapter opened with the battle over regulations from an ideological point of view—do they serve the public, or do they not? Regulations usually seek to protect the public from some industrial or economic danger or uncertainty. The Securities and Exchange Commission, for example, regulates the trading of stocks and bonds on the nation's stock markets, while the Food and Drug Administration regulates such things as how drugs must be tested before they can be marketed safely and what information must appear on the labels of processed foods and beverages sold throughout the country. Regulation usually pits the individual's freedom to do what he or she wants, or a business's drive to make a profit, against some vision of what is good for the public. As long as there are governments, such trade-offs will exist because it is for the purpose of managing citizens' collective lives that governments are formed. But the parties differ significantly on whether regulations are a good thing or an inhibition of individual freedom and entrepreneurship. How each trade-off is made among freedom, profit, and public safety is a question of ideology and public policy.

The number of agencies of the federal government whose principal job it is to issue and enforce regulations about what citizens and businesses can do, and how they have to do it, is something of a moving target.[16] Agencies are cut, redefined, and multiplied with new administrations. Given the scope of the undertaking, it is not surprising that regulation occasionally gets out of hand. If an agency exists to regulate, regulate it probably will, whether or not a clear case can be made for restricting action. The average cheeseburger in America, for instance, is the subject of over 40,000 federal and state

---

independent agencies government organizations independent of the departments but with a narrower policy focus

independent regulatory boards and commissions government organizations that regulate various businesses, industries, or economic sectors

regulations limitations or restrictions on the activities of a business or an individual

How the Federal Bureaucracy Grew So Much

The country started out with a minimum of agencies needed to support a nation: The Departments of State (diplomacy with other nations), War (now Defense, for when diplomacy fails), and Treasury (to collect taxes). As the nation grew, greater industrialization and urbanization inevitably produced new problems, which have resulted in a greater role for government—and new agencies—to regulate and maintain an increasingly complex society.

Number of Employees in Thousands, 2016

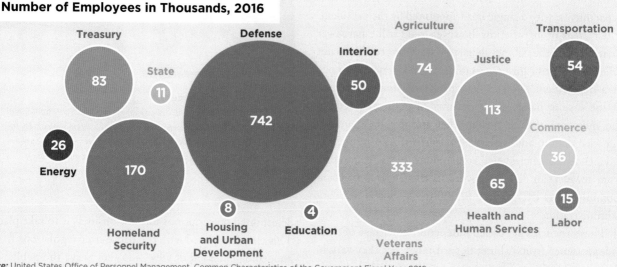

Treasury 83 · State 11 · Defense 742 · Interior 50 · Agriculture 74 · Justice 113 · Transportation 54 · Energy 26 · Homeland Security 170 · Housing and Urban Development 8 · Education 4 · Veterans Affairs 333 · Health and Human Services 65 · Commerce 36 · Labor 15

Source: United States Office of Personnel Management, Common Characteristics of the Government Fiscal Year 2016, www.opm.gov/policy-data-oversight/data-analysis-documentation/federal-employment-reports/common-characteristics-of-the-government/ccog2016.pdf.

Spending per Capita in Constant 2013 Dollars / Timeline of Department Creation

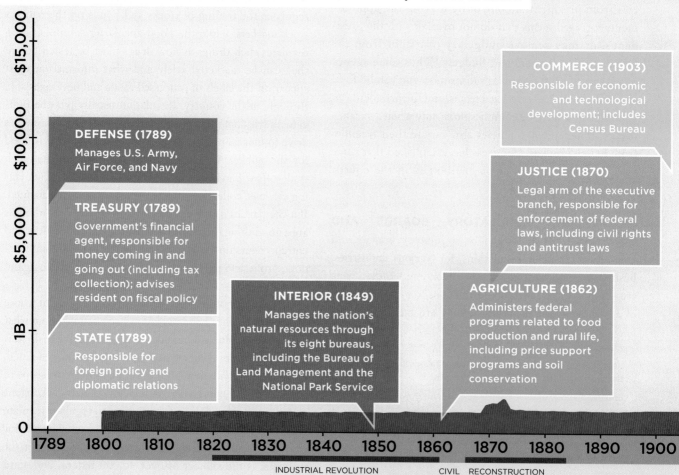

COMMERCE (1903)
Responsible for economic and technological development; includes Census Bureau

DEFENSE (1789)
Manages U.S. Army, Air Force, and Navy

JUSTICE (1870)
Legal arm of the executive branch, responsible for enforcement of federal laws, including civil rights and antitrust laws

TREASURY (1789)
Government's financial agent, responsible for money coming in and going out (including tax collection); advises resident on fiscal policy

INTERIOR (1849)
Manages the nation's natural resources through its eight bureaus, including the Bureau of Land Management and the National Park Service

AGRICULTURE (1862)
Administers federal programs related to food production and rural life, including price support programs and soil conservation

STATE (1789)
Responsible for foreign policy and diplomatic relations

INDUSTRIAL REVOLUTION · CIVIL WAR · RECONSTRUCTION

Sources: Table Ea636-643, Table Aa6-8, hsus.cambridge.org/HSUSWeb/HSUSEntryServlet, and U.S. Bureau of the Census, "Annual Population Estimates," NST-EST2012-01,

Annual Spending in Billions, 2017

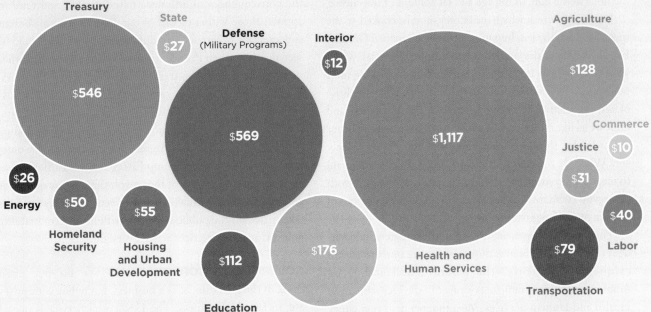

Treasury $546

State $27

Defense (Military Programs) $569

Interior $12

Agriculture $128

Energy $26

Homeland Security $50

Housing and Urban Development $55

Education $112

Veterans Affairs $176

Health and Human Services $1,117

Commerce $10

Justice $31

Labor $40

Transportation $79

Source: Office of Management and Budget, Historical Tables, Table 4.1: Outlays by Agency, www.whitehouse.gov/omb/budget/Historicals.

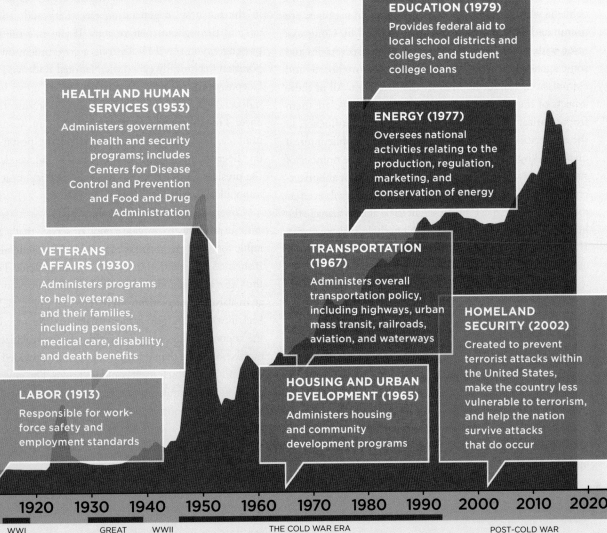

EDUCATION (1979)
Provides federal aid to local school districts and colleges, and student college loans

ENERGY (1977)
Oversees national activities relating to the production, regulation, marketing, and conservation of energy

HEALTH AND HUMAN SERVICES (1953)
Administers government health and security programs; includes Centers for Disease Control and Prevention and Food and Drug Administration

TRANSPORTATION (1967)
Administers overall transportation policy, including highways, urban mass transit, railroads, aviation, and waterways

HOMELAND SECURITY (2002)
Created to prevent terrorist attacks within the United States, make the country less vulnerable to terrorism, and help the nation survive attacks that do occur

VETERANS AFFAIRS (1930)
Administers programs to help veterans and their families, including pensions, medical care, disability, and death benefits

HOUSING AND URBAN DEVELOPMENT (1965)
Administers housing and community development programs

LABOR (1913)
Responsible for work-force safety and employment standards

1910 1920 1930 1940 1950 1960 1970 1980 1990 2000 2010 2020

WWI   GREAT DEPRESSION   WWII   THE COLD WAR ERA   POST-COLD WAR

Office of Management and Budget, "Historical Tables: Table 1.1, www.whitehouse.gov/omb/budget/historicals, www.census.gov/popest/data/national/totals/2012/index.html.

regulations, specifying everything from the vitamin content of the flour in the bun, to the age and fat content of the cheese, to the temperature at which the burger must be cooked, to the speed at which the ketchup must flow to be certified Grade A Fancy.[17] Some of these rules are undoubtedly crucial; we all want to be able to buy a cheeseburger without risking food poisoning and possible death. Others are informative; those of us on restrictive diets need to know what we are eating, and none of us likes to be ripped off by getting something other than what we think we are paying for. Others seem merely silly. When we consider that adult federal employees are paid to measure the speed of ketchup, we readily sympathize with those who claim that the regulatory function is getting out of hand in American government.

The regulatory agencies are set up to be largely independent of political influence, though some are bureaus within cabinet departments—the federal Food and Drug Administration, for example, is located in the Department of Health and Human Services. Most independent regulatory agencies are run by a commission of three or more people who serve overlapping terms, and the terms of office, usually between three and fourteen years, are set so that they do not coincide with presidential terms. Commission members are nominated by the president and confirmed by Congress, often with a bipartisan vote. Unlike cabinet secretaries and some agency heads, the heads of the regulatory boards and commissions cannot be fired by the president. All of these aspects of their organization are intended to insulate them from political pressures, including presidential influence, in the expectation that they will regulate in the public interest unaffected by current partisan preferences. The number of such agencies is growing, which places the national bureaucracy increasingly beyond the president's control, even as most Americans expect the president to be able to manage the bureaucracy to get things done.[18] Nonetheless, as we saw in *What's at Stake . . . ?*, a focused agenda by an administration can put pressure on the civil service, especially if it starves them for money or jeopardizes their job security, as the Trump administration has done, which can lead to ineffective agencies, demoralized personnel, and stalled initiatives.[19]

Congress wants to limit presidential influence of regulatory agencies because, as we have seen, not all presidential administrations view regulation in the same way, and as they approach the job of appointing regulatory officials accordingly, presidents can have an impact on how the agencies operate during their leaders' tenures in office. *What's at Stake . . . ?* showed us that, as holders of a conservative ideology that, in general, prefers to see less regulation and to leave control of industry to the market, Republican presidents tend to appoint businesspeople and others sympathetic to the industries being regulated. Democrats, by contrast, believe

that regulation by impartial experts can smooth out many of the consequences of an unregulated market and tend to appoint those with a record of regulatory accomplishment and scientific expertise. This difference in approach could be seen in action when President Barack Obama came into office in 2009. Reversing the trend set by President George W. Bush's administration, he reinvigorated the regulatory mission of agencies such as the EPA, the Occupational Safety and Health Administration, and the Securities and Exchange Commission, in what one progressive author called "the quiet revolution."[20] And the "Trump Effect" we saw earlier was to decisively reverse much of that revolution, just as quietly. A good deal of the lawmaking that affects our everyday lives takes place off the public stage and with little accountability unless Congress practices active oversight.

GOVERNMENT CORPORATIONS We do not often think of the government as a business, but public enterprises are, in fact, big business. The U.S. Postal Service is one of the larger businesses in the nation in terms of sales and personnel. The Tennessee Valley Authority and the Bonneville Power Administration of the northwestern states are both in the business of generating electricity and selling it to citizens throughout their regions. If you ride the rails as a passenger, you travel by Amtrak, a government-owned corporation (technically called the National Railroad Passenger Corporation). All these businesses are set up to be largely independent of both congressional and presidential influence. This independence is not insignificant. Consider, for example, how angry citizens are when the postal rates go up. Because the Postal Commission is independent, both the president and Congress avoid the political heat for such unpopular decisions.

Congress created these publicly owned government corporations primarily to provide a good or service that is not profitable for a private business to provide. The Federal Deposit Insurance Corporation (FDIC) is a good example. Following the Great Depression, during which financial institutions failed at an alarming rate, citizens were reluctant to put their money back into banks. A "government guarantee," through FDIC, of the safety of savings gave, and continues to give, citizens much more confidence than if the insurance were provided by a private company, which itself could go broke. The government's ownership of Amtrak came about because a national rail service did not prove profitable for private industry but was seen by Congress as a national resource that should not be lost.

government corporations companies created by Congress to provide to the public a good or service that private enterprise cannot or will not profitably provide

Similarly, the post office guarantees that mail reaches the most remote corners of the country, where delivery service might not be profitable for a private company. With competition from the private companies that do exist, like FedEx and UPS, however, as well as the declining demand for mail service as the country conducts more and more of its business electronically, the post office is in financial trouble and in 2012 announced plans to downsize in an effort to save money. In a twist, however, the rise of online shopping at private companies like Amazon has proved to be a boon to the postal service's survival. Ironically, in an effort to punish Amazon's owner, Jeff Bezos, President Trump has been putting pressure on the postal service to raise the rates it charges companies like Amazon, an effort that will likely hurt the post office much more than Amazon.[21]

> **Are some essential services now provided by the federal bureaucracy better left to the private sector?**

ROLES OF THE FEDERAL BUREAUCRACY

Federal bureaucrats at the broadest level are responsible for helping the president to administer the laws, policies, and regulations of government. The actual work the bureaucrat does depends on the policy area in which he or she is employed. Take another look at the titles of the cabinet departments and independent agencies displayed in *The Big Picture*. Some part of the bureaucracy is responsible for administering rules and policies on just about every imaginable aspect of social and economic life.

Bureaucrats are not confined to administering the laws, however. Although the principle of separation of powers—by which the functions of making, administering, and interpreting the laws are carried out by the legislative, executive, and judicial branches—applies at the highest level of government, it tends to dissolve at the level of the bureaucracy. In practice, the bureaucracy is an all-in-one policymaker. It administers the laws, but it also effectively makes and judges compliance with laws. It is this wide scope of bureaucratic power that creates the problems of control and accountability that we discuss throughout this chapter.

BUREAUCRACY AS ADMINISTRATOR We expect the agencies of the federal government to implement the laws passed by Congress and signed by the president. Operating under the ideal of neutral competence, a public bureaucracy serves the political branches of government in a professional, unbiased, and efficient manner. In many cases this is exactly what bureaucrats do, and with admirable ability and dedication. The rangers in the national parks help citizens enjoy our natural resources, police officers enforce the statutes of criminal law, social workers check for compliance with welfare regulations, and postal workers deliver letters and packages in a timely way. All these bureaucrats are simply carrying out the law that has been made elsewhere in government.

BUREAUCRACY AS RULE MAKER The picture of the bureaucrat as an impartial administrator removed from political decision making is an incomplete and unrealistic one. The bureaucracy has a great deal of latitude in administering national policy. Because it often lacks the time, the technical expertise, and the political coherence and leverage to write clear and detailed legislation, Congress frequently passes laws that are vague, contradictory, and overly general. To carry out or administer the laws, the bureaucracy must first fill in the gaps. Congress has essentially delegated some of its legislative power to the bureaucracy. Its role here is called **bureaucratic discretion**. Bureaucrats must use their own judgment, which under the ideal of neutral competence should remain minimal, in order to carry out the laws of Congress. Congress does not say how many park rangers should be assigned to Yosemite versus Yellowstone, for instance; the Park Service has to interpret the broad intent of the law and make decisions on this and thousands of other specifics. Bureaucratic discretion is not limited to allocating personnel and other "minor" administrative details. Congress cannot make decisions on specifications for military aircraft, dictate the advice the agricultural extension agents should give to farmers, or determine whether the latest sugar substitute is safe for our soft drinks. The appropriate bureaucracy must fill in all those details. For example, when Congress passed the Patient Protection and Affordable Care Act in 2010, a key provision barred insurers from implementing "unreasonable premium increases" unless they first submit justifications to federal and state officials. But Congress left it up to the bureaucracy to define "unreasonable," which would have enormous impact on how the law was implemented.

The procedures of administrative rule making are not completely insulated from the outside world, however. Before they become effective, all new regulations must first be publicized in the *Federal Register*, which is a primary source of information for thousands of interests affected by

---

bureaucratic discretion bureaucrats' use of their own judgment in interpreting and carrying out the laws of Congress

Federal Register the publication containing all federal regulations and notifications of regulatory agency hearings

Snapshot of America: *Who Are Our Federal Bureaucrats?*

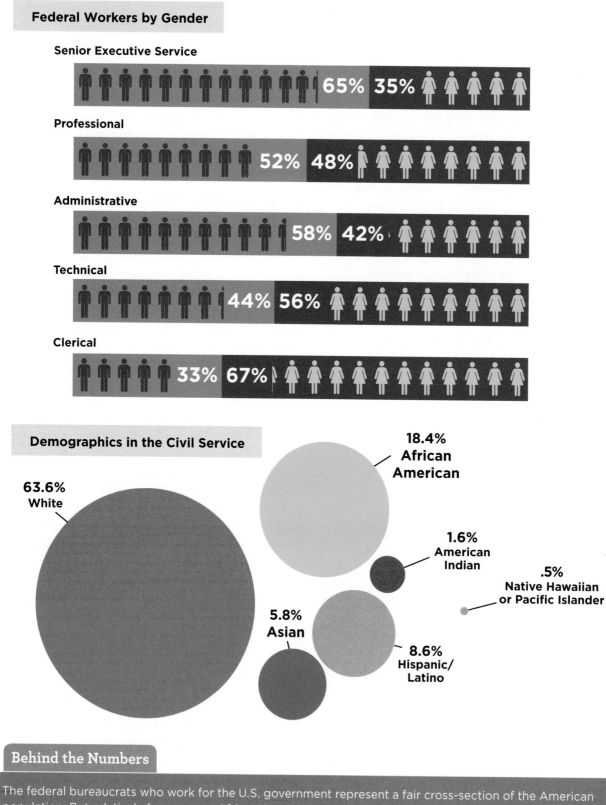

Federal Workers by Gender

Senior Executive Service

65% 35%

Professional

52% 48%

Administrative

58% 42%

Technical

44% 56%

Clerical

33% 67%

Demographics in the Civil Service

63.6%
White

18.4%
African
American

1.6%
American
Indian

.5%
Native Hawaiian
or Pacific Islander

5.8%
Asian

8.6%
Hispanic/
Latino

Behind the Numbers

The federal bureaucrats who work for the U.S. government represent a fair cross-section of the American population. But relatively few women, African Americans, or Hispanics reach the highest grade levels of the civil service ladder. Does this "glass ceiling" make a difference in the way the bureaucracy does its job?

Source: United States Office of Personnel Management, *Federal Equal Opportunity Recruitment Program (FEORP) Report to Congress,* Fiscal Year 2016, www.opm.gov/policy-data-oversight/diversity-and-inclusion/reports/feorp-2016.pdf.

decisions in Washington. Before adopting the rules, agencies must give outsiders—the public and interest groups—a chance to be heard. In the case of the rule making concerning the 2010 health care act, the bureaucracy became the focus of intense lobbying efforts by the health insurance industry, which wanted the rule to be defined as favorably for it as possible.[22]

BUREAUCRACY AS JUDGE The third major function of government is adjudication, or the process of interpreting the law in specific cases for potential violations and deciding the appropriate penalties when violations are found. This is what the courts do. However, a great deal of adjudication in America is carried out by the bureaucracy. For example, regulatory agencies not only make many of the rules that govern the conduct of business but also are responsible for seeing that individuals, but more often businesses, comply with their regulations. Tax courts, under the IRS, for instance, handle violations of the tax codes.

The adjudication functions of the agencies, while generally less formal than the proceedings of the courts, do have formal procedures, and their decisions have the full force of law. In most cases, if Congress does not like an agency ruling, it can work to change it, either by passing new legislation or by more subtle pressures. Nevertheless, agencies often issue rulings that could never have overcome the many hurdles of the legislative process in Congress.

WHO ARE THE FEDERAL BUREAUCRATS?

The full civilian workforce of the federal bureaucracy reflects the general workforce fairly accurately. For example, 46.8 percent of the U.S. civilian labor force is female and 42.6 percent of the civil service is female. African Americans make up 12.3 percent of the civilian workforce and 18.7 percent of the civil service.[23] The distributions are similar for other demographic characteristics such as ethnic origin or level of education. This representative picture is disturbed, however, by the fact that not all bureaucratic positions are equal. Policymaking is done primarily at the highest levels, and the upper grades are staffed predominantly by well-educated white males. As illustrated in *Snapshot of America: Who Are Our Federal Bureaucrats?*, women and minorities are distinctly underrepresented in the policymaking (and higher-paying) levels of the bureaucracy.[24]

---

bureaucratic culture the accepted values and procedures of an organization

---

Government exists, among other reasons, to solve citizens' common problems and to provide goods and services that the market does not or cannot provide. The apparatus for problem solving and service providing is primarily the bureaucracy. Congress and the president define the problems, make the initial decisions, and assign responsibility for solving them to a department, an agency, or a regulatory board.

Citizens or groups of citizens who want something from the government must deal with the bureaucracy as well. Finally, the bureaucrats themselves have a stake in performing their mandated jobs in a political context in which Congress and the president may hedge on the details of what those jobs actually are. Consequently, bureaucrats need to go beyond administering the laws to making them and judging compliance with them. Though we cautiously separate power, and check and balance it among all our elected officials, it is curious that where the officials are unelected and thus not accountable to the people, powers are fused and to a large extent unchecked. The bureaucracy is therefore a powerful part of the federal government.

In Your Own Words Outline the organization and roles of the federal bureaucracy.

POLITICS INSIDE THE BUREAUCRACY

Power struggles between political appointees and professional bureaucrats, constrained by cultural norms

Politicians and bureaucrats alike are wary about the effects of politics on decision making. They act as if fairness and efficiency could always be achieved if only the struggle over competing interests could be set aside through an emphasis on strict rules and hierarchical organization. We know, of course, that the struggle can't be set aside. As a fundamental human activity, politics is always with us, and it is always shaped by the particular rules and institutions in which it is played out. Politics within bureaucracies is a subset of politics generally, but it takes on its own cast according to the context in which it takes place.

BUREAUCRATIC CULTURE

The particular context in which internal bureaucratic politics is shaped is called **bureaucratic culture**—the accepted values and procedures of an organization. Consider any place you may have been employed. When you began your job, the accepted standards of behavior may not have been clear, but over time you figured out who had power, what your role was, which rules could be bent and which had to be followed strictly, and what the goals of the enterprise were. That's all a way of saying that you understood the accepted power narrative in your workplace. Chances are you came to share some of the values of your colleagues, at least with respect to your work. Those things add up to the culture of the workplace. Bureaucratic culture is just a specific instance of workplace culture.

Knowing the four main elements of bureaucratic culture will take us a long way toward understanding why bureaucrats and bureaucracies behave the way they do. Essentially these elements define what is at stake within a bureaucracy, and what bureaucrats need to do to ensure that they are winners and not losers in the bureaucratic world.

POLICY COMMITMENT Good bureaucrats develop a commitment to the policy issues their agency is tasked with. For instance, an employee of the USDA will eventually come to believe that agricultural issues are among the most important facing the country, even if he or she never thought much about farming before. In the same way, those working at the National Aeronautics and Space Administration place a priority on investigating outer space, and bureaucrats at the National Institutes of Health believe fervently in health research. They will share a commitment to their policy area not only because their jobs depend on it but also because all the people around them believe in it.

ADOPTION OF BUREAUCRATIC BEHAVIOR New bureaucrats will soon begin to see the logic of doing things bureaucratically; they may even start to sound like bureaucrats. **Bureaucratese**, the formal and often (to outsiders) amusing and sometimes confusing language that many bureaucrats use in their effort to convey information without controversy, may become their second tongue. Bureaucratese was developed in part because the use of acronyms and other linguistic shortcuts can make communication more efficient for those in the know. But the use of bureaucratese also seems to be an effort to avoid responsibility (for example, use of the passive voice means you don't say who performed the action) or to make the author appear more authoritative by using more and longer words than are really necessary.

Bureaucrats also develop a dependency on the rules because relying on the rules relieves them of the responsibility of relying on their own judgment. They learn that exercising such bureaucratic discretion, as we discussed earlier, can leave them vulnerable if their decisions are not clearly within the rules. They also adjust to the hierarchical organization in which they are dependent on their superiors for work assignments, promotions, budget allotments, and vacation authorizations. Those superiors will have the same relationships with their bosses.

Free spirits are not likely to thrive in a bureaucratic environment where deference, cooperation, and obedience are emphasized and rewarded, and the relentless rule orientation and hierarchy can wear down all but the most committed independent souls.

SPECIALIZATION AND EXPERTISE Departments, agencies, and bureaus have specific areas of responsibility. There is not a great deal of interagency hopping; most bureaucrats spend their whole professional lives working in the same area, often in the same department. Lawyers in the Justice Department, scientists at the National Science Foundation, physicians at the National Institutes of Health, and even soybean experts at the USDA all have specialized knowledge as the base of their power.

Because of specialization and expertise, bureaucrats come to know a lot more about their policy areas than do the public or even politicians who must make decisions relevant to those areas. Their possession of critical information gives bureaucrats considerable power in policymaking situations.

IDENTIFICATION WITH THE AGENCY The three characteristics of bureaucratic culture discussed so far lead to the fourth: identification with and protection of the agency. As bureaucrats become attached to the policy interests of their agencies, committed to the rules and structures of the bureaucracy, concerned with the fortunes of their superiors, and appreciative of their own and their colleagues' specialized knowledge, they identify their interests with those of their agencies. They will come to identify with the department, not just because their job depends on it but because they believe in what it does.

CONSEQUENCES OF THE BUREAUCRATIC CULTURE This pervasive bureaucratic culture has a number of political consequences. On the plus side, it holds the bureaucracy together, fostering values of commitment and loyalty to what could otherwise be seen as an impersonal and alienating work environment. It means that the people who work in the federal government, for the most part, really believe in what they do and do it well.

But bureaucratic culture can have negative consequences as well. As former FBI agent Coleen Rowley pointed out in testimony before the Senate Judiciary Committee in June 2002, this culture very likely had a role in the failure of our law enforcement and intelligence agencies to foresee and prevent the attacks of September 11, 2001. Rowley's office,

> **bureaucratese** the often unintelligible language used by bureaucrats to avoid controversy and lend weight to their words

in Minneapolis, had known that a possible terrorist, Zacarias Moussaoui, was seeking to take flying lessons. Finding his activities suspicious and worrisome, Minneapolis agents tried to get a warrant to search his computer but were unable to do so. In her testimony, Rowley targeted the FBI's hierarchical culture, with its implicit norm that said field agents did not go over the heads of their superiors, who frequently second-guessed their judgment. "There's a certain pecking order, and it's real strong," she told the committee. "Seven to nine levels is really ridiculous."[25]

Not only did bureaucratic culture keep the FBI from knowing what information it had prior to September 11, but it also kept the FBI and the Central Intelligence Agency from communicating with each other about the various pieces of the puzzle they had found. Between them they had much of the information needed to have discovered the plot, but no one "connected the dots." Why? The cultures are different. The FBI is primarily a law enforcement agency; agents are rewarded for making arrests. Its anti-terrorist activities prior to September 11 were focused on after-the-fact investigations of terrorist attacks (leading to convictions) but not on preventing such attacks against domestic targets.[26]

The CIA, by contrast, is focused on clandestine activity to develop information about non-American groups and nations. It is more secretive and less rule-bound, more focused on plans and intentions than on after-the-fact evidence and convictions. Agents focus on relationships, not individual achievement. One reporter covering the two agencies wrote that though the two agencies need to work with each other, "they have such different approaches to life that they remain worlds apart. In fact, they speak such different languages that they can barely even communicate."[27]

When an agency is charged with making the rules, enforcing them, and even adjudicating them, it is relatively easy to cover up less catastrophic agency blunders. If Congress, the media, or the public had sufficient information and the expertise to interpret it, this would not be as big a problem. However, specialization necessarily concentrates the expertise and information in the hands of the agencies, and this is one of the places where the channels of communication are narrow and restricted and news is limited. Perhaps for this reason, rumors and conspiracy theories about "the deep state" thrive on the Internet. Congress and the media are generalists. They can tell something has gone wrong when terrorists attack the United States seemingly without warning, but they cannot evaluate the hundreds of less obvious

problems that may have led to the failure to warn that only an expert would even recognize. And in the absence of facts, imaginations run wild.

> ### When is rocking the bureaucratic boat (blowing the whistle) a good thing, and when is it not?

Congress has tried to check the temptation for bureaucrats to cover up their mistakes by offering protection to whistleblowers. Whistleblowers, like Coleen Rowley, are employees who expose instances or patterns of error, corruption, or waste in their agencies. They are rarely popular with their bosses or their colleagues, as you can well imagine. The Whistleblower Protection Act of 1989 established an independent agency to protect employees from being fired, demoted, or otherwise punished for exposing wrongdoing. The act's intention to protect whistleblowers is one way to counteract the negative tendency of organizational behavior, but it does little to offset the pressure that bureaucrats are under to protect their programs and agencies from harm, embarrassment, and budget cuts. Moreover, the law has not worked anything like its supporters had hoped. Over the past ten years, complaints of agency punishment by whistleblowers have averaged 835 a year. In almost all these cases, the agency's decisions support the bureaucracy rather than the whistleblower, creating a great career disincentive to speak out when one's agency is guilty of corruption, wrongdoing, or simple incompetence.[28]

One problem with the phenomena of whistleblowers is separating valid claims of government wrongdoing from illegal behavior (see our discussion of Edward Snowden in Chapter 5), or distinguishing insider information that is used to feed partisan attacks on an administration from valid information about cover-ups or bureaucratic wrong-doing. For example, Republicans claimed the Obama administration impeded their House investigations into the September 11, 2012, attacks on the U.S. diplomatic compound in Benghazi, Libya.[29] The partisan noise made it difficult to determine if any of the claims had merit.

PRESIDENTIAL APPOINTEES AND THE CAREER CIVIL SERVICE

Another aspect of internal bureaucratic politics worth noting is the giant gulf between those at the very top of the department or agency who are appointed by the president and those in the lower ranks who are long-term civil service employees. Of the two million civilian employees in the U.S. civil service, about 3,500 are appointed by the president or his or her immediate subordinates.

> whistleblowers individuals who publicize instances of fraud, corruption, or other wrongdoing in the bureaucracy

Roberto Gonzalez/Getty Images

Low Morale

Government employees can come to strongly identify with the agency for which they work, supporting the mission they are tasked with and feeling protective of its legacy and turf. This can lead to low morale if the agency's mission is not a priority for a president, or, worse, if that mission runs counter to the president's own goals. The Trump administration's skepticism around climate change has led to anxiety at NASA and the EPA.

CONFLICTING AGENDAS Presidential appointees are sometimes considered "birds of passage" by the career service because of the regularity with which they come and go. Though generally quite experienced in the agency's policy area, appointees have their own careers or the president's agenda as their primary objective rather than the long-established mission of the agency. The rank-and-file civil service employees, in contrast, are wholly committed to their agencies. Minor clashes are frequent, but they can intensify into major rifts when the ideology of a newly elected president varies sharply from the central values of the operating agency. Researchers have found that presidents seek to put their own people, rather than career civil service managers, in the higher ranks of agencies that do not agree with their policy preferences.[30] So, for instance, when President Trump appointed Ryan Zinke as secretary of the interior, his agenda clashed with that of many of the career civil service in the Interior Department who were deeply committed to the preservation of national resources. Zinke reduced the emphasis on climate science in resource management, eliminated a ban on coal mining on federal lands, limited environmental protections in oil and gas extraction, and opened up most of the U.S. offshore areas to exploration for oil drilling. When he capped that by refusing to meet with his bipartisan National Parks Service Advisory Board, something no interior secretary had ever done, there was a mass resignation of the board, members figuring that their presence was doing no good.[31]

CONFLICTING TIME FRAMES As "birds of passage," political appointees have short-term outlooks.[32] The professionals, in contrast, serve long tenures in their positions. The average upper-level civil servant has worked in his or her agency for over seventeen years, and expects to remain there.[33] Chances are the professionals were there before the current president was elected, and they will be there after he or she leaves office. Thus, although the political appointees have the advantage of higher positions of authority, the career bureaucrats have time working on their side. Not surprisingly, the bureaucrat's best strategy when the political appointee presses for a new but unpopular policy direction is to stall, something easily achieved in a bureaucratic environment.

PRESIDENTIAL STRATEGIES Given the difficulty that presidents and their appointees can have in dealing with the entrenched bureaucracy, presidents who want to institute an innovative program are better off starting a new agency than trying to get an old one to adapt to new tasks. In the 1960s, when President John F. Kennedy wanted to start the Peace Corps, a largely volunteer organization that provided assistance to developing countries by working at the grassroots level with the people themselves, he could have added it to any number of existing departments. The problem was that either these existing agencies were unlikely to accept the idea that nonprofessional volunteers could do anything useful, or they were likely to subvert them to their own purposes, such as spying or managing aid. Thus President Kennedy was easily persuaded to have the Peace Corps set up as an independent agency, a frequent occurrence in the change-resistant world of bureaucratic politics.[34]

> **PAUSE AND REVIEW** Who, What, How
>
> Life inside the bureaucracy is clearly as political as life outside and has its own narrative within which many actors attempt to use the rules to advance themselves and the interests of their agency or clientele group.
>
> Individual bureaucrats want to succeed in their jobs and promote their agencies. In their favor are time, the bureaucratic culture, and the rigid nature of bureaucratic rules. Congress has helped bureaucrats who wish to challenge an agency to correct a perceived wrong or injustice by passing the Whistleblower Protection Act. The president has an enormous stake in what the bureaucracy does, as do the president's political appointees, who have their own agendas for advancement. But the entrenched civil service can often and easily outlast them, and ultimately prevail.

Jaime Schmidt

Courtesy of Jaime Schmidt

If you were thinking that a being a bureaucrat means being chained to a desk from 8 to 5 every day and filling out endless stacks of paperwork, meet Jaime Schmidt. Jaime is a passionate and devoted outdoorswoman, a steward of the recreational trails, and a conservator of the environment she loves. She is also a bureaucrat, and there is nothing stuffy about her.

Her actual title is U.S. Forest Service National Trail Information Coordinator, and she is focused on trail management. "[T]rails are such a wonderful analogy because they are linear and they connect, right? They connect people to each other. They connected me to my dad and my mom as we explored amazing places when I was young. They connect people to their communities. They connect people to their past, their present, their spiritual sense, and they connect all of us to our future. Trails are wonderful, they're wild, and they wind through beautiful places. So I feel incredibly lucky to be able to do what I do in my life and for a living."

Jaime's path to the job she loves began as the daughter of parents "who were very committed to volunteerism and service. My brother, sister and I grew up hiking and backpacking, volunteering, and with the expectation that we were going to contribute." She spent a couple of summers working at Glacier National Park, where she fell in love with another outdoor buff and, after graduating from college, the two joined the Peace Corps and headed out on a life of adventure.

It would be almost five years before they returned home again for good—three years in Honduras where, among other things, Jaime helped set up a program for underprivileged kids to spend time in the outdoors, eating healthy food, working hard and feeling valued—and then one year in Galapagos National Park, leading development of an environmental interpretive plan for the park. Then back stateside, where both of them were hired by the U.S. Forest Service, first in Idaho, then a dozen years in Alaska, and now back in Coeur d'Alene, Idaho, with occasional forays into the wilds of Washington, D.C. After years of managing hundreds of miles of trails from Montana to Alaska, Jaime now spends her time shaping national policy and programs and helping trail managers agency-wide in their work.

She so clearly loves her job that it's easy to forget that she is in fact a government employee—not something that fills every heart with joy and satisfaction. But for Jaime, the two go hand in hand.

About government service she says

"The students I went to school with and that I deal with now are generally conservation or environmentally-oriented. So they tend to see government as a mechanism to help manage public lands and effect change. They see government as one major way to get in there and make a difference. And if you don't like what government's doing, then get in there and help change it.

Which might be different from other students who, in general, might look from the outside towards the government and go 'ewwww … bureaucracy.' I guess what I would say to folks is, well, I see it as *our* government and we need government. Government gets us roads and health standards and great education systems. And if you don't like it or if you see problems, I think there's tremendous opportunity to get in there and help improve it."

And on keeping the republic

"We're all part of the Republic; we're each fortunate to be part of this Republic and we have a responsibility to contribute. I'm really big on service in any dimension, in any area of interest. For me, it's about the concept of citizen advocacy and citizen stewardship—to contribute to the greater good. And I think that we have a responsibility to do that, as opposed to the opposite of simply watching or criticizing.

Stewardship is recognizing and enjoying the opportunities and responsibilities we've inherited. For me, it's the great public lands and natural resources, clean air and healthy water, our trails and wilderness areas, our wild and scenic rivers. And knowing that, while we've inherited these resources, we also have a responsibility to take care of them and help make decisions that inform wise choices for their future management. We each have a responsibility to do something positive toward our future, whatever it is—our work, choices we make in the things we buy or don't buy, how we spend our weekends, how we vote. For the future—for our children, but also for the country and for the globe. That's the big piece. That's the hard piece. That's the important piece."

Source: Jaime Schmidt spoke with Christine Barbour in the summer of 2014.

EXTERNAL BUREAUCRATIC POLITICS

Turf wars among agencies and with the three branches of government

Politics affects relationships not only within bureaucratic agencies but also between those agencies and other institutions. The bureaucracy is not one of the official branches of government, since it falls technically within the executive branch, but it is often called the fourth branch of government because it wields so much power. It can be checked by other agencies, by the executive, by Congress, by the courts, or even by the public, but it is not wholly under the authority of any of those entities. In this section we examine the political relationships that exist between the bureaucracy and the other main actors in American politics.

INTERAGENCY POLITICS

As we have seen, agencies are fiercely committed to their policy areas, their rules and norms, and their own continued existence. The government consists of a host of agencies, all competing intensely for a limited amount of federal resources and political support. They all want to protect themselves and their programs, and they want to grow, or at least to avoid cuts in personnel and budgets.

To appreciate the agencies' political plight, we need to see their situation as they see it. Bureaucrats are a favorite target of the media and elected officials. Their budgets are periodically up for review by congressional committees and the president's budget department, the Office of Management and Budget. Consequently, agencies are compelled to work for their survival and growth. They have to act positively in an uncertain and changing political environment in order to keep their programs and their jobs.

CONSTITUENCY BUILDING One way agencies compete to survive is by building groups of supporters. Members of Congress are sensitive to voters' wishes, and because of this, support among the general public as well as interest groups is important for agencies. Congress will not want to cut an agency's budget, for instance, if doing so will anger a substantial number of voters or important interests.

As a result, agencies try to control some services or products that are crucial to important groups. In most cases, the groups are obvious, as with the clientele groups of, say, the USDA. Department of Agriculture employees work hard for farming interests, not just because they believe in the programs but also because they need strong support from agricultural clienteles to survive. Agencies whose work does not earn them a lot of fans—like the IRS, whose mission is tax collection—have few groups to support them. When Congress decided to reform the IRS in 1998, there were no defenders to halt the changes.[35] The survival incentives for bureaucratic agencies do not encourage agencies to work for the broader public interest but rather to cultivate special interests that are likely to be more politically active and powerful.

Even independent regulatory commissions run into this problem. Numerous observers have noted the phenomenon of **agency capture**, whereby commissions tend to become creatures of the very interests they are supposed to regulate. In other words, as the regulatory bureaucrats become more and more immersed in a policy area, they come to share the views of the regulated industries. The larger public's preferences tend to be less well formed and certainly less well expressed because the general public does not hire teams of lawyers, consultants, and lobbyists to represent its interests. The regulated industries have a tremendous amount at stake. Over time, regulatory agencies' actions may become so favorable to regulated industries that in some cases the industries themselves fight deregulation, as did the airlines when Congress and the Civil Aeronautics Board deregulated air travel in the 1980s.[36]

GUARDING THE TURF Agencies want to survive, and one way to stay alive is to offer services that no other agency provides. Departments and agencies are set up to deal with the problems of fairly specific areas. They do not want to overlap with other agencies because duplication of services might indicate that one of them is unnecessary, inviting congressional cuts. Thus, in many instances, agencies reach explicit agreements about dividing up the policy turf in an only partly successful effort to avoid competition and duplication.

This turf jealousy can undermine good public policy. Take, for example, the military. For years, the armed services successfully resisted a unified weapons procurement, command, and control system. Each branch wanted to maintain its traditional independence in weapons development, logistics, and communications technologies, costing

---

agency capture a process whereby regulatory agencies come to be protective of and influenced by the industries they were established to regulate

the taxpayers millions of dollars. Getting the branches to give up control of their turf was politically difficult, although it was accomplished eventually.

THE BUREAUCRACY AND THE PRESIDENT

As we discussed in Chapter 8, one of the president's several jobs is that of chief administrator. Organizational charts of departments and agencies suggest a clear chain of command, with the cabinet secretary at the top reporting directly to the president. But in this case, being "the boss" does not mean that the boss always, or even usually, gets his or her way. The long history of the relationship between the president and the bureaucracy is largely one of presidential frustration. President Kennedy voiced this exasperation when he said that dealing with the bureaucracy "is like trying to nail jelly to the wall." Presidents have more or less clear policy agendas that they believe they have been elected to accomplish, and with amazing consistency presidents complain that "their own" departments and agencies are uncooperative and unresponsive. The reasons for presidential frustration lie in the fact that, although the president has some authority over the bureaucracy, the bureaucracy's different perspectives and goals often thwart the chief administrator's plans.

Still, presidents can often use the mechanisms of the bureaucracy to accomplish some of their goals, primarily through executive orders, as we saw in Chapter 8, but also through other administrative suggestions, directives, and encouragement. Usually presidents gain their policy objectives by working with Congress, but when that proves too controversial, or, in the case of Barack Obama, simply impossible, presidents can resort to implementing existing laws so as to achieve some of their preferred polices. Thus Obama was able to make strides on climate change policy through the EPA, on immigration reform through directives to agencies in the Department of Homeland Security not to deport Dreamers or their families, and on marriage equality through the Justice Department's determination that the Defense of Marriage Act was not constitutional. In addition, he directed the Justice Department not to use its limited resources to challenge state marijuana laws that ran counter to federal

When Things Go Really Wrong
After Hurricane Maria tore across Puerto Rico in September 2017, virtually destroying its power grid, local officials, including the mayor of San Juan and the governor, requested that the president declare the island a federal disaster area. Federal Emergency Management Agency personnel arrived soon after to assess the damage and coordinate relief and aid, but the government response was criticized as insufficient and poorly managed, with blackouts lingering into 2018.

law, and he directed the Bureau of Alcohol, Tobacco, Firearms and Explosives to close the so-called gun show loophole, as discussed in Chapter 5. Likewise, as we saw in *What's at Stake . . . ?*, Trump reversed much of what Obama did by the simple expedient of undoing his directions to the bureaucracy, or canceling them. His 2018 decision to separate refugee families at the border was clearly his interpretation of a law that had never been used that way before even though he blamed Democrats for it. Such executive action is always subject to court challenge, especially if Congress is hostile, but a friendly bureaucracy, such as the Department of Justice in the refugee case, can help the president make such policy changes by not obstructing them. In addition, presidents have a few specific ways they can shape the bureaucracy.

APPOINTMENT POWER Presidents have some substantial powers at their disposal for controlling the bureaucracy. The first is the power of appointment. For the departments, and for quite a few of the independent agencies, presidents appoint the heads and the next layer or two of undersecretaries and deputy secretaries. These cabinet secretaries and agency administrators are responsible for running the departments and agencies. The president's formal power, though quite significant, is often watered down by the political realities of the appointment and policymaking processes.

Cabinet secretaries are supposed to set directions for the departments and agencies that serve the president's overall policy goals. The reality is that, although the president does select numerous political appointees, many also have to be approved by the Senate. The process begins at the start of the president's administration. At that time, the president is working to gain support for his or her overall program and doesn't want to make choices that are considered too controversial. This desire for early widespread support means presidents tend to play it safe and to nominate individuals with extensive experience in the policy areas they will oversee. Their backgrounds mean that the president's men and women have divided loyalties. They arrive on the job with some sympathy for the special interests and agencies they are to supervise on the president's behalf, as well as loyalty to the president.

As we mentioned, recent presidents have sought to achieve political control over agencies by expanding the numbers of their appointees at the top levels of agencies, especially those agencies whose missions are not consistent with the administration's policy agenda.[37] President George W. Bush was especially adept at this politicization of the bureaucracy. For instance, in his second term, he appointed one of his most trusted personal advisers to head the Department of Justice. Officials in the Justice Department fired existing U.S. attorneys and replaced them with conservatives who would be more sympathetic to Republican policy concerns, which blunted the agency's traditionally aggressive enforcement of civil rights laws.[38] This effort was not restricted to Justice, but a similar political housecleaning followed in the wake of the September 11 attacks and criticisms of the CIA's anti-terrorist preparations.[39]

President Obama's appointees were named with less of an eye to their ideological views than to their scientific expertise. As a Democrat, Obama attempted to reinvigorate the regulatory purpose and effective competence of the agencies in the bureaucracy, but Senate Republicans still refused to approve many of his recommendations because they generally disapprove of the agencies' regulatory mission. Rather than let agencies languish, Obama sought to get his nominations through with the use of recess appointments, a practice authorized by the Constitution that allows the president to make appointments without Senate approval when Congress is not in session. Intended to allow the president to deal with emergency appointments when the Senate cannot meet, presidents of both parties have used the strategy to get around recalcitrant Senates. In Obama's case the Republican House refused to agree to recess in order to thwart an impending Obama recess appointment, keeping both itself and the Senate in nominal session even while taking breaks. When the practice was challenged in court, the Supreme Court sided unanimously with the Senate, thus invalidating the president's appointment to the agency in question, the National Labor Relations Board, and tipping the balance toward Congress in the ongoing presidential-congressional battle for control of the bureaucracy.[40]

As we mentioned earlier, Trump has taken a somewhat scattershot approach to filling the bureaucratic branch. One hundred days into his administration, 87 percent of his executive branch positions were unstaffed.[41] He has had difficulty finding career bureaucrats who want to be associated with his administration's eccentric approach to governing, and they have experienced high turnover. He fills the positions in which he is interested, leaving others to languish or to be taken under the vice president's wing.

THE BUDGET PROPOSAL The second major power that presidents have in dealing with the bureaucracy is their key role in the budget process. About fifteen months before a budget request goes to Congress, the agencies send their preferred budget requests to the Office of Management and Budget, which can lower, or raise, departmental budget requests. Thus the president's budget, which is sent to Congress, is a good statement of the president's overall program for the national government, reflecting priorities, new initiatives, and intended cutbacks. The president's political appointees and the civil servants who testify before Congress are expected to defend the president's budget.

And they do defend the president's budget, at least in their prepared statements. However, civil servants have contacts with interest group leaders, congressional staff, the media, and members of Congress themselves. Regardless of what the president wants, the agencies' real preferences are made known to sympathetic members of the key authorizations and appropriations committees. Thus the president's budget is a beginning bargaining point, but Congress can freely add to or cut back presidential requests, and most of the time it does so. The president's budget powers, while not insignificant, are no match for an agency with strong interest group and congressional support. Presidential influence over the bureaucratic budget is generally more effective in terminating an activity that the president opposes than in implementing a program that the agency opposes.[42]

GOVERNMENT REORGANIZATION The president also can try to reorganize the bureaucracy, combining some agencies, eliminating others, and generally restructuring the way government responsibilities are handled. Such reorganization efforts have become a passion with some presidents, but they are limited in their efforts by the need for congressional approval.[43] President Trump has proposed a massive reorganization of bureaucracy to make the government more efficient to suit his ideological inclinations—the Departments of Labor and Education might be combined, for instance, and the word "welfare," which carries a social stigma, added to the name of the Department of Health and Human Services. Whether or not this effort is successful, Trump has reorganized the bureaucracy in another way—by repurposing it. The Department of the Interior is more a support to big business than to the preservation of natural resources, for instance, and the agency that runs Obamacare increasingly works to remove protections for affordable care.[44]

POWERS OF PERSUASION The final major power that presidents have over the bureaucracy is an informal one, the prestige of the office itself. The Office of the President impresses just about everyone. For presidents intent on change in an agency, their powers of persuasion and the sheer weight of the office can produce results. Few bureaucrats could stand face to face with the president of the United States and ignore a legal order. But presidents have limited time in office, their political pressures are many, and they need to choose their priorities carefully. The media, for example, will not permit presidents to spend a good part of each day worrying about programs that they think are trivial. A president who does so will be publicly criticized for wasting time on "minor matters." Thus the president and his or her top White House staff have to move on to other things. The temptation for a bureaucracy that does not want to cooperate with a presidential initiative is to wait it out, to take the matter under study, or to be "able" to accomplish only a minor part of the president's agenda. The agency or department can then begin the process of regaining whatever ground it lost. It, after all, will be there long after the current president is gone.

> iron triangles the phenomenon of a clientele group, congressional committee, and bureaucratic agency cooperating to make mutually beneficial policy

THE BUREAUCRACY AND CONGRESS

Relationships between the bureaucracy and Congress are not any more clear-cut than those between the agencies and the president, but in the long run individual members of Congress, if not the whole institution itself, have more control over what specific bureaucracies do than does the executive branch. This is not due to any particular grant of power by the Constitution, but rather to informal policy-making relationships that have grown up over time and are now all but institutionalized. That is, much of the influence over the bureaucracy is exercised by Congress, but in highly decentralized agency-by-agency and subcommittee-by-subcommittee sets of relationships.

IRON TRIANGLES Much of the effective power in making policy in Washington is lodged in what political scientists call **iron triangles**. An iron triangle is a tight alliance among congressional committees, interest groups or representatives of regulated industries, and bureaucratic agencies, in which policy comes to be made for the benefit of the shared interests of all three, not for the benefit of the greater public. Politicians are themselves quite aware of the pervasive triangular monopoly of power. Former secretary of health, education, and welfare John Gardner once declared before the Senate Government Operations Committee, "As everyone in this room knows but few people outside of Washington understand, questions of public policy nominally lodged with the Secretary are often decided far beyond the Secretary's reach by a trinity—not exactly a holy trinity—consisting of (1) representatives of an outside lobby, (2) middle-level bureaucrats, and (3) selected members of Congress."[45]

A good example of an iron triangle is the natural resources policy shown in Figure 9.1. In 2010, as oil gushed into the Gulf of Mexico from the ruined oil rig Deepwater Horizon, the Minerals Management Service (MMS), an obscure agency that few citizens had heard of, was blasted into the news. The MMS, which was in charge of issuing leases, collecting royalties, and overseeing the dangerous work of offshore drilling for oil and gas on America's continental shelf, was accused of having cozy and even illegal relationships with the industry it was charged with regulating. Agency employees were said to have accepted meals, gifts, and sporting trips from the oil industry, and some agency staff were accused of having had sex and using drugs with industry employees.

At the agency's top sat people like J. Steven Griles, who had worked as an oil industry lobbyist before joining the

FIGURE 9.1
The Oil Industry–BOEM Iron Triangle

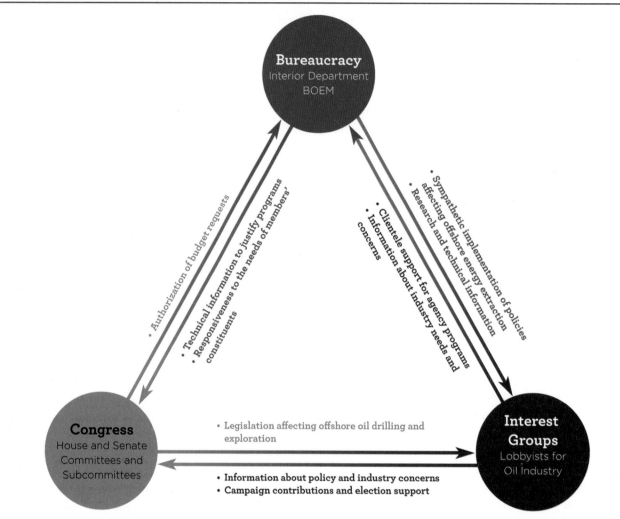

Iron triangles (involving Congress, the bureaucracy, and special interest groups) exist on nearly every subgovernment level. In this example, you can see how the BOEM (the Bureau of Ocean Energy Management), which depends on the House and the Senate for its budget, influences and is influenced by oil company lobbyists, who in turn influence and are influenced by House and Senate committees and subcommittees. This mutual interdependence represents a monopoly of power.

government. In middle management, the line between the industry and its regulators in the field was blurred.[46] As one MMS district manager put it, "Obviously we're all oil industry.... We're all from the same part of the country. Almost all our inspectors have worked for oil companies out on the [Gulf] platforms. They grew up in the same towns."[47] The industry and agency shared a goal of maximizing oil and gas production with hardly more than a whisper of concern for the effects of what was believed to be an unlikely accident. Not surprisingly, many key congressional leaders of the committees with jurisdiction over oil and gas drilling policies are from states with large petroleum interests. The House Committee on Natural

Resources and its subcommittee on Energy and Mineral Resources have several members whose districts have major financial interests in oil and gas production, and most of these members receive substantial contributions from the oil and gas industry. The oil- and gas-producing states of Louisiana, Texas, Oklahoma, Colorado, and New Mexico all have members of Congress who receive major contributions from oil and gas industry sources.[48]

Thus the oil industry, the MMS, and members of Congress with responsibility for overseeing the agency all possessed interests in protecting energy production that reinforced one another in a cozy triangle and disregarded the general public's interests in avoiding environmental catastrophe and receiving the appropriate royalties from oil and gas use. The drug and sex scandals, along with the media's relentless coverage of the Deepwater Horizon disaster, focused national attention on the problem and spurred the Obama administration to reorganize the agency, now called the Bureau of Ocean Energy Management (BOEM). However, the forces that created this situation—that is, the intertwined interests among members of Congress who serve on committees that oversee agencies that regulate the industries that affect voters in their districts—are a fundamental part of our political-economic system. As long as citizens and industry are free to "petition Congress for redress of grievances," as the First Amendment guarantees, iron triangles will remain.

The metaphor of the iron triangle has been refined by scholars, who speak instead of **issue networks**.[49] The iron triangle suggests a particular relationship among a fixed interest group and fixed agencies and fixed subcommittees. The network idea suggests that the relationships are more complex than a simple triangle. There are really clusters of interest groups, policy specialists, consultants, and research institutes ("think tanks") that are influential in policy areas. To continue with the offshore drilling example, environmental groups such as the League of Conservation Voters monitor the environmental records of members of Congress, and outside groups use existing laws to force agencies like the BOEM to change their procedures. So, for example, the Center for Biological Diversity sought to sue the Department of the Interior (of which the MMS was part) for failing to get appropriate environmental permits required by the Marine Mammal Protection Act and the Endangered Species Act.[50] Thus "outsiders" can use the courts, and they often lobby sympathetic members of Congress to contest the relationships that develop as iron triangles. Their participation shows that the concept of an iron triangle does not always incorporate all the actors in a particular policy area. That is, while the relationships identified by the iron triangle remain important, the full range of politics is frequently better captured by the concept of issue networks.

issue networks complex systems of relationships among groups that influence policy, including elected leaders, interest groups, specialists, consultants, and research institutes

congressional oversight efforts by Congress, especially through committees, to monitor agency rule making, enforcement, and implementation of congressional policies

Andrew Harrer/Bloomberg via Getty Images

Partisan-Fueled Oversight

The traditional role of oversight is for Congress to check on the executive branch, but partisan differences can also influence these investigations. Here, California senator Kamala Harris questions a witness on Capitol Hill in Washington, D.C., during a Senate Intelligence Committee hearing on social media influence in the 2016 U.S. elections. Many Republicans have sought to downplay the possible Russian interference, while Democrats are eager to investigate further now that they have a majority in the House.

CONGRESSIONAL CONTROL OF THE BUREAUCRACY

Congressional control of the bureaucracy is found more in the impact of congressional committees and subcommittees than in the actions of the institution as a whole. Congress, of course, passes the laws that create the agencies, assigns them their responsibilities, and funds their operations. Furthermore, Congress can, and frequently does, change the laws under which the agencies operate. Thus Congress clearly has the formal power to control the bureaucracy. It also has access to a good deal of information that helps members monitor the bureaucracy. This monitoring process, as we saw in Chapter 7, is called **congressional oversight**. Members learn about agency behavior through required reports, oversight hearings and testimony by experts, and reports by congressional agencies such as the Government Accountability Office, and from constituents and organized interests.[51] But Congress is itself often divided about what it wants to do and is unable to set clear guidelines for agencies. During the first six years of the George W. Bush administration, for example, the Republican majority was more intent on supporting the president than on protecting congressional prerogatives in the policy process. This aided the president's expansion of control of the bureaucracy.[52] Only when a congressional consensus exists on what an agency should be doing, or at least that Congress should monitor what the agency does, is congressional control fully effective.

In general, agencies are quite responsive to the congressional committees most directly involved with their authorizations and appropriations. The congressional control that committees and subcommittees exert on the bureaucracy is not the same as the control exercised by Congress as a whole. This is because the subcommittee policy preferences do not always reflect accurately the preferences of the full Congress. Members of Congress gravitate to committees in which they have a special interest—either because of the member's background and expertise or because of the committee's special relevance for the home constituency.[53] Thus, in being responsive to the relevant committees and subcommittees, usually with the support of the organized interests served by the agencies, bureaucrats are clearly less sensitive to the preferences of Congress as a whole, the president, and the general public.

THE BUREAUCRACY AND THE COURTS

Agencies can be sued by individuals and businesses for not following the law. If a citizen disagrees with an agency ruling on welfare eligibility, or the adequacy of inspections of poultry processing plants, or even a ruling by the IRS, he or she can take the case to the courts. In some cases the courts have been important. A highly controversial example involves the timber industry. Environmentalists sued the Department of the Interior and the U.S. Forest Service to prevent logging in some of the old-growth forests of the Pacific Northwest. They sought protection for the spotted owl under the terms of the Endangered Species Act. After a decade-long struggle, logging was greatly restricted in the area in 1992, despite opposition by the economically important timbering interests of the region. However, under the more business-friendly George W. Bush administration, the issue was once again on the agenda and, as the timber industry gained ground, the environmental groups were back in court. In 2009 the Obama administration reversed the Bush administration policy that had doubled the amount of logging allowed.[54] The Trump administration has undone regulations that preserved the federal forests.[55]

More often, though, the courts play only a modest role in controlling the bureaucracy. One of the reasons for this limited role is that, since the Administrative Procedure Act of 1946, the courts have tended to defer to the expertise of the bureaucrats when agency decisions are appealed. That is, unless a clear principle of law is violated, the courts usually support administrative rulings.[56] So, for example,

while the Supreme Court did restrict some aspects of the George W. Bush administration's policies of unlimited detention of "enemy combatants" held at Guantánamo Bay, it did not go nearly as far as civil liberties advocates wanted.[57]

Another reason is that Congress explicitly puts the decisions of numerous agencies, such as the Department of Veterans Affairs, beyond the reach of the courts. They do this, of course, when members expect they will agree with the decisions of an agency but are uncertain about what the courts might do. Some agencies, like the IRS and those dealing with immigration, have their own units to resolve disputes. Finally, even without these restrictions, the courts' time is extremely limited. The departments and independent agencies make thousands and thousands of important decisions each year; the courts can act on only those decisions about which someone feels sufficiently aggrieved to take the agency to court. Court proceedings can drag on for years, and meanwhile the agencies go about their business making new decisions. In short, the courts can, in specific instances, decide cases that influence how the bureaucracy operates, but such instances are the exception rather than the rule.

PAUSE AND REVIEW Who, What, How

All of Washington and beyond have something at stake in bureaucratic politics. The agencies themselves battle over scarce resources, using the tools of constituency building to keep pressure on Congress to maintain their funding levels, and keeping their functions separate from other agencies even if the result is redundancy and inefficiency.

Presidents can employ a variety of techniques to control the bureaucracy, but given time constraints and the weight of bureaucratic norms, they are generally unsuccessful at wresting control from the bureaucrats.

Congress has much at stake in its interactions with the bureaucracy. The bottom line in bureaucratic politics is that the bureaucracy is ultimately responsible to Congress. It is difficult to speak of Congress as a whole institution guided by a common interest, but individual members of Congress certainly have identifiable interests. Because policymaking in Congress so often takes place at the committee and subcommittee levels, and because those committees develop iron triangle relationships with interest groups and the bureaucracies that serve them, members of Congress have quite a lot of input into what the bureaucracy does.

In Your Own Words Outline the relationship between the federal agencies and the three branches of the federal government.

Political Cartoons

Political cartoons do more than elicit a laugh or a chuckle. Frequently they avoid humor altogether, going for outrage, indignation, ridicule, or scathing contempt. Often, they are aimed at well-known public figures—easy targets like the president, a major celebrity, or a well-known business leader. But cartoonists also use their pens (and their wits) to shine light on less glamorous and less recognizable aspects of the political ecosystem.

The bureaucracy, for example, is almost by definition an unsexy subject. Stories about federal agencies are a snore, and there is usually precious little that a photograph can say about what they do. But a cartoonist, communicating with both words and pictures and armed with an arsenal of devices—among them exaggeration, irony, sarcasm, symbolism, shock, and humor—can make profound and attention-grabbing statements about topics that otherwise might be ignored. With this barrage of weapons aimed at you, your critical thinking skills are crucial.[1]

Clay Bennett/© the Christian Science Monitor (www.CS Monitor.com). Reprinted with permission.

ASSISTANT TO THE AIDE OF THE DEPUTY VICE CHAIRMAN OF THE COMMITTEE TO REDUCE PENTAGON BUREAUCRACY

What to Watch Out For

- **What is the event or issue that inspired the cartoon?** Political cartoonists do not attempt to inform you about current events; they assume that you already know what has happened. Their job is to comment on the news, and so your first step in savvy cartoon readership is to be up on what's happening in the world. In this case, the situation being lampooned is the very nature of bureaucracy itself.

- **Who, or what, is the subject?** Are there any real people in the cartoon? Who are they? Many cartoonists do not confine their art to real people. Some will use a generic person sometimes labeled to represent a group (big business, the U.S. Senate, environmentalists, a political party, or a federal agency). The subject here is an almost-faceless bureaucrat, playing off the idea that bureaucrats are automatons without personal identity.

- **Are there symbols in the cartoon? What do they represent?** Without a key to the symbols that cartoonists use, their art can be incomprehensible. Uncle Sam stands in for the United States and is often used to depict specific federal agencies; donkeys are Democrats, and elephants are Republicans. Often these symbols are combined in unique ways. Again, the lack of a full face for the bureaucrat reduces him to his title, a symbol of bureaucracy run rampant.

- **What is the cartoonist's opinion about the topic of the cartoon?** Do you agree with it or not? Why? The cartoonist here is gently mocking the bureaucracy's typically bureaucratic efforts to make itself less bureaucratic.

---

1. Questions are based on the PoliticalCartoons.com teachers' guide, www.cagle.com/teacher.

THE CITIZENS AND THE BUREAUCRACY

The tension between transparency and efficiency

The picture that emerges from a look at the politics of the bureaucracy is one of a powerful arm of government, somewhat answerable to the president, more responsible to Congress, but with considerable discretion to do what it wants, often in response to the special interests of clientele groups or regulated industry. If anyone is forgotten in this policymaking arrangement, it is the American public, the average citizens and consumers who are not well organized and who may not even know that they are affected by an issue until the policy is already law. We can look at the relationship between the bureaucracy and the public to determine how the public interest is considered in bureaucratic policymaking.

First, we should figure out what the "public interest" in a democracy really means. Is it the majority preference? If so, then what happens to the minority? Is the public interest some unknown, possibly unpleasant goal that we would favor unanimously if only we could be detached from our particular interests—a sort of national equivalent of eating our spinach because it's good for us? We can imagine some interests that would be disadvantaged by any notion of the public good, no matter how benign. Industries that pollute are disadvantaged by legislation promoting clean air and water; manufacturers of bombs, warplanes, and tanks are disadvantaged by peace. The point here is not to argue that there is no such thing as a "public interest" but to point out that in a democracy it may be difficult to reach consensus on it.

To that end, the public interest can probably best be determined by increasing the number of people who have input into deciding what it is. The facts of political life are that the most organized, vocal, and well-financed interests usually get heard by politicians, including bureaucrats. When we speak of the public interest, we usually refer to the interest that would be expressed by the unorganized, less vocal, poorer components of society, if they would only speak. In this final section we look at efforts to bring more people into the bureaucratic policymaking process so as to make policy more responsive to more citizens.

To help increase bureaucratic responsiveness and sensitivity to the public, Congress has made citizen participation a central feature in the policymaking of many agencies. The opening up of media channels to increase transparency and engagement has made this easier, although it is still not an open democratic process. Much increased transparency has taken the form of **citizen advisory councils** that, by statute, subject key policy decisions of agencies to outside consideration by members of the public. There are more than 1,200 such committees and councils in the executive branch. The people who participate on these councils are not representative of the citizenry; rather, they are typically chosen by the agencies and have special credentials or interests relevant to the agencies' work. Thus citizen advisory councils are hardly a reflection of the general population.

Seven different types of citizen advisory councils have been called over the years (1937 through 1996) to make recommendations on the Social Security system. All have favored the existing programs and recommended expansion.

Why? Because members of the councils were carefully selected from among people who already thought highly of Social Security. What political scientist Martha Derthick concluded about the Social Security councils is probably true generally: "The outsiders tended to become insiders as they were drawn into the council's deliberations. . . . Typically, advisory council reports paved the way for program executives' own current recommendations."[58] The public is not immune to the same forces that create the convergence of interests within iron triangles.

Other reform efforts have attempted to make the bureaucracy more accessible to the public. Citizen access is enhanced by the passage of **sunshine laws** that require that meetings of policymakers be open to the public. Thus the Government in the Sunshine Act of 1976 requires important agency reviews, hearings, and decision-making sessions to be open to the public, along with most congressional committee and subcommittee meetings. However, most national security and personnel meetings and many criminal investigative meetings are exempted.

The right to attend a meeting is of little use unless one can find out that it is being held. The Administrative Procedure Act requires advanced published notices of all hearings, proposed rules, and new regulations so that the public can attend and comment on decisions that might affect them. These announcements appear in the *Federal Register*. In a separate section, the *Federal Register* also contains major presidential documents, including executive orders, proclamations, transcripts of speeches and news conferences, and other White House releases.

With all this information about every meeting, every proposed regulation, and more, the *Federal Register* becomes very large—more than 70,000 pages a year. Such size makes it quite forbidding to the average citizen; fortunately, a government booklet, "The Federal Register: What It Is and How to Use It," is generally available in libraries and on the Internet, and it greatly eases the task of navigating the *Register*. An online edition of the *Federal Register* is also available (www.gpo.gov/fdsys/browse/collection.action?collectionCode=FR).

A related point of access is the **Freedom of Information Act (FOIA)**, which was passed in 1966 and has been

citizen advisory councils citizen groups that consider the policy decisions of an agency; a way to make the bureaucracy responsive to the general public

sunshine laws legislation opening the process of bureaucratic policymaking to the public

Freedom of Information Act (FOIA) the 1966 law that allows citizens to obtain copies of most public records

amended several times since. This act provides citizens with the right to copies of most public records held by the agencies. These records include the evidence used in agency decisions, correspondence pertaining to agency business, research data, financial records, and so forth. The agency has to provide the information requested or let the applicant know which provisions of the FOIA allow the agency to withhold the information.

Citizens also receive protection under the **Privacy Act of 1974**, which gives them the right to find out what information government agencies have about them. It also sets up procedures so that erroneous information can be corrected and ensures the confidentiality of Social Security, tax, and related records.

These reforms may provide little practical access for most citizens. Few of us have the time, the knowledge, or the energy to plow through the *Federal Register* and to attend dull meetings. Similarly, while many citizens no doubt feel they are not getting the full story from government agencies, they also do not have much of an idea of what it is they don't know. Hence, few of us ever use the FOIA.

In fact, few Americans try to gain access to the bureaucracy because of the generally accepted narrative that tells us that it is too big, too remote, too complex, and too devoted to special interests. If you can't fight city hall, you certainly can't take on the federal government. The public does not think well of the bureaucracy or the government, although it does report favorably on its interactions with individual bureaucrats and agencies.[59] One reason for the public disaffection with the bureaucracy may be that it is so constantly under attack by a frustrated president and by members of Congress who highlight the failings of some aspects of government to divert attention from those that are serving their interests only too well. What citizens hear comes from the decidedly biased information channels of people with political points of view. Another reason may be the way that federal agencies and departments are portrayed in the media—exaggerated characters of bumbling, inefficient, depersonalized government bots. (See *Don't Be Fooled by . . . Political Cartoons* for tips on evaluating some media depictions of the bureaucracy.) Small wonder few Americans are predisposed to respect the bureaucracy or the job it does.

Political scientist Kenneth Meier suggests that although countries usually get bureaucracies no worse than they deserve,

AP Photo/Dee Marvin

"Freedom" of Information

The 1966 Freedom of Information Act (FOIA) allows citizens access to declassified documents at the state and federal levels. However, provisions contained within the act allow authorities to refuse access to specific information for various reasons. Officials can do this by blacking out content, as in the documents shown here, or by refusing to release them entirely. Critics say that it can be next to impossible to piece together the actual events or facts surrounding an event when access is denied so frequently, and that declassified should mean just that—that it is open to the public for review.

the United States has managed to get one that is much better than it deserves, given citizen attitudes and attentiveness toward it. He says that in terms of responsiveness and competency, the U.S. federal bureaucracy is "arguably the best in the world."[60] He places the responsibility for maintaining the quality of the system squarely with the citizens and, to some extent, with the media, suggesting that citizens contact bureaucratic agencies about issues of concern, vote with an elected official's bureaucratic appointments in mind, keep realistic expectations of what government can do, and encourage the media in its watchdog role. Keeping the republic may require public participation in bureaucracy as well as in democracy.

In Your Own Words Analyze the tension between transparency and efficiency in the federal bureaucracy.

Privacy Act of 1974 a law that gives citizens access to the government's files on them

LET'S REVISIT: *What's at Stake . . . ?*

At the beginning of this chapter we discussed the many regulations, mostly enacted by the Obama administration, that President Trump was intent on rolling back. In many cases he was successful – we mentioned a dozen but there were hundreds. We also said that regulations are controversial, but that they affect our lives (positively or negatively) every day in all kinds of ways.

Now that we know much more about regulations and the regulatory infrastructure that lets us swallow pills, eat dinner, or put our kids to sleep at night with a reasonable assurance that disaster will not befall us, we know that a wholly unregulated life is something most of us probably don't want to accept. Life can be hazardous and often government is the only one in a position to provide protection.

But like so many things in life, this is a line-drawing problem. Everyone wants to regulate murder and poisonous pills and flammable baby pajamas, but not everyone wants to protect the environment or limit the cost of college loans or police the loans made by banks. Just what is at stake in unrolling the regulations that the Obama administration put in place?

Most of the regulations of the Obama years, at least the ones targeted by Trump, were designed to safeguard the environment, protect the health of individuals, manage the economic crisis and keep the less fortunate segments of the population from being taken advantage of by the powerful segments. If you think about what those things have in common, most of them are costly to wealthy people while providing benefits to the less well off.

That means wealthier people have a stake in getting rid of them; there will be huge business savings and increased profits for many industries without government telling them to be socially responsible. Supporters argue that these savings and profits will trickle down and benefit workers and consumers too, though much ink has been spilled debating this point.

Fiscally conscious people have a stake in rolling back regulations because the bureaucracy is often inefficient and wasteful, and many things cost much more than they need to. But the flip side is that regulations can also save money in the long run even if they cost more in the short run. The *Clues to Critical Thinking* in this chapter makes that point, and we have evidence in the fact that under Obamacare health care costs were coming down for everyone. And saving the environment now is undoubtedly cheaper than trying to colonize space when we've depleted this planet.

Those who worry about the environment or the climate also have huge stakes in the rolling back of Obama regulations because scientists are convinced that the window for protecting the planet is rapidly closing.[61] Eliminating emissions standards and getting out of the Paris Climate Agreement are likely to be incredibly costly in the long run.

The stakes in regulation boil down to two issues – whether you think it is government's job to help protect individuals and the planet from the consequences of our or others' actions, and whether we would rather pay for those consequences, some of which are undeniable, in the short term, or hope for the best in the long term. The current administration's policy is to save now and hope individuals and the future can take care of themselves.

CLUES to Critical Thinking

"Why Corporate America Loves Donald Trump"

By *The Economist*, May 24, 2018

Deregulation is clearly a big issue for President Trump but as this Economist *article points out, and as we have seen in this chapter, it is not without costs.*

Most American elites believe that the Trump presidency is hurting their country. Foreign-policy mandarins are terrified that security alliances are being wrecked. Fiscal experts warn that borrowing is spiralling out of control. Scientists deplore the rejection of climate change. And some legal experts warn of a looming constitutional crisis.

Amid the tumult there is a striking exception. The people who run companies have made their calculations about the Age of Trump. On balance, they like it. Bosses reckon that the value of tax cuts, deregulation and potential trade concessions from China outweighs the hazy costs of weaker institutions and trade wars. And they are willing to play along with President Donald Trump's home-brewed economic vision, in which firms are freed from the state and unfair foreign competition, and profits, investment and, eventually, wages soar.

The financial fireworks on display in the first quarter of this year suggest that this vision is coming true. The earnings of listed firms rose by 22% compared with a year earlier; investment was up by 19%. But as our briefing explains, the investment surge is unlike any before—it is skewed towards tech giants, not firms with factories. When it comes to gauging the full costs of Mr Trump, America Inc is being short-sighted and sloppy.

The view from the C-suite

Since winning Congress and the White House, the Republicans have sought to unleash the power of business. After the election Mr Trump held summits with tycoons, televised live from the boardroom at Trump Tower, and later from his new HQ in the Oval Office. Though bosses have tired of this kind of pantomime, particularly after Mr Trump's equivocations over white-supremacist protests in Virginia last summer, they remain bullish. A reason is the Republican corporate-tax reform passed in December, the first on such a scale since 1986. It does several sensible things, including cutting headline rates to average European levels. The annual saving of $100bn is worth 6% of pre-tax profits (it accounts for a tenth of the fiscal deficit).

Deregulation is in full swing. This week saw a relaxation of banking rules. The leaders of many agencies have been replaced with Trump appointees. The change at the top, firms say, means officials are being more helpful. A surprising number of boardrooms support a muscular stance on trade with China. If, for argument's sake, China capitulated to American demands and imported $200bn more goods a year, it could boost the earnings of America Inc by a further 2%. The benefits for business of Mr Trump are clear, then: less tax and red tape, potential trade gains and a 6–8% uplift in earnings.

The trouble is that companies are often poor at assessing nebulous risks, and CEOs' overall view of the environment is fallible. During the Obama years corporate America was convinced it was under siege when in fact, judged by the numbers, it was in a golden era, with average profits 31% above long-term levels. Now bosses think they have entered a nirvana, when the reality is that the country's system of commerce is lurching away from rules, openness and multilateral treaties towards arbitrariness, insularity and transient deals.

As the contours of this new world become clearer, so will its costs to business in terms of complexity and predictability. Take complexity first. One of the ironies of the Trump team's agenda is that, although they want to get out of businesses' hair at home, when it comes to trade they want to regulate. When they tinker with tariffs, large numbers of firms have to scurry to respond because they have global supply chains. The steel duties proposed in March cover a mere 0.5% of American imports, but so far this month 200-odd listed American firms have discussed the financial impact of tariffs on their calls with investors. Over time, a mesh of distortions will build up.

Because trade is becoming more regulated, a new surveillance bureaucracy is sprouting. On May 23rd the Department of Commerce launched a probe of car imports. A bill in Congress envisages vetting all foreign investment into America to ensure that it does not jeopardise the country's "technological and industrial leadership in areas related to national security". American firms have $8trn of capital sunk abroad; foreign firms have $7trn in America; and there have been 15,000 inbound deals since 2008. The cost involved in monitoring all this activity could ultimately be vast. As America eschews global co-operation, its firms will also face more duplicative regulation abroad. Europe has already introduced new regimes this year for financial instruments and data.

The expense of re-regulating trade could even exceed the benefits of deregulation at home. That might be tolerable, were it not for the other big cost of the Trump era: unpredictability. At home the corporate-tax cuts will partly expire after 2022. America's negotiators are gunning for a five-year sunset clause in a new NAFTA deal, although Canada and Mexico would prefer something permanent. Bosses hope that the belligerence on trade is a ploy borrowed from "The Apprentice", and that stable agreements will emerge. But imagine that America stitches up a deal with China and the bilateral trade deficit then fails to shrink, or Chinese firms cease buying American high-tech components as they become self-sufficient, or Mr Trump is mocked for getting a bad deal. If so, the White House might rip the agreement up.

The new laws of the jungle

Another reason for the growing unpredictability is Mr Trump's urge to show off his power with acts of pure political discretion. He has just asked the postal service to raise delivery prices for Amazon, his bête noire and the world's second-most valuable listed firm. He could easily strike out in anger at other Silicon Valley firms—after all, they increasingly control the flow of political information. He wants the fate of ZTE, a Chinese telecoms firm banned in America for sanctions violations, to turn on his personal whim. Inevitably, other countries are playing rougher, too. China's antitrust police are blocking Qualcomm's $52bn

takeover of NXP, a rival semiconductor firm, as a bargaining chip. When policy becomes a rolling negotiation, lobbying explodes. The less predictable business environment that results will raise the cost of capital.

As America's expansion gets longer in the tooth, these arbitrary interventions could intensify. Mr Trump expects wages to rise, but 85% of firms in the S&P 500 are forecast to expand margins by 2019, reflecting a control of costs. Either shareholders, or workers and Mr Trump, are going to be disappointed. Given that interest rates are rising, a recession is likely in the next few years. In a downturn, American business may find that its fabled flexibility has been compromised because the politics of firing workers and slashing costs has become toxic.

Republicans are right that tax cuts and wise deregulation can boost firms' competitiveness. But little progress is being made on other priorities, including repairing infrastructure, ensuring small firms are not squashed by monopolies and reforming the education system. Most firms pride themselves on being level-headed, but at some point that bleeds into complacency. American business may one day conclude that this was the moment when it booked all the benefits of the Trump era, while failing to account properly for the costs. A strategy that assumes revenues but not expenses rarely makes sense.

Source: © The Economist Group Limited, London (May 24, 2018)

Consider the source and the audience: The *Economist* is a conservative British news weekly with a focus, as its name suggests, on the economy and the political context that affects it. It has a healthy circulation in the US as well as the UK. What kind of warning are they passing on here and why would their audience care?

Lay out the argument and the underlying values and assumptions: The *Economist* is all in favor of reduced corporate taxes and deregulation but they are wary of the way Trump is proceeding. They fear deregulation at home is being replaced with a regulatory structure to handle increased regulation of trade and that only certain businesses are benefiting. What is the author's view of fair trade and a healthy economy? What is the risk of "unpredictability?"

Uncover the evidence: This argument is based on expectations of what will happen to the economy based on historical experience. Is that a sound way to draw conclusions? What about the economic patterns they rely on (expecting a recession in a few years, for instance)? Should we trust that possibility?

Evaluate the conclusion: Essentially, the *Economist* is arguing that the Trump administration is replacing one regulatory structure with another that might work out well and might not. But only certain industries are benefiting and other priorities are falling behind. Do you agree?

Sort out the political implications: What are the costs of Trump's deregulatory policy in terms of things not done? Will we wish we had done them at some point? Will there still be time?

Review

What Is Bureaucracy?

Bureaucracies are everywhere today, in the private as well as the public spheres. They create a special problem for democratic politics because the desire for democratic accountability often conflicts with the desire to take politics out of the bureaucracy. We have moved from the spoils system of the nineteenth century to a civil service merit system with a more professionalized bureaucracy.

bureaucracy (p. 303)
neutral competence (p. 303)

accountability (p. 304)
red tape (p. 305)

The American Federal Bureaucracy

The U.S. bureaucracy has grown from just three cabinet departments at the founding to a gigantic apparatus of fifteen cabinet-level departments and hundreds of independent agencies, regulatory commissions, and government corporations. This growth has been in response to the expansion of the nation, the politics of special economic and social groups, and the emergence of new problems.

spoils system (p. 306)
patronage (p. 306)
civil service (p. 306)
Pendleton Act (p. 306)
Hatch Act (p. 306)

clientele groups (p. 308)
departments (p. 308)
independent agencies (p. 309)
independent regulatory boards and
     commissions (p. 309)

regulations (p. 309)
government corporations (p. 312)
bureaucratic discretion (p. 313)
Federal Register (p. 313)

Politics Inside the Bureaucracy

The culture of bureaucracy refers to how agencies operate—their assumptions, values, and habits. The bureaucratic culture increases employees' belief in the programs they administer, their commitment to the survival and growth of their agencies, and the tendency to rely on rules and procedures rather than goals.

Many observers believe that the bureaucracy should simply administer the laws the political branches have enacted. In reality, the agencies of the bureaucracy make government policy, and they play the roles of judge and jury in enforcing those policies. These activities are in part an unavoidable consequence of the tremendous technical expertise of the agencies because Congress and the president simply cannot perform many technical tasks.

bureaucratic culture (p. 315)

bureaucratese (p. 316)

whistleblowers (p. 317)

External Bureaucratic Politics

Agencies work actively for their political survival. They attempt to establish strong support outside the agency, to avoid direct competition with other agencies, and to jealously guard their own policy jurisdictions. Presidential powers are only modestly effective in controlling the bureaucracy. The affected clientele groups working in close cooperation with the agencies and the congressional committees that oversee them form powerful iron triangles.

agency capture (p. 320)
iron triangles (p. 323)

issue networks (p. 325)
congressional oversight (p. 325)

The Citizens and the Bureaucracy

Regardless of what the public may think, the U.S. bureaucracy is actually quite responsive and competent when compared with the bureaucracies of other countries. Citizens can increase this responsiveness by taking advantage of opportunities for gaining access to bureaucratic decision making.

citizen advisory councils (p. 328)
sunshine laws (p. 328)
Freedom of Information Act (FOIA) (p. 328)

Privacy Act of 1974 (p. 329)

In Your Own Words

After you've read this chapter, you will be able to

10.1 Describe the role that law plays in democratic societies.

10.2 Discuss the role of Congress and the Constitution in establishing the judiciary.

10.3 Explain how federalism plays out in the dual court system.

10.4 Outline the institutional rules and political influences that shape the Supreme Court and the decisions it makes.

10.5 Describe the relationship between citizens and the courts in America.

10

THE AMERICAN LEGAL SYSTEM AND THE COURTS

What's at Stake . . . When the Supreme Court Gets Involved in Partisan Politics?

THERE IS A CHERISHED NARRATIVE in American politics that says justice is blind and the Supreme Court is an apolitical, impartial dispenser of it. The marble pillars, red velvet drapes, and black robes are all in aid of keeping that narrative going. Don't let any of it fool you.

The Supreme Court is a thoroughly political institution. There is no more classic example of the Supreme Court dabbling in politics than the 2000 presidential election between George W. Bush and Al Gore and the resulting five-to-four decision in *Bush v. Gore*. The case must have set Alexander Hamilton spinning in his grave. In *The Federalist Papers*, the American founder gave life to the narrative when he wrote confidently that the Supreme Court would be the least dangerous branch of government. Having the power of neither the sword nor the purse, it could do little other than judge, and Hamilton blithely assumed that those judgments would remain legal ones, not matters of raw power politics.

More than two hundred years later, however, without military might or budgetary power, the Supreme Court took into its own hands the very political task of deciding who would be the next president of the United States and, what's more, made that decision right down party lines. On a five-to-four vote (five more conservative justices versus four more liberal ones), the Supreme Court overturned the decision of the Florida Supreme Court to allow a recount of votes in the contested Florida election and awarded electoral victory to Bush.

How had it come to this? The presidential vote in Florida was virtually tied, recounts were required by law in some locations, and voting snafus in several other counties had left untold numbers of votes uncounted. Whether those votes should, or even could, be counted or whether voter error and system failure had rendered them invalid was in dispute. Believing that a count of the disputed ballots would give him the few hundred votes he needed for victory, Al Gore wanted the recount. Bush did not. The Florida secretary of state, a Republican appointed by the governor, Bush's brother, ordered the vote counting finished. The Florida Supreme Court, dominated heavily by Democrats, ruled instead that a recount should go forward.

Bush appealed to the U.S. Supreme Court, asking it to overturn the Florida Supreme Court's decision and to stay, or suspend, the recount pending its decision. A divided Court issued the stay. Justice John Paul Stevens took the unusual route of writing a dissent from the stay, arguing that it was unwise to "stop the counting of legal votes." Justice Antonin Scalia wrote in response that the recount would pose "irreparable harm" to Bush by "casting a cloud on what he claims to be the legitimacy of his election."

The split between the justices, so apparent in the order for the stay, reappeared in the final decision, where six separate opinions ended up being written. On a five-to-four vote, the majority claimed that if the recount went forward under the Florida Supreme Court's order with different standards for counting the vote in different counties, it would amount to a denial of equal protection of the laws. The amount of work required to bring about a fair recount could not be accomplished before the December 12 deadline.

Robert King/Newsmakers

The Embattled Ballots

With the 2000 presidential election hinging on the outcome in too-close-to-call Florida, an election judge examines a punch card ballot during the vote recount in Broward County. The state recount was later ended by the Supreme Court ruling in Bush v. Gore, *which split the justices along party lines and effectively handed the election to George W. Bush despite Al Gore's lead in the popular vote.*

A three-person subset of the majority added that the Florida court's order was illegal in the first place.

The dissenters argued instead that the December 12 deadline was not fixed and that the recount could have taken place up to the meeting of the Electoral College on December 18, that there was no equal protection issue, that the Supreme Court should defer to the Florida Supreme Court on issues of state law, and that by involving itself in the political case, the Court risked losing public trust. While the winner of the election was in dispute, wrote Stevens, "the loser is perfectly clear. It is the nation's confidence in the judge as an impartial guardian of the rule of law."

Who was right here? The issue was debated by everyone from angry demonstrators outside the Court to learned commentators in scholarly journals, from families at the dinner table to editorial writers in the nation's press. Was Scalia correct that Bush had really already won and that it was up to the Court to save the legitimacy of his claim to power? Or was Stevens right: that by engaging in politics so blatantly, the Court had done itself irremediable damage in the eyes of the public? What was really at stake for the Court and for America in the five-to-four decision of *Bush v. Gore?* **《**

IMAGINE a world without laws. You careen down the road in your car, at any speed that takes your fancy. You park where you please and enter a drugstore that sells drugs of all sorts, from Prozac to LSD to vodka and beer. You purchase what you like—no one asks you for proof of your age or for a prescription—and there are no restrictions on what or how much you buy. There are no rules governing the production or usage of currency, either, so you hope that the dealer will accept what you have to offer in trade.

Life is looking pretty good as you head back out to the street, only to find that your car is no longer there. Theft is not illegal, and you curse yourself for forgetting to set the car alarm and for not using your wheel lock. There are no police to call, and even if there were, tracking down your car would be virtually impossible since there are no vehicle registration laws to prove you own it in the first place.

Rather than walk—these streets are quite dangerous, after all—you spot a likely car to get you home. You have to wrestle with the occupant, who manages to clout you over the head before you drive away. It isn't much of a prize, covered with dents and nicks from innumerable clashes with other cars jockeying for position at intersections where there are neither stop signs nor lights and the right of the faster prevails. Arriving home to enjoy your beer in peace and to gain a respite from the war zone you call your local community, you find that another family has moved in while you were shopping. Groaning with frustration, you think that surely there must be a better way!

And there is. As often as we might rail against restrictions on our freedom, such as not being able to buy beer if we are under twenty-one, or having to wear a motorcycle helmet, or not being able to speed down an empty highway, laws actually do us much more good than harm. British philosophers Thomas Hobbes and John Locke, whom we discussed in Chapter 1, both imagined a "prepolitical" world without laws. Inhabitants of Hobbes's state of nature found life without laws to be dismal or, as he put it, "solitary, poor, nasty, brutish and short." And although residents of Locke's state of nature merely found the lawless life to be "inconvenient," they had to mount a constant defense of their possessions and their lives. One of the reasons both Hobbes and Locke thought people would be willing to leave the state of nature for civil society, and to give up their freedom to do whatever they wanted, was to gain security, order, and predictability in life. Because we tend to focus on the laws that stop us from doing the things we want to do, or that require us to do things we don't want to do, we often forget the full array of laws that make it possible for us to live together in relative peace and to leave behind the brutishness of Hobbes's state of nature and the inconveniences of Locke's.

Laws occupy a central position in any political society, but especially in a democracy, where the distinguishing characteristic is that rule is ultimately by citizen-made law and not by the whim of a tyrant. Laws are the "how" in the formulation of politics as "who gets what, and how"—they dictate how our collective lives are to be organized, what rights we can claim, what principles we should live by, and how we can use the system to get what we want. Laws can also be the "what" in the formulation, as citizens and political actors use the existing rules to create new rules that produce even more favorable outcomes for themselves.

LAW AND THE AMERICAN LEGAL SYSTEM

Rules of the game that make collective living possible

Thinking about the law can be confusing. On the one hand, laws are the sorts of rules we have been discussing: limits and restrictions that get in our way, or that make life a little easier. On the other hand, we would like to believe in the narrative, reinforced by our founding, that our legal system is founded on rules that represent basic and enduring principles of justice, that create for us a higher level of civilization. The truth is a bit of both. Laws are products of the political process, created by political human beings to help them get valuable resources. Those resources may be civil peace and security, or a particular moral order, or power and influence, or even goods or entitlements. Thus, for security, we have laws that eliminate traffic chaos, enforce contracts, and ban violence. For moral order (and for security, as well!), we have laws against murder, incest, and rape. And for political advantage, we have laws like those that give large states greater power in the process of electing a president and those that allow electoral districts to be drawn by the majority party. Laws dealing with more concrete resources are those that, for example, give tax breaks to homeowners or subsidize dairy farmers.

Different political systems produce different systems of laws. In small communities where everyone shares values and experiences, formal legal structures may be unnecessary since everyone knows what is expected of him or her, and the community can force compliance with those expectations, perhaps by ostracizing nonconformists. In authoritarian systems, like those of Russia, North Korea, or China, laws exist primarily to serve the rulers and the state, and they are subject to sudden change at the whim of the rulers. In systems that merge church and state, such as the Holy Roman Empire, pre-Enlightenment Europe, or some Islamic countries today, laws are assumed to be God-given, and violations of the law are analogous to sin against an all-powerful creator. These sorts of legal systems are not much more convenient for the "ruled" than is Locke's state of nature, though they may be more secure.

In nonauthoritarian countries, where citizens are more than mere subjects and can make claims of rights against the government, laws are understood to exist for the purpose of serving the citizens. That is, laws make life more convenient, even if they have to restrict our actions to do so. But laws, and the courts that interpret and apply them, perform a variety of functions in democratic societies, some of which we commonly recognize, and others of which are less obvious.

THE ROLE OF LAW IN DEMOCRATIC SOCIETIES

For the purpose of understanding the role of law in democratic political systems, we can focus on five important functions of laws:[1]

- The most obvious function follows directly from Hobbes and Locke: laws provide security (for people and their property) so that we may go about our daily lives in relative harmony.
- Laws provide predictability, allowing us to plan our activities and business without fearing a random judgment that tells us we have broken a law we didn't know existed.
- The fact that laws are known in advance and that they identify punishable behaviors leads to the conflict-resolution function of laws in a democracy, through neutral third parties known as **courts.**
- Laws reflect and enforce conformity to society's values—for instance, that murder is wrong or that parents (or others) should not be allowed to abuse children.
- Laws distribute the benefits and rewards that society has to offer, and they allocate the costs of those good things, whether they are welfare benefits, civil rights protection, or tax breaks.

THE AMERICAN LEGAL TRADITION

We mentioned earlier that different political systems have different kinds of legal systems—that is, different systems

courts institutions that sit as neutral third parties to resolve conflicts according to the law

civil-law tradition a legal system based on a detailed comprehensive legal code, usually created by the legislature

common-law tradition a legal system based on the accumulated rulings of judges over time, applied uniformly—judge-made law

precedent a previous decision or ruling that, in common-law tradition, is binding on subsequent decisions

designed to provide order and resolve conflict through the use of laws. Most governments in the industrialized world, including many European countries, South America, Japan, the province of Quebec in Canada, and the state of Louisiana (because of its French heritage), have a legal system founded on a **civil-law tradition**, based on a detailed, comprehensive legal code usually generated by the legislature. Some of these codes date back to the days of Napoleon (1804). Such codified systems leave little to the discretion of judges in determining what the law is. Instead, the judge's job is to take an active role in getting at the truth. He or she investigates the facts, asks questions, and determines what has happened. The emphasis is more on getting the appropriate outcome than on maintaining the integrity of the procedures, although fair procedures are still important. While this system is well entrenched in much of the world, and has many defenders, the legal system in the United States is different in three crucial ways: it has a common-law tradition, it is an adversarial system, and it is a litigious system.

THE COMMON-LAW TRADITION The U.S. legal system, and that of all the states except Louisiana, is based on common law, which developed IN Great Britain and the countries that once formed the British Empire. The **common-law tradition** relied on royal judges making decisions based on their own judgment and on previous legal decisions, which were applied uniformly, or commonly, across the land. The emphasis was on preserving the decisions that had been made before, what is called relying on **precedent**, or *stare decisis* (Latin for "let the decision stand"). Judges in such a system have far more power in determining what the law is than do judges in civil-law systems, and their job is to determine and apply the law as an impartial referee, not to take an active role in discovering the truth.

The legal system in the United States, however, is not a pure common-law system. Legislatures do make laws, and attempts have been made to codify, or organize, them into a coherent body of law. American legislators, however, are less concerned with creating such a coherent body of law than with responding to the various needs and demands of their constituents. As a result, American laws have a somewhat haphazard and hodgepodge character. But the common-law nature of the legal system is reinforced by the fact that American judges still use their considerable discretion to decide what the laws mean, and they rely heavily on precedent and the principle of *stare decisis*. Thus, when a judge decides a case, he or she will look at the relevant law but will also consult previous rulings on the issue before making a ruling of his or her own.

"So Sue Me . . ."

Litigation is one avenue Americans sometimes take to address the risks of everyday life. The label on this coffee cup, "Caution . . . I'm Hot," is the result of one such lawsuit, in which a customer sued a chain for serving coffee that was determined to have been dangerously hot. The case was highly publicized in the media, drawing criticism that the verdict, which favored the plaintiff, was a gross representation of Americans' propensity for frivolous lawsuits. But others pointed to evidence that the elderly plaintiff suffered severe burns from the coffee, requiring skin grafts, and sued only after the company refused to pay her related medical bills.

THE UNITED STATES AS AN ADVERSARIAL SYSTEM

Related to its origins in the British common-law tradition, a second way in which the American legal system differs from many others in the world is that it is an adversarial system. By **adversarial system**, we mean that our trial procedures are "presumed to reveal the truth through the clash of skilled professionals vigorously advocating competing viewpoints."[2] The winner may easily be the side with the most skilled attorneys, not the side that is "right" or "deserving" or that has "justice" on its side. Judges have a primarily passive role; they apply the law, keep the proceedings fair, and make rulings when appropriate, but their role does not include that of active "truth seeker."

Other legal systems offer an alternative to the adversarial system, and a comparison with these **inquisitorial systems** can help us understand the strengths and weaknesses of our own. The difference can be summed up this way: adversarial systems are designed to determine whether a particular accused person is guilty, whereas inquisitorial systems are intended to discover "who did it."[3] While Britain shares our adversarial tradition, many civil-law European countries, like France and Germany, have trial procedures that give a much more active role to the judge as a fact-finder. In these systems, the judge questions witnesses and seeks evidence, and the prosecution (the side bringing the case) and the defense have comparatively minor roles.

In an era when American courtrooms have become theatrical stages and trials are often media extravaganzas, the idea of a system that focuses on finding the truth, that reduces the role of lawyers, that limits the expensive process of evidence gathering, and that makes trials cheaper and faster in general sounds very appealing. For both cultural and political reasons, we are unlikely to switch to a more inquisitorial system, however. It can be argued, for instance, that the adversarial system makes it easier to maintain that key principle of American law, "innocent until proven guilty." Once a judge in an inquisitorial system has determined that there is enough evidence to try someone, he or she is in fact assuming that the defendant is guilty.[4] In addition, the adversarial system fits with our cultural emphasis on individualism and procedural values, and it gives tremendous power to lawyers, who have a vested interest in maintaining such a system.[5]

THE UNITED STATES AS A LITIGIOUS SYSTEM Not only is the U.S. system adversarial, but it is also litigious, which is another way of saying that American citizens sue one another, or litigate, a lot. Legal scholars differ on whether Americans are more litigious than citizens of other nations. Certainly there are more lawyers per capita in the United States than elsewhere (three times as many as in England, for instance, and twenty times as many as in Japan), but other countries have legal professionals other than lawyers who handle legal work, and the number of actual litigators (lawyers who practice in court) is sometimes limited by professional regulations.

> **adversarial system** trial procedures designed to resolve conflict through the clash of opposing sides, moderated by a neutral, passive judge who applies the law
>
> **inquisitorial system** trial procedures designed to determine the truth through the intervention of an active judge who seeks evidence and questions witnesses

Your Day in Court

A cherished principle of our legal system is that everyone is entitled to his or her day in court. If you get into trouble, you are guaranteed access to the courts to redress your wrongs or to defend yourself against false claims. If you don't find yourself in court physically, you will certainly watch legal proceedings on television or read about someone's legal travails in a book, newspaper, or magazine. In a society with a heavy emphasis on due process rights, with a litigious disposition to boot, the legal system plays a prominent role in many of our lives at one time or another.

But the legal system is huge and complex, and it is run by lawyers who have a vested interest in that complexity: The more we cannot understand the language of the law, the more we need lawyers to tell us what it all means. We can't condense three years of law school vocabulary here, but we can arm you with some basics.

Both criminal and civil cases begin in an entry-level court. The questions to be decided in this court are (1) what is the relevant law and (2) is the person accused guilty of a crime or responsible for violating the civil law? The entry-level court produces a verdict based on the application of law to a finding of fact. If a party in such a case feels that a point of law was not applied properly, the case may wind up in appeals court, where cases are appealed only on points of law, not on interpretations of facts. If new facts are shown to be present, a new trial at the entry level can be ordered.

What to Watch Out For

At some point, you may very well find yourself headed to court. Here are a few questions to help you be prepared:

- **Does the dispute I am involved in need to be solved in a court of law?** If you have been arrested, you probably have little choice about whether you go to court, but if you are involved in a civil dispute, there are ways to solve conflicts outside the courtroom. Explore options involving mediation and arbitration if you want to avoid a lengthy and possibly acrimonious legal battle.
- **Do I need a lawyer?** It's one thing to draw up your own will but quite another to undertake your own criminal defense. Disputes such as divorce, child custody, and small claims fall somewhere in between, but as a general rule, if the person whose claims you are contesting has a lawyer, you might want one, too. Remember that the legal system has been designed by lawyers, and they are trained to know their way around it.
- **Is the case worth the potential cost in money, time, and emotional energy?** If you are charged with a crime, you may not have any choice over whether you go to court, but often people enter into civil disputes without a clear idea of the costs involved. Some lawyers will work on a contingency basis (taking a percentage, usually 30 percent, of the settlement he or she wins for you), but others will charge by the hour—which gets expensive very quickly. Cases can drag on for years, through multiple levels of appeals, and can become a major drain on one's energy and resources.
- **What is the judge's role?** The judge decides questions of law. Judges make rulings on points of law and instruct the jury on the law, so that the jurors will know how to use the facts they decide on. In some hearings where there is no jury, the judge finds facts and applies the law as well. In appeals courts, panels of judges rule on legal questions that are alleged to have arisen from an earlier trial. For example, if a defendant was not given the opportunity to speak to a lawyer, was that a violation of due process?
- **What's the jury's role?** The Constitution guarantees us a jury of our peers, or equals, and juries are intended to be a check by citizens on the power of the courts. Lawyers representing the two sides choose from a pool of citizens that is representative of the general population, according to a detailed set of rules, and those jurors decide on the facts in a case. Citizens can be asked to sit on grand juries (to decide if there is enough factual evidence to warrant bringing a case to trial) or trial juries (to decide whether or not someone is guilty as charged).
- **Should I serve on a jury if called?** Serving on a jury is a good opportunity to see how the system works from the inside, as well as to make a contribution to the nation. Finding a reason to be excused from jury duty sometimes seems like an attractive option when you are besieged by the demands of daily life, but there are real costs to avoiding this civic duty. Since all citizens are entitled to a jury trial, having an active pool of willing jurors is important to the nation's civic health.

Some evidence, however, suggests that Americans do file civil suits—that is, cases seeking compensation from actions that are not defined as crimes, such as medical malpractice or breach of contract—more often than do citizens of many other countries. While the American rate of filing civil suits is roughly the same as that of the English, Americans file 25 percent more civil cases per capita than do the Germans, and 30 to 40 percent more cases per capita than do the Swedes.[6] Comparisons aside, it remains true that forty-four lawsuits are filed annually for every thousand people in the population.[7] Why do Americans spend so much time in the courtroom? Scholars argue that the large number of lawsuits in the United States is a measure of our openness and democratic concern for the rights of all citizens,[8] and that litigation is unavoidable in democracies committed to individuals' freedoms and to citizens' rights to defend themselves from harm by others.[9] Americans also sue one another a lot because our society has traditionally failed to provide other mechanisms for providing compensation and security from risk. For instance, until health care reform kicked in fully in 2014, many Americans lacked health insurance, a basic security that in many other countries is provided by the government. Since premiums are skyrocketing due to lack of Republican support for the program, we may be returning to the days when litigation is the only way to deal with unexpected disaster in the form of a car accident, faulty production of appliances, or medical tragedy.

The large number of lawsuits in America, however, has a negative as well as a positive side. Some experts argue that Americans have come to expect "total justice," that everything bad that happens can be blamed on someone, who should compensate them for their harm.[10] In addition, our propensity to litigate means that the courts get tied up with what are often frivolous lawsuits, as when a prisoner filed a million-dollar lawsuit against New York's Mohawk Correctional Facility claiming "'cruel and unusual' punishment for incidents stemming from a guard's refusal to refrigerate the prisoner's ice cream."[11] Such suits are costly not only to the individuals or institutions that must defend themselves but also to taxpayers, who support the system as a whole, paying the salaries of judges and legal staff. Politicians make occasional attempts to limit lawsuits (for instance, the Republican effort to cap medical malpractice awards), but these efforts often have political motivations and usually come to nothing.

KINDS OF LAW

Laws are not all of the same type, and distinguishing among them can be difficult. It's not important that we understand all the shades of legal meaning. In fact, it often seems that lawyers speak a language all their own. Nevertheless, most of us will have several encounters with the law in our lifetimes, and it's important that we know what laws regulate what sorts of behavior. To get a better understanding of the various players in the court's legal arena, see *Don't Be Fooled by . . . Your Day in Court*.

SUBSTANTIVE AND PROCEDURAL LAWS We have used the terms *substantive* and *procedural* elsewhere in this book, and though the meanings we use here are related to the earlier ones, these are precise legal terms that describe specific kinds of laws. Substantive laws are those whose actual content or "substance" defines what we can and cannot legally do. Procedural laws, by contrast, establish the procedures used to conduct the law—that is, how the law is used, or applied, and enforced. Thus a substantive law spells out what behaviors are restricted—for instance, driving over a certain speed or killing someone. Procedural laws refer to how legal proceedings are to take place: how evidence will be gathered and used, how defendants will be treated, and what juries can be told during a trial. Because our founders were concerned with limiting the power of government to prevent tyranny, our laws are filled with procedural protections for those who must deal with the legal system—what we call guarantees of procedural due process. Given their different purposes, these two types of laws sometimes clash. For instance, someone guilty of breaking a substantive law might be spared punishment if procedural laws meant to protect him or her were violated because the police failed to read the accused his or her rights or searched the accused's home without a warrant. Such situations are complicated by the fact that not all judges interpret procedural guarantees in the same way.

CRIMINAL AND CIVIL LAWS Criminal laws prohibit specific behaviors that the government (state, federal, or both) has determined are not conducive to the public peace, behaviors as heinous as murder or as relatively innocuous as

substantive laws laws whose content, or substance, defines what we can or cannot do

procedural laws laws that establish how laws are applied and enforced—how legal proceedings take place

procedural due process procedural laws that protect the rights of individuals who must deal with the legal system

criminal laws laws prohibiting behavior the government has determined to be harmful to society; violation of a criminal law is called a crime

stealing an apple. Since these laws refer to crimes against the state, it is the government that prosecutes these cases, rather than the family of the murder victim or the owner of the apple. The penalty, if the person is found guilty, will be some form of payment to the public—for example, community service, jail time, or even death, depending on the severity of the crime and the provisions of the law. In fact, we speak of criminals having to pay their "debt to society" because, in a real sense, their actions are seen as a harm to society.

Civil laws, by contrast, regulate interactions between individuals. If one person sues another for damaging his or her property, or causing physical harm, or failing to fulfill the terms of a contract, it is not a crime against the state that is alleged but rather an injury to a specific individual. A violation of civil law is called a tort instead of a crime. The government's purpose here is not to prosecute a harm to society but to provide individuals with a forum in which they can peacefully resolve their differences. Apart from peaceful conflict resolution, government has no stake in the outcome.

Sometimes a person will face both criminal charges and a civil lawsuit for the same action. An example might be a person who drives while drunk and causes an accident that seriously injures a person in another car. The drunk driver would face criminal charges for breaking laws against driving while intoxicated and might be sued by the injured party to receive compensation for medical expenses, missed income, and pain and suffering. Such damages are called compensatory damages. The injured person might also sue the bar that served the alcohol to the drunk driver in the first place; this is because people suing for compensation often target the involved party with the deepest pockets—that is, the one with the best ability to pay. A civil suit might also include a fine intended to punish the individual for causing the injury. These damages are called punitive damages. Reflecting our notion that government poses a bigger threat to our liberties than we do to each other, the burden of proof is easier to meet in civil trials.

CONSTITUTIONAL LAW Constitutional law refers, of course, to the laws that are in the Constitution. These laws establish the basic powers of and limitations on government institutions and their interrelationships, and they guarantee the basic rights of citizens. In addition, constitutional law refers to the many decisions that have been made by lower court judges in the United States, as well as by the justices on the Supreme Court, in their attempts to decide precisely what the Constitution means and how it should be interpreted. Because of our common-law tradition, these decisions, once made, become part of the vast foundation of American constitutional law.

All the cases discussed in Chapters 5 and 6, on civil liberties and equal rights, are part of the constitutional law of this country. As we have seen, constitutional law evolves over time as circumstances change, justices are replaced, cases are overturned, and precedent is reversed.

STATUTORY LAW, ADMINISTRATIVE LAW, AND EXECUTIVE ORDERS Most laws in the country are made by Congress and the state legislatures, by the bureaucracy under the authority of Congress, and even by the president. Statutory laws are those laws that legislatures make at either the state or the national level. Statutes reflect the will of the bodies elected to represent the people, and they can address virtually any behavior. Statutes tell us to wear seatbelts, pay taxes, and stay home from work on Memorial Day. According to the principle of judicial review, judges may declare statutes unconstitutional if they conflict with the basic principles of government or the rights of citizens established in the Constitution.

Because legislatures cannot be experts on all matters, they frequently delegate some of their lawmaking power to bureaucratic agencies and departments. When these

More Than One Day in Court

The American justice system not only makes decisions on criminal cases but also allows citizens to seek compensation for injury or damage. In some cases, defendants may face both kinds of trials. In 2018 the actor Bill Cosby was convicted of criminal charges and sentenced to three to ten years in prison for drugging and sexually assaulting a woman, while he was simultaneously embroiled in several civil cases involving similar accusations.

civil laws laws regulating interactions between individuals; violation of a civil law is called a tort

constitutional law law stated in the Constitution or in the body of judicial decisions about the meaning of the Constitution handed down in the courts

statutory law law passed by a state or the federal legislature

bureaucratic actors exercise their lawmaking power on behalf of Congress, they are making **administrative law**. Administrative laws include the thousands of regulations that agencies create concerning how much coloring and other additives can be in the food we buy, how airports will monitor air traffic, what kind of material can be used to make pajamas for children, and what deductions can be taken legally when figuring your income tax. These laws, although made under the authority of elected representatives, are not, in fact, made by people who are directly accountable to the citizens of America. The implications of the undemocratic nature of bureaucratic decision making were discussed in Chapter 9.

> *Is justice a matter of enduring principles or the product of a political process?*

Finally, some laws, called **executive orders**, are made by the president. These laws, as we explained in Chapter 8, are made without any participation by Congress and need be binding only during the issuing president's administration. Famous executive orders include President Harry Truman's desegregation of the armed forces in 1948 and President Lyndon Johnson's initiation of affirmative action programs for companies doing business with the federal government in 1967.

PAUSE AND REVIEW Who, What, How

Citizens have a broad stake in a lawful society. They want security, predictability, peaceful conflict resolution, conformity to social norms, and a nondisruptive distribution of social costs and benefits, and they use laws to try to achieve these things. To accomplish their goals, they use the full array of laws and legal traditions available to them in the American legal system. The results of the legal process are shaped by the distinctive nature of the American system—its common-law roots and its adversarial and litigious nature.

In Your Own Words Describe the role that law plays in democratic societies.

CONSTITUTIONAL PROVISIONS AND THE DEVELOPMENT OF JUDICIAL REVIEW

The role of Congress and the Constitution in establishing the judiciary

Americans may owe a lot of our philosophy of law (called jurisprudence) to the British, but the court system we set up to administer that law is uniquely our own. Like every other part of the Constitution, the nature of the judiciary was the subject of hot debate during the nation's founding. Large states were comfortable with a strong court system as part of the strong national government they advocated; small states, cringing at the prospect of national dominance, preferred a weak judiciary. Choosing a typically astute way out of their quandary, the authors of the Constitution postponed it, leaving it to Congress to settle later.

Article III, Section 1, of the Constitution says simply this about the establishment of the court system: "The judicial power of the United States, shall be vested in one supreme court, and in such inferior courts as Congress may from time to time ordain and establish." It goes on to say that judges will hold their jobs as long as they demonstrate "good behavior"—that is, they are appointed for life—and that they will be paid regularly and cannot have their pay reduced while they are in office. The Constitution does not spell out the powers of the Supreme Court. It only specifies which cases must come directly to the Supreme Court (cases affecting ambassadors, public ministers and consuls, and states); all other cases come to it only on appeal. It was left to Congress to say how. By dropping the issue of court structure and power into the lap of a future Congress, the writers of the Constitution neatly sidestepped the brewing controversy. It would require an act of Congress, the Judiciary Act of 1789, to begin to fill in the gaps on how the court system would be organized. We turn to that act and its provisions shortly. First, we look at the controversy surrounding the birth of the one court that Article III does establish, the U.S. Supreme Court.

THE LEAST DANGEROUS BRANCH

The idea of an independent judiciary headed by a supreme court was a new one to the founders. No other country had one, not even England. Britain's highest court was also its Parliament, or legislature. To those who put their faith in the ideas of separation of powers and checks and balances, an independent judiciary was an ideal way to check the power of the president and the Congress, and an important part of the narrative they were creating about limited power. But to others it represented an unknown threat. To put those fears to rest, Alexander Hamilton penned *Federalist* No. 78, arguing that the judiciary was the least dangerous branch of government. It lacked the teeth of the other branches; it had neither the power

---

administrative law law established by the bureaucracy, on behalf of Congress

executive orders clarifications of congressional policy issued by the president and having the full force of law

of the sword (the executive power) nor the power of the purse (the legislative budget power), and consequently it could exercise "neither force nor will, but merely judgment."[12] For a while, Hamilton was right. The Court was thought to be such a minor player in the new government that several of George Washington's original appointees to that institution turned him down.[13] Many of those who served on the Court for a time resigned to take other positions thought to be more prestigious. Further indicating the Court's lack of esteem was the fact that when the capital was moved to Washington, D.C., city planners forgot to design a location for it. As a result, the highest court in the land had to meet in the basement office of the clerk of the U.S. Senate.[14]

JOHN MARSHALL AND JUDICIAL REVIEW

The low prestige of the Supreme Court was not to last for long, however, and its elevation was due almost single-handedly to the work of one man. John Marshall was the third chief justice of the United States and an enthusiastic Federalist. During his tenure in office, he found several ways to strengthen the Court's power (and the power of the national government along with it), the most important of which was having the Court create the power of **judicial review**. This is the power that allows the Court to review acts of the other branches of government and to invalidate them if they are found to run counter to the principles in the Constitution. For a man who attended law school for only six months (as was the custom in his day, he learned the law by serving as an apprentice), his legacy to American law is truly phenomenal.

FEDERALIST NO. 78 Marshall was not the first American to raise the prospect of judicial review. Although the Constitution was silent on the issue of the Court's power and Hamilton had been quick to reassure the public that he envisioned only a weak judiciary, he dropped a hint in *Federalist* No. 78 that he would approve of a much stronger role for the Court. Answering critics who declared that judicial review would give too much power to a group of unelected men to overrule the will of the majority as expressed through the legislature, Hamilton said that in fact the reverse was true. Since the Constitution was the clearest expression of the public will in America, by allowing that document to check the legislature, judicial review would actually place the true will of the people over momentary passions and interests that were reflected in Congress.

> **judicial review** the power of the courts to determine the constitutionality of laws
>
> *Marbury v. Madison* the landmark case that established the U.S. Supreme Court's power of judicial review

Freedom Fighter
Thurgood Marshall (center) secured his place in legal history when, as special counsel for the National Association for the Advancement of Colored People (NAACP), he convinced the Supreme Court to overturn segregation with the landmark 1954 ruling Brown v. Board of Education. *In 1967, Marshall himself became a Supreme Court justice, appointed by President Lyndon Johnson.*

MARBURY V. MADISON The Constitution does not give the power of judicial review to the Court, but it doesn't forbid the Court to have that power, either. Chief Justice John Marshall shrewdly engineered the adoption of the power of judicial review in *Marbury v. Madison* in 1803. This case involved a series of judicial appointments to federal courts made by President John Adams in the final hours of his administration. Most of those appointments were executed by Adams's secretary of state, but the letter appointing William Marbury to be justice of the peace for the District of Columbia was overlooked and not delivered. (In an interesting twist, John Marshall, who was finishing up his job as Adams's secretary of state, had just been sworn in as chief justice of the United States; he would later hear the case that developed over his own incomplete appointment of Marbury.) These "midnight" (last-minute) appointments irritated the new president, Thomas Jefferson, who wanted to appoint his own candidates, so he had his secretary of state, James Madison, throw out the letter, along with several other appointment letters. According to the

Judiciary Act of 1789, it was up to the Court to decide whether Marbury got his appointment, which put Marshall in a fix. If he exercised his power under the act and Jefferson ignored him, the Court's already low prestige would be severely damaged. If he failed to order the appointment, the Court would still look weak.

From a legal point of view, Marshall's solution was breathtaking. Instead of ruling on the question of Marbury's appointment, which was a no-win situation for him, he focused on the part of the act that gave the Court authority to make the decision. This he found to go beyond what the Constitution had intended; that is, according to the Constitution, Congress didn't have the power to give the Court that authority. So Marshall ruled that although he thought Marbury should get the appointment (he had originally made it, after all), he could not enforce it because the relevant part of the Judiciary Act of 1789 was unconstitutional and therefore void. He justified the Court's power to decide what the Constitution meant by saying "it is emphatically the province of the judicial department to say what the law is."[15]

THE IMPACT OF JUDICIAL REVIEW With the *Marbury* ruling, Marshall chose to lose a small battle in order to win a very large war. By creating the power of judicial review, he vastly expanded the potential influence of the Court and set it on the road to being the powerful institution it is today. While Congress and the president still have some checks on the judiciary through the powers to appoint, to change the number of members and jurisdiction of the Court, to impeach justices, and to amend the Constitution, the Court now has the ultimate check over the other two branches: the power to declare what they do to be null and void. What is especially striking about the gain of this enormous power is that the Court gave it to itself. What would have been the public reaction if Congress had voted to make itself the final judge of what is constitutional?

Aware of just how substantially their power was increased by the addition of judicial review, justices have tended to use it sparingly. The power was not used from its inception in 1803 until 1857, when the Court struck down the Missouri Compromise.[16] Since then it has been used only about 180 times to strike down acts of Congress, although it has been used much more frequently (more than 1,300 times) to invalidate acts of the state legislatures.[17]

> **What would American politics look like today if Chief Justice John Marshall hadn't adopted the power of judicial review?**

The Constitution is largely silent about the courts, leaving to Congress the task of designing the details of the judicial system. It was not the Constitution or Congress but John Marshall, the third chief justice, who used the common-law tradition of American law to give the Court the extraconstitutional power of judicial review. Once Marshall had claimed the power and used it in a ruling (*Marbury v. Madison*), it became part of the fundamental judge-made constitutional law of this country.

In Your Own Words   Discuss the role of Congress and the Constitution in establishing the judiciary.

FEDERALISM AND THE AMERICAN COURTS

The structure and organization of the dual court system

In response to the Constitution's open invitation to design a federal court system, Congress immediately got busy putting together the Judiciary Act of 1789. The system created by this act was too simple to handle the complex legal needs and the growing number of cases in the new nation, however, and it was gradually crafted by Congress into the very complex network of federal courts we have today. But understanding just the federal court system is not enough. Our federal system of government requires that we have two separate court systems, state and national—and, in fact, most of the legal actions in this country take place at the state level. Because of the diversity that exists among the state courts, some people argue that in truth we have fifty-one court systems. Since we cannot look into each of the fifty state court systems, we will take the "two-system" perspective and consider the state court system as a whole (see Figure 10.1).

UNDERSTANDING JURISDICTION

A key concept in understanding our dual court system is the issue of **jurisdiction**, the courts' authority to hear particular cases. Not all courts can hear all cases. In fact, the rules regulating which courts have jurisdiction over which cases are very specific. Most cases in the United States fall under the jurisdiction of state courts. As we will see, cases go to federal courts only if they qualify by virtue of the kind of question raised or the parties involved.

> **jurisdiction** a court's authority to hear certain cases

FIGURE 10.1

The Dual Court System

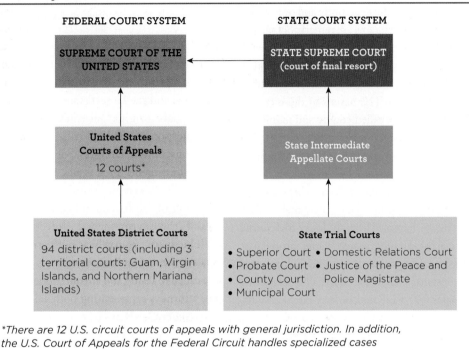

FEDERAL COURT SYSTEM

SUPREME COURT OF THE UNITED STATES

United States Courts of Appeals
12 courts*

United States District Courts
94 district courts (including 3 territorial courts: Guam, Virgin Islands, and Northern Mariana Islands)

STATE COURT SYSTEM

STATE SUPREME COURT (court of final resort)

State Intermediate Appellate Courts

State Trial Courts
- Superior Court • Domestic Relations Court
- Probate Court • Justice of the Peace and
- County Court   Police Magistrate
- Municipal Court

There are 12 U.S. circuit courts of appeals with general jurisdiction. In addition, the U.S. Court of Appeals for the Federal Circuit handles specialized cases (e.g., patents, international trade).

The choice of a court, though dictated in large part by constitutional rule and statutory law (both state and federal), still leaves room for political maneuvering. Four basic characteristics of a case help determine which court has jurisdiction over it: the involvement of the federal government (through treaties or federal statutes) or the Constitution, the parties to the case (if, for instance, states are involved), where the case arose, and how serious an offense it involves.[18] Once a case is in either the state court system or the federal court system, it almost always remains within that system. It is extremely rare for a case to start out in one system and end up in the other. Just about the only time this occurs is when a case in the highest state court is appealed to the U.S. Supreme Court, and this can happen only for cases involving a question of federal law.

Cases come to state and federal courts under either their original jurisdiction or their appellate jurisdiction. A court's **original jurisdiction** refers to those cases that can come

straight to it without being heard by any other court first. The rules and factors just discussed refer to original jurisdiction. **Appellate jurisdiction** refers to those cases that a court can hear on **appeal**—that is, when one of the parties to a case believes that some point of law was not applied properly at a lower court and asks a higher court to review it. Almost all the cases heard by the U.S. Supreme Court come to it on appeal. The Court's original jurisdiction is limited to cases that concern ambassadors and public ministers and to cases in which a state is a party—usually amounting to no more than two or three cases a year.

All parties in U.S. lawsuits are entitled to an appeal, although more than 90 percent of losers in federal cases accept their verdicts without appeal. After the first appeal, further appeals are at the discretion of the higher court; that is, the court can choose to hear them or not. The highest court of appeals in the United States is the U.S. Supreme Court, but its appellate jurisdiction is also discretionary. When the Court refuses to hear a case, it may mean, among other things, that the Court regards the case as frivolous or that it agrees with the lower court's judgment. Just because the Court agrees to hear a case, though, does not mean that it is going to overturn the lower court's ruling, although it does so about 70 percent of the time. Sometimes the Court hears a case in order to rule that it agrees with the lower court and to set a precedent that other courts will have to follow.

original jurisdiction the authority of a court to hear a case first

appellate jurisdiction the authority of a court to review decisions made by lower courts

appeal a rehearing of a case because the losing party in the original trial argues that a point of law was not applied properly

STATE COURTS

Although each state has its own constitution, and therefore its own set of rules and procedures for structuring and organizing its court system, the state court systems are remarkably similar in appearance and function (see Figure 10.1). State courts generally fall into three tiers, or layers. The lowest, or first, layer is the trial court, including major trial courts and courts where less serious offenses are heard. The names of these courts vary—for example, they may be called county and municipal courts at the minor level and superior or district courts at the major level. Here cases are heard for the first time, under original jurisdiction, and most of them end here as well.

Occasionally, however, a case is appealed to a higher decision-making body. In about three-fourths of the states, intermediate courts of appeals hear cases appealed from the lower trial courts. In terms of geographic organization, subject matter jurisdiction, and number of judges, courts of appeals vary greatly from state to state. The one constant is that these courts all hear appeals directly from the major trial courts and, on very rare occasions, directly from the minor courts as well.

Each of the fifty states has a state supreme court, although again the names vary. Since they are appeals courts, no questions of fact can arise, and there are no juries. Rather, a panel of five to nine justices, as supreme court judges are called, meet to discuss the case, make a decision, and issue an opinion. As the name suggests, a state's supreme court is the court of last resort, or the final court of appeals, in the state. All decisions rendered by these courts are final unless a case involves a federal question and can be heard on further appeal in the federal court system.

Judges in state courts are chosen through a variety of procedures specified in the individual state constitutions. The procedures range from appointment by the governor or election by the state legislature to the more democratic method of election by the state population as a whole. Thirty-nine states hold elections for at least some of their judges. Judicial elections are controversial, however. Supporters argue that they give people a voice, while holding judges accountable and keeping them in line with public opinion. Critics, however, say judicial elections can create a conflict of interest. For example, in 2002 the U.S. Chamber of Commerce and the Business Roundtable, two organizations that regularly appear in court, spent $25 million to influence judicial elections across the country.[19] Others argue that few people are able to cast educated votes in judicial elections and that the threat of defeat may influence judges' rulings.

FEDERAL COURTS

The federal system is also three-tiered. There is an entry-level tier called the district courts, an appellate level, and the Supreme Court at the very top (see Figure 10.1). In this section we discuss the lower two tiers and how the judges for those courts are chosen. Given the importance of the Supreme Court in the American political system, we discuss it separately in the following section.

DISTRICT COURTS The lowest level of the federal judiciary hierarchy consists of ninety-four U.S. federal district courts. These courts are distributed so that each state has at least one and the largest states each have four. The district courts have original jurisdiction over all cases involving any question of a federal nature or any issue that involves the Constitution, Congress, or any other aspect of the federal government. Such issues are wide-ranging but might include, for example, criminal charges resulting from a violation of the federal anticarjacking statute or a lawsuit against the Environmental Protection Agency.

The district courts hear both criminal and civil cases. In trials at the district level, evidence is presented, and witnesses are called to testify and are questioned and cross-examined by the attorneys representing both sides. In criminal cases the government is always represented by a U.S. attorney. U.S. attorneys, one per district, are appointed by the president, with the consent of the Senate. In district courts, juries are responsible for returning the final verdict.

U.S. COURTS OF APPEALS Any case appealed beyond the district court level is slated to appear in one of the U.S. courts of appeals. These courts are arranged in twelve circuits, essentially large superdistricts that encompass several of the district court territories, except for the twelfth, which covers just Washington, D.C. (see Figure 10.2). This Twelfth Circuit Court hears all appeals involving government agencies, and so its caseload is quite large even though its territory is small. (A thirteenth Federal Circuit Court hears cases on such specialized issues as patents and copyrights.) Cases are heard in the circuit that includes the district court where the case was heard originally. Therefore, a case that was tried initially in Miami, in the southern district in Florida, would be appealed to the Court of Appeals for the Eleventh Circuit, located in Atlanta, Georgia.

The jurisdiction of the courts of appeals, as their name suggests, is entirely appellate in nature. The sole function of these courts is to hear appeals from the lower federal district courts and to review the legal reasoning behind the decisions reached there. As a result, the proceedings involved in the appeals process differ markedly from those at the district court level. No evidence is presented, no new witnesses called, and no jury impaneled. Instead, the lawyers for both sides present written briefs summarizing their arguments and make oral arguments as well. The legal reasoning used to reach the decision in the district court is scrutinized, but the facts of the case are assumed to be the truth and are not debated. The decisions in the courts

FIGURE 10.2
The Federal Judicial Circuits

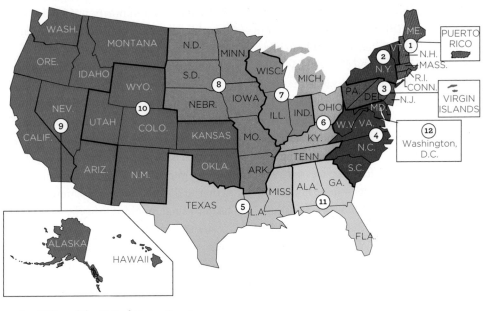

Source: Administrative Office of the United States Courts.

of appeals are made by a rotating panel of three judges who sit to hear the case. Although many more than three judges are assigned to each federal appeals circuit (for instance, the Court of Appeals for the Ninth Circuit, based in San Francisco, has twenty-two active judges), the judges rotate in order to provide a decision-making body that is as unbiased as possible. In rare cases when a decision is of crucial social importance, all the judges in a circuit will meet together, or *en banc*, to render a decision. Having all the judges present, not just three, gives a decision more legitimacy and sends a message that the decision was made carefully.

SELECTION OF FEDERAL JUDGES The Constitution is silent about the qualifications of federal judges. It specifies only that they shall be appointed by the president, with the advice and consent of the Senate, and that they shall serve lifetime terms under good behavior. They can be removed from office only if impeached and convicted by the House of Representatives and the Senate, a process that has resulted in only fifteen impeachments and eight convictions in more than two hundred years.

Traditionally, federal judgeships have been awarded on the basis of several criteria, including rewarding political friendship, supporting and cultivating future support, especially of a gender or ethnic or racial group, and ideology (see *Snapshot of America: Who Has Been Appointed to the Federal Courts?*). Throughout most of the country's history, the courts have been demographically uniform—white, male, and predominantly

Christian. President Jimmy Carter broke that trend, vowing to use his nominations to increase the diversity in the federal courts. President Bill Clinton renewed that commitment: nearly half of his appointees were women and minorities, compared to 35 percent under Carter, 14 percent under Ronald Reagan, and 27 percent under George H. W. Bush.[20] President George W. Bush, while not quite emulating Clinton's record, still made a point of nominating a diverse slate of candidates, especially increasing the number of Hispanics on the bench.[21] Barack Obama also made increasing the diversity on the courts a top priority. According to the White House counsel, Obama wanted "the federal courts to look like America."[22] Only 38 percent of Obama's appointments to district courts were white men (as opposed to 67 percent under Bush, 53 percent under Clinton, and 85 percent under Reagan). Nearly half, 43 percent, were women. Eleven were gay. Because the Obama administration cast a wider net, looking for diverse candidates but also for those with less traditional backgrounds (more government lawyers and law professors, for instance, than litigators), it was slower to fill the openings on the bench.[23] Without concerns about diversity, Trump was quick to start filling empty slots with candidates who were primarily white and male.[24]

These days an increasingly important qualification for the job of federal judge is the ideological or policy positions of the appointee. In the 1970s, Richard Nixon ran for president on the idea that the courts were liberal policymaking institutions, soft on crime and in need of conservative correction. Since that time, presidents have become more conscious of the political influence of the courts and have tried to use the nomination process to further their own political legacies. As presidents have taken advantage of the opportunity to shape the courts ideologically, the Senate confirmation process has become more rancorous. But the nomination process has been more important to conservatives than to liberals. Republican presidents Richard Nixon, Ronald Reagan, and George H. W. Bush made a conscious effort to redirect what they saw as the liberal tenor of court appointments in the years since the New Deal, and Democrat Jimmy Carter countered with liberal appointees, but the moderate ideology of most of Democratic president Bill Clinton's appointees meant that the courts did not swing back in a radically liberal direction.[25] Clinton's appointees were what one observer called "militantly moderate"—more liberal than Reagan's and Bush's, but less liberal than Carter's, and similar ideologically to the appointments of Republican president Gerald Ford.[26] By the end of George W. Bush's second term, 56.2 percent of the authorized judicial positions had been filled by Republicans, tilting the federal bench in a solidly conservative direction. Barack Obama, focused on the diversity of his appointees, had come under criticism from liberals for not filling seats quickly enough, and thus for failing to build a liberal judicial legacy, but at the end of his second term the federal bench had a narrow Democratic majority.[27]

This was despite the fact that the Republicans blocked votes on *all* Obama nominations, even moderate ones that would typically have enjoyed bipartisan support, in order to stall the Obama administration's efforts and to gain leverage for other things they wanted.[28] Ironically, when those nominations eventually came to a vote, they passed with the support of many of the Republicans who had engaged in the filibuster to delay the vote in the first place. These delay tactics scored the party a short-term political victory, and many federal judgeships went unfilled as a consequence. Because of the ensuing backlog of cases in the courts, then–Senate majority leader Harry Reid eventually invoked what is known as the nuclear option, eliminating the filibuster on non–Supreme Court federal nominees.

When Trump came into office, that slim Democratic majority on the courts was quickly undone. The Trump administration, urged on by Senate majority leader Mitch McConnell, has focused on filling the federal bench. McConnell said, "Obviously, this has been my top priority," and, unchecked by the filibuster they had helped to destroy, Republicans have made great strides in appointing conservative judges.[29]

The upshot is that, before the removal of the filibuster, the increasing politicization of the confirmation process meant that many of a president's nominees faced a grueling battle in the Senate, and even if they got through the Senate Judiciary Committee hearings, they were lucky to get as far as a vote on the floor. That is still the case if the president is of a different party than the Senate majority, as was Obama. A president with a Senate majority behind him can put a major stamp on the judiciary, however. Even before the recent changes in Senate procedure, including the end of a tradition that let members of the minority put holds on nominations, the Republicans were more effective at shaping the bench. Observers chalk this up to the greater discipline among Republican senators. Said one liberal advocate during George W. Bush's administration, "Republican senators have voted in lock step to confirm every judge that Bush has nominated. The Democrats have often broken ranks."[30] In addition, the Republican base has been more energized about the courts as a political issue because of concern about core issues like preserving gun rights and overturning abortion, affirmative action, and gay-friendly legislation; the Democrats have not had that single-minded focus.

Another, related influence on the appointment of federal judges is the principle of **senatorial courtesy**, which we discussed in Chapter 8. In reality, senators do most of the nominating of district court judges, often aided by applications made by lawyers and state judges. Traditionally, a president who nominated a candidate who failed to meet with the approval of the state's senators was highly unlikely to gain Senate confirmation of that candidate, even if the president was lucky enough to get the Senate Judiciary Committee to hold a hearing on the nomination. The practice of senatorial courtesy was weakened somewhat by George W. Bush's administration and Senate Republicans, who forced confirmation hearings despite the objections of Democratic home state senators.[31] Once Barack Obama was elected, however, Senate Republicans sought to restore the policy, sending a letter to the White House promising to block any appointments that didn't meet with the home state senator's approval, and even a member of Obama's own party put a hold on one of his nominees.[32] Under Trump and McConnell, the Republicans switched gears again, essentially rejecting the norm.[33]

The growing influence of politics in the selection of federal judges does not mean that merit is unimportant. As the nation's largest legal professional association, the American Bar Association (ABA) has had the informal role since 1946 of evaluating the legal qualifications of potential nominees. While poorly rated candidates are occasionally nominated and confirmed, perhaps because of the pressure of a senator or a president, most federal judges receive the ABA's professional blessing. The ABA's role has become more controversial in recent years, as Republicans are convinced that it has a liberal bias. In 2001 the Bush administration announced that

---

senatorial courtesy the tradition of granting senior senators of the president's party considerable power over federal judicial appointments in their home states

Snapshot of America: *Who Has Been Appointed to the Federal Courts?*

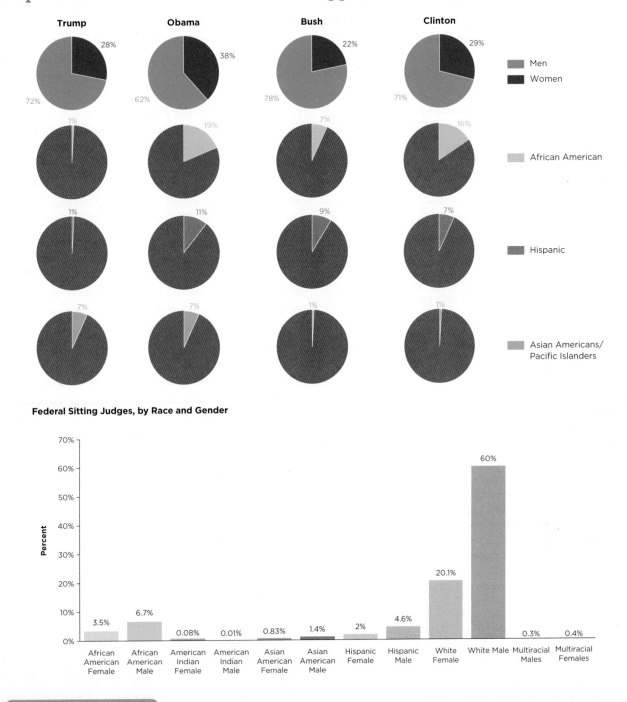

Trump Men 72% Women 28%
1% African American
1% Hispanic
7% Asian Americans/Pacific Islanders

Obama Men 62% Women 38%
19% African American
11% Hispanic
7% Asian Americans/Pacific Islanders

Bush Men 78% Women 22%
7% African American
9% Hispanic
1% Asian Americans/Pacific Islanders

Clinton Men 71% Women 29%
16% African American
7% Hispanic
1% Asian Americans/Pacific Islanders

Federal Sitting Judges, by Race and Gender

Category	Percent
African American Female	3.5%
African American Male	6.7%
American Indian Female	0.08%
American Indian Male	0.01%
Asian American Female	0.83%
Asian American Male	1.4%
Hispanic Female	2%
Hispanic Male	4.6%
White Female	20.1%
White Male	60%
Multiracial Males	0.3%
Multiracial Females	0.4%

Behind the Numbers

Just as America is becoming more diverse, so is our federal judiciary. President Obama nominated significantly more women and minorities to the federal bench than his predecessors. Does it increase the legitimacy of the courts when citizens see people like themselves in judges' robes? Are the decisions likely to be different?

Sources: Pew Research Center, "Trump has appointed a larger share of female judges than other GOP presidents, but lags Obama," October 2, 2018, http://www.pewresearch.org/fact-tank/2018/10/02/trump-has-appointed-a-larger-share-of-female-judges-than-other-gop-presidents-but-lags-obama/; Barry J. McMillion, "U.S. Circuit and District Court Judges: Profile of Select Characteristics," Congressional Research Service, August 2017, fas.org/sgp/crs/misc/R43426.pdf.

Note: Data from CRS Reports include nominations to territorial district courts in the U.S. Virgin Islands, Guam, and Northern Mariana Islands, as well as resubmitted nominations.

it would no longer seek the ABA's ratings of its nominees, breaking a tradition that went back to Dwight Eisenhower. The ABA continued to rate the nominees (and the Bush White House boasted that the vast majority of its nominees were rated qualified or well qualified), but it did so independently.[34] In March 2009 the Obama administration restored the ABA's traditional role in the nomination process, only to find that a number of Obama's potential nominees failed to rank as qualified, perhaps because they were less likely to have the traditional backgrounds as litigators that the litigator-heavy ABA panel may be looking for.[35] The administration's decision to drop those nominees who were not ranked as qualified was another reason it had a slower nominating process than its predecessors. Trump has ignored the ABA in making his appointments, resulting in a higher percentage of "unqualified" nominees.[36]

> How would the federal judiciary
> be different if judges were
> elected rather than appointed?

PAUSE AND REVIEW   Who, What, How

The dual court system in America is shaped by rules that ultimately determine who will win and who will lose in legal disputes. Because our common-law tradition gives the judge a great deal of power to interpret what the law means, the selection of judges is critical to how the rules are applied. Both the president and the Senate are involved in the selection of federal judges, and both have a stake in creating a federal judiciary that reflects the views they think are important—and that rewards the people they feel should be rewarded. The rules that determine whether the president or the Senate is successful come partly from the Constitution (the nomination and confirmation processes) and partly from tradition (senatorial courtesy).

In Your Own Words   Explain how federalism plays out in the dual court system.

THE SUPREME COURT

A political institution

At the very top of the nation's judicial system reigns the Supreme Court. The nine justices do not wear the elaborate wigs of their British colleagues in the House of Lords, the highest court of appeals in Britain, but they do don long black robes to hear their cases and sit against a majestic background of red silk, perhaps the closest thing to the pomp and circumstance of royalty that we have in American government. Polls show that even after its role in the contested presidential election of 2000, the Court gets higher ratings from the public than does Congress or the president, and that it doesn't suffer as much from the popular cynicism about government that afflicts the other branches.[37] The American public seems to believe the narrative that the Supreme Court is indeed above politics, as the founders wished them to believe. If the Court is seen as apolitical, its rulings will have greater force and legitimacy. Such a view, however, while gratifying to those who want to believe in the purity and wisdom of at least one aspect of their government, is not strictly accurate. The members of the Court themselves are preserved by the rule of lifetime tenure from continually having to seek reelection or reappointment, but they are not removed from the political world around them. It is more useful, and closer to reality, to regard the Supreme Court as an intensely political institution. In at least four critical areas—how its members are chosen, how those members choose which cases to hear, how they make decisions, and the effects of the decisions they make—the Court is a decisive allocator of who gets what, when, and how. Reflecting on popular idealizing of the Court, scholar Richard Pacelle says that "not to know the Court is to love it."[38] In the remainder of this chapter, we get to know the Court, not to stop loving it but to gain a healthy respect for the enormously powerful political institution it is.

HOW MEMBERS OF THE COURT ARE SELECTED

In a perfect world, the wisest and most intelligent jurists in the country would be appointed to make the all-important constitutional decisions faced by members of the Supreme Court. In a political world, however, the need for wise and intelligent justices needs to be balanced against the demands of a system that makes those justices the choice of an elected president, and confirmed by elected senators. The need of these elected officials to be responsive to their constituencies means that the nomination process for Supreme Court justices is often a battleground of competing views of the public good. To take a recent and prominent example, within hours of the announcement of Justice Antonin Scalia's death in February 2016, Senate majority leader Mitch McConnell had announced that the Senate would not hold hearings on anyone President Obama might nominate. The ostensible reason for his decision was that it was a presidential year and the people should have a chance to weigh in, yet a number of justices had been confirmed in election years, and in 2018, speaking about Anthony Kennedy's retirement, McConnell said he would move right away to replace him.[39] He followed through, and Brett Kavanaugh was confirmed just months before the midterm elections. McConnell's real reason for refusing to consider

Obama's nominee, as we saw earlier, was to try to hold out for the election of a Republican president who would nominate someone as conservative as Scalia had been. Merit is certainly important, but it is tempered by other considerations resulting from a democratic selection process.

On paper, the process of choosing justices for the Supreme Court is not a great deal different from the selection of other federal judges, though no tradition of senatorial courtesy exists at the high court level. Far too much is at stake in Supreme Court appointments to even consider giving any individual senator veto power. Because the job is so important, presidents get much more involved than they do in other federal judge appointments. As the box *Packing the Courts* highlights, the composition of the Court has long had serious political consequences.

More Than Half of the Population, Only a Third of the Court

Before Sandra Day O'Connor (on the left) became the first woman appointed to the U.S. Supreme Court in 1981, no woman had ever served on the nation's highest court. Today, a full third of the Court is female. Some observers note that women come to decisions differently than men, but the impact of the gender shift on the Court will not be clear for several years. Here, O'Connor joins current justices Sotomayor, Ginsburg, and Kagan for a panel discussion of the impact of O'Connor's trailblazing service.

The Constitution, silent on so much concerning the Supreme Court, does not give the president any handy list of criteria for making these critical appointments. But the demands of the president's job suggest that merit, shared ideology, political reward, and demographic representation all play a role in this choice.[40] We can understand something about the challenges that face a president making a Supreme Court appointment by examining each of these criteria briefly.

MERIT The president will certainly want to appoint the most qualified person and the person with the highest ethical standards who also meets the other prerequisites. Scholars agree that most of the people who have served the Court over the years have been among the best legal minds available, but they also know that sometimes presidents have nominated people whose reputations have proved questionable.[41] The ABA passes judgment on candidates for the Supreme Court, as it does for the lower courts, issuing verdicts of "well qualified," "qualified," "not opposed," and "not qualified." The FBI also checks out the background of nominees, although occasionally critical information is missed. In 1987 the Reagan administration, which had widely publicized its "Just Say No" campaign against drug use, was deeply embarrassed when National Public Radio reporter Nina Totenberg broke the

story that its Supreme Court nominee, appeals court judge Douglas Ginsburg, had used marijuana in college and while on the Harvard Law School faculty. Ginsburg withdrew his name from consideration. More controversial was the 1991 case of Clarence Thomas, already under attack for his lack of judicial experience and low ABA rating, who was accused of sexual harassment by a former employee, law professor Anita Hill. Thomas was confirmed, but the hearings brought to center stage ethical questions about Court nominees. We have already noted that Donald Trump does not consider the ABA ratings important in the nomination process.

POLITICAL IDEOLOGY Although presidents want to appoint well-qualified candidates to the Court, they are constrained by the desire to find candidates who share their views on politics and the law. Political ideology here involves a couple of dimensions. One is the traditional liberal-conservative dimension. Supreme Court justices, like all other human beings, have views on the role of government, the rights of individuals, and the relationship between the two. Presidents want to appoint justices who look at the world the same way they do, although they are occasionally surprised when their nominee's ideological stripes turn out to be different than they had anticipated. Republican president Dwight Eisenhower called the appointment of Chief Justice Earl Warren, who turned out to be quite liberal in his legal judgments, "the biggest

Packing the Courts

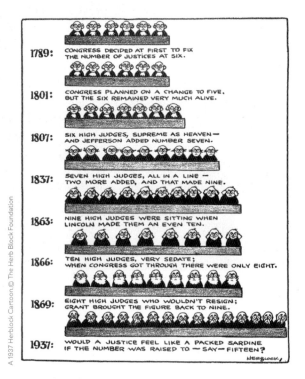

Precedent for the President
"Historical Figures"—a 1937 Herblock cartoon.

The Supreme Court was a thorn in President Franklin Roosevelt's side. Faced with the massive unemployment and economic stagnation that characterized the Great Depression of the 1930s, Roosevelt knew he would have to use the powers of government creatively, but he was hampered by a Court that was ideologically opposed to his efforts to regulate business and industry and skeptical of his constitutional power to do so. In Roosevelt's view, he and Congress had been elected by the people, and public opinion favored his New Deal policies, but a majority of the Supreme Court's "nine old men," as they were called, consistently stood in his way. Six of the justices were over age seventy, and Roosevelt had appointed none of them.

Roosevelt proposed to change the Court that continually thwarted him. The Constitution allows Congress to set the number of justices on the Supreme Court, and indeed the number has ranged from six to ten at various times in our history. Roosevelt's answer to the recalcitrant Court was to ask Congress to allow him to appoint a new justice for every justice over age seventy who refused to retire, up to a possible total of fifteen. Thus he would create a Court whose majority he had chosen and that he confidently believed would support his New Deal programs.

Most presidents try to pack the Court, building their own legacies with appointees who they hope will perpetuate their vision of government and politics. But Roosevelt's plan was dangerous because it threatened to alter the two constitutional principles of separation of powers and checks and balances. Roosevelt would have made into a truism Hamilton's claim that the judiciary was the least dangerous branch of government, while raising the power of the presidency to a height even Hamilton had not dreamed of. The American people reacted with dismay. Public opinion may have backed his policies, but it turned on him when he tried to pack the Court.

No other president has attempted to pack the Court as blatantly as Roosevelt did, and none has failed so ignominiously. The public backlash may have contributed to the slowing of the New Deal and the Republican victories in 1938 that left Roosevelt with a weakened Democratic majority in Congress. His audacious plan had risked the very policy success he was trying so hard to achieve.

In the end, Roosevelt was reelected two more times. The Court, ironically, did an about-face. One justice started voting with the Roosevelt supporters; another retired. Eventually he made eight appointments to the Supreme Court, putting his stamp on it more effectively than any other president since Washington. The Court was, in essence, packed by Roosevelt after all.

---

damn fool mistake I ever made."[42] Although there have been notable exceptions, most presidents appoint members of their own party in an attempt to get ideologically compatible justices. Overall, roughly 90 percent of Supreme Court nominees belong to the nominating president's party.

But ideology has another dimension when it refers to the law. Justices can take the view that the Constitution means exactly what it says it means and that all interpretations of it must be informed by the founders' intentions.

This approach, called **strict constructionism**, holds that if the meaning of the Constitution is to be changed, it must be done by amendment, not by judicial interpretation. Judge Robert Bork, a Reagan nominee who failed to be confirmed by the Senate, is a strict constructionist. During

> **strict constructionism** a judicial approach holding that the Constitution should be read literally, with the framers' intentions uppermost in mind

his confirmation hearings, when he was asked about the famous reapportionment ruling, in *Baker v. Carr*, that the Constitution effectively guarantees every citizen one vote, Bork replied that if the people of the United States wanted their Constitution to guarantee "one man one vote," they were free to amend the document to say so. In Bork's judgment, without that amendment, the principle was simply the result of justices' rewriting of the Constitution. When the senators asked him about the right to privacy, another right enforced by the Court but not specified in the Constitution, Bork simply laughed.[43] The opposite position to strict constructionism, what might be called **judicial interpretivism**, holds that the Constitution is a living document, that the founders could not possibly have anticipated all possible future circumstances, and that justices should interpret the Constitution in light of social changes. When the Court ruled in *Griswold v. Connecticut* that although there is no right to privacy in the Constitution, the Bill of Rights can be understood to imply such a right, it was engaging in judicial interpretation. Strict constructionists would deny that there is a constitutional right to privacy.

While interpretivism tends to be a liberal position because of its emphasis on change, and strict constructionism tends to be a conservative position because of its adherence to the status quo, the two ideological scales do not necessarily go hand in hand. For instance, even though the Second Amendment refers to the right to bear arms in the context of militia membership, many conservatives would argue that this needs to be understood to protect the right to bear arms in a modern context, when militias are no longer necessary or practical—not a strict constructionist reading of the Constitution. Liberals, by contrast, tend to rely on a strict reading of the Second Amendment to support their calls for tighter gun controls.

It is often hard for a president to know where a nominee stands on the strict constructionist–interpretivist scale, especially if that nominee does not have a large record of previous decisions in lower courts, but this ideological placement can be important in the decision-making process. This was the case, for instance, with President Nixon, who was convinced that interpretivist justices were rewriting the Constitution to give too many protections to criminal defendants, and with President Reagan, who faulted interpretivist justices for the *Roe v. Wade* decision legalizing

abortion on the grounds of the right to privacy. But in neither case have all of these presidents' appointees adhered to the desired manner of interpreting the Constitution.

In the George W. Bush administration, another ideological element rose in importance along with the strict constructionist–interpretivist divide. Bush was concerned with finding nominees who not only would interpret the Constitution strictly but also would support a strengthening of executive power. As we saw in Chapter 8, many members of the Bush administration supported the unitary theory of the executive, which claims that the Constitution permits only the president to wield executive power. Under this theory, efforts by Congress to create independent agencies outside of the president's purview are unconstitutional. The administration also objected to efforts by Congress and the courts to limit or interpret executive power in matters of national security. Both of the men Bush appointed to the Court, Chief Justice John Roberts and Samuel Alito, are supporters of a strong executive office.

President Obama's Supreme Court nominees reflected his own center-left, interpretivist ideology. His first nomination, Sonia Sotomayor, who joined the Court in September 2009, was more controversial for remarks she had made about her ethnicity and gender than for her judicial views. When former solicitor general Elena Kagan was nominated by Obama for the Court in 2010, however, her lack of a history of clear judicial rulings left her ideology something of a mystery, and many liberals feared that she would end up being a moderate voice on the Court.[44] Likewise, Merrick Garland, whom Obama nominated to replace Justice Scalia, was a more moderate judge who Obama hoped would meet with the approval of Republicans as a replacement for the conservative icon. After Senate Republicans refused to even hold hearings on Obama's nomination, Trump nominated and the Senate confirmed conservative, strict constructionist Neil Gorsuch to the Court. Gorsuch's conservatism is of the "plain text" variety—that is, the simple meaning of the words in laws is what matters, not their congressional or historical context.[45] Brett Kavanaugh, Trump's second appointee, is also conservative. He spent time as a political operative as well as a judge and has taken a more partisan stance to the Court, threatening those who were critical of his nomination, telling them "what comes around, comes around."[46]

The trend over the past few decades, since Nixon made a campaign issue of not appointing justices who were "soft on crime," is for Republican presidents to carefully pick conservative nominees, to avoid disappointments of the Eisenhower-Warren variety. Democratic presidents, however, particularly Bill Clinton and Barack Obama, have not seemed to share the urgency to put

judicial interpretivism a judicial approach holding that the Constitution is a living document and that judges should interpret it according to changing times and values

Mark Wilson/Getty Images

Justice in Waiting?

The unexpected death of conservative Justice Antonin Scalia in February 2016 left a hole in the Supreme Court that President Obama hoped to fill with the more moderate Merrick Garland (right). Many Republican lawmakers, however, preferred not to consider a new justice until after the 2016 presidential election in the hopes that a Republican would win the office. The unorthodox gamble paid off when Donald Trump won the presidency and appointed conservative Neil Gorsuch to the bench.

liberals on the Court; Clinton was not overly liberal himself and Obama was a constitutional scholar who weighed many issues other than ideology. The Trump-McConnell effort to get the maximum number of conservatives on the Court has only solidified the Court's move to the right; scholars have noted that both conservative and liberal justices have grown more conservative over time, shifting the Court to the right (see Figure 10.3).[47]

REWARD More than half of the people who have been nominated to the Supreme Court have been personally acquainted with the president.[48] Often nominees are friends or political allies of the president or other people the president wishes to reward in an impressive fashion. Harry Truman knew and had worked with all four of the men he appointed to the Court, Franklin Roosevelt appointed people he knew (and who were loyal to his New Deal), John F. Kennedy appointed his longtime friend and associate Byron White, and Lyndon Johnson appointed his good friend Abe Fortas.[49] While several FOBs (Friends of Bill) appeared on Clinton's short lists for his appointments, none was actually appointed. Though George W. Bush tried to appoint his friend and White House counsel Harriet Miers to the Court, she was forced to withdraw her name amid criticism that she wasn't sufficiently qualified. Barack Obama had a longtime working relationship with one of his nominees, Elena Kagan, who had been his first solicitor general.

REPRESENTATION Finally, presidents want to appoint people who represent groups they feel should be included in the political process, or whose support they want to gain. Lyndon Johnson appointed Thurgood Marshall at least in part because he wanted to appoint an African American to the Court. After Marshall retired, President George H. W. Bush appointed Clarence Thomas to fill his seat. Although Bush declared that he was making the appointment because Thomas was the person best qualified for the job, and not because he was black, few believed him. In earlier years, presidents also felt compelled to ensure that there was at least one Catholic and one Jew on the Court. This necessity has lost much of its force today as interest groups seem more concerned with the political than the denominational views of appointees, but Hispanic groups rejoiced when President Obama made Sonia Sotomayor the first Hispanic member of the Court in 2009. The issue of ethnic representation on the Court was put front and center during Sotomayor's confirmation hearings when she drew fire from Republicans who noted a line in a speech she had given in 2001, where she had argued that "I would hope that a wise Latina woman with the richness of her experiences would more often than not reach a better conclusion than a white male who hasn't lived that life."[50]

Table 10.1 shows the composition of the Supreme Court. There are six men on the Court and three women. Six justices are Catholic (though Gorsuch reportedly now belongs to an Episcopal church), and three Jewish; only Judeo-Christian religions have been represented on the Court so far. Five of the justices were appointed by Republicans, four by Democrats. They have attended an elite array of undergraduate institutions and law schools. There have never been any Native Americans or Asian Americans on the Court, and only two African Americans, whose terms did not overlap, and one Hispanic. The historically elite, white, male, Christian character of the Court raises interesting questions. We naturally want our highest judges to have excellent legal educations (although John Marshall barely had any). But should the nation's highest court represent demographically the people whose Constitution it guards? Some observers (including Justice Sotomayor) have suggested that women judges may be sensitive to issues that have not been salient to men and may alter behavior in the courtroom; the same may be true of minority judges. In a different vein, what message is sent to citizens when the custodians of national justice are composed primarily of a group that is itself fast becoming a minority in America?

CONFIRMATION BY THE SENATE As with the lower courts, the Senate must approve presidential appointments to the Supreme Court. We already mentioned the immediate

FIGURE 10.3

Changes in Ideology of Supreme Court Justices, 1937–2017

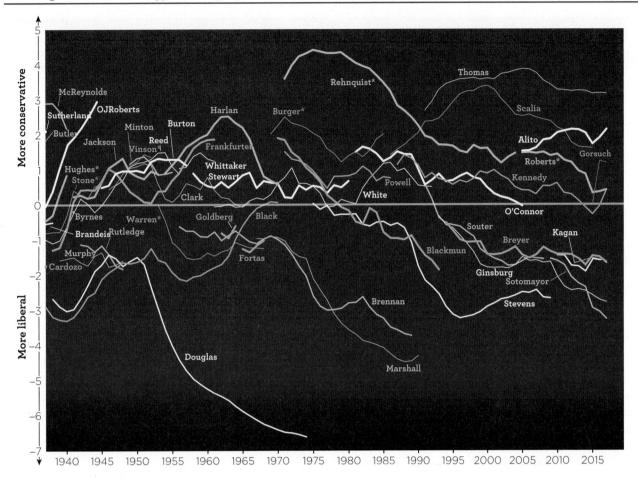

Source: Martin-Quinn Scores, Andrew W. Martin, and Kevin M. Quinn, "The 2017 Justice Data Files," mqscores.berkeley.edu/measures.php.

Note: Sotomayor and Kagan's 2010 ratings overlap. Justices' ideological ratings measured as Martin-Quinn scores. These calculations are due to Andrew Martin (Washington University School of Law) and Kevin M. Quinn (UC Berkeley School of Law) based on the Supreme Court Database (scdb.wustl.edu/documentation.php?var=decisionDirection). All cases before the Court are coded for liberal-conservative direction and outcomes, and justices' ideological voting scores over time are calculated based on their votes on the cases and relative to other justices.

Roberts's Court is growing more conservative.

and inflexible rejection by the Senate majority leader of any hearings for Obama's nominee to replace Scalia. Generally, however, the Senate Judiciary Committee plays the largest role, holding hearings and inviting the nominee, colleagues, and concerned interest groups to testify. Sometimes the hearings, and the subsequent vote in the Senate, are mere formalities, but increasingly, as the appointments have become more ideological and when the Senate majority party is not the party of the president, the hearings have had the potential to become political battlefields. Even when the president's party controls the Senate, the minority party can still influence the choice through the filibuster unless

the Senate Republicans renew their 2005 effort to halt this tradition. The Bork and Thomas hearings are excellent examples of what can happen when interest groups and public opinion get heavily involved in a controversial confirmation battle. These political clashes are so grueling because so much is at stake.

CHOOSING WHICH CASES TO HEAR

The introduction of political concerns into the selection process makes it almost inevitable that political considerations will also arise as the justices make their decisions. Politics makes an

TABLE 10.1

Composition of the Supreme Court, as of November 2018

JUSTICE	YEAR BORN	YEAR APPOINTED	POLITICAL PARTY	APPOINTING PRESIDENT	HOME STATE	COLLEGE/ LAW SCHOOL	RELIGION	POSITION WHEN APPOINTED
John G. Roberts Jr.	1955	2005	Rep.	G. W. Bush	Maryland	Harvard/ Harvard	Catholic	U.S. Appeals Court Judge
Clarence Thomas	1948	1991	Rep.	G. H. W. Bush	Georgia	Holy Cross/Yale	Catholic	U.S. Appeals Court Judge
Ruth Bader Ginsburg	1933	1993	Dem.	Clinton	New York	Cornell/ Columbia	Jewish	U.S. Appeals Court Judge
Stephen G. Breyer	1938	1994	Dem.	Clinton	California	Stanford, Oxford/ Harvard	Jewish	U.S. Appeals Court Judge
Samuel A. Alito Jr.	1950	2006	Rep.	G. W. Bush	New Jersey	Princeton/ Yale	Catholic	U.S. Appeals Court Judge
Sonia Sotomayor	1954	2009	Ind.	Obama	New York	Princeton/ Yale	Catholic	U.S. Appeals Court Judge
Elena Kagan	1960	2010	Dem.	Obama	New York	Oxford/ Harvard	Jewish	Solicitor General
Neil Gorsuch	1967	2017	Rep.	Trump	Colorado	Columbia/ Harvard	Catholic/ Episcopal*	U.S. Appeals Court Judge
Brett M. Kavanaugh	1965	2018	Rep.	Trump	Maryland	Yale/Yale	Catholic	U.S. Appeals Court Judge

Source: Supreme Court of the United States, "The Justices of the Supreme Court," www.supremecourtus.gov/about/biographies.aspx.

Gorsuch was raised Catholic but is currently a member of an Episcopal church

appearance at three points in the decision-making process, the first of which is in the selection of the cases to be heard.

The Supreme Court could not possibly hear the roughly eight thousand petitions it receives each year.[51] Intensive screening is necessary to reduce the number to the more manageable eighty to ninety that the Court finally hears. This screening process, illustrated in this chapter's *The Big Picture*, is a political one; having one's case heard by the Supreme Court is a scarce resource. What rules and which people determine who gets this resource and who doesn't?

PETITIONING THE SUPREME COURT Almost all the cases heard by the Court come from its appellate, not its original, jurisdiction, and of these virtually all arrive at the Court in the form of petitions for **writs of certiorari**, in which the losing party in a lower court case explains in writing why the Supreme Court should hear its case. Petitions to the Court are subject to strict length, form, and style requirements, and must be accompanied by a $300 filing fee. Those too poor to pay the filing fee are allowed to

petition the Court *in forma pauperis*, which exempts them not only from the filing fee but also from the stringent style and form rules. Approximately two-thirds of the 7,000–8,000 yearly case filings are *in forma pauperis*, but they are not heard in that proportion.[52] In 2015, twelve of eighty-one cases heard were *in forma pauperis*.[53] The Court's jurisdiction here is discretionary; it can either grant or deny a writ of certiorari. If it decides to grant certiorari and review the case, then the records of the case will be called up from the lower court where it was last heard.

For a case to be heard by the Court, it must be within the Court's jurisdiction, and it must present a real controversy that has injured the petitioner in some way, not just request the Court's advice on an abstract principle. In addition, it must be an appropriate question for the Court—that is, it must not be the sort of "political question" usually dealt with by the other

writs of certiorari formal requests by the U.S. Supreme Court to call up the lower court case it decides to hear on appeal

two branches of government. This last rule is open to interpretation by the justices, however, and they may not all agree on what constitutes a political question. But these rules alone do not narrow the Court's caseload to a sufficiently small number of cases, and an enormous amount of work remains for the justices and their staffs, particularly their law clerks.

THE ROLE OF LAW CLERKS Law clerks, usually recent graduates from law school who have served a year as clerk to a judge on a lower court, have tremendous responsibility over certiorari petitions, or "cert pets," as they call them. They must read all the petitions (thirty pages in length plus appendixes) and summarize each in a two- to five-page memo that includes a recommendation to the justices on whether to hear the case, all with minimal guidance or counsel from their justices.[54] Some justices join a "cert pool"—each clerk reads only a portion of the whole number of submitted petitions and shares his or her summaries and evaluations with the other justices. Seven of the nine current justices of the Court are in a pool; Samuel Alito and Neil Gorsuch require their clerks to read and evaluate all the petitions.

The memos are circulated to the justices' offices, where clerks read them again and make comments on the advisability of hearing the cases. The memos, with the clerks' comments, go on to the justices, who decide which cases they think should be granted cert and which denied. The chief justice circulates a weekly list of the cases he thinks should be discussed, which is known unimaginatively as the "discuss list." Other justices can add to that list the cases they think should be discussed in their Friday afternoon meetings.

THE RULE OF FOUR Once a case is on the discuss list, it takes a vote of four justices to agree to grant it certiorari. This **Rule of Four** means that it takes fewer people to decide to hear a case than it will eventually take to decide the case itself, and thus it gives some power to a minority on the Court. The denial of certiorari does not necessarily signal that the Court endorses a lower court's ruling. Rather, it simply means that the case was not seen as important or special enough to be heard by the highest court. Justices who believe strongly that a case should not be denied have, increasingly,

'Congress shall make no law'. . . now, I wonder what they meant by that . . .?

in recent years, engaged in the practice of "dissenting from the denial" in an effort to persuade other justices to go along with them (since dissension at this stage makes the Court look less consensual) and to put their views on record. Fewer than 5 percent of cases appealed to the Supreme Court survive the screening process to be heard by the Court.

OTHER INFLUENCES The decisions to grant cert, then, are made by novice lawyers without much direction, who operate under enormous time and performance pressures, and by the justices, who rely on the evaluations of these young lawyers while bringing to the process the full array of values and ideologies for which they were, in part, chosen. Naturally the product of this process will reflect these characteristics, but there are other influences on the justices and the decision-making process at this point as well.

One factor is whether the United States, under the representation of its lawyer, the **solicitor general**, is party to any of the cases before it. Between 70 and 80 percent of the appeals filed by the federal government are granted cert by the justices, a far greater proportion than for any other group.[55] Researchers speculate that this is because of the stature of the federal government's interests, the justices' trust in the solicitor general's ability to weed out frivolous lawsuits, and the experience the solicitor general brings to the job.[56] Justices are also influenced by **amicus curiae briefs**, or "friend of the court" documents, that are filed in support of about 8 percent of petitions for certiorari by interest groups that want to encourage the Court to grant or deny cert. The amicus briefs do seem to affect the likelihood that the Court will agree to hear a case, and since economic interest groups are more likely to be active here than are other kinds of groups, it is their interests that most often influence the justices to grant cert.[57] As we will see, amicus curiae briefs are also used later in the process.

Rule of Four the unwritten requirement that four Supreme Court justices must agree to grant a case certiorari in order for the case to be heard

solicitor general the Justice Department officer who argues the government's cases before the Supreme Court

amicus curiae briefs "friend of the court" documents filed by interested parties to encourage the Court to grant or deny certiorari or to urge it to decide a case in a particular way

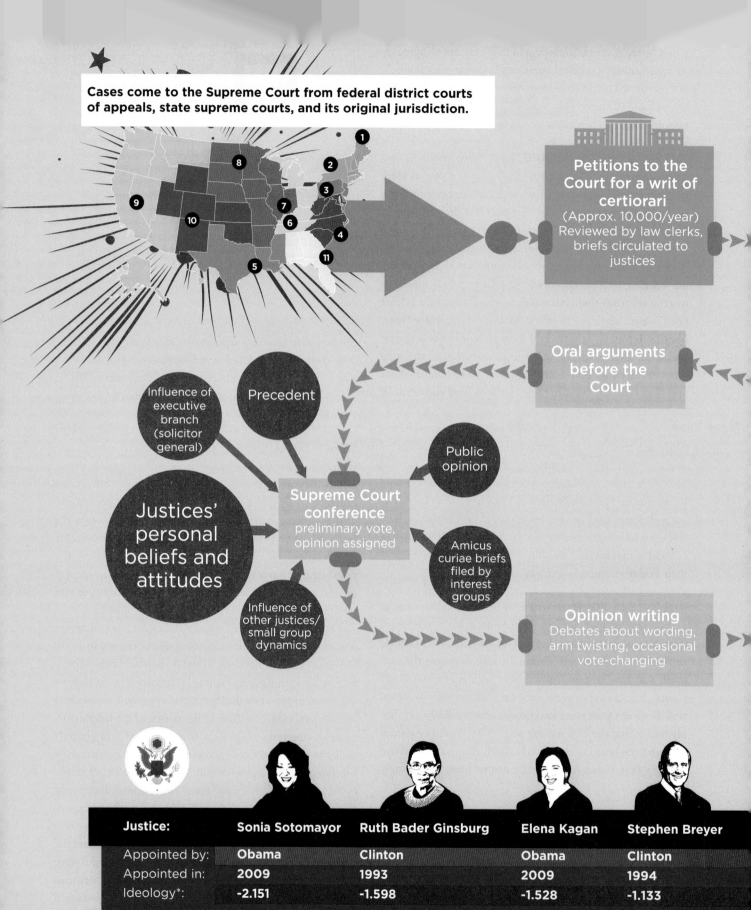

Cases come to the Supreme Court from federal district courts of appeals, state supreme courts, and its original jurisdiction.

Petitions to the Court for a writ of certiorari
(Approx. 10,000/year)
Reviewed by law clerks, briefs circulated to justices

Oral arguments before the Court

Influence of executive branch (solicitor general)

Precedent

Public opinion

Justices' personal beliefs and attitudes

Supreme Court conference
preliminary vote, opinion assigned

Amicus curiae briefs filed by interest groups

Influence of other justices/small group dynamics

Opinion writing
Debates about wording, arm twisting, occasional vote-changing

Justice:	Sonia Sotomayor	Ruth Bader Ginsburg	Elena Kagan	Stephen Breyer
Appointed by:	Obama	Clinton	Obama	Clinton
Appointed in:	2009	1993	2009	1994
Ideology*:	-2.151	-1.598	-1.528	-1.133

*Ideological identifications based on Martin-Quinn Scores, which use voting records to rate how liberal or conservative each justice is. Lower numbers are more liberal, higher numbers are more conservative. Shading gradation indicates degrees of liberal ideology (blue) to conservative (red).

The Supreme Court is the final court of appeal in the United States. Don't be fooled by the marble columns and velvet drapes—the Court is a political institution. Power is injected into the process when the justices decide which cases to hear, when they decide cases, and in the impact that those cases have on American lives. This is the political process by which a case gets to the Court.

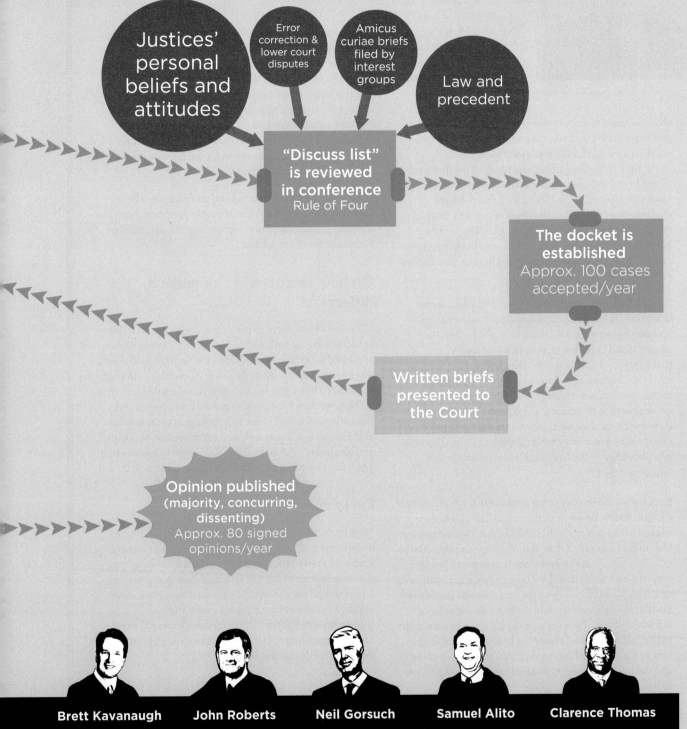

Brett Kavanaugh	**John Roberts**	**Neil Gorsuch**	**Samuel Alito**	**Clarence Thomas**
Trump	GW Bush	Trump	GW Bush	GHW Bush
2018	2005	2017	2005	1991
--**	1.05	1.503	1.677	3.578

** The Martin-Quinn score for Brett Kavanaugh was not available in November 2018.
Source: Administrative office of the United States Courts. Martin-Quinn Scores, http://mqscores.lsa.umich.edu/index.php.

PROFILES IN CITIZENSHIP
Sandra Day O'Connor

Even though she'd told the story many times, Sandra Day O'Connor's voice still echoed with the frustration of that first job hunt. Really, all she wanted then was to work as a lawyer. She was getting married that summer, and her husband-to-be still had a year left in law school. Since, she said dryly, they both liked to eat, she thought getting a job would be a good idea. Positions galore were posted on the jobs board at Stanford Law School, where she'd graduated third in her class of 102, but none of the firms was willing to hire a woman. The former Supreme Court justice's story sounded both ludicrous and poignant when we interviewed her the year before her retirement.

Sandra Day, soon to be Sandra Day O'Connor, set to work convincing the San Mateo County attorney to hire her; because he was engaged in public law, "he wasn't afraid to have a woman in his office." With that first job—initially undertaken without pay and in a shared office—she launched herself on a public career that coursed through years in the state attorney general's office in Arizona, the Arizona senate, and the state bench, and would finally hit its dramatic peak twenty-nine years later, when President Ronald Reagan appointed her as the first female justice on the U.S. Supreme Court.

But maybe it's too easy to blame Sandra Day O'Connor's extraordinary career in public law on the stubborn sexism of the private legal profession in 1950s America. She might have taken that path anyway—her decision to go to law school in the first place was in part idealistic, inspired by a professor she'd taken a law class from as an undergraduate. "He was the first one who persuaded me that the individual could make a difference in this big world of ours," she remembered. "The person at the bottom will sometimes have the best understanding of how to make something work. If you are sincere about it and determined enough, you can hang in there and see to it that it happens."

And those are the recurring themes in the life of Sandra Day O'Connor: sincerity in her efforts, determination to make a difference, persistence in the face of opposition, and independence in charting her path.

Perhaps all these qualities were honed from an early age, as she grew up on her family's Lazy B Ranch on the border of New Mexico and Arizona. As she has written, the ranch was "a place where the wind always blows, the sky forms a dome overhead, and the clouds make changing patterns against the blue, and where the stars at night are brilliant and constant, a place to see the sunrise and sunset, and always to be reminded how small we are in the universe but, even so, how one small voice can make a difference."[1]

And there is that idealism again, an optimism about the potential of human beings that is tempered, with a strong no-nonsense manner and a brisk practicality. Here is some of her advice:

On how one person can make a difference

"Of course [you] have to have courage, you have to learn to believe in yourself, and to do that you have to develop some skills. So learn to read fast, and to write well, that's what you need to learn to do as a student. I have to read something like 1,500 pages a day. Now I couldn't do that if I hadn't taken speed reading. And that's important. I'm serious. You don't realize how important it is to be able to read fast. Because if you can read fast, think of all you can learn . . . . And then have courage to believe that, yes, you are equipped to do something, and go do it."

On keeping the republic

"You know, I've always said that we don't inherit our knowledge and understanding through the gene pool. And every new generation has to learn all over again the foundations of our government, how it was set up and why, and what is every individual's role in it. And we have to convey that to every generation . . . [i]f every young generation of citizens [doesn't] have an understanding of this, we can't keep our nation in decent order for the future."

Source: Sandra Day O'Connor talked with Christine Barbour on March 3, 2005.

---

1. Sandra Day O'Connor and H. Alan Day, *Lazy B: Growing Up on a Cattle Ranch in the American Southwest* (New York: Random House 2002), 302.

DECIDING CASES

Once a case is on the docket, the parties are notified and they prepare their written briefs and oral arguments for their Supreme Court appearance. Lawyers for each side get only a half-hour to make their cases verbally in front of the Court, and they are often interrupted by justices who seek clarification, criticize points, or offer supportive arguments. The half-hour rule is generally followed strictly. In one case, two justices got up and walked out as the oral argument cut into their lunch hour, even though the lawyer who was speaking had been granted an extension by the chief justice.[58] The actual decision-making process occurs before and during the Supreme Court conference meeting. Conference debates and discussions take place in private, although justices have often made revealing comments in their letters and memoirs that give insight into the dynamics of conference decision making. A variety of factors affect the justices as they make decisions on the cases they hear. Some of those factors come from within the justices—their attitudes, values, and beliefs—and some are external.

JUDICIAL ATTITUDES Justices' attitudes toward the Constitution and how literally it is to be taken are clearly important, as we saw earlier in our discussion of interpretivism and strict constructionism. Judges are also influenced by the view they hold of the Court's role: whether it should be an active lawmaker and policymaker, or should keep its rulings narrow—that is, dealing with only the most specific legal issues—and leave broader lawmaking to the elected branches of government. Those who adhere to judicial activism are quite comfortable with the idea of overturning precedents, exercising judicial review, and otherwise making decisions that shape government policy. Practitioners of judicial restraint, by contrast, believe more strongly in the principle of *stare decisis* and reject any active lawmaking by the Court as unconstitutional.

These positions seem at first to line up with the positions of interpretivism and strict constructionism, and often they do. But exceptions exist, as when liberal justice Thurgood Marshall, who had once used the Constitution in activist and interpretivist ways to change civil rights laws, pleaded for restraint among his newer and more conservative colleagues who were eager to roll back some of the earlier decisions by overturning precedent and creating more conservative law.[59] In recent years, especially with respect to rulings that they see as socially liberal, conservatives

have lambasted what they call the activism or "legislating from the bench" of courts that they say takes decision making out of the hands of the people. But activism is not necessarily a liberal stance, and restraint is not necessarily conservative. Activism or restraint often seems to be more a function of whether a justice likes the status quo than of any steady point of principle.[60] A justice seeking to overturn the *Roe v. Wade* ruling allowing women to have abortions during the first trimester of pregnancy would be an activist conservative justice; Justice Thurgood Marshall ended his term on the Court as a liberal restraintist.

In addition to being influenced by their own attitudes, justices are influenced in their decision making by their backgrounds (region of residence, profession, place of education, and the like), their party affiliations, and their political attitudes, all of which the president and the Senate consider in selecting future justices.[61]

EXTERNAL FACTORS Justices are also influenced by external factors.[62] Despite the founders' efforts to make justices immune to politics and the pressures of public opinion by giving them lifetime tenure, political scientists have found that they usually tend to make decisions that are consistent with majority opinion in the United States. Of course, this doesn't mean that justices are reading public opinion polls over breakfast and incorporating their findings into judicial decisions after lunch. Rather, the same forces that mediate public opinion also shape the justices' opinions, and people who are elected by the public choose the justices they hope will help them carry out their agenda, usually one that is responsive to what the public wants.

Political forces other than public opinion exert an influence on the Court, however. The influence of the executive branch, discussed earlier, contributes to the high success rate of the solicitor general. Interest groups also put enormous pressure on the Supreme Court, although with varying success. Interest groups are influential in the process of nomination and confirmation of the justices, they file amicus curiae briefs to try to shape the decisions on the certiorari petitions, and they file an increasingly large number of briefs in support of one or the other side when the case is actually reviewed by the Court. According to one scholar, the number of amicus briefs filed by interest groups is increasing, although the Court does not release official numbers. Bloomberg News notes that the unofficial record for amicus briefs filed was 102 (for the 2003 affirmative action cases we discussed in Chapter 6) until the 2012 health care case, which inspired a whopping 136.[63] Interest groups also have a role in sponsoring cases when individual petitioners do not have the resources to bring a case before the Supreme Court. The National Association for the Advancement of Colored People (NAACP), the American Civil Liberties Union (ACLU), and the Washington Legal Foundation are

> judicial activism the view that the courts should be lawmaking, policymaking bodies
>
> judicial restraint the view that the courts should reject any active lawmaking functions and stick to judicial interpretations of the past

The Politics of Impartiality

Although the narrative around the Supreme Court is one of the impartial application of the law, in reality, the justices' views and attitudes about the law are shaped by the same forces that shape the public's views and attitudes. This can lead to highly partisan decisions, as in Citizens United v. Federal Election Commission, *which was so reviled by Democrats that President Obama took the unusual step of criticizing it during his State of the Union address in 2010.*

opinions are vitally important for how the nation will understand what the decision means. If, for instance, the opinion is written by the least enthusiastic member of the majority, it will be weaker and less authoritative than if it is written by the most passionate member. The same decision can be portrayed in different ways, stated broadly or narrowly, with implications for many future cases or for fewer. If the chief justice is in the majority, it is his or her job to assign the opinion-writing task. Otherwise, the senior member in the majority assigns the opinion. So important is the task that chief justices are known to manipulate their votes, voting with a majority they do not agree with in order to keep the privilege of assigning the opinion to the justice who would write the weakest version of the majority's conclusion.[65] Those

examples of groups that have provided funds and lawyers for people seeking to reach the Court. While interest group activity has increased tremendously since the 1980s, researchers are uncertain whether it has paid off in Court victories. Their support does seem to help cases get to the Court, however, and they may reap other gains, such as publicity.

A final influence worth discussing here is the justices' relationships with one another. While they usually (at least in recent years) arrive at their conference meeting with their minds already made up, they cannot afford to ignore one another. It takes five votes to decide a case, and the justices need each other as allies. One scholar who has looked at the disputes among justices over decisions, and who has evaluated the characterization of the Court as "nine scorpions in a bottle," says that the number of disagreements is not noteworthy.[64] On the contrary, what is truly remarkable is how well the justices tend to cooperate, given their close working relationship, the seriousness of their undertaking, and the varied and strong personalities and ideologies that go into the mix.

WRITING OPINIONS Once a decision is reached, or sometimes as it is being reached, the writing of the opinion is assigned. The **opinion** is the written part of the decision that states the judgment of the majority of the Court; it is the lasting part of the process, read by law students, lawyers, judges, and future justices. As the living legacy of the case, the written

justices who agree with the general decision, but who do so for reasons other than or in addition to those stated in the majority opinion, may write **concurring opinions**, and those who disagree may write **dissenting opinions**. These other opinions often have lasting impact as well, especially if the Court changes its mind, as it often does over time and as its composition changes. When such a reversal occurs, the reasons for the about-face are sometimes to be found in the dissent or the concurrence for the original decision.

THE POLITICAL EFFECTS OF JUDICIAL DECISIONS

The last area in which we can see the Supreme Court as a political actor is in the effects of the decisions it makes. These decisions, despite the best intentions of those who adhere to the philosophy of judicial restraint, often amount to the creation of public policies as surely as do acts of Congress. Chapters 5 and 6, on civil

opinion the written decision of the Court that states the judgment of the majority

concurring opinions documents written by justices expressing agreement with the majority ruling but describing different or additional reasons for the ruling

dissenting opinions documents written by justices expressing disagreement with the majority ruling

liberties and the struggle for equal rights, make clear that the Supreme Court, at certain points in its history, has taken an active lawmaking role. The history of the Supreme Court's policymaking role is the history of the United States, and we cannot possibly recount it here, but a few examples should show that rulings of the Court have had the effect of distributing scarce and valued resources among people, affecting decisively who gets what, when, and how.[66] It was the Court, for instance, under the early leadership of John Marshall, that greatly enhanced the power of the federal government over the states by declaring that the Court itself has the power to invalidate state laws (and acts of Congress as well) if they conflict with the Constitution;[67] that state law is invalid if it conflicts with national law;[68] that Congress' powers go beyond those listed in Article I, Section 8, of the Constitution;[69] and that the federal government can regulate interstate commerce.[70] In the early years of the twentieth century, the Supreme Court was an ardent defender of the right of business not to be regulated by the federal government, striking down laws providing for maximum working hours,[71] regulation of child labor,[72] and minimum wages.[73] The role of the Court in making civil rights policy is well known. In 1857 it decided that slaves, even freed slaves, could never be citizens;[74] in 1896 it decided that separate accommodations for whites and blacks were constitutional;[75] and then it reversed itself, declaring separate but equal to be unconstitutional in 1954.[76] It is the Supreme Court that has been responsible for the expansion of due process protection for criminal defendants,[77] for instituting the principle of one person–one vote in drawing legislative districts,[78] and for establishing the right of a woman to have an abortion in the first trimester of pregnancy.[79] And, of course, there was the case of *Bush v. Gore*, with which we began this chapter. Each of these actions has altered the distribution of power in American society in ways that some would argue should be done only by an elected body.

In many ways the Roberts Court promises to be as political as those that have come before, although there have been some surprising twists that keep Court-watchers guessing. In 2010 the Court ruled five to four that campaign finance legislation could not limit the money spent by corporations on election-eering broadcasts because corporations have First Amendment protections.[80] Although we don't yet understand the full impact of this case, as we will see in Chapter 14, the Super PACs it allows have changed the campaigning landscape. In 2012 the Court handed down rulings that, among other things, struck down most of Arizona's immigration law and upheld the constitutionality of President Obama's health care bill, albeit not on grounds that observers had anticipated. In that ruling, Chief Justice Roberts used creative reasoning to save the president's signature legislation, concluding the individual mandate in the bill was not a mandate, which would have fallen outside Congress's commerce clause power, but a tax, which was indisputably within Congress's tool box (see the *CLUES to Critical Thinking* feature at the end of the chapter).[81] In 2013 the Court rolled back parts of the historic Voting Rights Act and then the next week struck down the Defense of Marriage Act that defined marriage as being between a man and a woman. And in 2014 the Court limited the president's ability to make appointments during congressional recesses, struck down overall limits by individuals to campaigns, and ruled in a split decision that family-owned corporations do not have to provide health insurance that covers birth control to employees if it offends the owners' religious beliefs. The following year, they ruled that same-sex couples have a constitutional right to get married, and they supported an initiative giving citizens the right to take district redrawing out of the hands of state legislators and give it to an independent commission. In 2016 the Court upheld a University of Texas affirmative action program and struck down a Texas law limiting abortion, but the eight-person Court split four to four on President Obama's executive action delaying deportation for some undocumented immigrants, which left in place the lower court's ruling that struck it down.

Although this is by no means a comprehensive list of Supreme Court cases during Roberts's tenure, it shows that these decisions get right in the thick of determining who gets what and how they get it.

PAUSE AND REVIEW   Who, What, How

The Supreme Court is a powerful institution, and all Americans have a great stake in what it does. Citizens want to respect the Court and to believe that it is the guardian of American justice and the Constitution.

Presidents want to create a legacy and to build political support with respect to their Supreme Court appointments, and they want to place justices on the Court who reflect their political views and judicial philosophy. Occasionally they also want to influence the decisions made by the Court.

Members of the Senate also have an interest in getting justices on the Court who reflect their views and the views of their parties. They are also responsive to the wishes of their constituents and to the interest groups that support them. Confirmation hearings can consequently be quite divisive and acrimonious. Interest groups, which want members on the Court to reflect their views, can lobby the Senate before and during the confirmation hearings, and can prepare amicus curiae briefs in support of the parties they endorse in cases before the Court.

Finally, the justices themselves have a good deal at stake in the politics of the Supreme Court. They want a manageable caseload and are heavily reliant on their law clerks and the rules of court procedure. They want to make significant and respected decisions, which means they have to weigh their own decision-making criteria carefully.

In Your Own Words   Outline the institutional rules and political influences that shape the Supreme Court and the decisions it makes.

THE CITIZENS AND THE COURTS

Equal treatment and equal access?

In this chapter we have been arguing that the legal system and the American courts are central to the maintenance of social order and conflict resolution, and are also a fundamental component of American politics—who gets what, and how they get it. This means that a crucial question for American democracy is, who takes advantage of this powerful system for allocating resources and values in society? An important component of American political culture is the principle of equality before the law. We commonly take that principle to mean that all citizens should be treated equally by the law, but it also implies that all citizens should have equal access to the law. In this concluding section, we look at the questions of equal treatment and equal access.

EQUAL TREATMENT BY THE CRIMINAL JUSTICE SYSTEM

In Chapter 6, on civil rights, we examined in depth the issue of equality before the law in a constitutional sense. But what about the day-to-day treatment of citizens by the law enforcement and legal systems? Citizens are treated differently by these systems according to their race, their income level, and the kinds of crimes they commit. Experience has led African Americans and whites to develop very different narratives about the role the criminal justice system plays in their lives—narratives that are told and strengthened by the witness borne by social media, especially powerful when almost everyone has a video camera in his or her pocket. When law enforcement violations of civil rights are videotaped, posted in real time, and go viral before the official report has been made, the conventional, pro-law enforcement narratives are harder to maintain, although people's perception of the events is still often divided along racial lines.

The country was sadly reminded of that fact in the summer of 2014 through the very different reactions whites and blacks had to the shooting of Michael Brown, an unarmed teenager, by a police officer in Ferguson, Missouri. In the week following the killing, amid riots and demonstrations, curfews and the calling in of the National Guard by the governor, 80 percent of African Americans said they thought the incident raised important ideas about race. In contrast, 47 percent of whites said the issue of race was getting more attention than it deserved.[82] For African Americans, Brown was but the latest and not the last young man to be shot by police in suspect circumstances, highlighting the fear that many have that their sons are often targeted by the police out of fear or prejudice. Whites, by contrast, are accustomed to seeing the police as a source of safety rather than danger, and often fail to understand what such incidents look like from the other side of the racial divide. In fact, as Ferguson struggled for calm, sympathy for the police officer who shot Brown generated several online efforts to raise support and funds for him and his family. The Brown murder was not an exception but, as the social media–driven Black Lives Matter movement drove home, just one of a series of similar betrayals of the public trust by law enforcement officers who are predisposed to believe that black men are more dangerous than whites.

When San Francisco 49er Colin Kaepernick knelt during the national anthem in 2016 to protest police violence, he was ostracized within the NFL. Other players who followed his example were accused of protesting the flag or the anthem instead of the violence they were trying to highlight. President Trump weighed in targeting the players and the NFL owners followed suit with a decision to fine players who took a knee during the anthem. Trump's congratulatory tweet suggested that perhaps protesting players did not belong in the country at all.[83]

All this makes it is painfully clear that African Americans and white Americans do not experience our criminal justice system in the same ways, beginning with what is often the initial contact with the system, the police (see *Snapshot of America: How Confident Are We in the Police, by Race and Ethnicity?*). Blacks are often harassed by police or treated with suspicion without any real cause—consider the practice of "stop-and-frisk" tactics in black neighborhoods in New York City, for example, technically random in nature but affecting mostly black men. As a result, blacks, and black men especially, tend to perceive the police as persecutors rather than protectors. In New York, specifically, reactions to stop-and-frisk tended to reflect race, with 48 percent of whites calling the practice "acceptable," compared to a mere 35 percent of blacks.[84] Federal courts weighed in on the practice in 2013, ruling that stop-and-frisk violated the constitutional rights of minorities in the city and amounted to "indirect racial profiling." Stopping short of ending the practice entirely, Justice Shira A. Sheindlin called for a range of reforms and a federal monitor to oversee them.[85] Today the fact remains that blacks are more likely to be arrested than whites, and they are more likely to go to jail, where they serve harsher sentences. A study of marijuana use and arrests, for example, shows that while young whites use marijuana at higher rates than blacks, blacks are three times more likely to be arrested for marijuana possession.[86] Clearly, initial interactions with police play a role here—they are more likely to stop and frisk a black person. But race is not the only factor that divides American citizens in their experience of the criminal justice system.

Income also creates a barrier to equal treatment by the law. Over half of those convicted of felonies in the United States were defended by court-appointed lawyers.[87] These lawyers are likely to be less than enthusiastic about their assignments. For one thing, the pay is modest and sometimes irregular. Many lawyers do not like to provide free services *pro bono*

Snapshot of America: *How Confident Are We in the Police, by Race and Ethnicity?*

Equality of Police Treatment of Blacks and Whites*

All | White | Black | Hispanic

	treated equally	whites favored	most of them
All	35%	53%	2%
White	38%	50%	1%
Black	13%	81%	1%
Hispanic	35%	56%	3%

*Survey question reads "In general, do you think that the country's criminal justice system treats whites and blacks equally, or does it favor whites over blacks?"

Source: CNN/ORC Poll: 2016 Presidential Debates/Trump's Taxes/Racial Discrimination/Protests, Sept 28–Oct 2, 2016.

Public Assessment of Police Officers Who Are Prejudiced Against Blacks*

	most of them	some of them	only a few of them	almost none of them	unsure
All	5%	13%	24%	54%	0%
White	3%	9%	23%	59%	
Black	13%	30%	31%	23%	
Hispanic	8%	15%	22%	52%	3%

*Survey question reads "How confident are you that the police in this country are held accountable for any misconduct: very confident, somewhat confident, not so confident or not confident at all?"

Source: CNN/ORC Poll: 2016 Presidential Debates/Trump's Taxes/Racial Discrimination/Protests, Sept 28–Oct 2, 2016.

Public Assessment of Police Doing the Right Thing for Local Communities*

	always/often	sometimes	rarely/never	not confident at all	unsure
All	25%	41%	19%		1%
White	31%	43%	15%		1%
Black	4%	32%	38%	14%	1%
Hispanic	21%	37%	18%		3%

*Survey question reads "How much of the time do you think you can trust the police to do what is right for you and your community?

Source: Associated Press-NORC Center for Public Affairs Research Poll: Law Enforcement and Violence: The Divide Between Black and White Americans, July 17-19, 2015.

Behind the Numbers

Lady Justice, the statue that adorns many of the country's courthouses, wears a blindfold to signify that administration of the law is blind to differences in income, race, or who you know. In practice, however, the administration of justice is not color-blind. In the United States, whites and blacks have very different experiences with the police and the courts, and the police are the main contact that many have with the justice system. Look over the difference in the opinions of racial and ethnic groups in these charts. What kinds of experiences can account for these patterns? Is there anything that can be done to approach the ideal of a truly blind justice system?

Scott Olson/Getty Images

Emotions, Boiling Over

After local police shot and killed an unarmed teenager named Michael Brown in August 2014, protestors, both peaceful and disruptive, took to the streets of Ferguson, Missouri, to express their anger over what they saw as a pattern of unfair—and too often fatal—treatment along racial lines. Public reactions, especially heightened attention to the Black Lives Matter movement, brought renewed focus on issues of race relations in the United States.

publico ("for the public good") because they are afraid it will offend their regular corporate clients. Consequently the quality of the legal representation available to the poor is not of the same standard available to those who can afford to pay well. Yale law professor John H. Langbein is scathing on the role of money in determining the legal fate of Americans. He says, "Money is the defining element of our modern American criminal-justice system." The wealthy can afford crackerjack lawyers who can use the "defense lawyer's bag of tricks for sowing doubts, casting aspersions, and coaching witnesses," but "if you are not a person of means, if you cannot afford to engage the elite defense-lawyer industry—and that means most of us—you will be cast into a different system, in which the financial advantages of the state will overpower you and leave you effectively at the mercy of prosecutorial whim."[88]

EQUAL ACCESS TO THE CIVIL JUSTICE SYSTEM

Whereas the issue with respect to the criminal justice system is equal treatment, the issue for the civil justice system is equal access. Most of us in our lifetimes will have some legal problems. The Supreme Court has ruled that low-income defendants must be provided with legal assistance in state and federal criminal cases, but there is no such guarantee for civil cases. That doesn't mean, however, that less affluent citizens have no recourse for their legal problems. Both public and private legal aid programs exist. Among others,

the Legal Services Corporation (LSC), created by Congress in 1974, is a nonprofit organization that provides resources to over 138 legal aid programs around the country with more than 900 local offices. The LSC helps citizens and some immigrants with legal problems such as those concerning housing, employment, family issues, finances, and immigration. This program has been controversial, as conservatives have feared that it has a left-wing agenda. Trump proposed eliminating all funding for the program in the 2019 budget, but Congress did approve a $25 million increase.[89]

Does the fact that these services exist mean that more citizens get legal advice? Undoubtedly it does. Every year LSC programs handle nearly a million cases.[90] Still, there is no question that many of the legal needs of the less affluent are not being addressed through the legal system.[91] Clearly a bias in the justice system favors those who can afford to take advantage of lawyers and other means of legal assistance. And since people of color and women are much more likely to be poor than are white males (although white men are certainly represented among the poor), the civil justice system ends up discriminating as well.

These arguments do not mean that the U.S. justice system has made no progress toward a more equal dispensation of justice. Without doubt, we have made enormous strides since the days of *Dred Scott*, when the Supreme Court ruled that blacks did not have the standing to bring cases to court, and since the days when lynch mobs dispensed their brand of vigilante justice in the South. But the lives of African Americans are still at risk at multiple points in our justice system. Since Michael Brown's murder, the Black Lives Matter movement that we discussed in Chapter 1 has created and spread a counternarrative about the justice system in the United States that has helped to bring the experience of African Americans home to whites in a new way. Hillary Clinton helped put the public spotlight on that narrative when she invited the "Mothers of the Movement"—the moms of young black men slain by police or vigilantes—to the Democratic National Convention in 2016. The Mothers, who took the stage to the chants of "Black Lives Matter," also occasionally joined her on the campaign trail.

In Your Own Words Describe the relationship between citizens and the courts in America.

LET'S REVISIT: *What's at Stake...?*

In the years since the divisive outcome of *Bush v. Gore*, the nation has calmed down. The stunning national crisis that began with the terrorist attacks on September 11, 2001, put things into a broader perspective, and a Court-decided election no longer seemed as great a danger as the possibility of being caught without any elected leader at all at a critical time. Public opinion polls show that trust in all institutions of government, including the Supreme Court, ran high after September 11, and Bush's legitimacy no longer rested with the Court's narrow majority but rather with the approval ratings that hit unprecedented heights in the aftermath of the terrorist attacks and with his successful reelection in 2004. But changed national circumstances and subsequent elections do not mean that the Court's unusual and controversial move in resolving the 2000 election should go unanalyzed. What was at stake in this extraordinary case?

First, as Justice Stevens pointed out at the time, the long-term consequences of people's attitudes toward the Court were at risk. Indeed, polls have shown a somewhat steady decline in people's perceptions of the highest court in the land in the years since, but it remains unclear whether that is due to the Court's finding in *Bush v. Gore* or to later rulings—or to an overall decrease in faith in government institutions.[92] The Court, as we have seen, has often engaged in policymaking, and to believe that it is not a political institution would be a serious mistake. But part of its own legitimacy has come from the fact that most people do not perceive it as political, and it is far more difficult now to maintain that illusion. In the immediate aftermath of the decision, the justices, speaking around the country, tried to contain the damage and reassure Americans; some of the dissenting justices even emphasized that the decision was not made on political or ideological grounds. But fifteen years later, retired Justice Sandra Day O'Connor expressed some regrets, not about the ruling itself or her vote in it, but about the Court's decision to get involved at all. Noting that the case had earned the court "a less-than-perfect reputation," O'Connor wondered if "maybe the court should have said, 'We're not going to take it, goodbye.'"[93] Also at stake in such a deeply divided decision was the Court's own internal stability and ability to work together. While the confidentiality of the justices' discussions in arriving at the decision has been well guarded, the decision itself shows that they were acrimonious. Again, in the aftermath, the justices have tried to put a unified front on what was clearly a bitter split. Members of the majority have continued to socialize with dissenters, and as Justice Scalia himself told one audience, "If you can't disagree without hating each other, you better find another profession other than the law."[94] The stakes in this case may have been more directly political than in most other cases, but the members of the Supreme Court are used to disagreeing over important issues and probably handle the level of conflict more easily than do the Americans who look up to them as diviners of truth and right.

Another stake in the pivotal decision was the fundamental issue of federalism itself. The federal courts, as Justice Ruth Bader Ginsburg wrote in her dissent, have a long tradition of deferring to state courts on issues of state law. Indeed, many observers were astounded that the Court agreed to hear the case in the first place, assuming that the justices would have sent it back to be settled in Florida. Normally it would have been the ardent conservatives on the Court—Rehnquist, Scalia, and Thomas—whom one would have expected to leap to the defense of states' rights. Subsequent decisions have made clear, however, that the *Bush v. Gore* decision did not signal a reversal on their part.[95]

Some observers argue that the majority of the Court saw something else at stake that led them to set aside their strong beliefs in states' rights and to run the risk that they might be seen as more Machiavelli than King Solomon, more interested in power than wisdom. The majority saw the very security and stability of the nation at stake. Anticipating a long recount of the votes that might even then be inconclusive, they thought it was better to act decisively at the start rather than to wait until a circus-like atmosphere had rendered impossible the most important decision a voting public can make. Whether they were right in doing so, and whether the stakes justified the risks they took, politicians, partisans, and historians will continue to debate for years to come.

CLUES to Critical Thinking

"Welcome to the Roberts Court: How the Chief Justice Used Obamacare to Reveal His True Identity"

By Jeffrey Rosen, *The New Republic*, June 29, 2012

In the wake of the Supreme Court's five-to-four decision upholding most of President Obama's health care bill, Chief Justice John Roberts was praised by liberals and lambasted by conservatives. In this article, Professor Jeffrey Rosen explains that Roberts's vote was more complex than either side knew.

In 2006, at the end of his first term as Chief Justice, John Roberts told me that he was determined to place the bipartisan legitimacy of the Court above his own ideological agenda. But he recognized the difficulty of the task. "It's sobering to think of the seventeen chief justices," he said. "Certainly a solid majority of them have to be characterized as failures."

Specifically, he was concerned that his colleagues were too often handing down 5–4 decisions that divided along predictable party lines, which made it hard for the public to maintain faith in the Court as an institution that transcends politics. Roberts pledged to try to persuade his colleagues to avoid party line votes in the most divisive cases. Roberts said he would embrace as his model his judicial hero, John Marshall, who sometimes engaged in legal "twistifications," to use Thomas Jefferson's derisive phrase, in order to achieve results that would strengthen the institutional legitimacy of the Court.

In the health care case, Roberts produced a twistification of which Marshall would have been proud. He joined the four liberals in holding that the Affordable Care Act's individual mandate was justified by Congress's taxing power even though he also joined the four conservatives in holding that the mandate was not justified by Congress's power to regulate interstate commerce.

For bringing the Court back from the partisan abyss, Roberts deserves praise not only from liberals but from all Americans who believe that it's important for the Court to stand for something larger than politics. On Thursday, Roberts did precisely what he said he would do when he first took office: He placed the bipartisan legitimacy of the Court above his own ideological agenda. Seven years into his Chief Justiceship, the Supreme Court finally became the Roberts Court.

It would be easy, of course, to question the coherence of the combination of legal arguments that Roberts embraced,

but it would also be beside the point: Roberts's decision was above all an act of judicial statesmanship. On both the left and the right commentators are praising his "political genius" in handing the president the victory he sought even as he laid the groundwork for restricting congressional power in the future.

That's why it was foolish for conservatives to worry that Roberts could be intimidated by President Obama and other liberals who warned that a 5–4 Republican-Democratic vote striking down health care would represent a failure of Roberts's bipartisan vision. Roberts understood this on his own: Anyone who cared enough about his legacy to discuss it at the beginning of his tenure is far too savvy to be swayed by warnings from the left or right. Whether or not Roberts voted to uphold the mandate after the initial decisions were drafted, as some commentators are now suggesting, Roberts knew that the health care decision would be the defining moment of his early tenure, and he rose to the occasion.

That's not to say that Roberts has reinvented himself as a liberal: He has strong views that he's unwilling to compromise, and with his strategic maneuvering in the health care case, he has now increased the political capital that will allow him to continue to move the Court in a conservative direction in cases involving affirmative action and the voting rights act, both of which he may well strike down next year by 5–4 votes. Marshall achieved a similar act of judicial jujitsu in *Marbury v. Madison*, when he refused to confront president Jefferson over a question of executive privilege but laid the groundwork for expanding judicial power in the future.

But Roberts's career defining choice in the health care case calls to mind the bipartisan ambitions not only of John Marshall but also Barack Obama. Like Roberts, Obama came to Washington as a Harvard educated lawyer who was strongly identified with one side of the political spectrum but believed in the virtues of bipartisanship. Obama expressed that belief by endorsing a version of the health care mandate that had the imprimatur of conservatives ranging from Mitt Romney to the Heritage Foundation. But despite strenuously reaching out to Republicans in the health care debate, Obama was able to win only one Republican vote (that of Joseph Cao (R-LA)). And Obama found himself assailed on both his left and right flanks from ideological purists who saw any kind of moderation as a form of apostasy.

Roberts now faces similar attacks from the left and right over the health care case for the compromise he forged with the pragmatic liberals, Elena Kagan and Stephen Breyer, over the Medicaid expansion. All three justices concluded that it violated the Constitution by threatening states with the loss of their existing Medicaid funding, but could be saved by removing the threat. But by joining the liberals in upholding the mandate, Roberts was able to persuade them to join him in restricting Congressional power. On health care, both Obama and Roberts exercised something increasingly rare in a polarized age: bipartisan leadership, which inherently requires compromise.

In a sense, all of the justices in the health care case reached decisions that coincide with their judicial philosophies and temperaments. Roberts was more interested in institutional legitimacy than philosophical purity. The pragmatic liberals, Kagan and Breyer, were willing to meet him half way. The more civil libertarian liberals, Ginsburg and Sotomayor, were not. Among the conservative dissenters, the romantic libertarian, Anthony Kennedy, proved as unalterably opposed as ever to incursions on liberty, regardless of whether they came, in his view, from the right as from the left. The tea party conservative Clarence Thomas filed a separate statement making clear how radically he wanted to restrict federal power. And the newly minted devotee of states rights, Antonin Scalia, included sclerotic rhetoric warning of the apocalypse. Scalia, increasingly, sounds more like an angry pundit than a neutral judge, and in the process, he gives us a vision of what both the liberal and conservative wings might have sounded like if Roberts hadn't prevented them from polarizing entirely.

Of course, it didn't all come down to judicial temperament. In the most divisive constitutional cases, the substance of legal arguments will always play a part. Arguments by liberal scholars who care about constitutional text and history, such as

Neil Siegel of Duke Law School, were reflected in Chief Justice Roberts's opinion about the taxing power. Justice Ginsburg's defense of Congress's power to pass the mandate under the commerce clause adopted New Textualists arguments by Jack Balkin of Yale Law School about how the framers of Article VI of the Virginia Plan during the Constitutional Convention would have wanted Congress to coordinate economic action in areas where the states were powerless to act on their own. The majority opinion also vindicated Solicitor General Don Verrilli's decision to emphasize the breadth of Congress's taxing power. But in the end, there are good arguments on both sides of any constitutional question, and justices have broad discretion to pick and choose among competing legal arguments based on a range of factors—including concerns about text, history, precedent, or institutional legitimacy. The fact that Roberts chose to place institutional legitimacy front and center is the mark of a successful Chief.

As Roberts recognized, faith in the neutrality of the law and the impartiality of judges is a fragile thing. When I teach constitutional law, I begin by telling students that they can't assume that it's all politics. To do so misses everything that is constraining and meaningful and inspiring about the Constitution as a framework for government. There will be many polarizing decisions from the Roberts Court in the future, and John Roberts will be on the conservative side of many of them. But with his canny performance in the health care case, Roberts has given the country a memorable example of what it means to be a successful Chief Justice.

Source: Copyright Jeffrey Rosen. This article originally appeared in *The New Republic* and is reprinted by permission.

Consider the source and the audience: Jeffrey Rosen is a law professor at Georgetown University who supported the nomination of John Roberts as chief justice. He is writing in *The New Republic*, a longstanding center-left journal about politics. How are Rosen's own views reflected in this article?

Lay out the argument and the underlying values and assumptions: This article is about Chief Justice Roberts's efforts to be a "successful" chief justice. How do Roberts (and Rosen) define "success" in this context? How is it related to "institutional legitimacy"? And what does Rosen mean that the Court is now "the Roberts Court"?

Uncover the evidence: Rosen bases his insights into Roberts's thinking on his own interviews of Roberts, as well as his analysis of what Roberts argued in the health care case. Is that persuasive to you?

Evaluate the conclusion: Rosen argues that Roberts has used a "twistification" to get his way in the long run (reduced powers for Congress) while avoiding to seem like a partisan in the short run. Liberal critics like the short-term result but fear the long-term result. Conservative critics have the opposite view. Did Roberts's "nonpartisan" solution avoid politics?

Sort out the political implications: Roberts's decision here certainly sidestepped the kind of political controversy the Court generated when it decided *Bush v. Gore* in 2000 (see *What's at Stake...?*). Is avoiding that kind of dramatic taking-of-sides all that is necessary to restore "faith in the neutrality of the law and the impartiality of judges"?

Review

Law and the American Legal System

Laws serve five main functions in democratic societies. They offer security, supply predictability, provide for conflict resolution, reinforce society's values, and provide for the distribution of social costs and benefits. American law is based on legislation, but its practice has evolved from a tradition of common law and the use of precedent by judges. The American legal system is considered to be both adversarial and litigious in nature. The adversarial nature of our system implies that two opposing sides advocate their position with lawyers in the most prominent roles, while the judge has a relatively minor role, in comparison.

Laws serve many purposes and are classified in different ways. Substantive laws cover what we can or cannot do, while procedural laws establish the procedures used to enforce law generally. Criminal laws concern specific behaviors considered undesirable by the government, while civil laws cover interactions between individuals. Constitutional law refers to laws included in the Constitution as well as the precedents established over time by judicial decisions relating to these laws. Statutory laws, administrative laws, and executive orders are established by Congress and state legislatures, the bureaucracy, and the president, respectively.

courts (p. 337)
civil-law tradition (p. 337)
common-law tradition (p. 337)
precedent (p. 337)
adversarial system (p. 338)

inquisitorial system (p. 338)
substantive laws (p. 340)
procedural laws (p. 340)
procedural due process (p. 340)
criminal laws (p. 340)

civil laws (p. 341)
constitutional law (p. 341)
statutory laws (p. 341)
administrative law (p. 342)
executive orders (p. 342)

Constitutional Provisions and the Development of Judicial Review

The founders were deliberately vague in setting up a court system so as to avoid controversy during the ratification process. The details of design were left to Congress, which established a layering of district, state, and federal courts with differing rules of procedure. The Constitution never stated that courts could decide the constitutionality of legislation. The courts gained the extraconstitutional power of judicial review when Chief Justice John Marshall created it in *Marbury v. Madison*.

judicial review (p. 343)

Marbury v. Madison (p. 343)

Federalism and the American Courts

The political views of the judge and the jurisdiction of the case can have great impact on the verdict. The rules of the courtroom may vary from one district to another, and the American dual court system often leads to more than one court's having authority to deliberate.

jurisdiction (p. 344)
original jurisdiction (p. 345)

appellate jurisdiction (p. 345)
appeal (p. 345)

senatorial courtesy (p. 348)

The Supreme Court

The U.S. Supreme Court reigns at the top of the American court system. It is a powerful institution, revered by the American public but as political an institution as the other two branches of government. Politics is involved in how the Court is chosen, how it chooses which cases to hear, how it decides each case, and in the effects of its decisions.

strict constructionism (p. 352)
judicial interpretivism (p. 353)
writs of certiorari (p. 356)
Rule of Four (p. 357)

solicitor general (p. 357)
amicus curiae briefs (p. 357)
judicial activism (p. 361)
judicial restraint (p. 361)

opinion (p. 362)
concurring opinions (p. 362)
dissenting opinions (p. 362)

The Citizens and the Courts

Although the U.S. criminal justice system has made progress toward a more equal dispensation of justice, minorities and poor Americans have not always experienced equal treatment by the courts or had equal access to them.

Like

You and 1,000,000 people like this.

Image created by Patricia Mann; icon by Thomas Pajot/Shutterstock.com

In Your Own Words

After you've read this chapter, you will be able to

11.1 Explain the role of public opinion in a democracy.

11.2 Evaluate how well American citizens measure up to notions of an ideal democratic citizen.

11.3 Identify key factors that influence our individual and collective political opinions.

11.4 Describe different techniques used to gauge public opinion.

11.5 Give examples of ways in which public opinion enhances or diminishes the relationship between citizens and government.

11
PUBLIC OPINION

What's at Stake . . . When We Move to More Direct Democracy?

IT WAS LATE MAY 2018, and #hometovote was trending. Irish expats from all over the world were coming home to cast a constitutional vote on whether or not to repeal Ireland's Eighth Amendment banning abortions. Ireland's abortion laws were so restrictive that in 2012 a young woman, Savita Halappanavar, died of complications from a miscarriage after a hospital refused her a medically necessary abortion. Polls showed that the vote would be close, and so people were coming home to register their views. Because Ireland's voting laws for the most part require you to vote in person, in person they were voting, alongside many of their fellow countrypeople. Turnout was the highest it had been for a social issue in Ireland—64.1 percent of Irish voters showed up. And in the end, the close vote wasn't close after all. With a 66.4 percent majority, the Eighth Amendment was overturned, allowing for the passage of less restrictive laws.

It wasn't the first time a popular referendum had upended the social order in Ireland. In 2015, 61 percent of the country's voters turned out to decide, by a

Lauryn Canny
@LaurynCanny

Follow

I'm coming #HomeToVote ! Will be traveling 5,169 miles from LA to Dublin and will be thinking of every Irish woman who has had to travel to access healthcare that should be available in their own country. Let's do this, Ireland! #repealthe8th #VoteYes

6:40 PM - 22 May 2018

3,432 Retweets **24,472** Likes

◯ 212   ⟳ 3.4K   ♡ 24K

Home to Vote

Irish law requires in-person voting, so citizens living around the world traveled home to participate in the referendum to repeal the Eighth Amendment. Many of the travelers tweeted about their journeys, highlighting the distance they were willing to travel and many reflecting on the Irish women who had traveled to the United Kingdom in the past to obtain legal abortions.

62 percent majority, to allow marriage equality. In a country whose Constitution reflected the conservative principles of the Catholic Church, public opinion has been shifting faster than the wheels of government could turn. Politicians needed the Constitution amended to allow them to pass laws reflecting the shifts, and the people came out in droves to make it happen.

Direct votes on policy, like these two Irish referenda, are not unusual, but the results can be unpredictable and often shocking. For instance, on the morning of June 24, 2016, British citizens woke up to the unexpected news that they were on their way out of the European Union (EU)—an economic and political union of twenty-eight European countries that dated in some form back to the days after World War II. A nonbinding but politically important popular vote on whether the United Kingdom should withdraw from the EU (popularly called "Brexit") found that 51.9 percent of the U.K. voters (the United Kingdom consists of England, Scotland, Northern Ireland, Wales, and its overseas territory, Gibraltar) wanted out. Although Scotland, Northern Ireland, and Gibraltar voted to remain, they were stuck with the result.[1] By the evening of the 24th, Britain's prime minister, David Cameron, who had opposed Brexit but called the vote to appease political opponents, had resigned, the British pound was in free fall, several politicians who had advocated leaving were admitting they had played a little fast and loose with the facts about the consequences of a Brexit, and a number of British voters were expressing misgivings about the way they had voted. Some were so sure

the measure would fail they had voted for it as a "protest." Brexit remorse or "Bregret" was setting in quickly.[2]

Referenda can have unexpected consequences. Are they a good idea? "Letting the people decide" is an attractive idea in a country like the United States that prides itself on its democracy. But how much responsibility do you want to take for the way you are governed? Most of us are pretty comfortable with the idea that we should vote for those who make our rules (although we don't all jump at the chance to do it), but how about voting on the rules themselves? Citizens of some states—California, for instance— have become used to being asked for their votes on new state laws through referenda and voter initiatives. Other states, too, hold popular votes on issues it is hard to get politicians to take action on. In May 2018, for example, Ohio passed an initiative rejecting partisan gerrymandering in favor of a less partisan method of redistricting. But what about national politics—do you know enough or care enough to vote on laws for the country as a whole, just as if you were a member of Congress or a senator? Are you confident that your political strings aren't being pulled by the authors of the social media you tune in to? Should we be governed more by public opinion than by the opinions of our elected leaders? This is the question that drives the debate about whether U.S. citizens should be able to participate in such forms of direct democracy as the national referendum or initiative.

All American states employ some degree of direct democracy (although it is generally very weak in the South), but as we saw with Ireland and the United Kingdom, many other countries do as well. In the past several years alone, voters in Slovenia were asked to decide about the establishment of a tribunal to resolve a border dispute with Croatia, in Bolivia about whether there should be limits to individual landholdings, in Azerbaijan about amending the constitution, in Sierra Leone about choosing a president (in the first democratic elections since 1967), and in Iceland about terms of payment on the national debt.

Back in 1995, former senator Mike Gravel, D-Alaska, proposed that the United States join many of the world's nations in adopting a national plebiscite, or popular vote on policy. He argued that Americans should support a national initiative he called "Philadelphia II" (to evoke "Philadelphia I," which was, of course, the Constitutional Convention), which would set up procedures for direct popular participation in national lawmaking.[3] Such participation could take place through the ballot box (the Swiss go to the polls four times a year to vote on national policy) or even electronically, as some have suggested, with people voting on issues by computer at home. Experts agree that the technology exists for at-home participation in government. And public opinion is overwhelmingly in favor of proposals to let Americans vote for or against major national issues before they become law.[4]

Do you agree with Gravel and the roughly three-quarters of Americans who support more direct democracy at the national level? Should we have rule by public opinion in the United States? How would the founders have responded to this proposal? And what would be the consequences for American government if a national plebiscite were passed? Just what is at stake in the issue of direct democracy at the national level? **«**

IT is fashionable these days to denounce the public opinion polls that claim to tell us what the American public thinks about this or that political issue. The American people themselves are skeptical—65 percent of them think that the polls are "right only some of the time" or "hardly ever right."[5] (You might believe that finding, or you might not.) Politicians can be leery of polls, too—or even downright scornful of them. Disdainful of the Bill Clinton years, when the president's team of pollsters openly tested the public on various issues, including his approval ratings, the George W. Bush administration was cagey about the fact that they watched polls at all. Bush himself frequently said things like, "I really don't worry about polls or focus groups; I do what I think is right."[6] Matthew Dowd, the Bush administration's chief of polling at the Republican National Committee, echoed that stance with an emphatic "We don't poll policy positions. Ever."[7] Of course, the Bush administration did look at polls, and conducted them, too, just like every other administration has since the advent of modern polling—just as Barack Obama's administration did for eight years, and it's likely President Trump's does as well.[8]

These reactions to public opinion raise an interesting question. What is so bad about being ruled by the polls in a democracy, which, after all, is supposed to be ruled by the people? If politics is about who gets what, and how they get it, shouldn't we care about what the "who" thinks? **Public opinion** *is* just what the public thinks, although as we have argued throughout this book it is subject to mediation from a variety of sources. It is the aggregation, or collection, of individual attitudes and beliefs on one or more issues at any given time. **Public opinion polls** are nothing more than scientific efforts to measure that opinion—to estimate what an entire group of people thinks about an issue by asking a smaller sample of the group for its opinions. If the sample is large enough and chosen properly, we have every reason to believe that it will provide a reliable estimate of the whole. With today's technology, we can keep a constant finger on the pulse of America and know what its citizens are thinking at almost any given time. And yet, at least some Americans seem torn about the role of public opinion in government today. On the one hand, we want to believe that what we think matters, but on the other hand, we'd like to think that our elected officials are guided by unwavering principles. Reflected in this dilemma are not just different

Keeping in Touch With the People

Our elected officials may seem disconnected from popular opinion, but they are in fact keenly sensitive to their constituents, knowing that their votes on major bills may come back to haunt them when it's time for reelection. Members of Congress pay attention to public opinion polls, and most try to provide some face time in their districts as well. Here, Democratic senator Amy Klobuchar chats with constituents over coffee at a weekly "Minnesota Mornings" meet-and-greet event.

views of public opinion but also different narratives about what constitutes "good leadership."

In this chapter we argue that public opinion is important for the proper functioning of democracy, that the expression of what citizens think and what they want is a prerequisite for their ability to use the system and its rules to get what they want from it. But the quality of the public's opinion on politics—the degree to which it is influenced by our demographics, our circumstances, and the channels through which we get information—and the ways that it actually influences policy, may surprise us greatly.

THE ROLE OF PUBLIC OPINION IN A DEMOCRACY

Keeping the government of the people informed by the people

Public opinion is important in a democracy for at least two reasons. The first reason is normative: we believe public opinion should influence what government does. The second is empirical: a lot of people behave as if public opinion does matter, and thus, to the degree that they measure, record, and react to it, it does become a factor in American politics.

WHY PUBLIC OPINION *SHOULD* MATTER

The story of the American founding is about the rejection of aristocracy and monarchy and the rise of popular sovereignty—the idea that the people matter above all.

---

public opinion the collective attitudes and beliefs of individuals on one or more issues

public opinion polls scientific efforts to estimate what an entire group thinks about an issue by asking a smaller sample of the group for its opinion

The presence of "the people" is pervasive in the documents and narratives that create and support the American government. In the Declaration of Independence, Thomas Jefferson wrote that a just government must get its powers from "the consent of the governed." Our Constitution begins, "We, the People. . . ." And Abraham Lincoln's Gettysburg Address hails our nation as "government of the people, by the people, and for the people." What all of this tells us is that the very legitimacy of the U.S. government, like that of all other democracies, rests on the idea that government exists to serve the interests of its citizens.

Since the beginning of the republic, there has been a shift in our institutions toward a greater role for the citizenry in politics. We can see this in the Seventeenth Amendment to the Constitution (1913), which took the election of the U.S. Senate from the state legislatures and gave it to the citizens of the states. We can see it in the altered practice of the Electoral College. Once supposed to be a group of enlightened citizens who would exercise independent judgment, in recent decades it has almost always followed the vote of the people (with the dramatic exceptions of the 2000 and 2016 elections). We can see it in state politics, where the instruments of direct democracy—the initiative, referendum, and recall—allow citizens to vote on policies and even remove officials from office before their terms are up. These changes reflect views like those of political scientist V. O. Key, who observed, "Unless mass views have some place in the shaping of policy, all talk about democracy is nonsense."[9] But how to determine whose views should be heard? As we saw in Chapter 1, different theories of democracy prescribe different roles for "the people," in part because these theories disagree about how competent the citizens of a country are to govern themselves. Elitists suspect that citizens are too ignorant, ill-informed, or subject to manipulation to be trusted with major political decisions; pluralists trust groups of citizens to be competent on those issues in which they have a stake, but they think that individuals may be too busy to gather all the information they need to make informed decisions; and proponents of participatory democracy have faith that the people are both smart enough and able to gather enough information to be effective decision makers.

As Americans, we are also somewhat confused about what we think the role of the democratic citizen should be. We introduced these conflicting notions of citizenship in Chapter 1. One view, public-interested citizenship, which describes what we might call the ideal democratic citizen, is founded on the vision of a virtuous citizen activated by concern for the common good, who recognizes that democracy carries obligations as well as rights. In this familiar model, a citizen should be attentive to and informed about politics, exhibit political tolerance and a willingness to compromise, and practice high levels of participation in civic activities.

A competing view of self-interested citizenship holds that Americans are apolitical, self-absorbed actors. According to this view, Americans are almost the opposite of the ideal citizen: inattentive and ill-informed, politically intolerant and rigid, and unlikely to get involved in political life.

And in the current age, all forms of citizenship are subject to the power inherent in the channels through which we acquire information. An inquisitive citizen who reads widely, explores the web, and debates people with whom he or she disagrees is more likely to escape the perils of living in an information bubble and to demonstrate the values of public-interested citizenship. A citizen who ignores the news altogether or gets it only from sources he or she agrees with is more likely to be focused on less universal, more personal issues.

We argue in this chapter, as we have earlier, that the American public displays all of these visions of citizenship. But we also argue that there are mechanisms in American politics that buffer the impact of apolitical, self-interested behavior, so that Americans as a group often behave as ideal citizens, even though as individuals they do not.

WHY PUBLIC OPINION *DOES* MATTER

Politicians and media leaders act as though they agree with Key's conclusion, which is the practical reason why, regardless of the founding narrative, public opinion matters in American politics. Elected politicians have their own narrative, which is that the public is keeping tabs on them. When voting on major bills, members of Congress worry quite a lot about public opinion in their districts.[10] Presidents, too, pay close attention to public opinion. In fact, recent presidents have had in-house public opinion experts whose regular polls are used as an important part of presidential political strategies. And, indeed, the belief that the public is paying attention is not totally unfounded. Although the public does not often act as if it pays attention or cares very much about politics, it can act decisively if the provocation is sufficient. For instance, in the 2006 midterm election, voters showed their frustration with Republicans' support for the war in Iraq (despite polls that said a majority of Americans had come to oppose the war) by handing the Democrats enough seats in the House and the Senate to give them control in both chambers.[11] And in 2008 and 2010, elections were primarily about voter angst over a depressed economy, a worry that first enhanced and then diminished the Democrats' control of Congress. Multiple protest marches in the year and a half after Trump's inauguration made it clear that women's issues, immigration issues, and gun control were very much on the minds of millions of Americans. In special elections held to fill seats that unexpectedly became vacant, Democrats far outperformed Hillary Clinton's share of the presidential vote and Democrats succeeded in taking control of the House of Representatives in the 2018 midterms, as well as flipping seven governorships and six state legislative chambers.

Politicians are not alone in their tendency to monitor public opinion as they do their jobs. Leaders of the media also focus on public opinion, making huge investments in polls and devoting considerable coverage to reporting what the public is thinking. Polls are used to measure public attitudes toward all sorts of things and then are interpreted by the media, who set the narrative about what they mean. Of course, we are familiar with "horse race" polls that ask about people's voting intentions and lend drama to media coverage of electoral races. Sometimes these polls themselves become the story the media covers, with results tweeted and retweeted as soon as they are available, and competing narratives are quickly generated online to explain what they might mean. With the availability of a twenty-four-hour news cycle and the need to find something to report on all the time, it is not surprising that the media have fastened on their own polling as a newsworthy subject. Public opinion, or talk about it, seems to pervade the modern political arena.

Frederick M. Brown/Getty Images

Ironically Informative
John Oliver takes the biting humor he honed at the Daily Show *to an entirely new level on HBO's* Last Week Tonight, *which provides thoroughly researched reports that are at once informative, creative, interactive, sarcastic, and hilarious. The pay channel allows for free sharing of video and other material from the show—increasing its impact on public opinion as it makes the social media rounds.*

In Your Own Words Explain the role of public opinion in a democracy.

CITIZEN VALUES

How do we measure up?

In the preceding section, we reminded you of the two competing visions of citizenship in America: one, the ideal democratic citizen who is knowledgeable, tolerant, engaged in politics, and concerned about the common good, and two, the apolitical, self-interested actor who does not meet this ideal. Not surprisingly, our behavior frequently combines aspects of each. For instance, some citizens tune out political news but are tolerant of others and vote regularly. Many activist citizens are informed, opinionated, and participatory but are intolerant of others' views, which can make the give and take of democratic politics difficult. We are not ideal democratic citizens, but we know our founders did not expect us to be. As we will see by the end of this chapter, our democracy has so far survived fairly well despite our lapses.

POLITICAL KNOWLEDGE AND INTEREST

The ideal democratic citizen understands how government works, who the main actors are, and what major principles underlie the operation of the political system. Public opinion

PAUSE AND REVIEW Who, What, How

Public opinion is important in theory—in our views about how citizens and politicians should behave—and in practice—how they actually do behave. American political culture contains two views of citizenship, a public-interested and a self-interested view. These two views seem to be at odds, and Americans are ambivalent about the role public opinion should play in politics. The founders of the American polity developed constitutional rules to hold the power of citizens in check. Many of those rules, however, have changed over the intervening two hundred years as consensus has grown that citizens should play a stronger role in government.

Politicians and the media act as if they think the public is very powerful indeed. Politicians usually try to play it safe by responding to what the public wants, or what they think it will want in the future, while the media often cover public opinion as if it were a story in itself, and not just the public's reaction to a story.

pollsters periodically take readings on what the public knows about politics, and the conclusion is always the same: Americans are not very well informed about their political system.[12]

Knowledge of key figures in politics is important for knowing whom to thank—or blame—for government policy, key information if we are to hold our officials accountable. Virtually everyone (99 percent of Americans) can name the president, but knowledge falls sharply for less central offices.[13] In 2017, fewer than half (45 percent) knew that Neil Gorsuch was a justice on the Supreme Court (and that was after a scandalous story about McConnell blocking Obama's nominee had occupied the news for months) and only 62 percent knew that Paul Ryan was the Speaker of the House of Representatives, a position that is third in line for succession to the presidency, directly after the vice president.[14] Americans have a reasonable understanding of the most prominent aspects of the government system and the most visible leaders—and frequently about issues that receive a lot of media coverage—but they are ignorant about other central actors and key principles of political life.

Efforts to follow politics are also highly variable in the United States; only about a quarter of Americans say they follow public affairs "most of the time."[15] Taken together, the moderate levels of political knowledge and interest indicate that the American public does not approach the high levels of civic engagement recommended by civics texts, but neither is it totally ignorant and unconcerned.

TOLERANCE

A key democratic value is tolerance. In a democracy, with many people jockeying for position and competing visions of the common good, tolerance for ideas different from one's own and respect for the rights of others provide oil to keep the democratic machinery running smoothly. Tolerance is a prerequisite for compromise, which is an essential component of politics generally and of democratic politics particularly.

How do Americans measure up on the important democratic requirement of respect for others' rights? The record is mixed. As we saw in Chapters 5 and 6, America has a history of denying basic civil rights to some groups, but tolerance in general is on the rise since the civil rights movement of the 1960s. Small pockets of intolerance persist, primarily among extremist groups, although as we saw in the *What's at Stake . . . ?* in Chapter 6, more and more of it has bubbled to the surface since the 2016 election cycle. The anonymity of channels of communication on the Internet, from Twitter to Snapchat, allows people to express "socially inappropriate" and even downright racist views without fear of retribution. In fact, the idea that we should conform to respectful ways of referring to each other has been condemned as rampant political correctness, and its opposite blossoms on some social networks and even in one-to-one personal and social relationships.

In terms of general principles, most Americans support the values of freedom of speech, religion, and political equality. For instance, 90 percent of respondents told researchers they believed in "free speech for all, no matter what their views might be." Subsequent studies, such as those by the First Amendment Center, show similar data. However, when citizens are asked to apply these principles to particular situations in which specific groups have to be tolerated (especially unpopular groups like the American Nazi Party preaching race hatred or atheists preaching against God and religion), the levels of political tolerance drop dramatically.[16] In studies of political tolerance, the least politically tolerant are consistently the less educated and less politically sophisticated. For example, one study found that, on a civil liberties scale designed to measure overall support for First Amendment rights, only 24 percent of high school graduates earned high scores, compared with 52 percent of college graduates.[17] In practice, the mass public's record has not been bad, and some of the worst offenses of intolerance in our history, from slavery to the internment of Japanese Americans during World War II, were led by elites, not the mass public.

> *Of the three elements of the ideal citizen we discuss here—political knowledge, tolerance, and participation—which is most important for the health of democracy?*

PARTICIPATION

One of the most consistent criticisms of Americans by those concerned with the democratic health of the nation is that we do not participate enough. And indeed, as participation is usually measured, the critics are right. Figure 11.1 shows that for voter turnout in national elections, the United States ranks almost last among industrialized nations. Various explanations have been offered for the low U.S. turnout, including the failure of parties to work to mobilize turnout and obstacles to participation such as restrictive registration laws, limited voting hours, and the frequency of elections. We examine who votes and why in Chapter 14, but for now the fact remains that, among industrialized nations, the United States has one of the lowest levels of voter turnout in national elections, although greater levels of participation are seen among those with more education and higher income.

FIGURE 11.1
Comparison of Voter Turnout Among Select Nations

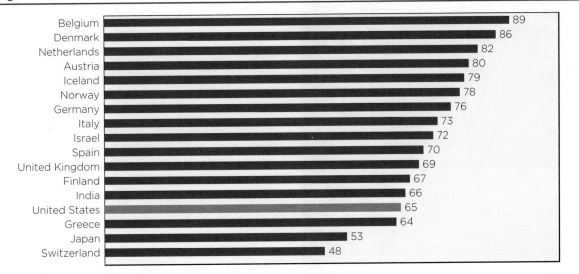

Source: Data calculated by authors with data from the Institute for Democracy and Electoral Assistance, www.idea.int/vt/.

PAUSE AND REVIEW Who, What, How

In a nation that claims to be ruled by the people, all American citizens have a stake in ensuring that "the people" are as close to being public-spirited ideal democratic citizens as they can be. It is also the case, however, that the primary incentive that drives each citizen is concern for his or her own interests, and that although many citizens do exhibit some of the characteristics of the ideal democratic citizen, they rarely exhibit all of them. Consequently, most citizens do not fit the model of the theoretical ideal. Those who do fit the model achieve that status through political education, the practice of toleration, and political participation.

In Your Own Words Evaluate how well American citizens measure up to notions of an ideal democratic citizen.

WHAT INFLUENCES OUR OPINIONS ABOUT POLITICS?

Sources of differing opinions in the American public

So far, we have learned that many, but by no means all, Americans approximate the characteristics of our so-called ideal democratic citizen. The elements of ideal democratic

> **political socialization** the process by which we learn our political orientations and allegiances

citizenship, however, are not distributed equally across the population. There are forces around us that bring most of us to consensus on the basics of the political culture we learned about in Chapter 2, and more complex forces that guide us into adopting the more divisive ideologies we studied in the same chapter.

MECHANISMS OF EARLY POLITICAL SOCIALIZATION: HOW WE LEARN SHARED NARRATIVES ABOUT THE RULES OF THE GAME

Democracies and, indeed, all other political systems depend for their survival on each new generation's picking up the values and allegiances of previous generations—beliefs in the legitimacy of the political system and its leaders, and a willingness to obey the laws and the commands of those leaders. The children in France or China support their leaders as surely as the children of the United States support theirs. Sharing an essential narrative about the founding of a country and the values that support it and deserve loyalty is key here.

We learn our earliest opinions through a process called **political socialization**, whereby values, beliefs, and attachments to political ideals are transferred from generation to generation. Early on, those values are supportive of the political system as we learn patriotism and good citizenship skills. The key agents of socialization are family, school, and houses of worship—all of which have an interest in turning out well-behaved children with loyalty to country. Socialization is

Little Patriots

Early political socialization can happen unintentionally. Parents take youngsters to parades to enjoy the music and the colorful pageantry. Once there, though, children begin to develop an emotional response to political celebrations (like the Fourth of July) and national symbols (like the American flag).

like mediation in the sense that the information we pick up comes through channels that may be controlled by people or organizations with interests in having us behave in particular ways. In the "olden days," of course, socialization was face to face, or maybe face to pastor or face to teacher, but now the possible agents of socialization have multiplied with the growth of the Internet and social media. Our fundamental values may be shaped in part by people we never see, never meet, and may not even be aware of.

The family is probably the biggest influence on our political development. Children typically develop an emotional response to some fundamental objects of government before they really understand much about those objects. They learn that the police are good (in most communities), the president is important, and the flag deserves respect. Thus one of the important orientations that develops in the preschool years is **patriotism**, a strong emotional attachment to the political community. Children saluting the flag or watching fireworks at Independence Day celebrations easily absorb the idea that being American is something special. Children also tend to choose the same political party as their parents.[18] Schools—where many children begin their day with the Pledge of Allegiance and where schoolbooks explicitly emphasize stirring narratives about national origins, founding heroes, and patriotism—are also an important agent of political learning and the development of citizen orientations. Most school districts

include as part of their explicit mission that the schools should foster good citizenship.[19] In many districts, U.S. history or civics is a required course, and some state legislatures require a course or two in U.S. and state politics for all college students in the state system. The media we are exposed to can also help build common values. When there were fewer television stations, most children watched the same cartoons, many of which reinforced patriotic themes, and even today they watch videos and play video games that do the same things.

The groups we belong to also foster in us basic values. Peer groups have a lot of influence on individuals' social and political attitudes. People who attend the same church tend to have similar political attitudes, as do individuals who live in the same neighborhoods. These tendencies can be traced in part to the ways people select themselves into groups, but they are reinforced by social contacts and by the social media connections that allow us to expand the numbers of peers we can contact and to build on and participate in the stories about who we are. The processes of talking, working, and worshiping together lead people to see the world similarly.[20] The appearance of consensus on rules of the game and basic values can be exaggerated by simple peer pressure. Researchers have documented a phenomenon they call the **spiral of silence**, a process by which minority voices silence themselves in the face of majority consensus.[21] This relative silence tends to embolden the advocates of the majority opinion to speak even more confidently. Thus, through this spiral of silence, what may begin as a bare majority for a group's position can become the overwhelming voice of the group.

DIFFERENCES IN PUBLIC OPINION

Political socialization produces a citizenry that largely agrees with the rules of the game and accepts the outcomes of the national political process as legitimate. That does not mean, however, that we are a nation in agreement on most or even very many things. As we get older and are exposed to more influences, our opinions become more complex. Our demographics (including race and ethnicity, gender, and age), partisanship and ideology, education, economic self-interest, and religion, as well as where we live all affect the way we come to see politics, what we believe we have at stake in the political process, and the kind of citizenship we practice. In the process, we move from consensus on the basics of American political culture to more divisive beliefs.

Those divisive beliefs work against the positive feelings toward government we build in our early years. In fact, at any given time,

patriotism a strong emotional attachment to one's political community

spiral of silence the process by which a majority opinion becomes exaggerated because minorities do not feel comfortable speaking out in opposition

large numbers of Americans express distrust in government to do the right thing, a reflection of the fact that the post–New Deal philosophy that there are public solutions to our problems means that when government acts there will be winners and losers. As conflict among different groups in society fluctuates, so do levels of trust that government will do the right thing. Occasionally we solidify behind our government and our leaders, especially when we perceive that we are under threat, as we did in the days after 9/11, but otherwise our trust in government reflects the divisions in our opinions and our loyalties to subgroups in the population.

RACE AND ETHNICITY As we saw in Chapter 6, race has been a deep and consistent cleavage in American politics. Even the early socialization experiences of whites and blacks are different, since for African American children it is not always clear that the police are their friends or that the system deserves their loyalty. Some of the most significant effects of the Obama presidency in this regard have been the opportunities for black kids to realize that the American dream of growing up to be president can actually belong to them, too.

Race has been a more divisive than unifying characteristic in this country. Only in recent decades have blacks achieved the same political rights as the white majority, and disparity in income between whites and blacks continues. When we compare by race the answers to a question about spending to improve the condition of blacks, the responses are quite different. African Americans are more favorable to such spending than are whites. We see a similar pattern in whether respondents would support a community bill to bar discrimination in housing. African Americans tend to favor such a law; whites are more likely to side with the owner's right to sell a house to whomever he or she chooses. These differences, some of which are shown in *Snapshot of America: What Do We Think, by Race and Ethnicity?*, are typical of a general pattern. On issues of economic policy and race, African Americans are substantially more liberal than whites. However, on social issues like abortion and prayer in schools, the racial differences are more muted.

The root of the differences between political attitudes of blacks and whites most certainly lies in the racial discrimination historically experienced by African Americans. Blacks tend to see much higher levels of discrimination and racial bias in the criminal justice system, in education, and in the job market.

Why Not Me?
President Obama bends over to allow the child of a White House staffer to pat his head and confirm that their hair feels the same. Children who have grown up with an African American president may feel very differently about their future prospects than those who came before them.

Official White House Photo by Pete Souza

Undeniably a large gulf exists between the races in their perceptions about the continuing frequency and severity of racial discrimination.[22] Finally, reflecting the very different stands on racial and economic issues the parties have taken, African Americans are the most solidly Democratic group in terms of both party identification and voting. Interestingly, as whites' income and other status indicators rise, they become more conservative and Republican until they achieve advanced degrees, when they tend to become Democrats. The same does not happen among African Americans. Better-educated and higher-income blacks actually have stronger racial identifications, which results in distinctly liberal positions on economic and racial issues and solid support for Democratic candidates.[23] Some signs indicate that this may be changing, however. The increasing number of black conservatives shows that the assumptions once made about African Americans and the Democratic Party are not universally true. This small but emerging pattern is exemplified by former secretary of state Condoleezza Rice; Supreme Court Justice Clarence Thomas; former California Board of Regents member Ward Connerly; former head of the Republican National Committee Michael Steele; Herman Cain, who briefly led in the polls for the Republican presidential nomination in 2012; Sen. Tim Scott, R-S.C., who threatened to impeach President Obama over the debt limit controversy; and most recently, Ben Carson, who ran for the Republican nomination in 2016 before serving as secretary of housing and urban development under Donald Trump.[24] Nevertheless, the rise of Obama to become the first black president of the United States has undoubtedly reinforced the bond between African Americans and the Democratic Party.

Snapshot of America: *What Do We Think, by Race and Ethnicity?*

Policies Supported by Race and Ethnicity

Legend: White* | Black | Hispanic | Asian

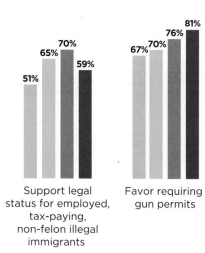
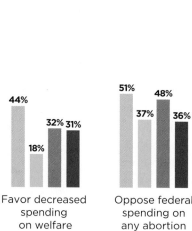
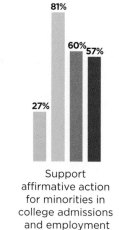

Support legal status for employed, tax-paying, non-felon illegal immigrants
- 51%
- 65%
- 70%
- 59%

Favor requiring gun permits
- 67%
- 70%
- 76%
- 81%

Support affirmative action for minorities in college admissions and employment
- 81%
- 27%
- 60%
- 57%

Favor decreased spending on welfare
- 44%
- 18%
- 32%
- 31%

Oppose federal spending on any abortion
- 51%
- 37%
- 48%
- 36%

Agree we are spending "too little" on improving the nation's education system
- 71%
- 77%
- 65%
- 61%

Source: Cooperative Congressional Survey, 2015 and 2016; General Social Survey 2016.

*Non-Hispanic whites.

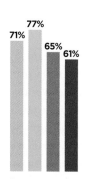

All four racial/ethnic groups agreed that **education** should be the top priority.

Behind the Numbers

Race and ethnicity stand for more than kinship; they also are markers for people's experiences in American society and politics. These experiences give rise to our policy preferences and even how we perceive the world. Looking at the differences in these charts, how can groups' experiences account for the differences you see?

Of course Americans differ by ethnicity as well as by race, and these factors interact in interesting ways to influence the opinions we hold on different policies. The *Snapshot of America* compares the views of non-Hispanic whites, blacks, Hispanics or Latinos, and Asians. Studies have shown that, although traditionally there has been little consensus among Asians as a group across a wide range of issues, in the hyperpartisan times in which we now live they are becoming much more liberal.[25] In general, whites, blacks, and Latinos are not consistent in terms of contemporary liberalism-conservatism. For example, whites are most conservative on the death penalty, with almost three-quarters favoring capital punishment, compared to about half of African Americans and Latinos. Blacks are most liberal in the belief that too little is spent on health care, but most conservative in favoring prayer in the schools. Latinos stand out in their opposition to abortion and in not favoring a reduction in the numbers of immigrants allowed into the country. Although the pattern is not one of ideological consistency, these differences make sense in terms of the particular histories and contexts of America's racial and ethnic mix.

GENDER For many years, one's gender had almost no predictive power in explaining opinions and behavior—except that women were less active in politics and usually less warlike in their political attitudes. Since the 1960s, however, there has been a revolution in our expectations about the role of women in society and in politics. As women gained more education and entered the workforce, they also increased their levels of participation in politics. Whereas in the 1950s women trailed men in voter turnout by over 12 percent, since 2006 women have voted at a slightly higher rate than men.[26]

Interestingly, in the last quarter of the twentieth century, as men and women approached equality in their levels of electoral participation, their attitudes on issues diverged. This tendency for men and women to take different issue positions or to evaluate political figures differently is called the **gender gap.**

> **gender gap** the tendency of men and women to differ in their political views on some issues

Snapshot of America: *What Do We Think, by Gender (and Marriage)?*

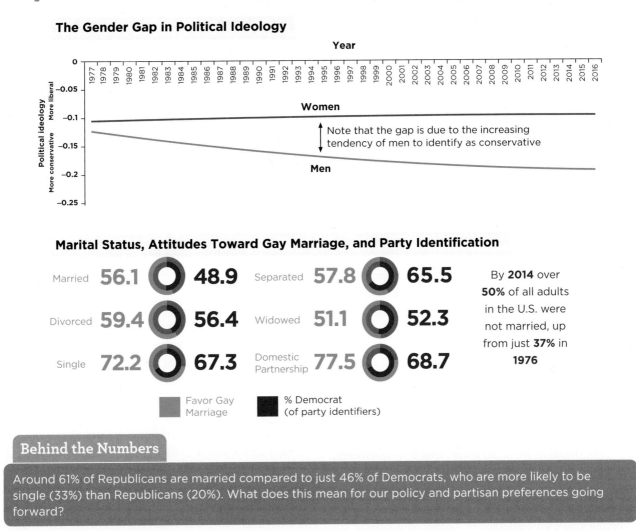

The Gender Gap in Political Ideology

Year

Political ideology (More liberal / More conservative)

Women

Note that the gap is due to the increasing tendency of men to identify as conservative

Men

Marital Status, Attitudes Toward Gay Marriage, and Party Identification

Married	56.1	48.9	Separated	57.8	65.5
Divorced	59.4	56.4	Widowed	51.1	52.3
Single	72.2	67.3	Domestic Partnership	77.5	68.7

By **2014** over **50%** of all adults in the U.S. were not married, up from just **37%** in **1976**

Favor Gay Marriage

% Democrat (of party identifiers)

Behind the Numbers

Around 61% of Republicans are married compared to just 46% of Democrats, who are more likely to be single (33%) than Republicans (20%). What does this mean for our policy and partisan preferences going forward?

Source: Calculated by the authors, Cooperative Congressional Elections Study, 2016, http://cces.gov.harvard.edu; Calculated by the authors, *CBS-New York Times* polls.

In almost all cases, it means that women are more liberal than men. The ideological stances of women overall have not changed significantly since the 1970s, but those of men have shifted steadily, as more call themselves conservatives [see *Snapshot of America: What Do We Think, by Gender (and Marriage?)*]. On a number of specific policy issues, the gender gap is substantial: women are more liberal on social welfare policies, that is, programs of aid for children, the elderly, and the poor; and women are less favorable to the death penalty and less willing than men to go war. On so-called women's issues, such as abortion or women having an equal role in business (where we might expect the greatest gender gap), the differences between the sexes are surprisingly small.[27] The gender gap has

> **marriage gap** the tendency of married and unmarried people to differ in their political views on some issues

important electoral consequences. Women are more likely than men to vote for Democratic candidates. In fact, in every presidential election from 1980 to 2016, women were more supportive of the Democratic candidate than were men, and interestingly, in recent elections, this gap has been largest among young people (those aged eighteen to twenty-nine).[28] The differences between men and women might be explained by their different socialization experiences and by the different life situations they face. The impact of one's life situation has emerged recently in what observers are calling the **marriage gap**. This refers to the tendency for different opinions to be expressed by those who are married or widowed versus those who have never been married. "Marrieds" tend toward more traditional and conservative values; "never marrieds" tend to have a more liberal perspective. The "never marrieds" are now sufficiently numerous that in many localities they constitute an important group that politicians must consider in deciding which issues to support.

STAGES OF LIFE We might expect that people change their opinions as they age, that our experiences over time affect how we see the political world. Although there is precious little evidence for the common view that masses of people progress from youthful idealism to mature conservatism, on some issues the differences across generations are striking (see *Snapshot of America: What Do We Think, by Age?*).

One important example is the finding of consistent age differences in political engagement. Middle-age and older citizens are typically more attentive to and more active in politics: they report more frequent efforts to persuade others, they vote more often, and they are more likely to write letters to public officials and to contribute to political campaigns. It seems that acting out one's political role may be part and parcel of the array of activities that we associate with "settling down," such as marrying, having children, and establishing a career. This exception was mitigated somewhat in 2008 with the unusual response of young people to Barack Obama's candidacy for president. The Obama candidacy brought record numbers of young people to the polls, and at the same time created one of the sharpest age-vote relationships we have seen, with younger voters supporting Obama in overwhelming numbers.[29] Similarly, but not quite as dramatically, in 2016 young voters chose Hillary Clinton over Donald Trump 55 to 27 percent.

Another area in which age plays a role in public opinion is in the creation of **political generations**, groups of citizens who have been shaped by particular events, usually in their youth, and whose shared experience continues to identify them throughout their lives. Growing up in the years after 9/11, for instance, can give a generation a set of shared values as surely as having grown up during the civil rights movement of the sixties, the Vietnam War, World War II, or the Great Depression.[30] One of the most distinctive of such groups was the New Deal generation—those who came of age during the 1930s. They were more Democratic in their party orientations than preceding generations, but they are also a generation that is almost gone.[31] They were followed by the Silent Generation and then the Baby Boomers—the huge eclectic group born in the postwar years from 1946 to 1964 who have entered late middle age and are beginning to collect Social Security and Medicare, expensive programs that end up being paid for in part by succeeding generations.

Larger even than the Baby Boomer generation are the millennials, born between roughly 1980 and 1997. Compared to their parents' generation, millennials are far more diverse, less religious, and more likely to be cynical about the media, possibly because they face a media landscape more complex, more multifaceted, and harder to master than any in history.[32] These young people do not fit the mold of their elders any more than previous generations did. Millennials, for example, favor legalization of marijuana, environmental protection, and LGBTQ

rights, whereas their elders find those issues more controversial. They are also more likely to vote Democratic.[33] As we can see in *Snapshot of America: What Do We Think, by Age?*, younger citizens are markedly more liberal on social issues than are older Americans, for whom accepted attitudes on these issues were rather different when they came of age politically. Political events and age thus intersect, forming lasting imprints on each new, young group as they develop political views and enter the electorate. As older groups die, overall opinion among the citizenry changes. This is the process of generational replacement.

PARTISANSHIP AND IDEOLOGY Much of the division in contemporary American public opinion can be described in ideological (liberal or conservative) or partisan (Democrat or Republican) terms. How we adopt the labels of current political conflict has a good deal of influence on the policy positions we take, and even on how we perceive political personalities and events.

As we saw in Chapter 2, ideologies are sets of ideas about politics, the economy, and society that help us deal with the political world. For many Americans today, liberalism stands for faith in government action to bring about equitable outcomes and social tolerance, while conservatism for many represents a preference for limited government and traditional social values. A whole host of policy controversies in contemporary American politics are widely discussed in liberal-conservative terms.

Party identification, as we will see in Chapter 12, refers to our relatively enduring allegiances to one of the major political parties; for many of us, it is part of what defines us and it comes from our very early years.[34] Party labels provide mental cues that we use in interpreting and responding to personalities and news.

Identification as a Democrat or a Republican strongly influences how we see the political world. Research shows that we resolve uncertainty about new policies or personalities or even objective events to be consistent with our partisanship. Toward the end of Republican president Ronald Reagan's second term in office, a poll asked Americans whether inflation and unemployment had gotten better or worse over the eight years of his administration. In fact, both had improved, but Democrats and Republicans were miles apart in their perceptions of the objective facts: a majority of the Democrats said inflation was worse and only 8 percent acknowledged it was better. By the end of Obama's second term, we saw the same phenomenon in reverse. Democrats recognized, accurately, that unemployment was way down; Republicans thought it had gone up.[35] Clearly we see the world through a partisan lens.

> **political generations** groups of citizens whose political views have been shaped by the common events of their youth

Snapshot of America: *What Do We Think, by Age?*

Policy Preference, by Age

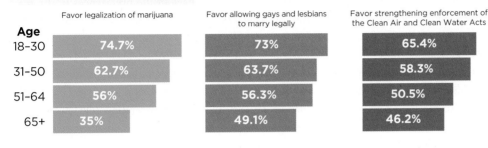

	Favor legalization of marijuana	Favor allowing gays and lesbians to marry legally	Favor strengthening enforcement of the Clean Air and Clean Water Acts	Favor deporting illegal immigrants
Age				
18–30	74.7%	73%	65.4%	31.5%
31–50	62.7%	63.7%	58.3%	43.5%
51–64	56%	56.3%	50.5%	49.4%
65+	35%	49.1%	46.2%	50.6%

On Some Policies, Age Does Not Matter Much

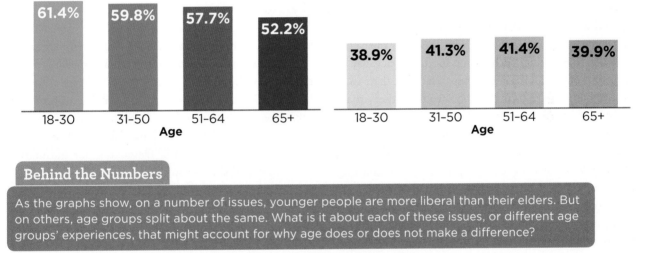

Agree that a woman should always be allowed to obtain an abortion as a matter of choice

18-30	31-50	51-64	65+
61.4%	59.8%	57.7%	52.2%

Age

Agree that we should make it easier to obtain concealed gun carry permits

18-30	31-50	51-64	65+
38.9%	41.3%	41.4%	39.9%

Age

Behind the Numbers

As the graphs show, on a number of issues, younger people are more liberal than their elders. But on others, age groups split about the same. What is it about each of these issues, or different age groups' experiences, that might account for why age does or does not make a difference?

Source: Calculated by the authors from the 2016 Cooperative Congressional Election Survey.

Because, as we have noted throughout this book, we are living in an age of hyperpartisanship, with party elites and candidates increasingly polarized, citizens have found it easier to sort themselves into one party or the other, especially as we are able to separate not just our residences and social lives but our cultures, news, and entertainment.[36] This process of **partisan sorting** means that average Democrats and Republicans are much further apart ideologically than was the case in previous decades (see Chapter 12, Figure 12.3). The impact on politics has been quite profound. For one thing, fewer people are likely to swing between candidates because fewer come to contemporary elections with a fully open mind.

> **partisan sorting** the process through which citizens align themselves ideologically with one of the two parties, leaving fewer citizens remaining in the center and increasing party polarization

We see this in the "red state versus blue state" phenomenon in presidential elections, in which the outcomes of all but a handful of states are perfectly predictable due to the states' being predominately Republican and conservative, or Democratic and liberal.[37] Another consequence of the great partisan sort is that citizens (following the lead of politicians and commentators) find it much easier to demonize the opposition. This has contributed to the nastiness, anger, and general incivility of contemporary politics, which in turn has contributed to citizens' disgust with politics in general, and those rising levels of distrust in government we saw earlier.[38]

EDUCATION As we suggested earlier in our discussion of the ideal democratic citizen, a number of political orientations change as a person attains more education. One important study looked in depth at how education influences aspects of citizenship, separating citizen values into "democratic enlightenment" and "democratic engagement."[39] Democratic enlightenment refers to a citizen's ability to hold democratic beliefs, including the idea that politics is about compromise and that sometimes the needs of the whole community will conflict with and override one's individual preferences. Democratic engagement refers to a citizen's ability to understand his or her own interests and how to pursue those interests in politics. As you might expect, both democratic dimensions are boosted by education: better-educated citizens are more likely to be informed about politics, to be tolerant and committed to democratic principles, and to vote and to participate at all levels of the political system (see *Snapshot of America: What Do We Think, by Education and Income?*).[40] Those who graduate from college have many more of the attributes of the idealized active democratic citizen than do those who do not graduate from high school.

ECONOMIC SELF-INTEREST People's political preferences often come from an assessment of what is best for them economically, from asking, "What's in it for me?" They may be the victims of manipulation by groups who don't share their interests but who are trying to convince them they are on their side, but the essential individual calculation is that they will be better off, even if they are mistaken. So, for instance, those in the lowest income brackets are the least likely to agree that too much is being spent on welfare or that they are paying too much in taxes; those with higher incomes are more likely to agree with these assessments. Similarly, those with lower incomes are generally more favorable than the wealthy to government attempts to narrow the income gap between rich and poor. These patterns are only tendencies, however. Some wealthy people favor the redistribution of wealth and more spending on welfare; some people living in poverty oppose these policies. Even on these straightforward economic questions, other factors are at work. (See *Snapshot of America: What Do We Think, by Education and Income?*)

RELIGION Many political issues touch on matters of deep moral conviction or values. In these cases the motivation for action or opinion formation is not self-interest but one's view of what is morally right. The question of morals and government, however, is tricky. Many people argue that it is not the government's business to set moral standards, although it is increasingly becoming the position of social conservatives that government policy ought to reflect traditional moral values. In addition, government gets into the morals business by virtue of establishing policies on issues of moral controversy, like abortion, assisted suicide, and organ transplants. These questions are often referred to as social issues, as opposed to economic issues, which center more on how to divide the economic pie.

Our views of morality and social issues are often rooted in our differing religious convictions and the values with which we were raised. Following the New Deal realignment, there were major political differences in the preferences of the major American religious groups: Protestants, Catholics, and Jews. Non-southern Protestants were predominantly Republican, and Catholics and Jews were much more likely to be Democrats and to call themselves liberals. Over the years those differences have softened quite a bit, but today Catholics are less conservative than Protestants, and more Democratic, while Jews and those calling themselves "not religious" are clearly more liberal and Democratic than the other groups.

Specific religious affiliations may no longer be the most important religious cleavage for understanding citizen opinions on social issues. Since the 1970s a new distinction has emerged in U.S. politics, between those in whose lives traditional religion plays a central role and those for whom it is less important. In this alignment, those who adhere to traditional religious beliefs and practices (frequent churchgoers, regular Bible readers, "born-again Christians," and those who pray frequently) tend to take conservative positions on an array of social issues (such as homosexuality and abortion), compared with more liberal positions taken on those issues by what may be called "seculars," those who say they have no religious affiliation. Among those who say they are agnostic, Democrats far outnumber Republicans and liberals outnumber conservatives.

GEOGRAPHIC REGION Where we live matters in terms of our political beliefs. People in the Farm Belt talk about different things than do city dwellers on the streets of Manhattan. Politicians who come from these areas represent people with different preferences, and much of the politics in Congress is about being responsive to differing geography-based opinions.[41] For instance, scholars have long argued that "the South is different." The central role of race and its plantation past for a long time gave rise to different patterns of public opinion compared to the non-southern states. The South today is not the Old South, but the region does retain some distinctive values. Opinions in the South—by which we mean the eleven states of the Confederacy—remain more conservative on civil rights but also on other social issues. (See *Snapshot of America: How Do We Differ From State to State?* in Chapter 4, which shows how the states vary in terms of political ideology.)

Whether we live in the city, the suburbs, or the country also has an effect on our opinions. City dwellers are more Democratic in their party affiliations and voting and are more liberal, both in their ideology and across most issues, from regulation of business to opposing capital punishment and favoring more environmental regulation (see Table 11.1). In fact, since the 1980s, the urban areas have become distinctly more Democratic while the Republican Party has gained strength in

Snapshot of America: *What Do We Think, by Education and Income?*

Democratic Enlightenment

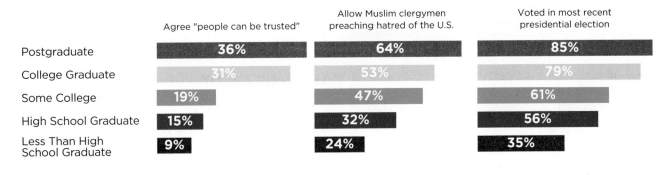

	Agree "people can be trusted"	Allow Muslim clergymen preaching hatred of the U.S.	Voted in most recent presidential election
Postgraduate	36%	64%	85%
College Graduate	31%	53%	79%
Some College	19%	47%	61%
High School Graduate	15%	32%	56%
Less Than High School Graduate	9%	24%	35%

Economic and Self-Interest

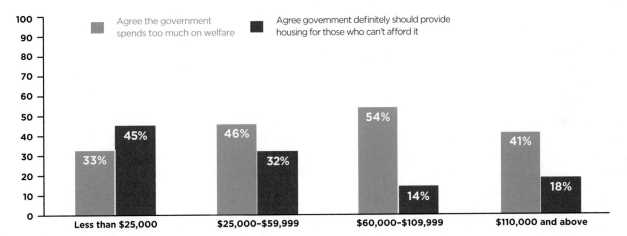

Agree the government spends too much on welfare

Agree government definitely should provide housing for those who can't afford it

	Less than $25,000	$25,000–$59,999	$60,000–$109,999	$110,000 and above
Agree the government spends too much on welfare	33%	46%	54%	41%
Agree government definitely should provide housing	45%	32%	14%	18%

*Some people think that the government in Washington should do everything possible to improve the standard of living of all poor Americans; other people think it is not the government's responsibility and that each person should take care of him- or herself.

Behind the Numbers

Americans' exercise of citizenship has long reflected a mix of concerns about community and self-interest. How do the democratic values of knowledge, participation, and enlightenment vary with levels of education? And can self-interest explain the differences in feelings about helping the poor and welfare among income groups?

Source: 2014 General Social Survey, calculated by authors.

the suburbs and rural areas.[42] This is consistent with analyses finding that rural areas have become the anchor for the contemporary Republican Party, with its stress on limited government, individual responsibility, and traditional values.

PAUSE AND REVIEW Who, What, How

Political socialization helps to fuel and maintain the political system by transferring fundamental democratic values from

one generation to the next. Less consensual values come from demographic characteristics such as race and ethnicity, gender, and age; our partisanship or political ideology; and other life experiences related to education, religious affiliation, and where we live.

As citizens find themselves in different circumstances, with differing political ideas, these differences are mined by interest groups, political parties, and candidates for office who are looking for support, either to further their causes or to get elected. Thus the differences in policy preferences that a complex society inevitably produces become the stuff of political conflict.

TABLE 11.1
Where We Live Makes a Difference

	URBAN	SUBURBAN	RURAL
PARTY IDENTIFICATION*			
Democrat[1]	62%	49%	37%
Republican	30	43	55
IDEOLOGY*			
Liberal[1]	33%	26%	20%
Conservative	29	34	51
PRESIDENTIAL APPROVAL			
Trump (April 2017)[1]	30%	44%	62%
Obama (April 2016)[2]	64	47	33
POLICY VIEWS			
Agree the government has gone too far regulating financial institutions and markets, making it harder for the economy to grow[3]	40%	39%	54%
Favor building a wall along the entire border with Mexico[3]	28	35	45
More important to control gun ownership than to protect the right of Americans to own guns[1]	63	52	34

Source: [1]Pew Research Center Poll, April 2017; [2]Pew Research Center Poll, April 2016; [3]Pew Research Center Survey, February 2017.

* The middle categories of "independent" and "moderate" for party identification and ideology are not shown but are included in the calculations.

In Your Own Words Identify key factors that influence our individual and collective political opinions.

MEASURING AND TRACKING PUBLIC OPINION

Using science to discover what people are thinking about political issues

Given the central role that public opinion plays in democracy, finding out what the public thinks is an important business, and one at which social scientists have gotten very adept over the years. Public opinion polls are sometimes discounted by politicians who don't like their results, but the truth is that today most social scientists and political pollsters conduct public opinion surveys according to the highest standards of scientific accuracy, and their results are for the most part reliable. In this section we look at the ways that we are able to gauge what the public thinks about issues important to our civic and political lives.

LEARNING ABOUT PUBLIC OPINION WITHOUT POLLS

You undoubtedly know what your friends and family think about many issues, even though you have never conducted an actual poll on their beliefs. We all reside in social communities that bring us into contact with various types of people. Simply by talking with them, we get a sense of their ideas and preferences, and most people are not shy about plastering their views all over their social media networks. But we do tend to hang around, communicate with, and listen to people who share our views and that can reinforce the idea that everyone in the world thinks like we do.

Politicians, whose careers depend on voters, have to try to avoid this pitfall, and they are necessarily good talkers and good listeners. They learn constituent opinion from the letters, phone calls, and emails they receive. They visit constituents, make speeches, attend meetings, and talk with community leaders and interest group representatives. Elected politicians also pick up signals from the size of the crowds that turn out to hear them speak and from the way those crowds respond to different themes. All these interactions give them a sense of what matters to people and how citizens are reacting to news events, economic trends, and social changes. Direct contact with people puts politicians in touch with concerns that could be missed entirely by the most scientifically designed public opinion poll. That poll might focus on issues of national news that are on the minds of national politicians or pollsters, but citizens might be far more concerned about the building of a dam upriver from their city or about teacher layoffs in their school district.

Members of Congress say they use a mix of sources to learn about public opinion, relying primarily on personal contacts including telephone calls and mail from constituents much more than opinion polls; however, most politicians try to gather as much polling data as they can when running for office.[43] Informal soundings of public opinion may be useful for some purposes, but they are not very reliable for gauging how everyone in a given population thinks because they may not be any more representative of the whole population than is a sampling of one's friends. That is, they may suffer from sample bias.

A **sample** is the portion of the population a politician or pollster surveys on an issue. Based on what that sample says, the surveyor then makes an estimation of what everyone else thinks. This may sound like hocus-pocus, but if the sample is scientifically chosen to be representative of the whole population, it actually works very well. Pollsters are trained to select a truly representative sample—that is, one that does not overrepresent any portion of the population and whose responses can therefore be safely generalized to the whole. When a sample is not chosen scientifically and has too many people in it from one portion of the population, we say it has a problem of **sample bias**. When trying to judge public opinion from what they hear among their supporters and friendly interest groups, politicians must allow for the bias of their own sampling. If they are not effective at knowing how those they meet differ from the full public, they will get a misleading idea of public opinion.

THE DEVELOPMENT OF MODERN PUBLIC OPINION POLLS

The scientific poll as we know it today was developed in the 1930s (for a history of polling, see this chapter's *The Big Picture*). However, newspapers and politicians have been trying to read public opinion as long as we have had democracies. The first efforts at actually counting opinions were the **straw polls**, dating from the first half of the nineteenth century and continuing in a more scientific form today.[44] The curious name for these polls comes from the fact that a straw, thrown up into the air, will indicate which way the wind is blowing.[45] These polls were designed to help politicians predict which way the political winds were blowing and, more specifically, who would win an upcoming election. Before the modern science of sampling was well understood, straw polls were conducted by a variety of hit-or-miss methods, and though their results were often correct, they were sometimes spectacularly wrong, as was the *Literary Digest*'s 1936 prediction (based on mail-in poll responses) that Alf Landon would beat Franklin Roosevelt and the 1948 polling fiasco that resulted in the now-iconic photo of a grinning

sample the portion of the population that is selected to participate in a poll

sample bias the effect of having a sample that does not represent all segments of the population

straw polls polls that attempt to determine who is ahead in a political race

Courtesy of Library of Congress, Prints and Photographs Division

Pollsters Get a Black Eye

Harry Truman laughed last and loudest after one of the biggest mistakes in American journalism. The Chicago Daily Tribune *relied on a two-week-old Gallup poll to predict the outcome of the 1948 presidential race, damaging the image of polling for decades. With polls today conducted all the way up to Election Day—and exit polls tracking how ballots are actually cast—similar goofs are much less likely.*

president-elect Harry Truman holding aloft a copy of the *Chicago Tribune* proclaiming "Dewey Defeats Truman."

THE SCIENCE OF OPINION POLLING TODAY

Today, polling is big business and a relatively precise science. Political polls are actually just a small offshoot of the marketing business, which spends a great deal of money trying to gauge what people want and are willing to buy. Many local governments also conduct surveys to find out what their citizens want and how satisfied they are with various municipal services. All polls face the same two challenges, however: (1) getting a good sample, which entails both sampling the right number of people and eliminating sample bias, and (2) asking questions that yield valid results.

HOW BIG DOES A SAMPLE NEED TO BE? No sample is perfect in matching the population from which it is drawn, but it should be close. Confronted with a critic who did not trust the notion of sampling, George Gallup is said to have responded, "Okay, if you do not like the idea of a sample, then the next time you go for a blood test, tell them to take it all!" It might seem counterintuitive, but statisticians have determined that a sample of only one thousand to

Public opinion polling is hard to get our minds around—how can we know what the public thinks without asking everyone? It seems beyond counterintuitive that we can estimate what an entire nation thinks by asking as few as 1,500 people, and yet, we can. While polling can feel mysterious, the truth is it is anything but—the science of polling allows us to make very educated estimates of what the public thinks.

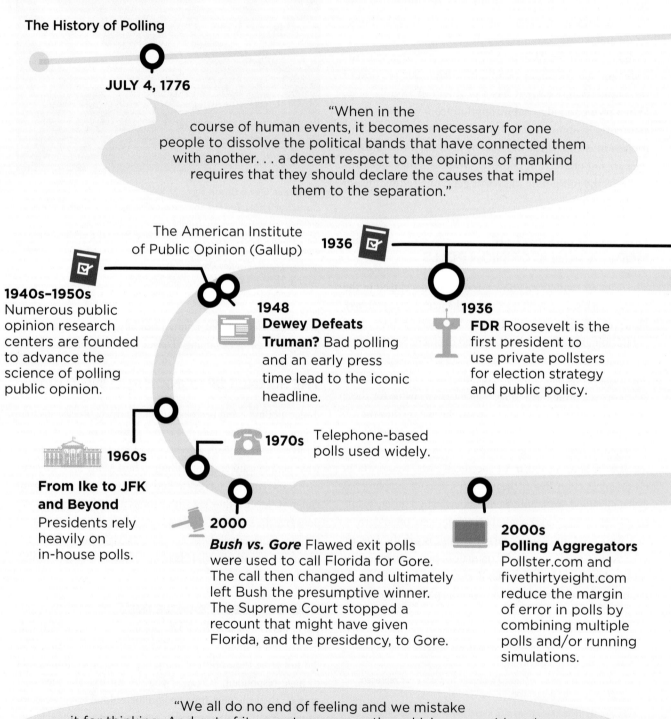

The History of Polling

JULY 4, 1776

"When in the course of human events, it becomes necessary for one people to dissolve the political bands that have connected them with another. . . a decent respect to the opinions of mankind requires that they should declare the causes that impel them to the separation."

The American Institute of Public Opinion (Gallup)

1936

1940s–1950s
Numerous public opinion research centers are founded to advance the science of polling public opinion.

1948
Dewey Defeats Truman? Bad polling and an early press time lead to the iconic headline.

1936
FDR Roosevelt is the first president to use private pollsters for election strategy and public policy.

1960s

From Ike to JFK and Beyond
Presidents rely heavily on in-house polls.

1970s Telephone-based polls used widely.

2000

Bush vs. Gore Flawed exit polls were used to call Florida for Gore. The call then changed and ultimately left Bush the presumptive winner. The Supreme Court stopped a recount that might have given Florida, and the presidency, to Gore.

2000s
Polling Aggregators
Pollster.com and fivethirtyeight.com reduce the margin of error in polls by combining multiple polls and/or running simulations.

"We all do no end of feeling and we mistake it for thinking. And out of it we get an aggregation which we consider a boon. Its name is public opinion. It is held in reverence. It settles everything. Some think it is the voice of God."
—Mark Twain, "Corn-pone Opinions," 1900

1824

First Straw Poll The poll showed a lead for Andrew Jackson over John Quincy Adams and two others. Jackson did win the popular vote but failed to get a majority in the Electoral College. The race was thrown to the House of Representatives, which picked Adams as the next president.

1936 George Gallup calls the election correctly for FDR, using probability theory to generalize from a small sample.

1920s-1930s
The Blossoming of Market Research Opinion researchers used sampling, survey techniques, and statistical methods to delve into consumers' minds.

1916-1936
Literary Digest **Straw Poll** The bigger the sample size, the better? The poll was sent to 10 million people in 1936, and the 2 million who responded indicated that Republican Alf Landon was winning the presidency. But it was a bad sample, drawn from a list of people more likely to be Republican.

2010s
Polling Techniques in Flux Cell phone-only households, call screening, low response rates, the rise of Internet polling, robo polling, and online panels are among the new considerations.

2012
Unskewing the Polls Convinced that turnout would not match that of 2008, Romney's pollsters assumed that polls showing an Obama lead must be wrong and altered their polls turnout model. Romney was reportedly "shell shocked" when he lost.

2016
The Polls Are Rigged Believing he would lose, Republican nominee Donald Trump tried to change the narrative by stressing to his base that the polls were "rigged," a claim that more than two-thirds of them believed.

two thousand people can be very representative of the entire United States with its more than 300 million residents.

A poll's reliability is indicated by its **sampling error**, which is a number that tells within what range the actual opinion of the whole population would fall. Typically a report of a poll will say that its "margin of error" is plus or minus 3 percent. This means that, based on sampling theory, there is a 95 percent chance that the real figure for the whole population is within 3 percent of that reported. For instance, when a poll reports a presidential approval rating of 60 percent and a 3 percent margin of error, there is a 95 percent chance that between 57 and 63 percent of the population approves of the president's job performance. A poll that shows one candidate leading another by 2 percent of the projected vote is really too close to call since the 2 percent might be due to sampling error. The larger the sample, the smaller the sampling error, but samples larger than two thousand add very little in the way of reliability. Surveying five thousand people is much more expensive and time consuming but does not substantially reduce the sampling error.

DEALING WITH THE PROBLEM OF SAMPLE BIAS Because of fiascos like the *Literary Digest* poll, modern polls now employ systematic **random samples** of the populations whose opinions they want to describe. In a systematic random sample, everyone should have the same chance to be interviewed. Since almost all households now have telephones, it is possible to get a representative sample in telephone polls. Some pollsters argue that respondents are more candid and cooperative when they are interviewed in person. But achieving a representative sample for in-person interviewing is much more difficult since it requires interviewers to make personal contact with specific individuals chosen in advance. And even phone polling is complicated by the fact that, increasingly, people rely on their cell phones rather than landlines, and cell phone polling is more difficult for pollsters since they are not allowed to autodial them.

Because reputable survey firms use scientific sampling strategies, sampling bias is not generally a problem that plagues modern pollsters, but there is one way it can sneak in through the back door. The chief form of sample bias in current surveys is **nonresponse bias**, which occurs when the opinions of those who choose to participate in a survey differ from the opinions of those who do not. Response rates to telephone surveys have dropped considerably over the years; in current surveys, sometimes as few as one-quarter of those intended to be included in surveys actually participate. The reasons for this drop include hostility to telemarketers; the increasing use of caller ID; the growing use of cell phones; and the simple fact that people are busier, are working more, and have less time and inclination to talk to strangers on the phone.[46] As a result, most telephone polls, unless corrected, will have too many elderly women and too few younger men because the former are typically at home to answer the phone when the interviewer calls, and the latter are more frequently out or have only a cell phone. One consequence of the nonresponse problem is that the most reluctant respondents—those likely to be missed in a typical survey—seem to be less racially tolerant than the average population, meaning that a standard survey might yield responses that are slightly more liberal on racial matters than might be the case for the population as a whole.[47] Pollsters deal with the problem of differential response rates, which yield a sample that does not look demographically like the population that is being sampled—perhaps there are too many whites or old people, or not enough college graduates or young adults—by **weighting** the sample to match what the census says the population looks like. This is done during the analysis of the results; under- or overrepresented groups are multiplied by values that bring them into line with their actual numbers in the population. Surprisingly, though, studies of differential response rates, which one might think would cause serious sample biases, find that well-constructed telephone polls continue to provide accurate information on citizens' responses to most questions about politics and issues.

NEW TECHNOLOGIES AND CHALLENGES IN POLLING

Technology is a pollster's friend, but it can also create unexpected challenges. With the advent of computer technology has come the substitution of computers for humans to do the telephone interviewing. The computers dial the numbers (autodialing) and deliver recorded messages, even "interacting" by asking questions that are answered by push-

sampling error a number that indicates within what range the results of a poll are accurate

random samples samples chosen in such a way that any member of the population being polled has an equal chance of being selected

nonresponse bias a skewing of data that occurs when there is a difference in opinion between those who choose to participate and those who do not

weighting adjustments to surveys during analysis so that selected demographic groups reflect their values in the population, usually as measured by the census

FIGURE 11.2
Asking the Right Question

Version A

Question: Do you favor or oppose allowing students and parents to choose a private school to attend at public expense?

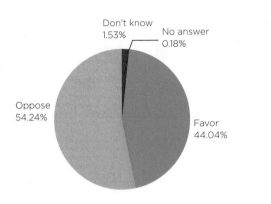

Don't know 1.53%
No answer 0.18%
Oppose 54.24%
Favor 44.04%

Version B

Question: A proposal has been made that would allow parents to send their school-age children to any public, private, or church-related school they choose. For those parents choosing non-public schools, the government would pay all or part of the tuition. Would you favor or oppose this proposal in your state?

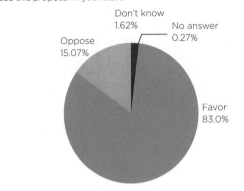

Don't know 1.62%
No answer 0.27%
Oppose 15.07%
Favor 83.0%

Comparison of results from two versions of school choice questions

Source: PDK/Gallup 33rd Annual Survey of the Public's Attitude Towards Public Schools, 2001.

ing buttons on a touch-tone phone. This technology, called "robo calling," is much cheaper than using human interviewers, but it is also controversial. It is easily abused, especially when combined with push poll methods (described in the next section).[48] Legitimate polling firms also use robo calls and have collected more information on more political subjects than has been available in the past, such as the state-by-state results provided by SurveyUSA.[49] Computers provide another challenge (and opportunity) for pollsters in the form of online surveys. Here we do not mean the polls that CNN or others put up asking for volunteers to click in their opinions on some issue. Pollsters create panels of Internet users who regularly log in to deliver their opinions on matters the pollsters select. Although some critics argue that the online polls have no scientific basis because they do not rely on strict probability samples, proponents argue that with appropriate adjustments, the Internet polls nicely match results from traditional telephone interviewing. They have the advantage of garnering fewer refusals, and for some kinds of questions, respondents to online surveys appear to be more candid in admitting to things that might be embarrassing to confess to a human interviewer.[50] Pollsters also face a growing challenge as increasing numbers of citizens, especially younger people, rely on cell phones. The U.S. Telephone Consumer Protection Act limits the technologies that can be used to contact cell phone users—forbidding autodialing, for instance. Those contacted by cell phones are

also more likely to refuse to answer polls. As pollsters adapt to these newer technologies, research and regulations are likely to lead to changes in how cell phone users are contacted.[51]

THE IMPORTANCE OF ASKING THE RIGHT QUESTIONS Asking the right questions in surveys is a surprisingly tricky business. Researchers have emphasized three main points with respect to constructing survey questions:

- **Respondents should be asked about things they know and have thought about.** Otherwise, they will often try to be helpful but will give responses based on whatever cues they can pick up from the context of the interview or the particular question, even if they have never heard of the subject of the question.[52] Researchers have also found that including a "don't know" category in the list of possible answers lessens the chance that survey participants will try to bluff their way through a question they know nothing about.[53]

- **Questions should not be ambiguous.** One highly controversial example comes from a 1992 survey that reported that over a third of the American public either did not believe or doubted that the Holocaust had even happened.[54] Media chaos ensued.[55] The

Doonesbury

uproar, however, was largely the product of a bad question. Respondents were asked, "Does it seem possible or does it seem impossible to you that the Nazi extermination of the Jews never happened?" To say that one believed the Holocaust happened, the respondent had to agree to a double negative—that it was "impossible" that it "never" happened. There was plenty of room for confusion. Other respondents were asked a more straightforward version of the question: "The term Holocaust usually refers to the killing of millions of Jews in Nazi death camps during World War II. Do you doubt that the Holocaust actually happened, or not?" With this wording, only 9 percent doubted the Holocaust had happened and 4 percent were unsure.[56]

- **Similar questions can yield surprisingly different answers.** For instance, do a majority of Americans support school choice, in which the government will pay the costs of children attending the schools their parents select? Notice in Figure 11.2 how two rather similar questions on this topic yield very different conclusions. In the shorter version, a majority are opposed to school choice, whereas in the longer version, which asks almost the same thing but with greater detail, an overwhelming majority are in favor of it.[57] Why do you think people would be more likely to answer more positively to the second wording?

There are still other considerations that pollsters should take into account. Studies have shown, for instance, that the order in which questions are asked can change the results, as can such a simple factor as the number of choices offered for responses. Clearly, good surveys can tell us a lot about public opinion, but they will hardly ever produce the final word.

And just as soon as they might, public opinion would probably shift again.

TYPES OF POLLS

Many people and organizations report the results of what they claim are measures of public opinion. To make sense of this welter of claims, it is useful to know some basic polling terminology and the characteristics of different types of polls.

NATIONAL POLLS National polls are efforts to measure public opinion within a limited period of time using a national representative sample. The time period of interviewing may be as short as a few hours, with the results reported the next day, or extended over a period of weeks, as in academic polls. The underlying goal, however, is the same: to achieve scientifically valid measures of the knowledge, beliefs, or attitudes of the adult population.

Many national polls are conducted by the media in conjunction with a professional polling organization. These polls regularly measure attitudes on some central item, such as how the public feels about the job that the president or Congress is doing. Several of these organizations make their polls available through the Internet.[58] Some of the polls that regularly collect data in large national samples include the following: the ABC News/*Washington Post* poll, the CBS News/*New York Times* poll, the NBC News/*Wall Street Journal* poll, and the CNN/*USA Today*/Gallup poll. With the growing numbers of polls have come "polls of polls," which seek to average the results of multiple polling organizations' efforts. These can be found online, at sites like elections.huffingtonpost.com/pollster, www.pollingreport.com, fivethirtyeight.com, and www.realclearpolitics.com. Other polling organizations provide more in-depth surveys than these media polls. Some are designed to see how people feel about particular topics or to find out how people develop attitudes and evaluate politics more generally. Two of these in particular, the General Social Survey and the National Election Studies, provide much of the data for academic research on public opinion in America (and much of what we say in this chapter about public opinion).[59]

CAMPAIGN POLLS A lot of polling is done for candidates in their efforts to win election or reelection. Most well-funded campaigns begin with a **benchmark poll**, taken of a sample of the population, or perhaps just of the potential voters, in a state or district to gather baseline information on how well the candidate is known, what issues people associate with the candidate, and what issues people are concerned about, as well as assessments of the opposition, especially if the opponent is an incumbent. Benchmark polls are instrumental in designing campaign strategy.

Presidential campaigns and a few of the better-funded statewide races (for example, those for governor or U.S. senator) conduct **tracking polls**. These follow changes in attitudes toward the candidates by having ongoing sets of interviews. Such daily samples are too small to allow for reliable generalization, but groups of these interviews averaged over time are extremely helpful. The oldest interviews are dropped as newer ones are added, providing a dynamic view of changes in voters' preferences and perceptions.

A sudden change in a tracking poll might signal that the opponent's new ads are doing damage or that interest group endorsements are having an effect. Campaign strategies can be revised accordingly. More recently, the news media have undertaken tracking polls as part of their election coverage. By 2008 there were up to nine pollsters reporting daily results, and several websites were aggregating the polls. The averaging process of the aggregators helps smooth out individual pollsters' house effects (biases or patterns that might be built in to an individual pollster's methodology) and differences in their assumptions about turnout. Their "track record" was a good one—the folks at the *Huffington Post* site

(which was then called pollster.com) and fivethirtyeight. com missed the individual state results by less than 2.5 points. In 2012 there were at least ninety polls in the field at least once, and twenty-four trackers were in the field at least five times in the last three weeks of the campaign. Most of these underestimated Obama's support, though some, like the well-known Gallup and Rasmussen polls, were particularly off-base. There was a good deal of back and forth in the media about what the electorate was likely to look like, with some Republicans arguing that the public polls were "skewed" because there were too many Democrats in the samples (a demographic distribution that proved correct on Election Day, however), but it was the polling aggregators that got it right again. In 2016 the polling averages came close to predicting the popular vote, which went to Hillary Clinton slightly short of the three points the polls predicted. But the models failed to estimate turnout correctly when it came to the states, leading most analysts to think that Clinton would win the Electoral College as well. Only Nate Silver of fivethirtyeight.com felt there was uncertainty in the predictions, given the third-party vote and a relatively high number of undecided voters (see this chapter's *Profiles in Citizenship*). In the end, enough states that were predicted to go to Clinton slid over to Trump by just one point, and he won the Electoral College vote.[60]

On election night the media commentators often "call" a race, declaring one candidate a winner, sometimes as soon as the voting booths in a state are closed but well before the official vote count has been reported. These predictions are made, in part, on the basis of **exit polls**, which are short questionnaires administered to samples of voters in selected precincts after they vote. Exit polls focus on vote choice, a few demographic questions, some issue preferences, and evaluations of candidates. In addition to helping the networks predict the winners early, exit polls are used by network broadcasters and journalists to add explanatory and descriptive material to their election coverage. Because exit polls are expensive to conduct, media organizations have banded together in recent years to share the costs of conducting national exit polls.

Exit polls, however, have a mixed record in recent elections, leading news agencies to become cautious about how the results are used.[61] The challenges faced by those conducting exit polls are the same as those the preelection pollsters must contend with: it is very difficult to obtain a fully representative sample of voters. As a result of these problems, networks are now relatively cautious in declaring winners without corroborating evidence from the actual vote returns; there were no mistakes in "calling" the states in the 2004 presidential election, although exit poll results led the

---

benchmark poll an initial poll on a candidate and issues on which campaign strategy is based and against which later polls are compared

tracking polls an ongoing series of surveys that follow changes in public opinion over time

exit polls election-related questions asked of voters right after they vote

PROFILES IN CITIZENSHIP
Nate Silver

David E. Klutho/Sports Illustrated/Getty Images

Public opinion polls generated a lot of controversy in the days leading up to the 2012 presidential election. Most professional pollsters and the Obama campaign said that their polls forecast an Obama victory; the Romney campaign claimed those polls over-sampled Democrats. At the center of the controversy was Nate Silver, whose forecasting model steadily predicted a likely win for Obama. Republicans said he was shilling for the Democrats, but he ultimately nailed the Electoral College vote.

But then, Nate Silver is a very smart guy, a guy who deals in numbers and mathematical models and predictions all the time. He wasn't long out of college before he had developed the PECOTA (Player Empirical Comparison and Optimization Test Algorithm) system—a model for predicting the performance of baseball players that became associated with a web site called Baseball Prospectus that Silver managed. Baseball is a long way from politics, however, and by 2008 Silver had given up Baseball Prospectus and was concentrating his mathematical prowess on primaries and electoral votes, writing on the new blog that he called fivethirtyeight.com (after the total number of votes in the Electoral College).

If you ask him how he got to here from there, the answer is about what you'd expect from this young, brilliant, and quirky man. He got into politics because of Internet poker, of course. Doesn't everyone?

Some context here is that Silver is the son of a political scientist, so the world was one he was well familiar with and he liked it. "I was more into politics as compared to a normal person," he says, "because it was interesting, kind of like a big game show." But still, Internet poker?

"In 2006 I was playing poker mostly online. The outgoing Republican Congress passed a law where they basically made online poker illegal, but it was not very effective. What they technically did, more or less, is say you can play poker, but you can't deposit money in and out, so that had a chilling effect on the game . . . that got me following congressional procedure." Besides, he had gone to the University of Chicago, and a member of the Chicago law faculty, Sen. Barack Obama, was running for president. "That was kind of cool," he says. "I actually had like a hometown candidate now."

Silver started blogging on the liberal Daily Kos site under the pseudonym Poblano, and then he started fivethirtyeight.com. What Silver added that other analysts didn't was a model that aggregated the existing polling and, based on those numbers as well as demographic and other data, ran computerized simulations of the various primary and general election races. His predictions were uncannily accurate, and soon Silver's readership soared and he was on cable TV, analyzing polls and races.

In 2010 Silver signed a three-year contract with the *New York Times,* and then left to start his own web empire at ESPN, where you can currently find fivethirtyeight.com. There, he blogs regularly on politics and elections—with occasional forays into sports, economics, and popular culture. He's also written a book, *The Signal and the Noise: Why So Many Predictions Fail—But Some Don't.*

What does he want people to get from his work? "I want to inform people, I want people to think more critically about things. Basically, I want people to not be intimidated by numbers and statistics, to not just assume that something that they hear, whether it's from a politician or from Fox News or from [another] writer in the *New York Times,* is necessarily true. I just want to encourage people to use their brains."

Here's some other advice from Nate Silver:

On patriotism

"You probably have some family members who have their flaws and idiosyncrasies and probably a few distant relatives who are even fairly screwed-up people, but you still love them, anyway. I think that's what patriotism is really, saying, 'Look, this is where I was born, or I migrated to the United States, this is where my loyalty is. . . .' You don't have a choice, it doesn't matter how unhappy you are, you know? It's your family, and you are stuck with it."

On keeping the republic

"People just have to be willing to put in the work. It's a big, complicated world now, and as many people that there are, there are more things to be done. Don't underestimate your ability to come up with an idea that nobody else has. It happens all the time. Quit being a consumer and be a producer. Start your own blog, start your own political organization. Have fun with it—there is nothing wrong with that at all."

Source: Nate Silver spoke with Christine Barbour in July 2010.

Kerry campaign to think they had won early in the evening.[62] In 2008 and 2012 the exit polls did not lead to any surprises, although by 2012 the media consortium sponsoring the polls had decided not to poll some of the less populated and less competitive states.

PSEUDO-POLLS A number of opinion studies are wrongly presented as polls. More deceptive than helpful, these pseudo-polls range from potentially misleading entertainment to outright fraud. Self-selection polls are those, like the *Literary Digest*'s, in which respondents, by one mechanism or another, select themselves into a survey rather than being chosen randomly. Examples of self-selection polls include viewer or listener call-in polls and Internet polls. These polls tell you only how a portion of the media outlet's audience (self-selected in the first place by their choice of a particular outlet) who care enough to call in or click a mouse (self-selected in the second place by their willingness to expend effort) feel about an issue.

When the CNN web site asks users to record their views on a current issue, the audience is limited, first, to those who own or have access to computers; second, to those who care enough about the news to be on the CNN site; and third, to those who want to pause in their news viewing for the short time it takes for their vote to be counted and the results to appear on the screen. Further, nothing stops individuals from recording multiple votes to make the count seem greater than it is. Results of such polls are likely to be highly unrepresentative of the population as a whole. They should be presented with caution and interpreted with a great deal of skepticism.

Another, increasingly common kind of pseudo-poll is the **push poll**, which poses as a legitimate information-seeking effort but is really a shady campaign trick to change people's attitudes. Push polls present false or highly negative information, often in a hypothetical form, and ask respondents to react to it. The information, presented as if true or at least possible, can raise doubts about a candidate and even change a voter's opinion about him or her. Insofar as they have a legitimate function, "push questions" are used on a limited basis by pollsters and campaign strategists to find out how voters might respond to negative information about the candidate or the opposition. This is the kind of information

> **push polls** polls that ask for reactions to hypothetical, often false, information in order to manipulate public opinion

that might be gathered in a benchmark poll, for example. Less scrupulous consultants, working for both political parties, however, sometimes use the format as a means of propaganda. As an example, a pollster put this question to Florida voters:

> Please tell me if you would be more likely or less likely to vote for Lt. Governor Buddy MacKay if you knew that Lt. Gov. Buddy MacKay plans to implement a new early-release program for violent offenders who have served a mere 60 percent of their sentences if he is elected governor?[63]

MacKay had no such plans, and to imply that he did was false. Moreover, the goal of this "poll" was not to learn anything but rather to plant negative information in the minds of thousands of people. By posing as a legitimate poll, the push poll seeks to trick respondents into accepting the information as truthful and thereby to influence the vote. Such polls are often conducted without any acknowledgment of who is sponsoring them (usually the opponents of the person being asked about). The target candidate often never knows that such a poll is being conducted, and because push polls frequently pop up the weekend before an election, he or she cannot rebut the lies or half-truths. A key characteristic of push polls is that they seek to call as many voters as they can with little regard to the usual care and quality of a legitimate representative sample. "Push polling for me is marketing," said Floyd Ciruli, a Denver-based pollster. "You call everybody you can call and tell them something that may or may not be true."[64]

Legislation against push polling has been introduced in several state legislatures, and the practice has been condemned by the American Association of Political Consultants.[65] There is a real question, however, about whether efforts to regulate push polls can survive a First Amendment test before the Supreme Court.

SURVEY EXPERIMENTS A final category of polls are those conducted by social scientists not so much to gauge and measure public opinion about elections or current events as to deepen our understanding of public attitudes, especially on controversial issues such as race, gender, and civil liberties, where respondents know what the socially acceptable answers to the survey questions are and so are less likely to disclose their true opinions. In survey experiments, the survey questions are manipulated in an effort to get respondents to disclose more information than they think they are disclosing.

A pioneering example of such work is an experiment in the study of racial attitudes in which researchers sought to find out if the way a question is framed affects how respondents feel about a particular group. In this case, researchers wondered if the mention of affirmative action, which many people do not like, would influence respondents' attitudes toward African Americans. A sample of white respondents were randomly put into two groups, a control group that was only asked a question about their feelings toward blacks, and a group that first was asked about their view of affirmative action and then their attitude toward blacks. The mere mention of affirmative action excited more negative responses toward blacks in the second group,[66] which helped researchers to understand the complex sets of issues that lie behind racial attitudes in American public opinion and told them something about the impact of framing on racial attitudes. The number of survey experiments is increasing because the technology of the Internet allows the use of images, sounds, and other multimedia in addition to the words used in a typical survey.[67]

HOW ACCURATE ARE POLLS?

For many issues, such as attitudes toward the environment or presidential approval, we have no objective measure against which to judge the accuracy of public opinion polls. With elections, however, polls do make predictions, and we can tell by the vote count whether the polls are correct. The record of most polls is, in general, quite good. For example, almost all the major polls have predicted the winner of presidential elections correctly since 1980, except in the incredibly close 2000 election. Even in 2016 they had Hillary Clinton's popular victory margin within one point, although several of the states were slightly off. They are not correct to the percentage point, nor would we expect them to be, given the known levels of sampling error, preelection momentum shifts, and the usual 15 percent of voters who claim to remain undecided up to the last minute. Polls taken closer to Election Day typically become more accurate as they catch more of the late deciders.[68] Even in the 2000 presidential election, most of the polls by the election's eve had done a fairly good job of predicting the tightness of the race. Read *Don't Be Fooled by . . . Public Opinion Polls* for some tips on how you can gauge the reliability of poll results you come across.

> ### Do frequent opinion polls enhance or diminish democracy?

Citizens, politicians and their staffs, the media, and professional polling organizations are all interested in the business of measuring and tracking public opinion. Citizens rely on polls to monitor elections and get a sense of where other Americans stand on particular issues. Their interest is in fair polling techniques that produce reliable results.

To win elections, politicians must know what citizens think and what they want from their officials. They need to know how various campaign strategies are playing publicly and how they are faring in their races against other candidates. Politicians and their campaign consultants evaluate face-to-face contact with voters and their correspondence and calls, but they also pay attention to national media and party or campaign polls.

The media want current and accurate information on which to base their reporting. They also have an interest in keeping and increasing the size of their audiences. To build their markets, they create and publish polls that encourage their audiences to see elections as exciting contests.

Finally, professional pollsters have an interest in producing accurate information for their clients. The quality of their surveys rests with good scientific polling techniques.

In Your Own Words Describe different techniques used to gauge public opinion.

THE CITIZENS AND PUBLIC OPINION

Informational shortcuts that save democracy from our lack of care and attention

Politicians may act as if citizens are informed and attentive, but we have seen ample evidence that only some Americans live up to our model of good citizenship, and those who do often belong disproportionately to the ranks of the well-educated, the well-off, and the older portions of the population. This disparity between our ideal citizen and reality raises some provocative questions about the relationships among citizens, public opinion, and democracy. Were the founders right to limit the influence of the masses on government? Do we want less informed and less coherent opinions represented in politics? Can democracy survive if it is run only by an educated elite? Can it work if many of us are subject to "fake news" or live in information bubbles, untouched by the issues and values that affect our fellow citizens?

Earlier in this chapter we suggested that all would not be lost for American democracy if only some of us turned out to be ideal citizens, and that although Americans as individuals

Public Opinion Polls

In October 2015, social media was buzzing over a poll posted on CNN's Facebook page that showed two-thirds of Democratic voters saying Bernie Sanders had beaten Hillary Clinton in the first debate. Yet pundits—and a bevy of other polls released in the following days—handed the win to Clinton.[1]

Why the discrepancy? A quality poll is very different from an online survey. Anyone can set up a poll on Facebook, but it will not produce the random sample that is key in public opinion polls. Online polls are open to anyone, and those with skin in the game (like Sanders's supporters) are more likely to take part.

There are lots of polls out there, ranging from those conducted carefully by reputable polling organizations to online marketing surveys to polls designed to further particular political purposes. How are we to know which results are reliable indications of what the public thinks? One thing we can do is bring our critical thinking skills to bear.

What to Watch Out For[2]

- **What kind of poll is it?** A good poll relies on a random sample of people. If polling participants self-select—that is, if they clicked their own way to the survey—it's not a random sample, and it's not a good poll. Before you believe poll results, ask yourself: Is this really a randomized poll, or is it a popularity contest in which only those with an ax to grind bothered to answer?[3]
- **Who sponsored the poll—and who conducted it?** Some polling firms are better than others. Even if the poll was conducted by a professional polling company, it may still have been commissioned on behalf of a candidate or company. Ask yourself: Does the sponsor have an agenda? How might that agenda influence the poll, the question wording, or the sponsor's interpretation of events?
- **Who was sampled?** Remember that registered voters are not necessarily likely voters. A reputable polling organization will weight responses according to the likelihood that the respondent will actually vote in order to come up with a better prediction of the election result. And, depending on what information they are trying to pinpoint, some polls survey only members of one party, readers of a particular magazine, or people of a certain age.

- **What questions were asked?** Polls that ask, "If the election were tomorrow . . ." make great headlines, but they're essentially meaningless, because they pressure undecided voters to give an answer when they are still, well, undecided and when, in reality, they still have plenty of time to make a decision.
- **How are the questions worded?** Are loaded or vague terms used? Are the questions available with the poll results? If not, why not? Do the questions seem to lead you to respond one way or the other? Do they oversimplify issues or complicate them? If the survey claims to have detected change over time, be sure the same questions were used consistently.
- **Are the survey topics ones that people are likely to have information and opinions about?** Respondents rarely admit that they don't know how to answer a question, so responses on obscure or technical topics are less reliable.
- **What is the poll's response rate?** A lot of "don't knows," "no opinions," or refusals to answer can have a decided effect on the results.
- **How do the poll results compare to other polls?** A headline touting "shocking" results might get lots of clicks, but polling results that seem to come out of left field are usually way off.
- **Where's the data?** News organizations like to spin polls into attention-grabbing headlines, so they'll likely report on the most sensational polls. When you see a report on a poll, ask yourself: Who is doing the interpreting? What are that person's motives? Search for the original and complete poll data and try interpreting the results yourself—and if the data are not available, ask yourself why.

1. Katie Sanders, "No, Internet, CNN Did Not Delete Its Poll Showing Bernie Sanders Won the Democratic Debate," *PunditFact*, October 19, 2015, www.politifact.com/punditfact/statements/2015/oct/19/nowthis/no-internet-cnn-did-not-delete-its-poll-showing-be/.
2. Some of these questions are based in part on similar advice given to poll watchers in Herbert Asher, *Polling and the Public: What Every Citizen Should Know,* 7th ed. (Washington, D.C.: CQ Press, 2007), 206–209.
3. Ryan Struck, "Good Poll or Bad Poll: How to Tell the Difference," The Post Calvin blog, October 25, 2015, thepostcalvin.com/good-poll-or-bad-poll-how-to-tell-the-difference/; and National Public Radio, "The Breaking News Consumers' Handbook: Election Polls Edition," On the Media, December 18, 2015.

Sathi Soma via AP, File

Fake News, Real Consequences

The Internet has long been fertile ground for conspiracy theories, but fake news web sites like InfoWars have given these ideas credibility and helped them to spread quickly, with real-world consequences. In December 2016, Edgar Welch was arrested after firing an assault-style rifle at a Washington, D.C., pizzeria. He had read online that the restaurant was a front for a child sex-slavery ring with links to Hillary Clinton.

might not fit the ideal, Americans as a group might behave as that ideal would predict. How is such a trick possible?

The argument goes like this: It may not be rational for all people to be deeply immersed in the minutiae of day-to-day politics. Our jobs, families, hobbies, and other interests leave us little time for in-depth study of political issues, and unless we get tremendous satisfaction from keeping up with politics (and some of us certainly do), it might be rational for us to leave the political information gathering to others. Social scientists call this idea **rational ignorance.**

This does not mean that we are condemned to make only ignorant or mistaken political decisions. Citizens are generally pretty smart. In fact, studies show that voters can behave much more intelligently than we could ever guess from their answers to surveys about politics. A great many of us, sometimes without thinking about it, use shortcuts, called heuristics, to get political information. Such heuristics often serve us quite well, in the sense that they help us make the same decisions we might have made had we invested considerable time and energy in collecting that political information ourselves.[69]

One such shortcut is the **on-line processing** of information.[70] (On-line here does not refer to time spent on the Internet, as you will see, although the Internet can be instrumental in the process.) Many of the evaluations we make of people, places, and things in our lives (including political figures and ideas) are made on the fly. We assemble impressions and reactions while we are busy leading our lives. When queried, we might not be able to explain why we like or dislike a thing or a person, and we might sound quite ignorant in the sense of not seeming to have reasons for our

beliefs. But we do have reasons, and they may make a good deal of sense, even if we can't identify what they are.

A second important mental shortcut that most of us use is the **two-step flow of information.** Politicians and the media send out massive amounts of information—multiple narrative streams that compete for our attention. We can absorb only a fraction of this information, and even then it is sometimes hard to know how to interpret it. In these circumstances, we tend to rely on **opinion leaders**, people who are more or less like us, who share our values, but who know more about the subject than we do, to mediate the information and make sense of it for us.[71] Opinion leaders and followers can be identified in all sorts of realms besides politics. When we make an important purchase, say, a computer or a car, most of us do not research all the scientific data and technical specifications. We ask people who are like us, who we think should know, and whom we can trust. We get others' opinions online, from those we follow on social media, from blogs, and from comments and reviews made by others; technology allows us to gather information from multiple "experts."[72] We compile their advice, consult our own intuition, and buy. The result is that we get pretty close to making an optimal purchase without having to become experts ourselves. The same thing happens politically. The two-step flow allows us to behave as though we feel that we are very well informed without requiring us to expend all the resources that being informed entails.

Given the effectiveness of this process, something to consider is that, as part of the college-educated elite and a person who has taken an American politics class, you may be the opinion leader for your family or friends. Throughout the book, we have emphasized the many ways that technology allows you to construct and disseminate narratives that compete with the powerful. Consider that with this status and opportunity comes responsibility as well, to be sure that the stories you create and pass on are factually correct and well (and critically) thought out.

> **Is a democracy that depends on citizen "shortcuts" weaker than one that does not?**

rational ignorance the state of being uninformed about politics because of the cost in time and energy

on-line processing the ability to receive and evaluate information as events happen, allowing us to remember our evaluation even if we have forgotten the specific events that caused it

two-step flow of information the process by which citizens take their political cues from more well-informed opinion leaders

opinion leaders people who know more about certain topics than we do and whose advice we trust, seek out, and follow

The upshot of our use of political shortcuts is that we end up being smarter as a group than we might be if we were evaluated purely on an individual basis. Even though many voters may be confused about which candidates stand where on specific issues, groups of voters do a great job of sorting out which party or candidate best represents their interests. Members of the religious right vote for Republicans, and members of labor unions vote for Democrats, for instance. Even though there are undoubtedly quite a few confused voters in the electorate in any particular election, they tend to cancel each other out in the larger scheme of things, although some biases remain.[73] As a whole, from the politician's point of view, the electorate appears to be responsive to issues and quite rational in evaluating an incumbent's performance in office.[74] So even though citizens do not spend a lot of time learning about politics, politicians are smart to assume that the electorate is attentive and informed. In fact, this is precisely what most of them do. For example, studies have shown that state legislators vote in accordance with the ideological preferences of their citizens, just as if the citizens were instructing them on their wishes.[75] The states with the most liberal citizens—for example, New York, Massachusetts, and California—have the most liberal policies. And the most conservative states, those in the South and the Rocky Mountains, have the most conservative policies. Other studies confirm a similar pattern in national elections.[76]

We began this chapter by asking why polling is routinely disparaged by politicians. Why don't we have more confidence in being ruled by public opinion? After all, in a democracy where the people's will is supposed to weigh heavily with our elected officials, we have uncovered some conflicting evidence. Many Americans do not model the characteristics of the ideal democratic citizen, but remember that the United States has two traditions of citizenship—one much more apolitical and self-interested than the public-spirited ideal. The reality in America is that the ideal citizen marches side by side with the more self-interested citizen, who, faced with many demands, does not put politics ahead of other daily responsibilities. But we have also argued that there are mechanisms and shortcuts that allow even some of the more apolitical and self-interested citizens to cast intelligent votes and to have their views represented in public policy. This tells us that at least one element of democracy—responsiveness of policies to public preferences—is in good working order, if the people the majority choose can make it through the institutional barriers to power (for example, gerrymandering, the Electoral College).

In Your Own Words Give examples of ways in which public opinion enhances or diminishes the relationship between citizens and government.

LET'S REVISIT: *What's at Stake . . . ?*

We have argued in this chapter that public opinion is important in policymaking and that politicians respond to it in a variety of ways. But what would happen if we more or less bypassed elected officials altogether and allowed people to participate directly in national lawmaking through the use of a national referendum or initiative? What is at stake in rule by public opinion?

On the one hand, voters would seem to have something real to gain in such lawmaking reform. It would give new meaning to government "by the people," and decisions would have more legitimacy with the public. Certainly it would be harder to point the finger at those in Washington as being responsible for bad laws. In addition, as has been the experience in states with initiatives, citizens might succeed in getting legislation passed that legislators themselves refuse to vote for. Prime examples are term limits and balanced budget amendments. Term limits would cut short many congressional careers, and balanced budget amendments would force politicians into hard

choices about taxation and spending cuts that they prefer to avoid.

On the other side of the calculation, however, voters might be worse off. While policies like the two just mentioned clearly threaten the jobs of politicians, they also carry unintended consequences that might or might not be very good for the nation as a whole. The Irish referenda show how voters can free politicians to pass laws in line with changing times and values; the experience of the Brexiteers in the United Kingdom provides an example of the kind of decision that citizens make when they want to send a message but do not, perhaps, want to live with all the consequences.[77] Not only policymaking but also the protection of individual freedoms might suffer under increased direct democracy; the majority is not always the best safeguard of civil liberties and civil rights.

Who should decide—politicians who make a career out of understanding government, or people who pay little attention to politics and current events and who vote from instinct and outrage? Politicians who have a vested interest in keeping their jobs, or the public who can provide a check on political greed and self-interest? The answer changes with the way you phrase the question, but the public might well suffer if left to its own mercy on questions of policy it does not thoroughly understand.

There is no doubt that the founders of the Constitution, with their limited faith in the people, would have rejected such a national referendum wholeheartedly. Not only does it bring government closer to the people, but it wreaks havoc with their system of separation of powers and checks and balances. Popular opinion was supposed to be checked by the House and the Senate, which were in turn to be checked by the other two branches of government. Bringing public opinion to the fore upsets this delicate balance.

In addition, many scholars warn that the hallmark of democracy is not just hearing what the people want, but allowing the people to discuss and deliberate over their political choices. Home computer voting or trips to the ballot box do not necessarily permit such key interaction.[78] Majority rule without the tempering influence of debate and discussion can deteriorate quickly into majority tyranny, with a sacrifice of minority rights.

The flip side may also be true, however. Since voters tend to be those who care more intensely about political issues, supporters of a national referendum also leave themselves open to the opposite consequence of majority tyranny: the tyranny of an intense minority who care enough to campaign and vote against an issue that a majority prefer, but only tepidly.

Finally, there are political stakes for politicians in such a reform. As we have already seen, the passage of laws they would not have themselves supported would make it harder for politicians to get things done. But on the positive side, a national referendum would allow politicians to avoid taking the heat for decisions that are bound to be intensely unpopular with some segment of the population. One of the reasons national referenda are often used in other countries is to diffuse the political consequences for leaders of unpopular or controversial decisions.

Direct democracy at the national level would certainly have a major impact on American politics, but it is not entirely clear who the winners and losers would be, or even if there would be any consistent winners. The new rules would benefit different groups at different times. The American people believe they would enjoy the power, and various groups are confident they would profit, but in the long run the public interest might be damaged in terms of the quality of American democracy and the protections available to minorities. Politicians have very little to gain. If such a reform ever does come about, it will be generated not by the elite but by public interest groups, special interest groups, and reformers from outside Washington.

CLUES to Critical Thinking

"Does 'Tribalism' End in a Compromise or a Fight?"

By Laila Lalami, June 26, 2018

Public opinion in the United States seems to have less and less to do with the issues and more to do with what the people you identify with think. We talked about how identity affects opinion, but just as partisanship can place party over country, public opinion can place identity over issues, creating the state of tribalism that this author describes.

Early in June, the valedictorian at Bell County High School in southeastern Kentucky delivered a graduation speech filled with inspirational quotations that, he said with a twinkle in his eye, he'd found on Google. One line, in particular, drew wild applause from the crowd in this conservative part of the country: "'Don't just get involved. Fight for your seat at the table. Better yet, fight for a seat at the head of the table.' —Donald J. Trump." As people cheered, though, the valedictorian issued a correction: "Just kidding, that was Barack Obama." Right away, the applause died down, and a boo could be heard. The identity of the messenger, it was painfully evident, mattered more than the content of the message.

When Americans hear about "tribalism," they often imagine a faraway land where one ethnic or religious faction mercilessly persecutes another for generations. Only recently have many in this country begun to appraise the extent of the tribalism at home. Writing for The Times's Op-Ed page in February, Amy Chua, the Yale law professor who once extolled the merits of "tiger moms," warned about the dangers of a "zero-sum tribalist contest." Jonah Goldberg, the conservative columnist and pundit who once railed against "liberal fascism," recently went on NPR's "Morning Edition" to sound the alarm on "a cheap form of tribalism," telling the host Steve Inskeep that "people are retreating into their little cocoons." And in a Wall Street Journal op-ed, Senator Orrin Hatch lamented that identity politics—"tribalism by another name"—could turn the nation into "a divided country of ideological ghettos."

In its first sense, tribalism refers to the organization of people along lines of common ancestry or joint identity for the purpose of exercising political power— as the indigenous people of many parts of the world, including the Americas, have long done. But over time, as new forms of governance appeared—city-states, kingdoms and especially empires, which controlled vast colonies with different races, cultures and languages— tribalism came to be seen as crude and antiquated, a political structure that could never hope to address the challenges of large states. And now, in the modern era, the word is used almost exclusively in its second, derogatory sense, to suggest an irrational loyalty to your people.

The impulse to belong to a clan is deeply human, however, and new tribes continue to form, organized not around ancestry but along fuzzier lines of ideology or demography. Modern tribes, like ancient ones, have idiosyncratic languages; one faction might speak of "illegal aliens," "traditional families" and "the life of the unborn," while the other talks of "undocumented workers," "marriage equality" and "my body, my choice." They rule over separate territories, listen to different oracles, uphold distinct values and dismiss contradictory information as unreliable propaganda or "fake news.

Above all, tribe members protect one another from perceived attacks by outsiders. Last April, when the MSNBC host Joy Reid was found to have posted homophobic content on a now-defunct blog (and claimed, dubiously, to have been hacked), many liberals rallied to her side anyway, pointing out that the posts were more than 10 years old and urging others to accept her profuse apologies. Had such posts been attributed to a Fox News personality, however, it's almost certain those same liberals would have offered no opportunity for forgiveness. The gift of absolution is given within a tribe, and rarely outside it.

Political tribes can organize along stark lines: the working class versus the 1 percent, baby boomers versus millennials, city dwellers versus rural people. But they can also be more nebulous, forming around subtleties of education, lifestyle or cultural taste. Some years ago, when Howard Dean was the front-runner for the Democratic nomination for the presidency, the conservative PAC Club for Growth ran a TV ad in Iowa featuring an elderly white couple being asked about Dean's tax proposal. "What do I think?" the husband says. "I think Howard Dean should take his tax-hiking, government-expanding, latte-drinking, sushi-eating, Volvo-driving, New York Times-reading—" Then his wife interrupts: "body-piercing, Hollywood-loving, left-wing freak show back to Vermont, where it belongs."

The question was at least putatively about Dean's plan to repeal George W. Bush's tax cuts, but instead of eliciting a coherent opinion on how much tax should reasonably be withheld, from whom and for what services, it provoked a rant against a particular group of people, who were characterized almost entirely through their lifestyle and consumer choices. There was no need to talk policy, because the policy was reframed as an embrace of one tribe and a rejection of the other.

In principle, the United States is a country where various tribes are supposed to work in coalition to form what the founders called "a more perfect union." Americans also pride themselves on having a "melting pot" model of immigration, in which each new group is thrown into the mix, contributing to the overall sustenance of the nation. But the reality is that, for most of this country's history, one tribe has held power, deciding who was allowed to settle the land and who could be dispossessed, who was free and who was enslaved, who had the right to vote and who did not. The hegemony of white landowners prompted few, if any, complaints about tribalism in the national conversation. It was only when other factions began to demand justice and recognition—the "seat at the table" that Trump, but not Obama, was applauded for encouraging people to seek—that the debate about which tribe holds power became explicit rather than implicit.

It is not a coincidence, then, that use of the word "tribalism" in print increased significantly during the civil rights struggles, anti-war protests and cultural clashes of the 1960s, reaching a peak in 1972, when Richard Nixon campaigned for and won a second term. That era was characterized by turmoil, both abroad and here in the United States, where tribes rebelled against one another in nearly every public arena, from draft offices to college campuses to lunch counters. After Nixon's resignation and the end of the Vietnam War, complaints about tribalism declined steadily, only to rise again in the 1990s.

Why the 1990s? Over the course of his presidency, Bill Clinton moved the Democratic Party to the right: He deregulated banks, cut welfare programs, signed the Defense of Marriage Act into law, built a border wall between San Diego and Tijuana and expanded mass incarceration. These are not progressive ideas, which left Republicans with few concrete policies that could distinguish them from Democrats. Republicans did, however, have culture—and, eventually, character. When Clinton's affair with Monica Lewinsky surfaced in 1998, conservatives attacked him as the symbol of a lost and immoral society, while liberals minimized his offenses and portrayed the young intern as a harlot. Twenty years later, the two tribes would switch sides, with liberals denouncing Donald Trump for sexual predation while conservatives, including white evangelicals, rallied around him.

Political tribes often display similar group behavior, but this doesn't mean that the values they hold are equivalent. Tearing migrant children away from their parents, for instance, is not a morally neutral policy. In moments like these, complaints about tribalism can be politically expedient—a way of making even the most consequential debate seem like a mere spat between loyalists on either side. (Where was this passion for the fates of asylum seekers, some conservatives have asked, during the Obama administration?) By reducing every question to tribalist point-scoring, it becomes easier to escape the moral implications of taking an asylum-seeking child from his or her mother and incarcerating them hundreds of miles apart.

Some people think that dialogue and debate can help the United States defeat its current tribalism. If only we could calmly talk about our differences, the argument goes, we would reach some compromise. But not all disagreements are bridgeable. The Union and the Confederacy did not resolve their differences through dialogue; it was a civil war that put an end to slavery. Jim Crow laws were defeated through mass protests and civil disobedience. Schools were desegregated though a Supreme Court decision, which had to be implemented with the help of the National Guard. The Chinese Exclusion Act was repealed as a political necessity during World War II. Some fights are not talked away; they are, in the end, either won or lost.

This is not to say that tribal impasses of the moment can't be broken. But it is generally not a good idea to expect people on the receiving end of brutal policies—like families broken apart by police violence, immigration raids, travel bans or anti-L.G.B.T. discrimination—to hash out a compromise over sweet tea. "Maybe we pushed too far," Barack Obama is quoted as saying in a new memoir by Benjamin Rhodes, one of his closest aides. "Maybe people just want to fall back into their tribe." What the ever-compromising Obama doesn't consider is that resolution sometimes requires pushing even further.

Source: Lalami, Laila. "Does American 'Tribalism' End in a Compromise, or a Fight?" The New York Times. June 26, 2018. https://www.nytimes.com/2018/06/26/magazine/does-american-tribalism-end-in-a-compromise-or-a-fight.html.

Consider the Source and the Audience: Laila Lalami is a Moroccan-American novelist who teaches at the University of California, Riverside. She was born in Morocco, got an MA in London, and a Ph.D. in California. How might being an immigrant help her see divisions of opinion in the U.S. more clearly? How might it make it harder for her to understand those divisions?

Layout the Argument, the Values and the Assumptions: Lalami posits that it is human nature to form tribes, that western civilization only thought it was beyond tribalism because one big tribe held so much power that all other tribes were squashed into submission. How have changing demographics in the United States altered that power dynamic? Lalami says tribes can form over all sort of differences—why don't they form alliances more often?

Uncover the evidence: Lalami's argument is anthropological, historical, and political. What kind of evidence does she offer from each of these areas? Do you find the evidence convincing? Is tribalism part of our nature?

Evaluate the Conclusion: The larger part Lalami's argument is mostly descriptive and informative—explaining the reasons for and examples of our tribal nature. It is only toward the end that she makes an explicitly political argument—that tribalism is on the rise as groups challenge the all-powerful position of white, western male-dominated culture. Has she provided adequate evidence for this conclusion? Does our everyday experience of politics bear it out?

Sort out the Political Significance: Lalami implies that Obama's compromising nature did not suit the challenge of making a place for new tribes at the table. She suggests that fighting, not compromise, is the way to resolve the current contest among competing tribes. What kind of fighting do you think she refers to: physical or political? Would one lead to the other?

Review

The Role of Public Opinion in a Democracy

The role of public opinion in politics has been hotly debated throughout American history. The founders devised a Constitution that would limit the influence of the masses. Today some changes in the rules have given the public a greater role in government. Politicians and the media watch public opinion very closely. Elected officials look for job security by responding to immediate public desires or by skillfully predicting future requests. The media make large investments in polls, sometimes covering public attitudes on a candidate or an issue as a story in itself.

public opinion (p. 373)　　　　　　**public opinion polls** (p. 373)

Citizen Values

There are two competing visions of citizenship in America. The ideal democratic citizen demonstrates political knowledge, tolerates different ideas, and votes consistently. At the other extreme lies the apolitical, self-interested citizen. Most Americans fall somewhere between these extremes.

What Influences Our Opinions About Politics?

Political socialization—the transfer of fundamental democratic values from one generation to the next—produces a citizenry that largely agrees with the rules of the game and accepts the outcomes of the national political process as legitimate. Despite this agreement, opinions about politics vary widely. These opinions are affected by demographic characteristics such as race, gender, and age; by political ideology; and by other factors such as education, income, religion, and geographic region. Interest groups, political parties, and candidates all attempt to determine the political ideas shared by various groups in order to gain their support.

political socialization (p. 377)　　**gender gap** (p. 380)　　　　　　**partisan sorting** (p. 383)
patriotism (p. 378)　　　　　　　　**marriage gap** (p. 381)
spiral of silence (p. 378)　　　　　**political generations** (p. 382)

Measuring and Tracking Public Opinion

Most politicians pay attention to their own informal samplings of opinion, but they have also come to rely on professional polling. Such polls are based on scientific polling methods that focus on getting a good sample and asking questions that yield valid results.

sample (p. 387)

sample bias (p. 387)

straw polls (p. 387)

sampling error (p. 390)

random samples (p. 390)

nonresponse bias (p. 390)

weighting (p. 390)

benchmark poll (p. 393)

tracking polls (p. 393)

exit polls (p. 393)

push polls (p. 395)

The Citizens and Public Opinion

Even though Americans do not measure up to the ideal of the democratic citizen, much evidence supports the idea that public opinion does play a large role in government policy. Some citizens may seem apolitical and disinterested, but many others use rational information shortcuts to make their voting decisions. Policymakers have responded by staying generally responsive to public preferences.

rational ignorance (p. 398)

on-line processing (p. 398)

two-step flow of information (p. 398)

opinion leaders (p. 398)

12
POLITICAL PARTIES

In Your Own Words

After you've read this chapter, you will be able to

12.1 Describe the role that parties play in making government policy.

12.2 Explain the tension between the party base and the general electorate regarding their influence on issue positions.

12.3 Outline the evolution of the party system in the United States.

12.4 Explain the ways in which parties connect citizens and government.

12.5 Describe how the American party system works.

12.6 Give examples of how parties serve (or fail to serve) citizens in American politics.

What's at Stake . . . When "Outsiders" Challenge Establishment Party Candidates?

IT HAPPENED TO BOTH PARTIES IN 2016, albeit in different ways and with different results.

In the Democratic Party, it was at the primary stage—the early elections to determine who the party's presidential nominee would be. Hillary Clinton entered the race as the front-runner—the one everyone expected to win easily. When it came to party ideology, she was a moderate left Democrat, a liberal at heart who had been toughened to practicality by years of service to her party as first lady, senator from New York, and secretary of state under Barack Obama. In terms of her ties to her party, Clinton was as establishment as they come. Not only had she helped shape its modern identity, but she was well connected, well liked, and the clear party favorite.

JUSTIN SAGLIO/AFP/Getty Images

Justin Sullivan/Getty Images

Insiders, Outsiders

Both the Democratic and Republican Party establishments were challenged by outsiders in the 2016 presidential election, with Vermont senator Bernie Sanders (top), an independent-turned-Democrat, running against Hillary Clinton (top, right) in the primary and businessman Donald Trump (bottom, left) disrupting a cadre of Republican hopefuls, including former Florida governor Jeb Bush (bottom).

The challenge Clinton didn't predict came from her left. The independent senator from Vermont, Bernie Sanders, declared his intention to run in the Democratic primary on April 30, 2015. Running in a major party's primary instead of as an independent comes with huge advantages—media attention, a debate stage, ballot position. What it doesn't do is make you loyal to the party's goals or make the party establishment loyal to you.

Although Clinton won the nomination eventually, Sanders's challenge was serious. He did particularly well with young voters, the white working class, and voters who themselves did not identify with a party. His best states were those where the candidate selection mechanism was the caucus—a discussion-based process that rewards intensity of support and willingness to spend time to choose the candidate—or the open primary—an election in which non–party members are allowed to participate. Sanders attacked Clinton's positions on trade and ended up pulling her to the left on a number of policy issues, such as college tuition, trade, and Wall Street reform, to name a few.

In the process, Sanders left Clinton battle scarred, with a reputation for being inauthentic and untrustworthy on important issues that some of his supporters never forgave. Despite his subsequent endorsement and his enthusiastic campaigning on Clinton's behalf, many of the young people who backed Sanders never enthusiastically transferred their support to her, and a number defected to third-party candidates. The white working-class support Sanders had drawn appealed to Democrats who felt the party had ignored them in favor of propping up banks and corporations and supporting social programs to aid minorities. Many of them were angry and resentful, ripe for the picking by an anti-establishment candidate, and when Sanders left the stage, there was another in the wings.

The same outsider infiltration that happened to the Democrats was happening to the Republicans. A crowded field of primary hopefuls seeking the nomination was already deeply divided, like their party, between establishment economic conservatives (Jeb Bush, Chris Christie, Rand Paul, Carly Fiorina, Lindsey Graham, John Kasich, Scott Walker, and George Pataki) and social conservative, Tea Party/Freedom Caucus types (Marco Rubio, Ted Cruz, Ben Carson, Mike Huckabee, Bobby Jindal, Rick Perry, and Rick Santorum). As the establishment candidates took aim at each other, another outsider, a former Democrat turned original birther, a successful real estate developer and reality-show host, stepped in and stole the show.

The field barely had a chance. Donald Trump's entertainment value was such that he garnered hours of free media time as the cable stations covered his rallies, hoping he would say something outrageous as he sought to persuade voters that he was running against the "political correctness" that kept them from expressing their true feelings. Aiming straight for the disaffected voters who felt abandoned by the party that had promised them much (control of immigration, the repeal of Obamacare, the end of abortion and gay marriage) but delivered little, Trump promised to "make America great again," and in the process decimated the field. With withering scorn, he called Jeb Bush, the establishment favorite, front-runner, and heir to the Bush family dynasty, "low energy," and Bush's quiet and restrained demeanor seemed to prove him right. "Little Marco" diminished Rubio, "Lyin' Ted Cruz" took care of the Texan, as one by one Trump mocked them and bullied them and knocked them out of the race.

There was a policy debate to be had in the Republican Party, an important one between the establishment and the Freedom Caucus that had been brewing for years and immobilizing Congress, but it never got a hearing. Instead, the primary was reduced to a clown show of name calling and one-upmanship as each candidate tried to outdo himself or herself on the issues Trump brought front and center—mainly immigration (he promised to build a huge wall between the United States and Mexico that Mexico would pay for) and the undoing of the Obama agenda. Trump's rallies drew large crowds, drawn to hear him talk about how he would deport undocumented workers, ban Muslims from entering the country, and bring back jobs he claimed were stolen by the Chinese, all while generally signaling disrespect for social norms of respectful language and politically correct behavior. Those signals, as we noted in *What's at Stake . . . ?* in Chapter 6, were interpreted as not-so-subtle dog whistles that freed up an underbelly of American culture to use crude sexist, racist, anti-Semitic, and xenophobic language at his rallies and in social media forums that Trump did not repudiate. Social media became an echo chamber that repeated the sentiments, or gave them attention by disparaging them. In either case, social media amplified them.

But like Sanders, Trump's outsider, anti-establishment stance appealed to those who felt that Washington had gotten too corrupt and full of itself, too dysfunctional and too removed from their concerns. He drew support not just from bigots but also from the same white working class to which Sanders appealed. By the end of the primary season, against everyone's best guesses and predictions, Trump was the Republican Party's nominee, and he went on to win the Electoral College in a squeaker of a surprise victory in November.

What happened here? How did two outside candidates have such an impact on the nomination process of parties to which they had barely any ties? What impact is that having on the parties' futures? Just what is at stake when party establishments are challenged from outside like this? We will return to that question after we look more closely at the role parties play in American politics and how they work. ◀◀

A political party is a group of citizens united under a commitment to common ideas and policies who want to make those policies happen by controlling government. The means to that end are recruiting, nominating, and electing candidates for office. Naturally, that's a business that can look pretty divisive much of the time. For one party to win, another has to lose. Not surprisingly, Americans have always been of two minds about parties. Partisan passions can burn long and brightly, fueling public service and civic action. But we are also cynical about partisan bickering and the **political gridlock**, or stalemate, that can result when rival parties stubbornly refuse to budge from their positions to achieve a compromise in the public interest.

Skepticism about political parties, in fact, has been a major feature of American politics since the drafting of the Constitution. When James Madison wrote in *Federalist* No. 10 that "liberty is to faction what air is to fire," he conceded that factions, whether in the form of interest groups or political parties, are a permanent fixture within our representative system, but he hoped to have limited their effects by creating a large republic with many and varied interests. President George Washington echoed Madison's concerns when he warned "against the baneful effects of the spirit of party generally" in his farewell address as president in 1796.

But it was already too late. There were parties in Madison's day, as there are in our own. In fact, despite popular disenchantment with political parties and politicians' occasional frustration with them, most political observers and scholars believe that parties are essential to the functioning of democracy in general, and American democracy in particular. The fact is, parties have not damaged the Constitution. They provide an extraconstitutional framework of rules and institutions that enhance the way the Constitution works. Who wins and who loses in American politics is determined not just by the Constitution but also by more informal rules, and chief among these are the rules produced by the political parties. In this chapter you will learn more about parties themselves, their role in American politics, their history, and the characteristics of the American party system.

WHY POLITICAL PARTIES?

Organizations seeking to influence government policy by controlling the apparatus of government

Probably because Madison hoped that they would not thrive, political parties—unlike Congress, the presidency, the Supreme Court, and even the free press—are not mentioned in the Constitution. As we will see, in fact, many of the rules that determine the establishment and role of the parties have been created by party members themselves. Although the founding documents of American politics are silent on the place of political parties, keen political observers have long appreciated the fundamental role that political parties play in our system of government.[1] According to one scholar, "Political parties created democracy, and . . . democracy is unthinkable save in terms of parties."[2]

> **political party** a group of citizens united by ideology and seeking control of government in order to promote their ideas and policies
>
> **political gridlock** the stalemate that occurs when political rivals, especially parties, refuse to budge from their positions to achieve a compromise in the public interest

THE ROLE OF PARTIES IN A DEMOCRACY

Our definition of parties—as organizations that seek, under a common banner, to promote their ideas and policies by gaining control of government through the nomination and election of candidates for office—underscores a key difference between parties and interest groups. Although both interest groups and parties seek to influence government policies, only parties gain this influence by sponsoring candidates in competitive elections. For political parties, winning elections represents a means to the end of controlling democratic government.

Parties are crucial to the maintenance of democracy for three reasons:

- **Political linkage.** Parties provide a linkage between voters and elected officials, helping to tell voters what candidates stand for and providing a way for voters to hold their officials accountable for what they do in office, both individually and collectively.
- **Unification of a fragmented government.** Parties help overcome some of the fragmentation in government that comes from separation of powers and federalism. The founders' concern, of course, was to prevent government

from becoming too powerful. But so successful were they in dividing up power that without the balancing effect of party to provide some connection between state and national government, for instance, or between the president and Congress, American government might find it very hard to achieve anything at all. Parties can lend this coherence, however, only when they control several branches or several levels of government.

- **A voice for the opposition.** Parties provide an articulate opposition to the ideas and policies of those elected to serve in government. Some citizens and critics may decry the **partisanship**, or taking of political sides, that sometimes seems to be motivated by possibilities for party gain as much as by principle or public interest. Others, however, see partisanship as providing the necessary antagonistic relationship that, like our adversarial court system, keeps politicians honest and allows the best political ideas and policies to emerge.

To highlight the multiple tasks that parties perform to make democracy work and to make life easier for politicians, political scientists find it useful to divide political parties into three separate components: the party organization, the party-in-government, and the party-in-the-electorate.[3]

FIGURE 12.1

Organizational Structure of the Party System

National party organization
National committees
Members are elected by national conventions or state committees.

State party organizations
State party committees
Members are elected by party voters or by lower-level committees.

Local party organizations
County committees, or state senate, judicial, and congressional district committees
Members are elected by voters in primary elections.
Precinct and ward organizations
Members are party activists.

Party members
Registered voters; vote in party primaries.

FIGURE 12.2

Party Identification, 1952–2018

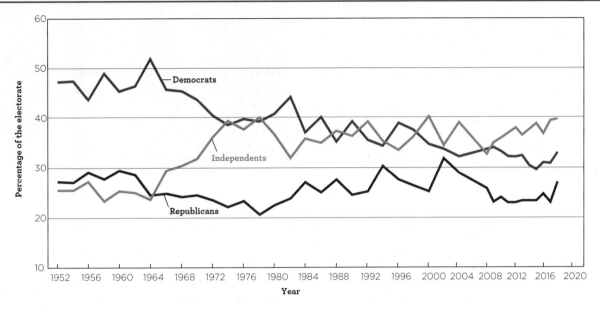

Source: American National Election Studies, University of Michigan; data made available by the Inter-University Consortium for Political and Social Research; for 2009–2013, data from Pew Research Center, "Party Identification," www.pewresearch.org/data-trend/political-attitudes/party-identification/. Extended with authors' calculations using Pew Research Center national adult surveys, 2014 and 2016. Data accessed through the Roper Center for Public Opinion Research.

PARTY ORGANIZATION The **party organization** is what most people think of as a political party. The party organization represents the system of central committees at the national, state, and local levels. At the top of the Democratic Party organization is the Democratic National Committee, and the Republican National Committee heads the Republican Party. Underneath these national committees are state-level party committees, and below them are county-level party committees, or county equivalents (see Figure 12.1). These party organizations raise money for campaigns, recruit and nominate candidates, organize and facilitate campaigns, register voters, mobilize voters to the polls, conduct party conventions and caucuses, and draft party platforms. This may seem like a lot; however, this is only a fraction of what party organizations do, as we will see later in the chapter.

partisanship loyalty to a political cause or party

party organization the official structure that conducts the political business of parties

party-in-government party members who have been elected to serve in government

party-in-the-electorate ordinary citizens who identify with the party

party identification voter affiliation with a political party

PARTY-IN-GOVERNMENT The **party-in-government** comprises all the candidates for national, state, and local office who have been elected. The president, as the effective head of his or her party; the Speaker of the House of Representatives; the majority and minority leaders in the House and the Senate; the party whips in Congress; and state governors are all central actors in the party-in-government, which plays an important role in organizing government and in translating the wishes of the electorate into public policies.

PARTY-IN-THE-ELECTORATE The **party-in-the-electorate** represents ordinary citizens who identify with or have some feeling of attachment to one of the political parties. Public opinion surveys determine **party identification**, or party ID, by asking respondents if they think of themselves as Democrats, Republicans, or independents. You can see two clear trends in party identification over time in Figure 12.2. Overall, voter attachments to the parties have declined; the percentage identifying as independent has increased substantially from less than 30 percent through the mid-1960s to around 40 percent since the mid-1970s. The second trend to note in Figure 12.2 is the loss of the large numerical advantage the Democratic Party had among identifiers in the 1950s. The parties were about even by 2002, but the Democrats have recovered and held a modest lead in party affiliation that has grown slightly since 2016.

Most voters who identify with one of the political parties "inherit" their party IDs from their parents, as we suggested in our discussion of political socialization in Chapter 11.[4] Party identifiers generally support the party's basic ideology and policy principles. These policy principles usually relate to each party's stance on the use of government to solve various economic and social problems.

Voters in most states can choose to register their party preferences for the purpose of voting in party primaries (elections to choose candidates for office). These voters are not required to perform any special activities, to contribute money to the political party, or, for that matter, even to vote in the primaries. Although voters do not have a strong formal role to play in the party organization, parties use identifiers as a necessary base of support during elections. In virtually every presidential election, both of the major-party candidates win the votes of an overwhelming percentage of those who identify with their respective parties. But just capturing one's **party base** is not sufficient to win a national election since neither party has a majority of the national voters. As we will see later in this chapter, candidates are often pulled between the ideological preferences of their base and the more moderate preferences of independents.

> ### Can we have a democracy without political parties?

THE RESPONSIBLE PARTY MODEL

Earlier we said that one of the democratic roles of parties is to provide a link between the voters and elected officials, or, to use the terms we just introduced, between the party-in-the-electorate and the party-in-government. There are many ways in which parties can link voters and officials, but for the link to truly enhance democracy—that is, the control of leaders by citizens—certain conditions have to be met. Political scientists call the fulfillment of the following conditions the **responsible party model:**[5]

- Each party should present a coherent set of programs to the voters, consistent with its ideology and clearly different from those of the other party.
- The candidates for each party should pledge to support their party's platform and to implement their party's program if elected.

Getting the House in Order
Nancy Pelosi was elected the first woman Speaker of the House of Representatives in 2007 and maintained discipline in her caucus—and her leadership role—even after losing the majority in 2010. Through she has been criticized for neglecting to develop younger leaders, and has said she considers herself a "transitional Speaker," there is little doubt she will take up the Speaker's gavel again in 2019.

- Voters should make their choices based on which party's program most closely reflects their own ideas, and they should hold the parties responsible for promises not kept by voting their members out of office.
- While governing, each party should exercise control over its elected officials to ensure that party officials are promoting and voting for its programs, thereby providing accountability to the voters.

The responsible party model proposes that democracy is strengthened when voters are given clear alternatives and hold the parties responsible for keeping their promises. Voters can, of course, hold officials accountable without the assistance of parties, but it takes a good deal more of their time and attention. Furthermore, several political scientists have noted that although individuals can be held accountable for their own actions, many, if not most, government actions are the product of many officials. Political parties give us a way of holding officials accountable for what they do collectively as well as individually.[6]

> **party base** members of a political party who consistently vote for that party's candidates
>
> **responsible party model** party government when four conditions are met: clear choice of ideologies, candidates pledged to implement ideas, party held accountable by voters, and party control over members

The responsible party model fits some systems, especially parliamentary systems such as in Great Britain, quite well. Strong, disciplined, and determined parties are appropriate for a parliamentary system where the majority party controls, by definition, both the legislative and the executive branches, and can control the government without minority obstruction like our Senate filibuster. The model is more problematic when used, as political scientists in the past have done, to critique the American parties, which during the middle decades of the twentieth century were seen as too unfocused and undisciplined to fit the model.[7]

Changes in our system over the past twenty years or so have brought the American parties closer to a responsible party model—especially in the distinctive policy programs the parties have come to represent. But even as the parties have become more highly polarized, there is a growing disconnect between their behavior and the demands of our constitutional system of checks and balances and separation of powers. This means that the parties often share power and must cooperate to get things done, yet having such polarized parties in our system of shared powers is a recipe for gridlock and frustration—which is pretty much what most Americans see today in their national government.[8] In practice the American system also falls short of the idealized responsible party model because American voters don't fit the model's conditions; they do not vote solely on party or issues, relying on other considerations like candidate experience and personality. Still, even though it doesn't fit the American case perfectly, the responsible party model is valuable because it underscores the importance of voters holding the parties accountable for governing, and it provides a useful yardstick for understanding fundamental changes in the U.S. two-party system.

| PAUSE AND REVIEW | Who, What, How |

Political parties seek to control government and to promote their ideologies and policies. They do this by creating rules that allow them to control the nomination, campaign, and election processes and by trying to control the actions of their members elected to office. Politicians obviously have something at stake here, too. Parties provide a mechanism that helps them get nominated for office, win elections, and run government—but winning requires the support of nonparty members as well.

American citizens also have a big stake in what political parties do. Parties provide a link between citizens and government, cohesion among levels and branches of government, and an articulate opposition to government policy.

In Your Own Words   Describe the role that parties play in making government policy.

DO AMERICAN PARTIES OFFER VOTERS A CHOICE?

The party base and the general electorate as countervailing forces on a party's issue positions

A key feature of the responsible party model is that the parties should offer voters a choice between different visions of how government should operate. Barry Goldwater, the 1964 Republican presidential nominee, stated this more bluntly: political parties, he said, should offer "a choice, not an echo." Offering voters a choice is the primary means through which parties make representative democracy work. In America the policy differences between the two major parties, the Democrats and the Republicans (often also called the GOP for "Grand Old Party"), are narrower than in some democracies around the world, particularly those with many parties spread across the ideological spectrum. Increasingly, however, voters do see clear policy choices between the two parties.[9] In this section we investigate what the two major parties stand for, including competing forces that draw the parties apart to ideologically distinct positions or push them together to take more moderate stances.

WHAT DO THE PARTIES STAND FOR?

Cynical voters may think that members of the two parties are not very different from each other once they are elected to office, but the parties really are quite distinct in their ideologies, their memberships, and the policies they stand for.

PARTY IDEOLOGY   Each major party represents a different ideological perspective about the way that government should be used to solve problems. Ideologies, as we have said before, are broad sets of ideas about politics that help to organize our views of the political world, the information that regularly bombards us, and the positions we take on various issues. Parties are important mediators of those views—passing them on to us and letting us know which views are acceptable from the party's perspective and which are not. As we saw in Chapter 2, liberalism and conservatism today are ideologies that divide the country sharply over issues such as the role of government in the economy, in society, and in citizens' private lives. In general, conservatives look to government to provide social and moral order, but they want the economy to remain as unfettered as possible in the distribution of material resources. Liberals encourage government action to solve economic and social problems but want government to stay out of their personal, religious, and moral lives, except as a protector of their basic rights.

FIGURE 12.3
Party Identification and Ideology

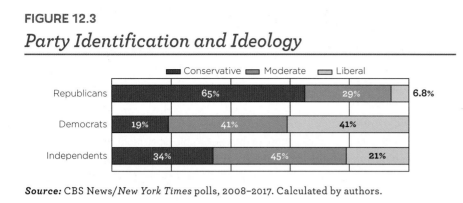

Source: CBS News/*New York Times* polls, 2008–2017. Calculated by authors.

At least since the New Deal of the 1930s, the Democratic Party, especially outside the South, has been aligned with a liberal ideology and the Republican Party with a conservative perspective.[10] Since the 1960s the parties have become more consistent internally with respect to their ideologies. The most conservative region in the country is the South, but because of lingering resentment of the Republican Party for its role in the Civil War, the South was for decades tied tightly to the Democratic Party. In the 1960s, however, conservative southern Democratic voters began to vote for the Republican Party, and formerly Democratic politicians were switching their allegiances as well. By the 1990s the South had become predominantly Republican. This swing made the Democratic Party more consistently liberal and the Republicans more consistently conservative and, as we explained in Chapter 7, the parties became more polarized.

To illustrate these shifts, in 1977 only about one-third of party identifiers were "consistents" (liberal Democrats and conservative Republicans), compared to the one-fifth who were "inconsistents" (conservative Democrats and liberal Republicans). The forces for polarization and **partisan sorting** (the recent tendency for people to line up with the party that shares their ideological views and issue positions) have yielded much more consistency in party and ideological identifications: currently over half of party identifiers are consistents, whereas only about one in ten are inconsistents.[11] The stronger activist core is able to exert more internal pressure within the parties, nominating candidates through primaries but also calling for ideological conformity in the parties in Congress. This leads to the phenomenon of **hyperpartisanship**, discussed in Chapter 7, which has brought Congress to a standstill recently. As a result, there is no overlap in the House of Representatives between the parties: all Republicans are more conservative than the most conservative Democrat, yielding two completely distinct ideological encampments with little basis for compromise. The differences among the public are not as great, but

they are still notable. Figure 12.3 shows the ideological composition of Democrats, Republicans, and independents. Notice that, although the conservative label is more popular, the likelihood of identifying oneself as a conservative is much greater among Republicans. It is not, of course, the case that all Democrats think the same or that all Republicans think the same. Each party has its ideological and moderate factions, but the divisions between partisans in the electorate are greater today than they used to be.[12]

PARTY MEMBERSHIP Party ideologies attract and are reinforced by different coalitions of voters. This means that the Democrats' post–New Deal liberal ideology reflects the preferences of its coalition of working- and lower-class voters, including union members, minorities, women, the elderly, and more educated urban dwellers. The Republicans' conservative ideology, by contrast, reflects the preferences of upper- to middle-class whites, those who are in evangelical and Protestant religions, and rural and suburban voters. The *Snapshot of America: Who Belongs to What Party?* shows how each party's coalition differs based on group characteristics. There is nothing inevitable about these coalitions, however, and they are subject to change as the parties' stances on issues change and as the opposing party offers new alternatives. Working-class whites (non-Hispanic whites without a college education) were once the bedrock constituency of the Democratic Party. However, the Republicans' more conservative appeals on racial and social issues have won over enough of this group that are they are as likely to support Republicans in a given election,[13] although as we saw by their choice of Donald Trump as their candidate in the 2016 primaries, they do not feel that the establishment party has been responsive to their concerns.

POLICY DIFFERENCES BETWEEN THE PARTIES When the parties run slates of candidates for office, those candidates run on a **party platform**—a list of

partisan sorting the process through which citizens align themselves ideologically with one of the two parties, leaving fewer citizens remaining in the center and increasing party polarization

hyperpartisanship a commitment to party so strong that it can transcend other commitments

party platform a list of policy positions a party endorses and pledges its elected officials to enact

Snapshot of America: *Who Belongs to What Party?*

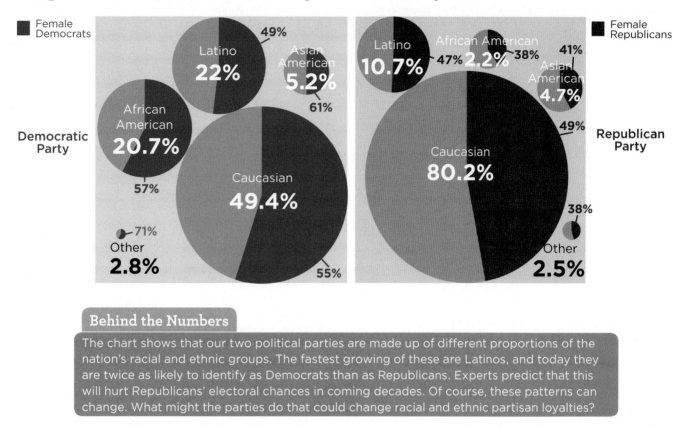

Female Democrats · **Democratic Party**

- Latino **22%** — 49%
- Asian American **5.2%** — 61%
- African American **20.7%** — 57%
- Caucasian **49.4%** — 55%
- Other **2.8%** — 71%

Female Republicans · **Republican Party**

- Latino **10.7%** — 47%
- African American **2.2%** — 38%
- Asian American **4.7%** — 41%
- Caucasian **80.2%** — 49%
- Other **2.5%** — 38%

Behind the Numbers

The chart shows that our two political parties are made up of different proportions of the nation's racial and ethnic groups. The fastest growing of these are Latinos, and today they are twice as likely to identify as Democrats than as Republicans. Experts predict that this will hurt Republicans' electoral chances in coming decades. Of course, these patterns can change. What might the parties do that could change racial and ethnic partisan loyalties?

Source: American National Election Studies Time Series Survey 2016. Authors' calculations with racial and ethnic groups weighted to match 2015 Census data (www.statista.com/statistics/270272/percentage-of-us-population-by-ethnicities/).

policy positions the party endorses and pledges its elected officials to enact as policy. A platform is the national party's campaign promises, usually made only in a presidential election year. If the parties are to make a difference politically, then the platforms have to reflect substantial differences that are consistent with their ideologies. The responsible party model requires that the parties offer distinct platforms, that voters know about them and vote on the basis of them, and that the parties ensure that their elected officials follow through in implementing them.

The two major parties' stated positions on some key issues from their 2016 platforms appear in *Don't Be Fooled by . . . Political Party Platforms*. These differences between the Democratic and Republican platforms in 2016 are typical, and they are what make it possible for the electorate to bring about meaningful policy changes. When the parties' programs are clearly different, electing a new majority party to Congress can result in substantial changes in the policy directions pursued by the national government.

That is, party differences are necessary for popular control of the overall direction of government policy.

FORCES DRAWING THE PARTIES APART AND PUSHING THEM TOGETHER

Political parties in our system have a dilemma—how to keep the core ideological base satisfied while appealing to enough more moderate voters that they can win elections in diverse constituencies. This is not likely to be a problem in a small, homogeneous district. Conservative Republicans and liberal Democrats can be nominated and elected and party members are happy. As constituencies get larger and more diverse, parties have a choice. They can be moderate and win elections, or stay ideologically pure and lose. In other words, there are internal forces that draw the parties away from each other, to the opposite ends of the ideological spectrum, but external, electoral forces can push them together. These forces are central to understanding electoral politics in America today. In this section we look more closely at these complex relationships.

Political Party Platforms

Are you a member of a political party, or thinking about becoming one? If so, you've got some homework to do. Each major party (and most minor ones, too) has put together a party platform—a document that outlines the party's political positions and agenda for the coming years. You can think of the party platform as a political dating profile, filled with information that can help you make sound decisions about whether you want to pursue a relationship with one party or another.

Before you become "involved" with a party, we encourage you to take a few moments to read the platform of your preferred party—and consider alternatives as well. You can find the full text of each party's 2016 platform on the parties' national committee web sites; we've included here a few highlights from the two major-party platforms.

What to Watch Out For

When you read a party's platform, keep these questions in mind:

- **Whose platform is it?** Established parties like the Democratic and Republicans Parties are likely to want to excite their base, while upstarts like the Greens and the Libertarians might be more concerned with attracting new members. Consider how these goals might influence how each party presents itself in its party platform.
- **Who is the platform directed to?** Is it catering to the mainstream party members or to the party's more extreme factions? Where do you fit in along that continuum?
- **How did the political climate affect this platform?** Platforms are created as part of the national conventions—which come at the tail end of the presidential primary season. Do you think the events (and players) of this party's primary influenced the platform? If so, how does that influence relate to you and your political priorities?

- **What does this party—and the other parties!—have to say about issues you care about?** The beauty of digital information is that you can quickly and easily search for key words that matter most to you. Do a quick search for terms that are high on your political priority list—for example, health care, abortion, firearms, terrorism, taxes, the Supreme Court—to find out where each party stands on the issue.
- **Do you think the party can deliver on its policy proposals?** What resources—money, power, and so on—would it need? Can it get them? Would enacting the promised policies achieve what the party claims it would? Who would win, and who would lose?
- **Does this platform deserve your support?** Membership in a political party is a form of political power: by voting in party primaries, you can help to shape the party of the future, along with its agenda. Think carefully about how you can best wield that power. Supporting a party need not mean that you endorse the party line on every single issue—but it is a useful way of identifying a clear set of priorities for political action.
- **What are your alternatives?** In the end, you may determine that membership in a party is not important to you at all, and that you wish to remain an independent voter. But remember that, come November, you will be choosing among candidates who are affiliated with parties. Knowing what each party stands for can help you to make better decisions in the voting booth—especially in state and local elections where you may not have access to the kind of information made available about national candidates.

© enchanted_glass, via iStock

Here are a few highlights from each party's platform:

ISSUE	DEMOCRATIC PARTY	REPUBLICAN PARTY
Abortion	"We believe unequivocally...that every woman should have access to quality reproductive health care services, including safe and legal abortion...."	"...we assert the sanctity of human life and affirm that the unborn child has a fundamental right to life which cannot be infringed."
Education	"...every student should be able to go to college debt-free, and working families should not have to pay any tuition to go to public colleges and universities. We will also make community college free..."	"In order to bring down college costs and give students access to a multitude of financing options, private sector participation in student financing should be restored. Any regulation that increases college costs must be challenged to balance its worth against its negative economic impact on students and their families, and tuition tax credits."
Federal Debt	"We will also ensure that new spending and tax cuts are offset so that they do not add to the nation's debt over time. We will tackle waste, fraud, and abuse to make sure government dollars are spent wisely and efficiently."	"We must impose firm caps on future debt, accelerate the repayment of the trillions we now owe in order to reaffirm our principles of responsible and limited government, and remove the burdens we are placing on future generations."
Health Care	"Democrats believe that health care is a right, not a privilege, and our health care system should put people before profits...."	"Any honest agenda for improving healthcare must start with repeal of the dishonestly named Affordable Care Act of 2010: Obamacare....In its place we must combine what worked best in the past with changes needed for the future."
Gun Rights	"...we will expand and strengthen background checks and close dangerous loopholes in our current laws; repeal the Protection of Lawful Commerce in Arms Act (PLCAA) to revoke the dangerous legal immunity protections gun makers and sellers now enjoy; and keep weapons of war...off our streets."	"We uphold the right of individuals to keep and bear arms...Lawful gun ownership enables Americans to exercise their God-given right of self-defense for the safety of their homes, their loved ones, and their communities."
Taxes	"At a time of massive income and wealth inequality, we believe the wealthiest Americans and largest corporations must pay their fair share of taxes. Democrats will claw back tax breaks for companies that ship jobs overseas, eliminate tax breaks for big oil and gas companies, and crack down on inversions and other methods companies use to dodge their tax responsibilities."	"Republicans consider the establishment of a pro-growth tax code a moral imperative.... Wherever tax rates penalize thrift or discourage investment, they must be lowered. Wherever current provisions of the code are disincentives for economic growth, they must be changed....We will eliminate as many special interest provisions and loopholes as possible and curb corporate welfare..."
Terrorism	"We will strengthen our homeland security, deal wisely and firmly with those who seek to imperil America or our partners, deter aggression, and promote peace. We will use all the tools of American power, especially diplomacy and development, to confront global threats and ensure war is the last resort."	"The Republican Party stands united with all victims of terrorism and will fight at home and abroad to destroy terrorist organizations and protect the lives and fundamental liberties of all people."

Source: Democratic Party platform, https://democrats.org/about/party-platform/; Republican Party platform, https://gop.com/platform/.

THE PULL TOWARD EXTREMISM As we have seen so far in this chapter, major forces within the parties keep them distinct: the needs to placate party activists, to raise money, and to keep the candidates true to their own beliefs as well as to those of their base. On key issues, although presidents seek to portray their proposals as serving the interests of the general public, in fact the specific policy solutions are almost always consistent with their party's ideological perspective and policy agenda.

The main players in political parties are often called the "party faithful," or **party activists**, people who are especially committed to the values and policies of the party, and who devote more of their resources, in both time and money, to the party's cause. The activists are part of the party base, but their support for the party goes beyond simply voting. They also volunteer their time, donate their money, and stay actively involved in party politics. Although these party activists are not an official organ of the party, they represent a party's lifeblood. Compared to the average voter, party activists tend to be more ideologically extreme (more conservative or more liberal even than the average party identifier) and to care more intensely about the party's issues. Their influence has had significant effects on the ideological character of both parties.[14] Party activists play a key role in keeping the parties ideologically distinct because one of the primary goals of their participation and support is to ensure that the party advocates for their issue positions. Because they tend to be concerned with keeping the party pure, they can be reluctant to compromise on their issues,[15] although they also care a great deal about winning.[16]

Liberal activists kept the Democratic Party to the left of most Americans during the 1970s and 1980s. Republicans sought to keep alive the impression that the Democrats were a party of crazed left-wing activists in 1988 by making *liberal*, or "the L-word" as they referred to it, such a derogatory term that Democrats would not use it to describe themselves for fear of turning off voters. The Democratic Party dealt with this problem by giving more weight to moderates like Bill Clinton and Al Gore and by relabeling themselves as "progressives" with fewer and fewer candidates and on-air leftists embracing the "liberal" label.[17] Even under President Obama, the party stayed relatively moderate through 2016, although the candidacy of Vermont senator Bernie Sanders revealed strength on the left, especially among younger voters, reflected in the policy positions that Hillary Clinton ultimately championed. As we saw in *What's at Stake . . . ?*, the Republicans have been struggling with an establishment at odds with its most conservative members, first, in the religious right and, later, in the Tea Party. The 2016 primaries revealed internal schisms among party activists divided between those holding economic conservative views, those holding social conservative views, and a new populism that found its voice in supporting the candidacy of Donald Trump. Since the election, the party as a whole has lost some identifiers who felt strongly about their ideological principles, and the ones who remain have moved closer to Trump's positions.[18] (See this chapter's *Profiles in Citizenship*.)

The need to please party activists gives candidates a powerful incentive to remain true to the party's causes. Activists are poised to work hard for candidates who promote their political, social, economic, or religious agendas and, conversely, to work just as hard against any candidate who does not pass their litmus test.[19] This means that candidates who moderate too much or too often risk alienating the activists who are a key component of their success, and it keeps candidates from converging to the ideological position of the moderate voter (see Figure 12.4, top). Consequently, fewer politicians are willing to be truly moderate and work with the other side, and those who are out of step with their party's most extreme members may find it hard to represent both constituents and party in certain regions of the country. The trend against bipartisanship in an increasingly polarized Senate led Sen. Olympia Snowe of Maine to retire in 2012 and caused Sen. John McCain of Arizona to take his fellow senators to task in a speech in defense of legislative norms in 2017 (see the *CLUES to Critical Thinking* feature in Chapter 7).[20]

THE PUSH TOWARD MODERATION Ideological purists do not always win the day, however. Obviously, if a candidate is going to win an election, he or she must appeal to more voters than does the opposing candidate. On any policy or set of policies, voters' opinions range from very liberal to very conservative; however, in the American two-party system, most voters tend to be in the middle, holding a moderate position between the two ideological extremes (see Figure 12.4, bottom). In diverse districts, the party that appeals best to the moderate and independent voters usually wins most of the votes. Thus, even though the ideologies of the parties are distinct, the pressures related to winning a majority of votes can lead both parties to campaign on the same issue positions, making

party activists the "party faithful"; the rank-and-file members who carry out the party's electioneering efforts

them look similar to voters.[21] As a result, at various times the Republicans moved from their initial opposition to join the majority of voters in supporting Social Security, Medicare, and Medicaid. Similarly, the Democrats, while wanting to expand health care coverage, did not until recently embrace a government "single-payer" plan that would necessarily cover everyone. In an age of extreme polarization such as the one in which we find ourselves today, the forces that work toward moderation are weaker than they usually are. They are weakened further by a

recent trend toward what political scientists call **negative partisanship**, the tendency to hate the other party even more than one likes one's own.[22] In an environment of negative partisanship, it is hard to find a unifying policy position because the parties are like two rival sports teams whose rabid fans can't stand each other and they don't *want* to find common ground. This is different from both polarization and hyperpartisanship because it goes beyond commitment to the party's ideological or policy positions; partisanship actually becomes part of one's personal identity.

Under normal circumstances, the parties can deal with the tension between activists and the larger body of moderates in ways other than by changing the party positions. One strategy is simply to emphasize partisan issues that are

> **negative partisanship** loyalty to a party driven by hatred of the other party

FIGURE 12.4

External and Internal Forces on the Parties

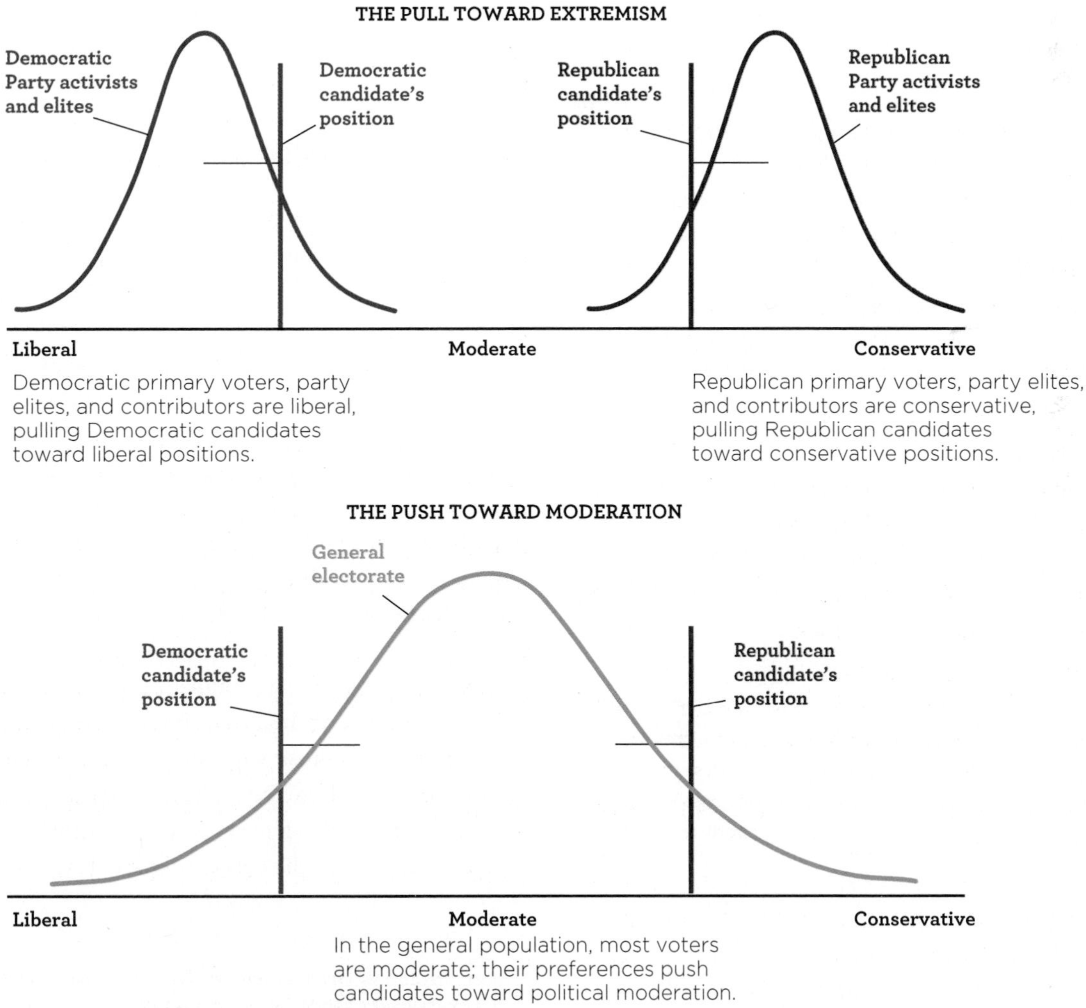

THE PULL TOWARD EXTREMISM

Democratic Party activists and elites

Democratic candidate's position

Republican candidate's position

Republican Party activists and elites

Liberal   Moderate   Conservative

Democratic primary voters, party elites, and contributors are liberal, pulling Democratic candidates toward liberal positions.

Republican primary voters, party elites, and contributors are conservative, pulling Republican candidates toward conservative positions.

THE PUSH TOWARD MODERATION

General electorate

Democratic candidate's position

Republican candidate's position

Liberal   Moderate   Conservative

In the general population, most voters are moderate; their preferences push candidates toward political moderation.

popular with moderates or to reframe the issues in ways that are palatable to more voters. In the 2004 election, George W. Bush focused on the dangers inherent in the war on terror, on which moderates favored him strongly over John Kerry; however, in 2008 and 2012 the need to appease the party base kept John McCain and Mitt Romney to the right of center for most of their campaigns. In 2008 Barack Obama appealed to moderates with his insistence that politics need not be ideological and divisive, but in 2012, after four years of partisan gridlock in Washington, he ran instead on helping the middle class, and his campaign focused on turning out the Democratic base. By 2016 we were well outside the bounds of party politics as usual. Hillary Clinton tried to find a unifying theme with her "Stronger Together" message, but she had to spend much of her time reacting to the things said and done by Donald Trump. Trump made little effort to run to the middle or to dissociate himself from the base that had given him his primary victory. Negative partisanship, for the most part, kept both parties in their lanes, but so many other variables were at work in that election that it is hard to fit it into the usual party narratives.

> **Does partisanship have to lead to divisiveness?**

PAUSE AND REVIEW Who, What, How

The rules of electoral politics create incentives for the parties to take moderate positions that appeal to the majority of voters, but party activists, primary voters, and big-money donors, who tend to be more ideological and issue oriented, pull party policy agendas back toward their extremes. As a consequence, parties and their candidates tend to remain true to their respective party's ideological perspective, promoting policy solutions that are consistent with the party's ideology. Thus Democratic candidates espouse a policy agenda that reflects the liberal interests of the coalition of groups that represent their most ardent supporters. Likewise, Republican candidates advocate a policy agenda that reflects the conservative interests of the coalition of groups that are their most ardent supporters. In this way, both parties, in most elections, offer voters "a choice, not an echo," but they also contribute to the growing partisanship of American politics. The real losers in this situation may be the party moderates and independents who, less intense and active than the party base, find themselves poorly represented at the end of the day.

In Your Own Words Explain the tension between the party base and the general electorate regarding their influence on issue positions.

THE HISTORY OF PARTIES IN AMERICA

From party machines to effective political organizations

For James Madison, parties were just an organized version of that potentially dangerous political association, the faction. He had hoped their influence on American politics would be minimal, but scarcely was the ink dry on the Constitution before the founders were organizing themselves into groups to promote their political views. In the 1790s a host of disagreements among these early American politicians led Alexander Hamilton and John Adams to organize the Federalists, the group of legislators who supported their views. Later, Thomas Jefferson and James Madison would do the same with the Democratic-Republicans. Over the course of the next decade, these organizations expanded beyond their legislative purposes to include recruiting candidates to run as members of their party for both Congress and the presidency. The primary focus, however, was on the party-in-government and not on the voters.[23]

THE EVOLUTION OF AMERICAN PARTIES

The history of political parties in the United States is dominated by ambitious politicians who have shaped their parties in order to achieve their goals.[24] Chief among those goals, as we have seen, are getting elected to office and running government once there. In 1828 Martin Van Buren and Andrew Jackson turned the Democratic Party away from a focus on the party-in-government, creating the country's first mass-based party and setting the stage for the development of the voter-oriented party machine. **Party machines** were tightly organized party systems at the state, city, and county levels that kept control of voters by getting them jobs, helping them out financially when necessary, and in fact becoming part of their lives and their communities. This mass organization was built around one principal goal: taking advantage of the expansion of voting rights to all white men (even those without property) to elect more Democratic candidates.[25] The Jacksonian Democrats enacted a number of party and government reforms designed to enhance the control of party leaders, known as

> **party machines** mass-based party systems in which parties provided services and resources to voters in exchange for votes

party bosses, over the candidates, the officeholders, and the campaigns. During the nomination process, the party bosses would choose the party's candidates for the general election. The most common means for selecting candidates was the party caucus, a special meeting of hand-picked party leaders who appointed the party's nominees. Any candidate seeking elective office (and most offices were elective) would have to win the boss's approval by pledging his loyalty to the party boss and supporting policies that the party boss favored.

Winning candidates were expected to hire only other party supporters for government positions and reward only party supporters with government contracts. This largesse expanded the range of people with a stake in the party's electoral success. The combination of candidates and people who had been given government jobs and contracts meant that the party had an army of supporters to help recruit and mobilize voters to support the party. Moreover, because party bosses controlled the nomination process, any candidate who won elective office but did not fulfill his pledges to the party boss would be replaced by someone who would. This system of patronage, which we discussed in Chapter 9 (on bureaucracy), rewarded faithful party supporters with public office, jobs, and government contracts and ensured that a party's candidates were loyal to the party or at least to the party bosses.

Because the Democratic Party machine was so effective at getting votes and controlling government, the Whig Party (1830s through 1850s), and later the Republican Party (starting in the mid-1850s), used these same techniques to organize. Party bosses and their party machines were exceptionally strong in urban areas in the East and Midwest. The urban machines, while designed to further the interests of the parties themselves, had the important democratic consequence of integrating into the political process the masses of new immigrants coming into the urban centers at the turn of the twentieth century. Because parties were so effective at mobilizing voters, the average participation rate exceeded 80 percent in most U.S. elections prior to the 1900s.

"THAT'S WHAT'S THE MATTER."

Boss Tweed. "As long as I count the Votes, what are you going to do about it? say?"

Set to Win
Party bosses, like New York City's Boss Tweed, controlled the political process and ruled the ballot box.

However, the strength of these party machines was also their weakness. In many cases, parties would do almost anything to win, including directly buying the votes of people, mobilizing new immigrants who could not speak English, and resurrecting dead people from their graves to vote in the elections. In addition, the whole system of patronage, based on doling out government jobs, contracts, and favors, came under attack by reformers in the early 1900s as representing favoritism and corruption. Political reforms such as the party primary, in which the party-in-the-electorate rather than the party bosses chose among competing party candidates for a party's nomination, and civil service reform, under which government jobs were filled on the basis of merit instead of party loyalty, did much to ensure that party machines went the way of the dinosaur.

A BRIEF HISTORY OF PARTY ERAS

A striking feature of American history is that, although we have not had a revolutionary war in America since the 1700s, we have several times changed our political course in rather dramatic ways. One of the many advantages of a democratic form of government is that dramatic changes in policy direction can be effected through the ballot box

party bosses party leaders, usually in an urban district, who exercised tight control over electioneering and patronage

patronage a system in which successful party candidates reward supporters with jobs or favors

party primary an election in which party candidates are nominated by registered party members rather than party bosses

rather than through bloody revolution. Over the course of two centuries, the two-party system in the United States has been marked by periods of relative stability lasting twenty-five to forty years, with one party tending to maintain a majority of congressional seats and controlling the presidency. These periods of stability are called **party eras**. Short periods of large-scale change—peaceful revolutions, as it were, signaled by one major **critical election** in which the majority of people shift their political allegiance from one party to another—mark the end of one party era and the beginning of another. Scholars call such a shift in party dominance a **realignment**. In these realignments the coalitions of groups supporting each of the parties change to a new alignment of groups. Though it is not always the case, realignments generally result in parallel changes in government policies, reflecting the policy agenda of each party's new coalition. Realignments have been precipitated by major critical events like the Civil War and the Great Depression. Sometimes decisive realignments are not apparent, but rather the old period of stability gradually breaks down without a critical precipitating event in a period of **dealignment**, slowly re-forming into a new and different party era. The United States has gone through six party eras in its two-hundred-years-plus history. *The Big Picture* in this chapter summarizes the six party eras and the realigning elections associated with the transitions between them.

THE PARTIES TODAY

As *The Big Picture* in this chapter indicates, the New Deal coalition supporting the fifth party era has changed, but no single critical election has marked a clear realignment. Rather, we have had an incremental realignment across a relatively long series of elections that has included the massive migration of white southerners to the Republican Party and the less massive but still notable trend for Catholics to be less solidly Democratic than they were at the formation of the New Deal. Similarly, African Americans have shifted from somewhat favoring the Democratic Party to overwhelming Democratic identification, a trend solidified with Barack Obama's nomination as the Democratic candidate for the presidency in 2008. The geographic bases of the parties have also changed: the South used to be solidly Democratic; it is now the most dependable region for the Republican Party in presidential elections. In recent elections, Democrats have been more likely to win in New England and the mid-Atlantic states—areas where the Republicans were stronger in the 1940s.

However, since the 1980s, party identification has strengthened, but along more consistent ideological and less regional lines.[26] In recent years these changes have been labeled as differences between "Red" and "Blue" America, which refers to the southern, midwestern, and mountain states (red states) support for the Republican Party set against a pattern of coastal and industrial Northeast (blue states) support for Democrats (see *Snapshot of America: How Did We Vote in the 2016 Presidential Election?* in Chapter 14).

The current party era is thus characterized by major changes that have mobilized women, African Americans, Latinos, Asian Americans, and other minorities into the Democratic Party and southern whites into the Republican Party, and a system in which neither party has a clear, enduring majority. These phenomena have led to a much higher incidence of divided government at the national and state levels, with the executive and legislative branches in the hands of different parties. Political scientist Bruce Cain speculates on possible outcomes for this party era in the *CLUES to Critical Thinking* feature at the end of the chapter.

PAUSE AND REVIEW Who, What, How

Early political leaders designed parties as elite-driven institutions that served their own interests in governing. Laws that gave the vote to all white males, however, meant that politics was less of an elite activity and inspired leaders to create the mass-based political machine. These machines continued to allow leaders total control over the party, but with the perhaps unexpected consequence of politicizing new generations of American immigrants and strengthening American democracy.

Reformers wanted more political accountability—more power for the voters and less for the party bosses. They broke the machines with civil service reform and primary elections. The American party system, though not perfect, has allowed citizens to repeatedly change their government, at times radically, without resort to violence or bloodshed.

In Your Own Words Outline the evolution of the party system in the United States.

> **party eras** extended periods of relative political stability in which one party tends to control both the presidency and Congress
>
> **critical election** an election signaling a significant change in popular allegiance from one party to another
>
> **realignment** a substantial and long-term shift in party allegiance by individuals and groups, usually resulting in a change in policy direction
>
> **dealignment** a trend among voters to identify themselves as independents rather than as members of a major party

WHAT DO PARTIES DO?

Running elections in order to control government and execute policy agendas

We have said that, in general, parties play an important role in American democracy by providing a link between citizens and government, coherence in government, and a vocal opposition. These roles are tied closely to the two main activities of parties: electioneering and governing. Generally, party organizations handle tasks related to electioneering, and the party-in-government handles tasks related to governing. In this section we look at each of these two essential party functions.

ELECTIONEERING

Electioneering involves recruiting and nominating candidates, defining policy agendas, and getting candidates elected. According to an old saying in politics, "before you can save the world, you must save your seat." One of the primary reasons for the existence of party organizations is to help candidates get and save their seats.

RECRUITING CANDIDATES Each party's electioneering activities begin months before the general election when they begin recruiting strong candidates to run. There is usually no shortage of ambitious politicians eager to run for high-profile offices like state governor and U.S. senator, but the local parties have to work hard to fill less visible and desirable elective offices like those in the state legislature and county government. It is especially difficult to recruit candidates to run against a current officeholder because incumbents, having previously assembled a winning coalition and having a name voters recognize, are hard to beat. Incumbents also tend to have a financial advantage; donors and interest groups are more likely to give money to candidates who have proven themselves by winning than to challengers who are largely untested.[27]

In response to this reality, parties focus on races they think they can win and devote their resources to those elections. Although they generally try to run candidates in most races, they will target as especially winnable those contests where the seat is open (no incumbent is running), where the

Mudslinging Back in the Fourth Party Era
Tough campaigns aren't new to American politics. During the 1896 presidential race, this very partisan novelty item attempted to show what a vote for either candidate would mean: a vote for William McKinley, "Protection to American Industries"; a vote for William Jennings Bryan, "Repudiation, Bankruptcy, and Dishonor."

incumbent is plagued by scandal or mishap, or where strong electoral indicators or trends suggest that the party has a good chance of winning the seat. The party attempts to recruit quality candidates—perhaps known community leaders—and to direct campaign contributions and aid to the targeted contests.[28] One reason the 2018 midterm elections were notable is for the extensive recruiting job Democrats did, even in districts where they did not expect to win, and the high number of Republican retirements that left seats without incumbents.

NOMINATING CANDIDATES The nomination phase is a formal process through which the party chooses a candidate for each elective office to be contested that year. The nomination phase can unite the party behind its candidates, or it can lead to division within the party among the competing factions that support different candidates and different policy agendas. Consequently the nomination phase is one of the most difficult and important tasks for the party.

Today party primaries are the dominant means for choosing candidates for congressional, statewide, state legislative, and local offices. In most states the primary election occurs three to four months prior to the general election. In these primaries, party members select their party's nominees for the

> **electioneering** the process of getting a person elected to public office

James Madison may have been suspicious of political parties, lumping them in with the dreaded "factions" that he thought were so destructive to liberty, but the fact is that they have always been with us, even in Madison's time. What has varied over time is not the tendency of Americans to form umbrella groups with their ideological fellows to try to effect political change from inside the system, but the particular configurations of those parties. This *Big Picture* shows how American parties have evolved over time and, since 1879, when data on the current parties begin, just how polarized those parties have been at various times in our history.

First Party Era

In the U.S. party system's elite-driven formative stage, the issue of federal versus states' rights provided the central political cleavage. The Federalists, supporters of a stronger national government, were led by John Adams and Alexander Hamilton, while the Democratic-Republicans (also called Jeffersonian Republicans) supported states' rights and were led by Thomas Jefferson and James Madison.

Second Party Era

Buoyed by an explosion in the number of voters—which swelled from 350,000 in 1824 to well over a million in 1828—Andrew Jackson prevailed in the bitter election of 1828, solidifying the coalition of states' rights supporters (lower classes and southern states) over those advocating more power for the national government (business interests and northern states). From the ashes of Adams's failed candidacy came a new party—the Whigs, led by Henry Clay and Daniel Webster, who competed with the Democrats until the mid-1850s.

Third Party Era

Republicans took control of the House of Representatives in 1858, and by 1860 the party's presidential candidate, Abraham Lincoln, had won the presidency as well. After the Civil War, an era of regionalism pitted Republicans (northern and western states) against Democrats (southern and pro-slavery states). Presidential elections were closely contested, but the Republicans tended to hold the edge.

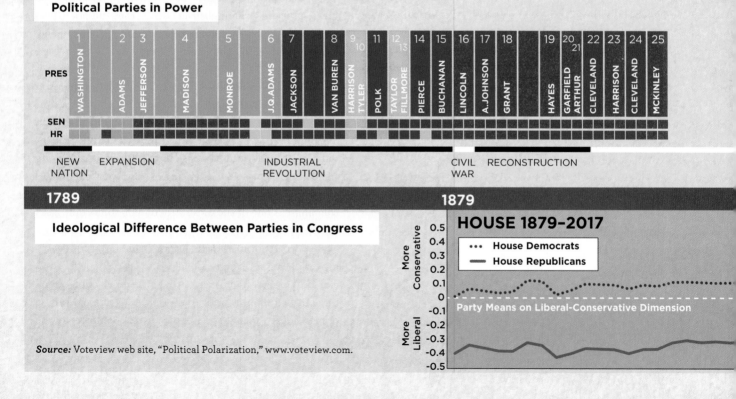

Political Parties in Power

PRES — 1 WASHINGTON — 2 ADAMS — 3 JEFFERSON — 4 MADISON — 5 MONROE — 6 J.Q.ADAMS — 7 JACKSON — 8 VAN BUREN — 9/10 HARRISON TYLER — 11 POLK — 12/13 TAYLOR FILLMORE — 14 PIERCE — 15 BUCHANAN — 16 LINCOLN — 17 A.JOHNSON — 18 GRANT — 19 HAYES — 20/21 GARFIELD ARTHUR — 22 CLEVELAND — 23 HARRISON — 24 CLEVELAND — 25 MCKINLEY

SEN
HR

NEW NATION   EXPANSION   INDUSTRIAL REVOLUTION   CIVIL WAR   RECONSTRUCTION

1789   1879

Ideological Difference Between Parties in Congress

HOUSE 1879–2017

More Conservative
0.5
0.4
0.3
0.2
0.1
0

···· House Democrats
—— House Republicans

Party Means on Liberal-Conservative Dimension

-0.1
More Liberal
-0.2
-0.3
-0.4
-0.5

Source: Voteview web site, "Political Polarization," www.voteview.com.

Fourth Party Era

Although William Jennings Bryan, a Nebraska Democrat, attempted to merge the Democratic Party with the People's Party in the presidential election of 1896, he failed to amass enough farmers and industrial labor voters to win. The splitting of votes between the People's Party and the Democrats strengthened the Republican Party. As economic issues subsided in the late 1890s, the regional bases of Republicans and Democrats intensified.

Fifth Party Era

The coalition of voters supporting the New Deal included southern Democrats, Catholic immigrants, blue-collar workers, and farmers. Republicans maintained support among business owners and industrialists, and strengthened their regional support in the Northeast and Plains states.

Sixth Party Era

While there is much controversy about whether we have entered a new partisan era at all, and no single critical election has marked the realignment, incremental changes have occurred that are large and so far long-lasting. A realigning process has mobilized African Americans and other minorities into the Democratic Party and southern whites into the Republican Party, creating a greater consistency between partisanship and ideological and issue preferences. The current era is characterized by a narrowly divided nation, intense party competition, and increased gridlock in government.

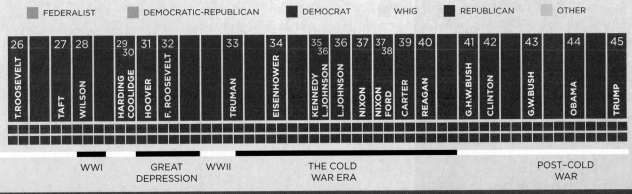

FEDERALIST   DEMOCRATIC-REPUBLICAN   DEMOCRAT   WHIG   REPUBLICAN   OTHER

| 26 | | 27 | 28 | 29 30 | 31 | 32 | | 33 | | 34 | 35 36 | 36 | 37 | 37 38 | 39 | 40 | | 41 | 42 | | 43 | | 44 | | 45 |

T. ROOSEVELT · TAFT · WILSON · HARDING COOLIDGE · HOOVER · F. ROOSEVELT · TRUMAN · EISENHOWER · KENNEDY L. JOHNSON · L. JOHNSON · NIXON · NIXON FORD · CARTER · REAGAN · G.H.W. BUSH · CLINTON · G.W. BUSH · OBAMA · TRUMP

WWI   GREAT DEPRESSION   WWII   THE COLD WAR ERA   POST–COLD WAR

2018

offices on the ballot. There are a number of different types of primaries. Generally, in a **closed primary**, only voters who have registered as a member of a given party are allowed to vote in that party's primary. In an **open primary**, voters simply request one party's ballot on the day of the primary or choose which party's primary they wish to participate in after they enter the polling booth.[29] Many party officials complain about the open primary system because it permits members of the other party to get involved in the nomination process.[30] Because voters who are not necessarily loyal to a party are allowed to vote, open primaries can weaken political parties.[31] By contrast, Vermont senator Bernie Sanders, running for the 2016 Democratic presidential nomination even though his own previous party identification was independent, argued that there should be more open primaries since the ones that allowed only Democrats to vote shut out many of his supporters.

In presidential primaries, voters do not choose the actual candidates they want to run for president; rather, they elect delegates. Delegates are usually party activists who support a candidate and run for the opportunity to go to the party's national **nominating convention** the summer before the election and cast a vote for him or her. We discuss the mechanics of presidential election nominating conventions in more detail in Chapter 14.

In addition to nominating candidates, party conventions have the important function of bringing together the party faithful to set the policy priorities of the party, to elect party officers, and, not least, to provide a sense of solidarity and community for the activists. After working long and hard all year in their communities, party activists find it rejuvenating to come together with like-minded people to affirm the principles and policies they hold in common.

The primary process and the practice of televising convention proceedings have dramatically changed the nature of these national conventions. Before reforms in the late 1960s ensured that candidates would be chosen by elected delegates rather than party bosses, national conventions were filled with political bargaining and intrigue and conflict over platform issues. Delegates going into the convention did not always know who would be the party's nominee.[32] By 1972, when many states had adopted the primary system, delegates were committed to presidential candidates before the convention began, meaning there was little question about who would get the nomination. Floor battles at the convention can still happen, however, as they did in 1980 during the late Massachusetts senator Ted Kennedy's challenge to President Jimmy Carter for the Democratic

nomination. The prospect of such a divisive move can throw party members into a panic, as it did toward the end of the primaries in 2016, when Democrats feared Bernie Sanders would take his battle for the nomination all the way to the July convention. But generally speaking, today's presidential nominating conventions merely rubber-stamp the primary victor.

Even though skirmishes between the ideological wings within both parties flare up occasionally, for the most part conventions have turned into choreographed events, designed to show, in prime time, that the party is unified behind its presidential candidate and to launch the official campaigns. In fact, conventions have generally become so routine and predictable that since 2000, to the parties' chagrin, the television networks have devoted little prime-time coverage to them, although the cable stations have picked up the slack. In 2008, however, things were a little more exciting and networks and cable stations alike showed the major convention speeches, with Obama's and McCain's acceptance speeches garnering more than 38 million viewers each.[33] Ratings were down again in 2012 and 2016, even though the 2016 Republican National Convention, reflecting the unconventional nature of its candidate, was atypical fare. Donald Trump spoke every night, as did members of his family; plagiarism charges were leveled at the campaign as parts of Melania Trump's speech about her husband appeared to have been lifted from Michelle Obama's 2008 speech about hers; and internal party dissension shook the gathering when Sen. Ted Cruz spoke and instead of endorsing Trump urged Republicans to "vote their conscience." The Democratic National Convention, by contrast, was a more typical pageant studded with political and show-business stars, in the mode of past conventions. And, despite disruptions by his supporters, Bernie Sanders endorsed Clinton. It will probably be remembered chiefly, however, for a stirring speech by a Gold Star father whose Muslim American son had lost his life in defense of his country. The father, Khizr Khan, challenged Donald Trump to read the Constitution and set off a multiday clash between the family and the Republican

closed primary a primary election in which only registered party members may vote

open primary a primary election in which eligible voters do not need to be registered party members

nominating convention the formal party gathering to choose candidates

presidential nominee over Trump's proposed ban on Muslims coming into the country.

DEFINING POLICY AGENDAS After a political party nominates its candidates, one of the party's main roles is to develop a policy agenda, which represents policies that a party's candidates agree to promote when campaigning and to pursue when governing. The development of such an agenda involves much politicking and gamesmanship as each faction of the party tries to get its views written into the party platform, which we discussed earlier. Whoever wins control over the party platform has decisive input on how the campaign proceeds. In 2016, when Sanders lost the Democratic primary, the Democratic National Committee allowed him to fill some slots on the platform committee and the resulting document reflected compromise between his policy preferences and those of nominee Hillary Clinton.

GENERAL ELECTIONS In the election phase, the role of the party changes from choosing among competing candidates within the party and developing policy agendas to getting its nominated candidates elected.

As the Bruce Cain article at the end of the chapter indicates, social media have revolutionized the ways that parties relate to their supporters (see *CLUES to Critical Thinking*). Rather than a party having to be the main source of voter education about a candidate, candidates can effectively run their own campaigns with their own staffs. Creating ads that can go viral, fundraising on the Internet, maintaining web sites, and tweeting out announcements to followers allows candidates to present themselves on their own terms rather than having everything filtered through the eyes of others. But even though candidates are less dependent on the parties for the nuts and bolts of their campaigns, voters themselves are guided more by their party affiliations, which constrains candidates from getting too far out of step from the party line.

Today's political parties primarily offer candidate services, including fundraising and training in campaign tactics, instruction on compliance with election laws, and public opinion polling and professional campaign assistance.[34]

Money, of course, is central in such a capital-intensive campaign, and the parties are major fundraising organizations.

It's a Party for the Party

The national nominating conventions have evolved into full-blown spectacles, as carefully orchestrated as a Super Bowl halftime show or the Oscars. Here, Ronald Reagan and his vice president, George H. W. Bush, stand with their wives, watching balloons drop to celebrate the end of the 1984 Republican National Convention in Dallas.

Because of a loophole in the campaign finance laws that allowed parties—but not candidates—to collect contributions of unlimited size from donors, parties became major banks for candidates in the 1990s (see Chapter 14). These unlimited funds, called **soft money**, were used by the parties for party-building efforts such as voter registration and issue development activities.[35] Both parties distributed money to candidates either by giving cash directly to them or by supplementing the campaign efforts of candidates with television and radio issue advertising. Although this issue advertising was supposed to represent an "independent" expenditure of money—candidates were not allowed to participate in the decisions about how the money was spent or to direct the content of the issue ads—in practice, there was generally much correspondence between the parties' issue ads and the candidates' campaign ads, because parties simply mimicked the ads of their candidates.

Soft money raising was seriously limited in 2002 by the Bipartisan Campaign Reform Act, or BCRA. In 2010, however, as we will see in Chapter 14, the Supreme Court fundamentally changed the financial and political landscape of electoral politics in America with its decision in *Citizens United v. Federal Elections Commission*. The Court's decision allows individuals and organizations to give unlimited amounts of money to so-called Super PACs (political action committees), which are independent of the candidates' and even the parties' campaign efforts. It means that those with deep pockets and a willingness to spend have the ability to exercise enormous influence in the electoral arena—and to do so anonymously. It is too early to gauge the full impact of

> **soft money** unregulated campaign contributions by individuals, groups, or parties that promote general election activities but do not directly support individual candidates

the decision, but legions of critics argue that the Court's *Citizens United* decision is a fundamental threat to democratic equality.[36] Getting the decision overturned became one of Bernie Sanders's signature issues in the 2016 Democratic primary.

In congressional elections, both parties spend a great deal of money on the targeted contests we discussed earlier.[37] For targeted seats, the parties supplement their issue ads by sending party leaders into the district to raise money for the candidate. This move has the added benefit of giving the candidate greater media visibility. When presidents have high popularity ratings, they are a positive campaign presence for their party's congressional candidates. If their approval ratings have fallen by the midterm, their congressional campaign appearances are more limited to fundraising events for their party's congressional candidates in closed gatherings of the party faithful with whom they typically remain a big draw. For the party that does not control the presidency, congressional leaders and presidential hopefuls (sometimes one and the same) usually fill this void.

GOVERNING

Once a party's candidates have been elected to office, attention turns to the matter of governance. **Governing** involves the two major jobs of controlling government by organizing and providing leadership for the legislative and/or executive branches and enacting the party's policy agendas. Party governance gives voters a means to make officeholders accountable for both failed and successful governing policies,[38] and it can provide an extraconstitutional framework that can lend some coherence to the fragmentation produced by separation of powers and federalism.

CONTROLLING GOVERNMENT When a party "controls" government at the national level and in the states, it means that the party determines who occupies the leadership positions in the branch of government in which the party has a majority. Thus, when Donald Trump won the presidency in 2016, he—and, by extension, the Republicans—controlled the top leadership positions in the executive branch of the government (cabinet secretaries and undersecretaries of agencies and the White House staff). The Republican Party also controlled the legislative branch. This means the Republicans selected the majority leader in the Senate and the Speaker of the House, controlled committee assignments, selected chairs of legislative committees, had a majority of seats on each committee, and generally got their way. Controlling government also means that the legislative leadership controls the legislative calendar and the rules governing legislative debate and amendments (especially in the House).

The job of party governance in Congress has been made more challenging in recent years by the increasingly frequent use of the filibuster by the minority party in the Senate to stop everything from simple nominations to fill executive agency offices and staff the federal courts to legislation with clear majority (but less than three-fifths) support in the chamber. It is much more difficult to govern with polarized parties in a system in which power is checked at almost every turn. With divided government, the job of governing becomes even more difficult for both parties.

EXECUTION OF POLICY AGENDAS AND ACCOUNTABILITY The ultimate goal of a political party is not only to choose who occupies the leadership positions in government but also to execute its policy agenda—the party's solutions to the nation's problems. Whether the problem is defined as a lack of affordable health care, insufficient national security, high taxes, distressed communities, unemployment, illegal immigration, or a failing economy, each party represents an alternative vision for how to approach and solve problems.

We have already noted that significant differences exist between the platforms and policy agendas of the two major parties. The question here is whether the parties actually implement their policy agendas. On this score, parties do

> **governing** activities directed toward controlling the distribution of political resources by providing executive and legislative leadership, enacting agendas, mobilizing support, and building coalitions

David Frum

Courtesy of FrumForum.com

David Frum is a waiter. And no, that doesn't mean the former Bush speechwriter, author of eight books and editor of the *Frum Forum,* a web site "dedicated to the modernization and renewal of the Republican party and the conservative movement,"[1] has opted for a second career in restaurant service.

According to Frum the political world is divided into two types of people: waiters and chasers.

"A waiter is somebody who has a vision of where his country is going and parks himself at that position to wait for the country. Churchill was a waiter, Reagan was a waiter, but also Lyndon LaRouche was a waiter—it's not necessarily a good thing to be a waiter . . . The chasers are those always trying to catch up to where they think the people are at that moment."

Chasers—Frum mentions Newt Gingrich, Bill Clinton, and Rush Limbaugh—adopt the values of the constituency they want to lead; waiters believe the world will eventually come around to adopting their view. It is being a waiter that enables Frum to be at once an ardent member of the Republican Party and also one of its toughest critics.

Born into a liberal Canadian family (he became a U.S. citizen in 2007), Frum moved right in college "under the impact of events." He says, "The late 1970s felt like the end of the world, the end of western civilization. . . . Then came the Reagan years and the battle to turn that situation around, and all of us young Reaganites felt that the Reagan people did a very good job of keeping us mobilized and motivated. . . ." He went on to law school at Harvard, and by the late 1980s he had become an editorial writer at the *Wall Street Journal.* It was there that he got his first taste of running counter to party orthodoxy, exploring the criticism of U.S. economic trends that it had benefited the wealthiest Americans but had left the least wealthy falling farther behind. His work on the successes and limits of the Reagan Revolution resulted in his first book, *Dead Right.*

His writing brought him to the attention of the incoming George W. Bush administration in 2000, and he was offered a job as a White House speechwriter, where he was credited with the famous "axis of evil" phrase that justified Bush's foreign policy. His willingness to criticize the administration of which he had once been a part made him a target in Republican circles, chiefly on Fox News, where the attacks got

personal. It cemented Frum's role as a waiter, a role he maintains today. Unlike some disaffected Republicans, who continue to call themselves conservative but who have left the Republican Party behind, Frum says, "I have not given up on the movement. I am not going to." Though he adds ruefully, "They may give up on me."

While he waits, here are some of his observations on American politics:

On partisanship

"It's a question about in whose interest do you govern, how do you govern, how do you solve problems, how do you work with people that disagree with you? How important is consensus? This is not a parliamentary political system, and if you try to run it like a parliamentary system, you wreck it. In a parliamentary system the government has enormous power. . . . The job of the other side is to shoot you down, embarrass you, and trip you up—but the other side of the political aisle cannot interfere with the working of the government. There's no filibuster, there's no veto, and the government governs. The other side tries to bring them down and they usually succeed, and at that point you have these very rapid alternations of power. . . .

In the congressional system, the ability to sabotage, to stop the government from governing is very great, and the American system appears to work best with a high degree of consensus. It's not that partisanship is intrinsically evil; in Britain it's fine. In Britain it's indispensable; if you didn't have intense partisanship in Britain, the government would be too strong. But in America, partisanship is a problem because the government can't govern."

On keeping the republic

"Do not entrap yourself in a closed information system. Closed information systems require the complicity of the audience because information now is so abundant that it takes great effort to avoid coming into contact with it. Political science suggests that people are working harder and harder to avoid coming into contact with unwelcome information. And as I look at the Republican Party, many of these problems are not problems of leadership but of followership and the citizens also need to work harder at their job."

Source: David Frum spoke with Christine Barbour and Gerald Wright on September 17, 2010.

1. "About," *FrumForum,* www.frumforum.com/about.

Party Chairs on the Hot Seat

Though party chairs, like Democrat Debbie Wasserman Schultz (left) and Republican Ronna Romney McDaniel (right), are lower profile than the party leaders, they are essential in recruiting candidates, fundraising, and managing internal party politics.

fairly well. The party that controls the presidency typically implements about two-thirds of its platform promises.[39]

The classic example of a party fulfilling its campaign promises was the first hundred days of the New Deal under the Democratic Party. Running on a platform that called for an activist national government, Franklin Roosevelt and the congressional Democrats were elected in a landslide in 1932. Under Roosevelt's leadership, Congress proceeded to pass New Deal legislation designed to regulate the economy and banking industry, and to provide government programs to help farmers and the unemployed. After maintaining control of Congress in 1934, the Democrats went on to pass one of the most important pieces of legislation in American history, the Social Security Act (1935). Similarly, recent presidents have been successful in passing the signature issues of their campaigns. Important examples include President George W. Bush's tax cuts and the No Child Left Behind Act, President Obama's Patient Protection and Affordable Care Act and the financial reform bill, and Trump's efforts to undo them. These were major changes in the direction of national policy.

The greater competitiveness of the parties in the current era, however, means that divided government happens much more frequently than in earlier party systems, and as we saw in Chapter 8, presidential success typically plummets when the president's party loses control of Congress. This was certainly the case for Presidents Bush, Clinton, and Obama following the midterm elections that brought them divided government for parts of their administrations. The same will probably be true for President Trump post-2018, unless he decides to work with the Democrats.

Within the context of the responsible party model, the ability of a party to accomplish its stated agenda is extremely important for voter accountability. As the party in power promotes its policy agenda and its ideas for how government should solve problems, it provides voters with an opportunity to hold the party responsible for its successes or failures. Voters then determine if a party's candidates should be rewarded through reelection or punished by "throwing the rascals out." In 1932 the persistence of the Depression convinced voters that the GOP policies had failed and led them to replace the Republicans with the Democrats and their solutions. After seeing Democrats implement the New Deal in 1933 and 1934, the voters cast their ballots to keep Roosevelt and his party in power, thus rewarding the party for its efforts to deal with the Great Depression. As we have pointed out, such clear accountability is more difficult under divided government, when voters do not know which party to hold accountable.

PAUSE AND REVIEW　Who, What, How

It is hard to imagine any actors in American politics not having a stake in the activities of electioneering and governing. For political parties, the stakes are high. They want electoral victory for their candidates and control of government. They try to achieve these goals by using the rules they themselves have created, as well as the electoral rules imposed by the state and federal governments.

Candidates seeking to get elected to office, and to build a reputation once there, engage in candidate-centered campaigns with the assistance of the party organization and the party-in-the-electorate. They also encourage the election of other members of their party.

Party activists want to gain and keep control of the party's agenda, to ensure that it continues to serve the causes they believe in. They participate in primaries and hold elected officials accountable.

Citizens value their limited government, but paradoxically they also get impatient when government seems to grind to a halt in a morass of partisan bickering. The policy efficiency and coherence that parties can create can dissolve the gridlock, but this comes at the potential cost of a more powerful government. When voters elect a divided government, gridlock is almost inevitable.

CHARACTERISTICS OF THE AMERICAN PARTY SYSTEM

Two parties, increasingly polarized and decentralized

Party systems vary tremendously around the world. In some countries, the government structure has only one major party. This single party usually maintains its power through institutional controls that forbid the development of opposition parties (totalitarian states like China and the old Soviet Union), or through corruption and informal means of physical coercion (Mexico, until recently), or through military control (Burma, Libya, and Sudan). These systems essentially prevent any meaningful party competition. Without choices at the ballot box, democracy is impossible. Some countries, by contrast, have so many parties that often no single party can amass enough votes to control government. When that happens, the parties may try to cooperate with other parties, governing together as a coalition. Parties can represent ideological positions, social classes, or even more informal group interests. Parties can put tight constraints on what elected leaders can do, making them toe the "party line," or they can give only loose instructions that leaders can obey as they please. The truth is, there is no single model of party government.

Among all the possibilities, the American party system is distinctive, but it too fails to fit a single model. It is predominantly a two-party system, although third-party movements have come and gone throughout our history. For decades, political scientists observed that the American system tended toward ideological moderation, at least compared with other multiple-party countries. However, the parties have changed and today they are at least as far apart ideologically as they have been at any point in our long national history. This polarization has grown in a highly decentralized party system with fluctuating levels of party discipline. We explore each of these characteristics in this section.

TWO PARTIES

As we have seen, the United States has a two-party system. Throughout most of the United States' history, in fact, two specific parties, the Democrats and the Republicans, have been the only parties with a viable chance of winning the vast majority of elective offices. As a consequence, officeholders representing these two parties dominate the governing process.

WHY A TWO-PARTY SYSTEM? The United States—along with countries like Great Britain and New Zealand—stands in sharp contrast to other democratic party systems around the world, such as those found in Sweden, France, Israel, and Italy, which have three, four, five, or more major political parties, respectively. The United States has experienced few of the serious political splits—stemming from such divisive issues as language, religion, or social conflict—that are usually responsible for multiple parties. The lack of multiple deep and enduring cleavages among the American people is reinforced by the longevity of the Democratic and Republican Parties themselves. Both parties predate the Industrial Revolution, the urbanization and suburbanization of the population, and the rise of the information age, and they have weathered several wars, including the Civil War and two world wars, as well as numerous economic recessions and depressions. One scholar compared each party to a "massive geological formation composed of different strata, with each representing a constituency or group added to the party in one political era and then subordinated to new strata produced in subsequent political eras." Proponents from one era may continue to support a political party even if it undergoes changes in issue positions. These political parties persist not just because of the support they can attract today but also because of the accumulation of support over time.[40]

But the most important reason the United States maintains a two-party system is that the rules of the system, in most cases designed by members of the two parties themselves, make it very difficult for third parties to do well on a permanent basis.[41] As we saw in Chapter 4, for instance, democracies that have some form of proportional representation are more likely to have multiple parties. These governments distribute seats in the legislature to parties by virtue of the proportion of votes that each party receives in the election. For example, if a party receives 20 percent of the vote, it will receive roughly 20 percent of the seats in the legislature. Countries with proportional representation systems have more parties than do those with single-member plurality-vote systems, because small parties can still participate in government even though they do not get a majority of the votes. In the United States, in contrast, we use the single-member-district electoral system. This means that the candidate who receives the most votes in a defined district (generally with only one seat) wins that seat, and the loser gets nothing, except perhaps some campaign debt. This type of winner-take-all system creates strong incentives for voters to cast their ballots for one of the two established parties because voters know they are

George Frey/Getty Images

Never Trump

Donald Trump's surprising victory in the Republican primary race led to the rise of "Never Trumpers," Republicans opposed to their party's nominee and his brash, norm-breaking style. Perhaps most prominent of these was Evan McMullin, who launched an independent bid for the presidency and spoke out against Trump throughout the 2016 campaign. Although McMullin claimed 21 percent of the vote in his home state of Utah, he was unable to break through nationwide.

effectively throwing away their votes when they vote for a third-party candidate.

The United States has other legal barriers that reinforce the two-party system. In most states, legislators from both parties have created election laws that regulate each major party's activities, but these laws also protect the parties from competition from other parties. For example, state election laws ensure the place of both major parties on the ballot and make it difficult for third parties to gain ballot access. Many states require that potential independent or third-party candidates gather a large number of signature petitions before their names can be placed on the ballot. Another common state law requires a third party to have earned some minimum percentage of the votes in the previous election before it can conduct a primary to select its candidate.

Third parties are also hampered by existing federal election laws. These laws regulate the amount of campaign contributions that presidential candidates can receive from individuals and PACs and provide dollar-for-dollar federal matching money for both major parties' presidential campaigns, if the candidates agree to limit their spending to a predetermined amount. However, third-party candidates cannot claim federal campaign funds until after the election is over, and even then their funds are limited by the percentage of past and current votes they received. As an additional hurdle, they need to have gained about 5 percent or more of the national vote in order to be eligible for federal funds.[42] Access to the national media can also be a problem for third parties. Even though regulations are in place to ensure that the broadcast media give candidates equal access to the airwaves, Congress has insisted on a special exception that allows participation in televised debates to be limited to candidates from the two major parties, and the Debate Commission requires candidates to reach 15 percent in the polls before they are invited. Consequently, Libertarian Gary Johnson, Green Party candidate Jill Stein, and independent Evan McMullin were unable to participate in 2016.

THIRD-PARTY MOVEMENTS Just because the Democrats and the Republicans have dominated our party system does not mean that they have gone unchallenged. Over the years, numerous third-party movements have tried to alter the partisan make-up of American politics. These parties have usually arisen either to represent specific issues that the parties failed to address, like Prohibition in 1869, or to promote ideas that were not part of the ideological spectrum covered by the existing parties, like socialist parties, never very popular here, or the Libertarian Party. In general, third parties have sprung up from the grassroots or have broken off from an existing party (the latter are referred to as splinter parties). In the case of the current Tea Party movement, the new party is not actually distinct from the Republican Party (most Tea Party members identify themselves as conservative Republicans), and as long as the Republican Party adopts most of the issues the Tea Partiers care about, they are not likely to separate and form an organized party of their own. In many cases, third parties have been headed up by a strong leader who carries much of the momentum for the party's success on his or her own shoulders (for example, Teddy Roosevelt, George Wallace, and Ross Perot).

Third parties can have a dramatic impact on presidential election outcomes. When the winning margins are large, third parties may be merely a blip on the screen, but when the electorate is narrowly divided, the presence of third-party candidates is fraught with peril for Democrats and Republicans. When Ralph Nader ran in 2000, as a Green Party member, some joked that GREEN stood for "Get Republicans Elected Every November." Did Ralph Nader cost Al Gore the election? Perhaps he did, but that oversimplifies a complex event. As one analyst put it, Nader undoubtedly cost Gore many votes, but Pat Buchanan's Reform Party candidacy cost Bush as well. Although Buchanan won only 450,000 votes overall, had he not been in the race, Bush arguably could have won narrow victories in Iowa, New Mexico, Oregon, and Wisconsin, and won the Electoral College without the help of Florida.[43] The 2016 election was so close it is entirely likely that candidacies by Johnson and Stein may have had an impact at the margin. Third-party challenges are not just a lose-lose proposition for the major parties, however. In an effort to prevent third parties from taking crucial support away from them, many major-party candidates, as we saw earlier, try to appropriate their issues, thereby broadening their base of support. Although third parties are in most cases short lived, they nonetheless fill a significant role in the American party system.

> **Are the American people well represented by a two-party system?**

INCREASING IDEOLOGICAL POLARIZATION

Compared to many other party systems—for instance, India, the global leader in political parties, which in 2015 had at least 1,866 registered partisan groups—the United States has traditionally had a rather limited menu of viable parties: the moderately liberal Democratic Party versus a moderately conservative Republican Party. Both parties continue to agree on the fundamental features of American politics—including the Bill of Rights, the Constitution, and a capitalist free-enterprise system—but the policy differences between the parties have grown. Rather than the 1950s characterization of the parties as "Tweedledum and Tweedledee," today there stands, as we saw in Chapter 2, an ideological gulf between the parties on a host of central issues of the economy, the distribution of the nation's resources, and the role of government in our private lives. As much as ever in our history, the Democratic Party holds that government policy should actively promote the welfare of the middle class and the poor, largely by extending the enlarged role of the state that defined the New Deal. Today's Republicans, in contrast, want to greatly reduce the role of government in the market and let individual initiative and the workings of unfettered capitalism settle questions of resource allocation while giving the states a stronger role in legislating conformance to "traditional family values." The result is a country that has consensus on the fundamentals of government structure but with parties that are divided sharply over the role of government in the economy and our lives.

DECENTRALIZED PARTY ORGANIZATIONS

In American political parties, local and state party organizations make their own decisions. They have affiliations with the national party organization but no obligations to obey its dictates other than by selecting delegates to the national convention. Decision making is dispersed across the organization rather than centralized at the national level; power tends to move from the bottom up instead of from the top down. This means that local concerns and politics dominate the lower levels of the party, molding its structure, politics, and policy agendas. Local parties and candidates can have a highly distinctive character and may look very different from the state or national parties. Political scientists refer to this as a fragmented party organization.

American parties are organized (or disorganized) into several major divisions spread across the national, state, and local levels. Most visible are the national committees, the Republican National Committee (RNC) and the Democratic National Committee (DNC). They are responsible for taking care of the national parties' business between their national presidential nominating conventions. They provide a good deal of campaign support and fundraising assistance, especially to presidential candidates. After these are the congressional campaign committees, one for each party in the House and in the Senate, which are responsible for trying to elect party members with the goal of keeping or gaining party control.

At the subnational level are state and local party organizations. Since the 1970s the state organizations have become more professionally organized and staffed, providing increased levels of support, often with funds from the national committees. Increasingly, the state legislative leaders have what are called "leadership PACs," which they use to gather funds from activists and interest groups and funnel those into competitive contests in their efforts to gain partisan majorities in the state legislatures. Finally, there are local party organizations, which are generally much weaker, often existing only on a part-time basis staffed by volunteers. The local organizations have such a structure because the vast majority of local elections, like those for city councils and school boards, are nonpartisan.[44] The decentralized character of American parties means that the national organization does not have financial or, especially, ideological control of the state and local organizations. This makes it possible for new factions within the parties to capture local and then state organizations as a base for influencing the directions of the parties more generally. Consider, for example, the successful efforts of the Christian Right in the Republican Party in the late 1980s. Building on dedicated local volunteers and church networks, the movement established itself as a powerful force in the Republican Party nationally. The Tea Party movement today, with its Freedom Caucus in Congress, is attempting to follow a similar strategy, although national media attention helps it focus its efforts at nonlocal levels as well.

The consequences of decentralization can also be seen in the occasional frustration of national officials when an embarrassing candidate is able to pull off a primary victory.

BIPARTISANSHIP

Among many examples is David Duke, a former Ku Klux Klan member who ran for governor of Louisiana in 1991 and for the state's senator in 2016. Donald Trump ran in a crowded field in 2016 and pulled off the nomination and the presidency against the interests and desires of the party establishment. Without centralized control they were limited in their efforts to stop him. Usually, in these cases, the embarrassing candidate just loses and is forgotten.

The biggest reason for the fragmentation of control of American parties is federalism and political reforms like the direct primary. All of our candidates, even the president and vice president, are elected in state (or local) elections that are to some extent governed by state laws. Thus members of the state legislatures and Congress are attached primarily to the state parties that constitute much of the electoral base. Of course, even their ability to run depends on their surviving the local context of contested district or state primary elections, and the national parties have at best only indirect influence on these.

Decentralization, however, does not mean that local parties are necessarily different from their national counterparts. Consider the possible effect of party activists. Although their influence means that the base may control the leadership (decentralization), rather than the other way around, power may be less fragmented as the base strengthens its hold on the entire party. The more conservative base of the Republican Party has long had greater control at the local level, but national Republican policy was tempered by the need to get along with Democrats in Congress and to appeal to the moderate voter in national elections. When the party took control of Congress in 1994, however, members of Congress were better able to impose their more ideological perspective at the upper levels of the party.

CHANGES IN PARTY DISCIPLINE OVER TIME

Historically, American party organizations have been notable for their lack of a hierarchical (top-down) power structure, and the officials elected to government from the two parties have not felt compelled to take their orders from the top. This looseness within the parties was a continuing source of frustration for the advocates of the responsible party model of government. They wished for greater **party discipline**— the ability of party leaders to keep members voting together in a cohesive way—which was more typical of European parliamentary parties. This lack of party unity among legislators in the United States reflected the diversity of opinions within the parties, among both activists and rank-and-file identifiers. We have seen, however, that significant changes have occurred in the parties' base coalitions, especially in the movement of southern conservatives from the Democratic to the Republican Party. This shift, with similar but less dramatic ideological alignment in the non-southern states, has resulted in a party system in which we have greater ideological agreement within the parties and greater ideological distance between them.

These changes in the electoral environment of Congress have helped create the conditions for greatly heightened partisanship in Congress. One factor is simply the greater ideological agreement within the parties coupled with an increased (and seemingly increasing) ideological gulf between the parties. This is reinforced by stronger party leadership made possible by rules changes in the House of Representatives in the 1970s.[45] For example, in 2006, Democrat Nancy Pelosi became the first woman Speaker of the House and led the Democrats with a firm and expert hand. She gained a reputation among some as "one of the most powerful Speakers in modern history."[46] Pelosi's ability to lead the House Democrats and to pass President Obama's program was made possible by the increased ideological homogeneity within the Democratic Party that is an important aspect of the polarized political parties of the contemporary era.[47] The Republican victories in 2010 made John Boehner, of Ohio, the new Speaker of the House. His freshman class was largely supported by the Tea Party movement (now known as the Freedom Caucus), and their energy and unbending commitment to conservative principles repeatedly made it difficult for Boehner to reach compromises with his Democratic colleagues or the Obama administration, frequently causing him to back off

> **party discipline** the ability of party leaders to bring party members in the legislature into line with the party program

of positions he had taken to keep his party base happy.[48] He finally quit in frustration in 2015 and was replaced by Paul Ryan, of Wisconsin, who himself decided to resign the post in 2018.

PAUSE AND REVIEW Who, What, How

The United States' two-party system is a direct result of, first, the kind of electoral system that the founders designed and, second, the rules that lawmakers in the two parties have put into place to make it difficult for third parties to thrive. This does not stop the drive for third parties, however, when dissatisfied voters seek representation of ideas and issues that the two major parties do not address.

The American parties are, in general, ideologically moderate. Activists want parties to take more extreme stances and to act on their principles. Voting in primaries has enabled them to pull the parties in a more extreme, but also more disciplined, direction. The losers here are the general voting public, who cannot always find a moderate alternative to vote for.

In Your Own Words Describe how the American party system works.

THE CITIZENS AND POLITICAL PARTIES

*Learning to tolerate
the messiness of democracy*

We began this chapter by noting that, for all their importance to the success of democracy, political parties have been perennially unpopular with the public. Scholars tell us that one reason for this unpopularity is that voters are turned off by partisan bickering and each party's absorption with its own ideological agenda instead of a concern for the public interest.[49] In this section we suggest the possibility that politics is about bickering, and that bickering may itself be a major safeguard of American democracy.

We defined politics at the start of this book as the struggle over who gets what and how they get it in society, a process that involves cooperation, bargaining, compromise, and trade-offs. We remarked at the outset that Americans often see politics as a dirty business, but that it is really our saving grace since it allows us to resolve conflict without violence. The difficulty is that Americans do not see politics as our saving grace. Perhaps we have enjoyed relative domestic tranquility for so long that we do not know what it is like to have to take our disagreements to the streets and the battlefields to resolve them. Some researchers have found that

when Americans look at government, they do not focus primarily on the policy outcomes but on the political process itself. Although policies themselves are increasingly complex and difficult to grasp, most of us are able to understand the ways in which the policies are created, the give and take, the influence of organized interests, and the rules of the game. In other words, finding the what of politics to be complicated, most citizens focus their attention and evaluation on the how. We are not helped out here by the media, which, rather than explaining the substance of policy debate to American citizens, instead treat politics like one long, bitterly contested sporting event. With the nearly unlimited challenges and opportunities that our mediated world presents, parties are in some ways overshadowed by a host of other political forces that we allow into our lives and are also extremely vulnerable to being manipulated by those outside forces, as the Russian attack on our electoral system made clear.

Given citizen dissatisfaction with partisan politics in America, where do we go from here? What is the citizen's role in all this, if it is not to stand on the sidelines and be cynical about partisan politics? Political scientists John Hibbing and Elizabeth Theiss-Morse argue that the problem lies with a lack of citizen education—education not about the facts of American government but about the process. "Citizens' big failure," they claim, "is that they lack an appreciation for the ugliness of democracy."[50] Democratic politics is messy by definition; it is authoritarian government that is neat, tidy, and efficient. Perhaps the first thing we as citizens should do is to recognize that partisanship is not a failure of politics; it is the heart of politics.

At the beginning of this chapter, we said there were three ways in which parties enhanced democracy in America. We have given considerable attention to the first two: the linkage between citizen and government and the coherence among the branches of government that parties can provide. The third way parties serve democracy is in providing for a vocal opposition, an adversarial voice that scrutinizes and critiques the opposite side, helping to keep the process and the people involved honest. This is akin to the watchdog function the media are said to serve, but it is more institutionalized, a self-monitoring process that keeps both parties on their toes. To be sure, this self-monitoring certainly can, and does, deteriorate into some of the uglier aspects of American democracy, but it also serves as the guardian of political freedom. Where such partisan squabbling is not allowed, political choice and democratic accountability cannot survive either.

There are three things citizens can do to offset their frustration with the partisan course of American politics:

- **Get real.** Having realistic expectations of the process of democratic government can certainly help head off disillusionment when those expectations are not met.
- **Get involved.** Parties, because of their decentralized nature, are one of the places in American politics to which citizens have easy access. The only reason the more extreme ideologues hold sway in American politics is that the rest of us allow them to, by leaving the reins in their hands.

- **Don't split your ticket.** If you are truly disturbed by what you see as government paralysis, try voting for a straight party ticket. Even if you vary the party from election to election, you will be able to hold the party accountable for government's performance.

In Your Own Words   Give examples of how parties serve (or fail to serve) citizens in American politics.

LET'S REVISIT: *What's at Stake . . . ?*

We began this chapter by looking at the way two outside candidates had an outsized impact on the 2016 election results. Bernie Sanders helped weaken Hillary Clinton in ways she was unable to recover from, and Donald Trump decimated his primary field and ended up winning the presidency. That's a lot of power for people outside a party establishment to leverage—clearly both candidates spoke to something in the electorate that the establishment candidates missed. We asked what was at stake when outside candidates take on the establishment.

For the parties, the answer is clearly, a lot. That's why party machines thrived—they could keep an iron check on insurrection, and the establishment *was* the party. Democratic reforms of the party system helped rid the parties of corruption, made them more transparent and democratic, but also rendered them more fragile, more open to the influence of outside challengers. That's why, even though open primaries can help recruit new members, parties are cautious about them, and why the Democrats, despite having dispatched the party machines that kept them in power in so many places, have continued to allow the establishment to put its thumb on the scale.

For the Democratic Party, the Sanders campaign opened up a schism that had long simmered beneath the surface but had been relatively quiet since the Bill Clinton years—a division between those who sought more radical economic transformation to overturn the existing power structure and those who were focused on more incremental change to expand rights and economic security. Those who take the former view argue that Democrats have forgotten their roots as supporters of the working class and have instead become a detached party of intellectual and entertainment elites. More moderate Democrats argue that the way to get things done is by working closer to the middle and trying to find compromise solutions that bring Americans together. Hidden in this split is a disagreement about whether economic transformation would bring with it racial and gender equality or whether those problems are systemic and must be addressed as such. On this point, too, Bernie Sanders and Hillary Clinton

disagreed, with Clinton focusing much more on race and diversity, and perhaps further alienating the white working class who felt ignored by the party.

Those divisions in the Democratic Party, which have been quiet for several decades, are likely to be more explosive now that Sanders supporters are blaming Hillary Clinton for the loss of an election they think their candidate would have won. (Since no one seriously ran against Sanders, we can't know how that hypothetical match would have turned out.) But it is difficult to respond simultaneously to white working-class constituencies who feel some degree of racial grievance, and communities of color who have been one of the stalwart supporters of the party.

For the Republican Party, the stakes of the Trump election are mixed. On the one hand, they won! Republicans of all stripes are thrilled to be in charge of two branches of government, with the prospect of cementing their control over the third. On the other hand, few Republicans wanted Trump to be their nominee. They don't want the racial and gender baggage he brings with him. And they know that a long-term breach with Hispanics is bad for the party given the changing national demographics. Their agenda is not Trump's agenda, and they can only hope that he doesn't care enough to challenge them on the policies they want to pass. However, Trump doesn't think he owes the party anything (and in most respects, he's right), so he probably feels little obligation to play nice if his will conflicts with theirs. Trump's electoral behavior would not indicate that playing nice is one of his strengths, and the party is likely to be the loser if conflict ensues.

At the same time, the Trump election is a distraction from the party's internal divisions that it's been struggling to resolve. As we saw in Chapter 2, the Republican Party houses both procedural economic conservatives and more substantive social conservatives, and their preferred policies are not the same. Some of the social conservatives are the white working class that chose Trump as the nominee and voted for his election—possibly some of the same people who supported Bernie Sanders, since we know that Hillary Clinton lost some white working-class support to Trump. Clearly those internal divisions are not harming the party's existence now, and if the

GOP hangs on to state legislatures in 2020 and continues to gerrymander its way to a secure congressional majority, they may not in the future.

But the Republican Party is a party that has lost the popular vote in six of the last seven presidential elections. Only the vagaries of the Electoral College have given them the presidencies in two of those elections. If their goal is to build an enduring majority, they need to follow the advice of their 2012 "autopsy" report to be more inclusive,

something a Trump presidency so far does not seem to have in the cards.

The stakes in outside infiltration of parties clearly vary by party. For voters, it can open up more choices. But for a system that depends on two strong parties to work, it carries risks of weakening the parties internally, or undermining their agendas altogether. Our history shows that the parties have survived worse threats, but we are certainly in challenging times today.

---

⑤SAGE edge™
for CQ Press

Want a better grade?

Get the tools you need to sharpen your study skills. **SAGE edge** offers practice quizzes, eFlashcards, video, and multimedia at **edge.sagepub.com/barbour9e.**

CLUES to Critical Thinking

"The Trump Precedent: The Future of Political Parties in Three Movements"

By Bruce E. Cain, *The American Interest*, May 21, 2018

The presidency of Donald Trump has provided political scientists with puzzles to solve, and his very unpredictability means that political scientists are not in agreement on what his presidency means. Here Bruce Cain, a Stanford political scientist, picks three possible impacts that Trump could have on our party system.

Assuming that the current political situation reflects something deeper about our current politics, what will our democracy look like in the future?

No U.S. political leader in recent memory has stirred quite as much concern about the health of the U.S. political system as Donald Trump. Of course, his administration may eventually prove to be just a one-off episode in the United States' history, a fluky, non-replicable byproduct of populist backlash and the Electoral College. But it is also possible that Trump's ascent signifies something more fundamental than that, a harbinger of impending party realignment or a major shift in the way politics is conducted. In the words of

Buffalo Springfield, "There's something happening here. What it is ain't exactly clear."

Count me as one who is sure that there are deeper issues at play but unsure as to how they will actually play out in the long run. The biggest surprise to me is not Donald Trump the man. He revealed himself to us many years ago. I was more astonished that the Republican Party would acquiesce so meekly to policies that blatantly contradict conservative principles of fiscal restraint, free trade, and residual Cold War opposition to Russia.

That they have done so raises lots of TBD questions. Has the Republican Party actually changed its policy orientation, or is it temporarily going along with the President in order to avoid internal strife? To what extent is the weakness of the Republican Congressional leaders a reflection of the strength of the underlying ideological tensions in the party's coalition? And are the Democrats headed in a similar direction, splitting between progressive and moderate wings and united only in opposition to all things Republican?

Assuming for the moment that the current political situation actually reflects something deeper about our current politics and is not just the temporary chaos caused by one unusual political figure, where might this lead us? I think that it could go in three different directions.

The first is the usual story of American politics in transition: Party coalitions are shifting as they have in the past, but the American political party system will retain its same duopolistic form and function. The education, racial, and gender divide sharpens over time with women and college grads continuing to migrate towards the Democrats while Republicans solidify their appeal to rural and exurban whites.

Donald Trump gets political credit for spotting the opportunity to garner the support of those who feel left behind by automation, free trade and competition from immigrant labor. But to turn this into a permanent realignment, the Republicans will eventually need to figure out how to deliver some tangible returns to the downwardly mobile segment of Trump's base constituency.

In this scenario, there is no radical break from two-party politics. All the coalitional movement takes place within the existing party structures.

Efforts to create a third party will most likely be quickly extinguished by the single member simple plurality electoral system and the deeply embedded accumulation of other rules that favor the current duopoly (e.g. anti-fusion laws, high ballot access thresholds, sore loser prohibitions, etc.). The only real hope for a third party to gain a foothold would be if the white nationalist base could become regionally concentrated and therefore dominant in some section of the country such as the interior mountain or plains states. But even then, the odds are against any party that bases its appeal on a population that is dwindling due to prevailing demographic trends.

A second direction our party system could take is a more serious departure from politics as usual based on changes in the way we communicate and organize politically. Perhaps President Trump's populism is not just about particular economic and racial resentments, but represents a fundamental shift in the way we conduct politics.

There is nothing new about a populist leader whipping up fervor in the base to consolidate political power and pursue a particular policy agenda, but in the past it required capturing, owning or suppressing the traditional media. Now the traditional media are fading and are increasingly replaced by social media

and the internet. Capturing the entire media space is unnecessarily inefficient. It is more expedient to target messages through social media to a winning coalition of supporters. Big data and the internet enable a much greater capacity to communicate directly with the blocs of voters you need support from. Voters can be identified and mobilized much more easily than ever before. Governing coalitions could thus arise and fade more quickly behind emerging political entrepreneurs. The party duopoly would no longer be necessary and would be replaced by a more fluid and responsive politics.

This may seem implausible at first glance, but it is consistent with certain modern trends. In recent decades, referendums and initiatives have been on the rise in mature democracies. The UK made its momentous decision to withdraw from the European Union based on a vote of the people. The Five Star Party in Italy has emerged out of nowhere to become a governing party by means of an internet platform. Perhaps traditional institutionalized parties will fade and be replaced by direct democracy hybrids.

Unlike the first scenario, this second one involves not just movement across coalitional boundaries, but a radical transformation in the form and function of the party system as a whole. While there is some plausibility to this scenario, there are many reasons to think that it could fail to fully develop. Parties arose because it was necessary to coordinate voters and office holders in order to win elections and govern successfully. Time will tell whether the Five Star party can govern and hold itself together. The notion that "the people" have the time, energy, motivation and knowledge to govern effectively has to date proven illusory.

I am more inclined to think that U.S. politics is headed down a third path where we retain the duopoly form and the essential intermediating function of political parties, but the party as organization moves into the largely unregulated internet space. The history of U.S. political reform is that political activity gravitates into the areas of least legal resistance. This is no clearer example of that principle than campaign finance reform. We imposed stricter restrictions on campaign donations after Watergate, and it eventually gave rise to PACs, independent spending, and now Super PACs. We passed disclosure regulations, and big money found safer ground in nonprofit 501c4s. We tried to offset private campaign money with public subsidies, but the restrictions proved too burdensome, and presidential candidates now avoid the public finance system entirely.

In this third scenario, the Democratic and Republican parties are still dominant and favored in many ways by state and federal laws. But the political parties continue the present trend of morphing into networks of party affiliated groups that spend "independently" on behalf of candidates. Outside groups and social media figures with large followings enforce party discipline rather than Congressional leaders.

This might work effectively as a strategy for forging a winning electoral coalition, but will it lead to effective government? The latter requires aggregating separate interests into some collective consensus. Log-rolling is the politically easiest way to aggregate, but it is not always possible and can lead to disjointed, inconsistent,

and excessively costly policies in the end. Bargaining to compromise is better, but harder to do unless there are strong pressures to participate and make concessions. If we are headed toward a politics dominated by a loose coalition of affiliated groups, then where will the centripetal forces that can bind the party coalition in office together come from?

The rhetoric of populism focuses on the swamp of inside players and elected officials. The reality of achieving effective governance may increasingly reside with outside groups. Navigating that civil society morass might prove even more difficult than working in the DC swamp.

Source: Cain, Bruce E., "The Trump Precedent: The Future of Political Parties in Three Movements," By Bruce E. Cain, The American Interest, May 21, 2018. Reprinted with permission from the author.

Consider the source and the audience: Cain is writing in *The American Interest*, a moderately conservative journal that deals mostly with global and international affairs. Of course global affairs are deeply impacted by what the United States and its leaders do. Who is Cain talking to here and what kinds of information is he trying to provide?

Lay out the argument and the underlying values and assumptions: Why does Cain think the American party system is on the verge or in the midst of major change? What role does Trump play in this, and what role the Republican Party? Cain is not so much making a single argument here, as positing that one of three scenarios is likely to happen: the Republicans have narrowed their base to a dwindling population and the two party system limps along; Trump forms a populist movement that transforms politics and the two party system itself becomes defunct; or the two parties continue in some version of their current form, co-opting public space that is not already regulated to expand their power. How does he see the media influencing the outcome?

Uncover the evidence: Although Cain provides three possibilities here, he thinks that one is more likely than the other two. Why is that? Is that conclusion based on hard evidence or his suppositions? What are those suppositions? Do you agree with his concerns about effective governance?

Evaluate the conclusion: Cain thinks that the most likely impression the Trump phenomenon will leave on the two party system is to leave it similar in form but controlled by outside forces. Do you agree with his reasons for discarding his first two possibilities? Are there any possibilities he has overlooked?

Sort out the political implications: Suppose that Cain is right and that the two major parties, instead of being the compromising, cooperating institutions John McCain hopes for in the Chapter 7 *CLUES to Critical Thinking*, become tools of wealthy outside groups. What does that mean for democracy? Is this a form of pluralism or has it gone too far? What would Madison say?

Review

Why Political Parties?

Political parties make a major contribution to American government by linking citizens and government, overcoming some of the fragmentation of government that separation of powers and federalism can produce, and creating an articulate opposition.

political party (p. 407)

political gridlock (p. 407)

partisanship (p. 408)

party organization (p. 409)

party-in-government (p. 409)

party-in-the-electorate (p. 409)

party identification (p. 409)

party base (p. 410)

responsible party model (p. 410)

Do American Parties Offer Voters a Choice?

American political parties offer the average voter a choice in terms of ideology, membership, and policy positions (platform). The differences may not always be evident, however, because electoral forces create incentives for parties to take moderate positions, pushing the parties together. At the same time, party activists who are committed to the values and policies of a particular party play a key role in drawing the parties apart and keeping them ideologically distinct.

partisan sorting (p. 412)

hyperpartisanship (p. 412)

party platform (p. 412)

party activists (p. 416)

negative partisanship (p. 417)

The History of Parties in America

American history reveals six party eras. These are periods of political stability when one party has a majority of congressional seats and controls the presidency. A realignment, or new era, occurs when a different party assumes control of government. Party politics today may be undergoing both a realignment and a dealignment, resulting in greater numbers of voters identifying themselves as independents.

party machines (p. 418)

party bosses (p. 419)

patronage (p. 419)

party primary (p. 419)

party eras (p. 420)

critical election (p. 420)

realignment (p. 420)

dealignment (p. 420)

What Do Parties Do?

The two primary activities of parties are electioneering (getting candidates elected) and governing (all the activities related to enacting party policy agendas in government).

electioneering (p. 421)

closed primary (p. 424)

open primary (p. 424)

nominating convention (p. 424)

soft money (p. 425)

governing (p. 426)

Characteristics of the American Party System

America's two-party system is relatively moderate, decentralized, and increasingly disciplined. The rules are designed to make it hard for third parties to break in, but numerous third-party movements have arisen at different times to challenge the two dominant parties.

party discipline (p. 432)

The Citizens and Political Parties

Although most Americans dislike the partisan bickering that characterizes politics in the United States, those disagreements are a central part of a functioning democracy.

13
INTEREST GROUPS

In Your Own Words

After you've read this chapter, you will be able to

13.1 Explain how and why interest groups form.

13.2 Identify four types of interest groups and the kinds of interests they represent.

13.3 Describe how interest groups use lobbying and campaign activities to get the public policy they want.

13.4 Identify specific resources that interest groups bring to bear when attempting to influence public policy.

13.5 Summarize the relationships among citizens, interest groups, and government.

What's at Stake . . . When Business Groups Face Off Against Public Interest Groups?

WHAT DID THE CHICKEN that laid your breakfast egg have for its breakfast? Was your hamburger once on drugs? And just what is the pedigree of the french fries you ate at lunch? Do you care? Some people do. Those who worry about eating vegetables that have been grown with the aid of pesticides or chemical fertilizers, or meat from animals that were given hormones or antibiotics, or who are concerned about the environmental effects of such practices, form part of a growing number of consumers who look for the label *organic* before they buy food. One estimate says that Americans spent more than $45.2 billion on organic foods in 2017.[1]

What does it mean to be organic? Once upon a time there was no standardized definition, so states, localities, and private agencies were free to define organic as they wished. Usually the standards were stringent. For example, many

Organic or Not?

What makes a food organic, and who gets to decide? Organic farming is now big business, and small changes in the definition of organic can mean the gain or loss of millions of dollars.

groups required organic farmers to use land on which no artificial or synthetic fertilizers, pesticides, or herbicides had been used for five years. Such farming techniques favored the small, committed organic farmer and were difficult for large agribusinesses to apply.[2]

In an effort to eliminate the patchwork of local regulations and to assure consumers that organic food purchased anywhere in the country was equally safe, groups representing the organic food industry repeatedly asked the U.S. Department of Agriculture (USDA) to nationalize standards. When the USDA revealed its standardized definition of organic, however, it was a definition traditional organic farmers and consumers didn't recognize. USDA standards proposed in December 1997 would have allowed the use of genetic engineering, irradiation, antibiotics and

hormones, and sewage sludge—techniques that run directly counter to the values of organic farming—in the production of foods to be labeled organic. Though strongly supported by the conventional food manufacturers—known in the media as Big Agriculture—and the developers of biotechnology, these standards were bitterly opposed by the organic food industry and its consumers.

Before they issue new regulations, however, all federal agencies must give interested parties and the public the opportunity to be heard. In the battle to win USDA support, the conventional food industry and the food preparers associations had—and used—all the resources of big business; at the time the organic food industry had none of those. Searching for another strategy for influencing the enormous bureaucracy of the USDA, they began a grassroots lobbying campaign, encouraging consumers to write to the USDA objecting to the new standards. Natural food stores posted information and distributed fliers on the proposed regulation, and Horizon Organic Dairy used the back panels of its milk cartons to pass on the information and urge consumer action.[3]

The campaign was successful. The USDA received nearly 300,000 letters and emails opposing the proposal. Even Congress went on record against it.[4] The result was that Secretary of Agriculture Dan Glickman eliminated the provision allowing genetic engineering, crop irradiation, and the use of sewage sludge as fertilizer. Said Glickman, "Democracy will work. We will listen to the comments and will, I am sure, make modifications to the rule."[5]

Depending on where you stand, the moral of this story varies. It might be a David-and-Goliath success, or just a quirky tale about a handful of food fanatics. What is really at stake in the issue of which groups have power in shaping the policymaking process? **«**

FRENCH observer Alexis de Tocqueville, traveling in America in the early 1830s, noted a peculiar (he thought) tendency of Americans to join forces with their friends, neighbors, and colleagues. He said, "Americans of all ages, all conditions, and all dispositions, constantly form associations. They have not only commercial and manufacturing companies, in which all take part, but associations of a thousand other kinds—religious, moral, serious, futile, general or restricted, enormous or diminutive."[6] And that was *before* the invention of social media! Today we are connected in ways Tocqueville could not have imagined, instantly able to locate likeminded people, and translate those associations into activity. As the *Snapshot of America: How Many of Us Belong, and to What?* shows, Americans are indeed among the top "joiners" in the world.

Tocqueville's remarks did not refer specifically to political groups, but James Madison noted the American propensity to form political associations, or what he called factions. As we saw in Chapter 3, Madison defined a **faction** as a group of citizens united by some common passion or interest, and opposed to the rights of other citizens or to the interests of the whole community.[7] He feared that factions would weaken and destabilize a republic, but he also believed, as he argued in *Federalist* No. 10 (see the *CLUES to Critical Thinking* feature at the end of the chapter), that a large republic could contain

> **faction** a group of citizens united by some common passion or interest and opposed to the rights of other citizens or to the interests of the whole community

the effects of factions by making it hard for potential members to find one another and by providing for so many potential political groups that, if they did find each other and organize, their very numbers would cancel each other out.

Modern political scientists have a different take on factions, which they call by the more neutral term *interest groups*. An **interest group** (like the agribusiness and organic food groups in *What's at Stake . . . ?*) is an organization of individuals who share a common political goal and unite for the purpose of influencing public policy decisions.[8] (Parties, as we noted in Chapter 12, also seek to influence policy, but they do so by sponsoring candidates in elections and running governments.) The one major difference between this definition and Madison's is that many political scientists do not believe that all interest groups are opposed to the broad public interest. Rather, they hold that interest groups can play an important role in our democracy, ensuring that the views of organized interests are heard in the governing process.[9] That is, interest groups are an essential part of the "who" in our formulation of politics as who gets what and how. Interest groups play a central role in the pluralist theory of democracy, which argues that democracy is enhanced when citizens' interests are represented through group membership. The group interaction ensures that members' interests are represented but also that no group can become too powerful.

Although they have long existed, interest groups, unlike political parties, were not a major force in American politics until the beginning of the twentieth century. When the Progressive reformers at the turn of the century opened up the political process to the people, political parties were weakened and interest groups were correspondingly strengthened. By the 1960s, Washington, D.C., was awash in interest group activity as the federal government continued to expand its New Deal and Great Society programs,[10] and the growth has continued to the present day.

The increase in the number of interest groups accelerated after 1971, when the Federal Election Campaign Act was passed in an effort to curb campaign spending abuses. Seeking to regulate the amount of money an interest group could give to candidates for federal office, the law provided for **political action committees (PACs)** to serve as fundraisers for interest groups. As we will see later in this chapter, PACs are limited in how much money they can donate to a candidate, but a number of loopholes allow them to get around some of the restrictions. Recent court cases have allowed the existence of what are called **Super PACs**, which can spend unlimited amounts of money on a candidate's behalf but are not allowed to coordinate with the candidate's campaign.[11] Many PACs are creatures of interest groups, but others are independent and act as interest groups in their own right. PACs have become extremely powerful players in American politics, typically contributing a substantial portion of candidates' campaign funds, although the role of Super PACs remains controversial. The question of just how much campaign money should be supplied by outside groups and to what extent it obligates candidates to do the groups' bidding became an issue in the 2016 primaries.

The explosion of interest group activity has probably caused Madison and the other founders to roll over in their graves. After all, Madison believed that he had secured the republic against what he called the "mischiefs of faction." He could not have envisioned a day when mass transportation and communication systems would virtually shrink the large size of the republic that he had believed would isolate interest groups. In today's world, dairy farmers in Wisconsin can easily form associations with dairy farmers in Pennsylvania; coal producers in the East can organize with coal producers in the Midwest; citrus growers in Florida can plan political strategy with citrus growers in California. Nor would Madison have foreseen the development of the Internet, which allows hundreds of thousands of people to organize and to voice their concerns to their representatives almost instantaneously.

Critics argue that interest groups have too much power, that they unduly influence officials who want their financial support, that they don't effectively represent the interests of groups that don't organize (the poor, the homeless, or the young, for instance), and that they clog up the vital arteries of American democracy, leading to gridlock and stagnation.[12] Supporters echo Madison's pluralist hopes—that group politics can preserve political stability by containing and regulating conflict and by providing checks on any one group's power—and they argue that interest groups have a positive role to play in the democratic process. The two narratives about the power of interest groups routinely battle it out in American electoral politics, but the truth is that neither party can really afford to ignore them.

THE FORMATION AND ROLE OF INTEREST GROUPS

Organizing around common political goals to influence policy from outside the apparatus of government

Whether we approve or disapprove of the heavy presence of interest groups in the United States, it is undeniable that they

---

interest group an organization of individuals who share a common political goal and unite for the purpose of influencing government decisions

political action committees (PACs) the fundraising arms of interest groups

Super PACs special PACs that can spend unlimited amounts of money on a candidate's behalf but are not allowed to coordinate their efforts with those of the candidate's campaign

Snapshot of America: *How Many of Us Belong, and to What?*

Kinds of Groups American Adults Are Active In

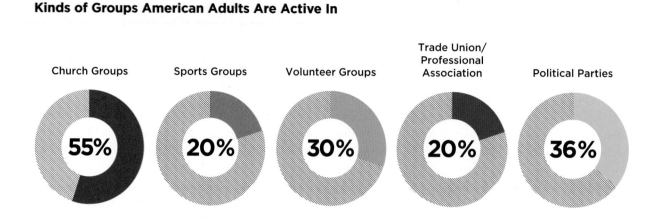

Church Groups	Sports Groups	Volunteer Groups	Trade Union/ Professional Association	Political Parties
55%	20%	30%	20%	36%

How Americans Are Asked to Take Part in Civic Actions

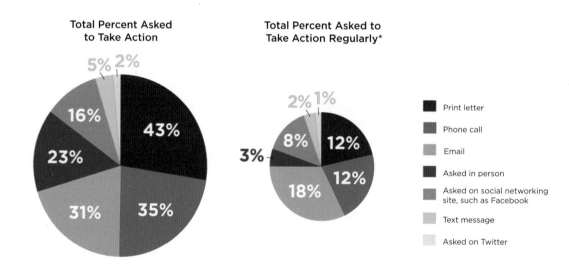

Total Percent Asked to Take Action

5% 2%
16%
23%
43%
31% 35%

Total Percent Asked to Take Action Regularly*

2% 1%
3% 8% 12%
18% 12%

- ■ Print letter
- ■ Phone call
- ■ Email
- ■ Asked in person
- ■ Asked on social networking site, such as Facebook
- ■ Text message
- ■ Asked on Twitter

*Regularly defined as daily, every few days, or once a week

Behind the Numbers

Americans are active in groups. And about half of those asked were contacted via Internet or social media. Notice the wide range of types of groups we join. What sorts of issues or controversies might cause the members of each of these groups to become active in local, state, or even national politics?

Source: General Social Survey, 2014. Calculated by the authors; Pew Research Center, Civic Engagement in the Digital Age, April 25, 2013, www.pewinternet.org/2013/04/25/civic-engagement-in-the-digital-age/.

play a significant role in determining who gets what in American politics. In this section we look at why interest groups form in the first place and the various political roles that they play.

WHY DO PEOPLE JOIN GROUPS?

Most of us are aware of public problems that we think need to be addressed—everything from potholes that need filling to streets that are too dark at night to tuition that is too high to glaciers that are melting. But despite our country's reputation as a nation of joiners, most of us never act to solve a problem, never organize a group, and never even join one. Social scientists call this a **collective action problem**: the difficulty in getting people to work together to achieve a common goal when the solution is costly and no one individual has an incentive to use resources to make it happen. Collective action problems usually involve a **collective good**, that is, a good or benefit that, once provided, cannot be denied to others. Safe roads, public safety, better education, and the sustainability of the planet are all examples of collective goods that once produced can be enjoyed by anyone. When collective goods are involved, it is difficult to persuade people to join groups because they are going to reap the benefits anyway. These folks are called **free riders**: people who refuse to spend time, money, or effort on the collective solution because they can reap the benefits whether they join or not.[13] The larger the number of potential members involved, the more this holds true, because each will have trouble seeing that his or her efforts will make a difference.

The problem of collective action can be overcome, in part, by the shared perception of a serious common problem or threat, an abundance of time and money to support a cause, and effective leadership.

COMMON PROBLEM OR THREAT Most interest groups seem to be organized around shared interests, but many people who share interests never come together at all. One noted scholar believes the key triggering mechanism for interest group formation is a disturbance in the political, social, or economic environment that threatens the members of a group—for instance, government action to regulate businesses and professions.[14] This threat alerts the group's members that they need to organize to protect their interests through political action. Often, the formation of one group to promote a particular interest is seen as the threat that triggers the formation of a group on the opposite side.

RESOURCE ADVANTAGE Researchers have long observed that some interest groups organize more easily than others even absent an external threat.[15] The resources available to prospective interest group members seem to be the key. Those with more money can pay for the web sites, social media campaigns, publicity, legal assistance, and professional lobbying that get the message to Washington and the public that the group means business. Perhaps just as important, those with greater resources are more likely to understand the political process, to have the confidence to express their views, and to appreciate the value of organizing into an interest group to push their policy positions.[16] All of this means that individuals with more wealth and more knowledge of the political system have a natural advantage in using the interest group process to pursue their policy goals, and it helps explain why there are so few groups to represent the homeless, welfare recipients, and the unemployed.

EFFECTIVE LEADERSHIP Effective and charismatic leaders can also help spur the formation of an interest group. The strong, effective leadership of what one scholar has called interest group entrepreneurs can be crucial to a group's ability to organize, no matter what its resources are.[17] These entrepreneurs have a number of important characteristics, among them that they shoulder much of the initial burden and costs of organizing the group, and that they can convince people that the interest group will be able to promote the group's interests and influence the policies that affect it.[18] Such inspirational leaders have included Cesar Chavez, who organized the United Farm Workers; Ralph Nader, who began a number of consumer interest groups; and Candy Lightner, who established Mothers Against Drunk Driving (MADD).

SELECTIVE INCENTIVES External threats, financial resources, and effective leadership can spur interest group formation, but they are usually not enough to overcome what we earlier called the problem of collective action. Groups frequently use **selective incentives**—different kinds of benefits available to their members that are not available to the general population—as an inducement to get people to join.[19] These incentives include material benefits, solidary benefits, and expressive benefits.

---

collective action problem the difficulty in getting people to work together to achieve a common goal when the solution is costly and no one individual has an incentive to use resources to make it happen

collective good a good or service that, by its very nature, cannot be denied to anyone who wants to consume it

free riders people who refuse to spend time, money, or effort on the collective solution because they can reap the benefits whether they join or not

selective incentives benefits that are available only to group members as an inducement to get them to join

Courtesy of Sylvan Mishima Brackett; Peko Peko Japanese. Illustration by James Montgomery Flagg via Library of Congress

Tasty Benefits

Slow Food USA is an interest group that represents people who want to preserve local, authentic ways of growing and preparing food. The organization holds local and international events dedicated to eating regionally, seasonally, and convivially. These events serve as selective incentives to attract new members.

- **Material benefits** are tangible rewards that members can use. One of the most common material benefits is information. For example, many groups publish a magazine or a newsletter packed with information about issues important to the group and pending legislation relevant to the group's activities. In addition to information, interest groups often offer material benefits in the form of group activities, group benefit policies, or gifts. The National Rifle Association (NRA) sponsors hunting and shooting competitions and offers discounted insurance policies. The Sierra Club offers a package of benefits that includes over 300 nature treks throughout the United States. The Arbor Day Foundation gives members ten free trees when they join.

- **Solidary benefits** come from interaction and bonding among group members. For many individuals, politics is an enjoyable activity, and the social interactions occurring through group activities provide high levels of satisfaction and, thus, are a strong motivating force. Solidary incentives can come from local chapter meetings, lobbying missions to Washington or the state capital, or group-sponsored activities. The significant point is that the interest group provides the venue through which friendships are made and social interactions occur.

- **Expressive benefits** are those rewards that come from doing something that you strongly believe in, from affiliating yourself with a purpose to which you are deeply committed—essentially from the expression of your values and interests. Many people, for example, are attracted to the American Civil Liberties Union (ACLU) because they believe passionately in protecting individual civil liberties. People who join the National Right to Life Committee believe strongly in making all abortions illegal in the United States. Their membership in the group is a way of expressing their views and ideals.

Group leaders often use a mixture of incentives to recruit and sustain members. Thus the NRA recruits many of its members because they are committed to the cause of protecting an individual's right to bear arms. The NRA reinforces this expressive incentive with material incentives like its magazine and with solidary incentives resulting from group fellowship. The combination of these incentives helps make the NRA one of the strongest interest groups in Washington, D.C.

> **Does it distort democracy for interest groups to bring different resources to the political process?**

ROLES OF INTEREST GROUPS

As Madison guessed, interest groups have become an integral part of American politics, but as we suggested earlier, many observers of American politics disagree with his verdict that they are a curse upon the system, to be contained and neutralized. In this section we go beyond the negative stereotypes of interest groups to discuss the important roles they play in political representation, participation, education, agenda building, provision of program alternatives, and program monitoring.[20]

> **material benefits** selective incentives in the form of tangible rewards
>
> **solidary benefits** selective incentives related to the interaction and bonding among group members
>
> **expressive benefits** selective incentives that derive from the opportunity to express values and beliefs and to be committed to a greater cause

- **Representation.** It's entirely possible that the most important thing about you is not where you live, and yet congressional representation pretty much sticks to our interests as they are related to the place we call home. Interest groups help represent their members' views to Congress, the executive branch, and administrative agencies on a whole host of other dimensions. Whether they represent teachers, manufacturers of baby food, people concerned with the environment, or the elderly, interest groups ensure that their members' concerns are adequately heard in the policymaking process. The activity of persuading policymakers to support their members' positions is called **lobbying**. Lobbying is the central activity of interest groups and, as we will see, it encompasses a variety of ways of bringing pressure to bear on government.

- **Participation.** Like our representation, opportunities for participation in government are limited by the Constitution. Interest groups provide an avenue for citizen participation in politics that goes beyond voting in periodic elections. They are a mechanism for people who share the same interests or who are pursuing the same policy goals to pool resources and channel their efforts for collective action. Whereas individual political action might seem futile, participation in the group can be much more effective.

- **Education.** One of the more important functions of interest groups is to educate policymakers regarding issues that are important to the interest group, and then to educate their members about the issues that are important to them. Members of Congress must deal with many issues and generally cannot hope to become experts on all of them. Consequently they often find themselves legislating about matters where they have scant knowledge. Interest groups can fill this void by providing details in hearings and briefings on issues about which they are often the experts. In addition, sometimes interest groups must educate their members about new laws or developments on important issues that may affect them. Accordingly, they maintain web sites, social media, and mailing lists that allow them to inform their members of relevant news and call them to action when necessary.

- **Agenda building.** The issues that Congress, the executive branch, or administrative agencies will address constitute an informal political agenda. Interest groups work to get the issues they care about onto that agenda and to make them a high priority for action.

- **Provision of program alternatives.** Once issues have been put on the agenda, interest groups can supply alternative suggestions for how they should be dealt with. From this mix of proposals, political actors choose a solution.[21]

- **Program monitoring.** Once laws are enacted, interest groups keep tabs on their consequences, informing Congress and the regulatory agencies about the effects, both expected and unexpected, of federal policy.[22] Program monitoring helps the government decide whether to continue or change a policy, and it also helps to keep politicians accountable by ensuring that someone is paying attention to what they do.

PAUSE AND REVIEW Who, What, How

If all of the benefits of interest group membership are collective goods, then potential members may free ride on the efforts of others while still enjoying the product of the group's success. Thus forming an interest group and persuading people to join is a challenge, eased by external threats, resources, charismatic leadership, and selective incentives. Interest groups may have any number of goals, but they primarily want to influence policy. To accomplish this goal, they employ representation, participation, education, agenda building, alternative policy proposals, and program monitoring. Several of these functions enhance the opportunities for citizens to be represented and to participate in their own governance.

In Your Own Words Explain how and why interest groups form.

TYPES OF INTEREST GROUPS

Organizing around shared interests, passions, and identities

There are potentially as many interest groups in America as there are interests, which is to say the possibilities are unlimited. Therefore, it is helpful to divide them into different types, based on the kind of benefit they seek for their members. Here we distinguish among economic, equal opportunity, public, and government (both foreign and domestic) interest groups. Depending on the definitions they use, scholars have come up with different schemes for classifying interest groups, so do not be too surprised if you come across these groups with different labels at various times.

ECONOMIC INTEREST GROUPS

Economic interest groups seek to influence government for the economic benefit of their members. Generally these are players in the productive and professional activities of the

---

lobbying interest group activities aimed at persuading policymakers to support the group's positions

economic interest groups groups that organize to influence government policy for the economic benefit of their members

nation—businesses, unions, other occupational associations, agriculturalists, and so on. The economic benefits they seek may be higher wages for a group or an industry, lower tax rates, bigger government subsidies, or more favorable regulations. What all economic interest groups have in common is that they are focused primarily on pocketbook issues.

CORPORATIONS AND BUSINESS ASSOCIATIONS

Given that government plays a key role in regulating the economy and defining the ground rules for economic competition, it should not surprise us that 70 percent of all the interest groups that have their own lobbies in Washington, D.C., or hire professionals there, are business related.[23] Corporations and business groups, which have huge stakes in the outcome of the economic-policymaking process and spend heavily to influence it, are the most numerous and the most powerful of all interest groups (see Figure 13.1). An example of what this means in practical terms is Wall Street's average spending of $1.5 million a day to influence the implementation of the Dodd-Frank Wall Street Reform and Consumer Protection Act (passed in 2010).[24] Those expenditures continued and were a powerful reason that Trump eased some of the Dodd-Frank restrictions in 2018. The primary issues that these interest groups pursue involve taxes, labor, and regulatory issues. However, business interests have also been active in the areas of education, welfare reform, and health insurance.

Economic interest groups may be corporations like BP or Monsanto, which lobby government directly. More than six hundred corporations keep full-time Washington offices to deal with government relations, and that doesn't count the companies that hire out this function to independent lobbyists, or whose attempts to influence policy are made in cooperation with other businesses.[25] Such cooperation may take the form of industry associations, like the Tobacco Institute, the American Sportfishing Association, or the National Frozen Pizza Institute. At a more general level, businesses may join together in associations like the National Association of Manufacturers or the Business Roundtable, representing major corporations.[26] The most diverse of these major business lobbies is the Chamber of Commerce, which represents a whole host of businesses (over three million) ranging from small mom-and-pop stores to large employers.[27]

Increasingly in the post–*Citizens United* world, rich individuals are spending politically—either on behalf of the industries that made them rich or for pet causes they have come to support. Billionaires like the brothers who own Koch Industries have spent millions themselves or through various foundations to fight environmental regulation and to fuel the anti-establishment wing of the Republican Party, and the Robert Mercer family has poured millions into conservative causes. Tom Steyer and George Soros are their liberal counterparts—hugely rich men who spend freely, not necessarily to influence specific policies but to put a government into power that will gratefully support their policy stances.

UNIONS AND PROFESSIONAL ASSOCIATIONS

Interest groups often organize in response to one another. The business groups we just discussed organized not only as a way to deal with the increased regulatory powers of the federal government but also because labor was organized. Although labor organizations do not represent the force in society that they once did (membership has declined dramatically since the early 1950s, when over 35 million workers were unionized),[28] they can still be a formidable power when they decide to influence government, especially at the state level. The American Federation of Labor–Congress of Industrial Organizations (AFL-CIO) is by far the largest American union organization, with 12.5 million members from fifty-five trade and industrial unions.[29] In 2005, the year of the AFL-CIO's fiftieth anniversary, two of its most influential member unions, the Brotherhood of Teamsters and Service Employees International Union, left the AFL-CIO with two other unions, depriving the organization of one-third of its members.[30] The United Auto Workers and the United Mine Workers of America also represent major segments of the labor force.[31]

Public employees are another large segment of America's union-represented workforce. The American Federation of Government Employees represents federal workers, while the American Federation of State, County and Municipal Employees represents workers at lower levels of government. Teachers, firefighters, police, and postal workers, among others, also have large unions that wield significant influence on matters of policy in their particular areas of interest. In recent years, however, public employee unions have taken a hit as Republican governors like Wisconsin's Scott Walker have targeted them as part of a budget-cutting strategy. Because unions have been a legendary force in organizing and getting out the vote for the Democrats, the Republican restrictions on public unions have had the side benefit (for them) of reducing Democratic resources as well as cutting the budget. The resulting reduction in union power was demonstrated in June 2012, when a recall election failed to remove Walker from power.[32] A 2018 Supreme Court decision refusing to make public union dues mandatory will weaken unions even further.[33]

Unions are not the only organizations to represent economic interests along occupational lines. Many occupations that require much training or education have formed professional associations. Their basic purposes are to protect the profession's interests and to promote policies that enhance its position. For example, the American Medical Association has lobbied vigorously to lower the amount of medical malpractice awards.[34] The American Bar Association not only represents

FIGURE 13.1

Contributions to Political Parties, by Economic Sector, 2014

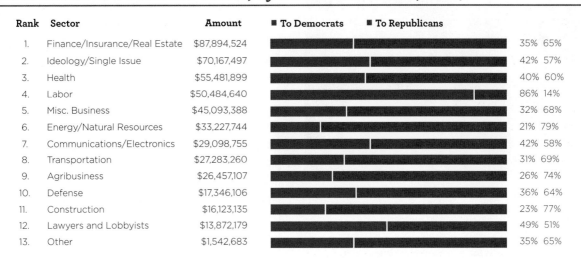

Rank	Sector	Amount	To Democrats	To Republicans
1.	Finance/Insurance/Real Estate	$87,894,524	35%	65%
2.	Ideology/Single Issue	$70,167,497	42%	57%
3.	Health	$55,481,899	40%	60%
4.	Labor	$50,484,640	86%	14%
5.	Misc. Business	$45,093,388	32%	68%
6.	Energy/Natural Resources	$33,227,744	21%	79%
7.	Communications/Electronics	$29,098,755	42%	58%
8.	Transportation	$27,283,260	31%	69%
9.	Agribusiness	$26,457,107	26%	74%
10.	Defense	$17,346,106	36%	64%
11.	Construction	$16,123,135	23%	77%
12.	Lawyers and Lobbyists	$13,872,179	49%	51%
13.	Other	$1,542,683	35%	65%

Which economic sectors are financing our elected officials? This figure shows how much different sectors of the economy are contributing to which political parties. Although contributions do not necessarily guarantee politicians' votes or support, they certainly let politicians know what issues their political friends are concerned about. Notice that the finance/insurance/real estate sector outspends any other group by a wide margin. What is this likely to mean when issues of financial reform or consumer protection legislation are considered?

Source: Center for Responsive Politics, "PACs by Industry," www.opensecrets.org/pacs/list.php.

attorneys' interests (as do groups like the Association of Trial Lawyers of America) but, over the years, also has actively promoted structural and procedural reforms of the courts.

AGRICULTURAL INTEREST GROUPS Farming occupies an unusual place in American labor politics. It is the one occupation on which everyone in the nation depends for food, but it is also the one most subject to the vagaries of climate and other forces beyond human control. To keep farmers in business and the nation's food supply at affordable levels, the U.S. government has long regulated and subsidized agriculture. Consequently, although less than 2 percent of the U.S. workforce is involved in farming, a large network of interest groups has grown up over the years to pursue policies favorable to agriculture. These include the American Farm Bureau, the largest national organization representing farmers, and other groups like the American Agriculture Movement and the National Farmers Union, which represents the interests of small-scale farmers.[35]

The agricultural community has evolved over the years to include agribusiness interests ranging from growers' associations (wheat, corn, fruit) to large multinational corporations like Archer Daniels Midland (a major grain processor), the Altria Group (which includes Philip Morris, other tobacco and cigarette companies, and a wine maker), and Conagra Brands. These agribusiness interests are not very different from the corporate interests we discussed earlier, even though their business is agriculture.

EQUAL OPPORTUNITY INTEREST GROUPS

Equal opportunity interest groups organize to promote the civil rights of groups that do not believe their members' interests are being adequately represented and protected in national politics through traditional means. These groups also advocate for their members because, in many cases, they are economically disadvantaged or are at risk of becoming so. Equal opportunity groups believe that their members are underrepresented not because of what they do but because of who they are. They may be the victims of discrimination or see themselves as threatened. These groups have organized on the basis of age, race, ethnic group, gender, or sexual orientation. Membership is not limited to people who are part of the demographic group because many people believe that promoting the interests and rights of various groups in society is in the broader interest of all. For this reason, some scholars classify these groups as public interest groups, a type we explore in the next section.

Because their members often feel that they have been marginalized by and excluded from the system, they may seek to

---

equal opportunity interest groups groups that organize to promote the civil and economic rights of underrepresented or disadvantaged groups

March Like a Girl

The election of Donald Trump, despite allegations of sexual misconduct, inspired a series of Women's Marches around the world. Held the day after Trump's inauguration, the marches drew millions of people worldwide. They are part of a renewed push for equality for women.

influence policy by going around traditional channels and using less conventional means like protests, sit-ins, and demonstrations. As we will see toward the end of this chapter, just recently, Black Lives Matter protests, demonstrations in support of young undocumented immigrants who were brought to the country when they were children, the Women's Marches, and the social media #MeToo protest have become powerful social movements that policy makers pay close attention to because they energize so many voters.

> ### Are there ways to get people to pay for collective goods?

AGE One of the fastest-growing segments of the U.S. population is composed of people aged sixty-five and older, as we saw in Chapter 2. Established in 1961, the American Association of Retired Persons (now known simply as AARP) has a membership of nearly 38 million Americans, more than one-half of all Americans over fifty years old. Despite its original name, ironically, almost half of AARP's members still work.[36] Why does a group that claims to represent retired Americans have so many workers? Because a mere $16 a year is all it takes to become a member of AARP and to enjoy its numerous material benefits, like reduced health insurance rates and travel discounts.

With the motto of "Leave No Child Behind," the Children's Defense Fund (CDF) is strikingly different from AARP, and not just in the ages of those it represents. The CDF is funded from foundation grants and private donations. Indeed, because its constituents are not adults, it does not have any formal members. To combat this, the CDF regularly holds media events in

which it issues reports and displays the results of its sponsored research. Through these media events, the CDF hopes to draw the public's attention to the plight of children in poverty and to enhance the public's support for programs that address their needs.[37] The CDF does not have the support of a legion of dues-paying members to get its proposed legislation passed. Supporters of children's rights and well-being suggest that this lack of effective advocates is precisely the reason that children are the largest group in the United States living in poverty.

RACE AND ETHNICITY Many equal opportunity groups promote the interests of racial or ethnic minorities. While newer groups like Black Lives Matter are in the headlines more often, none can match the longevity and success of the National Association for the Advancement of Colored People (NAACP). Founded in 1909 in response to race riots in Springfield, Illinois (the home of Abraham Lincoln), the NAACP has had a long history of fighting segregation and promoting the cause of equal opportunity and civil rights for African Americans. Its Legal Defense and Educational Fund is responsible for litigating most of the precedent-setting civil rights cases, including the famous *Brown v. Board of Education*. (See Chapter 6 for details on the struggle for equal rights.) Today the NAACP is by far the largest race-based equal opportunity group, with a membership of over 500,000.[38]

Many other equal opportunity interest groups are similar to the NAACP but focus on the civil rights of other races or ethnic minorities. The League of United Latin American Citizens (LULAC) has worked for over ninety years to advocate the rights of Hispanics in the United States with respect to issues such as education, employment, voter registration, and housing.[39] The Mexican American Legal Defense and Educational Fund (MALDEF) is dedicated to the protection of Latinos in the United States, working through the courts and the legislatures on issues of language, immigration, employment, and education.[40] The National Council of La Raza has focused on immigration reform since 1968.

In a similar vein, the American Indian Movement (AIM) has promoted and protected the interests of Native Americans since the late 1960s. Founded on a philosophy of self-determination, AIM has worked to support legal rights, educational opportunities, youth services, job training, and other programs designed to eliminate the exploitation and oppression of Native Americans.[41] Likewise, numerous groups represent the concerns of Asian Americans. For example, the Southeast Asia Resource Action Center (SEARAC) is an umbrella organization coordinating the efforts of several networks supporting Asian Americans. SEARAC is a national and regional advocate for Cambodian, Laotian, and Vietnamese Americans on public policies concerning health care, economic growth, civil rights, and increased political participation.[42]

GENDER Issues dealing with the equal treatment of women are a major feature of the American political landscape. Among women's groups, the National Organization for Women (NOW) is the largest, with over 500,000 members nationwide.[43] Funded by membership dues, NOW maintains an active lobbying effort in Washington and in many state capitals, builds coalitions with other women's rights groups, and conducts leadership training for its members. NOW has been a lightning rod for controversy among women because of its strong support for women's reproductive rights. Other groups that have drawn fire for having a feminist ideological agenda include EMILY's List, which stands for Early Money Is Like Yeast (it makes the dough rise). EMILY's List is a PAC that contributes money to Democratic women candidates.

Whereas NOW and groups like EMILY's List have ties to liberal interests, other groups, like the National Women's Political Caucus, have sprung up to support the efforts of all women to be elected to public office, no matter what their partisan affiliation. Still others are conservative. For every group like NOW or EMILY's List, there is a conservative counterpart that actively opposes most, if not all, of what is seen as a liberal feminist agenda. For instance, Republican women have formed WISH (Women in the Senate and House). Other prominent conservative women's group are the Eagle Forum, which since 1972 has campaigned against reproductive rights, the Equal Rights Amendment, and the societal trend of women working outside the home; and the Susan B. Anthony List, which supports antiabortion candidates.[44]

In addition to these women's groups, there are groups that promote equal opportunity for men. The American Coalition for Fathers and Children, for example, formed around the issue of promoting divorced men's custodial rights.[45] The men's groups pale in comparison, however, to the women's groups when it comes to funding, membership, and national exposure.

SEXUAL ORIENTATION With the sexual revolution of the late 1960s and early 1970s, a number of gay and lesbian groups formed to fight discriminatory laws and practices based on sexual orientation. Their activities represent a two-tier approach to advocating equal opportunities for gays and lesbians. First, there is a focus on local and state governments to pass local ordinances or state laws protecting the civil rights of gays and lesbians. Groups that have made efforts at the local and state levels include the Gay and Lesbian Activists Alliance, which has been active in the mid-Atlantic states around Washington, D.C., since 1971,

Paul Zimmerman/Getty Images For EMILY's List

Raising the Bar, and the Money
Elizabeth Warren, Ellen Malcolm, Debbie Stabenow, Deborah Roos, Tammy Duckworth, Katie McGinty, Jeanne Shaheen and Val Demmings attend EMILY's List Breaking Through Gala in 2016. EMILY's List is a gender-equality-focused interest group that works toward a very specific goal: to encourage—both socially and financially—women to run for public office.

and the GLBTQ Legal Advocates & Defenders (GLAD), a group composed of individuals from New England. On the national level, groups like the National LGBTQ Task Force and the Human Rights Campaign tend to focus their efforts on opposing federal policies that are intolerant of gays and lesbians (for example, exclusion of gays and lesbians from the military or a constitutional amendment to ban gay marriage) and on promoting funding for AIDS research.

While most gay and lesbian groups are officially nonpartisan, many have close ties to the Democratic Party. To promote gay and lesbian issues within the Republican Party, activists within the GOP have formed groups like the Log Cabin Republicans and the now-defunct GOProud to provide campaign contributions to GOP candidates who support equal opportunity for gays and lesbians, and to lobby Republican representatives and senators on gay and lesbian issues.[46]

PUBLIC INTEREST GROUPS

Public interest groups try to influence government to produce noneconomic benefits that cannot be restricted to the interest groups' members or denied to any member of the general public. The benefits of clean air, for instance, are available to all, not just the members of the environmental group that fought for them. In a way, all interest group benefits are collective goods that all members of the group can enjoy, but public interest groups seek collective goods that are open to all members of society or, in some cases, the entire world.

Public interest group members are usually motivated by a view of the world that they think everyone would be better off to adopt. They believe that the benefit they seek is good for

> **public interest groups** groups that organize to influence government to produce collective goods or services that benefit the general public

AP Photo/Matt Rourke

Activism for Animals
People for the Ethical Treatment of Animals (PETA) promotes animal welfare and a vegan lifestyle, often with attention-grabbing stunts, including locking activists in cages outside a fur coat store in Philadelphia.

everyone, even if individuals outside their group may disagree or even reject the benefit. Few people would dispute the value of clean air, peace, and the protection of human rights internationally, but no such consensus exists about protecting the right to an abortion, or the right to carry concealed weapons, or the right to smoke marijuana. Yet each of these issues has public interest groups dedicated to procuring and enforcing these rights for all Americans. Because they are involved in the production of collective goods for very large populations and the individual incentive to contribute may be particularly difficult to perceive, public interest groups are especially vulnerable to the free rider problem. That has not stopped them from organizing, however. The number of these groups grew dramatically in the 1960s and again in the 1980s.[47] People are drawn to public interest groups because they support the groups' values and goals; that is, expressive benefits are the primary draw for membership. Often when events occur that threaten the goals of a public interest group, membership increases. For example, fearing that the Republicans would dismantle environmental laws after Ronald Reagan was elected president, new members flocked to environmental interest groups like the Sierra Club and the National Wildlife Federation; these organizations gained about 150,000 members from 1980 to 1985.[48] Likewise, after President Clinton signed the Brady Bill in 1993—which required a waiting period before gun purchases, among other regulations—the NRA saw its membership increase by half a million, and it surged again in 2008 when, in anticipation of Barack Obama's election to the presidency, the NRA claimed that Obama would ban guns if elected (even though Obama's record on gun rights was hardly one designed to please gun control advocates).[49] Although many members are initially attracted by expressive benefits, public interest groups seek to keep them active by offering material benefits and services ranging from free subscriptions to the group's magazine to discount insurance packages.

ENVIRONMENTAL GROUPS Starting with Earth Day in 1970, environmentally based interest groups have been actively engaged in promoting environmental policies. The Clean Air and Water Acts, the Endangered Species Act, and the creation of the Environmental Protection Agency all represent examples of their successes during the 1970s. Today the Sierra Club, National Audubon Society, and Natural Resources Defense Council maintain active and professional lobbying efforts in Washington, as do environmental groups such as Greenpeace. On the extreme fringes of the environmental movement are more confrontational groups like Earth First! Their members take a dim view of attempts to lobby members of Congress for "green" laws. Instead, their calls for direct action have included building and living in aerial platforms in old-growth redwood forests in California so as to dissuade the timber industry from felling the trees. Activists have also protested by taking over the offices of local members of Congress.[50]

CONSUMER GROUPS The efforts of Ralph Nader and his public interest group Public Citizen became synonymous with the cause of consumer protectionism early on. Nader exposed the hazards of a variety of consumer products and addressed unsafe practices in the nuclear power, automobile, airline, and health care industries.[51] His book with Donald Ross, *Action for a Change*, gave rise to the PIRGs (Public Interest Research Groups) that can be found in many states and on many college campuses today. Another consumer advocacy group is Consumers Union, the nonprofit publisher of *Consumer Reports* magazine. Consumers Union testifies before state and federal government agencies, petitions government, and files lawsuits to protect consumer interests.[52]

RELIGIOUS GROUPS Religious groups in America have had a long history of interest group activity, dating back to the abolitionist movement. In more recent times, religious groups have developed and grown in response to what they describe as the moral decay and decadence of American society. The Christian Coalition, for example, whose million-plus members make it the most powerful religious fundamentalist group in American politics,[53] lobbies on political issues and provides members with voters' guides. Pat Robertson, who had chaired the Christian Coalition's board, also developed the Christian Broadcasting Network in 1976, which, along with other large Christian media sources like James Dobson's Focus on the Family radio broadcast, helps to educate and mobilize evangelical Christians on political issues nationwide. These groups have become a major force in national politics and an important part of the coalition supporting the Republican Party.[54]

Fundamentalist Christian groups are not the only religiously affiliated interest groups. The United States

Conference of Catholic Bishops also lobbies on particular issues like health care and birth control, and the Anti-Defamation League promotes a broad set of foreign, domestic, and legal issues that combat worldwide anti-Semitism and discrimination against Jewish Americans.

SECOND AMENDMENT GROUPS Based on its interpretation of the Second Amendment to the Constitution, the NRA is opposed to almost any effort to control and regulate the sale and distribution of firearms. As we saw in Chapter 5, overall, the NRA has had considerable policy success. Despite public opinion polls that show a clear majority of Americans favoring gun control, the level of regulation of gun purchases remains minimal. The NRA's success can be credited to its highly dedicated members who are willing to contribute their time, resources, and votes to those candidates who support the NRA's positions—and, conversely, to a credible threat of retribution to officeholders who cross the NRA. In the 1994 elections, one year after passage of the Brady Bill, NRA voters contributed to the coalition of voters who ousted moderate Democratic representatives, and Brady supporters, across the South.[55]

One group that has challenged the power of the NRA is Handgun Control, Inc., an interest group founded by Brady Bill namesake James Brady, who was severely wounded in the 1981 attempted assassination of President Reagan, and his wife, Sarah. Handgun Control, Inc., now known as the Brady Campaign to Prevent Gun Violence, was instrumental in getting waiting-period legislation passed in 1993. In 1994 Congress followed the Brady Bill with the Violent Crime Control and Law Enforcement Act, which banned nineteen types of automatic or semiautomatic assault rifles.[56] With the election of a Republican majority in 1994, gun control efforts had less success in Congress, and when the assault weapons ban lapsed in 2004, they were able to keep it from being renewed.[57]

In the wake of the massacre at Sandy Hook Elementary School, a new gun control lobby has sprung up to take on the NRA: Everytown for Gun Safety, a combined effort of the financial grassroots foot soldiers of Moms Demand Action for Gun Sense.[58] Following the 2018 shootings at Marjory Stoneman Douglas High School in Parkland, Florida, the students took matters into their own hands through their March for Our Lives campaign, using social media to organize protests around the country, registering students to vote, and planning to put heavy pressure on those running for office.

REPRODUCTIVE RIGHTS GROUPS The Supreme Court's decision in *Roe v. Wade* (1973), granting women the right to an abortion, generated a number of interest groups. On the pro-choice side of this debate are the National Abortion Rights Action League (NARAL) and Planned Parenthood. These

Lobbying at Home and Abroad

Lobbying by foreign governments can take many forms, including preferential treatment. Since Donald Trump took office, he and his family have been granted several Chinese trademarks, including several that had previously rejected and three for Ivanka Trump's businesses.

groups have mounted a public relations campaign aimed at convincing policymakers that a majority of Americans want women to have the right to choose safe and legal abortions.[59] In 2012 many of these same groups were involved in defending the Obama administration's position that health care plans had to include birth control coverage.

On the pro-life side of the debate are the National Right to Life Committee and its more confrontational partner, Operation Rescue. The National Right to Life Committee lobbies Congress and state legislatures to limit abortions, hoping ultimately to secure the passage of a constitutional amendment banning them altogether. Operation Rescue attempts to prevent abortions by blocking access to abortion clinics, picketing clinics, and intercepting women who are considering abortions. In recent years, pro-life groups have shifted from a single focus on abortion to other issues they see as similar, such as opposing stem cell research.

Conservative groups won an important victory in a 2014 Supreme Court ruling in favor of Hobby Lobby. The family-held corporation had argued that the Affordable Care Act's requirement that insurance plans must include birth control coverage violated its religious values because they perceived some forms of birth control as causing very early abortions.[60] The case illustrated how interest groups can use the courts as well as the legislative process to achieve their policy goals.

OTHER PUBLIC INTEREST GROUPS Other public interest groups target the issue of human rights. The ACLU is a nonprofit, nonpartisan defender of individual rights against the encroachment of a powerful government. The ACLU supports the rights of disadvantaged minorities and claims to be the "nation's guardian of liberty."[61]

Wayne Pacelle

Paul Markow Photography

In the midst of one of his finest moments, Wayne Pacelle got himself thrown out of the gallery of the House of Representatives. He was watching the vote on a budget amendment he had lobbied hard for, and he needed 218 votes to win, and everyone thought they were going to be trounced. He watched the scoreboard light up with vote after vote. When they got to 232, he couldn't help it. He let out a yell and pumped his fist. But the House frowns on emotional displays in the gallery, and out he went. Was he abashed? Hardly. "It didn't take the smile off my face," he says, grinning even now at the memory.

It was a great win, but every single triumph matters to Pacelle—this is how he feeds his spirit and keeps himself going in the face unimaginable stories of animal abuse in his job as CEO of the Humane Society of the United States. Each law enacted by Congress to protect animals, each state bill passed, each statewide ballot measure approved, each animal life saved, each creature relieved of pain and suffering—he tallies them all.

"For us, it's not an all-or-nothing game," he explains. "We can't solve all of the issues in the world, we never will. . . But if we solve it for a million, or 10 million, or a billion creatures, that's a 100-percent victory for each of those animals. And just that one act of merciful behavior or the shielding of an animal from abuse or cruelty can mean all the difference between a good quality of life and a miserable, tormented existence for that creature."

Pacelle has felt that kind of enormous, compassionate connection to animals ever since he was two or three years old. He carried that empathy and awareness with him as he got older and, as he read philosophy and learned more about the world, he began to fit it into a broader context of what it meant to him to be a responsible citizen. "I'm broadly interested in making the world a better place," he says. "That's the bottom line. Public policy is just the means to achieve the end of a more fair, a more just society."

How has he kept that idealism and commitment in the face of the giant sums of money that Washington lobbyists traffic in these days? He may be an optimist, but he's a realist, too. "You'd be naive to think money doesn't have an impact," he says. "It does. It gains access, and it builds loyalty. But, ultimately, money is a means to an end. Money is there to have resources to deliver a message to influence voting behavior. So if you've got people who can organize around a principle and you can deliver votes based on that set of ideas, then you don't need money." Well, maybe not as much, anyway.

Here are some of his thoughts:

On the positive side of lobbying

"There's a reason in Washington, D.C., that there are thousands of lobbyists and thousands of interest groups. They're not here for fun; it's not just a big party. They're here because it does make a difference, and participation can have a measurable impact on public policy. . . I mean when we're not on defense, we're on the offense. It's almost a very crusading sort of attitude. I don't like to infuse it with religious sorts of notions, but it's a powerful, ethical construct. And having enough imagination to see that things can be different. That we're not just locked into our present set of social relationships and circumstances, that we can aspire to do things better."

On keeping the republic

"No one's going to hand you a key to change everything, but if you're smart and if you're determined you can make a real difference in the world. I've seen it happen thousands and thousands of times. And anybody who tells me differently just isn't paying attention to what's going on. And don't count on somebody else to do it, you know, don't count on a group like the Humane Society of the United States to do it. When I go around and I talk to people I say, 'Listen, we can help.' And our staff of four hundred, we've got great experts and we do a lot of amazing stuff, but you make the difference. It's the collective action of people of conscience that really can have a meaningful impact on society. And again, the history is of people stepping up and calling themselves to action. And leadership and citizenship are such important values in this culture. And if not them, who?"

Source: Wayne Pacelle talked with Christine Barbour on March 10, 2005.

Another human rights group, Amnesty International, promotes human rights worldwide, with over three million members in 150 countries. In the United States, Amnesty International lobbies on issues such as the death penalty, arms control, and globalization.[62] It has been especially active in the face of action or threats by the Trump administration with respect to immigrant and refugee rights, rights of the LGBTQ community, and press freedom.

Interest groups have also taken up the cause of animal rights. The most well-known of these groups is the Humane Society. Beyond providing local animal shelters, the Humane Society researches animal cruelty and lobbies governments at all levels on issues ranging from domestic pet overpopulation and adoption to farm animal treatment and wildlife habitat protection (see *Profiles in Citizenship: Wayne Pacelle*). In recent years a number of actors and actresses have used their celebrity status to protect animals. People for the Ethical Treatment of Animals (PETA) is a leading national interest group promoting the rights of animals. Its grassroots campaigns include attacking major health and beauty corporations like Procter & Gamble for using animals for product testing, assailing circuses and rodeos for using animals as entertainment, and condemning fur coat manufacturers for the cruel ways they kill animals.[63] Other groups like the Animal Liberation Front also advocate animal rights. Animal rights activists often use civil disobedience in their attempts to stop hunting and end the use of animals for biomedical and product safety tests.[64]

GOVERNMENT INTEREST GROUPS

Government interest groups—representing both foreign and domestic governments—also lobby Congress and the president. Typically some lobbyists' most lucrative contracts come from foreign governments seeking to influence foreign trade policies. The Japanese government maintains one of the more active lobbying efforts in Washington, hiring former members of Congress and bureaucrats to aid in their efforts to keep U.S. markets open to Japanese imports.[65] In recent years, ethics rules have been initiated to prevent former government officials from working as foreign government lobbyists as soon as they leave office, but lobbying firms continue to hire them when they can because of their contacts and expertise.[66] Donald Trump's presidency has presented new challenges to ethics laws since he has refused to divest himself of his wide business interests, many of which require the cooperation of foreign governments. As the many scandals haunting members of his family business and his administration make clear,

government interest groups groups that organize to represent foreign or domestic governments, and to lobby Congress and the president on their behalf

foreign governments found the Trumps to be attractive and potentially lucrative lobbying targets.[67]

Domestic governments have become increasingly involved in the business of influencing federal policy. With the growing complexities of American federalism, state and local governments have an enormous stake in what the federal government does and often try to gain resources, limit the impact of policy, and otherwise alter the effects of federal law. All fifty states have government relations offices in Washington to attempt to influence federal policy directly.[68]

PAUSE AND REVIEW   Who, What, How

All citizens stand to win or lose a great deal from government action. If it goes their way, producing policy that benefits them, they win. But if it produces policy that helps other citizens at their expense, or passes the cost of expensive policy on to them, or reduces their ability to use the system to get what they want, then they lose. Economic actors want to protect their financial interests; members of disadvantaged or threatened groups want to protect their legal and economic interests; ideologically motivated people want to promote their vision of the good society; and governments want a good relationship with the U.S. federal government. All these actors promote their goals through the formation of different types of interest groups.

In Your Own Words   Identify four types of interest groups and the kinds of interests they represent.

INTEREST GROUP POLITICS

Strategies for influencing different branches of government

The term *lobbying* comes from seventeenth-century England, where representatives of special interests would meet members of the English House of Commons in the large anteroom, or lobby, outside the Commons floor to plead their cases.[69] Contemporary lobbying, however, reaches far beyond the lobby of the House or the Senate. Interest groups do indeed contact lawmakers directly, but they no longer confine their efforts to chance meetings in the legislative lobby.

Today, lobbyists target all branches of government and the American people as well. The ranks of those who work with lobbyists have also swelled. Beginning in the 1980s, interest groups, especially those representing corporate interests, have been turning to a diverse group of political consultants, including professional Washington lobbyists, campaign specialists, advertising and media experts, pollsters, and academics. Lobbying today is a big business in its own right, creating narratives to persuade the public, weaponizing social media, and backing candidates whose narratives fit with their own (see *The Big Picture: Campaign Spending Before and After* Citizens United).

No More Free Lunches
These days, rules and regulations prevent some activities between lobbyists and lawmakers, but that wasn't always the case. While lobbyists can no longer treat government workers to free meals, they once wined and dined lawmakers. Old Ebbitt Grill in Washington, D.C., was a popular meeting place for meals, drinks, and schmoozing.

There are two main types of lobbying. **Direct lobbying** (sometimes called inside lobbying) is interaction with actual decision makers within government institutions. We tend to think of Congress as the typical recipient of lobbying efforts, but the president, the bureaucracy, and even the courts are also the focus of heavy efforts to influence policy. **Indirect lobbying** (or outside lobbying) attempts to influence policymakers by mobilizing interest group members or the general public to contact elected representatives on an issue. Some groups have resorted to more confrontational indirect methods, using political protests, often developing into full-blown social movements, to make their demands heard by policymakers. Recently, corporations and other, more traditional interest groups have been combining tactics—joining conventional lobbying methods with the use of email, computerized databases, talk radio, and twenty-four-hour cable television—to bring unprecedented pressure to bear on the voting public to influence members of government.

DIRECT LOBBYING: CONGRESS

When interest groups lobby Congress, they rarely concentrate on all 435 members of the House or all 100 members of the Senate. Rather, lobbyists focus their efforts on congressional committees, where most bills are written and revised. Because the committee leadership is relatively stable from one Congress to the next (unless a different party wins a majority), lobbyists can develop long-term relationships with committee members and their staffs.

STRATEGIES FOR CONGRESSIONAL LOBBYING

Interest groups use many strategies to influence members of Congress:

- **Personal contacts.** Personal contacts, including appointments, banquets, parties, lunches, or simply casual meetings in the hallways of Congress, are the most common and the most effective form of lobbying.
- **Professional lobbyists.** Interest groups frequently need professional help to navigate the increasingly complex world of government regulations and benefits. As a result, much of modern lobbying involves the use of professional lobbyists, either in-house employees dedicated to advancing the interests of a particular group, or contract lobbyists who work for lobbying firms that address a variety of groups' needs.

Because access to power and knowledge about how government works is key to successful lobbying, some of the most effective lobbyists are former government officials. Rotating into lobbying jobs from elected or other government positions is known as passing through the **revolving door**, a concept we meet again in Chapter 15. It refers to public officials who leave their posts to become interest group representatives (or media figures), parlaying the special knowledge and contacts they gathered in government into lucrative salaries in the private sector. Such assistance can be so invaluable to their clients that even legislative aides can make their fortune lobbying, commanding starting salaries of more than $300,000 a year.[70] One study has found that 56 percent of the revenue generated by private lobbying firms can be traced to people who once had some involvement with the federal government.[71] Current law passed in 2007 requires that senators wait two years before lobbying Congress; members of the House must wait just one year. Former Senate staffers cannot lobby the Senate for a year after they leave their positions, and House staffers cannot lobby the actual offices or committees where they worked.

Other government officials also face new restrictions on when they can lobby the agencies for which they once worked.[72] President Obama felt so strongly that the revolving door was a breach of the public trust that early in his administration he signed an executive order prohibiting presidential appointees from working as lobbyists for two years after leaving their posts and from returning to

direct lobbying direct interaction with public officials for the purpose of influencing policy decisions

indirect lobbying attempts to influence government policymakers by encouraging the general public to put pressure on them

revolving door the tendency of public officials, journalists, and lobbyists to move between public- and private-sector (media, lobbying) jobs

lobby the executive branch during his time in office.[73] In support of his oft-repeated intention to "drain the swamp," Donald Trump signed an executive order requiring administration appointees to pledge not to lobby the agencies for which they worked for five years. Nonetheless, one investigation found that of the nearly 200 people who left his administration in his first year and a half in office, several had gone on to lobbying jobs by obtaining waivers allowing them to do so, by working part time so that they didn't have to register as lobbyists, or, in one case, by refusing to sign the pledge at all.[74] On the flip side of the revolving door, ProPublica, a nonprofit public watchdog, found that 187 members of the Trump administration had previously tried to influence the agencies they were now hired to lead.[75] In one particularly flagrant case, Trump appointed as Environmental Protection Agency head Scott Pruitt, an Oklahoma attorney general who had sued the EPA over climate change.[76] Pruitt finally resigned in July 2018, after repeated scandals came to light.

The reason revolving-door activity is subject to occasional attempts at regulation and frequent ethical debate is because it raises questions about whether people should be able to convert public service into private profit, and whether such an incentive draws people into public office for motives other than serving the public interest.

- **Expert testimony.** Interest groups lobby decision makers by providing testimony and expertise, and sometimes they even draft legislation on the many issue areas in which policymakers cannot take the time to become expert.[77] Information is one of the most important resources lobbyists can bring to their effort to influence Congress. Providing valid information to representatives and staffers becomes a tool that lobbyists use to build long-term credibility with members of Congress.

For example, in 2003, with support from a president and a vice president who were former energy company executives, Republicans in Congress worked closely with energy companies to develop legislation that would increase oil exploration, coal mining, and nuclear plant development. One industry lobbyist said of the energy bill: "This is the mother lode."[78] Democrats, locked out of the conference committee that was considering the bill, were so frustrated by the influence of the energy lobbyists that then-senator Bob Graham, D-Fla., fumed, "at this point, industry lobbyists are effectively writing this bill."[79] Of course, in their turn, energy companies had been frustrated with the Clinton administration's pro-environmental positions on energy exploration, claiming that they listened only to conservationists and environmental groups.[80]

- **Campaign contributions.** Giving money to candidates is another lobbying technique that helps interest groups

gain access and a friendly ear. The 1974 Federal Election Campaign Act was aimed at regulating the amount of money an interest group could give to candidates for federal office, by providing for PACs to serve as fundraisers for interest groups. Subsequent campaign finance legislation has limited how much money PACs can donate to candidates, but loopholes let them circumvent the restrictions in order to support the candidates of their choice. These loopholes have been enhanced since 2012, when the Supreme Court's ruling in *Citizens United v. Federal Election Commission* essentially removed any limits on political expenditures by corporations and unions. Figures 13.2 and 13.3 show how the major types of PACs divide their money between the Democratic and Republican Parties. As groups have adjusted to the new rules, expenditures by what are now called Super PACs have soared.[81] These groups use the money not only to support or oppose specific candidates but also to define the issues and tenor of the campaigns—which, given the volume of money at their disposal, they are increasingly able to do.

- **Coalition formation.** Interest groups attempt to bolster their lobbying efforts by forming coalitions with other interest groups. Although these coalitions tend to be based on single issues, building coalitions in favor of or against specific issues has become an important strategy in lobbying Congress. In recent years, for instance, liberal and conservative groups came together in an unlikely coalition to stop legislation in the House and the Senate that aimed to stop online piracy.[82]

ATTEMPTS AT LOBBYING REFORM Many attempts have been made to regulate the tight relationship between lobbyist and lawmaker. The difficulty, of course, is that lawmakers benefit from the relationship with lobbyists in many ways and are not enthusiastic about curtailing their opportunities to get money and support. In 1995 Congress completed its first attempt in half a century to regulate lobbying when it passed the Lobbying Disclosure Act. The act required lobbyists to report how much they are paid, by whom, and what issues they are promoting.[83] Also in 1995, the Senate and the House passed separate resolutions addressing gifts and travel given by interest groups to senators and representatives.[84] Partly in reaction, in September 2007, after the Democrats took back the majority in the House and the Senate in 2006, Congress passed and President George W. Bush signed the Honest Leadership and Open Government Act, which tightened travel and gift restrictions and included, among other things, the following provisions:[85]

- Prohibits senators, members of the House, and their aides from receiving any gifts, meals, or travel in violation of their chamber's rules. While these rules are

BEFORE

At Issue

Is corporate political spending a form of free speech protected under the First Amendment? Do corporations have the same free speech protections as people? Who should have such rights?

THE CASE

Citizens United

federal prohibitions on election spending violated First Amendment protections of free speech

Individuals and corporations could contribute unlimited amounts to nonprofits and 527s. Neither organization could advocate directly for the election or defeat of a candidate. Corporations could not directly spend on political ads.

Individuals

Corporations

Nonprofits

527s

Federal PACs

National Parties

—— Unlimited Contributions

—— FEC-Regulated Contributions

THE RULING

The Supreme Court

Anthony Kennedy   John Roberts   Antonin Scalia   Samuel Alito   Clarence Thomas

Sonya Sotomayor   Ruth Bader Ginsburg   Stephen Breyer   John Paul Stevens

In favor of
Citizens United

5-4

"Corporations are people too." This phrase was first heard after the Supreme Court's 2010 ruling in *Citizens United v. Federal Election Commission*, which extended the First Amendment's protections of free speech to include corporate campaign spending. Critics charge that unlimited corporate spending will drown out the voices of individuals. Can you tell which campaign ads you see on TV are from a corporate-funded super PAC? Would knowing the source make a difference in how you reacted to an ad?

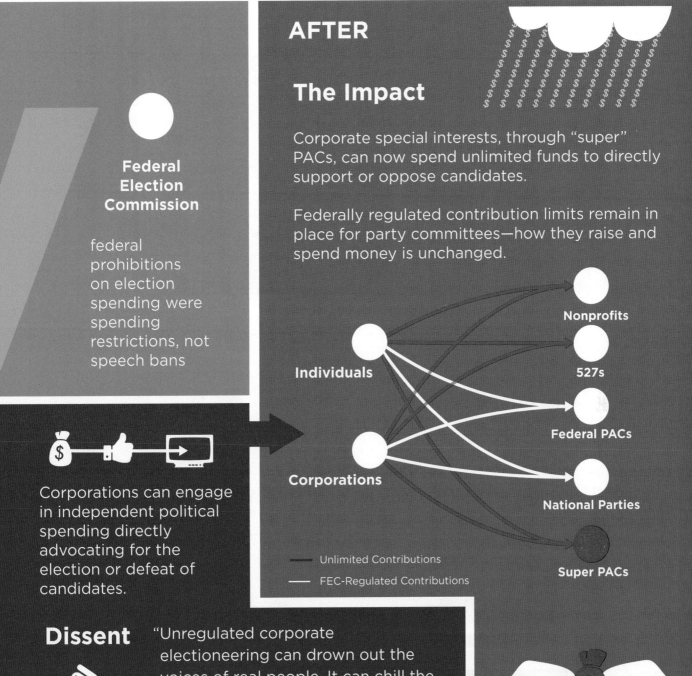

AFTER

The Impact

Corporate special interests, through "super" PACs, can now spend unlimited funds to directly support or oppose candidates.

Federally regulated contribution limits remain in place for party committees—how they raise and spend money is unchanged.

Federal Election Commission

federal prohibitions on election spending were spending restrictions, not speech bans

Corporations can engage in independent political spending directly advocating for the election or defeat of candidates.

Individuals

Corporations

Nonprofits

527s

Federal PACs

National Parties

Super PACs

—— Unlimited Contributions

—— FEC-Regulated Contributions

Dissent

"Unregulated corporate electioneering can drown out the voices of real people. It can chill the speech of those who hold office and decrease the willingness and capacity of citizens to participate in self-government."

—Justice John Paul Stevens

The ban on corporate spending was reversed.

FIGURE 13.2

Spending by Type of PAC, 1989–2016 (in millions)

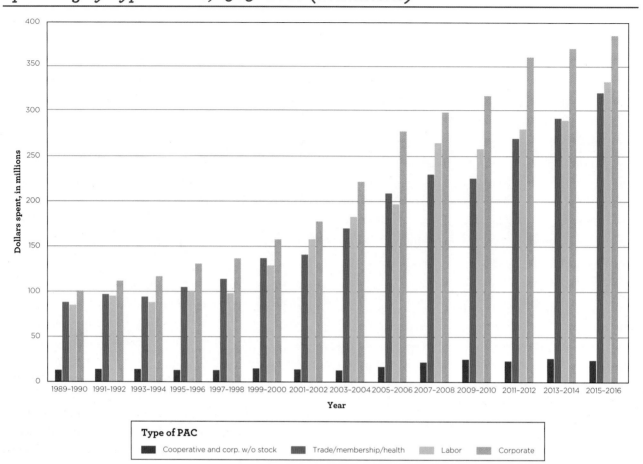

Source: Harold W. Stanley and Richard G. Niemi, "Table 2-11: Spending, by Type of PAC, 1997–2014," Vital Statistics on American Politics 2015–2016 (Washington, D.C.: CQ Press, 2015), 97; Federal Election Commission 2015–2016 Election Cycle Data Summaries, Table 1, transition.fec.gov/press/summaries/2016/ElectionCycle/24m_PAC.shtml.

FIGURE 13.3

PAC Contributions to All Congressional Candidates, by Type of PAC and Candidate Party, 2015–2016

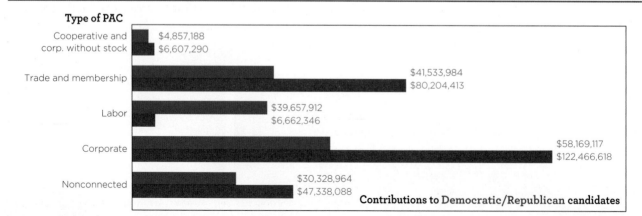

Source: Federal Election Commission, "PAC Table 2: PAC Contributions to Candidates: January 1, 2015 through December 31, 2016," https://transition.fec.gov/press/summaries/2016/tables/pac/PAC2_2016_24m.pdf.

complex, basically any gifts from registered lobbyists are forbidden and gifts from other sources must have a monetary value of under $50.

- Increases the frequency with which lobbyist disclosures must be filed.
- Requires lawmakers to disclose when lobbyists "bundle" or collect from clients more than $15,000 in campaign contributions in a six-month period.
- Requires disclosure of "earmarks"—that is, special projects of individual legislators often hidden in legislation, and their sponsors.
- Forbids members of Congress to influence lobbying firms to hire members of a particular party.

Ethics reforms can cast a definite chill on lobbyist activity. The combination of the 2007 reform and President Obama's limitations on lobbyists' access to the White House led to a significant drop in lobbying. The number of registered lobbyists dropped from 14,840 to 12,340 between 2007 and 2013.[86] Nevertheless, members of Congress and lobbyists quickly learn where they can bend the rules.[87] As soon as the 2007 reform was passed, lobbying groups scrambled to find new ways to provide travel for lawmakers they wanted to influence, and ways to make free meals acceptable (perhaps calling them receptions, which are legal if widely attended, or fundraisers).[88]

DIRECT LOBBYING: THE PRESIDENT

Lobbyists also target the president and the White House staff to try to influence policy. As with Congress, personal contacts within the White House are extremely important, and the higher up in the White House, the better. Nor has the White House been exempt from the revolving-door phenomenon. Despite even Obama's seemingly uncompromising stance against the revolving door, he had to relax his rules to fill some executive branch positions.[89] Part of the difficulty is that the practice of the revolving door is so pervasive—with one party's appointees joining lobbying firms while their party is out of power—that a president is hard pressed to find stellar appointees who haven't been lobbyists at some point.

The official contact point between the White House and interest groups is the Office of Public Engagement. Its basic purpose is to foster good relations between the White House and interest groups in order to mobilize these groups to support the administration's policies. Given the highly partisan and ideologically charged nature of most presidencies, it should not be surprising that each White House administration cultivates the groups with which it feels most ideologically comfortable.

In the case of the Trump White House, lobbying is slightly different because the president has retained his private business interests. It is relatively easy for groups seeking to gain access to the president to do so by staying at one of his many properties, especially Mar-a-Lago, where he himself spends so much of his time. Public Citizen, a public watchdog group, found that in the president's first year in office, sixty-four industry groups, corporations, foreign governments, and political groups and candidates spent money at Trump properties.[90] It is probably impossible to trace any explicit quid pro quo arrangements without seeing more financial records, but one of the reasons presidents have historically divested themselves of their financial interests or put them into blind trusts is to avoid any appearance of conflict of interest.

DIRECT LOBBYING: THE BUREAUCRACY

Opportunities for lobbying the president may be somewhat limited, but opportunities for lobbying the rest of the executive branch abound. Interest groups know that winning the legislative battle is only the first step. The second, and sometimes most important, battle takes place in the bureaucracy, where Congress has delegated rule-making authority to federal agencies that implement the law.[91] When, for instance, the Occupational Safety and Health Administration (OSHA) decreed that workplace design must take into account the physical abilities of workers in order to avoid repetitive motion injuries, groups like organized labor supported the effort, although they believed the new standards did not go far enough; by contrast, business groups lobbied heavily against it, claiming that the standards were unnecessary, unsupported by medical evidence, and expensive to implement.[92] Interest groups often try to gain an advantage by developing strong relations with regulating agencies. Because many of the experts on a topic are employed by the interests being regulated, it is not unusual to find lobbyists being hired by government agencies, or vice versa, in an extension of the revolving-door situation we discussed earlier. The close relationships that exist between the regulated and the regulators, along with the close relationships between lobbyists and congressional staffers, lead to the creation of the iron triangles we talked about in Chapter 9 (see especially Figure 9.1 on page 326). In addition to iron triangles working against an open policymaking environment by limiting the participation of actors not in the triangle, they also have the potential for presenting conflicts of interest. Although recent laws prevent former government employees from lobbying their former agencies for five years after they leave their federal jobs, government agencies are sometimes forced to recruit personnel from within the businesses they are regulating because that is often where the experts are to be found.

DIRECT LOBBYING: THE COURTS

Interest groups also try to influence government policy by challenging the legality of laws or administrative regulations in the courts. These legal tactics have been used by groups like the NAACP (challenging segregation laws), the ACLU (freedom of speech, religion, and civil liberties cases), the Sierra Club (environmental enforcement), and Common Cause (ethics in government). As soon as the Bipartisan Campaign Reform Act (BCRA) of 2002 (also called the McCain-Feingold Act) was passed, the NRA, the ACLU, the AFL-CIO, and other groups immediately went into action to challenge the new law in court. Sometimes groups bring cases directly, and sometimes they file amicus curiae ("friend of the court") briefs asking the courts to rule in ways favorable to their positions. Many of the groups that challenged campaign finance reform returned to chime in with amicus briefs in the *Citizens United* case that ultimately rendered the heart of the BCRA unconstitutional.[93]

INDIRECT LOBBYING: THE PUBLIC

One of the most powerful and fastest-growing kinds of lobbying is indirect lobbying, in which the lobbyists use public opinion to put pressure on politicians to do what they want.[94] Much of indirect lobbying consists of telling a compelling story and getting the public to buy it so that they react by pressuring government to do what the interest group wants. Then the group focuses on educating the public by disseminating information and research, mobilizing direct citizen lobbying efforts, and organizing demonstrations or protests. In a mediated world, the possibilities for informing and activating citizens have exploded.

EDUCATING THE PUBLIC Education involves building and disseminating a compelling narrative. To say that it is a narrative isn't to imply that it is false, but it is a preferred frame through which interest groups want the public to view an issue. Many interest group leaders are sure that the public will rally to their side once they know "the truth" about their causes.[95] Interest groups often begin their campaigns by using research to show that the problem they are trying to solve is a legitimate one. For example, the Tax Foundation is a conservative group promoting tax cuts. To dramatize its point that American taxes are too high, every year the foundation announces "Tax Freedom Day"—the day on which the average wage earner finishes paying the amount of taxes he or she will owe and starts working for his or her own profit. In 2018 that day was April 19.[96] The foundation believes that this information is so compelling that the public will jump to the conclusion that their taxes are too high.

Of course, all the research in the world by the Tax Foundation, or any other interest group, does no good if the public is unaware of it. For this reason, interest groups cultivate press coverage. They know that people are more likely to take their research seriously if it is reported by the media as legitimate news, but getting news coverage can be difficult for interest groups because they are in competition with every other group, not to mention with actual news stories. Many of them turn to expensive public relations firms to help them get their message out,

using tactics ranging from TV commercials to social media campaigns (see *Don't Be Fooled by . . . the Donate Button*).

A popular way for interest groups to get out their message is through the use of **issue advocacy ads**. These commercials encourage constituents to support or oppose a certain policy or candidate without directly telling citizens how to vote. In the past, as long as these ads did not specifically promote the election or defeat of a particular candidate, issue advocacy ads were not subject to any limitations, meaning a PAC could spend all the money it wanted on ads promoting an issue and, by implication, the candidates of its choice. The passage of the BCRA put a temporary chill on these ads, but several recent Supreme Court rulings, culminating with the 2010 decision in *Citizens United*, have lifted the restrictions, and in fact, issue advocacy ads can now directly advocate for or against candidates as well as for their issue positions.[97]

Groups can also get information to the public through the skillful use of the Internet, whether through carefully designed advocacy web sites and blogs, social media posts, or web-based videos, creating messages that go "viral," spreading quickly by email and hitting targeted audiences. Internet-savvy interest groups are increasingly turning to YouTube for a cheap and efficient way to get their message out.

MOBILIZING THE PUBLIC The point of disseminating information, hiring public relations firms, creating web sites, and running issue ads is to motivate the public to lobby politicians themselves. On most issues, general public interest is low, and groups must rely on their own members for support. As you might suspect, groups like AARP, the Christian Coalition, and the NRA, which have large memberships, have an advantage because they can mobilize a large contingent of citizens from all over the country to lobby representatives and senators. Generally this mobilization involves encouraging members to write letters, send emails or faxes, or make phone calls to legislators about a pending issue.

Professional lobbyists freely admit that their efforts are most effective when the people "back home" are contacting representatives about an issue.[98] Considerable evidence indicates that members of Congress do monitor their mail and respond to the wishes of their constituents, but as these tactics have become more prevalent, they are being met with increasing skepticism and resistance on Capitol Hill.[99] To combat congressional skepticism, many interest groups have begun to deliver on their threats to politicians by mobilizing their members to vote. The religious right has long been able to do this, mobilizing conservative voters from the pulpit, but more recently liberals—for example, the "netroots," liberal activist groups like MoveOn.org, Organizing

> **issue advocacy ads** advertisements that support issues or candidates without telling constituents how to vote

The Donate Button

The NRA knows who you are—but it's not gunning for you; it's after your money. So are the Brady Campaign to Prevent Gun Violence, the Humane Society, the Sierra Club, and the Red Cross. Once upon a time, fundraising meant boots on the ground, with solicitors for interest groups ringing doorbells and stuffing envelopes in hopes of getting support—and donations. But in the age of the Internet, they can let an algorithm do much of the work for them: Spend a few minutes browsing the web for hiking boots, and soon thereafter you'll start seeing targeted ads for sports outfitters, and before long, you've caught the attention of the NRA or the Sierra Club, both of which hope that outdoorsy people support their causes.

Of course, supporting causes that are important to you is a valuable way to take part in democracy. But how can you be sure that you're not being manipulated or taken advantage of? When presented with a plea for funds, it is worth doing a little homework before you part with any cash.

What to Watch Out For

- **Who are they, and what have they actually done in the past?** Bear in mind that much of the information about groups on the web—including what you find on the organization's web site and even on Wikipedia—originates from the groups themselves. Seek out objective information from reputable news sources and nonpartisan watchdog groups like OpenSecrets.org.
- **What's the rush?** Fundraising campaigns are designed to get you to break out your credit card and hit "Donate" *now*. Many messages seem to imply that Armageddon is imminent, and that the world will soon self-destruct without your donation. As often happens after an impulse buy, you may find yourself regretting laying out your hard-earned money on something that might not be worthwhile. Take your time and do your homework. A worthy cause will be just as happy to receive your donation tomorrow as it is today.
- **What's their agenda?** Always ask yourself, "What is this group? What does it stand for?"

Professional fundraisers often spend a lot of time telling you what they are against, or whom they oppose, in the hopes that you will share their animosities and therefore support them. But it's equally important to know what they're for—what specific causes, policies, and activities do they support, and how do they support them?

- **What do they want from you?** Be clear about what you are being asked for—it's not always money. A group may ask you to write your congressperson, make a phone call, wear a ribbon, or otherwise show support for a cause. Use your web search skills to see what causes the group supports and to get a sense of how effectively it has lobbied for those causes in the past. Make sure you know what you are committing to do, and that you really agree with the cause.
- **Where does the money go?** Even if you are fully on board with a group's mission, it's worth your time to investigate how much of your money will actually go toward fulfilling it. CharityNavigator.org can tell you how a nonprofit group spends its money. If most of the money it collects goes to administrative costs, you won't be furthering your cause much by contributing your dollars. OpenSecrets.org offers detailed accounting of how much money a group raised—and where they spent it.
- **What's in it for you?** What material benefits does the group offer? Do you receive a newsletter? Discounts on products or services? Special offers for the group? Would membership provide solidary benefits or expressive benefits that are important to you? We are not advising free ridership here, but it is wise to know exactly what you are getting before you part with your cash.
- **Are they making an emotional plea?** Interest groups routinely up their game during times of crisis—after a national disaster or tragedy, for example. Groups will capitalize on heightened emotions, and not always in the most altruistic ways. They might be promoting a cause that is related only tangentially to recent events. Even worse, scam artists will join the fray by pretending to represent legitimate interest groups in hopes of getting your cash for themselves.

Ralph Freso/Getty Images

Going to Bat Against Breast Cancer
Interest groups don't just lobby government—they lobby the public, too, in hopes of educating us about (and rallying us behind) their causes. The Susan G. Komen Foundation for Breast Cancer Research has increased public awareness of breast cancer largely through public events like Major League Baseball's annual Mother's Day event, during which players, coaches, and umpires across the league sport pink bats, gloves, and other equipment.

for Action, People for the American Way, and ActBlue that challenge establishment politicians and interest groups—have gotten into the game via the Internet.

UNCONVENTIONAL METHODS: SOCIAL PROTEST AND MASS MOVEMENTS A discussion of interest group politics would not be complete without mention of the unconventional technique of social protest. Throughout our history, groups have turned to **social protest**—activities ranging from planned, orderly demonstrations to strikes and boycotts, to acts of civil disobedience—when other techniques have failed to bring attention to their causes.

Like other grassroots lobbying techniques, the techniques of social protest provide a way for people, often those closed out from more traditional avenues of political action, to publicly disseminate a narrative expressing their disagreement with a government policy or action. Thus demonstrations and protests have frequently served an important function for those who have been excluded from the political process because of their minority, social, or economic status. Although social protest may have the same objective as other types of indirect lobbying—that is, spreading the narrative, educating the public, and mobilizing

the group's members—demonstrations and spontaneous protests also aim to draw in citizens who have not yet formed an opinion or to change the minds of those who have. Such actions may turn a political action into a mass movement, attracting formerly passive or uninterested observers to the cause.

Social protest in the United States has brought about major changes, from the labor movement of the late nineteenth century to the women's suffrage movement of the late nineteenth and early twentieth centuries, to the civil rights movement of the 1960s, but the potential for mediated citizens to organize and spread the narratives that support these movements has changed dramatically in recent years. High-tech flash campaigns have helped groups like Censure and Move On (now MoveOn.org, a citizen action group formed in 1998 to pressure Congress not to impeach President Clinton) to mobilize hundreds of thousands of citizens to lobby Congress by setting up relatively inexpensive and efficient "cyberpetitions" on their web sites.[100] The early Tea Party rallies, Occupy Wall Street, and Black Lives Matter are all good examples of such social media–driven movements, even though they also take advantage of more traditional media outlets.

More recently, women engaged in social demonstrations against the Trump administration's policies toward women by marching the day after his inauguration and again one year later. The #MeToo movement focused on holding men (or, more rarely, women) accountable for sexual harassment and sexual assault spread through social media and resulted in the indictments or firings of such powerful men as Hollywood producer Harvey Weinstein, NBC anchor Matt Lauer, and PBS and CBS host Charlie Rose. These movements have energized women to become politically involved, running for office in numbers the United States has never seen. In 2018, following the shootings at Marjory Stoneman Douglas High School, students organized walkouts from schools and a day of national protest against the ease with which military-style assault weapons could be obtained. As we saw in Chapter 1, organized under the hashtag #NeverAgain, thousands of people marched to bring awareness to the problem of the easy accessibility of assault-style weapons. The March for Our Lives students spent the summer crossing the country, registering young people to vote and creating a social movement that is becoming part of the American political environment. Although it isn't possible to gauge the impact they had on the 2018 election turnout, young voters turned out at a rate that was usually high for a midterm election, which many often skip.

> **social protest** public activities designed to bring attention to political causes, usually generated by those without access to conventional means of expressing their views

"ASTROTURF" POLITICAL CAMPAIGNS: DEMOCRATIC OR ELITE DRIVEN?

The indirect lobbying we have discussed is often called **grassroots lobbying**, meaning that it addresses people in their roles as ordinary citizens. It is the wielding of power from the bottom (roots) up, rather than from the top down. Most of what we refer to as grassroots lobbying, however, does not spring spontaneously from the people but is orchestrated by elites, leading some people to call it **astroturf lobbying**—indicating that it is not genuine. Often the line between real grassroots and astroturf lobbying is blurred, however. The organic food movement we saw in *What's at Stake . . . ?* had an impassioned public that was organized but not manipulated by the organic food industry. A movement may be partly spontaneous but partly orchestrated. After MoveOn.org's success as a spontaneous expression of popular will spread by "word of mouse" over the Internet, its organizers began other flash campaigns, notably one called "Gun Safety First," urging people to support gun control measures. This was less clearly a spontaneous popular movement, but it still involved mobilizing citizens to support a cause they believed in. Similarly, the current Tea Party movement has been, in part, the project of Dick Armey, a former Republican House majority leader whose organization, FreedomWorks for America, promotes low taxes and small government. FreedomWorks and several other conservative groups, as well as prominent individuals, including some commentators at Fox News, have lent their organizational expertise to the Tea Partiers but deny that they are orchestrating an astroturf movement.[101] Regardless of how it started out, the Tea Party movement has certainly acquired a life and mind, perhaps several minds, of its own.

At the astroturf extreme, there was nothing spontaneous at all about the pharmaceutical industry's 2003 efforts to oppose the importation of cheaper drugs from Canada. The Pharmaceutical Research and Manufacturers Association (PhRMA), the industry's lobbying group, spent over $4 million on such tactics as persuading seniors that their access to medicine would be limited if reimportation of these American-made drugs were allowed and convincing members of a Christian advocacy group that prescription drug importation might lead to easier access to the controversial morning-after pill.[102] Concerned citizens were then coached by a PhRMA-hired public relations firm on how to contact legislators to weigh in against the proposed law. Such a strategy is obviously an attempt to create an opinion that might not otherwise even exist, playing on popular fears about drug availability and sentiments about abortion to achieve corporate ends.

Although pure grassroots efforts are becoming increasingly rare, a good deal of indirect lobbying is done to promote what a group claims is the public interest, or at least the interest of the members of some mass-based group like AARP. One observer who works for a public interest group says- "Grassroots politics has become a top-down corporate enterprise," and speculates that there is very little genuine grassrootstype lobbying left.[103] More often than not, astroturf lobbying uses the support of the public to promote the interest of a corporation or business. In many cases the clients of astroturf lobbying efforts are large corporations seeking tax breaks, special regulations, or simply the end of legislation that may hurt the corporation's interest. To generate public support, clients employ armies of lobbyists, media experts, and political strategists to conduct polls, craft multimedia advertising campaigns, and get the message out to "the people" through cable and radio news talk shows, the Internet, outbound call centers, fax machines, or some combination of these. Astroturf campaigns are very expensive.

> ### Are there any lobbying techniques that should be off limits in a democracy?

One prominent campaign media consultant predicts that direct lobbying will become less important as indirect lobbying gains in effectiveness and popularity.[104] Although indirect lobbying seems on its face to be more democratic, to the extent that it manipulates public opinion, it may in fact have the opposite effect. On the other hand, to the extent that Americans can become more sophisticated mediated citizens, there are ever more tools for them to create their own narratives and to take on powerful interests, as the kids from Parkland have done with the NRA.

PAUSE AND REVIEW Who, What, How

Interest groups exist to influence policy. Because of the complexity of the American system, these groups can accomplish their goals in a number of ways. They can engage in direct lobbying, by working from inside the government to influence what the government does, or by working on the public rather than on government officials to influence policy. Sometimes interest group organizers will inspire their members to use unconventional methods to try to influence government, including social protests, mass resistance or demonstrations, and Internet communication. Increasingly, lobbyists are combining strategies and taking advantage of the new communication technologies to create innovative, expensive, and often successful campaigns to influence public policy.

> **grassroots lobbying** indirect lobbying efforts that spring from widespread public concern
>
> **astroturf lobbying** indirect lobbying efforts that manipulate or create public sentiment, "astroturf" being artificial grassroots

In Your Own Words Describe how interest groups use lobbying and campaign activities to get the public policy they want.

INTEREST GROUP RESOURCES

Using money, leadership skills, membership size and intensity, and information to make their voices heard

Interest group success depends in large part on the resources a group can bring to the project of influencing government (see Table 13.1). The pluralist defense of interest groups is that all citizens have the opportunity to organize, and thus all can exercise equal power. But all interest groups are not created equal. Some have more money, more effective leadership, more members, or better information than others, and these resources can translate into real power differences that give groups a better chance of influencing government policy than, say, the Children's Defense Fund. In this section we examine the resources that interest groups can draw on to exert influence over policymaking: money, leadership, membership, and information.

MONEY

Interest groups need money to conduct the business of trying to influence government policymakers. Money can buy an interest group the ability to put together a well-trained staff, to hire outside professional assistance, and to make campaign contributions in the hopes of gaining access to government officials. Having money does not guarantee favorable policies, but not having money just about guarantees failure.

STAFF One of the reasons money is important is that it enables an interest group to hire a professional staff, usually an executive director, assistants, and other office support staff. The main job of this professional staff is to take care of the day-to-day operations of the interest group, including pursuing policy initiatives; recruiting and maintaining membership; providing membership services; and, of course, raising more money through direct mailings, telemarketing,

TABLE 13.1
Ten of the Most Influential Lobbies in Washington

INDUSTRY OR GROUP	MAJOR PLAYERS	KEY POLICY AREAS	LOBBYING EXPENDITURES FOR 2016
Finance	Insurance, securities and investing, real estate, banks, finance/credit companies	Financial regulation and reforms	$501.5 million
Pharmaceuticals	Pfizer, Eli Lilly & Co., Merck	Health care regulation	$247.4 million
Defense	Lockheed Martin, Boeing, General Dynamics	Defense, military	$137.2 million
Agribusiness	Food industry (Kraft, Unilever, Monsanto); tobacco companies (Philip Morris); biofuel producers and logging companies	Food labeling, environmental regulation, biofuel production	$127.8 million
Technology	Apple, Microsoft, Google, Amazon, Facebook	Corporate tax rates, cybersecurity, net neutrality	$121.3 million
Oil	Exxon Mobile, Koch Industries, Chevron Corporation, Royal Dutch Shell	Environmental regulation	$119.3 million
Mining	The coal industry	Environmental regulation	$13.9 million
Gun rights	National Rifle Association (NRA)	Second Amendment rights, gun control and regulation	$10.6 million
Retirees	AARP	Health care, Medicare, Social Security, retirement, age discrimination	$8.7 million
Pro-Israel	American Israel Public Affairs Committee	Foreign policy	$4.5 million

Source: Compiled by the authors using rankings by BusinessPundit.com, www.businesspundit.com/10-of-the-biggest-lobbies-in-washington/, April 26, 2011, and figures from the Center for Responsive Politics, www.opensecrets.org/lobby/top.php?indexType=c&showYear=2016.

FIGURE 13.4

PAC Contributions to Congressional Campaigns by Type of Contest, 1998–2016

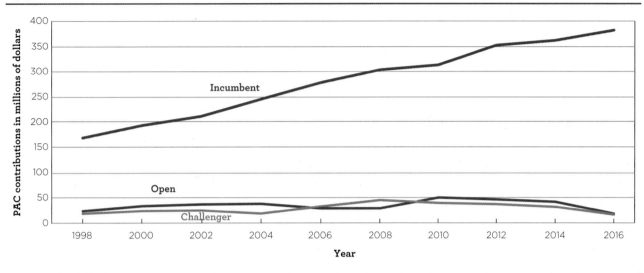

Source: Federal Election Commission, "Campaign Finance Statistics," www.fec.gov/press/campaign_finance_statistics.shtml.

web site donations, and organizational functions. Money is important for creating an organizational infrastructure that can in turn be used to raise additional support and resources.

PROFESSIONAL ASSISTANCE Money also enables the interest group to hire the services of professionals, such as a high-powered lobbying firm. These firms have invested heavily to ensure that they have connections to members of Congress.[105] A well-endowed group can also hire a skilled person to handle Internet operations and a public relations firm to help shape public opinion on a policy.

CAMPAIGN CONTRIBUTIONS Interest groups live by the axiom that to receive, one must give—and give a lot to important people. The maximum that any PAC can give to a congressional campaign is $5,000 for each separate election. Although some PACs give millions to campaigns, most PACs give less than $50,000 to candidates for each election cycle, focusing their contributions on members of the committees responsible for drafting legislation important to their groups.[106] In the wake of the *Citizens United* decision, however, considerable money can be spent by groups on a candidate's behalf, and the groups don't have to disclose the donors' identities. It has become apparent that although *Citizens United* made only small changes to campaign finance law, it had the psychological effect of giving a "green light" to those who wanted to spend lavishly on an election.[107] In 2016 the so-called Super PACs unleashed by *Citizens United* spent more than one billion dollars, although it wasn't clear

that all that money had a real impact on the outcome of the election, at least in the presidential and Senate races.[108]

PAC spending is usually directed toward incumbents of both parties, with incumbents in the majority party, especially committee chairs, getting the greatest share. This dramatic difference is shown in Figure 13.4, which illustrates not only that most of the PAC money goes to incumbents but also that this huge imbalance has increased over the past decade. About 80 percent of PAC contributions go to incumbent members of Congress.[109] Most PACs want to curry favor with incumbents of either party, but some tend to channel their money to one party. For instance, business interests, the American Medical Association, pro-life groups, Christian groups, and the NRA tend to support Republican candidates; and labor groups, the Association of Trial Lawyers of America, the National Education Association, and environmental and pro-choice groups give primarily to Democrats.

The ability to make sizable and strategically placed campaign contributions buys an interest group access to government officials.[110] Access gives the interest group the ability to talk to a representative and members of his or her staff and to present information relevant to the policies they seek to initiate, change, or protect. Access is important because representatives have any number of competing interests vying for their time. Money is meant to oil the door hinge of a representative's office so that it swings open for the interest group. For instance, Bill Clinton's administration was well known in its early years for allowing major donors to stay in the Lincoln bedroom of the White House. The access bought by campaign contributions is usually less blatant, but officials know who has supported their campaigns, and they are unlikely to forget it when the interest group comes knocking at their doors.

The relationship between money and political influence is extremely controversial. Many critics argue that this money buys more than just access; rather, they charge, it buys votes. The circumstantial evidence is strong. For instance, in the Senate deliberations on a public option in health care, which would have provided individuals with an alternative to private health care insurance, the thirty senators who supported the public option had received an average of $15,937 in contributions from the health care industry in the previous six years, compared to the $37,322, on average, received by the seventy senators who opposed it.[111]

However, in the matter of vote buying, systematic studies of congressional voting patterns are mixed. These studies show that the influence of campaign contributions is strongest in committees, where most bills are drafted. However, once the bill reaches the floor of the House or the Senate, there is no consistent link between campaign contributions and roll-call voting.[112] This suggests that campaign contributions influence the process of creating and shaping the legislation, and thus defining the policy alternatives. Nonetheless, the final outcome of a bill is determined by political circumstances that go beyond the campaign contributions of interest groups.

LEADERSHIP

Leadership is an intangible element in the success or failure of an interest group. We mentioned earlier that an effective and charismatic leader or interest group entrepreneur can help a

group organize even if it lacks other resources. In the same way, such a leader can keep a group going when it seems to lack the support from other sources. Candy Lightner's role in MADD and Cesar Chavez's leadership of the United Farm Workers are excellent cases in point. But professional interest group leadership can come at a cost. As the mass-membership interest groups that characterized this country in the past century give way to highly professional groups whose power comes more from their organizational skills than from their active members, some observers have argued that the groups no longer serve as training grounds for citizenship and are more elite driven than democratic. Says one, "The result is a new civic America largely run by advocates and managers without members and marked by yawning gaps between immediate involvements and larger undertakings."[113] Ultimately, professional group leadership can leave the mass citizenry with fewer paths to civic engagement, eliminating one of the characteristics of interest group politics that leads pluralists, for instance, to claim that interest groups can enhance democracy.

MEMBERSHIP: SIZE AND INTENSITY

The membership of any interest group is an important resource in terms of its size, but the level of intensity that members exhibit in support of the group's causes is also critical. Members represent the lifeblood of the interest group because they generally fund its activities. When an interest group is trying to influence policy, it can use its members to write letters, send emails, and engage in other forms of personal contact with legislators or administrative officials. Interest groups often try to reinforce their PAC contributions by encouraging their members to give personal campaign contributions to favored candidates.

Larger groups generally have an advantage over smaller ones. For instance, with nearly 38 million members, AARP can mobilize thousands of people in an attempt to influence elected officials' decisions regarding issues like mandatory retirement, Social Security, or Medicare. In addition, if an interest group's members are spread throughout the country, as are AARP's, that group can exert its influence on almost every member of Congress.

If a group's members are intensely dedicated to the group's causes, then the group may be far stronger than its numbers would indicate. Intense minorities, because of their willingness to devote time, energy, and money to a

Michael Rougier/The LIFE Picture Collection/Getty Images

Leaders Inspire Leaders

The success of the United Farm Workers Union rested largely on the shoulders of Cesar Chavez, whose charismatic and effective leadership caught the attention of powerful Americans like Robert F. Kennedy and brought national attention to the plight of farm workers. Here, Kennedy lends his support to Chavez (center) during the activist's prolonged hunger strike in 1968.

cause they care passionately about, can outweigh more apathetic majorities in the political process. For instance, although a majority of Americans favor some form of gun control, they are outweighed in the political process by the intense feeling of the just over four million members who the NRA claims strongly oppose gun control.[114]

INFORMATION AND COMMUNICATION

Information is one of the most powerful resources in an interest group's arsenal. Often the interest group's members are the only sources of information on the potential or actual impact of a law or regulation. The long struggle to regulate tobacco is a case in point. Although individuals witnessed their loved ones and friends suffering from lung diseases, cancer, and heart problems, it took public health interest groups like the American Cancer Society, the Public Health Cancer Association, and the American Heart Association to conduct the studies, collect the data, and show the connection between these life-threatening illnesses and smoking habits. Of course, the tobacco industry and its interest group, the Tobacco Institute, presented their own research to counter these claims. Not surprisingly, the tobacco industry's investigations showed "no causal relationship" between tobacco use and these illnesses.[115] Eventually, the volume of information showing a strong relationship overwhelmed industry research suggesting otherwise. In 1998 the tobacco industry reached a settlement with states to pay millions of dollars for the treatment of tobacco-related illnesses.

But information that isn't circulated cannot be a powerful tool. In a mediated era like ours—when most of us experience politics, if not life itself, through channels we do not control—it is imperative for those wanting to lobby government effectively to master the use of those channels. For a group to build and disseminate a moving narrative, it has to know who its audience is and how that audience accesses and shares information. There are increasing generational effects at work—while older people remain glued to the local news or maybe a cable outlet like Fox News, younger people curate the information they get. Cracking the code and using all available media will increasingly be crucial to an interest group's success at getting what it wants.

PAUSE AND REVIEW Who, What, How

There is no mystery about what interest groups want: they seek to influence the policymaking process. Some interest groups are clearly more successful than others because the rules of interest group politics reward some group characteristics—such as money, effective leadership, membership size and intensity, and the possession of information—more than others (perhaps social conscience or humanitarianism). It is certainly possible to imagine reforms or rule changes that would change the reward structure and, in so doing, change the groups that would be successful.

In Your Own Words Identify specific resources that interest groups bring to bear when attempting to influence public policy.

THE CITIZENS AND INTEREST GROUPS

The people versus the powerful

Defenders of pluralism believe that interest group formation helps give more power to more citizens, and we have seen that it certainly can enhance democratic life. Interest groups offer channels for representation, participation, education, public agenda building, and defining policy solutions, and they help to keep politicians accountable. Pluralists also believe that the system as a whole benefits from interest group politics. They argue that if no single interest group commands a majority, interest groups will compete with one another and ultimately must form coalitions to create a majority. In the process of forming coalitions, interest groups compromise on policy issues, leading to final policy outcomes that reflect the general will of the people as opposed to the narrow interests of specific interest groups.[116] In this final section we examine the claims of critics of interest group politics who argue that it skews democracy—giving more power to some people than to others—and particularly discriminates against segments of society that tend to be underrepresented in the first place (the poor and the young, for instance).

We have seen in this chapter that a variety of factors—money, leadership, membership, information, and mastery of the media—can make an interest group successful. But this raises red danger flags for American democracy. In American political culture, we value political equality, which is to say the principle of one person, one vote. And as far as voting goes, this is how we practice democracy. Anyone who attempts to visit the polls twice on Election Day is turned away, no matter how rich that person is, how intensely he or she feels about the election, or how eloquently he or she begs for another vote. But policy is made not only at the ballot box. It is also made in the halls and hearing rooms of Congress; in the conference rooms of the bureaucracy; and in corporate boardrooms, private offices, restaurants, and bars. In these places interest groups speak loudly, and since some groups are vastly more successful than others, they have the equivalent of extra votes in the policymaking process.

We are not terribly uncomfortable with the idea that interest groups with large memberships should have more power. After all, democracy is usually about getting the most votes in order to win. But when it comes to the idea that the wealthy have an advantage, or those who feel intensely, or those who have more information, we start to balk. What about the rest of us? Should we have relatively less power over who gets what because we lack these resources?

It is true that groups with money, and business groups in particular, have distinct advantages of organizational access. Many critics suggest that business interests represent a small, wealthy, and united set of elites who dominate the political process,[117] and much evidence supports the view that business interests maintain a special relationship with government and tend to unite behind basic conservative issues (less government spending and lower taxes). Other evidence, however, suggests that business interests are often divided regarding government policies and that other factors can counterbalance their superior monetary resources.

Because business interests are not uniform and tightly organized, groups with large memberships can prevail against them. Corporate money may buy access, but politicians ultimately depend on votes. Groups with large memberships have more voters. A good example of this principle occurred in 1997 when President Clinton proposed trimming $100 billion in Medicare spending over five years. Instead of raising premiums on the elderly, the Clinton administration proposed cuts in Medicare reimbursements to hospitals and doctors. This proposal sparked an intensive lobbying campaign pitting the American Medical Association and the American Hospital Association, two of the most powerful and well-financed lobbies in Washington, against AARP, representing nearly 38 million older Americans. Fearing the voting wrath of AARP, the Republican-led Congress struck a deal with the administration to cut Medicare reimbursements for hospitals and doctors.[118] As this example suggests, when a group's membership is highly motivated and numerous, it can win despite the opposition's lavish resources.[119] Interest group politics in America clearly contains some biases, but it is not the case that any one group or kind of group always gets its way. After years of collecting government subsidies and benefiting from favorable policies, the tobacco industry has at last been stripped of its privilege, illustrating that even corporate giants can be brought low.[120] Similarly, the less wealthy but very intense NRA, which kept gun control off the American law books for decades, has finally been confronted by angry citizens' groups that have put the issue of gun control firmly on the public's agenda, though with mixed success.[121]

What has helped to equalize the position of these groups in American politics is the willingness on the part of citizens to fight fire with fire, politics with politics, organization with organization—an effort made more accessible with the widespread use of the Internet. It is, finally, the power of participation and democracy that can make pluralism fit the pluralists' hopes. For some groups, such as the poor, such advice may be nearly impossible to follow. Lacking knowledge of the system and the resources to organize in the first place, poor people are often the last to be included in interest group politics. Neighborhood-level organizing, however, can counteract this tendency. Other groups left out of the system, such as the merely indifferent, or young people who often regard current issues as irrelevant, will pay the price of inattention and disorganization when the score cards of interest group politics are finally tallied.

In Your Own Words Summarize the relationships among citizens, interest groups, and government.

LET'S REVISIT: *What's at Stake . . . ?*

Let's go back to the question of what's at stake in the dispute over the USDA's organic food regulation. Remember that regulations are a form of rules, and rules determine who the winners and losers are likely to be. Regulations can serve a variety of interests. They could serve the "public interest," simply making it easier for consumers to buy organic food by standardizing what it means to be organic. But other definitions of the public interest might go beyond what consumers prefer, to ask what is best for the environment, for the economy, for farmers. In this case, there were competing business interest groups as well. Agribusiness and the food preparation industry wanted to use regulations to break into a lucrative market previously closed to them because of the labor-intensive nature of organic farming. For the traditional organic farmers, the proposed regulations spelled disaster.

As far as big business was concerned, this case was like many others. Businesses in the United States are able to lobby the government freely to try to get rules and regulations passed that enhance their positions, and to try to stop those that will hurt them. The larger sums of money that big business can bring to the lobbying effort usually give them an edge in influencing government. If the larger businesses were allowed to compete as organic food producers, the small businesses would lose the only advantage they had, and they would have been forced out of business. In this case, the small businesses were aided by citizen action in the form of grassroots lobbying—ironically, in this case, with a little astroturf thrown in. Because those consumers who choose to eat organic foods were a focused, committed, and assertive segment of the population, they were able to follow through with political action.

Today, the playing field has changed. Organic food groups are now almost as powerful as their "agribusiness" counterparts, many traditional food industries have organic divisions, and some traditional food interest groups, like the Grocery Manufacturers Association, are weakening.[122] New consumer groups, like the Organic Consumers Organization, were founded in the wake of the battle over how organic was to be defined.[123] Powerful interests within the organic food industry face their own divisions, for instance over whether organic farming must be done in dirt or can be hydroponic.[124] Interest group power can be fluid, and success by unconventional means can breed new and strong industry groups.

CLUES to Critical Thinking

Federalist *No. 10*

By James Madison, November 23, 1787

Of all the Federalist Papers, *perhaps none has received as much scrutiny and discussion as Madison's* Federalist No. 10 *and his claim that interest groups—or factions, as he calls them—can potentially threaten the very health of a society.*

To the People of the State of New York:

Among the numerous advantages promised by a well constructed Union, none deserves to be more accurately developed than its tendency to break and control the violence of faction. The friend of popular governments never finds himself so much alarmed for their character and fate, as when he contemplates their propensity to this dangerous vice....

By a faction, I understand a number of citizens, whether amounting to a majority or a minority of the whole, who are united and actuated by some common impulse of passion, or of interest, adversed to the rights of other citizens, or to the permanent and aggregate interests of the community.

There are two methods of curing the mischiefs of faction: the one, by removing its causes; the other, by controlling its effects.

There are again two methods of removing the causes of faction: the one, by destroying the liberty which is essential to its existence; the other, by giving to every citizen the same opinions, the same passions, and the same interests.

It could never be more truly said than of the first remedy, that it was worse than the disease. Liberty is to faction what air is to fire, an aliment without which it instantly expires. But it could not be less folly to abolish liberty, which is essential to political life, because it nourishes faction, than it would be to wish the annihilation of air, which is essential to animal life, because it imparts to fire its destructive agency.

The second expedient is as impracticable as the first would be unwise. As long as the reason of man continues fallible, and he is at liberty to exercise it, different opinions will be formed. As long as the connection subsists between his reason and his self-love, his opinions and his passions will have a reciprocal influence on each other; and the former will be objects to which the latter will attach themselves. The diversity in the faculties of men, from which the rights of property originate, is not less an insuperable obstacle to a uniformity of interests. The protection of these faculties is the first object of government. From the protection of different and unequal faculties of acquiring property, the possession of different degrees and kinds of property immediately results; and from the influence of these on the sentiments and views of the respective proprietors, ensues a division of the society into different interests and parties.

The latent causes of faction are thus sown in the nature of man; and we see them everywhere brought into different degrees of activity, according to the different circumstances of civil society.... But the most common and durable source of factions has been the various and unequal distribution of property. Those who hold and those who are without property have ever formed distinct interests in society. Those who are creditors, and those who are debtors, fall under a like discrimination. A landed interest, a manufacturing interest, a mercantile interest, a moneyed interest, with many lesser interests, grow up of necessity in civilized nations, and divide them into different classes, actuated by different sentiments and views. The regulation of these various and interfering interests forms the principal task of modern legislation, and involves the spirit of party and faction in the necessary and ordinary operations of the government....

It is in vain to say that enlightened statesmen will be able to adjust these clashing interests, and render them all subservient to the public good. Enlightened statesmen will not always be at the helm. Nor, in many cases, can such an adjustment be made at all without taking into view indirect and remote considerations, which will rarely prevail over the immediate interest which one party may find in disregarding the rights of another or the good of the whole.

The inference to which we are brought is, that the CAUSES of faction cannot be removed, and that relief is only to be sought in the means of controlling its EFFECTS.

If a faction consists of less than a majority, relief is supplied by the republican principle, which enables the majority to defeat its sinister views by regular vote. It may clog the administration, it may convulse the society; but it will be unable to execute and mask its violence under the forms of the Constitution. When a majority is included in a faction, the form of popular government, on the other hand, enables it to sacrifice to its ruling passion or interest both the public good and the rights of other citizens. To secure the public good and private rights against the danger of such a faction, and at the same time to preserve the spirit and the form of popular government, is then the great object to which our inquiries are directed. Let me add that it is the great desideratum by which this form of government can be rescued from the opprobrium under which it has so long labored, and be recommended to the esteem and adoption of mankind.

By what means is this object attainable? Evidently by one of two only. Either the existence of the same passion or interest in a majority at the same time must be prevented, or the majority, having such coexistent passion or interest, must be rendered, by their number and local situation, unable to concert and carry into effect schemes of oppression. If the impulse and the opportunity be suffered to coincide, we well know that neither moral nor religious motives can be relied on as an adequate control. They are not found to be such on the injustice and violence of individuals, and lose their efficacy in proportion to the number combined together, that is, in proportion as their efficacy becomes needful.

From this view of the subject it may be concluded that a pure democracy, by which I mean a society consisting of a small number of citizens, who assemble and administer the government in person, can admit of no cure for the mischiefs of faction. A common passion or interest will, in almost every case, be felt by a majority of the whole; a communication and concert result from the form of government itself; and there is nothing to check the inducements to sacrifice the weaker party or an obnoxious individual. Hence it is that such democracies have ever been spectacles of turbulence and contention; have ever been found incompatible with personal security or the rights of property; and have in general been as short in their lives as they have been violent in their deaths. Theoretic politicians, who have patronized this species of government, have erroneously supposed that by reducing mankind to a perfect equality in their political rights, they would, at the same time, be perfectly equalized and assimilated in their possessions, their opinions, and their passions.

A republic, by which I mean a government in which the scheme of representation takes place, opens a different prospect, and promises the cure for which we are seeking. Let us examine the points in which it varies from pure democracy, and we shall comprehend both the nature of the cure and the efficacy which it must derive from the Union.

The two great points of difference between a democracy and a republic are: first, the delegation of the government, in the latter, to a small number of citizens elected by the rest; secondly, the greater number of citizens, and greater sphere of country, over which the latter may be extended.

The effect of the first difference is, on the one hand, to refine and enlarge the public views, by passing them through the medium of a chosen body of citizens, whose wisdom may best discern the true interest of their country, and whose patriotism and love of justice will be least likely to sacrifice it to temporary or partial considerations. Under such a regulation, it may well happen that the public voice, pronounced by the representatives of the people, will be more consonant to the public good than if pronounced by the people themselves, convened for the purpose. On the other hand, the effect may be inverted. Men of factious tempers, of local prejudices, or of sinister designs, may, by intrigue, by corruption, or by other means, first obtain the suffrages, and then betray the interests, of the people. The question resulting is, whether small or extensive republics are more favorable to the election of proper guardians of the public weal; and it is clearly decided in favor of the latter by two obvious considerations:

In the first place, it is to be remarked that, however small the republic may be, the representatives must be raised to a certain number, in order to guard against the cabals of a few; and that, however large it may be, they must be limited to a certain number, in order to guard against the confusion of a multitude. Hence, the number of representatives in the two cases not being in proportion to that of the two constituents, and being proportionally greater in the small republic, it follows that, if the proportion of fit characters be not less in the large than in the small republic, the former will present a greater option, and consequently a greater probability of a fit choice.

In the next place, as each representative will be chosen by a greater number of citizens in the large than in the small republic, it will be more difficult for unworthy candidates to practice with success the vicious arts by which elections are too often carried; and the suffrages of the people being more free, will be more likely to centre in men who possess the most attractive merit and the most diffusive and established characters.

It must be confessed that in this, as in most other cases, there is a mean, on both sides of which inconveniences will be found to lie. By enlarging too much the number of electors, you render the representatives too little acquainted with all their local circumstances and lesser interests; as by reducing it too much, you render him unduly attached to these, and too little fit to comprehend and pursue great and national objects. The federal Constitution forms a happy combination in this respect; the great and aggregate interests being referred to the national, the local and particular to the State legislatures.

The other point of difference is, the greater number of citizens and extent of territory which may be brought within the compass of republican than of democratic government; and it is this circumstance principally which renders factious combinations less to be dreaded in the former than in the latter. The smaller the society, the fewer probably will be the distinct parties and interests composing it; the fewer the distinct parties and interests, the more frequently will a majority be found of the same party; and the smaller the number of individuals composing a majority, and the smaller the compass within which they are placed, the more easily will they concert and execute their plans of oppression. Extend the sphere, and you take in a greater variety of parties and interests; you make it less probable that a majority of the whole will have a common motive to invade the rights of other citizens; or if such a common motive exists, it will be more difficult for all who feel it to discover their own strength, and to act in unison with each other. Besides other impediments, it may be remarked that, where there is a consciousness of unjust or dishonorable purposes, communication is always checked by distrust in proportion to the number whose concurrence is necessary.

Hence, it clearly appears, that the same advantage which a republic has over a democracy, in controlling the effects of faction, is enjoyed by a large over a small republic,—is enjoyed by the Union over the States composing it. Does the advantage consist in the substitution of representatives whose enlightened views and virtuous sentiments render them superior to local prejudices and schemes of injustice? It will not be denied that the representation of the Union will be most likely to possess these requisite endowments. Does it consist in the greater security afforded by a greater variety of parties, against the event of any one party being able to outnumber and oppress the rest? In an equal degree does the increased variety of parties comprised within the Union, increase this security? Does it, in fine, consist in the greater obstacles opposed to the concert and accomplishment of the secret wishes of an unjust and interested majority? Here, again, the extent of the Union gives it the most palpable advantage.

The influence of factious leaders may kindle a flame within their particular States, but will be unable to spread a general conflagration through the other States. A religious sect may degenerate into a political faction in a part of the Confederacy; but the variety of sects dispersed over the entire face of it must secure the national councils against any danger from that source. A rage for paper money, for an abolition of debts, for an equal division of property, or for any other improper or wicked project, will be less apt to pervade the whole body of the Union than a particular member of it; in the same proportion as such a malady is more likely to taint a particular county or district, than an entire State.

In the extent and proper structure of the Union, therefore, we behold a republican remedy for the diseases most incident to republican government. And according to the degree of pleasure and pride we feel in being republicans, ought to be our zeal in cherishing the spirit and supporting the character of Federalists.

PUBLIUS.

Source: Library of Congress, http://thomas.loc.gov/home/histdox/ fed_10.html.

Consider the source and the audience: *The Federalist Papers* were anonymous editorials, written to persuade the citizens of New York to sign on to the Constitution. *Federalist* No. 10 was especially aimed at people who feared the possibilities for corruption in a large country. How is Madison responding to those fears?

Lay out the argument and the underlying values and assumptions: How does Madison define factions, and why are they problematic? Why does he think the root causes of factions cannot be controlled, but the effects of factions can? How will the new republic do that?

Uncover the evidence: Does Madison provide any evidence to support his arguments? Is there any other type of evidence he could have added to make his argument more persuasive?

Evaluate the conclusion: Was Madison right? Are factions the source of instability in American politics? Can they be contained?

Sort out the political implications: What would Madison say if he could come back today? Would he think his expectations in *Federalist* No. 10 had been borne out? Would his argument change in the altered technological environment of today?

Review

The Formation and Role of Interest Groups

Government will always distribute resources in ways that benefit some at the expense of others. People form interest groups in order to influence the way that government policy decisions are made. To accomplish their goals, interest groups lobby elected officials, rally public opinion, offer policy suggestions, and keep tabs on policy once enacted. Interest groups also must organize and convince others to join, often offering selective benefits to members.

faction (p. 440)
interest group (p. 441)
political action committees (PACs) (p. 441)
Super PACs (p. 441)

collective action problem (p. 443)
collective good (p. 443)
free riders (p. 443)
selective incentives (p. 443)
material benefits (p. 444)

solidary benefits (p. 444)
expressive benefits (p. 444)
lobbying (p. 445)

Types of Interest Groups

Interest groups come in all different types. Economic groups like business associations or trade unions want to protect and improve their status. Public interest groups advocate their vision of society, and equal opportunity groups organize to gain, or at least improve, economic status and civil rights. Governments form associations to improve relations among their ranks.

economic interest groups (p. 445)
equal opportunity interest groups (p. 447)

public interest groups (p. 449)
government interest groups (p. 453)

Interest Group Politics

Lobbyists are the key players of interest groups. They influence public policy either by approaching the three branches of government (direct lobbying) or by convincing the people to pressure the government (indirect lobbying).

direct lobbying (p. 454)
indirect lobbying (p. 454)
revolving door (p. 454)

issue advocacy ads (p. 460)
social protest (p. 462)
grassroots lobbying (p. 463)

astroturf lobbying (p. 463)

Interest Group Resources

The success of individual interest groups is often affected by factors like funding, quality of leadership, membership size and intensity, and access to information.

The Citizens and Interest Groups

Critics of interest groups fear that the most powerful groups are simply those with the most money, and that this poses a danger to American democracy. However, interest group formation may also be seen as a way to give more power to more citizens, offering a mechanism to keep politicians accountable by offering additional channels for representation, participation, education, public agenda building, and creation of policy solutions.

John Sommers II/Getty Images

14

VOTING, CAMPAIGNS, AND ELECTIONS

What's at Stake . . . in the Electoral College?

OH, THE IRONY! The candidate who throughout the election accused the process of being rigged won in the end, not because he got more votes but because of an ancient and vestigial appendage of election law that distorted the popular vote results so that his losing margin was enough to deliver to him the presidency.

For Republicans who watched election results late into the night on November 8, 2016, it was a lightning bolt of good luck that managed to strike twice in twenty years, though it had happened only four times in our history. For Democrats it felt like the crazy, upending election of 2000 all over again, minus the Supreme Court and the recount. A candidate who had trailed in the national poll averages for the entire election cycle and who continued to trail in the popular vote was about to win the presidency of the United States. When all the votes were counted, Donald Trump was nearly three million popular votes behind Hillary Clinton. Yet he—not she—became president of the United States.

By President_Rutherford_Hayes_1870_-_1880.jpg: Mathew Bradyderivative work: UpstateNYer, via Wikimedia Commons

By Pach Brothers - photographAdam Cuerden - restoration, via Wikimedia Commons

Saul Loeb/AFP/Getty Images

Chip Somodevilla/Getty Images

Winning and Losing at the Same Time

Donald J. Trump won a majority of Electoral College votes—and thus the presidency—despite receiving nearly three million fewer popular votes than Hillary Clinton. This may seem shocking, but it has happened four times in American history, in the cases of Rutherford B. Hayes, Benjamin Harrison, George W. Bush, and, of course, Trump himself.

How does that happen? Stunned and tearful Democrats were in shock, feeling their votes hadn't counted, feeling disenfranchised. Crowds took to the streets in cities across the nation to protest the election results. Petitions circulated demanding that the people's vote be honored.

Jubilant Republicans thanked their lucky stars for an institution they often felt was rigged against them but that had managed to give them the presidency in three of the last seven elections, even though they had won the popular vote in only one of them.

The Democrats' demon and the Republicans' savior? The Electoral College.

The Electoral College is like the appendix of American politics. It's an organ you don't really need any more and that is generally so quiet and unobtrusive you don't even realize it's there. But when it gets inflamed, it's painful, and if it bursts, it threatens a systemwide failure.

The emergency caused by the Electoral College has so far not threatened the life of the republic, but it can pose a crisis of legitimacy. Twice in this very young century, Democratic winners of the popular vote had to give gracious concession speeches, respecting the procedures of American politics and the results they produced, even while they and their supporters felt robbed of a victory that seemed by every other rule of democracy to be theirs.

What is this evolutionary appendage that intervenes periodically to save the bacon of the party that lost the popular vote and throw the winning party into mourning? Where did it come from, and why doesn't some political surgeon just remove it before it causes more chaos?

The U.S. founders faced a dilemma about how the executive of the new republic should be chosen. Remember, in the days after Shays's Rebellion, they were filled with doubt about the wisdom that the people could be counted on to exercise. Direct popular election of the president felt too risky—they might pick a rabble-rousing demagogue like Daniel Shays, who wouldn't demonstrate the wisdom and stability that

the founders valued. Besides, the South would object; since slaves were not citizens and couldn't vote, the North would always have a population advantage. But the alternative, giving Congress the ability to choose the executive like in a parliamentary system, meant doing away with their cherished principle of separation of powers. The Electoral College seemed to be one of those compromises that had worked so well for them throughout the constitution-writing process.

Electors would be chosen at the state level, originally by state legislators (who had been elected by the people) and eventually by the people themselves. The number of electors awarded to each state would be based on the total number of representatives that that state had in Congress (House plus Senate). This removed any objections the South would have since it had already been decided that slaves would count as three-fifths of a person for purposes of determining how many representatives a state received. Electors would cast votes for the presidency based on their independent judgment about who would be the better presidential candidate. In the 68th *Federalist Paper*, Alexander Hamilton wrote, "A small number of persons, selected by their fellow-citizens from the general mass, will be most likely to possess the information and discernment requisite to such complicated [tasks]."

And that is the ancient history of today's Electoral College. Since then our ideas about democracy have changed. We no longer see the people as the threat to stability that the founders worried about, and we have introduced more popular control into our political process. We amended the Constitution to directly elect senators, when once they too were chosen by state legislators, so that the entire Congress is directly elected by the people.

Even the Electoral College has evolved a bit. In the early 1800s, states figured they would have more leverage if, rather than voting independently, their electors all voted the same way. When they began to cast their votes for the popular vote winner in their state, the founders who felt this violated the check provided by independent electors were dismayed. Some very unorthodox election results ensued when states were using different methods of elector selection, including Andrew Jackson winning both the popular vote for president and the Electoral College in 1824 and *still* losing the presidency in the House of Representatives. By the late 1800s, all states were choosing their electors by popular vote.

Still, even with electors popularly chosen, the matter of how to distribute them remains, and that too is up to the states. Today all states but two give all their votes to the popular vote winner in their state. The other two, Maine and Nebraska, use a system based on congressional districts. In this chapter's *The Big Picture,* we show you how different state rules for distributing the votes could have resulted in different winners in the 2012 presidential election.

Ironically, the winner-take-all distribution of electoral votes generally exaggerates the advantage of the winner, turning even a slight popular vote lead into a landslide in the Electoral College. In the few cases like 2000 and 2016, however, it has a different, antidemocratic consequence. Since Hillary Clinton lost some crucial states, such as Wisconsin, Florida, and Pennsylvania, by a point or less, and won other, big states like California and New York by millions of votes, her popular vote number was enough to win easily, but she lost the Electoral College vote by a narrow margin in enough places to lose out on the presidency.

Coincidentally, back when Al Gore lost the Electoral College vote while winning the popular majority in 2000, the newly elected junior senator from New York, Hillary Clinton, said, "I believe strongly that in a democracy, we should respect the will of the people and to me that means it's time to do away with the Electoral College and move to the popular election of our president."[1] In fact, in 2012, Trump himself called the Electoral College "a disaster for a democracy."[2] There have been schemes for change that avoid the complicated and unlikely process of constitutional amendment, such as the National Popular Vote Interstate Compact that aims to create a contract among states controlling at least 270 electoral votes. Under the compact they would cast their votes for the popular vote winner. It has been enacted in twelve states controlling 172 electoral votes and is pending in several others (see www. nationalpopularvote.com). Yet, until enough states sign on, the Electoral College is still with us and still thwarting the popular will at awkward intervals.

So in this "enlightened democratic" day and age, the question is why? Why do we still have this archaic institution whose original purpose, like that of the human appendix, has long since been lost to history, but, like the appendix, still flares up occasionally in unexpected ways? For a voter who cast a ballot for a person who won more votes but lost the election, it can feel a bit like a democratic backfire. What is at stake in keeping the Electoral College after all this time? We will return to this question after we look more closely at how voting and elections work in American politics. **«**

ALTHOUGH we pride ourselves on our democratic

government, Americans seem to have a love-hate relationship with the idea of campaigns and voting. As a result, we engage in competing narratives about the worth of elections. On the one hand, many citizens believe that elections do not accomplish anything, that elected officials ignore the wishes of the people, and that government is rigged to benefit the elite at the expense of the many. There are exceptions, of course, but typically only about half of the eligible electorate votes.

On the other hand, when it is necessary to choose a leader or make a decision, whether picking the captain of a football team, or deciding where to go to dinner, the first instinct of many Americans is to call an election. Even though there are other ways to choose leaders—picking the oldest, the wisest, or the strongest; holding a lottery; or asking for volunteers—Americans almost always prefer an election. We elect over half a million public officials in America.[3] This means we have a lot of elections—more elections more often for more officials than in any other democracy. In this chapter we examine the complicated place of elections in American politics and American culture.

VOTING IN A DEMOCRATIC SOCIETY

A nonviolent means for political change

Until the last couple hundred years, it was virtually unimaginable that the average citizen should have any say in who would govern. Leaders were chosen by birth, by the church, by military might, by the current leaders, but not by the mass public. Real political change, when it occurred, was usually ushered in with violence and bloodshed.

Today, global commitment to democracy is on the rise. Americans and, increasingly, other citizens around the world buy into the narrative that government with the consent of the governed is superior to government imposed on unwilling subjects and that political change is best accomplished through the ballot box rather than on the battlefield or in the streets. The mechanism that connects citizens with their governments, by which they signify their consent and through which they accomplish peaceful change, is elections. Looked at from this perspective, elections are an amazing innovation—they provide a method for the peaceful transfer of power. Radical political changes can take place without blood being shed, an accomplishment that would confound most of our political ancestors.

As we saw in Chapter 1, however, proponents of democracy can have very different ideas about how much power citizens should exercise over government. Elite theorists believe that citizens should confine their role to choosing among competing elites; pluralists think citizens should join groups that fight for their interests in government on their behalf; and participatory democrats call for more active and direct citizen involvement in politics. Each of these views has consequences for how elections should be held. How many officials should be chosen by the people? How often should elections be held? Should people choose officials directly, or through representatives whom they elect? How accountable should officials be to the people who elect them? Who should be allowed to vote? We have already seen, in Chapter 11, that though Americans hardly resemble the informed, active citizens prescribed by democratic theory, that does not mean they are unqualified to exercise political power.

THE FOUNDERS' INTENTIONS

The founders were of two minds about this, of course. The Constitution reflects their fears that people could not reliably exercise wise and considered judgment about politics. Consequently the founders built a remarkable layer of insulation between the national government and the will of the people. The president was to be elected not directly by the people but by an **Electoral College**, which was expected to be a group of wiser-than-average men who would use prudent judgment. In fact, only the House of Representatives, one-half of one-third of the government, was to be popularly elected. The Senate and the executive and judicial branches were to be selected by different types of political elites who could easily check any moves that might arise from the whims of the masses. In the founders' view, the government needed the support of the masses, but it could not afford to be led by what they saw as the public's shortsighted and easily misguided judgment.

Despite the founders' reluctance to entrust much political power to American citizens, we have since altered our method of electing senators to make these elections direct, and the Electoral College, as we shall see, almost always endorses the popular vote for president. Elections have become a central part of American life, even if our participation in them is somewhat uneven.

THE FUNCTIONS OF ELECTIONS

Theorists argue that elections fulfill a variety of functions in modern democratic life: selecting leaders, giving direction to policy, developing citizenship, informing the public, containing conflict, and legitimizing and stabilizing the system. Here we examine and evaluate how well elections fill these functions.

SELECTION OF LEADERS Like our founders, many philosophers and astute political observers have had doubts about whether elections are the best way to choose wise and capable leaders. Philosophers from Plato to John Stuart Mill have expressed doubts about citizen capability, arguing that you cannot trust the average citizen to make wise choices in the voting booth.[4] A skilled demagogue can manipulate voters by making emotional appeals to their anger, fear, or resentment. More recent critics also focus on the other side of the equation, claiming that democratic elections often fail to produce the best leaders because the electoral process scares off some of the most capable candidates. Running for office is a hard, expensive, and bruising enterprise. Many qualified people are put off by the process, though they might be able to do an excellent job and have much to offer through public service. The simple truth is that elections ensure only that the leader chosen is the most popular on the ballot. There is no guarantee that the best candidate will run, or that the people will choose the wisest, most honest, or most capable leader from the possible candidates.

> ### Are elections the best way to choose our leaders?

POLICY DIRECTION Democracy and elections are only partially about choosing able leadership. The fears of the founders notwithstanding, today we also expect that the citizenry will have a large voice in what the government actually does. Competitive elections are intended in part to keep leaders responsive to the concerns of the governed, since they can be voted out of office if voters are displeased.

The policy impact of elections, however, is indirect. For instance, at the national level, we elect individuals and, by association, the policies they promise to enact, but we do not vote on actual policies. Although citizens in about half the states can make policy directly through initiatives and referenda, the founders left no such option at the national level. Thus the different parts of the national government respond to different publics at different times. The voice of the people

---

Electoral College an intermediary body that elects the president

Vote Smart

Volunteer members of Project Vote Smart, liberals and conservatives alike, reach out to citizens to inform them about the voting records and backgrounds of thousands of candidates and elected officials so that voters can make informed decisions. The group accepts no funding from any organization, special interest group, or industry as part of its effort to maintain its neutral, nonbiased platform.

is muted and modulated. Occasionally, however, especially when there is a change in the party that controls the government, elections do produce rather marked shifts in public policy.[5] The New Deal of the 1930s is an excellent case in point. The election of a Democratic president and Congress allowed a sweeping political response to the Depression, in sharp contrast to the previous Republican administration's hands-off approach to the crisis.

The electoral process does a surprisingly good job of directing policy in less dramatic ways as well. Research demonstrates, for example, that in the states, elections achieve a remarkable consistency between the general preferences of citizens and the kinds of policies that the states enact.[6] At the congressional level, members of the House and the Senate are quite responsive to the overall policy wishes of their constituents, and those who are not tend to lose their jobs.[7] Scholars have found that, for the most part, presidents also deliver on the promises that they make and that the national parties accomplish much of what they set out in their platforms.[8] Elections speed up the process by which changes in public preferences for a more activist or less activist (more liberal or more conservative) government are systematically translated into patterns of public policy.[9]

> **political efficacy** citizens' feelings of effectiveness in political affairs

CITIZEN DEVELOPMENT Some theorists argue that participation in government in and of itself—regardless of which leaders or policy directions are chosen—is valuable for citizens and that elections help citizens feel fulfilled and effective.[10] When individuals are unable to participate in politics, their sense of **political efficacy**, of being effective in political affairs, suffers. People who participate more, whether in elections or through other means, feel more powerful and have higher senses of political efficacy.[11] Elections thus provide a mechanism by which individuals can move from being passive subjects who feel pushed and pulled by forces larger than themselves to being active citizens fulfilling their potential to have a positive effect on their own lives.

INFORMING THE PUBLIC When we watch the circus of the modern presidential campaign, it may seem a bit of a stretch to say that an important function of campaigns and elections is to educate the public. But ideally the campaign is a time of deliberation when alternative points of view are aired openly so that the citizenry can judge the truth and desirability of competing claims and the competence of competing candidates and parties. The evidence is that people do learn a good deal of useful political information from campaign advertisements and for the most part choose the candidates who match their values and policy preferences.[12] As citizens, we probably know and understand a lot more about our government because of our electoral process than we would without free and competitive elections.

CONTAINING CONFLICT Elections help us influence policy, but in other ways they also limit our options for political influence.[13] If elections help reduce our political conflicts to electoral contests, they also operate as a kind of safety valve for citizen discontent. There is always a relatively peaceful mechanism through which unhappy citizens can vent their energy. Elections can change officials, replacing Democrats with Republicans or vice versa, but they do not fundamentally alter the underlying character of the system. Without the electoral vent, citizens might eventually turn to more threatening behaviors like boycotts, protests, civil disobedience, and rebellion.

LEGITIMATION AND SYSTEM STABILITY A final important function of elections is to make political outcomes acceptable to participants. By participating in the process of elections, we implicitly accept, and thereby legitimize, the results. The genius here is that participation tends to make political results acceptable even to those who lose. They do not take to the streets, set up terrorist cells, or stop paying their taxes. Rather, in the overwhelming majority of instances, citizens who lose in the electoral process shrug their shoulders, obey the rules made by the winning representatives, and wait for their next chance to elect candidates whose policies are more to their liking. Even in 2000 and 2016, when Al Gore and Hillary Clinton won the popular vote but lost in the Electoral College, their supporters largely accepted the results peacefully, if regretfully (see the *CLUES to Critical Thinking* feature at the end of the chapter). The beauty of elections is that they can bring about change but without grave threats to the stability of the system.

WHAT IF WE DON'T VOTE?

Despite all the good reasons for doing so, many people do not vote. Does it matter? There are two ways to tackle this question. One approach is to ask whether election outcomes would be different if nonvoters were to participate. The other approach is to ask whether higher levels of nonvoting indicate that democracy is not healthy. Both questions, of course, concern important potential consequences of low participation in our elections.

CONSEQUENCES FOR ELECTION OUTCOMES Studies of the likely effects of nonvoting come up with contradictory answers. The upshot is that it is unclear whether it would benefit one party or the other if more

people voted. Republicans tend to fear that encouraging more people to vote would result in more Democrats in the electorate since they are drawn disproportionally from demographic groups who do not vote. There is some evidence that this might be the case. One political scholar found some evidence of this for the 1980 presidential election and concluded that a much higher turnout among nonvoters would have made the election closer and that Jimmy Carter might even have won reelection.[14] Similarly, when political scientists have run simulations to test whether full turnout would alter the results in elections for the U.S. Senate, the share of the vote for Democratic candidates is increased, but given that these elections are not particularly close, the extra votes would seldom change the winner of the elections.[15]

Undermining this interpretation are findings from most other presidential elections that nonvoters' preferences are quite responsive to short-term factors, so they disproportionately prefer the winning candidate. Because these voters are less partisan and have less intensely held issue positions, they are moved more easily by the short-term campaign factors favoring one party or the other. In most presidential elections, nonvoters' participation would have increased the winner's margin only slightly or not changed things at all.[16] Interviews taken shortly after recent presidential elections suggest that those who did not vote would have broken for the winner, regardless of party.[17]

CONSEQUENCES FOR DEMOCRACY Low turnout might not affect who wins an election, but elections do more than simply select leaders. How might nonvoting affect the quality of democratic life in America? Nonvoting can influence the stability and legitimacy of democratic government. The victor in close presidential elections, for example, must govern the country, but as little as 25 percent of the eligible electorate may have voted for the winner. When a majority of the electorate sits out of an election, the entire government process may begin to lose legitimacy in society at large. Nonvoting can also have consequences for the nonvoter. To the extent that nonvoters have different policy goals, they are underrepresented by not voting. Politicians are more attentive to the voice of voters (and contributors). And then psychologically, as we have noted, failure to participate politically can aggravate already low feelings of efficacy and produce higher levels of political estrangement. To the extent that being a citizen is an active pursuit, unhappy, unfulfilled, and unconnected citizens seriously damage the quality of democratic life for themselves and for the country as a whole.

Those with the greatest stake in the continued existence of elections in America are the citizens who live under their rule. At stake for citizens is the important question of which candidates and parties will govern. However, by viewing elections in a broader perspective, we can see that elections also contribute to the quality of democratic life: they help to define a crucial relationship between the governed and those they choose as leaders, to influence public policy, to educate the citizenry, to contain conflict, and to legitimize political outcomes and decisions.

Not participating in elections has consequences. To the extent that this affects one party disproportionally, a whole set of preferences may receive less representation. Many politicians would like to attend to the needs of all constituents equally, but when push comes to shove and they have to make hard choices, voters are going to be heeded more than silent nonvoters. Also at stake in low and declining turnout rates is the quality of democratic life—and the stability and legitimacy of the system. Nonvoting is tied to citizen estrangement from the political process, and in this view the quality of democratic life itself depends on active citizen participation.

In Your Own Words Explain the function of elections, both as intended by the founders and in practice.

EXERCISING THE RIGHT TO VOTE IN AMERICA

Overcoming multiple barriers to participation

We argued in Chapter 11 that even without being well informed and following campaigns closely, Americans can still cast intelligent votes reflecting their best interests. But in a typical presidential election, barely half of the adult population votes, and in off-year congressional elections, primaries, and many state and local elections, the rates of participation drop even lower. Some observers argue that that is just fine—ill-informed voters *should* stay home. The question of how easy we should make voting is one with important philosophical and partisan implications.

REGULATING THE ELECTORATE

One factor with a significant impact on whether people exercise their right to vote is the legal obstacle course they face. Voter turnout provides a dramatic illustration of our theme that rules make a difference in who wins and who loses in politics. Election rules define who can vote and how easy it will be for those legally eligible to vote to actually do so. In many countries the government takes responsibility for registering citizens to vote, and in some—Australia, Belgium, and Italy,

> **regulating the electorate** the process of setting rules that define who can vote and how difficult or easy it will be to cast a ballot in an election

for example—voting is required by law. As a result, turnout rates in these countries are high.[18] Traditionally the United States has had a set of rules that put a brake on voting participation by making registration a burdensome activity and by making voting more difficult than it is in other places. Election rules act as a set of valves that make it easier or harder for people to vote, a process we call **regulating the electorate**.

HOW EASY SHOULD VOTING BE? A PARTISAN DIVIDE Even people who are deeply committed to democratic norms debate whether voting ought to be made so easy that uninformed voters go to the polls. For those who think voters should pass some minimum threshold of involvement in the system, the existence of some hurdles, in the form of registration laws and limited voting opportunities, helps to weed out those who really do not know much about the issues or the candidates they are voting for. Those who reject this idea say that everyone who is obligated under the law ought to have easy access to making that law, and that individuals might not know the nuances of public policy but they do know their own interests best. This is a philosophical debate that is unlikely to be solved any time soon.

Alongside this philosophical debate is an ongoing and recently intensified partisan battle about who should be encouraged to vote. At the heart of this debate (if not in its rhetoric) is not so much what is good for the democracy as a whole, as much as what is most beneficial to each political party. Substantial demographic differences are found in the primary supporters of the parties: In general, Republicans have been wealthier, whiter, and better educated; Democrats less wealthy, less educated, and much more diverse. In recent years, those with more education have swung to the Democratic Party, especially those with advanced degrees. Republicans are still more likely to vote, and restrictions on voting like voter ID laws, fewer voting hours, or longer registration periods are widely believed to have a greater impact on Democratic supporters. Thus, at least since the battle over the Voting Rights Act of 1965, there has been a consistent split between Democrats, who tend to favor laws that make voting easier, since their voters are those most likely to be dissuaded by cumbersome regulations, and Republicans, who favor tighter rules, knowing that most of their voters will turn out anyway. This battle has intensified in recent years as the parties have become more polarized.

And so, the debate over how easy it should be to exercise one's right to vote, instead of being fought over philosophical grounds about the nature of democracy, has become a partisan power struggle. When Democrats were in charge of Congress in the 1990s, they attempted to address the problem at the federal level. In 1993, for instance, Congress

A Hard-Won Right

Black voters in Peachtree, Alabama, lined up to vote a year after the passage of the Voting Rights Act of 1965. While Americans cherish their right to choose their leaders and representatives, the ease with which they can do so has always been influenced by politics.

passed the so-called **Motor Voter Act**, which requires the states to take a more active role in registering people to vote, including providing registration opportunities when people are applying for driver's licenses or at the welfare office. A number of states followed up with laws that allowed extended periods of early voting, same-day registration, and, in the case of Oregon, voting by mail. Each reform has marginally increased the numbers of people voting, but on the whole the results have been a disappointment to Democratic reformers. An exhaustive review of the research concluded that, even with obstacles to voting removed, "for many people, voting remains an activity from which there is virtually no gratification—instrumental, expressive, or otherwise."[19] Even though regulating the electorate makes little apparent difference to electoral outcomes, it has not gone away as a partisan issue.

STATE CONTROL OF ELECTIONS AND THE ROLE OF THE SUPREME COURT Although constitutional amendments set fundamental voting protections based on race, gender, and age, and federal legislation like the Motor Voter Act is the law of the land, the Constitution gives to the states the primary responsibility for determining how elections are held. Most of the rules that regulate the electorate—how early and where voters need to register, whether early voting or voting by mail is permitted, how long polls are open, and the like—are made at the state level, and over time we have seen substantial fluctuations in how easy various states make it for citizens to exercise their constitutional right to vote.

Since 2008, and especially following the 2010 Republican successes in state elections, state laws have been passed that require various forms of identification to vote and that cut back on the existing trend of permitting early voting. The Supreme Court cleared the way for the election rule battles in its 2008 decision that Indiana's voter ID law—at the time the strictest in the nation—does not violate the Constitution. Encouraged by that decision, almost half of the states, mostly those under Republican control, have instituted voting restrictions. These include various voter ID requirements, restrictions of voter registration drives, elimination of election-day registration, and a cutting back on opportunities for early voting.[20] (See *Snapshot of America: How Did We Vote in the 2016 Presidential Election?*)

The Voting Rights Act of 1965 put some southern states under scrutiny to be sure they were not continuing to discriminate against African Americans. But in 2013 the drive to tighten the voting rules was made much easier by the Supreme Court's decision in *Shelby County v. Holder*, which blunted the Voting Right Act's requirement for states with histories of racial discrimination to have changes in their election laws cleared by the federal courts or the Department of Justice. Following that decision, a number of states in the deep South implemented restrictive provisions that would be or had been denied under the preclearance requirement. Recent changes in Virginia provide an illustration of the measures the Republican-controlled state governments have adopted: the state eliminated same-day registration, reduced the early voting period, ended preregistration for sixteen- and seventeen-year-olds, and instituted a photo ID requirement. Republicans insist that these measures are intended to reduce voter fraud, but there is little or no evidence that such fraud exists and the real agenda is clearly to restrict the voting of constituents (minorities, the poor, and the young) who are seen as sympathetic to Democrats.

But the electoral rules are not settled. Citizen and partisan groups are contesting efforts to restrict voting in the legislatures and in the courts. Although the justification for greater restrictions is generally stated in terms of ensuring the integrity of the electoral process—a goal few would disagree with, whether Democrats or Republicans—the sharp partisan divide on electoral restrictions supports the idea that this is

Motor Voter Act legislation allowing citizens to register to vote at the same time they apply for a driver's license or other state benefit

really a battle to regulate the electorate for partisan advantage. Before the 2016 election the courts struck down restrictive state election laws in Texas, North Carolina, Wisconsin, Kansas, and North Dakota. But the Supreme Court struck down a North Carolina voter ID law as too restrictive, and it has signaled its intent to leave all but the most egregious cases to the states. With the firm conservative majority on the Court, that is unlikely to change.[21]

WHO VOTES AND WHO DOESN'T?

Many political observers, activists, politicians, and political scientists worry about the extent of nonvoting in the United States.[22] When people do not vote, they have no voice in choosing their leaders, their policy preferences are not registered, and they do not develop as active citizens. Some observers fear that their abstention signals an alienation from the political process.

From survey data, we know quite a lot about who votes and who doesn't in America in terms of their age, gender, income, education, and racial and ethnic make-up. For instance, older citizens consistently vote at higher rates than younger ones do. Gender also makes a difference. Since 1984, women have been voting at a higher rate than men, although the differences are typically only 3 or 4 percent. The likelihood of voting goes up steadily with income and education. Finally, race and ethnicity matter. Turnout among members of racial and ethnic minority groups has traditionally been lower than that of whites. But that changed in 2008 (and 2012), with an African American as the Democratic nominee.

When we add these characteristics together, the differences are substantial. For example, the turnout among eighteen- to twenty-four-year-old males with less than a high school education is about a third the rate of the turnout rate for females aged sixty-five to seventy-four years with advanced degrees.[23] By virtue of their different turnout rates, some groups in American society are receiving much better representation than others. The upshot is that our elected officials are indebted to and hear much more from the higher socioeconomic ranks in society. They do not hear from and are not elected by the low-participation "have nots."[24]

MICHAEL B. THOMAS/AFP/Getty Images

Exercising the Right to Vote
Students wait in line to vote on the campus of the University of Central Arkansas in 2016. Young people tend to vote at lower rates than older citizens, while women vote at higher rates than men. Many people, however, don't vote, and convenience, such as having a polling station nearby, may be a contributing factor.

In Your Own Words Summarize the influences on who votes and who doesn't.

HOW AMERICA DECIDES

Choosing whether and how to vote

Given the important functions of democracy we have just discussed, the costs of nonvoting, and the tremendous struggle many groups have had to achieve the right to vote, the decision not to vote might seem surprising. But voting varies dramatically in its importance to different citizens. For some, it is a significant aspect of their identities as citizens: 87 percent of American adults believe that voting in elections is a "very important obligation" for Americans, although about half that many actually vote.[25] They make their decisions about whether and how to vote based on a variety of factors.

If we do choose to go to the polls, a number of considerations go into our decision about how to vote, including our partisan identification and social group membership; our gender, race, and ethnicity; our stance on the issues and our evaluation of the job government has been doing generally; and our opinions of the candidates. In this section we examine how these factors play out in the simple act of voting.

DECIDING WHETHER TO VOTE

Deciding whether and how to vote is enormously complex. Although we may not consciously consider each of these factors, most play a role in our final decision. One choice is whether to vote at all. As we have noted elsewhere, compared with citizens

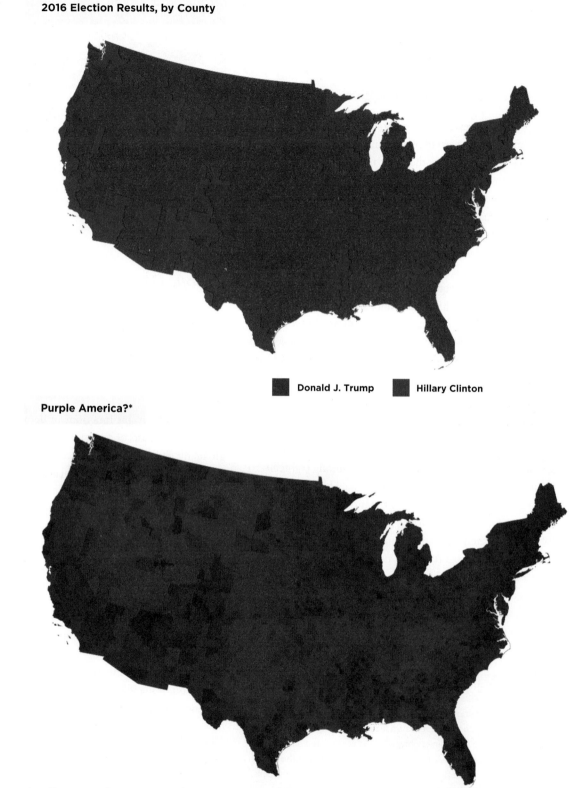

2016 Election Results, by County

Donald J. Trump   Hillary Clinton

Purple America?*

Note: Counties in purple reflect a mix of Democratic and Republican votes.

Source: Map by M. E. J. Newman, http://www-personal.umich.edu/~mejn/election/2016/. Licensed under Creative Commons CC-BY-2.0: https://creativecommons.org/licenses/by/2.0/.

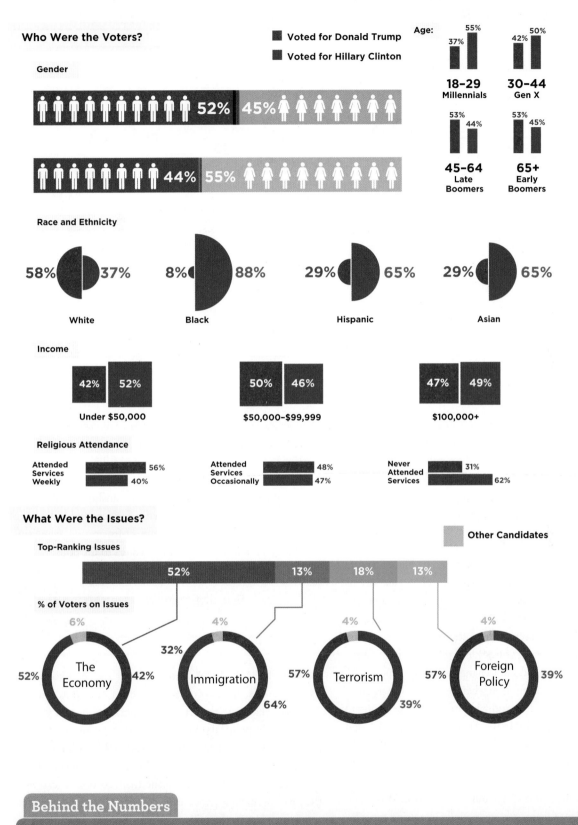

Who Were the Voters?

■ Voted for Donald Trump
■ Voted for Hillary Clinton

Gender

🚹🚹🚹🚹🚹🚹🚹🚹🚹 **52%** **45%** 🚺🚺🚺🚺🚺🚺

🚹🚹🚹🚹🚹🚹 **44%** **55%** 🚺🚺🚺🚺🚺🚺🚺🚺🚺

Age:

18–29 Millennials — 37% / 55%	**30–44** Gen X — 42% / 50%
45–64 Late Boomers — 53% / 44%	**65+** Early Boomers — 53% / 45%

Race and Ethnicity

58% / **37%** — White

8% / **88%** — Black

29% / **65%** — Hispanic

29% / **65%** — Asian

Income

42% / **52%** — Under $50,000

50% / **46%** — $50,000–$99,999

47% / **49%** — $100,000+

Religious Attendance

Attended Services Weekly — 56% / 40%

Attended Services Occasionally — 48% / 47%

Never Attended Services — 31% / 62%

What Were the Issues?

Other Candidates

Top-Ranking Issues

52% | **13%** | **18%** | **13%**

% of Voters on Issues

The Economy — 6% / 52% / 32% / 42%

Immigration — 4% / 57% / 64%

Terrorism — 4% / 57% / 39%

Foreign Policy — 4% / 57% / 39%

Behind the Numbers

We hear a lot about Red and Blue America, but it is more complicated. On the maps, notice most states are a mix of Democratic and Republican counties. Within this, which groups tend to be Democratic or Republican? Can you think of any issues that could be the basis for the partisan tendencies between different groups of voters?

Source: CNN Exit Polls, November 9, 2016, http://www.cnn.com/election/results/exit-polls

FIGURE 14.1

Voter Turnout in Presidential and Midterm House Elections, 1932–2018

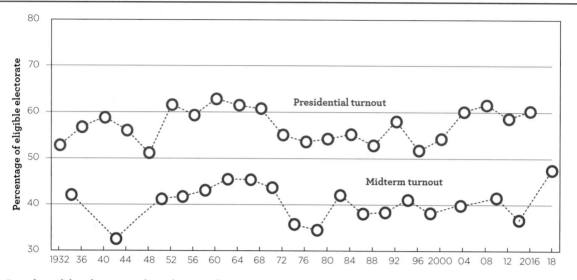

Source: Presidential data from 2000 through 2005, *The New York Times Almanac,* 114; midterm data through 1998 from U.S. Census Bureau, 2000 Statistical Abstract, 291; 2004 data and beyond from United States Election Project, www.electproject.org/home/voter-turnout/voter-turnout-data.

of other democratic nations, Americans have markedly lower voter turnout levels. Despite overall increases in education, age, and income, which generally increase the number of voters, presidential election turnout rates have barely gotten over the 60-percent mark for more than thirty years (and midterm congressional turnout rates have been much lower)[26] (see Figure 14.1).

ATTITUDE CHANGES Political scientists have found that some of the low voter turnout we can see in Figure 14.1 is accounted for by changes over time in psychological orientations or attitudes toward politics.[27] For one thing, if people feel that government is corrupt, or the system is rigged, or they cannot make a difference, they often don't bother to vote. Lower feelings of political efficacy lead to less participation.

Attitudes, of course, do not change without some cause; they reflect citizens' reactions to what they see in the political world. It is easy to understand why attitudes have changed since the relatively tranquil 1950s. Amid repeated scandals and increasing partisanship, our public airwaves have been dominated by negative information about and images of the leadership in Washington, D.C. Turnout was down, for instance, in the generation that came of age during the Nixon Watergate scandal. President Obama ran successfully by raising expectations for a more inclusive, cleaner, and less partisan politics, and the United States saw the highest turnout levels in decades. However, the hyperpartisanship that followed lowered people's estimation of the president, Congress, and politics in general.

Democratic voter turnout was down in 2010, especially among young voters, as discussed earlier, in part because midterm election turnout always drops but also possibly reflecting frustration with Obama's inability to change the tone as he had promised and with the continued partisanship in politics. In 2016, both Vermont senator Bernie Sanders and billionaire Donald Trump appealed to feelings of frustration, cynicism, and rancor and drew some of these voters to the polls.

Should there be penalties for those who don't vote?

VOTER MOBILIZATION Another factor that political scientists argue has led to lower turnout from the 1960s into the 2000s is a change in the efforts of politicians, interest groups, and especially political parties to make direct contact with people during election campaigns.[28] **Voter mobilization** includes contacting people—especially supporters—to inform them about the election and to persuade them to vote. It can take the form of making phone calls, knocking on doors, or even supplying rides to the polls. As the technology of campaigns,

> **voter mobilization** a party's efforts to inform potential voters about issues and candidates and to persuade them to vote

especially the use of television, developed and expanded in the 1980s and 1990s, fewer resources were used for the traditional shoe-leather efforts of direct contact with voters, but solid evidence now indicates that personal contacts do a better job of getting out the vote than do mass mailing and telephone calls.[29] Both Democrats and Republicans have invested heavily in high-tech, sophisticated get-out-the-vote (GOTV) efforts that have led to increases in participation, at least in presidential elections (see Figure 14.1).[30]

DECREASE IN SOCIAL CONNECTEDNESS Some of the overall decline in voter turnout toward the end of the last century is due to larger societal changes rather than to citizen reactions to parties and political leaders. **Social connectedness** refers to the number of organizations people participate in and how tightly knit their communities and families are—that is, how well integrated they are into the society in which they live. As people increasingly leave the communities in which they grew up, live alone, and join fewer groups like religious and social organizations, they lose their ties to the larger community and have less of a stake in participating in communal decisions. Lower levels of social connectedness have been an important factor in accounting for the low turnout in national elections.[31]

THE RATIONALITY OF VOTING A final element in the decision of whether or not to vote is whether it is a rational act for a given individual. The definition of rational means that the benefits of an action outweigh the costs. It is rational for us to do those things from which we get back more than we put in. Voting demands our resources, time, and effort. Given those costs, if someone views voting primarily as a way to influence government and sees no other benefits from it, it becomes a largely irrational act.[32] That is, no one individual's vote can change the course of an election unless the election would otherwise be a tie, and the probability of that happening in a presidential election is small (though, as the 2000 election showed, it is not impossible).

For many people, however, the benefits of voting go beyond the likelihood that they will affect the outcome of the election. In fact, studies have demonstrated that turnout decisions are not really based on our thinking that our votes will determine the outcome. Rather, we achieve other kinds of less tangible benefits from voting. Just like the expressive benefits that many people get from joining an interest group, there are expressive benefits from voting as well. It feels good to do what we think we are

> **social connectedness** citizens' involvement in groups and their relationships to their communities and families

Souls to the Polls

Congregants from Day Springs Missionary Baptist Church in Gainesville, Florida, head to polling sites to cast their ballots in October 2012, one of many "souls to the polls" events organized by black churches. Voters are more likely to cast ballots when barriers to voting—including transportation to polling sites—are low. Strong social connections such as those provided by membership in a church or civic group also increase voter participation.

supposed to do or to help, however little, the side or the causes we believe in.[33] Plus, we get social rewards from our politically involved friends for voting (and avoid sarcastic remarks for not voting). These benefits accrue no matter which side wins.

It is useful to remember, however, that even these psychological benefits are not distributed equally in the electorate. For example, the social pressures to be engaged and the rewards from voting are substantially higher for those in the middle class than for the working class and the unemployed. That is, the socially (and economically) connected receive greater expressive as well as "instrumental" or policy benefits from voting.

> ### Is our democracy stronger if more Americans vote?

DECIDING WHOM TO VOTE FOR

The decision to vote is only part of the voter's calculus. There is also the question of whom to vote for, a decision that is shaped by party loyalty and group identity as much as by the candidates and the issue positions they take.

PARTISANSHIP AND SOCIAL GROUP MEMBERSHIP

The single biggest factor accounting for how people decide to vote is party identification, a concept we discussed in Chapter 12. For most citizens, party ID is relatively stable, carrying over from one election to the next in what one scholar has called "a standing decision."[34] In 2016, 89 percent of those identifying with the Democratic Party voted for Hillary Clinton, and 90

Guac the Vote

The U.S. Hispanic Chamber of Commerce lent its support to a voter registration effort dubbed "Guac the Vote," which aimed to make taco trucks a center for signing up more voters during the 2016 presidential campaign. The effort got under way after a Latino supporter of Republican candidate Donald Trump noted that the nation would have a "taco truck on every corner" if immigration from Mexico went unchecked.

percent of those identifying with the Republican Party voted for Donald Trump.[35]

Scholars have demonstrated that party ID also has an important indirect influence on voting decisions, because voters' party ID also colors their views on policy issues and their evaluation of candidates, leading them to judge their party's candidate and issue positions as superior.[36] Under unusual circumstances, social group characteristics can exaggerate or override traditional partisan loyalties. The 1960 election, for instance, was cast in terms of whether the nation would elect its first Catholic president. In that context, religion was especially salient, and fully 82 percent of Roman Catholics supported John F. Kennedy, compared to just 37 percent of Protestants—a difference of 45 percentage points. Compare that to 1976, when the Democrats ran a devout Baptist, Jimmy Carter, for president. The percentage of Catholics voting Democratic dropped to 58 percent, while Protestants voting Democratic increased to 46 percent. The difference shrank to just 12 percent.

GENDER, RACE, AND ETHNICITY The impact of gender on voting decisions is not clear. In Chapter 11 we discussed the gender gap in the positions men and women take on the issues, which has generally led women to be more likely to support the Democratic candidate. Since 1964, women have been more supportive of the Democratic candidate in every presidential election but one (they were not more likely to support Carter in 1976), and the Democrats clearly wanted to put women's issues at the forefront during the 2016 campaign.[37] But women do not vote monolithically; for instance, married women are more conservative than single women.

It's an open question whether the gender of a candidate affects the women's vote. Despite the speculation that the nomination of Sarah Palin as the Republican vice presidential candidate might have swayed some women to support the McCain-Palin ticket, there was little evidence in the 2008 exit polls to support that idea. According to exit polls, Hillary Clinton benefited from a gender gap, but no larger than Barack Obama's. College-educated women voted for her in much greater numbers than those without a degree.

African Americans have tended to vote Democratic since the civil rights movement of the 1960s. In fact, just under 90 percent of African American voters cast votes for the Democratic candidate in recent presidential elections (1988 to 2004).[38] The nomination of Barack Obama, the first African American to receive a major party's presidential nomination, increased the solidarity of the African American vote even further. African American support for the Democratic ticket reached a record 95 percent in 2008 and 93 percent in 2012.[39] That fell to 88 percent for Clinton in 2016.

Ethnicity is less predictive of the vote than race, partly because ethnic groups in the United States become politically diverse as they are assimilated into the system. Although immigrant groups have traditionally found a home in the Democratic Party, dating back to the days when the party machine would provide a one-stop shop for new immigrants seeking jobs, homes, and social connections, recent immigrant groups today include Asians and Hispanics, both of which comprise diverse ethnic communities with distinct identities and varying partisan tendencies.[40] These diverse groups tend to support the Democratic Party, but each has subgroups that are distinctly more Republican: Vietnamese, in the case of Asians; and Cubans, among Latino groups.[41] That said, in 2016, Clinton received the overwhelming majority of Hispanic votes. Nationally, 65 percent of Latino voters supported Clinton (down from 71 percent for Obama in 2012), as did 65 percent of Asian Americans, and 56 percent of all other racial and ethnic minorities. One observer calls these groups the "coalition of the ascendant," meaning that these are growing portions of the population whose support for the Democratic Party spells trouble for the Republicans if they cannot broaden their appeal.[42] Even so, Trump was able to make up the difference with white support in 2016.

ISSUES AND POLICY An idealized view of elections would have highly attentive citizens paying careful attention to the different policy positions offered by the candidates and then, perhaps aided by informed policy analyses from the media, casting their ballots for the candidates who best represent their preferred policy solutions. In truth, as we know by now, American citizens are not "ideal," and the role played by issues is less obvious and more complicated than the ideal model would predict. The apparent role of issues in electoral decision making is limited by the following factors:

- People are busy and, in many cases, rely on party labels to tell them what they need to know about the candidates.[43]
- People know where they stand on "easy" issues like capital punishment or gay marriage, but some issues, like economic and tax policy, health care, Social Security reform, or foreign policy in the Middle East, are complicated. Many citizens tend to tune out these more complicated issues or, confused, fail to vote in their own interests.[44]
- The media do not generally cover issues in depth. Instead, they much prefer to focus on the horse-race aspect of elections, looking at who is ahead in the polls rather than what substantive policy issues mean for the nation.[45]
- As we discussed in Chapter 11, people process a lot of policy-relevant information in terms of their impressions of candidates (on-line processing) rather than as policy information. They are certainly influenced by policy information, but they cannot necessarily articulate their opinions and preferences on policy.

Although calculated policy decisions by voters are rare, policy considerations do have a real impact on voters' decisions. To see that, it is useful to distinguish between prospective and retrospective voting. The idealized model of policy voting with which we opened this section is **prospective voting**, in which voters base their decisions on what will happen in the future if they vote for a candidate—what policies will be enacted, what values will be emphasized in policy. Prospective voting requires a good deal of information that average voters, as we have seen, do not always have or even want. Although all voters do some prospective voting and, by election time, are usually aware of the candidates' major issue positions, it is primarily party activists and political elites who engage in the full-scale policy analysis that prospective voting entails.

Instead, most voters supplement their spotty policy information and interest with their evaluation of how they think the country is doing, how the economy has performed, and how well the incumbents have carried out their jobs. They engage in **retrospective voting**, casting their votes as signs of approval based on past performance to signal their desire for more of the same or for change.[46]

In presidential elections this means that voters look back at the state of the economy; at perceived successes or failures in

Arnold Sachs/Getty Images

The Shake That Launched a Dream?

Having the opportunity to shake the hand of a sitting president—especially one he particularly admired—clearly meant a lot to the teenaged Bill Clinton, and the moment became a cornerstone of the story of his campaign.

foreign policy; and at domestic issues like education, gun control, or welfare reform. In 1980 Ronald Reagan skillfully focused on voter frustration in the presidential debate by asking voters this question: "[A]re you better off than you were four years ago?"[47] Politicians have been reprising that question ever since.

In 2012 the central strategic campaign objective of the Republican challenger, Mitt Romney, was to cast the election as a referendum on Obama's culpability for a slow economic recovery, hoping that this strategy would push voters to cast a ballot for change. The Obama campaign had the challenge of changing the subject and making the election a choice between the president's and Romney's visions for the country. The Obama campaign began a concerted effort to shape public views of Romney in the summer of 2012, running commercials that painted the Republican as a rich venture capitalist who was out of touch with middle-class America. By the time Romney began to answer those ads in the fall campaign, many people had made up their minds. Similarly, Hillary Clinton ran in 2016 on the strength of the Obama record and sought to make Trump's temperament and experience the focal point in her campaign. In the end, it turned out that a sufficient number of voters recognized his flaws but voted for him anyway because they either didn't like Clinton or believed that Trump would shake up Washington.

---

prospective voting basing voting decisions on well-informed opinions and consideration of the future consequences of a given vote

retrospective voting basing voting decisions on reactions to past performance; approving the status quo or a desire for change

Retrospective voting is considered to be "easy" decision making, as opposed to the more complex decision making involved in prospective voting because one only has to ask, "How have things been going?" as a guide to whether to support the current party in power. Retrospective voting is also seen as a useful way of holding politicians accountable, not for what they said or are saying in a campaign, but for what they or members of their party in power did. Some scholars believe that this type of voting is all that is needed for democracy to function well.[48] In practice, voters combine elements of both voting strategies.

THE CANDIDATES In addition to considerations of party, personal demographics, and issues, voters also base their decisions on judgments about candidates as individuals. What influences voters' images of candidates? Some observers have claimed that voters view candidate characteristics much as they would a beauty or personality contest. There is little support, however, for the notion that voters are won over merely by good looks or movie-star qualities. Consider, for example, that Richard Nixon almost won against John F. Kennedy, who had good looks, youth, and a quick wit in his favor. Then, in 1964, the awkward, gangly Lyndon Johnson defeated the more handsome and articulate Barry Goldwater in a landslide. In fact, ample evidence indicates that voters form clear opinions about candidate qualities that are relevant to governing, such as trustworthiness, competence, experience, and sincerity. Citizens also make judgments about the ability of the candidates to lead the nation and withstand the pressures of the presidency. Ronald Reagan, for example, was admired widely for his ability to stay above the fray of Washington politics and to see the humor in many situations. By contrast, his predecessor, Jimmy Carter, seemed overwhelmed by the job.

Voters do not make up their minds about the candidates in isolation, however. Each campaign works hard to define its own candidate in positive terms and to create a negative narrative about the opponent. In 2012, voters had had four years of Obama as president and generally liked him, even in an economy that virtually everyone agreed had not recovered fast enough. In January 2012, one poll found that fully 71 percent agreed that the president was "warm and friendly" rather than "cold and aloof."[49] Similarly, Obama stacked up well as a "good communicator" and one who "cares about people like me." Obama's challenger, Mitt Romney, decided early on to stress his success in business as qualification for dealing with the economy, but even before Romney had wrapped up the nomination, the Obama campaign began to define him as a rich plutocrat who was unconcerned about the average person. The negative image that many people formed of Romney in the early summer of 2012 stuck and was reinforced during the campaign, despite his best efforts to present himself differently.

In 2016 the Clinton campaign similarly started early to define Donald Trump as a man who was temperamentally unsuited to the presidency and who was xenophobic, racist, and sexist. At the same time, Trump was using the methods that had served him well during the primary—seizing on a perceived weakness in his opponent and reinforcing it with name-calling ("Lyin' Ted Cruz," "Little Marco Rubio," "Low Energy Jeb Bush")—to start calling her "Crooked Hillary Clinton," sometimes just shortened due to the limitations of Twitter to "Crooked." Although polls showed that voters did mistrust Clinton, something that she reinforced with her secretive disposition, they also thought that she was far more qualified to hold office than he was. Exit polls showed her winning on most presidential characteristics, and, indeed, she won the popular vote but failed to clear the hurdles of the Electoral College.

PAUSE AND REVIEW Who, What, How

All political actors are not equal on Election Day. Some reduce their power considerably by failing to turn out to vote for a variety of reasons. But citizens have a strong interest in seeing that good and effective leaders are elected and that power transfers peacefully from losers to winners. By the standard of highly informed voters carefully weighing the alternative policy proposals of competing candidates, the electorate may seem to fall short. However, by a realistic standard that considers the varying abilities of people and the frequent reluctance of candidates and the media to be fully forthcoming about policy proposals, the electorate does not do too badly. Voters come to their decisions through a mix of partisan considerations, membership in social groups, policy information, candidate image, and campaign narratives.

In Your Own Words Describe factors that affect citizens' decisions on whether and how to vote.

PRESIDENTIAL CAMPAIGNS

*The long, expensive
road to the White House*

Being president of the United States is undoubtedly a difficult challenge, but so is getting the job in the first place. In this section we examine the long, expensive, and grueling "road to the White House," as the media like to call it.

GETTING NOMINATED

Each of the major parties (and the minor parties, too) needs to come up with a single viable candidate from the long list of party members with ambitions to serve in the White House. How the candidate is chosen will determine the sort of candidate chosen. Remember, in politics the rules are always central to shaping the outcome. Prior to 1972, primary election results were mostly considered "beauty contests" because their results were not binding. But since 1972, party nominees for the presidency have been chosen in primaries, taking the power away from the party elite and giving it to the activist members of the party who care enough to turn out and vote in the party primaries.

THE PRE-PRIMARY SEASON It is hard to say when a candidate's presidential campaign actually begins. Potential candidates may begin planning and thinking about running for the presidency in childhood. Bill Clinton is said to have wanted to be president since high school, when he shook President Kennedy's hand. At one time or another, many people in politics consider going for the big prize, but there are several crucial steps between wishful thinking and running for the nomination. Candidates vary somewhat in their approach to the process, but most of those considering a run for the White House go through the following steps:

1. Potential candidates usually test the waters unofficially. They talk to friends and fellow politicians to see just how much support they can count on, and they often leak news of their possible candidacy to the press to see how it is received in the media. This period of jockeying for money, lining up top campaign consultants, generating media buzz, and getting commitments of potential support from party and interest group notables—even before candidates announce they are running—is called the **invisible primary**. Some candidates may have an interest but find during the invisible primary that there is not enough early support among the powerful or the public to support a presidential run.[50] Candidate trips to Iowa or New Hampshire (the early caucus and primary states) a year or two before the primaries often indicate that a potential candidate is well into his or her own invisible primary.

2. If the first step has positive results, candidates file with the Federal Election Commission (FEC) to set up a committee to receive funds so that they can officially explore their prospects. The formation of an **exploratory committee** legally allows the candidate to collect money to determine if he or she wants to run, but it is also useful as a form of campaigning itself. Announcing the creation of such a committee can be exploited as a media event by the candidate, using the occasion to get

Dan Wasserman Editorial Cartoon/TNS

free publicity for the launching of the still-unannounced campaign and for signaling to the political community that the presidential primary landscape has changed.

3. It costs a lot of money for a candidate to be taken seriously. Some well-positioned candidates are able to raise large amounts of money before they officially enter the race, whereas others are forced to scramble to catch up. Those with the most pre-primary funds are more likely to win.[51] CNN analyst Paul Begala notes that "Napoleon said god is on the side of big battalions. Voters are usually on the side of big money."[52] This is especially the case in party primaries, where the ideological differences between candidates are not huge and often the candidates are not well-known.

4. The potential candidate must use the pre-primary season to position himself or herself as a credible prospect with the media. It is no coincidence that in most election years (2016 was a notable exception), both parties' nominees have all held prominent government offices and have entered the field with some media credibility. Incumbents especially have a huge advantage here.

5. The final step of the pre-primary season is the official announcement of candidacy. Like the formation of the exploratory committee, this statement is part of the campaign itself. Promises are made to supporters, agendas are set, media attention is captured, and the process is under way.

PRIMARIES AND CAUCUSES The actual fight for the nomination takes place in the state party caucuses and primaries, in which delegates to the parties' national conventions are chosen. The form the process takes can have a lot to do with who wins it. With the rules having such an impact on who wins and who loses, it is wise to look at them carefully.

---

invisible primary early attempts to raise money, line up campaign consultants, generate media attention, and get commitments for support even before candidates announce they are running

exploratory committee a committee formed to determine the viability of one's candidacy for office; activities may include polling, travel, and other communications relevant to the purpose

It Always Starts in Iowa

Candidates eyeing the presidential nominations of their parties tend to spend a lot of time in Iowa, where crucial first votes take place. In 2018, Congressman John Delaney, D-Md., became the first candidate to visit the state ahead of the 2020 election. Unlike many of his peers in years past, Delaney was clear about his reason for the trip, which earned him some respect among election-weary Iowans.

In a party **caucus**, grassroots members of the party in each community gather in selected locations to discuss the current candidates. They then vote for delegates from that locality who will be sent to the national convention, or who will go on to larger caucuses at the state level to choose the national delegates. Attending a caucus is time consuming, and participation rates are frequently in the single digits, which, critics argue, makes them less democratic.[53] Most states still hold primary elections, but in recent years there has been a trend toward caucuses, the method used in fifteen states.[54] In the 2016 Democratic primary race, Vermont senator Bernie Sanders did especially well in caucus states for several reasons. Among them, his supporters were more enthusiastic and likely take the time necessary to caucus, and the caucus states tended to be the northern and western, mostly white states where he excelled.

The most common device for choosing delegates to the national conventions is the **presidential primary**. Primary voters cast ballots that send delegates committed to voting for a particular candidate to the conventions. Presidential primaries can be either open or closed, depending on the rules the state party organizations adopt, and these can change from year to year. Any registered voter may vote in an **open primary**, regardless of party affiliation. At the polling place, the voter chooses the ballot of the party whose primary he or she wants to vote in. Only registered party members may vote in a **closed primary**. A subset of this is the semi-open primary, open only to registered party members and those not registered as members of other parties.

The Democrats also send elected state officials, including Democratic members of Congress and governors, to their national conventions. Some of these officials are "superdelegates,"

able to vote as free agents, but the rest must reflect the state's primary vote.[55] In 2016 Bernie Sanders railed against what he called a rigged system, believing that closed primaries shut out his independent voters and that superdelegates supported the establishment candidate. It's important to note, however, that the party makes its rules to secure a winning candidate. They don't want nonparty members voting to throw off their results, and although the superdelegates have always voted with the popular vote winner, they exist as a check on a voter choice that the party thinks isn't viable. During the drafting of the 2016 Democratic Party platform, Clinton and Sanders supporters agreed to form a commission to study the issue of the superdelegate role, even as many Republicans voiced the wish that they had had superdelegates in 2016 to offset the vote for Trump.

In addition to varying in terms of whom they allow to vote, the parties' primary rules also differ in how they distribute delegates among the candidates. The Democrats generally use a method of proportional representation, in which the candidates get the percentage of delegates equal to the percentage of the primary vote they win (provided they get at least 15 percent). Republican rules run from proportional representation, to winner-take-all (the candidate with the most votes gets all the delegates, even if he or she does not win an absolute majority), to direct voting for delegates (the delegates are not bound to vote for a particular candidate at the convention), to the absence of a formal system (caucus participants may decide how to distribute the delegates).

State primaries also vary in the times at which they are held, with various states engaged in **front-loading**, vying to hold their primaries first in order to gain media maximum exposure and influence over the nomination. By tradition and state law, the Iowa caucus and the New Hampshire primary are the first contests for delegates. As a result, they get tremendous attention, from both candidates and the media—much more than their contribution to the delegate count would justify. This is why, in 1998, other states began moving their primaries earlier in the season.[56] In 2016 the parties pushed back on the process, with the Iowa caucuses held on February 1, nearly a month later than in 2012, and fifteen states and territories (down from twenty-three in 2012) having held primaries or caucuses by March 1, 2016, the day of

caucus a local gathering of party members to choose convention delegates

presidential primary an election by which voters choose convention delegates committed to voting for a certain candidate

open primary a primary election in which eligible voters need not be registered party members

closed primary a primary election in which only registered party members may vote

front-loading the process of scheduling presidential primaries early in the primary season

Super Tuesday, on which the largest number of primaries are held.

The consequence of front-loading and the reason that the parties have pushed back on the states that practice it is that it favors candidates who have a substantial war chest and are prepared to campaign nationally from the beginning. In a non-front-loaded system, winners of early primaries could use that success to raise more campaign funds to continue the battle. With the primaries stacked at the beginning, however, this becomes much harder. The process favors well-known, well-connected, and, especially, well-funded candidates. Incumbents, of course, have an enormous advantage here.

No incumbent has been seriously opposed from within his own party since Ronald Reagan gave Gerald Ford a good scare in 1976, although Bernie Sanders thought seriously about challenging Barack Obama in 2012. Since then, of the two major parties' nominees, all but one had previously served as governor, senator, vice president, or secretary of state. Only Donald Trump came to the race with no prior political office-holding experience. Governors, with executive experience and the ability to claim that they are untainted by the gridlock politics of Washington, tend to have an edge, with four of six former governors going on to win the presidency since 1976.

The primary campaigns involve a lot of speeches and television ads and extensive use of social media for information and fundraising purposes, but debates among the contenders for a party's nomination are also key. These are televised nationally, giving the whole country exposure to each party's candidates. It is arguable that the many debates among candidates for the 2008 Democratic nomination gave Barack Obama national media exposure and that the united effort of the candidates to weaken Hillary Clinton in those debates was costly to her as well. Consequently, when she ran in 2016, she held out for far fewer debates, much to Bernie Sanders's chagrin. In 2016 the crowded debate stage enabled Donald Trump to lay low while the other candidates battled each other. Meanwhile, Hillary Clinton found a surprisingly

Justin Sullivan/Getty Images

A Solemn End

Former senator, secretary of state, and Democratic presidential candidate Hillary Clinton gives her final speech in the 2016 election, conceding to Republican rival Donald J. Trump on November 9, 2016. Her running mate Tim Kaine (right) and husband and former president Bill Clinton (left) stand alongside her.

adept debate opponent in Sanders, which helped boost his candidacy to prominence.

Fundraising prowess, early endorsements, solid organization, and good debate performances all help build a narrative in a crowded field that one or another candidate is a **front-runner**. Early front-runner status garners a candidate more media coverage and reinforces everyone's expectations that a candidate is a winner. But front-runners are punished if they fail to live up to the hype they and the media create. The imperative for all the other candidates is to attack the front-runner hard to drive down his or her support, while maneuvering into position as the chief alternative. Challengers to the front-runner generally hold on as long as they can in case the head of the pack stumbles, each hoping to emerge as the new leader. In 2016 Hillary Clinton and Jeb Bush were the early front-runners. Clinton faced an unexpectedly strong challenge from Sanders. Although she held on to win the nomination, the media speculated endlessly on why she could not put away a challenge by a seventy-five-year-old self-avowed democratic socialist. Bush did not survive the primary process. Despite all the advantages he brought to the race, he went down under a withering onslaught from Donald Trump, as did, ultimately, the other fifteen Republican candidates.

Clearly, a chief goal of a candidate's campaign has to be to control the narrative and not let the media take it over. The campaign wants to define its candidate in the best terms; define the other candidates as unelectable; and give the impression of **momentum**, the idea that the candidate is on a roll, and that polls, primary victories, endorsements, and

front-runner the leading candidate and expected winner of a nomination or an election

momentum the widely held public perception that a candidate is gaining electoral strength

Rallying at the Convention

Pakistani American Khizr Khan speaks at the 2016 Democratic National Convention in Philadelphia with his wife, Ghazala, at his side. Khan voiced his anger with Republican candidate Donald Trump's statements about America's Muslim population and challenged the candidate by asking, "Have you even read the U.S. Constitution?" Trump's reaction, including a flurry of tweets and interview statements criticizing the Khans, set off a wave of controversy.

THE CONVENTION

Since 1972, delegates attending the national conventions have not had to decide who the parties' nominees would be. However, two official actions continue to take place at the conventions. First, as we discussed in Chapter 12, the parties hammer out and approve their platforms, the documents in which parties set out their distinct issue positions. Second, the vice presidential candidate is officially named. The choice of the vice president is up to the presidential nominee. Traditionally (although not always) the choice is made to balance the ticket—ideologically, regionally, or even by gender or experience. In 2008 Barack Obama chose Delaware senator Joe Biden as his running mate, going for an experienced hand with a foreign policy background to shore up his own—at

funding are all coming his or her way. But the narrative has to be backed up with performance. Bernie Sanders was able to stay in the race until the end despite Clinton's front-runner status because he did well in debates and won a respectable number of caucuses and primaries. In the crowded Republican field, no one candidate could develop a convincing narrative that he or she was ahead before Trump began amassing victories. Bush had more money, but he could not translate that into debate or primary victories, and his establishment status and fundraising prowess was not sufficient to sustain the narrative that he was a winning candidate.

Interestingly, who actually "wins" in the primaries is as much a product of the prevailing narrative as whether the candidate actually comes in first in the balloting. That narrative, shaped by the campaign but also by the media and the competition, determines whether the candidate is seen to be improving or fading. Much of the political credit that a candidate gets for an apparent "win" depends on who else is running in that primary and the media expectations of that candidate's performance. It was the genius of Donald Trump that he was able to create a narrative early on that his opponents were losers—Jeb Bush was low energy, Ted Cruz was a liar, and so on—that stuck with voters. In a real sense the voters' decision-making process, in addition to party loyalty and personal identity, ends up being a choice among the competing candidates' narratives. Voters then share through social media the elements of those narratives that they find most compelling, which is why it is so important to examine carefully all the information you receive about a candidate (see *Don't Be Fooled by . . . Viral Media* later in this chapter).

that time relatively thin—record. Democrats applauded his pick of Biden as one that balanced the ticket and showcased Obama's own judgment and decision-making skills. They had barely finished cheering their new nominee, however, when John McCain upstaged Obama with his own pick, Alaska governor Sarah Palin, who he felt would bolster his maverick credentials, help him energize his base, and bolster his standing with women. The choice was immediately controversial; wildly popular with religious conservatives, it was viewed with surprise and skepticism by Democrats and media commentators. In 2016 Donald Trump picked Indiana governor Mike Pence, to satisfy Republican party elites who were worried about the lack of serious governing experience on the ticket. Hillary Clinton made the safe but popular choice of former Virginia governor, and then senator, Tim Kaine, saying her top criterion was someone who could step in and govern if need be.

There is no clear evidence that the vice presidential choice has significant electoral consequences, but the presidential nominees weigh it carefully nonetheless. If nothing else, the caliber of the nominee's choice for vice president is held to be an indication of the kind of appointments the nominee would make if elected. Although McCain's pick of Sarah Palin as his running mate in 2008 was popular initially, with 20 percent more of the public having more positive than negative feelings toward her, a cascade of bad news stories about her soon engulfed the McCain campaign. By the time of the election, Palin's negatives were 7 percent higher than her positives. This all rebounded on the campaign amid charges that McCain could hardly have been following his slogan of "putting country first" with such a selection.

The conventions typically provide the nominee with a "convention bump" in the preelection polls. Media coverage of the carefully orchestrated party harmony, the enthusiasm of party supporters, and even the staged theatrics seem to have a positive impact on viewers. The result is that candidates have usually, though not always, experienced a noticeable rise in the polls immediately following the conventions. Both Obama and McCain received bounces from their conventions in 2008, though McCain's was slightly larger. McCain briefly achieved a lead in the polls after his convention, but the negative publicity surrounding Palin and then the economic crisis that began in mid-September put Obama back on top, where he stayed through the election. Following the 2012 conventions, Romney gained a small bump that was lost quickly in the larger bounce for Obama that followed the Democratic convention. In 2016 Hillary Clinton's bounce was higher and lasted longer than Donald Trump's, in part because of Trump's lackluster convention and his self-inflicted damage in taking on a Gold Star father who spoke at the Democratic National Convention. Even given that, the polls were back to their preconvention level within a month.

THE GENERAL ELECTION CAMPAIGN

After the candidates are nominated in late summer, there is a short break, at least for the public, before the traditional fall campaign. When the campaign begins, the goal of each side is to convince supporters to turn out and to get undecided voters to choose its candidate. Most voters, the party identifiers, will usually support their party's candidate, although they need to be motivated by the campaign to turn out and cast their ballots. Most of the battle in a presidential campaign is for the **swing voters**, the one-third or so of the electorate who have not made up their minds at the start of the campaign and who are open to persuasion by either side. This means that for both parties the general election strategy differs considerably from the strategy used to win a primary election. Traditionally the logic has been that to win the general election the campaigns move away from the sharp ideological tone used to motivate the party faithful in the primaries and "run to the middle" by making less ideological appeals. However, in this era of polarized parties, especially since the second George W. Bush campaign, there are fewer citizens in the middle, and those who are there are much less likely to vote.[57] Thus the tendency has been for a campaign to stay with the party's ideological message, putting at least as much emphasis on mobilizing its base as on appealing to independents and uncommitted voters. Besides keeping the parties' bases involved, staying with more

A Formal Tally
Senate pages carry bound wooden boxes containing Electoral College votes from the fifty states into the U.S. House of Representatives chamber. The votes are tallied during a joint session of Congress, although as we've seen twice in the twenty-first century, the Electoral College votes do not always match the popular vote.

ideological appeals can help candidates avoid being charged with "flip-flopping" on the issues.

In the general campaign, each side seeks to get its message across, to define the choice in terms that give its candidate the advantage. This massive effort to influence the information to which citizens are exposed requires a clear strategy, which begins with a plan for winning the states where the candidate will be competitive. The campaign in 2016 broke with most political scientists' ideas about how campaigns work. Hillary Clinton ran a by-the-book professional effort, while it looked like Donald Trump was inventing the rules as he went along. For all the political heavyweights on her team, however, the Clinton campaign missed the white working-class anger in traditionally blue states like Michigan, Wisconsin, Pennsylvania, and Ohio that gave Trump a thin edge in those states.

THE ELECTORAL COLLEGE As we saw in *What's at Stake . . . ?*, the presidential election is not a national race; it is a race between the candidates in each of the fifty states and the District of Columbia (see *Snapshot of America: How Did We Vote in the 2016 Presidential Election?*). The reasons for the Electoral College's existence may seem outdated sometimes, but it nevertheless drives campaign strategy. Because our founders feared giving too much power to the volatile electorate, we do not actually vote for the president and vice president in presidential elections. Rather, we cast our votes in November for electors (members of the Electoral College), who in turn vote for the president in December. The Constitution provides for each state to have as many electoral votes as it does senators and representatives in Congress. Thus Alaska has three electoral votes (one for each of the state's U.S. senators and one for its

swing voters the approximately one-third of the electorate who are undecided at the start of a campaign

The founding fathers intended the Electoral College to be a compromise between direct election of the president (they weren't sure they trusted us!) and selection of the president by Congress (they didn't want him to be indebted). Consequently, the Electoral College is selected once every four years, those members meet in November to choose the president, and then they disband, never to meet again. Good idea, or bad? Look at how it works and decide for yourself.

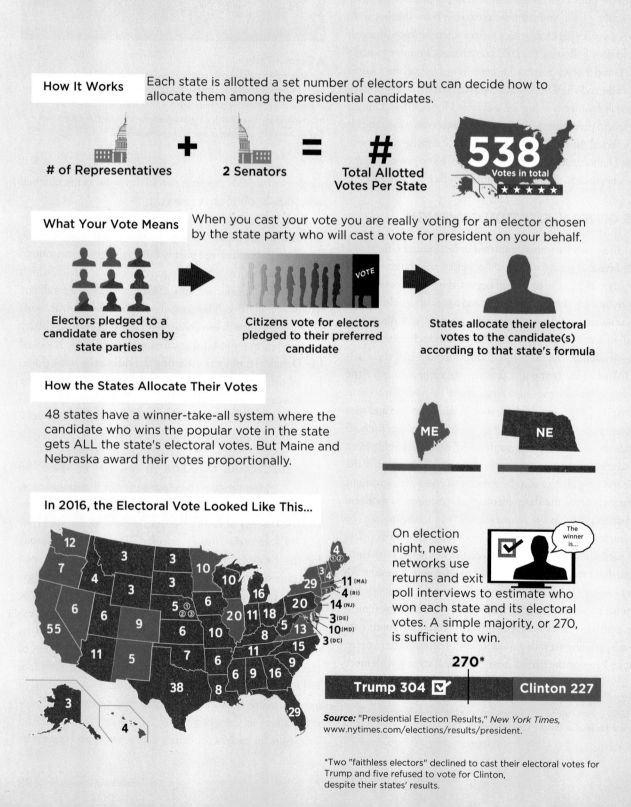

How It Works

Each state is allotted a set number of electors but can decide how to allocate them among the presidential candidates.

# of Representatives + **2 Senators** = **# Total Allotted Votes Per State**

538 Votes in total

What Your Vote Means

When you cast your vote you are really voting for an elector chosen by the state party who will cast a vote for president on your behalf.

Electors pledged to a candidate are chosen by state parties

Citizens vote for electors pledged to their preferred candidate

States allocate their electoral votes to the candidate(s) according to that state's formula

How the States Allocate Their Votes

48 states have a winner-take-all system where the candidate who wins the popular vote in the state gets ALL the state's electoral votes. But Maine and Nebraska award their votes proportionally.

ME   NE

In 2016, the Electoral Vote Looked Like This...

On election night, news networks use returns and exit poll interviews to estimate who won each state and its electoral votes. A simple majority, or 270, is sufficient to win.

The winner is...

270*

Trump 304   **Clinton 227**

Source: "Presidential Election Results," *New York Times*, www.nytimes.com/elections/results/president.

*Two "faithless electors" declined to cast their electoral votes for Trump and five refused to vote for Clinton, despite their states' results.

But It Could Be Different The winner-take-all system seems unfair to some people, and it concentrates presidential contests in just a few "battleground states." But states could allocate their votes differently. Here are a few of the options, with a look at how they would have affected the results of the 2016 election.

In 2016, the Electoral Vote Looked Like This...

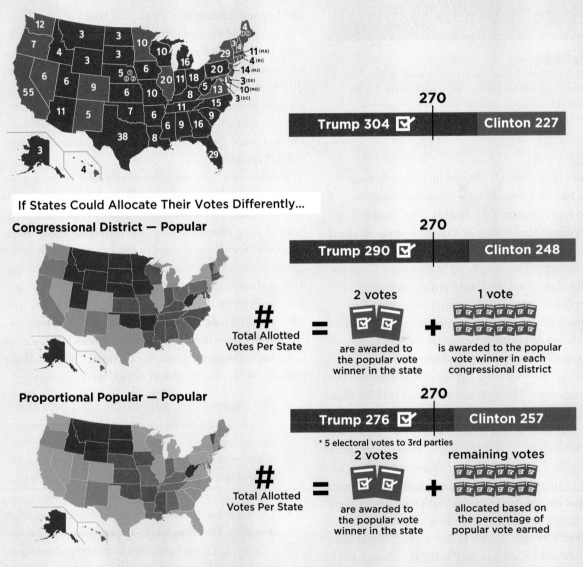

270

| Trump 304 ☑ | Clinton 227 |

If States Could Allocate Their Votes Differently...

Congressional District — Popular

270

| Trump 290 ☑ | Clinton 248 |

#
Total Allotted
Votes Per State

=

2 votes
are awarded to the popular vote winner in the state

+

1 vote
is awarded to the popular vote winner in each congressional district

Proportional Popular — Popular

270

| Trump 276 ☑ | Clinton 257 |

* 5 electoral votes to 3rd parties

#
Total Allotted
Votes Per State

=

2 votes
are awarded to the popular vote winner in the state

+

remaining votes
allocated based on the percentage of popular vote earned

Popular Vote — Eliminate the Electoral College (because the popular vote winner has lost 5 times!)

| Trump 62,979,636 (48.88%) | Clinton 65,844,610 (51.11%) ☑ |

National Popular Vote Interstate Compact A budding agreement among the states would commit each state to cast all of its electoral votes for the national popular vote winner, ensuring that the popular vote winner becomes president, but without amending the Constitution. It will take effect if states with 270 combined electoral votes commit to be bound by it. As of 2018, twelve states plus the District of Columbia, accounting for more than half of the required 270 votes, had passed legislation to join the compact.

Source: 270toWin, www.270towin.com/alternative-electoral-college-allocation-methods/

Michael Nagle/Bloomberg via Getty Images

Drumming Up Support

A volunteer for the Trump campaign makes a phone call at the candidate's campaign headquarters inside Trump Tower in New York. Campaign work is big business, from the paid staff to the scores of volunteers who promote the candidate across the nation and help get out the vote.

sole member of the House of Representatives). By contrast, California has fifty-five electoral votes (two senators and fifty-three representatives). In addition, the Twenty-third Amendment gave the District of Columbia three electoral votes. There are 538 electoral votes in all; 270 are needed to win the presidency. This chapter's *The Big Picture* shows the distribution of electoral votes among the states today; they are reapportioned every ten years, after each new Census.

Electors are generally activist members of the party whose presidential candidate carried the state. In December, following the election, the electors meet and vote in their state capitals. In the vast majority of cases, they vote as expected, but there are occasional "faithless electors" who vote for their own preferences. The results of the electors' choices in the states are then sent to the Senate, where the ballots are counted when the new session opens. If no candidate achieves a majority in the Electoral College, the Constitution calls for the House of Representatives to choose from the top three electoral vote winners. In this process, each state has one vote. If the vote goes to the House, then the Senate decides on the vice president, with each senator having a vote. This has happened only twice (the last time was in 1824), although some observers of the 2000 election speculated that that election, too, could have been decided in the House of Representatives if Florida's election had not been decided in the courts.

The importance of the Electoral College is that all the states but Maine and Nebraska operate on a winner-take-all basis. Thus the winner in California, even if he or she has less than a majority of the popular vote, wins all of the state's fifty-five electoral votes. The loser in California may have won 49 percent of the popular vote but gets nothing in the Electoral College. It is possible, as we have seen, for the popular vote

winner to lose in the Electoral College. This has happened only four times in our history. Usually, however, the opposite happens: the Electoral College exaggerates the candidate's apparent majority. The 2012 election is typical of this exaggeration of the victory margin in the Electoral College. Obama got more than 51 percent of the two-party popular vote, but his majority in the Electoral College was 61.7 percent. This exaggeration of the winning margin has the effect of legitimizing winners' victories and allowing them to claim that they have a mandate—a broad popular endorsement—even if they won by a smaller margin of the popular vote.

The rules of the Electoral College give greater power to some states over others. The provision that all states get at least three electoral votes in the Electoral College means that citizens in the smaller-population states get proportionately greater representation in the Electoral College. Alaska, for example, sent one elector to the Electoral College for every 240,000 people, while California had one elector for every 679,000 residents.

However, this "advantage" is probably offset by the practice of winner-take-all, which focuses the candidates' attention on the largest states with the biggest payoffs in electoral votes, especially the competitive, or "battleground," states. Small states with few electoral votes or those that are safely in the corner of one party or the other are ignored. In 2016 the battleground map expanded to include Florida, North Carolina, Virginia, Pennsylvania, Nevada, and Colorado, as well as typically red and blue states that usually don't find themselves close.

Over the years, hundreds of bills have been introduced in Congress to reform or abolish the Electoral College.[58] Major criticisms of the current system include the following:

- The Electoral College is undemocratic because it is possible for the popular winner not to get a majority of the electoral votes.
- In a very close contest, the popular outcome could be dictated by a few "faithless electors" who vote their consciences rather than the will of the people of their states.
- The Electoral College distorts candidates' campaign strategies. The winner-take-all provision in all but two states puts a premium on a few large, competitive states, which get a disproportionate share of the candidates' attention.

Few people deny the truth of these charges, and hardly anyone believes that if we were to start all over, the current Electoral College would be chosen as the best way to elect a president. Nevertheless, it's not clear it will ever be changed.

WHO RUNS THE CAMPAIGN? Running a modern presidential campaign has become a highly specialized profession. Most presidential campaigns are led by an "amateur," a nationally prestigious chairperson who may serve as an adviser and assist in fundraising. However, the real work of the campaign is done by the professional staff the candidate hires, and who themselves become important figures not only in the campaigns but often in the administrations as advisers and, later, as political commentators. For example, James Carville, Bill Clinton's campaign strategist, continues to appear frequently on television as a campaign commentator, as does Karl Rove, who ran both of George W. Bush's successful campaigns and worked as a policy adviser in the Bush White House. Obama's campaign trust included David Axelrod, who continued as a political adviser in the White House (see *Profiles in Citizenship*); Robert Gibbs, who took the job as Obama's first press secretary; and David Plouffe, who served as the 2008 Obama campaign manager and then White House adviser. Jim Messina, an Obama White House staffer, joined on as campaign manager in 2012. Campaign work at the beginning of the twenty-first century is big business. Donald Trump's campaign was not an orthodox one and broke many of the rules of modern campaigning. He relied heavily on his children, especially his son-in-law; on his campaign CEO (which is not a traditional position), Steve Bannon from Breitbart News; on his campaign manager, Kellyanne Conway; and on Republican National Committee chair Reince Priebus.

Some of the jobs include not only the well-known ones of campaign manager and strategist but also more specialized components tailored to the modern campaign's emphasis on information and money. For instance, candidates need to hire research teams to prepare position papers on issues so that the candidate can answer any question posed by potential supporters and the media. But researchers also engage in the controversial but necessary task of **oppo research**—delving into the background and vulnerabilities of the opposing candidate with an eye to exploiting his or her weaknesses. Central to the modern campaign's efforts to get and control the flow of information, oppo research has become a central component in all elections, contributing to the negative campaigning so prevalent in recent years.[59] Astute candidates also have oppo research done on themselves; knowing that their opponent will be studying them, they work to be prepared to deal with attacks that might be coming.

Candidates also need advance teams to plan and prepare their travel agendas, to arrange for crowds (and the signs they wave) to greet the candidates at airports, and even to reserve accommodations for the press. Especially in the primaries, staff devoted to fundraising are essential to ensure the constant flow of money necessary to grease the wheels of any presidential campaign. They work with big donors and engage in direct-mail and Internet campaigns to solicit money from targeted groups.

Finally, of course, candidates need to hire a legal team to keep their campaigns in compliance with the regulations of the FEC and to file the required reports. In general, campaign consultants are able to provide specialized technical services that the parties' political committees cannot.[60]

PRESENTING THE CANDIDATE An effective campaign begins with a clear understanding of how the candidate's strengths fit with the context of the times and the mood of the voters, on which the campaign narrative is built. To sell a candidate effectively, the claims to special knowledge, competence, or commitment must be credible.[61] The 2008 Obama presidential campaign is considered by many observers to be one of the best-run campaigns in modern American politics. It paired nearly complete control of the campaign narrative with an unprecedented use of technology and a massive and very well-organized volunteer component.

In 2012 the Obama campaign again won plaudits for its organization and excellent technological innovation. Sometimes lost in the general awe of the data-crunching and GOTV operation is the strategic effort the campaign made early on to frame the narrative of the election as a choice between two candidates offering very different visions for America rather than as a referendum on the president. Given slow economic growth and the Republicans' success in denying the president any legislative victories in the two years preceding the election, the campaign felt it would lose the latter, so as soon as the campaign was sure that Romney would be the Republican nominee, it began to define him as a wealthy plutocrat out of touch with middle-class American concerns. Inexplicably, the Romney campaign let the Obama campaign have the stage to itself in the summer before the election. By the time Romney's campaign began to introduce Romney as it wanted voters to see him, as a bipartisan economic problem solver, it was too late. Many voters' perceptions were locked in. Again, in 2016, the Trump campaign broke with all the conventional wisdom. The candidate did not release his tax returns; produced a superficial medical report; spoke offensively about women, Latinos, and Muslims; and refused to acknowledge that Barack Obama was a citizen. Shortly after he kicked off his campaign, Trump was recorded mocking a disabled reporter. And tapes surfaced in which he had earlier bragged in a radio interview about walking in on beauty

oppo research investigation of an opponent's background for the purpose of exploiting weaknesses or undermining credibility

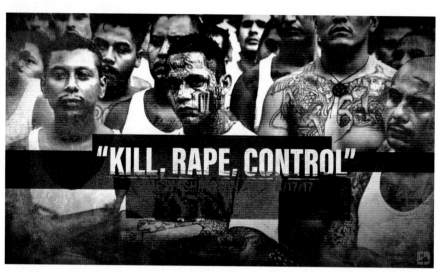

A Strong Position

The race for governor of Virginia in 2017 turned ugly when Republican candidate Ed Gillespie ran campaign ads equating support for sanctuary cities by his Democratic opponent, Ralph Northam, with support for undocumented immigrant members of the violent Salvadoran gang MS-13. Northam supporters and others accused Gillespie of drawing on the tradition of the famous Willie Horton ad and playing on some white voters' fears of Latinos and immigrants.

pageant contestants while they were undressed and in which he boasted that his fame allowed him to assault women without any consequences. Trump's supporters mostly acknowledged that those things happened but either admired them or just didn't care.[62]

THE ISSUES Earlier we indicated that issues matter to voters as they decide how to vote. This means that issues must be central to the candidate's strategy for getting elected. From the candidate's point of view, there are two kinds of issues to consider when planning a strategy: valence issues and position issues.

Valence issues are policy matters on which the voters and the candidates share the same preference. These are what we might call "motherhood and apple pie" issues, because no one opposes them. Everyone is for a strong, prosperous economy; for America having a respected leadership role in the world; for fighting terrorism; for thrift in government; and for a clean environment. Similarly, everyone opposes crime and drug abuse, government waste, political corruption, and immorality.

Position issues have two sides. On abortion, there are those who are pro-life and those who are pro-choice. On military engagements such as Vietnam, Iraq, or Afghanistan, there are those who favor pursuing a military victory and those who favor just getting out. Many of the hardest decisions for candidates are on position issues—although a clear stand means that they will gain some friends, it also guarantees that they will make some enemies. Realistic candidates who want to win as many votes as possible try to avoid being

clearly identified with the losing side of important position issues. For instance, activists in the Republican Party fought to keep their strong pro-life plank in the party platform in 2000. However, because a majority of the electorate is opposed to the strong pro-life position, candidates generally deemphasize that in the general election. In 2016, issues did not play a major role, but immigration was one on which candidates took vastly different positions. Trump promised to deport 11 million undocumented workers and to build a wall to keep them out. Clinton favored immigration reform with a path to citizenship.

When candidates or parties do take a stand on a difficult position issue, the other side often uses it against them as a wedge issue. A **wedge issue** is a position issue on which the parties differ and that proves controversial within the ranks of a particular party. For a Democrat, expanding Social Security benefits is not a controversial position. For a Republican, though, it is dicey, because many working-class members of the base support it but traditional small-government Republicans do not. An astute strategy for a Democratic candidate, then, is to raise the issue, hoping to drive a wedge between the Republicans and to recruit to his or her side the Republican supporters of Social Security.

The idea of **issue ownership** helps to clarify the role of policy issues in presidential campaigns. Because of their past stands and performance, each of the parties is widely perceived as better able to handle certain kinds of problems. For instance, the Democrats may be seen as better able to deal with education matters, and the Republicans as more effective at solving crime-related problems. If education is pressing, a voter might go with the Democratic candidate; if crime is more important,

> **valence issues** issues on which most voters and candidates share the same position
>
> **position issues** issues on which the parties differ in their perspectives and proposed solutions
>
> **wedge issue** a controversial issue that one party uses to split the voters in the other party
>
> **issue ownership** the tendency of one party to be seen as more competent in a specific policy area

David Axelrod

Courtesy of Jamie Manley and Axelrod Strategies

David Axelrod got involved in his first campaign pamphleteering for Bobby Kennedy when he was nine years old, and from then through his days as communications director for Barack Obama's senate and presidential campaigns, to a stint in the White House as senior advisor to the president, to his current gig as founding director at the University of Chicago's Institute of Politics, he has pretty much lived his dream.

Though he grew up in New York, Axelrod has been an adopted Chicagoan since his days as an undergrad at University of Chicago. He quickly fell in love with the city and with Chicago politics—talking himself into an internship at the *Chicago Tribune*, where he spent two and a half years covering local politics on the night shift, and more years in the trenches before landing a coveted column. When Axelrod left the paper to set up his own consulting business, it was a leap of faith; he had been bitten, hard, by the campaign bug.

Campaigns are like a narcotic, says the man who has been instrumental in running so many of them. "They are these existential experiences, where you are running full speed for months, sometimes years, and all for one day. And when they end, you feel let down and you're looking for the next challenge . . . There is something really invigorating, inspiring about being part of an effort too, to make change, to make a difference." Axelrod's story is all about finding inspiration not just in volunteers and students but in the authentic figures who can see themselves clearly in relation to their times, and who believe in the transformative power of good government to make people's lives better.

For him, authenticity is the key to making a public figure inspiring and, indeed, electable. "I think that authenticity is an essential ingredient for successful candidates and successful leaders," he says. "If you don't feel comfortable in your own skin then voters are not going to feel comfortable with you." In fact, it was the seeming lack of authenticity he was finding in those seeking out his services that caused him to work with Barack Obama. "He was considering a race for the Senate—this seemed to me like a way to recharge my batteries . . . I always liked him. He was very public spirited, he seemed like a good guy. He always knew why he wanted to be in public life and what he wanted to do."

He says, "My job whenever I talk to young people, but certainly at the University, is to make the point that whatever equity you care about, whether it's human rights, climate change, deficits, education . . . it's going to be impacted dramatically by the decisions that are made in Washington, in state capitals, and in capitals around the world. And you can walk away and let other people make those decisions, but then you have to live with the consequences of those."

On patriotism

"I was the son of an immigrant who came here with nothing; I ended up as the Senior Advisor to the President. I grew up in a housing development and my sister and I shared a room in a rental apartment that was probably about as big as from here to the kitchen. And I've lived my dreams. My father came here in 1922. If he'd tried to come in '23 when the very harsh immigration laws were put in place, he probably wouldn't have been here. And his life would have been different and I think less good. So I believe in America. I believe in what America has been. I believe in the values that have been time honored and I think fighting for those is a worthy cause. And I hope young people pick that torch up because they're the ones who are going to have the greatest—by far the greatest—stake here."

On keeping the republic

"The greatest admonition I can give to young people is don't take what we have for granted. Democracy requires participation. I'm biased in this regard because I'm devoting my life to it—to this project—but I think they should get in the arena. And getting in the arena doesn't necessarily mean running for public office, although it could. It doesn't necessarily mean working in campaigns . . . As messy and as troubled and as challenged as it is, I really believe it's the best path forward...This is the best vehicle to influence your future and the future of your community, the country, and the world . . . don't, don't surrender to the cynicism. That would be a tragic thing to do because I've seen it. You *can* bring about real fundamental change."

Source: David Axelrod spoke with Christine Barbour and Gerald C. Wright on August 18, 2014.

the voter might choose the Republican.[63] From the candidate's point of view, the trick is to convince voters that the election is about the issues that his or her party "owns."

Because valence issues are relatively safe, candidates stress them at every opportunity. They also focus on the position issues that their parties "own" or on which they have majority support. What this suggests is that the real campaign is not about debating positions on issues—how to reduce the deficit or whether to restrict abortion—but about which issues should be considered. Issue campaigning is to a large extent about setting the agenda and then creating a narrative that convinces voters to care about it.

THE MEDIA As we have noted, it is impossible to understand the modern political campaign without appreciating the pervasive role of the media. With twenty-four-hour television news stations, talk radio, and the incredible web of the Internet, mediated citizens are bombarded with information from reporters and pollsters, pundits and late night comedians, bloggers and tweeters, Facebook sharers and email forwarders, your textbook authors, and your professor. In fact, you yourself can become part of the vast network of people passing along information and crowdsourcing a story about how a campaign is taking place, and creating a narrative about what it all means. It is the daunting task of the campaign to try to manage that incredible flow of information—to control the story that is being told so that it advantages their candidate—while also taking advantage of all that the modern information network has to offer in the way of getting their message out. It's a lot like trying to dance with a bear without getting your head bitten off.

There are two kinds of information in any campaign—the kind you pay for (and have some modicum of control over) and the kind you don't. Campaign ads are paid for. Even though many voters tend to ignore them—or at least they tell survey interviewers that they do—we know that campaign advertising matters. And advertising is no longer confined to television and radio. Internet ads, which can be carefully targeted, are an excellent use of a campaign's money, especially when they are tied to fundraising sites and allow a campaign to gather email addresses. Studies show that advertising provides usable information for voters. Political ads can heighten the loyalty of existing supporters, and they can educate the public about what candidates stand for and what issues candidates believe are most important.

The proliferation of social media has changed the game considerably. Campaigns still produce advertisements, of course, but they don't have to pay to get them in front of voters—if the message is intriguing, provocative, inflammatory,

or, occasionally, inspiring enough, a few "likes" or "shares" from key influencers can send it viral, inserting it into personal newsfeeds across the Internet, and often getting coverage in the mainstream news as well.[64] Further complicating the messaging mix is the fact that videos, memes, blog posts, tweets, and status updates can be created by anyone, and, again, particularly compelling content can and often does go viral without campaigns or interest groups having to lift a finger (see *Don't Be Fooled by . . . Viral Media*). All of these messages can help to establish or reinforce the narrative on which voters base their choice of candidates.

One of the best examples of negative messaging came before the Internet was a factor in campaign advertising. Because Republican vice president George H. W. Bush was behind in the polls in 1988, his campaign sought to change the way people were thinking about him and his Democratic opponent, Massachusetts governor Michael Dukakis. They came up with an effective ad showing criminals walking in and out of a prison through a turnstile. A voice-over claimed that Dukakis's "revolving door prison policy" had permitted first-degree murderers to leave on weekend furloughs. At the same time, a pro-Bush group called the National Security PAC ran the more controversial "Willie Horton" ad, which focused on the mug shot of Horton, who was black, while explaining that he was a convict serving a life sentence for murder who had obtained a weekend pass from prison and raped his girlfriend. The commercial combined the claim that Dukakis was soft on crime with the more subtle dog whistle of racism.[65] The Dukakis campaign failed to respond to this one-two punch, a fatal error in modern politics, and subsequent surveys showed that those who saw the commercials came to think of crime as an important issue in the campaign. Bush's standings began to climb, and, of course, he went on to win the election.[66]

Today, such a campaign strategy seems quaint. Sometimes the most effective commercials don't ever have to get on TV—by going viral they show up in voters' curated media feeds and can get to targeted audiences. They are also harder to respond to because they spread so fast and the recipient may never hear the response. Controlling the message is a new challenge in our intensely mediated era.

Negative advertising about one's opponent, like the Willie Horton ad, may turn off some voters and give the perception that politics is an unpleasant business. But as long as it does not go too far, an attack ad that highlights

---

negative advertising campaign advertising that emphasizes the negative characteristics of opponents rather than one's own strengths

Viral Media

Verbal accusations, negative attacks, and rumor mongering have characterized American election campaigns since the days of George Washington. *George Washington?* His opponents called him a "dictator" who would "debauch the nation."[1] Thomas Jefferson was accused of having an affair with a slave, a controversy that has outlived any of the people involved; and Abraham Lincoln was claimed to have had an illegitimate child.

Like it or not (and most Americans say they do not), in the Internet age such negative and deeply personal attacks are more prevalent than ever. Once, negative attacks were limited to soap box speeches and debates, and quotes that accusers hoped would get picked up by the news media. The age of television made attack advertisements—sometimes paid for by candidates but more often by third parties—a choice weapon in the battle for the hearts and minds of the electorate. Today such groups don't need to pay for airtime or space in newspapers—they can just create videos, memes, or even just pithy but potent tweets, and release them into the wild. The more outrageous the claims made in them, the more likely they are to go viral. And they're effective: people remember negative messages far more than they do positive ones. Tracking polls show that after a voter has seen a negative ad eight times, he or she begins to move away from the attacked candidate.[2]

Candidates, operatives, and interest groups usually claim that their messages are not really negative, but rather that they are "comparative," and indeed a candidate often needs to compare his or her record with another's in order to make the case that he or she is the superior choice. But negative ads and media attacks are nonetheless unpopular with voters, who often see them as nasty, unfair, and false. In fact, claims that are proven untrue can frequently backfire on the person making them.

What to Watch Out For

How is a savvy media consumer to know what to believe? Be careful, be critical, and be fair in your assessment of the messages that pop up on your screens. Ask yourself these questions:

- **How did this message find you?** Did it come up in your social media feeds? Was it a paid advertisement? Was it forwarded, posted, or tweeted by a friend? As we've discussed elsewhere, social media are designed to connect you with content that will appeal to you and your deeply held beliefs. If a claim seems to be tailor made to make you feel outraged, consider whether you are being manipulated by an algorithm.

- **Who created the message?** If it's a glossy video, chances are it was professionally produced—and someone had to pay for it. Was it paid for by a candidate's campaign? What do they have at stake, and how might that affect their charges? If it's a rougher or more rudimentary meme (the kind that your nephew could create on his phone in about thirty seconds), think hard before you lend it any credence at all. If you can't tell who created it, you should probably dismiss it.

- **Are the accusations relevant to the campaign or the office in question?** If character is a legitimate issue, questions of adultery or drug use might have bearing on the election. If not, they might just be personal details used to smear this candidate's reputation. Ask yourself, What kind of person should hold the job? What kinds of qualities are important?

- **Is the accusation or attack timely?** If a person is accused of youthful experimentation or indiscreet behavior in his or her twenties but has been an upstanding lawyer and public servant for twenty-five years, do the accusations have bearing on how the candidate will do the job?

- **Does the message convey a fair charge that can be answered, or does it evoke unarticulated fears and emotions?** A 1964 ad for Lyndon Johnson's presidential campaign showed a little girl counting as she plucked petals from a daisy. An adult male voice gradually replaced hers, counting down to an explosion resulting in a mushroom cloud that obliterated the picture. The "Daisy" commercial never even mentioned Johnson's opponent, Barry Goldwater, though the clear implication was that the conservative, pro-military Goldwater was likely to lead the nation to a nuclear war. The ad was aired only once, but it became a classic example of the sort of ad that seeks to play on the fears of its viewers.

- **Is there any truth to the message?** Before you click "share" on that scathing accusation against a candidate you don't like, study the message and evaluate its truthfulness. Valuable resources for fact-checking messages in the media—including ads, reporting, claims made by candidates and their surrogates, and viral messages—include FactCheck.org, Snopes.com, and Politifact.com.

---

1. Alexandra Marks, "Backlash Grows Against Negative Political Ads," *Christian Science Monitor*, September 28, 1995, 1.
2. Ibid.

negative aspects of an opponent's record actually registers more quickly and is remembered more frequently and longer by voters than are positive ads.[67] Experts have suggested that requiring candidates to appear in their own ads would discourage negativity. Negative ads, however, continue to be the rule, rather than the exception, though not all candidates resort to them equally. Hillary Clinton spent far more on all advertising than did Donald Trump in 2016, most of it to highlight Trump's own behavior and words.

Because paid media coverage is so expensive, a campaign's goal is to maximize opportunities for free coverage while controlling, as much as possible, the kind of coverage it gets. The major parties' presidential candidates are accompanied by a substantial entourage of reporters who need to file stories on a regular basis, not only for the nation's major newspapers and television networks but also to keep busy the reporters and commentators on the cable news stations, like CNN, MSNBC, and Fox. These media have substantial influence in setting the narrative—determining what issues are important and, hence, which candidates' appeals will resonate with voters.[68] As a result, daily campaign events are planned more for the press and the demands of the evening news than for the in-person audiences, who often seem to function primarily as a backdrop for the candidates' efforts to get favorable airtime each day. The campaigns also field daily conference calls with reporters to attack their opponents and defend their candidates and to try to control, or "spin," the way they are covered.

In 2008, campaign managers finally figured out how to use the Internet to good advantage at the same time that it really came into its own as a source of news. Mainstream media outlets like the *New York Times*, the *Washington Post*, *Time* magazine, and the major networks maintained blogs that joined independent bloggers like Josh Marshall of talkingpointsmemo.com and *National Review Online* in updating campaign news and poll results throughout the day. And now that there's a cell phone in every pocket, YouTube has helped to transform the electoral landscape as well. A recorded gaffe or misstatement by a candidate or a campaign surrogate could go viral—reaching millions of viewers with the quick swipes of many fingers. Politicians accustomed to a more conventional way of campaigning were often caught in the YouTube trap. Bill Clinton, for instance, campaigning for his wife in the Democratic primary in 2008, was several times recorded saying something ill-advised that spread quickly before he could attempt damage control. And Mitt Romney was recorded in 2012 at a private fundraiser speaking about how 47 percent of Americans, who pay no taxes, would

never vote for him or be persuaded to take responsibility for their lives. His poll numbers dipped after this, and although they improved after the first debate, he was haunted by the image of being unsympathetic to the plight of almost half of Americans. In 2016 there seemed to be nothing Donald Trump could say that would offend his supporters enough to change their votes, and many admired his brash authenticity.

Although the candidates want the regular exposure, they do not like the norms of broadcast news, which they see as perpetuating horse-race journalism, focusing on who is ahead rather than on substantive issues.[69] In addition, the exhausting nature of campaigns, and the mistakes and gaffes that follow, are a source of constant concern because of the media's tendency to zero in on them and replay them endlessly. The relationship between the campaigns and the media is testy. Each side needs the other, but the candidates want to control the message, and the media want stories that are "news"—controversies, changes in the candidates' standings, or stories of goofs and scandals. Hillary Clinton's dislike for the news media dated back to her days as first lady; and Donald Trump, who had a real entertainer's talent for scoring free news coverage, lost no time banning reporters he did not like from his campaign events and threatening to shut down some press freedoms if he were elected. We discuss the complex relationship between the media and the candidates at greater length in Chapter 15.

Candidates in recent elections have turned increasingly to "soft news" and entertainment programming to get their messages across. Candidates have been especially effective at appealing across party lines to reach less engaged voters in the soft news formats. Since Bill Clinton appeared on *The Arsenio Hall Show* to play his saxophone in 1992, candidates have made late night television one of their go-to places to show their human side and demonstrate their senses of humor. NBC's *Saturday Night Live*, Comedy Central's *The Daily Show* (previously with Jon Stewart and now with Trevor Noah), and *The Late Show with Stephen Colbert* have been favored destinations for candidates (even Michelle Obama stopped in to visit *The Daily Show with Jon Stewart* and *The Colbert Report*). During the 2016 campaign, both Hillary Clinton and Donald Trump made appearances on SNL and various talk shows, and Clinton even appeared on *Between Two Ferns* with Zach Galifianakis.

PRESIDENTIAL DEBATES Since 1976 the presidential debates have become one of the major focal points of the campaign. The first televised debate was held in 1960

Presidential Debates, Then and Now

The 1960 presidential debate between Vice President Richard Nixon and Sen. John F. Kennedy was the first to be televised—and many believe that it benefited the young, charismatic Kennedy, who appeared poised and relaxed in comparison to a brooding Nixon. A half-century later, many analysts argue that debates have little influence on election outcomes. For instance, although many people felt that Hillary Clinton won the 2016 presidential debates, she lost the election to opponent Donald Trump.

between Sen. John F. Kennedy and Vice President Richard Nixon. The younger and more photogenic Kennedy came out on top in those televised debates, but interestingly, those who heard the debates on the radio thought that Nixon did a better job.[70] In general, leading candidates find it less in their interest to participate in debates because they have more to lose and less to win, and so for years debates took place on a sporadic basis.

More recently, however, media and public pressure have all but guaranteed that at least the major-party candidates will participate in debates, although the number, timing, and format of the debates are renegotiated for each presidential election season. Recent elections have generated two or three debates, with a debate among the vice presidential contenders worked in as well. Third-party candidates, who have the most to gain from the free media exposure and the legitimacy that debate participation confers on a campaign, lobby to be included but rarely are. Ross Perot was invited in 1992 because both George H. W. Bush and Bill Clinton hoped to woo his supporters but neither Gary Johnson nor Jill Stein made the 15 percent polling threshold to participate in 2016. However, some of the debates, especially those identified with significant candidate errors or positive performances, have moved vote intentions 2 to 4 percent, which in a close race could be significant.[71] In addition, a good deal of evidence indicates that citizens learn about the candidates and their issue positions from the debates.[72] In 2012 President Obama was familiar to voters, but his challenger, Mitt Romney, was known mostly as the plutocratic caricature

that had been painted of him in Obama advertisements. During their first debate, Romney looked relaxed, confident, and presidential, while the president looked grumpy and passive. You could watch pundits on Twitter come to the rapid-fire conclusion that the president had blown it, and commentators immediately went on TV to share the more or less collective judgment. Polls showed a huge win for Romney, and many of the Republican-leaning voters who had been turned off by Romney's 47 percent gaffe returned to his camp. Mad at himself for his sleepy performance in the first debate, Obama snapped back in the second and third debates, and polls showed that voters considered him the winner. By Election Day, he had returned to his pre-debate standing in the polls.

Hillary Clinton and Donald Trump faced off in three debates in 2016, with Clinton a strong winner in all the scientific post-debate polls. Her extensive debate prep paid off, and she was able to needle the less prepared Trump into making responses that made him seem short-tempered and irritable. Since she was trying to make the election about temperament, this played well into her narrative.

Unfortunately, the debates were generally thin on substance, and although several debate moderators made the difficult decision to take an active role in fact-checking some of Trump's claims, others did not. The election was ultimately about the emotional response voters had to the two candidates rather than a rational evaluation of their preparation, and Clinton's victories didn't help get her over the Electoral College finish line.

MONEY Winning—or even losing—a presidential campaign involves serious money. The two major-party presidential candidates in 2016 spent over a billion dollars, money that was supplemented by PAC spending. The data in Figure 14.2 show this striking upward trend, which came about despite significant fundraising limits put in place by the Bipartisan Campaign Reform Act (BCRA).

This torrent of cash is used to cover the costs of all the activities just discussed: campaign professionals, polling, and travel for the candidates and often their spouses (along with the accompanying staff and media), with the biggest share going to the production and purchase of media advertising.

Where does all this money come from? To make sense of the changing world of election campaign finance, we need to start by defining the different kinds of campaign contributions, each with different sources and regulations:

- **Government matching funds** are money given, in the primary and general election campaigns, to qualified presidential candidates who choose to accept them and to spend only that money. The funds came from citizens who checked the box on their tax returns that sent $3 ($6 on joint returns) to fund presidential election campaigns. The idea behind the law was to more easily regulate big-money influence on campaign finances, to ensure a fair contest, and to free up candidates to communicate with the public. For primary elections, if a candidate raises at least $5,000 in each of twenty states and agrees to abide by overall spending limits (almost $55 million in 2012), as well as state-by-state limits, the federal government matches every contribution up to $250.

  This same fund has in the past fully financed both major-party candidates' general election campaigns and continues to subsidize the two national party nominating conventions. John McCain opted to participate in the 2008 federal campaign financing and faced a spending limit of $84.1 million. Barack Obama was the first presidential nominee not to participate in the general election federal financing, arguing that by relying on small donations over the Internet, his campaign was essentially publicly funded anyway. This meant that his campaign had to raise all the funds it would spend rather than receiving the federal subsidy, but it also meant that the Obama campaign was not limited in the amount it could spend. If presidential candidates accept this public funding, they may not raise any other funds or use any leftover funds raised during the primary campaign. With the adroit use of the Internet, mediated citizenship spread to mediated campaign funding, with social media contacts urging each other to give, signing up for automatic weekly or monthly donations, and being hit up for solicitations by similar candidates with whom the candidate they initially supported shared lists.

  Obama's decision to self-fund pretty much spelled the death of public funding of presidential general election campaigns as neither candidate in 2012 or 2016 accepted it, and few taxpayers were donating funds to keep it going, in any case.[73]

- **Hard money** refers to the funds given directly to candidates by individuals, political action committees (PACs), the political parties, and the government. The spending of hard money is under candidates' control, but its collection is governed by the rules of the Federal Election Campaign Act (FECA) of 1971, 1974, and its various amendments. This act established the FEC and was intended to stop the flow of money from large contributors (and thus limit their influence) by outlawing contributions by corporations and unions, and by restricting contributions from individuals. In 2015–2016, individuals could give a federal candidate up to $2,700 per election.[74] The limit on the parties' hard money contributions to candidates was held to be unconstitutional in a 1999 Colorado district federal court decision but was later upheld in a five-to-four Supreme Court decision.[75]

  However, in the 2010 decision in *Citizens United v. Federal Election Commission*,[76] the Supreme Court struck down a provision of BCRA that prohibited corporations (and, by implication, unions and interest groups) from sponsoring broadcast ads for or against specific candidates. Corporations, unions, and individual citizens are thus free to engage in broadcast campaigns, although provisions requiring disclosure and limitations on direct contributions to candidates were retained. A new loophole is being exploited by what are called 501c groups (after the section of the tax codes under which they are chartered). Experts disagreed about the likely consequences of the far-reaching

---

government matching funds money given by the federal government to qualified presidential candidates in the primary and general election campaigns

hard money campaign funds donated directly to candidates; amounts are limited by federal election laws

decision, but mirroring the Court's five-to-four breakdown on the ruling, it was generally decried by liberals and supported by conservatives.[77] What is not controversial is that the decision opened the floodgates for vast sums of money, much of it coming through what are known as Super PACs funded by very wealthy individuals, corporations, and unions.[78]

- **Soft money** is unregulated money collected by parties and interest groups in unlimited amounts to spend on party-building activities, GOTV drives, voter education, or issue position advocacy. Prior to the passage of campaign finance reform in 2002, as long as the money was not spent to tell people how to vote or coordinated with a specific candidate's campaign, the FEC could not regulate soft money. This allowed corporate groups, unions, and political parties to raise unlimited funds often used for television and radio advertising, especially in the form of issue advocacy ads. As we discussed in Chapter 13, **issue advocacy ads**

are television or radio commercials run during an election campaign that promote a particular issue, usually by attacking the character, views, or position of the candidate the group running the ad wishes to defeat. The courts have considered these ads protected free speech and have held that individuals and organizations could not be stopped from spending money to express their opinions about issues, or even candidates, so long as they did not explicitly tell viewers how to vote.

FIGURE 14.2

Increase in Total Spending in Presidential Campaigns, 1976–2016

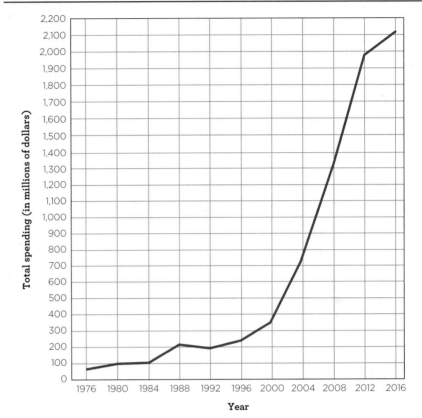

Source: Center for Responsive Politics, "Presidential Fund-raising and Spending, 1976–2008," www.opensecrets.org/pres08/totals.php?cycle=2008; "Banking on Becoming President," www.opensecrets.org/pres08/index.php; "2012 Presidential Race," www.opensecrets.org/pres12/index.php?q3; "2016 Presidential Race," www.opensecrets.org/pres16/.

Most observers thought that BCRA would remove unregulated money from campaigns and curb negative advertising. Although it limited the spending of PACs and parties, new groups, called 527 groups after the loophole (section 527) in the Internal Revenue Code that allows them to avoid the regulations imposed by BCRA, sprang up in their stead. Like groups that raised and spent soft money prior to BCRA, 527s can raise unlimited funds for issue advocacy or voter mobilization so long as they do not openly promote or try to defeat any particular candidate. BCRA does forbid all groups, even 527s, from running such ads funded by soft money within sixty days of a general election, or within thirty days of a primary election. The 2010 *Citizens United* ruling loosened the regulations further, lifting the sixty-day limit. Interest groups, corporations, and unions have greater leeway in how and when they campaign for candidates. They are still limited in

---

soft money unregulated campaign contributions by individuals, groups, or parties that promote general election activities but do not directly support individual candidates

issue advocacy ads advertisements paid for by soft money, and thus not regulated, that promote certain issue positions but do not endorse specific candidates

making direct (hard money) contributions, but most of their efforts will be as independent expenditures (efforts that cannot be coordinated with the candidates' campaigns). Given that such contributors do not share a single common ideology or set of issue preferences, some observers argue that any effects will largely cancel each other out, but there is no doubt that we have seen a huge influx of private money into elections.[79]

GETTING OUT THE VOTE Get-out-the-vote (GOTV) drives refer to the voter mobilization efforts we discussed earlier in this chapter, an increasingly important part of any presidential campaign. In the 1980s and 1990s, such efforts concentrated mostly on television advertising. The expense of these "air wars" meant that parties and campaigns worried less about knocking on doors and the shoe-leather efforts associated with a campaign's "ground war." Parties mistakenly associated GOTV with "get on television" rather than its traditional meaning of "get out the vote."[80] Beginning in 1998 the campaigns renewed efforts to contact potential voters face-to-face. This is consistent with research that shows that decreased party mobilization efforts were a substantial part of the reason that voter turnout had been decreasing.[81]

In 2008 and 2012, however, the Obama campaign rewrote the strategy book for modern campaigns. Not only did it reawaken efforts at direct contacting, but it tied such contact to advances in Internet technology and social networking, from regular ads on YouTube, to recurring emails and text messages to contributors, to highly sophisticated and coordinated volunteer efforts at voter mobilization.[82] The Clinton team had followed suit in 2016, opening hundreds of offices, and deploying thousands of volunteers in places across all the battleground states. With many of the Obama team, they ran a high-tech professional campaign. Donald Trump did not have a ground game, relying on his rallies to build enthusiasm and the Republican National Committee, which had made a major effort to up its game after 2012.

What is particularly interesting about these grassroots efforts is that they are not just a return to a bygone era. Rather, mobilization efforts combine old-school door-to-door campaigning with modern technology.[83] Vast computer databases tell volunteers whose doors to knock on, and these volunteers often have hand-held personal electronic devices that have detailed information on each voter.[84] This allows parties and groups to target swing voters and their base voters. Campaigns and interest groups also flood supporters' email in-boxes and tie up the phone lines. In their zeal to seek out all possible voters, campaigns have reached out to poorer voters in both urban and rural areas who have not received either party's attention in recent decades.[85]

INTERPRETING ELECTIONS

After the election is over, when the votes are counted, and we know who won, it would seem that the whole election season is finally finished and the narrative spinning is over. In reality, the outcomes of our collective decisions cry for interpretation. Probably the most important interpretation is the one articulated by the victor. The winning candidate in presidential elections inevitably claims an **electoral mandate**, a kind of narrative based on the belief that the people want the president to do the things he or she campaigned on and that the election is all about the voters' preference for the president's leadership and policy programs. Presidents who can sell the interpretation that their election to office is a ringing endorsement of their policies can work with Congress from a favored position.[86] To the extent that presidents are able to sell their interpretation, they will be more successful in governing. In contrast, the losing party will try to argue that its loss was due to the characteristics of its candidate or specific campaign mistakes. Party members will, predictably, resist the interpretation that the voters rejected their message and their vision for the nation. In general, Congress responds less to presidential declarations of a mandate and more to indications of changes in public preferences signaled by a change in which party wins the presidency or a large legislative seat turnover, especially one that produces a change in party control of Congress.[87]

The media also develop their narratives about the meaning of elections. In fact, research shows that of the many possible explanations that are available, the mainstream media quickly—in just a matter of weeks—home in on an agreed-upon standard explanation of the election.[88] In 2016 it was that both candidates were unlikable and that the campaign was negative, exhausting, and issue free. The media's difficulty calling Trump out on his many fabrications and their attempts to create a false equivalence in their treatment of the two were in part due to Clinton's long, difficult

get-out-the-vote (GOTV) drives efforts by political parties, interest groups, and the candidate's staff to maximize voter turnout among supporters

electoral mandate the perception that an election victory signals broad support for the winner's proposed policies

relationship with the media and what they perceive as her secretiveness, as well as the fact that, believing Clinton would win, few in the media took Trump seriously until the very end. When investigative reports finally began to dig into Trump's background, it was late in the game. Then, ten days before Election Day, FBI director James Comey said he was looking into Clinton's emails again, and that became the focus of the media coverage. By the time Comey cleared her a week later, many people had already voted.

PAUSE AND REVIEW — Who, What, How

In the matter of presidential elections, the parties, their elites, party activists, and the candidates all have something vital at stake. The traditional party leaders fared best under the old rules and closed-door decision making that yielded seasoned and electable politicians as the parties' nominees. Activists, with a broader agenda than simply winning power, seek control of the platform and the nomination, and may well have goals other than electability in mind. The primary system allows them to reap the fruits of the considerable time and resources they are willing to invest in politics.

Candidates seeking the nomination must answer to both traditional party leaders and activist members. This often puts them in a difficult position. Once nominated and pursuing a national bipartisan victory, the candidate needs to hold on to party supporters while drawing in those not already committed to the other side. Here the candidate makes use of the rules of the Electoral College, professional staff, strategic issue positions, the media, fundraising, and voter mobilization.

In Your Own Words Identify the organizational and strategic tactics employed in presidential campaigns.

THE CITIZENS AND ELECTIONS

*Do too many informed voters
lead to too much conflict?*

We have acknowledged that the American citizen does not look like the ideal citizen of classical democratic theory. Nothing we have learned in this chapter has convinced us otherwise, but that does not mean that Americans are doomed to an undemocratic future. The modern mediated era does not look like the world of classical Greek democracy either—it is more diverse, more equal, more interconnected, and much more complex. In the first chapter of this book, we considered three models of citizen activity in democracies, which we revisit here.

The first model we discussed is the elite model, which argues that as citizens we can do no more (or are fit to do

no more) than choose the elites who govern us, making a rather passive choice from among remote leaders. The second model of democratic politics, the pluralist model, sees us as participating in political life primarily through our affiliation with different types of groups. Finally, the participatory model of democracy is perhaps more prescriptive than the other two models, which it rejects because it believes that it is unsatisfactory for the majority of the citizenry to play a largely passive role in the political system. This model holds that we grow and develop as citizens through being politically active. In fact, rather than fitting any of these models exclusively, the American citizen's role in elections seems to borrow elements from all three models in a way that might be called a fourth model. American citizens, though they do not meet the ideals of democratic theory, do make a difference in American politics through the mechanism of elections.

A FOURTH MODEL?

Early studies of voting that used survey research found that most citizens had surprisingly low levels of interest in presidential election campaigns. These studies of the 1944 and 1948 presidential elections found that most citizens had their minds made up before the campaigns began and that opinions changed only slightly in response to the efforts of the parties and candidates. Instead of people relying on new information coming from the campaigns, people voted according to the groups to which they belonged. That is, income, occupation, religion, and similar factors structured who people talked to, what they learned, and how they voted.

The authors of these studies concluded that democracy is probably safer without a single type of citizen who matches the civic ideal of high levels of participation, knowledge, and commitment.[89] In this view, such high levels of involvement would indicate a citizenry fraught with conflict. Intense participation comes with intense commitment and strongly held positions, which make for an unwillingness to compromise. This revision of the call for classic "good citizens" holds that our democratic polity is actually better off when it has lots of different types of citizens: some who care deeply, are highly informed, and participate intensely; many more who care moderately, are a bit informed, and participate as much out of duty to the process as commitment to one party or candidate; and some who are less aware of politics until some great issue or controversy awakens their political slumber.

The virtue of modern democracy in this political specialization view is that citizens play different roles and that together these roles combine to form an electoral system that has the attributes we prefer: it is reasonably stable; it responds to changes of issues and candidates, but not too much; and the electorate as a whole cares, but not so intensely that any significant portion of the citizenry will challenge the results of an election. Its most obvious flaw is that it is biased against the interests of those who are least likely to be the activist or pluralist citizens—the young, the poor, the uneducated, and minorities.[90]

DO ELECTIONS MAKE A DIFFERENCE?

If we can argue that most Americans do take more than a passive role in elections and that, despite being less-than-ideal democratic citizens, most Americans are involved "enough," then we need to ask whether the elections they participate in make any difference. Do they?

- At a minimal but nevertheless important level, elections in the United States do achieve electoral accountability. By this we mean only that, by having to stand for reelection, our leaders are more or less constantly concerned with the consequences of their present actions for their next election. The fact that citizens tend to vote retrospectively provides incumbent administrations with a lot of incentive to keep things running properly, and certainly to avoid policies that citizens may hold against them. Thus we begin by noting that elections keep officeholders attentive to what they are doing.
- Elections also matter because it makes a difference who wins. Today the parties stand on opposite sides of many issues, and given the chance, they will move national policy in the direction they believe in. Looking at elections over time, scholars observe a direct relationship between national elections and the policies that government subsequently enacts. Electing Democrats results in more liberal policies; electing Republicans results in more conservative policies.[91] This same generalization can be seen in the politics of the American states, where we find that more liberal states enact more liberal policies and more conservative states enact more conservative policies.[92] There is much solid evidence that elections are indeed crucial in bringing about a degree of policy congruence between the electorate and what policymakers do.
- Finally, elections matter because they give mediated citizens points of activity around which to rally. When Republicans were angry at the passage of the Affordable Care Act in 2009, they targeted the 2010 midterms as a way to express their disappointment and anger. After the election of Donald Trump, Democrats similarly focused on the 2018 midterms, recruiting candidates and honing their message. Elections can provide a structure for citizen activity, and with the connections the mediated age provides us, we have more opportunities than ever to take advantage of them if we choose.

Just because elections seem to work to bring policy into rough agreement with citizen preferences does not mean that all citizens know what they want and that candidates know this and respond. Some citizens do know what they want; others do not. Some candidates heed the wishes of constituents; others pay more attention to their own consciences or to the demands of ideological party activists and contributors. Averaged over all these variables, however, we do find that policy follows elections. Citizens, even with the blunt instrument of the ballot, can and do change what government does.[93]

In Your Own Words Recognize the importance of elections for citizens.

LET'S REVISIT: *What's at Stake . . . ?*

We began this chapter asking how, in a modern democracy, an archaic constitutional institution, long altered from its original purpose, managed to throw an election from a popular vote winner to her opponent. What is at stake in keeping the Electoral College in an age when its use seems to have outlived the intentions and concerns of the founders and when, in fact, it might have preserved the fate of exactly the unexperienced, populist kind of candidate they were seeking to avoid?

As we have seen in this chapter, and all through this book, politics is about rules, and jockeying to get the rules that give you an advantage. To understand the stakes in keeping the Electoral College, we need to be clear on the fact that its major job is to produce winners and losers.

There is the most agitation to change a rule when it is perceived to produce a result that makes you a loser. Then you have a stake in changing it. In the case of the Electoral College, when it produces a president other than the popular vote winner, there is one side losing and feeling aggrieved, ready to change the rules, but there is also a side that won, and, what's more, a side that won *only* because of the Electoral College. That side has a stake in keeping the institution. Finding consensus for change at that point is impossible.

There is far less agitation to change the rules when, like a quiet appendix, it's not causing any trouble. At that time we hardly notice it. And when change probably means a constitutional amendment, which is hard work even during times of passionate desire for transformation, it's even less likely.

Uncontested states—the non-swing states that generally go consistently for one party or the other—would normally have a stake in changing the Electoral College because most of them receive hardly any attention by campaigners for the White House. The National Public Vote project claims that 94 percent of the 2016 campaign was fought in just twelve states.[94]

But that means that the twelve states that received all the attention have a large stake in keeping things just as they are. Candidate visits, promises, ad spending, rallies, news coverage—all those are pluses to the states that are used to figuring as the important swing states.

What was curious about the 2016 election is that the electoral map began to shift in subtle ways. With demographic changes it's possible that today's solid red or blue states will be tomorrow's swing states, and that gives all states a stake in waiting to see how things turn out.

One clear possessor of stakes in this process is the American people, who, as we have seen, are by and large proceduralists, accepting the outcome of the rules whether they like them or not, because they recognize that a rule-based procedural system is preferable to the alternative. At the same time, we *are* a democracy. And we have a stake in having rules that are seen as fair and representative of the people's will—which may be why the National Popular Vote Interstate Compact continues to gather support, and why the 2016 election resulted in renewed calls for reform.

CLUES to Critical Thinking

Al Gore's concession speech, December 13, 2000

The 2000 presidential election was unusual on several counts (see What's at Stake . . . ? *in Chapter 10). A state's election results were contested, amid accusations of fraud and misleading ballot design; that state's supreme court was overruled by the U.S. Supreme Court in the matter of recounts; and the results of that contested state election gave an Electoral College victory to a candidate who had lost the popular vote. This concession speech by Al Gore, who won the popular vote even as he lost the Electoral College, highlights how elections, even as odd as that one, serve to legitimate government when people agree on the rules.*

Good evening

Just moments ago, I spoke with George W. Bush and congratulated him on becoming the 43rd president of the United States, and I promised him that I wouldn't call him back this time.

I offered to meet with him as soon as possible so that we can start to heal the divisions of the campaign and the contest through which we just passed.

Almost a century and a half ago, Senator Stephen Douglas told Abraham Lincoln, who had just defeated him for the presidency, "Partisan feeling must yield to patriotism. I'm with you, Mr. President, and God bless you."

Well, in that same spirit, I say to President-elect Bush that what remains of partisan rancor must now be put aside, and may God bless his stewardship of this country.

Neither he nor I anticipated this long and difficult road. Certainly neither of us wanted it to happen. Yet it came, and now it has ended, resolved, as it must be resolved, through the honored institutions of our democracy.

Over the library of one of our great law schools is inscribed the motto, "Not under man but under God and law." That's the ruling principle of American freedom, the source of our democratic liberties. I've tried to make it my guide throughout this contest as it has guided America's deliberations of all the complex issues of the past five weeks.

Now the U.S. Supreme Court has spoken. Let there be no doubt, while I strongly disagree with the court's decision, I accept it. I accept the finality of this outcome which will be ratified next Monday in the Electoral College. And tonight, for the sake of our unity of the people and the strength of our democracy, I offer my concession.

I also accept my responsibility, which I will discharge unconditionally, to honor the new president elect and do everything possible to help him bring Americans together in fulfillment of the great vision that our Declaration of Independence defines and that our Constitution affirms and defends.

Let me say how grateful I am to all those who supported me and supported the cause for which we have fought. Tipper and I feel a deep gratitude to Joe and Hadassah Lieberman who brought passion and high purpose to our partnership and opened new doors, not just for our campaign but for our country.

This has been an extraordinary election. But in one of God's unforeseen paths, this belatedly broken impasse can point us all to a new common ground, for its very closeness can serve to remind us that we are one people with a shared history and a shared destiny.

Indeed, that history gives us many examples of contests as hotly debated, as fiercely fought, with their own challenges to the popular will.

Other disputes have dragged on for weeks before reaching resolution. And each time, both the victor and the vanquished have accepted the result peacefully and in the spirit of reconciliation.

So let it be with us.

I know that many of my supporters are disappointed.

I am too. But our disappointment must be overcome by our love of country.

And I say to our fellow members of the world community, let no one see this contest as a sign of American weakness. The strength of American democracy is shown most clearly through the difficulties it can overcome.

Some have expressed concern that the unusual nature of this election might hamper the next president in the conduct of his office. I do not believe it need be so.

President-elect Bush inherits a nation whose citizens will be ready to assist him in the conduct of his large responsibilities.

I personally will be at his disposal, and I call on all Americans—I particularly urge all who stood with us to unite behind our next president. This is America. Just as we fight hard when the stakes are high, we close ranks and come together when the contest is done.

And while there will be time enough to debate our continuing differences, now is the time to recognize that that which unites us is greater than that which divides us.

While we yet hold and do not yield our opposing beliefs, there is a higher duty than the one we owe to political party. This is America and we put country before party. We will stand together behind our new president.

As for what I'll do next, I don't know the answer to that one yet. Like many of you, I'm looking forward to spending the holidays with family and old friends. I know I'll spend time in Tennessee and mend some fences, literally and figuratively.

Some have asked whether I have any regrets and I do have one regret: that I didn't get the chance to stay and fight for the American people over the next four years, especially for those who need burdens lifted and barriers removed, especially for those who feel their voices have not been heard. I heard you and I will not forget.

I've seen America in this campaign and I like what I see. It's worth fighting for and that's a fight I'll never stop.

As for the battle that ends tonight, I do believe as my father once said, that no matter how hard the loss, defeat might serve as well as victory to shape the soul and let the glory out.

So for me this campaign ends as it began: with the love of Tipper and our family; with faith in God and in the country

I have been so proud to serve, from Vietnam to the vice presidency; and with gratitude to our truly tireless campaign staff and volunteers, including all those who worked so hard in Florida for the last 36 days.

Now the political struggle is over and we turn again to the unending struggle for the common good of all Americans and for those multitudes around the world who look to us for leadership in the cause of freedom.

In the words of our great hymn, "America, America": "Let us crown thy good with brotherhood, from sea to shining sea."

And now, my friends, in a phrase I once addressed to others, it's time for me to go.

Thank you and good night, and God bless America.

Source: CNN.com transcripts, http://transcripts.cnn.com/TRANSCRIPTS/0012/14/se.06.html.

Consider the source and the audience: Gore is speaking to several audiences here. Who are they? Why does he address "our fellow members of the world community"? At the time, Gore was certainly considering a run for the presidency in the future. How might that have shaped his message? How could he have used this speech to rally supporters if he had wanted to?

Lay out the argument and the underlying values and assumptions: What personal values of Gore's become apparent in this speech? How do they affect his political views? What is Gore's view of the common good here? How does that differ from partisan advantage, and when should the former take precedence over the latter? When should a political outcome be accepted even when one doesn't like it? How do the "honored institutions of our democracy" help to resolve contests like this? In what context does Gore refer to the Supreme Court and the Electoral College?

Uncover the evidence: What kinds of evidence does Gore use to support his argument that the result of the election process should be accepted even if one doesn't agree with it, and that George W. Bush is the legitimate president of the United States?

Evaluate the conclusion: Did Gore's use of symbolism and references to history, law, and religion convince supporters to accept the election result? Did they convince the world that the United States was a stable and solid nation? Did they convince the nation to put the trauma of the partisan backbiting behind it and move on?

Sort out the political implications: Many electoral reforms were debated following the election, but few were enacted. Who would have resisted reform, and why?

Review

Voting in a Democratic Society

Elections represent the core of American democracy, serving several functions: selecting leaders, giving direction to policy, developing citizenship, informing the public, containing conflict, and stabilizing the political system.

Electoral College (p. 476)   **political efficacy (p. 477)**

Exercising the Right to Vote in America

Voting enhances the quality of democratic life by legitimizing the outcomes of elections. However, American voter turnout levels are typically among the lowest in the world and may endanger American democracy. Even so, debate exists—often along party lines—over how easy it should be to vote, and state laws and the Supreme Court have played large roles in the outcome of that debate. Factors such as age, gender, income, education, and race and ethnicity affect whether a person is likely to vote.

regulating the electorate (p. 479)   voter mobilization (p. 484)
Motor Voter Act (p. 480)   social connectedness (p. 485)

How America Decides

Candidates and the media often blur issue positions, and voters realistically cannot investigate policy proposals on their own. Therefore, voters decide by considering party identification and peer viewpoints, prominent issues, and campaign images.

prospective voting (p. 487)   retrospective voting (p. 487)

Presidential Campaigns

The "road to the White House" is long, expensive, and grueling. It begins with planning and early fundraising in the pre-primary phase and develops into more active campaigning during the primary phase, which ends with each party's choice of a candidate, announced at the party conventions. During the general election, the major-party candidates are pitted against each other in a process that relies increasingly on the media and getting out the vote. Much of the battle at this stage is focused on attracting voters who have not yet made up their minds.

The Electoral College demonstrates well the founders' desire to insulate government from public whims. Citizens do not vote directly for the president or vice president but rather for an elector who has already pledged to vote for that candidate. Except in Maine and Nebraska, the candidate with the majority of votes in a state wins all the electoral votes in that state.

invisible primary (p. 489)   momentum (p. 491)   government matching funds (p. 504)
exploratory committee (p. 489)   swing voters (p. 493)   hard money (p. 504)
caucus (p. 490)   oppo research (p. 497)   soft money (p. 505)
presidential primary (p. 490)   valence issues (p. 498)   issue advocacy ads (p. 505)
open primary (p. 490)   position issues (p. 498)   get-out-the-vote (GOTV) drives (p. 506)
closed primary (p. 490)   wedge issue (p. 498)   electoral mandate (p. 506)
front-loading (p. 490)   issue ownership (p. 498)
front-runner (p. 491)   negative advertising (p. 500)

The Citizens and Elections

Although American citizens do not fit the mythical ideal of the democratic citizen, elections still seem to work in representing the voice of the people in terms of citizen policy preferences.

In Your Own Words

After you've read this chapter, you will be able to

15.1 Discuss changes over the past several decades in the ways in which Americans get their news and information.

15.2 Describe the ways in which media ownership and government regulation influence the news we get.

15.3 Explain the roles and responsibilities of journalists and the tools they use to shape and perpetuate political narratives.

15.4 Identify the strategies politicians use to counter the influence of the media and shape and perpetuate their own political narratives.

15.5 Summarize the relationship between citizens and the media.

15
MEDIA, POWER, AND POLITICAL COMMUNICATION

What's at Stake . . . in Living in an Information Bubble?

FROM THE MOMENT AMERICANS WOKE UP ON JUNE 12, 2016, to the horrific news that forty-nine people had been shot at the Pulse nightclub in Orlando, Florida, two competing stories about the tragedy took root in the American psyche. Spawned by the ideological assumptions we began with, fed by the media sources we turned to for information, and nurtured by the social media connections through which we shared what we learned, the stories grew. They were symbolized by two very different speeches by the 2016 presidential candidates and perfectly illustrated by the ongoing chatter on two competing morning talk shows throughout the week: *Morning Joe* on MSNBC and *Fox & Friends* on Fox.

Phil Hands

Choose Your Own Narrative

In the rush to cover emerging events in Orlando, news media outlets tended to focus on one of three basic narratives, framing the issue around gun control, immigration and terrorism, or gay rights.

One story said that the shooter was a mentally disturbed American of Afghan heritage, born in New York, conflicted about his own sexuality, violent at home, and unpopular at work for his homophobic and racist language. The big question for the people for whom this narrative made sense was how this unbalanced man, three times interviewed by the FBI for possible terrorist sympathies and on the terror watch list for a period of time, was able to be licensed as a security guard and managed to buy the AR-15 assault weapon that allowed him to mow down partiers at Pulse.

In her speech, presumptive Democratic nominee Hillary Clinton embraced the LGBTQ community, emphasized the importance of reaching out to the American Muslim population to enlist their cooperation in detecting radicalized "lone-wolf" terrorists, and talked about the importance of putting an assault weapon ban in place so that the same weapon that had been used in multiple mass shootings could not be easily purchased by people with suspicious backgrounds or histories of mental illness.

The themes Clinton set out were talked about, repeated, and woven into a common story about the Orlando shooting that was discussed endlessly on MSNBC's *Morning Joe*, as well as on innumerable other shows and through newspaper stories and social media communications that were shared like wildfire, for days after the massacre.

But that was not the only narrative. A competing story said that the shooting was conducted by a member of ISIS, committed to exterminating gays and other Americans

in an act of radical Islamic terrorism. In this view the president of the United States was complicit in the attack by not using the phrase "radical Islamic terrorism" and perhaps for suspected Muslim sympathies. The big question for people persuaded by this narrative was how the shooter had gotten into the country in the first place and how he and people like him could be kept out. In his speech, given shortly after Clinton's, presumptive Republican nominee Donald Trump also expressed sympathy for the LGBTQ community, but he reiterated his call for a ban on immigration from countries where there was a perceived threat to Americans. He referred to the shooter as an Afghan born to immigrant parents, not as an American, and said the major problem we faced was that Hillary Clinton wanted to let huge numbers of Muslim immigrants into the country without proper vetting. He deplored a lack of leadership that he said was destroying the country.

Trump was not lauded by his party leadership for his accusations about President Obama or his call for a ban on Muslim immigration, but his views clearly resonated with his base. The morning show *Fox & Friends* reinforced the narrative, as did other Fox shows and talk radio, and it too took off on wings of social media.

A Gallup poll captured the difference: 60 percent of Democrats saw the issue as gun violence; 70 percent of Republicans said it was terrorism.[1]

Two narratives, focused on one objective event, explaining the world in diametrically opposed ways (and neither one true, apparently, as more evidence emerged in later years).[2] If you lived in one world, you would not even recognize the other. Your media-viewing habits, your connections with family and friends, and the news you would forward to each other would create the impression that all right-thinking people saw the world the way you did. You would be in an information bubble, the kind we discussed back in Chapter 1, a closed loop of self-reinforcing evidence supporting a particular interpretation of events.

Does it make a difference to your life or to the republic we all try to keep if citizens are living in virtually separate worlds of so-called facts and information? Do democracies require that we share some fundamental understanding of the world? Are information bubbles merely a version of the ideologies we have discussed throughout this book, or do they threaten the integrity of the common political culture itself? Can we communicate without the common foundation provided by referencing the same understanding of facts? Just what is at stake in a world of citizens locked in information bubbles? «

IN this book we have seen that a major component of power is control of information, or the way information is assembled into narratives, and we have come to recognize the truth right under all of our noses—information is no longer a scarce resource. It is abundant and the clamour of the information marketplace is the sound of many people seeking to tell and sell their narratives at increasing volume. The phenomenal increase of channels through which information can flow—that is, the explosion of the media in the last century but especially in the digital age—has made understanding the relationships among power, narratives, and political communication all the more central. Indeed, as citizens and scholars, we ignore it at our peril.

In every chapter in this book we have tried to be clear that power is not just something that is leveraged at us, but something that we, as citizens, can lay claim to. It may not be easy, the decks may be stacked against us, but it is possible. In the mediated age in which we now live, that is truer than ever, which is why we began our discussion of the media in Chapter 1—so that you would be able to think about how the channels through which information is delivered affect all of our lives and how we, in turn, can affect it. This chapter, more so than most in this book, is almost as much about us as it is about institutions and process.

Today we are bombarded by a constant competition of narratives spewing from every television and radio show, web site, blog, Twitter feed, Facebook page, or Instagram story. In this chapter we look at the modern media world, the impact it has on shaping our political beliefs, and the ways in which we can take hold of the narrative ourselves to be more critical consumers of the information we receive.

WHERE DO WE GET OUR INFORMATION?

A hybrid of traditional and interactive sources

Narratives are built from information, and increasingly we get that information from a wide array of media sources. *Media* is the plural of *medium*, meaning in this case an agency through which communication between two different

---

mass media the means of conveying information to large public audiences cheaply and efficiently

media convergence the merging of traditional media with digital communication technologies such as telecommunications and the Internet

---

entities can take place. Just as a medium can be a person who claims to transmit messages from the spiritual world to earthbound souls, today's **mass media**, whether through printed word or electronic signal, convey information cheaply and efficiently from the upper reaches of the political world to everyday citizens. Today we do far more than just watch and listen to the media, which are increasingly multimedia, digital, available on demand, and often interactive in nature. Communication scholars refer to this merging of traditional and digital media as **media convergence**, and it has implications for our political as well as social lives.[3] Politicians scramble to stay on top of electronic innovations that continually shape and alter the political world. And what is just as important in a democratic society, the media help carry information back from citizens to the politicians who lead, or seek to lead, them. The news media in the twenty-first century increasingly rely on new technology. The printing press may have been invented in China over a thousand years ago, but almost all of the truly amazing innovations in information technology—telegraphs, telephones, photography, radio, television, computers, faxes, cell phones, and the Internet—have been developed in the past two hundred years, and just over half of them have come into common use only in the past fifty. What that means is that our technological capabilities sometimes outrun our sophistication about how that technology ought to be used or how it may affect the news it transfers.

Understanding who gets information, where it comes from, and how that information is affected by the technology that brings it to us is crucial to being a knowledgeable student of politics, not to mention an effective democratic citizen. In this section we examine the sources that we in America turn to for the news and the consequences that follow from our choices.

THE MASS MEDIA TODAY

Once upon a time, news entered the average American's life at only a couple of neatly defined and very predictable points during the day. The local morning paper arrived before dawn, there to be read over coffee and breakfast. The afternoon paper (yes, most cities had two papers back then) was waiting for you when you came home from work. Big-city papers like the *New York Times* and the *Washington Post* were available only to those who lived in New York or Washington, D.C., unless you ordered a copy of the paper to be mailed to you, at great expense, arriving several days late (no FedEx, no overnight delivery). In 1960 the evening news came on all three TV stations at 7:30 p.m., and TV-owning America (87 percent of households in 1960) got their last news of the day

From One Nightly News Hour to 24/7

In 1968, television news was limited to evening broadcasts on the three networks—only a few relatively powerful people, like President Lyndon Johnson, had the luxury of tuning in to all three of them simultaneously. Today it's possible to create your own custom media diet from a variety of sources—and carry them all around in your pocket, but ironically the president was one of the later adopters of this new technology, due to security concerns.

from Chet Huntley and David Brinkley on NBC, John Daly on ABC, or Douglas Edwards on CBS (Edwards was to be followed two years later by Walter Cronkite, also known as "Uncle Walter," dubbed by his employer, CBS, as the most trusted face in news). That was pretty much it for news in 1960s America, unless a special event (a space shot, for instance) or a tragedy (like John F. Kennedy's assassination) occurred that required a special bulletin.

Today media convergence defines how we get our news—we get at least a little news from a lot of sources. Only 18 percent of Americans report often getting news from print newspapers, 25 percent from radio, 33 percent from news web sites and apps, 26 percent from network news, 28 percent from cable TV, and 37 percent from local TV.[4] But overall, 67 percent of adults get some news on social media, 50 percent sometimes or often. They are likeliest to get news from, in descending order, Twitter, Reddit, Facebook, Tumblr, YouTube, Snapchat, Instagram, LinkedIn, and WhatsApp, although Facebook is by far the most popular social media site in general, followed by YouTube, Instagram, LinkedIn, and Snapchat.[5]

There are sharp generational divides in these habits. Millennials (those born between about 1980 and 1997) are far more likely to rely on Facebook for news than are their elders (although they are less likely to be interested in political news); Baby Boomers (born between 1946 and 1964) rely more on local television; and Gen Xers (born in between) split the difference.[6] Consider what this means. Younger generations are more likely to get their news from sources they curate themselves—that is, they choose the source of the news directly, or they choose the people with whom they associate, who in turn share the news with them. By contrast, older Americans watch whatever is served up to them by the

media elite. That means that younger people are participating in the choice of narratives they wish to engage in, but they also have the option of eliminating all the ones they don't like. *Snapshot of America: Where Do We Get Our News?* shows the demographics behind this changing media landscape.

Although most of the American public is exposed to some news, and some people are exposed to quite a lot of it, levels of political information in this country are not high. In one study, only about half of the public could correctly answer basic questions about domestic politics and public figures.[7] These politically informed people are not evenly distributed throughout the population, either. Older Americans, those with more education, and men were more likely to answer the questions correctly.[8]

THE DEMISE OF THE PRINT MEDIA

No less a grand thinker than Thomas Jefferson said, "The basis of our governments being the opinion of the people, the very first object should be to keep that right; and were it left to me to decide whether we should have a government without newspapers or newspapers without a government, I should not hesitate a moment to prefer the latter."[9] A look at some survey results, however, shows that print media are in deep trouble. Whereas a third of Americans bought a daily paper in 1941, only 13 percent did so in 2009.[10] From 1991 to 2012, the number of Americans who said they bought a newspaper the previous day plummeted by 50 percent, from 56 percent to 23 percent.[11] Readership continued to fall through 2017, although the pace of decline has moderated somewhat as the economy picked up, mostly due to new, unearned revenue, such as venture capital investments and philanthropy.[12] Although this influx of cash, much of it from the tech industry

Snapshot of America: *Where Do We Get Our News?*

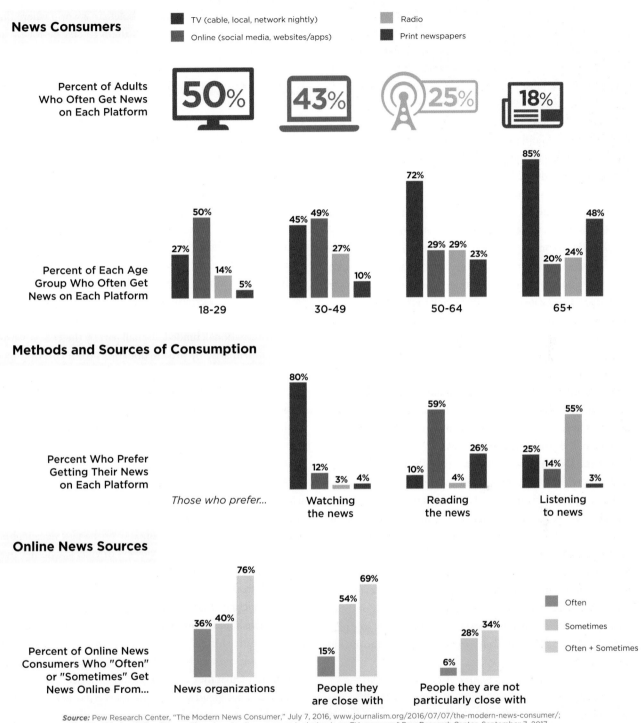

News Consumers

Legend:
- TV (cable, local, network nightly)
- Online (social media, websites/apps)
- Radio
- Print newspapers

Percent of Adults Who Often Get News on Each Platform
- 50%
- 43%
- 25%
- 18%

Percent of Each Age Group Who Often Get News on Each Platform

18-29: 27%, 50%, 14%, 5%
30-49: 45%, 49%, 27%, 10%
50-64: 72%, 29%, 29%, 23%
65+: 85%, 20%, 24%, 48%

Methods and Sources of Consumption

Percent Who Prefer Getting Their News on Each Platform

Those who prefer...

Watching the news: 80%, 12%, 3%, 4%
Reading the news: 10%, 59%, 4%, 26%
Listening to news: 25%, 14%, 55%, 3%

Online News Sources

Percent of Online News Consumers Who "Often" or "Sometimes" Get News Online From...

Legend:
- Often
- Sometimes
- Often + Sometimes

News organizations: 36%, 40%, 76%
People they are close with: 15%, 54%, 69%
People they are not particularly close with: 6%, 28%, 34%

Source: Pew Research Center, "The Modern News Consumer," July 7, 2016, www.journalism.org/2016/07/07/the-modern-news-consumer/; Jeffrey Gottfried and Elisa Shearer, "Americans' online news use is closing in on TV news use," Pew Research Center, September 7, 2017, www.pewresearch.org/fact-tank/2017/09/07/americans-online-news-use-vs-tv-news-use/.

Behind the Numbers

The Pew Research Center derived these categories of news consumers from their surveys. Given the descriptions of each, where do you fit? In what ways does where one gets one's news affect one's knowledge of political leaders?

(such as the sale of the *Washington Post* to Amazon.com founder and CEO Jeff Bezos in 2013[13]) signals the potential for a shift in the news model, print editions continue to struggle, and 2015 was the worst year for newspapers since the Great Recession.[14] Many venerable newspapers have ceased publication or moved to a print-online hybrid or simply an online existence, most notably the *Christian Science Monitor*.[15] Today most towns have only one paper, if they have any at all.

Midway through the second decade of the century, it is not unusual to hear people say that the day of the print media is over.[16] If you are feeling inclined to irony, you can Google "newspapers are dead" and you will get over 60,000,000 hits, all with people insisting (1) that it is true, (2) that it isn't, (3) that it matters, and (4) that it doesn't. In further irony, many of the most thriving news web sites—from "viral news sites" like *BuzzFeed* to online journals like the *Drudge Report* and the *Huffington Post* that traffic in "breaking news"—are often merely linking to reporting done by those same dinosaur newspapers whose deaths they are quick to proclaim.

The demise of those newspapers carries a cost that has little to do with whether their reporting is accessed at a newsstand or on a phone. As Internet expert and writer Clay Shirky says, "Society doesn't need newspapers. What we need is journalism."[17] By this he means information, well researched and objective, about the world we live in, about the things our elected officials are doing in our name, and about the consequences of the public choices we make.

That kind of journalism has traditionally been paid for by newspapers that have either had their own news bureaus around the world or subscribed to and supported a news service like the Associated Press (AP). The money they paid for news-gathering came from advertisers who had no other way to reach their markets—not only from big advertisers, but from local classified ads, job listings, and real estate listings. Today all those advertisers have multiple, cheap, or even free outlets through which to reach customers. The loss of those crucial revenue streams hit newspapers—and thus journalism—hard (see *Don't Be Fooled by . . . Clickbait* later in this chapter).

> **What aspects of journalism are fundamental to keeping the republic?**

Shirky argues that we are in the midst of a revolution "where the old stuff gets broken faster than the new stuff is put in its place,"[18] so we don't know what journalism will look like in a new, post-newspaper age. But Shirky thinks it's a mistake to assume that we aren't transitioning to such an age, that those who proclaim loudly that the old newspaper model can be saved are whistling past the graveyard, refusing to acknowledge that printing presses are costly to run and that the model of newspaper-centered news is obsolete in a world where the Internet makes it impossible for them to charge for or to retain control over the work they do.

RADIO AND TELEVISION

Radios, once state-of-the-art communication, have become commonplace. Most American households have at least one, and 91 percent of Americans say they listen to radio weekly.[19] More than 15,000 radio stations broadcast over the airwaves in the United States, offering entertainment and news shows through commercial networks and their local affiliates and satellite stations.[20] Since the 1980s, "talk radio" has provided an interactive political platform, allowing the radio hosts and their guests, as well as the audience, to air their opinions on politics and creating a sense of political community among their primarily conservative listeners. There are also two noncommercial networks, National Public Radio and Public Radio International, funded in small part by the U.S. government but primarily by private donations from corporations and individuals.[21] But the impact of radio on the American public, initially dramatic, cannot compare with the effects of television. American ownership of television sets skyrocketed from 9 percent of households in 1950 to 97 percent in 1975, a statistic that continues to hold firm. In fact, 58 percent of American homes have one or two television sets and 39 percent own three or more; about 84 percent of U.S. adults subscribe to cable or satellite services, although that percentage is falling as streaming services become more popular.[22] Live television viewership has declined over the past decade, but Americans remain voracious viewers of videos, whether live on television, delayed on a digital recording device, or streamed from the Internet. Nielsen, a marketing firm that tracks audience share, reports that the average American watches five hours of live television each day and another half hour of "time shifted" television.[23] That doesn't count the hours they spend watching videos, many of which originated for television, that they stream on another device. Considering that Americans spend six to eight hours a day at school or at work, this is an astounding figure, accounting for much of America's leisure time.

Television is primarily an entertainment medium; news has always been a secondary function. Whereas the earliest news offerings consisted simply of "talking heads" (reporters reading their news reports), many newscasts now fall into the category of "infotainment," news shows dressed up with drama and emotion to entice viewers to tune in. Once given a choice of only three networks, the typical American home today receives nearly 189 television channels, although each might watch only about 17 of them.[24] Rather than pursuing broad markets, stations are now often focusing on specific audiences such as people interested in health and fitness, sports, or travel. This practice of targeting a small, specialized broadcast market is called **narrowcasting**.[25] The competition for viewers is fierce, and as we will see, the quality of the news available can suffer as a consequence.

Politicians were quick to realize that, even more than radio, television allowed them to reach a broad audience without having to deal with print reporters and their adversarial questions. The Kennedy administration was the first to make real use of television, a medium that might have been made for the young, telegenic president. And it was television that brought the nation together in a community of grief when Kennedy was assassinated. Television carried the Vietnam War (along with its protesters) and the civil rights movement into Americans' homes, and the images that it created helped build popular support to end the war abroad and segregation at home. Television can create global as well as national communities, an increasingly familiar experience to many Americans as they watch their TVs in the wake of jubilant international celebrations, natural disasters, or human-made mayhem.

A number of television shows today focus on politics. Many cable stations and C-SPAN, sometimes called "America's Town Hall," offer news around the clock, although not all the news concerns politics. Weekend shows like *Meet the Press* highlight the week's coverage of politics, and the cable news stations frequently showcase debates between liberals and conservatives on current issues.

Political shows target particular age groups or ideologies. And politics is often the subject of the jokes on such shows as *Full Frontal, Saturday Night Live, The Daily Show, The Late Show,* and *Last Week Tonight.* Since at least 2000, the major presidential candidates and their wives have appeared on these comedy/entertainment shows to try to show that they are regular, likable people and to reach audiences that might not otherwise tune in to politics. President Obama was particularly adept at using unorthodox outlets, for instance, appearing on the online show *Between Two Ferns* to encourage young people to sign up for health insurance. In 2016, Donald Trump let Jimmy Fallon tousle his hair, revealing an extensive comb-over, and Hillary Clinton showed up on *Between Two Ferns* while suffering from pneumonia. These appearances have the effect of humanizing the candidates and making them seem approachable, often by getting them to laugh at themselves.

THE INTERNET

The reach of print media, radio, and television is dwarfed by the scope and possibilities of the Internet, which connects home or business computers to a global network of digital sites and an ever-expanding array of media content. In 2018 some 89 percent of American adults used the Internet (up from 46 percent in 2000).[26] A full 65 percent of households have a broadband connection at home, down from a high of 70 percent in 2016, and more than 80 percent of Americans are able to access the Internet from smartphones and other devices.[27] We have already seen the numbers of Americans who get news online and particularly from social media. Thirty-seven percent of Internet users have socially interacted with others concerning the news—creating it, commenting on it, or disseminating it through social networking sites like Facebook or Twitter.[28] The Internet has revolutionized the way we get information.

The digital age in which we live today has made politics immediate and personal. For much of our history, we haven't known our fellow citizens outside of our own communities, we have been unable to directly investigate the issues ourselves, and we've had no idea what actions our government has taken to deal with issues unless the media told us. We are still dependent on the mass media to connect us to our government and to create the only real space we have for public deliberation of issues. But technological developments make possible ever-newer forms of political community and more immediate access to information. Government officials can communicate with us directly, bypassing the traditional press. Networking sites like Facebook, LinkedIn, and Twitter allow people to reach out and interact socially, and politicians have not been shy about using such strategies to create networks of supporters. Chat rooms and blogs allow people with common interests to find each other from the far reaches of the world, allowing debate and discussion on a scale never before imagined.

Some visionaries talk of the day when we will all vote electronically on individual issues from our home computers (or maybe even our phones). If we have not yet arrived at that day of direct democratic decision making, changes in the media are nonetheless revolutionizing the possibilities of democracy, much as the printing press and television did earlier, bringing us closer to the Athenian ideal of political community in cyberspace, if not in real space.

Today, most major **news organizations**—including all the major newspapers and broadcast news organizations—are multimedia ventures. All the major newspapers, magazines, and news networks (both TV and radio), along with news services like the AP, have web sites where all or most of the news in their

---

narrowcasting the targeting of specialized audiences by the media

news organizations businesses (and occasionally nonprofits) devoted to reporting and disseminating news via print, broadcast, or digital media—or a multimedia combination.

print versions can be found, often with additional content, including *blogs* and *podcasts*. Access to these sites is sometimes available for free, although that clearly provides a disincentive for people to subscribe, thus damaging these news organizations' bottom line and hindering their ability to report the news. Increasingly, they are putting most of their content behind a pay wall, like the *New York Times* and *Wall Street Journal* have done, as they search for a viable business model that will keep them solvent. By searching for the topics we want and connecting to links with related sites, we can customize our web news. Politics buffs can bypass nonpolitical news, and vice versa. True politics junkies can go straight to the source: the federal government makes enormous amounts of information available at its www.whitehouse.gov, www.house.gov, and www.senate.gov sites.

The web has also provided fertile ground for myriad other sources of news to take root. While print and broadcast media were faced with a scarcity of space and airtime, the wide open web has space for seemingly endless content and a low barrier to entry for new voices seeking a platform. For example, online news sites like *Slate, Vox, Salon*, the *Huffington Post*, and the *Drudge Report* exist solely on the Internet and may or may not adopt the conventions, practices, and standards of the more traditional media. Also in the mix are **news aggregators**—sites and software that cull content from other web sites to produce "newsfeeds." Editors on some news aggregators, like *Google News*, the *Huffington Post, BuzzFeed*, and *theSkimm*, choose articles from other sites to share with their readers, sometimes in combination with original content. Other news aggregators allow readers to customize their own news feeds through web-based applications. Anyone with a smartphone can set up a blog, podcast, or video channel via simple and inexpensive (or even free) applications such as WordPress, Stitcher, and YouTube. This new technology provides open platforms for individuals to create content that is personal, political, cultural, or anything in between—running the gamut from individual diaries to investigative journalism. The proliferation of web sites professing to provide news can make processing the information on the web challenging. As we discussed in Chapter 1, these overlapping sources give us access to more information than ever before, but the task of sorting and evaluating that information is solely our own responsibility.

Not only does the web provide information, but it is also interactive to a degree that far surpasses talk radio or television. Most social media, web sites, and blogs offer discussion opportunities where all sorts of information can be shared, topics debated, and people met. Likewise, most online news sources enable readers to comment on articles and posts. Although this can allow the formation of communities based on specialized interests or similar views, it can also make it very easy for people with fringe or extreme views to find each other and organize.[29] Political campaigns began to take advantage of this in 2008,

using online technology and social networking principles to organize, raise funds, and get out the vote. Barack Obama's campaign proved to be skilled at using the new technology, setting the gold standard for future candidates to beat.[30] The Internet has the potential to increase the direct participation of citizens in political communities and political decisions, though the fact that not all Americans have equal access to the web means that multiple classes of citizenship could form. (See *Snapshot of America: Who Participates in Social Media?*)

Some observers believe that the new media landscape is fertile ground for positive changes. Media critic Dan Gillmor argues that a powerful, citizen-driven journalism is taking the place of a complacent, ratings-driven corporate journalism, that information is gathered and disseminated in real time with multiple researchers on the job to correct and assist each other, a sort of Wikipedia journalism, perhaps.[31] This is the model, for instance, of Andrew Sullivan, who "live blogged" the Iranian uprising in 2009, passing on to his readers information tweeted to him from the front lines, information that could not have been easily gathered even with a news bureau in Tehran. Sullivan would agree with Gillmor, arguing that blogging is "the first journalistic model that actually harnesses rather than exploits the true democratic nature of the web."[32] (See *Profiles in Citizenship* for more from Andrew Sullivan.)

For Sullivan, the demise of the old media and the rise of the new was a positive development, making him more hopeful for democracy, not less. He said,

> But what distinguishes the best of the new media is what could still be recaptured by the old: the mischievous spirit of journalism and free, unfettered inquiry. Journalism has gotten too pompous, too affluent, too self-loving, and too entwined with the establishment of both wings of American politics to be what we need it to be.
>
> We need it to be fearless and obnoxious, out of a conviction that more speech, however much vulgarity and nonsense it creates, is always better than less speech. In America, this is a liberal spirit in the grandest sense of that word—but also a conservative one, since retaining that rebelliousness is tending to an ancient American tradition, from the Founders onward.[33]

Shirky is optimistic as well:

> For the next few decades, journalism will be made up of overlapping special cases. Many of these models will rely

---

news aggregators web sites, applications, and software that cull content from other digital sources

Snapshot of America: *Who Participates in Social Media?*

Social Networking Use, by Age

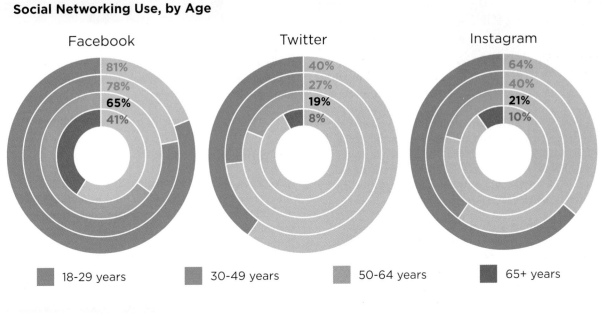

Facebook
- 81%
- 78%
- **65%**
- 41%

Twitter
- 40%
- 27%
- **19%**
- 8%

Instagram
- 64%
- 40%
- **21%**
- 10%

Legend:
- ■ 18-29 years
- ■ 30-49 years
- ■ 50-64 years
- ■ 65+ years

Monthly Active Users

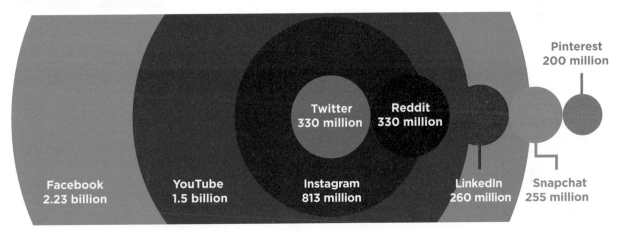

- **Facebook** 2.23 billion
- **YouTube** 1.5 billion
- **Instagram** 813 million
- **Twitter** 330 million
- **Reddit** 330 million
- **LinkedIn** 260 million
- **Snapchat** 255 million
- **Pinterest** 200 million

Overall Use Over Time, by Age

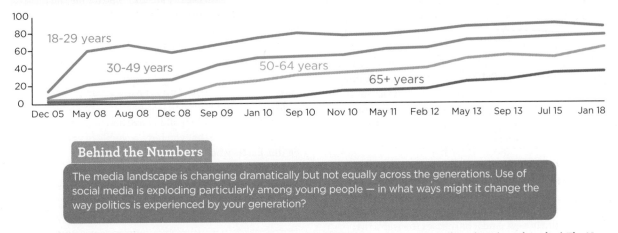

- 18-29 years
- 30-49 years
- 50-64 years
- 65+ years

X-axis: Dec 05, May 08, Aug 08, Dec 08, Sep 09, Jan 10, Sep 10, Nov 10, May 11, Feb 12, May 13, Sep 13, Jul 15, Jan 18

Behind the Numbers

The media landscape is changing dramatically but not equally across the generations. Use of social media is exploding particularly among young people — in what ways might it change the way politics is experienced by your generation?

Source: Pew Research Center Social Media Fact Sheet, February 2018, http://www.pewinternet.org/fact-sheet/social-media/; The Next Web, "Reddit now has more monthly users than Twitter," April 2018, https://thenextweb.com/contributors/2018/04/19/reddit-now-active-users-twitter-engaging-porn/.

Andrew Sullivan

Andrew H. Walker/Getty Images

Andrew Sullivan was a blogging pioneer, a man who described his job as "having a conversation with 1.2 million people a month." His job broke down traditional boundaries between journalism and political activism, reporting and analysis, and the personal and the public. By the time her retired his blog in 2015, he had transformed the way a writer could crowd-source information and interact with an audience.

In the beginning, it seemed to be a perfect medium for Sullivan. He was Oxford educated, with a Ph.D. in government from Harvard, and before turning thirty, he was the editor of the *New Republic*. Blogging let him combine advocacy and fact-sifting in a form of journalism that broke with the old models of news-gathering and dissemination.

Sullivan was not at all shy about airing his opinions—he was a Catholic, a conservative, British-born, America-loving, married gay man who considered himself a libertarian with a deep thread of compassion and humanitarianism running through it all. But while opinionated, he was not partisan. He refused to appear on partisan cable television shows, and he showed a remarkable ability to change his mind about deeply held views if new evidence appeared or was met with a persuasive counterargument.

What Sullivan called his "readership of extraordinarily smart and humane and interesting people" was the lifeblood of his blog. When he sought information, they provided it; when he was wrong, they corrected him; when something was happening in the world that he cared about, they gathered round in a virtual community to share the news. After the 2009 Iranian election resulted in streets full of green-garbed protesters demonstrating against the regime, his site became the go-to place for updates. Facing local news blackouts, demonstrators blogged, tweeted, and texted information that found its way to Sullivan. He says: "My colleagues Patrick and Chris, we took eight-hour shifts around twenty-four hours. . . . it was totally an organic process in which we were essentially a filter and I think it was a breakthrough moment for the media."

For Sullivan, blogging was a democratic as well as a journalistic phenomenon. In 2002 he wrote in the *London Times* that "what bloggers do is completely new—and cannot be replicated on any other medium. It's genuinely new. And it harnesses the web's real genius—its ability to empower anyone to do what only a few in the past could genuinely pull off.

In that sense, blogging is the first journalistic model that actually harnesses rather than merely exploits the true democratic nature of the web. It's a new medium finally finding a unique voice."[1]

Here are some other thoughts from Andrew Sullivan:

On patriotism

"It's not the same thing as nationalism. It is not that your country is always right. . . . I think at some level it is simply loving—and I mean that in a deep sense—the culture, tradition, constitution, and people of the place you call home. In a way I must say I have two patriotisms—of the country I came from and the country I'm still trying to become a citizen of. And patriotism, yes, does mean sometimes dissenting from one's country's leadership, but I think it's too facile to say it's the highest form. I think another equally valid form is supporting your country when the chips are down, even when it isn't perfect, even when it does make mistakes, because it's yours."

On keeping the republic

"America is actually in I think a quite extraordinary crisis right now—spiritually, politically, and economically. I don't think it's been this acute since maybe the late 70s or 60s. . . . I do think people have to understand if they are not there the discourse will be captured by someone else. And you have a responsibility—I've lived long enough to understand that. And it's easy to insulate oneself and delude oneself into thinking it doesn't really matter or I don't have to do something—but in fact you do.

One of the ways this really struck home for me was, personally, in the late 80s, early 90s, the AIDS crisis. I realized if I didn't help these people who were dying no one would. . . . And then when I contracted it, and thought I was given a few years, I sat down and wrote [his book] *Virtually Normal*, because I wanted to leave behind a contribution to an argument [about gay rights]. . . . I had nothing to lose because I thought I was going to die. But why should I have had to get to that point? So imagine that you have a couple of years left on this Earth, what are you waiting for?"

Source: Andrew Sullivan talked with Christine Barbour in August 2010.

---

1. Andrew Sullivan, "A Blogger's Manifesto," *Sunday Times of London*, February 24, 2002.

on amateurs as researchers and writers. Many of these models will rely on sponsorship or grants or endowments instead of revenues. Many of these models will rely on excitable 14 year olds distributing the results. Many of these models will fail. No one experiment is going to replace what we are now losing with the demise of news on paper, but over time, the collection of new experiments that do might give us the journalism we need.[34]

And then again, they may not—Shirky's optimism does not seem misplaced in light of the work of writers such as Gillmor and Sullivan, but it's undeniable that the changing ways in which information is shared will have some effects on our democracy. The jury is out on this one, but the open, innovative nature of the medium allows each of us to engage in the experimentation and work that might bring the answers. The late media critic Marshall McLuhan wrote in the 1960s that "the medium is the message." In the Internet age, that has the potential to be true as never before.

PAUSE AND REVIEW Who, What, How

From newspapers to radio, television, and, most recently, the Internet, Americans have moved eagerly to embrace the new forms of technology that entertain them and bring new ways of communicating information. But the deluge of political information requires consumers to sort through and critically analyze the news they get—often a costly exercise in terms of time, effort, and financial resources. Consequently, although the amount of political information available to Americans has increased dramatically, Americans do not seem to be particularly well informed about their political world.

In Your Own Words Discuss changes over the past several decades in the ways in which Americans get their news and information.

HOW DOES MEDIA OWNERSHIP AFFECT CONTROL OF THE NARRATIVE?

A complex system of corporate and independent gatekeepers

As we saw in Chapter 1, the people who control the news we get are **gatekeepers**—they are in charge of what information

> **gatekeepers** journalists and media elite who determine which news stories are covered and which are not

gets to us. We have also seen that the gatekeeping structure of the American media has changed radically since the days of the nation's founding. Back then, newspapers were partisan instruments dependent on government for their very existence. But today, most news comes from—or at least through—massive, corporate-owned sources—whether through conventional news sources like the *New York Times* and CBS or via Facebook and Google. In this section we look at ownership of the modern media complex, the ways in which government regulates (or does not regulate) the media, and how it all affects the gatekeeping function of the media.

WHO OWNS THE MEDIA?

Today the media are big business, but on a scale undreamed of by such early journalism entrepreneurs as Joseph Pulitzer and William Hearst, whose fiercely competitive tabloid wars in 1890s New York gave birth to what is known as *yellow journalism*, as each rushed to attract readers with sensational headlines and stories. Today's media get the bulk of their revenue from advertising rather than from circulation. Logic dictates that advertisers will want to spend their money where they can get the biggest bang for their buck: the papers with the most readers, the stations with the largest audiences, the web sites with the most clicks (see *Don't be Fooled by . . . Clickbait*). Because advertisers go after the most popular media outlets, competition is fierce and outlets that cannot promise advertisers wide enough exposure fail to get the advertising dollars and go out of business.

The traditional mainstream media still exists, but all the major circulation newspapers in this country, as well as commercial radio and television networks, are owned by major conglomerates and have huge digital presences. Overall this has meant that there are fewer and fewer media outlets owned by fewer and fewer corporations, with content more and more the same.[35] In fact, just six corporations—Time-Warner (currently in the process of merging with AT&T), Disney, Viacom, CBS Corporation, News Corp, and Comcast—own most of the major national newspapers, the leading news magazines, the national television networks including CNN and other cable stations, as well as publishing houses, movie studios, telephone companies, entertainment firms, and other multimedia operations. Most of these corporations are also involved in other businesses, as their familiar names attest. Often editorial decisions are matters of corporate policy, not individual judgment. And if profit was an overriding concern for the editor-entrepreneurs a century ago, it is gospel for the conglomerates today. *The Big Picture* in this chapter gives you an idea

Clickbait

You're trolling through your newsfeeds and see a link that is just irresistible: a revolutionary diet secret, a terrifying news headline, or a top ten list just begging you to select the "five greatest" songs/athletes/movies of all time. Do you click? Do you read? Do you share?

Web sites depend on web traffic to generate revenue, and web traffic is measured in clicks. Much of the content on the Internet today is designed specifically to go viral—to be circulated widely and quickly. And it's not just cat videos that go viral—sometimes, it's news. Donald Trump's use of Twitter is a case in point: the reality star propelled himself to the front of the Republican presidential field on the back of tweets that provoked either outrage or praise, and which were quickly reposted, parsed, and commented on by a news media hungry for clicks.[1] By the end of the election, Trump's campaign had gotten nearly $6 billion in free media coverage, much of it in viral coverage.[2]

What to Watch Out For

Here are a few tips for savvy web surfing:

- **Is this headline manipulating you?** Savvy headline writers know that writers can drum up what researchers call "manufactured emotions" over what is often pretty benign content. The most effective headlines will provoke anxiety, outrage, fear, or curiosity.[3] That doesn't mean that there's no real news hidden behind clickbait headlines—but it doesn't mean that there *is* real news there, either.
- **Is this news, or is it fluff?** Some important news stories can rise to the top on the back of clicks, making their way from independent publications or citizen journalists into the mainstream media. Videos capturing police shootings are just one example of real news stories that spread via viral sharing. But sometimes important news stories can fall through the cracks while the Internet explodes over viral stories, such as the "what color is this dress?" meme that seemed to take over the web in 2015.[4] There's nothing wrong with entertainment on the web—just make sure you're not missing out on real news.
- **Is this "sponsored content"?** Seeking to shore up diminishing revenue streams, many news outlets (not to mention your social media feeds) include advertising, often presented in the same style and format as the site's original content. Many articles with buzzy headlines, sitting alongside regular reporting on respected news sites, are actually long-form advertisements, written specifically to change perceptions about a product or company, and are designed to be shared via social media.[5] Look out for tags like "sponsored content," "recommended post," or "advertisement."
- **Is this troll fodder?** Internet trolls—individuals who intentionally disrupt online discourse with arguments and commentary that is inflammatory, abusive, or off-topic—don't generate much sympathy. But they do generate clicks, and publishers know it. Even sites that malign or claim to ban such activity simultaneously try to attract trolls, knowing that an online controversy will push even more browsers toward their site.[6] Trolling can be a political tool, as well—late in the election season of 2016, the news broke that Russia had hired Internet trolls to try to sway American public opinion.[7] Avoid getting sucked into online sparring matches with Internet trolls.
- **Is this an article, or a listicle?** There's something about a top five list that's just hard to resist. Psychologists theorize that we like lists because they pique our curiosity (we want to see if we can guess what's on it) and because of the ease with which we can scan and digest information when it's presented in this easy and predictable format.[8] If you look for listicles that offer links to deeper sources of information, you'll find they can be a useful jumping-off point.[9] More often than not they are just another route to lure you to advertising and multiple clicks, however.
- **Are people reading this, or just sharing it?** A 2016 study showed that more than half of the links shared on social media were not actually clicked on—that is, people shared the story without having read it. The study also found that this kind of sharing plays an outsize role in shaping political narratives and agendas.[10] Don't engage in blind sharing: before you recommend (or comment on) a story, read it!

1. Michael Barbaro, "Pithy, Mean and Powerful: How Donald Trump Mastered Twitter for 2016," *New York Times*, October 5, 2015, www.nytimes.com/2015/10/06/us/politics/donald-trump-twitter-use-campaign-2016.html.
2. Nicholas Confessore and Karen Yourish, "$2 Billion Worth of Free Media for Donald Trump," *New York Times*, March 15, 2016, www.nytimes.com/2016/03/16/upshot/measuring-donald-trumps-mammoth-advantage-in-free-media.html.

3. Bryan Gardiner, "You'll Be Outraged at How Easy It Was to Get You to Click on This Headline," *Wired*, December 18, 2015, www.wired.com/2015/12/psychology-of-clickbait/.

4. Johnathan Mahler, "The White and Gold (No, Blue and Black) Dress That Melted the Internet," *New York Times*, February 27, 2015, www.nytimes.com/2015/02/28/business/a-simple-question-about-a-dress-and-the-world-weighs-in.html.

5. Jeff Sonderman and Millie Tran, "The Definition of 'Sponsored Content'," American Press Institute, November 13, 2013, www.americanpressinstitute.org/publications/reports/white-papers/the-definition-of-sponsored-content/.

6. Lene Bech Sillesen, "Trolls Make Good Clickbait," *Columbia Journalism Review*, August 21, 2014, www.cjr.org/behind_the_news/trolls_make_good_clickbait_-_t.php.

7. Natasha Bertrand, "It Looks Like Russia Hired Internet Trolls to Pose as Pro-Trump Americans," *Business Insider*, July 27, 2016, www.businessinsider.com/russia-internet-trolls-and-donald-trump-2016-7.

8. Claudia Hammond, "Nine Psychological Reasons Why We Love Lists," BBC, April 13, 2015, www.bbc.com/future/story/20150410-9-reasons-we-love-lists.

9. Rachel Edidin, "5 Reasons Listicles Are Here to Stay, and Why That's OK," *Wired*, January 8, 2014, www.wired.com/2014/01/defense-listicle-list-article/.

10. Caitlin Dewey, "6 in 10 of You Will Share This Link Without Reading It, a New, Depressing Study Says," *Washington Post*, June 16, 2016, www.washingtonpost.com/news/the-intersect/wp/2016/06/16/six-in-10-of-you-will-share-this-link-without-reading-it-according-to-a-new-and-depressing-study/.

of what this corporate ownership of the media looks like, but keep in mind that it is a constantly changing picture. What troubles many critics is that many Americans don't know that most of their news and entertainment comes from just a few corporate sources and are unaware of the consequences that this corporate ownership structure has for all of us.[36]

But the modern conventional media have a lot of competition in the area of creating narratives. Startups like *VICE*, *Vox*, *FiveThirtyEight*, *BuzzFeed*, and the *Huffington Post* on the center-left—all of which have developed fresh, diverse, often edgy brands—have become media empires themselves or been gobbled up by other outlets. Sites like *Breitbart* have done the same on the far right. Many journalists who began as bloggers have found their way into the bigger media picture as well. And corporate forces like Google, Facebook, and Apple, while not journalistic producers in their own right, aggregate and distribute news via algorithms that decide who gets what information. As we suggested earlier, social media are rapidly becoming favored news sources, even though they are not news producers. Though sites like Facebook, Twitter, and YouTube are big business and may use their own formulas to decide what news to expose us to, they, as well as blogs and crowd-sourced sites, like Medium, allow citizen participation to an unprecedented degree.

Importantly, even though social media outlets post articles and news on our pages that their formulas think we will be interested in, they are based on our own profiles—we decide who our friends are on Facebook or whose tweets fill our feed or who we follow on Instagram—and the algorithms are based on what the social media outlets judge to be our taste. We end up creating, with a little artificial intelligence assistance, a curated base of knowledge that essentially tells us what we have decided we want to hear. We are not helpless, but in order not to be caught in a bubble, we cannot be passive, either.

The Pew Center's Project for Excellence in Journalism, which has studied YouTube in particular, finds that

the data reveal that a complex, symbiotic relationship has developed between citizens and news organizations on YouTube, a relationship that comes close to the continuous journalistic "dialogue" many observers predicted would become the new journalism online. Citizens are creating their own videos about news and posting them. They are also actively sharing news videos produced by journalism professionals. And news organizations are taking advantage of citizen content and incorporating it into their journalism. Consumers, in turn, seem to be embracing the interplay in what they watch and share, creating a new kind of television news.[37]

In addition, the growing number of cell phone users offers another way for people to access their customized news streams (a whopping 92 percent of millennials own smartphones), with owners of smartphones notable for their heavy news consumption and people who access their news on mobile devices spending longer with the news and getting it from more sources.[38] The fact that these tech-savvy news readers are disproportionately well educated and young suggests that America's news-reading habits may be changing dramatically, and that the web may come closer to realizing its potential for offering a truly democratic, practical, and "free" alternative to the corporate-produced news we now receive.

HOW DOES MEDIA OWNERSHIP IMPACT THE NEWS WE GET?

What does the concentrated corporate ownership of the traditional mass media mean to us as consumers of the news? We should be aware of at least five major consequences:

THE BIG PICTURE:
Who Owns (and Controls) Today's Information Networks?

Today most of our news comes from a handful of powerful sources. While some, like the *New York Times*, are still independent, others are part of massive media conglomerates, or like the *Washington Post*, owned by Amazon's Jeff Bezos, tied in other ways to the information world. What implication does this ownership structure have for the news we get?

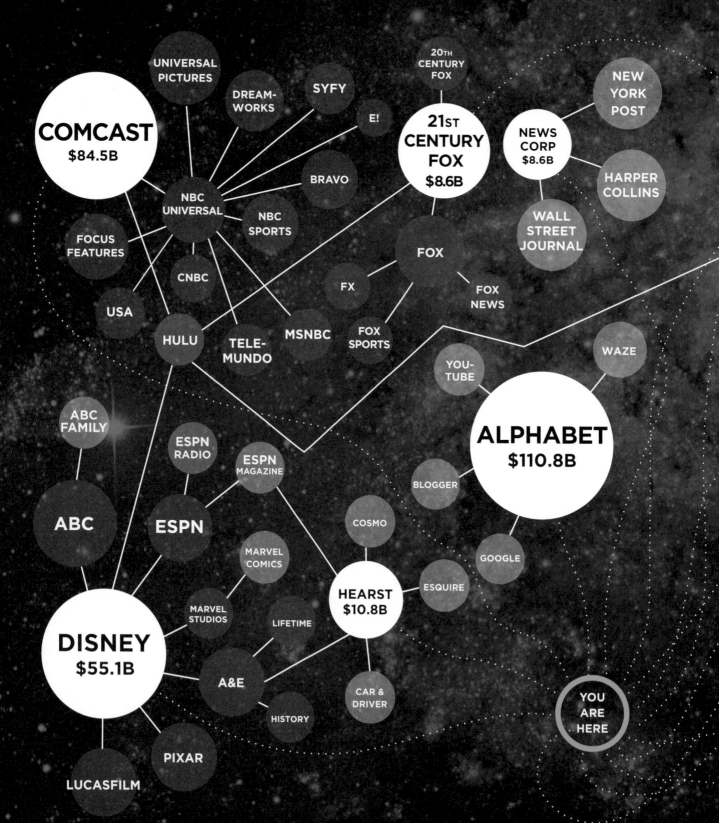

Source: Compiled by the authors from company filings.

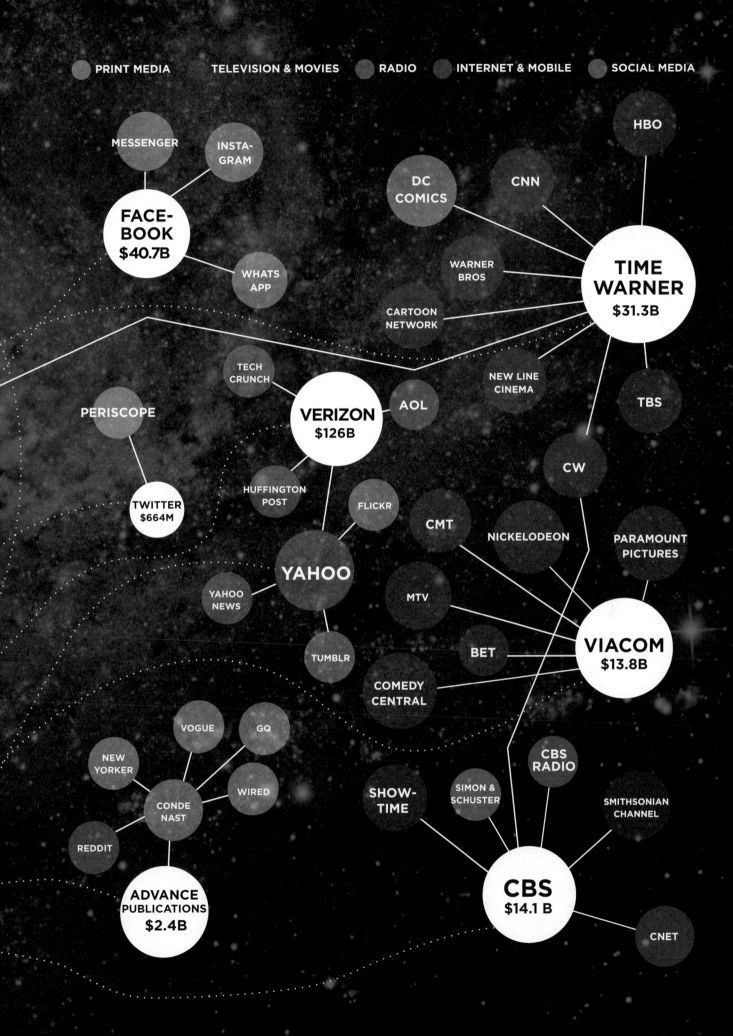

PRINT MEDIA   TELEVISION & MOVIES   RADIO   INTERNET & MOBILE   SOCIAL MEDIA

MESSENGER
INSTA-GRAM

FACE-BOOK
$40.7B

WHATS APP

HBO

DC COMICS
CNN

WARNER BROS

CARTOON NETWORK

TIME WARNER
$31.3B

TECH CRUNCH

PERISCOPE

VERIZON
$126B

AOL

NEW LINE CINEMA

TBS

TWITTER
$664M

HUFFINGTON POST

FLICKR

CMT

CW

NICKELODEON

PARAMOUNT PICTURES

YAHOO

MTV

YAHOO NEWS

TUMBLR

BET

VIACOM
$13.8B

COMEDY CENTRAL

VOGUE
GQ

NEW YORKER

WIRED

CONDE NAST

SHOW-TIME

SIMON & SCHUSTER

CBS RADIO

SMITHSONIAN CHANNEL

REDDIT

ADVANCE PUBLICATIONS
$2.4B

CBS
$14.1 B

CNET

Extremes Go Mainstream

Breitbart Media was founded in 2007 as a "Huffington Post of the right" but went mainstream under executive chairman Steve Bannon, who in 2016 aligned the site with Republican presidential candidate Donald Trump. Bannon's bet paid off, and he soon—but briefly—became a senior counselor to the president.

- There is a **commercial bias** in the media today toward what will increase advertiser revenue and audience share. Because people tune in (or click) to watch scandals, crime stories, and disasters, extensive coverage of similar events appears relentlessly on the front pages of most newspapers and news sites. Journalistic judgment and ethics are often at odds with the imperative to turn a profit.

- The effort to get and keep large audiences, and to make way for increased advertising, means a reduced emphasis on political news. This is especially true at the local television level, where older Americans, in particular, tend to get their information, and where the bulk of the coverage goes to weather, sports, disasters, human interest stories, and "happy talk" among the newscasters.[39] The content of the news we get is lightened up, dramatized, and streamlined to keep audiences tuned in.[40] As in the days of yellow journalism, market forces encourage sensational coverage of the news, especially in the wake of natural or human-made disasters. Some sources specialize in "infotainment," so-called because of its efforts to make the delivery of information more attractive by dressing it up as titillating or engaging. Some web sites like *BuzzFeed* specialize in **clickbait** pieces—sensational headlines that tease you into clicking a link to find some information that sounds intriguing. Other news web sites tell you in advance how many minutes it will take to read an article so that you know what you are committing to before you start.

- The corporate ownership of today's media means that the media outlets frequently face conflicts of interest in deciding what news to cover or how to cover it. For instance, after Disney acquired ABC, several ABC employees, including a news commentator who had been critical of Disney in the past, were fired.[41] And with Rupert Murdoch's News Corp supporting Republican candidates and causes, who would be surprised at the Republican-friendly coverage of its news operations like *Fox News*, the *New York Post*, and the *Wall Street Journal*?[42] In fact, 33 percent of newspaper editors in America said they would not feel free to publish news that might harm their parent company,[43] a statistic that should make us question what is being left out of the news we receive.

- Breaking a news story has always been a point of pride for editors and journalists. (It is the *Washington Post* that gets kudos for breaking the Watergate scandal—nobody remembers the second newspaper to chime in.) Thus journalists have always had to walk a fine line between the time spent reporting—that is, investigating and verifying stories—and getting those stories published before their competition does. This tension has become even more intense as daily deadlines for print or nightly broadcast have given way to the modern twenty-four-hour news cycle. In the rush to avoid getting "scooped" by another station or newspaper, reporters and editors alike have sometimes jumped the gun, disseminating incorrect information or flat-out lies without taking the time to fact check or analyze them. For example, when the U.S. Supreme Court's hotly anticipated decision on the Affordable Care Act was handed down in 2012, both Fox and CNN rushed to report on it without having read Chief Justice John Roberts's decision in its entirety—and told viewers incorrectly that Obamacare had been struck down.[44] Even more troubling, perhaps, is the number of journalists and editors at online outlets who have retweeted or reblogged to their readers clearly made-up stories from news satire sites.[45] (See *Don't Be Fooled by . . . Parody News Sites* in Chapter 5.) Even when the

---

commercial bias the tendency of the media to make coverage and programming decisions based on what will attract a large audience and maximize profits

clickbait sensational headlines designed to tempt Internet users to click through to a specific web site

story is true, the rush to publish first can itself become part of the story. In June 2016, the Associated Press reported that, on the basis of their canvasing of superdelegates, Hillary Clinton had sewn up the Democratic nomination the night before the California primaries. Bernie Sanders supporters were furious, seeing further evidence that the system was rigged and claiming that the announcement had suppressed the Sanders turnout. At the same time, the Clinton campaign was frustrated that her victory was portrayed as the product of elite decision-making and not the result of her earning more than three million more votes than Sanders.

ALTERNATIVES TO THE CORPORATE MEDIA

Today the giant corporate media conglomerations do not define all of our alternatives for getting news, and they cannot control all the narratives as effectively as they once did. We have already discussed startup alternatives like *Vox* and *BuzzFeed*, although some of these are among the new models most driven to tempt people to click on seductive-sounding links. Still, the explosion of online publishing gives more people more alternatives for getting (and sharing) information that is not subject to a corporate agenda. Because the drive for profit affects the news we get in serious ways, it's important to note that some forms of media have chosen a different route to financial survival. Government-owned radio and television, of course, can provide an alternative to the for-profit media world. Americans tend to assume that media wholly owned or controlled by the government serve the interests of government rather than the citizens, and, as we have seen, privately owned media are not necessarily free from advertiser (or "supporter") influence, either. But countries like the United Kingdom demonstrate that government-owned sources like the BBC can be bastions of creativity and innovation and well-respected gatekeepers in the bargain.

> ### Can a corporate-owned press be a free press?

A small independent press does continue to thrive outside the for-profit world. A few investigative magazines, like *Mother Jones* (published by the Foundation for National Progress) and *Consumer Reports* (published by Consumers Union), and web sites like factcheck.org (University of Pennsylvania) and ProPublica rely on funding from subscribers and members of their nonprofit parent organizations.[46] However, unless they are completely free of advertising (as is *Consumer Reports*), even these independent publications are not entirely free from corporate influence.

REGULATION OF THE MEDIA

The media in America are almost entirely privately owned, but they do not operate without some public control. Although the principle of freedom of the press keeps the print media nearly free of restriction (see Chapter 5), the broadcast media have been treated differently and control of the Internet has become controversial and complex. In the early days of radio, great public enthusiasm for the new medium resulted in so many radio stations that signal interference threatened to damage the whole industry. Broadcasters asked the government to impose some order, which it did with the passage of the Federal Communications Act, creating the Federal Communications Commission (FCC), an independent regulatory agency, in 1934. Because access to the airwaves was considered a scarce public resource, the government acted to ensure that radio and television serve the public interest by representing a variety of viewpoints. Accordingly, the 1934 bill contained three provisions designed to ensure fairness in broadcasting—the equal time rule (if one candidate speaks, all must have the opportunity), the fairness doctrine (requiring stations to give free airtime to issues of public concern), and the right of rebuttal (allowing people whose reputations were damaged on air to respond)—all of which have been limited or eliminated since.

These rules remain somewhat controversial. Politicians would like to have the rules enforced because they help them to air their views publicly. Media owners see these rules as forcing them to air unpopular speakers who damage their ratings and as limiting their abilities to decide station policy. They argue that access to broadcast time is no longer such a scarce resource, given all the cable and satellite outlets, and that the broadcast media should be subject to the same legal protections as the print media.

Many of the limitations on station ownership that the original act established were abolished with the 1996 Telecommunications Act in order to open up competition and promote diversity in media markets. The act failed to rein in the media giants, however, and ended up facilitating mergers that concentrated media ownership even more. The law permits ownership of multiple stations as long as they do not reach more than 35 percent of a market, and nothing prevents the networks themselves from reaching a far larger market through their collective affiliates. The 1996 legislation also opened up the way for ownership of cable stations by network owners, and it allows cable companies to offer many services previously supplied only by telephone companies. The overall effect of this deregulation has been to increase dramatically the possibilities for media monopoly.

As we saw in the *What's at Stake . . . ?* in Chapter 5, some Internet users favor a policy of net neutrality that would ensure that telecommunication companies cannot use their control over Internet access to restrict or limit content with price discrimination, and would keep the Internet unfettered and open to innovation. Opponents argue that such a policy would reduce incentives for companies to innovate. In 2015, at President Obama's urging, the FCC ruled in favor of net neutrality, ensuring that all Internet traffic must be treated equally. Although the ruling had no chance of becoming law, the Republican House immediately voted to oppose it and the ruling was challenged in court as well. The Trump administration overturned it in 2018.

PAUSE AND REVIEW Who, What, How

The ownership of the media has historically influenced whether the news is objective, and thus serves the public interest, or is slanted to serve a particular political or economic interest. Democratic theory and American political tradition tell us that democracy requires a free press to which all citizens have access. We have a free press in this country, and we also have a free market, and these two worlds produce clashing rules in which the press has largely been the loser to economic imperative.

In Your Own Words Describe the ways in which media ownership and government regulation influence the news we get.

SPINNING POLITICAL NARRATIVES

The stories we tell
that legitimize or delegitimize power

Think about the narrative that northerners tell about the Civil War and the one told by native southerners: was it a war to end slavery and restore national unity, or a war of secession because states' rights were violated? Same war, different narrative, in a battle of competing meanings that has not yet been settled today.

When Walter Cronkite went to Vietnam in 1968 and said we were losing the war there, that report clashed with the narrative the government was telling. President Lyndon Johnson knew he'd lost the support of the country because Cronkite was seen as a trustworthy gatherer and reporter of the facts. Today there is no consensus on who is the trusted reporter of facts. The saying that "you are entitled to your own opinion but not your own facts," once the gold standard of debate, is laughable in the face of some of today's realities. Some candidates and officials, and indeed, the president of the United States, lie so fast that the fact checkers can't keep up with them; cable stations, web sites, and commentators on Twitter herald facts based on very different assumptions of reality; and many journalists follow an ethic that "fairness" requires finding "equivalence" between two sides, which are often not equivalent at all.

We like to think that journalism is all about facts and, in its purest sense, it is. A fact is simply a verifiable piece of information that can be shown to be empirically true. If it isn't true, it isn't a fact. Control of the facts itself can confer power. Discovering and reporting facts in a timely way is power. What we think of as the job of the news media is a powerful part of a democratic society. Without the facts, we cannot make the good, informed decisions about our governance that we need to make.

But control of the facts can be directed toward goals other than the health of a democracy. Withholding factual information that someone needs to make a decision, or releasing that information at a strategic time, or refusing to invest resources in uncovering the facts—all of those are powerful actions that do not lead to good, informed decision making. The thing about facts is that by themselves they don't always tell us what we need to know. They often need to be put into context and interpreted so that we know what to make of them, and at that point, they begin to be part of a narrative, a story that imparts meaning and value. In this section we look at the major weavers of political narratives and the ways in which political narratives are shaped.

THE FACT GATHERERS

The basic fabric of our national narratives is woven by journalists—professional reporters or fact gatherers whose job it is to tell us *what happened*. They may interpret facts, but they don't speculate, or insert their own judgment for that of their audience or traffic in known untruths. If they make a mistake, which happens, they correct it. Journalists aren't perfect—their demographic profile alone suggests they may be predisposed to see the world in one way or another (see *Snapshot of America: Who Are the Journalists?*), but their job is to try to discover and disseminate the facts. The risk we run when journalism as a

Snapshot of America: *Who Are the Journalists?*

How Journalists Compare to the Rest of Us

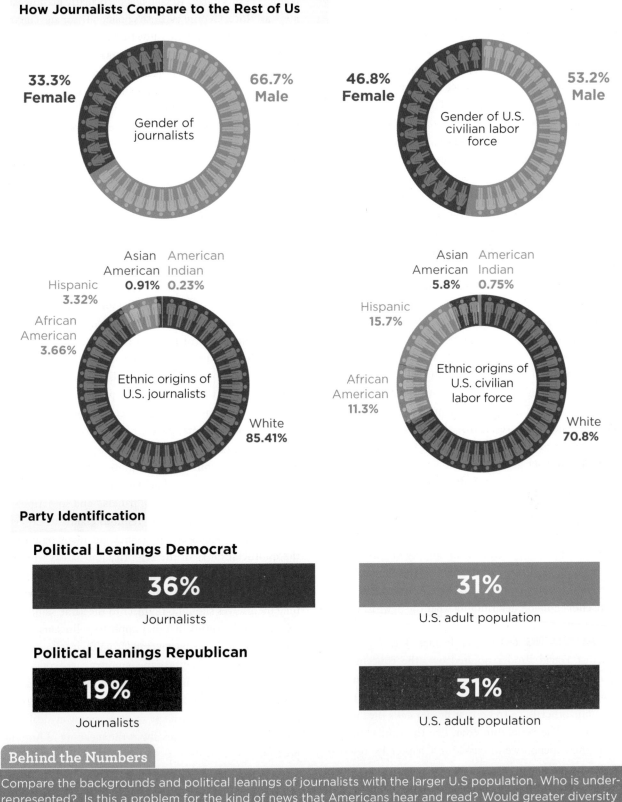

33.3% Female   **66.7% Male**
Gender of journalists

46.8% Female   **53.2% Male**
Gender of U.S. civilian labor force

Asian American **0.91%**   American Indian **0.23%**
Hispanic **3.32%**
African American **3.66%**
Ethnic origins of U.S. journalists
White **85.41%**

Asian American **5.8%**   American Indian **0.75%**
Hispanic **15.7%**
African American **11.3%**
Ethnic origins of U.S. civilian labor force
White **70.8%**

Party Identification

Political Leanings Democrat

36%
Journalists

31%
U.S. adult population

Political Leanings Republican

19%
Journalists

31%
U.S. adult population

Behind the Numbers

Compare the backgrounds and political leanings of journalists with the larger U.S population. Who is under-represented? Is this a problem for the kind of news that Americans hear and read? Would greater diversity among journalists affect how events are reported and interpreted in the news?

Source: Lars Willnat and David H. Weaver. *The American Journalist in the Digital Age: Key Findings.* Bloomington, IN: School of Journalism, Indiana University. 2014.

profession is not seen by society as worth supporting is spelled out in the *CLUES to Critical Thinking* feature at the end of the chapter.

THE ANALYSTS

Some journalists take great pride in sticking to reporting but the greater the access to and contact with those in power, the harder it is to maintain a distance and to refrain from putting one's analysis in with the facts. Providing analysis doesn't mean a journalist is not reporting facts, it just means that the journalist's own expertise, values, ideas, beliefs, understandings, and even political agenda might get included in the narrative. It can be very difficult for experts not to want to share their expertise—great humility does not generally spring from contact with great power.

At the top echelon of American journalists are those who cover the national political beat in Washington. National politics takes place in Washington—not just the interactions of Congress, the president, and the courts but also the internal workings of political parties and the rival lobbying of interest groups, including states, major corporations, and other national organizations. For a political reporter, Washington is the coveted place to be and, by and large, it, along with New York City, is where the weaving of the media narratives take place.

What is fascinating about living in an age of widespread social networks, however, is that although the media elite have an easier time of controlling the narrative than the rest of us, the Internet gives everyone with a computer or a smartphone a bit part in spreading a compelling story, or even attempting to challenge it. The extensive sharing, tweeting, clicking, and even trolling that we have noted throughout this chapter means that the mainstream corporate media do not maintain the monopoly of control they once had. And we have seen already that the democratizing effects of the Internet have weakened the mainstream corporate chokehold on determining what the news is.

THE REVOLVING DOOR As former *Washington Post* journalist David Broder pointed out, the concentration of politics, politicians, and reporters in Washington leads to "a complex but cozy relationship between journalists and public officials," a trend that Broder calls the "revolving door."[47] The **revolving door**, like the similar interest group phenomenon we discussed in Chapter 13, refers to the practice of journalists taking positions in government and then returning to journalism again, or vice versa, perhaps several times over.

The number of prominent journalists who have gone through this revolving door is legion, as any glimpse of a cable news panel will make obvious. These folks, in permanent or temporary exile from politics themselves, are only sometimes agenda-free as they help weave narratives about what current political events mean. To take one particularly glaring example, Karl Rove, George W. Bush's policy advisor and currently a commentator on Fox, even while he heads a Republican PAC, was heavily invested in the narrative that Mitt Romney would win the 2012 election, an outcome he had put considerable money behind. His adherence to his own narrative led him to support the story that the polls showing Obama ahead were wrong and, when Fox called the state of Ohio and thus the election for Obama on election night, he blew an on-air fuse, calling for a retraction and forcing anchor Megyn Kelly to reconfirm the results. In 2016, CNN hired former Trump campaign aide Corey Lewandowski as a commentator, even as he was still under contractual ties to Trump.

THE ROLE OF THE PUNDIT Many of those analysts who return to the media through the revolving door find themselves joining the ranks of the journalists and academics who have earned the unofficial and slightly tongue-in-cheek title of **pundit**. A pundit is traditionally a learned person, someone professing great wisdom. In contemporary media parlance, it has come to mean a professional observer and commentator on politics—a person skilled in the ways of the media and of politics who can make trenchant observations and predictions about the political world and help us untangle the complicated implications of political events.

The twenty-four-hour news cycle and the growth in cable news shows means there is a nearly insatiable demand for bodies to fill the political "panels," and sometimes the ones who appear have pretty tenuous claims to expertise. Because of the media attention they get, many pundits join the unofficial ranks of the celebrity journalists who cross over from reporting on public figures to being public figures themselves, thus raising a host of questions about whether they themselves should be subject to the same standards of criticism and scrutiny that they apply to politicians. Because they receive wide media coverage from their fellow journalists, the pronouncements of the punditry carry considerable power. The pundits, as journalists, are meant to be a check on the power of politicians, but it is arguable that there is no check on the pundits, except an increasingly cynical public as they weave their stories about the meaning of American politics.

revolving door the tendency of public officials, journalists, and lobbyists to move between public- and private-sector (media, lobbying) jobs

pundit a professional observer and commentator on politics

THE CREATION OF POLITICAL NARRATIVES

The media are among the main agents of what we called *political socialization* in Chapter 11: they help to transfer political values from one generation to the next and to shape political views in general by the narratives they create about the meaning of politics. We have already looked at the question of bias in the media and noted not only that there is a corporate or commercial bias but also that Americans are increasingly convinced that the news media are ideologically biased. Political scientists acknowledge that ideological bias may exist, but they conclude that it isn't so much that the media tell us what to think as that they tell us what to think *about* and how to think about it. Scholars have documented several kinds of related media effects on our thinking: agenda setting, framing, persuasion by professional communicators, and a tendency to reduce politics to issues of conflicts and superficial image rather than substantive policy disputes.[48]

AGENDA SETTING Even the Internet is limited in the number of the many daily political events it can cover, which means that reporters, especially television reporters, perform the function of **agenda setting**—defining for the public the relative importance of an issue through the amount and prominence of coverage it receives.[49] When television reporters choose to cover an event, they are telling us that out of all the events happening, this one is important and we should pay attention. They are priming us to focus on it and to evaluate politicians in light of it. It gives our national storytellers immense power to decide what is important enough for us to pay attention to, although the Internet dilutes that effect somewhat.

FRAMING Just as a painting's appearance can be altered by changing its frame, a political event can look different to us depending on the media's **framing** of the event—that is, what they choose to emphasize in their coverage. For example, people view a war differently depending on whether the coverage highlights American casualties or military victories. To return to the issue we opened this chapter with, the media can portray a massacre in a nightclub as the action of a disturbed young man with a gun he should not have been able to buy, or as the action of an international terrorist who had no business

> **agenda setting** the media's role in defining the relative importance of an issue or event via the amount and prominence of coverage they devote to it
>
> **framing** the process through which the media emphasize particular aspects of a news story, thereby influencing the public's perception of the story

being in this country. The important point about framing is that how the media present a political issue or event may affect how the public perceives that issue, whether they see it as a problem, and who they view as responsible for solving it.

PERSUASION BY PROFESSIONAL COMMUNICATORS Some political scientists argue that the media affect public opinion because viewers, who often don't have the time or background to research issues themselves, rely on opinion leaders (see Chapter 11).[50] Often, however, especially in the age of Internet news, social media, twenty-four-hour cable, and multiple broadcast choices, the communicators on whom the media rely are people who regularly pass through the revolving door and whose objectivity cannot be taken for granted. And even when the media offer a near-unanimous opinion, as the editorial pages did in endorsing Clinton in 2016, the public may ignore their lead (see Figure 15.1).

REDUCTION OF POLITICS TO SOUND AND FURY Reporting on the details of policy wonkery is hard work, and delving into the nitty gritty of a story requires diligence and toughness. Some journalists have these qualities and demonstrate them daily, whether they are *Vox*'s Ezra Klein giving full rein to his inner policy wonk in an evaluation of economic policy, or NPR's Sarah Koenig doing long-form investigations on the hit podcast *Serial*. But such hard work is just that, and in a nonstop, twenty-four-hour news cycle, journalists don't always

FIGURE 15.1

Newspaper Endorsements of Presidential Candidates, 1932–2016

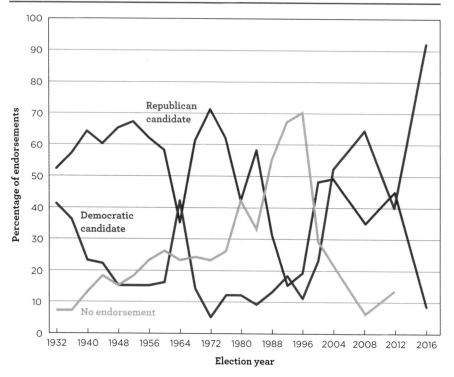

Source: Harold W. Stanley and Richard G. Niemi, *Vital Statistics on American Politics, 2009–2010* (Washington, D.C.: CQ Press, 2010), Table 14.7; 2012 data from editorandpublisher.com/election/.

keep bored reporters engaged, but it's a narrative that trivializes what is at stake in campaigns, or partisan battles in Congress, or disputes between the president and Congress, and it doesn't help educate the American public.

Television is primarily an entertainment medium and, by its nature, is focused on image: what people look like, what they sound like, and how an event is staged and presented. Television, and to some extent its competition in the print and digital media, concentrates on doing what it does well: giving us pictures of politics instead of delving beneath the surface. Political players respond by focusing on **optics**—the way a situation, person, or event is presented by the media and perceived by the public—rather than on substantive issues. This, along with the horse-race metaphor we just mentioned, has the effect of leading us to value the more superficial aspects of politics, even if only subconsciously.

In a similar way, the necessities of the media turn the words of politicians into the audio equivalent of a snapshot, the **sound bite**. A sound bite is a short block of speech by a politician that makes it on the news. The amount of time that the electronic media devote to the actual words a politician utters is shrinking. In 2000 the average length for a sound bite from a presidential candidate on the nightly network news was 7.3 seconds, down from 10 seconds in 1992 and 42 seconds in 1968.[51] Journalists use the extra time to interpret what we have heard and often to put it into the horse-race metaphor we just discussed.[52] In an implicit acknowledgment that the attention span of the public has been trained to instant and speedy gratification, social media cater to this penchant for bite-sized ideas. Instagram and Snapchat encourage people to communicate through single (and, in the case of Snapchat,

have to ability or the luxury to do the long-form piece or the deep dive into a story. Being under constant pressure to produce something that people will tune in to or click on means that a lot of what is reported is shallow and meaningless, unless reporters can peg it to a quick and dirty narrative. Who is ahead? How does it look? Is she corrupt? Did he cheat? These are default narratives that consume much of American political coverage and cause a weary public to view it with a cynical eye.

Horse-race journalism refers to the media's tendency to see politics as a competition between individuals. Rather than reporting on the policy differences between politicians or the effects their proposals will have on ordinary Americans, today's media tend to create narratives based on who is ahead, what they need to do to catch up, and what various events will do to the poll numbers, the visible (though not always reliable) indicator of who is ahead. When you report on politics as if it were a battle between individual gladiators or a game of strategy and wit but not substance, it tends to increase citizen cynicism, as if politicians cared only to score victories off one another in a never-ending fight to promote their own self-interests, and it also ignores the concerns that citizens have about politics. The obsession with who is winning may

> **horse-race journalism** the media's focus on the competitive aspects of politics rather than on actual policy proposals and political decisions
>
> **optics** the way a situation, person, or event is presented by the media and perceived by the public
>
> **sound bite** a brief, snappy excerpt from a public figure's speech that is easy to repeat on the news

transient) images, and Twitter has managed to turn a bug into a feature, forcing politicians and journalists alike to condense their thoughts to a mere 280 characters.

The emphasis on image and simplified narratives also means that reporters tend to concentrate on developing scandals to the exclusion of other, possibly more relevant, news events. Political scientist Larry Sabato refers to this behavior as a **feeding frenzy**: "the press coverage attending any political event or circumstance where a critical mass of journalists leap to cover the same embarrassing or scandalous subject and pursue it intensely, often excessively, and sometimes uncontrollably."[53] Many such feeding frenzies have been over scandals that have proved not to be true or seemed insignificant with the passing of time, and yet the media have treated them with the seriousness of a world crisis. After such attacks, the media frequently indulge in introspection and remorse, until the next scandal starts to brew.

Political scientist Thomas Patterson argues that the zest for catching politicians in a lie or a "gaffe" means that most presidents and presidential candidates are treated by the press as fundamentally untrustworthy, when in fact most do precisely what they say they are going to do. Because it takes time and energy to investigate all the claims that a president or a candidate makes, the media evaluate political claims not with their own careful scrutiny but with statements from political opponents. This makes politics appear endlessly adversarial and, as Patterson says, replaces investigative journalism with attack journalism.[54]

THE POWER OF THE MAINSTREAM MEDIA'S NARRATIVE

The effects of agenda setting; framing; expert persuasion; and shallow, overly dramatized reporting should not be taken to mean that we are all unwitting dupes of the media. In the first place, these are not iron-clad rules; they are tendencies that scholars have discovered and confirmed with experimentation and public opinion surveys. That means they hold true for many but not all people. Members of the two major political

'...Political campaigns have become so simplistic and superficial... In the 20 seconds we have left, could you explain why?..'

parties, for instance, are less affected by agenda setting than are independents, perhaps because the latter do not have a party to rely on to tell them what is important,[55] although as the media become more partisan, the partisan narratives can themselves be reinforced by media effects.

Second, we bring our own armor to the barrage of media effects we face regularly. We all filter our news watching through our own narratives constructed on the ideas, values, and distinct perspectives we bring to politics. That is, we exercise **selective perception**.[56] If people do not seem to be well informed on the issues emphasized by the media, it may be that they do not see them as playing a role in a narrative they value or as having an effect on their lives. The point is that, as consumers, we do more than passively absorb the messages and values provided by the media.

A serious consequence of the superficial and negative content of political coverage is that voters' opinions of candidates have sunk, and citizen dissatisfaction with the electoral process has risen.[57] Not only is the public becoming more cynical about the political world, but it is also becoming more cynical about the media. A recent public opinion poll shows that half or more of the American public now thinks that the news is too biased, sensationalized, and manipulated by special interests, and that reporters offer too many of their own opinions, quote unnamed sources, and are negative.[58] If people cease to trust the media, the media become less effective in playing their legitimate roles as well as their more controversial ones, and democracy becomes more difficult to sustain.

It would be good for democracy if the growing dominance of online media sources could counteract some of the media's negativity by allowing interactivity, but all it takes is a look at the comments on an online article or blog post to realize that much

feeding frenzy excessive press coverage of an embarrassing or scandalous subject

selective perception the phenomenon of filtering incoming information through personal values and interests

of the media's negative view of politics either reflects or has animated a similar public perspective. The difference, of course, is that the mainstream media tend to be negative about the process in general and the animus of members of the public tends to be more tribal—elevating the party or side they agree with and being vitriolic about the one they don't. In fact, although researchers have tried to look at whether the ideological slant of a news source makes a difference to one's perception of the news, it is a difficult question to answer since people seem to gravitate to the sources with which they agree. Are their views shaped by bias in the news, or do they choose the bias they prefer to be exposed to? A 2003 study looking at misperceptions about the Iraq war (specifically, beliefs that there was evidence of links between al Qaeda and Saddam Hussein, that weapons of mass destruction had been found in Iraq, and that world opinion favored U.S. action in Iraq) concluded that the frequency with which those beliefs were held varied dramatically with the primary source of a person's news. Watchers of Fox News (which tended to be more supportive of the Bush administration) held those misperceptions much more frequently than did those who got their news from other sources.[59]

PAUSE AND REVIEW Who, What, How

Journalists, of course, are people like us—they have values and beliefs that shape their ideas of what is important to cover, even though most make an effort to be objective. In addition, they want bylines or airtime, the respect of their peers, and professional acclaim, at the same time that they want to help keep their news organizations competitive and profitable. Many of them must produce stories, whether something new is happening or not, and feel pressure to get the story that they feel politicians are withholding. All of these factors mean that what is at stake for journalists is not always serving the public.

Citizens, however, require sound knowledge about what is happening in the political world so that they can make informed decisions and vote for the people who will represent their interests. Even if journalists provided a single narrative, they would have a stake in investigating its accuracy. With multiple, conflicting stories to assess, that stake becomes all the more important.

In Your Own Words Explain the roles and responsibilities of journalists and the tools they use to shape and perpetuate political narratives.

POLITICS AS PUBLIC RELATIONS

Waging the permanent campaign

There is no doubt that the media portray politics in a negative light and that news reporting emphasizes personality, superficial image, and conflict over substantive policy issues. Some media figures argue, however, that this is not the media's fault,

but rather the responsibility of politicians and their press officers who are so obsessed with their own images on television that they limit access to the media, speak only in prearranged sound bites, and present themselves to the public in carefully orchestrated "media events."[60] That is, in their own effort to control the political narrative, politicians are limiting the ability of journalists to do their jobs properly.

Media events are designed to limit the ability of reporters to put their own interpretation on the occasion. The rules of American politics, which require a politician to have high public approval to maximize his or her clout, mean that politicians have to try to get maximum exposure for their ideas and accomplishments while limiting the damage the media can do with their intense scrutiny, investigations, and critical perspectives. This effort to control the media can lead to an emphasis on short-term gain over long-term priorities and the making of policy decisions with an eye to their political impact—a tendency that has come to be known as the **permanent campaign**.[61]

NEWS MANAGEMENT

News management describes the chief mechanism of the permanent campaign, the efforts of a politician's staff—media consultants, press secretaries, pollsters, campaign strategists, and general advisers—to control the news about the politician. The staff want to put their own issues on the agenda, determine for themselves the standards by which the politician will be evaluated, frame the issues, and supply the sources for reporters, so that they will put their client, the politician, in the best possible light. In contemporary political jargon, they want to put a **spin**, or an interpretation, on the news that will be most flattering to the politician whose image is in their care, to build the narrative that the media representatives will repeat as fact. To some extent, modern American politics has become a battle between the press and the politicians and among the politicians themselves to control the agenda and the narratives that reach the public. It has become a battle of the "spin doctors."

The classic example of news management is the rehabilitation of the image of Richard Nixon after he lost the 1960 election to the more media-savvy Kennedy campaign. Inspired by the way the Kennedy administration had managed the image of Kennedy as war hero, patriot, devoted father, and faithful husband, when at least one of those characterizations wasn't true, Nixon

permanent campaign the idea that governing requires a continual effort to convince the public to sign on to the program, requiring a reliance on consultants and an emphasis on politics over policy

news management the efforts of a politician's staff to control news about the politician

spin an interpretation of a politician's words or actions, designed to present a favorable image

speechwriter Ray Price saw his mission clearly. Noting that Nixon was personally unpopular with the public, he wrote in a 1967 memo, "We have to be very clear on this point: that the response is to the image, not to the man, since 99 percent of the voters have no contact with the man. It's not what's there that counts, it's what's projected—and it's not what he projects but rather what the voter receives. It's not the man we have to change, but rather the received impression."[62] With the help of an advertising executive and a television producer, among others, Nixon was repackaged and sold to voters as the "New Nixon." He won election as president in 1968 and 1972, and that he had to resign in 1974 is perhaps less a failure of his image makers than the inevitable revelation of the "real" Nixon underneath.

National Archives

News That Would Not Be Managed

The Nixon administration ran a tight ship when it came to managing the president's image, but even they could not spin the story after Watergate broke. Here, Nixon press secretary Ron Ziegler and staffers Frank Gannon and Diane Sawyer catch their breath after the president announced his resignation in 1974. (Sawyer passed through the revolving door to journalism and is former anchor of ABC World News.)

NEWS MANAGEMENT TECHNIQUES

The techniques of political communication that Nixon's handlers developed for managing his image have become part of the basic repertoire of political staffs, particularly in the White House but even to some extent for holders of lesser offices. They can include any or all of the following:[63]

- **Tight control of information.** Staffers pick a "line of the day"—for instance, a focus on education or child care—and orchestrate all messages from the administration around that theme. This strategy frustrates journalists who are trying to follow independent stories. But it recognizes that the staff must "feed the beast" by giving the press something to cover, or they may find the press rebelling and covering stories they don't want covered at all.[64]
- **Tight control of access to the politician.** If the politician is available to the press for only a short period of time and makes only a brief statement, the press corps is forced to report the appearance as the only available news.
- **Elaborate communications bureaucracy.** The Nixon White House had four offices handling communications. In addition to the White House press secretary, who was frequently kept uninformed so that he could

more credibly deny that he knew the answers to reporters' questions, there was an Office of Communications, an Office of Public Liaison, and a speechwriting office.

- **A concerted effort to bypass the White House press corps.** During Nixon's years this meant going to regional papers that were more easily manipulated. Today it can also include television talk shows and late-night television, and other forums that go directly to the public, such as town hall meetings and digital opportunities to reach the public through outlets like Facebook, Reddit, and YouTube. Part and parcel of this approach is the strategy of rewarding media outlets that provide friendly coverage and punishing those that do not.
- **Prepackaging the news in sound bites.** If the media are going to allow the public only a brief snippet of political language, the reasoning goes, let the politician's staff decide what it will be. In line with this, the press office will repeat a message often, to be sure the press and the public pick up on it, and it will work on phrasing that is catchy and memorable. Not incidentally, almost every serious politician now has a Twitter account that he, she, or the staff uses regularly.
- **Leaks.** A final and effective way that politicians attempt to control the news is with the use of **leaks**, secretly revealing confidential information to the press. Leaks can serve a variety of purposes. For instance, a leak can be a **trial balloon**, in which an official leaks a policy or plan in order to gauge public reaction to it. If the reaction is negative, the official denies he or she ever mentioned it, and if it is positive, the policy can go ahead without risk.

---

leaks confidential information secretly revealed to the press

trial balloon an official leak of a proposal to determine public reaction to it without risk

---

NEWS MANAGEMENT SINCE NIXON

Not all presidential administrations are equally accomplished at using these techniques of news management, of course. Nixon's was successful, at least in his first administration, and Ronald Reagan's has been referred to as a model of public relations.[65] President Bill Clinton did not manage the media effectively in the early years of his first administration; consequently, he was at the mercy of a frustrated and annoyed press corps. Within a couple of years, however, the Clinton staff had become much more skilled, and by his second administration they were adeptly handling scandals that would have daunted more seasoned public relations experts.

The George W. Bush administration did a superb job of news management, especially in Bush's first term. For instance, most of Bush's public events were open only to Bush supporters; where there was audience interaction, he received questions only from those who endorsed his programs and goals, and reporters who could be trusted to ask supportive questions were favored in White House news briefings and press conferences.[66] Supporters defended the Bush White House's news management strategy as efficient

Spin Matters

Press secretaries, as an administration's liaison to the press, are often a target of criticism. President Trump's first press secretary, Sean Spicer, was roundly mocked for his insistence that Trump's inauguration crowd was larger than Obama's, despite photo evidence indicating otherwise, leading to a memorable impersonation of him by Melissa McCarthy on Saturday Night Live. *Trump was reportedly infuriated that Spicer was played by a woman.*

and praiseworthy. Critics, by contrast, claimed that the White House had become a "propaganda machine" to serve the president's political goals.[67] Barack Obama's White House was as disciplined as Bush's, although his public events were not vetted for supporters and the president faced more negative questions because of it. During the presidential campaign, the Obama camp was famous for avoiding leaks and controlling its message, and although that perfect discipline was not maintained in the White House, it was still remarkably free of public infighting and leaks. Obama's first press secretary, Robert Gibbs, was a senior adviser to the president and had uncommon access and a dedication to protecting Obama's interests, though his second, Jay Carney, and his third, Josh Earnest, were more traditional spokespeople.[68] One difference between the Obama administration and its predecessors was the elaborate electronic communication network it had set up, which allowed administration officials to talk directly to supporters and to bypass the traditional media if they wanted to, texting and tweeting as well as sending emails and posting information, videos, and pictures to the White House web site.

Donald Trump did not begin his presidency on a good footing with the press.[69] During his campaign he had made them a target, limiting the access of outlets whose coverage he didn't like, telling them he would sue them, and calling them out at his rallies, saying they were dishonest. Trump has always preferred to provide his own coverage of events via Twitter, a habit that did not change with his ascension to the presidency. More than any other president, he has felt free to create his own narratives, even when they bear no relationship to widely validated facts, to chart his own course, and to suggest that media coverage of him that is unflattering is false and that journalists should be punished for publishing what he calls fake news. Trump's supporters delight in his brash disregard for the norms of truth telling and free speech and sometimes there is entertainment value in his politics as performance art—but even more than the Nixon administration's news management, it also poses a real threat to the fundamental principles of democratic governance.

REDUCTION IN POLITICAL ACCOUNTABILITY

There is a real cost to the transformation of politics into public relations, no matter whose administration is engaging in the practice (and with varying degrees of expertise, they all do). Not only does it mean that politicians must spend time and energy on image considerations that do not really help them serve the public, but the skills required by an actor and a statesperson are not the same. The current system may encourage us to choose the wrong leaders for the wrong reasons and discourage the right people from running at all.

The transformation of politics into professional storytelling also means that we suffer from a loss of **political accountability**. Such accountability is the very hallmark of democracy: political leaders must answer to the public for their actions. If our leaders do something we do not like, we can make them bear the consequences of their actions by voting them out of office. The threat of being voted out of office is supposed to encourage them to do what we want in the first place. If politics is reduced to image, if we don't know what our leaders are doing, and if it becomes a game of cat and mouse with the media over what story should be told to the public, then accountability is weakened and so is democracy.[70]

PAUSE AND REVIEW Who, What, How

The professional goals of journalists clash with those of politicians, who need to communicate with the public; to present themselves as attractive, effective leaders; and to make their ideas and proposed policies clear to voters. The clash of journalists' and politicians' goals means that politicians have had to develop their own strategies for getting their story out to the public.

What is at stake for citizens is not only their ability to get information on which to base their political decisions, but also their ability to see good as well as bad in government, to know their leaders as they really are and not just their public relations images, and to hold them accountable. The rules put the burden of responsibility on citizens to be critical consumers of the media.

In Your Own Words
Identify the strategies politicians use to counter the influence of the media and shape and perpetuate their own political narratives.

THE CITIZENS AND THE MEDIA

Growing citizen access increases engagement but blurs lines of journalism

In this chapter we have been unable to talk about the media without talking about citizenship. Citizens have been a constant "who" in our analysis because the media exist largely to give

> **political accountability** the democratic principle that political leaders must answer to the public for their actions

information to citizens and to mediate their relationship to government. But if we evaluate the traditional role of the media with respect to the public, the relationship that emerges is not a particularly responsive one. Almost from the beginning, control of the American media has been in the hands of an elite group, whether party leaders, politicians, wealthy entrepreneurs, or corporate owners. Financial concerns have meant that the media in the United States have been driven more by profit motive than by public interest. Not only are ownership and control of the media far removed from the hands of everyday Americans, but the reporting of national news is done mostly by reporters who do not fit the profile of those "average" citizens and whose concerns often do not reflect the concerns of their audience.

Citizens' access to the media has been correspondingly remote. The primary role available to them has been passive: that of reader, listener, or watcher. The power they wield is the power of switching newspapers or changing channels, essentially choosing among competing elites; but this is not an active, participatory role. While freedom of the press is a right technically held by all citizens, there is no right of access to the press. Citizens have difficulty making their voices heard, and, of course, most do not even try. Members of the media holler long and loud about their right to publish what they want, but only sporadically and briefly do they consider their obligations to the public to provide the sort of information that can sustain a democracy. If active democracy requires a political community in which the public can deliberate about important issues, it would seem that the American media are failing miserably at creating that community.

> **Should the media be driven by what consumers want to know or by what they need to know?**

The rapid changes in information technology that we have discussed throughout this chapter offer some hope that the media can be made to serve the public interest more effectively. The media are in flux and, while the future of the print media is in question, some of the new media that are replacing it are remarkably more open and responsive. Along with social networks, some of these new media—such as cable news, specialized television programs, and Internet news—allow citizens to get fast-breaking reports of events as they occur and even to customize the news that they get. Talk radio and call-in television shows—new uses of the "old" media—allow citizen interaction, as do Internet chat rooms and other online forums. Many web

Capturing History With a Cell Phone

The arrest of two black men in a Philadelphia Starbucks—they were waiting for a friend before ordering—was captured in this blurry photo, which was taken from a bystander's phone. Widespread use of smartphones and access to mass audiences through social networking platforms has enabled citizen journalists to shed light on events and experiences that the traditional news media either ignored or had difficulty reporting.

sites allow users to give their opinions of issues in unscientific straw polls (see Chapter 11). Some analysts speculate that it is only a matter of time until we can all vote on issues from our home computers. The one thing that the new media have in common is that they bypass the old, making the corporate journalistic establishment less powerful than it was but perhaps giving rise to new elites and raising new questions about participation and how much access we really want citizens to have.

One of the most significant developments in the new media is the proliferation of **citizen journalism**, reporting and commentary by everyday citizens unaffiliated with traditional media outlets, and distributed via the web in the form of blogs, podcasts, and video sharing. These new platforms are, essentially, the modern equivalent of giving citizens their own printing presses and the means to publish their views. Although these resources can be devoted to any subject, the ones that interest us here are the ones that focus on politics and media criticism. As is true of any unregulated media source, a good deal of inaccurate and unsubstantiated information is posted on the web. There is no credentialing process for citizen reporters or bloggers, they are not usually admitted to the White House or other official news conferences unless they also report for a more traditional media outlet, and they generally lack the resources required to do a great deal of investigative reporting.

In Your Own Words Summarize the relationship between citizens and the media.

> **citizen journalism** reporting and commentary by everyday citizens unaffiliated with traditional media outlets, and distributed via the web in the form of blogs, podcasts, or video uploads

LET'S REVISIT: *What's at Stake . . . ?*

We began this chapter by asking what's at stake to the job of keeping the republic if we're locked in separate media bubbles, curating our own news, and creating or believing narratives that fit our preconceived ideas rather than challenging us to think critically. Are we just divided ideologically, or is the integrity of the political culture we share at stake?

The results of the contentious 2016 election were so close that, even though Hillary Clinton won by the metric of the popular vote, the official rules of the Electoral College gave the

presidency to Donald Trump. Having survived that election, barely, it is tempting to answer the question of what's at stake by saying that living in our closed information bubbles brings us very close to losing the common understanding and shared beliefs about the political world that make a peaceful resolution of our differences possible.

Perhaps the best example is a fundamental one. Donald Trump's campaign slogan was "Make America Great Again," or #MAGA as he frequently tweeted out to his many supporters. He elaborated on the narrative of what that slogan stood for at rallies of people who fully shared his views: immigration was destroying the country, trade had stolen our jobs, Muslims threatened our security, the military was terrible, inner cities were war zones, and we were a loser of a country. Only Trump could fix this mess of a nation and restore us to greatness.

Supporting Trump's narrative were Trump himself, in rallies, on Twitter, and on Fox News's *The Sean Hannity Show*; other commentators on Fox; the rightwing Breitbart News, whose publisher left to become CEO of Trump's campaign; and innumerable social media sites. It was a gloomy, downright scary apocalyptic vision. To half the population, that vision was as alien as Mars. But it resonated with Trump's supporters, figuratively if not literally. Their America wasn't great any more. There were too many people who looked different, too many people not speaking English, too many people telling them that the language they used to describe their life experiences was off-limits and crude, too many people upending gender roles and the very idea of gender itself, too many people getting fat off of government without doing any work. Too many people looking down on them for being who they were, when who they were—upstanding white, working-class citizens—used to mean something. Making America great again meant restoring their dignity, making them whole, and soothing the sense of grievance that convinced them the rules of life were rigged against them.

Clinton's supporters, by contrast, were in an entirely different bubble. Also supported through social media as well as in most outlets of popular culture, their idea was that, sure, America had a ways to go, but it was so much *greater* than it

had been. The picture was rosy. A popular African American president was leaving office after two full terms, breaking a barrier many thought they would never see. People of color were optimistic about their futures. Cops were still killing black men, but Black Lives Matter had organized and there was power in that organization. A woman was running for president, and many people thought she might win. Diversity meant interesting people, widened horizons, great restaurants, a vivid and colorful world. Gays were free to marry, transgender people were free to be themselves, people could even smoke pot legally in a handful of states. With a Democrat in the White House for four more years (they hoped), many of the changes that Obama had enacted to protect the environment, provide security to immigrants, and provide health care to all would be locked in, and liberals on the Supreme Court would secure reproductive rights for women and rights for gays. America was a wonderful country; it seemed it could only get better.

How on earth to reconcile these two narratives? Ironically, the great equalizer was the election. Both sides could feel that their narrative won, but only one side could claim the presidency, and with Trump on his way to the White House, the optimistic, rose-colored-glasses people began to feel that maybe they did, in fact, live in an apocalyptic world. And things for the Trump supporters began to look brighter. Whether the two narratives would meet somewhere in the middle or pass each other on forever-separate paths is an open question with open consequences. The stakes of living in separate narrative bubbles are critical to us all.

Want a better grade?

Get the tools you need to sharpen your study skills. **SAGE edge** offers practice quizzes, eFlashcards, video, and multimedia at **edge.sagepub.com/barbour9e.**

CLUES to Critical Thinking

"The Strange, Sad Death of Journalism"

By Michael Gerson, *Washington Post*, November 27, 2009

In this article a conservative laments changes in the profession of journalism. Is this a partisan or a bipartisan issue?

Like the nearby Smithsonian National Museum of Natural History, the Newseum—Washington's museum dedicated to journalism—displays dinosaurs. On a long wall near the entrance, the front pages of newspapers from around the country are electronically posted each morning—the artifacts of a declining industry. Inside, the high-tech exhibits are nostalgic for a lower-tech time when banner headlines and network news summarized the emotions and exposed the scandals of the nation. Lindbergh Lands Safely. One Small Step. Nixon Resigns. Cronkite removes his glasses to announce President Kennedy's death at 1 p.m. Central Standard Time.

Behind a long rack of preserved, historic front pages, there is a kind of journalistic mausoleum, displaying the departed. The *Ann Arbor News*, closed July 23 after 174 years in print. The *Rocky Mountain News*, taken at age 150. The *Seattle Post-Intelligencer*, which passed quietly into the Internet.

What difference does this make? For many conservatives, the "mainstream media" is an epithet. Didn't the Internet expose the lies of Dan Rather? Many on the left also shed few tears, preferring to consume their partisanship raw in the new media.

But a visit to the Newseum is a reminder that what is passing is not only a business but also a profession—the journalistic tradition of nonpartisan objectivity. Journalists, God knows, didn't always live up to that tradition. But they generally accepted it, and they felt shamed when their biases or inaccuracies were exposed. The profession had rules about facts and sources and editors who enforced standards. At its best, the profession of journalism has involved a spirit of public service and adventure— reporting from a bomber during a raid in World War II, or exposing the suffering of Sudan or Appalachia, or rushing to the site of the World Trade Center moments after the buildings fell.

By these standards, the changes we see in the media are also a decline. Most cable news networks have forsaken objectivity entirely and produce little actual news, since makeup for guests is cheaper than reporting. Most Internet sites display an endless hunger to comment and little appetite for verification. Free markets, it turns out, often make poor fact-checkers, instead feeding the fantasies of conspiracy theorists from "birthers" to Sept. 11, 2001, "truthers." Bloggers in repressive countries often show great courage, but few American bloggers have the resources or inclination to report from war zones, famines and genocides.

The democratization of the media—really its fragmentation—has encouraged ideological polarization. Princeton University professor Paul Starr traced this process recently in the *Columbia Journalism Review*.

After the captive audience for network news was released by cable, many Americans did not turn to other sources of news. They turned to entertainment. The viewers who remained were more political and more partisan. "As Walter Cronkite prospered in the old environment," says Starr, "Bill O'Reilly and Keith Olbermann thrive in the new one. As the diminished public for journalism becomes more partisan, journalism itself is likely to shift further in that direction."

Cable and the Internet now allow Americans, if they choose, to get their information entirely from sources that agree with them—sources that reinforce and exaggerate their political predispositions.

And the whole system is based on a kind of intellectual theft. Internet aggregators (who link to news they don't produce) and bloggers would have little to collect or comment upon without the costly enterprise of newsgathering and investigative reporting. The old-media dinosaurs remain the basis for the entire media food chain. But newspapers are expected to provide their content free on the Internet. A recent poll found that 80 percent of Americans refuse to pay for Internet content. There is no economic model that will allow newspapers to keep producing content they don't charge for, while Internet sites repackage and sell content they don't pay to produce.

I dislike media bias as much as the next conservative. But I don't believe that journalistic objectivity is a fraud. I was a journalist for a time, at a once-great, now-diminished newsmagazine. I've seen good men and women work according to a set of professional standards I respect—standards that serve the public. Professional journalism is not like the buggy-whip industry, outdated by economic progress, to be mourned but not missed. This profession has a social value that is currently not reflected in its market value.

What is to be done? A lot of good people are working on it. But if you currently have newsprint on your hands, thank you.

Consider the source and the audience: Michael Gerson, as he indicates in his column, is a conservative. A former speechwriter and adviser to President George W. Bush (as well as other Republicans), he now writes a syndicated column that appears, among other places, in the widely read *Washington Post*. How might this background affect his views of the media and journalism?

Lay out the argument and the underlying values and assumptions: Gerson is nostalgic in this column for the *profession* of journalism. How does he define that? What does he mean by the "democratization" of the media? What damage does he think it has done? In what way is it based on "intellectual theft"?

Uncover the evidence: Does Gerson offer any evidence for his view in this column? Does the fact that most of his audience probably watches TV, reads some news, and participates in social media mean that he doesn't need to do more than to refer to their shared culture?

Evaluate the conclusion: Gerson, like many others, concludes that objective news gathering as an honorable profession is getting lost in the scrum of sloppy and parasitic cable TV shows, blogs, and tweets. Is he right? Can the profession of journalism endure in that environment?

Sort out the political significance: If Gerson is right, what is to be done? Is there a business model that will keep journalism alive while allowing the myriad voices that have been generated in the modern media to thrive? If it is in all of our interests to have people doing good, solid reporting on the events of the day, how is it to be paid for?

Review

Where Do We Get Our Information?

An increasing number of Americans have access to the Internet via any number of devices, and the convergence of mass media in the digital age means that we have more information at our fingertips than ever before. More media outlets and more information means that Americans must devote ever-increasing amounts of time and effort to sorting out what is relevant to them. Traditional news media—especially newspapers—struggle to survive in an era of free online content, with revenue streams shrinking while demands for content increase.

mass media (p. 515)   narrowcasting (p. 519)   news aggregators (p. 520)
media convergence (p. 515)   news organizations (p. 519)

How Does Media Ownership Affect Control of the Narrative?

Today's media is largely profit driven, and although small and independent news sources are gaining traction through digital media, the biggest news organizations are still owned by a few large corporate interests. The modern new media landscape allows for more content and more diverse voices, but those voices are still largely intertwined with big media on many levels. The government also plays a role, with regulations on broadcast media. The 1934 Federal Communications Act, which created the Federal Communications Commission, imposed order on multiple media outlets and attempted to serve the public interest through three provisions: the equal time rule, the fairness doctrine, and the right of rebuttal. However, the impact of the FCC is shifting in the media age, with more news coming from unregulated sources like the web and cable news sources.

gatekeepers (p. 523)   commercial bias (p. 528)   clickbait (p. 528)

Spinning Political Narratives

Journalists, playing four roles, have great influence over news content and presentation. Gatekeepers decide what is news and what is not. Disseminators determine relevant news and get it out to the public quickly. The investigator role involves verifying the truth of various claims or analyzing particular policies. Finally, as public mobilizers, journalists try to report the people's interests rather than their own. Some critics believe the homogeneous background of journalists—mostly male, white, and well educated—biases the press, as does their predominantly liberal ideology.

Public skepticism of the media has increased in recent decades. Others claim that the revolving door, the practice of journalists taking government positions but later returning to reporting, severely damages news objectivity. The media affect our thinking about politics through agenda setting, framing, persuasion by professional communicators, and a tendency to reduce politics to issues of conflicts and superficial image rather than substantive policy disputes.

revolving door (p. 532)

pundit (p. 532)

agenda setting (p. 533)

framing (p. 533)

horse-race journalism (p. 534)

optics (p. 534)

sound bite (p. 534)

feeding frenzy (p. 535)

selective perception (p. 535)

Politics as Public Relations

Politicians themselves—and their campaigns—try hard to avoid being caught in media narratives about them by managing the news and trying to communicate directly with voters. The resulting tension probably doesn't help the media's negative coverage of politics. When the narratives by which voters evaluate politicians are not accurate, political accountability suffers.

permanent campaign (p. 536)

news management (p. 536)

spin (p. 536)

leaks (p. 537)

trial balloon (p. 537)

political accountability (p. 539)

The Citizens and the Media

Citizens historically have played a passive role in the media as consumers of information. But the rise of new, interactive media and the growth of the civic journalism movement may help to transform citizens into more active media participants.

citizen journalism (p. 540)

APPENDIX MATERIAL

1

ARTICLES OF CONFEDERATION

To all to whom these Presents shall come, we the under-signed Delegates of the States affixed to our Names send greeting.

Articles of Confederation and perpetual Union between the states of New Hampshire, Massachusetts-bay Rhode Island and Providence Plantations, Connecticut, New York, New Jersey, Pennsylvania, Delaware, Maryland, Virginia, North Carolina, South Carolina and Georgia.

ARTICLE I

The Stile of this Confederacy shall be "The United States of America".

ARTICLE II

Each state retains its sovereignty, freedom, and independence, and every power, jurisdiction, and right, which is not by this Confederation expressly delegated to the United States, in Congress assembled.

ARTICLE III

The said States hereby severally enter into a firm league of friendship with each other, for their common defense, the security of their liberties, and their mutual and general welfare, binding themselves to assist each other, against all force offered to, or attacks made upon them, or any of them, on account of religion, sovereignty, trade, or any other pretense whatever.

ARTICLE IV

The better to secure and perpetuate mutual friendship and intercourse among the people of the different States in this Union, the free inhabitants of each of these States, paupers, vagabonds, and fugitives from justice excepted, shall be entitled to all privileges and immunities of free citizens in the several States; and the people of each State shall free ingress and regress to and from any other State, and shall enjoy therein all the privileges of trade and commerce, subject to the same duties, impositions, and restrictions as the inhabitants thereof respectively, provided that such restrictions shall not extend so far as to prevent the removal of property imported into any State, to any other State, of which the owner is an inhabitant; provided also that no imposition, duties or restriction shall be laid by any State, on the property of the United States, or either of them.

If any person guilty of, or charged with, treason, felony, or other high misdemeanor in any State, shall flee from justice, and be found in any of the United States, he shall, upon demand of the Governor or executive power of the State from which he fled, be delivered up and removed to the State having jurisdiction of his offense.

Full faith and credit shall be given in each of these States to the records, acts, and judicial proceedings of the courts and magistrates of every other State.

ARTICLE V

For the most convenient management of the general interests of the United States, delegates shall be annually appointed in such manner as the legislatures of each State shall direct, to meet in Congress on the first Monday in November, in every year, with a power reserved to each State to recall its delegates, or any of them, at any time within the year, and to send others in their stead for the remainder of the year.

No State shall be represented in Congress by less than two, nor more than seven members; and no person shall be capable of being a delegate for more than three years in any term of six years; nor shall any person, being a delegate, be capable of holding any office under the United States, for which he, or another for his benefit, receives any salary, fees or emolument of any kind.

Each State shall maintain its own delegates in a meeting of the States, and while they act as members of the committee of the States.

In determining questions in the United States in Congress assembled, each State shall have one vote.

Freedom of speech and debate in Congress shall not be impeached or questioned in any court or place out of Congress, and the members of Congress shall be protected in their persons from arrests or imprisonments, during the time of their going to and from, and attendence on Congress, except for treason, felony, or breach of the peace.

ARTICLE VI

No State, without the consent of the United States in Congress assembled, shall send any embassy to, or receive any embassy from, or enter into any conference, agreement, alliance or treaty with any King, Prince or State; nor shall any person holding any office of profit or trust under the United States, or any of them, accept any present, emolument, office or title of any kind whatever from any King, Prince or foreign State; nor shall the United States in Congress assembled, or any of them, grant any title of nobility.

No two or more States shall enter into any treaty, confederation or alliance whatever between them, without the consent of the United States in Congress assembled, specifying accurately the purposes for which the same is to be entered into, and how long it shall continue.

No State shall lay any imposts or duties, which may interfere with any stipulations in treaties, entered into by the United States in Congress assembled, with any King, Prince or State, in pursuance of any treaties already proposed by Congress, to the courts of France and Spain.

No vessel of war shall be kept up in time of peace by any State, except such number only, as shall be deemed necessary by the United States in Congress assembled, for the defense of such State, or its trade; nor shall any body of forces be kept up by any State in time of peace, except such number only, as in the judgement of the United States in Congress assembled, shall be deemed requisite to garrison the forts necessary for the defense of such State; but every State shall always keep up a well-regulated and disciplined militia, sufficiently armed and accoutered, and shall provide and constantly have ready for use, in public stores, a due number of filed pieces and tents, and a proper quantity of arms, ammunition and camp equipage.

No State shall engage in any war without the consent of the United States in Congress assembled, unless such State be actually invaded by enemies, or shall have received certain advice of a resolution being formed by some nation of Indians to invade such State, and the danger is so imminent as not to admit of a delay till the United States in Congress assembled can be consulted; nor shall any State grant commissions to any ships or vessels of war, nor letters of marque or reprisal, except it be after a declaration of war by the United States in Congress assembled, and then only against the Kingdom or State and the subjects thereof, against which war has been so declared, and under such regulations as shall be established by the United States in Congress assembled, unless such State be infested by pirates, in which case vessels of war may be fitted out for that occasion, and kept so long as the danger shall continue, or until the United States in Congress assembled shall determine otherwise.

ARTICLE VII

When land forces are raised by any State for the common defense, all officers of or under the rank of colonel, shall be appointed by the legislature of each State respectively, by whom such forces shall be raised, or in such manner as such State shall direct, and all vacancies shall be filled up by the State which first made the appointment.

ARTICLE VIII

All charges of war, and all other expenses that shall be incurred for the common defense or general welfare, and allowed by the United States in Congress assembled, shall be defrayed out of a common treasury, which shall be supplied by the several States in proportion to the value of all land within each State, granted or surveyed for any person, as such land and the buildings and improvements thereon shall be estimated according to such mode as the United States in Congress assembled, shall from time to time direct and appoint.

The taxes for paying that proportion shall be laid and levied by the authority and direction of the legislatures of the several States within the time agreed upon by the United States in Congress assembled.

ARTICLE IX

The United States in Congress assembled, shall have the sole and exclusive right and power of determining on peace and war, except in the cases mentioned in the sixth article— of sending and receiving ambassadors—entering into treaties and alliances, provided that no treaty of commerce shall be made whereby the legislative power of the respective States shall be restrained from imposing such imposts and duties on foreigners, as their own people are subjected to, or from prohibiting the exportation or importation of any species of goods or commodities whatsoever—of establishing rules for deciding in all cases, what captures on land or water shall be legal, and in what manner prizes taken by land or naval forces in the service of the United States shall be divided or appropriated—of granting letters of marque and reprisal in times of peace—appointing courts for the trial of piracies and felonies commited on the high seas and establishing courts for receiving and determining finally appeals in all cases of captures, provided that no member of Congress shall be appointed a judge of any of the said courts.

The United States in Congress assembled shall also be the last resort on appeal in all disputes and differences now subsisting or that hereafter may arise between two or more States concerning boundary, jurisdiction or any other causes whatever; which authority shall always be exercised in the manner following. Whenever the legislative or executive authority or lawful agent of any State in controversy with another shall present a petition to Congress stating the matter in question and praying for a hearing, notice thereof shall be given by order of Congress to the legislative or executive authority of the other State in controversy, and a day assigned for the appearance of the parties by their lawful agents, who shall then be directed to appoint by joint consent, commissioners or judges to constitute a court for hearing and determining the matter in question: but if they cannot agree, Congress shall name three persons out of each of the United States, and from the list of such persons each party shall alternately strike out one, the petitioners beginning, until the number shall be reduced to thirteen; and from that number not less than seven, nor more than nine names as Congress shall direct, shall in the presence of Congress be drawn out by lot, and the persons whose names shall be so drawn or any five of them, shall be commissioners or judges, to hear and finally determine the controversy, so always as a major part of the judges who shall hear the cause shall agree in the determination: and if either party shall neglect to attend at the day appointed, without showing reasons, which Congress shall judge sufficient, or being present shall refuse to strike, the Congress shall proceed to nominate three persons out of each State, and the secretary of Congress shall strike in behalf of such party absent or refusing; and the judgement and sentence of the court to be appointed, in the manner before prescribed, shall be final and conclusive; and if any of the parties shall refuse to submit to the authority of such court, or to appear or defend their claim or cause, the court shall nevertheless proceed to pronounce sentence, or judgement, which shall in like manner be final and decisive, the judgement or sentence and other proceedings being in either case transmitted to Congress, and lodged among the acts of Congress for the security of the parties concerned: provided that every commissioner, before he sits in judgement, shall take an oath to be administered by one of the judges of the supreme or superior court of the State, where the cause shall be tried, 'well and truly to hear and determine the matter in question, according to the best of his judgement, without favor, affection or hope of reward': provided also, that no State shall be deprived of territory for the benefit of the United States.

All controversies concerning the private right of soil claimed under different grants of two or more States, whose jurisdictions as they may respect such lands, and the States which passed such grants are adjusted, the said grants or either of them being at the same time claimed to have originated antecedent to such settlement of jurisdiction, shall on the petition of either party to the Congress of the United States, be finally determined as near as may be in the same manner as is before prescribed for deciding disputes respecting territorial jurisdiction between different States.

The United States in Congress assembled shall also have the sole and exclusive right and power of regulating the alloy and value of coin struck by their own authority, or by that of the respective States—fixing the standards of weights and measures throughout the United States—regulating the trade and managing all affairs with the Indians, not members of any of the States, provided that the legislative right of any State within its own limits be not infringed or violated—establishing or regulating post offices from one State to another, throughout all the United States, and exacting such postage on the papers passing through the same as may be requisite to defray the expenses of the said office—appointing all officers of the land forces, in the service of the United States, excepting regimental officers—appointing all the officers of the naval forces, and commissioning all officers whatever in the service of the United States—making rules for the government and regulation of the said land and naval forces, and directing their operations.

The United States in Congress assembled shall have authority to appoint a committee, to sit in the recess of Congress, to be denominated 'A Committee of the States', and to consist of one delegate from each State; and to appoint such other committees and civil officers as may be necessary for managing the general affairs of the United States under their direction—to appoint one of their members to preside, provided that no person be allowed to serve in the office of president more than one year in any term of three years; to ascertain the necessary sums of money to be raised for the service of the United States, and to appropriate and apply the same for defraying the public expenses—to borrow money, or emit bills on the credit of the United States, transmitting every half-year to the respective States an account of the sums of money so borrowed or emitted—to build and equip a navy—to agree upon the number of land forces, and to make requisitions from each State for its quota, in proportion to the number of white inhabitants in such State; which requisition shall be binding, and thereupon the legislature of each State shall appoint the regimental officers, raise the men and cloath, arm and equip them in a solid-like manner, at the expense of the United States; and the officers and men so cloathed, armed and equipped shall march to the place appointed, and within the time agreed on by the United States in Congress assembled. But if the United States in Congress assembled shall, on consideration of circumstances judge proper that any State should not raise men, or should raise a smaller number of men than the quota thereof, such extra number shall be raised, officered, cloathed, armed and equipped in the same manner as the quota of each State, unless the legislature of such State shall judge that such extra number cannot be safely spread out in the same, in which case they shall raise, officer, cloath, arm and equip as many of such extra number as they judge can be safely spared. And the officers and men so cloathed, armed, and equipped, shall march to the place appointed, and within the time agreed on by the United States in Congress assembled.

The United States in Congress assembled shall never engage in a war, nor grant letters of marque or reprisal in time of peace, nor enter into any treaties or alliances, nor coin money, nor regulate the value thereof, nor ascertain the sums and expenses necessary for the defense and welfare of the United States, or any of them, nor emit bills, nor borrow money on the credit of the United States, nor appropriate money, nor agree upon the number of vessels of war, to be built or purchased, or the number of land or sea forces to be raised, nor appoint a commander in chief of the army or navy, unless nine States assent to the same: nor shall a question on any other point, except for adjourning from day to day be determined, unless by the votes of the majority of the United States in Congress assembled.

The Congress of the United States shall have power to adjourn to any time within the year, and to any place within the United States, so that no period of adjournment be for a longer duration than the space of six months, and shall publish the journal of their proceedings monthly, except such parts thereof relating to treaties, alliances or military operations, as in their judgement require secrecy; and the yeas and nays of the delegates of each State on any question shall be entered on the journal, when it is desired by any delegates of a State, or any of them, at his or their request shall be furnished with a transcript of the said journal, except such parts as are above excepted, to lay before the legislatures of the several States.

ARTICLE X

The Committee of the States, or any nine of them, shall be authorized to execute, in the recess of Congress, such of the powers of Congress as the United States in Congress assembled, by the consent of the nine States, shall from time to time think expedient to vest them with; provided that no power be delegated to the said Committee, for the exercise of which, by the Articles of Confederation, the voice of nine States in the Congress of the United States assembled be requisite.

ARTICLE XI

Canada acceding to this confederation, and adjoining in the measures of the United States, shall be admitted into, and entitled to all the advantages of this Union; but no other colony shall be admitted into the same, unless such admission be agreed to by nine States.

ARTICLE XII

All bills of credit emitted, monies borrowed, and debts contracted by, or under the authority of Congress, before the assembling of the United States, in pursuance of the present confederation, shall be deemed and considered as a charge against the United States, for payment and satisfaction whereof the said United States, and the public faith are hereby solemnly pledged.

ARTICLE XIII

Every State shall abide by the determination of the United States in Congress assembled, on all questions which by this confederation are submitted to them. And the Articles of this Confederation shall be inviolably observed by every State, and the Union shall be perpetual; nor shall any alteration at any time hereafter be made in any of them; unless such alteration be agreed to in a Congress of the United States, and be afterwards confirmed by the legislatures of every State.

And Whereas it hath pleased the Great Governor of the World to incline the hearts of the legislatures we respectively represent in Congress, to approve of, and to authorize us to ratify the said Articles of Confederation and perpetual Union. Know Ye that we the undersigned delegates, by virtue of the power and authority to us given for that purpose, do by these presents, in the name and in behalf of our respective constituents, fully and entirely ratify and confirm each and every of the said Articles of Confederation and perpetual Union, and all and singular the matters and things therein contained: And we do further solemnly plight and engage the faith of our respective constituents, that they shall abide by the determinations of the United States in Congress assembled, on all questions, which by the said Confederation are submitted to them. And that the Articles thereof shall be inviolably observed by the States we respectively represent, and that the Union shall be perpetual.

In Witness whereof we have hereunto set our hands in Congress. Done at Philadelphia in the State of Pennsylvania the ninth day of July in the Year of our Lord One Thousand Seven Hundred and Seventy-Eight, and in the Third Year of the independence of America.

Agreed to by Congress 15 November 1777
In force after ratification by Maryland, 1 March 1781

2

DECLARATION OF INDEPENDENCE

On June 11, 1776, the responsibility to "prepare a declaration" of independence was assigned by the Continental Congress, meeting in Philadelphia, to five members: John Adams, Benjamin Franklin, Thomas Jefferson, Robert Livingston, and Roger Sherman. Impressed by his talents as a writer, the committee asked Jefferson to compose a draft. After modifying Jefferson's draft the committee turned it over to Congress on June 28. On July 2 Congress voted to declare independence; on the evening of July 4, it approved the Declaration of Independence.

In Congress, July 4, 1776.

The unanimous Declaration of the thirteen United States of America,

When in the Course of human events, it becomes necessary for one people to dissolve the political bands which have connected them with another, and to assume among the Powers of the earth, the separate and equal station to which the Laws of Nature and of Nature's God entitle them, a decent respect to the opinions of mankind requires that they should declare the causes which impel them to the separation.

We hold these truths to be self-evident, that all men are created equal, that they are endowed by their Creator with certain unalienable Rights, that among these are Life, Liberty and the pursuit of Happiness. That to secure these rights, Governments are instituted among Men, deriving their just powers from the consent of the governed. That whenever any form of Government becomes destructive of these ends, it is the Right of the People to alter or to abolish it, and to institute new Government, laying its foundation on such principles and organizing its powers in such form, as to them shall seem most likely to effect their Safety and Happiness. Prudence, indeed, will dictate that Government long established should not be changed for light and transient causes; and accordingly all experience hath shown, that mankind are more disposed to suffer, while evils are sufferable, than to right themselves by abolishing the forms to which they are accustomed. But when a long train of abuses and usurpations, pursuing invariably the same Object evinces a design to reduce them under absolute Despotism, it is their right, it is their duty, to throw off such Government, and to provide new

Guards for their future security. Such has been the patient sufferance of these Colonies; and such is now the necessity which constrains them to alter their former Systems of Government. The history of the present King of Great Britain is a history of repeated injuries and usurpations, all having in direct object the establishment of an absolute Tyranny over these States. To prove this, let Facts be submitted to a candid world.

He has refused his Assent to Laws, the most wholesome and necessary for the public good.

He has forbidden his Governors to pass Laws of immediate and pressing importance, unless suspended in their operation till his Assent should be obtained; and when so suspended, he has utterly neglected to attend to them.

He has refused to pass other Laws for the accommodation of large districts of people, unless those people would relinquish the right of Representation in the Legislature, a right inestimable to them and formidable to tyrants only.

He has called together legislative bodies at places unusual, uncomfortable, and distant from the depository of their Public Records, for the sole purpose of fatiguing them into compliance with his measures.

He has dissolved Representative Houses repeatedly, for opposing with manly firmness his invasions on the rights of the people.

He has refused for a long time, after such dissolutions, to cause others to be elected; whereby the Legislative Powers, incapable of Annihilation, have returned to the People at large for their exercise; the State remaining in the mean time exposed to all the dangers of invasion from without, and convulsions within.

He has endeavored to prevent the population of these States; for that purpose obstructing the Laws of Naturalization of Foreigners; refusing to pass others to encourage their migration hither, and raising the conditions of new Appropriations of Lands.

He has obstructed the Administration of Justice, by refusing his Assent to Laws for establishing Judiciary Powers.

He has made Judges dependent on his Will alone, for the tenure of their offices, and the amount and payment of their salaries.

He has erected a multitude of New Offices, and sent hither swarms of Officers to harass our People, and eat out their substance.

He has kept among us, in times of peace, Standing Armies without the Consent of our legislature.

He has affected to render the Military independent of and superior to the Civil Power.

He has combined with others to subject us to a jurisdiction foreign to our constitution, and unacknowledged by our laws; giving his Assent to their acts of pretended legislation:

For quartering large bodies of armed troops among us:

For protecting them, by a mock Trial, from Punishment for any Murders which they should commit on the Inhabitants of these States:

For cutting off our Trade with all parts of the world:

For imposing taxes on us without our Consent:

For depriving us in many cases, of the benefits of Trial by Jury:

For transporting us beyond Seas to be tried for pretended offences:

For abolishing the free System of English Laws in a neighbouring Province, establishing therein an Arbitrary government, and enlarging its Boundaries so as to render it at once an example and fit instrument for introducing the same absolute rule into these Colonies:

For taking away our Charters, abolishing our most valuable Laws, and altering fundamentally the Forms of our Governments:

For suspending our own Legislature, and declaring themselves invested with Power to legislate for us in all cases whatsoever.

He has abdicated Government here, by declaring us out of his Protection and waging War against us.

He has plundered our seas, ravaged our Coasts, burnt our towns, and destroyed the lives of our people.

He is at this time transporting large armies of foreign mercenaries to compleat the works of death, desolation and tyranny, already begun with circumstances of Cruelty & perfidy scarcely parallel in the most barbarous ages, and totally unworthy the Head of a civilized nation.

He has constrained our fellow Citizens taken Captive on the high Seas to bear Arms against their Country, to become the executioners of their friends and Brethren, or to fall themselves by their Hands.

He has excited domestic insurrections amongst us, and has endeavoured to bring on the inhabitants of our frontiers, the merciless Indian Savages, whose known rule of warfare, is an undistinguished destruction of all ages, sexes and conditions.

In every stage of these Oppressions We have Petitioned for Redress in the most humble terms: Our repeated Petitions have been answered only by repeated injury. A Prince, whose character is thus marked by every act which may define a Tyrant, is unfit to be the ruler of a free People.

Nor have We been wanting in attention to our British brethren. We have warned them from time to time of attempts by their legislature to extend an unwarrantable jurisdiction over us. We have reminded them of the circumstances of our emigration and settlement here. We have appealed to their native justice and magnanimity, and we have conjured them by the ties of our common kindred to disavow these usurpations, which would inevitably interrupt our connections and correspondence. They too have been deaf to the voice of justice and of consanguinity. We must, therefore, acquiesce in the necessity, which denounces our Separation, and hold them, as we hold the rest of mankind, Enemies in War, in Peace Friends.

We, therefore, the Representatives of the United States of America, in General Congress, Assembled, appealing to the Supreme Judge of the world for the rectitude of our intentions, do, in the Name, and by Authority of the good People of these Colonies, solemnly publish and declare, That these United Colonies are, and of Right ought to be Free and Independent States; that they are Absolved from all Allegiance to the British Crown, and that all political connection between them and the State of Great Britain, is and ought to be totally dissolved; and that as Free and Independent States, they have full Power to levy War, conclude Peace, contract Alliances, establish Commerce, and to do all other Acts and Things which Independent States may of right do. And for the support of this Declaration, with a firm reliance on the Protection of Divine Providence, we mutually pledge to each other our Lives, our Fortunes and our sacred Honor.

John Hancock

New Hampshire:
Josiah Bartlett,
William Whipple,
Matthew Thornton.

Massachusetts-Bay:
Samuel Adams,
John Adams,

Robert Treat Paine,
Elbridge Gerry.

Rhode Island:
Stephen Hopkins,
William Ellery.

Connecticut:
Roger Sherman,

Samuel Huntington,
William Williams,
Oliver Wolcott.

New York:
William Floyd,
Philip Livingston,
Francis Lewis,

Lewis Morris.

Pennsylvania:
Robert Morris,
Benjamin Harris,
Benjamin Franklin,
John Morton,
George Clymer,

James Smith,
George Taylor,
James Wilson,
George Ross.

Delaware:
Caesar Rodney,
George Read,
Thomas McKean.

Georgia:
Button Gwinnett,

Lyman Hall,
George Walton.

Maryland:
Samuel Chase,
William Paca,
Thomas Stone,
Charles Carroll of Carrollton.

Virginia:
George Wythe,
Richard Henry Lee,

Thomas Jefferson,
Benjamin Harrison,
Thomas Nelson Jr.,
Francis Lightfoot Lee,
Carter Braxton.

North Carolina:
William Hooper,
Joseph Hewes,
John Penn.

South Carolina:

Edward Rutledge,
Thomas Heyward Jr.,
Thomas Lynch Jr.,
Arthur Middleton.

New Jersey:
Richard Stockton,
John Witherspoon,
Francis Hopkinson,
John Hart,
Abraham Clark.

3

CONSTITUTION OF THE UNITED STATES

The United States Constitution was written at a convention that Congress called on February 21, 1787, for the purpose of recommending amendments to the Articles of Confederation. Every state but Rhode Island sent delegates to Philadelphia, where the convention met that summer. The delegates decided to write an entirely new constitution, completing their labors on September 17. Nine states (the number the Constitution itself stipulated as sufficient) ratified by June 21, 1788.

The framers of the Constitution included only six paragraphs on the Supreme Court. Article III, Section 1, created the Supreme Court and the federal system of courts. It provided that "[t]he judicial power of the United States, shall be vested in one supreme Court," and whatever inferior courts Congress "from time to time" saw fit to establish. Article III, Section 2, delineated the types of cases and controversies that should be considered by a federal—rather than a state—court. But beyond this, the Constitution left many of the particulars of the Supreme Court and the federal court system for Congress to decide in later years in judiciary acts.

We the People of the United States, in Order to form a more perfect Union, establish Justice, insure domestic Tranquility, provide for the common defence, promote the general Welfare, and secure the Blessings of Liberty to ourselves and our Posterity, do ordain and establish this Constitution for the United States of America.

ARTICLE I

Section 1. All legislative Powers herein granted shall be vested in a Congress of the United States, which shall consist of a Senate and House of Representatives.

Section 2. The House of Representatives shall be composed of Members chosen every second Year by the People of the several States, and the Electors in each State shall have the Qualifications requisite for Electors of the most numerous Branch of the State Legislature.

No Person shall be a Representative who shall not have attained to the age of twenty five Years, and been seven Years a Citizen of the United States, and who shall not, when elected, be an Inhabitant of that State in which he shall be chosen.

[Representatives and direct Taxes shall be apportioned among the several States which may be included within this Union, according to their respective Numbers, which shall be determined by adding to the whole Number of free Persons, including those bound to Service for a Term of Years, and excluding Indians not taxed, three fifths of all other Persons.][1] The actual Enumeration shall be made within three Years after the first Meeting of the Congress of the United States, and within every subsequent Term of ten Years, in such Manner as they shall by Law direct. The Number of Representatives shall not exceed one for every thirty Thousand, but each State shall have at Least one Representative; and until such enumeration shall be made, the State of New Hampshire shall be entitled to chuse three, Massachusetts eight, Rhode-Island and Providence Plantations one, Connecticut five, New-York six, New Jersey four, Pennsylvania eight, Delaware one, Maryland six, Virginia ten, North Carolina five, South Carolina five, and Georgia three.

When vacancies happen in the Representation from any State, the Executive Authority thereof shall issue Writs of Election to fill such Vacancies.

The House of Representatives shall chuse their Speaker and other Officers; and shall have the sole Power of Impeachment.

Section 3. The Senate of the United States shall be composed of two Senators from each State, [chosen by the Legislature thereof,][2] for six Years; and each Senator shall have one Vote.

Immediately after they shall be assembled in Consequence of the first Election, they shall be divided as equally as may be into three Classes. The Seats of the Senators of the first Class shall be vacated at the Expiration of the second Year, of the second Class at the Expiration of the fourth Year, and of the third Class at the Expiration of the sixth Year, so that one third may be chosen every second Year; [and if Vacancies happen by Resignation, or otherwise, during the Recess of the Legislature of any State, the Executive thereof may make temporary Appointments until the next Meeting of the Legislature, which shall then fill such Vacancies.][3]

No Person shall be a Senator who shall not have attained to the Age of thirty Years, and been nine Years a Citizen of the United States, and who shall not, when elected, be an Inhabitant of that State for which he shall be chosen.

The Vice President of the United States shall be President of the Senate, but shall have no Vote, unless they be equally divided.

The Senate shall chuse their other Officers, and also a President pro tempore, in the Absence of the Vice President, or when he shall exercise the Office of President of the United States.

The Senate shall have the sole Power to try all Impeachments. When sitting for that Purpose, they shall be on Oath or Affirmation. When the President of the United States is tried, the Chief Justice shall preside: And no Person shall be convicted without the Concurrence of two thirds of the Members present.

Judgment in Cases of Impeachment shall not extend further than to removal from Office, and disqualification to hold and enjoy any Office of honor, Trust or Profit under the United States: but the Party convicted shall nevertheless be liable and subject to Indictment, Trial, Judgment and Punishment, according to Law.

Section 4. The Times, Places and Manner of holding Elections for Senators and Representatives, shall be prescribed in each State by the Legislature thereof; but the Congress may at any time by Law make or alter such Regulations, except as to the Places of chusing Senators.

The Congress shall assemble at least once in every Year, and such Meeting shall [be on the first Monday in December],[4] unless they shall by Law appoint a different Day.

Section 5. Each House shall be the Judge of the Elections, Returns and Qualifications of its own Members, and a Majority of each shall constitute a Quorum to do Business; but a smaller Number may adjourn from day to day, and may be authorized to compel the Attendance of absent Members, in such Manner, and under such Penalties as each House may provide.

Each House may determine the Rules of its Proceedings, punish its Members for disorderly Behaviour, and, with the Concurrence of two thirds, expel a Member.

Each House shall keep a Journal of its Proceedings, and from time to time publish the same, excepting such Parts as may in their Judgment require Secrecy; and the Yeas and Nays of the Members of either House on any question shall, at the Desire of one fifth of those Present, be entered on the Journal.

Neither House, during the Session of Congress, shall, without the Consent of the other, adjourn for more than three days, nor to any other Place than that in which the two Houses shall be sitting.

Section 6. The Senators and Representatives shall receive a Compensation for their Services, to be ascertained by Law, and paid out of the Treasury of the United States. They shall in all Cases, except Treason, Felony and Breach of the Peace, be privileged from Arrest during their Attendance at the Session of their respective Houses, and in going to and returning from the same; and for any Speech or Debate in either House, they shall not be questioned in any other Place.

No Senator or Representative shall, during the Time for which he was elected, be appointed to any civil Office under the Authority of the United States, which shall have been created, or the Emoluments whereof shall have been encreased during such time; and no Person holding any Office under the United States, shall be a Member of either House during his Continuance in Office.

Section 7. All Bills for raising Revenue shall originate in the House of Representatives; but the Senate may propose or concur with Amendments as on other Bills.

Every Bill which shall have passed the House of Representatives and the Senate, shall, before it become a Law, be presented to the President of the United States; If he approve he shall sign it, but if not he shall return it, with his Objections to that House in which it shall have originated, who shall enter the Objections at large on their Journal, and proceed to reconsider it. If after such Reconsideration two thirds of that House shall agree to pass the Bill, it shall be sent, together with the Objections, to the other House, by which it shall likewise be reconsidered, and if approved by two thirds of that House, it shall become a Law. But in all such Cases the Votes of both Houses shall be determined by yeas and Nays, and the Names of the Persons voting for and against the Bill shall be entered on the Journal of each House respectively. If any Bill shall not be returned by the President within ten Days (Sundays excepted) after it shall have been presented to him, the Same shall be a Law, in like Manner as if he had signed it, unless the Congress by their Adjournment prevent its Return, in which Case it shall not be a Law.

Every Order, Resolution, or Vote to which the Concurrence of the Senate and House of Representatives may be necessary (except on a question of Adjournment) shall be presented to the President of the United States; and before the Same shall take Effect, shall be approved by him, or being disapproved by him, shall be repassed by two thirds of the Senate and House of Representatives, according to the Rules and Limitations prescribed in the Case of a Bill.

Section 8. The Congress shall have Power To lay and collect Taxes, Duties, Imposts and Excises, to pay the Debts and provide for the common Defence and general Welfare of the United States; but all Duties, Imposts and Excises shall be uniform throughout the United States;

To borrow Money on the credit of the United States;

To regulate Commerce with foreign Nations, and among the several States, and with the Indian Tribes;

To establish an uniform Rule of Naturalization, and uniform Laws on the subject of Bankruptcies throughout the United States;

To coin Money, regulate the Value thereof, and of foreign Coin, and fix the Standard of Weights and Measures;

To provide for the Punishment of counterfeiting the Securities and current Coin of the United States;

To establish Post Offices and post Roads;

To promote the Progress of Science and useful Arts, by securing for limited Times to Authors and Inventors the exclusive Right to their respective Writings and Discoveries;

To constitute Tribunals inferior to the supreme Court;

To define and punish Piracies and Felonies committed on the high Seas, and Offences against the Law of Nations;

To declare War, grant Letters of Marque and Reprisal, and make Rules concerning Captures on Land and Water;

To raise and support Armies, but no Appropriation of Money to that Use shall be for a longer Term than two Years;

To provide and maintain a Navy;

To make Rules for the Government and Regulation of the land and naval Forces;

To provide for calling forth the Militia to execute the Laws of the Union, suppress Insurrections and repel Invasions;

To provide for organizing, arming, and disciplining, the Militia, and for governing such Part of them as may be employed in the Service of the United States, reserving to the States respectively, the Appointment of the Officers, and the Authority of training the Militia according to the discipline prescribed by Congress;

To exercise exclusive Legislation in all Cases whatsoever, over such District (not exceeding ten Miles square) as may, by Cession of particular States, and the Acceptance of Congress, become the Seat of the Government of the United States, and to exercise like Authority over all Places purchased by the Consent of the Legislature of the State in which the Same shall be, for the Erection of Forts, Magazines, Arsenals, dock-Yards, and other needful Buildings;—And

To make all Laws which shall be necessary and proper for carrying into Execution the foregoing Powers, and all other Powers vested by this Constitution in the Government of the United States, or in any Department or Officer thereof.

Section 9. The Migration or Importation of such Persons as any of the States now existing shall think proper to admit, shall not be prohibited by the Congress prior to the Year one thousand eight hundred and eight, but a Tax or duty may be imposed on such Importation, not exceeding ten dollars for each Person.

The Privilege of the Writ of Habeas Corpus shall not be suspended, unless when in Cases of Rebellion or Invasion the public Safety may require it.

No Bill of Attainder or ex post facto Law shall be passed.

No Capitation, or other direct, Tax shall be laid, unless in Proportion to the Census or Enumeration herein before directed to be taken.[5]

No Tax or Duty shall be laid on Articles exported from any State.

No Preference shall be given by any Regulation of Commerce or Revenue to the Ports of one State over those of another; nor shall Vessels bound to, or from, one State, be obliged to enter, clear, or pay Duties in another.

No Money shall be drawn from the Treasury, but in Consequence of Appropriations made by Law; and a regular Statement and Account of the Receipts and Expenditures of all public Money shall be published from time to time.

No Title of Nobility shall be granted by the United States: And no Person holding any Office of Profit or Trust under them, shall, without the Consent of the Congress, accept of any present, Emolument, Office, or Title, of any kind whatever, from any King, Prince, or foreign State.

Section 10. No State shall enter into any Treaty, Alliance, or Confederation; grant Letters of Marque and Reprisal; coin Money; emit Bills of Credit; make any Thing but gold and silver Coin a Tender in Payment of Debts; pass any Bill of Attainder, ex post facto Law, or Law impairing the Obligation of Contracts, or grant any Title of Nobility.

No State shall, without the Consent of the Congress, lay any Imposts or Duties on Imports or Exports, except what may be absolutely necessary for executing its inspection Laws: and the net Produce of all Duties and Imposts, laid by any State on Imports or Exports, shall be for the Use of the Treasury of the United States; and all such Laws shall be subject to the Revision and Control of the Congress.

No State shall, without the Consent of Congress, lay any Duty of Tonnage, keep Troops, or Ships of War in time of Peace, enter into any Agreement or Compact with another State, or with a foreign Power, or engage in War, unless actually invaded, or in such imminent Danger as will not admit of delay.

ARTICLE II

Section 1. The executive Power shall be vested in a President of the United States of America. He shall hold his Office during the Term of four Years, and, together with the Vice President, chosen for the same Term, be elected, as follows:

Each State shall appoint, in such Manner as the Legislature thereof may direct, a Number of Electors, equal to the whole Number of Senators and Representatives to which the State may be entitled in the Congress: but no Senator or Representative, or Person holding an Office of Trust or Profit under the United States, shall be appointed an Elector.

[The Electors shall meet in their respective States, and vote by Ballot for two Persons, of whom one at least shall not be an Inhabitant of the same State with themselves. And they shall make a List of all the Persons voted for, and of the

Number of Votes for each; which List they shall sign and certify, and transmit sealed to the Seat of the Government of the United States, directed to the President of the Senate. The President of the Senate shall, in the Presence of the Senate and House of Representatives, open all the Certificates, and the Votes shall then be counted. The Person having the greatest Number of Votes shall be the President, if such Number be a Majority of the whole Number of Electors appointed; and if there be more than one who have such Majority, and have an equal Number of Votes, then the House of Representatives shall immediately chuse by Ballot one of them for President; and if no Person have a Majority, then from the five highest on the list the said House shall in like Manner chuse the President. But in chusing the President, the Votes shall be taken by States, the Representation from each State having one Vote; A quorum for this Purpose shall consist of a Member or Members from two thirds of the States, and a Majority of all the States shall be necessary to a Choice. In every Case, after the Choice of the President, the Person having the greatest Number of Votes of the Electors shall be the Vice President. But if there should remain two or more who have equal Votes, the Senate shall chuse from them by Ballot the Vice President.][6]

The Congress may determine the Time of chusing the Electors, and the Day on which they shall give their Votes; which Day shall be the same throughout the United States.

No Person except a natural born Citizen, or a Citizen of the United States, at the time of the Adoption of this Constitution, shall be eligible to the Office of President; neither shall any Person be eligible to that Office who shall not have attained to the Age of thirty five Years, and been fourteen Years a Resident within the United States.

In Case of the Removal of the President from Office, or of his Death, Resignation, or Inability to discharge the Powers and Duties of the said Office,[7] the Same shall devolve on the Vice President, and the Congress may by Law provide for the Case of Removal, Death, Resignation or Inability, both of the President and Vice President, declaring what Officer shall then act as President, and such Officer shall act accordingly, until the Disability be removed, or a President shall be elected.

The President shall, at stated Times, receive for his Services, a Compensation, which shall neither be encreased nor diminished during the Period for which he shall have been elected, and he shall not receive within that Period any other Emolument from the United States, or any of them.

Before he enter on the Execution of his Office, he shall take the following Oath or Affirmation:—"I do solemnly swear (or affirm) that I will faithfully execute the Office of President of the United States, and will to the best of my Ability, preserve, protect and defend the Constitution of the United States."

Section 2. The President shall be Commander in Chief of the Army and Navy of the United States, and of the Militia of the several States, when called into the actual Service of the United States; he may require the Opinion, in writing, of the principal Officer in each of the executive Departments, upon any Subject relating to the Duties of their respective Offices, and he shall have Power to grant Reprieves and Pardons for Offences against the United States, except in Cases of Impeachment.

He shall have Power, by and with the Advice and Consent of the Senate, to make Treaties, provided two thirds of the Senators present concur; and he shall nominate, and by and with the Advice and Consent of the Senate, shall appoint Ambassadors, other public Ministers and Consuls, Judges of the supreme Court, and all other Officers of the United States, whose Appointments are not herein otherwise provided for, and which shall be established by Law: but the Congress may by Law vest the Appointment of such inferior Officers, as they think proper, in the President alone, in the Courts of Law, or in the Heads of Departments.

The President shall have Power to fill up all Vacancies that may happen during the Recess of the Senate, by granting Commissions which shall expire at the End of their next Session.

Section 3. He shall from time to time give to the Congress Information of the State of the Union, and recommend to their Consideration such Measures as he shall judge necessary and expedient; he may, on extraordinary Occasions, convene both Houses, or either of them, and in Case of Disagreement between them, with Respect to the Time of Adjournment, he may adjourn them to such Time as he shall think proper; he shall receive Ambassadors and other public Ministers; he shall take Care that the Laws be faithfully executed, and shall Commission all the Officers of the United States.

Section 4. The President, Vice President and all civil Officers of the United States, shall be removed from Office on Impeachment for, and Conviction of, Treason, Bribery, or other high Crimes and Misdemeanors.

ARTICLE III

Section 1. The judicial Power of the United States, shall be vested in one supreme Court, and in such inferior Courts as the Congress may from time to time ordain and establish. The Judges, both of the supreme and inferior Courts, shall hold their Offices during good Behaviour, and shall, at stated Times, receive for their Services, a Compensation, which shall not be diminished during their Continuance in Office.

Section 2. The judicial Power shall extend to all Cases, in Law and Equity, arising under this Constitution, the Laws of the United States, and Treaties made, or which shall be made, under their Authority; —to all Cases affecting Ambassadors, other public Ministers and Consuls; —to all Cases of admiralty and maritime Jurisdiction; —to Controversies to which the United States shall be a Party; —to Controversies between two or more States; —between a State and Citizens of another State; —between Citizens of different States; —between Citizens of the same State claiming Lands under Grants of different States, and between a State, or the Citizens thereof, and foreign States, Citizens or Subjects.[8]

In all Cases affecting Ambassadors, other public Ministers and Consuls, and those in which a State shall be Party, the supreme Court shall have original Jurisdiction. In all the other Cases before mentioned, the supreme Court shall have appellate Jurisdiction, both as to Law and Fact, with such Exceptions, and under such Regulations as the Congress shall make.

The Trial of all Crimes, except in Cases of Impeachment, shall be by Jury; and such Trial shall be held in the State where the said Crimes shall have been committed; but when not committed within any State, the Trial shall be at such Place or Places as the Congress may by Law have directed.

Section 3. Treason against the United States, shall consist only in levying War against them, or in adhering to their Enemies, giving them Aid and Comfort. No Person shall be convicted of Treason unless on the Testimony of two Witnesses to the same overt Act, or on Confession in open Court.

The Congress shall have Power to declare the Punishment of Treason, but no Attainder of Treason shall work Corruption of Blood, or Forfeiture except during the Life of the Person attainted.

ARTICLE IV

Section 1. Full Faith and Credit shall be given in each State to the public Acts, Records, and judicial Proceedings of every other State. And the Congress may by general Laws prescribe the Manner in which such Acts, Records and Proceedings shall be proved, and the Effect thereof.

Section 2. The Citizens of each State shall be entitled to all Privileges and Immunities of Citizens in the several States.

A Person charged in any State with Treason, Felony, or other Crime, who shall flee from Justice, and be found in another State, shall on Demand of the executive Authority of the State from which he fled, be delivered up, to be removed to the State having Jurisdiction of the Crime.

[No Person held to Service or Labour in one State, under the Laws thereof, escaping into another, shall, in Consequence of any Law or Regulation therein, be discharged from such Service or Labour, but shall be delivered up on Claim of the Party to whom such Service or Labour may be due.][9]

Section 3. New States may be admitted by the Congress into this Union; but no new State shall be formed or erected within the Jurisdiction of any other State; nor any State be formed by the Junction of two or more States, or Parts of States, without the Consent of the Legislatures of the States concerned as well as of the Congress.

The Congress shall have Power to dispose of and make all needful Rules and Regulations respecting the Territory or other Property belonging to the United States; and nothing in this Constitution shall be so construed as to Prejudice any Claims of the United States, or of any particular State.

Section 4. The United States shall guarantee to every State in this Union a Republican Form of Government, and shall protect each of them against Invasion; and on Application of the Legislature, or of the Executive (when the Legislature cannot be convened) against domestic Violence.

ARTICLE V

The Congress, whenever two thirds of both Houses shall deem it necessary, shall propose Amendments to this Constitution, or, on the Application of the Legislatures of two thirds of the several States, shall call a Convention for proposing Amendments, which, in either Case, shall be valid to all Intents and Purposes, as Part of this Constitution, when ratified by the Legislatures of three fourths of the several States, or by Conventions in three fourths thereof, as the one or the other Mode of Ratification may be proposed by the Congress; Provided [that no Amendment which may be made prior to the Year One thousand eight hundred and eight shall in any Manner affect the first and fourth Clauses in the Ninth Section of the first Article; and][10] that no State, without its Consent, shall be deprived of its equal Suffrage in the Senate.

ARTICLE VI

All Debts contracted and Engagements entered into, before the Adoption of this Constitution, shall be as valid against the United States under this Constitution, as under the Confederation.

This Constitution, and the Laws of the United States which shall be made in Pursuance thereof; and all Treaties made, or which shall be made, under the Authority of the United States, shall be the supreme Law of the Land; and the Judges in every State shall be bound thereby, any Thing in the Constitution or Laws of any State to the Contrary notwithstanding.

The Senators and Representatives before mentioned, and the Members of the several State Legislatures, and all executive and judicial Officers, both of the United States and of the several States, shall be bound by Oath or Affirmation, to support this Constitution; but no religious Test shall ever be required as a Qualification to any Office or public Trust under the United States.

ARTICLE VII

The Ratification of the Conventions of nine States, shall be sufficient for the Establishment of this Constitution between the States so ratifying the Same.

Done in Convention by the Unanimous Consent of the States present the Seventeenth Day of September in the Year of our Lord one thousand seven hundred and Eighty seven and of the Independence of the United States of America the Twelfth. IN WITNESS whereof We have hereunto subscribed our Names,

George Washington, President and deputy from Virginia, and thirty-eight other delegates.

[The language of the original Constitution, not including the Amendments, was adopted by a convention of the states on September 17, 1787, and was subsequently ratified by the states on the following dates: Delaware, December 7, 1787; Pennsylvania, December 12, 1787; New Jersey, December 18, 1787; Georgia, January 2, 1788; Connecticut, January 9, 1788; Massachusetts, February 6, 1788; Maryland, April 28, 1788; South Carolina, May 23, 1788; New Hampshire, June 21, 1788.

Ratification was completed on June 21, 1788.

The Constitution subsequently was ratified by Virginia, June 25, 1788; New York, July 26, 1788; North Carolina, November 21, 1789; Rhode Island, May 29, 1790; and Vermont, January 10, 1791.]

AMENDMENTS

AMENDMENT I

(First ten amendments ratified December 15, 1791.)

Congress shall make no law respecting an establishment of religion, or prohibiting the free exercise thereof; or abridging the freedom of speech, or of the press; or the right of the people peaceably to assemble, and to petition the Government for a redress of grievances.

AMENDMENT II

A well regulated Militia, being necessary to the security of a free State, the right of the people to keep and bear Arms, shall not be infringed.

AMENDMENT III

No Soldier shall, in time of peace be quartered in any house, without the consent of the Owner, nor in time of war, but in a manner to be prescribed by law.

AMENDMENT IV

The right of the people to be secure in their persons, houses, papers, and effects, against unreasonable searches and seizures, shall not be violated, and no Warrants shall issue, but upon probable cause, supported by Oath or affirmation, and particularly describing the place to be searched, and the persons or things to be seized.

AMENDMENT V

No person shall be held to answer for a capital, or otherwise infamous crime, unless on a presentment or indictment of a Grand Jury, except in cases arising in the land or naval forces, or in the Militia, when in actual service in time of War or public danger; nor shall any person be subject for the same offence to be twice put in jeopardy of life or limb; nor shall be compelled in any criminal case to be a witness against himself, nor be deprived of life, liberty, or property, without due process of law; nor shall private property be taken for public use, without just compensation.

AMENDMENT VI

In all criminal prosecutions, the accused shall enjoy the right to a speedy and public trial, by an impartial jury of the State and district wherein the crime shall have been committed, which district shall have been previously ascertained by law, and to be informed of the nature and cause of the accusation; to be confronted with the witnesses against him; to have compulsory process for obtaining witnesses in his favor, and to have the Assistance of Counsel for his defence.

AMENDMENT VII

In Suits at common law, where the value in controversy shall exceed twenty dollars, the right of trial by jury shall be preserved, and no fact tried by a jury, shall be otherwise re-examined in any Court of the United States, than according to the rules of the common law.

AMENDMENT VIII

Excessive bail shall not be required, nor excessive fines imposed, nor cruel and unusual punishments inflicted.

AMENDMENT IX

The enumeration in the Constitution, of certain rights, shall not be construed to deny or disparage others retained by the people.

AMENDMENT X

The powers not delegated to the United States by the Constitution, nor prohibited by it to the States, are reserved to the States respectively, or to the people.

AMENDMENT XI
(RATIFIED FEBRUARY 7, 1795)

The Judicial power of the United States shall not be construed to extend to any suit in law or equity, commenced or prosecuted against one of the United States by Citizens of another State, or by Citizens or Subjects of any Foreign State.

AMENDMENT XII
(RATIFIED JUNE 15, 1804)

The Electors shall meet in their respective states and vote by ballot for President and Vice-President, one of whom, at least, shall not be an inhabitant of the same state with themselves; they shall name in their ballots the person voted for as President, and in distinct ballots the person voted for as Vice-President, and they shall make distinct lists of all persons voted for as President, and of all persons voted for as Vice-President, and of the number of votes for each, which lists they shall sign and certify, and transmit sealed to the seat of the government of the United States, directed to the President of the Senate; — The President of the Senate shall, in the presence of the Senate and House of Representatives, open all the certificates and the votes shall then be counted; — The person having the greatest number of votes for President, shall be the President, if such number be a majority of the whole number of Electors appointed; and if no person have such majority, then from the persons having the highest numbers not exceeding three on the list of those voted for as President, the House of Representatives shall choose immediately, by ballot, the President. But in choosing the President, the votes shall be taken by states, the representation from each state having one vote; a quorum for this purpose shall consist of a member or members from two-thirds of the states, and a majority of all the states shall be necessary to a choice. [And if the House of Representatives shall not choose a President whenever the right of choice shall devolve upon them, before the fourth day of March next following, then the Vice-President shall act as President, as in the case of the death or other constitutional disability of the President. —][11] The person having the greatest number of votes as Vice-President, shall be the Vice-President, if such number be a majority of the whole number of Electors appointed, and if no person have a majority, then from the two highest numbers on the list, the Senate shall choose the Vice-President; a quorum for the purpose shall consist of two-thirds of the whole number of Senators, and a majority of the whole number shall be necessary to a choice. But no person constitutionally ineligible to the office of President shall be eligible to that of Vice-President of the United States.

AMENDMENT XIII
(RATIFIED DECEMBER 6, 1865)

Section 1. Neither slavery nor involuntary servitude, except as a punishment for crime whereof the party shall have been duly convicted, shall exist within the United States, or any place subject to their jurisdiction.

Section 2. Congress shall have power to enforce this article by appropriate legislation.

AMENDMENT XIV
(RATIFIED JULY 9, 1868)

Section 1. All persons born or naturalized in the United States, and subject to the jurisdiction thereof, are citizens of the United States and of the State wherein they reside. No State shall make or enforce any law which shall abridge the privileges or immunities of citizens of the United States; nor shall any State deprive any person of life, liberty, or property, without due process of law; nor deny to any person within its jurisdiction the equal protection of the laws.

Section 2. Representatives shall be apportioned among the several States according to their respective numbers, counting the whole number of persons in each State, excluding Indians not taxed. But when the right to vote at any election for the choice of electors for President and Vice President of the United States, Representatives in Congress, the Executive and Judicial officers of a State, or the members of the Legislature thereof, is denied to any of the male inhabitants of such State, being twenty-one years of age,[12] and citizens of the United States, or in any way abridged, except for participation in rebellion, or other crime, the basis of representation therein shall be reduced in the proportion which the number of such male citizens shall bear to the whole number of male citizens twenty-one years of age in such State.

Section 3. No person shall be a Senator or Representative in Congress, or elector of President and Vice President, or hold any Office, civil or military, under the United States, or under any State, who, having previously taken an oath, as a member of Congress, or as an officer of the United States, or as a member of any State legislature, or as an executive or judicial officer of any State, to support the Constitution of the United States, shall have engaged in insurrection or rebellion against the same, or given aid or comfort to the enemies thereof. But Congress may by a vote of two-thirds of each House, remove such disability.

Section 4. The validity of the public debt of the United States, authorized by law, including debts incurred for payment of pensions and bounties for services in suppressing insurrection or rebellion, shall not be questioned. But neither the United States nor any State shall assume or pay any debt or obligation incurred in aid of insurrection or rebellion against the United States, or any claim for the loss or emancipation of any slave; but all such debts, obligations and claims shall be held illegal and void.

Section 5. The Congress shall have power to enforce, by appropriate legislation, the provisions of this article.

AMENDMENT XV
(RATIFIED FEBRUARY 3, 1870)

Section 1. The right of citizens of the United States to vote shall not be denied or abridged by the United States or by any State on account of race, color, or previous condition of servitude.

Section 2. The Congress shall have power to enforce this article by appropriate legislation.

AMENDMENT XVI
(RATIFIED FEBRUARY 3, 1913)

The Congress shall have power to lay and collect taxes on incomes, from whatever source derived, without apportionment among the several States, and without regard to any census or enumeration.

AMENDMENT XVII
(RATIFIED APRIL 8, 1913)

The Senate of the United States shall be composed of two Senators from each State, elected by the people thereof, for six years; and each Senator shall have one vote. The electors in each State shall have the qualifications requisite for electors of the most numerous branch of the State legislatures.

When vacancies happen in the representation of any State in the Senate, the executive authority of such State shall issue writs of election to fill such vacancies: Provided, That the legislature of any State may empower the executive thereof to make temporary appointments until the people fill the vacancies by election as the legislature may direct.

This amendment shall not be so construed as to affect the election or term of any Senator chosen before it becomes valid as part of the Constitution.

AMENDMENT XVIII
(RATIFIED JANUARY 16, 1919)

Section 1. After one year from the ratification of this article the manufacture, sale, or transportation of intoxicating liquors within, the importation thereof into, or the exportation thereof from the United States and all territory subject to the jurisdiction thereof for beverage purposes is hereby prohibited.

Section 2. The Congress and the several States shall have concurrent power to enforce this article by appropriate legislation.

Section 3. This article shall be inoperative unless it shall have been ratified as an amendment to the Constitution by the legislatures of the several States, as provided in the Constitution, within seven years from the date of the submission hereof to the States by the Congress.[13]

AMENDMENT XIX
(RATIFIED AUGUST 18, 1920)

The right of citizens of the United States to vote shall not be denied or abridged by the United States or by any State on account of sex.

Congress shall have power to enforce this article by appropriate legislation.

AMENDMENT XX
(RATIFIED JANUARY 23, 1933)

Section 1. The terms of the President and Vice President shall end at noon on the 20th day of January, and the terms of Senators and Representatives at noon on the 3d day of January, of the years in which such terms would have ended if this article had not been ratified; and the terms of their successors shall then begin.

Section 2. The Congress shall assemble at least once in every year, and such meeting shall begin at noon on the 3d day of January, unless they shall by law appoint a different day.

Section 3.[14] If, at the time fixed for the beginning of the term of the President, the President elect shall have died, the Vice President elect shall become President. If a President shall not have been chosen before the time fixed for the beginning of his term, or if the President elect shall have failed to qualify, then the Vice President elect shall act as President until a President shall have qualified; and the Congress may by law provide for the case wherein neither a President elect nor a Vice President elect shall have qualified, declaring who shall then act as President, or the manner in which one who is to act shall be selected, and such person shall act accordingly until a President or Vice President shall have qualified.

Section 4. The Congress may by law provide for the case of the death of any of the persons from whom the House of Representatives may choose a President whenever the right of choice shall have devolved upon them, and for the case of the death of any of the persons from whom the Senate may choose a Vice President whenever the right of choice shall have devolved upon them.

Section 5. Sections 1 and 2 shall take effect on the 15th day of October following the ratification of this article.

Section 6. This article shall be inoperative unless it shall have been ratified as an amendment to the Constitution by the legislatures of three-fourths of the several States within seven years from the date of its submission.

AMENDMENT XXI
(RATIFIED DECEMBER 5, 1933)

Section 1. The eighteenth article of amendment to the Constitution of the United States is hereby repealed.

Section 2. The transportation or importation into any State, Territory, or possession of the United States for delivery or use therein of intoxicating liquors, in violation of the laws thereof, is hereby prohibited.

Section 3. This article shall be inoperative unless it shall have been ratified as an amendment to the Constitution by conventions in the several States, as provided in the Constitution, within seven years from the date of the submission hereof to the States by the Congress.

AMENDMENT XXII
(RATIFIED FEBRUARY 27, 1951)

Section 1. No person shall be elected to the office of the President more than twice, and no person who has held the office of President, or acted as President, for more than two years of a term to which some other person was elected President shall be elected to the office of the President more than once. But this Article shall not apply to any person holding the office of President when this Article was proposed by the Congress, and shall not prevent any person who may be holding the office of President, or acting as President, during the term within which this Article becomes operative from holding the office of President or acting as President during the remainder of such term.

Section 2. This article shall be inoperative unless it shall have been ratified as an amendment to the Constitution by the legislatures of three-fourths of the several States within seven years from the date of its submission to the States by the Congress.

AMENDMENT XXIII
(RATIFIED MARCH 29, 1961)

Section 1. The District constituting the seat of Government of the United States shall appoint in such manner as the Congress may direct:

A number of electors of President and Vice President equal to the whole number of Senators and Representatives in Congress to which the District would be entitled if it were a State, but in no event more than the least populous State; they shall be in addition to those appointed by the States, but they shall be considered, for the purposes of the election of President and Vice President, to be electors appointed by a State; and they shall meet in the District and perform such duties as provided by the twelfth article of amendment.

Section 2. The Congress shall have power to enforce this article by appropriate legislation.

AMENDMENT XXIV
(RATIFIED JANUARY 23, 1964)

Section 1. The right of citizens of the United States to vote in any primary or other election for President or Vice President, for electors for President or Vice President, or for Senator or Representative in Congress, shall not be denied or abridged by the United States or any State by reason of failure to pay any poll tax or other tax.

Section 2. The Congress shall have power to enforce this article by appropriate legislation.

AMENDMENT XXV
(RATIFIED FEBRUARY 10, 1967)

Section 1. In case of the removal of the President from office or of his death or resignation, the Vice President shall become President.

Section 2. Whenever there is a vacancy in the office of the Vice President, the President shall nominate a Vice President who shall take office upon confirmation by a majority vote of both Houses of Congress.

Section 3. Whenever the President transmits to the President pro tempore of the Senate and the Speaker of the House of Representatives his written declaration that he is unable to discharge the powers and duties of his office, and until he transmits to them a written declaration to the contrary, such powers and duties shall be discharged by the Vice President as Acting President.

Section 4. Whenever the Vice President and a majority of either the principal officers of the executive departments or of such other body as Congress may by law provide, transmit to the President pro tempore of the Senate and the Speaker of the House of Representatives their written declaration that the President is unable to discharge the powers and duties of his office, the Vice President shall immediately assume the powers and duties of the office as Acting President.

Thereafter, when the President transmits to the President pro tempore of the Senate and the Speaker of the House of Representatives his written declaration that no inability exists, he shall resume the powers and duties of his office unless the Vice President and a majority of either the principal officers of the executive departments or of such other body as Congress may by law provide, transmit within four days to the President pro tempore of the Senate and the Speaker of the House of Representatives their written declaration that the President is unable to discharge the powers and duties of his office. Thereupon Congress shall decide the issue, assembling within forty-eight hours for that purpose if not in session. If the Congress, within twenty-one days after receipt of the latter written declaration, or, if Congress is not in session, within twenty-one days after Congress is required to assemble, determines by two-thirds vote of both Houses that the President is unable to discharge the powers and duties of his office, the Vice President shall continue to discharge the same as Acting President; otherwise, the President shall resume the powers and duties of his office.

AMENDMENT XXVI (RATIFIED JULY 1, 1971)

Section 1. The right of citizens of the United States, who are eighteen years of age or older, to vote shall not be denied or abridged by the United States or by any State on account of age.

Section 2. The Congress shall have power to enforce this article by appropriate legislation.

AMENDMENT XXVII (RATIFIED MAY 7, 1992)

No law varying the compensation for the services of the Senators and Representatives shall take effect, until an election of Representatives shall have intervened.

Source: U.S. Congress, House, Committee on the Judiciary, The Constitution of the United States of America, as Amended, 100th Cong., 1st sess., 1987, H Doc 100–94.

NOTES

1. The part in brackets was changed by section 2 of the Fourteenth Amendment.
2. The part in brackets was changed by the first paragraph of the Seventeenth Amendment.
3. The part in brackets was changed by the second paragraph of the Seventeenth Amendment.
4. The part in brackets was changed by section 2 of the Twentieth Amendment.
5. The Sixteenth Amendment gave Congress the power to tax incomes.
6. The material in brackets was superseded by the Twelfth Amendment.
7. This provision was affected by the Twenty-fifth Amendment.
8. These clauses were affected by the Eleventh Amendment.
9. This paragraph was superseded by the Thirteenth Amendment.
10. Obsolete.
11. The part in brackets was superseded by Section 3 of the Twentieth Amendment.
12. See the Nineteenth and Twenty-sixth Amendments.
13. This amendment was repealed by Section 1 of the Twenty-first Amendment.
14. See the Twenty-fifth Amendment.

NOTES

CHAPTER 1

1. Emily Witt, "How the Survivors of Parkland Began the Never Again Movement," *The New Yorker*, February 19, 2018, https://www.newyorker.com/news/news-desk/how-the-survivors-of-parkland-began-the-never-again-movement.

2. Dahlia Lithwick, "They Were Trained for This Moment," *Slate*, February 28, 2018, https://slate.com/news-and-politics/2018/02/the-student-activists-of-marjory-stoneman-douglas-high-demonstrate-the-power-of-a-full-education.html.

3. Asma Khalid, "A New Generation's Political Awakening," NPR, April 21, 2018, https://www.npr.org/2018/04/ 21/604293152/a-new-generations-political-awakening.

4. Jonathan Bernstein, "Let Teenagers Vote," Bloomberg, February 21, 2018, https://www.bloomberg.com/view/articles/2018-02-21/expand-u-s-voting-rights-to-teenagers; Jonathan Bernstein, "Democracy Demands We Let Teenagers Vote," Bloomberg, March 13, 2018, https://www.bloomberg.com/view/articles/2018-03-13/democracy-demands-we-let-teenagers-get-the-vote.

5. E. J. Dionne, *Why Americans Hate Politics* (New York: Simon & Schuster, 1991), 354, 355.

6. Harold D. Lasswell, *Politics: Who Gets What, When, How* (New York: McGraw-Hill, 1938).

7. Joseph A. Schumpeter, *Capitalism, Socialism, and Democracy*, 3rd ed. (New York: Harper Colophon Books, 1950), 269–296.

8. Robert A. Dahl, *Pluralist Democracy in the United States* (Chicago, Ill.: Rand McNally, 1967).

9. Carole Pateman, *Participation and Democratic Theory* (New York: Cambridge University Press, 1970).

10. For an explanation of this view, see, for example, Russell L. Hanson, *The Democratic Imagination in America: Conversation With Our Past* (Princeton, N.J.: Princeton University Press, 1985), 55–91; and Gordon Wood, *The Creation of the American Republic, 1776–1787* (New York: Norton, 1969).

11. Eli Pariser, "Beware Online 'Filter Bubbles,'" March 2011, www.ted.com/talks/eli_pariser_beware_online_filter_bubbles?language=en; Mandy Zibart, "How to Escape Your News Bubble," January 21, 2016, medium.com/extra-extra/how-to-escape-your-news-bubble-3187c83fa481#.5wbplmiye.

12. "The Danger of the Social Media Information Bubble," *Science Daily*, democracychronicles.com/social-media-information/.

13. Pariser, "Beware Online 'Filter Bubbles.'"

CHAPTER 2

1. Chris Cillizza, "Three Sentences on Immigration Reform That Will Haunt Republicans in 2016," *Washington Post*, July 1, 2014, www.washingtonpost.com/blogs/the-fix/wp/2014/07/01/three-sentences-on-immigration-that-will-haunt-republicans-in-2016/.

2. Ashley Parker and Jonathan Martin, "Senate, 68–32, Passes Overhaul for Immigration," *New York Times*, June 27, 2013, www.nytimes.com/2013/06/28/us/politics/immigration-bill-clears-final-hurdle-o-senate-approval.html?_r=0.

3. Richard Gonzales, "Federal Appeals Court Deals Trump Another Setback On DACA," NPR, November 8, 2018, https://www.npr.org/2018/11/08/665916995/federal-appeals-court-deals-trump-another-setback-on-daca.

4. Tal Kopan, "How Trump changed the rules to arrest more non-criminal immigrants," CNN, March 2, 2018, https://www.cnn.com/2018/03/02/politics/ice-immigration-deportations/index.html.

5. Michele Norris, "As America Changes, Some Anxious Whites Feel Left Behind," *National Geographic*, April 2018, https://www.nationalgeographic.com/magazine/2018/04/race-rising-anxiety-white-america/.

6. Jerry Markon, "U.S. Illegal Immigrant Population Falls Below 11 Million, Continuing Nearly Decade-Long Decline, Report Says," *Washington Post*, January 20, 2016.

7. Max Bearak, "Even Before Trump, More Mexicans Were Leaving the U.S. Than Arriving," *Washington Post*, January 27, 2017, https://www.washingtonpost.com/news/worldviews/wp/2017/01/27/even-before-trump-more-mexicans-were-leaving-the-us-than-arriving/.

8. *Graham v. Richardson*, 403 U.S. 532 (1971).

9. See, for instance, Nicole Cusano, "Amherst Mulls Giving Non-citizens Right to Vote," *Boston Globe*, October 26, 1998, B1; "Casual Citizenship?" Editorial, *Boston Globe*, October 31, 1998, A18.

10. David M. Kennedy et al., *The American Pageant*, 12th ed. (Boston, Mass.: Houghton Mifflin, 2002), 731.

11. Jonathan Blitzer, "In Rural Tennessee, a Big ICE Raid Makes Some Conservative Voters Rethink Trump's Immigration Agenda," *New Yorker*, April 19, 2018, https://www.newyorker.com/news/dispatch/in-rural-tennessee-a-big-ice-raid-makes-some-conservative-voters-rethink-trumps-immigration-agenda.

12. Adam Liptak, "Blocking Parts of Arizona Law, Justices Allow Its Centerpiece," *New York Times*, June 26, 2012, www.nytimes.com/2012/06/26/us/supreme-court-rejects-part-of-arizona-immigration-aw.html?_r=1.

13. Brian Lawson, "UA Economist Finds Immigration Law Could Cost Alabama Millions in Lost Taxes, Billions in Lost GDP," *Huntsville Times*, January 31, 2012, blog.al.com/breaking/2012/01/ua_economist_finds_immigration.html.

14. Kate Zernike and Megan Thee-Brenan, "Poll Finds Tea Party Backers Wealthier and More Educated," *New York Times*, April 14, 2010.

15. Major Garrett, "Top Priority: Make Obama a One-Term President," *National Review*, October 23, 2010, www.nationaljournal.com/member/magazine/top-gop-priority-make-obama-a-one-term-president-20101023.

16. Amanda Taub, "The Rise of American Authoritarianism," *Vox*, March 1, 2016, www.vox.com/2016/3/1/11127424/trump-authoritarianism.

17. NYU professor Jonathan Haidt, quoted in Taub, "The Rise of American Authoritarianism."

18. Matt Grossmann, "Racial Attitudes and Political Correctness in the 2016 Presidential Election," Niskanen Center, May 10, 2018, https://niskanencenter.org/blog/racial-attitudes-and-political-correctness-in-the-2016-presidential-election/.

19. Benjamin R. Barber, "Foreword," in Grant Reeher and Joseph Cammarano, eds., *Education for Citizenship: Ideas and Innovations in Political Learning* (New York: Rowman & Littlefield, 1997), ix.

20. Alexa Ura, "Fiery Anti-Immigration GOP Nominee Dan Patrick Shifts Tome to Appeal to Hispanic Voters," *Huffington Post*, May 29, 2014, www.huffingtonpost.com/2014/05/29/dan-patrick-hispanic-voters-_n_5411060.html.

21. Carrie Budoff Brown, Jake Sherman, and Manu Raju, "2012 Election Puts Spotlight on Immigration Reform," *Politico*, November 11, 2012, www.politico.com/news/stories/1112/83552.html.

CHAPTER 3

1. Kirk Johnson, Richard Pérez-Peña, and Erik Eckholm, "Cautious Response to Armed Oregon Protest," *New York Times*, January 4, 2016, www.nytimes.com/2016/01/05/us/in-oregon-law-enforcement-faces-dilemma-in-confronting-armed-group.html; Julie Turkewitz and Kirk Johnson, "Ammon Bundy and 7 Oregon Protesters Held; La Voy Finicum Is Reported Dead," *New York Times*, January 27, 2016, www.nytimes.com/2016/01/27/us/oregon-armed-group-arrest-bundy.html; Associated Press, "In Total Surrender, Ammon Bundy Urges Followers to Stand Down," *New York Post*, January 28, 2016, nypost.com/2016/01/28/in-total-surrender-ammon-bundy-urges-followers-to-stand-down/.

2. David Barstow, "Tea Party Lights Fuse for Rebellion on Right," *New York Times*, February 15, 2010, www.nytimes.com/2010/02/16/us/politics/16teaparty.html?emc=eta1.

3. Tea Party, "About Us," www.teaparty.org/about-us/.

4. "Lubbock Co. Judge Warns of Potential Danger If Obama Is Re-elected," Fox 34 News, August 23, 2012, www.myfoxlubbock.com/news/local/story/Lubbock-tom-head-tax-rates-president-obama/PeO4Q8GeGEiy_FpxheUnmA.cspx.

5. Toni Lucy, "Anti-Government Forces Still Struggle to Recover From Oklahoma City Fallout," *USA Today*, May 9, 2000, 9A; Evan Thomas and Eve Conant, "Hate: Antigovernment Extremists Are on the Rise—and on the March," *Newsweek*, April 19, 2010.

6. See, for example, Jamelle Bouie, "How Trump Happened," March 13, 2016, www.slate.com/articles/news_and_politics/cover_story/2016/03/how_donald_trump_happened_racism_against_barack_obama.single.html.

7. There are many good illustrations of this point of view. See, for example, Gordon Wood, *The Creation of the American Republic, 1776–1787* (New York: Norton, 1969); Lawrence Henry Gipson, *The Coming of the Revolution, 1763–1775* (New York: Harper Torchbooks, 1962); Bernard Bailyn, *The Ideological Origins of the American Revolution*

(Cambridge, Mass.: Belknap, 1967); and Jack P. Greene, ed., *The Reinterpretation of the American Revolution, 1763–1789* (New York: Harper & Row, 1968).

8. Robert Darcy, Susan Welch, and Janet Clark, *Women, Elections, and Representation* (Lincoln: University of Nebraska Press, 1994), 5–6.

9. Donald R. Wright, *African Americans in the Colonial Era* (Arlington Heights, Ill.: Harlan Davidson, 1990), 52.

10. Ibid., 56.

11. Ibid., 57–58.

12. Lawrence Henry Gipson, "The American Revolution as an Aftermath of the Great War for the Empire, 1754–1765," in Edmund S. Morgan, ed., *The American Revolution* (Englewood Cliffs, N.J.: Prentice Hall, 1965), 160.

13. Bailyn, *The Ideological Origins of the American Revolution*, 160–229.

14. Gipson, "The American Revolution," 163.

15. James L. Roark, et al., *The American Promise: A History of the United States*, 3rd ed. (Boston, Mass.: Bedford/St. Martin's, 2005).

16. Thomas Paine, *Common Sense and Other Political Writings* (Indianapolis, Ind.: Bobbs-Merrill, 1953).

17. Cited in John L. Moore, *Speaking of Washington* (Washington, D.C.: Congressional Quarterly, 1993), 102–103.

18. John Locke, *Second Treatise of Government*, C. B. Macpherson, ed. (Indianapolis, Ind.: Hackett, 1980), 31.

19. Garry Wills, *Inventing America* (New York: Doubleday, 1978), 377.

20. Wright, *African Americans in the Colonial Era*, 122.

21. Ibid., 152.

22. Mary Beth Norton et al., *A People and a Nation* (Boston, Mass.: Houghton Mifflin, 1994), 159.

23. Darcy, Welch, and Clark, *Women, Elections, and Representation*, 8.

24. See, for example, Sally Smith Booth, *The Women of '76* (New York: Hastings House, 1973); and Charles E. Claghorn, *Women Patriots of the American Revolution: A Biographical Dictionary* (Metuchen, N.J.: Scarecrow Press, 1991).

25. Carl Holliday, *Woman's Life in Colonial Days* (Boston, Mass.: Cornhill, 1922), 143.

26. Wood, *The Creation of the American Republic*, 398–399.

27. Ibid., 404.

28. Alexander Hamilton, James Madison, and John Jay, *The Federalist Papers*, Clinton Rossiter, ed. (New York: New American Library, 1961), 84.

29. Adrienne Koch, "Introduction," in James Madison, *Notes of Debates in the Federal Convention of 1787* (New York: Norton, 1969), xiii.

30. Moore, *Speaking of Washington*, 9.

31. James Madison, *Notes of Debates in the Federal Convention of 1787 Reported by James Madison*, reissue ed. (New York: Norton, 1987).

32. There are many collections of Anti-Federalist writings. See, for example, W. B. Allen and Gordon Lloyd, eds., *The Essential Antifederalist* (Lanham, Md.: University Press of America, 1985); Cecilia Kenyon, ed., *The Antifederalists* (Indianapolis, Ind.: Bobbs Merrill, 1966); and Ralph Ketcham, *The Anti-Federalist Papers and the Constitutional Convention Debates* (New York: New American Library, 1986).

33. Hamilton, Madison, and Jay, *The Federalist Papers*, 322.

34. Ketcham, *The Anti-Federalist Papers*, 14.

35. Carl Hulse, "Recalling 1995 Bombing, Clinton Sees Parallels," *New York Times*, April 16, 2010.

CHAPTER 4

1. Andrew Harris, "Marijuana Mayhem Splits U.S. in Two as States Like Idaho Bust Travelers," *Idaho Statesman*, August 22, 2014, www.idahostatesman.com/2014/08/22/3336621/marijuana-mayhem-splits-us-in.html.

2. Dave Phillips, "Bid to Expand Medical Marijuana Business Faces Federal Hurdles," *New York Times*, August 23, 2014, www.nytimes.com/2014/08/24/us/bid-to-expand-medical-marijuana-business-faces-federal-hurdles.html; Joel Warner, "Charlotte's Web: Untangling One of Colorado's Biggest Cannabis Success Stories," *Westword*, December 3, 2014, http://www.westword.com/news/charlottes-web-untangling-one-of-colorados-biggest-cannabis-success-stories-6050830; Saundra Young, "Marijuana Stops Child's Severe Seizures," CNN, August 7, 2013, https://www.cnn.com/2013/08/07/health/charlotte-child-medical-marijuana/index.html.

3. James Higdon, "How a Pair of Kentucky Pols Are About to Legalize Hemp," *Politico*, August 4, 2018, https://www.politico.com/magazine/story/2018/08/04/mcconnell-comer-legalize-hemp-marijuana-kentucky-219156.

4. Carrie Johnson, "U.S. Eases Stance on Medical Marijuana," *Washington Post*, October 20, 2009.

5. Matt Laslo, "Why Is the White House Contradicting Trump's Pot Policy?," *Rolling Stone*, August 30, 2018, https://www.rollingstone.com/politics/politics-news/why-is-the-white-house-contradicting-trumps-pot-policy-717524/.

6. Lindsey Seavert, "Mom Charged After Giving Son Medical Marijuana," KARE (NBC affiliate), Minneapolis, MN, August 20, 2014, www.kare11.com/story/news/local/2014/08/20/mn-mom-charged-after-giving-son-medical-marijuana/14372025/.

7. Juliet Lapidos, "The Public Lightens Up About Weed," *New York Times*, July 26, 2014, www.nytimes.com/2014/07/27/opinion/sunday/high-time-the-public-lightens-up-about-weed.html.

8. Alexander Hamilton, James Madison, and John Jay, *The Federalist Papers*, Clinton Rossiter, ed. (New York: New American Library, 1961), 82.

9. James Madison, *Notes of Debates in the Federal Convention of 1787*, reissue ed. (New York: Norton, 1987), 86.

10. David M. Olson, *The Legislative Process* (Cambridge, Mass.: Harper & Row, 1980), 21–23.

11. Richard F. Fenno Jr., *The United States Senate: A Bicameral Perspective* (Washington, D.C.: American Enterprise Institute for Public Policy Research, 1982), 5.

12. Madison, *Notes of Debates in the Federal Convention of 1787*, 136, 158.

13. Hamilton, Madison, and Jay, *The Federalist Papers*, 465.

14. Lawrence S. Graham et al., *Politics and Government: A Brief Introduction*, 3rd ed. (Chatham, N.J.: Chatham House Publishers, 1994), 172–173.

15. Baron de Montesquieu, *The Spirit of the Laws*, Thomas Nugent, trans. (New York: Hafner Press, 1949), 152.

16. Hamilton, Madison, and Jay, *The Federalist Papers*, 322.

17. Ibid., 84.

18. Ibid., 322.

19. Ibid., 321–322.

20. For a full explanation of the bakery metaphors, see Morton Grodzins, *The American System* (Chicago, Ill.: Rand McNally, 1966). A more updated discussion of federalism can be found in Joseph Zimmerman, *Contemporary American Federalism: The Growth of National Power* (New York: Praeger, 1992).

21. Justice Louis Brandeis, *New State Ice Co. v. Liebmann*, 285 U.S. 262 (1932).

22. Eliza Griswold, "The Fracturing of Pennsylvania," *New York Times*, November 11, 2011; Wenonah Hauter, "For Democrats Nationwide, Pennsylvania Offer a Lens on the Widening Rift Over Fracking," *Huffington Post Politics*, September 25, 2013, www.huffingtonpost.com/wenonah-hauter/for-democrats-nationwide-_b_3981518.html.

23. Maxine Joselow, "If Elected, Democratic Governors Could Adopt California's Car Rules," November 6, 2018, *Scientific American*, https://www.scientificamerican.com/article/if-elected-democratic-governors-could-adopt-californias-car-rules/.

24. Elizabeth Weise, "Amazon's Second Headquarters Search Hits Crunch Time; One Group Warns 'It's a Race to the Bottom,'" *USA Today*, April 2, 2018, https://www.usatoday.com/story/tech/2018/04/02/amazons-second-headquarters-search-hits-crunch-time-one-group-warns-its-race-bottom/473705002/.

25. James Dao, "Red, Blue and Angry All Over," *New York Times*, January 16, 2005.

26. *McCulloch v. Maryland*, 4 Wheat. 316 (1819).

27. *Gibbons v. Ogden*, 9 Wheat. 1 (1824).

28. *Cooley v. Board of Wardens of Port of Philadelphia*, 53 U.S. (12 How.) 299 (1851).

29. *Dred Scott v. Sanford*, 60 U.S. 393 (1857).

30. *Pollock v. Farmer's Loan and Trust Company*, 1157 U.S. 429 (1895).

31. *Lochner v. New York*, 198 U.S. 45 (1905).

32. *Hammer v. Dagenhart*, 247 U.S. 251 (1918).

33. John Kincaid, "State-Federal Relations: Dueling Policies," in *The Book of the States 2008* (Lexington, Ky.: The Council of State Governments, 2008), 19.

34. Ibid.

35. Morris Fiorina, *Congress: Keystone of the Washington Establishment*, 2nd ed. (New Haven, Conn.: Yale University Press, 1989); John E. Chubb, "Federalism and the Bias for Centralization," in John E. Chubb and Paul E. Peterson, eds., *The New Directions in American Politics* (Washington, D.C.: Brookings Institution, 1985), 273–306.

36. U.S. Census Bureau, *Statistical Abstract of the United States, 2010* (Washington, D.C.: U.S. Census Bureau), Table 419.

37. Quote from Rochelle L. Stanfield, "Holding the Bag," *National Journal*, September 9, 1995, 2206.

38. Kincaid, "State-Federal Relations: Dueling Policies."

39. Martha Derthick, "Madison's Middle Ground in the 1980s," *Public Administration Review* (January–February 1987): 66–74.

40. Donald F. Kettl, "Mandates Forever," *Governing* (August 2003): 12; Tom Diemer, "Unfunded Mandate Bill Working Well," *Cleveland Plain Dealer*, February 8, 1998, 20A; Jonathan Walters, "The Accidental Tyranny of Congress," *Governing* (April 1997): 14.

41. "Keeping America Healthy," www.medicaid.gov/Medicaid-CHIP-Program-Information/By-Topics/Financing-and-Reimbursement/Financing-and-Reimbursement.html.

42. Alison Vekshin, "Tea Party Opposition to Stimulus Will Harm States, Kramer Says," *Business Week*, September 15, 2010, www.businessweek.com/news/2010-09-15/tea-party-opposition-to-stimulus-will-harm-states-kramer-says.html; Jeff Brady, "Stimulus Money Meets Mixed Reactions From States," *Weekend Edition*, National Public Radio, February 19, 2009, www.npr.org/templates/story/story.php?storyId=100731571; National Conference of State Legislatures, "State Budget Update, March 2011," www.ncsl.org/issues-research/budget/state-budget-update-march-2011.aspx.

43. Stephen C. Fehr, "Recession Could Reshape State Governments in Lasting Ways," Pew Center for

the States, February 11, 2010, www.stateline.org/live/details/story?contentId=454018.

44. Ibid.

45. Pickerill J. Mitchell and Cynthia J. Bowling, "Polarized Parties, Politics, and Policies: Fragmented Federalism in 2013–2014," *Publius: The Journal of Federalism* 44 (2014): 369–398; Shanna Rose and Cynthia J. Bowling, "The State of American Federalism 2014–15: Pathways to Policy in an Era of Party Polarization," *Publius: The Journal of Federalism* 45 (2015): 351–379.

46. "America Might See a New Constitutional Convention in a Few Years," *The Economist*, September 30, 2017, https://www.economist.com/news/briefing/21729735-if-it-did-would-be-dangerous-thing-america-might-see-new-constitutional-convention; Dennis Welch, "Lawmakers Converge on State Capitol to Talk Constitutional Convention," AZ Family, September 12, 2017, http://www.azfamily.com/story/36351851/lawmakers-converge-on-state-capitol-to-talk-constitutional-convention.

47. Hamilton, Madison, and Jay, *The Federalist Papers*, 278.

48. *Gonzales v. Raich*, 545 U.S. 1 (2005).

49. Johnson, "U.S. Eases Stance on Medical Marijuana."

50. Jacob Sullum, "The Power to Regulate Anything," *Los Angeles Times*, April 22, 2008.

51. Warren Richey, "Showdown Over Medical Marijuana," *Christian Science Monitor*, November 29, 2004.

CHAPTER 5

1. The White House, "Net Neutrality, President Obama's Plan for a Free and Open Internet," obamawhitehouse.archives.gov/node/323681.

2. "FCC Approves Sweeping Internet Regulation Plan, Obama Accused of Meddling," Foxnews.com, February 26, 2015, www.foxnews.com/politics/2015/02/26/fcc-approves-sweeping-internet-regulation-plan-obama-accused-meddling .html.

3. The White House, "Net Neutrality."

4. Mario Trujillo, "House Passes Bill Barring FCC From Regulating Internet Rates," April 15, 2016, thehill.com/policy/technology/276454-house-passes-bill-barring-fcc-from-regulating-internet-rates.

5. "FCC Approves Sweeping Internet Regulation Plan."

6. Trujillo, "House Passes Bill Barring FCC From Regulating Internet Rates."

7. Jim Puzzanghera, "Senate Takes First Step to Save Net Neutrality Rules, Voting to Overturn FCC Action," *Los Angeles Times*, May 16, 2018, www.latimes.com/business/la-fi-net-neutrality-senate-20180516-story.html.

8. Harper Neidig, "Dems Push to Restore Net Neutrality Rules," *The Hill*, May 6, 2016, thehill.com/policy/technology/386313-dems-push-to-restore-net-neutrality-rules.

9. *West Virginia Board of Education v. Barnette*, 319 U.S. 624 (1943).

10. *Hamdi v. Rumsfeld*, 124 S. Ct. 2633 (2004); *Rasul v. Bush*, 124 S. Ct. 2686 (2004).

11. *Hamdan v. Rumsfeld*, 548 U.S. 557 (2007).

12. *Korematsu v. United States*, 323 U.S. 214 (1944).

13. Associated Press, *The Cold War at Home and Abroad 1945–1953* (New York: Grollier, 1995), 145.

14. Robert Frederick Burk, *The Eisenhower Administration and Black Civil Rights* (Knoxville: University of Tennessee Press, 1984), 204.

15. Ben Conery, "Administration Seeks Patriot Act Extensions; Defies Liberties Groups," *Washington Times*, September 16, 2009, 1.

16. Jack N. Rakove, "James Madison and the Bill of Rights," in *This Constitution: From Ratification to the Bill of Rights*, American Political Science Association and American Historical Association (Washington, D.C.: Congressional Quarterly, 1988), 165.

17. David M. O'Brien, *Constitutional Law and Politics*, vol. 2 (New York: Norton, 1995), 300.

18. Ann Bowman and Richard Kearney, *State and Local Government*, 3rd ed. (Boston: Houghton Mifflin, 1996), 39.

19. *Barron v. The Mayor and City Council of Baltimore*, 7 Peters 243 (1833).

20. *Gitlow v. New York*, 268 U.S. 652 (1920), cited in O'Brien, *Constitutional Law and Politics*, 304. *Chicago, Burlington & Quincy Railroad Co. v. Chicago*, 166 U.S. 226 (1897).

21. Peter Irons, *Brennan vs. Rehnquist: The Battle for the Constitution* (New York: Knopf, 1994), 116.

22. O'Brien, *Constitutional Law and Politics*, 646.

23. Ibid., 647.

24. Ibid., 645; Henry J. Abraham and Barbara A. Perry, *Freedom and the Court* (New York: Oxford University Press, 1994), 223.

25. Ibid., 648.

26. Irons, *Brennan vs. Rehnquist*, 137.

27. *Abington School District v. Schempp*, 374 U.S. 203, 83 S. Ct. 1560 (1963); *Abington School District v. Schempp*; *Murray v. Curlett*, 374 U.S. 203 (1963); *Engel v. Vitale*, 370 U.S. 421, 82 S. Ct. 1261 (1962); *Epperson v. Arkansas*, 393 U.S. 97 (1968).

28. *Lemon v. Kurtzman*, 403 U.S. 602, 91 S. Ct. 2105 (1971).

29. O'Brien, *Constitutional Law and Politics*, 661.

30. *Lynch v. Donnelly*, 465 U.S. 668 (1984); *Wallace v. Jaffree*, 472 U.S. 38 (1985); *Edwards v. Aguillard*, 482 U.S. 578 (1987); *Board of Education of Westside Community Schools v. Mergens*, 496 U.S. 226 (1990); *Lee v. Weisman*, 112 S. Ct. 2649 (1992); *Santa Fe Independent School District v. Doe*, 530 U.S. 290 (2000); *Locke v. Davey*, 124 S. Ct. 1307 (2004); *Town of Greece v. Galloway*, 572 U.S.__ (2014).

31. Charles C. Hayes, "State Lawmakers Reignite School Wars Over Religion," The First Amendment Center, at Vanderbilt University and the Newseum, April 6, 2012, www.firstamendmentcenter.org/state-lawmakers-reignite-school-wars-over-religion.

32. *Cantwell v. Connecticut*, 310 U.S. 296 (1940).

33. *Minersville School District v. Gobitis*, 310 U.S. 586 (1940); *West Virginia State Board of Education v. Barnette*, 319 U.S. 624 (1943).

34. *Sherbert v. Verner*, 374 U.S. 398 (1963).

35. *Employment Division, Department of Human Resources v. Smith*, 494 U.S. 872 (1990).

36. *City of Boerne v. Flores*, 521 U.S. 507, 1997.

37. *Gonzales v. O Centro Espirata Beneficente Uniao do Vegetal*, 546 U.S. 418 (2006).

38. Adam Liptak, "Religious Groups Given 'Exception' to Work Bias Law," *New York Times*, January 11, 2012, www.nytimes.com/2012/01/12/us/supreme-court-recognizes-religious-exception-to-job-discrimination-laws.html.

39. Rodney K. Smith, "Does Obama Really Care About Religious Freedom in America?" *Christian Science Monitor*, February 17, 2012, www.csmonitor.com/Commentary/Opinion/2012/0217/Does-Obama-really-care-about-religious-freedom-in-America.

40. John L. Sullivan, James Piereson, and George Marcus, *Political Tolerance and American Democracy* (Chicago, Ill.: University of Chicago Press, 1982), 203.

41. John Cassidy, "Demonizing Edward Snowden: Which Side Are You on?" *New Yorker* blog, June 24, 2013, www.newyorker.com/online/blogs/johncassidy/2013/06/demonizing-edward-snowden-which-side-are-you-on.html.

42. O'Brien, *Constitutional Law and Politics*, 373; Samuel Walker, *In Defense of American Liberties: A History of the ACLU* (New York: Oxford University Press, 1990), 29.

43. Cited in Walker, *In Defense of American Liberties*, 14.

44. *Schenck v. United States*, 249 U.S. 47 (1919); *Debs v. United States*, 249 U.S. 211 (1919); *Frowerk v. United States*, 249 U.S. 204 (1919); *Abrams v. United States*, 250 U.S. 616 (1919).

45. *Whitney v. California*, 274 U.S. 357 (1927).

46. *Brandenburg v. Ohio*, 395 U.S. 444 (1969).

47. *Tinker v. Des Moines*, 393 U.S. 503 (1969).

48. *Street v. New York*, 394 U.S. 576 (1969).

49. *Texas v. Johnson*, 491 U.S. 397 (1989).

50. *United States v. Eichman*, 110 S. Ct. 2404 (1990).

51. *Virginia v. Black*, 538 U.S. 343 (2003).

52. *National Association for the Advancement of Colored People v. Alabama*, 357 U.S. 449 (1958).

53. *Sheldon v. Tucker*, 364 U.S. 516 (1960).

54. *Heart of Atlanta Motel v. United States*, 379 U.S. 241 (1964).

55. *Roberts v. United States Jaycees*, 468 U.S. 609 (1984).

56. *Jacobellis v. Ohio*, 378 U.S. 476 (1964).

57. *Miller v. California*, 413 U.S. 15 (1973).

58. *Cohen v. California*, 403 U.S. 15 (1971).

59. *Brown vs. Entertainment Merchants Association*, 564 U.S. (2011).

60. *Chaplinsky v. New Hampshire*, 315 U.S. 568 (1942).

61. *Terminello v. Chicago*, 337 U.S. 1 (1949).

62. *Cohen v. California*, 403 U.S. 15 (1971).

63. *Doe v. University of Michigan*, 721 F. Supp. 852 (E. D. Mich. 1989); *UMW Post v. Board of Regents of the University of Wisconsin*, 774 F. Supp. 1163, 1167, 1179 (E. D. Wis. 1991).

64. *R.A.V. v. City of St. Paul*, 60 LW 4667 (1992).

65. *Near v. Minnesota*, 283 U.S. 697 (1930).

66. *New York Times Company v. United States*, 403 U.S. 670 (1971).

67. Anthony Lewis, *Make No Law: The Sullivan Case and the First Amendment* (New York: Vintage Books/Random House, 1991).

68. *New York Times v. Sullivan*, 376 U.S. 254 (1964).

69. Christina Zhao, "Michael Cohen Threatened The Onion With Cease and Desist Letter Over Satirical Article About Trump's Death," *Newsweek*, May 22, 2018, www.newsweek.com/michael-cohen-threatened-onion-cease-and-desist-letter-over-fake-satirical-938950.

70. *Nebraska Press Association v. Stuart*, 427 U.S. 539 (1976).

71. *Daily Currant*, March 22, 2016.

72. David Weigel, "'I Want to Believe': Why Does the Media Keep Running Fake Stories From a Joke-Free Satire Site?" *Slate*, March 11, 2013, www.slate.com/articles/news_and_politics/politics/2013/03/daily_currant_satire_the_fake_news_website_keeps_fooling_journalists.html.

73. Max Read, "Breitbart Fooled by Joke News Site After Blasting Writer for Being Fooled by Same Joke News Site," *Gawker*, March 11, 2013, gawker.com/5989887/breitbart-fooled-by-joke-news-site-after-blasting-writer-for-being-fooled-by-same-joke-news-site.

74. Alex Goldman, "Facebook Attempts to Teach Its Users to Recognize Satire—With a 'Satire' Tag," *On the Media*, August 18, 2014, www.onthemedia.org/story/facebook-attempts-teach-its-users-recognize-satire-satire-tag/.

75. Ibid.

76. *Reno v. ACLU*, 521 U.S. 1113 (1997).

77. *Ashcroft v. ACLU*, 124 S. Ct. 2783 (2004).

78. *United States v. American Library Association, Inc.*, 539 U.S. 194 (2003).

79. Pamela LiCalzi O'Connell, "Compressed Data: Law Newsletter Has to Sneak Past Filters," *New York Times*, April 2, 2001, C4.

80. Jeffery Seligno, "Student Writers Try to Duck the Censors by Going On-line," *New York Times*, June 7, 2001, G6.

81. Chloe Albanesius, "After Blackout, Congress Postpones Action on SOPA, PIPA," *PC Magazine*, January 20, 2012, www.pcmag.com/article2/0,2817,2399132,00.asp.

82. *United States v. Lopez*, 514 U.S. 549 (1995); *Printz v. United States*, 521 U.S. 898 (1997).

83. Walter Hickey, "How the NRA Became the Most Powerful Special Interest in Washington," *Business Insider*, December 18, 2012, www.businessinsider.com/nra-lobbying-money-national-rifle-association-washington-2012–12.

84. Karen McVeigh, "Sandy Hook: One Year on, Campaigners Prepare for New Push on Gun Control," *The Guardian*, December 13, 2013, www.theguardian.com/world/2013/dec/13/sandy-hook-campaigners-push-gun-control.

85. White House Fact Sheet, "New Executive Actions to Reduce Gun Violence and Make Our Communities Safer," January 4, 2016, www.whitehouse.gov/the-press-office/2016/01/04/fact-sheet-new-executive-actions-reduce-gun-violence-and-make-our.

86. Jugal K. Patel, "After Sandy Hook, More Than 400 People Have Been Shot in Over 200 School Shootings," *New York Times*, February 15, 2018, www.nytimes.com/interactive/2018/02/15/us/school-shootings-sandy-hook-parkland.html.

87. Robert J. Spitzer, *The Politics of Gun Control* (Chatham, N.J.: Chatham House, 1995), 49.

88. Ibid., 47.

89. *United States v. Cruikshank*, 92 U.S. 542 (1876); *Presser v. Illinois*, 116 U.S. 252 (1886); *Miller v. Texas*, 153 U.S. 535 (1894); *United States v. Miller*, 307 U.S. 174 (1939).

90. Warren Richey, "Supreme Court Asserts Broad Gun Rights," *Christian Science Monitor*, June 27, 2008.

91. Robert Barnes and Dan Eggen, "Supreme Court Affirms Fundamental Right to Bear Arms," *Washington Post*, June 29, 2010, www.washingtonpost.com/wp-dyn/content/article/2010/06/28/AR2010062802134.html.

92. *Katz v. United States*, 389 U.S. 347 (1967).

93. *United States v. Jones*, 565 U.S.__ (2012).

94. Adam Liptak, "Major Ruling Shields Privacy of Cellphones," *New York Times*, June 25, 2014, www.nytimes.com/2014/06/26/us/supreme-court-cellphones-search-privacy.html.

95. *Skinner v. Railway Labor Executive Association*, 489 U.S. 602 (1989).

96. *Veronia School District v. Acton*, 515 U.S. 646 (1995).

97. Associated Press, "Supreme Court Upholds Invasive Strip Searches," National Public Radio, April 2, 2012, www.npr.org/2012/04/02/149849568/supreme-court-upholds-invasive-strip-searches.

98. *Weeks v. United States*, 232 U.S. 383 (1914).

99. *Wolf v. Colorado*, 338 U.S. 25 (1949).

100. *Mapp v. Ohio*, 367 U.S. 643 (1961).

101. *United States v. Calandra*, 414 U.S. 338 (1974).

102. *United States v. Janis*, 428 U.S. 433 (1976).

103. *Massachusetts v. Sheppard*, 468 U.S. 981 (1984); *United States v. Leon*, 468 U.S. 897 (1984); *Illinois v. Krull*, 480 U.S. 340 (1987).

104. *Herring v. United States*, 492 F. 3d 1212 (2009).

105. *Miranda v. Arizona*, 382 U.S. 925 (1965); *Dickerson v. United States*, 530 U.S. 428, 120 S. Ct. 2326; 2000 U.S. LEXIS 4305.

106. *Johnson v. Zerbst*, 304 U.S. 458 (1938).

107. *Gideon v. Wainwright*, 372 U.S. 335 (1963).

108. *Ross v. Moffitt*, 417 U.S. 600 (1974); *Murray v. Giarratano*, 492 U.S. 1 (1989).

109. Henry Weinstein, "Many Denied Right to Counsel, Group Says," *Los Angeles Times*, July 13, 2004, A10.

110. *In re Kemmler*, 136 U.S. 436 (1890).

111. *Atkins v. Virginia*, 536 U.S. 304 (2002).

112. *Roper v. Simmons*, 543 U.S. 551 (2005).

113. *Kennedy v. Louisiana*, 554 U.S. 407 (2008).

114. *Furman v. Georgia, Jackson v. Georgia, Branch v. Texas*, 408 U.S. 238 (1972).

115. *Gregg v. Georgia*, 428 U.S. 153 (1976); *Woodson v. North Carolina*, 428 U.S. 280 (1976); *Roberts v. Louisiana*, 428 U.S. 325 (1976).

116. *McCleskey v. Kemp*, 481 U.S. 279 (1987).

117. *McCleskey v. Zant*, 111 S. Ct. 1454 (1991).

118. *Baze v. Rees*, 553 U.S. 35 (2008).

119. Jack Hitt, "The Moratorium Gambit," *New York Times Magazine*, December 9, 2001, 82.

120. Keith Richburg, "New Jersey Approves Abolition of Death Penalty," *Washington Post*, December 14, 2007, A3.

121. Baxter Oliphant, "Support for Death Penalty Lowest in More Than Four Decades," Pew Research Center, September 29, 2016, www.pewresearch.org/fact-tank/2016/09/29/support-for-death-penalty-lowest-in-more-than-four-decades/; Frank Newport, "In U.S., Two-Thirds Continue to Support Death Penalty," October 13, 2009, www.gallup.com/poll/123638/In-U.S.-Two-Thirds-Continue-Support-Death-Penalty.aspx.

122. Samuel D. Warren and Louis D. Brandeis, "The Right to Privacy," *Harvard Law Review* 4 (1890).

123. "In Major Privacy Win, Supreme Court Rules Police Need Warrant to Track Your Cellphone," NPR, June 22, 2018, www.npr.org/2018/06/22/605007387/supreme-court- rules-police-need-warrant-to-get-location-information- from-cell-to.

124. *Griswold v. Connecticut*, 391 U.S. 145 (1965).

125. *Eisenstadt v. Baird*, 405 U.S. 438 (1972).

126. *Roe v. Wade*, 410 U.S. 113 (1973).

127. *Harris v. McRae*, 448 U.S. 297 (1980).

128. See, for example, *Webster v. Reproductive Health Services*, 492 U.S. 4090 (1989) and *Rust v. Sullivan*, 111 S. Ct. 1759 (1991).

129. *Gonzales v. Carhart*, 550 U.S. 124 (2007).

130. Erik Eckholm, "Push for 'Personhood' Amendment Represents New Tack in Abortion Fight," *New York Times*, October 25, 2011, www.nytimes.com/2011/10/26/us/ politics/personhood-amendments-would-ban-nearly-all-abortions.html.

131. Andrew Sullivan, "An Anti-Abortion Frenzy in the States," *The Daily Dish*, April 25, 2012, dish.andrewsullivan.com/2012/04/25/an-anti-abortion-frenzy-in-the-states/, Erik Eckholm and Kim Severson, "Virginia Senate Passes Ultrasound Bill as Other States Take Notice," *New York Times*, February 28, 2012, www.nytimes.com/2012/02/29/us/virginia-senate-passes-revised-ultrasound-bill.html.

132. Ariane de Vogue, Tal Kopan, Dan Berman, "Supreme Court Strikes Down Texas Abortion Access Law," CNN.com, June 27, 2016, www.cnn.com/2016/06/27/politics/supreme-court-abortion-texas/.

133. *Bowers v. Hardwick*, 478 U.S. 186 (1986).

134. *Commonwealth of Kentucky v. Wasson*, 842 S.W.2d 487 (1992).

135. *Lawrence v. Texas*, 539 U.S. 558 (2003).

136. *Romer v. Evans*, 517 U.S. 620 (1996).

137. *Cruzan v. Director, Missouri Department of Health*, 497 U.S. 261 (1990).

138. Frank Newport, "The Terri Schiavo Case in Review: Support for Her Being Allowed to Die Consistent," Gallup News Service, April 1, 2005, news.gallup.com/poll/15475/terri-schiavo-case-review.aspx.

139. *Washington v. Glucksberg*, 521 U.S. 702 (1997); *Vacco v. Quill*, 521 U.S. 793 (1997).

140. Soumya Karlamangla, "California's Physician-Assisted Suicide Law Is Overturned—At Least for Now," *Los Angeles Times*, May 25, 2018, www.latimes.com/health/la-me-ln-end-of-life-option-act-20180525-htmlstory.html.

141. Stephen Adler and Wade Lambert, "Just About Everyone Violates Some Laws, Even Model Citizens," *Wall Street Journal*, March 12, 1993, 1.

CHAPTER 6

1. Rosie Gray, "Inside a White Nationalist Conference Energized by Trump's Rise," *Buzzfeed*, May 26, 2016, www.buzzfeed.com/rosiegray/inside-a-white-nationalist-conference-energized-by-trumps-ri.

2. Rosie Gray, "How 2015 Fueled the Rise of the Freewheeling, White Nationalist Alt Right Movement," *Buzzfeed*, December 27, 2015, www.buzzfeed.com/rosiegray/how-2015-fueled-the-rise-of-the-freewheeling-white-nationali.

3. Carly Mallenbaum, "Former KKK Grand Wizard David Duke Keeps Tweeting Support for Trump," *USA Today*, November 9, 2016, www.usatoday.com/story/news/politics/onpolitics/2016/11/09/david-duke-donald-trump-tweet/93526394/

4. Conor Friedersdorf, "How to Take 'Political Correctness' Away From Donald Trump," *The Atlantic*, February 23, 2016, www.theatlantic.com/politics/archive/2016/02/how-to-take-political-correctness-away-from-donald-trump/470271/.

5. Carly Wayne, Nicholas Valentino, and Marzia Oceno, "How Sexism Drives Support for Donald Trump," *Washington Post*, October 23, 2016, www.washingtonpost.com/news/monkey-cage/wp/2016/10/23/how-sexism-drives-support-for-donald-trump/.

6. Sarah Posner and David Neiwert, "How Trump Took Hate Groups Mainstream," *Mother Jones*, October 14, 2016, www.motherjones.com/politics/2016/10/donald-trump-hate-groups-neo-nazi-white-supremacist-racism/.

7. Ben Jacobs and Oliver Laughland, "Charlottesville: Trump Reverts to Blaming Both Sides Including 'Violent Alt-Left'," *The Guardian*, August 16, 2017, www.theguardian.com/us-news/2017/aug/15/donald-trump-press-conference- far-right-defends-charlottesville.

8. Cited in Ronald Brownstein, "Trump's Rhetoric of White Nostalgia," *The Atlantic*, June 2, 2016, www.theatlantic.com/politics/archive/2016/06/trumps-rhetoric-of-white-nostalgia/485192/.

9. Carol Graham, "Unhappiness in America," Brookings, May 27, 2016, www.washingtonpost.edu/research/opinions/2016/05/27-unhappiness-in-america-graham.

10. Olga Khazan, "Middle-Aged White Americans Are Dying of Despair," *The Atlantic*, November 4, 2015, www.theatlantic.com/health/archive/2015/11/boomers-deaths-pnas/413971/.

11. Matthew Macwilliams, "The One Weird Trait That Predicts Whether You're a Trump Supporter," *Politico*, January 17, 2016, www.politico.com/magazine/story/2016/01/donald-trump-2016-authoritarian-213533.

12. Wendy Rahn and Eric Oliver, "Trump's Voters Aren't Authoritarians, New Research Says. So What Are They?" *Washington Post*, March 9, 2016, www.washingtonpost.com/news/monkey-cage/wp/2016/03/09/trumps-voters-arent-authoritarians-new-research-says-so-what-are-they/.

13. Michael Tesler, "In a Trump-Clinton Match-up, Racial Prejudice Makes a Striking Difference," *Washington Post*, May 25, 2016, www .washingtonpost.com/news/monkey-cage/ wp/2016/05/25/in-a-trump-clinton-match-up- theres-a-striking-effect-of-racial-prejudice/; Michael Tesler, "Trump Is the First Modern Republican to Win the Nomination Based on Racial Prejudice," *Washington Post*, August 1, 2016, www.washingtonpost.com/news/monkey-cage/ wp/2016/08/01/trump-is-the-first-republican- in-modern-times-to-win-the-partys-nomination- on-anti-minority-sentiments/.

14. Kathy Kiely, "These Are America's Governors. No Blacks. No Hispanics," *USA Today*, January 21, 2002, 1A.

15. "Senators of the United States: 1789–Present," https://www.senate.gov/artandhistory/history/ resources/pdf/chronlist.pdf.

16. Graham, "Unhappiness in America."

17. David O'Brien, *Constitutional Law and Politics*, vol. 2 (New York: Norton, 1991), 1265.

18. American Civil Liberties Union, "Felon Enfranchisement and the Right to Vote," www.aclu .org/votingrights/exoffenders/index.html; National Conference of State Legislatures, "Felon Voting Rights," April 30, 2017, www.ncsl.org/research/ elections-and-campaigns/felon-voting-rights.aspx.

19. *Dred Scott v. Sanford*, 19 How. (60 U.S.) 393 (1857).

20. Scholars are divided about Lincoln's motives in issuing the Emancipation Proclamation. Whether he genuinely desired to end slavery or merely used political means to shorten the war is hard to tell at this distance. Donald G. Nieman, *Promises to Keep: African-Americans and the Constitutional Order, 1776 to the Present* (New York: Oxford University Press, 1991), 55.

21. Bernard A. Weisberger, *Many Papers, One Nation* (Boston, Mass.: Houghton Mifflin Company, 1987), 200.

22. Nieman, *Promises to Keep*, 107.

23. *The Civil Rights Cases*, 109 U.S. 3 (1883).

24. *Plessy v. Ferguson*, 163 U.S. 537 (1896).

25. Weisberger, *Many Papers, One Nation*, 205–206.

26. *Guinn v. United States*, 238 U.S. 347 (1915).

27. *Missouri ex rel Gaines v. Canada*, 305 U.S. 337 (1938).

28. *Sweatt v. Painter*, 339 U.S. 629 (1950).

29. *Korematsu v. United States*, 323 U.S. 214 (1944).

30. *Brown v. Board of Education of Topeka (I)*, 347 U.S. 483 (1954).

31. *Brown v. Board of Education of Topeka (II)*, 349 U.S. 294 (1955).

32. *Gayle v. Browder*, 352 U.S. 903 (1956).

33. *Heart of Atlanta Motel, Inc. v. United States*, 379 U.S. 241 (1964); *Katzenbach v. McClung*, 379 U.S. 294 (1964); *Harper v. Virginia Board of Elections*, 383 U.S. 663 (1966).

34. Nieman, *Promises to Keep*, 179.

35. Ibid., 180.

36. *Swann v. Charlotte-Mecklenberg Board of Education*, 402 U.S. 1 (1971).

37. *Milliken v. Bradley*, 418 U.S. 717 (1974).

38. "*Brown v. Board*'s Goals Unrealized," *Atlanta Journal-Constitution*, May 16, 2004, 6C; Gary Orfield and Chungmei Lee, "*Brown* at 50: King's Dream or *Plessy*'s Nightmare?" Report conducted by the Harvard Civil Rights Project, 2004, www .civilrightsproject.harvard.edu/research/reseg04/ brown50.pdf.

39. *Regents of the University of California v. Bakke*, 438 U.S. 265 (1978).

40. See, for example, *United Steelworkers of America v. Weber*, 443 U.S. 193 (1979); *Fullilove v. Klutznick*, 448 U.S. 448 (1980); *Firefighters Local Union No.*

1784 v. Stotts, 467 U.S. 561 (1984); and *Wygant v. Jackson Board of Education*, 476 U.S. 267 (1986).

41. *Patterson v. McLean Credit Union*, 491 U.S. 164 (1989); *Wards Cove Packing, Inc. v. Atonio*, 490 U.S. 642 (1989); *City of Richmond v. J. A. Croson*, 488 U.S. 469 (1989).

42. Carmen DeNavas-Walt and Bernadette D. Proctor, "Income and Poverty in the United States: 2014," www.census.gov/content/dam/Census/library/ publications/2015/demo/p60-252.pdf; Ruth Simon and Tom McGinty, "Loan Rebound Misses Black Businesses," *Wall Street Journal*, March 14, 2014, www.wsj.com/articles/SB10001424052702304585 0457941702157159661 0.

43. Joel Dresang, "Black Professional Men Paid Less Than White Peers," *Milwaukee Journal Sentinel*, August 16, 2001, 1D.

44. Andrea Orr, "Why Do Black Men Earn Less?" Economic Policy Institute, March 3, 2011, www .epi.org/publication/why_do_black_ men_earn_less/.

45. Pew Research Center for the People and the Press, "Blacks Upbeat About Black Progress, Prospects," January 12, 2010, www.people-press.org/ reports/576; Gallup, "One Third in US See Improved Race Relations Under Obama," August 24, 2011, www.gallup.com/poll/149141/one-third- improved-race-relations-obama.aspx; "Race in America: Key Data Points," Pew Research Center, August 27, 2013, www.pewresearch.org/key-data- points/race-in-america-key-data-points/.

46. Josiah Ryan, "'This Was a Whitelash,' Van Jones' Take on the Election Results," CNN, November 9, 2016, www.cnn.com/2016/11/09/politics/ van-jones-results-disappointment-cnntv/.

47. Adam Liptak, "Supreme Court Invalidates Key Part of Voting Rights Act," *New York Times*, June 25, 2013, www.nytimes.com/2013/06/26/us/ supreme-court-ruling.html?pagewanted=all.

48. Adam Liptak and Michael Wines, "Strict North Carolina Voter ID Law Thwarted After Supreme Court Rejects Case," May 15, 2017, https://www .nytimes.com/2017/05/15/us/politics/voter-id- laws-supreme-court-north-carolina.html.

49. National Conference of Black Mayors, "Leadership Development Program," www.aphia06dbl.org/ files/NCBM.pdf.

50. Pew Research Center for the People and the Press, "Public Backs Affirmative Action but Not Minority Preferences," June 2, 2009, pewresearch.org/ pubs/1240/sotomayor-supreme- court-affirmative-action-minority-preferences.

51. Jodi Wilgoren, "U.S. Court Bars Race as Factor in School Entry," *New York Times*, March 28, 2001, A1.

52. Jacques Steinberg, "Redefining Diversity," *New York Times*, August 29, 2001, A14.

53. *Gratz v. Bollinger*, 539 U.S. 244 (2003).

54. *Grutter v. Bollinger*, 539 U.S. 306 (2003).

55. Nick Anderson, "How Supreme Court's Michigan Affirmative Action Ruling Affects Colleges," *Washington Post*, April 23, 2014, www .washingtonpost.com/local/education/how- supreme-courts-michigan-affirmative-action- ruling-affects-colleges/2014/04/23/7b0c79ae- cad7-11e3-93eb-6c0037dde2ad_story.html.

56. Adam Liptak, "Supreme Court Upholds Affirmative Action Program at University of Texas," *New York Times*, June 24, 2016, www.nytimes.com/2016/06/24/us/politics/ supreme-court-affirmative-action-university-of- texas.html.

57. Ward Connerly, "Up From Affirmative Action," *New York Times*, April 29, 1996.

58. David K. Shipler, "My Equal Opportunity, Your Free Lunch," *New York Times*, March 5, 1995.

59. *Cherokee Nation v. Georgia*, 30 U.S. (5 Pet.) 1, 20 (1831).

60. Vine Deloria Jr. and Clifford M. Lytle, *The Nations Within: The Past and Future of American Indian Sovereignty* (New York: Pantheon, 1984), 17.

61. J. Bretting and B. Morris, "Fry-Bread Federalism Revisited: A Model of American Indian Intergovernmental Relations," paper presented at the 2005 annual meeting of the Western Political Science Association, Oakland, Calif.

62. *Lyng v. Northwest Indian Cemetery Protective Association*, 485 U.S. 439 (1988).

63. *Employment Division v. Oregon*, 494 U.S. 872 (1990).

64. U.S. Census Bureau, "American Indian and Alaskan Native Heritage Month," November 2017, www .census.gov/newsroom/facts-for-features/2017/ aian-month.html.

65. Ibid.

66. Nicholas Kristof, "Poverty's Poster Child," May 10, 2012, www.nytimes.com/2012/05/10/opinion/ kristof-poverty sposter-child.html.

67. *Seminole Tribe of Florida v. Butterworth*, 658 F.2d 310 (1981), cert. denied, 455 U.S. 1020 (1982); *State of California v. Cabazon Band of Mission Indians*, 480 U.S. 202 (1987).

68. National Indian Gaming Commission web site, "2016 Indian Gaming Revenues Increased 4.4%," July 17, 2017, www.nigc.gov/news/ detail/2016-indian-gaming- revenues- increased-4.4.

69. Americana Gaming Association, *State of the States: The AGA Survey of the Casino Industry*, 2017, www .americangaming.org/sites/default/files/research_ files/2017%20State%20of%20the%20States.pdf.

70. National Caucus of Native American State Legislators web site, www. nativeamericanlegislators.org/Public%20 Documents/Caucus%20Membership.aspx.

71. U.S. Census Bureau, "Hispanic Heritage Month 2017," October 17, 2017, https://www.census.gov/ content/dam/Census/newsroom/facts-for- features/2017/cb17-ff17.pdf.

72. U.S. Census Bureau, "2010 Census Shows Nation's Hispanic Population Grew Four Times Faster Than US Population," May 26, 2011, www.census .gov/newsroom/releases/archives/2010_census/ cb11-cn146.html.

73. Pew Hispanic Center, "Country of Origin Profiles," May 26, 2011, www.pewhispanic. org/2011/05/26/country-of-origin-profiles/.

74. Pew Research Center, "5 Facts About Latinos and Education," July 28, 2016, www.pewresearch.org/ fact-tank/2016/07/28/5-facts-about-latinos-and- education/.

75. Mark Falcoff, "Our Language Needs No Law," *New York Times*, August 5, 1996.

76. Gustavo López, Neil G. Ruizs, and Eileen Patten, "Key Facts About Asian Americans, a Diverse and Growing Population," Pew Research Center, September 8, 2017, http://www.pewresearch.org/ fact-tank/2017/09/08/key-facts-about- asian-americans/.

77. Ibid.

78. Ronald Takaki, *Strangers From a Different Shore* (Boston, Mass.: Little, Brown, 1989), 363–364.

79. *Hirabayashi v. United States*, 320 U.S. 81 (1943); *Korematsu v. United States*, 323 U.S. 214 (1944).

80. U.S. Census Bureau, "Income, Poverty and Health Insurance Coverage: 2010," www.census.gov/ newsroom/releases/archives/income_wealth/ cb11-157.html.

81. Data from harvard.edu, stanford.edu, mit.edu, and berkeley.edu, compiled by the authors June 19, 2018.

82. Takaki, *Strangers From a Different Shore*, 479.

83. Chris Fuchs, "Two Sides in Harvard Affirmative Action Case Set to Meet in Court Over Sealed Records," NBC News, April 9, 2018, https://www

.nbcnews.com/news/asian-america/
two-sides-harvard-affirmative-action-case-set-
meet-court-over-n864031.

84. López, Ruiz, and Patten, "Key Facts About Asian Americans."

85. Lena H. Sun, "Getting Out the Ethnic Vote," *Washington Post*, October 7, 1996, B5; K. Connie Kang, "Asian Americans Slow to Flex Their Political Muscle," *Los Angeles Times*, October 31, 1996, A18.

86. Mac Tan, "Why Is Asian American Voter Turnout So Low?", Quora, October 27, 2015, www.quora.com/Why-is-Asian-American-voter-turnout-so-low.

87. Sun, "Getting Out the Ethnic Vote"; Kang, "Asian Americans Slow to Flex Their Political Muscle."

88. Eleanor Flexner, *Century of Struggle: The Woman's Rights Movement in the United States* (New York: Atheneum, 1973), 148–149.

89. Nancy E. McGlen and Karen O'Connor, *Women's Rights: The Struggle for Equality in the 19th and 20th Centuries* (New York: Praeger, 1983), 272–273.

90. *Bradwell v. Illinois*, 16 Wall. 130 (1873).

91. Quoted in Flexner, *Century of Struggle*, 178.

92. Ibid., 296.

93. McGlen and O'Connor, *Women's Rights*, 83.

94. Jane Mansbridge, *Why We Lost the ERA* (Chicago, Ill.: Chicago University Press, 1986), 13.

95. *Reed v. Reed*, 404 U.S. 71 (1971); *Craig v. Boren*, 429 U.S. 190 (1976).

96. *Weinberger v. Wiesenfeld*, 420 U.S. 636 (1975); *Califano v. Goldfarb*, 430 U.S. 199 (1977); *Califano v. Westcott*, 443 U.S. 76 (1979); *Orr v. Orr*, 440 U.S. 268 (1979).

97. Shelley Donald Coolidge, "Flat Tire on the Road to Pay Equity," *Christian Science Monitor*, April 11, 1997, 9; National Committee on Pay Equity, "The Wage Gap Over Time; In Real Dollars, Women See a Continuing Gap," www.pay-equity.org/info-time.html.

98. *Ledbetter v. Goodyear Tire & Rubber Co.*, 550 U.S. 618 (2007).

99. Clare O'Connor, "Trump Halting Equal Pay Measure 'A Blatant Attack on Women,' Activists Say," *Forbes*, August 30, 2017, www.forbes.com/sites/clareoconnor/2017/08/30/trump-halting-equal-pay-measure-a-blatant-attack-on-women-activists-say/#3a197352395b.

100. Joseph E. Abboud, "Salary History Not a Defense to Equal Pay Act Claims, 9th Circuit Says," May 16, 2018, https://www.lexology.com/library/detail.aspx?g=7e17b8c1-680c-452c-b81f-b1339680c8fd.

101. *Johnson v. Transportation Agency, Santa Clara, California*, 480 U.S. 616 (1987).

102. Barbara Noble, "At Work: And Now the Sticky Floor," *New York Times*, November 22, 1992, 23.

103. Kenneth Gray, "The Gender Gap in Yearly Earnings: Can Vocational Education Help?" *Office of Special Populations' Brief*, vol. 5, no. 2. National Center for Research in Vocational Education, University of California, Berkeley, Office of Special Populations, University of California, Berkeley.

104. U.S. Equal Employment Opportunity Commission, "EEOC Updated Pregnancy Discrimination Guidance," press release, June 25, 2015, www.eeoc.gov/eeoc/newsroom/release/6-25-15.cfm.

105. Barbara Burrell, "Campaign Finance: Women's Experience in the Modern Era," in Sue Thomas and Clyde Wilcox, eds., *Women and Elective Office: Past, Present, and Future* (New York: Oxford University Press, 1998), 27.

106. Gary F. Moncrief, Peverill Squire, and Malcolm E. Jewell, *Who Runs for the Legislature?* (Upper Saddle River, N.J.: Prentice Hall, 2001), 98–99.

107. CQ Weekly, "Guide to the New Congress," November 6, 2014, www.cq.com/graphics/weekly/2014/11/06/wr20141106_CQWeekly.pdf;

108. Center for American Women and Politics, fact sheets, www.cawp.rutgers.edu/fast_facts/.

109. Hillary Clinton, "Hillary's Remarks in Washington, DC," June 7, 2008, www.hillaryclinton.com.

110. Amy Caiazza, "Does Women's Representation in Elected Office Lead to Women-Friendly Policy?" Research in Brief, Institute for Women's Policy Research, May 2002, www.thecocklebur.com/wp-content/uploads/2010/12/One-2002-report.pdf; Kimberly Cowell-Meyers and Laura Langbein, "Linking Women's Descriptive and Substantive Representation in the United States," *Politics and Gender*, 5 (2009): 491–518.

111. Kristin Eliasberg, "Making a Case for the Right to Be Different," *New York Times*, June 16, 2001, B11.

112. *Bowers v. Hardwick*, 478 U.S. 186 (1986).

113. *Lawrence v. Texas*, 539 U.S. 558 (2003).

114. *Goodridge v. Dept. of Pub. Health*, 440 Mass. 309 (2003).

115. Ariane de Vogue, "Supreme Court Rules for Colorado Baker in Same-Sex Wedding Cake Case," CNN, June 4, 2018, https://www.cnn.com/2018/06/04/politics/masterpiece-colorado-gay-marriage-cake-supreme-court/index.html.

116. David W. Dunlap, "Gay Survey Raises a New Question," *New York Times*, October 18, 1994, B8.

117. U.S. Department of Labor, "Amended Regulations: Executive Order 11246 Prohibiting Discrimination Based on Sexual Orientation and Gender Identity," www.dol.gov/ofccp/lgbt .html.

118. Pew Research Center, "Changing Attitudes on Gay Marriage," June 26, 2017, http://www.pewforum.org/fact-sheet/changing-attitudes-on-gay-marriage/.

119. *Massachusetts Board of Retirement v. Murgia*, 427 U.S. 307 (1976).

120. *Massachusetts Board of Retirement v. Murgia; Vance v. Bradley*, 440 U.S. 93 (1979); *Gregory v. Ashcroft*, 501 U.S. 452 (1991).

121. *Alabama v. Garrett*, 531 U.S. 356 (2001).

122. *Graham v. Richardson*, 403 U.S. 365 (1971).

123. *Pyler v. Doe*, 457 U.S. 202 (1982).

124. Robert J. Samuelson, "Immigration and Poverty," *Newsweek*, July 15, 1996, 43.

125. Sanford J. Ungar, "Enough of the Immigrant Bashing," *USA Today*, October 11, 1995, 11A.

126. Theda Skocpol, "Advocates Without Members: The Recent Transformation of American Civil Life," in Theda Skocpol and Morris P. Fiorina, eds., *Civic Engagement in American Democracy* (Washington, D.C., and New York: Brookings Institution and the Russell Sage Foundation, 1999), 470–472.

CHAPTER 7

1. Burgess Everett and Glenn Thrush, "McConnell Throws Down the Gauntlet: No Scalia Replacement Under Obama," *Politico*, February 13, 2016, www.politico.com/story/2016/02/mitch-mcconnell-antonin-scalia-supreme-court-nomination-219248#ixzz48Bb32rNc.

2. Burgess Everett, "Flake Says It Might Be Garland Time," *Politico*, October 20, 2016, www.politico.com/story/2016/10/jeff-flake-merrick-garland-vote-supreme-court-230109.

3. John R. Hibbing and Elizabeth Theiss-Morse, *Congress as Public Enemy* (New York: Cambridge University Press, 1995), chs. 2, 3.

4. Glenn R. Parker and Roger H. Davidson, "Why Do Americans Love Their Congressmen So Much More Than Their Congress?" *Legislative Studies Quarterly* (February 1979): 52–61.

5. Heinz Eulau and Paul D. Karps, "The Puzzle of Representation: Specifying Components of Responsiveness," *Legislative Studies Quarterly* 2 (1977): 233–254.

6. Richard Fenno, *Homestyle* (Boston, Mass.: Little, Brown, 1978), ch. 3.

7. Gary Jacobson, *The Politics of Congressional Elections*, 4th ed. (New York: Longman, 1997), ch. 8.

8. Pew Research Center poll, cited in John Avalon, "Hyper-partisanship Dragging Down Nation," June 7, 2012, www.cnn .com/2012/06/07/opinion/avlon-partisan-pew/index.html.

9. Keith Poole and Howard Rosenthal, "The Polarization of the Political Parties," May 10, 2012, voteview.com/political_polarization.asp.

10. David W. Brady, Hahrie Han, and Jeremy C. Pope, "Primary Elections and Candidate Ideology: Out of Step With the Primary Electorate?" *Legislative Studies Quarterly* 32 (2007): 79–105.

11. Thomas E. Mann and Norman J. Ornstein, *It's Even Worse Than It Looks: How the American Constitutional System Collided With the New Politics of Extremism* (New York: Basic Books, 2012); Thomas E. Mann and Norman J. Ornstein, "Let's Just Say It: The Republicans Are the Problem," *Washington Post*, April 27, 2012, www.washingtonpost.com/opinions/lets-just-say-it-the-republicans-are-the-problem/2012/04/27/gIQAxCVUIT_print.html.

12. Mann and Ornstein, "Let's Just Say It."

13. Ibid.

14. Charles Mahtesian and Jim VandeHei, "Congress: It's Going to Get Worse," *Politico*, May 1, 2012, www.politico.com/news/stories/0412/75771.html; Steve LaTourette, "The Senate's 'Manchurian Candidates,'" *Politico*, November 11, 2012, www.politico.com/news/stories/1112/83703.html.

15. Megan Slack, "Here's How a Government Shutdown Hurts the American People," *The White House Blog*, September 30, 2013, www.whitehouse.gov/blog/2013/09/30/heres-how-government-shutdown-hurts-american-people; Jonathan Weisman and Ashley Parker, "Republicans Back Down, Ending Crisis Over Shutdown and Debt Limit," *New York Times*, October 16, 2013, www.nytimes.com/2013/10/17/us/congress-budget-debate.html.

16. Jonathan Miller, "Mourdock: Compromise Is Democrats Agreeing With Republicans," *National Journal*, May 9, 2012, www.nationaljournal.com/congress/mourdock-compromise-is-democrats-agreeing-with-republicans-20120509.

17. "Moderate GOP Rep. LaTourette Announces Retirement," MSNBC, July 31, 2012, www.msnbc.com/the-daily-rundown/moderate-gop-rep-latourette-announces.

18. Ella Nilsen, "'None of This Is Normal': Read the Full Transcript of Sen. Jeff Flake's Blistering Retirement Speech," *Vox*, October 24, 2017, www.vox.com/2017/10/24/16537284/full-transcript-flake-retirement-speech.

19. Ross K. Baker, *House and Senate* (New York: Norton, 1989).

20. D. C. W. Parker and M. Dull, "Divided We Quarrel: The Politics of Congressional Investigations, 1947–2004," *Legislative Studies Quarterly* 34 (2009): 319–345.

21. Jonathan Alter, "Obama Miracle Is White House Free of Scandal," Bloomberg News, October 27, 2011, www.bloomberg .com/news/2011-10-27/obama-miracle-is-white-house-free-of-scandal-commentary-by-jonathan-alter.html.

22. Tim Fernholz, "Democrats, Meet Darrell Issa, Likely the Man With the Subpoena," *Newsweek*, September 7, 2010, www.thedailybeast.com/newsweek/2010/09/07/darrell-issa-could-investigate-president-obama.html; Paul Waldman, "What Benghazi Is About: Scandal Envy," *The*

American Prospect, November 15, 2012, prospect.org/article/what-benghazi-about-scandal-envy.

23. David M. Herszenhorn, "House Benghazi Report Finds No New Evidence of Wrongdoing by Hillary Clinton," *New York Times*, June, 28, 2016, www.nytimes.com/2016/06/29/us/politics/hillary-clinton-benghazi.html.

24. Neil A. Lewis, "Justice Dept. Nominee Avoids Confrontation at Hearing," *New York Times*, February 26, 2009, 23; Charlie Savage, "Long After Nomination, An Obama Choice Withdraws," *New York Times*, April 10, 2010, 16.

25. Gail Russell Chaddock, "Congress Girds Up for Return to Oversight," *Christian Science Monitor*, April 9, 2007, 1; Elizabeth Williamson, "Revival of Oversight Role Sought; Congress Hires More Investigators, Plans Subpoenas," *Washington Post*, April 25, 2007, A1.

26. Richard Painter and Michael Gerhardt, "Time to Support the President on Judicial Nominations," *The Hill's Congress Blog*, March 12, 2012, thehill.com/blogs/congress-blog/judicial/215445-time-to-support-the-president-on-judicial-nominations.

27. Adam Liptak, "Supreme Court Rebukes Obama on Right of Appointment," *New York Times*, June 24, 2014, www.nytimes.com/2014/06/27/us/supreme-court-president-recess-appointments.html.

28. Charles Cameron, Albert Cover, and Jeffrey Segal, "Senate Voting on Supreme Court Nominations," *American Political Science Review* 84 (1990): 525–534.

29. David Mayhew, *Congress: The Electoral Connection* (New Haven, Conn.: Yale University Press, 1974).

30. *Baker v. Carr*, 396 U.S. 186 (1962); *Westberry v. Sanders*, 376 U.S. 1 (1964).

31. Sandhya Somashekhar and Aaron Blake, "Census Data Realigns Congressional Districts in Key Political States," *Washington Post*, December 21, 2010, www.washingtonpost.com/wp-dyn/content/article/2010/12/21/AR2010122103084.html.

32. Sam Wang, "The Great Gerrymander of 2012," *New York Times*, February 2, 2013, www.nytimes.com/2013/02/03/opinion/sunday/the-great-gerrymander-of-2012.html.

33. Christopher Ingraham, "Pennsylvania Supreme Court draws 'much more competitive' district map to overturn Republican gerrymander," *Washington Post*, February 20, 2018, https://www.washingtonpost.com/news/wonk/wp/2018/02/19/pennsylvania-supreme-court-draws-a-much-more-competitive-district-map-to-overturn-republican-gerrymander/?utm_term=.1fd6c0aedefb.

34. Roger H. Davidson and Walter J. Oleszek, *Congress and Its Members*, 9th ed. (Washington, D.C.: CQ Press, 2004), 48.

35. Charles Cameron, David Epstein, and Sharyn O'Halloran, "Do Majority-Minority Districts Maximize Substantive Black Representation in Congress?" *American Political Science Review* 90 (December 1996): 794–812; Kevin Hill, "Does the Creation of Majority Black Districts Aid Republicans? An Analysis of the 1992 Congressional Election in Eight Southern States," *Journal of Politics* 57 (May 1995): 384–401; D. Lublin, "Racial Redistricting and African-American Representation: A Critique of 'Do Majority-Minority Districts Maximize Substantive Black Representation in Congress?'" *American Political Science Review* 93 (1999): 183–186.

36. "How to Rig an Election," *The Economist*, April 25, 2002; Aaron Blake, "Name That District! (Gerrymandering Edition)," *Washington Post*, July 27, 2011, www.washingtonpost.com/blogs/the-fix/post/name-that-district-gerrymandering-edition/2011/07/25/gIQA17HucI_blog.html.

37. Richard L. Hasen, "Suppression of Minority Voting Rights Is About to Get Way Worse," *Slate*, June 25, 2018, slate.com/news-and-politics/2018/06/the-abbott-v-perez-case-echoes-shelby-county-v-holder-as-a-further-death-blow-for-the-voting-rights-act.html.

38. *Shaw v. Reno*, 509 U.S. 630 (1993); *Miller v. Johnson*, 115 S. Ct. 2475 (1995).

39. Hasen, "Suppression of Minority Voting Rights Is About to Get Way Worse."

40. Peter Urban, "Congress Gets Lavish Benefits," *Connecticut Post*, January 16, 2005; Debra J. Saunders, "Perks of Office" Editorial, *San Francisco Chronicle*, November 19, 2000, 9.

41. Commission on the Executive, Legislative and Judicial Salaries, *Fairness for Public Servants* (Washington, D.C.: U.S. Government Printing Office, 1988), 23.

42. Eric Uslaner, *The Decline of Comity in Congress* (Ann Arbor: University of Michigan Press, 1993); Ezra Klein, "Olympia Snowe Is Right About American Politics. Will We Listen?" Wonkblog, *Washington Post*, February 28, 2012.

43. Gary Jacobson, *The Politics of Congressional Elections*, 3rd ed. (New York: HarperCollins, 1992); Peverill Squire, "Challengers in Senate Elections," *Legislative Studies Quarterly* 14 (1989): 531–547; David Cannon, *Actors, Athletes and Astronauts: Political Amateurs in the United States Congress* (Chicago, Ill.: University of Chicago Press, 1990).

44. Calculated by the authors from the Campaign Finance Institute data table, "Expenditures of House Incumbents and Challengers, by Election Outcome, 1974–2008," www.cfinst.org/pdf/vital/VitalStats_t3.pdf.

45. Harold Stanley and Richard Niemi, *Vital Statistics on American Politics*, 5th ed. (Washington, D.C.: CQ Press, 1995).

46. Edward R. Tufte, *Political Control of the Economy* (Princeton, N.J.: Princeton University Press, 1978); Robert S. Erikson, "The Puzzle of the Midterm Loss," *Journal of Politics* 50 (November 1988): 1011–1029; Robert S. Erikson and Gerald C. Wright, "Voters, Candidates, and Issues in Congressional Elections," in Lawrence Dodd and Bruce Oppenheimer, eds., *Congress Reconsidered*, 10th ed. (Washington, D.C.: CQ Press, 2013), 91–116.

47. Kyla Calvert Mason, "Percentage of Americans With College Degrees Rises, Paying for Degrees Tops Financial Challenges," PBS, April 22, 2014, https://www.pbs.org/newshour/education/percentage-americans-college-degrees-rises-paying-degrees-tops-financial-challenges; Reid Wilson, "Census: More Americans Have College Degrees Than Ever Before," *The Hill*, April 3, 2017, thehill.com/homenews/state-watch/326995- census-more-americans-have-college-degrees-than-ever-before.

48. Peter Whoriskey, "Growing Wealth Widens Distance Between Lawmakers and Constituents," *Washington Post*, December 26, 2011.

49. Kathleen Dolan, "Voting for Women in the 'Year of the Woman,'" *American Journal of Political Science* 42 (1998): 272–293; Jennifer Lawless and Richard Fox, *It Takes a Candidate: Why Women Don't Run for Office* (New York: Cambridge University Press, 2005).

50. Richard E. Cohen, "Is It an Earthquake, or Only a Tremor?" *National Journal*, July 8, 1995, 1786; Richard Fausset, "Supreme Court Won't Intervene in North Carolina Election Fight," *New York Times*, February 19, 2016; Adam Liptak, "Justices Hear Arguments on Devising District Maps," *New York Times*, March 22, 2016.

51. Sabrina Vourvoulias, "Donald Trump's Kryptonite: Millions of Active—and Furious—Latino Voters," *The Guardian*, May 9, 2016, www.theguardian.com/commentisfree/2016/may/09/latino-voter-turnout-trump-kryptonite; Larid W. Bergad, "Could Latinos Choose the Next President? States in Which Latinos Could Determine the Margin of Victory in the 2016 Presidential Election," Center for Latin American, Caribbean & Latino Studies, City University of New York, Report 2, February 2016.

52. Larry M. Bartels, *Unequal Democracy: The Political Economy of the New Gilded Age* (New York/Princeton, N.J.: Russell Sage Foundation/Princeton University Press, 2008); Martin Gilens, *Affluence and Influence: Economic Inequality and Political Power in America* (New York/Princeton, N.J.: Russell Sage Foundation/Princeton University Press, 2012); Elizabeth Rigby and Gerald C. Wright, "Political Parties and Representation of the Poor in the American States," *American Journal of Political Science* 57 (2013): 552–565.

53. Nicholas Carnes, "Does the Numerical Underrepresentation of the Working Class in Congress Matter?" *Legislative Studies Quarterly* 37 (2012): 5–34.

54. Jane Mansbridge, "Should Blacks Represent Blacks and Women Represent Women? A Contingent 'Yes,'" *Journal of Politics* 61 (1999): 628–657; Claudine Gay, "The Effect of Black Congressional Representation on Political Participation," *American Political Science Review* 95 (2001): 589–602.

55. Cindy Simon Rosenthal, "The Role of Gender in Descriptive Representation," *Political Research Quarterly* 48 (1995): 599–611; Jennifer L. Lawless, "Politics of Presence? Congresswomen and Symbolic Representation," *Political Research Quarterly* 57 (2004): 81–99; Michele Swers, *The Difference Women Make: The Policy Impact of Women in Congress* (Chicago, Ill.: University of Chicago Press, 2002).

56. Katherine Tate, *Black Faces in the Mirror: African Americans and Their Representatives in the U.S. Congress* (Princeton, N.J.: Princeton University Press, 2003); Kenny J. Whitby, *The Color of Representation: Congressional Behavior and Black Interests* (Ann Arbor: University of Michigan Press, 1997).

57. David Canon, *Race, Redistricting, and Representation: The Unintended Consequences of Black Majority Districts* (Chicago, Ill.: University of Chicago Press, 1999); Lublin, *The Paradox of Representation*; John D. Griffin, "When and Why Minority Legislators Matter," *Annual Review of Political Science* 17 (2014): 327–336.

58. Mansbridge, "Should Blacks Represent Blacks and Women Represent Women?"

59. Carnes, "Does the Numerical Underrepresentation of the Working Class in Congress Matter?"

60. Mann and Ornstein, *It's Even Worse Than It Looks*.

61. Glenn Parker, *Characteristics of Congress: Patterns in Congressional Behavior* (Englewood Cliffs, N.J.: Prentice Hall, 1989), 17–18, ch. 9.

62. Davidson and Oleszek, *Congress and Its Members*, 9th ed., 155–156.

63. Leroy Rieselbach, *Congressional Reform in the Seventies* (Morristown, N.J.: General Learning Press, 1977); Leroy Rieselbach, *Congressional Reform* (Washington, D.C.: CQ Press, 1986).

64. Ed Gillespie and Bob Schellhas, eds., *Contract With America: The Bold Plan by Rep. Newt Gingrich, Rep. Dick Armey and the House Republicans to Change the Nation* (New York: Random House, 1994); James G. Gimpel, *Legislating the Revolution* (Boston, Mass.: Allyn & Bacon, 1996).

65. Perry Bacon Jr., "Don't Mess With Nancy Pelosi," *Time*, August 27, 2006.

66. Edward Epstein, "Pelosi's Action Plan for Party Unity," *CQ Weekly*, March 30, 2009, 706.

67. Ronald Peters, coauthor of *Speaker Nancy Pelosi and the New American Politics*, quoted in Edward Epstein, "Pelosi Gets Good Marks in Two New Books," *CQ Weekly*, May 10, 2010, 1128.

68. Bill Weiss, "Call for Resignation of Speaker John Boehner," petitions.moveon.org/sign/call-for-resignation; Sean Davis, "Is It Time for John Boehner to Resign as Speaker?" *The Federalist*, October 16, 2013, thefederalist.com/2013/10/16/time-john-boehner-resign-speaker/.

69. Alex Wayne, "Senate Passes Sweeping Health Overhaul," *CQ Weekly*, December 28, 2009, 2944.

70. Davidson and Oleszek, *Congress and Its Members*, 9th ed., 193.

71. Matthew McCubbins and Thomas Schwartz, "Congressional Oversight Overlooked: Police Patrols Versus Fire Alarms," *American Journal of Political Science* (February 1984): 165–179.

72. Barbara Sinclair, "Party Leaders and the New Legislative Process," in Lawrence Dodd and Bruce Oppenheimer, eds., *Congress Reconsidered*, 6th ed. (Washington, D.C.: CQ Press, 1997), 229–245.

73. Richard Fenno, *Congressmen in Committees* (Boston, Mass.: Little, Brown, 1973); Glenn R. Parker, *Characteristics of Congress* (Englewood Cliffs, N.J.: Prentice Hall, 1989).

74. Davidson and Oleszek, *Congress and Its Members*, 9th ed., 204.

75. Steven Smith and Eric Lawrence, "Party Control of Committees in the Republican Congress," in Lawrence Dodd and Bruce Oppenheimer, eds., *Congress Reconsidered*, 6th ed. (Washington, D.C.: CQ Press, 1997), 163–192.

76. Davidson and Oleszek, *Congress and Its Members*, 9th ed., 219–220.

77. Copies of these and hundreds of other GAO reports are available online at www.gao.gov.

78. Ramsey Cox, "Senate Rejects Amendment to End Tobacco Farm Subsidies," *The Hill*, May 23, 2013, thehill.com/blogs/floor-action/senate/301645-senate-rejects-amendment- to-end-tobacco-farm-subsidies.

79. Barbara Sinclair, *The Transformation of the U.S. Senate* (Baltimore, Md.: Johns Hopkins University Press, 1989).

80. Nick Gas, "Boehner: Cruz Is 'Lucifer in the Flesh,'" *Politico*, April 28, 2016, www.politico.com/story/2016/04/john-boehner-ted-cruz-lucifer-222570.

81. Susan Herbst, *Rude Democracy: Civility and Incivility in American Politics* (Philadelphia, Penn.: Temple University Press, 2010).

82. Janet Reitman, "Meet the Senator Who Filibustered for 15 Hours on Gun Control," *Rolling Stone*, June 20, 2016, www.rollingstone.com/politics/news/meet-the-senator- who-filibustered-for-15-hours-on-gun-control- 20160620.

83. Roger H. Davidson, Walter J. Oleszek, and Frances E. Lee, eds., *Congress and Its Members*, 11th ed. (Washington, D.C.: CQ Press, 2008), 276.

84. John Stewart, "A Chronology of the Civil Rights Act of 1964," in Robert Loevy, ed., *The Civil Rights Act of 1964: The Passage of the Law That Ended Racial Segregation* (Albany: State University of New York Press, 1997), 358.

85. Ibid., 358–360.

86. David Herszenhorn, "How the Filibuster Became the Rule," *New York Times*, December 3, 2007, www.nytimes.com/2007/12/02/weekinreview/02herszenhorn.html.

87. Burgess Everett and Seung Min Kim, "Senate Goes for 'Nuclear Option,'" *Politico*, November 21, 2013, www.politico.com/story/2013/11/harry-reid-nuclear-option-100199.html.

88. Sahil Kapur, "Nuclear Option Triggered: Dems Make Historic Change to Filibuster Rules," *Talking Points Memo*, November 21, 2013, talkingpointsmemo.com/dc/harry-reid-nuclear-option-senate.

89. Barbara Sinclair, "The New World of U.S. Senators," in Lawrence C. Dodd and Bruce I. Oppenheimer, eds., *Congress Reconsidered*, 8th ed. (Washington, D.C.: CQ Press, 2005), 11; Richard Beth and Stanley Bach, "Filibusters and Cloture in the Senate," Congressional Research Service, March 28, 2003, www.senate.gov/reference/resources/pdf/RL30360 .pdf.

90. Emily Pierce, "Cloture, Filibusters Spur Furious Debate," *Roll Call*, March 5, 2008; U.S. Senate Virtual Reference Desk, "Senate Action on Cloture Motions," www.senate.gov/ pagelayout/reference/cloture_motions/clotureCounts.htm.

91. Barbara Sinclair, *Unorthodox Lawmaking: New Legislative Processes in the U.S. Congress*, 4th ed. (Washington, D.C: CQ Press, 2011).

92. Donald R. Matthews and James A. Stimson, *Yeas and Nays* (New York: Wiley, 1975).

93. Richard Smith, "Interest Group Influence in the U.S. Congress," *Legislative Studies Quarterly* 20 (February 1995): 89–140.

94. Richard S. Dunham, "Power to the President—Courtesy of the GOP," *Business Week*, October 20, 1997, 51.

95. Stephen C. Craig, *The Malevolent Leaders: Popular Discontent in America* (Boulder, Colo.: Westview Press, 1993); David Easton, "A Reassessment of the Concept of Political Support," *British Journal of Political Science* 5 (1975): 435–457; Glenn Parker, "Some Themes in Congressional Unpopularity," *American Journal of Political Science* 21 (1977): 93–110; E. J. Dionne Jr., *Why Americans Hate Politics* (New York: Simon & Schuster, 1991).

96. Seymour M. Lipset and William Schneider, *The Confidence Gap: Business, Labor, and Government in the Public Mind* (Baltimore, Md.: Johns Hopkins University Press, 1987).

97. Nina Totenberg, "Sen. McCain Says Republicans Will Block All Court Nominations If Clinton Wins," NPR, October 17, 2016, www.npr.org/2016/10/17/498328520/sen-mccain- says-republicans-will-block-all-court-nominations-if-clinton-wins.

98. Everett, "Flake Says It Might Be Garland Time."

CHAPTER 8

1. Jonathan Bernstein, "Trump Has Already Abdicated His Role as Head of State," Bloomberg, August 21, 2017, www.bloomberg.com/view/articles/2017-08-21/trump-has-already-abdicated-his-role-as-head-of-state-j6m413br; "Normalizing Trump: An Incredibly Brief Explainer," PressThink, September 17, 2017, pressthink.org/2017/09/normalizing-trump-incredibly-brief-explainer/.

2. Bruce Miroff, "Monopolizing the Public Space: The President as a Problem for Democratic Politics," in Bruce Miroff, Raymond Seidelman, and Todd Swanstrom, eds., *Debating Democracy* (Boston, Mass.: Houghton Mifflin, 1997), 294–303.

3. Max Farrand, *The Framing of the Constitution of the United States* (New Haven, Conn.: Yale University Press, 1913), 163.

4. Skip Thurman, "One Man's Impeachment Crusade," *Christian Science Monitor*, November 18, 1997, 4.

5. David Montgomery, "S.D. Republican Party Calls for Obama Impeachment," *Sioux Falls Argus Leader*, June 23, 2014; Impeach Obama Petition, www.teaparty.org/impeach-obama-petition/; Reid J. Epstein, "Impeach Obama,

Says Michael Burgess," *Politico*, August 9, 2011; Igor Volsky, "Top Republican Senator Suggests Impeaching Obama Over Immigration Policies," Think Progress, June 26, 2012, thinkprogress.org/politics/2012/06/26/506195/top-republican-senator-suggests-impeaching-obama-over-immigration-policies/; Jennifer Steinhauer, "Ignoring Qualms, Some Republicans Nurture Dreams of Impeaching Obama," *New York Times*, August 24, 2013; Tal Kopan, "Kerry Bentivolio: Impeachment 'a Dream,'" *Politico*, August 21, 2013.

6. Robert DiClerico, *The American President*, 4th ed. (Englewood Cliffs, N.J.: Prentice Hall, 1995), 374; Susan Milligan, "Democrats Scuttle Proposal to Impeach Bush: Move Avoids House Debate," *Boston Globe*, June 12, 2008, A5.

7. Joseph A. Pika and John Anthony Maltese, *The Politics of the Modern Presidency*, 6th ed. (Washington, D.C.: CQ Press, 2004), 3; Jeffrey K. Tulis, "The Two Constitutional Presidencies," in Michael Nelson, ed., *The Presidency and the Political System* (Washington, D.C.: CQ Press, 1994), 91–123.

8. Loch Johnson and James M. McCormick, "The Making of International Agreements: A Reappraisal of Congressional Involvement," *Journal of Politics* 40 (1978): 468–478.

9. Pika and Maltese, *The Politics of the Modern Presidency*, 6th ed., 374; and author calculations from Library of Congress, thomas.loc.gov/home/treaties/treaties.html.

10. Lawrence Margolis, *Executive Agreements and Presidential Power in Foreign Policy* (New York: Praeger, 1985).

11. D. Roderick Kiewiet and Mathew D. McCubbins, "Presidential Influence on Congressional Appropriations Decisions," *American Political Science Review* 32 (1988): 713–736.

12. Joseph J. Schatz, "With a Deft and Light Touch, Bush Finds Ways to Win," *CQ Weekly*, December 11, 2004, 2900–2904.

13. William G. Powell, *Power Without Persuasion: The Politics of Direct Presidential Action* (Princeton, N.J.: Princeton University Press, 2003).

14. Kenneth R. Mayer, *With the Stroke of a Pen: Executive Orders and Presidential Power* (Princeton, N.J.: Princeton University Press, 2002), 88–89.

15. Adam L. Warber, *Executive Orders and the Modern Presidency: Legislating From the Oval Office* (Boulder, Colo.: Lynne Rienner Publishers, 2006); William G. Howell, *Power Without Persuasion: The Politics of Direct Presidential Action* (Princeton, N.J.: Princeton University Press, 2003).

16. Robert A. Carp, Ronald Stidham, and Kenneth L. Manning, *Judicial Process in America*, 6th ed. (Washington, D.C.: CQ Press, 2004), 168.

17. Amy Goldstein, "Civil Rights Organizations Question Nominee Elena Kagan's Record on Race," *Washington Post*, June 27, 2010.

18. Charlie Savage, "Obama Backers Fear Opportunities to Reshape Judiciary Are Slipping Away," *New York Times*, November 14, 2009, https://www.nytimes.com/2009/11/15/us/politics/15judicial.html.

19. Jennifer Bendery, "Obama Leaving His Mark on Judiciary as Senate Confirms Gay, Black Judges," *Huffington Post*, June 24, 2014, www.huffingtonpost.com/2014/06/17/obama-judges_ n_5503075.html.

20. Jennifer Bendery, "Trump Is Remaking the Courts in His Image: White, Male and Straight," *Huffington Post*, March 11, 2018, www.huffingtonpost.com/entry/trump-judicial-nominees-white-male-straight_ us_5aa2b9bee4b07047bec6107c.

21. Quoted in Henry Abramson, *Justices and Presidents: A Political History of Appointments to the Supreme Court*, 2nd ed. (New York: Oxford University Press, 1985), 263.

22. Gerald Boyd, "White House Hunts for a Justice, Hoping to Tip Ideological Scales," *New York Times*, June 30, 1987; Alan I. Abramowitz and Jeffrey A. Segal, *Senate Elections* (Ann Arbor: University of Michigan Press, 1992), 1–6.

23. David Plotz, "Advise and Consent (Also, Obstruct, Delay, and Stymie): What's Still Wrong With the Appointments Process," *Slate Magazine*, March 19, 1999, www.slate.com/StrangeBedfellow/99–03–19/StrangeBedfellow.asp.

24. Jennifer Bendery, "As Senate Runs Out of Judges to Confirm, Dozens of Courts Still Sit Empty With No Nominees," *Huffington Post*, June 4, 2014, www.huffingtonpost.com/2014/06/04/obama-judicial-nominees_n_5439100.html.

25. Mary Kate Cary, "Obama Wrong to Criticize the Supreme Court," *USNews.com* blog, www.usnews.com/opinion/blogs/mary-kate-cary/2010/01/29/obama-was-wrong-to-criticize-the-supreme-court.

26. Rebecca Mae Salokar, *The Solicitor General: The Politics of Law* (Philadelphia, Penn.: Temple University Press, 1992), 29.

27. Bob Woodward, *Shadow: Five Presidents and the Legacy of Watergate* (New York: Simon & Schuster, 1999), 212–217.

28. Chris Cillizza, "Another Day, Another Clemency—What Trump's Pardons Are Really Saying," CNN, June 6, 2018, www.cnn.com/2018/06/06/politics/donald-trump-alice-johnson-pardon/index.html.

29. Cited in David O'Brien, *Constitutional Law and Politics* (New York: Norton, 1991), vol. 1, 218.

30. *In re Neagle*, 135 U.S. 546 (1890); *In re Debs*, 158 U.S. 564 (1895); *United States v. Curtiss-Wright Export Corp.*, 299 U.S. 304, 57 S. Ct. 216 (1936); *Youngstown Sheet & Tube v. Sawyer*, 343 U.S. 579 (1952).

31. Lyn Ragsdale, *Presidential Politics* (Boston, Mass.: Houghton Mifflin, 1993), 55.

32. *Historical Statistics of the United States: Colonial Times to 1970* (Washington, D.C.: U.S. Government Printing Office, 1975).

33. *Inaugural Addresses of the United States* (Washington, D.C.: U.S. Government Printing Office, 1982), quoted in Ragsdale, *Presidential Politics*, 71.

34. Suzanne Bilyeu, "FDR: How He Changed America—and Still Affects Your Life Today," *New York Times Upfront*, January 14, 2008.

35. *United States v. Curtiss-Wright Export Corp.*, 299 U.S. 304, 57 S. Ct. 216 (1936).

36. Arthur M. Schlesinger Jr., *The Imperial Presidency* (Boston, Mass.: Mariner Books, 2004).

37. Richard Nixon interview with David Frost, May 20, 1977, cited in Charles Savage, *Takeover: The Return of the Imperial Presidency and the Subversion of American Democracy* (New York: Little, Brown, 2007), 21.

38. Roger H. Davidson and Walter J. Oleszek, *Congress and Its Members*, 9th ed. (Washington, D.C.: CQ Press, 2004), 407.

39. *Clinton v. Jones*, 520 U.S. 681 (1997).

40. Charlie Savage, "Bush Challenges Hundreds of Laws," *Boston Globe*, April 30, 2006.

41. Philip Cooper, cited in Savage, "Bush Challenges Hundreds of Laws."

42. Carrie Budoff Brown and Jennifer Epstein, "President Obama's 'Year of Action' Falls Short," *Politico*, October 8, 2014, www.politico.com/story/2014/10/president-obama-executive-action-111687.html.

43. Alexander Burns, Jonathan Martin, and Maggie Haberman, "Pence Is Trying to Control Republican Politics. Trump Aides Aren't Happy," *New York Times*, May 14, 2018, www.nytimes.com/2018/05/14/us/politics/pence-trump-midterms.html.

44. Richard E. Neustadt, *Presidential Power and the Modern Presidents* (New York: Free Press, 1990), 10.

45. Ibid.

46. George Edwards III, *The Strategic President: Persuasion and Opportunity in Presidential Leadership* (Princeton, N.J.: Princeton University Press, 2009).

47. Samuel Kernell, *Going Public: New Strategies of Presidential Leadership*, 2nd ed. (Washington, D.C.: CQ Press, 1996).

48. Barbara Hinckley, *The Symbolic Presidency* (London: Routledge, 1990), ch. 2.

49. Jackie Calmes, "Obama Counts on Power of Convening People for Change," *New York Times*, January 11, 2014, A10.

50. See Hedrick Smith, *The Power Game: How Washington Works* (New York: Random House, 1988), 405–406, for similar reports on the Nixon and Reagan administrations.

51. Lee Sigelman, "Gauging the Public Response to Presidential Leadership," *Presidential Studies Quarterly* 10 (Summer 1980): 427–433; James A. Stimson, "Public Support for American Presidents: A Cyclical Model," *Public Opinion Quarterly* 40 (Spring 1976): 1–21; Michael MacKuen, "Political Drama, Economic Conditions, and the Dynamics of Presidential Popularity," *American Journal of Political Science* 27 (February 1983): 165–192.

52. John R. Hibbing and Elizabeth Theiss-Morse, *Stealth Democracy: Americans' Beliefs About How Government Should Work* (New York: Cambridge University Press, 2002).

53. Paul Brace and Barbara Hinckley, *Follow the Leader: Opinion Polls and the Modern Presidents* (New York: Basic Books, 1992), ch. 5.

54. Ibid., ch. 6.

55. Neustadt, *Presidential Power and the Modern Presidents*, 50–72.

56. Mark A. Peterson, *Legislating Together: The White House and Capitol Hill From Eisenhower to Reagan* (Cambridge, Mass.: Harvard University Press, 1990); George Edwards, *At the Margins: Presidential Leadership of Congress* (New Haven, Conn.: Yale University Press, 1989), ch. 9.

57. James L. Sundquist, "Needed: A Political Theory for a New Era of Coalition Government in the United States," *Political Science Quarterly* 103 (Winter 1988–1989): 613–635.

58. *Congressional Quarterly Weekly Report*, December 21, 1996, 3455.

59. Shawn Zeller, "Historic Success, at No Small Cost," *CQ Weekly*, January 11, 2010, 112.

60. David Mayhew, *Divided We Govern: Party Control, Lawmaking, and Investigations, 1946–1990* (New Haven, Conn.: Yale University Press, 1991).

61. Ragsdale, *Presidential Politics*, 1–4.

62. Terry Moe, "Presidents, Institutions, and Theory," in George C. Edwards III, John H. Kessel, and Bert A. Rockman, eds., *Researching the Presidency: Vital Questions, New Approaches* (Pittsburgh, Penn.: University of Pittsburgh Press, 1993), 370.

63. Ibid.

64. The President's Committee on Administrative Management, *Report of the Committee* (Washington, D.C.: U.S. Government Printing Office, 1937).

65. Jane Meyer and Doyle McManus, *Landslide: The Unmaking of the President, 1984–1988* (Boston, Mass.: Houghton Mifflin, 1988).

66. Tom Hamburger and Christi Parsons, "President Obama's Czar System Concerns Some," *Los Angeles Times*, March 5, 2009; Zachary Coile, "Obama's Big Task: Managing the Best, Brightest," *San Francisco Chronicle*, January 11, 2009; James Risen, "Obama Takes on Congress Over Policy Czar Positions," *New York Times*, April 16, 2011.

67. White House, "2013 Annual Report to Congress on White House Staff," www.whitehouse.gov/briefing-room/disclosures/annual-records/2013.

68. James P. Pfiffner, *The Modern Presidency*, 2nd ed. (New York: St. Martin's, 1998), 91.

69. Harold Relyea, "Growth and Development of the President's Office," in David Kozak and Kenneth Ciboski, eds., *The American Presidency* (Chicago, Ill.: Nelson Hall, 1985), 135; Pfiffner, *The Modern Presidency*, 2nd ed., 122.

70. Sid Frank and Arden Davis Melick, *The Presidents: Tidbits and Trivia* (Maplewood, N.J.: Hammond, 1986), 103.

71. Timothy Walch, ed., *At the President's Side: The Vice-Presidency in the Twentieth Century* (Columbia: University of Missouri Press, 1997), 45.

72. Ann Devroy and Stephen Barr, "Reinventing the Vice Presidency: Defying History, Al Gore Has Emerged as Bill Clinton's Closest Political Advisor," *Washington Post National Weekly Edition*, February 27–March 5, 1995, 6–7.

73. See, for example, Stephen F. Hayes, *Cheney: The Untold Story of America's Most Powerful and Controversial Vice President* (New York: HarperCollins, 2007); Bruce Kluger, David Slavin, and Tim Foley, *Young Dick Cheney: Great American* (San Francisco, Calif.: AlterNet Books, 2008); John Nichols, *Dick: The Man Who Is President* (New York: The New Press, 2004); Lou Dubose and Jake Bernstein, *Vice: Dick Cheney and the Hijacking of the American Presidency* (New York: Random House, 2006).

74. Evan Thomas, "Inconvenient Truth Teller; From Health-Care Reform to Afghanistan, Joe Biden Has Bucked Obama—as Only a Good Veep Can," *Newsweek*, October 19, 2009, 30+; Howard Kurtz, "Finding Virtue in Vice; Despite Gaffes, Biden Has Blossomed as Obama's Most Recent Prime Spokesman," *Washington Post*, June 10, 2010, C01.

75. Michelle Obama, "As Barack's First Lady, I Would Work to Help Working Families and Military Families," *U.S. News & World Report*, October 1, 2008.

76. Jeffrey M. Jones, "Michelle Obama Remains Popular in U.S.," www.gallup.com/poll/154952/michelle-obama-remains-popular.aspx.

77. Robert K. Murray and Tim H. Blessing, "The Presidential Performance Study: A Progress Report," *Journal of American History* 70 (December 1983): 535–555.

78. Jon R. Bond and Richard Fleisher, *The President in the Legislative Arena* (Chicago, Ill.: University of Chicago Press, 1990); George C. Edwards III, *Presidential Influence in Congress* (San Francisco, Calif.: Freeman, 1980).

79. James David Barber, *The Presidential Character*, 4th ed. (Englewood Cliffs, N.J.: Prentice Hall, 1992).

80. See Michael Nelson, "James David Barber and the Psychological Presidency," in David Pederson, ed., *The "Barberian" Presidency: Theoretical and Empirical Readings* (New York: Peter Lang, 1989), 93–110; Alexander George, "Assessing Presidential Character," *World Politics* (January 1974): 234–283; Jeffrey Tulis, "On Presidential Character," in Jeffrey Tulis and Joseph Bessette, eds., *Presidency and the Constitutional Order* (Baton Rouge: Louisiana State University Press, 1981).

81. Joseph Califano, *A Presidential Nation* (New York: Norton, 1975), 184–188.

82. Claire Lomas, "Donald Trump: Being Presidential 'Would Be Boring,'" *The Telegraph*, April 5, 2016, www.telegraph.co.uk/news/2016/04/05/donald-trump-being-presidential-would-be-boring/.

83. Joel Achenbach, "In a Heated Race, Obama's Cool Won the Day," *Washington Post*, November 6, 2008, A47.

84. Ed Pilkington, "Feel the love, feel the hate - my week in the cauldron of Trump's wild rallies," *The Guardian*, November 1, 2018, https://www.theguardian.com/us-news/2018/nov/01/trump-rallies-america-midterms-white-house.

85. Laila Lalalmi, "Does American 'Tribalism' End in a Compromise, or a Fight?," *New York Times*, June 26, 2018, https://www.nytimes.com/2018/06/26/magazine/does-american-tribalism-end-in-a-compromise-or-a-fight.html.

CHAPTER 9

1. John Whitesides, "Beyond the Daily Drama and Twitter Battles, Trump Begins to Alter American Life," Reuters, September 28, 2017, www.reuters .com/article/us-trump-effect-rules/beyond-the-daily-drama-and-twitter-battles-trump-begins-to-alter-american-life-idUSKCN1C3261; Chase Gunter, "How Big Is the Federal Workforce, Really?" FCW, October 5, 2017, fcw.com/articles/2017/10/05/federal-workforce-volker-size .aspx; Clyde Wayne Crews, Jr., "Trump's 2018 Regulatory Reform Agenda by the Numbers," Forbes, May 10, 2018, www.forbes.com/sites/waynecrews/ 2018/05/10/trumps-2018-regulatory-reform-agenda-by-the-numbers/#36f294187cd2; Danny Vinik, "The Radical Idea Buried in Trump's State of the Union," Politico, February 1, 2018, www .politico.com/agenda/story/2018/02/01/trump-civil-service-reform-state-of-the-union-000635.

2. John Whitesides, "Beyond the daily drama and Twitter battles, Trump begins to alter American life," Reuters, September 28, 2017, https://www.reuters .com/article/us-trump-effect-rules/beyond-the-daily-drama-and-twitter-battles-trump-begins-to-alter-american-life-idUSKCN1C3261.

3. Clyde Wayne Crews, "Trump's 2018 Regulatory Reform Agenda By the Numbers," Forbes, May 10, 2018, https://www.forbes.com/sites/waynecrews/2018/05/10/trumps-2018-regulatory-reform-agenda-by-the-numbers/#5d7366d97cd2; Noam Scheiber, "Trump Moves to Ease the Firing of Federal Workers," New York Times, May 25, 2018.

4. H. H. Gerth and C. Wright Mills, eds., From Max Weber (New York: Oxford University Press, 1946), 196–199.

5. Herbert Kaufman, "Emerging Conflicts in the Doctrines of Public Administration," American Political Science Review 50 (December 1956): 1057–1073.

6. Morris P. Fiorina, Congress: Keystone of the Washington Establishment (New Haven, Conn.: Yale University Press, 1977).

7. Herbert Kaufman, Red Tape, Its Origins, Uses, and Abuses (Washington, D.C.: Brookings Institution, 1977).

8. Louis Jacobson, "Taking the Measure of the Federal Workforce Under Donald Trump," PolitiFact, January 22, 2018, www.politifact.com/truth-o-meter/article/2018/jan/22/taking-measure-federal-workforce/.

9. Kenneth J. Meier and John Bohte, Politics and the Bureaucracy, 5th ed. (Belmont, Calif.: Thompson/Wadsworth), 2007.

10. Ibid.

11. U.S. National Debt Clock, accessed July 2, 2018, www.usdebtclock.org.

12. White House, "The Cabinet," www.whitehouse .gov/administration/cabinet.

13. Best Places to Work in the Federal Government, "FEC," bestplacestowork.org/BPTW/rankings/detail/LF00; "Social Security Administration," bestplacestowork.org/BPTW/rankings/detail/SZ00.

14. William G. Howell and David E. Lewis, "Agencies by Presidential Design," Journal of Politics 64 (2002): 1095–1114.

15. Dennis D. Riley, Controlling the Federal Bureaucracy (Philadelphia, Penn.: Temple University Press, 1987), 139–142.

16. Office of Management and Budget, "2017 Report to Congress on the Benefits and Costs of Federal Regulations and Agency Compliance With the Unfunded Mandates Reform Act," www .whitehouse.gov/wp-content/uploads/2017/12/draft_2017_cost_benefit_report.pdf; Clyde Wayne Crews Jr., "How Many Federal Agencies Exist? We Can't Drain the Swamp Until We Know," Forbes, July 5, 2017, www.forbes.com/sites/waynecrews/2017/07/05/how-many-federal-agencies-exist-we-cant-drain-the-swamp-until-we-know/#15141ae81aa2.

17. U.S. News and World Report, February 11, 1980, 64.

18. David E. Lewis, "The Adverse Consequences of the Politics of Agency Design for Presidential Management in the United States: The Relative Durability of Insulated Agencies," British Journal of Political Science 34 (2004): 377–404.

19. Noam Scheiber, "Trump Moves to Ease the Firing of Federal Workers," New York Times, May 25, 2018, www.nytimes.com/ 2018/05/25/business/economy/trump-federal-workers.html.

20. John B. Judis, "The Quiet Revolution: Obama Has Reinvented the State in More Ways Than You Can Imagine," New Republic, February 1, 2010, www.tnr .com/article/politics/the-quiet-revolution.

21. Emily Stephenson, "Postal Service Downsizing Plan Cuts 35,000 Jobs," February 23, 2012, www .msnbc.msn.com/id/46501840/ns/business-us_business/t/postal-service-downsizing-plan-cuts-jobs/#.T80IVr9Xsb1; Emily Stewart, "Trump's Trying to Fight Amazon and Jeff Bezos From the White House," Vox, May 21, 2018, www.vox.com/policy-and-politics/2018/5/19 /17371780/donald-trump- amazon-jeff- bezos-postal-service.

22. Robert Pear, "Health Insurance Companies Try to Shape Rules," New York Times, May 15, 2010.

23. Bureau of Labor Statistics, "Employment Projections: Civilian Labor Force by Age, Sex, Race and Ethnicity," https:// www.bls.gov/emp/tables/civilian-labor-force-detail.htm; Partnership for Public Service, "Fed Figures," https://ourpublicservice.org/research/fed-figures.php.

24. Ibid.

25. Quoted in Donald F. Kettl, System Under Stress: Homeland Security and American Politics (Washington, D.C.: CQ Press, 2004), 48.

26. "The 9/11 Commission Report: Final Report of the National Commission on Terrorist Attacks Upon the United States, Executive Summary," www.c-span.org/pdf/911final reportexecsum.pdf.

27. Quoted in Kettl, System Under Stress, 53.

28. Catherine Rampell, "Whistle-blowers Tell of Cost of Conscience," USA Today, November 24, 2006, 13A; Peter Eisler, "Whistle-blowers' Rights Get Second Look; Bills to Strengthen Protections Now Have Better Chance to Pass, Backers Say," USA Today, March 15, 2010, 6A.

29. Dana Hughes, "Obama Administration Denies Benghazi Whistleblowers Being Kept Quiet," ABC News, May 1, 2013, abcnews.go.com/blogs/politics/2013/05/obama-administration-denies-benghazi-whistleblowers-being-kept-quiet/; Adam Clark Estes, "Fox News Says Obama Muzzled Benghazi Whistleblowers," TheWire.com, April 29, 2013, www.thewire.com/politics/2013/04/fox-news-says-obama-muzzled-benghazi-whistleblowers/64705/.

30. David E. Lewis, "Staffing Alone: Unilateral Action and the Politicization of the Executive Office of the President, 1988–2004," Presidential Studies Quarterly 35 (2005): 496–514.

31. Keith Schneider, "How Interior Secretary Ryan Zinke Prompted a Mass Resignation From His National Park Service Advisory Board," Los Angeles Times, January 17, 2018, www.latimes.com/nation/la-na-national-park-zinke-oil-gas-20180117-story.html.

32. Terry Moe, "The President's Cabinet," in James Pfiffer and Roger J. Davidson, eds., Understanding the Presidency, 3rd ed. (New York: Longman, 2003), 208.

33. Office of Personnel Management, Federal Workforce Statistics: The Fact Book 2003 Edition (Washington, D.C.: OPM, 2003), 10, www.opm.gov/feddata/03factbk.pdf.

34. Francis E. Rourke, Bureaucracy, Politics and Public Policy, 3rd ed. (Boston, Mass.: Little, Brown, 1984), 106.

35. Albert B. Crenshaw, "Cash Flow," Washington Post, June 28, 1998, H1.

36. Anthony E. Brown, The Politics of Airline Regulation (Knoxville: University of Tennessee Press, 1987).

37. Lewis, "Staffing Alone."

38. Charlie Savage, "Bush Aide Admits Hiring Boasts; Says He Broke No Rules Giving Jobs to Conservatives," Boston Globe, June 6, 2007, A9; Charlie Savage, "Scandal Puts Spotlight on Christian Law School; Grads Influential in Justice Dept.," Boston Globe, April 8, 2007, A1; Eric Lipton, "Colleagues Cite Partisan Focus by Justice Officials," New York Times, May 12, 2007, A1.

39. Walter Pincus, "CIA Director Cuts Meetings on Terrorism; Coordinating Sessions Reduced to 3 a Week," Washington Post, January 10, 2005, A15; Walter Pincus, "Changing of the Guard at the CIA; Goss's Shake-Ups Leave Some Questioning Agency's Role," Washington Post, January 6, 2005, A3.

40. Robert Barnes, "Supreme Court Rebukes Obama on Recess Appointments," Washington Post, June 26, 2014.

41. Sonam Sheth and Skye Gould, "Who's Running the Government?" Business Insider, April 22, 2017, www.businessinsider.com/whos-running-the-government-trump-unfilled-executive-branch-positions-2017-4.

42. Riley, Controlling the Federal Bureaucracy, ch. 2.

43. Harold Seidman and Robert Gilmour, Politics, Position, and Power: From the Positive to the Regulatory State, 4th ed. (New York: Oxford University Press, 1986), 3; Mark Landler and Annie Lowrey, "Obama Bid to Cut Government Tests Congress," New York Times, January 13, 2012, www.nytimes .com/2012/01/14/us/politics/obama-to-ask-congress-for-power-to-merge-agencies.html.

44. Jimmy Tobias, "The Zinke effect: how the US interior department became a tool of big business," The Guardian, November 12, 2018, https://www.theguardian.com/us-news/2018/nov/12/the-zinke-effect-how-the-us-interior-department-became-a-tool-of-industry.

45. Quoted in Riley, Controlling the Federal Bureaucracy, 43.

46. Edmund L. Andrews, "Blowing the Whistle on Big Oil," New York Times, December 3, 2006.

47. Quoted in Jason DeParle, "Minerals Service Had a Mandate to Produce Results," New York Times, August 7, 2010.

48. Center for Responsive Politics, "Oil and Gas," www .opensecrets.org/industries/indus.php?ind=e01.

49. Hugh Heclo, "Issue Networks and the Executive Establishment," in Anthony King, ed., The New American Political System (Washington, D.C.: American Enterprise Institute, 1978), 87–124.

50. Deborah Zabarenko, "Environmental Group to Sue U.S. Over Oil Permits," May 14, 2010, www .reuters.com/article/idUSTRE64D64320100515.

51. Matthew McCubbins and Thomas Schwartz, "Congressional Oversight Overlooked: Police Patrols Versus Fire Alarms," American Journal of Political Science 28 (1984): 16–79.

52. Thomas E. Mann, Molly Reynolds, and Peter Hoey, "Is Congress on the Mend?" New York Times, April 28, 2007.

53. Kenneth Shepsle and Barry Weingast, "The Institutional Foundations of Committee Power," American Political Science Review 81 (1987): 85–104.

54. Felicity Barringer, "Limits on Logging Are Reinstated," New York Times, July 16, 2009, www .nytimes.com/2009/07/17/science/earth/17forest.html.

55. Emily Shugerman, "Donald Trump Signs Executive Order That Could Allow Companies to Mine and Drill for Oil at National Monuments," Independent, April 26, 2017, www.independent.co .uk/news/world/americas/donald-trump-order-national-monuments-oil-mining-logging-federal-land-protections-latest-a7703866.html.

56. Matthew Crenson and Francis E. Rourke, "By Way of Conclusion: American Bureaucracy Since World War II," in Louis Galambois, ed., *The New American State: Bureaucracies and Policies Since World War II* (Baltimore: Johns Hopkins University Press, 1987), 137–177.

57. Charles Lane, "High Court Rejects Detainee Tribunals: 5 to 3 Ruling Curbs President's Claim of Wartime Power," *Washington Post*, June 30, 2006, A1; Robert Barnes, "Justices Say Detainees Can Seek Release," *Washington Post*, June 13, 2008, A1.

58. Martha Derthick, *Policymaking for Social Security* (Washington, D.C.: Brookings Institution, 1979), reprinted in "The Art of Cooptation: Advisory Councils in Social Security," in Francis E. Rourke, ed., *Bureaucratic Power in National Policy Making*, 3rd ed. (Boston, Mass.: Little, Brown, 1986), 109.

59. Charles T. Goodsell, *The Case for Bureaucracy* (Chatham, N.J.: Chatham House, 1993), ch. 3; Robert L. Kahn, Barbara A. Gutek, Eugenia Barton, and Daniel Katz, "Americans Love Their Bureaucrats," in Francis E. Rourke, ed., *Bureaucracy, Politics, and Public Policy*, 4th ed. (Boston, Mass.: Little, Brown, 1988).

60. Meier and Bohte, *Politics and the Bureaucracy*, 5th ed., 210–211.

61. UN Environment, "Rapid and unprecedented action required to stay within 1.5°C says UN's Intergovernmental Panel on Climate Change," October 8, 2018, https:// www.unenvironment.org/ newsand-stories/press-releaserapid-and-unprecedented-action-requiredstay-within-15oc-says-uns.

CHAPTER 10

1. This list is based loosely on the discussion of the functions of law in James V. Calvi and Susan Coleman, *American Law and Legal Systems* (Upper Saddle River, N.J.: Prentice Hall, 1997), 2–4; Steven Vago, *Law and Society* (Upper Saddle River, N.J.: Prentice Hall, 1997), 16–20; and Lawrence Baum, *American Courts: Process and Policy*, 4th ed. (Boston, Mass.: Houghton Mifflin, 1998), 4–5.

2. Christopher E. Smith, *Courts, Politics, and the Judicial Process* (Chicago, Ill.: Nelson-Hall, 1993), 179.

3. Henry Abraham, *The Judicial Process* (New York: Oxford University Press, 1993), 97.

4. Ibid., 96–97.

5. Smith, *Courts, Politics, and the Judicial Process*, 329.

6. Jethro K. Lieberman, *The Litigious Society* (New York: Basic Books, 1981), 6.

7. Smith, *Courts, Politics, and the Judicial Process*, 324.

8. Ibid., 324, 327.

9. Lieberman, *The Litigious Society*, 168–190.

10. Lawrence Friedman, *Total Justice: What Americans Want From the Legal System and Why* (Boston, Mass.: Beacon Press, 1985), 31–32, cited in Smith, *Courts, Politics, and the Judicial Process*, 323.

11. "Prison Suits," *Reader's Digest*, August 1994, 96.

12. Alexander Hamilton, James Madison, and John Jay, *The Federalist Papers*, ed. Clinton Rossiter (New York: New American Library, 1961).

13. Robert A. Carp and Ronald Stidham, *The Federal Courts* (Washington, D.C.: CQ Press, 1991), 4.

14. Lawrence Baum, *The Supreme Court*, 5th ed. (Washington, D.C.: CQ Press, 1995), 13.

15. *Marbury v. Madison*, 5 U.S. (1 Cranch) 137 (1803).

16. *Dred Scott v. Sanford*, 60 U.S. (19 How.) 393.

17. Lawrence Baum, *The Supreme Court*, 12th ed. (Washington, D.C.: CQ Press, 2016), 159, 162.

18. Baum, *The Supreme Court*, 5th ed., 22–24.

19. Matthew J. Streb, "Just Like Any Other Election? The Politics of Judicial Elections," in Matthew J. Streb, ed., *Law and Election Politics: The Rules of the Game* (Boulder, Colo.: Lynne Rienner, 2005).

20. Joan Biskupic, "Making a Mark on the Bench," *Washington Post National Weekly Edition*, December 2–8, 1996, 31.

21. Sheldon Goldman, Sara Schiavoni, and Elliot Slotnick, "George W. Bush's Judicial Philosophy: Mission Accomplished," *Judicature* 92 (May/June 2009): 276.

22. John Schwartz, "For Obama, a Record on Diversity but Delays on Judicial Confirmations," *New York Times*, August 6, 2011, www.nytimes .com/2011/08/07/us/politics/07courts .html?_r=2.

23. Max Ehrenfreund, "The Number of White Dudes Becoming Federal Judges Has Plummeted Under Obama," *Washington Post*, February 18, 2016, www. washingtonpost.com/news/wonk/wp/2016/02/18/ the-number-of-white-dudes-becoming-federal-judges-has-plummeted-under-obama/; Charlie Savage, "Ratings Shrink President's List for Judgeships," *New York Times*, November 22, 2011, www.nytimes.com/2011/11/23/us/politics/ screening-panel-rejects-many-obama-picks-for-federal-judgeships.html.

24. Rorie Spill Solberg and Eric N. Waltenburg, "Trump's Judicial Nominations Would Put a Lot of White Men on Federal Courts," *Washington Post*, November 28, 2017, www.washingtonpost.com/ news/monkey-cage/wp/2017/11/28/this-is-how-trump-is-changing-the-federal-courts/; John Gramlich, "Trump's Appointed Judges Are a Less Diverse Group Than Obama's," Pew Research Center, March 20, 2018, www.pewresearch.org/ fact-tank/2018/03/20/trumps-appointed-judges-are-a-less-diverse-group-than-obamas/.

25. Biskupic, *Making a Mark on the Bench*.

26. Ibid.

27. Jeffrey Toobin, "Obama's Unfinished Judicial Legacy," *New Yorker*, July 31, 2012, www.newyorker .com/online/blogs/comment/2012/07/why-judges-matter.html; Savage, "Ratings Shrink President's List for Judgeships"; Ehrenfreund, "The Number of White Dudes."

28. Doug Kendall, "The Bench in Purgatory: The New Republican Obstructionism on Obama's Judicial Nominees," *Slate*, October 26, 2009, www .slate.com/id/2233309/.

29. Susan Davis and Kelsey Snell, "Mitch McConnell on Filling the Federal Bench: 'This Is My Top Priority,'" NPR, May 24, 2018, www.npr. org/2018/05/24/614228261/mitch-mcconnell-on-filling-the-federal-bench-this-is-my-top-priority.

30. David G. Savage, "Conservative Courts Likely Bush Legacy," *Los Angeles Times*, January 2, 2008, A11.

31. David M. O'Brien, "Ironies and Disappointments: Bush and Federal Judgeships," in Colin Campbell and Bert Rockman, eds., *The George W. Bush Presidency* (Washington, D.C.: CQ Press, 2004), 139–143.

32. Manu Raju, "Republicans Warn Obama on Judges," *Politico*, March 2, 2009, www.politico.com/news/ stories/0309/19526.html; Ted Sherman, "Sen. Menendez Blocking Federal Judge's Appointment to Powerful Court of Appeals," NJ.com, January 6, 2012, www.nj.com/news/index.ssf/2012/01/sen_ menendez_blocks_federal_ju.html.

33. Al Weaver, "Schumer Blasts 'Appalling' Senate GOP Flip-Flop on Judicial Nominees," *Washington Examiner*, May 7, 2018, www.washingtonexaminer .com/news/congress/schumer-blasts-appalling-senate-gop-flip-flop-on-judicial-nominees.

34. Greg Gordon, "Federal Courts, Winner Will Make a Mark on the Bench," *Minneapolis Star Tribune*, September 27, 2004, 1A.

35. Savage, "Ratings Shrink President's List for Judgeships."

36. Allan Smith, "Trump Is Bypassing Judicial Ratings Agencies Before Making His Nominations—and It Has Led to a Substantial Increase in 'Not Qualified' Nominees," *Business Insider*, November 15, 2017, www .businessinsider.com/trump-judicial-nominees-increase-in-aba-not-qualified-ratings-2017-11.

37. Linda Greenhouse, "The Nation: Vote Count Omits a Verdict on the Court," *New York Times*, November 18, 2001, sec. 4, 4; Jeffrey M. Jones, "Trust in Judicial Branch Up, Executive Branch Down," The Gallup Organization, September 20, 2017, news.gallup.com/poll/219674/trust-judicial-branch-executive-branch-down.aspx.

38. Cited in Robert Marquand, "Why America Puts Its Supreme Court on a Lofty Pedestal," *Christian Science Monitor*, June 25, 1997, 14.

39. Susan Davis and Kelsey Snell, "Mitch McConnell On Filling The Federal Bench: 'This Is My Top Priority,'" NPR, May 24, 2018, www.npr. org/2018/05/24/614228261/mitch-mcconnell-on-filling-the-federal-bench-this-is-my-top-priority.

40. Although the president has no official "list" of criteria, scholars are mostly agreed on these factors. See, for instance, Henry J. Abraham, *The Judiciary* (New York: New York University Press, 1996), 65–69; Lawrence Baum, *American Courts: Process and Policy*, 4th ed. (Boston, Mass.: Houghton Mifflin, 1998), 105–106; Philip Cooper and Howard Ball, *The United States Supreme Court: From the Inside Out* (Upper Saddle River, N.J.: Prentice Hall, 1996), 49–60; and Thomas G. Walker and Lee Epstein, *The Supreme Court of the United States* (New York: St. Martin's Press, 1993), 34–40.

41. Baum, *American Courts*, 4th ed., 105.

42. From the filmstrip *This Honorable Court* (Washington, D.C.: Greater Washington Educational Telecommunications Association, 1988), program 1.

43. Ibid.

44. Peter Baker, "Kagan Nomination Leaves Longing on the Left," *New York Times*, May 10, 2010, www .nytimes.com/2010/05/11/us/politics/11nominees. html?scp=1&sq=Elena%20Kagan%201iberal&st=cse.

45. Oyez, "Neil Gorsuch," https://www.oyez.org/ justices/neil_gorsuch.

46. CBS News, September 29, 2018, "Brett Kavanaugh's attack on Democrats could pose risk to Supreme Court," https://www.cbsnews.com/ news/brett-kavanaugh-attack-on-democrats-poses-risk-to-supreme-court/.

47. Dave Gilson, "Charts: The Supreme Court's Rightward Shift," *Mother Jones*, June 29, 2012, www.motherjones.com/politics/2012/06/ supreme-court-roberts- obamacare-charts.

48. Baum, *American Courts*, 4th ed., 105.

49. Walker and Epstein, *The Supreme Court of the United States*, 40.

50. Sonia Sotomayor, "A Latina Judge's Voice," address at U.C. Berkeley, October 26, 2001, www.berkeley.edu/ news/media/releases/2009/05/26_sotomayor.shtml.

51. Lawrence Baum, *The Supreme Court*, 8th ed. (Washington, D.C.: CQ Press, 2004), 103.

52. U.S. Supreme Court, "2013 Year-End Report on the Federal Judiciary," www.supremecourt.gov/ publicinfo/year-end/2013year-endreport.pdf.

53. Federal Judicial Center, "Supreme Court Caseloads, 1880–2015," www.fjc.gov/history/ exhibits/graphs-and-maps/ supreme-court-caseloads-1880-2015.

54. Cooper and Ball, *The United States Supreme Court*, 104.

55. Ibid., 134.

56. Walker and Epstein, *The Supreme Court of the United States*, 90.

57. Ibid., 91–92.

58. David O'Brien, *Storm Center* (New York: Norton, 1990), 272.

59. Walker and Epstein, *The Supreme Court of the United States*, 129–130.

60. Adam Cohen, "Psst . . . Justice Scalia . . . You Know, You're an Activist Too," *New York Times*, April 19, 2005, web version.

61. Walker and Epstein, *The Supreme Court of the United States*, 126–130.

62. What follows is drawn from the excellent discussion in Walker and Epstein, *The Supreme Court of the United States*, 131–139.

63. Greg Stohr, "Record Number of Amicus Briefs Filed in Health Care Cases," *Bloomberg News*, March 15, 2012, go.bloomberg.com/health-care-supreme-court/2012-03-15/record-number-of-amicus-briefs-filed-in-health-care-cases/.

64. Max Lerner, *Nine Scorpions in a Bottle: Great Judges and Cases of the Supreme Court* (New York: Arcade Publishing, 1994).

65. Philip J. Cooper, *Battles on the Bench: Conflict Inside the Supreme Court* (Lawrence: University Press of Kansas, 1995), 42–46.

66. For a provocative argument that the Court does not, in fact, successfully produce significant social reform and actually damaged the civil rights struggles in this country, see Gerald N. Rosenberg, *The Hollow Hope: Can Courts Bring About Social Change?* (Chicago, Ill.: University of Chicago Press, 1991).

67. *Marbury v. Madison*, 5 U.S. (1 Cranch) 137 (1803).

68. *Martin v. Hunter's Lessee*, 14 U.S. 304 (1816).

69. *McCulloch v. Maryland*, 4 Wheat. 316 (1819).

70. *Gibbons v. Ogden*, 9 Wheat. 1 (1824).

71. *Lochner v. New York*, 198 U.S. 45 (1905).

72. *Hammer v. Dagenhart*, 247 U.S. 251 (1918).

73. *Adkins v. Children's Hospital*, 261 U.S. 525 (1923).

74. *Dred Scott v. Sanford*, 19 How. 393 (1857).

75. *Plessy v. Ferguson*, 163 U.S. 537 (1896).

76. *Brown v. Board of Education*, 347 U.S. 483 (1954).

77. For example, *Mapp v. Ohio*, 367 U.S. 643 (1961); *Gideon v. Wainwright*, 372 U.S. 335 (1963); and *Miranda v. Arizona*, 382 U.S. 925 (1965).

78. *Baker v. Carr*, 396 U.S. 186 (1962).

79. *Roe v. Wade*, 410 U.S. 113 (1973).

80. *Citizens United v. Federal Election Commission*, 558 U.S. ___ (2010).

81. Jeffrey Rosen, "Welcome to the Roberts Court: How the Chief Justice Used Obamacare to Reveal His True Identity," *New Republic*, June 29, 2012, www.tnr.com/blog/plank/104493/welcome-the-roberts-court-who-the-chief-justice-was-all-along.

82. Pew Research Center for the People and the Press, "Stark Racial Divisions in Reactions to Ferguson Police Shooting," August 18, 2014, www.people-press.org/2014/08/18/stark-racial-divisions-in-reactions-to-ferguson-police-shooting/.

83. Jeremy Stahl, "The NFL Just Gave Donald Trump Everything He Wanted," *Slate*, May 23, 2018, slate.com/culture/2018/05/the-nfls-new-anthem-policy-is-a-political-gift-from-roger-goodell-to-donald-trump.html; Tom Schad, "'#Winning': Mike Pence Hails NFL's New Anthem Policy as a Victory for Donald Trump," *USA Today*, May 23, 2018, www.usatoday.com/story/sports/nfl/2018/05/23/mike-pence-nfl-new-national-anthem-policy-win-donald-trump/637826002/.

84. "New Yorkers' Views of the Mayor and the Police," *New York Times*, August 20, 2012, www.nytimes.com/interactive/2012/08/20/nyregion/new-yorkers-views-of-the-mayor-and-the-police.html.

85. Joseph Goldstein, "Judge Rejects New York's Stop and Frisk Policy," *New York Times*, August 12, 2013, www.nytimes.com/2013/08/13/nyregion/stop-and-frisk-practice-violated-rights-judge-rules.html.

86. Dylan Matthews, "The Black/White Marijuana Arrest Gap, in Nine Charts," *Washington Post Wonkblog*, June 4, 2013, www.washingtonpost.com/blogs/wonkblog/wp/2013/06/04/the-blackwhite-marijuana-arrest-gap-in-nine-charts/.

87. Bureau of Justice Statistics, "Indigent Defense Systems," www.bjs.gov/index.cfm?ty=tp&tid=28#top.

88. John H. Langbein, "Money Talks, Clients Walk," *Newsweek*, April 17, 1995, 32.

89. Legal Services Corporation, "LSC Receives $25 Million Spending Boost From Congress," March 23, 2018, www.lsc.gov/media-center/press-releases/2018/lsc-receives-25-million-spending-boost-congress.

90. Legal Services Corporation, "Fact Sheet: What Is LSC?", www.lsc.gov/about/factsheet_whatislsc.php.

91. Consortium on Legal Services and the Public, *Agenda for Success: The American People and Civil Justice* (Chicago, Ill.: American Bar Association, 1996); see also Legal Services Corporation, "Serving the Civil Legal Needs of Low-Income Americans," April 30, 2000, www.lsc.gov/pressr/exsum.pdf.

92. Justin McCarthy, "Americans Losing Confidence in All Branches of U.S. Government," Gallup Politics, June 30, 2014, www.gallup.com/poll/171992/americans-losing-confidence-branches-gov.aspx.

93. Dahleen Glanton, "O'Connor Questions Court's Decision to Take Bush v. Gore," *Chicago Tribune*, April 27, 2013, articles.chicagotribune.com/2013-04-27/news/ct-met-sandra-day-oconnor-edit-board-20130427_1_o-connor-bush-v-high-court.

94. Linda Greenhouse, "*Bush v. Gore*: A Special Report," *New York Times*, February 20, 2001.

95. Tom McCarthy, "The Supreme Court Has Already Reshaped America—Here's How," *Guardian*, July 2, 2018, www.theguardian.com/law/2018/jul/02/supreme-court-donald-trump-anthony-kennedy-conservative-nominee-republicans

CHAPTER 11

1. Brian Wheeler and Alex Hunt, "Brexit: All You Need to Know About the UK Leaving the EU," BBC, August 10, 2016, www.bbc.com/news/uk-politics-32810887.

2. Lizzie Dearden, "Brexit Research Suggests 1.2 Million Leave Voters Regret Their Choice in Reversal That Could Change Result," *Independent*, July 1, 2016, www.independent.co.uk/news/uk/politics/brexit-news-second-eu-referendum-leave-voters-regret-bregret-choice-in-millions-a7113336.html.

3. Mike Gravel, "Philadelphia II: National Initiatives," *Campaigns and Elections* (December 1995/January 1996): 2.

4. According to a September 1994 Roper poll, 76 percent favor a national referendum.

5. Survey by Fox News and Opinion Dynamics, May 24–May 25, 2000, iPOLL database, Roper Center for Public Opinion Research, University of Connecticut, www.ropercenter.uconn.edu/ipoll.html.

6. "Exchange With Reporters in Waco, Texas, August 7, 2001," *Public Papers of the Presidents: George W. Bush—2001*, vol. 2, 945; U.S. Government Printing Office via GPO Access.

7. Joshua Green, "The Other War Room," *Washington Monthly*, April 2002, 16.

8. Sam Stein, "Obama Mocks Polls but Spends More on Them ($4.4M) Than Bush," *Huffington Post*, July 29, 2010, www.huffingtonpost.com/2010/07/29/obama-mocks-polls-but-spe_n_663553.html.

9. V. O. Key Jr., *Public Opinion and American Democracy* (New York: Knopf, 1961), 7.

10. John Kingdon, *Congressmen's Voting Decisions*, 2nd ed. (New York: Harper & Row, 1981), ch. 2.

11. Gary C. Jacobson, "The War, the President, and the 2006 Midterm Congressional Elections," paper presented at the annual meeting of the Midwest Political Science Association, Chicago, April 12–15, 2007.

12. Many works repeat this theme of the uninformed and ignorant citizen. See, for example, Bernard Berelson, Paul F. Lazarsfeld, and William N.

McPhee, *Voting: A Study of Opinion Formation in a Presidential Campaign* (Chicago, Ill.: University of Chicago Press, 1954); Angus Campbell, Philip E. Converse, Warren E. Miller, and Donald E. Stokes, *The American Voter* (New York: Wiley, 1960); W. Russell Neuman, *The Paradox of Mass Politics* (Cambridge, Mass.: Harvard University Press, 1986); and Michael X. Delli Carpini and Scott Keeter, *What Americans Know About Politics and Why It Matters* (New Haven, Conn.: Yale University Press, 1996).

13. Delli Carpini and Keeter, *What Americans Know About Politics*, 70–75.

14. Pew Research Center, "From Brexit to Zika: What Do Americans Know?", July 25, 2017, www.people-press.org/2017/07/25/from-brexit-to-zika-what-do-americans-know/.

15. Ibid.

16. Herbert McClosky and Alida Brill, *Dimensions of Tolerance* (New York: Russell Sage Foundation, 1983), 50.

17. Ibid., 250.

18. M. Kent Jennings and Richard G. Niemi, *The Political Character of Adolescence* (Princeton, N.J.: Princeton University Press, 1974); Robert C. Luskin, John P. McIver, and Edward Carmines, "Issues and the Transmission of Partisanship," *American Journal of Political Science* 33 (May 1989): 440–458; Christopher H. Achen, "Parental Socialization and Rational Party Identification," *Political Behavior* 24 (June 2002): 151–170.

19. Shirley Engle and Anna Ochoa, *Education for Democratic Citizenship: Decision Making in the Social Studies* (New York: Teachers College of Columbia University, 1988).

20. Kenneth D. Wald, Dennis E. Owen, and Samuel S. Jill Jr., "Political Cohesion in Churches," *Journal of Politics* 52 (1990): 197–215; Robert Huckfeldt, Paul Allen Beck, Russell J. Dalton, and Jeffrey Levine, "Political Environments, Cohesive Social Groups, and the Communication of Public Opinion," *American Journal of Political Science* 39 (1995): 1025–1054; David C. Leege, Kenneth D. Wald, Brian S. Krueger, and Paul D. Mueller, *The Politics of Cultural Differences: Social Change and Voter Mobilization in the Post–New Deal Period* (Princeton, N.J.: Princeton University Press, 2002).

21. Elisabeth Noelle-Neumann, *The Spiral of Silence: Public Opinion, Our Social Skin* (Chicago, Ill.: University of Chicago Press, 1984).

22. Lee Sigelman and Susan Welch, *Black Americans' Views of Racial Equality—The Dream Deferred* (Cambridge, U.K.: Cambridge University Press, 1991).

23. Katherine Tate, "Black Political Participation in the 1984 and 1988 Presidential Elections," *American Political Science Review* 85 (December 1991): 1159–1176.

24. Amanda Terkle, "Rep. Tim Scott Floats Impeachment If Obama Invokes 14th Amendment on Debt Limit (VIDEO)," *HuffPost Politics*, July 6, 2011, www.huffingtonpost.com/2011/07/06/tim-scott-impeachment-obama-14-amendment-debt_n_891521.html.

25. Thomas B. Edsall, "Why Are Asian-Americans Such Loyal Democrats?" *New York Times*, November 4, 2015, www.nytimes.com/2015/11/04/opinion/why-are-asian-americans-such-loyal-democrats.html?_r=0.

26. Figure calculated by the authors from National Election Studies data.

27. Rosalee A. Clawson and Zoe M. Oxley, *Public Opinion: Democratic Ideal and Democratic Practice*, 2nd ed. (Washington, D.C.: CQ Press, 2013).

28. Matthew Yglesias, "The Partisan Gender Gap Among Millennials Is Staggeringly Large," *Vox*, May 22, 2018, www.vox.com/policy-and-

politics/2018/3/22/17146534/
millennial-gender-gap-partisan.

29. Scott Helman, "Obama Strikes Chord With Generation Next: Campaign Targets Youth Vote in Ind," *Boston Globe*, May 3, 2008; Cynthia Burton and Joseph A. Gambardello, "Turnout for N.J. Primary Highest in Half a Century," *Philadelphia Inquirer*, February 7, 2008.

30. Paul R. Abramson and Ada W. Finifter, "On the Meaning of Political Trust: New Evidence From Items Introduced in 1978," *American Journal of Political Science* 25 (May 1981): 295–306; Arthur H. Miller, "Is Confidence Rebounding?" *Public Opinion* (June/July 1983); Erikson and Tedin, *American Public Opinion*, 7th ed., 162–166.

31. Warren E. Miller and J. Merrill Shanks, *The New American Voter* (Cambridge, Mass.: Harvard University Press, 1996), ch. 7.

32. Hannah Fingerhut, "Millennials' Views of News Media, Religious Organizations Grow More Negative," Pew Research Center, January 4, 2016, www.pewresearch.org/fact-tank/2016/01/04/millennials-views-of-news-media-religious-organizations-grow-more-negative/; David Masci, "Q&A: Why Millennials Are Less Religious Than Older Americans," Pew Research Center, January 8, 2016, www.pewresearch.org/fact-tank/2016/01/08/qa-why-millennials-are-less-religious-than-older-americans/; Eileen Patten, "The Nation's Latino Population Is Defined by Its Youth," Pew Research Center, April 20, 2016, www.pewhispanic.org/2016/04/20/the-nations-latino-population-is-defined-by-its-youth/.

33. "A Deep Dive Into Party Affiliation," Pew Research Center, April 7, 2015, www.people-press.org/2015/04/07/a-deep-dive-into-party-affiliation/.

34. Campbell et al., *The American Voter*; Donald P. Green, Bradley Palmquist, and Eric Schickler, *Partisan Hearts and Minds: Political Parties and the Social Identities of Voters* (New Haven, Conn.: Yale University Press, 2002).

35. Janell Ross, "How Come 53% of Republicans Think the Unemployment Rate Has Risen Under Obama?" *Washington Post*, November 20, 2015, www.washingtonpost.com/news/the-fix/wp/2015/11/20/the-amount-of-misinformation-about-our-economy-is-amazing/.

36. M. J. Hetherington, "Resurgent Mass Partisanship: The Role of Elite Polarization," *American Political Science Review* 95 (2001): 619–631; Alan Abramowitz, *The Disappearing Center: Engaged Citizens, Polarization and American Democracy* (New Haven, Conn.: Yale University Press, 2010); Matthew S. Levendusky, *The Partisan Sort: How Liberals Became Democrats and Conservatives Became Republicans* (Chicago, Ill.: University of Chicago Press, 2010).

37. Gerald C. Wright and Nathan Birkhead, "The Macro Sort of State Partisanship," *Political Research Quarterly* 67 (2014): 426–439.

38. Lilliana Mason, *Uncivil Agreement: How Politics Became Our Identity* (Chicago: University of Chicago Press, 2018).

39. Norman H. Nie, Jane Junn, and Kenneth Stehlik-Barry, *Education and Democratic Citizenship in America* (Chicago, Ill.: University of Chicago Press, 1996).

40. For more on the effects of education, see Delli Carpini and Keeter, *What Americans Know About Politics*, 188–189; Robert S. Erikson and Kent L. Tedin, *American Public Opinion*, 7th ed. (New York: Pearson-Longman, 2005), 152–159; and Herbert H. Hyman, Charles R. Wright, and John Shelton Reed, *The Enduring Effects of Education* (Chicago, Ill.: University of Chicago Press, 1975). For a dissenting view that formal education is just a mask for intelligence and native cognitive ability, see Robert Luskin, "Explaining Political Sophistication," *Political Behavior* 12 (1990): 3298–3409.

41. Robert S. Erikson, Gerald C. Wright, and John P. McIver, *Statehouse Democracy* (New York: Cambridge University Press, 1993).

42. Philip Bump, "There Really Are Two Americas, An Urban One and a Rural One," *Washington Post*, October 21, 2014, www.washingtonpost.com/news/the-fix/wp/2014/10/21/there-really-are-two-americas-a-urban-one-and-a-rural-one/.

43. Pew Research Center for People and the Press, "Public Appetite for Government Misjudged: Washington Leaders Wary of Public Opinion," www.people-press.org/files/legacy-pdf/92.pdf.

44. Susan Herbst, *Numbered Voices: How Opinion Polling Has Shaped American Politics* (Chicago, Ill.: University of Chicago Press, 1993), ch. 4.

45. William Safire, *Safire's New Political Dictionary: The Definitive Guide to the New Language of Politics* (New York: Random House, 1993), 764.

46. Richard Morin, "Don't Ask Me: As Fewer Cooperate on Polls, Criticism and Questions Mount," *Washington Post*, October 28, 2004, C1.

47. Pew Research Center for the People and the Press, "Opinion Poll Experiment Reveals Conservative Opinions Not Underestimated, But Racial Hostility Missed," March 27, 1998, www.people-press.org/content.htm; Andrew Rosenthal, "The 1989 Elections: Predicting the Outcome; Broad Disparities in Votes and Polls Raising Questions," *New York Times*, November 9, 1989, A1; Adam Clymer, "Election Day Shows What the Opinion Polls Can't Do," *New York Times*, November 12, 1989, sec. 4, 4; George Flemming and Kimberly Parker, "Race and Reluctant Respondents: Possible Consequences of Non-Response for Pre-Election Survey," May 16, 1998, www.people-press.org/content.htm.

48. William Saletan, "Phoning It In," *Slate*, December 7, 2007, www.slate.com/iod/2179395/.

49. SurveyUSA home page, www.surveyusa.com.

50. David Sanders, Harold D. Clarke, Marianne C. Stewart, and Paul Whiteley, "Does Mode Matter for Modeling Political Choice? Evidence From the 2005 British Election Study," *Political Analysis* 15 (2007): 257–285; Robert P. Berrens, Alok K. Bohara, Hank Jenkins-Smith, Carol Silva, and David L. Weimer, "The Advent of Internet Surveys for Political Research: A Comparison of Telephone and Internet Samples," *Political Analysis* 11 (2003): 1–22; Taylor Humphrey, "The Case for Publishing (Some) Online Polls," *Polling Report*, January 15, 2007; Linchiat Chang and Jon A. Krosnick, "National Surveys via RDD Telephone Interviewing Versus the Internet," *Public Opinion Quarterly* 2009 (73): 641–678.

51. J. Michael Brick, Pat D. Brick, Sarah Dipko, Stanley Presser, Clyde Tucker, and Yangyang Yuan, "Cell Phone Survey Feasibility in the U.S.: Sampling and Calling Cell Numbers Versus Landline Numbers," *Public Opinion Quarterly* 71 (Spring 2007): 23–39. See the special issue of *Public Opinion Quarterly* (Winter 2007) for perspectives on the challenges that cell phones pose for surveys.

52. George F. Bishop et al., "Pseudo-Opinions on Public Affairs," *Public Opinion Quarterly* 44 (Summer 1980): 198–209.

53. Graham Kalton and Howard Schuman, "The Effect of the Question on Survey Responses: A Review," *Journal of the Royal Statistical Society. Series A (General)* 145 (1982): 42–73; Howard Schuman and Stanley Presser, *Questions and Answers in Attitude Surveys* (New York: Academic Press, 1981), 148–160.

54. This was a Roper Starch Worldwide poll conducted in November 1992 for the American Jewish Committee, and it was reported in conjunction with the dedication of the Holocaust Memorial Museum.

55. Debra J. Saunders, "Poll Shows Americans in Deep Dumbo," *San Francisco Chronicle*, April 23, 1993, A30; Leonard Larsen, "What's on Americans' Mind? Not Much, History Poll Finds," *Sacramento Bee*, June 2, 1993, B7, cited in David W. Moore and Frank Newport, "Misreading the Public: The Case of the Holocaust Poll," *Public Perspective* (March–April 1994).

56. Moore and Newport, "Misreading the Public," 29.

57. John Zaller, *The Nature and Origins of Mass Opinion* (New York: Cambridge University Press, 1992).

58. See, for example, www.langerresearch.com/category/abc-news-polls/, www.cbsnews.com/latest/opinion/, www.washingtonpost.com/politics/polling/, www.nytimes.com/search?query=Polls+and+Public+Opinion, www.people-press.org, and for an excellent roundup of political polls, see www.pollingreport.com.

59. Two recent additions to the large-scale surveys are the National Annenberg Elections Surveys, which launched large, complex, in-person surveys of voter attitudes and decision making in the 2000, 2004, and 2008 elections (www.annenbergpublicpolicycenter.org/political-communication/naes/) and the recurring (since 2006) Cooperative Congressional Elections studies, which are Internet-based surveys. Each carries questions by teams of scholars from dozens of universities exploring a wide variety of questions about political behavior; see https://cces.gov.harvard.edu/.

60. Nate Silver, "Which Polls Fared Best, and Worst, in the 2012 Presidential Race," November 10, 2012, fivethirtyeight.blogs.nytimes.com/2012/11/10/which-polls-fared-best-and-worst-in-the-2012-presidential-race/.

61. Most of the exit poll reporting is based on surveys done by Edison Media Research and Mitofsky International for the National Election Pool. This is a consortium of ABC News, Associated Press, CBS News, CNN, Fox News, and NBC News. Each of the media organizations has its own analysts who then highlight different aspects of the exit poll data.

62. Adam Lisberg, "Exit Polls Out of Whack: Early Numbers Told Wrong Story," *New York Daily News*, November 4, 2002, 11; "Evaluation of Edison/Mitofsky Election System 2004," prepared by Edison Media Research and Mitofsky International for the National Election Pool (NEP), January 19, 2005.

63. Quoted in "Planting Lies With 'Push Polls,'" *St. Petersburg Times*, June 7, 1995, 10A.

64. Quoted in Betsy Rothstein, "Push Polls Utilized in Final Weeks," *The Hill*, October 28, 1998, 3.

65. "Pollsters Seek AAPC Action," *Campaigns and Elections* (July 1996): 55.

66. Paul Sniderman and Thomas Piazza, *The Scar of Race* (Cambridge: Harvard University Press, 1995).

67. TESS Time-Sharing Experiments for the Social Sciences, tessexperiments.org.

68. Erikson and Tedin, *American Public Opinion*, 5th ed. (Boston, Mass.: Allyn & Bacon), 42–47.

69. Research suggests that the use of information shortcuts does allow the electorate to make decisions that are more in line with their values than if they did not have such shortcuts; see Samuel Popkin, *The Reasoning Voter* (Chicago, Ill.: University of Chicago Press, 1991); and Paul Sniderman, Richard Brody, and Philip Tetlock, *Reasoning and Choice: Exploration in Political Psychology* (New York: Cambridge University Press, 1991). However, this is not the same as saying that,

if fully informed, everyone would make the same decision that he or she does without information. Indeed, information really does count; see Larry Bartels, "Uninformed Votes: Information Effects in Presidential Elections," *American Journal of Political Science* 40 (February 1996): 194–230; and Scott Althaus, "Information Effects in Collective Preferences," *American Political Science Review* 92 (September 1998): 545–558.

70. Milton Lodge, Kathleen McGraw, and Patrick Stroh, "An Impression-Driven Model of Candidate Evaluation," *American Political Science Review* 82 (June 1989): 399–419.

71. Berelson, Lazarsfeld, and McPhee, *Voting*, 109–115.

72. Philip Meyer, "The Elite Newspaper of the Future," *American Journalism Review* (October/November 2008), www.ajr.org/article.asp?id=4605.

73. Larry M. Bartels, "Uninformed Votes: Information Effects in Presidential Elections," *American Journal of Political Science* 40 (1996): 194–230.

74. Gerald C. Wright, "Level of Analysis Effects on Explanations of Voting," *British Journal of Political Science* 18 (July 1989): 381–398; Samuel Popkin, *The Reasoning Voter* (Chicago, Ill.: University of Chicago Press, 1991); Benjamin Page and Robert Shapiro, *The Rational Public* (Chicago, Ill.: University of Chicago Press, 1993).

75. Erikson, Wright, and McIver, *Statehouse Democracy*.

76. Michael B. MacKuen, Robert S. Erikson, and James A. Stimson, "Macropartisanship," *American Political Science Review* 89 (December 1989): 1125–1142.

77. Dearden, "Brexit Research Suggests 1.2 Million Leave Voters Regret Their Choice."

78. Jean Bethke Elshtain, "A Parody of True Democracy," *Christian Science Monitor*, August 13, 1992, 18.

CHAPTER 12

1. See, for example, James Bryce, *The American Commonwealth* (Chicago, Ill.: Sergel, 1891), vol. 2, pt. 3.

2. E. E. Schattschneider, *Party Government* (New York: Holt, Rinehart, and Winston, 1942), 1.

3. This division and the following discussion are based on Frank Sorauf, *Party Politics in America* (Boston, Mass.: Little, Brown, 1964), ch. 1; and V. O. Key Jr., *Politics, Parties, and Pressure Groups*, 5th ed. (New York: Corwell, 1964).

4. Richard G. Niemi and M. Kent Jennings, "Issues of Inheritance in the Formation of Party Identification," *American Journal of Political Science* 35 (1991): 970–988.

5. The discussion of the responsible party model is based on Austin Ranney, *The Doctrine of the Responsible Party Government* (Urbana: University of Illinois Press, 1962), chs. 1, 2.

6. Morris P. Fiorina, "The Decline of Collective Responsibility in American Politics," *Daedalus* 109 (Summer 1980): 25–45; John H. Aldrich, *Why Parties? The Origin and Transformation of Party Politics in America* (Chicago, Ill.: University of Chicago Press, 1995), 3.

7. American Political Science Association, "Toward a More Responsible Two-Party System: A Report of the Committee on Political Parties of the American Political Science Association," *American Political Science Review* 44 (1950; 3, pt. 2): 1–99.

8. Thomas E. Mann and Norman J. Ornstein, *It's Even Worse Than It Looks: How the American Constitutional System Collided With the New Politics of Extremism* (New York: Basic Books, 2012).

9. Alan I. Abramowitz, "Exploring the Bases of Partisanship in the American Electorate: Social Identity vs. Ideology," *Political Research Quarterly* 59 (2006): 175–187.

10. Alan I. Abramowitz and Kyle L. Saunders, "Ideological Realignment in the U.S. Electorate," *Journal of Politics* 60 (1998): 634–652; Geoffrey C. Layman and Thomas M. Carsey, "Party Polarization and 'Conflict Extension' in the American Electorate," *American Journal of Political Science* 46 (2002): 786–802; Geoffrey C. Layman et al., "Activists and Conflict Extension in American Party Politics," *American Political Science Review* 104 (2010): 324–346.

11. Calculated by the authors using data from CBS News/*New York Times* national surveys; Abramowitz and Saunders report the same basic pattern in their analysis of white party identifiers using data from the American National Election Studies, Abramowitz and Saunders, "Ideological Realignment of the U.S. Electorate," 186.

12. Edward G. Carmines and Geoffrey C. Layman, "Issue Evolution in Postwar American Politics: Old Certainties and Fresh Tensions," in Byron E. Shafer, ed., *Present Discontents: American Politics in the Very Late Twentieth Century* (Chatham, N.J.: Chatham House, 1997), 89–134.

13. Ruy A. Teixeira and Joel Rogers, *America's Forgotten Majority: Why the White Working Class Still Matter* (New York: Basic Books, 2000); Thomas Frank, *What's the Matter With Kansas? How Conservatives Won the Heart of America* (New York: Metropolitan Books, 2004).

14. John H. Aldrich, "A Downsian Spatial Model With Party Activism," *American Political Science Review* 77 (1983): 974–990; David W. Brady, Hahrie Han, and Jeremy C. Pope, "Primary Elections and Candidate Ideology: Out of Step With the Primary Electorate?" *Legislative Studies Quarterly* 27 (2007): 79–105; Layman et al.; James L. Gibson and Susan E. Scarrow, "State Organizations in American Politics," in Eric M. Uslaner, ed., *American Political Parties: A Reader* (Itasca, Ill.: F. F. Peacock, 1993), 234.

15. James Q. Wilson, *The Amateur Democrat: Club Politics in Three Cities* (Chicago, Ill.: University of Chicago Press, 1965).

16. Walter J. Stone and Alan I. Abramowitz, "Winning May Not Be Everything, But It's More Than We Thought: Presidential Party Activists in 1980," *American Political Science Review* 77 (1983): 945–956.

17. Godfrey Hodgson, *The Myth of American Exceptionalism* (New Haven, Conn.: Yale University Press, 2009).

18. Thomas Carsey, Geoffrey Layman and Mark Brockway, "Donald Trump and Conflict Extension in American Public Opinion" Paper presented at the annual meeting of the Southern Political Science Association, New Orleans, January 4–6, 2017.

19. Joseph A. Aistrup, *The Southern Strategy Revisited: Republican Top-Down Advancement in the South* (Lexington: University of Kentucky Press, 1996), 148–151; Robert S. Erikson, Gerald C. Wright, and John P. McIver, *Statehouse Democracy: Public Opinion and Policy in the American States* (Cambridge, U.K.: Cambridge University Press, 1993), ch. 5.

20. Keith T. Poole and Howard Rosenthal, "The Polarization of American Politics," *Journal of Politics* 46 (1984): 1061–1079; Alan Abramowitz, *The Disappearing Center: Engaged Citizens, Polarization, and American Democracy* (New Haven, Conn.: Yale University Press, 2010); "WATCH: Senate Has 'Become More Partisan, More Tribal Than at Any Time I Can Remember,' McCain Says," PBS NewsHour, July 25, 2017, www.pbs.org/newshour/politics/watch-senate-become-partisan-tribal-time-can-remember-mccain-says.

21. Anthony Downs, *An Economic Theory of Democracy* (New York: Harper & Row, 1957).

22. Alan Abramowitz and Steven Webster, "'Negative Partisanship' Explains Everything," *Politico Magazine*, September/October 2017, www.politico.com/magazine/story/2017/09/05/negative-partisanship-explains-everything-215534.

23. Aldrich, *Why Parties?*

24. Ibid., 5.

25. This discussion of the Jacksonian Democrats and machine politics and patronage is based on Aldrich, *Why Parties?*, ch. 4; Leon D. Epstein, *Political Parties in the American Mold* (Madison: University of Wisconsin Press, 1986), 134–143; and Frank J. Sorauf and Paul Allen Beck, *Party Politics in America*, 6th ed. (Glenview, Ill.: Scott, Foresman, 1988), 83–91.

26. Gerald C. Wright, John P. McIver, Robert S. Erikson, and David B. Holian, "Stability and Change in State Electorates, Carter Through Clinton," paper presented at the Midwest Political Science Association meetings, Chicago, 2000; Larry Bartels, "Partisanship and Voting Behavior, 1952–1996," *American Journal of Political Science* 44 (2000): 35–50.

27. Gary C. Jacobson, *The Electoral Origins of Divided Government* (Boulder, Colo.: Westview Press, 1990), and *The Politics of Congressional Elections*, 6th ed. (New York: Longman, 2003).

28. Xandra Kayden and Eddie Mahe Jr., "Back From the Depths: Party Resurgence," in Uslaner, *American Political Parties*, 192, 196; Aistrup, *The Southern Strategy Revisited*, ch. 4.

29. Sarah McCally Morehouse and Malcolm E. Jewell, *State Politics, Parties, & Policy*, 2nd ed. (Lanham, Md.: Rowman & Littlefield, 2003), 127–133.

30. Alec MacGillis and Peter Slevin, "Did Rush Limbaugh Tilt Result in Indiana? Conservative Host Urged 'Chaos' Votes," *Washington Post*, May 8, 2008, A01.

31. David E. Price, *Bring Back the Parties* (Washington, D.C.: Congressional Quarterly, 1984), 130–132.

32. Sorauf and Beck, *Party Politics in America*, 6th ed., 218–233.

33. Jill Serjeant, "John McCain Speech Draws Record TV Ratings," September 5, 2008, www.washingtonpost.com.

34. C. P. Cotter, J. L. Gibson, J. F. Bibby, and R. J. Huckshorn, *Party Organizations in American Politics* (New York: Praeger, 1984); John J. Coleman, "Resurgent or Just Busy? Party Organizations in Contemporary America," in John Green and Daniel Shea, eds., *The State of the Parties* (Lanham, Md.: Rowman & Littlefield, 1996), ch. 22.

35. Jill Abramson, "Democrats and Republicans Step Up Pursuit of 'Soft Money,'" *New York Times*, May 13, 1998, 2; Jill Abramson, "Cost of '96 Campaign Sets Record at $2.2 Billion," *New York Times*, November 25, 1997, 1.

36. "Living in a Citizens United World: When Other Voices Are Drowned Out," *New York Times*, March 26, 2012 (editorial); Adam Liptak, "Viewing Free Speech Through Election Law Haze," *New York Times*, May 4, 2010; Adam Liptak, "Former Justice O'Connor Sees Ill in Election Finance Ruling," *New York Times*, January 27, 2010; Rebekah Metzler, "Progressives Push Amendment to Overturn Citizens United," USNEWS.com, April 18, 2012; Jeffrey Tobin, "Money Talks," *New Yorker*, April 11, 2011; Jaime Fuller, "Big Sky's the Limit," *The American Prospect*, June 2012; Rebekah Metzler, "McCain Calls SCOTUS Decision on Campaign Spending 'Stupid,'" USNEWS.com, March 27, 2012.

37. Aistrup, *The Southern Strategy Revisited*, 76; Paul S. Herrnson, *Congressional Elections: Campaigning at Home and in Washington*, 2nd ed. (Washington, D.C.: CQ Press, 1998), ch. 4.

38. Sorauf and Beck, *Party Politics in America*, 6th ed.

39. Gerald Pomper with Susan Lederman, *Elections in America* (New York: Longman, 1980), 145–150, 167–173.

40. Samuel Huntington, "The Visions of the Democratic Party," *Public Interest* (Spring 1985): 64; Layman and Carsey, "Party Polarization and 'Conflict Extension.'"

41. This section is based on Alan Ware, *Political Parties and Party Systems* (New York: Oxford University Press, 1996).

42. L. Sandy Maisel, *Parties and Elections in America*, 2nd ed. (New York: McGraw-Hill, 1993), ch. 10; Epstein, *Political Parties in the American Mold*; Price, *Bring Back the Parties*, 284.

43. David Leonhardt, "The Election: Was Buchanan the Real Nader?" *New York Times*, December 10, 2000, sec. 4, 4.

44. Gerald C. Wright, "Charles Adrian and the Study of Nonpartisan Elections," *Political Research Quarterly* 61 (2008): 13–16.

45. Joseph Cooper and David W. Brady, "Institutional Context and Leadership Style: The House From Cannon to Rayburn," *American Political Science Review* 75 (1981): 411–425; John H. Aldrich and David W. Rohde, "The Logic of Conditional Party Government: Revisiting the Electoral Connection," in Lawrence Dodd and Bruce Oppenheimer, eds., *Congress Reconsidered*, 7th ed. (Washington, D.C.: CQ Press, 2001).

46. Michelle Cottle, "House Broker," *New Republic*, June 11, 2008, www.tnr.com.

47. Aldrich and Rohde, "The Logic of Conditional Party Government."

48. Ed Hornick, "The 'Big Headache': Boehner Backed Into Corner by Tea Party, Obama," CNN News, July 26, 2011, articles.cnn.com/ 2011-07-26/politics/tea.party.boehner_1_tea- party-debt-ceiling-debt-limit-vote?_s=PM:POLITICS.

49. See, for example, Fiorina, *Divided Government*; and John R. Hibbing and Elizabeth Theiss-Morse, *Congress as Public Enemy: Public Attitudes Toward American Political Institutions* (Cambridge, U.K.: Cambridge University Press, 1995).

50. Hibbing and Theiss-Morse, *Congress as Public Enemy*, 157.

CHAPTER 13

1. Organic Trade Association, "Maturing U.S. Organic Sector Sees Steady Growth of 6.4 Percent in 2017," press release, May 18, 2018, https://ota.com/news/press-releases/20201.

2. Dann Denny, "Defining 'Organic,'" *Bloomington Herald Times*, April 16, 1998, D1.

3. Marian Burros, "Eating Well: U.S. Proposal on Organic Food Gets a Grass-Roots Review," *New York Times*, March 25, 1998, F10.

4. Gene Kahn, "National Organic Standard Will Aid Consumers," *Frozen Food Age* 47 (September 1998): 18.

5. Burros, "Eating Well," F10.

6. Alexis de Tocqueville, *Democracy in America*, Richard D. Heffner, ed. (New York: New American Library, 1956), 198.

7. James Madison, "*Federalist* No. 10," in Roy P. Fairfield, ed., *The Federalist Papers*, 2nd ed. (Baltimore, Md.: Johns Hopkins University Press, 1981), 16.

8. This definition is based on Jeffrey M. Berry, *The Interest Group Society*, 3rd ed. (New York: Longman, 1997); and David Truman, *The Governmental Process: Political Interest and Public Opinion*, 2nd ed. (New York: Knopf, 1971).

9. Berry, *The Interest Group Society*, 3rd ed.; Truman, *The Governmental Process*; Allan J. Cigler and Burdett A. Loomis, eds., *Interest Group Politics*, 6th ed. (Washington, D.C.: CQ Press, 2002).

10. Burdett A. Loomis and Allan J. Cigler, "Introduction: The Changing Nature of Interest Group Politics," in Cigler and Loomis, *Interest Group Politics*, 6th ed., 2–5, 21–22.

11. Michael Luo, "Money Talks Louder Than Ever in Midterms," *New York Times*, October 7, 2010, www.nytimes.com/2010/10/08/us/politics/08donate.html.

12. On this last point, see Jonathan Rauch, *Demosclerosis: The Silent Killer of American Government* (New York: Crown, 1994), 39.

13. Mancur Olson Jr., *The Logic of Collective Action* (New York: Schocken, 1971).

14. Truman, *The Governmental Process*, 66–108.

15. Berry, *The Interest Group Society*, 3rd ed., 66.

16. Jeffrey Berry, Kent E. Portney, and Ken Thomson, *The Rebirth of Urban Democracy* (Washington, D.C.: Brookings Institution, 1993).

17. Robert Salisbury, "An Exchange Theory of Interest Groups," *Midwest Journal of Political Science* 13 (1969): 1–32.

18. For a full description of these incentives, see Peter B. Clark and James Q. Wilson, "Incentive Systems: A Theory of Organizations," *Administrative Science Quarterly* 6 (1961): 129–166.

19. The idea of selective incentives is Olson's (1971, 51). This discussion comes from the work of Clark and Wilson (1961), 129–166, as interpreted in Salisbury. Clark and Wilson use the terms *material*, *solidary*, and *purposive* benefits, while Salisbury prefers *material*, *solidary*, and *expressive*. We follow Salisbury's interpretation and usage here.

20. Berry, *The Interest Group Society*, 3rd ed., 6–8; John W. Kingdon, *Agendas, Alternatives, and Public Policy* (Boston, Mass.: Little, Brown, 1984).

21. Kingdon, *Agendas, Alternatives, and Public Policy*.

22. Children's Defense Fund, 2005, www.childrensdefense.org.

23. John P. Heinz et al., *The Hollow Core* (Cambridge, Mass.: Harvard University Press, 1993), 1–3.

24. Benjamin Goad, "Wall Street Spending $1.5M a Day on Lobbying, Campaigns," *The Hill*, July 25, 2014, thehill.com/regulation/finance/213342-wall-street-spending-15m-a-day-on-lobbying-politics.

25. Ronald G. Shaiko, "Making the Connection: Organized Interests, Political Representation, and the Changing Rules of the Game in Washington Politics," in Paul S. Herrnson, Ronald G. Shaiko, and Clyde Wilcox, eds., *The Interest Group Connection* (Washington, D.C.: CQ Press, 2005), 6.

26. Foundation for Public Affairs, *Public Interest Group Profiles, 2004–2005* (Washington, D.C.: CQ Press, 2004), 486–488.

27. U.S. Chamber of Commerce, "About Us," www.uschamber.com/about.

28. Dan Eggen, "Chamber and Democrats Battle Over the Midterms and Election Spending," *Washington Post*, October 8, 2010, www.washingtonpost.com/wp-dyn/content/article/2010/10/08/AR2010100804145_pf.html.

29. AFL-CIO, "Our Unions and Allies," https://aflcio.org/about-us/our-unions-and-allies.

30. "Labor Pains," *Houston Chronicle*, July 28, 2005, B10; Amanda Paulson, "Union Split: Sign of Decline or Revival," *Christian Science Monitor*, July 27, 2005, 2.

31. International Brotherhood of Teamsters, www.teamsters.org; United Auto Workers, www.uaw.org; United Mine Workers of America, www.umwa.org.

32. David Kocieniewski, "Unions at Center of Wisconsin Recall Vote, Suffer a New Setback in Its Outcome," *New York Times*, June 6, 2012, www.nytimes.com/2012/06/07/us/politics/scott-walkers-win-in-wisconsin-casts-doubts-on-union-power.html.

33. Alana Semuels, "Is This the End of Public-Sector Unions in America?" *The Atlantic*, June 27, 2018, www.theatlantic.com/politics/archive/2018/06/janus-afscme-public-sector-unions/563879/.

34. Steve Lohr, "Bush's Next Target: Malpractice Lawyers," *New York Times*, February 27, 2005, sec. 3, 1.

35. American Farm Bureau Federation, "We Are Farm Bureau," www.fb.org/about/home/; American Agriculture Movement, www.aaminc.org; National Farmers Union, www.nfu.org.

36. AARP, "Our Mission," www.aarp.org/about-aarp/.

37. Children's Defense Fund, www.childrensdefense.org.

38. Foundation for Public Affairs, *Public Interest Group Profiles, 2004–2005*, 483–485; NAACP, *NAACP: 2016 Annual Report*, www.naacp.org/wp-content/uploads/2018/01/NAACP2016AnnualReportWEB.pdf.

39. League of United Latin American Citizens, lulac.org/about/history/.

40. Foundation for Public Affairs, *Public Interest Group Profiles, 2004–2005*, 460–462.

41. American Indian Movement, www.aimovement.org.

42. Southeast Asia Resource Action Center, www.searac.org.

43. National Organization for Women, "How Many Members Does NOW Currently Have?" now.org/faq/how-many-members-does-now-currently-have/.

44. Eagle Forum, www.eagleforum.org; Susan B. Anthony List, www.sba-list.org.

45. American Coalition for Fathers and Children, www.acfc.org; National Congress for Fathers and Children, www.fathersmanifesto.net/ncfc.htm.

46. Log Cabin Republicans, "About Log Cabin," www.logcabin.org/about-us/.

47. Allan J. Cigler and Anthony J. Nowns, "Public Interest Entrepreneurs and Group Patrons," in Allan J. Cigler and Burdett A. Loomis, eds., *Interest Group Politics*, 4th ed. (Washington, D.C.: CQ Press, 1995), 77–78.

48. Christopher J. Bosso, "The Color of Money," in Cigler and Loomis, *Interest Group Politics*, 4th ed., 104.

49. Ben Smith, "NRA: Obama Most Anti-Gun Candidate Ever; Will Ban Guns," *Politico*, August 6, 2008, www.politico.com/blogs/bensmith/0808/NRA_Obama_most_antigun_candidate_ever_will_ban_guns.html.

50. William Booth, "Logging Protester Killed by Falling Redwood Tree," *Washington Post*, September 19, 1998, A2; Ed Henry, "Earth First! Activists Invade Riggs's California Office. In Aftermath, Congressman Considers Bill to Strengthen Penalty for Assaulting Congressional Staffers," *Roll Call*, October 27, 1997.

51. For a discussion of coalition politics involving Ralph Nader, see Loree Bykerk and Ardith Maney, "Consumer Groups and Coalition Politics on Capitol Hill," in Cigler and Loomis, *Interest Group Politics*, 4th ed., 259–279.

52. Consumers Union, www.consumersunion.org.

53. Foundation for Public Affairs, *Public Interest Group Profiles, 2004–2005*, 197–199.

54. See James Guth et al., "Onward Christian Soldiers: Religious Activist Groups in American Politics," in Cigler and Loomis, *Interest Group Politics*, 4th ed., 55–75; Guth et al., "A Distant Thunder?" in Cigler and Loomis, *Interest Group Politics*, 6th ed., 162–165.

55. Joseph A. Aistrup, *Southern Strategy Revisited* (Lexington: University Press of Kentucky, 1996), 56–61.

56. Adam Clymer, "Decision in the Senate: The Overview; Crime Bill Approved 61–38, but Senate Is Going Home Without Acting on Health Care," *New York Times*, August 26, 1994, 1.

57. Sheryl Gay Stolberg, "Effort to Renew Weapons Ban Falters on Hill," *New York Times*, September 9,

2004, A1; Edward Epstein, "Supporters of Gun Ban Lament Its Expiration," *San Francisco Chronicle*, September 10, 2004, A1.

58. Chris Arnold, "A Million Mom Army and a Billionaire Take on the NRA," NPR, June 17, 2016, www.npr.org/2016/06/17/482343185/a-million-mom-army-and-a-billionaire-take-on-the-nra.

59. Jon Jeter, "Jury Says Abortion Opponents Are Liable; Efforts to Close Clinics Violate Racketeering Law," *Washington Post*, April 21, 1998, A1; "Operation Rescue Founder Files for Bankruptcy Due to Lawsuits," *Washington Post*, November 8, 1998, A29.

60. Adam Liptak, "Court Limits Birth Control Rule," *New York Times*, July 1, 2014, 1.

61. American Civil Liberties Union, "About Us," www.aclu.org/about/aboutmain.cfm.

62. Amnesty International, "About Us," www.amnestyusa.org/about-us/who-we-are.

63. Loomis and Cigler, *Interest Group Politics*, 6th ed., 22–23; People for the Ethical Treatment of Animals, www.peta.org.

64. Animal Rights Law Project, www.animal-law.org; Animal Liberation Front, www.animalliberationfront.com; "Deaths of More Baby Rats on Shuttle Prompt Protests," *Los Angeles Times*, April 29, 1998, A14; Daniel B. Wood, "Animal Activists vs. Furriers: Now It's All in the Label," *Christian Science Monitor*, November 27, 1998, 2; Brad Knickerbocker, "Activists Step Up War to 'Liberate' Nature," *Christian Science Monitor*, January 20, 1999, 4.

65. Ronald J. Hrebenar and Clive S. Thomas, "The Japanese Lobby in Washington: How Different Is It?" in Cigler and Loomis, *Interest Group Politics*, 4th ed., 349–368.

66. Pamela Fessler, "Ethics Standards Announced," *Congressional Quarterly Weekly Report*, December 12, 1992, 3792; Allison Mitchell, "A New Form of Lobbying Puts Public Face on Private Interests," *New York Times on the Web*, September 30, 1998.

67. Nyshka Chandran, "Foreign Officials From Four Countries Tried to Figure Out Ways to Manipulate Jared Kushner, Report Says," CNBC, February 28, 2018, www.cnbc.com/2018/02/28/foreign-officials-want-to-influence-jared-kushner-report.html; Chris Riotta, "Jared Kushner Hid One of His Companies on a Disclosure Form—Then Profited," *Newsweek*, October 12, 2017, www.newsweek.com/jared-kushner-ivanka-trump-white-house-forms-omissions-cadre-millions-679231; Jeremy Venook, "Is Kushner Companies Taking Advantage of Its Connection to the President?," *The Atlantic*, May 9, 2017, www.theatlantic.com/business/archive/2017/05/jared-kushner-conflict-of-interest/ 525897/.

68. Beverly A. Cigler, "Not Just Another Special Interest: Intergovernmental Representation," in Cigler and Loomis, eds., *Interest Group Politics*, 4th ed., 134–135.

69. William Safire, *Safire's New Political Dictionary* (New York: Random House, 1993), 417–418.

70. Jeffrey H. Birnbaum, "The Road to Riches Is Called K Street," *Washington Post*, June 22, 2005, A1; Matt Kelley, "Pull of Lobbyists' Revolving Door: Salary vs. Service," *USA Today*, December 25, 2008, www.usatoday.com/news/washington/2008–12–25-revolvingdoor-inside_N.htm.

71. Jeffrey H. Birnbaum, "When Candidates Decry Lobbying, Ex-Lawmakers Embrace It," *Washington Post*, January 8, 2008, A17; Jordi Blanes I Vidal, Mirko Draca, and Christian Fons-Rosen, "Revolving Door Lobbyists," May 2011, personal.lse.ac.uk/blanesiv/revolving.pdf.

72. Bart Jansen, "Lobbying Bill Signed Into Law," *CQ Today*, CQPolitics.com, September 14, 2007; see also www.common cause.org.

73. Dan Eggen and R. Jeffrey Smith, "Lobbying Rules Surpass Those of Previous Administrations, Experts Say," *Washington Post*, January 22, 2009, www.washington post.com/wp-dyn/content/article/2009/01/21/AR2009012103472.html.

74. Derek Kravitz and Alex Mierjeski, "Trump Promised His Appointees Wouldn't Become Lobbyists. Guess How That Turned Out," *Mother Jones*, May 6, 2018, www.motherjones.com/politics/2018/05/trump-promised-his-appointees-wouldnt-become-lobbyists-guess-how-that-turned-out/.

75. Ben Mathis-Lilley, "Swamp-Draining Trump Administration Has Hired 187 Lobbyists, New Report Finds," *Slate*, March 7, 2018, slate.com/news-and-politics/2018/03/trump-administration-has-hired-187-lobbyists-propublic-finds-swamp-much.html.

76. Chris Mooney, Brady Dennis, and Steven Mufson, "Trump Names Scott Pruitt, Oklahoma Attorney General Suing EPA on Climate Change, to Head the EPA," *Washington Post*, December 8, 2016, www.washingtonpost.com/news/energy-environment/wp/2016/12/07/trump-names-scott-pruitt-oklahoma-attorney-general-suing-epa-on-climate-change-to-head-the-epa/.

77. See Diana M. Evans, "Lobbying the Committee: Interest Groups and the House Public Works and Transportation Committee," in Allan J. Cigler and Burdett A. Loomis, eds., *Interest Group Politics*, 3rd ed. (Washington, D.C.: CQ Press, 1991), 264–265. For a graphic example of this practice, see Michael Weisskopf and David Maraniss, "Forging an Alliance for Deregulation; Rep. DeLay Makes Companies Full Partners in the Movement," *Washington Post*, March 12, 1995, A1.

78. Carl Hulse, "Tough Going as Negotiators Hammer Out Energy Bill," *New York Times*, September 30, 2003, A20.

79. Ibid.

80. Mike Soraghan, "Measure Stresses Drilling in Rockies; Energy Bill Gets OK, May Go to House Today," *Denver Post*, November 18, 2003, A1.

81. Ashley Parker, "Outside Money Drives a Deluge of Political Ads," *New York Times*, July 27, 2014.

82. "Stopping SOPA: A Backlash From the Internet Community Against Attempts to Rein in Content Thieves," *The Economist*, January 21, 2012, www.economist.com/node/21543173.

83. Adam Clymer, "Congress Passes Bill to Disclose Lobbyists' Roles," *New York Times*, November 30, 1995, 1.

84. Adam Clymer, "Senate, 98–0, Sets Tough Restriction on Lobbyist Gifts," *New York Times*, July 29, 1995, 1; "House Approves Rule to Prohibit Lobbyists' Gifts," *New York Times*, November 17, 1995, 1.

85. Jeff Zeleny and David D. Kirkpatrick, "House, 411–8, Passes a Vast Ethics Overhaul," *New York Times*, August 1, 2007, www.nytimes.com.

86. Megan R. Wilson, "Bombshell: Ethics Office Alleges Illegal Lobbying," *The Hill*, July 25, 2014, thehill.com/business-a-lobbying/business-a-lobbying/213394-bombshell-ethics-office-alleges-illegal-lobbying.

87. Jeffrey H. Birnbaum, "Seeing the Ethics Rules, and Raising an Exception," *Washington Post*, October 23, 2007, A17.

88. Ibid.

89. Kenneth P. Vogel, "President Obama's Lobbying Reforms Praised by Congressional Research Service," *Politico*, December 3, 2009, www.politico.com/news/stories/1209/30185.html; Peter Baker, "Obama's Pledge to Reform Ethics Faces an Early

Test," *New York Times*, February 2, 2009, www.nytimes.com/2009/02/03/us/politics/03lobby.html.

90. Alan Zibel, "Presidency for Sale: 64 Trade Groups, Companies, Candidates, Foreign Governments and Political Groups Spending Money at Trump's Properties," Public Citizen, January 16, 2018, https://corporatepresidency.org/presidencyforsale/.

91. See Douglas Yates, *Bureaucratic Democracy* (Cambridge, Mass.: Harvard University Press, 1982), ch. 4.

92. Cindy Skrzcki, "OSHA Set to Propose Ergonomics Standards; Long-Studied Rules Repeatedly Blocked," *Washington Post*, February 19, 1999.

93. Supreme Court of the United States Blog, "Citizens United v. Federal Election Commission," www.scotusblog.com/case-files/cases/citizens-united-v-federal-election-commission/.

94. Samuel Kernell, *Going Public: New Strategies of Presidential Leadership* (Washington, D.C.: CQ Press, 1986), 34.

95. Berry, *The Interest Group Society*, 3rd ed., 121–122.

96. The Tax Foundation, "Tax Freedom Day 2018 Is April 19th," https://taxfoundation.org/tax-freedom-day-2018/.

97. Luo, "Money Talks Louder Than Ever"; *Citizens United v. Federal Election Commission*, 558 U.S. 50 (2010).

98. William B. Browne, "Organized Interests, Grassroots Confidants, and Congress," in Cigler and Loomis, *Interest Group Politics*, 4th ed., 288; John W. Kingdon, *Congressmen's Voting Decisions*, 2nd ed. (New York: Harper & Row, 1981).

99. Evans, "Lobbying the Committee," 269.

100. *Censure and Move On* (news release), October 15, 1998, www.moveon.org.

101. Chris Good, "The Tea Party Movement: Who's in Charge?" *The Atlantic*, April 13, 2009, www.theatlantic.com/politics/archive/2009/04/the-tea-party-movement-whos-in-charge/13041/.

102. Mark Brunswick, "Prescription Politics; Drug Lobby Intensifies Fight on Price Controls and Imports," Minneapolis *Star Tribune*, November 16, 2003, 1A; Jim VandeHei and Juliet Eilperin, "Drug Firms Gain Church Group's Aid; Claim About Import Measure Stirs Anger," *Washington Post*, July 23, 2003, A1.

103. John Stauber, director of the Center for Media & Democracy, quoted in J. A. Savage, "Astroturf Lobbying Replaces Grassroots Organizing: Corporations Mask Their Interests by Supporting Supposed Grassroots Organizations," *Business and Society Review*, September 22, 1995, 8.

104. Mike Murphy in Mitchell, "A New Form of Lobbying," A1.

105. Bill McAllister, "Rainmakers Making a Splash," *Washington Post*, December 4, 1997, A21.

106. Federal Election Commission, "PAC's Grouped by Total Spent," April 13, 2005, www.fec.gov/press/press2005/20050412pac/groupbyspending2004.pdf; Richard L. Hall and Frank W. Wayman, "Buying Time: Money Interests and the Mobilization of Bias in Congressional Committees," *American Political Science Review* 84 (1990): 797–820.

107. Luo, "Money Talks Louder Than Ever"; *Citizens United v. Federal Election Commission*.

108. Robert Maguire, "$1.4 Billion and Counting in Spending by Super PACs, Dark Money Groups," Open Secrets, November 9, 2016, www.opensecrets.org/news/2016/11/1-4-billion-and-counting-in-spending-by-super-pacs-dark-money-groups.

109. Jeffrey H. Birnbaum, "To Predict Losers in a Power Shift, Follow the Money," *Washington Post*, October 16, 2006, D1.

110. Andrew Bard Schmookler, "When Money Talks, Is It Free Speech?" *Christian Science Monitor*,

November 11, 1997, 15; Nelson W. Polsby, "Money Gains Access. So What?" *New York Times*, August 13, 1997, A19.

111. "Senators Supporting Public Option Received Half as Much Money From Health Insurers," October 9, 2009, maplight.org/senators-supporting-public-option-got-half-as-much-money-from-health-insurers.

112. See John R. Wright, *Interest Groups and Congress* (Boston, Mass.: Allyn & Bacon, 1996), 136–145; "Contributions, Lobbying, and Committee Voting in the U.S. House of Representatives," *American Political Science Review* 84 (1990): 417–438; Richard L. Hall and Frank W. Wayman, "Buying Time: Money Interests and the Mobilization of Bias in Congressional Committees," *American Political Science Review* 84 (1990): 797–820.

113. Theda Skocpol, *Diminished Democracy: From Membership to Management in American Civic Life* (Norman: University of Oklahoma Press, 2003); Theda Skocpol, "Advocates Without Members: The Recent Transformation of American Civic Life," in Theda Skocpol and Morris Fiorina, eds., *Civic Engagement in American Democracy* (Washington, D.C.: Brookings Institution, 1999).

114. Kelly D. Patterson and Matthew M. Singer, "The National Rifle Association in the Face of the Clinton Challenge," in Cigler and Loomis, *Interest Group Politics*, 6th ed., 62–63; Dave Gilson, "The NRA Says It Has 5 Million Members; Its Magazines Tell Another Story," *Mother Jones*, March 7, 2018, www.motherjones.com/politics/2018/03/nra-membership-magazine-numbers-1/.

115. Lee Fritscheler and James M. Hoefler, *Smoking and Politics*, 5th ed. (Upper Saddle River, N.J.: Prentice Hall, 1996), 20–35.

116. Truman, *The Governmental Process*, 519.

117. See C. Wright Mills, *The Power Elite* (New York: Oxford University Press, 1956); G. William Domhoff, *The Powers That Be* (New York: Vintage, 1979).

118. David S. Hilzenrath, "Health Care Factions Clashing on Medicare Battlefield," *Washington Post*, July 19, 1997, C1; Ruth Marcus, "Some Swat Home Runs, Others Strike Out on Budget Deal," *Washington Post*, August 3, 1997, A1; Jennifer Mattos, "Clinton Proposes Medicare Cuts," *Time Daily*, January 14, 1997.

119. The problem is that there are a relatively small number of groups with large memberships. Labor unions, some environmental groups like the Sierra Club, some social movements revolving around abortion and women's rights, and the NRA currently have large memberships spread across a number of congressional districts.

120. Linda Greenhouse, "Justices to Rule on Tobacco," *New York Times*, May 2, 1999, sec. 4, 2; David E. Rosenbaum, "The Tobacco Bill: The Overview," *New York Times*, June 18, 1999, 1.

121. Katie Hafner, "Screen Grab: Mobilizing on Line for Gun Control," *New York Times*, May 20, 1999, G5; Francis X. Clines, "Guns and Schools: In Congress—Sketchbook," *New York Times*, June 17, 1999, 30.

122. Helena Bottemiller Evich and Catherine Boudreau, "The Big Washington Food Fight," *Politico*, November 26, 2017, www.politico.com/story/2017/11/26/food-lobby-consumer-tastes-washington-190528.

123. Organic Consumers Association, https://www.organicconsumers.org/.

124. Tamar Haspel, "Organic Food Fight!" *Slate*, November 14, 2017, www.slate.com/articles/technology/future_tense/2017/11/a_battle_over_hydroponics_shows_that_the_usda_organic_certification_program.html.

CHAPTER 14

1. Jonathan Mahler and Steven Edder, "The Electoral College is Hated by Many. So Why Does It Endure?" *The New York Times*, November 201, 2016, www.nytimes.com/2016/11/11/us/politics/the-electoral-college-is-hated-by-many-so-why-does-it-endure.html.

2. Ibid.

3. Gerald Pomper, *Elections in America* (New York: Dodd, Mead, 1970), 1.

4. John Stuart Mill, *Considerations on Representative Government* (New York: Liberal Arts Press, 1958), 114.

5. David W. Brady, *Critical Elections and Congressional Policy Making* (Palo Alto, Calif.: Stanford University Press, 1988); Barbara Sinclair, "Party Realignment and the Transformation of the Political Agenda: The House of Representatives, 1925–1938," *American Political Science Review* 71 (September 1977): 940–954.

6. Robert S. Erikson, Gerald C. Wright, and John P. McIver, *Statehouse Democracy* (New York: Cambridge University Press, 1993).

7. Robert Erikson and Gerald Wright, "Voters, Candidates, and Issues in Congressional Elections," in Lawrence Dodd and Bruce Oppenheimer, eds., *Congress Reconsidered*, 6th ed. (Washington, D.C.: CQ Press, 1997); Gerald C. Wright and Michael Berkman, "Candidates and Policy Position in U.S. Senate Elections," *American Political Science Review* 80 (June 1986): 576–590; Robert S. Erikson, Michael MacKuen, and James A. Stimson, *The Macro Polity* (New York: Cambridge University Press, 2002).

8. Gerald Pomper with Susan Lederman, *Elections in America*, 2nd ed. (New York: Longman, 1980), chs. 7 and 8; Benjamin Ginsberg, *The Consequences of Consent* (Reading, Mass.: Addison Wesley Longman, 1982); Ian Budge and Richard I. Hofferbert, "Mandates and Policy Outputs: U.S. Party Platforms and Federal Expenditures, 1950–1985," *American Political Science Review* 84 (March 1990): 248–261.

9. Erikson, MacKuen, and Stimson, *The Macro Polity*.

10. Carole Pateman, *Participation and Democratic Theory* (Cambridge, U.K.: Cambridge University Press, 1970).

11. Sidney Verba and Norman H. Nie, *Participation in America* (New York: Harper, 1972).

12. Robert S. Erikson, Costas Panagopoulos, and Christopher Wlezien, "The Crystallization of Voter Preferences During the 2008 Presidential Campaign," *Presidential Studies Quarterly* 40 (2010): 482–496; Robert Andersen, James Tilley, and Anthony F. Heath, "Political Knowledge and Enlightened Preferences: Party Choice Through the Electoral Cycle," *British Journal of Political Science* 35 (2005): 285–302; Steven F. Finkel, "Reexamining the 'Minimal Effects' Model in Recent Presidential Elections," *Journal of Politics* 55 (February 1993): 1–21.

13. Ginsberg, *The Consequences of Consent*.

14. John Petrocik, "Voter Turnout and Electoral Preference: The Anomalous Reagan Elections," in Kay Lehman Schlozman, ed., *Elections in America* (Boston, Mass.: Allen & Unwin, 1987), 239–260.

15. Jack Citrin, Eric Schickler, and John Sides, "What If Everyone Voted? Simulating the Impact of Increased Turnout in Senate Elections," *American Journal of Political Science* 47 (January 2003): 75–90.

16. Petrocik, "Voter Turnout and Electoral Preference," 243–251; Stephen Earl Bennett and David Resnick, "The Implications of Nonvoting for Democracy in the United States," *American Journal of Political Science* 34 (August 1990): 795.

17. Calculated by the authors from the 2004 and 2008 Pre- and Post-American National Election Studies.

18. International Institute for Democracy and Electoral Assistance, "Turnout in the World, Country by Country Performance," 2005, www.idea.int/vt/survey/voter_turnout_pop2.cfm.

19. Benjamin Highton, "Voter Registration and Turnout in the United States," *Perspectives on Politics* 2 (2004): 507–515.

20. "States With New Voting Restrictions Since 2010 Election," www.brennancenter.org/new-voting-restrictions-2010- election.

21. Camila Domonoske, "As November Approaches, Courts Deal Series of Blows to Voter ID Laws," NPR, August 2, 2016, www.npr.org/sections/thetwo-way/2016/08/02/488392765/as-november-approaches-courts-deal-series-of-blows-to-voter-id-laws; Ariane de Vogue, "Voting Challenges Head Toward the Supreme Court: 4 Cases to Watch," CNN, July 19, 2016, www.cnn.com/2016/07/19/politics/voting-rights-supreme-court/; Adam Liptak and Michael Wines, "Strict North Carolina Voter ID Law Thwarted After Supreme Court Rejects Case," *New York Times*, May 15, 2017, www.nytimes.com/2017/05/15/us/politics/voter-id-laws-supreme-court-north-carolina.html; Joan Biskupic, "How the Supreme Court Is Changing the Rules on Voting," CNN, June 26, 2018, www.cnn.com/2018/06/25/politics/supreme-court-voting-rights-gerrymandering/index.html.

22. Steven J. Rosenstone and John Mark Hansen, *Mobilization, Participation, and Democracy in America* (New York: Macmillan, 1993); Ruy A. Teixeira, *The Disappearing American Voter* (Washington, D.C.: Brookings Institution, 1992); Raymond E. Wolfinger and Steven J. Rosenstone, *Who Votes?* (New Haven, Conn.: Yale University Press, 1980); Richard J. Timpone, "Structure, Behavior, and Voter Turnout in the United States," *American Political Science Review* 92 (March 1998): 145–158.

23. Ibid.

24. Kay Lehman Schlozman, Sidney Verba, and Henry E. Brady, "Civic Participation and the Inequality Problem," in *Civic Engagement in American Democracy*, Theda Skocpol and Morris P. Fiorina, eds. (New York: Russell Sage, 1999); Henry E. Brady, Kay Lehman Schlozman, and Sidney Verba, "Prospecting for Participants: Rational Expectations and the Recruitment of Political Activists," *American Political Science Review* 93 (1999): 153–168.

25. Roper Center for Public Opinion Research, Community Consensus Survey, February 12–14, 1999.

26. Richard Brody, "The Puzzle of Political Participation in America," in Anthony King, ed., *The New American Political System* (Washington, D.C.: American Enterprise Institute, 1978), 287–324.

27. Teixeira, *The Disappearing American Voter*, ch. 2; Paul R. Abramson, John H. Aldrich, and David W. Rohde, *Change and Continuity in the 1996 and 1998 Elections* (Washington, D.C.: CQ Press, 1999).

28. Rosenstone and Hansen, *Mobilization, Participation, and Democracy in America*.

29. Alan S. Gerber and Donald P. Green, "The Effects of Canvassing, Direct Mail, and Telephone Contact on Voter Turnout: A Field Experiment," *American Political Science Review* 94 (2000): 653–663.

30. Gerald Pomper, "The Presidential Election: The Ills of American Politics After 9/11," in Michael Nelson, ed., *The Elections of 2004* (Washington, D.C.: CQ Press, 2005), 46.

31. Teixeira, *The Disappearing American Voter*, 36–50; Robert Putnam, *Bowling Alone: The Collapse and Revival of American Community* (New York: Simon & Schuster, 2000), 31–47.

32. Anthony Downs, *An Economic Theory of Democracy* (New York: Harper & Row, 1957), 260–276.

33. Morris P. Fiorina, "The Voting Decision: Instrumental and Expressive Aspects," *Journal of Politics* 38 (1976): 390–415.

34. V. O. Key Jr., *The Responsible Electorate: Rationality in Presidential Voting, 1936–1960* (Cambridge, Mass.: Harvard University Press, 1966); Warren E. Miller and J. Merrill Shanks, *The New American Voter* (Cambridge, Mass.: Harvard University Press, 1996), ch. 7.

35. "Election 2016: Exit Polls," http://edition.cnn.com/election/results/exit-polls/national/president.

36. Angus Campbell, Phillip Converse, Warren Miller, and Donald Stokes, *The American Voter* (New York: Wiley, 1960); Donald Green, Bradley Palmquist, and Eric Schickler, *Partisan Hearts and Minds* (New Haven, Conn.: Yale University Press, 2002); Larry M. Bartels, "Beyond the Running Tally: Partisan Bias in Political Perceptions," *Political Behavior* 24 (2002): 117–150.

37. M. Margaret Conway, Gertrude A. Steuernagel, and David W. Ahern, *Women and Political Participation: Cultural Change in the Political Arena*, 2nd ed. (Washington, D.C.: CQ Press, 2005).

38. Calculated from Harold W. Stanley and Richard G. Niemi, *Vital Statistics on American Politics, 2007–2008* (Washington, D.C.: CQ Press, 2008), 127.

39. These figures are taken from media exit polls for the 2004 and 2008 presidential elections; Ron Brownstein, "The American Electorate Has Changed, and There's No Turning Back," *National Journal*, November 8, 2012, www.nationaljournal.com/magazine/the-american-electorate-has-changed-and-there-s-no-turning-back-20121108.

40. Wendy K. Tam, "Asians—A Monolithic Voting Bloc?" *Political Behavior* 17 (1995): 223–249; Pie-Te Lein, M. Margaret Conway, and Janelle Wong, *The Politics of Asian-Americans: Diversity and Community* (New York: Routledge, 2004); Atiya Kai Stokes, "Latino Group Consciousness and Political Participation," *American Politics Research* 41 (2003): 361–378; Benjamin Highton and Arthur L. Burris, "New Perspectives on Latino Voter Turnout in the United States," *American Politics Research* 30 (2002): 285–306.

41. Pei-Te Lien, Christian Collet, Janelle Wong, and S. Karthick Ramakrishnan, "Asian Pacific American Public Opinion and Participation," *PS: Political Science and Politics* 34 (2001): 628; David L. Leal, Matt A. Barreto, Jongho Lee, and Rodolfo O. De la Garza, "The Latino Vote in the 2004 Election," *PS: Political Science and Politics* 38 (2005): 41–49.

42. CNN, "Election 2016: Exit Polls," http://edition.cnn.com/election/results/exit-polls/national/president.

43. Downs, *An Economic Theory of Democracy*.

44. Edward Carmines and James Stimson, "Two Faces of Issue Voting," *American Political Science Review* 74 (March 1980): 78–91; Larry Bartels, *Unequal Democracy* (Princeton, N.J.: Princeton University Press, 2008).

45. James Fallows, "Why Americans Hate the Media," *Atlantic Monthly*, February 1996, 45–64.

46. Morris P. Fiorina, *Retrospective Voting in American National Elections* (New Haven: Yale University Press, 1981).

47. "The Candidates' Confrontation: Excerpts From the Debate," *Washington Post*, October 30, 1980, A14.

48. Fiorina, "The Voting Decision"; Benjamin I. Page, *Choice and Echoes in Presidential Elections* (Chicago, Ill.: University of Chicago Press, 1978).

49. Pew Poll cited in John Sides and Lynn Vavreck, *The Gamble: Choice and Chance in the 2012 Presidential Election* (Princeton, N.J.: Princeton University Press, 2012), 28.

50. Linda Feldmann, "Before Any Votes: A 'Money Primary,'" *Christian Science Monitor*, February 26, 2007, 1; Craig Gilbert, "'Invisible Primary' Already Begun: Some Think Presidential Field Narrowing Too Soon," *Milwaukee Journal Sentinel*, March 5, 2007; Chris Cillizza and Michael A. Fletcher, "Candidates Woo Bush Donors for 'Invisible Primary,'" *Washington Post*, December 10, 2006, A01.

51. Michael J. Goff, *The Money Primary: The New Politics of Early Presidential Nomination Process* (Lanham, Md.: Rowman & Littlefield, 2004); Randall E. Adkins and Andrew J. Dowdle, "The Money Primary: What Influences the Outcome of Pre-Primary Presidential Nominating Fundraising?" *Presidential Studies Quarterly* 32 (June 2002): 256–275.

52. Jonathan Mann, "Money Talks in Republican Presidential Primaries," CNN Politics, February 1, 2012, articles.cnn.com/2012-02-01/politics/politics_mann-florida-romney-money_1_mitt-romney-super-pacs-super-political-action-committees?_s= PM:POLITICS.

53. Thomas R. Marshall, "Turnout and Representation: Caucuses Versus Primaries," *American Journal of Political Science* 22 (1978): 169–182; Gerald C. Wright, "Rules and the Ideological Character of Primary Electorates," in Steven S. Smith and Melanie J. Springer, eds., *Reforming the Presidential Nomination Process* (Washington, D.C.: Brookings Institution, 2009).

54. Barry Burden, "The Nominations: Technology, Money, and Transferable Momentum," in Nelson, *The Elections of 2004*, 21–22.

55. Max Follmer, "Everything You've Ever Wanted to Know About Delegates and Superdelegates," *Huffington Post*, February 13, 2008, www.huffingtonpost.com/2008/02/13/everything-youve-ever-wa_n_86335.html.

56. Burden, "The Nominations," 21.

57. Alan Abramowitz, *The Polarized Public?* (Upper Saddle River, N.J.: Pearson, 2013).

58. Shlomo Slonim, "The Electoral College at Philadelphia," *Journal of American History* 73 (June 1986): 35.

59. Ruth Shalit, "The Oppo Boom," *New Republic*, January 3, 1994, 16–21; Adam Nagourney, "Researching the Enemy: An Old Political Tool Resurfaces in a New Election," *New York Times*, April 3, 1996, D20.

60. Robin Kolodny and Angela Logan, "Political Consultants and the Extension of Party Goals," *PS: Political Science & Politics* (June 1998): 155–159.

61. Patrick Sellers, "Strategy and Background in Congressional Campaigns," *American Political Science Review* 92 (March 1998): 159–172.

62. Jenna Johnson, "Trump Demanded Obama's Records; But He's Not Releasing His Own," *Washington Post*, August 12, 2016, www.washingtonpost.com/politics/trump-demanded-obamas-records-now-more-are-asking-where-are-trumps/2016/08/12/b536925a-5ff3-11e6-9d2f-b1a3564181a1_story.html; Tom McCarthy, "Trump Dictated Note Saying He Was 'Astonishingly' Healthy, Doctor Says," *Guardian* (UK), May 2, 2018, https://www.theguardian.com/us-news/2018/may/01/trump-dictated-doctors-note-harold-bornstein; Michael Finnegan and Mark Z. Barabak, "'Shithole' and Other Racist Things Trump Has Said—So Far," *Los Angeles Times*, January 12, 2018, www.latimes.com/politics/la-na-trump-racism-remarks-20180111-htmlstory.html; Glenn Kessler, "Donald Trump's Revisionist History of Mocking a Disabled Reporter," *Washington Post*, August 2, 2016, www.washingtonpost.com/news/fact-checker/wp/2016/08/02/donald-trumps-revisionist-history-of-mocking-a-disabled-reporter/; "Transcript: Donald Trump's Taped Comments About Women," *New York Times*, October 8, 2016, www.nytimes.com/2016/10/08/us/donald-trump-tape-transcript.html; Caitlin Yilek, "Trump Told Stern He Walked Backstage When Beauty Queens Were Naked," *The Hill*, October 9, 2016, thehill.com/blogs/ballot-box/presidential-races/300093-trump-confirms-he-walked-backstage-when-beauty-queens.

63. John Petrocik, "Issue Ownership in Presidential Elections, With a 1980 Case Study," *American Journal of Political Science* 40 (August 1996): 825–850.

64. See Malcolm Gladwell, *The Tipping Point: How Little Things Can Make a Big Difference* (Boston, Mass.: Little, Brown, 2000); Jonah Berger, *Contagious: Why Things Catch On* (New York: Simon & Schuster, 2013).

65. American Museum of the Moving Image, "The Living Room Candidate: Presidential Campaign Commercials 1952–2004," livingroomcandidate.movingimage.us/index.php.

66. Darrell M. West, *Air Wars: Television Advertising in Election Campaigns, 1952–2004* (Washington, D.C.: CQ Press, 2005).

67. Kathleen Hall Jamieson, "Shooting to Win; Do Attack Ads Work? You Bet—and That's Not All Bad," *Washington Post*, September 26, 2004, B1.

68. Shanto Iyengar and Donald Kinder, *News That Matters: Television and American Opinion* (Chicago, Ill.: University of Chicago Press, 1987); James N. Druckman, "Priming the Vote: Campaign Effects in a U.S. Senate Election," *Political Psychology* 25, no. 4 (2004): 577–594.

69. Thomas Patterson, *Out of Order* (New York: Knopf, 1993); Fallows, "Why Americans Hate the Media," 45–64.

70. Elihu Katz and Jacob Feldman, "The Debates in Light of Research," in Sidney Kraus, ed., *The Great Debates* (Bloomington: Indiana University Press, 1962), 173–223.

71. Thomas Holbrook, "Campaigns, National Conditions, and U.S. Presidential Elections," *American Journal of Political Science* 38 (November 1994): 986–992; John Geer, "The Effects of Presidential Debates on the Electorate's Preferences for Candidates," *American Politics Quarterly* 16 (1988): 486–501; David Lanoue, "The 'Turning Point': Viewers' Reactions to the Second 1988 Presidential Debate," *American Politics Quarterly* 19 (1991): 80–89.

72. David Lanoue, "One That Made a Difference: Cognitive Consistency, Political Knowledge, and the 1980 Presidential Debate," *Public Opinion Quarterly* 56 (Summer 1992): 168–184; Carol Winkler and Catherine Black, "Assessing the 1992 Presidential and Vice Presidential Debates: The Public Rationale," *Argumentation and Advocacy* 30 (Fall 1993): 77–87; Lori McKinnon, John Tedesco, and Lynda Kaid, "The Third 1992 Presidential Debate: Channel and Commentary Effects," *Argumentation and Advocacy* 30 (Fall 1993): 106–118; Mike Yawn, Kevin Ellsworth, and Kim Fridkin Kahn, "How a Presidential Primary Debate Changed Attitudes of Audience Members," *Political Behavior* 20 (July 1998): 155–164; Annenberg Public Policy Center, "Voters Learned Positions on Issues Since Presidential Debates," NAES04 National Annenberg Election Survey, www.annenbergpublicpolicycenter.org/Down loads/Political_Communication/naes/.

73. Tarini Parti, "Will 2012 Be the End of the Presidential Public Financing System?" www.opensecrets.org/news/2011/08/the-end-of-presidential-public-financing.html.

74. Federal Election Commission, "FEC Chart: 2015–16 Campaign Cycle Contribution Limits," www.fec.gov/press/press2015/news_releases/20150320release.shtml.

75. Susan Glasser, "Court's Ruling in Colorado Case May Reshape Campaign Finance; Limits on Political Parties' 'Hard Money' Spending Nullified," *Washington Post*, March 28, 1999, A6; *FEC v. Colorado Republican Federal Campaign Committee*, 121 S. Ct. 2351, 2371 (2001).

76. *Citizens United v. Federal Election Commission*, 558 U.S. 50 (2010).

77. "How Corporate Money Will Reshape Politics: Restoring Free Speech in Elections," *New York Times*, January 21, 2010, room fordebate.blogs.nytimes.com/2010/01/21/how-corporate-money-will-reshape-politics.

78. Spencer MacColl, "Citizens United Decision Profoundly Affects Political Landscape," May 5, 2011, www.opensecrets.org/news/2011/05/citizens-united-decision-profoundly-affects-political-landscape.html.

79. "The Court's Blow to Democracy," *New York Times*, January 21, 2010; Warren Richey, "Supreme Court: Campaign-Finance Limits Violate Free Speech," *Christian Science Monitor*, January 21, 2010; John Samples and Ilya Shapiro, "Supreme Court: Free Speech for All," *Washington Examiner*, January 21, 2010.

80. Dan Balz and David S. Broder, "Close Election Turns on Voter Turnout," *Washington Post*, November 1, 2002, A1.

81. Steven J. Rosenstone and John Mark Hansen, *Mobilization, Participation, and Democracy in America* (New York: Macmillan, 1993).

82. Adam Nagourney, "The '08 Campaign: A Sea Change for Politics as We Know It," *New York Times*, November 4, 2008, A1.

83. Craig Gilbert, "Personal Touch in Political Race; Bush, Kerry Sides Try to Rally Support Like Never Before," Milwaukee *Journal Sentinel*, June 28, 2004, 1A.

84. Blumenthal, "Down to the Wire."

85. Ibid.

86. Lawrence J. Grossman, David A. M. Peterson, and James A. Stimson, *Mandate Politics* (New York: Cambridge University Press, 2006).

87. Lawrence J. Grossback, David A. M. Peterson, and James A. Stimson, "Comparing Competing Theories on the Causes of Mandate Perceptions," *American Journal of Political Science* 49 (2005): 406–419.

88. Marjorie Hershey, "The Constructed Explanation: Interpreting Election Results in the 1984 Presidential Race," *Journal of Politics* 54 (November 1992): 943–976.

89. Bernard Berelson, Paul Lazarsfeld, and William N. McPhee, *Voting* (Chicago, Ill.: University of Chicago Press, 1954), ch. 10.

90. Sidney Verba, Kay Lehman Schlozman, Henry Brady, and Norman H. Nie, "Race, Ethnicity and Political Resources: Participation in the United States," *British Journal of Political Science* 23 (1993): 453–497.

91. Erikson, MacKuen, and Stimson, *The Macro Polity*; James A. Stimson, Michael B. MacKuen, and Robert S. Erikson, "Dynamic Representation," *American Political Science Review* 89 (September 1995): 543.

92. Erikson, Wright, and McIver, *Statehouse Democracy*.

93. Paul Burstein, "The Impact of Public Opinion on Public Policy: A Review and an Agenda," *Political Research Quarterly* 56 (2003): 29–40; David Jones and Monika McDermott, *Americans, Congress, and Democratic Responsiveness: Public Evaluations of Congress and Electoral Consequences* (Ann Arbor: University of Michigan Press, 2009); Stephen Ansolabehere and Phillip Edward Jones, "Constituents' Responses to Congressional Roll Call Voting," *American Journal of Political Science* 54 (2010): 58–97.

94. National Popular Vote, www.nationalpopularvote.com/

CHAPTER 15

1. "Republicans, Democrats Interpret Orlando Incident Differently," Gallup Poll, June 17, 2016, www.gallup.com/poll/192842/republicans-democrats-interpret-orlando-incident-differently.aspx.

2. Jane Coaston, "New Evidence Shows the Pulse Nightclub Shooting Wasn't About Anti-LGBTQ Hate," *Vox*, April 5, 2018, www.vox.com/policy-and-politics/2018/4/5/17202026/pulse-shooting-lgbtq-trump-terror-hate.

3. Dan O'Hair and Mary Weimann, *Real Communication*, 2nd ed. (New York: Bedford/St. Martin's, 2012), 543.

4. Elisa Shearer and Jeffrey Gottfried, "News Use Across Social Media Platforms: 2017," Pew Research Center, September 7, 2017, www.journalism.org/2017/09/07/news-use-across-social-media-platforms-2017/.

5. Ibid.

6. Amy Mitchell, Jeffery Gottfried, and Katerina Eva Matsa, "Millennials and Political News: Social Media—The Local TV for the Next Generation?" Pew Research Center, June 1, 2015, www.journalism.org/2015/06/01/millennials-political-news/.

7. Pew Research Center for the People and the Press, "The Times Mirror News Interest Index: 1989–1995," www.people-press.org.

8. Pew Research Center for the People and the Press, "Audience Segments in a Changing News Environment," August 17, 2008, www.people-press.org/files/legacy-pdf/444.pdf, 44.

9. Thomas Jefferson to Edward Carrington, 1787, ME 6:57, Thomas Jefferson on Politics and Government, etext.virginia.edu/jefferson/quotations/jeff1600.htm.

10. Frank Ahrens, "The Accelerating Decline of Newspapers," *Washington Post*, October 27, 2009, www.washingtonpost.com/wp-dyn/content/article/2009/10/26/AR2009102603272.html.

11. Russell Heimlich, "In Changing News Landscape, Even Television Is Vulnerable," Pew Center for People and the Press, October 11, 2012, www.pewresearch.org/daily-number/number-of-americans-who-read-print-newspapers-continues-decline/.

12. Rick Edmonds, Emily Guskin, Tom Rosenstiel, and Amy Mitchell, "Newspapers: Building Digital Revenues Proves Painfully Slow," Pew Center Project for Excellence in Journalism, April 11, 2012, stateofthemedia.org/2012/newspapers-building-digital-revenues-proves-painfully-slow/; Pew Research Journalism Project, "Newspaper Fact Sheet," June 13, 2018, www.journalism.org/fact-sheet/newspapers/.

13. Paul Farhi, "Washington Post to Be Sold to the Founder of Amazon," *Washington Post*, August 5, 2013.

14. Michael Barthel, "5 Key Takeaways About the State of the News Media in 2016," Pew Research Center, June 15, 2016, www.pewresearch.org/fact-tank/2016/06/15/state-of-the-news-media-2016-key-takeaways/.

15. Newspaper Death Watch, newspaperdeathwatch.com.

16. Jack Shafer, "The Great Newspaper Liquidation," June 5, 2012, blogs.reuters.com/jackshafer/2012/06/05/the-great-newspaper-liquidation/; David Carr, "The Fissures Are Growing for Newspapers," *New York Times*, July 8, 2012, www.nytimes.com/2012/07/09/business/media/newspapers-are-running-out-of-time-to-adapt-to-digital-future.html.

17. Clay Shirky, "Newspapers and Thinking the Unthinkable," March 13, 2009, www.shirky.com/weblog/2009/03/newspapers-and-thinking-the-unthinkable/.

18. Ibid.

19. Pew Research Journalism Project, "Audio and Podcasting Fact Sheet," June 16, 2017, www.journalism.org/fact-sheet/audio-and-podcasting/.

20. Jennifer Waits, "FCC Reports That the Number of Radio Stations in the U.S. Increased Last Quarter," July 11, 2014, www.radiosurvivor.com/2014/07/11/fcc-reports-non-commercial-fm-stations-lpfm-stations-fm-translators-u-s-rise-last-quarter/.

21. NPR, "Public Radio Finances," www.npr.org/about-npr/178660742/public-radio-finances; Public Radio International, "How Is PRI Funded?" www.pri.org/faqs#funding.

22. U.S Energy Information Administration, "Average Number of Televisions in U.S. Homes Declining," February 28, 2017, www.eia.gov/todayinenergy/detail.php?id=30132; Lee Rainie, "About 6 in 10 Young Adults in U.S. Primarily Use Online Streaming to Watch TV," Pew Research Center, September 13, 2017, www.pewresearch.org/fact-tank/2017/09/13/about-6-in-10-young-adults-in-u-s-primarily-use-online-streaming-to-watch-tv/; Todd Spangler, "Cord-Cutting Explodes: 22 Million U.S. Adults Will Have Canceled Cable, Satellite TV by End of 2017," *Variety*, September 13, 2017, variety.com/2017/biz/news/cord-cutting-2017-estimates-cancel-cable-satellite-tv-1202556594/.

23. David Hinckley, "Average American Watches 5 Hours of TV Per Day, Report Shows," *New York Daily News*, March 5, 2014, www.nydailynews.com/life-style/average-american-watches-5-hours-tv-day-article-1.1711954.

24. Megan Geuss, "On Average, Americans Get 189 Cable TV Channels and Only Watch 17," *Arstechnica*, May 6, 2014, arstechnica.com/business/2014/05/on-average-americans-get-189-cable-tv-channels-and-only-watch-17/.

25. For an in-depth study of the negative effects of this sort of advertising on national community, see Joseph Turow, *Breaking Up America: Advertisers and the New Media World* (Chicago, Ill.: University of Chicago Press, 1997).

26. Monica Anderson, Andrew Perrin, and JingJing Jiang, "11% of Americans Don't Use the Internet. Who Are They?" Pew Research Center, March 5, 2018, www.pewresearch.org/fact-tank/2018/03/05/some-americans-dont-use-the-internet-who-are-they/.

27. Pew Research Center, "Internet/Broadband Fact Sheet," www.pewinternet.org/fact-sheet/internet-broadband/; Andrew Perrin and JingJing Jiang, "About a Quarter of U.S. Adults Say They Are 'Almost Constantly' Online," Pew Research Center, March 14, 2018, www.pewresearch.org/fact-tank/2018/03/14/about-a-quarter-of-americans-report-going-online-almost-constantly/.

28. Monica Anderson and Andrea Caumont, "How Social Media Is Reshaping News," Pew Research Center, September 24, 2014, www.pewresearch.org/pubs/1508/internet-cell-phone-users-news-social-experience.

29. Robert Marquand, "Hate Groups Market to the Mainstream," *Christian Science Monitor*, March 6, 1998, 4.

30. Philip Rucker, "Romney Advisors, Aiming to Pop Obama's Digital Balloon, Pump Up Online Campaign," *Washington Post*, July 13, 2012, www.washingtonpost.com/politics/romney-advisers-aiming-to-pop-obamas-digital-balloon-pump-up-online-campaign/2012/07/13/gJQAsbc4hW_story.html.

31. Dan Gillmor, *We the Media: Grassroots Journalism by the People, for the People* (Sebastopol, Calif.: O'Reilly Media, 2008).

32. Andrew Sullivan, "A Blogger Manifesto: Why Online Weblogs Are One Future for Journalism," *Sunday Times of London*, February 24, 2002.

33. Andrew Sullivan, "Happy 4th," *Daily Dish*, July 4, 2010, andrewsullivan.theatlantic.com/the_daily_dish/2010/07/happy-4th.html.

34. Shirky, "Newspapers and Thinking the Unthinkable."

35. Ben H. Bagdikian, *The Media Monopoly*, 5th ed. (Boston, Mass.: Beacon Press, 1997), xv.

36. Bagdikian, ix.

37. Michael Barbaro, "Pithy, Mean and Powerful: How Donald Trump Mastered Twitter for 2016," *New York Times*, October 5, 2015, www.nytimes.com/2015/10/06/us/politics/donald-trump-twitter-use-campaign-2016.html.

38. Pew Research Center, "New Devices, Platforms Spur More News Consumption," March 19, 2012, pewresearch.org/pubs/2222/news-media-network-television-cable-audioo-radio-digital-platforms-local-mobile-devices-tablets-smartphones-native-american-community-newspapers; JingJing Jiang, "Millennials Stand Out For Their Technology Use, but Older Generations Also Embrace Digital Life," Pew Research Center, May 2, 2018, www.pewresearch.org/fact-tank/2018/05/02/millennials-stand-out-for-their-technology-use-but-older-generations-also-embrace-digital-life.

39. Robert Entman, *Democracy Without Citizens* (New York: Oxford University Press, 1989), 110–111.

40. Walter Goodman, "Where's Edward R. Murrow When You Need Him?" *New York Times*, December 30, 1997, E2.

41. Bagdikian, xxii.

42. Neil King Jr. and Louise Radnofsky, "News Corp. Gives $1 Million to GOP," *Wall Street Journal*, August 18, 2010, online.wsj.com/article/SB10001424052748703824304575435922310302654.html.

43. Bagdikian, 217.

44. Brian Stetler, "CNN and Fox Trip Up in Rush to Get the News on the Air," *New York Times*, June 28, 2012, www.nytimes.com/2012/06/29/us/cnn-and-foxs-supreme-court-mistake.html.

45. David Weigel, "I Want to Believe: Why Does the Media Keep Running Fake Stories From a Joke-Free Satire Site?" *Slate*, March 11, 2013, www.slate.com/articles/news_and_politics/politics/2013/03/daily_currant_satire_the_fake_news_website_keeps_fooling_journalists.html.

46. Journalism.org, "Nonprofit News Outlets," features.journalism.org/nonprofit-news-outlets/.

47. David Broder, *Behind the Front Page* (New York: Simon & Schuster, 1987), 148.

48. Dom Bonafede, "Crossing Over," *National Journal*, January 14, 1989, 102; Michael Kelly, "David Gergen, Master of the Game," *New York Times Magazine*, October 31, 1993, 64ff; Jonathan Alter, "Lost in the Big Blur," *Newsweek*, June 9, 1997, 43.

49. Shanto Iyengar, *Is Anyone Responsible?* (Chicago, Ill.: University of Chicago Press, 1991), 2.

50. Shanto Iyengar and Donald R. Kinder, *News That Matters* (Chicago, Ill.: University of Chicago Press, 1987).

51. Benjamin I. Page, Robert Y. Shapiro, and Glenn R. Dempsey, "What Moves Public Opinion?" *American Political Science Review* (March 1987): 23–43. The term *professional communicator* is used by Benjamin Page, *Who Deliberates? Mass Media in Modern Democracy* (Chicago: University of Chicago Press, 1996), 106–109.

52. Center for Media and Democracy, "Sound Bites Get Shorter," *O'Dwyer's PR Newsletter*, November 11, 2000, www.prwatch.org/node/384.

53. Thomas E. Patterson, *Out of Order* (New York: Vintage Books, 1994), 74.

54. Larry J. Sabato, *Feeding Frenzy: How Attack Journalism Has Transformed American Politics* (New York: Free Press, 1991), 6.

55. Ibid., 245.

56. Iyengar and Kinder, *News That Matters*, 93.

57. W. Russell Neuman, Marion R. Just, and Ann N. Crigler, *Common Knowledge: News and the Construction of Political Meaning* (Chicago, Ill.: University of Chicago Press, 1996), 106–119.

58. Ibid., 23.

59. Judith Valente, "Do You Believe What Newspeople Tell You?" *Parade Magazine*, March 2, 1997, 4.

60. Steven Kull, "Misperceptions, the Media, and the Iraq War," PIPA/Knowledge Networks Poll, Program on International Policy Attitudes, October 2, 2003, 13–16, www.pipa.org/OnlineReports/Iraq/Media_10_02_03_Report.pdf.

61. Walter Cronkite, "Reporting Political Campaigns: A Reporter's View," in Doris Graber, Denis McQuail, and Pippa Norris, eds., *The Politics of News, the News of Politics* (Washington, D.C.: CQ Press, 1998), 57–69.

62. Joe Klein, "The Perils of the Permanent Campaign," *Time*, October 30, 2005.

63. Kelly, "David Gergen, Master of the Game," 7.

64. Ibid.

65. Kenneth T. Walsh, *Feeding the Beast: The White House Versus the Press* (New York: Random House, 1996).

66. Hertsgaard, *On Bended Knee*, 6.

67. Johanna Neuman, "An Identity Crisis Unfolds in a Not-So-Elite Press Corps," *Los Angeles Times*, February 25, 2005, 18.

68. Jack Shafer, "The Propaganda President: George W. Bush Does His Best Kim Jong-il," *Slate*, February 3, 2005, www.slate.com/articles/news_and_politics/press_box/2005/02/the_propaganda_president.html.

69. Jeff Zeleny, "Robert Gibbs," *New York Times*, November 6, 2008.

70. John Dickerson, "Always Be Selling," *Slate*, December 4, 2013, www.slate.com/articles/news_and_politics/politics/2013/12/barack_obama_needs_to_sell_obamacare_again_the_president_is_trying_to_save.html.

GLOSSARY

abolitionists a coalition of free blacks and northern whites working to end slavery prior to the Civil War (6)

accommodationists supporters of government nonpreferential accommodation of religion (5)

accountability the principle that bureaucratic employees should be answerable for their performance to supervisors, all the way up the chain of command (9)

administrative law law established by the bureaucracy, on behalf of Congress (10)

advanced industrial democracy a system in which a democratic government allows citizens a considerable amount of personal freedom and maintains a free-market (though still usually regulated) economy (1)

adversarial system trial procedures designed to resolve conflict through the clash of opposing sides, moderated by a neutral, passive judge who applies the law (10)

advice and consent the constitutional obligation that the Senate approve certain executive appointments (7)

affirmative action a policy of creating opportunities for members of certain groups as a substantive remedy for past discrimination (6)

agency capture a process whereby regulatory agencies come to be protective of and influenced by the industries they were established to regulate (9)

agenda setting the media's role in defining the relative importance of an issue or event via the amount and prominence of coverage they devote to it (15)

allocative representation congressional work to secure projects, services, and funds for the represented district (7)

amendability the provision for the Constitution to be changed, so as to adapt to new circumstances (4)

amicus curiae briefs "friend of the court" documents filed by interested parties to encourage the Court to grant or deny certiorari or to urge it to decide a case in a particular way (10)

anarchy the absence of government and law (1)

Anti-Federalists advocates of states' rights who opposed the Constitution (3)

appeal a rehearing of a case because the losing party in the original trial argues that a point of law was not applied properly (10)

appellate jurisdiction the authority of a court to review decisions made by lower courts (10)

Articles of Confederation the first constitution of the United States (1777) creating an association of states with weak central government (3)

astroturf lobbying indirect lobbying efforts that manipulate or create public sentiment, "astroturf" being artificial grassroots (13)

asylum protection or sanctuary, especially from political persecution (2)

authoritarian capitalism a system in which the state allows people economic freedom but maintains stringent social regulations to limit noneconomic behavior (1)

authoritarian governments systems in which the state holds all power over the social order (1)

authoritarian populism a radical right-wing movement that appeals to popular discontent but whose underlying values are not democratic (2)

authority power that is recognized as legitimate, or right (1)

bad tendency test the rule used by the courts that allows speech to be punished if it leads to punishable actions (5)

benchmark poll an initial poll on a candidate and issues on which campaign strategy is based and against which later polls are compared (11)

bicameral legislature a legislature with two chambers (4, 7)

Bill of Rights a summary of citizen rights guaranteed and protected by a government; added to the Constitution as its first ten amendments in order to achieve ratification (3)

bills of attainder laws under which specific persons or groups are detained and sentenced without trial (5)

black codes a series of laws in the post–Civil War South designed to restrict the rights of former slaves before the passage of the Fourteenth and Fifteenth Amendments (6)

block grant federal funds provided for a broad purpose and unrestricted by detailed requirements and regulations (4)

boycott the refusal to buy certain goods or services as a way to protest policy or force political reform (6)

Brown v. Board of Education of Topeka the Supreme Court case that rejected the idea that separate could be equal in education (6)

bureaucracy an organization characterized by hierarchical structure, worker specialization, explicit rules, and advancement by merit (9)

bureaucratese the often unintelligible language used by bureaucrats to avoid controversy and lend weight to their words (9)

bureaucratic culture the accepted values and procedures of an organization (9)

bureaucratic discretion bureaucrats' use of their own judgment in interpreting and carrying out the laws of Congress (9)

busing achieving racial balance by transporting students to schools across neighborhood boundaries (6)

cabinet a presidential advisory group selected by the president, made up of the vice president, the heads of the federal executive departments, and other high officials to whom the president elects to give cabinet status (8)

capitalist economy an economic system in which the market determines production, distribution, and price decisions, and property is privately owned (1)

casework legislative work on behalf of individual constituents to solve their problems with government agencies and programs (7)

categorical grant federal funds provided for a specific purpose and restricted by detailed instructions, regulations, and compliance standards (4)

caucus a local gathering of party members to choose convention delegates (14)

checks and balances the principle that allows each branch of government to exercise some form of control over the others (4)

chief administrator the president's executive role as the head of federal agencies and the person responsible for the implementation of national policy (8)

chief foreign policy maker the president's executive role as the primary shaper of relations with other nations (8)

chief of staff the person who oversees the operations of all White House staff and is traditionally expected to control access to the president (8)

citizen advisory councils citizen groups that consider the policy decisions of an agency; a way to make the bureaucracy responsive to the general public (9)

citizen journalism reporting and commentary by everyday citizens unaffiliated with traditional media outlets, and distributed via the web in the form of blogs, podcasts, or video uploads (15)

citizens members of a political community with both rights and responsibilities (1)

civil laws laws regulating interactions between individuals; violation of a civil law is called a tort (10)

civil liberties individual freedoms guaranteed to the people primarily by the Bill of Rights (5)

civil rights citizenship rights guaranteed to the people (primarily in the Thirteenth, Fourteenth, Fifteenth, Nineteenth, and Twenty-sixth Amendments) and protected by the government (5, 6)

civil service nonmilitary employees of the government who are appointed through the merit system (9)

civil-law tradition a legal system based on a detailed comprehensive legal code, usually created by the legislature (10)

classical liberalism a political ideology dating from the seventeenth century emphasizing individual rights over the power of the state (1)

clear and present danger test the rule used by the courts that allows language to be regulated only if it presents an immediate and urgent danger (5)

clickbait sensational headlines designed to tempt Internet users to click through to a specific web site (15)

clientele groups groups of citizens whose interests are affected by an agency or a department and who work to influence its policies (9)

closed primary a primary election in which only registered party members may vote (12, 14)

cloture a vote to end a Senate filibuster; requires a three-fifths majority, or sixty votes (7)

coattail effect the added votes received by congressional candidates of a winning presidential party (7)

collective action problem the difficulty in getting people to work together to achieve a common goal when the solution is costly and no one individual has an incentive to use resources to make it happen (13)

collective good a good or service that, by its very nature, cannot be denied to anyone who wants to consume it (13)

commander-in-chief the president's role as the top officer of the country's military establishment (8)

commercial bias the tendency of the media to make coverage and programming decisions based on what will attract a large audience and maximize profits (15)

Common Sense the pamphlet written by Thomas Paine in 1776 that persuaded many Americans to support the revolutionary cause (3)

common-law tradition a legal system based on the accumulated rulings of judges over time, applied uniformly—judge-made law (10)

communist democracy a utopian system in which property is communally owned and all decisions are made democratically (1)

communitarians those who favor a strong, substantive government role in the economy and the social order so that their vision of a community of equals may be realized (2)

compelling state interest a fundamental state purpose, which must be shown before the law can limit some freedoms or treat some groups of people differently (5)

concurrent powers powers that are shared by the federal and state governments (4)

concurring opinions documents written by justices expressing agreement with the majority ruling but describing different or additional reasons for the ruling (10)

confederal system government in which local units hold all the power (4)

confederation a government in which independent states unite for common purpose but retain their own sovereignty (3)

conference committees temporary committees formed to reconcile differences in House and Senate versions of a bill (7)

congressional oversight efforts by Congress, especially through committees, to monitor agency rule making, enforcement, and implementation of congressional policies (7, 9)

conservatives people who generally favor limited government and are cautious about change (2)

constituency the voters in a state or district (7)

constitution the rules that establish a government (3)

Constitutional Convention the assembly of fifty-five delegates in the summer of 1787 to recast the Articles of Confederation; the result was the U.S. Constitution (3)

constitutional law law stated in the Constitution or in the body of judicial decisions about the meaning of the Constitution handed down in the courts (10)

cooperative federalism the federal system under which the national and state governments share responsibilities for most domestic policy areas (4)

Council of Economic Advisers the organization within the Executive Office of the President that advises the president on economic matters (8)

courts institutions that sit as neutral third parties to resolve conflicts according to the law (10)

criminal laws laws prohibiting behavior the government has determined to be harmful to

society; violation of a criminal law is called a crime (10)

critical election an election signaling a significant change in popular allegiance from one party to another (12)

cycle effect the predictable rise and fall of a president's popularity at different stages of a term in office (8)

de facto discrimination discrimination that is the result not of law but rather of tradition and habit (6)

de jure discrimination discrimination that arises from or is supported by the law (6)

dealignment a trend among voters to identify themselves as independents rather than as members of a major party (12)

Declaration of Independence the political document that dissolved the colonial ties between the United States and Britain (3)

democracy government that vests power in the people (1)

departments one of the major subdivisions of the federal government, represented in the president's cabinet (9)

descriptive representation the idea that an elected body should mirror demographically the population it represents (7)

devolution the transfer of powers and responsibilities from the federal government to the states (4)

digital native an individual born after the advent of digital technology who is proficient in and dependent on its use (1)

direct lobbying direct interaction with public officials for the purpose of influencing policy decisions (13)

dissenting opinions documents written by justices expressing disagreement with the majority ruling (10)

divided government the situation that exists when political rule is split between two parties, in which one controls the White House and the other controls one or both houses of Congress (8)

divine right of kings the principle that earthly rulers receive their authority from God (1)

dual federalism the federal system under which the national and state governments are responsible for separate policy areas (4)

due process of law the guarantee that laws will be fair and reasonable and that citizens suspected of breaking the law will be treated fairly (5)

earmarks legislative provisions to allocate spending to a specific purpose or project (7)

economic conservatives those who favor a strictly procedural government role in the economy and the social order (2)

economic interest groups groups that organize to influence government policy for the economic benefit of their members (13)

economic liberals those who favor an expanded government role in the economy but a limited role in the social order (2)

economics production and distribution of a society's material resources and services (1)

electioneering the process of getting a person elected to public office (12)

Electoral College an intermediary body that elects the president (4, 14)

electoral mandate the perception that an election victory signals broad support for the winner's proposed policies (14)

English-only movements efforts to make English the official language of the United States (6)

enumerated powers of Congress congressional powers specifically named in the Constitution (Article I, Section 8) (4)

equal opportunity interest groups groups that organize to promote the civil and economic rights of underrepresented or disadvantaged groups (13)

Equal Rights Amendment a constitutional amendment passed by Congress but never ratified that would have banned discrimination on the basis of gender (6)

establishment clause the First Amendment guarantee that the government will not create and support an official state church (5)

ex post facto laws laws that criminalize an action after it occurs (5)

exclusionary rule the rule created by the Supreme Court that evidence seized illegally may not be used to obtain a conviction (5)

executive agreements presidential arrangements with other countries that create foreign policy without the need for Senate approval (8)

executive the branch of government responsible for putting laws into effect (4)

Executive Office of the President the collection of organizations that help the president with policy and political objectives (8)

executive orders clarifications of congressional policy issued by the president and having the full force of law (8, 10)

exit polls election-related questions asked of voters right after they vote (11)

expectations gap the gap between popular expectations of what modern presidents can and should do, and their constitutional powers to get things done (8)

exploratory committee a committee formed to determine the viability of one's candidacy for office; activities may include polling, travel, and other communications relevant to the purpose (14)

expressive benefits selective incentives that derive from the opportunity to express values and beliefs and to be committed to a greater cause (13)

faction a group of citizens united by some common passion or interest and opposed to the rights of other citizens or to the interests of the whole community (3, 13)

Federal Register the publication containing all federal regulations and notifications of regulatory agency hearings (9)

federalism a political system in which power is divided between the central and regional units (3)

The Federalist Papers a series of essays written to build support for ratification of the Constitution (3)

Federalists supporters of the Constitution who favored a strong central government (3)

feeding frenzy excessive press coverage of an embarrassing or scandalous subject (15)

fighting words speech intended to incite violence (5)

filibuster a practice of unlimited debate in the Senate in order to prevent or delay a vote on a bill (7)

framing the process through which the media emphasize particular aspects of a news story, thereby influencing the public's perception of the story (15)

franking the privilege of free mail service provided to members of Congress (7)

free exercise clause the First Amendment guarantee that citizens may freely engage in the religious activities of their choice (5)

free press a press that is able to report fully on government's activities (5)

free riders people who refuse to spend time, money, or effort on the collective solution because they can reap the benefits whether they join or not (13)

freedom of assembly the right of the people to gather peacefully and to petition government (*5*)

Freedom of Information Act (FOIA) the 1966 law that allows citizens to obtain copies of most public records (9)

French and Indian War a war fought between France and England, and allied Indians, from 1754 to 1763; resulted in France's expulsion from the New World (3)

front-loading the process of scheduling presidential primaries early in the primary season (14)

front-runner the leading candidate and expected winner of a nomination or an election (14)

fusion of powers an alternative to separation of powers, combining or blending branches of government (4)

gatekeepers journalists and the media elite who determine which news stories are covered and which are not (1, 15)

gender gap the tendency of men and women to differ in their political views on some issues (11)

gerrymandering redistricting to benefit a particular group (7)

get-out-the-vote (GOTV) drives efforts by political parties, interest groups, and the candidate's staff to maximize voter turnout among supporters (14)

Gibbons v. Ogden Supreme Court ruling (1824) establishing national authority over interstate business (4)

going public a president's strategy of appealing to the public on an issue, expecting that public pressure will be brought to bear on other political actors (8)

governing activities directed toward controlling the distribution of political resources by providing executive and legislative leadership, enacting agendas, mobilizing support, and building coalitions (12)

government a system or organization for exercising authority over a body of people (1)

government corporations companies created by Congress to provide to the public a good or service that private enterprise cannot or will not profitably provide (9)

government interest groups groups that organize to represent foreign or domestic governments, and to lobby Congress and the president on their behalf (13)

government matching funds money given by the federal government to qualified presidential candidates in the primary and general election campaigns (14)

grandfather clauses provisions exempting from voting restrictions the descendants of those able to vote in 1867 (6)

grassroots lobbying indirect lobbying efforts that spring from widespread public concern (13)

Great Compromise the constitutional solution to congressional representation: equal votes in the Senate, votes by population in the House (3)

habeas corpus the right of an accused person to be brought before a judge and informed of the charges and evidence against him or her (5)

hard money campaign funds donated directly to candidates; amounts are limited by federal election laws (14)

hashtag activism a form of political engagement that occurs by organizing individuals online around a particular issue (1)

Hatch Act the 1939 law that limited the political involvement of civil servants to protect them from political pressure and keep politics out of the bureaucracy (9)

head of government the political role of the president as leader of a political party and chief arbiter of who gets what resources (8)

head of state the apolitical, unifying role of the president as symbolic representative of the whole country (8)

honeymoon period the time following an election when a president's popularity is high and congressional relations are likely to be productive (8)

horse-race journalism the media's focus on the competitive aspects of politics rather than on actual policy proposals and political decisions (15)

House Rules Committee the committee that determines how and when debate on a bill will take place (7)

hyperpartisanship a commitment to party so strong that it can transcend other commitments (7, 12)

identity politics the assertion of power, or discrimination, *by* a group—or an appeal for support *to* a group—based on their common perception of who they are (2)

ideologies sets of beliefs about politics and society that help people make sense of their world (2)

immigrants citizens or subjects of one country who move to another country to live or work (2)

imminent lawless action test the rule used by the courts that restricts speech only if it is aimed at producing or is likely to produce imminent lawless action **(5)**

impeachment a formal charge by the House that the president (or another member of the executive branch) has committed acts of "Treason, Bribery, or other high Crimes and Misdemeanors," which may or may not result in removal from office (8)

incorporation Supreme Court action making the protections of the Bill of Rights applicable to the states (5)

incumbency advantage the electoral edge afforded to those already in office (7)

independent agencies government organizations independent of the departments but with a narrower policy focus (9)

independent regulatory boards and commissions government organizations that regulate various businesses, industries, or economic sectors (9)

indirect lobbying attempts to influence government policymakers by encouraging the general public to put pressure on them (13)

individualism the belief that what is good for society is based on what is good for individuals (2)

information bubble a closed cycle, sometimes self-created, in which all the information we get reinforces the information we already have, solidifying our beliefs without reference to outside reality checks (1)

inherent powers presidential powers implied but not stated explicitly in the Constitution (8)

initiative citizen petitions to place a proposal or constitutional amendment on the ballot, to be adopted or rejected by majority vote, bypassing the legislature (4)

inquisitorial system trial procedures designed to determine the truth through the intervention of an active judge who seeks evidence and questions witnesses (10)

institutions organizations in which government power is exercised (1)

interest group an organization of individuals who share a common political goal and unite for the purpose of influencing government decisions (13)

intermediate standard of review a standard of review used by the Court to evaluate laws that make a quasi-suspect classification (6)

intersectionality the interdependent discrimination and oppression that results when an individual is a member of more than one oppressed or minority group (6)

invisible primary early attempts to raise money, line up campaign consultants, generate media attention, and get commitments for support even before candidates announce they are running (14)

iron triangles the phenomenon of a clientele group, congressional committee, and bureaucratic agency cooperating to make mutually beneficial policy (9)

issue advocacy ads advertisements paid for by soft money, and thus not regulated, that promote certain issue positions but do not endorse specific candidates (13, 14)

issue networks complex systems of relationships among groups that influence policy, including elected leaders, interest groups, specialists, consultants, and research institutes (9)

issue ownership the tendency of one party to be seen as more competent in a specific policy area (14)

Jim Crow laws southern laws designed to circumvent the Thirteenth, Fourteenth, and Fifteenth Amendments and to deny blacks rights on bases other than race (6)

joint committees combined House-Senate committees formed to coordinate activities and expedite legislation in a certain area (7)

judicial activism the view that the courts should be lawmaking, policymaking bodies (10)

judicial interpretivism a judicial approach holding that the Constitution is a living document and that judges should interpret it according to changing times and values (10)

judicial power the power to interpret laws and judge whether a law has been broken (4)

judicial restraint the view that the courts should reject any active lawmaking functions and stick to judicial interpretations of the past (10)

judicial review the power of the courts to determine the constitutionality of laws (4, 10)

jurisdiction a court's authority to hear certain cases (10)

laissez-faire capitalism an economic system in which the market makes all decisions and the government plays no role (1)

leaks confidential information secretly revealed to the press (15)

legislative agenda the slate of proposals and issues that representatives think it worthwhile to consider and act on (7)

legislative liaison executive personnel who work with members of Congress to secure their support in getting a president's legislation passed (8)

legislative supremacy an alternative to judicial review; the acceptance of legislative acts as the final law of the land (4)

legislature the body of government that makes laws (4)

legitimate accepted as "right" or proper (1)

Lemon **test** the three-pronged rule used by the courts to determine whether the establishment clause is violated (5)

libel written defamation of character (5)

liberals people who generally favor government action and view change as progress (2)

libertarians those who favor a minimal government role in any sphere (2)

literacy tests tests requiring reading or comprehension skills as a qualification for voting (6)

lobbying interest group activities aimed at persuading policymakers to support the group's positions (13)

majority party the party with the most seats in a house of Congress (7)

Marbury v. Madison the landmark case that established the U.S. Supreme Court's power of judicial review (10)

marriage gap the tendency of married and unmarried people to differ in their political views on some issues **(11)**

mass media the means of conveying information to large public audiences cheaply and efficiently (15)

material benefits selective incentives in the form of tangible rewards (13)

McCulloch v. Maryland Supreme Court ruling (1819) confirming the supremacy of national over state government (4)

media the channels—including television, radio, newspapers, and the Internet—through which information is sent and received (1)

media convergence the merging of traditional media with digital communication technologies such as telecommunications and the Internet (15)

mediated citizens those for whom most personal and commercial relationships; access to information about the world and recreational or professional activities; and communication with others passes through third-party channels, which may or may not modify or censor that information (1)

midterm loss the tendency for the presidential party to lose congressional seats in off-year elections (7)

Miller **test** the rule used by the courts in which the definition of obscenity must be based on local standards (5)

minimum rationality test a standard of review used by the Court to evaluate laws that make a nonsuspect classification (6)

modern presidency the trend toward a higher degree of executive power since the 1930s (8)

momentum the widely held public perception that a candidate is gaining electoral strength (14)

Motor Voter Act legislation allowing citizens to register to vote at the same time they apply for a driver's license or other state benefit (14)

narrowcasting the targeting of specialized audiences by the media (15)

National Association for the Advancement of Colored People (NAACP) an interest group founded in 1910 to promote civil rights for African Americans (6)

national lawmaking the creation of policy to address the problems and needs of the entire nation (7)

National Security Council (NSC) the organization within the Executive Office of the President that provides foreign policy advice to the president (8)

nativism the belief that the needs of citizens ought to be met before those of immigrants (2)

naturalization the legal process of acquiring citizenship for someone who has not acquired it by birth (2)

necessary and proper clause constitutional authorization for Congress to make any law required to carry out its powers (4)

negative advertising campaign advertising that emphasizes the negative characteristics of opponents rather than one's own strengths (14)

negative partisanship loyalty to a party driven by hatred of the other party (12)

net neutrality the idea that Internet providers should provide access to all websites without preference or prejudice (5)

neutral competence the principle that bureaucracy should be depoliticized by making it more professional (9)

New Jersey Plan a proposal at the Constitutional Convention that congressional representation be equal, thus favoring the small states (3)

news aggregators web sites, applications, and software that cull content from other digital sources (15)

news management the efforts of a politician's staff to control news about the politician (15)

news organizations businesses (and occasionally nonprofits) devoted to reporting and disseminating news via print, broadcast, or digital media—or a multimedia combination (15)

nominating convention the formal party gathering to choose candidates (12)

nonresponse bias a skewing of data that occurs when there is a difference in opinion between those who choose to participate and those who do not (11)

normative a term used to describe beliefs or values about how things should be or what people ought to do rather than what actually is (2)

norms informal, unwritten expectations that guide behavior and support formal rule systems; often most noticeable when broken (1)

nuclear option a controversial Senate maneuver by which a simple majority could decide to allow a majority to bypass the filibuster for certain kinds of votes (7)

nullification declaration by a state that a federal law is void within its borders (4)

Office of Management and Budget the organization within the Executive Office of the President that oversees the budgets of departments and agencies (8)

omnibus legislation a large bill that contains so many important elements that members can't afford to defeat it and the president can't afford to veto it, even if the bill contains elements they dislike (7)

on-line processing the ability to receive and evaluate information as events happen, allowing us to remember our evaluation even if we have forgotten the specific events that caused it (11)

open primary a primary election in which eligible voters need not be registered party members (12, 14)

opinion the written decision of the Court that states the judgment of the majority (10)

opinion leaders people who know more about certain topics than we do and whose advice we trust, seek out, and follow (11)

oppo research investigation of an opponent's background for the purpose of exploiting weaknesses or undermining credibility (14)

optics the way a situation, person, or event is presented by the media and perceived by the public (15)

original jurisdiction the authority of a court to hear a case first (10)

pardoning power a president's authority to release or excuse a person from the legal penalties of a crime (8)

parliamentary system government in which the executive is chosen by the legislature from among its members and the two branches are merged (4)

partisan gerrymandering redistricting controlled by the majority party in a state's legislature, to increase the number of districts that party can expect to carry (7)

partisan sorting the process through which citizens align themselves ideologically with one of the two parties, leaving fewer citizens remaining in the center and increasing party polarization (11, 12)

partisanship loyalty to a party that helps shape how members see the world, define problems, and identify appropriate solutions (7, 12)

party activists the "party faithful"; the rank-and-file members who carry out the party's electioneering efforts (12)

party base members of a political party who consistently vote for that party's candidates (12)

party bosses party leaders, usually in an urban district, who exercised tight control over electioneering and patronage (12)

party discipline the ability of party leaders to bring party members in the legislature into line with the party program (12)

party eras extended periods of relative political stability in which one party tends to control both the presidency and Congress (12)

party identification voter affiliation with a political party (12)

party machines mass-based party systems in which parties provided services and resources to voters in exchange for votes (12)

party organization the official structure that conducts the political business of parties (12)

party platform a list of policy positions a party endorses and pledges its elected officials to enact (12)

party polarization greater ideological (liberal versus conservative) differences between the parties and increased ideological consensus within the parties (7)

party primary an election in which party candidates are nominated by registered party members rather than party bosses (12)

party-in-government party members who have been elected to serve in government (12)

party-in-the-electorate ordinary citizens who identify with the party (12)

patriotism a strong emotional attachment to one's political community (11)

patronage a system in which a successful candidate rewards friends, contributors, and party loyalists for their support with jobs, contracts, and favors (9, 12)

Pendleton Act the 1883 civil service reform that required the hiring and promoting of civil servants to be based on merit, not patronage (9)

permanent campaign the idea that governing requires a continual effort to convince the public to sign on to the program, requiring a reliance on consultants and an emphasis on politics over policy (15)

Plessy v. Ferguson the Supreme Court case that established the constitutionality of the principle "separate but equal" (6)

pocket veto presidential authority to kill a bill submitted within ten days of the end of a legislative session by not signing it (7)

police power the ability of the government to protect its citizens and maintain social order (5)

policy entrepreneurship the practice of legislators becoming experts and taking leadership roles in specific policy areas (7)

policy representation congressional work to advance the issues and ideological preferences of constituents (7)

political accountability the democratic principle that political leaders must answer to the public for their actions (15)

political action committees (PACs) the fundraising arms of interest groups (13)

political correctness the idea that language shapes behavior and therefore should be regulated to control its social effects (2, 5)

political culture the broad pattern of ideas, beliefs, and values that a population holds about its citizens and government (2)

political efficacy citizens' feelings of effectiveness in political affairs (14)

political generations groups of citizens whose political views have been shaped by the common events of their youth (11)

political gridlock the stalemate that occurs when political rivals, especially parties, refuse to budge from their positions to achieve a compromise in the public interest (12)

political narrative a persuasive story about the nature of power, who should have it and how it should be used (1)

political party a group of citizens united by ideology and seeking control of government in order to promote their ideas and policies (12)

political socialization the process by which we learn our political orientations and allegiances (11)

politics who gets what, when, and how; a process of determining how power and resources are distributed in a society without recourse to violence (1)

poll taxes taxes levied as a qualification for voting (6)

popular sovereignty the concept that the citizens are the ultimate source of political power (1, 3)

popular tyranny the unrestrained power of the people (3)

populism social movements based on the idea that power has been concentrated illegitimately among elites at the people's expense (1)

pork barrel projects public works projects and grants for specific districts paid for by general revenues (7)

position issues issues on which the parties differ in their perspectives and proposed solutions (14)

power the ability to get other people to do what you want (1)

power to persuade a president's ability to convince Congress, other political actors, and the public to cooperate with the administration's agenda (8)

precedent a previous decision or ruling that, in common-law tradition, is binding on subsequent decisions (10)

presidential primary an election by which voters choose convention delegates committed to voting for a certain candidate (14)

presidential style the image that presidents project that represents how they would like to be perceived at home and abroad (8)

presidential system government in which the executive is chosen independently of the legislature and the two branches are separate (4)

presidential veto a president's authority to reject a bill passed by Congress; may be overridden only by a two-thirds majority in each house (8)

prior restraint censorship of or punishment for the expression of ideas before the ideas are printed or spoken (5)

Privacy Act of 1974 a law that gives citizens access to the government's files on them (9)

procedural due process procedural laws that protect the rights of individuals who must deal with the legal system (10)

procedural guarantees government assurance that the rules will work smoothly and treat everyone fairly, with no promise of particular outcomes (1, 2)

procedural laws laws that establish how laws are applied and enforced—how legal proceedings take place (10)

prospective voting basing voting decisions on well-informed opinions and consideration of the future consequences of a given vote (14)

public interest groups groups that organize to influence government to produce collective goods or services that benefit the general public (13)

public opinion the collective attitudes and beliefs of individuals on one or more issues (11)

public opinion polls scientific efforts to estimate what an entire group thinks about an issue by asking a smaller sample of the group for its opinion (11)

public-interested citizenship a view of citizenship focused on action to realize the common good (1)

pundit a professional observer and commentator on politics **(15)**

push polls polls that ask for reactions to hypothetical, often false, information in order to manipulate public opinion (11)

racial gerrymandering redistricting to enhance or reduce the chances that a racial or ethnic group will elect members to the legislature (7)

racism institutionalized power inequalities in society based on the perception of racial differences (3, 6)

random samples samples chosen in such a way that any member of the population being polled has an equal chance of being selected (11)

ratification the process through which a proposal is formally approved and adopted by vote (3)

rational ignorance the state of being uninformed about politics because of the cost in time and energy (11)

realignment a substantial and long-term shift in party allegiance by individuals and groups, usually resulting in a change in policy direction (12)

reapportionment a reallocation of congressional seats among the states every ten years, following the census (7)

recall elections votes to remove elected officials from office (4)

Reconstruction the period following the Civil War during which the federal government took action to rebuild the South (6)

red tape the complex procedures and regulations surrounding bureaucratic activity (9)

redistricting the process of dividing states into legislative districts (7)

referendum an election in which a bill passed by the state legislature is submitted to voters for approval (4)

refugees individuals who flee an area or a country because of persecution on the basis of race, nationality, religion, group membership, or political opinion (2)

regulated capitalism a market system in which the government intervenes to protect rights and make procedural guarantees (1)

regulating the electorate the process of setting rules that define who can vote and how difficult or easy it will be to cast a ballot in an election (14)

regulations limitations or restrictions on the activities of a business or an individual (9)

representation the efforts of elected officials to look out for the interests of those who elect them (7)

republic a government in which decisions are made through representatives of the people (1, 4)

responsible party model party government when four conditions are met: clear choice of ideologies, candidates pledged to implement ideas, party held accountable by voters, and party control over members (12)

retrospective voting basing voting decisions on reactions to past performance; approving the status quo or a desire for change (14)

revolving door the tendency of public officials, journalists, and lobbyists to move between public- and private-sector (media, lobbying) jobs (13, 15)

roll call votes publicly recorded votes on bills and amendments on the floor of the House or the Senate (7)

Rule of Four the unwritten requirement that four Supreme Court justices must agree to grant a case certiorari in order for the case to be heard (10)

rules directives that specify how resources will be distributed or what procedures govern collective activity (1)

sample the portion of the population that is selected to participate in a poll (11)

sample bias the effect of having a sample that does not represent all segments of the population (11)

sampling error a number that indicates within what range the results of a poll are accurate (11)

sedition speech that criticizes the government to promote rebellion (5)

segregation the practice and policy of separating races (6)

select committee a committee appointed to deal with an issue or a problem not suited to a standing committee (7)

selective incentives benefits that are available only to group members as an inducement to get them to join (13)

selective perception the phenomenon of filtering incoming information through personal values and interests (15)

self-interested citizenship a view of citizenship focused on action to realize an individual citizen's interests (1)

senatorial courtesy the tradition of granting senior senators of the president's party considerable power over federal judicial appointments in their home states (8, 10)

seniority system the accumulation of power and authority in conjunction with the length of time spent in office (7)

separation of powers the institutional arrangement that assigns legislative, executive, and judicial powers to different persons or groups, thereby limiting the powers of each (4)

separationists supporters of a "wall of separation" between church and state (5)

sexual harassment unwelcome sexual speech or behavior that creates a hostile work environment (6)

Shays's Rebellion a grassroots uprising (1787) by armed Massachusetts farmers protesting foreclosures (3)

signing statements statements recorded along with signed legislation clarifying the president's understanding of the constitutionality of the bill (8)

slavery the ownership, for forced labor, of one people by another (3)

social connectedness citizens' involvement in groups and their relationships to their communities and families (14)

social conservatives those who endorse limited government control of the economy but considerable government intervention to realize a traditional social order; based on religious values and hierarchy rather than equality (2)

social contract the notion that society is based on an agreement between government and the governed in which people agree to give up some rights in exchange for the protection of others (1)

social democracy a hybrid system combining a capitalist economy and a government that supports equality (1)

social liberals those who favor greater control of the economy and the social order to bring about greater equality and to regulate the effects of progress (2)

social order the way we organize and live our collective lives (1)

social protest public activities designed to bring attention to political causes, usually generated by those without access to conventional means of expressing their views (13)

socialist economy an economic system in which the state determines production, distribution, and price decisions, and property is government owned (1)

soft money unregulated campaign contributions by individuals, groups, or parties that promote general election activities but do not directly support individual candidates (12, 14)

solicitor general the Justice Department officer who argues the government's cases before the Supreme Court (8, 10)

solidary benefits selective incentives related to the interaction and bonding among group members (13)

sound bite a brief, snappy excerpt from a public figure's speech that is easy to repeat on the news (15)

Speaker of the House the leader of the majority party who serves as the presiding officer of the House of Representatives (7)

spin an interpretation of a politician's words or actions, designed to present a favorable image (15)

spiral of silence the process by which a majority opinion becomes exaggerated because minorities do not feel comfortable speaking out in opposition (11)

spoils system the nineteenth-century practice of firing government workers of a defeated party and replacing them with loyalists of the victorious party (9)

standing committees permanent committees responsible for legislation in particular policy areas (7)

State of the Union address a speech given annually by the president to a joint session of Congress and to the nation announcing the president's agenda (8)

statutory law law passed by a state or the federal legislature (10)

strategic politicians office-seekers who base the decision to run on a rational calculation that they will be successful (7)

straw polls polls that attempt to determine who is ahead in a political race (11)

strict constructionism a judicial approach holding that the Constitution should be read literally, with the framers' intentions uppermost in mind (10)

strict scrutiny a heightened standard of review used by the Supreme Court to assess the constitutionality of laws that limit some freedoms or that make a suspect classification (6)

subjects individuals who are obliged to submit to a government authority against which they have no rights (1)

substantive guarantees government assurance of particular outcomes or results (1)

substantive laws laws whose content, or substance, defines what we can or cannot do (10)

sunshine laws legislation opening the process of bureaucratic policymaking to the public (9)

Super PACs special PACs that can spend unlimited amounts of money on a candidate's behalf but are not allowed to coordinate their efforts with those of the candidate's campaign (13)

supremacy clause constitutional declaration (Article VI) that the Constitution and laws made under its provisions are the supreme law of the land (4)

suspect classification a classification, such as race, for which any discriminatory law must be justified by a compelling state interest (6)

swing voters the approximately one-third of the electorate who are undecided at the start of a campaign (14)

symbolic representation efforts of members of Congress to stand for American ideals or to identify with common constituency values (7)

Three-fifths Compromise the formula for counting five slaves as three people for purposes of representation, which reconciled northern and southern factions at the Constitutional Convention (3)

totalitarian a system in which absolute power is exercised over every aspect of life (1)

tracking polls an ongoing series of surveys that follow changes in public opinion over time (11)

traditional presidency the founders' vision of limited executive power (8)

treaties formal agreements with other countries; negotiated by the president and requiring approval by two-thirds of the Senate (8)

trial balloon an official leak of a proposal to determine public reaction to it without risk (15)

two-step flow of information the process by which citizens take their political cues from more well-informed opinion leaders (11)

unfunded mandate a federal order mandating that states operate and pay for a program created at the national level (4)

unicameral legislature a legislature with one chamber (4)

unitary system government in which all power is centralized (4)

valence issues issues on which most voters and candidates share the same position (14)

values the central ideas, principles, or standards that most people agree are important (2)

veto override reversal of a presidential veto by a two-thirds vote in both houses of Congress (7)

Virginia Plan a proposal at the Constitutional Convention that congressional representation be based on population, thus favoring the large states (3)

voter mobilization a party's efforts to inform potential voters about issues and candidates and to persuade them to vote (14)

weak presidency a term that refers to presidents who do not excel at managing their executive offices (8)

wedge issue a controversial issue that one party uses to split the voters in the other party (14)

weighting adjustments to surveys during analysis so that selected demographic groups reflect their values in the population, usually as measured by the census (11)

whistleblowers individuals who publicize instances of fraud, corruption, or other wrongdoing in the bureaucracy (9)

White House Office the more than four hundred employees within the EOP who work most closely and directly with the president (8)

writs of certiorari formal requests by the U.S. Supreme Court to call up the lower court case it decides to hear on appeal (10)

INDEX

Fortas, Abe, 354
42 (2013), 182
Foundation for National Progress, 529
Founding fathers, 3, 14, 17, 74, 263, 474, 476
Fourteenth Amendment (U.S. Constitution)
　due process rights, 154, 162
　equal protection clause, 159, 162, 173, 179
　guaranteed civil rights, 117, 129, 136–137, 184, 197
　right to privacy, 160
　state-federal balance of power, 104, 108, 110, 137
Fourth Amendment (U.S. Constitution), 136*t*, 155–156, 160
Fourth Party Era, 423
Fox & Friends, 513, 514
Fox News, 463, 467, 502, 513, 528, 541
Fragmentation, 244
Framing, 533
Franking privileges, 217, 228
Franklin, Benjamin, 3, 17, 73
Free blacks, 66, 69, 70, 178
Freedom, 48, 56
Freedom Caucus, 54, 220, 406, 431
Freedom of assembly, 136*t*, 145
Freedom of expression/speech, 136*t*, 141–145, 147–151
Freedom of Information Act (1966), 328, 329
Freedom of religion, 136*t*, 137–141, 191, 192, 206
Freedom of the press, 136*t*, 142, 147, 148–151
FreedomWorks, 463
Free exercise clause, 140–141
Free press, 142
Free rider problem, 443, 450
Free speech protections, 136*t*
　see also Freedom of expression/speech
French and Indian War, 66–67
Frum, David, 427
Fry-bread federalism, 191
Fugitive Slave Act (1850), 178
Fugitive slaves, 175
Full Frontal With Samantha Bee, 294, 519
Fundamentalist Christian groups, 450–451
Funny or Die, 294
Furman v. Georgia (1972), 159
Fusion of powers, 102

Galifianakis, Zach, 503
Gallup, George, 387, 389
Gallup poll, 392, 393
Gambling, 192
Gardiner, Bryan, 524
Gardner, Cory, 90
Gardner, John, 323
Garland, Merrick, 214, 220, 240, 254–255, 269, 353
Garner, John Nance, 289
Gatekeepers, 7, 523
Gates, Robert, 286
Gay and Lesbian Activists Alliance, 449
Gay community
　see LGBTQ community
Gay rights, 161–162, 206–207, 363
Gender
　affirmative action policies, 202
　civilian workforce, 314, 315
　congressional representation, 230–232, 233, 234
　denial of rights, 196–200, 202–205
　differential treatment, 176–177
　equal opportunity interest groups, 449
　gender gap, 380–381
　income gaps, 200, 201
　journalist demographics, 531
　judicial appointments, 349
　party member demographics, 413
　public opinion differences, 380–381
　sexual harassment, 203
　stereotypical portrayals, 296
　2016 presidential election, 296–297, 483
　voter turnout, 481, 486
　see also Women
General Dynamics, 464*t*
General election campaign
　candidate presentation, 495, 498
　citizen participation, 477–478, 507–508
　debates, 503
　Electoral College votes, 493–495
　financial resources and expenditures, 425–426, 503–505, 506*f*
　issues and policies, 498, 500, 508
　media coverage, 500–503

presidential debates, 503
public interest, 507
staffing resources, 495
swing voters, 493
voter mobilization efforts, 505–506
General Social Survey, 393
Generational opinion differences, 382, 383
Generations, political, 382
Gen Xers, 18, 36, 483, 516
Geographic-based public opinions, 384–385, 386*t*
George III (King of England), 69
Germany
　federalist system, 107
　voter turnout, 377*f*
Gerry, Elbridge, 93, 227*f*
Gerrymandering, 225–228, 227*f*
Gerson, Michael, 541–543
Get-out-the-vote (GOTV) drives, 495, 505–506
Gibbons v. Ogden (1824), 109
Gibbs, Robert, 495, 538
Gideon, Clarence Earl, 157
Gideon v. Wainwright (1963), 136*t*, 157
Giffords, Gabrielle, 151
Gilbert v. Minnesota (1920), 136*t*
Gillmor, Dan, 520, 523
Gilmore, Gary, 159
Gingrich, Newt, 54, 82, 238
Ginsburg, Douglas, 351
Ginsburg, Ruth Bader, 356*t*, 358, 367, 456
Gitlow v. New York (1925), 136*t*, 137
Glass Ceiling Commission, 202
Glass ceiling theory, 202, 296–297, 314
GLBTQ Legal Advocates & Defenders (GLAD), 449
Glendening, Parris, 159
Glickman, Dan, 440
Going public strategy, 279–282
Goldwater, Barry, 411, 488, 503
Gone With the Wind (1939), 182
Gonzales, Alberto, 194
Gonzales v. Raich (2005), 122
Gonzalez-Barrera, Ana, 43
González, Emma, 2, 3, *3*
Good faith exception, 156
Good sportsmanship, 94
Google, 4, 22, 150, 218, 464*t*, 525, 526
Google News, 520
GOProud, 449
Gore, Al
　concession speech, 509–511
　party support, 416
　popular vote, 475, 478
　presidential election, 334–335, 367
　third-party candidates, 55, 430
　vice-presidential role, 268, 289
Governing function, 426, 428
Government
　Articles of Confederation, 71–73, 78
　challenges to authority, 60–61
　citizens' rights and responsibilities, 14, 41, 47, 374–375
　definition, 5
　divided government impacts, 116
　gridlock situations, 116, 407, 411
　influence strategies, 111–114
　political process, 5
　rules and institutions, 6, 91–92
　see also Bill of Rights; Policymaking process
Government Accountability Office (GAO), 243–244, 325
Government corporations, 312–313
Government interest groups, 453
Government matching funds, 504
Graham, Bob, 455
Graham, Lindsey, 406
Grandfather clauses, 179, 180
Grand juries, 340
Grants
　block grants, 111, 112
　categorical grants, 111, 112
Graphs and visual displays, 37
Grassley, Chuck, 255
Grassroots lobbying, 440, 461, 463
Gravel, Mike, 372
Gray, Rosie, 169–170
Great Britain
　Brexit, 105, 372, 399

unitary systems, 104
voter turnout, 377*f*
Great Compromise, 76, 79
Great Depression
　New Deal programs, 109, 274–275, 352
　realignments, 420
　voter turnout, 428
　see also Social Security system
Greatest Generation, 36
Great Law of Peace, 17
Great Society, 275
Greece, 377*f*
Green Party, 51*f*, 55, 430
Greenpeace, 450
Gregory v. Ashcroft (1991), 177
Gridlock situations, 116, 407, 411
Griles, J. Steven, 323
Griswold, Estelle, 160
Griswold v. Connecticut (1965), 160, 353
Grocery Manufacturers Association, 469
Group power, 407, 441
　see also Interest groups; Lobbying/lobbyists
Guess Who's Coming to Dinner (1967), 182
Gulf War, 281
Gun ownership, 152, 415
Gun ownership regulation, 2, 151, 153, 353, 450

Habeas corpus, 133
Halappanavar, Savita, 371
Haley, Nikki, 196
Hamdan v. Rumsfeld (2006), 276
Hamdi v. Rumsfeld (2004), 276
Hamilton, Alexander
　on bills of rights, 81, 133, 165–166
　defense of standing armies, 153
　on the Electoral College, 474
　Federalist Paper No. 68, 474
　Federalist Paper No. 70, 263
　Federalist Paper No. 78, 97, 98, 342–343
　Federalist Paper No. 84, 81, 133, 165–166
　Federalist Papers, 80
　judicial powers, 97, 98, 334–335, 342–343
　party organization, 418, 422
　Philadelphia Convention, 73
　presidential term of office, 95
Hamilton v. Regents of California (1934), 136*t*
Hammer v. Dagenhart (1918), 109
Hammond, Claudia, 525
Hammond, Darrell, 294
Hancock, John, 68
Handgun Control, Inc., 153, 451
Handguns, 151, 153, 154
Hardball With Chris Matthews (television show), 77
Hard money, 504–505
Hardwick, Michael, 162
Harlan, John Marshall, 145, 179
Harris, Kamala, 172
Hashtag activism, 2–3, 21
#BlackLivesMatter, 21
Hastert, Dennis, 238
Hasty generalizations, 115
Hatch Act (1939), 306
Head of government, 263–264
Head of state, 263
Head, Tom, 62
Health care policies, 106, 114, 415, 528
Hearst Corporation, 526
Hearst, William, 523
Helgeland, Brian, 182
The Help (2011), 182
Hemp Farming Act (2018), 90
Henry, Patrick, 73, 81, 129
Hibbing, John, 433
Hierarchy, 303
Hill, Anita, 351
Hispanic Americans
　civilian workforce, 314
　congressional districts, 227
　congressional representation, 232, 233, 234
　demographic makeup, 36, 43
　denial of rights, 192–194, 208
　equality of police treatment, 366
　equal opportunity interest groups, 448
　equal rights, 172, 193
　immigration issues, 34, 40–41, 42, 192–194